CONSTITUTIONAL LAW FOR A CHANGING AMERICA

RIGHTS, LIBERTIES, AND JUSTICE

CONSTITUTIONAL LAW FOR A CHANGING AMERICA

RIGHTS, LIBERTIES, AND JUSTICE

SECOND EDITION

LEE EPSTEIN
Washington University

THOMAS G. WALKER
Emory University

A DIVISION OF
CONGRESSIONAL QUARTERLY INC.
WASHINGTON, D.C.

Book design by Kachergis Book Design, Pittsboro, North Carolina.

SECOND PRINTING

Library of Congress Cataloging-in-Publication Data
Epstein, Lee, 1958-
      Constitutional law for a changing America :
   rights, liberties, and justice / Lee Epstein,
   Thomas G. Walker - 2nd ed.
            p.   cm.
      Includes bibliographical references and index.
      ISBN 0-87187-830-5
      1. Civil rights-United States.   2. United States-
   Constitutional law.   3. Judicial process-United States.
   4. United States. Supreme Court.   I. Walker, Thomas G.
   II. Title.
   KF4749.E67   1995
   342.73'085-dc20   94-33980
   [347.30285]   CIP

In honor of our parents
Ann and Kenneth Spole
Josephine and George Walker

CONTENTS

TABLES, FIGURES, AND BOXES

PREFACE

Three years have passed since *Constitutional Law for a Changing America: Rights, Liberties, and Justice* made its debut in a discipline already supplied with many fine casebooks by law professors, historians, and social scientists. We believed then, as we do now, that there was a need for a fresh approach because, as political science professors who regularly teach courses on public law, and as scholars concerned with judicial processes, we saw a growing disparity between what we were teaching and what our research taught us.

We had adopted books for our classes that focused primarily on Supreme Court decisions and how the Court applied the resulting legal precedents to subsequent disputes, but as scholars we knew that the law is only one slice of the pie. A host of political factors—internal and external—influence the Court's decisions and shape the development of constitutional law. Among the more significant forces at work are the ways that lawyers and interest groups frame legal disputes, the ideological and behavioral propensities of the justices, the politics of judicial selection, public opinion, and the positions taken by elected officials, to name just a few.

Because we thought no existing book adequately combined the lessons of the legal model with the influences of the political process, we wrote one. In most respects, our book follows tradition: readers will find, for example, that we include the classic cases that best illustrate the development of constitutional law. But our focus—and even the appearance of this volume—is different. We emphasize the arguments raised by lawyers and interest groups, and we include tables and figures on Court trends, profiles of influential justices and organizations, and other materials that bring out the rich political context in which decisions are reached. As a result, students and instructors will find this work both similar to and different from casebooks they may have read before.

Integrating traditional teaching and research concerns was only one of our goals. Another was to animate the subject of public law. As instructors, we find our subject inherently interesting—to us public law is exciting stuff. The typical constitutional law book, however, could not be less inviting in design, presentation, or prose. That kind of book seems to dampen enthusiasm. We have written a book that we hope mirrors the excitement we feel for our subject. Along with cases excerpted in the traditional manner, we have included full descriptions of the events that led to the suits, photographs of litigants, and relevant exhibits from the cases. We hope these materials demonstrate to students that Supreme Court cases are more than just legal names and citations, that they involve real people engaged in real disputes. Readers will also find reference material designed to enhance their understanding of the law—information on the Supreme Court decision-making process, the structure of the federal judiciary, material on briefing court cases, a glossary of legal terms, and biographical information on the justices.

In preparing this second edition, we have strengthened the distinctive features of the first. Readers will find changes at all three levels of the book—overall organization, chapters, and cases. Beginning with the organization of the volume, we restructured the material on Supreme Court decision making, adding new information on legal and political approaches and creating a separate chapter, "Approaches to Supreme Court Decision Making." This addition eliminates the need for supplemental readings on the various theories that have been offered to explain Court decisions. The new chapter also sets the stage for an important theme developed throughout the book—many factors, not just precedent, influence the direction and content of Court decisions. Another organizational change involved the "Freedom of Expression" chapter. It is now divided into three chapters dealing, respectively, with speech, press, and obscenity and libel, which should make for more manageable reading and instruction.

Readers will find the most significant changes within individual chapters. All the chapters have been thoroughly updated, containing opinions handed down during the 1991, 1992, and 1993 terms. In some, we have added a few oldies but goodies, including *Duncan v. Louisiana, Sherbert v. Verner,* and *Goldman v. Weinberger.* Where relevant, we also updated the narrative to take into account recent events in the legal and political environments. The chapter on obscenity and libel, for example, now includes a discussion of feminist arguments against pornography; hate speech

also plays a prominent role in our examination of freedom of expression.

Several chapters have been completely revised—with "Religion: Exercise and Establishment" the most prominent example. There, we rewrote the Free Exercise section to emphasize major doctrinal changes occurring over the past three decades and to highlight the interaction between Congress and the Court. Readers will also find changes in the Establishment section. There, we modified the chronological approach to stress instead the substance of the cases.

In the privacy chapter we streamlined the discussion of cases outside the reproductive realm, while reorganizing the material on abortion. Excerpts on reproductive choice now focus exclusively on the legal standard articulated in *Roe v. Wade;* they demonstrate how the *Roe* standard has changed over time and speculate on why alterations have occurred. In making this change, we do not neglect cases involving parental consent and funding of abortions: they receive treatment in the narrative. And abortion protest—a subject of contemporary concern—receives coverage in the Freedom of Expression chapter.

Finally, readers will note two kinds of changes in our presentation of Court cases. First, we added excerpts from many dissenting and concurring opinions; in fact, virtually all cases analyzed in the text now include one or the other or both. Although these opinions lack the force of precedent, they are useful in helping students to see alternative points of view. Second, to retain the historical flavor of the decisions, we reprinted verbatim the original language used in the *U.S. Reports* to introduce opinions. Students will see that during most of its history, the Court used the term "Mr." to refer to justices, as in "Mr. Justice Holmes delivered the opinion of the Court" or "Mr. Justice Harlan, dissenting." In 1980 the Court dropped the "Mr." This point may seem minor, but we think it is evidence that the justices, like other Americans, have updated their usage to reflect fundamental changes in American society—in this case, the emergence of women as a force in the legal profession and shortly thereafter on the Court itself.

One thing has not changed—our intention to keep the text up to date with an annual supplement containing the latest important opinions. A separate volume, the supplement will be packaged with the text (the first will appear in August 1995), and will be cumulative until the next edition of the book is published. Making the supplement available at the beginning of the fall semester means the new cases can be included in the syllabus whether the course is taught in the fall or spring.

ACKNOWLEDGMENTS

Although the first edition of this volume was published only three years ago, it had been in the works for many more. During those developmental years, numerous people provided guidance, but none as much as Joanne Daniels, a former editor at CQ Press. It was Joanne who conceived of a constitutional law book that would be accessible, sophisticated, and contemporary. And it was Joanne who brought that concept to our attention and helped us develop it into a book. We are forever in her debt.

Since this new edition charts the same course as the original volume, we remain grateful to all of those who had a hand in the first. They include David Tarr and Jeanne Ferris at CQ Press, Joseph A. Kobylka of Southern Methodist University, and our many colleagues who reviewed and commented on it: Judith A. Baer, Ralph Baker, Lawrence Baum, John Brigham, Gregory A. Caldeira, Robert A. Carp, Phillip J. Cooper, John B. Gates, Wayne McIntosh, John A. Maltese, Richard J. Pacelle, Jr., C. K. Rowland, and Donald R. Songer.

We have accumulated equally as many, if not more, debts in producing this edition. First and foremost, we owe much to two editors at CQ Press, Brenda Carter and Carolyn Goldinger. Brenda brought a (much needed) fresh eye to the project. She had many ideas about the direction the revision should take and

managed to convey them in such a way as to make them seem like ours, not hers. But we know better and herein acknowledge her major contribution to the volume. In the preface to the previous edition, we said that Carolyn Goldinger, our copy editor, was "nothing short of a saint," and her halo has not slipped. Her imprint is everywhere: she managed to translate our (too often) jargonistic writing into accessible prose; she (correctly) questioned our interpretation of certain events and opinions; she even made our tables and figures understandable. We also are grateful to Jamie R. Holland for her skill and persistence in tracking down elusive photographs.

We thank our colleagues who offered valuable suggestions for revision: Bradley C. Canon, Sue Davis, John Fliter, Edward V. Heck, Kevin McGuire, Susan Mezey, and Harry P. Stumpf. Many thanks go to Jeffrey A. Segal for his frank appraisal of the earlier work and his willingness to discuss even half-baked ideas for changes. Jack Knight, who read drafts of several chapters, also deserves special acknowledgment.

Our home institutions provided substantial support, not complaining when presented with astronomical telephone bills, postal fees, and copying expenses. For this and all the moral support they provide, we thank our department chairs, John Sprague (Washington University) and Harvey E. Klehr (Emory University).

Finally, we acknowledge the support of our friends and families. We are forever grateful to our former professors for instilling in us their genuine interest in and curiosity about things judicial and legal, and to our parents for their unequivocal support. Walker expresses his special thanks to Aimee and Emily for always being there; and Epstein to her husband Jay for enduring all that he does not have to (but does, anyway), without complaining (much).

Any errors of omission or commission remain our sole responsibility. We encourage students and instructors alike to comment on the book and to inform us of any errors.

PART I
THE LIVING CONSTITUTION

I**N MAY 1787** the Founders of our nation met in Philadelphia "for the sole and express purpose of revising the Articles of Confederation," but within a month they dramatically altered their mission. Viewing the articles as unworkable, they decided to start afresh. What emerged just four months later, on September 17, was an entirely new government scheme embodied in the U.S. Constitution.

The Framers were quite pleased with their handiwork, so much so that after they completed it, they "adjourned to City Tavern, dined together and took cordial leave of each other."[1] Most of the delegates were ready to go home after the long, hot summer in Philadelphia. And they did so, confident that the new document would receive speedy passage by the states. At first, it appeared as if their optimism was justified. As Table 1-1 depicts, before the year was out four states had ratified the Constitution—three by unanimous votes. But after January 1788, "the pace . . . slowed considerably."[2] By this time, a movement opposed to ratification was growing and marshaling arguments to deter state convention delegates. Most of all, these opponents, the so-called Anti-Federalists, feared the Constitution's new balance of power. They

believed that strong state governments provided the only "sure defense of their liberties against a potentially tyrannical central authority," and that the Constitution tipped the scales in favor of federal power.[3] These fears were countered by the Federalists, who favored passage of the Constitution. Although their arguments and writings took many forms, among the most important was a series of eighty-five articles published in New York newspapers, under the pen name Publius. Written by John Jay, James Madison, and Alexander Hamilton, *The Federalist Papers* continues to provide insight into the objectives and intent of the Founders.

Debates between the Federalists and their opponents often were highly philosophical in tone, with emphasis on the appropriate roles and powers of national institutions. In the states, however, ratification drives were full of the stuff of ordinary politics. Massachusetts provides a case in point. According to one account, the following events transpired there:

> Of the 355 delegates, 60 percent or more probably came to Boston on January 9 opposed. If the Federalists were to have any chance at all, they would need the hearty support of Samuel Adams, their already legendary Revolutionary

---

1. *1787*, compiled by historians of the Independence National Historical Park (New York: Exeter Books, 1987), 191.

2. Daniel A. Farber and Suzanna Sherry, *A History of the American Constitution* (St. Paul, Minn.: West Publishing, 1990), 177.

3. Melvin I. Urofsky, *A March of Liberty* (New York: Knopf, 1988), 96–98.

TABLE I-1 The Ratification of the Constitution

State	Date of Action	Decision	Margin
Delaware	December 7, 1787	ratified	30:0
Pennsylvania	December 12, 1787	ratified	46:23
New Jersey	December 18, 1787	ratified	38:0
Georgia	December 31, 1787	ratified	26:0
Connecticut	January 8, 1788	ratified	128:40
Massachusetts	February 6, 1788	ratified with amendments	187:168
Maryland	April 26, 1788	ratified	63:11
South Carolina	May 23, 1788	ratified with amendments	149:73
New Hampshire	June 21, 1788	ratified with amendments	57:47
Virginia	June 25, 1788	ratified with amendments	89:79
New York	July 26, 1788	ratified with amendments	30:27
North Carolina	August 2, 1788	rejected	184:84
	November 21, 1789	ratified with amendments	194:77
Rhode Island	May 29, 1790	ratified with amendments	34:32

SOURCE: Daniel A. Farber and Suzanna Sherry, *A History of the American Constitution* (St. Paul, Minn.: West Publishing, 1990), 216.

hero, and of governor John Hancock, of Declaration immortality. Adams was tepid; Hancock, aloof and cool, preferring to wait and see which way the political tides might flow.

After three weeks of heated debate a delegation headed by Adams climbed Beacon Hill to knock on the door of the wealthy and gouty Hancock. They proposed that the governor declare for ratification on condition that a series of amendments be tacked on for the consideration of the Congress.

The price for Hancock's support? The presidency, if Virginia failed to ratify or if Washington declined to serve. Otherwise, the vice presidency or, some say, the promise of Bowdoin's support in the next governor's race.

Hancock agreed to the bribe and, his feet swathed in bandages, was carried theatrically to the rostrum to make his "Conciliatory Proposition" as though it were his own brainchild. Adams, still the darling of both sides, seconded the resolution to consider the amendments, and a few days later added several of his own.

The Constitution carried on February 6, 187 to 168, making Massachusetts the sixth state to ratify.[4]

This compromise, the call for a bill of rights, caught on. As one scholar noted, "It worked so well that Madison now advocated its use wherever the vote promised to be close."[5] As it turned out, he and other Federalists needed to do so quite often: as Table I-1 indicates, of the nine states ratifying after January 1788, sev-en recommended that the new Congress consider amendments. Indeed, New York and Virginia probably would not have agreed to the Constitution without such an addition; Virginia actually called for a second constitutional convention for that purpose. Other states began devising their own wish lists—enumerations of specific rights they wanted put into the document.

Why were states so reluctant to ratify the Constitution without a bill of rights? Some viewed the new government scheme with downright suspicion, bemoaning "the great and extensive powers granted to the new government over the lives, liberties, and property of every citizen."[6] But more tended to agree with Thomas Jefferson's sentiment expressed in a letter to Madison:

4. J. T. Keenan, *The Constitution of the United States: An Unfolding Story,* 2d ed. (Chicago: Dorsey Press, 1988), 32–33.

5. Alpheus T. Mason, *The States Rights Debate,* 2d ed. (New York: Oxford University Press, 1972), 92–93.

6. Address of the Albany Antifederal Committee, April 26, 1788, quoted in Farber and Sherry, *American Constitution,* 180.

I like the organization of the government into legislative, Judiciary, and Executive.... I will now add what I do not like ... the omission of a bill of rights providing clearly and without the aid of sophisms for freedom of religion, freedom of press, protection against standing armies....[7]

What Jefferson's remark suggests is that many thought well of the new system of government, but were troubled by the lack of a declaration of rights. Remember that at the time, Americans clearly understood concepts of *fundamental* and *inalienable* rights, those that inherently belonged to them and that no government could deny. Even England, the country with which they had fought a war for their freedom, had such guarantees. The Magna Charta of 1215 and the Bill of Rights of 1689 gave Britons the right to a jury trial, to protection against cruel and unusual punishments, and so forth. Moreover, after the Revolution, virtually every state constitution included a philosophical statement about the relationship between citizens and their government and/or a listing of fifteen to twenty inalienable rights such as religious freedom and electoral independence. Small wonder that the call for such a statement or enumeration of rights became a battle cry for those opposed to ratification. It was so widespread, we might ask why the Framers failed to include it in the original document. Did they not anticipate the reaction?

Records of the 1787 constitutional debates indicate that, in fact, the delegates considered specific individual guarantees on at least four separate occasions.[8] On August 20 Charles Pinckney submitted a proposal that included several guarantees, such as freedom of the press and the eradication of religious tests, but the various committees never considered his plan. On three separate occasions toward the closing days of the convention, September 12, 14, and 16, some tried, again without success, to convince the delegates to enumerate specific guarantees. At one point, George Mason averred that a bill of rights "would give great quiet to the people; and with the aid of the state delegations, a bill might be prepared in a few hours." This motion was unanimously defeated by those remaining in attendance. On the convention's last day, Edmund Randolph made a desperate plea that the delegates allow the states to submit amendments and then convene a second convention. To this, Pinckney responded, "Conventions are serious things, and ought not to be repeated."

Why these suggestions received such unwelcome receptions by the majority of delegates is a matter of scholarly debate. Some suggest that the pleas came too late, that the Framers wanted to complete their mission by September 15 and "were not physically or psychologically prepared to stay on in Philadelphia even an extra day."[9] Others disagree, arguing that the Framers were more concerned with the structure of government than with individual rights,[10] and that the plan they devised—one based on enumerated, not unlimited powers—would foreclose the need for a bill of rights. Hamilton wrote, "The Constitution is itself ... a Bill of Rights."[11] Under it the government could exercise only those functions specifically bestowed upon it; all remaining rights lay with the people. He also asserted that "independent of those which relate to the structure of government," the Constitution did, in fact, contain some of the more necessary specific guarantees.[12] For example, Article I, Section 9, prohibits bills of attainder, ex post facto laws, and the suspension of writs of habeas corpus. Hamilton and others further argued that the specification of rights was not only unnecessary, but also could "even be dangerous" because no such listing could be inclusive.[13] As James

7. Quoted in Alpheus T. Mason and D. Grier Stephenson, Jr., *American Constitutional Law,* 10th ed. (Englewood Cliffs, N.J.: Prentice-Hall, 1993), 349.

8. The following discussion comes from Farber and Sherry, *American Constitution,* 221–222. This book reprints verbatim debates over the Constitution and the Bill of Rights.

9. *1787,* 183.

10. Gerald Gunther, *Individual Rights in Constitutional Law,* 4th ed. (Mineola, N.Y.: Foundation Press, 1986), 72.

11. *The Federalist Papers,* No. 84, Isaac Kramnick, ed. (New York: Penguin Books, 1987), 477.

12. Ibid., 473.   13. Ibid., 476.

Wilson asserted before the Pennsylvania ratifying convention:

> A Bill of Rights annexed to a constitution is an *enumeration of the powers* reserved. If we attempt an enumeration, everything that is not enumerated is presumed to be given. The consequence is, that an imperfect enumeration would throw all implied power into the scale of government, and the rights of the people would be rendered incomplete.[14]

Despite these misgivings, the reality of the political environment caused many Federalists to change their views on the inclusion of a bill of rights. They realized that if they did not accede to state demands, either the Constitution would not be ratified or a new convention would be necessary. Since neither alternative was particularly attractive, they agreed to amend the Constitution as soon as the new government came into power.

One month after the start of the first Congress, in May 1789, Madison announced to the House of Representatives that he would draft a bill of rights and submit it within the coming month. As it turned out, the task proved a bit more onerous than Madison thought; the states had submitted nearly 200 amendments for Congress's consideration, and some of them would have decreased significantly the power of the national government.[15] After sifting through these lists, Madison at first thought it might be best to incorporate the amendments into the Constitution's text, but he soon changed his mind.[16] Instead, he presented the House with the following statement, echoing the views expressed in the Declaration of Independence:

> That there be prefixed to the Constitution a declaration, that all power is originally vested in, and consequently derived from, the people.[17]

The legislators rejected this proposal, preferring a

TABLE 1-2 The Ratification of the Bill of Rights

State	Date of Action	Ratified	Rejected
New Jersey	November 20, 1789	I, III–XII	II
Maryland	December 19, 1789	I–XII	
North Carolina	December 22, 1789	I–XII	
South Carolina	January 19, 1790	I–XII	
New Hampshire	January 25, 1790	I, III–XII	II
Delaware	January 28, 1790	II–XII	I
New York	February 24, 1790	I, III–XII	II
Pennsylvania	March 10, 1790	III–XII	I, II
Rhode Island	June 7, 1790	I, III–XII	II
Vermont	November 3, 1791	I–XII	
Virginia	November 3, 1791	I	
	December 15, 1791	II–XII	
Massachusetts	March 2, 1939	III–XII	I, II
Georgia	March 18, 1939	III–XII	I, II
Connecticut	April 19, 1939	III–XII	I, II

SOURCE: Daniel A. Farber and Suzanna Sherry, *A History of the American Constitution* (St. Paul, Minn.: West Publishing, 1990), 244.

NOTE: Roman numerals in the "Ratified" and "Rejected" columns refer to the original articles, not those within the eventual Bill of Rights.

listing of rights to a philosophical statement. Madison returned to his task, eventually fashioning a list of seventeen amendments. When he took it back to the House, however, the list was greeted with suspicion and opposition. Some members of Congress, even those who had argued for a bill of rights, now did not want to be bothered with the proposals, insisting that they had more important business to settle. One suggested that other nations would not see the United States "as a serious trading partner as it was still tinkering with its constitution instead of organizing its government."[18]

Finally, in July 1789, after Madison had prodded and even begged, the House considered his proposals. A special committee scrutinized them and reported a few days later; and the House adopted, with some

14. Quoted in Farber and Sherry, *American Constitution*, 224.

15. Urofsky, *March of Liberty*, 108.

16. C. Herman Pritchett, *The American Constitution* (New York: McGraw-Hill, 1959), 368.

17. Quoted in Urofsky, *March of Liberty*, 108.

18. Quoted in Farber and Sherry, *American Constitution*, 231.

modification, Madison's seventeen amendments. The Senate, however, considered some and rejected others so that by the time President George Washington submitted the Bill of Rights to the states on October 2, 1789, only twelve remained.[19]

As shown in Table 1-2, the states ratified ten of those twelve. The amendments that did not receive approval were the first two on the list (the original Articles I and II). Article I concerned the number of representatives:

After the first enumeration required by the first article of the Constitution, there shall be one Representative for every thirty thousand, until the number shall amount to one hundred, after which the proportion shall be so regulated by Congress, that there shall be not less than one hundred Representatives, nor less than one Representative for every forty thousand persons, until the number of Representatives shall amount to two hundred; after which the proportion shall be so regulated by Congress, that there shall not be less than two hundred Representatives, nor more than one Representative for every fifty thousand persons.

Article II contained the following provision:

No law varying the compensation for the services of the Senators and Representatives shall take effect, until an election of Representatives shall have intervened.

19. Among those rejected was the one Madison "prized above all others": that the states would have to abide by many of the enumerated guarantees. See Chapter 2 on incorporation of the Bill of Rights.

This article also failed to garner sufficient support from the states in the 1790s and did not become a part of the Bill of Rights. Unlike the original Article I, however, this provision eventually took its place in the Constitution. In 1992, more than 200 years after it was first proposed, it was ratified by the states, thereby becoming the Twenty-seventh Amendment to the U.S. Constitution.

Why the states originally refused to pass this amendment, along with the original Article I, is something of a mystery, for few records of state ratification proceedings exist. What we do know is that two years later, on December 15, 1791, when Virginia ratified, the Bill of Rights became part of the U.S. Constitution.

THE AMENDMENT PROCESS

That Congress proposed and the states ratified the first ten amendments to the Constitution in three years is truly remarkable: since then only seventeen others have been added! Undoubtedly, this reticence would have pleased the writers of the Constitution. They wanted to create a government that would have some permanence, but they also recognized the need for flexibility. One of the major flaws in the Articles of Confederation, some thought, was the amending process: changing that document required the unanimous approval of the thirteen colonies. The Framers imag-

TABLE 1-3 Methods of Amending the Constitution

Proposed By	Ratified By	Used For
Two-thirds vote in both houses of Congress	State legislatures in three-fourths of the states	26 amendments
Two-thirds vote in both houses of Congress	Ratifying conventions in three-fourths of the states	21st amendment
Constitutional convention (called at the request of two-thirds of the states)	State legislatures in three-fourths of the states	Never used
Constitutional convention (called at the request of two-thirds of the states)	Ratifying conventions in three-fourths of the states	Never used

BOX I-1 AMENDMENTS PROPOSED BY CONGRESS
BUT REJECTED BY THE STATES

■ The first would have empowered Congress to regulate the proportion of members of the House of Representatives once the population went beyond 100,000 persons per Representative.

■ This amendment, proposed in the second session of the 11th Congress, reflected a suspicion of all things royal dating back to Plymouth Rock. It would have stripped citizenship from anyone who "shall accept, claim, receive or retain any title of nobility or honour, or shall, without the consent of Congress, accept and retain any present pension, office or emolument of any kind whatever, from emperor, king, prince or foreign power...."

■ On March 2, 1861, two days before Abraham Lincoln's inauguration, proslavery forces gathered the votes to propose an amendment that would have "settled" the issue of slavery. It read: "No Amendment shall be made to the Constitution which will authorize or give to Congress the power to abolish or interfere, within any state, with the domestic institutions thereof, including that of persons held to labor or service by the laws of said State."

Five weeks later, Union forces at Fort Sumter were fired upon, and a Civil War was under way over slavery, a domestic institution concerning persons held to labor or service by the laws of certain states.

■ The Child Labor Amendment was proposed June 2, 1924. It would have given Congress power to "limit, regulate, and prohibit the labor of persons under 18 years of age." Section 2 would have suspended any state laws that might contravene regulations established by Congress.

Subsequent federal controls accepted by the Supreme Court, such as the Fair Labor Standards Act of 1938, have pretty much obviated the need for such an amendment. However, a retired top-ranking labor leader said in 1986 that President Ronald Reagan's proposal to establish a lowered minimum wage to help unskilled teenagers obtain summer employment was "proof that a Child Labor Amendment is still needed."

■ The Equal Rights Amendment (ERA), stating that "equality of rights under the law shall not be denied or abridged by the United States or by any State on account of sex," was proposed in March 1972. A seven-year deadline was given an unprecedented three-year extension. That deadline expired in 1982.

■ An amendment to give the District of Columbia representation in Congress was proposed by Congress in 1978. It read: "For purposes of representation in the Congress, election of the President and Vice President, and Article V of this Constitution, the District [of Columbia] ... shall be treated as though it were a State."

The amendment also would have obviated the Twenty-third Amendment, which gave D.C. residents the right to vote in presidential elections. The measure expired August 22, 1985.

SOURCE: From *The Constitution of the United States: An Unfolding Story,* 2d ed., by J. T. Keenan, 45–46. Copyright © 1988 by The Dorsey Press. Reprinted by permission of the publisher, Brooks/Cole, Pacific Grove, Calif.

ined an amending procedure that would be "bendable but not trendable, tough but not insurmountable, responsive to genuine waves of popular desire, yet impervious to self-serving campaigns of factional groups."[20] Hence, in Article V, they specified procedures for altering the Constitution *(see Table 1-3).* The Constitution can be amended in one of four ways. But, perhaps because the First Congress chose the con-

gressional proposing and state legislative ratification method for the Bill of Rights, that way has been used most often. Indeed, all but the Twenty-first Amendment, which repealed prohibition, followed that approach.

That only twenty-seven amendments have made it through Congress and the states and that twenty-six have done so through one route should not be taken to mean that other amendments or other approaches have not been proposed. In fact, through 1994 Con-

20. Keenan, *Constitution of the United States,* 41.

gress had considered more than 10,000 amendments and sent 33 of them to the states *(see Box 1-1)*. Attempts at using other proposal methods are not unusual.[21] At present, the states are only two votes short of requesting Congress to create a national convention to consider a balanced budget amendment.

THE SUPREME COURT AND THE AMENDMENT PROCESS

So far, our discussion of the amendment process has not mentioned the president or the Supreme Court. The reason is that neither has any formal constitutional role in it. We do not want to suggest, however, that these institutions have nothing to do with the process; both have significant, albeit informal, functions. Presidents often instigate and support proposals for constitutional amendments. Indeed, virtually every chief executive has wanted some alteration to the Constitution. In his first inaugural address, George Washington urged adoption of a bill of rights;[22] 200 years later, George Bush urged quick ratification of an amendment to prohibit flag desecration. The Court also has played at least two important roles in the process. First, it has served as an "instigator." Of the seventeen additions to the Constitution after the Bill of Rights, Congress proposed four specifically to overturn Supreme Court decisions *(see Box 1-2)*. Many consider one of these—the Fourteenth—the single most important addition since 1791.

Many of the 10,000 or so proposals considered by Congress were aimed at similar objectives, among them the failed Child Labor[23] and Equal Rights amend-

ments, both of which emanated, at least in part, from Supreme Court rulings rejecting their premises. These two ultimately were passed by Congress, but not ratified by the states. More recently, Congress has considered the following amendments, all of which were aimed at overturning Court decisions: a human life amendment that would make abortions illegal (in response to *Roe v. Wade,* 1973); a school prayer amendment that would allow public school children to engage in prayer (in response to *Engel v. Vitale,* 1962, and *School District of Abington Township v. Schempp,* 1963); and a flag desecration amendment that would prohibit mutilation of the American flag (in response to *Texas v. Johnson,* 1989).

Second, the Court has been asked to interpret Article V, which deals with the amendment process, but it has been hesitant to do so. Consider *Coleman v. Miller* (1939), which involved the actions of the Kansas legislature over the Child Labor Amendment. Proposed by Congress in 1924, the amendment stated, "The Congress shall have power to limit, regulate, and prohibit the labor of persons under eighteen years of age." In January 1925 Kansas legislators rejected the Child Labor Amendment. The issue arose again, however, when the state senate reconsidered the amendment in January 1937. At that time, the legislative body split, 20-20, with the lieutenant governor casting the decisive vote in favor of the amendment. Members of the Kansas legislature (mostly those who had opposed the proposal) challenged the 1937 vote on two grounds: they questioned the ability of the lieutenant governor to break the tie and, more generally, the reconsideration of an amendment that previously had been rejected. In particular, the legislators asserted that the amendment had "lost its vitality" because "of that rejection and the failure of ratification within a reasonable time limit." Writing for the Court, Chief Justice Charles Evans Hughes refused to address this point. Rather, he asserted that the suit raised questions, particularly those pertaining to recision, that were political and, thus, nonjusticiable. In his words,

---

21. Perhaps the most widely reported was Sen. Everett Dirksen's effort to get the states to request a national convention with the purpose of overturning *Reynolds v. Sims,* the Supreme Court's 1964 reapportionment decision. He failed, by one state, to do so.

22. See Pritchett, *American Constitution,* 368.

23. In 1916 Congress passed a child labor law that prohibited the shipment in interstate commerce of anything made by children under age fourteen. When the Court struck down this act (and another like it) as an unconstitutional use of congressional power (*Hammer v. Dagenhart,* 1918), Congress proposed a Child Labor Amendment. See Clement E. Vose, *Constitutional Change* (Lexington, Mass.: Lexington Books, 1972).

BOX 1–2 FOUR AMENDMENTS THAT OVERTURNED SUPREME COURT DECISIONS

THE ELEVENTH

When Chisholm sued Georgia in 1793 and the Supreme Court dropped a bombshell on states-righters by agreeing to hear the case, Anti-Federalists were outraged. Congress responded swiftly by proposing the Eleventh Amendment, which was ratified by the requisite three-fourths of the states within a year, though not declared ratified until 1798. The amendment protects states against suits by citizens of another state or of another country.

THE FOURTEENTH

Congress and the High Court tangled again after the *Dred Scott v. Sandford* (sometimes spelled Dread Scott by abolitionists) case of 1857. Nine separate decisions were rendered on this case, but Chief Justice Roger B. Taney spoke for the "majority" in declaring that slaves could not be citizens and that Congress had exceeded its purview in prohibiting slavery in the territories. A Civil War and a few years of Reconstruction intervened before the Fourteenth Amendment, which conferred citizenship on all persons born or naturalized in the United States, could correct the Scott ruling.

THE SIXTEENTH

Congress next "got around the Supreme Court" through the passage of the Sixteenth Amendment, which legalized the income tax. In 1895 the Court turned down a federal income tax law on grounds that the Constitution requires taxes to be apportioned among the states proportionately according to population. But, in a spirit of cooperation, the Court invited Congress to overthrow the objection by means of an amendment. Congress proposed the Sixteenth Amendment in 1909, and the states ratified it in 1913.

THE TWENTY-SIXTH

President Richard Nixon, although signing a change in the Voting Rights Act that allowed eighteen-year-olds to vote in federal, state, and local elections, expressed doubt that the law was constitutional. Suit was speedily arranged, and the Court confirmed the president's misgivings in a 5–4 rejection that said, in effect: "The Congress does not have jurisdiction over state and local elections."

At a time when eighteen-year-olds were losing their lives in Vietnam, the Twenty-sixth Amendment had wide popular approval. In record time it was proposed by Congress in March 1971 and ratified in June, giving eighteen-year-olds the right to vote in national, state, and local elections.

SOURCE: From *The Constitution of the United States: An Unfolding Story,* 2d ed., by J. T. Keenan, 42–43. Copyright © 1988 by The Dorsey Press. Reprinted by permission of the publisher, Brooks/Cole, Pacific Grove, Calif.

"the ultimate authority" over the amendment process was Congress, not the Court.

As one authority noted, "From the opinions filed in ... *Coleman* ... it would seem that the Court regards all questions relating to the interpretation of [Article V] as 'political questions,' and hence as addressed exclusively by Congress."[24] That observation was borne out in one of the Court's most recent Article V cases, *NOW v. Idaho* (1982). At issue was a 1978 act of Congress that extended the original deadline for state ratification of the Equal Rights Amendment from 1979 to 1982 and rejected a clause "that would have allowed state legislatures to rescind their prior approval."[25] In the wake of a strong anti-ERA movement, Idaho, which had passed the amendment in the early 1970s, decided to ignore federal law and retract its original vote.[26] The National Organization for Women challenged the state's action, and in 1982 the Court docketed the case for argument. But, upon the request of the solicitor

24. Harold Chase and Craig Ducat, *Edwin Corwin's The Constitution* (Princeton, N.J.: Princeton University Press, 1978), 268.

25. Nancy McGlen and Karen O'Connor, *Women's Rights* (New York: Praeger, 1983), 379.

26. Three other states, Nebraska, Kentucky, and Tennessee, also rescinded.

general, it dismissed the suit as moot: the congressionally extended time period for ratification had run out, and the controversy was no longer viable.

Before the decade is over, the Court might be confronted with even more difficult questions. If the drive for a balanced budget amendment succeeds in attaining the support of two-thirds of the states, the Court might be in a position to consider issues relating to the creation of a second constitutional convention. Would the delegates to such a convention deliberate only the amendments under consideration or would they be able to take up any or all parts of the Constitution? Addressing this question might be one of the most significant tasks the Supreme Court has ever faced. Remember that the 1787 Philadelphia delegates met solely to amend the Articles of Confederation, but ended by reframing the entire system of government. Perhaps that is why those same men were so vehemently opposed to the notion of holding another convention to propose a bill of rights. As Jefferson wrote, a second such convention could "endanger the most valuable parts of the system" and significantly weaken our government.[27]

In any event, it may be a while before the Court must address this delicate issue. Since 1983 no state has passed the balanced budget amendment, a situation some credit to the formation of an anticonvention movement that strongly opposes any organized tinkering with the original document. And, in a way, as one writer notes, the success of this countermovement "is testimony to the success of the first convention."[28] Undoubtedly this assertion is so: as the Bill of Rights enters its third century, we have only to remind ourselves that it is the heart of the world's oldest surviving ruling charter.

27. Quoted in *The Origins of the American Constitution*, ed. Michael Kammen (New York: Penguin Books, 1986), 372.

28. Richard Lacayo, "Is It Broke: Should We Fix It?" *Time*, July 6, 1987, 55.

CHAPTER 1
APPROACHES TO SUPREME COURT DECISION MAKING

T H E   B A L A N C E of this book is devoted to narrative and opinion excerpts that show how the U.S. Supreme Court has interpreted many of the amendments to the Constitution. As a student approaching civil liberties, rights, and justice, perhaps for the first time, you may think it is odd that the subject requires 836 pages of text. After all, in length, the Constitution and the amendments to it could fit easily into many Court decisions. Moreover, the document itself—its language—seems so clear.

First appearances, however, can be deceiving. Even apparently clear constitutional scriptures do not necessarily lend themselves to clear constitutional interpretation. For example, according to the First Amendment, "Congress shall make no law ... prohibiting the free exercise" of religion. Sounds simple enough. But could you, based on those words, answer the following questions, all of which have been posed to the Court?

• May a state refuse to give unemployment benefits to an individual who quits her job because her employer wants her to work on Saturdays, the day of rest in her religion?
• May the military retain a policy that forbids Jews in service from wearing yarmulkes?
• May a city prohibit the sacrificing of animals for religious purposes?
• May a school board force students to salute the flag and recite the pledge of allegiance, practices that violate their religious beliefs?

What these and other questions arising from the different guarantees contained in the Constitution illustrate is that a gap sometimes exists between the document's words and reality. Although the language may seem quite explicit, its meaning can be elusive and difficult to follow. Accordingly, justices have developed various approaches to resolving disputes. In this chapter, we consider those approaches, as well as those that have been suggested by generations of scholars who have sought to unravel the mysteries of judicial decision making and to isolate those factors that determine case outcomes.

As you might imagine, there is no shortage of explanations for Court decisions, but they can be categorized into two groups: the legally relevant and the extralegal. Here, we review these approaches, strains of which appear in the justices' opinions in the chapters that follow.

LEGALLY RELEVANT APPROACHES

Legally relevant approaches to U.S. Supreme Court decision making emanate from expectations of how our society expects justices to behave, particularly what they should and should *not* consider to reach decisions. Under this school of thought, jurists are supposed to shed all their personal biases, preferences, and partisan attachments when they take their seats on the bench, for those things, it is argued, should have no bearing on Court decisions. Rather, justices ought to reach decisions in accord with factors that have some grounding in the law.

Because the justices themselves consider legally relevant factors appropriate criteria for reaching decisions, they often say they use them to resolve disputes. Whether they actually do is for you to determine as you read the cases to come. That is, you will need to think about this question: Do the justices use legally relevant approaches to reach decisions or do they reach their decisions first and then use legally relevant approaches to justify them? Before you can address this question, however, it is important to have some sense of specific factors that comprise the legally relevant category. Below, we discuss six of the most important and describe the judicial philosophies that support their use in decision making.

The Doctrine of Original Intent

In a famous Supreme Court case, *Barron v. Baltimore* (1833), Chief Justice John Marshall rejected the view that the Bill of Rights covered state actions. His reasoning: the Framers of the Constitution did not intend for it to do so. About 150 years later, Chief Justice William H. Rehnquist used the same grounds to find that cartoon parodies, however obnoxious, constitute protected expression.

Undoubtedly, between Marshall and Rehnquist, other chief justices and associate justices have looked to the intent of the Framers of the Constitution and its amendments to reach conclusions about extant disputes.[1] But why? What possible relevance could their intentions have for today's controversies? Advocates of this approach offer several answers. First, they assert that the Framers acted in a calculated manner. That is, they knew what they were doing, so why should we disregard their precepts? One adherent said, "Those who framed the Constitution chose their words carefully; they debated at great length the most minute points. The language they chose meant something. It is incumbent upon the Court to determine what that meaning was."[2]

Second, if they scrutinize the intent of the Framers, justices can deduce "constitutional truths," which they can apply to cases. Doing so, as Robert Bork and others argue, would produce neutral principles of law and eliminate value-laden decisions.[3] Consider, for example, speech advocating the violent overthrow of the government. Suppose the government enacted a law prohibiting such expression and arrested members of a radical political party for violating it. Justices could scrutinize such a law in several ways. An ideologue—say, a liberal—might conclude solely because of these liberal values that the First Amendment prohibits such a ban on expression. Conservative jurists might reach the opposite conclusion, again, because their ideology dictates such an outcome.

Neither would be proper jurisprudence in Bork's opinion, because both are value laden, and ideological preferences should not creep into the law. Bork favors an examination of the Framers' intent as a way to keep the law value free. In 1971 he wrote,

> Speech advocating violent overthrow is ... not [protected] "political speech" ... as that term must be defined by a Madisonian system of government. It is not political speech because it violates constitutional truths about processes and because it is not aimed at a new definition of political truth by a legislative majority.[4]

Finally, supporters of this mode of analysis argue that it fosters stability in law. According to some ob-

---

1. Given the subject of this volume, we deal here exclusively with the intent of the Framers of the U.S. Constitution and its amendments. One also could apply this approach to statutory construction by considering the intent of those who drafted the laws in question.

2. Edwin Meese III, Address Before the American Bar Association, July 9, 1983, Washington, D.C.

3. See Robert Bork, "Neutral Principles and Some First Amendment Problems," *Indiana Law Journal* 47 (1971): 1–35.

4. Ibid., 31.

servers, the law today is far too fluid; it changes with the ideological whims of the justices, creating havoc for those who must implement and interpret Court decisions. Lower court judges, lawyers, and even ordinary citizens do not know if today's rights will be there tomorrow. Following a jurisprudence of original intent would eliminate such confusion because "by seeking to judge policies in light of principles, rather than remodel principles in light of policies, the Court could avoid both the charge of incoherence and the charge of being either too conservative or too liberal."[5]

Although many Supreme Court opinions contemplate the original intent of the Framers, and arguments in favor of such an approach seem to have merit, this view is not without its critics. One reason for the controversy is that the doctrine became quite politicized during the Reagan presidency. Those who advocated it, particularly former attorney general Edwin Meese and defeated Supreme Court nominee Bork, were widely viewed as conservatives who were using the doctrine to attain their own ideological ends.

Others, however, have raised several more concrete objections to this jurisprudence. Some argue that if the justices employed only this approach, the Constitution would lose its applicability and be rendered useless. Justice William J. Brennan, Jr., has asserted:

We current Justices read the Constitution in the only way that we can: as Twentieth Century Americans. We look to the history of the time of the framing and to the intervening history of interpretation. But the ultimate question must be, what do the words of the text mean in our time. For the genius of the Constitution rests not in any static meaning it might have had in a world that is dead and gone, but in the adaptability of its great principles to cope with current problems and current needs. What the constitutional fundamentals meant to the wisdom of other times cannot be their measure to the vision of our time. Similarly, what those fundamentals mean for us, our descendants will learn, cannot be the measure to the vision of their time.[6]

A second criticism is that the Constitution embodies not one intent, but many. Political scientists Jeffrey A. Segal and Harold J. Spaeth pose some interesting questions: "Who were the Framers? All fifty-five of the delegates who showed up at one time or another in Philadelphia during the summer of 1787? Some came and went.... Some probably had not read it. Assuredly, they were not all of a single mind. Apart from the delegates who refused to sign, should not the delegates to the various state conventions that were called to ratify the Constitution also be counted as Framers?"[7] Historian Arthur Schlesinger, Jr., provided a poignant example of this ambiguity when he noted that Meese attacked "the Dred Scott decision [holding that blacks did not enjoy the same constitutional status as whites] as a violation of original intent. Yet Chief Justice Roger B. Taney based his decision squarely on 'original intent.'" Such a discrepancy led Schlesinger to ask: "Whose version of original intent are we to believe: Roger Taney's in 1857 or Edwin Meese's in 1985."[8]

Finally, from which sources should justices divine the original intentions of the Framers? Obviously, they could look at the records of the constitutional debates and at the Founders' journals and papers, but those documents often fail to provide a single clear message. Justice Robert H. Jackson wrote in *Youngstown Sheet and Tube Co. v. Sawyer* (1952):

Just what our forefathers did envision, or would have envisioned had they foreseen modern conditions, must be divined from materials almost as enigmatic as the dreams Joseph was called upon to interpret for Pharaoh. A century and a half of partisan debate and scholarly specification yields no net result but only supplies more or less apt quotations from respected sources on each side of any question. They largely cancel each other.

5. Meese, Address.

6. William J. Brennan, Jr., Address to the Text and Teaching Symposium, Georgetown University, October 12, 1985, Washington, D.C.

7. Jeffrey A. Segal and Harold J. Spaeth, *The Supreme Court and the Attitudinal Model* (Cambridge: Cambridge University Press, 1993), 39.

8. Arthur Schlesinger, Jr., "On 'Original Intent,'" *Wall Street Journal*, January 17, 1986.

Literalism

On the surface, literalism resembles the doctrine of original intent: it puts a premium on the Constitution. But this is where the similarity ends. In an effort to prevent the infusion of new meanings from sources outside the text of the Constitution, original intent adherents seek to deduce constitutional truths by examining the intended meanings behind the words. Literalists consider only the plain meaning of the words in the Constitution (their literal meaning) and apply them to disputes. This distinction can lead to some extraordinary differences in case outcomes. If we use again the example of speech aimed at overthrowing the U.S. government, original intent advocates would hold that the meaning behind the First Amendment prohibits such expression. Literalists, on the other hand, would scrutinize the words of the First Amendment—"Congress shall make no law ... abridging freedom of speech"—and read them literally: *no law* means *no law.* Hence, any statute infringing on speech, even a law that prohibits expression advocating the overthrow of the government, would violate the First Amendment.

These two views sometime overlap. When it comes to the right to privacy, particularly its use to create other rights, such as legalized abortion, some original intent adherents and literalists would reach the same conclusion: that it does not exist. The former would argue that it was not the intent of the Framers to confer privacy; the latter, that because the Constitution fails to guarantee explicitly such a right, Americans do not automatically possess it.

Although strains of literalism run through the opinions of many justices, Hugo Black is most closely associated with this view. During his thirty-four-year tenure on the Court, Black reiterated the literalist philosophy. His own words best describe his position:

My view is, without deviation, without exception, without any ifs, buts, or whereases, that freedom of speech means that government shall not do anything to people ... either for the views they have or the views they express or the words they speak or write. Some people would have you believe that this is a very radical position, and maybe it is. But all I am doing is following what to me is the clear wording of the First Amendment.... As I have said innumerable times before I simply believe that "Congress shall make no law" means Congress shall make no law.... Thus we have the absolute command of the First Amendment that no law shall be passed by Congress abridging freedom of speech or the press.[9]

Why did Black advocate literalism? Like original intent adherents, he viewed it as a value-free form of jurisprudence. If justices looked only at the words of the Constitution, their decisions would not reflect ideological or political values, but rather those of the document. Black's opinions provide good illustrations. Although he almost always supported claims of free *speech* against government challenges, he refused to extend constitutional protection to *expression* that was not precisely speech. For example, he asserted that activities such as flag burning and the wearing of arm bands, even if designed to express political views, fell outside of the speech protected by the First Amendment.

Despite the high regard scholars have for Black, many have actively attacked his jurisprudence. One asserts that it led him to "quixotic" views, particularly of the coverage of the First Amendment.[10] For example, most analysts and justices—even those considered liberal—agree that obscene materials fall outside of First Amendment protection and that states can prohibit their dissemination. But, in opinion after opinion, Black clung to the view that no publication could be banned on the grounds that it was obscene. In *Smith v. California* (1959) Black wrote separately to express his displeasure with the use of legal standards

9. Hugo L. Black, *A Constitutional Faith* (New York: Knopf, 1969), 45–46.
10. See John Hart Ely, *Democracy and Distrust* (Cambridge: Harvard University Press, 1980).

BOX 1-1 HUGO LAFAYETTE BLACK (1937–1971)

THE EIGHTH child of a Baptist store-keeper and farmer, Hugo Black was born February 27, 1886, in Harlan, Alabama, and spent the first years of his life in the hill country near there. When he was still a youngster, his family moved to Ashland, a larger community where his father's business prospered. Black attended the local schools in Ashland and, after trying one year at Birmingham Medical College, decided to study law. At eighteen he entered the University of Alabama Law School at Tuscaloosa.

Receiving his LL.B. in 1906, Black returned to Ashland and set up his first law practice. The following year a fire destroyed his office and library, and Black decided to move to Birmingham. There he quickly established a relationship with labor by defending the United Mine Workers strikers in 1908. Black also developed an expertise for arguing personal injury cases.

BLACK was named a part-time police court judge in Birmingham in 1910 and was elected county solicitor (public prosecutor) for Jefferson County in 1914. As solicitor, he gained a measure of local fame for his investigation of reports of the brutal means police employed while questioning suspects at the notorious Bessemer jail. When he left the solicitor's post in 1917 to join the World War I effort, Black had succeeded in emptying a docket that had once held as many as 3,000 pending cases.

His brief military career kept him within the borders of the United States. He returned to practice law in Birmingham in 1918 and continued to expand his practice, still specializing in labor law and personal injury cases. He married Josephine Foster, February 23, 1921. They had two sons and one daughter. In 1923 Black joined the Ku Klux Klan, but resigned from the organization two years later just before he ran for the Democratic nomination for the Senate seat held by Democrat Oscar Underwood. Campaigning as the poor man's candidate, Black won the party's endorsement and the subsequent election. He entered the Senate in 1927 and immediately began to study history and the classics at the Library of Congress to compensate for his lack of a liberal education.

During his two terms in the Senate Black used committee hearings to investigate several areas, including abuses of marine and airline subsidies and the activities of lobbying groups. In 1933 he introduced a bill to create a thirty-hour work week. This legislation, after several alterations, was finally passed in 1938 as the Fair Labor Standards Act. One of the Senate's strongest supporters of President Franklin Roosevelt, Black spoke out in favor of his 1937 Court-packing scheme and other New Deal programs. Black's support for the administration and his strong liberal instincts led the president to pick him as his choice to fill the Supreme Court seat vacated by the retirement of Willis Van Devanter. Black was confirmed by the Senate, 63–16, on August 17, 1937.

Black's previous affiliation with the Ku Klux Klan was widely reported in the national news media after his confirmation. The furor quickly quieted, however, when the new justice admitted in a dramatic radio broadcast that he had indeed been a member of the Klan but added that he had resigned many years before and would comment no further. During his Court career, Black always carried in his pocket a copy of the United States Constitution.

Black's first wife died in 1951, and he married Elizabeth Seay DeMerritte, September 11, 1957. He retired from the Court September 17, 1971, after suffering an impairing stroke. He died eight days later in Washington.

SOURCE: Adapted from Elder Witt, *Guide to the U.S. Supreme Court*, 2d ed. (Washington, D.C.: Congressional Quarterly, 1990), 860.

that may allow for the suppression of obscene material. He asserted:

Certainly the First Amendment's language leaves no room for interference that abridgments of speech and press can be made just because they are slight. That Amendment provides, in simple words, that "Congress shall make no law . . . abridging the freedom of speech, or of the press." I read "no law . . . abridging" to mean *no law abridging*. The First Amendment, which is the supreme law of the land, has thus fixed its own value on freedom of speech and press by putting these freedoms wholly "beyond the reach" of *federal* power to abridge. No other provision of the Constitution purports to dilute the scope of the unequivocal commands of the First Amendment. Consequently, I do not believe that any federal agencies, including Congress and the Court, have power or authority to subordinate speech and press to what they think are "more important interests." The contrary notion is, in my judgment, court-made not Constitution-made.[11]

Even those who *generally* agreed with literalism thought such a view went a bit too far.

A second objection raised is that literalism can result in wholly inconsistent outcomes. For example, is it really sensible for a literalist to hold that obscenity is constitutionally protected, while the desecration of the flag is not? Segal and Spaeth raise yet a third problem with literalism: it supposes a precision in the English language that simply does not exist. Not only may words, including those used by the Framers, have multiple meanings, but also the meanings themselves may be quite contrary. For example, the common legal word *sanction*, as Segal and Spaeth note, means to punish *and* to reward.[12] How, then, would a literalist construe it?

Meaning of the Words

The "meaning of the words" approach to constitutional interpretation, most associated with W. W. Crosskey, has its roots in both literalism and original-

ism: it emphasizes the words of the Constitution at the time the Framers wrote them.[13] But there are differences. While literalists stress the words themselves, this mode emphasizes their meaning; and while originalism "places a premium upon reasoning that is historically grounded, the meaning of the words focuses on lexicographic skill."[14] In other words, "the 'meaning' mode attempts to define the words of the Constitution according to what they meant at the time the document or its amendment was written."[15]

The merits of this approach are similar to those of literalism and originalism. By focusing on how the Framers defined their own words and then applying their definitions to disputes over those constitutional provisions containing them, this approach seeks to generate value-free and ideology-free jurisprudence. Of even greater importance, its adherents argue, is that it attempts to "preserve some sense of stability and continuity in the agreements and understandings on which legitimate governmental power is based."[16]

Chief Justice Marshall's opinion in *Gibbons v. Ogden* (1824), which, in part, involved a dispute over the congressional power to regulate interstate commerce, provides a particularly good illustration of the value of this approach. As part of his decision, Marshall felt it necessary to determine the meaning of the word *commerce*. Rather than fashion his own definition, Marshall turned to how the Framers defined it at the time they wrote it:

All America understands, and has uniformly understood, the word "commerce" to comprehend navigation. It was so understood, and must have been so understood, when the constitution was framed. The power over commerce, including navigation, was one of the primary objects for which the people of America adopted their government, and must have been contemplated in forming it.

---

11. Smith v. California, 361 U.S. 147 at 157–158 (1959).
12. Segal and Spaeth, *The Supreme Court and the Attitudinal Model*, 34.

13. See W. W. Crosskey, *Politics and the Constitution in the History of the United States* (Chicago: University of Chicago Press, 1953).
14. David W. Rohde and Harold J. Spaeth, *Supreme Court Decision Making* (San Francisco: W. H. Freeman, 1976), 41.
15. Ibid.
16. C. Herman Pritchett, *Constitutional Law of the Federal System* (Englewood Cliffs, N.J.: Prentice-Hall, 1984), 37.

Even modern-day justices occasionally invoke this approach. In *Nixon v. United States* (1993), the Rehnquist Court considered a challenge to the procedures the Senate used to impeach a federal judge, Walter L. Nixon, Jr. Rather than having the entire Senate try the case, a special twelve-member committee heard the case and reported to the full body. Nixon argued that this procedure violated Article I of the Constitution, which states, "The Senate shall have the sole power to try all Impeachments." But before he addressed Nixon's claim, Chief Justice Rehnquist sought to determine whether courts had any business resolving such disputes. In so doing, he used a meaning of the words approach to consider the word *try* in Article I:

Petitioner argues that the word "try" in the first sentence imposes by implication an additional requirement on the Senate in that the proceedings must be in the nature of a judicial trial.... There are several difficulties with this position which lead us ultimately to reject it. The word "try," both in 1787 and later, has considerably broader meanings than those to which petitioner would limit it. Older dictionaries define try as "[t]o examine" or "[t]o examine as a judge." See 2 S. Johnson, A Dictionary of the English Language (1785). In more modern usage the term has various meanings. For example, try can mean "to examine or investigate judicially," "to conduct the trial of," or "to put to the test by experiment, investigation...." Webster's Third New International Dictionary (1971).

Like the other modes we have examined, the meaning of the words approach is not without its critics. One objection is similar to that leveled at originalism: it is too static. Political scientist C. Herman Pritchett noted that like originalism, it can "make a nation the prisoner of its past, and reject any constitutional development save constitutional amendment."[17] Because sea-faring vessels were the primary instruments of commerce in 1787, it was easy for Marshall to conclude that commerce "comprehend[s]" navigation. Although one could try to make an equally compelling case today for, say, airplanes, it would be a far more difficult task.

Another criticism is that the "original meaning may be as difficult to establish as original intent."[18] In our discussion of originalism, we pointed out that it was often impossible to determine the intent of the Framers. Attempting to understand what they meant by each word can be just as daunting, requiring the development of a specialized dictionary, which could take years of research to compile and still not have any value—determinate or otherwise. Even Chief Justice Marshall seemed to recognize this, when he wrote:

A Constitution ... [which] would partake of the prolixity of a legal code ... could scarcely be embraced by the human mind. It would, probably, never be understood by the public. Its nature, therefore, requires that only its great outlines should be marked, its important objects designated, and the minor ingredients which compose those objects be deduced from the nature of the objects themselves.[19]

Logical Reasoning

Unlike originalism or the meaning of the words approach, logical reasoning is not necessarily dependent on historical interpretations of particular constitutional provisions. Rather, it suggests that judges do "what all intelligent people do when obliged to interpret a document: analyze its terms, then try to discern the premises of its arguments, and the conclusions to which they lead."[20] Logical analysis often takes the form of a syllogism, consisting of a major premise, which "sets forth a proposition"; a minor premise, which "contains an assertion related to the major premise"; and a conclusion, which "logically follows" from both major and minor premises.[21]

Marshall's opinion in *Marbury v. Madison* (1803), provides an oft-cited example of logical reasoning in action:

17. Ibid.

18. Ibid.

19. *McCulloch v. Maryland*, 4 Wheat. 316 (1819).

20. Walter F. Murphy, James E. Fleming, and William F. Harris, *American Constitutional Interpretation* (Mineola, N.Y.: Foundation Press), 302–303.

21. Rohde and Spaeth, *Supreme Court Decision Making*, 42.

MAJOR PREMISE: A law repugnant to the Constitution is void.

MINOR PREMISE: This law is repugnant to the Constitution.

CONCLUSION: Therefore, this law is void.

The beauty of logical analysis, as this example illustrates, is that the resulting decision takes on an objective, perhaps even a scientific, aura. In other words, Marshall's syllogism suggests that anybody with a logical mind would reach the same conclusion. But is this necessarily so? Consider another syllogism:

MAJOR PREMISE: Sweden has many storks.

MINOR PREMISE: Storks deliver babies.

CONCLUSION: Therefore, Sweden has many babies.

We know that storks do not deliver babies, and therein lies the major problem with logical analysis: it "exists independently of factual or empirical analysis." Therefore, "almost any conclusion can be given logical form."[22] To understand why this assertion is correct, compare the two syllogisms. If we assume that the major premises of both are accurate, then the soundness of their conclusions rests with the factual accuracy of their minor premises. Obviously, storks do not deliver babies, but is Marshall's minor premise any more believable or, more to the point, logically driven? Put another way, can logic reveal whether a particular law is repugnant to the Constitution?

To many the answer is no. Political scientists David Rohde and Harold Spaeth suggest that logical reasoning "enables judges to make decisions compatibly with their policy preferences and at the same time causing their opinions and decisions to exhibit a semblance of order and a quality of connectedness."[23] Justice Oliver Wendell Holmes, Jr., put it this way:

The life of the law has not been logic: it has been experience. The felt necessities of the time, the prevalent moral and political theories, intuitions of public policy, avowed or unconscious, even the prejudices which judges share with their fellow-men, have had a good deal more to do than the syllogism in determining the rules by which men should be governed.[24]

Stare Decisis

Translated from Latin, stare decisis means "to abide by, or adhere to, decided cases." What the term suggests is that, as a general rule, jurists should decide cases on the basis of previously established precedent. In shorthand terms, judicial tribunals should "honor prior rulings."[25] Many assert that Chief Justice Earl Warren did just that in *Watkins v. United States* (1957) to resolve one of Watkins's claims, that some questions put to him by a congressional committee violated his First Amendment rights. Warren used an earlier precedent, *United States v. Rumely*, to reach a decision favorable to Watkins:

The Court recognized the restraints of the Bill of Rights upon congressional investigations in United States v. Rumely.... It was concluded that, when First Amendment rights are threatened, the delegation of power to [a] committee [to conduct investigations] must be clearly revealed in its charter.[26]

The benefits of this approach are fairly evident. Ralph Rossum and G. Alan Tarr wrote, "Reliance on precedent ... adds stability, continuity, and predictability to the entire legal profession."[27] Chief Justice Harlan F. Stone acknowledged the value of precedent in a somewhat more ironic way: "the rule of *stare decisis* embodies a wise policy because it is often more important that a rule of law be settled than that it be settled right."[28] The message, however, is the same: if the Court adheres to past decisions, it provides some

24. *The Common Law,* quoted by Max Lerner in *The Mind and Faith of Justice Holmes* (New York: Modern Library, 1943), 51–52.

25. Louis Fisher, *Constitutional Dialogues* (Princeton, N.J.: Princeton University Press, 1988), 80.

26. *Watkins v. United States,* 354 U.S. 178, at 198 (1957).

27. Ralph A. Rossum and G. Alan Tarr, *American Constitutional Law,* 3d ed. (New York: St. Martin's, 1991), 4.

28. *United States v. Underwriters Association,* 322 U.S. 533, 579 (1944).

22. Ibid., 43.   23. Ibid.

direction to all who labor in the legal enterprise. Lower court judges know how they should and should not decide cases; lawyers can frame their arguments in accord with the lessons of past cases; legislators understand what they can and cannot enact or regulate, and so forth. In addition, as Sheldon Goldman notes, the "rule of precedent symbolizes that we are dealing with a court of law as distinguished from a legislative body."[29] It is one of the features that makes the judiciary unique.

Precedent, then, is an important and useful factor in Supreme Court decision making. It is interesting to note that the Court rarely reverses itself (only about 250 times over its entire history).[30] Even modern-day Courts, as Table 1-1 shows, have been loath to overrule precedents. In the thirty-eight terms covered in Table 1-1, the Court has overturned only 105 precedents or about 2.8 per term. "By comparison," Segal and Spaeth point out, "it declared more than four times as many laws unconstitutional during this same period."[31] What is more, the justices almost always cite previous rulings in their decisions; indeed, it is the rare Court opinion that does *not* mention other cases.[32] Finally, several scholars have verified that precedent helps to explain Court decisions in some areas of the law. In one study, analysts found that the Court reacted quite consistently to legal doctrine presented in more than fifteen years of death penalty litigation. Put differently, using precedent from past cases, the researchers could correctly categorize the outcomes (for or against the death penalty) in 75 percent of sixty-four cases decided since 1972.[33] Scholarly work considering

TABLE 1-1 Precedents Overruled, 1953–1990 Terms

Chief Justice	Number of Terms Served	Number of Overruled Precedents	Average Number of Overrulings Per Term
Warren	16	42	2.6
Burger	17	44	2.6
Rehnquist	5	19	3.8
Total	38	105	2.8

SOURCE: Jeffrey A. Segal and Harold J. Spaeth, *The Supreme Court and the Attitudinal Model* (Cambridge: Cambridge University Press, 1993), 51.

precedent in search and seizure litigation had similar success.[34]

Despite these data, we should not conclude that the justices necessarily follow this approach. Many allege that judicial appeal to precedent often is mere window dressing, used to hide ideologies and values, rather than a substantive form of analysis. There are several reasons for this allegation.

First, the Supreme Court has generated so much precedent that it is usually possible to find support for any conclusion. By way of proof, turn to any page of any opinion in this book and you probably will find the writers—both for the majority and the dissenters—citing precedent.

Second, it may be difficult to locate the rule of law emerging in a majority opinion and "technically, a court is bound to follow not everything stated in relevant precedent, but only the rule of law that was necessary for decision in that case, what is called the *ratio decidendi*."[35] Other points made in a given opinion— *obiter dicta*—have no legal weight, and judges are not bound by it. It is up to courts to separate the *ratio deci-*

29. Sheldon Goldman, *Constitutional Law*, 2d ed. (New York: Harper-Collins, 1991), 13.

30. Stephen L. Wasby, *The Supreme Court in the Federal Judicial System*, 4th ed. (Chicago: Nelson-Hall, 1993), 275.

31. Segal and Spaeth, *The Supreme Court and the Attitudinal Model*, 50.

32. Wasby, *The Supreme Court in the Federal Judicial System*, 275. It is also the rare justice who says that he or she does not use precedent as a guide. Most unusual, then, was Justice William O. Douglas, who frequently admitted that he would rather create a precedent than follow one.

33. Tracey E. George and Lee Epstein, "On the Nature of Supreme Court Decision Making," *American Political Science Review* 86 (1992): 323–337.

34. Jeffrey A. Segal, "Predicting Supreme Court Cases Probabilistically: The Search and Seizure Cases, 1962–1984," *American Political Science Review* (1984): 891–900.

35. Lawrence Baum, *The Supreme Court*, 3d ed. (Washington, D.C.: CQ Press, 1989), 123.

dendi from *dicta*. Doing so can be difficult, but it provides a way for justices to skirt precedent with which they do not agree. All they need to do is declare "portions of the reasoning upon which the previous decision was based to be *dicta*."[36] By the same token, justices can brush aside even the *ratio decidendi* when it suits their interests. Because the Supreme Court, at least today, is so selective about the cases it chooses to decide, it probably would not take a case for which clear precedent existed. Even in the past, two cases that were precisely identical would probably not be accepted.

What this means is that justices can always deal with "problematic" *ratio decidendi* by distinguishing the case at hand from those that have already been decided. The Court's later interpretation of the *Watkins* decision provides a good example. Just two years after it ruled in favor of John Watkins, the Court heard *Barenblatt v. United States* (1959), in which it looked again at whether a congressional committee could question an individual about his political beliefs and associations. Like Watkins, Barenblatt alleged that he could refuse to answer such questions because they infringed on his First Amendment rights. Nonetheless, the Court "distinguished the *Watkins* precedent by authorizing investigating committees to 'balance' the competing ... interests."[37]

Third, and most interesting, many justices recognize the limits of *stare decisis* in cases involving constitutional interpretation. As Justice William O. Douglas once wrote, a judge should support the Constitution, "not the gloss which his predecessors may have put on it."[38] But Justice Black may have said it best:

Ordinarily it is sound policy to adhere to prior decisions but this practice has quite properly never been a blind, inflexible rule. Courts are not omniscient. Like every other human agency, they too can profit from trial and error, from experience and reflection. As others have demonstrated, the principle commonly referred to as *stare decisis* has never been thought to extend so far as to prevent the courts from correcting their own errors.... Indeed, the Court has a special responsibility where questions of constitutional law are involved to review its decisions from time to time and where compelling reasons present themselves to refuse to follow erroneous precedents; otherwise mistakes in interpreting the Constitution are extremely difficult to alleviate and needlessly so.[39]

And, in fact, of the 105 precedents overruled between the 1953 and 1990 terms *(see Table 1-1)*, 68.6 percent involved constitutional issues.

Balancing Approaches

So far we have examined five modes of analysis that are not case specific, meaning that conclusions reached by literalists and original intent advocates, for example, on points of law would not waiver with the facts of a given case. Presumably, the original intent advocates would always hold that the First Amendment does not protect speech advocating the violent overthrow of the government, and the literalists would always reach precisely the opposite conclusion, regardless of the specific controversy at hand. Supporters of a balancing approach take a position that is more case specific than philosophical; that is, in each case they balance the interests of the individual against those of the government. Their decisions can vary because at times an individual's activity outweighs the government's interest in prohibiting it, while at other times the reverse holds true.

The balancing approach, however, is not monolithic. Some justices take a very strict view of balancing, giving the interests of individuals and governments equal weight. They justify doing so on constitutional and philosophical grounds, saying, for example, that while the First Amendment protects individual speech, the text of the Constitution gives legislatures the power to enact laws, which may sometimes interfere with such speech. The Court, according to this

---

36. Rohde and Spaeth, *Supreme Court Decision Making*, 36.
37. Ibid, 37.
38. William O. Douglas, "Stare Decisis," *Columbia Law Review* 49 (1949), 736.

39. *Green v. United States*, 356 U.S. 165, 195 (1958).

view, should initially give equal weight to both and then balance them to determine which should fall. Justice John Marshall Harlan's opinion in *Barenblatt* demonstrates this theory in practice. Among the issues raised was whether a congressional committee could question an individual about his political beliefs and associations. Barenblatt alleged that he could refuse to answer such questions because they infringed on his First Amendment rights. Harlan wrote:

Where First Amendment rights are asserted to bar governmental interrogation, resolution of the issue always involves a balancing by the courts of the competing private and public interests at stake in the particular circumstances shown.

He held that, in this instance, the scale favored the government over Barenblatt.

Balancing also can take at least two other forms. While some opinions, such as Harlan's in *Barenblatt*, weigh equally the claims of governments and individuals, others give preference to one above the other. In accordance with a philosophy of judicial restraint, Justice Felix Frankfurter often balanced government interests versus individual interests but with a finger on the scale: he gave preference to the state over the individual. He did so in the belief that a body made up of unelected judges should not lightly overturn laws passed by legislatures composed of representatives elected by the populace. In his view,

the framers of the Constitution denied ... legislative powers to the federal judiciary. They chose instead to insulate the judiciary from the legislative function. They did not grant to this Court supervision over legislation.... [Thus,] the removal of unwise laws from the statute books ... lies not to the court but to the ballot and to the processes of democratic government.[40]

In contrast to Frankfurter's perspective is the preferred freedoms position, which also balances interests, but tips the scale to favor the individual's rights

and liberties.[41] According to this view, "freedom of expression is so vital in its relationship to the objectives of the Constitution that inevitably it must stand in a preferred position ... [and, therefore,] legislation claimed to impinge on rights of free speech and thought should be inspected more critically by the judiciary."[42] In other words, the Court should regard any laws touching upon First Amendment rights with a good deal of suspicion. Why? Justice Jackson provides some justifications:

The very purpose of a Bill of Rights was to withdraw certain subjects from the vicissitudes of political controversy, to place them beyond the reach of majorities and officials and to establish them as legal principles to be applied by the courts. One's right to life, liberty, and property, to free speech, a free press, freedom of worship and assembly, and other fundamental rights may not be submitted to vote: they depend on the outcome of no elections.[43]

Critiques of the various forms of balancing are often less pointed than those we have already examined and more philosophical in orientation.[44] Debates over this mode of analysis generally have centered on views about the role of the Supreme Court in a democratic society. Those opposed to the equal balancing of Harlan and to the judicial restraint of Frankfurter contend that each ignores the Court's role of protecting minority interests. According to this argument, justices, because they are not elected officials, are in the best position to protect groups and individuals who hold unpopular views. As Justice Brennan wrote in *NAACP v. Button* (1963),

Groups which find themselves unable to achieve their objectives through the ballot frequently turn to the courts.... *And, under the conditions of modern government, litigation may well be the sole practicable avenue open to a minority to petition for redress of grievances.... For such a group, association for lit-*

---

40. *West Virginia v. Barnette*, 319 U.S. 624 (1943). For a fuller version of Frankfurter's dissent in this case, see pages 292–293.

41. As Pritchett wrote: "Advocates of the preferred position ... also allowed for balancing, but [put] freedom's thumb on the scale." *Constitutional Civil Liberties* (Englewood Cliffs, N.J.: Prentice-Hall, 1984), 30.

42. Robert B. McKay, "The Preference for Freedom," *New York University Law Review* 34 (1959): 1182.

43. *West Virginia v. Barnette* (1943).

44. But, for more specific criticisms of balancing, see Laurent B. Frantz, "The First Amendment in the Balance," *Yale Law Journal* 71 (1962): 1424–50. On the preferred freedoms approach, see Felix Frankfurter's dissent in *Kovacs v. Cooper* (1949).

igation may be the most effective form of political association (emphasis added).

Brennan opposed doctrines like absolute balancing because they almost always lead to decisions in favor of the majority. Consider the outcome in *Barenblatt:* Would it have been possible for Justice Harlan to weigh the interests of all against those of one man and reach any other conclusion?

Frankfurter and others chastise adherents of a position giving special treatment to individual rights and liberties. In Frankfurter's view, that posture is "mischievous" because its application gives the Court too much power. When Congress and other legislative bodies enact laws that reflect the will of the people, why should the Court—composed of unelected officials—strike them down? In this light, the Court should be seen as part of the ruling regime, willing to reflect its wishes.

EXTRALEGAL APPROACHES

Thus far in our discussion we have not mentioned the justices' ideologies, their political party affiliations, or their personal views on various public policy issues. The reason is legally relevant approaches to Supreme Court decision making do not admit that such factors play a role in the how the Court arrives at its decisions. Instead, they suggest that justices divorce themselves from their personal and political biases and settle disputes based upon the law.

Extralegal approaches posit a quite different vision of Supreme Court decision making. They argue that the forces that drive the justices are anything but legal in composition. Put in different terms, extralegal approaches suggest that it is unrealistic to expect justices to shed all their preferences and values and to ignore public opinion when they put on their black robes. Rather, under those black robes remains a person, a person—like all of us—whose biases and partisan attachments are strong and pervasive.

Justices usually do not admit that they are swayed by the public or that they vote the way they do because of their ideologies. Hence, our discussion of extralegal approaches is distinct from the section on legally relevant factors. In it you will find little in the way of supporting statements from the justices, for it is an unusual justice indeed who admits to following anything but legally relevant criteria in deciding cases. Instead, we have included the results of decades of research by scholars who think that non–legally relevant forces shape judicial decisions. We organize these approaches into three categories: policy-based, strategic, and political. Whether you are persuaded by these scholarly accounts is a question to consider not only as you read the discussion that follows but also as you turn to the opinion excerpts in the later chapters.

Policy-Based Approaches

Adherents to policy-based approaches argue that justices hold certain values they would like to see reflected in the outcomes of Court cases. The two most prevalent policy-based approaches stress the importance of judicial *attitudes* and *roles*.

Attitudes. Attitudinal approaches emphasize the importance of the justices' ideologies. Typically, scholars examining the ideologies of the justices discuss the degree to which a justice is conservative or liberal—as in "Justice X holds conservative views on issues of criminal law" or "Justice Y holds liberal views on free speech." This school of thought holds that when a case comes before the Court each justice evaluates the facts of the dispute and arrives at a decision consistent with his or her personal ideology.

One of the first scholars to study the importance of the personal attitudes of the justices was C. Herman Pritchett.[45] Examining the Court during the New Deal period, Pritchett was not satisfied with traditional le-

45. C. Herman Pritchett, *The Roosevelt Court* (New York: Macmillan, 1948); and Pritchett, "Divisions of Opinion Among Justices of the U.S.

FIGURE 1-1 Left-Right Continuum of Justices Serving Between 1939 and 1941

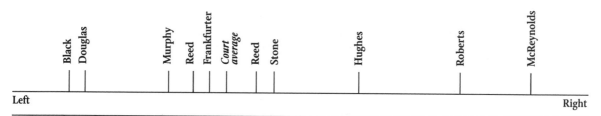

SOURCE: C. Herman Pritchett, "Divisions of Opinion Among Justices of the U.S. Supreme Court, 1939–1941," *American Political Science Review* 35 (1941): 894.

NOTE: Reed appears twice because his dissents were "equally divided" between the liberal and conservative wings of the Court. See Pritchett, "Divisions of Opinion Among Justices," 895.

gal explanations of judicial decisions. If the law drove Court rulings, why did various justices in interpreting the same legal provisions consistently reach different conclusions on the important legal questions of the day? Pritchett concluded that the law alone was unable to explain why the justices voted the way they did. He found that personal attitudes have a strong influence on judicial decisions. Based on their voting patterns, Pritchett was able to place the justices of that era on a left-right continuum (*see Figure 1–1*).

Pritchett's findings touched off an explosion of research on the influence of attitudes on Supreme Court decision making.[46] Much of this scholarship describes how liberal or conservative the various justices have been and attempts to predict their voting behavior based on their attitudinal preferences. To understand some of these differences, consider the material in Table 1-2. This table presents the voting records of the present chief justice, William Rehnquist, and his two immediate predecessors, Warren Burger and Earl Warren. The data report the percentage of times each

voted in the liberal direction in three different issue areas: civil liberties, economic liberties, and federalism.

The data show dramatic differences among these three important jurists, especially in civil liberties. Cases in this category include disputes over issues such as the First Amendment freedoms of religion, speech and press, the right to privacy, the rights of the criminally accused, and illegal discrimination. The liberal position in such cases is a vote in favor of the individual who is claiming a denial of these basic rights. Warren supported the liberal side almost 80 percent of the time, but Burger and Rehnquist did so in less than 30 percent of such cases.

Economics cases involve challenges to the government's authority to regulate the economy. The liberal position supports an active role by the government in controlling business and economic activity. Here again the three justices show different ideological positions. Warren is the most liberal of the three, ruling in favor of government regulatory activity in better than 80 percent of the cases, while Burger and Rehnquist support such government activity in less than half the cases. Finally, there are the federalism cases, which deal with disputes between the federal government and the states. Warren and Burger favor the federal government in about two-thirds of such cases, but Rehnquist

Supreme Court, 1939–1941." *American Political Science Review* 35 (1941): 890–898.

46. The classic works in this area are Pritchett, *The Roosevelt Court*; Glendon Schubert, *The Judicial Mind* (Evanston, Ill.: Northwestern University Press, 1965); and Rohde and Spaeth, *Supreme Court Decision Making*. For a lucid, modern-day treatment, see Segal and Spaeth, *The Supreme Court and the Attitudinal Model*, chap. 6.

TABLE 1-2 Liberal Voting of the Chief Justices, 1953–1991

| | Issue Areas | | | | | |
| | Civil Liberties | | Economics | | Federalism | |
	Number of cases	Percentage Liberal	Number of cases	Percentage Liberal	Number of cases	Percentage Liberal
Warren	771	78.5	443	81.9	94	69.1
Burger	1,430	29.6	423	42.6	111	63.1
Rehnquist	1,665	20.4	413	42.2	155	38.7

SOURCE: Lee Epstein, Jeffrey A. Segal, Harold J. Spaeth, and Thomas G. Walker, *The Supreme Court Compendium: Data, Decisions, and Developments* (Washington, D.C.: Congressional Quarterly, 1994), Table 6-1. This source can be consulted for voting data over twelve issue areas for all of the justices who sat on the Court from 1953 to 1991.

NOTE: The data in this table are based on decisions reached during the following tenures: Earl Warren, 1953–1968; Warren Burger, 1969–1985; William Rehnquist, justice, 1972–1986; chief justice, 1986– .

does so in less than 40 percent. These data are representative of the findings of most such studies. Within given issue areas, individual justices tend to show consistent ideological predispositions.

Moreover, we often hear that a particular Court is ideologically predisposed toward one side or the other. For example, in September 1993 the *Wall Street Journal* ran a story entitled "The Right Rules Supreme—America's Highest Court Was Dominated by Conservatives in the '92–'93 Term."[47] Sometimes an entire Court era is described in attitudinal terms, such as the "liberal" Warren Court or the "conservative" Rehnquist Court. Figure 1-2 confirms that these labels have some basis in fact. Looking at the two lines from left to right, from the 1950s through the 1990s, you will note the downward trend, indicating the increased conservatism of the Court in economics and civil liberties cases.

How valuable are the ideological terms used to describe particular justices or Courts in helping us understand judicial decision making? On the one hand, knowledge of justices' ideologies can lead to fairly accurate predictions about their voting behavior. Suppose, for example, that the Rehnquist Court hands down a decision dealing with the death penalty and that the vote in the case is 8–1 in favor of the criminal defendant. The most conservative member of the Court (at least on death penalty cases) is Justice Antonin Scalia—he almost always votes against the defendant. If we predicted that it was Justice Scalia who dissented in our hypothetical death penalty case, we would almost certainly be right.[48]

On the other hand, preference-based approaches are not foolproof. First, how do we know if a particular justice is liberal or conservative? The answer is that we know a justice is liberal or conservative because he or she casts liberal or conservative votes. For example, Justice Scalia favors conservative positions on the Court because he is a conservative; we know he is a conservative because he favors conservative positions

47. Robert Rice, "The Right Rules Supreme," *Wall Street Journal*, September 14, 1993, 14.

48. We adapt this example from Segal and Spaeth, *The Supreme Court and the Attitudinal Model*, 223.

FIGURE 1-2 Court Decisions on Economics and Civil Liberties Cases, 1953–1991 Terms

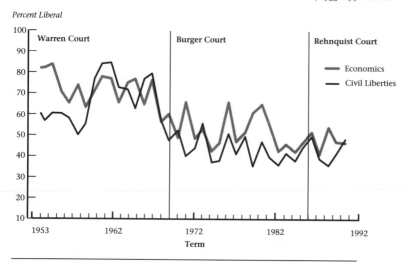

Percent Liberal

SOURCE: Lee Epstein, Jeffrey A. Segal, Harold J. Spaeth, and Thomas G. Walker, *The Supreme Court Compendium: Data, Decisions, and Developements* (Washington, D.C.: Congressional Quarterly, 1994), Table 3-8.

in the cases he decides. This is circular reasoning indeed.[49] Second, knowing that a justice is liberal or conservative or that the Court decided a case in a liberal or conservative way does not tell us much about the Court's (or the country's) policy positions. To say that *Roe v. Wade* (1973) is a liberal decision is to say little about the policies governing abortion in the United States. If it did, this book would be nothing more than a list of cases labeled liberal or conservative. But such labels would give us no sense of 200 years of constitutional interpretation.

Finally, we must understand that ideological labels are occasionally time dependent, that they are bound to particular historical eras. For example, in your class you might read *Muller v. Oregon* (1908), in which the Supreme Court upheld a state law that set a maximum

number on the hours women (but not men) could work. How would you, as a student in the 1990s, view such an opinion? You probably would classify it as conservative because it seems to patronize and protect women. But in the context of the early 1900s, most considered *Muller* to be a liberal ruling that permitted the government to put an end to sweatshop conditions facing women in the workplace.

A related problem is that some decisions do not fall neatly on a single conservative-liberal dimension. Consider the 1993 case of *Wisconsin v. Mitchell*, in which the Court upheld a state law that increased the sentence for crimes if the defendant "intentionally selects the person against whom the crime is committed" on the basis of race, religion, national origin, sexual orientation, and other similar criteria. Is this ruling liberal or conservative? If you view the law as penalizing racial or ethnic hatred, you would likely see it as a liberal decision. However, if you see the law as treating criminal defendants more harshly and penalizing a person because of what he or she believes or says, the ruling is conservative.

49. Some scholars have sought to determine justices' ideology from sources independent of their votes. Jeffrey A. Segal and Albert D. Cover, for example, used newspaper editors' assessments of judicial candidates to derive ideological scores for some of the more recent justices. See "Ideological Values and the Votes of U.S. Supreme Court Justices," *American Political Science Review* 83 (1989): 557. This approach works well enough, but because editors paid little attention to judicial nominations prior to the 1930s, it cannot be extended very far back in time.

TABLE 1-3 Votes in Support of and Opposition to Decisions Declaring Legislation Unconstitutional, 1953–1991 Terms

Justice	Votes on State, Local Laws	Percentage	Votes on Federal Laws	Percentage
Black	128–33	79.5	24–6	80.0
Blackmun	224–69	76.5	22–9	71.0
Brennan	370–12	96.9	51–3	94.4
Burger	154–72	68.1	20–8	71.4
Burton	16–7	69.6	0–3	0.0
Clark	88–23	79.3	6–8	42.9
Douglas	225–10	95.7	30–3	90.9
Fortas	35–3	92.1	11–0	100.0
Frankfurter	32–8	80.0	3–3	50.0
Goldberg	49–3	94.2	6–0	100.0
Harlan	98–56	63.6	16–14	53.3
Jackson	8–0	100.0	0–0	—
Kennedy	35–3	92.1	4–0	100.0
Marshall	271–14	95.1	35–5	87.5
Minton	11–2	84.6	0–0	—
O'Connor	70–33	68.0	15–1	93.8
Powell	171–20	89.5	20–3	87.0
Reed	13–2	86.7	0–0	—
Rehnquist	87–146	37.3	14–14	50.0
Scalia	30–18	62.5	7–0	100.0
Souter	11–1	91.7	2–0	100.0
Stevens	148–22	87.1	14–7	66.7
Stewart	235–45	83.9	29–10	74.4
Thomas	4–4	50.0	1–0	100.0
Warren	129–6	95.6	18–6	75.0
White	297–73	80.3	30–22	57.7
Whittaker	20–3	87.0	2–2	50.0

SOURCE: Lee Epstein, Jeffrey A. Segal, Harold J. Spaeth, and Thomas G. Walker, *The Supreme Court Compendium: Data, Decisions, and Developments* (Washington, D.C.: Congressional Quarterly, 1994), Table 6-7.

NOTE: Includes only those cases in which a majority voted to declare legislation unconstitutional. Figures to the left of the dash indicate the number of votes in favor of striking down legislation; figures to the right indicate the number of votes in favor of upholding the legislation. The other columns give the percentages of cases in which the justice voted with the majority to declare legislation unconstitutional.

Roles. Another concept within the policy-based category of preferences is the judicial role, which scholars have defined as the "norms of behavior which constrain the activities of the role occupant."[50] In other words, some students of the Court argue that each jurist has a view of his or her role, a view that is based upon fundamental beliefs of what a good judge should do or what the proper role of the Court should be. The belief is that jurists vote in accordance with these role conceptions.

Analysts typically discuss judicial roles in terms of activism and restraint. An activist justice believes that the proper role of the Court is to assert independent positions in deciding cases, to review the actions of the other branches vigorously, to strike down unconstitutional acts willingly, and to impose far-reaching remedies for legal wrongs whenever necessary. Restraint-oriented justices take the opposite position. Courts should not become involved in the operations of the other branches unless absolutely necessary. The benefit of the doubt should be given to actions taken by elected officials. Courts should impose remedies that are narrowly tailored to correct a specific legal wrong.

Based on these definitions, we might expect to find activist justices more willing than their opposites to strike down legislation. Therefore, a natural question to ask is this: To what extent have specific jurists practiced judicial activism or restraint? The data in Table 1-3 address this question by reporting the votes of justices on the Court between 1953 and 1991 in cases in which the majority declared federal, state, or local legislation unconstitutional. Note the wide variation among the justices, even for those who sat together and therefore heard many of the same cases. For example, compare Justice Powell's rate of nearly 90 percent (meaning that he almost always voted with the majority to strike down laws) with Chief Justice Burger's 68 percent—a difference of more than twenty percentage points, despite the fact that Burger's and Powell's ten-

50. James L. Gibson, "Judges' Role Orientations, Attitudes, and Decisions," *American Political Science Review* 72 (1978): 917.

ures on the Court almost completely overlapped! Perhaps most interesting is the behavior of Justice Frankfurter. In many Supreme Court opinions, Frankfurter declared his adherence to the doctrine of judicial restraint. But the data—although limited to the last nine years of his service on the bench—reveal a justice who did not hesitate to vote with the majority to overturn legislation.

The Frankfurter example should make clear that what justices say they do and what they actually do may be two different things.[51] But it also illustrates a less obvious point: judicial activism and restraint do not necessarily equal judicial liberalism and conservatism. An activist judge need not be liberal, and a judge who practices restraint need not be conservative. As for Frankfurter, Segal and Spaeth argue that in his voting behavior he was "a staunch economic conservative" who was willing to strike down laws that impinged on his policy preferences.[52] Among the twenty-seven justices who served on the Court between 1953 and 1992, only two—Harlan and Whittaker—supported liberal outcomes in economic cases at a rate lower than Frankfurter's 39 percent. In other words, in some areas of the law, Frankfurter was a conservative activist.

It is also true that so-called liberal Courts are no more likely to strike down legislation than are conservative Courts. Consider Figure 1-3, which shows the number of federal, state, and local laws struck down since 1789. Note the relatively high numbers of statutes declared unconstitutional during the 1920s and by the Burger and Rehnquist Courts. We have already learned that the 1970s and 1980s were periods of relative conservatism on the Court; the 1920s was also a conservative period. Such activism calls into question a strong relationship between ideology and judicial role.

51. For a more detailed examination of Frankfurter's voting, see Harold J. Spaeth, "The Judicial Restraint of Mr. Justice Frankfurter—Myth or Reality." *American Journal of Political Science* 8 (1964): 22.
52. See Segal and Spaeth, *The Supreme Court and the Attitudinal Model*, 236–237.

FIGURE 1-3 Provisions of Federal, State, and Local Laws and Ordinances Held Unconstitutional by the Supreme Court, 1789–1992

Number Held Unconstitutional

SOURCE: Harold W. Stanley and Richard G. Niemi, *Vital Statistics on American Politics*, 4th ed. (Washington, D.C.: CQ Press, 1994), 308.
NOTE: The last period includes only three years rather than a full decade, which may explain the apparent decline.

We have shown that one can use measures, such as the number of laws struck down, to assess the extent to which justices practice judicial activism or restraint. But does such information help us understand Supreme Court decision making? This question is difficult to answer because few scholars have studied the relationship between roles and voting in a systematic way.

The paucity of scholarly work on judicial roles leads to one criticism of the approach: it is virtually impossible to separate roles from attitudes. When Justice Frankfurter voted to uphold an economically conservative law, can we necessarily conclude that he was practicing restraint? The answer, quite clearly, is no. It may have been his conservative attitude toward economic cases—not restraint—that led him to uphold the law.

Another criticism of role approaches is similar to that leveled at attitudinal factors—they tell us very little about the resulting policy in a case. Again, to say that *Roe v. Wade* was an activist decision (it did, after all, strike down abortion laws in all fifty states) is to say nothing about the policy content of the opinion.

Strategic Approaches

As a class, strategic approaches argue that justices are rational decision makers who have certain *preferences* about the outcomes of Court decisions and seek to join opinions that reflect those preferences. While policy-based approaches focus on the individual justice, suggesting that he or she reaches decisions in a vacuum, strategic approaches contend that we ought to consider that each justice operates in a setting with eight colleagues. As a consequence, a justice's vote may well depend upon what the other justices do or what they are expected to do.[53]

Such approaches to Supreme Court decision mak-

ing seem to be sensible: after all, justices can do very little on their own. It takes a majority vote to decide a case and a majority agreeing on a single opinion to set precedent. Under such conditions, human interaction is important and case outcomes—not to mention the rationale of decisions—can be influenced by the nature of relations among the members of the group.

Although scholars have not considered strategic approaches to the same degree that they have studied, say, judicial attitudes, a number of influential works point to their importance. Research conducted by Walter F. Murphy, David J. Danelski, and J. Woodford Howard into the private papers of the former justices consistently has shown that through intellectual persuasion, effective bargaining over opinion writing, informal lobbying, and so forth, justices have influenced the actions of their colleagues.[54]

How does strategic behavior manifest itself? One way is the frequency of vote changes. During the deliberations that occur shortly after oral argument, the justices discuss the case and vote on it. But these votes do not become final until several months later when the opinions are completed and the decision is made public *(see the Appendix for information on Court procedures).* Research has shown that between the initial vote on the merits of cases and the official announcement of the decision at least one vote switch occurs more than 50 percent of the time.[55] This figure indicates that justices change their minds—a phenomenon that attitudinal-based approaches cannot explain.

Consider an example unearthed from the papers of Justice Thurgood Marshall. During the 1990 term the justices unanimously voted in conference to affirm the

---

53. Strategic approaches are not limited to what a justice expects his or her colleagues to do. They also take into account expectations concerning other political institutions (for example, the president, Congress). We take these up later in the chapter.

54. Walter F. Murphy, *Elements of Judicial Strategy* (Chicago: University of Chicago Press, 1964); David J. Danelski, "The Influence of the Chief Justice in the Decisional Process of the Supreme Court," in *The Federal Judicial System,* ed. Thomas P. Jahnige and Sheldon Goldman (New York: Holt, Rinehart and Winston, 1968); J. Woodford Howard, "On the Fluidity of Judicial Choice," *American Political Science Review* 62 (1968): 43–56.

55. Saul Brenner, "Fluidity on the Supreme Court, 1956–1967," *American Journal of Political Science* 26 (1982): 388; and Brenner, "Fluidity on the United States Supreme Court: A Re-examination," *American Journal of Political Science* 24 (1980): 526. His data are for the Vinson and Warren Courts only.

lower court judgment in the case of *Owen v. Owen*. Chief Justice Rehnquist assigned the majority opinion to Justice Scalia. Scalia circulated his draft on December 3 with an accompanying memo: "I was as firm as any of you in my opinion that the judgment in this case had to be an affirmance. I found it impossible, however, to write it that way.... I hope that you may agree with me, but otherwise the opinion will have to reassigned." In other words, Scalia was telling his colleagues that he changed his mind and had written to reverse the lower court opinion.

Justice Marshall scribbled NO!!! and WAIT in large letters across the Scalia draft; the chief justice responded with a rather curt note to Scalia, asserting that he should not have written the opinion since he had changed his mind; rather, he should have asked to have it reassigned immediately. Rehnquist decided to have a go at it himself. In the meantime, just four days later Justice O'Connor indicated that she could "join something along [the] lines" Scalia proposed. Suddenly, the nine-person majority to affirm had dwindled to seven.

Another defection from the majority came in February, when Rehnquist sent the following memo to the others: "After Nino [Scalia] circulated his draft opinion coming out to 'reverse' rather than to 'affirm,' I reassigned this case to myself.... After having made this effort, I have decided that Nino was correct.... Anyone else wishing to do so, of course, is free to try their hand at the same task which I attempted.... I therefore assign the case back to Nino and join his revised opinion." By the end of March, every justice, save John Paul Stevens, had agreed to sign Scalia's opinion. And even Stevens was open to persuasion. During the early days of April he and Scalia exchanged several memos on possible revisions to the opinion. In the end, Scalia could not accommodate Stevens, and Stevens ended up writing a lone dissent that took the position the entire group of nine originally had expressed in conference.

Over a few short months, a 9–0 vote to affirm became an 8–1 decision to reverse. Surely, such a large vote shift is unusual. But our perusal of the Thurgood Marshall papers leads us to conclude, like previous scholars, that it is not unusual for justices to reevaluate their initial positions or to succumb to the persuasion of their colleagues. Nor is it atypical for colleagues to attempt to persuade each other of the merits of their positions.

Vote shifts are just one manifestation of the interdependence of the Court's decision-making process. Another is the revision of opinions that occurs in almost every Court case. As opinion writers seek to accommodate their colleagues' wishes, their drafts may undergo five, ten, even fifteen revisions. Such bargaining over the content of an opinion is quite important because it can alter significantly the policy ultimately expressed. *Griswold v. Connecticut* (1965), in which the Court considered the constitutionality of a state law that prohibited the dissemination of birth control devices and information, even to married couples, provides a clear example. In his initial draft of the majority opinion, Justice Douglas struck down the law on the grounds that it interfered with the First Amendment's right to association. A memorandum from Justice Brennan, however, convinced Douglas to alter his rationale and to establish the foundation for a right to privacy. "Had the Douglas draft been issued as the *Griswold* opinion of the Court, the case would stand as a precedent on the freedom of association," rather than serve as the landmark ruling it became.[56]

While strategic approaches have their uses, *Griswold* points to a problem with them: to date, scholarly treatments have been ad hoc or case specific. We do not know the extent to which a case like *Griswold* represents the rule or the anomaly. Until analysts begin to study interdependent decision making more systematically, which manuscript collections such as Thurgood

---

56. See Bernard Schwartz, *The Unpublished Opinions of the Warren Court* (New York: Oxford University Press, 1985), chap. 7.

Marshall's make possible, the general value of this approach will remain unknown.

Political Factors

In the previous section we considered how strategic approaches take into account internal bargaining on the Court. But they also consider political pressures that come from outside the Court. In what follows, we consider three sources of such influence: public opinion, partisan politics, and interest groups.

For these factors, it is important to keep in mind that the justices do not have to face reelection. Indeed, one of the fundamental differences between the Supreme Court and the political branches is that there is no direct electoral connection between the justices and the public. Once appointed, justices may serve for life. They are not accountable to the public and are not required to undergo any periodic reevaluation of their decisions. Therefore, an ever-present question is why they would let the stuff of ordinary politics, such as public opinion and interest groups, influence their opinions.

Public Opinion. The president and members of Congress are always trying to keep in touch with what the people are thinking. Conducting and analyzing public opinion polls is a never-ending task. There is good reason for this activity. The political branches are supposed to represent the people, and the incumbents' reelection prospects can be jeopardized by straying too far from what the public wants. But federal judges—including Supreme Court justices—are not dependent upon pleasing the public to stay in office, and they do not serve in the same kind of representative capacity that legislators do.

But does that mean that the justices are not affected by public opinion? Certainly, we can think of times when the Court has handed down rulings that fly in the face of what the public wants. The most obvious example occurred after Franklin D. Roosevelt's 1932 election to the presidency. By choosing Roosevelt (as

well as electing many Democrats to Congress) the people were sending a clear signal that they wanted the government to take vigorous action to end the Great Depression. The president and Congress responded with many laws—the so-called New Deal legislation—but the Court remained unmoved by the public's endorsement of Roosevelt and his legislation. In case after case (at least until 1937), the justices struck down many of the laws and administrative programs designed to get the nation's economy moving again.

In contrast, there have been times when the Court seems to have embraced public opinion, especially under conditions of extreme national stress. One example occurred during World War II. In *Korematsu v. United States* (1944), the justices endorsed the government's program to move all Japanese Americans from the Pacific Coast states to inland relocation centers. The justices clearly were swept away in the same wartime apprehensions as the rest of the nation.

In addition to studying specific cases, scholars also conduct more systematic research. What conclusions have they reached? Many analysts indicate that particular Court rulings do not deviate significantly from the views of the citizenry. As political scientist Thomas Marshall wrote, "Most modern Court decisions reflect public opinion. When a clear-cut poll majority or plurality exists, over three-fifths of the Court's decisions reflect the polls. By all arguable evidence the modern Supreme Court appears to reflect public opinion about as accurately as other policy makers."[57] Moreover, some argue that Court decisions also may reflect more general societal trends. Figure 1-4 plots the ideological mood of the public against the ideological direction of Supreme Court decisions. Two researchers claim a correspondence between decision and mood trends: the justices "are broadly aware of fundamental trends in ideological tenor of public opinion, and that at least some justices, consciously or not, may adjust their decisions at the margins to accommodate such funda-

57. Thomas Marshall, *Public Opinion and the Supreme Court* (New York: Unwin Hyman, 1989), 97.

mental trends."[58] However, as you look at the figure, note that the relationship is not exact; in other words, public opinion and Court decisions are not the same at any given point in time. Rather, the Court seems to lag behind public opinion.

Let us assume that these scholars are correct and that Supreme Court decisions track the public opinion polls. That assumption raises a question: Why do justices consider the views of the public in deciding cases when their jobs do not depend upon winning public approval?[59] Scholars offer a number of reasons. First, because they are political appointees, nominated and approved by popularly elected officials, it is logical that the justices will reflect, however subtly, the views of the majority. It is probably true, for example, that an individual radically out of step with either the president or the Senate would not be nominated, much less confirmed. A second reason relates to the institutional setting of the Court. Put simply, the justices lack any real mechanism for enforcing their decisions. Instead, they depend not only on other political officials to support their positions but also on general public compliance, especially when controversial Court opinions will have ramifications well beyond the particular concerns of the parties to the suit. Finally, the Court, at least occasionally, views public opinion as a legitimate guide for decisions. It has even gone so far as to incorporate that dimension into some of its jurisprudential standards. For example, in evaluating whether certain kinds of punishments violate the Eighth Amendment's prohibition against cruel and unusual punishment, the Court proclaimed that it would look toward "evolving standards of decency," as defined by public sentiment.[60]

Some scholars, however, remain unconvinced of the role of public opinion in Court decision making. In

FIGURE 1-4 The Supreme Court and Public Opinion

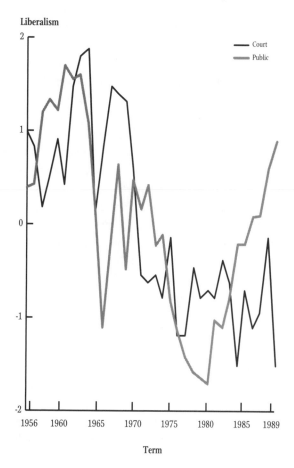

Term

SOURCE: William Mishler and Reginald S. Sheehan, "The Supreme Court as a Counter-Majoritarian Institution? The Impact of Public Opinion on Supreme Court Decisions," *American Political Science Review* 87 (1993): 91.

NOTE: The two series are a public mood score and percentage of Supreme Court decisions decided in the liberal direction. For purposes of presentation, we have standardized the two series.

58. William Mishler and Reginald S. Sheehan, "The Supreme Court as a Counter-Majoritarian Institution? The Impact of Public Opinion on Supreme Court Decisions," *American Political Science Review* 87 (1993): 89.

59. We adopt this discussion from Lee Epstein and Joseph F. Kobylka, *The Supreme Court and Legal Change: Abortion and the Death Penalty* (Chapel Hill: University of North Carolina Press, 1992), 21–22.

60. *Trop v. Dulles*, 356 U.S. 349 (1958).

part, this disbelief emanates from a concern about the nature of the research that has been conducted. Helmut Norpoth and Jeffrey Segal, for example, criticized the study that produced the data depicted in Figure 1-4.[61] In reexamining that study's methodology, they reach the following conclusion: "Does public opinion influence Supreme Court decisions? If the model of influence is of the sort where the justices set aside their own (ideological) preferences and abide by what they divine as the vox populi, our answer is a resounding no." What Norpoth et al find instead is that Court appointments made by Richard Nixon in the early 1970s caused a "sizable ideological shift" in the direction of Court decisions (see Figure 1-4). Therefore, it was the entry of conservative justices that created the illusion that the Court was echoing public opinion rather than sitting justices who modified their voting patterns in order to conform to the changing views of the public.

This finding reinforces yet another criticism of this approach: that public opinion affects the Court only indirectly through presidential appointments, and not through the justices reading the public opinion polls. This distinction is important, for if justices were truly influenced by the public, their decisions would change with the ebb and flow of opinion. But if they merely share their appointing president's ideology (which must mirror the majority of the citizens *at the time of the election*) then their decisions will remain constant over time. Thus, they would not necessarily fluctuate, as public opinion often does.

Partisan Politics. As Jonathan Casper wrote, we cannot overestimate "the importance of the political context in which the Court does its work." In his view, the statement that the Court follows the election returns "recognizes that the choices the Court makes are related to developments in the broader

political system."[62] In other words, the political environment has an effect on Court behavior. In fact, many assert that the Court is responsive to the influence of partisan politics, both internally and externally.

On the inner workings of the Court, social scientists long have argued that political creatures inhabit the Court, that justices are not simply neutral arbiters of the law. Since 1789, the beginning of constitutional government in the United States, those who have ascended to the bench have come from the political institutions of government or, at the very least, have affiliated with a particular political party. Judicial scholars recognize that justices bring with them the philosophies of those partisan attachments. Just as the members of the present Court tend to reflect the views of the Republican or Democratic parties, so too did the justices who came from the ranks of the Federalist and Jeffersonian parties. As one might expect, justices who affiliate with the Democratic party tend to be more liberal in their decision making than those who are Republicans.[63]

The Court also faces political pressure from the outside. Although the justices have no electoral connection or mandate of responsiveness, we recognize that the other institutions of government have some influence on judicial behavior; and, naturally, the direction of that influence will reflect the partisan composition of those branches. For example, the Court has always had a "multifaceted relationship" with the president, a relationship that provides the president with "several sources of potential influence."[64] Some of those sources directly link the president and the Court, including (1) the president's power to nominate jus-

---

61. Helmut Norpoth and Jeffrey A. Segal, "Popular Influence in Supreme Court Decisions," *American Political Science Review* 88 (September 1994): 711–716.

62. Jonathan Casper, *The Politics of Civil Liberties* (New York: Harper and Row, 1972), 293.

63. See C. Neal Tate, "Personal Attribute Models of Voting Behavior of U.S. Supreme Court Justices: Liberalism in Civil Liberties and Economics Decisions, 1946–1978," *American Journal of Political Science* 75 (1981): 355–367.

64. Lawrence Baum, *The Supreme Court*, 4th ed. (Washington, D.C.: CQ Press, 1992), 143.

tices and, thereby, the ability to shape the Court; (2) the relationships many presidents have enjoyed with sitting justices, including Franklin Roosevelt's with James Byrnes, Lyndon Johnson's with Abe Fortas, and Richard Nixon's with Warren Burger; and (3) the notion that the president, having been elected within the previous four years, may carry a popular mandate, reflecting the preferences of the people, which would affect the environment within which the Court operates.[65]

A less direct source of influence is the executive branch, which operates under the president's command. The bureaucracy can assist the Court in implementing its policies, or it can hinder the Court by refusing to do so, a fact of which the justices are well aware. As a judicial body, the Supreme Court cannot implement or execute its own decisions. The Court often must depend on the executive branch to give its decisions legitimacy through action. The Court, therefore, may act strategically, anticipating the wishes of the executive branch and responding accordingly to avoid a confrontation that could threaten its legitimacy. Along these lines, *Marbury v. Madison* (1803), in which the Court enunciated the doctrine of judicial review, provides a classic example. Some scholars suggest that the justices knew if they ruled in a certain direction, the administration would not carry out their orders. Because the Court felt that such a failure would threaten the legitimacy of judicial institutions, it crafted its opinion in a way that would not force the administration to take any action, but would send a message about its displeasure with the administration's politics.

Another indirect source of presidential influence is the U.S. solicitor general, a presidential appointee whose office presents the position of the federal government in written briefs and oral arguments and represents the interests of the United States in Supreme

TABLE 1-4 Success Rate of the Solicitor General as an Amicus Curiae, by President, 1952–1990 Terms

President	Total Number of Cases[a]	Percentage Won
Eisenhower	42	83.3
Kennedy	48	87.5
Johnson	41	82.9
Nixon	79	70.9
Ford	38	71.1
Carter	86	65.1
Reagan[b]	123	67.5
Bush[c]	99	75.8

SOURCE: Lee Epstein, Jeffrey A. Segal, Harold J. Spaeth, and Thomas G. Walker, *The Supreme Court Compendium: Data, Decisions, and Developments* (Washington, D.C.: Congressional Quarterly, 1994), Table 7-12.

a. Includes all cases where the solicitor general filed amicus curiae briefs and the Court decided the case with an opinion on the merits.

b. Includes 1980–1982 and 1986–1987 terms.

c. Includes 1988–1990 terms.

Court litigation. The solicitor general's office can affect two aspects of Supreme Court decision making. First, the office may express an opinion on whether the Court should grant an appealed case a full hearing. The Court relies on these arguments as a preconference screening device, as a way to filter out insignificant petitions. To the extent that the office helps the Court set its agenda, the solicitor general is able to ensure that the justices consider the administration's political goals and priorities. Second, through written briefs and oral arguments, the justices expect that solicitors general will share their expertise with them, thereby becoming the Court's "tenth justice." This participation occurs both when the federal government is an actual party to an appeal and when the solicitor general acts as an amicus curiae (friend of the Court) expressing views on an appeal in which the government has an interest but is not a formal litigant. In fact, as Table 1-4 indicates, the solicitor general is a most successful amici in Supreme Court litigation, regardless of the particular administration in office at the time. Data on the government's participation as a

---

65. For more on the relationship between the president and the justices, see Henry J. Abraham, *Justices and Presidents*, 3d ed. (New York: Oxford University Press, 1992).

party also point to its ability to convince the justices to adopt its preferred positions.[66]

That the president and the executive branch are in a position to affect Supreme Court decision making is undoubtedly true. What also seems to be the case is that the particular party affiliation of the president has a great deal to do with the ideological direction of that influence. Presidents want to see their views, usually reflecting those of their party, translated into law. Such motivation tells us a great deal about the justices they nominate and reflects a partisan pattern of judicial selection politics that began with George Washington's packing the Court with Federalists and has extended through Bill Clinton's appointments.

Presidential influence is also demonstrated in the kinds of arguments their solicitors general bring into the Court. That is, solicitors general representing Democratic administrations tend to present more liberal arguments; those from the ranks of the Republican party, more conservative arguments. The transition from the Bush administration to Clinton's provides an interesting illustration. Bush's solicitor general had filed amicus curiae briefs—many of which took a conservative position—in a number of cases heard by the Court during the 1993–1994 term. Drew S. Days III, Clinton's solicitor general, rewrote at least four of those briefs to reflect the new administration's more liberal posture. For example, Days argued that the Civil Rights Act of 1991 should be applied retroactively, whereas the Bush administration suggested that it should not be; in another case, Days claimed that jurors cannot be dismissed on the basis of sex; his predecessor argued that such dismissals were constitutional.[67]

Congress, too—or so some argue—can influence Supreme Court decision making. Like the president, the legislature has many powers over the Court that

the justices cannot ignore.[68] Some of these resemble those of the president—the Senate's role in confirmation proceedings, the implementation of judicial decisions—but there are others. Congress can restrict the Court's jurisdiction to hear cases, enact legislation or even propose constitutional amendments to recast Court decisions, and hold judicial salaries constant. In addition, the "goal of deterring or ending a congressional attack on the Court may influence the Court's policy choices."[69] Often cited examples include the Court's willingness to defer to the Radical Republican Congress after the Civil War and to approve New Deal legislation after Franklin Roosevelt proposed his Court-packing plan in 1937. As these—and many other—examples illustrate, relations between the Court and Congress are hardly random. The partisan composition of the legislature vis-à-vis the Court plays a major role in determining the course of those relations, be they antagonistic or amiable.

The effect that partisan politics has on the Court has been widely explored. For the most part, analysts agree that it influences the justices or, at least, the environment in which they work. Still, the same criticism that is leveled against public opinion research *may* apply here: partisan politics only indirectly affects the Court through presidential appointments and, perhaps, through the office of the solicitor general. What is more, some would argue that the Court has no reason to respond strategically to Congress, in particular, since it is so rare that the legislature threatens, much less takes action, against the judiciary. Only once, for example, has Congress retaliated against the Court by removing its jurisdiction over a class of cases—and that occurred more than 100 years ago.[70] This argument needs to be kept in mind as you read the cases that pit the Court against Congress and the president.

---

66. See Lee Epstein, Jeffrey A. Segal, Harold J. Spaeth, and Thomas G. Walker, *The Supreme Court Compendium: Data, Decisions, and Developments* (Washington, D.C.: Congressional Quarterly, 1994), Tables 7–10 and 7–11.

67. William H. Freivogel, "Ginsburg May Alter Balance in Key Civil Rights Cases," *St. Louis Post-Dispatch*, October 3, 1993, 1B.

68. Baum, *The Supreme Court*, 4th ed., 141. See also William N. Eskridge, Jr., "Overriding Supreme Court Statutory Interpretation Decisions," *Yale Law Journal* 101 (1991): 331.

69. Ibid., 142.

70. For a different view, see Eskridge, "Overriding Supreme Court Statutory Interpretation Decisions."

Interest Groups. In *The Federalist Papers,* No. 78, Alexander Hamilton wrote that the U.S. Supreme Court was "to declare the sense of the law" through "inflexible and uniform adherence to the rights of the constitution and individuals." Despite this expectation, Supreme Court litigation has become political over time.[71] We see manifestations of politics in virtually every aspect of the Court's work, from the nomination and confirmation of justices to the factors that influence their decisions. But perhaps the most striking example of this politicization is the incursion of organized interests into the judicial process.

Naturally, interest groups may not attempt to persuade the Supreme Court the same way lobbyists deal with Congress. It would be grossly improper for the representatives of an interest group to approach a Supreme Court justice directly. Instead, interest groups try to influence Court decisions by submitting written legal arguments called amicus curiae briefs *(see Box 1-2).* This procedure allows interest groups to make their views known to the Court, even when the group is not a direct party to the litigation. As Figure 1-5 shows, interest groups are now a major presence in Supreme Court litigation. The data indicate that the majority of cases contain at least one amicus curiae brief filed by an organized interest. On average, 84.4 percent of all full opinion cases decided between 1986 and 1991 contained at least one amicus curiae brief, and the average amicus case contained 4.4 briefs. During the 1990 term more than 4.5 amici cosigned the typical amicus curiae brief, for a total of about 1,800 organized participants. In addition to participating as amici, groups are sponsoring cases—that is, providing litigants with attorneys and the money necessary to pursue their cases—in record numbers.

The explosion of interest group participation in Supreme Court litigation raises two questions. First, why do groups, in ever-increasing numbers, go to the

FIGURE 1-5 The Percentage of the Supreme Court's Full Opinion Cases Containing at Least One Amicus Curiae Brief, 1953–1990 Terms

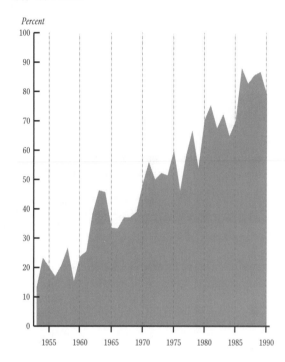

SOURCE: Lee Epstein, "Interest Group Litigation During the Rehnquist Court Era," *The Journal of Law and Politics* 9 (1993): 645.

Court? One answer is obvious: they want to influence the Court's decisions. But groups also go to the Supreme Court to achieve other, more subtle ends. One of these is the setting of institutional agendas. In other words, by filing amicus curiae briefs at the case-selection stage or by simply bringing cases to the Court's attention, organizations seek to influence the justices' decisions on which disputes they will hear.[72] Group participation also may serve as a counterbalance to other interests that have competing goals *(see Table 1-5).* Table 1-5 lists two sets of groups filing briefs in support of the pro-choice and pro-life positions in

---

71. Some of the views expressed in this section come from Lee Epstein, "Interest Group Litigation During the Rehnquist Court Era," *Journal of Law and Politics* 9 (1993): 639–717.

72. See Gregory A. Caldeira and John R. Wright, "Organized Interests and Agenda Setting in the U.S. Supreme Court," *American Political Science Review* 82 (1988): 1109–27.

BOX 1-2 AMICUS CURIAE PARTICIPATION

In the

Supreme Court of the United States

October Term, 1975

NO. 75-5444

————•————

Erlich Anthony Coker, *Petitioner*

—v.—

State of Georgia, *Respondent*

———

ON WRIT OF CERTIORARI TO THE SUPREME COURT OF GEORGIA

....

BRIEF AMICI CURIAE OF THE AMERICAN CIVIL LIBERTIES UNION, THE CENTER FOR CONSTITUTIONAL RIGHTS, THE NATIONAL ORGANIZATION FOR WOMEN LEGAL DEFENSE AND EDUCATION FUND, THE WOMEN'S LAW PROJECT, THE CENTER FOR WOMEN POLICY STUDIES, THE WOMEN'S LEGAL DEFENSE FUND, AND EQUAL RIGHTS ADVOCATES, INC.

....

Ruth Bader Ginsburg
Melvin L. Wulf
Kathleen Willert Peratis
Susan Deller Ross
Marjorie Mazen Smith
American Civil Liberties Union
22 East 40th Street
New York, New York 10016

Elizabeth M. Schneider
Nancy Stearns
Center for Constitutional Rights
853 Broadway
New York, New York 10003
Attorneys for Amici Curiae

....

The amicus curiae practice probably originates in Roman law. A judge would often appoint a *consilium* (officer of the court) "to advise him on points on which he [was] in doubt."[1] That may be why the term amicus curiae translates from the Latin as "friend of the court." But today it is the rare amicus who is a friend of the court. Rather, contemporary briefs almost always are a friend of a party, supporting one side over the other.[2] Consider the brief filed in *Coker v. Georgia* (1977), the cover of which is reprinted here. In that case, attorneys for the American Civil Liberties Union (including Ruth Bader Ginsburg) and other organizations supported Coker, who had received a sentence of death for rape. They argued that such a sentence amounted to cruel and unusual punishment. In other words, these groups were anything but neutral participants.

How does an organization become an amicus curiae participant in the Supreme Court of the United States? Under the Court's rules, groups wishing to file an amicus brief must obtain the written consent of the parties to the litigation (the federal and state governments are exempt from this requirement). If the parties refuse to give their consent, the group can file a motion with the Court asking for its permission. The Court today almost always grants these motions.

1. Frank Covey, Jr., "Amicus Curiae: Friend of the Court," *De Paul Law Review* 9 (1959): 33.

2. See Samuel Krislov, "The Amicus Curiae Brief: From Friendship to Advocacy," *Yale Law Journal* 72 (1963): 694–721, for a history of amicus curiae practice in the United States.

TABLE 1-5 Amici Curiae in *Webster v. Reproductive Health Services* by Two Group Types

Group Type	Pro-Choice Amici	Pro-Life Amici
Religious	American Jewish Congress, Board of Homeland Ministries—United Church of Christ, National Jewish Community Advisory Council, Presbyterian Church USA, Religious Coalition for Abortion Rights, St. Louis Catholics for a Choice, Albuquerque Monthly Meeting of Religious Society Friends, American Friends Service Committee, American Humanist Association, American Jewish Committee, Americans for Religious Liberty, Anti-Defamation League, Commission on Social Action of Reformed Judaism, Episcopal Diocese of Massachusetts—Women in Crisis Committee, Episcopal Diocese of New York, Episcopal Women's Caucus, Federation of Reconstructionists Congregations and Havurot, General Board of Church and Society—United Methodist Church, Health Institute of Women Today, Jewish Labor Committee, NA'MAT, National Assembly of Religious Women, North American Federation of Temple Youth, Union of American Hebrew Congregations, Unitarian Universalists Women's Federation, United Church of Christ Coordinating Center for Women, Washington Ethical Center of the American Ethical Union, Women in Ministry—Garrett Evangelical Seminary, Women in Mission and Ministry—Episcopal Church USA, Women's League for Conservative Judaism, 8 Episcopal Bishops Americans United for Separation of Church and State Catholics for a Free Choice, Chicago Catholic Women, National Coalition of American Nuns, Women in Spirit of Colorado Task Force	Agudeth Israel of America Catholics United for Life, National Organization of Episcopalians for Life, Baptists for Life, Lutherans for Life, Moravians for Life, United Church of Christ Friends for Life, Task Force of United Methodists on Abortion Sexuality, Christian Action Council Catholic Health Association Christian Advocates Serving Evangelism Covenant House, Good Council Holy Orthodox Church Lutheran Church—Missouri Synod, Christian Life Commission of the Southern Baptist Conference, National Association for Evangelicals Missouri Catholic Conference New England Christian Action Council Rutherford Institute and Rutherford Institutes in eighteen states U.S. Catholic Conference New England Christian Action Council
Science/ Medical/ Hospital	American Medical Association, American Academy of Child and Adolescent Medicine, American Academy of Pediatrics, American College of Obstetricians and Gynecologists, American Fertility Society, American Medical Women's Association, American Psychiatric Association, American Society of Human Genetics, American Public Health Association, Alan Guttmacher Institute, American College of Preventive Medicine, California Physicians for Choice, California Republicans for Choice, City of New York, Massachusetts Department of Public Health, Berkeley School of Public Health, National Abortion Federation, New York State Republican Family Committee, three deans/chairs American Psychological Association 167 Scientists and Physicians National Association of Public Hospitals American Nurses Association, Nurses Association of the ACOG	American Academy of Medical Ethics American Association of Pro-Life Ob-Gyns, American Association of Pro-Life Pediatricians Doctors for Life, Missouri Doctors for Life, Missouri Citizens for Life, Lawyers for Life

SOURCE: Adapted from Lee Epstein and Joseph F. Kobylka, *The Supreme Court and Legal Change: Abortion and the Death Penalty* (Chapel Hill: University of North Carolina Press, 1992), Appendix 2 and Table 6-10. See also *U.S. Supreme Court Records and Briefs*, Congressional Information Service, no. 88-605.

NOTE: This table lists only a fraction of the briefs filed in *Webster*. Overall, there were seventy-eight amicus curiae briefs submitted (forty-six on the pro-life side and thirty-two on the pro-choice side). Even more impressive is that a total of 5,681 individuals and groups signed on to these briefs. In the table, a cluster of groups represents a single brief.

TABLE 1-6 Justices' Citations to Amicus Curiae Briefs, 1953–1991 Terms

Justice	Number of Citations to Amicus Curiae Briefs	Number of Citations to Amicus Curiae Briefs Divided by Total Opinions Written
Black	297	.53
Blackmun	531	.69
Brennan	755	.65
Burger	337	.68
Burton	17	.21
Clark	109	.36
Douglas	416	.45
Fortas	43	.44
Frankfurter	74	.29
Goldberg	87	.39
Harlan	252	.37
Jackson	10	.63
Kennedy	82	.65
Marshall	505	.71
Minton	8	.20
O'Connor	292	.77
Powell	458	.77
Reed	20	.33
Rehnquist	453	.53
Scalia	157	.62
Souter	10	.29
Stevens	607	.71
Stewart	363	.51
Thomas	7	.35
Warren	99	.40
White	660	.66
Whittaker	28	.25

SOURCE: Lee Epstein, Jeffrey A. Segal, Harold J. Spaeth, and Thomas G. Walker, *The Supreme Court Compendium: Data, Decisions, and Developments* (Washington, D.C.: Congressional Quarterly, 1994), Table 7-22.

NOTE: Justices' opinions include opinions of the Court, judgments, and dissenting and concurring opinions. Data for the justices cover the terms from 1953 to 1991. Therefore, for those justices joining the Court prior to 1953, data are not completely descriptive of their careers.

Webster v. Reproductive Health Services, a 1989 abortion case. While the groups depicted here represent only a small fraction of those filing in the case (a record-setting seventy-eight briefs were submitted), the balancing goal is evident: pro-choice and pro-life sides matched constituency for constituency, at least in the areas of religion and science. Finally, groups go to the Court to publicize their causes and their organizations. The NAACP Legal Defense Fund's legendary litigation campaigns in housing access and school desegregation cases provide excellent examples: they resulted not only in favorable policy decisions and moved civil rights issues to the forefront of the policy agenda, but also they established the LDF as the foremost organizational litigant of these issues.

A second and more relevant question is this: Can groups influence the outcomes of Supreme Court decisions? This question is difficult to answer. On the one hand, there is evidence that cases sponsored by interest groups have a greater chance of success than those brought by private parties. This seems to be the lesson of the litigation campaigns of the NAACP Legal Defense Fund and, more recently, of those conducted by the Women's Rights Project of the American Civil Liberties Union (ACLU), which has had an unusual degree of success in sex discrimination litigation. Some scholars argue that groups help shape the way the Court resolves issues and can set the context in which the justices do their work.[73] Perhaps the justices, like members of Congress, view groups as the sources of important information that otherwise would not have come to their attention. Table 1-6 lists the number of times justices cited amicus curiae briefs in their opinions from 1953 to 1991. It is interesting to note that the proportion of written opinions citing at least one brief has grown appreciably over the past few decades. The average citation rate for the Warren Court justices was .42; that figure rose to .66 for those serving on the Burger Court; and to .68 for Rehnquist

73. See Susan E. Lawrence, *The Poor in Court* (Princeton, N.J.: Princeton University Press, 1990).

Court jurists.[74] Why this increase has occurred is open to speculation; what is clear is that the justices—now more than ever—are at least learning enough from amicus curiae briefs to cite them in their opinions.

On the other hand, there is equally compelling evidence suggesting that groups are no more successful than other interests. One study paired similar cases decided by the same district court judge, the same year, with the only major difference being that one case was sponsored by a group, the other by a nongroup. The study found no major differences between the two.[75] Research by Donald Songer and Reginald Sheehan reached almost the same conclusion about the effectiveness of amicus curiae briefs in Supreme Court litigation. In seeking to assess the impact of amicus curiae briefs on all written Court decisions from 1967 to 1987, Songer and Sheehan devised a statistical model that considered many factors, such as the Court's ideological makeup, relevant to decision making.[76] Ultimately, they found that briefs had a "differential impact."

Briefs filed by state and local governments appear to have little effect on the outcome of cases heard by the Supreme Court. Briefs filed by other amicus parties have the potential for a moderate impact on the chances for litigant success as long as they are not opposed by the United States as either a direct party or as amicus curiae. In contrast briefs filed for the United States by the solicitor general were shown to have a major impact on Court decisions even after the effects of [other variables] were taken into account.[77]

In short, the debate over the influence of interest groups continues. And it is one that you will be able to enter, for within the case excerpts we often provide information on the arguments of amici and attorneys. Accordingly, you will be able to assess the extent to which they influence the justices.

There is, as you now know, considerable disagreement in the scholarly and legal communities over the reasons why justices decide cases the way they do. As you read the narrative and opinion excerpts that follow, try to keep these different approaches in mind. They and variations of them will show up in many of the Court's opinions. Ask yourself which of the approaches the justices seem to be adopting. And, when it comes to legal approaches in particular, consider whether the justices use them to reach decisions or whether the justices—as extralegal approaches would suggest—reach conclusions first and then invoke legal factors to justify them.

READINGS

Barnum, David G. *The Supreme Court and American Democracy.* New York: St. Martin's, 1993.

Baum, Lawrence. *The Supreme Court,* 4th ed. Washington, D.C.: CQ Press, 1992.

Carter, Lief H. *Contemporary Constitutional Lawmaking.* New York: Pergamon Press, 1985.

Casper, Jonathan D. *The Politics of Civil Liberties.* New York: Harper & Row, 1972.

Crosskey, W. W., and William Jeffrey, Jr. *Politics and the Constitution in the History of the United States.* Chicago: University of Chicago Press, 1980.

Emerson, Thomas I. *Toward a General Theory of the First Amendment.* New York: Random House, 1966.

Epstein, Lee, Jeffrey A. Segal, Harold J. Spaeth, and Thomas G. Walker. *The Supreme Court Compendium: Data, Decisions, and Developments.* Washington, D.C.: Congressional Quarterly, 1994.

Eskridge, William N., Jr., and John Ferejohn. "The Article I, Section 7 Game." *Georgetown Law Journal* 80 (1992): 523–564.

Fisher, Louis. *Constitutional Dialogues.* Princeton, N.J.: Princeton University Press, 1988.

Goldstein, Leslie Friedman. *In Defense of the Text.* Savage, Md.: Rowman and Littlefield, 1991.

---

74. This figure excludes Thomas and Souter, who have not written enough opinions for meaningful analysis.

75. Lee Epstein and C. K. Rowland, "Debunking the Myth of Interest Group Invincibility in the Courts," *American Political Science Review* 85 (1991): 205–217.

76. Donald R. Songer and Reginald S. Sheehan, "The Impact of Amicus Briefs on Decisions on the Merits" (paper presented at the annual meeting of the American Political Science Association, San Francisco, August 30, 1990).

77. Ibid., 12.

Lawrence, Susan E. *The Poor in Court*. Princeton, N.J.: Princeton University Press, 1990.

Marshall, Thomas. *Public Opinion and the Supreme Court*. New York: Unwin Hyman, 1989.

Murphy, Walter J. *Elements of Judicial Strategy*. Chicago: University of Chicago Press, 1964.

Pritchett, C. Herman. *The Roosevelt Court*. New York: Macmillan, 1948.

Segal, Jeffrey A., and Harold J. Spaeth. *The Supreme Court and the Attitudinal Model*. Cambridge: Cambridge University Press, 1993.

Walker, Thomas G., and Lee Epstein. *The Supreme Court of the United States: An Introduction*. New York: St. Martin's Press, 1992.

Wasby, Stephen L. *The Supreme Court in the Federal Judicial System*, 4th ed. Chicago: Nelson-Hall, 1993.

CHAPTER 2

INCORPORATION OF THE BILL OF RIGHTS

THE FIRST AMENDMENT of the U.S. Constitution contains a clear prohibition: "Congress shall make no law ... abridging the freedom of speech." Note that the wording specifically and exclusively limits the powers of Congress, reflecting the fact that the Bill of Rights was added to the Constitution because of fear that the *federal* government might become too powerful and encroach upon individual rights. Does this language mean that state legislatures *may* enact laws curtailing their citizens' free speech? For more than 100 years it did. The U.S. Supreme Court, following historical interpretations and emphasizing the intention of the Framers of the Constitution, refused to nationalize the Bill of Rights by making its protections as binding on the state governments as they are on the federal government. Not being restricted by the federal Bill of Rights, the states were free to recognize those freedoms they deemed important and to develop their own guarantees against state violations of those rights.

Through a principle called selective incorporation, however, this interpretation is no longer valid. Beginning at the turn of the century, the Supreme Court slowly, but steadfastly, informed state governments that they too must abide by most guarantees contained in the first eight amendments of the federal Constitution. Today we take for granted that the states

in which we live must not infringe on our right to exercise our religion freely, to feel safe in our homes against unwarranted government intrusions, and so forth. But the process by which we obtained these rights was long, with most litigants clamoring for incorporation (in the major cases) actually losing their disputes. The process caused acrimonious debates among Supreme Court justices along the way. In fact, the question of whether states must honor the guarantees contained in the Bill of Rights is almost as old as the nation and has been debated by modern Courts as well.

MUST STATES ABIDE BY THE BILL OF RIGHTS? INITIAL RESPONSES

In drafting the original version of the Constitution of 1787, the delegates to the convention did not include a bill of rights, believing that such a listing was unnecessary.[1] When some delegates clamored for a specification of rights, however, James Madison submitted to the First Congress a list of seventeen articles (amendments), mostly aimed at safeguarding personal freedoms against tyranny by the federal government.

---

1. Before the Framers adjourned, "It was moved and seconded to appoint a Committee to prepare a Bill of Rights." The motion, however, was defeated.

In a speech to the House, he suggested that "in revising the Constitution, we may throw into that section, which interdicts the abuse of certain powers of the State legislatures, some other provisions of equal, if not greater importance than those already made." To that end, Madison's fourteenth amendment said that "no State shall violate the equal right of conscience, freedom of the press, or trial by jury in criminal cases."[2] This article failed to garner congressional approval and was never considered by the states.

Although scholars now agree that Madison viewed his fourteenth amendment as the most significant among the seventeen he proposed, Congress's refusal to adopt it may have meant that the Founders of our nation never intended for the Bill of Rights to be applied to the states or their local governments. Chief Justice John Marshall's opinion in *Barron v. Baltimore* (1833), the first case in which the U.S. Supreme Court considered nationalizing the Bill of Rights, supports such a conclusion. While reading *Barron,* note the relative ease with which Marshall reached his conclusion that historical circumstances could not possibly have implied that states were bound by the federal Bill of Rights.

Barron v. Baltimore

32 U.S. (7 PET.) 243 (1833)

Vote: 6 (Duvall, Johnson, Marshall, McLean, Story, Thompson)
    0

Opinion of the Court: Marshall
Not participating: Baldwin

The story of this case begins in Baltimore, a city undergoing major economic changes in the early 1800s.[3] Because of its busy harbor, Baltimore was becoming a major hub of economic activity in the United States.

Such growth necessitated constant construction and excavation. While entrepreneurs erected new buildings, the city began to repair its badly worn streets.

Most of Baltimore's residents welcomed such activity, but a group of wharf owners saw problems. They noticed that the city's street construction altered the flow of streams coming into Baltimore Harbor. This redirection of water, the owners argued in a letter to the city, led to the accumulation of large masses of sand and earth near their wharves, causing the surrounding water to become too shallow for ships. Because their livelihood depended on accommodating large ships, which unloaded goods on the wharves for storage in nearby warehouses, the owners wanted the city to dredge the sand and dirt at its expense.

Baltimore officials paid no heed to the wharf owners, and within five years city construction had ruined John Barron and John Craig's business. The water surrounding their dock had become too shallow to service large ships. In 1822 they brought city representatives to county court in Maryland, asking for $20,000 in damages. The court ordered it to pay them $4,500. A state appellate court, however, reversed the county court's decision, and a determined Barron appealed to the U.S. Supreme Court.

Barron's lawyer tried to discuss the specific issue of the wharf, but the justices asked him to confine his argument to constitutional issues. The attorney responded by arguing that the Fifth Amendment of the U.S. Constitution, which guarantees that "private property cannot be taken for public use, without just compensation" should apply to states, and not just the federal government.[4] Baltimore's attorney, Roger Brooke Taney, a future chief justice, must have thought otherwise, but the Court never gave him a chance to speak. As soon as he got up to argue the city's case, the Court cut him off, apparently having made up its mind.

Writing for a unanimous Court, in one of his

2. James Madison, Speech before the House of Representatives, June 7, 1789.

3. For a full account of this case, see Fred Friendly and Martha J. H. Elliot, *The Constitution: That Delicate Balance* (New York: Random House, 1984).

4. See Friendly and Elliot, *The Constitution,* 11.

Conditions in Baltimore Harbor, depicted in 1830 by William J. Bennett, lead to the 1833 Supreme Court decision in *Barron v. Baltimore.* Chief Justice John Marshall's majority opinion in *Barron* explained why state and local governments were not constrained by the federal Bill of Rights.

last major opinions, Chief Justice Marshall, who previously had shown a propensity to enlarge the powers of national government, sent a clear message to the states on the question of nationalizing the Bill of Rights.

MR. CHIEF JUSTICE MARSHALL delivered the opinion of the Court.

The constitution was ordained and established by the people of the United States for themselves, for their own government, and not for the government of the individual states. Each state established a constitution for itself, and, in that constitution, provided such limitations and restrictions on the powers of its particular government as its judgment dictated. The people of the United States framed such a government for the United States as they supposed best adapted to their situation, and best calculated to promote their interests. The powers they conferred on this government were to be exercised by itself; and the limitations on power, if expressed in general terms, are naturally, and, we think, necessarily applicable to the government created by the instrument. They are limitations of power granted in the instrument itself; not of distinct governments, framed by different persons and for different purposes.

If these propositions be correct, the fifth amendment must be understood as restraining the power of the general government, not as applicable to the states. In their several constitutions they have imposed such restrictions on their respective governments as their own wisdom suggested;

such as they deemed most proper for themselves. It is a subject on which they judge exclusively, and with which others interfere no farther than they are supposed to have a common interest....

Had the people of the several states, or any of them, required changes in their constitutions; had they required additional safeguards to liberty from the apprehended encroachments of their particular governments: the remedy was in their own hands, and would have been applied by themselves. A convention would have been assembled by the discontented state, and the required improvements would have been made by itself. The unwieldy and cumbrous machinery of procuring a recommendation from two-thirds of congress, and the assent of three-fourths of their sister states, could never have occurred to any human being as a mode of doing that which might be effected by the state itself. Had the framers of these amendments intended them to be limitations on the powers of the state governments, they would have imitated the framers of the original constitution, and have expressed that intention. Had congress engaged in the extraordinary occupation of improving the constitutions of the several states by affording the people additional protection from the exercise of power by their own governments in matters which concerned themselves alone, they would have declared this purpose in plain and intelligible language.

But it is universally understood, it is a part of the history of the day, that the great revolution which established the constitution of the United States, was not effected without immense opposition. Serious fears were extensively entertained that those powers which the patriot statesmen, who then watched over the interests of our country, deemed essential to union, and to the attainment of those invaluable objects for which union was sought, might be exercised in a manner dangerous to liberty. In almost every convention by which the constitution was adopted, amendments to guard against the abuse of power were recommended. These amendments demanded security against the apprehended encroachments of the general government not against those of the local governments.

In compliance with a sentiment thus generally expressed, to quiet fears thus extensively entertained, amendments were proposed by the required majority in congress, and adopted by the states. These amendments contain no

expression indicating an intention to apply them to the state governments. This court cannot so apply them.

We are of opinion that the provision in the fifth amendment to the constitution, declaring that private property shall not be taken for public use without just compensation, is intended solely as a limitation on the exercise of power by the government of the United States, and is not applicable to the legislation of the states. We are therefore of opinion that there is no repugnancy between the several acts of the general assembly of Maryland, given in evidence by the defendants at the trial of this cause, in the court of that state, and the constitution of the United States. This court, therefore, has no jurisdiction of the cause; and it is dismissed.

INCORPORATION THROUGH THE FOURTEENTH AMENDMENT: EARLY INTERPRETATIONS

Marshall quipped that the Court did not have "much difficulty" in addressing the question at issue in *Barron*. But the question of the applicability of the Bill of Rights to state and local governments would not disappear with similar ease. Indeed, in the years immediately preceding the Civil War, several Court decisions clearly showed the nature of a polity without universal application of national rights. Among the most significant of these was *Scott v. Sandford* (1857), in which the justices ruled that the Constitution did not grant citizenship to blacks. Not surprisingly, the debate over incorporation heated up after ratification of the Fourteenth Amendment in 1868. Given that this amendment was ratified three years after the Civil War, the goals of its framers seemed clear: to secure the Union and to ensure equality for blacks. Some lawyers, however, saw additional opportunities under the Fourteenth Amendment. They viewed one of its provisions, the Privileges and Immunities Clause, as a vehicle by which to nationalize the Bill of Rights. The wording of this clause makes such an interpretation possible: "No State shall make or enforce any law which shall abridge the privileges or immunities of citizens of the United States." Asserting that the privileges and immunities of U.S. citizenship included all those rights stipulated in the federal Bill of Rights, these attorneys argued that this provision of the Fourteenth Amendment "incorporated" the constitutional guarantees and obliged the states to conform to them.

The Supreme Court had its first opportunity to scrutinize this claim in *The Slaughterhouse Cases* (1873). This litigation grew out of the industrial revolution—an economic diversification that touched the whole country. Although this revolution changed the United States for the better in many ways, it also had negative effects. In Louisiana, for example, the state legislature claimed that the Mississippi River had become polluted because New Orleans butchers continually dumped garbage into it. To remedy this problem (or, as some have suggested, to use it as an excuse to form a monopolistic enterprise), the legislature created a company, the Crescent City Live Stock Landing & Slaughter House Company, to receive and slaughter all city livestock for twenty-five years.

Because they were forced to use its facilities and pay top dollar for the privilege, the butchers of New Orleans despised this new corporation. They formed their own organization, the Butchers' Benevolent Association, and hired an attorney, former U.S. Supreme Court justice John A. Campbell, to sue the corporation for depriving them of their right to pursue their business, a basic guarantee, they argued, granted by the Fourteenth Amendment's Privileges and Immunities Clause. After a state district court and the Louisiana Supreme Court ruled in favor of the corporation, the butchers' association appealed to the U.S. Supreme Court.

Writing for a slim, five-person majority, Justice Samuel F. Miller affirmed the judgment of the Louisiana court. As he put it:

Was it the purpose of the fourteenth amendment, by the simple declaration that no State should make or enforce any law which shall abridge the privileges and immunities of *citizens of the United States*, to transfer the security and protection of all the civil rights which we have mentioned, from the States to the Federal government? And where it is declared that Congress shall have the power to enforce that article, was it intended to bring within the power of Congress the entire domain of civil rights heretofore belonging exclusively to the States?

All this and more must follow, if the proposition of the plaintiffs ... be sound. For not only are these rights subject to the control of Congress whenever in its discretion any of them are supposed to be abridged by State legislation, but that body may also pass laws in advance, limiting and restricting the exercise of legislative power by the States, in their most ordinary and usual functions, as in its judgment it may think proper on all such subjects. And still further, such a construction followed by the reversal of the judgments of the Supreme Court of Louisiana in these cases, would constitute this court a perpetual censor upon all legislation of the States, on the civil rights of their own citizens, with authority to nullify such as it did not approve as consistent with those rights, as they existed at the time of the adoption of this amendment. The argument we admit is not always the most conclusive which is drawn from the consequences urged against the adoption of a particular construction of an instrument. But when, as in the case before us, these consequences are so serious, so far-reaching and pervading, so great a departure from the structure and spirit of our institutions; when the effect is to fetter and degrade the State governments by subjecting them to the control of Congress, in the exercise of powers heretofore universally conceded to them of the most ordinary and fundamental character; when in fact it radically changes the whole theory of the relations of the State and Federal governments to each other and of both these governments to the people; the argument has a force that is irresistible, in the absence of language which expresses such a purpose too clearly to admit of doubt.

We are convinced that no such results were intended by the Congress which proposed these amendments, nor by the legislatures of the States which ratified them....

Justice Miller's majority opinion had at least two major effects on the development of the law. First, its severely limited interpretation rendered the Privileges and Immunities Clause of the Fourteenth Amendment almost useless, a condition that has changed little over the past century. Second and most relevant to our understanding of incorporation, the Court made clear that it would not use this clause as a vehicle by which to nationalize the Bill of Rights.

With the *Slaughterhouse Cases* sounding the death knell for incorporation via the Privileges and Immunities Clause, attorneys turned to yet another section of the Fourteenth Amendment, the Due Process Clause, which says, "Nor shall any State deprive any person of life, liberty, or property, without due process of law." The advocates of nationalizing the Bill of Rights hoped to convince the Court that the words *due process of law* incorporated those rights protected by the first eight amendments. If this argument proved successful, the Due Process Clause would prohibit the states from violating any of the liberties protected under the federal Bill of Rights. But would the justices be willing to use this section as a mechanism for incorporation?

In its first opportunity to evaluate this claim, *Hurtado v. California* (1884), the Court rejected such an interpretation of the Due Process Clause. While reading the opinions in *Hurtado,* consider two questions. First, did the Court completely shut the door on the use of this clause to incorporate the Bill of Rights? Second, how did Justice John Marshall Harlan's lone dissent differ from the views of the Court's majority?

Hurtado v. California

110 U.S. 516 (1884)
*Vote: 7 (Blatchford, Bradley, Gray, Matthews, Miller,
        Waite, Woods)
    1 (Harlan)
Opinion of the Court: Matthews
Dissenting opinion: Harlan
Not participating: Field*

Joseph Hurtado and his wife, Susie, lived in Sacramento, California, where they were friendly with Jose Antonio Estuardo, an immigrant from Chile. The friendship disintegrated, however, when Hurtado learned of Estuardo's affair with Susie. Hurtado asked his former crony to leave the city, but Estuardo contin-

ued to court Susie until Hurtado sent her to live with her parents. This arrangement proved only temporary; when Susie returned to Sacramento, Estuardo again pursued her. Faced with this continuing threat, Hurtado assaulted Estuardo in a bar, and police arrested him on battery charges. After his trial was postponed, Hurtado shot and killed his wife's lover.[5] The state charged Hurtado with murder, an offense punishable by death.

At the time, many states provided for grand jury hearings before a defendant went to trial. Typically, such bodies listen exclusively to the prosecutor's side of a case and decide whether enough evidence exists to go to trial. The California Constitution of 1879, however, specified that prosecutors could initiate trials from an information (a document issued by the prosecutor, officially charging an individual with criminal violations), reviewed by a judge in lieu of a grand jury. Such was the case in *Hurtado.* Based on an information, the state brought Hurtado to trial for murder. He was found guilty and received the death penalty. The California Supreme Court affirmed this sentence, and a date was set for his execution. Hurtado's counsel objected on the grounds that the state denied the condemned man his right to a grand jury hearing and to due process of law. Because these guarantees applied to federal proceedings under the Fifth Amendment, he argued that they also should apply to the states under the Fourteenth Amendment's Due Process and Privileges and Immunities clauses. The state responded that since *Barron v. Baltimore* it was settled law that the states were not constitutionally obliged to observe the provisions of the federal Bill of Rights. After Hurtado lost this point in the California Supreme Court, he sought a writ of error to the U.S. Supreme Court, urging the justices to incorporate the Fifth Amendment right to a grand jury hearing into the Due Process Clause and thus make it binding on the states.

---

5. For more details on this case, see Richard C. Cortner, *The Supreme Court and the Second Bill of Rights* (Madison: University of Wisconsin Press, 1981).

MR. JUSTICE MATTHEWS delivered the opinion of the Court.

It is claimed on behalf of the prisoner that the conviction and sentence are void, on the ground that they are repugnant to that clause of the Fourteenth Article of Amendment of the Constitution of the United States which is in these words:

"Nor shall any State deprive any person of life, liberty, or property without due process of law."

The proposition of law we are asked to affirm is that an indictment or presentment by a grand jury, as known to the common law of England, is essential to that "due process of law," when applied to prosecutions for felonies, which is secured and guaranteed by this provision of the Constitution of the United States, and which accordingly it is forbidden to the States respectively to dispense with in the administration of criminal law.

The question is one of grave and serious import, affecting both private and public rights and interests of great magnitude, and involves a consideration of what additional restrictions upon the legislative policy of the States has been imposed by the Fourteenth Amendment to the Constitution of the United States....

We are to construe this phrase in the Fourteenth Amendment by the *usus loquendi* [common usage of ordinary speech] of the Constitution itself. The same words are contained in the Fifth Amendment. That article makes specific and express provision for perpetuating the institution of the grand jury, so far as relates to prosecution for the more aggravated crimes under the laws of the United States....

According to a recognized canon of interpretation, especially applicable to formal and solemn instruments of constitutional law, we are forbidden to assume, without clear reason to the contrary, that any part of this most important amendment is superfluous. The natural and obvious inference is, that in the sense of the Constitution, "due process of law" was not meant or intended to include, *en vi termini* [by the force of the term], the institution and procedure of a grand jury in any case. The conclusion is equally irresistible, that when the same phrase was employed in the Fourteenth Amendment to restrain the action of the States, it was used

in the same sense and with no greater extent; and that if in the adoption of that amendment it had been part of its purpose to perpetuate the institution of the grand jury in all the States, it would have embodied, as did the Fifth Amendment, express declarations to that effect. Due process of law in the latter refers to that law of the land which derives its authority from the legislative powers conferred upon Congress by the Constitution of the United States, exercised within the limits therein prescribed, and interpreted according to the principles of the common law. In the Fourteenth Amendment, by parity of reason, it refers to that law of the land in each State, which derives its authority from the inherent and reserved powers of the State, exerted within the limits of those fundamental principles of liberty and justice which lie at the base of all our civil and political institutions, and the greatest security for which resides in the right of the people to make their own laws, and alter them at their pleasure....

But it is not to be supposed that these legislative powers are absolute and despotic, and that the amendment prescribing due process of law is too vague and indefinite to operate as a practical restraint. It is not every act, legislative in form, that is law. Law is something more than mere will exerted as an act of power. It must be not a special rule for a particular person or a particular case, but ... "the general law, a law which hears before it condemns, which proceeds upon inquiry, and renders judgment only after trial," so "that every citizen shall hold his life, liberty, property and immunities under the protection of the general rules which govern society," and thus excluding, as not due process of law, acts of attainder, bills of pains and penalties, acts of confiscation, acts reversing judgments, and acts directly transferring one man's estate to another, legislative judgments and decrees, and other similar special, partial and arbitrary exertions of power under the forms of legislation. Arbitrary power, enforcing its edicts to the injury of the persons and property of its subjects, is not law, whether manifested as the decree of a personal monarch or of an impersonal multitude. And the limitations imposed by our constitutional law upon the action of the governments, both State and national, are essential to the preservation of public and private rights, notwithstanding the representative character of our political institutions. The enforcement of these limitations by judicial process is the device of self-governing communities to protect the rights of individuals and minorities, as well against the power of numbers, as against the violence of public agents transcending the limits of lawful authority, even when acting in the name and wielding the force of the government....

It follows that any legal proceeding enforced by public authority, whether sanctioned by age and custom, or newly devised in the discretion of the legislative power, in furtherance of the general public good, which regards and preserves these principles of liberty and justice, must be held to be due process of law....

Tried by these principles, we are unable to say that the substitution for a presentment or indictment by a grand jury of the proceeding by information, after examination and commitment by a magistrate, certifying to the probable guilt of the defendant, with the right on his part to the aid of counsel, and to the cross-examination of the witnesses produced for the prosecution, is not due process of law. It is ... an ancient proceeding at common law, which might include every case of an offence of less grade than a felony, except misprision of treason; and in every circumstance of its administration, as authorized by the statute of California, it carefully considers and guards the substantial interest of the prisoner. It is merely a preliminary proceeding, and can result in no final judgment, except as the consequence of a regular judicial trial, conducted precisely as in cases of indictments....

For these reasons, finding no error therein, the judgment of the Supreme Court of California is

Affirmed.

MR JUSTICE HARLAN, dissenting.

My brethren concede that there are principles of liberty and justice, lying at the foundation of our civil and political institutions, which no State can violate consistently with that due process of law required by the Fourteenth Amendment in proceedings involving life, liberty, or property. Some of these principles are enumerated in the opinion of the court. But, for reasons which do not impress my mind as satisfactory, they exclude from that enumeration the exemption from prosecution, by information, for a public offence involving life. By what authority is that exclusion made?...

[I]t is said that the framers of the Constitution did not suppose that due process of law necessarily required for a capital offence the institution and procedure of a grand jury, else they would not in the same amendment prohibiting the deprivation of life, liberty, or property, without due process of law, have made specific and express provision for a grand jury where the crime is capital or otherwise infamous; therefore, it is argued, the requirement by the Fourteenth Amendment of due process of law in all proceedings involving life, liberty, and property, without specific reference to grand juries in any case whatever, was not intended as a restriction upon the power which it is claimed the States previously had, so far as the express restrictions of the national Constitution are concerned, to dispense altogether with grand juries.

This line of argument, it seems to me, would lead to results which are inconsistent with the vital principles of republican government. If the presence in the Fifth Amendment of a specific provision for grand juries in capital cases, alongside the provision for due process of law in proceedings involving life, liberty, or property, is held to prove that "due process of law" did not, in the judgment of the framers of the Constitution, necessarily require a grand jury in capital cases, inexorable logic would require it to be, likewise, held that the right not to be put twice in jeopardy of life and limb for the same offence, nor compelled in a criminal case to testify against one's self—rights and immunities also specifically recognized in the Fifth Amendment—were not protected by that due process of law required by the settled usages and proceedings existing under the common and statute law of England at the settlement of this country. More than that, other amendments of the Constitution proposed at the same time, expressly recognize the right of persons to just compensation for private property taken for public use; their right, when accused of crime, to be informed of the nature and cause of the accusation against them, and to a speedy and public trial, by an impartial jury of the State and district wherein the crime was committed; to be confronted by the witnesses against them; and to have compulsory process for obtaining witnesses in their favor.... If the argument of my brethren be sound, those rights—although universally recognized at the establishment of our institutions as secured by that due process of law which for centuries had been the foundation of Anglo-Saxon liberty—were not deemed by our fathers as essential in the due process of law prescribed by our Constitution; because,—such seems to be the argument—had they been regarded as involved in due process of law they would not have been specifically and expressly provided for, but left to the protection given by the general clause forbidding the deprivation of life, liberty, or property without due process of law. Further, the reasoning of the opinion indubitably leads to the conclusion that but for the specific provisions made in the Constitution for the security of the personal rights enumerated, the general inhibition against deprivation of life, liberty, and property without due process of law would not have prevented Congress from enacting a statute in derogation of each of them....

It seems to me that too much stress is put upon the fact that the framers of the Constitution made express provision for the security of those rights which at common law were protected by the requirement of due process of law, and, in addition, declared, generally, that no person shall "be deprived of life, liberty or property without due process of law." The rights, for the security of which these express provisions were made, were of a character so essential to the safety of the people that it was deemed wise to avoid the possibility that Congress, in regulating the processes of law, would impair or destroy them. Hence, their specific enumeration in the earlier amendments of the Constitution, in connection with the general requirement of due process of law, the latter itself being broad enough to cover every right of life, liberty or property secured by the settled usages and modes of proceeding existing under the common and statute law of England at the time our government was founded....

[D]ue process of law protects the fundamental principles of liberty and justice, adjudges, in effect, that an immunity or right, recognized at the common law to be essential to personal security, jealously guarded by our national Constitution against violation by any tribunal or body exercising authority under the general government, and expressly or impliedly recognized, *when the Fourteenth Amendment was adopted,* in the Bill of Rights or Constitution of every State in the Union, is, yet, not a fundamental principle in governments established, as those of the States of the Union are, to

secure to the citizen liberty and justice, and, therefore, is not involved in that due process of law required in proceedings conducted under the sanction of a State. My sense of duty constrains me to dissent from this interpretation of the supreme law of the land.

Although it failed to adopt Hurtado's claims, the Court did not completely preclude the possibility of incorporation. The majority reasoned that because due process is explicitly part of the Fifth Amendment, it could not be the equivalent of the entire Bill of Rights. In other words, the Due Process Clause could not be used to apply the entire Bill of Rights to the states. But, as Richard C. Cortner points out, the Court ruled that the Due Process Clause "did protect against state encroachment those 'fundamental principles of liberty and justice which lie at the base of all our civil and political institutions.'"[6] For the legal community and citizens of the United States, however, the Court left unresolved a critical question: Did "fundamental principles" include those guarantees contained under the Bill of Rights?

Chicago, Burlington & Quincy Railroad v. Chicago (1897), one of the most important cases to come to the Court after *Hurtado,* involved an economic issue rather than criminal procedure. This case, like *Barron* and *The Slaughterhouse Cases,* grew out of a controversy caused by industrialization, this time in Chicago. As that city began to expand, it bought, under the principle of eminent domain, large pieces of property belonging to railroad companies and private citizens. Based on local ordinances, the city offered property owners what it considered just compensation for the land. If the owners considered the offers unacceptable, they could challenge the city in county court. In many instances, owners took advantage of litigation, challenging offers made by the city as inequitable. But, in this particular county court, an interesting pattern emerged: individual property owners received almost

6. Cortner, *The Supreme Court,* 21.

$13,000 for their lands, while the railroad companies got only $1.

Viewing this apparent inequity as a violation of the Fifth Amendment's guarantee that private property shall not "be taken for public use, without just compensation," one railroad company took its case to the Illinois Supreme Court. When the judges affirmed the county court's decision, the company appealed to the U.S. Supreme Court, asking the justices to interpret the Fifth Amendment the same way John Barron had sixty-four years before: that the Just Compensation (or Takings) Clause should apply to states. The railroads, however, had a weapon nonexistent in Barron's day— the Fourteenth Amendment's Due Process Clause. And this Court did what the justices under John Marshall had refused to do: it ruled that the states must abide by the Fifth Amendment's commands regarding public use of private property. Writing for the majority, Justice Harlan had an opportunity to see the logic of his dissent in *Hurtado* become the basis for the opinion of the Court:

In determining what is due process of law regard must be had to substance, not to form.... If compensation for private property taken for public use is an essential element of due process of law as ordained by the Fourteenth Amendment, then the final judgment of a state court ... is to be decreed the act of the State within the meaning of that amendment.

Harlan added that just compensation indeed constituted "a vital principle of republican institutions" without which "almost all other rights would become worthless."

Finally, then, the Court incorporated, via the Fourteenth Amendment, a clause contained in the Bill of Rights. In so deciding, however, the Court failed to bridge the apparent contradictions between *Hurtado* and *Chicago Railroad*, leaving open the question of which would provide controlling precedent in this area. Stated another way, why was the Court willing to incorporate the Fifth Amendment's guarantee of just compensation, but not the grand jury provision?

The next incorporation case, *Maxwell v. Dow* (1900), did little to shed light on this puzzling question. At issue were the antics of Charles L. "Gunplay" Maxwell, who robbed a Utah bank in 1898. Under the state's newly adopted constitution, an individual charged with a noncapital offense, such as armed robbery, could be tried by a jury of eight persons instead of the traditional twelve, and no provision was made for a defendant's right to a grand jury hearing. After an eight-person jury found him guilty and he was sentenced to eighteen years in prison, Maxwell hired an experienced criminal lawyer, J. W. N. Whitecotton, to represent him in the state supreme court. Whitecotton argued that the state's denial of grand jury proceedings and its jury trial system deprived Maxwell of his federal Fifth and Sixth Amendment rights, which should be incorporated under the Fourteenth Amendment's Due Process Clause and Privileges and Immunities Clause. Utah's highest court rejected this claim, and Maxwell filed for a writ of error with the U.S. Supreme Court, asking the justices specifically to rectify contradictions of interpretation between *Hurtado* and *Chicago Railroad*. The Court, 8–1, refused to do so and, in fact, virtually ignored the entire incorporation argument. Writing for the majority, Justice Rufus W. Peckham noted, "Trial by jury has never been affirmed to be a necessary requisite of due process of law."

Thus, the three major cases following the *Slaughterhouse* decision—*Hurtado*, *Chicago Railroad*, and *Maxwell*—provided no clear answers to a legal community seeking direction on incorporation. If anything, more questions than answers remained because of the apparent contradictions among these decisions.

NEW LIFE FOR INCORPORATION

As legal scholars debated incorporation, the Court took a case that eventually provided the ultimate solution. In *Twining v. New Jersey* (1908) the Court moved one cautious step closer to enunciating the doctrine of selective incorporation. While reading *Twining*, consider the following questions: First, and most important, what did the Court suggest about incorporation-based arguments? Second, how did it reconcile contradictions between *Hurtado* and *Chicago Railroad?*

Twining v. New Jersey

211 U.S. 78 (1908)

Vote: 8 (Brewer, Day, Fuller, Holmes, McKenna, Moody,
Peckham, White)
   1 (Harlan)

Majority opinion: Moody
Dissenting opinion: Harlan

New Jersey initiated several actions, all involving fraud, against Albert Twining and other officers of a bank trust. The state trial and appellate courts dismissed all but one, which involved the false reporting of a bank stock deal by Twining.

At his trial in state court, Twining refused to take the stand, invoking his guarantee against self-incrimination. The judge allowed him to do this, but in his charge to the jury he made reference to Twining's refusal to testify, insinuating that it implied guilt. If the federal Fifth Amendment provision against self-incrimination were applicable to the states, such comments clearly would be impermissible.

Twining's attorney appealed to the state's high court, alleging that the judge's words denied Twining due process of law. But the New Jersey Supreme Court upheld the judge's right to highlight in his instructions to the jury a defendant's refusal to testify. Twining appealed to the U.S. Supreme Court, asking it to incorporate the Fifth Amendment protection against self-incrimination.

MR. JUSTICE MOODY delivered the opinion of the Court.

The defendants ... appeal to [a] clause of the Fourteenth Amendment, and insist that the self-incrimination, which they allege the instruction to the jury compelled, was a denial of due process of law.... It is possible that some of the personal rights safeguarded by the first eight Amendments against National action may also be safeguarded against state action, because a denial of them would be a denial of due process of law. If this is so, it is not because those rights are enumerated in the first eight Amendments, but because they are of such a nature that they are included in the conception of due process of law. Few phrases of the law are so elusive of exact apprehension as this. Doubtless the difficulties of ascertaining its connotation have been increased in American jurisprudence, where it has been embodied in constitutions and put to new uses as a limit on legislative power. This court has always declined to give a comprehensive definition of it, and has preferred that its full meaning should be gradually ascertained by the process of inclusion and exclusion in the course of the decisions of cases as they arise. There are certain general principles well settled, however, which narrow the field of discussion and may serve as helps to correct conclusions....

But ... we prefer to rest our decision on broader grounds, and inquire whether the exemption from self-incrimination is of such a nature that it must be included in the conception of due process. Is it a fundamental principle of liberty and justice which inheres in the very idea of free government and is the inalienable right of a citizen of such a government? If it is, and if it is of a nature that pertains to process of law, this court has declared it to be essential to due process of law. In approaching such a question it must not be forgotten that in a free representative government nothing is more fundamental than the right of the people through their appointed servants to govern themselves in accordance with their own will, except so far as they have restrained themselves by constitutional limits specifically established, and that in our peculiar dual form of government nothing is more fundamental than the full power of the State to order its own affairs and govern its own people, except so far as the Federal Constitution expressly or by fair implication has withdrawn that power. The power of the people of the States to make and alter their laws at pleasure is the greatest security for liberty and justice, this court has said in *Hurtado v. California.* We are not invested with the jurisdiction to pass upon the expediency, wisdom or justice of the laws of the States as declared by their courts, but only to determine their conformity with the Federal Constitution and the paramount laws enacted pursuant to it. Under the guise of interpreting the Constitution we must take care that we do not import into the discussion our own personal views of what would be wise, just and fitting rules of government to be adopted by a free people and confound them with constitutional limitations. The question before us is the meaning of a constitutional provision which forbids the States to deny to any person due process of law. In the decision of this question we have the authority to take into account only those fundamental rights which are expressed in that provision, not the rights fundamental in citizenship, state or National, for they are secured otherwise, but the rights fundamental in due process, and therefore an essential part of it. We have to consider whether the right is so fundamental in due process that a refusal of the right is a denial of due process. One aid to the solution of the question is to inquire how the right was rated during the time when the meaning of due process was in a formative state and before it was incorporated in American constitutional law. Did those who then were formulating and insisting upon the rights of the people entertain the view that the right was so fundamental that there could be no due process without it? It has already appeared that, prior to the formation of the American Constitutions, in which the exemption from compulsory self-incrimination was specifically secured, separately, independently, and side by side with the requirement of due process, the doctrine was formed, as other doctrines of the law of evidence have been formed, by the course of decision in the courts covering a long period of time. Searching further, we find nothing to show that it was then thought to be other than a just and useful principle of law. . . .

The decisions of this court, though they are silent on the precise question before us, ought to be searched to discover if they present any analogies which are helpful in its decision. The essential elements of due process of law, already established by them, are singularly few, though of wide application and deep significance. We are not here concerned with the effect of due process in restraining substantive laws, as, for example, that which forbids the taking of private property for public use without compensation. We need notice now only those cases which deal with the principles which must be observed in the trial of criminal and civil causes. Due process requires that the court which assumes to determine the rights of parties shall have jurisdiction and

that there shall be notice and opportunity for hearing given the parties. Subject to these two fundamental conditions, which seem to be universally prescribed in all systems of law established by civilized countries, this court has up to this time sustained all state laws, statutory or judicially declared, regulating procedure, evidence and methods of trial, and held them to be consistent with due process of law.

Among the most notable of these decisions are those sustaining the denial of jury trial both in civil and criminal cases, the substitution of informations for indictments by a grand jury, the enactment that the possession of policy slips raises a presumption of illegality, and the admission of the deposition of an absent witness in a criminal case. The cases proceed upon the theory that, given a court of justice which has jurisdiction and acts, not arbitrarily but in conformity with a general law, upon evidence, and after inquiry made with notice to the parties affected and opportunity to be heard, then all the requirements of due process, so far as it relates to procedure in court, and methods of trial and character and effect of evidence, are complied with. . . .

We have assumed only for the purpose of discussion that what was done in the case at bar was an infringement of the privilege against self-incrimination. We do not intend, however, to lend any countenance to the truth of that assumption. The courts of New Jersey, in adopting the rule of law which is complained of here, have deemed it consistent with the privilege itself and not a denial of it. . . . We think that the exemption from compulsory self-incrimination in the courts of the States is not secured by any part of the Federal Constitution.

Judgment affirmed.

Even though it ruled against Twining's claim, the Court cracked opened the door for the application of some rights to the states: a majority of the justices held that the Fourteenth Amendment's Due Process Clause "might protect against state action of some rights similar to those contained in the Bill of Rights"—those rights that were fundamental and inalienable.[7] But note the Court's cautiousness. It refused to rule that

7. Ibid., 48.

the entire Bill of Rights was applicable to the states through the Due Process Clause; in other words, due process of law is not the equivalent of the first eight Amendments. Quite the contrary. Recall the Court's words: rights akin to those in the Bill of Rights might fall under the protection of the Due Process Clause "not because those rights are enumerated in the first eight Amendments, but because they are of such a nature that they are included in the conception of due process of law." As Cortner writes, "The Court thus seemed to be indicating that if the Due Process Clause protected rights similar to some of those in the Bill of Rights, such rights would be only similar and not identical in scope and meaning to their counterparts in the Bill of Rights."[8]

In the final analysis, the opinion in *Twining* is narrow in its approach to incorporation. The Court refused to make the entire Bill of Rights applicable to the states and it denied that the specific right at issue—the exemption from compulsory self-incrimination—should be protected against state action. Still, it is an important decision because it created the *possibility* of incorporation by future Courts, if they could identify rights deemed fundamental and inalienable. In any event, the application to the states of such rights apparently was to occur selectively, on a case-by-case basis.

INCORPORATION IN THE WAKE OF *TWINING*

In his opinion in *Twining,* Justice William H. Moody provided several examples of fundamental and inalienable rights: a court must have jurisdiction to hear a case, it must provide adequate notice of trial dates and charges, and it must grant a trial for those accused of committing a crime. Beyond these, Moody did not specify what other guarantees might fall under the rubric of fundamental and inalienable. This gap put a

8. Ibid.

burden on lawyers litigating claims of civil rights, civil liberties, and criminal justice to bring cases testing the boundaries of *Twining.* These lawyers had a vested interest in securing the vast federal guarantees for their clients for whom such rights remained inapplicable in state courts. They recognized that cases involving free speech, religion, and search and seizure, which they were losing in state trial courts, could turn into winners if the Court agreed that these and other rights were fundamental. It is not surprising that one of the earlier cases assessing the boundaries of *Twining* involved a free speech claim brought to the Court's attention by the American Civil Liberties Union.

The issues in *Gitlow v. New York* (1925) arose during the early 1900s (and in the 1950s) when the United States was gripped by a fear of communist subversion. To combat the "Red Menace," several states, including New York, created commissions to investigate subversive organizations. The New York commission in 1919 raided one such group, arresting 500 Socialist and Communist party leaders and seizing their materials. Among the publications taken was the *Left Wing Manifesto,* a journal edited by Benjamin Gitlow, who was elected to the state legislature on the Socialist party ticket. The journal called for mass action to overthrow the capitalist system in the United States. Gitlow was prosecuted in a New York trial court for violating the state's criminal anarchy law. Under the leadership of Clarence Darrow, Gitlow's defense attorneys alleged that the statute violated the First Amendment's guarantee of free speech, a fundamental right deserving incorporation under the Due Process Clause.

In a 7–2 decision the Supreme Court affirmed Gitlow's conviction. But, in doing so, it adopted Darrow's argument and incorporated the Free Speech Clause. As Justice Edward T. Sanford wrote for the majority,

For present purposes we may and do assume that freedom of speech and of the press ... are among the fundamental personal rights and "liberties" protected by the due process clause of the Fourteenth Amendment from impairment by the states.... Reasonably limited ... this freedom is an inestimable privilege in a free government.

The Court went no further: once again, it refused to provide a more general principle by which to identify fundamental rights.

Even so, *Gitlow* is an important case for two reasons. First, the justices moved a step beyond *Twining*. In *Twining* the Court "indicated that the Due Process Clause might guarantee certain 'fundamental' rights similar to those in the Bill of Rights"[9]; in *Gitlow,* the Court made applicable to the states the specific First Amendment guarantees of free speech and press. Second, *Gitlow* was a portent. Although the Court did not explicate a particular approach to incorporation, its willingness to apply speech and press guarantees to the states because these rights are fundamental generated a doctrine called *selective incorporation.* Under this approach, the Court would proceed on a case-by-case, right-by-right basis in determining whether various provisions of the Bill of Rights met the fundamental and inalienable rights criterion for incorporation. Again, *Twining*—with its emphasis on the selective application of rights—foreshadowed this development. But it was in *Gitlow* that the Court took a concrete step toward selective incorporation.

Although the Court seemed implicitly to adopt this doctrine of selective incorporation, applying several other guarantees contained in the First Amendment to the states, it waited almost fifteen years before it provided any further indication of what it meant by "fundamental rights." This time *Palko v. Connecticut* (1937), a case involving the Fifth Amendment's prohibition against double jeopardy, provided the vehicle. While reading *Palko,* consider the signals it sent to lawyers across the nation. How did it help them to determine which rights were fundamental?

9. Ibid., 62.

Palko v. Connecticut

302 U.S. 319 (1937)

Vote: 8 (Black, Brandeis, Cardozo, Hughes, McReynolds, Roberts, Stone, Sutherland)
   1 (Butler)

Opinion of the Court: Cardozo

The story of Frank Palko begins in Connecticut, where he robbed a store and shot and killed two police officers. Arrested in Buffalo, New York, Palko confessed to the killings. At his trial for first degree murder, the Connecticut judge refused to admit Palko's confession, and, in the absence of such evidence, the jury found him guilty only of second degree murder. State prosecutors appealed to the Connecticut Supreme Court of Errors, which reversed the trial judge's exclusion of Palko's confession and ordered a new trial. Palko's attorney objected, claiming that a new trial violated the Fifth Amendment's prohibition of double jeopardy. Nevertheless, Palko was tried and convicted again, but this time of first degree murder. When his appeal to the Connecticut high court failed, Palko brought suit in the U.S. Supreme Court, asking it to incorporate double jeopardy.

MR. JUSTICE CARDOZO delivered the opinion of the Court.

The argument for appellant is that whatever is forbidden by the Fifth Amendment is forbidden by the Fourteenth also. The Fifth Amendment, which is not directed to the states, but solely to the federal government, creates immunity from double jeopardy. No person shall be "subject for the same offense to be twice put in jeopardy of life or limb." The Fourteenth Amendment ordains, "nor shall any State deprive any person of life, liberty, or property, without due process of law." To retry a defendant, though under one indictment and only one, subjects him, it is said, to double jeopardy in violation of the Fifth Amendment, if the prosecution is one on behalf of the United States. From this the consequence is said to follow that there is a denial of life or liberty without due process of law, if the prosecution is one on behalf of the People of a State....

We have said that in appellant's view the Fourteenth Amendment is to be taken as embodying the prohibitions of the Fifth. His thesis is even broader. Whatever would be a violation of the original bill of rights (Amendments I to VIII) if done by the federal government is now equally unlawful by force of the Fourteenth Amendment if done by a state. There is no such general rule.

The Fifth Amendment provides, among other things, that no person shall be held to answer for a capital or otherwise infamous crime unless on presentment or indictment of a grand jury. This court has held that, in prosecutions by a state, presentment or indictment by a grand jury may give way to information at the instance of a public officer. The Fifth Amendment provides also that no person shall be compelled in any criminal case to be a witness against himself. This court has said that, in prosecutions by a state, the exemption will fail if the state elects to end it. The Sixth Amendment calls for a jury trial in criminal cases and the Seventh for a jury trial in civil cases at common law where the value in controversy shall exceed twenty dollars. This court has ruled that consistently with those amendments trial by jury may be modified by a state or abolished altogether....

On the other hand, the due process clause of the Fourteenth Amendment may make it unlawful for a state to abridge by its statutes the freedom of speech which the First Amendment safeguards against encroachment by the Congress, or the like freedom of the press, or the free exercise of religion, or the right of peaceable assembly, without which speech would be unduly trammeled, or the right of one accused of crime to the benefit of counsel. In these and other situations immunities that are valid as against the federal government by force of the specific pledges of particular amendments have been found to be implicit in the concept of ordered liberty, and thus, through the Fourteenth Amendment, become valid as against the states.

The line of division may seem to be wavering and broken if there is a hasty catalogue of the cases on the one side and the other. Reflection and analysis will induce a different view. There emerges the perception of a rationalizing principle which gives to discrete instances a proper order and co-

herence. The right to trial by jury and the immunity from prosecution except as the result of an indictment may have value and importance. Even so, they are not of the very essence of a scheme of ordered liberty. To abolish them is not to violate a "principle of justice so rooted in the traditions and conscience of our people as to be ranked as fundamental." Few would be so narrow or provincial as to maintain that a fair and enlightened system of justice would be impossible without them. What is true of jury trials and indictments is true also, as the cases show, of the immunity from compulsory self-incrimination. This too might be lost, and justice still be done. Indeed, today as in the past there are students of our penal system who look upon the immunity as a mischief rather than a benefit, and who would limit its scope, or destroy it altogether. No doubt there would remain the need to give protection against torture, physical or mental. Justice, however, would not perish if the accused were subject to a duty to respond to orderly inquiry. The exclusion of these immunities and privileges from the privileges and immunities protected against the action of the states has not been arbitrary or casual. It has been dictated by a study and appreciation of the meaning, the essential implications, of liberty itself.

We reach a different plane of social and moral values when we pass to the privileges and immunities that have been taken over from the earlier articles of the federal bill of rights and brought within the Fourteenth Amendment by a process of absorption. These in their origin were effective against the federal government alone. If the Fourteenth Amendment has absorbed them, the process of absorption has had its source in the belief that neither liberty nor justice would exist if they were sacrificed. This is true, for illustration, of freedom of thought, and speech. Of that freedom one may say that it is the matrix, the indispensable condition, of nearly every other form of freedom. With rare aberrations a pervasive recognition of that truth can be traced in our history, political and legal. So it has come about that the domain of liberty, withdrawn by the Fourteenth Amendment from encroachment by the states, has been enlarged by latter-day judgments to include liberty of the mind as well as liberty of action. The extension became, indeed, a logical imperative when once it was recognized, as long ago it was, that liberty is something more than exemption from physical restraint, and that even in the field of substantive rights and duties the legislative judgment, if oppressive and arbitrary, may be overridden by the courts. Fundamental too in the concept of due process, and so in that of liberty, is the thought that condemnation shall be rendered only after trial. The hearing, moreover, must be a real one, not a sham or a pretense. . . .

Our survey of the cases serves, we think, to justify the statement that the dividing line between them, if not unfaltering throughout its course, has been true for the most part to a unifying principle. On which side of the line the case made out by the appellant has appropriate location must be the next inquiry and the final one. Is that kind of double jeopardy to which the statute has subjected him a hardship so acute and shocking that our polity will not endure it? Does it violate those "fundamental principles of liberty and justice which lie at the base of all our civil and political institutions"? The answer surely must be "no." What the answer would have to be if the state were permitted after a trial free from error to try the accused over again or to bring another case against him, we have no occasion to consider. We deal with the statute before us and no other. The state is not attempting to wear the accused out by a multitude of cases with accumulated trials. It asks no more than this, that the case against him shall go on until there shall be a trial free from the corrosion of substantial legal error. This is not cruelty at all, nor even vexation in any immoderate degree. If the trial had been infected with error adverse to the accused, there might have been review at his instance, and as often as necessary to purge the vicious taint. A reciprocal privilege, subject at all times to the discretion of the presiding judge, has now been granted to the state. There is here no seismic innovation. The edifice of justice stands, its symmetry, to many, greater than before. . . .

The judgment is

Affirmed.

In 1937 protection against double jeopardy was not a fundamental right in the states. But did the Court provide attorneys with any further guidance as to what this elusive term included? To some extent it did. It defined fundamental rights as those without which liberty and justice could not exist. But the process by which the Court planned to make known exactly which rights fall into that category remained unchanged from *Gitlow*. The majority of justices adopted the doctrine of selective incorporation, from which they would determine fundamental rights on a case-by-case basis.

IN THE AFTERMATH OF *PALKO*: INCORPORATION AND THE WARREN COURT

What happened after *Palko*? As Table 2-1 shows, the Court continued to incorporate the various guarantees contained in the Bill of Rights. At first, the Court limited itself to those rights contained in the First Amendment; it was not until the 1960s that it began to incorporate guarantees the Constitution affords to the rights of the criminally accused.

Selective incorporation of these guarantees in the 1960s came as a part of the Warren Court's revolution in the area of defendants' rights. It was this Court, for example, that guaranteed indigents the right to counsel in certain kinds of cases and forced police to read suspected offenders a set of statements, called the "Miranda warnings." In the coming chapters we shall have much more to say about the Warren Court and its liberalizing decisions in this area and in other matters involving rights and liberties. Here, we just point out that the impact of the Warren Court revolution would have been less far-reaching had it not incorporated these guarantees. Only indigents involved in federal—not state—crimes would receive attorneys; only federal agents—not state or local police officers—would be forced to read Miranda warnings, and so on. Because federal prosecutions amount to such a small percentage of the total number of prosecutions (the vast majority originate in states), these decisions would have affected few defendants. Instead, with incorporation, all levels of government must abide by the selected constitutional guarantees.

TABLE 2-1 Cases Incorporating Provisions of the Bill of Rights into the Due Process Clause of the Fourteenth Amendment

Constitutional Provision	Case	Year
First Amendment		
Freedom of speech and press	*Gitlow v. New York*	1925
Freedom of assembly	*DeJonge v. Oregon*	1937
Freedom of petition	*Hague v. CIO*	1939
Free exercise of religion	*Cantwell v. Connecticut*	1940
Establishment of religion	*Everson v. Board of Education*	1947
Fourth Amendment		
Unreasonable search and seizure	*Wolf v. Colorado*	1949
Exclusionary rule	*Mapp v. Ohio*	1961
Fifth Amendment		
Payment of compensation for the taking of private property	*Chicago, Burlington and Quincy R. Co. v. Chicago*	1897
Self-incrimination	*Malloy v. Hogan*	1964
Double jeopardy	*Benton v. Maryland*	1969
When jeopardy attaches	*Crist v. Bretz*	1978
Sixth Amendment		
Public trial	*In re Oliver*	1948
Due notice	*Cole v. Arkansas*	1948
Right to counsel (felonies)	*Gideon v. Wainwright*	1963
Confrontation and cross-examination of adverse witnesses	*Pointer v. Texas*	1965
Speedy trial	*Klopfer v. North Carolina*	1967
Compulsory process to obtain witnesses	*Washington v. Texas*	1967
Jury trial	*Duncan v. Louisiana*	1968
Right to counsel (misdemeanor when jail is possible)	*Argersinger v. Hamlin*	1972
Eighth Amendment		
Cruel and unusual punishment	*Louisiana ex rel. Francis v. Resweber*	1947
Ninth Amendment		
Privacy[a]	*Griswold v. Connecticut*	1965

Note: Provisions the Court has not incorporated: Second Amendment right to keep and bear arms; Third Amendment right against quartering soldiers; Fifth Amendment right to a grand jury hearing; Seventh Amendment right to a jury trial in civil cases; and Eighth Amendment right against excessive bail and fines.

a. The word *privacy* does not appear in the Ninth Amendment (nor anywhere in the text of the Constitution). In *Griswold* several members of the Court viewed the Ninth Amendment as guaranteeing (and incorporating) that right.

A second development after *Palko* is that justices continued to advocate different solutions to this long-standing problem. Some justices, such as John Marshall Harlan (II)[10] and Potter Stewart, have endorsed an approach that, according to observers, is close to *Twining*. These justices viewed the term "due process of law" as requiring only that criminal trials, for example, "be fundamentally fair." Their solution, as Harlan writes, involves

a much more discriminating process of adjudication than does 'incorporation.' ... It entails a 'gradual process of judicial inclusion and exclusion,' seeking, with due recognition of constitutional tolerance for state experimentation and disparity, to ascertain those immutable principles of justice which inhere in the very idea ... of free government which no member of the Union may disregard.[11]

Other justices—indeed, a majority of the Warren Court—espoused the principles of selective incorporation. Still others, such as Hugo Black and William O. Douglas, supported the first John Marshall Harlan's total incorporation approach, which suggests that all guarantees enumerated in the Bill of Rights should apply to the states through the Fourteenth Amendment.[12]

These two developments after *Palko*—the Warren Court's use of selective incorporation and the support for distinct approaches to incorporation—are well illustrated in *Duncan v. Louisiana* (1968). As you read the case, consider how the various opinions encapsulate a historical range of perspectives on the incorporation of the Bill of Rights.

---

10. Two justices have shared the name John Marshall Harlan. To distinguish them, scholars and other writers call the elder John Marshall Harlan I. He served on the Court from 1877 to 1911. His grandson, identified as John Marshall Harlan II, served from 1955 to 1971. Harlan I took quite liberal positions on issues such as incorporation and civil rights, often dissenting from his colleagues on the bench. Harlan II assumed a more conservative posture on the issues of his day, frequently dissenting from liberal Warren Court rulings.

11. Justice Harlan, dissenting in *Duncan v. Louisiana* (1968).

12. In addition, Justices Frank Murphy and William O. Douglas articulated a total incorporation plus doctrine, which held that all rights—enumerated, implied, and evolving—should apply to the states.

Duncan v. Louisiana

391 U.S. 145 (1968)

Vote: 7 (Black, Brennan, Douglas, Fortas, Marshall, Warren, White)

    2 (Harlan, Stewart)

Opinion of the Court: White

Concurring opinions: Black, Fortas

Dissenting opinion: Harlan

In October 1966, Gary Duncan, a nineteen-year-old black man, was driving down a highway when he spotted two of his younger cousins on the side of the road with four white youths. Duncan apparently became alarmed because his cousins had recently transferred to a formerly all-white school where "racial incidents" had occurred. He pulled over and asked his cousins to get into his car. What happened next is in dispute. The white youths asserted that Duncan slapped one of them, Herman M. Landry, Jr., before getting back into his car; Duncan and his cousins maintained that he "touched" Landry rather than slapped him.

Just after Duncan pulled away, P. E. Lathum, the principal of a private school formed in response to the desegregation of the area's public schools, called the police. He had observed the encounter and alleged that Duncan had hit Landry. The police questioned Duncan, but let him go in the belief that he had not committed an offense. But, just a few days later, they arrested Duncan on the charge of cruelty to juveniles.[13]

Believing that their son's arrest was racially motivated, Duncan's parents contacted Richard Sobol, an attorney for the Lawyers Constitutional Defense Committee, a civil rights organization with offices in New Orleans. Sobol agreed to represent Duncan after he became convinced that "Duncan's case was part of a pattern of anti–civil rights intimidation and harassment" in the area.[14]

---

13. We adopt this paragraph and those that follow from Cortner, *The Supreme Court*, 248–251.

14. Ibid., 249.

Sobol filed a motion with a state trial court judge to dismiss the charge against Duncan. He asserted that Louisiana law permitted cruelty to juveniles convictions only against individuals having supervision over the youngster, which Duncan did not have over Landry. The prosecuting attorney reported to Landry's family that they would not be able to win the case.

Rather than see Duncan set free, Landry's mother asked the police to rearrest him on charges of simple battery, a misdemeanor punishable in Louisiana by a maximum of two years in jail and a $300 fine. Sobol went back to court, this time to request that Duncan be tried by a jury. The judge refused, citing the Louisiana Constitution, which grants jury trials only in cases involving punishments of hard labor or death.

The state supreme court also rejected Sobol's request, and he appealed to the U.S. Supreme Court. His argument was simple: the Due Process Clause of the Fourteenth Amendment should be used to apply the Sixth Amendment's jury trial guarantee to all state prosecutions where a sentence of two or more years could be imposed. The state countered with a reference to *Maxwell v. Dow* in which the Court held that trial by jury has "never been affirmed to be a necessary requisite of due process of law."

MR. JUSTICE WHITE delivered the opinion of the Court.

... The test for determining whether a right extended by the Fifth and Sixth Amendments with respect to federal criminal proceedings is also protected against state action by the Fourteenth Amendment has been phrased in a variety of ways in the opinions of this Court. The question has been asked whether a right is among those " 'fundamental principles of liberty and justice which lie at the base of all our civil and political institutions,'" ... whether it is "basic in our system of jurisprudence," ... and whether it is "a fundamental right, essential to a fair trial."... The claim before us is that the right to trial by jury guaranteed by the Sixth Amendment meets these tests. The position of Louisiana, on the other hand, is that the Constitution imposes upon the States no duty to give a jury trial in any criminal case, regardless of the seriousness of the crime or the size of the punishment which may be imposed. Because we believe that trial by jury in criminal cases is fundamental to the American scheme of justice, we hold that the Fourteenth Amendment guarantees a right of jury trial in all criminal cases which—were they to be tried in a federal court—would come within the Sixth Amendment's guarantee. Since we consider the appeal before us to be such a case, we hold that the Constitution was violated when appellant's demand for jury trial was refused.

The history of trial by jury in criminal cases has been frequently told. It is sufficient for present purposes to say that by the time our Constitution was written, jury trial in criminal cases had been in existence in England for several centuries and carried impressive credentials traced by many to Magna Carta. Its preservation and proper operation as a protection against arbitrary rule were among the major objectives of the revolutionary settlement which was expressed in the Declaration and Bill of Rights of 1689....

Jury trial came to America with English colonists, and received strong support from them. Royal interference with the jury trial was deeply resented.... The Declaration of Independence stated solemn objections to the King's making "Judges dependent on his Will alone, for the tenure of their offices, and the amount and payment of their salaries," to his "depriving us in many cases, of the benefits of Trial by Jury," and to his "transporting us beyond Seas to be tried for pretended offenses." The Constitution itself, in Art. III, § 2, commanded:

"The Trial of all Crimes, except in Cases of Impeachment, shall be by Jury; and such Trial shall be held in the State where the said Crimes shall have been committed."

Objections to the Constitution because of the absence of a bill of rights were met by the immediate submission and adoption of the Bill of Rights. Included was the Sixth Amendment which, among other things, provided:

"In all criminal prosecutions, the accused shall enjoy the right to a speedy and public trial, by an impartial jury of the State and district wherein the crime shall have been committed."

The constitutions adopted by the original States guaranteed jury trial. Also, the constitution of every State entering the Union thereafter in one form or another protected the right to jury trial in criminal cases.

Even such skeleta. history is impressive support for considering the right to jury trial in criminal cases to be fundamental to our system of justice....

We are aware of prior cases in this Court in which the prevailing opinion contains statements contrary to our holding today that the right to jury trial in serious criminal cases is a fundamental right and hence must be recognized by the States as part of their obligation to extend due process of law to all persons within their jurisdiction. Louisiana relies especially on *Maxwell v. Dow* (1900); *Palko v. Connecticut* (1937); and *Snyder v. Massachusetts* (1934). None of these cases, however, dealt with a State which had purported to dispense entirely with a jury trial in serious criminal cases. *Maxwell* held that no provision of the Bill of Rights applied to the States—a position long since repudiated—and that the Due Process Clause of the Fourteenth Amendment did not prevent a State from trying a defendant for a noncapital offense with fewer than 12 men on the jury. It did not deal with a case in which no jury at all had been provided. In neither *Palko* nor *Snyder* was jury trial actually at issue, although both cases contain important dicta asserting that the right to jury trial is not essential to ordered liberty and may be dispensed with by the States regardless of the Sixth and Fourteenth Amendments. These observations, though weighty and respectable, are nevertheless dicta, unsupported by holdings in this Court that a State may refuse a defendant's demand for a jury trial when he is charged with a serious crime.... Respectfully, we reject the prior dicta regarding jury trial in criminal cases.

The guarantees of jury trial in the Federal and State Constitutions reflect a profound judgment about the way in which law should be enforced and justice administered. A right to jury trial is granted to criminal defendants in order to prevent oppression by the Government. Those who wrote our constitutions knew from history and experience that it was necessary to protect against unfounded criminal charges brought to eliminate enemies and against judges too responsive to the voice of higher authority. The framers of the constitutions strove to create an independent judiciary but insisted upon further protection against arbitrary action. Providing an accused with the right to be tried by a jury of his peers gave him an inestimable safeguard against the corrupt or overzealous prosecutor and against the compliant, biased, or eccentric judge. If the defendant preferred the common-sense judgment of a jury to the more tutored but perhaps less sympathetic reaction of the single judge, he was to have it. Beyond this, the jury trial provisions in the Federal and State Constitutions reflect a fundamental decision about the exercise of official power—a reluctance to entrust plenary powers over the life and liberty of the citizen to one judge or to a group of judges. Fear of unchecked power, so typical of our State and Federal Governments in other respects, found expression in the criminal law in this insistence upon community participation in the determination of guilt or innocence. The deep commitment of the Nation to the right of jury trial in serious criminal cases as a defense against arbitrary law enforcement qualifies for protection under the Due Process Clause of the Fourteenth Amendment, and must therefore be respected by the States....

The judgment below is reversed and the case is remanded for proceedings not inconsistent with this opinion.

Reversed and remanded.

MR. JUSTICE BLACK, with whom MR. JUSTICE DOUGLAS joins, concurring.

The Court today holds that the right to trial by jury guaranteed defendants in criminal cases in federal courts by Art. III of the United States Constitution and by the Sixth Amendment is also guaranteed by the Fourteenth Amendment to defendants tried in state courts. With this holding I agree for reasons given by the Court. I also agree because of reasons given in my dissent in *Adamson v. California*. In that dissent, I took the position, contrary to the holding in *Twining v. New Jersey*, that the Fourteenth Amendment made all of the provisions of the Bill of Rights applicable to the States. This Court in *Palko v. Connecticut*, decided in 1937, ... explain[ed] ... that certain Bill of Rights' provisions were made applicable to the States by bringing them "within the Fourteenth Amendment by a process of absorption." Thus *Twining v. New Jersey* refused to hold that any one of the Bill of Rights' provisions was made applicable to the States by the Fourteenth Amendment, but *Palko*, which must be read as overruling *Twining* on this point, concluded that the Bill of Rights Amendments that are "implicit in the concept of ordered liberty" are "absorbed" by the Fourteenth as protections against state invasion. In this situation I said in *Adamson v. California* that, while "I would ... extend to all the people of the nation the complete protection of the Bill of Rights," that "if the choice must be between the selective process of the *Palko* decision applying some of the Bill of Rights to the States, or the *Twining* rule applying none of them, I would choose the *Palko* selective process." ... And I am very happy to support this selective process through which our Court has since the *Adamson* case held most of the specific Bill of Rights' protections applicable to the States to the same extent they are applicable to the Federal Government. Among these are the right to trial by jury decided today, the right against compelled self-incrimination, the right to counsel, the right to compulsory process for witnesses, the right to confront witnesses, the right to a speedy and public trial, and the right to be free from unreasonable searches and seizures.

All of these holdings making Bill of Rights' provisions applicable as such to the States mark, of course, a departure from the *Twining* doctrine holding that none of those provisions were enforceable as such against the States. The dissent in this case, however, makes a spirited and forceful defense of that now discredited doctrine....

While I do not wish at this time to discuss at length my disagreement with Brother HARLAN's forthright and frank restatement of the now discredited *Twining* doctrine, I do want to point out what appears to me to be the basic difference between us. His view, as was indeed the view of *Twining,* is that "due process is an evolving concept" and therefore that it entails a "gradual process of judicial inclusion and exclusion" to ascertain those "immutable principles ... of free government which no member of the Union may disregard." Thus the Due Process Clause is treated as prescribing no specific and clearly ascertainable constitutional command that judges must obey in interpreting the Constitution, but rather as leaving judges free to decide at any particular time whether a particular rule or judicial formulation embodies an "immutable principl[e] of free government" or is "implicit in the concept of ordered liberty," or whether certain conduct "shocks the judge's conscience" or runs counter to some other similar, undefined and undefinable standard. Thus due process, according to my Brother HARLAN, is to be a phrase with no permanent meaning, but one which is found to shift from time to time in accordance with judges' predilections and understandings of what is best for the country. If due process means this, the Fourteenth Amendment, in my opinion, might as well have been written that "no person shall be deprived of life, liberty or property except by laws that the judges of the United States Supreme Court shall find to be consistent with the immutable principles of free government." It is impossible for me to believe that such unconfined power is given to judges in our Constitution that is a written one in order to limit governmental power.

Another tenet of the *Twining* doctrine as restated by my Brother HARLAN is that "due process of law requires only fundamental fairness." But the "fundamental fairness" test is one on a par with that of shocking the conscience of the Court. Each of such tests depends entirely on the particular judge's idea of ethics and morals instead of requiring him to depend on the boundaries fixed by the written words of the Constitution. Nothing in the history of the phrase "due process of law" suggests that constitutional controls are to depend on any particular judge's sense of values.... [Rather] the Due Process Clause gives all Americans, whoever they are and wherever they happen to be, the right to be tried by independent and unprejudiced courts using established procedures and applying valid pre-existing laws. There is not one word of legal history that justifies making the term "due process of law" mean a guarantee of a trial free from laws and conduct which the courts deem at the time to be "arbitrary," "unreasonable," "unfair," or "contrary to civilized standards." The due process of law standard for a trial is one in accordance with the Bill of Rights and laws passed pursuant to constitutional power, guaranteeing to all alike a trial under the general law of the land.

Finally I want to add that I am not bothered by the argument that applying the Bill of Rights to the States, "according to the same standards that protect those personal rights against federal encroachment," interferes with our concept of federalism in that it may prevent States from trying novel social and economic experiments. I have never believed that under the guise of federalism the States should be able to experiment with the protections afforded our citizens through the Bill of Rights.... It seems to me totally inconsistent to advocate, on the one hand, the power of this Court to strike down any state law or practice which it finds "unreasonable" or "unfair" and, on the other hand, urge that the States be given maximum power to develop their own laws and procedures. Yet the due process approach of my Brother HARLAN... does just that since in effect it restricts the States to practices which a majority of this Court is willing to approve on a case-by-case basis....

In closing I want to emphasize that I believe as strongly as ever that the Fourteenth Amendment was intended to make the Bill of Rights applicable to the States. I have been willing to support the selective incorporation doctrine, however, as an alternative, although perhaps less historically supportable than complete incorporation. The selective incorporation process, if used properly, does limit the Supreme Court in the Fourteenth Amendment field to specific Bill of Rights' protections only and keeps judges from roaming at will in their own notions of what policies outside the Bill of Rights are desirable and what are not. And, most importantly for me, the selective incorporation process has the virtue of having already worked to make most of the Bill of Rights' protections applicable to the States.

MR. JUSTICE HARLAN, whom MR. JUSTICE STEWART joins, dissenting.

The States have always borne primary responsibility for operating the machinery of criminal justice within their borders, and adapting it to their particular circumstances. In exercising this responsibility, each State is compelled to conform its procedures to the requirements of the Federal Constitution. The Due Process Clause of the Fourteenth Amendment requires that those procedures be fundamentally fair in all respects. It does not, in my view, impose or encourage nationwide uniformity for its own sake; it does not command adherence to forms that happen to be old; and it does not impose on the States the rules that may be in force in the federal courts except where such rules are also found to be essential to basic fairness.

The Court's approach to this case is an uneasy and illogical compromise among the views of various Justices on how the Due Process Clause should be interpreted. The Court does not say that those who framed the Fourteenth Amendment intended to make the Sixth Amendment applicable to the States. And the Court concedes that it finds nothing unfair about the procedure by which the present appellant was tried. Nevertheless, the Court reverses his conviction: it holds, for some reason not apparent to me, that the Due Process Clause incorporates the particular clause of the Sixth Amendment that requires trial by jury in federal criminal cases—including, as I read its opinion, the sometimes trivial accompanying baggage of judicial interpretation in federal contexts. I have raised my voice many times before against the Court's continuing undiscriminating insistence upon fastening on the States federal notions of criminal justice, and I must do so again in this instance. With all respect, the Court's approach and its reading of history are altogether topsy-turvy....

... In my view, often expressed elsewhere, the first section of the Fourteenth Amendment was meant neither to incorporate, nor to be limited to, the specific guarantees of the first eight Amendments. The overwhelming historical evidence ... demonstrates, to me conclusively, that the Congressmen and state legislators who wrote, debated, and ratified the Fourteenth Amendment did not think they were "incorporating" the Bill of Rights and the very breadth and generality of the Amendment's provisions suggest that its authors did not suppose that the Nation would always be limited to mid-19th century conceptions of "liberty" and "due process of law" but that the increasing experience and evolving conscience of the American people would add new "intermediate premises." In short, neither history, nor sense, supports using the Fourteenth Amendment to put the States in a constitutional straitjacket with respect to their own development in the administration of criminal or civil law.

Although I therefore fundamentally disagree with the total incorporation view of the Fourteenth Amendment, it seems to me that such a position does at least have the virtue, lacking in the Court's selective incorporation approach, of internal consistency: we look to the Bill of Rights, word for word, clause for clause, precedent for precedent because, it is said, the men who wrote the Amendment wanted it that way. For those who do not accept this "history," a different source of "intermediate premises" must be found. The Bill of Rights is not necessarily irrelevant to the search for guidance in interpreting the Fourteenth Amendment, but the reason for and the nature of its relevance must be articulated.

Apart from the approach taken by the absolute incorporationists, I can see only one method of analysis that has any internal logic. That is to start with the words "liberty" and "due process of law" and attempt to define them in a way that accords with American traditions and our system of government. This approach, involving a much more discriminating process of adjudication than does "incorporation," is, albeit difficult, the one that was followed throughout the 19th and most of the present century. It entails a "gradual process of judicial inclusion and exclusion," seeking, with due recognition of constitutional tolerance for state experimentation and disparity, to ascertain those "immutable principles ... of free government which no member of the Union may disregard." Due process was not restricted to rules fixed in the past, for that "would be to deny every quality of the law but its age, and to render it incapable of progress or improvement." Nor did it impose nationwide uniformity in details, for

"[t]he Fourteenth Amendment does not profess to secure to all persons in the United States the benefit of the same laws and the same remedies. Great diversities in these respects may exist in two States separated only by an imaginary line. On one side of this line there may be a right of trial by jury, and on the other side no such right. Each State prescribes its own modes of judicial proceeding."

Through this gradual process, this Court sought to define "liberty" by isolating freedoms that Americans of the past and of the present considered more important than any suggested countervailing public objective. The Court also, by interpretation of the phrase "due process of law," enforced the Constitution's guarantee that no State may imprison an individual except by fair and impartial procedures.

The relationship of the Bill of Rights to this "gradual process" seems to me to be twofold. In the first place it has long been clear that the Due Process Clause imposes some restrictions on state action that parallel Bill of Rights restrictions on federal action. Second, and more important than this accidental overlap, is the fact that the Bill of Rights is evidence, at various points, of the content Americans find in the term "liberty" and of American standards of fundamental fairness....

Today's Court still remains unwilling to accept the total incorporationists' view of the history of the Fourteenth Amendment. This, if accepted, would afford a cogent reason for applying the Sixth Amendment to the States. The Court is also, apparently, unwilling to face the task of deter-

mining whether denial of trial by jury in the situation before us, or in other situations, is fundamentally unfair. Consequently, the Court has compromised on the ease of the incorporationist position, without its internal logic. It has simply assumed that the question before us is whether the Jury Trial Clause of the Sixth Amendment should be incorporated into the Fourteenth, jot-for-jot and case-for-case, or ignored. Then the Court merely declares that the clause in question is "in" rather than "out."

The Court has justified neither its starting place nor its conclusion. If the problem is to discover and articulate the rules of fundamental fairness in criminal proceedings, there is no reason to assume that the whole body of rules developed in this Court constituting Sixth Amendment jury trial must be regarded as a unit. The requirement of trial by jury in federal criminal cases has given rise to numerous subsidiary questions respecting the exact scope and content of the right. It surely cannot be that every answer the Court has given, or will give, to such a question is attributable to the Founders; or even that every rule announced carries equal conviction of this Court; still less can it be that every such subprinciple is equally fundamental to ordered liberty....

Even if I could agree that the question before us is whether Sixth Amendment jury trial is totally "in" or totally "out," I can find in the Court's opinion no real reasons for concluding that it should be "in." The basis for differentiating among clauses in the Bill of Rights cannot be that only some clauses are in the Bill of Rights, or that only some are old and much praised, or that only some have played an important role in the development of federal law. These things are true of all. The Court says that some clauses are more "fundamental" than others, but it turns out to be using this word in a sense that would have astonished Mr. Justice Cardozo and which, in addition, is of no help. The word does not mean "analytically critical to procedural fairness" for no real analysis of the role of the jury in making procedures fair is even attempted. Instead, the word turns out to mean "old," "much praised," and "found in the Bill of Rights." The definition of "fundamental" thus turns out to be circular....

The argument that jury trial is not a requisite of due process is quite simple. The central proposition of *Palko,* a proposition to which I would adhere, is that "due process of law" requires only that criminal trials be fundamentally fair.

As stated above, apart from the theory that it was historically intended as a mere shorthand for the Bill of Rights, I do not see what else "due process of law" can intelligibly be thought to mean. If due process of law requires only fundamental fairness, then the inquiry in each case must be whether a state trial process was a fair one. The Court has held, properly I think, that in an adversary process it is a requisite of fairness, for which there is no adequate substitute, that a criminal defendant be afforded a right to counsel and to cross-examine opposing witnesses. But it simply has not been demonstrated, nor, I think, can it be demonstrated, that trial by jury is the only fair means of resolving issues of fact....

... [T]here is a wide range of views on the desirability of trial by jury, and on the ways to make it most effective when it is used; there is also considerable variation from State to State in local conditions such as the size of the criminal caseload, the ease or difficulty of summoning jurors, and other trial conditions bearing on fairness. We have before us, therefore, an almost perfect example of a situation in which the celebrated dictum of Mr. Justice Brandeis should be invoked. It is, he said,

"one of the happy incidents of the federal system that a single courageous State may, if its citizens choose, serve as a laboratory...."

This Court, other courts, and the political process are available to correct any experiments in criminal procedure that prove fundamentally unfair to defendants. That is not what is being done today: instead, and quite without reason, the Court has chosen to impose upon every State one means of trying criminal cases; it is a good means, but it is not the only fair means, and it is not demonstrably better than the alternatives States might devise.

I would affirm the judgment of the Supreme Court of Louisiana.

As *Duncan* illustrates, the Court continued to abide by the compromise position of selective incorporation, applying only those rights about which the justices believed "that neither liberty nor justice would exist if they were sacrificed." But, *in practice*, the total incorporation approach favored by the first John Marshall Harlan and Hugo Black has predominated. As depicted in Table 2-1, between 1897 and 1969 the Court incorporated almost every guarantee contained in the Bill of Rights, in several cases reversing earlier precedents denying the incorporation of specific provisions. In fact, the Court has done what Harlan advocated in his lone dissent in *Hurtado:* it has applied virtually all guarantees contained in the first eight amendments to the states. The last right incorporated, ironically, was double jeopardy.

The theory of selective incorporation, in concept, emerged the victor; but, for all practical purposes and with only a few exceptions, total nationalization has prevailed. As a result, present reading of the Constitution now ensures that the basic civil liberties of citizens of the United States are uniformly protected against infringement by any government entity—federal, state, or local.

READINGS

Berger, Raoul. *Government by Judiciary.* Cambridge, Mass.: Harvard University Press, 1977, chap. 8.

Cortner, Richard C. *The Supreme Court and the Second Bill of Rights.* Madison: University of Wisconsin Press, 1981.

Fairman, Charles. "Does the Fourteenth Amendment Incorporate the Bill of Rights?" *Stanford Law Review* 2 (1949): 5.

Frankfurter, Felix. "Memorandum on 'Incorporation' of the Bill of Rights into the Due Process Clause of the Fourteenth Amendment." *Harvard Law Review* 78 (1965): 746.

Green, John R. "The Bill of Rights, the Fourteenth Amendment, and the Supreme Court." *Michigan Law Review* 46 (1948): 869.

Henkin, Louis. "Selective Incorporation in the Fourteenth Amendment." *Yale Law Journal* 73 (1963): 74.

Levy, Leonard. *Introduction to the Fourteenth Amendment and the Bill of Rights: The Incorporation Theory.* New York: Da Capo, 1970.

Walker, Frank H. "Constitutional Law—Was It Intended That the Fourteenth Amendment Incorporate the Bill of Rights?" *North Carolina Law Review* 42 (1964): 925.

PART II
CIVIL LIBERTIES

PART II
APPROACHING CIVIL LIBERTIES

THE NEXT FIVE chapters explore Supreme Court interpretation of guarantees contained in the First Amendment and those that have been seen as relating to the right of privacy. As a student approaching civil liberties, perhaps for the first time, you might be wondering why we devote so much space in Chapter 3 (Religion) and Chapters 4 through 6 (Expression) to the following few phrases:

Congress shall make no law respecting an establishment of religion, or prohibiting the free exercise thereof; or abridging the freedom of speech, or of the press; or the right of the people peaceably to assemble, and to petition the Government for a redress of grievances.

After all, the guarantees contained in the First Amendment seem specific enough—or do they? Suppose we read about a religion that required its members to ingest LSD before religious services, or about students who were so fed up with university policies they burned down the administration building, or about a radio station that regularly allowed its announcers to use profanity. Taking the words of the First Amendment, "Congress shall make *no* law," to heart, we might conclude that its language—the guarantees of freedom of religion, speech, and press—protects these activities. Is that conclusion correct? Is society obliged to condone forms of expression such as those in our examples?

What these and the subsequent case examples illustrate is that a gap sometimes exists between the words of the First Amendment and reality. Although the language of the amendment may seem explicit, its meaning can be elusive and therefore difficult to apply to actual circumstances.

Supreme Court formulation and interpretation of a right to privacy, as we shall see in Chapter 7, present even more difficulties, primarily because the Constitution contains no explicit mention of such a guarantee. Even though most justices agree that it exists, they have disagreed over various questions, including from what provision of the Constitution the right to privacy arises and how far it extends.

It is the gap between what the Constitution says (or does not say) and the kinds of questions litigants ask the Court to address that explains why we devote so much space to civil liberties. Because the meaning of those rights is less than crystal clear, the institution charged with interpreting and applying them—the Supreme Court of the United States—has approached its task in a somewhat erratic way. Throughout the Court's history, different justices have brought different modes of interpretation to the guarantees of religion, expression, and the press, and to the right to privacy, which in turn have significantly affected the way citizens enjoy those rights.

FIGURE II-1 The Supreme Court's Support for First Amendment Claims, 1953–1991 Terms

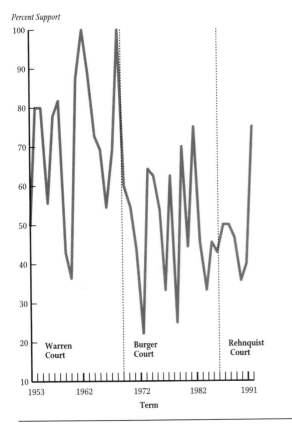

Percent Support

Warren Court

Burger Court

Rehnquist Court

Term

SOURCE: Lee Epstein, Jeffrey A. Segal, Harold J. Spaeth, and Thomas G. Walker, *The Supreme Court Compendium: Data, Decisions, and Developments* (Washington, D.C.: Congressional Quarterly, 1994),Table 3-8.

NOTE: First Amendment cases include all disputes involving free expression and religious liberty.

Figure II-1 provides one way of looking at how differently the Court has treated First Amendment claims over a period of forty years. The Court led by Earl Warren was generally supportive of such claims, ruling in favor of the party alleging some abridgment of his or her rights in more than two-thirds of the cases. The Court under Chief Justice Warren Burger moved in the opposite direction, with its support of the individual rights position well below that of its predecessor. It may be too soon to reach any conclu-

sions about the Rehnquist Court, but, based on the data displayed in Figure II-1, it seems that the present justices will not be any less supportive of First Amendment rights than those who sat on the Burger Court.

Figure II-1 helps to reinforce the point that the First Amendment is open to interpretation, that the words of the Constitution alone do not necessarily provide a sufficient guidepost for the justices as they go about resolving cases. Even so, the data raise many questions. Why does the Burger Court—and perhaps the Rehnquist Court—evince patterns of decision making distinctly different from the Warren Court? Is it merely because recent Courts have had more conservative members? Or have the cases and the precedent governing their resolution changed? Perhaps the more recent justices have invoked different modes of analysis to resolve these disputes. Might it also be that the Court has responded to the public or to the other institutions of government? Another possibility is that the Warren Court was far more supportive of First Amendment claims than its predecessors and the Burger and Rehnquist Courts, in turn, rebalanced the scales. Finding the answers to these questions will require careful study of the cases to come.

This task is important because since 1942 more of the Court's docket has been taken up by civil liberties disputes. Figure II-2 details this growth, showing the percentage of the agenda the Court has allocated to cases involving First Amendment and privacy claims. In the 1930s these disputes took up a paltry 2 percent to 3 percent of the Court's time; today that figure is around 15 percent, but it reached as high as 25 percent in the early 1970s.

What accounts for this emphasis on civil liberties? Scholars have offered many different answers including the changes in legal standards governing this area; the growing presence of interest groups; the fact that states, under the selective incorporation of the Bill of Rights (*see Chapter 2*), must now guarantee all First Amendment rights to their citizens, and so forth.

Another answer is that the legal standards in this area have changed. These kinds of changes often occur when scholars and attorneys develop new ways of framing old problems; occasionally, governments codify these new approaches and/or lawyers present them to the Court for its consideration. The so-called hate speech laws provide an example. In the belief that certain kinds of expression pose a threat to compelling societal interests, some state and local governments have passed laws forbidding racist and sexist language, the placement of symbols (such as a swastika or burning cross) that might arouse anger, and so forth. However well intended such laws might be, they pose complex problems for the Supreme Court because they could run counter to the First Amendment's guarantee of freedom of speech.

Another illustration comes from the writings of one of the Court's most recent additions, Ruth Bader Ginsburg. Eight years before she took her seat on the Supreme Court, Ginsburg advocated a distinct approach to abortion jurisprudence. Rather than locating the right to obtain an abortion in privacy or due process guarantees (the course, as you shall see, that the Court had taken), she argued that it could be based in notions of equality. This approach may be reasonable, but it would require the justices to rethink at least twenty years of constitutional litigation.

In the coming pages, we examine hate speech laws, Ginsburg's arguments, and several other newer approaches to older problems, including obscenity and pornography. For now, we remind you that the recent spate of frameworks by which to (re)consider issues of civil liberties provides another explanation for the length of this section of the book. Every now and then, they have provided the fodder for litigation, causing the Court to rethink previously well-entrenched principles of law. And while the justices do not always adopt these approaches, it is important

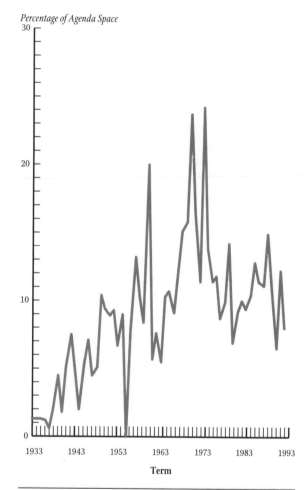

FIGURE II-2 Percentage of Agenda Space Allocated to Substantive Rights Cases, 1933–1992 Terms

Percentage of Agenda Space

SOURCES: 1933–1987: Richard L. Pacelle, Jr., *The Transformation of the Supreme Court's Agenda* (Boulder, Colo.: Westview Press, 1991), Figure 6-3. 1988–1992: Provided to the authors by Richard L. Pacelle, Jr.

NOTE: Substantive rights cases center on First Amendment and privacy (including abortion) issues.

for us to think about them. Not only does their rejection (or acceptance) have bearing on the ultimate state of the law in a given area, but also they provide a unique window from which to view some of the most interesting legal, societal, and political controversies of our day.

CHAPTER 3
RELIGION: EXERCISE AND ESTABLISHMENT

O N   M Y   A R R I V A L in the United States," wrote Alexis de Tocqueville in the 1830s, "the religious aspect of the country was the first thing that struck my attention; and the longer I stayed there, the more I perceived the great political consequences resulting from this new state of things. In France I had almost always seen the spirit of religion and the spirit of freedom marching in opposite directions. But in America I found they were intimately united and that they reigned in common over the same country."[1] Writing in the 1990s, political commentator Garry Wills asserted: "We may not realize that we live in the most religious nation in the developed world. But nine out of ten Americans say that they have never doubted the existence of God, and internationally, Americans rank second (behind only Malta) when rating the importance of God in their lives. So why is it surprising when the decisions we make in the voting booth reflect our basic religious values?"[2]

Two of the most astute observers of American politics, writing 155 years apart, reached similar conclusions: religion plays an important role in the lives of most Americans. In a nation where 60 percent to 75 percent of the population belong to one of the more than 340,000 churches, temples, and synagogues, it is not surprising, therefore, to find chaplains reading invocations before legislative sessions, states erecting Christmas displays, or members of the Supreme Court singing carols.[3]

Indeed, as Tocqueville observed, Americans have always been a religious people. We all learned in elementary school that the first settlers came to America to escape religious persecution in Europe and to practice their religion freely in a new land. What we often forget, however, is that as the colonies developed during the seventeenth century, they too became intolerant toward "minority" religions: many passed anti-Catholic laws or imposed ecclesiastical views on their citizens. Prior to the adoption of the Constitution, only two states (Maryland and Rhode Island, later joined by Virginia) provided full religious freedoms—the remaining eleven had some restrictive laws, and six of those had established state religions. Puritanism was the official faith of the Massachusetts Bay Colony, for instance, while Virginia established itself under the Church of England.

---

1. Alexis de Tocqueville, *Democracy in America*, vol. 1 (New York: Vintage Books, 1954), 319.

2. Garry Wills, *Under God* (New York: Simon & Schuster, 1990), book jacket.

3. For excellent reviews of the role religion plays in American political culture, see Kenneth D. Wald, *Religion and Politics in the United States*, 2d ed. (Washington, D.C.: CQ Press, 1992); and Wills, *Under God*.

More tolerant attitudes toward religious liberty developed with time. After independence was declared, some states adopted constitutions that contained guarantees of religious freedom. For example, North Carolina's 1776 constitution proclaimed that "All men have a natural and unalienable right to worship Almighty God according to the dictates of their own consciences." But other constitutions continued to favor some religions over others. While Delaware provided that "[t]here shall be no establishment of any religious sect in this State in preference to another," it forced all state officers to "profess faith in God the Father, and in Jesus Christ His Only Son."

It would be fair to say that when the Framers gathered in Philadelphia, they—like modern-day Americans—held divergent views about the relationship between religion and the state. Even so, the subject of religion arose only occasionally during the course of the debates. After one particularly difficult session, Benjamin Franklin moved that the delegates pray "for the assistance of Heaven, and its blessings on our deliberations." With virtual unanimity, the delegates attacked Franklin, arguing that a prayer session might offend some members and that it would require them to pay a minister "to officiate in [the] service."[4] In the end, the Founders mentioned religion only once in the Constitution. Article VI provides that all government officials must take an oath to "support this Constitution; but no religious Test shall ever be required as a Qualification to any Office or public Trust under the United States."

Opponents of the new Constitution objected to its lack of any guarantees of religious liberty. New York Anti-Federalists, for example, condemned the document for "not securing the rights of conscience in matters of religion, of granting the liberty of worshipping God agreeable to the mode thereby dictated."[5]

Many states proposed amendments to the Constitution that centered on religious liberty. When James Madison drew up what would become the Bill of Rights, he included a section on religion: "The Civil Rights of none shall be abridged on account of religious belief or worship, nor shall any national religion be established, nor shall the full and equal rights of conscience be in any manner, or on any pretext, infringed." After several rounds of changes, the following phrases became the first two guarantees contained in the First Amendment of the Constitution:

> Congress shall make no law respecting an establishment of religion, or prohibiting the free exercise thereof. . . .

About 150 years after the Bill of Rights was ratified, a Supreme Court justice wrote, "No provision of the Constitution is more closely tied to or given content by its generating history than the religious clause of the First Amendment. It is at once the refined product and the terse summation of that history."[6] Surely, this assessment accurately describes attitudes toward religion yesterday and today: religion motivated many to come to America, and it continues to play a major role in our political culture.

But how has the Court interpreted the Religious Establishment and Free Exercise clauses? Are their meanings the same today as when the Framers wrote them? In this chapter, we examine these and other questions, and we begin with a basic question that has bearing for both clauses: What is religion?

DEFINING RELIGION

Suppose some prisoners form a religion that holds that God requires them to eat filet mignon and drink Cabernet Sauvignon every day. Members of this new religion ask prison officials to serve them such food and drink, but, believing that the religion is nothing

---

4. Quoted in *A History of the American Constitution* by Daniel A. Farber and Suzanna Sherry (St. Paul, Minn.: West Publishing, 1990), 122–123.

5. Address of the Albany Antifederal Committee, April 26, 1788, excerpted in Farber and Sherry, *A History of the American Constitution*, 181.

6. Dissenting opinion of Justice Wiley B. Rutledge in *Everson v. Board of Education* (1947).

more than a ploy to get expensive meat and wine, the officials refuse the request. The prisoners, arguing that the government is depriving them of their right to exercise freely their religion, file a lawsuit to force the prison to comply.

This dispute may strike you as easy to resolve; after all, it seems clear that the prisoners formed this religion only to obtain steak and wine. But how would you distinguish their "religion" from others that also seek to obtain benefits for their members at society's expense? For example, if an Orthodox Jew is fired from her job because she refuses to work on Saturdays, should the state deny her unemployment benefits? Is she using her religion to take money from the state? You would probably answer no to both questions because you perceive a difference between the religion of the prisoners and the religion of the unemployed worker. But what is that difference? How do we distinguish a genuine religion from a sham?

These questions are critical to our discussion because if a religion is not genuine or *bona fide,* it is not entitled to protection under the religion clauses of the First Amendment. But the cases that come before the Supreme Court are never as obvious as our gourmet prisoners' lawsuit, and, in fact, the Court has had a good deal of difficulty in defining religion in terms of the First Amendment. Its first attempt came in 1879 in *Reynolds v. United States.* In the next section, which deals with the free exercise of religion, we discuss this case in some detail. Here, it is enough to say that it involved the Mormon church, whose adherents—at the time of this dispute—lived mostly in the Utah territory. Apparently, because the church was relatively new (it had formed in 1830) and its practices (particularly polygamy) were unfamiliar, if not distasteful, to the Court, the justices felt the need to consider whether it was a religion at all. Writing for the Court, Chief Justice Morrison R. Waite suggested the following:

The word "religion" is not defined in the Constitution. We must go elsewhere, therefore, to ascertain its meaning, and nowhere more appropriately, we think, than to the history of the times in the midst of which the provision was adopted.

Using this approach, Waite did not declare that the Mormons were not a religion; but he did say that the government could outlaw one of its teachings—the practice of polygamy—because there was no support for it at the time of the founding of our nation.

In fact, at the time the Mormon religion was founded, its adherents were persecuted and even attacked by hostile mobs. Many Mormons moved to the West because other states would not tolerate their presence. For example, in 1838 Missouri called out the militia because, as the state governor wrote, "The Mormons must be treated as enemies, and must be exterminated."[7] As *Reynolds* indicates, government efforts to undermine the religion did not stop after the Mormons settled in Utah. In addition to the anti-polygamy law, Congress in 1887 passed an act that allowed the government to "disenfranchise Mormon voters, remove corporate status from the Mormon church, and confiscate all church property."[8] About 1,300 Mormons were arrested.

A decade or so after the decision in *Reynolds,* the Court had an opportunity to reconsider it when a Mormon challenged a law that disqualified individuals from voting if they refused to take an oath "abjuring bigamy or polygamy." But in *Davis v. Beason* (1890), the Court only reinforced *Reynolds,* this time with a statement about beliefs in God and "morals":

The term "religion" has reference to one's views of his relations to his Creator, and to the obligations they impose of reverence for his being and character, and of obedience to his will. . . . With man's relations to his Maker and the obligations he may think they impose, and the manner in which an expression shall be made by him of his belief on those subjects, no interference can be permitted, provided always the laws of society, designed to secure its peace and prosperity, and the morals of its people, are not interfered with.

7. Quoted in *American Constitutional Law* by Laurence Tribe (Mineola, N.Y.: Foundation Press, 1988), 1271.
8. Ibid.

These are narrow approaches to religion; *Reynolds* suggests that religious practices that are new or were unknown to the Framers can be regulated by the government. When we consider that during the eighteenth century there were only a few dozen major religions or sects compared with more than 250 today— to say nothing of the hundreds of small "fringe" groups, we can see why this ruling was so under-inclusive.[9] *Davis* binds religion to a belief in God, a belief that some religions do not hold or about which some "religious" individuals are skeptical. It also permits regulation of religious practices if those practices interfere with the "morals" of the people. In short, through the nineteenth century courts defined religion, as legal scholar Laurence Tribe has written, in terms of "theistic notions respecting divinity, morality, and worship. In order to be considered legitimate, religions had to be viewed as 'civilized' by Western standards."[10]

Fortunately for adherents of non-mainstream religions, *Reynolds* and *Davis* were not the Court's last words on the subject. Since the 1940s two types of cases have provided the Court with opportunities to reconsider Waite's approach. The first centers on religions that appear to be shams and is well exemplified by *United States v. Ballard* (1944). Guy Ballard and his wife asserted that St. Germain had chosen him as a "divine messenger." According to Ballard, to carry out the saint's wishes, he founded the "I Am" religion in California. As the spiritual leader of I Am, Ballard claimed supernatural healing powers and told his followers that he needed money to continue his work. To collect these funds, Ballard used the postal service, making a good deal of money along the way.

Asserting that the I Am sect was not a religion, the federal government accused Ballard of using the mails to defraud people. When the case reached the Supreme Court, it addressed the question of what a jury could consider in determining whether to convict Ballard. The trial court judge had told the jury that it could not take into account the *truth* of Ballard's views (for example, whether St. Germain had chosen Ballard as a messenger); rather, it could consider only the *sincerity* with which Ballard held his views. The Supreme Court agreed with this approach. Writing for the majority, Justice Douglas asserted:

Men may believe what they cannot prove. They may not be put to the proof of their religious doctrines or beliefs. Religious experiences which are as real as life to some may be incomprehensible to others. Yet the fact that they may be beyond the ken of mortals does not mean that they can be made suspect before the law. Many take their gospel from the New Testament. But it would hardly be supposed that they could be tried before a jury charged with the duty of determining whether those teachings contained false representations. The miracles of the New Testament, the Divinity of Christ, life after death, the power of prayer are deep in the religious convictions of many. If one could be sent to jail because a jury in a hostile environment found those teachings false, little indeed would be left of religious freedom.

As for the Ballards, Douglas had this to say:

The religious views espoused by [Ballard] might seem incredible, if not preposterous, to most people. But if those doctrines are subject to trial before a jury charged with finding their truth or falsity, then the same can be done with the religious beliefs of any sect. When the triers of fact undertake that task, they enter a forbidden domain.

Under the *Ballard* approach, as one observer notes, "the test of a genuine religious belief is the sincerity with which it is held," and not the truth of a person's convictions.[11] For our gourmet prisoners, then, we would ask if they sincerely held their religious views, rather than if those views were factually accurate.

The second category of cases in which the Court has considered the question of what religion is involves conscientious objector exemptions from the

9. These figures were quoted in ibid., 1179.
10. Ibid.

11. Peter Woll, *Constitutional Law* (Englewood Cliffs, N.J.: Prentice-Hall, 1981), 785.

military. In the Universal Military Training and Service Act of 1940, Congress provided exemptions from military combat to individuals "who, by reason of religious training and belief, [are] conscientiously opposed to participation in war in any form." The law defined religious training and belief as "an individual's belief in a relation to a Supreme Being involving duties superior to those arising by any human relation but [not including] essentially political, sociological, or philosophical views or a merely personal moral code."

Using Congress's definition, members of some organized religions, such as the Quakers, would qualify easily for exemptions. But what about those who are not members of a traditional, organized religion or those who do not necessarily frame their religious views with reference to a supreme being? Could they obtain religious exemptions from military service?

As the Vietnam War raged on in the 1960s, several cases presented the Court with an opportunity to answer these questions. In *United States v. Seeger* (1965) the justices considered whether three individuals, who were not members of an organized religion, could obtain a military exemption on religious grounds. The appellee, Seeger, asserted that while he opposed participation in the war on the basis of his religious belief, that "he preferred to leave the question as to his belief in a Supreme Being open 'rather than answer yes or no.'" Did his declared "skepticism or disbelief in the existence of God" disqualify him from a religious exemption. Writing for the Court, Justice Tom C. Clark said it did not, for

Congress, in using the expression "Supreme Being" rather than the designation "God," was merely clarifying the meaning of religious training and belief so as to embrace all religions and to exclude essentially political, sociological, or philosophical views.

Clark then provided a standard to govern future litigation, a standard that again stressed the sincerity of the beliefs held:

[T]he test of belief "in relation to a Supreme Being" is whether a given belief that is sincere and meaningful occupies a place in the life of its possessor parallel to ... the orthodox belief in God.

In response to the Court's ruling in *Seeger*, Congress removed from the 1940 law the words "in relation to a Supreme Being." But more litigation ensued. In *Welsh v. United States* (1970) the Court considered another section of the law, which excluded from exemption coverage individuals whose views were "essentially political, sociological, or philosophical." In a judgment for the Court,[12] Justice Black wrote:

We certainly do not think that [the law's] exclusion of those persons with "essentially political, sociological, or philosophical views or a merely personal moral code" should be read to exclude those who hold strong beliefs about our domestic and foreign affairs or even those whose conscientious objection to participation in all wars is founded to a substantial extent upon considerations of public policy. The two groups of registrants that obviously do fall within these exclusions from the exemption are those whose beliefs are not deeply held and those whose objection to war does not rest at all upon moral, ethical, or religious principle but instead rests solely upon considerations of policy, pragmatism, or expediency. In applying [the law's] exclusion of those whose views are "essentially political, sociological, or philosophical" or of those who have "a merely personal moral code," it should be remembered that these exclusions are definitional and do not therefore restrict the category of persons who are conscientious objectors by "religious training and belief."

In other words, the Court expanded its ruling in *Seeger:* even if a draftee's objection to the war was not based strictly on traditional religious grounds, he could obtain a religious exemption if his moral and ethical beliefs were sincerely held—as sincerely held as traditionally defined religious beliefs. For if those views are so strong, they take on a religious character falling within the protection of the law.

---

12. A judgment represents the view of a plurality, not a majority, of the Court's members. Unlike a majority opinion (or "opinion of the Court"), a judgment lacks precedential value.

At least in the conscientious objector cases, the Court moved away from the strictly theistic view of religion it had expressed in *Reynolds.* To be "religious," that is, to come under the protection of the Free Exercise Clause, one's religion need not be based in a belief in God. Rather, the Court's inquiries have focused on the sincerity (but not the truth) with which someone (or one's religion) holds a particular view.

These approaches to defining religion have not satisfied everyone. Some scholars argue that courts should avoid this issue altogether. As one analyst put it:

Any definition of religion would seem to violate religious freedom in that it would dictate to religions, present and future, what they must [be like]. Furthermore, an attempt to define religion, even for purposes of increasing freedom for religions, would run afoul of the "establishment" clause as excluding some religions, or even as establishing a notion respecting religion.[13]

Scholars at the other end of the spectrum argue that courts still retain a westernized, theistic bias toward religion. A noted theologian has argued:

[C]ourts [often] turn to some vague "man-in-the-street" idea of what "religion" should be. [But] a man-in-the-street approach would surely have ruled out early Christianity, which seemed both subversive and atheistic to the religious Romans of the day. The truth is that one man's "bizarre cult" is another's true path to salvation, and the Bill of Rights was designed to safeguard minorities from the man-on-the-street's uncertain capacity for tolerance.[14]

The cases and narrative to come provide you with many opportunities to assess these claims. In particular, as you read, ask yourself whether the Court still evinces a bias toward established, major religions or has it significantly changed its approach in response to the growth of religions in the United States? You may also want to consider the competing charge that the Court has gone too far, that it extends First Amendment coverage to religions that are undeserving. How, for example, would the Court treat our prisoners' religion? Under the case law we have just reviewed, would the Court rule in their favor or in the favor of the prison officials?

FREE EXERCISE OF RELIGION

Imagine a religious sect that forced its members to handle poisonous snakes in the belief that such activity served two purposes: it tested the sincerity of members and helped to recruit new members. Should a court of law prohibit such activity because it is dangerous? Or should it rule that snake handling falls under the umbrella of the free exercise of religion and thus constitutes legitimate behavior?[15] A literal approach to the Free Exercise Clause would suggest the latter; that is, religious denominations can pursue any exercise of their religion they desire. It seems clear that the majority of Americans did not think the free exercise of religion meant any such thing at the time the clause was framed. While we do not know specifically what the Framers intended by the words "free exercise" (congressional debates over religious guarantees tended to focus on the Establishment, rather than the Free Exercise Clause), writings and documents of the day point to a universally accepted limit.[16] As Thomas Jefferson set it out in an 1802 letter to the Danbury Baptist Association: [I believe] "that religion is a matter which lies solely between man and his God; that he owes account to none other for his faith or his worship; that the legislative powers of the

---

13. Jonathan Weiss, "Privilege, Posture and Protection—'Religion' in the Law," *Yale Law Journal* (1964) 73: 604.

14. Harvey Cox of Harvard Divinity School, quoted in *The First Amendment* by Steven Shiffrin and Jesse H. Choper (St. Paul, Minn.: West, 1991), 733–734.

15. In *Harden v. Tennessee* (1949), the Tennessee Supreme Court decided to outlaw such activity on the grounds that it was "dangerous to the life and health of people." We draw this example from M. Glenn Abernathy, *Civil Liberties Under the Constitution*, 3d ed. (New York: Harper & Row, 1977).

16. For an interesting view, see Michael W. McConnell, "Free Exercise as the Framers Understood It," in *The Bill of Rights* by Eugene W. Hickok, Jr. (Charlottesville: University of Virginia Press, 1991).

Government reach actions only, and not opinion."[17] In other words, the free exercise of religion is not limitless, as a literal reading of the amendment would suggest. Rather, at least under Jefferson's interpretation, governments can regulate "actions."

Like Jefferson, the Court has never taken a literal approach to the Free Exercise Clause. Rather, in its first major decision in this area, it seized on his words to proclaim that some religious activities lie beyond First Amendment protections.[18] As we mentioned, that case was *Reynolds v. United States,* which involved the Mormon practice of polygamy. Mormons believed that males "had the duty . . . to practice polygamy" and that failure to do so would result in "damnation in the life to come." Word of this practice found its way to the U.S. Congress, which was charged with governing the Utah territory, where many Mormons lived. In 1874 Congress outlawed polygamy. After he took his second wife, Mormon follower George Reynolds was charged with violating the law. In his defense, Reynolds argued that he was following the dictates of his faith, a right reserved to him under the Free Exercise Clause.

The U.S. Supreme Court disagreed. In a unanimous opinion, the justices rejected an absolutist interpretation of the clause and instead sought to draw a distinction between the behavior it did and did not protect. Chief Justice Waite's opinion for the Court asserted: "Congress was deprived of all legislative power over mere opinion, but was left free to reach actions which were in violation of social duties or subversive of the good order." This distinction between opinions (or beliefs) and actions (or practices) became, as we shall see, the centerpiece for several future religion cases. Some suggest that the Court used it here as a means to strike down the unpopular practice of polygamy. Constitutional law scholar John Brigham notes, "More significant than the distinction between belief and action . . . seems to be the fact that the Mormon practice was not viewed with equanimity by the rest of the population including the Supreme Court."[19]

Because it involved a practice considerably less problematic than polygamy, and an older, more established religion than the Mormon church, *Pierce v. Society of Sisters* (1925) illustrates the validity of Brigham's observation. In 1922 Oregon passed a compulsory public school education act, requiring children between the ages of eight and sixteen to attend public school. A diverse body of interests supported this measure for equally varying reasons: Progressives hailed it as a necessary step for the assimilation of immigrants, while the Ku Klux Klan backed it because it was viewed as anti-Catholic. Indeed, the ultimate effect of the Oregon law was to force closure of the state's privately run schools, several of which were Roman Catholic. The Society of Sisters, organized in 1880 to provide secular and religious instruction to children, faced dissolution because it derived more than $30,000 of its annual income from its school. Rather than shut its doors, the society chose to sue the state, arguing that the law impinged on its free exercise rights. The sisters received support from organizations representing the spectrum of religions in the United States. Jews, Lutherans, Episcopalians, and Seventh-Day Adventists also had a vested interest in the case's outcome—most ran private schools. In addition, they wanted to show their unified distaste

---

17. Letter to the Danbury Baptist Association, 1802, quoted in *Reynolds v. United States* (1879).

18. As we shall soon see, in its religious establishment cases the Court also seized upon another phrase used in Jefferson's Danbury Baptist Association letter—a "wall of separation." The Court's reliance on Jefferson's thinking has been questioned by some analysts because he was in France at the time the First Amendment was drafted. See John S. Baker, Jr., "The Establishment Clause as Intended" in Hickok, *The Bill of Rights.* On the other hand, Jefferson and Madison, the author of the Bill of Rights, corresponded frequently during this period. See Leonard W. Levy, *Constitutional Opinions* (New York: Oxford University Press, 1986).

19. John Brigham, *Civil Liberties and American Democracy* (Washington, D.C.: CQ Press, 1984), 77.

BOX 3-1   THE JEHOVAH'S WITNESSES

The Jehovah's Witnesses began in the 1870s in Pittsburgh, Pennsylvania. Starting as a Bible study class directed by Charles Taze Russell, the sect became a powerful grass-roots movement. By the late 1930s, under the leadership of Joseph Franklin Rutherford, the Witnesses were preaching all over the United States and in several foreign countries.

Members see themselves as evangelical ministers with the mission to preach about Jehovah's struggle with Satan. They denounce organized religion, particularly Catholicism. In the past, their views made them very unpopular, and they were often in trouble with the law. Because they preached on street corners and distributed their literature door-to-door, the Witnesses could be prosecuted for violating city ordinances.

The Supreme Court decided the following cases:

Lovell v. City of Griffin (1938). May a town prohibit the distribution of pamphlets unless a permit has been obtained? No. The Court struck down the prohibition on First Amendment prior restraint grounds.

Cantwell v. Connecticut (1940). May a state prohibit the solicitation of money for any cause without first obtaining a license from a public official? No. The Court asserted that the law, as implemented, violated the Free Exercise Clause.

Jones v. Opelika (1942). May a town place a tax on those selling any goods door-to-door? Yes. The Court upheld the tax on the grounds that it covered commercial activity, which fell beyond First Amendment protection.

Murdock v. Pennsylvania (1943). May a city place a tax on those selling any goods door-to-door? No. The Court overruled *Jones v. Opelika* and held that the ordinance violated religious liberty guarantees.

Martin v. Struthers (1943). May a city prohibit all forms of door-to-door solicitation? No. The Court held that the ordinance violated First Amendment free speech guarantees.

for the Klan-backed law, believing it repressed "pluralism in education."[20]

In a unanimous opinion, the Court held for the Society of Sisters. But the Court virtually ignored the *Reynolds* belief-action distinction; instead, it rested its ruling on the view that the society (as opposed to the Mormons) engaged in a "useful and meritorious" undertaking. In the eyes of the justices,

The inevitable practical result of enforcing the act ... would be the destruction of appellees' primary schools.... Appellees are engaged in a kind of undertaking not inherently harmful but long regarded as useful and meritorious. Certainly, there is nothing in the present record to indicate that they have failed to discharge their obligations to patrons, students, or the state.

It was not until 1940, in fact, that the Court returned to and embellished upon the belief-action dichotomy. That year the Court for the first time specifically applied the Free Exercise Clause to state action, in this instance, taken against the Jehovah's Witnesses *(see Box 3-1)*. The Jehovah's Witnesses denomination considers itself "ministers of the gospel to the 'gentiles,'" and, as such, distributes pamphlets and solicits money, activities regulated by laws in many states.[21] In *Cantwell v. Connecticut*, among other cases, the Witnesses asked the Court to strike down such regulation as infringements upon their right to practice their religion freely.

Cantwell v. Connecticut

310 U.S. 296 (1940)

Vote: 9 (Black, Douglas, Frankfurter, Hughes, McReynolds, Murphy, Reed, Roberts, Stone)

    0

Opinion of the Court: Roberts

Newton Cantwell and his two sons, Jesse and Russell, members of the Jehovah's Witnesses sect, were

---

20. For more details on this case, see Clement E. Vose, *Constitutional Change* (Lexington, Mass.: Lexington Books, 1972).

21. Richard E. Morgan, *The Law and Politics of Civil Rights and Liberties* (New York: Knopf, 1985), 185.

playing records and distributing pamphlets to citizens walking the streets in New Haven, Connecticut, in an area that was predominately Catholic. Two passersby took offense at the anti-Catholic messages of the material and complained. The next day, police arrested the Cantwells for violating a state law prohibiting individuals "from soliciting money for any cause" without a license. The law required those who wanted to solicit to obtain a "certificate of approval" from the state's secretary of the Public Welfare Council. The state charged this official with determining whether "the cause is a religious one" or one of a *"bona fide* object of charity."[22] If the official found neither, he was authorized to withhold the necessary certificate.

Although this law was neutral—that is, it applied to all those engaging in solicitation—the Witnesses challenged it as a restriction on their free exercise rights. Hayden Covington, their attorney and ACLU (American Civil Liberties Union) member, argued that the law "deprived the Cantwells of their right of freedom to worship Almighty God."

MR. JUSTICE ROBERTS delivered the opinion of the Court.

The First Amendment declares that Congress shall make no law respecting an establishment of religion or prohibiting the free exercise thereof. The Fourteenth Amendment has rendered the legislatures of the states as incompetent as Congress to enact such laws. The constitutional inhibition of legislation on the subject of religion has a double aspect. On the one hand, it forestalls compulsion by law of the acceptance of any creed or the practice of any form of worship. Freedom of conscience and freedom to adhere to such religious organization or form of worship as the individual may choose cannot be restricted by law. On the other hand, it safeguards the free exercise of the chosen form of religion. Thus the Amendment embraces two concepts—freedom to believe and freedom to act. The first is absolute but, in the nature of things, the second cannot be. Conduct remains

subject to regulation for the protection of society. The freedom to act must have appropriate definition to preserve the enforcement of that protection. In every case the power to regulate must be so exercised as not, in attaining a permissible end, unduly to infringe the protected freedom. No one would contest the proposition that a state may not, by statute, wholly deny the right to preach or to disseminate religious views. Plainly such a previous and absolute restraint would violate the terms of the guarantee. It is equally clear that a state may by general and non-discriminatory legislation regulate the times, the places, and the manner of soliciting upon its streets, and of holding meetings thereon; and may in other respects safeguard the peace, good order and comfort of the community, without unconstitutionally invading the liberties protected by the Fourteenth Amendment. The appellants are right in their insistence that the Act in question is not such a regulation. If a certificate is procured, solicitation is permitted without restraint but, in the absence of a certificate, solicitation is altogether prohibited.

The appellants urge that to require them to obtain a certificate as a condition of soliciting support for their views amounts to a prior restraint on the exercise of their religion within the meaning of the Constitution. The State insists that the Act, as construed by the Supreme Court of Connecticut, imposes no previous restraint upon the dissemination of religious views or teaching but merely safeguards against the perpetration of frauds under the cloak of religion. Conceding that this is so, the question remains whether the method adopted by Connecticut to that end transgresses the liberty safeguarded by the Constitution.

The general regulation, in the public interest, of solicitation, which does not involve any religious test and does not unreasonably obstruct or delay the collection of funds, is not open to any constitutional objection, even though the collection be for a religious purpose. Such regulation would not constitute a prohibited previous restraint on the free exercise of religion or interpose an inadmissible obstacle to its exercise.

It will be noted, however, that the Act requires an application to the secretary of the public welfare council of the State; that he is empowered to determine whether the cause is a religious one, and that the issue of a certificate depends upon his affirmative action. If he finds that the cause is not

---

22. For more details, see Henry J. Abraham, *Freedom and the Court,* 5th ed. (New York: Oxford University Press, 1988), 298.

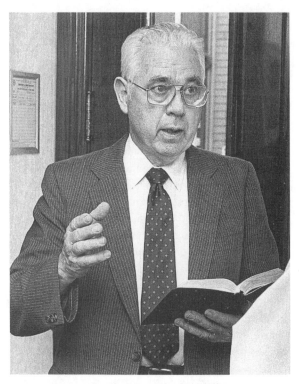

Russell Cantwell raising funds for the Jehovah's Witnesses in Brooklyn in 1991. He, his brother Jesse, and his father Newton Cantwell were convicted for soliciting without a license; the Supreme Court overturned the convictions in 1940.

state may protect its citizens from fraudulent solicitation by requiring a stranger in the community, before permitting him publicly to solicit funds for any purpose, to establish his identity and his authority to act for the cause which he purports to represent. The state is likewise free to regulate the time and manner of solicitation generally, in the interest of public safety, peace, comfort, or convenience. But to condition the solicitation of aid for the perpetuation of religious views or systems upon a license, the grant of which rests in the exercise of a determination by state authority as to what is a religious cause, is to lay a forbidden burden upon the exercise of liberty protected by the Constitution. . . .

The judgment affirming the convictions . . . is reversed and the cause is remanded for further proceedings not inconsistent with this opinion. So ordered.

Reversed and remanded.

that of religion, to solicit for it becomes a crime. He is not to issue a certificate as a matter of course. His decision to issue or refuse it involves appraisal of facts, the exercise of judgment, and the formation of an opinion. He is authorized to withhold his approval if he determines that the cause is not a religious one. Such a censorship of religion as the means of determining its right to survive is a denial of liberty protected by the First Amendment and included in the liberty which is within the protection of the Fourteenth. . . .

Nothing we have said is intended even remotely to imply that, under the cloak of religion, persons may, with impunity, commit frauds upon the public. Certainly penal laws are available to punish such conduct. Even the exercise of religion may be at some slight inconvenience in order that the state may protect its citizens from injury. Without doubt a

In this opinion, Justice Owen Roberts returned to the belief-action dichotomy, but treated it in a slightly different manner. He claimed that although the Free Exercise Clause covered belief and action, "The first is absolute but, in the nature of things, the second cannot be." How then would the Court distinguish protected action from illegal action? Under the principles articulated in *Cantwell,* which some analysts refer to as the "valid secular policy" test, the Court looks at the particular legislation or policy adopted by the government.[23] If the policy serves a legitimate nonreligious governmental goal, not directed at any particular religion, the Court will uphold it, even if the legislation has the effect of conflicting with religious practices. In *Cantwell* the Court said that the state could regulate the collection of funds, even if those funds were for a religious purpose, because it has a valid interest in protecting its citizens from fraudulent solicitation. If Connecticut's law had not empowered a government official to determine whether a cause is religious or not, the Court probably would have upheld it as a legitimate secular policy.

23. See Richard C. Cortner, *The Supreme Court and Civil Liberties Policy* (Palo Alto, Calif.: Mayfield, 1975), 145–147.

Had the Court upheld the law, the Jehovah's Witnesses would have found it more difficult to carry out the dictates of their religion. By the same token, all other would-be solicitors—charitable organizations and the like—would be similarly affected. In other words, the religious and the nonreligious would be subject to the regulations. Looking at *Cantwell* this way reveals an important underpinning of the logic of the valid secular policy test: neutrality. If the government has a valid secular reason for its policy, then in the eyes of the justices, religions should not be exempt from its coverage simply because they are religions. Exempting them would be to give religion an elevated position in society. One could argue that there is a difference between making it more difficult for a religion to carry out its mandate and a charity to collect funds. But, by adopting the valid secular policy test, the Court suggested that the effect on the Jehovah's Witnesses amounts to only an incidental intrusion on religion that comes about as the government pursues a legitimate interest.

Application of the Valid Secular Policy Test

How has this test worked? In particular, what constitutes a valid secular policy, a legitimate state interest? In *Cantwell*, Justice Roberts provided some clues as to what these concepts might encompass: the prevention of fraud, the regulation of the time and manner of solicitation, and actions involving the interest of "public safety, peace, comfort or convenience." Shortly after *Cantwell*, the Court added to Roberts's list when it reviewed cases involving mandatory flag salutes and child labor laws.

At issue in the first flag salute case, *Minersville School District v. Gobitis* (1940), were the recitation of the Pledge of Allegiance and the hand gesture or salute that accompanied it. For most individuals, particularly school children, the pledge and salute are noncontroversial routines that illustrate their loyalty to the basic tenets of American society. Such is not the case for the Jehovah's Witnesses, who exalt religious laws over all others. They claim that the salute and the pledge violates a teaching from Exodus:

Thou shalt not make unto thee any graven image, or any likeness of anything that is in heaven above, or that is in earth beneath, or that is in the water under the earth; thou shalt not bow down thyself to them, nor serve them.

Accordingly, Jehovah's Witnesses do not want their children to recite the pledge and salute the flag. The problem, at the time of this case, was that schools made the pledge and salute to the flag mandatory for all public school children. Flag salute laws became particularly pervasive after World War I as a show of patriotism. Before the war only five states required flag salutes; by 1935 that figure had risen to eighteen, with many local school boards compelling the salute in absence of state legislation.[24]

Beginning in the mid-1930s, the Witnesses actively campaigned to do away with the salutes. The campaign began in Nazi Germany, where Jehovah's Witnesses refused to salute Hitler with raised palms and were punished by imprisonment in concentration camps.[25] Joseph Rutherford, who was the Witnesses' leader in the United States, spoke out against the American flag salute, which, at the time, was regularly done with a straight, extended arm, resembling the Nazi-Fascist salute. He asserted that Witnesses "do not 'Heil Hitler' nor any other creature."

After Rutherford's speech, some members of the Jehovah's Witnesses asked their children not to salute the flag. Among these was Walter Gobitas,[26] whose two children—twelve-year-old Lillian and her younger brother William—attended a Pennsylvania public school with a mandatory flag salute policy. When they refused to salute the flag, they were expelled. Represented by attorneys from the Witnesses, including Hayden Covington, Gobitas brought suit against the school board, arguing that the expulsion

24. We derive this account from Peter Irons, *The Courage of Their Convictions* (New York: Free Press, 1988), 17–24.

25. Ibid., 16.

26. The family name, Gobitas, was misspelled in the records.

Walter Gobitas sued the Minersville, Pennsylvania, school district after his children, William and Lillian, were expelled for refusing to salute the flag because of their Jehovah's Witnesses faith.

violated his children's free speech and free exercise of religion rights. In Chapter 4, we explore the free speech component of Gobitas's claim. For now, it is important to note that the Supreme Court rejected these arguments. Writing for the Court, Justice Frankfurter asserted that:

[T]he ultimate foundation of a free society is the binding tie of cohesive sentiment.... The flag is the symbol of our national unity, transcending all internal differences.... To stigmatize legislative judgment in providing for this universal gesture of respect for the symbol of our national life ... would amount to no less than the pronouncement of pedagogical and psychological dogma in a field where courts possess ... no controlling competence.

To put it in terms of the valid secular policy test, Frankfurter was claiming that the state had a legitimate secular reason for requiring flag salutes: to foster patriotism. That the law affected the religious practice of the Jehovah's Witnesses did not, in Frankfurter's view, detract from its constitutionality. Besides, Frankfurter believed that the Court should not interfere with local policies because that "would in effect make [the Court] the school board for the country."

Some of these same arguments—particularly those centered on national unity—were raised in the 1980s by attorneys seeking to convince the Court to uphold state regulations prohibiting the desecration of the American flag. (We shall consider these cases in the next chapter.) Here, it is worth noting that there were extraordinary repercussions from the Court's decision in *Gobitis*. Not surprising, after the ruling many states either retained or passed laws requiring flag salutes and pledges for all public school children and threatening to expel anyone who did not comply. What was startling was the violence against Jehovah's Witnesses. "Within two weeks of the Court's decision," two federal officials later wrote, "hundreds of attacks upon the Witnesses were reported to the Department of Justice."[27] Viewing their refusal to salute the flag as unpatriotic—especially as the country fought in World War II—mobs throughout the United States stoned, kidnapped, beat, and even castrated Jehovah's Witnesses.

These episodes of violence prompted many newspapers and major organizations, such as the American Bar Association, to condemn the Court's ruling. They also propelled the Witnesses to look for yet another suit by which to mount a constitutional challenge to the mandatory flag salutes. With the help of lawyer Hayden Covington and attorneys from the ACLU, the Jehovah's Witnesses located the Barnette family—Jehovah's Witnesses who had been harassed by the West Virginia school system for failure to participate in the flag salute ritual. One of the Barnette children had been expelled.[28]

Despite the Supreme Court's decision in *Gobitis*, which said the flag salute laws were constitutional, a three-judge district court, in *West Virginia Board of Education v. Barnette,* sympathized with the Barnette family's plight. According to John J. Parker, the well-respected circuit court judge, "The salute to the United States' flag is an expression of the homage of the soul. To force it upon one who has conscientious scruples against giving it is petty tyranny unworthy of the spirit of the Republic, and forbidden, we think, by the United States Constitution."[29]

The Supreme Court agreed. In a 6–3 decision, handed down on Flag Day in 1943, the Court overturned *Gobitis*. The Court centered its decision squarely in free expression, rather than free exercise, guarantees. Justice Jackson wrote for the majority:

[The issue does not] turn on one's possession of particular religious views or the sincerity with which they are held. While religion supplies appellees' motive for enduring the discomforts of making the issue in this case, many citizens who do not share these religious views hold such a compulsory rite to infringe constitutional liberty of the individual. It is not necessary to inquire whether non-conformist beliefs will exempt from the duty to salute unless we first find power to make the salute a legal duty.

Because the Court found that the state did not have the power to impose a flag salute on public school children, it did not need to make such an inquiry.

We revisit *Barnette* in the next chapter because it is important to an understanding of the development of free expression guarantees. Two questions, however, should be addressed here. The first is obvious: Why did the Court undergo a major change of heart, overruling *Gobitis* just three years after it had been announced? Some scholars suggest that extrajudicial factors were at work. For example, the legal community widely criticized the *Gobitis* opinion: of the twenty-two law review-type articles published about the case

---

27. Irons, *The Courage of Their Convictions*, 22–23.

28. For more details on this case, see David Manwaring, *Render Unto Caesar: The Flag Salute Controversy* (Chicago: University of Chicago Press, 1962).

29. Chief Judge John Parker of the Fourth Circuit, as Henry J. Abraham notes, was a "prominent and distinguished Republican leader in North Carolina for many years and an outstanding jurist." Parker was nominated to the Supreme Court, but a coalition of organized interests (most notably the AFL-CIO and NAACP) and anti-Hoover Progressive senators blocked his appointment by a two-vote margin. See Abraham, *Justices and Presidents*, 3d ed. (New York: Oxford University Press, 1992), 42–43.

between 1940 and 1941, only two agreed with the justices. In addition, state courts generally did not follow the precepts of *Gobitis;* none that heard related cases affirmed the expulsion of children against challenges on religious grounds. Some rejected the Court's logic outright.[30] Moreover, the Court may have been reacting to the atrocities of Nazi Germany, where patriotism was taken to obscene ends. Recall that Justice Frankfurter, in *Gobitis,* viewed patriotism as a legitimate government end. But in *Barnette,* Jackson had a different point of view. Note, in particular, his implicit reference to Nazism and fascism:

National unity as an end which officials may foster by persuasion and example is not in question. The problem is whether under our Constitution compulsion as here employed is a permissible means for its achievement.

Struggles to coerce uniformity of sentiment in support of some end thought essential to their time and country have been waged by many good as well as by evil men.... Those who begin coercive elimination of dissent soon find themselves exterminating dissenters. Compulsory unification of opinion achieves only the unanimity of the graveyard.

It seems trite but necessary to say that the First Amendment ... was designed to avoid these ends by avoiding these beginnings.

Finally, the Court experienced some turnover in membership between *Gobitis* and *Barnette.* Two members of the *Gobitis* majority were replaced by Jackson and Wiley Rutledge. Also, Hugo Black, William Douglas, and Frank Murphy—all of whom had joined *Gobitis*—indicated in 1942 that they had changed their thinking on the issue.[31]

A second question concerns the valid secular policy test. The Court used it to uphold mandatory flag salutes in *Gobitis,* so did the justices banish it in *Barnette*

by striking down the same laws? The answer is no, as you may be able to see from the excerpt of Jackson's opinion. In fact, the very next year in *Prince v. Massachusetts* (1944), the Court invoked the valid secular policy test to rule against the Witnesses.

Prince involved a Massachusetts law prohibiting minors (girls under eighteen and boys under twelve) from selling "upon the streets or in other public places, any newspaper, magazines, periodicals, or other articles of merchandise." It further specified that any parent or guardian allowing minors to perform such activity would be engaging in criminal behavior. Sarah Prince, a Jehovah's Witness, allowed her nine-year-old niece, Betty Simmons, for whom Prince was the legal guardian, to help her distribute religious pamphlets. Prince knew she was violating the law— she had been warned by school authorities—but she continued and was arrested.

At the trial court level, there was some doubt as to whether the child actually had sold materials, but when the case reached the Supreme Court, it dealt exclusively with this question: Did the state law violate First Amendment principles? A divided Court held that it did not. Writing for a five-person majority, Justice Rutledge asserted:

The State's authority over children's activities is broader than over like actions of adults. This is peculiarly true of public activities and in matters of employment. A democratic society rests ... upon the healthy, well-rounded growth of young people into full maturity as citizens.... It may secure this against impeding restraints and dangers, within a broad range of selection. Among evils most appropriate for such action are the crippling effects of child employment ... and the possible harms arising from other activities subject to all the diverse influences of the street. It is too late now to doubt that legislation appropriately designed to reach such evils is within the state's police power, whether against the parent's claim to control of the child or one that religious scruples dictate contrary action.

Clearly, legislatures can regulate religious practices of potential harm to children as well as those of ques-

30. See the amicus curiae brief filed by the Bill of Rights Committee of the American Bar Association in *Barnette.* Also, in note 15 of his opinion, Jackson cites some of the writings critical of *Gobitis.*

31. As Henry J. Abraham notes, the trio filed a memorandum (in another Jehovah's Witness case, *Jones v. Opelika,* 1942) stating that "since we joined in the opinion in the *Gobitis* case, we think this is an appropriate occasion to state that we now believe that it was also wrongly decided." See Abraham, *Freedom and the Court,* 303.

tionable morality and safety. Such laws, in the eyes of the justices, present a reasonable use of state police power, which is the ability of states to regulate in the best interests of their citizens. In other words, child labor laws represent a valid secular policy and, when in opposition to a free exercise claim, the free exercise claim falls.

The Demise of the Valid Secular Policy Test

Most of the cases we have examined have several traits in common: they were brought by Jehovah's Witnesses, a minority religion; they were decided during the 1940s, a period when the Court was neither particularly conservative nor liberal in ideological outlook; and they involved arguments that combined free expression and free exercise claims. By the same token, the Court's approaches to the cases were relatively consistent. The Court remained true to the belief-action dichotomy set out in *Reynolds* and, when a religion's actions were at stake, it invoked the valid secular policy test to resolve the disputes. These approaches occasionally led the justices to strike down state policies *(Cantwell)*, as well as to uphold them *(Gobitis, Prince)*.

In the 1960s, however, major changes began to occur in the direction of precedent governing free exercise claims and in the kinds of cases the Court decided. The first signs came in *Braunfeld v. Brown*, which was one of several cases the Court heard in 1961 involving "blue" or Sunday closing laws. At issue in *Braunfeld* was Pennsylvania's blue law, which allowed only certain kinds of stores to remain open on Sunday. Abraham Braunfeld, an Orthodox Jew, owned a retail clothing and home furnishing store in Philadelphia. Because such stores were not among those permitted to remain open on Sunday, Braunfeld wanted the Court to issue a permanent injunction against the law. His religious principles dictated that he could not work on Saturday, the Jewish sabbath, but he needed to be open six days a week for economic reasons. He challenged the law as a violation

of, among other things, his right to exercise his religion.

In a judgment, Chief Justice Earl Warren upheld the constitutionality of blue laws and restated the belief-action dichotomy:

Certain aspects of religious exercise cannot, in any way, be restricted or burdened by either federal or state legislation. Compulsion by law of the acceptance of any creed or the practice of any form of worship is strictly forbidden. The freedom to hold religious beliefs and opinions is absolute....

However, the freedom to act, even where the action is in accord with one's religious convictions, is not totally free from legislative restrictions.... [L]egislative power over mere opinion is forbidden but it may reach people's action when they are found to be in violation of important social duties or subversive of good order, even when the actions are demanded by one's religion.

But, according to many observers, Warren's opinion veered significantly from established precedent. Consider the following passage:

Of course, to hold unassailable all legislation regulating conduct which imposes solely an indirect burden on the observance of religion would be a gross oversimplification. If the purpose or effect of a law is to impede the observance of one or all religions or is to discriminate invidiously between religions, that law is constitutionally invalid even though the burden may be characterized as being only indirect. But if the State regulates conduct by enacting a general law within its power, the purpose and effect of which is to advance the State's secular goals, the statute is valid despite its indirect burden on religious observance *unless the State may accomplish its purpose by means which do not impose such a burden* (emphasis added).

In some ways, this statement merely restates the logic of *Cantwell* and the valid secular policy test. But note the italicized phrase: it represents an important addition to the test because it suggests that the state must show that its legislation achieves an important secular end *and* that it could not have achieved those ends with less restrictive legislation, that is, legislation that would place less of a burden on religious freedom.

Sunday closing laws, Warren reasoned, met both these standards. According to the chief justice, in passing blue laws, the state intended to set up a day of "rest, repose, recreation and tranquillity—a day which all members of the family and community have the opportunity to spend and enjoy together." In other words, the Sunday closing laws reflect a valid secular purpose. They also are the least restrictive way of accomplishing that purpose. Even though the laws indirectly burden members of some religions (for example, Orthodox Jews), Warren reasoned that the states had adopted a relatively unburdensome way of accomplishing their goal of creating a uniform "weekly respite from all labor."

Other members of the Court took issue with Warren's analysis; as a judgment, after all, his opinion represented the views of only a plurality of the justices. Especially memorable were dissents by William Brennan, and Potter Stewart. Brennan thought the Court had taken a misguided approach to the issue: "I would approach this case differently, from the point of view of the individuals whose liberty is— concededly—curtailed by these enactments. For the values of the First Amendment ... look primarily towards the preservation of personal liberty, rather than towards the fulfillment of collective goals." In a one-paragraph dissent, Stewart put the issue even more starkly:

> Pennsylvania has passed a law which compels an Orthodox Jew to choose between his religious faith and his economic survival. That is a cruel choice. It is a choice which I think no State can constitutionally demand. For me this is not something that can be swept under the rug and forgotten in the interest of enforced Sunday togetherness. I think the impact of this law upon the appellants grossly violates their constitutional right to free exercise of their religion.

The divided opinion over *Braunfeld* created something of a quandary for legal scholars: Was the Court— through its adoption of a least restrictive means approach—signaling a change in the way it would resolve free exercise disputes? Or was *Braunfeld* an aberration? Consider these questions as you read *Sherbert v. Verner* (1963).

Sherbert v. Verner

374 U.S. 398 (1963)

Vote: 7 (Black, Brennan, Clark, Douglas, Goldberg, Stewart, Warren)
  2 (Harlan, White)

Opinion of the Court: Brennan
Concurring opinions: Douglas, Stewart
Dissenting opinion: Harlan

Adell Sherbert was spool tender in a Spartanburg, South Carolina, textile mill, a job she had held for thirty-five years. Sherbert worked Monday though Friday from 7 a.m. to 3 p.m. She had the option of working Saturdays, but chose not to. Sherbert was a member of the Seventh-Day Adventist church, which held that no work be performed between sundown on Friday and sundown on Saturday. In other words, Saturday was her church's sabbath.

On June 5, 1959, Sherbert's employer informed her that, beginning June 6, work on Saturdays would no longer be voluntary: to retain her job she would need to report to the mill every Saturday. Sherbert continued to work Monday through Friday but, in accord with her religious beliefs, failed to show up on six successive Saturdays. Her employer fired her July 27.

Between June 5 and July 27, Sherbert had tried to find a job at three other textile mills, but they too operated on Saturdays. Sherbert filed for state unemployment benefits. Under South Carolina law, a claimant who is eligible for benefits must be "able to work ... and available for work"; a claimant is ineligible for benefits if he or she has "failed, without good cause ... to accept available suitable work when offered him by the employment office or the employer." The benefits examiner in charge of Sherbert's claim turned her down on the grounds that she failed, without good cause, to accept "suitable work when offered" by her employer. In other words, her religious preference was an insufficient justification for her refusal of a job.

Sherbert and her lawyers filed suit in a state court, which ruled in favor of the employment office, as did the state supreme court. When Sherbert's attorneys asked the U.S. Supreme Court to review the case, they raised several claims emanating from the Court's previous rulings on the free exercise of religion. First, after reviewing the belief-action distinction of *Reynolds* and *Cantwell*, they tried to show that the state's denial actually impinged on the forbidden territory of beliefs. They illustrated the fine line that separates beliefs from actions: the South Carolina law "conditions [Sherbert's] eligibility for benefits ... upon being willing to accept work on Saturday and disqualified her for her refusal to accept a job involving work on Saturday. In effect this requires her to repudiate her religious belief by professing a willingness to do something in conflict with the tenets of her church. This is not mere regulation of conduct. It invades the sphere of belief and intellect." In essence, the attorneys were adopting a page out of Stewart's dissent in *Braunfeld*: the state was using economic coercion to force Sherbert to give up a religious belief.

Second, Sherbert's attorneys tried to use *Braunfeld*, a precedent seemingly adverse to their client's interests, by flipping *Braunfeld* so that it worked for her. "The right to observe the Sabbath by abstaining from labor is of the essence. Take away that right or stifle it, and there is no freedom of religion so far as a Saturday Sabbatarian is concerned. Most Sunday-observing Christians probably feel as strongly with respect to their right similarly to refrain from labor in observance of Sunday as the Lord's Day."

The state had an easier task, or so it seemed. It could rely on *Braunfeld* to show that South Carolina, just like Pennsylvania, had not criminalized religious beliefs. Moreover, it offered—as did Pennsylvania in *Braunfeld*—a secular and, in its view, "legitimate governmental purposes for the law." According to the state, it sought to encourage "stable employment" and to discourage fraudulent behavior in those seeking unemployment benefits. Finally, while the state admitted that its denial of benefits financially burdened Sherbert, it argued that the burden was no more direct or greater than the economic hardship Braunfeld had alleged.

So the question for the Court to settle was the following: May a state deny unemployment benefits to persons whose religious beliefs preclude working on Saturdays?

MR. JUSTICE BRENNAN delivered the opinion of the Court.

The door of the Free Exercise Clause stands tightly closed against any governmental regulation of religious beliefs as such, *Cantwell v. Connecticut*.... On the other hand, the Court has rejected challenges under the Free Exercise Clause to governmental regulation of certain overt acts prompted by religious beliefs or principles, for "even when the action is in accord with one's religious convictions, [it] is not totally free from legislative restrictions." *Braunfeld v. Brown.* The conduct or actions so regulated have invariably posed some substantial threat to public safety, peace or order. See, *e.g.*, *Reynolds v. United States*; *Prince v. Massachusetts*....

Plainly enough, appellant's conscientious objection to Saturday work constitutes no conduct prompted by religious principles of a kind within the reach of state legislation. If, therefore, the decision of the South Carolina Supreme Court is to withstand appellant's constitutional challenge, it must be either because her disqualification as a beneficiary represents no infringement by the State of her constitutional rights of free exercise, or because any incidental burden on the free exercise of appellant's religion may be justified by a "compelling state interest in the regulation of a subject within the State's constitutional power to regulate...."

We turn first to the question whether the disqualification for benefits imposes any burden on the free exercise of appellant's religion. We think it is clear that it does. In a sense the consequences of such a disqualification to religious principles and practices may be only an indirect result of welfare legislation within the State's general competence to enact; it is true that no criminal sanctions directly compel appellant to work a six-day week. But this is only the beginning, not the end, of our inquiry. For "if the purpose or effect of a law is to impede the observance of one or all religions or is to discriminate invidiously between religions, that law is constitutionally invalid even though the burden may be characterized as being only indirect." *Braunfeld v. Brown.* Here not only is it apparent that appellant's declared ineligibility for benefits derives solely from the practice of her religion, but the pressure upon her to forego that practice is unmistakable. The ruling forces her to choose between following the precepts of her religion and forfeiting benefits, on the one hand, and abandoning one of the precepts of her religion in order to accept work, on the other hand. Governmental imposition of such a choice puts the same kind of burden upon the free exercise of religion as would a fine imposed against appellant for her Saturday worship.

Nor may the South Carolina court's construction of the statute be saved from constitutional infirmity on the ground that unemployment compensation benefits are not appellant's "right" but merely a "privilege." It is too late in the day to doubt that the liberties of religion and expression may be infringed by the denial of or placing of conditions upon a benefit or privilege. . . .

We must next consider whether some compelling state interest enforced in the eligibility provisions of the South Carolina statute justifies the substantial infringement of appellant's First Amendment right. It is basic that no showing merely of a rational relationship to some colorable state interest would suffice; in this highly sensitive constitutional area, "[o]nly the gravest abuses, endangering paramount interests, give occasion for permissible limitation." . . . No such abuse or danger has been advanced in the present case. The appellees suggest no more than a possibility that the filing of fraudulent claims by unscrupulous claimants feigning religious objections to Saturday work might not only dilute the unemployment compensation fund but also hinder the scheduling by employers of necessary Saturday work. But that possibility is not apposite here because no such objection appears to have been made before the South Carolina Supreme Court, and we are unwilling to assess the importance of an asserted state interest without the views of the state court. Nor, if the contention had been made below, would the record appear to sustain it; there is no proof whatever to warrant such fears of malingering or deceit as those which the respondents now advance. Even if consider-

ation of such evidence is not foreclosed by the prohibition against judicial inquiry into the truth or falsity of religious beliefs, *United States v. Ballard,* . . . it is highly doubtful whether such evidence would be sufficient to warrant a substantial infringement of religious liberties. For even if the possibility of spurious claims did threaten to dilute the fund and disrupt the scheduling of work, it would plainly be incumbent upon the appellees to demonstrate that no alternative forms of regulation would combat such abuses without infringing First Amendment rights. . . .

In these respects, then, the state interest asserted in the present case is wholly dissimilar to the interests which were found to justify the less direct burden upon religious practices in *Braunfeld v. Brown.* The Court recognized that the Sunday closing law which that decision sustained undoubtedly served "to make the practice of [the Orthodox Jewish merchants'] . . . religious beliefs more expensive." But the statute was nevertheless saved by a countervailing factor which finds no equivalent in the instant case—a strong state interest in providing one uniform day of rest for all workers. That secular objective could be achieved, the Court found, only by declaring Sunday to be that day of rest. Requiring exemptions for Sabbatarians, while theoretically possible, appeared to present an administrative problem of such magnitude, or to afford the exempted class so great a competitive advantage, that such a requirement would have rendered the entire statutory scheme unworkable. In the present case no such justifications underlie the determination of the state court that appellant's religion makes her ineligible to receive benefits. . . .

The judgment of the South Carolina Supreme Court is reversed and the case is remanded for further proceedings not inconsistent with this opinion.

It is so ordered.

MR. JUSTICE STEWART, concurring in the result.

My . . . difference with the Court's opinion is that I cannot agree that today's decision can stand consistently with *Braunfeld v. Brown.* The Court says that there was a "less direct burden upon religious practices" in that case than in this. With all respect, I think the Court is mistaken, simply as a matter of fact. The *Braunfeld* case involved a state *criminal* statute. The undisputed effect of that statute, as pointed out by MR. JUSTICE BRENNAN in his dissenting opinion in that case, was that "'Plaintiff, Abraham Braunfeld, will be unable to continue in his business if he may not stay open on Sunday and he will thereby lose his capital investment.' In other words, the issue in this case—and we do not understand either appellees or the Court to contend otherwise—is whether a State may put an individual to a choice between his business and his religion."

The impact upon the appellant's religious freedom in the present case is considerably less onerous. We deal here not with a criminal statute, but with the particularized administration of South Carolina's Unemployment Compensation Act. Even upon the unlikely assumption that the appellant could not find suitable non-Saturday employment, the appellant at the worst would be denied a maximum of 22 weeks of compensation payments. I agree with the Court that the possibility of that denial is enough to infringe upon the appellant's constitutional right to the free exercise of her religion. But it is clear to me that in order to reach this conclusion the Court must explicitly reject the reasoning of *Braunfeld v. Brown.* I think the *Braunfeld* case was wrongly decided and should be overruled, and accordingly I concur in the result reached by the Court in the case before us.

MR. JUSTICE HARLAN, whom MR. JUSTICE WHITE joins, dissenting.

Today's decision is disturbing both in its rejection of existing precedent and in its implications for the future. The significance of the decision can best be understood after an examination of the state law applied in this case.

South Carolina's Unemployment Compensation Law was enacted in 1936 in response to the grave social and economic problems that arose during the depression of that period.... [T]he purpose of the legislature was to tide people over, and to avoid social and economic chaos, during periods when *work was unavailable.* But at the same time there was clearly no intent to provide relief for those who for purely personal reasons were or became *unavailable for work.* In accordance with this design, the legislature provided that "an unemployed insured worker shall be eligible to receive benefits with respect to any week *only* if the Commission finds that ... [h]e is able to work and is available for work...." (Emphasis added.)

The South Carolina Supreme Court has uniformly applied this law in conformity with its clearly expressed pur-

pose. It has consistently held that one is not "available for work" if his unemployment has resulted not from the inability of industry to provide a job but rather from personal circumstances, no matter how compelling....

... What the Court is holding is that if the State chooses to condition unemployment compensation on the applicant's availability for work, it is constitutionally compelled to *carve out an exception*—and to provide benefits—for those whose unavailability is due to their religious convictions. Such a holding has particular significance in two respects.

First, despite the Court's protestations to the contrary, the decision necessarily overrules *Braunfeld v. Brown,* which held that it did not offend the "Free Exercise" Clause of the Constitution for a State to forbid a Sabbatarian to do business on Sunday. The secular purpose of the statute before us today is even clearer than that involved in *Braunfeld.* And just as in *Braunfeld*—where exceptions to the Sunday closing laws for Sabbatarians would have been inconsistent with the purpose to achieve a uniform day of rest and would have required case-by-case inquiry into religious beliefs—so here, an exception to the rules of eligibility based on religious convictions would necessitate judicial examination of those convictions and would be at odds with the limited purpose of the statute to smooth out the economy during periods of industrial instability. Finally, the indirect financial burden of the present law is far less than that involved in *Braunfeld.* Forcing a store owner to close his business on Sunday may well have the effect of depriving him of a satisfactory livelihood if his religious convictions require him to close on Saturday as well. Here we are dealing only with temporary benefits, amounting to a fraction of regular weekly wages and running for not more than 22 weeks. Clearly, any differences between this case and *Braunfeld* cut against the present appellant.

Second, the implications of the present decision are far more troublesome than its apparently narrow dimensions would indicate at first glance. The meaning of today's holding, as already noted, is that the State must furnish unemployment benefits to one who is unavailable for work if the unavailability stems from the exercise of religious convictions. The State, in other words, must *single out* for financial assistance those whose behavior is religiously motivated, even though it denies such assistance to others whose identical behavior (in this case, inability to work on Saturdays) is not religiously motivated.

It has been suggested that such singling out of religious conduct for special treatment may violate the constitutional limitations on state action. My own view, however, is that at least under the circumstances of this case it would be a permissible accommodation of religion for the State, if it chose to do so, to create an exception to its eligibility requirements for persons like the appellant. The constitutional obligation of "neutrality," ... is not so narrow a channel that the slightest deviation from an absolutely straight course leads to condemnation. There are too many instances in which no such course can be charted, too many areas in which the pervasive activities of the State justify some special provision for religion to prevent it from being submerged by an all-embracing secularism. The State violates its obligation of neutrality when, for example, it mandates a daily religious exercise in its public schools, with all the attendant pressures on the school children that such an exercise entails.... But there is, I believe, enough flexibility in the Constitution to permit a legislative judgment accommodating an unemployment compensation law to the exercise of religious beliefs such as appellant's.

For very much the same reasons, however, I cannot subscribe to the conclusion that the State is constitutionally compelled to carve out an exception to its general rule of eligibility in the present case. Those situations in which the Constitution may require special treatment on account of religion are, in my view, few and far between, and this view is amply supported by the course of constitutional litigation in this area.... Such compulsion in the present case is particularly inappropriate in light of the indirect, remote, and insubstantial effect of the decision below on the exercise of appellant's religion and in light of the direct financial assistance to religion that today's decision requires.

For these reasons I respectfully dissent from the opinion and judgment of the Court.

Does Brennan's majority opinion represent a significant break from past free exercise claims? Some analysts suggest that it does. Although Brennan affirmed the belief-action dichotomy, he agreed with Sherbert's attorney that the lines were blurred. Accordingly, he made it far more difficult for states to regulate "action." No longer would a secular legislative purpose suffice; rather, under *Sherbert*, when the government enacts a law that burdens free exercise of religion, it must show that it was protecting an important, compelling government interest and in the least restrictive manner possible. *Sherbert* also represented a step away from previous free exercise cases in which the Court insisted on neutrality, for here the Court was striking down a law that was neutral in application on the grounds that it burdened the free exercise of religion with a less-than-compelling interest. Other analysts argue that *Sherbert* represented a logical step from *Braunfeld*. It was in *Braunfeld* that Warren first articulated the least restrictive manner standard on which Brennan relied to strike the South Carolina law.

Either way, *Sherbert* raises several questions. First, if *Braunfeld* and *Sherbert*, taken together, indicated a turning point in the standards governing free exercise cases, why did the Court decide the cases so differently? In *Braunfeld*, the Court found against the religious claimant to uphold Sunday closing laws, but in *Sherbert* it struck down the state's unemployment benefits policy. How can we explain the inconsistency? Some of the justices (for example, Harlan in dissent and Stewart in concurrence) argued that because this discrepancy could not be resolved, *Sherbert* effectively overruled *Braunfeld*. But the majority claimed that the difference between the two was obvious: Pennsylvania had achieved its goal of creating a uniform day of rest in the least intrusive way possible, while South Carolina could have protected its interest in preventing fraud in other, less restrictive ways.

Second, how would the Court use the new standard? In theory, the Court would now balance the interests of the state against those of the free exercise claimant. In practice, according to some analysts, such balancing—given the compelling interest-least restrictive means approach—would almost always result in a victory for the free exercise claimant. After all, governments would have to demonstrate that policies burdening religion are of "sufficient magnitude to override the interest claiming protection"[32] and cast in the least restrictive possible manner, a difficult task, as indicated by *Sherbert*. The next section examines whether this prediction—that governments would be unable to prevail in these cases—accurately describes Court resolution of the post-*Sherbert* cases.

Free Exercise Claims During the Burger Court, 1969–1986

The Warren Court ushered in the change in free exercise standards in *Braunfeld* and *Sherbert*, but it was up to the justices of the Court led by Chief Justice Warren Burger to apply those standards, as the Warren Court heard very few free exercise cases after *Sherbert*.

The opportunity for the Burger Court to put its stamp on this area of the law arose early in the new chief's tenure. In 1972, with two of the four Nixon appointees (Burger and Harry A. Blackmun) participating, the Court decided *Wisconsin v. Yoder*. As you read the excerpt from *Yoder*, consider how the Burger Court dealt with the standard it inherited from its predecessor. Do you detect any differences in approach? Or does Burger's opinion parallel Warren's in *Braunfeld* and Brennan's in *Sherbert*?

Wisconsin v. Yoder

406 U.S. 205 (1972)
Vote: 6 (Blackmun, Brennan, Burger, Marshall,
    Stewart, White)
    1 (Douglas)
Opinion of the Court: Burger
Concurring opinions: Stewart, White
Dissenting in part: Douglas
Not participating: Powell, Rehnquist

Like many states, Wisconsin had a compulsory education law, mandating that children attend public

or private schools until the age of sixteen. This kind of law violated the norms of the Amish, who were among the first religious groups to arrive in the United States. As a simple people, who eschew technology, including automobiles and electricity, they do not permit their children to attend school after the eighth grade, believing that they will be adversely exposed "to worldly influences in terms of attitudes, goals, and values contrary to their beliefs." Instead, they prefer to educate their older children at home.

For several decades prior to the 1970s, the Amish had many skirmishes with education officials over this issue. After one particularly nasty incident in Iowa, "a group of ministers, bankers, lawyers, and professors formed a group called the National Committee for Amish Religious Freedom (NCARF)" to provide legal defense for the Amish. NCARF's leaders included the general counsel of the American Jewish Committee, the dean of Boston University Law School, and the executive director of the Commission on Religious Liberty of the National Council of Churches.[33]

Among the suits for which NCARF provided legal assistance was a controversy emanating from New Glarus, Wisconsin, where the school district administrator brought a complaint against Amish families for not sending their older children to school. When the parents were fined $5 by the county court, they claimed that the compulsory attendance law violated their First and Fourteenth Amendment rights.

At the heart of this case, attorney William Ball argued, were two fundamental issues. First, he claimed that the Amish did not want their children to be uneducated or ignorant. In fact, the teenagers pursued rigorous home study after their public school education. Second, because education was continuing at home, the state could demonstrate no compelling reason to require the children to attend public school. Amicus curiae briefs, "representing the full spectrum

---

32. *Wisconsin v. Yoder* (1972).

33. For more details, see Cortner, *The Supreme Court and Civil Liberties Policy,* 153–182.

of American religious beliefs," supported Ball's view. In contrast, the attorney general of Wisconsin compared this case to *Prince v. Massachusetts (see page 86)*, in which the Court upheld child labor regulations. He claimed that the two laws were similar because both were enacted out of a legitimate "concern for the welfare of" children.

MR. CHIEF JUSTICE BURGER delivered the opinion of the Court.

On petition of the State of Wisconsin, we granted the writ of certiorari in this case to review a decision of the Wisconsin Supreme Court holding that respondents' convictions for violating the State's compulsory school-attendance law were invalid under the Free Exercise Clause of the First Amendment to the United States Constitution made applicable to the States by the Fourteenth Amendment. For the reasons hereafter stated we affirm the judgment of the Supreme Court of Wisconsin....

Amish objection to formal education beyond the eighth grade is firmly grounded in ... central religious concepts. They object to the high school, and higher education generally, because the values they teach are in marked variance with Amish values and the Amish way of life; they view secondary school education as an impermissible exposure of their children to a "worldly" influence in conflict with their beliefs. The high school tends to emphasize intellectual and scientific accomplishments, self-distinction, competitiveness, worldly success, and social life with other students. Amish society emphasizes informal learning-through-doing; a life of "goodness," rather than a life of intellect; wisdom, rather than technical knowledge; community welfare, rather than competition; and separation from, rather than integration with, contemporary worldly society.

Formal high school education beyond the eighth grade is contrary to Amish beliefs, not only because it places Amish children in an environment hostile to Amish beliefs with increasing emphasis on competition in class work and sports and with pressure to conform to the styles, manners, and ways of the peer group, but also because it takes them away from their community, physically and emotionally, during the crucial and formative adolescent period of life. During this period, the children must acquire Amish atti-

tudes favoring manual work and self-reliance and the specific skills needed to perform the adult role of an Amish farmer or housewife....

The Amish do not object to elementary education through the first eight grades as a general proposition because they agree that their children must have basic skills in the "three R's" in order to read the Bible, to be good farmers and citizens, and to be able to deal with non-Amish people when necessary in the course of daily affairs. They view such a basic education as acceptable because it does not significantly expose their children to worldly values or interfere with their development in the Amish community during the crucial adolescent period. While Amish accept compulsory elementary education generally, wherever possible they have established their own elementary schools in many respects like the small local schools of the past. In the Amish belief higher learning tends to develop values they reject as influences that alienate man from God....

There is no doubt as to the power of a State, having a high responsibility for education of its citizens, to impose reasonable regulations for the control and duration of basic education.... [But] a State's interest in universal education, however highly we rank it, is not totally free from a balancing process when it impinges on fundamental rights and interests, such as those specifically protected by the Free Exercise Clause of the First Amendment, and the traditional interest of parents with respect to the religious upbringing of their children so long as they ... "prepare them for additional obligations."

It follows that in order for Wisconsin to compel school attendance beyond the eighth grade against a claim that such attendance interferes with the practice of a legitimate religious belief, it must appear either that the State does not deny the free exercise of religious belief by its requirement, or that there is a state interest of sufficient magnitude to override the interest claiming protection under the Free Exercise Clause....

The essence of all that has been said and written on the subject is that only those interests of the highest order and those not otherwise served can overbalance legitimate claims of free exercise of religion. We can accept it as settled, therefore, that, however, strong the State's interest in universal compulsory education, it is by no means absolute to the exclusion or subordination of all other interests. *E.g., Sherbert v. Verner* (1963)....

We come then to the quality of the claims of the respondents concerning the alleged encroachment of Wisconsin's compulsory school-attendance statute on their rights and the rights of their children to the free exercise of the religious beliefs they and their forebears have adhered to for almost three centuries. In evaluating those claims we must be careful to determine whether the Amish religion and their mode of life are, as they claim, inseparable and interdependent. A way of life, however virtuous and admirable, may not be interposed as a barrier to reasonable state regulation of education if it is based on purely secular considerations: to have the protection of the Religion Clauses, the claims must be rooted in religious belief....

Giving no weight to ... secular considerations ... we see that the record in this case abundantly supports the claim that the traditional way of life of the Amish is not merely a matter of personal preference, but one of deep religious conviction, shared by an organized group, and intimately related to daily living....

... The conclusion is inescapable that secondary schooling, by exposing Amish children to worldly influences in terms of attitudes, goals, and values contrary to beliefs, and by substantially interfering with the religious development of the Amish child and his integration into the way of life of the Amish faith community at the crucial adolescent stage of development, contravenes the basic religious tenets and practice of the Amish faith, both as to the parent and the child....

In sum ... the State's requirement of compulsory formal education after the eighth grade would gravely endanger if not destroy the free exercise of respondents' religious beliefs.

Neither the findings of the trial court nor the Amish claims as to the nature of their faith are challenged in this Court by the State of Wisconsin. Its position is that the State's interest in universal compulsory formal secondary education to age 16 is so great that it is paramount to the undisputed claims of respondents that their mode of preparing their youth for Amish life, after the traditional elementary education, is an essential part of their religious belief and practice. Nor does the State undertake to meet the claim that the Amish mode of life and education is in-

separable from and a part of the basic tenets of their religion—indeed, as much a part of their religious belief and practices as baptism, the confessional, or a sabbath may be for others.

Wisconsin concedes that under the Religion Clauses religious beliefs are absolutely free from the State's control, but it argues that "actions," even though religiously grounded, are outside the protection of the First Amendment. But our decisions have rejected the idea that religiously grounded conduct is always outside the protection of the Free Exercise Clause.... This case, therefore, does not become easier because respondents were convicted for their "actions" in refusing to send their children to the public high school; in this context belief and action cannot be neatly confined in logic-tight compartments....

Nor can this case be disposed of on the grounds that Wisconsin's requirement for school attendance to age 16 applies uniformly to all citizens of the State and does not, on its face, discriminate against religions or a particular religion, or that it is motivated by legitimate secular concerns. A regulation neutral on its face may, in its application, nonetheless offend the constitutional requirement for governmental neutrality if it unduly burdens free exercise of religion. *Sherbert v. Verner*....

We turn, then, to the State's broader contention that its interest in its system of compulsory education is so compelling that even the established religious practices of the Amish must give way. Where fundamental claims of religious freedom are at stake, however, we cannot accept such a sweeping claim; despite its admitted validity in the generality of cases, we must searchingly examine the interests that the State seeks to promote by its requirement for compulsory education to age 16, and the impediment to those objectives what would flow from recognizing the claimed Amish exemption....

The State advances two primary arguments in support of its system of compulsory education. It notes ... that some degree of education is necessary to prepare citizens to participate effectively and intelligently in our open political system if we are to preserve freedom and independence. Further, education prepares individuals to be self-reliant and self-sufficient. We accept these propositions.

However, the evidence adduced by the Amish in this case is persuasively to the effect that an additional one or two years of formal high school for Amish children in place of their long-established program of informal vocational education would do little to serve those interests.... It is one thing to say that compulsory education for a year or two beyond the eighth grade may be necessary when its goal is the preparation of the child for life in modern society as the majority live, but it is quite another if the goal of education be viewed as the preparation of the child for life in the separated agrarian community that is the keystone of the Amish faith....

The State attacks respondents' position as one fostering "ignorance" from which the child must be protected by the State. No one can question the State's duty to protect children from ignorance but this argument does not square with the facts disclosed in the record. Whatever their idiosyncrasies as seen by the majority, this record strongly shows that the Amish community has been a highly successful social unit within our society, even if apart from the conventional "mainstream." Its members are productive and very law-abiding members of society....

Insofar as the State's claim rests on the view that a brief additional period of formal education is imperative to enable the Amish to participate effectively and intelligently in our democratic process, it must fall. The Amish alternative to formal secondary school education has enabled them to function effectively in their day-to-day life under self-imposed limitations on relations with the world, and to survive and prosper in contemporary society as a separate, sharply identifiable and highly self-sufficient community for more than 200 years in this country. In itself this is strong evidence that they are capable of fulfilling the social and political responsibilities of citizenship without compelled attendance beyond the eighth grade at the price of jeopardizing their free exercise of religious belief. When Thomas Jefferson emphasized the need for education as a bulwark of a free people against tyranny, there is nothing to indicate he had in mind compulsory education through any fixed age beyond a basic education. Indeed, the Amish communities singularly parallel and reflect many of the virtues of Jefferson's ideal of the "sturdy yeoman" who would form the basis of what he considered as the ideal of a democratic society. Even their idiosyncratic separateness exemplifies the diversity we profess to admire and encourage....

Finally, the State, on authority of *Prince v. Massachusetts*, argues that a decision exempting Amish children from the State's requirement fails to recognize the substantive right of the Amish child to a secondary education, and fails to give due regard to the power of the State as *parens patriae* to extend the benefit of secondary education to children regardless of the wishes of their parents. Taken at its broadest sweep, the Court's language in *Prince* might be read to give support to the State's position. However, the Court was not confronted in *Prince* with a situation comparable to that of the Amish as revealed in this record; this is shown by the Court's severe characterization of the evils that it thought the legislature could legitimately associate with child labor, even when performed in the company of an adult....

This case, of course, is not one in which any harm to the physical or mental health of the child or to the public safety, peace, order, or welfare has been demonstrated or may be properly inferred. The record is to the contrary, and any reliance on that theory would find no support in the evidence....

For the reasons stated we hold, with the Supreme Court of Wisconsin, that the First and Fourteenth Amendments prevent the State from compelling respondents to cause their children to attend formal high school to age 16. Our disposition of this case, however, in no way alters our recognition of the obvious fact that courts are not school boards or legislatures, and are ill-equipped to determine the "necessity" of discrete aspects of a State's program of compulsory education. This should suggest that courts must move with great circumspection in performing the sensitive and delicate task of weighing a State's legitimate social concern when faced with religious claims for exemption from generally applicable educational requirements....

Affirmed

MR. JUSTICE DOUGLAS, dissenting in part.

I agree with the Court that the religious scruples of the Amish are opposed to the education of their children beyond the grade schools, yet I disagree with the Court's conclusion that the matter is within the dispensation of parents alone. The Court's analysis assumes that the only interests at stake in the case are those of the Amish parents on the one hand, and those of the State on the other. The difficulty with this approach is that, despite the Court's claim, the parents are seeking to vindicate not only their own free exercise claims, but also those of their high-school-age children....

... [I]t is essential to reach the question to decide the case ... because no analysis of religious-liberty claims can take place in a vacuum. If the parents in this case are allowed religious exemption, the inevitable effect is to impose the parent's notions of religious duty upon their children. Where the child is mature enough to express potential conflicting desires, it would be an invasion of the child's rights to permit such an imposition without canvassing his views.... As the child has no other effective forum, it is in this litigation that his rights should be considered. And, if an Amish child desires to attend high school, and is mature enough to have that desire respected, the State may well be able to override the parents' religiously motivated objections....

What are we to make of Chief Justice Burger's first major statement on the free exercise of religion? He cited *Sherbert* with approval and invoked its approach to find that the state's interest was not sufficiently compelling to outweigh the free exercise claim. That Burger found for the religious claimants lends support to those analysts who argue that the *Sherbert* standard would almost always lead to such a conclusion. But some scholars allege that Burger grounded his opinion on respect for the history and the practices of the Amish rather than the logic of *Sherbert*. If Burger did follow such a course, he would not be the first nor probably the last to do so. Remember Chief Justice Waite's opinion in *Reynolds*? Did it not rest as much on his Court's perception of the Mormons as a strange and bizarre sect as it did on legal factors?

Whatever Burger's motivation, it seemed as if the Court would continue to apply the compelling interest standard to free exercise claims. Less than a decade after *Yoder*, the justices decided *Thomas v. Review Board of Indiana Employment Security Division* (1981), the facts of which a bore a marked resem-

blance to *Sherbert*. Thomas was a Jehovah's Witness who worked in a steel mill. When the owners closed the mill down, they transferred Thomas to another plant. Because his new job required him to make tanks for use by the military, Thomas quit on religious grounds and filed for unemployment benefits, which the state denied. Writing for the Court, Chief Justice Burger acknowledged the parallels between *Sherbert* and this dispute: "Here, as in *Sherbert*, the employee was put to a choice between fidelity to his religious beliefs or cessation of work; the coercive impact on Thomas is indistinguishable from *Sherbert....*" Accordingly, he said, "Unless we are prepared to overrule *Sherbert*, Thomas can not be denied the benefits due him."

Two years after *Thomas*, in *Bob Jones University v. United States* (1983), the Supreme Court examined yet another free exercise question: May the government punish a sectarian institution for its religiously divined racist policy? Bob Jones University was not affiliated with any denomination but described itself as "dedicated to the teaching and propagation of ... fundamentalist Christian beliefs." These beliefs included, among others, a strong prohibition against interracial dating and marriage. To enforce this particular tenet, the school excluded blacks until 1971, when it accepted applications from married blacks only. Litigation forced the school to begin admitting unmarried blacks in 1976, but only if they adhered to a strict set of rules; for example, interracial dating or marriage would lead to expulsion. The school continued to deny admission to individuals in interracial marriages. The Internal Revenue Service (IRS) revoked Bob Jones's tax-exempt status on the grounds that the school's policies were racist. The university challenged the decision, saying that the IRS action punished the practice of religious beliefs. Therefore, one of the issues before the Court was whether the government's interest in prohibiting race discrimination was sufficiently compelling to abridge free exercise guarantees.

Writing for the Court, Chief Justice Burger once again applied the compelling interest-least restrictive means standard of *Sherbert* to rule against Bob Jones:

The governmental interest at stake here is compelling.... [T]he government has a fundamental, overriding interest in eradicating racial discrimination in education—discrimination that prevailed ... for the first 165 years of this Nation's constitutional history. That governmental interest substantially outweighs whatever burden denial of tax benefits places on petitioners' exercise of their religious beliefs. The interests asserted by petitioners cannot be accommodated with that compelling governmental interest, and no "less restrictive means" are available to achieve the governmental interest....

Burger also noted that this policy—unlike the one at issue in *Yoder*—would not prevent Bob Jones from practicing its religion. Seen in this way, the IRS policy was more akin to Sunday closing laws. In *Braunfeld*, Chief Justice Warren acknowledged that while blue laws would place an economic burden on some Orthodox Jews, they would not stop them from practicing their religion. Here Burger wrote: "Denial of tax benefits will inevitably have a substantial impact on the operation of private religious schools, but will not prevent these schools from observing their religious tenets."

Bob Jones is interesting for a number of reasons, not the least of which is that it demonstrates Court use of the compelling interest standard to *uphold* a government policy that allegedly infringes on the free exercise of religion. The eradication of racism, in the eyes of the justices, represents one example of an important governmental objective.

The Demise of Sherbert and the Compelling Interest Standard?

Despite the Burger Court's application of the compelling interest standard in *Bob Jones*, there were signs in the early to mid-1980s that some of the justices wanted to rethink that standard or, at the very least, make it easier for the state to respond to free exercise

challenges. *United States v. Lee*—decided in 1982, a year before *Bob Jones*—was the first of these signs.

Lee, a member of the Amish faith, owned a farm and a carpentry shop. In violation of federal law, he refused to withhold Social Security taxes or pay the employers' share of those taxes, arguing that the payment of taxes and the receipt of Social Security benefits violated his religious tenets. To support his argument, Lee's attorneys pointed out that Congress had provided a Social Security tax exemption to self-employed Amish. And, while Lee did not fall under that specific exemption—he employed others—the very existence of the exemption demonstrated Congress's sensitivity toward the Amish.

In a short opinion for the Court, Chief Justice Burger disagreed. To be sure, Burger conceded, "compulsory participation" in the Social Security system interferes with the free exercise rights of the Amish. But the government was able to justify that burden on religion by showing that compulsory participation is "essential to accomplish an overriding governmental interest" in the maintenance of the Social Security system in the United States. As Burger put it: "To maintain an organized society that guarantees religious freedom to a great variety of faiths requires that some religious practices yield to the common good."

Why do some scholars cite *Lee* as a first cut into the compelling interest standard of *Sherbert*? After all, Burger did adopt it to resolve the dispute. What they see is a discrepancy between *Lee* and *Yoder*. Why was Burger willing to exempt the Amish from mandatory education laws but unwilling to exempt them from compulsory participation in the Social Security system? In *Lee* Burger tried to address this question when he wrote: "It would be difficult to accommodate the comprehensive Social Security system with myriad exceptions flowing from a wide variety of religious beliefs." But this point caused observers to suggest that the Burger Court was willing to override an important governmental interest if only a few groups would be affected or if the impact of the religious exemption would be fairly negligible, as was the case in *Yoder.*

Goldman v. Weinberger (1986), one of the last major free exercise cases of the Burger Court era, did little to quell these and other suspicions about the direction of Court doctrine. As you read this case, ask yourself whether the Warren Court, under the *Sherbert* standard, would have decided it the same way. Why or why not?

―――――――――――

Goldman v. Weinberger

475 U.S. 503 (1986)
Vote: 5 (Burger, Powell, Rehnquist, Stevens, White)
  4 (Blackmun, Brennan, Marshall, O'Connor)
Opinion of the Court: Rehnquist
Concurring opinion: Stevens
Dissenting opinions: Blackmun, Brennan, O'Connor

S. Simcha Goldman was an Orthodox Jew and an ordained rabbi. In 1973 he received an armed forces scholarship to study clinical psychology at Loyola University in Chicago. He completed the Ph.D. program and in September 1977 entered the service as a captain in the Air Force. He was stationed at March Air Force Base (AFB) in Riverside, California, as a clinical psychologist in the base hospital. From the time Goldman began his service at the base, he wore a yarmulke (skull cap) while in and out of uniform. Goldman did so because his religion requires its adherents to keep their heads covered at all times.

For the first three and a half years of Goldman's stint at March, no one objected to or even questioned his right to wear the yarmulke. But on May 8, 1981, the hospital commander, Col. Joseph Gregory, told Goldman that the yarmulke violated Air Force Dress Code Regulation (AFR) 35-10, a 190-page regulation "that describes in minute detail all of the various items of apparel that constitute the Air Force Uniform." Relevant here is that 35-10 gives military commanders the discretion to permit individuals to wear

religious apparel in certain locations, and it states that a member of the Air Force has the "right, within limits, to express individuality through his or her appearance. However, the image of a disciplined service member who can be relied on to do his or her job excludes the extreme, the unusual, and the fad." Under his reading of 35-10, and despite Goldman's arguments about the free exercise of religion, Gregory concluded that Goldman could no longer wear the yarmulke indoors while in uniform anywhere on the base except the hospital.

Goldman refused to heed Gregory's request and, two weeks later, contacted Air Force attorneys. They tried to resolve the matter through negotiations with March AFB personnel but failed. After the negotiations had broken down, Gregory revised his order to Goldman: on June 23, 1981, Goldman was told that he could no longer wear his yarmulke anywhere on the base including the hospital. The very next day, Gregory sent Goldman a formal reprimand threatening him with court-martial. Gregory also told Goldman that he was withdrawing a positive recommendation on Goldman's application to stay in the military another year.

At this point, Goldman brought suit against the secretary of defense, arguing that the Air Force regulation violated his First Amendment free exercise rights. A U.S. district court agreed, but a panel of judges on the Court of Appeals for the District of Columbia reversed. When Goldman asked for an en banc hearing,[34] the appellate court denied the request above the dissents of only three judges.[35] But what an interesting trio they made! Judge Kenneth Starr, who would later serve as solicitor general, said, "The treatment of Dr. Goldman seems to me patently unconscionable." Two future Supreme Court justices, Ruth Bader Ginsburg and Antonin Scalia, wrote in dissent:

―――――――――――

34. U.S. Courts of Appeals typically hear cases in panels of three judges. An *en banc* hearing is one in which all the judges of the court participate.

35. *Goldman v. Secretary of Defense,* 739 F. 2d 657 (1984).

S. Simcha Goldman ... has long served his country as an Air Force officer with honor and devotion. A military commander has now declared intolerable the yarmulke Dr. Goldman has worn without incident throughout his several years of military service. At the least, the declaration suggests "callous indifference" to Dr. Goldman's faith, and it runs counter to "the best of our traditions" to "accommodate the public service to the spiritual needs [of our people]." ... *cf.* Braunfeld v. Brown (Stewart, J., dissenting) (commenting on state law exposing Orthodox Jew to "cruel choice" between "his religious faith and his economic survival").... I believe that the court en banc should measure the command suddenly and lately championed by the military against the restraint imposed even on an armed forces commander by the Free Exercise Clause of the First Amendment.

With the court of appeals' rejection, Goldman's attorneys, some of whom worked for the National Jewish Commission on Law and Public Affairs, brought the case to the Supreme Court. There, they argued that Goldman's conduct was of a nonintrusive nature that "interferes with no one else, does not harm the public health, and imposes no burden on accommodation." They were attempting to show that Goldman's behavior was markedly different from activities the Court had struck down in *Reynolds* (polygamy) and *Prince* (solicitation by children in violation of child labor laws). They also maintained that the Air Force lacked any overriding governmental interest that would justify such a major intrusion into Goldman's religious practice; after all, he had worn the yarmulke for three and a half years with no effect on the national defense.

The government's response was that "[t]here can be no serious doubt that uniform dress and appearance standards serve the military interest in maintaining discipline, moral, and esprit de corps" and that enforcement of the dress code "is a necessary means to the undeniably critical ends of molding soldiers into an effective fighting force." According to the government, wearing a yarmulke may be a non-intrusive religious practice for civilians but "in the military, the smallest departure from the uniform dress code is an occasion for comment. It sets the wearer apart from his fellow soldiers and serves as a public assertion of individuality in a context in which cohesion and group identify are essential." The government also urged the justices to consider what might happen if they allowed Goldman to wear his yarmulke: other religions could request exemptions to wear turbans, dreadlocks, kum kums (red dots on foreheads), and so forth.

JUSTICE REHNQUIST delivered the opinion of the Court.

Petitioner S. Simcha Goldman contends that the Free Exercise Clause of the First Amendment to the United States Constitution permits him to wear a yarmulke while in uniform, notwithstanding an Air Force regulation mandating uniform dress for Air Force personnel.... We granted certiorari because of the importance of the question, and now affirm....

Petitioner argues that AFR 35-10, as applied to him, prohibits religiously motivated conduct and should therefore be analyzed under the standard enunciated in *Sherbert v. Verner* (1963).... But we have repeatedly held that "the military is, by necessity, a specialized society separate from civilian society."... "[T]he military must insist upon a respect for duty and a discipline without counterpart in civilian life" ... in order to prepare for and perform its vital role....

Our review of military regulations challenged on First Amendment grounds is far more deferential than constitutional review of similar laws or regulations designed for civilian society. The military need not encourage debate or tolerate protest to the extent that such tolerance is required of the civilian state by the First Amendment; to accomplish its mission the military must foster instinctive obedience, unity, commitment, and esprit de corps.... The essence of military service "is the subordination of the desires and interests of the individual to the needs of the service."...

These aspects of military life do not, of course, render entirely nugatory in the military context the guarantees of the First Amendment.... But "within the military community there is simply not the same [individual] autonomy as there is in the larger civilian community."... In the context of the present case, when evaluating whether military needs justify a particular restriction on religiously motivated conduct, courts must give great deference to the professional judgment of military authorities concerning the relative importance of a particular military interest.... Not only are courts "'ill-equipped to determine the impact upon discipline that any particular intrusion upon military authority might have,'" ... but the military authorities have been charged by the Executive and Legislative Branches with carrying out our Nation's military policy. "[J]udicial deference ... is at its apogee when legislative action under the congressional authority to raise and support armies and make rules and regulations for their governance is challenged."...

The considered professional judgment of the Air Force is that the traditional outfitting of personnel in standardized uniforms encourages the subordination of personal preferences and identities in favor of the overall group mission. Uniforms encourage a sense of hierarchical unity by tending to eliminate outward individual distinctions except for those of rank. The Air Force considers them as vital during peacetime as during war because its personnel must be ready to provide an effective defense on a moment's notice; the necessary habits of discipline and unity must be developed in advance of trouble. We have acknowledged that "[t]he inescapable demands of military discipline and obedience to orders cannot be taught on battlefields; the habit of immediate compliance with military procedures and orders must be virtually reflex with no time for debate or reflection."...

To this end, the Air Force promulgated AFR 35-10, a 190-page document, which states that "Air Force members will wear the Air Force uniform while performing their military duties, except when authorized to wear civilian clothes on duty."...

Petitioner Goldman contends that the Free Exercise Clause of the First Amendment requires the Air Force to make an exception to its uniform dress requirements for religious apparel unless the accouterments create a "clear danger" of undermining discipline and esprit de corps. He asserts that in general, visible but "unobtrusive" apparel will not create such a danger and must therefore be accommodated. He argues that the Air Force failed to prove that a specific exception for his practice of wearing an unobtru-

sive yarmulke would threaten discipline. He contends that the Air Force's assertion to the contrary is mere *ipse dixit*, with no support from actual experience or a scientific study in the record, and is contradicted by expert testimony that religious exceptions to AFR 35-10 are in fact desirable and will increase morale by making the Air Force a more humane place.

But whether or not expert witnesses may feel that religious exceptions to AFR 35-10 are desirable is quite beside the point. The desirability of dress regulations in the military is decided by the appropriate military officials, and they are under no constitutional mandate to abandon their considered professional judgment. Quite obviously, to the extent the regulations do not permit the wearing of religious apparel such as a yarmulke, a practice described by petitioner as silent devotion akin to prayer, military life may be more objectionable for petitioner and probably others. But the First Amendment does not require the military to accommodate such practices in the face of its view that they would detract from the uniformity sought by the dress regulations. The Air Force has drawn the line essentially between religious apparel that is visible and that which is not, and we hold that those portions of the regulations challenged here reasonably and evenhandedly regulate dress in the interest of the military's perceived need for uniformity. The First Amendment therefore does not prohibit them from being applied to petitioner even though their effect is to restrict the wearing of the headgear required by his religious beliefs.

The judgment of the Court of Appeals is

Affirmed.

JUSTICE BRENNAN, with whom JUSTICE MARSHALL joins, dissenting.

Simcha Goldman invokes this Court's protection of his First Amendment right to fulfill one of the traditional religious obligations of a male Orthodox Jew—to cover his head before an omnipresent God. The Court's response to Goldman's request is to abdicate its role as principal expositor of the Constitution and protector of individual liberties in favor of credulous deference to unsupported assertions of military necessity. I dissent....

Dr. Goldman has asserted a substantial First Amendment claim, which is entitled to meaningful review by this

Court. The Court, however, evades its responsibility by eliminating, in all but name only, judicial review of military regulations that interfere with the fundamental constitutional rights of service personnel.

Our cases have acknowledged that in order to protect our treasured liberties, the military must be able to command service members to sacrifice a great many of the individual freedoms they enjoyed in the civilian community and to endure certain limitations on the freedoms they retain.... Notwithstanding this acknowledgment, we have steadfastly maintained that "'our citizens in uniform may not be stripped of basic rights simply because they have doffed their civilian clothes.'"... And, while we have hesitated, due to our lack of expertise concerning military affairs and our respect for the delegated authority of a coordinate branch, to strike down restrictions on individual liberties which could reasonably be justified as necessary to the military's vital function, ... we have never abdicated our obligation of judicial review.

Today the Court eschews its constitutionally mandated role. It adopts for review of military decisions affecting First Amendment rights a subrational-basis standard—absolute, uncritical "deference to the professional judgment of military authorities." If a branch of the military declares one of its rules sufficiently important to outweigh a service person's constitutional rights, it seems that the Court will accept that conclusion, no matter how absurd or unsupported it may be.

A deferential standard of review, however, need not, and should not, mean that the Court must credit arguments that defy common sense. When a military service burdens the free exercise rights of its members in the name of necessity, it must provide, as an initial matter and at a minimum, a *credible* explanation of how the contested practice is likely to interfere with the proffered military interest. Unabashed *ipse dixit* cannot outweigh a constitutional right.

In the present case, the Air Force asserts that its interests in discipline and uniformity would be undermined by an exception to the dress code permitting observant male Orthodox Jews to wear yarmulkes. The Court simply restates these assertions without offering any explanation how the exception Dr. Goldman requests reasonably could interfere with the Air Force's interests. Had the Court given actual consideration to Goldman's claim, it would have been compelled to decide in his favor.

The Government maintains in its brief that discipline is jeopardized whenever exceptions to military regulations are granted....

The contention that the discipline of the Armed Forces will be subverted if Orthodox Jews are allowed to wear yarmulkes with their uniforms surpasses belief. It lacks support in the record of this case, and the Air Force offers no basis for it as a general proposition. While the perilous slope permits the services arbitrarily to refuse exceptions requested to satisfy mere personal preferences, before the Air Force may burden free exercise rights it must advance, at the *very least,* a rational reason for doing so....

The Government also argues that the services have an important interest in uniform dress, because such dress establishes the preeminence of group identity, thus fostering esprit de corps and loyalty to the service that transcends individual bonds. In its brief, the Government characterizes the yarmulke as an assertion of individuality and as a badge of religious and ethnic identity, strongly suggesting that, as such, it could drive a wedge of divisiveness between members of the services.

...[T]he purported interests of the Air Force in complete uniformity of dress and in elimination of individuality or visible identification with any group other than itself are belied by the service's own regulations. The dress code expressly abjures the need for total uniformity:

..."Appearance in uniform is an important part of this image.... Neither the Air Force nor the public expects absolute uniformity of appearance. Each member has the right, within limits, to express individuality through his or her appearance. However, the image of a disciplined service member who can be relied on to do his or her job excludes the extreme, the unusual, and the fad." AFR 35-10.

It cannot be seriously contended that a serviceman in a yarmulke presents so extreme, so unusual, or so faddish an image that public confidence in his ability to perform his duties will be destroyed. Under the Air Force's own standards, then, Dr. Goldman should have and could have been granted an exception to wear his yarmulke....

Finally, the Air Force argues that while Dr. Goldman describes his yarmulke as an "unobtrusive" addition to his uniform, obtrusiveness is a purely relative, standardless judgment. The Government notes that while a yarmulke might not seem obtrusive to a Jew, neither does a turban to a Sikh, a saffron robe to a Satchidananda Ashram-Integral Yogi, nor dreadlocks to a Rastafarian. If the Court were to require the Air Force to permit yarmulkes, the service must also allow all of these other forms of dress and grooming.

The Government dangles before the Court a classic parade of horribles, the specter of a brightly-colored, "ragtag band of soldiers." Although turbans, saffron robes, and dreadlocks are not before us in this case and must each be evaluated against the reasons a service branch offers for prohibiting personnel from wearing them while in uniform, a reviewing court could legitimately give deference to dress and grooming rules that have a *reasoned* basis in, for example, functional utility, health and safety considerations, and the goal of a polished, professional appearance. It is the lack of any reasoned basis for prohibiting yarmulkes that is so striking here.

Furthermore, contrary to its intimations, the Air Force has available to it a familiar standard for determining whether a particular style of yarmulke is consistent with a polished, professional military appearance—the "neat and conservative" standard by which the service judges jewelry. No rational reason exists why yarmulkes cannot be judged by the same criterion. Indeed, at argument Dr. Goldman declared himself willing to wear whatever style and color yarmulke the Air Force believes best comports with its uniform....

The Court and the military services have presented patriotic Orthodox Jews with a painful dilemma—the choice between fulfilling a religious obligation and serving their country. Should the draft be reinstated, compulsion will replace choice. Although the pain the services inflict on Orthodox Jewish servicemen is clearly the result of insensitivity rather than design, it is unworthy of our military because it is unnecessary. The Court and the military have refused these servicemen their constitutional rights; we must hope that Congress will correct this wrong.

JUSTICE BLACKMUN, dissenting.

I would reverse the judgment of the Court of Appeals, but for reasons somewhat different from those respectively enunciated by JUSTICE BRENNAN and JUSTICE O'CONNOR. I feel that the Air Force is justified in considering not only the costs of allowing Captain Goldman to cover his head indoors, but also the cumulative costs of accommodating constitutionally indistinguishable requests for religious exemptions. Because, however, the Government has failed to make any meaningful showing that either set of costs is significant, I dissent from the Court's rejection of Goldman's claim.

The Government concedes that Goldman wears his yarmulke out of sincere religious conviction. For Goldman, as for many other Jews, "a yarmulke is an expression of respect for God ... intended to keep the wearer aware of God's presence." If the Free Exercise Clause of the First Amendment means anything, it must mean that an individual's desire to follow his or her faith is not simply another personal preference, to be accommodated by government when convenience allows. Indeed, this Court has read the Clause, I believe correctly, to require that "only those interests of the highest order and those not otherwise served can overbalance legitimate claims to the free exercise of religion." *Wisconsin v. Yoder* (1972). In general, government "may justify an inroad on religious liberty [only] by showing that it is the least restrictive means of achieving some compelling state interest." ... *Sherbert v. Verner* (1963). The clear import of *Sherbert* ... is that this showing must be made even when the inroad results from the "evenhanded" application of a facially neutral requirement. "Rules are rules" is not by itself a sufficient justification for infringing religious liberty.

Nor may free exercise rights be compromised simply because the military says they must be. To be sure, application of the First Amendment to members of the Armed Services must take into account "the different character of the military community and of the military mission." ... AS JUSTICE BRENNAN and JUSTICE O'CONNOR point out, however, military personnel do not forfeit their constitutional rights as a price of enlistment. Except as otherwise required by "interests of the highest order," soldiers as well as civilians are entitled to follow the dictates of their faiths.

In my view, this case does not require us to determine the extent to which the ordinary test for inroads on religious freedom must be modified in the military context, because the Air Force has failed to produce even a mini-mally credible explanation for its refusal to allow Goldman to keep his head covered indoors. I agree with the Court that deference is due the considered judgment of military professionals that, as a general matter, standardized dress serves to promote discipline and esprit de corps. But Gold-man's modest supplement to the Air Force uniform clearly poses by itself no threat to the Nation's military readiness. Indeed, the District Court specifically found that Goldman has worn a yarmulke on base for years without any adverse effect on his performance, any disruption of operations at the base, or any complaints from other personnel....

The Air Force argues that it has no way of distinguishing fairly between Goldman's request for an exemption and the potential requests of others whose religious practices may conflict with the appearance code, perhaps in more con-spicuous ways....

The problem with this argument, it seems to me, is not doctrinal but empirical. The Air Force simply has not shown any reason to fear that a significant number of en-listed personnel and officers would request religious ex-emptions that could not be denied on neutral grounds such as safety, let alone that granting these requests would no-ticeably impair the overall image of the service.... The Air Force contends that the potential for such disruption was demonstrated at trial through the introduction of an Army publication discussing the beliefs and practices of a variety of religious denominations, some of which have traditions or requirements involving attire. But that publication pro-vides no indication whatsoever as to how many soldiers belong to the denominations it describes, or as to how many are likely to seek religious exemptions from the dress code.

In these circumstances, deference seems unwarranted. Reasoned military judgments, of course, are entitled to re-spect, but the military has failed to show that this particu-lar judgment with respect to Captain Goldman is a rea-soned one. If, in the future, the Air Force is besieged with requests for religious exemptions from the dress code, and those requests cannot be distinguished on functional grounds from Goldman's, the service may be able to argue credibly that circumstances warrant a flat rule against any

visible religious apparel. That, however, would be a case different from the one at hand.

JUSTICE O'CONNOR, with whom JUSTICE MARSHALL joins, dissenting.

... I believe that the Court should attempt to articulate and apply an appropriate standard for a free exercise claim in the military context, and should examine Captain Gold-man's claim in light of that standard.

Like the Court today in this case involving the military, the Court in the past has had some difficulty, even in the ci-vilian context, in articulating a clear standard for evaluat-ing free exercise claims that result from the application of general state laws burdening religious conduct. In *Sherbert v. Verner* (1963) and *Thomas v. Review Bd. of Indiana Em-ployment Security Div.* (1981), the Court required the States to demonstrate that their challenged policies were "the least restrictive means of achieving some compelling state interest" in order to deprive claimants of unemployment benefits when the refusal to work was based on sincere re-ligious beliefs. In *Wisconsin v. Yoder* (1972) the Court noted that "only those interests of the highest order and those not otherwise served can overbalance legitimate claims to the free exercise of religion" in deciding that the Amish were exempt from a State's requirement that children attend school through the age of 16. In *United States v. Lee* (1982) the Court stated that "[t]he State may justify a limitation on religious liberty by showing that it is essential to accom-plish an overriding governmental interest," and held that the Amish could not exempt themselves from the Social Se-curity system on religious grounds....

These tests, though similar, are not identical. One can, however, glean at least two consistent themes from this Court's precedents. First, when the government attempts to deny a free exercise claim, it must show that an unusually important interest is at stake, whether that interest is de-nominated "compelling," "of the highest order," or "over-riding." Second, the government must show that granting the requested exemption will do substantial harm to that interest, whether by showing that the means adopted is the "least restrictive" or "essential," or that the interest will not "otherwise be served." These two requirements are entirely

RELIGION: EXERCISE AND ESTABLISHMENT 105

sensible in the context of the assertion of a free exercise claim. First, because the government is attempting to override an interest specifically protected by the Bill of Rights, the government must show that the opposing interest it asserts is of special importance before there is any chance that its claim can prevail. Second, since the Bill of Rights is expressly designed to protect the individual against the aggregated and sometimes intolerant powers of the state, the government must show that the interest asserted will in fact be substantially harmed by granting the type of exemption requested by the individual.

There is no reason why these general principles should not apply in the military, as well as the civilian, context. As this Court has stated unanimously, "'our citizens in uniform may not be stripped of basic rights simply because they have doffed their civilian clothes.'"... Furthermore, the test that one can glean from this Court's decisions in the civilian context is sufficiently flexible to take into account the special importance of defending our Nation without abandoning completely the freedoms that make it worth defending.

The first question that the Court should face here, therefore, is whether the interest that the Government asserts against the religiously based claim of the individual is of unusual importance. It is perfectly appropriate at this step of the analysis to take account of the special role of the military. The mission of our Armed Services is to protect our Nation from those who would destroy all our freedoms. I agree that, in order to fulfill that mission, the military is entitled to take some freedoms from its members. As the Court notes, the military "'must insist upon a respect for duty and a discipline without counterpart in civilian life.'" The need for military discipline and esprit de corps is unquestionably an especially important governmental interest.

But the mere presence of such an interest cannot, as the majority implicitly believes, end the analysis of whether a refusal by the Government to honor the free exercise of an individual's religion is constitutionally acceptable. A citizen pursuing even the most noble cause must remain within the bounds of the law. So, too, the Government may, even in pursuing its most compelling interests, be subject to specific restraints in doing so. The second question in the analysis of a free exercise claim under this Court's precedents must also be reached here: will granting an exemption of the type requested by the individual do substantial harm to the especially important governmental interest?

I have no doubt that there are many instances in which the unique fragility of military discipline and esprit de corps necessitates rigidity by the Government when similar rigidity to preserve an assertedly analogous interest would not pass constitutional muster in the civilian sphere.... Nonetheless, as JUSTICE BRENNAN persuasively argues, the Government can present no sufficiently convincing proof in this case to support an assertion that granting an exemption of the type requested here would do substantial harm to military discipline and esprit de corps.

First, the Government's asserted need for absolute uniformity is contradicted by the Government's own exceptions to its rule.... Furthermore, the Government does not assert, and could not plausibly argue, that petitioner's decision to wear his yarmulke while indoors at the hospital presents a threat to health or safety....

In the rare instances where the military has not consistently or plausibly justified its asserted need for rigidity of enforcement, and where the individual seeking the exemption establishes that the assertion by the military of a threat to discipline or esprit de corps is in his or her case completely unfounded, I would hold that the Government's policy of uniformity must yield to the individual's assertion of the right of free exercise of religion. On the facts of this case, therefore, I would require the Government to accommodate the sincere religious belief of Captain Goldman. Napoleon may have been correct to assert that, in the military sphere, morale is to all other factors as three is to one, but contradicted assertions of necessity by the military do not on the scales of justice bear a similarly disproportionate weight to sincere religious beliefs of the individual.

I respectfully dissent.

The Court decision in *Goldman* fueled debate in political and academic circles. Taking up Brennan's invitation, members of Congress introduced legislation to overturn the ruling. The bill allowed members of the armed forces "to wear an item of religious apparel while in uniform" so long the item is "neat and conservative" and does not "interfere with the performance" of military duties. In the debate over the bill supporters made poignant arguments about religious freedom. As Rep. Benjamin Gilman, R-N.Y., put it, "To deny religious individuals the opportunity to serve because of the necessity of wearing an unobtrusive part of their apparel would be a disservice to so many loyal, patriotic Americans." Another New York representative, Democrat Stephen Solarz, said, "I need hardly remind you that the most effective military force in the Middle East, the Israel Defense Forces, permits its members to wear yarmulkes. I do not think it has handicapped their ability to overcome their enemies in battle." Opponents were equally adamant. Sen. John Glenn, D-Ohio, put into the record letters from the secretary of defense and the joint chiefs of staff expressing serious reservations about the legislation. They feared that officers would have difficulty determining whether attire was "neat and conservative."[36] But Congress, unlike the Supreme Court, resisted military claims and passed the law in September 1987. *Goldman* was effectively overturned.

Debate in academic and legal circles centered less on the Court's holding in *Goldman* and more on the rationale it invoked to resolve the dispute. Was *Goldman* a substantial break from the *Sherbert* standard? Clearly, the four dissenters saw it that way. O'Connor's opinion is particularly interesting. After noting that Court cases in this area adopted slightly different versions of a similar standard, she set out the "two consistent themes" running through Court precedent from *Sherbert* to *Lee*. First, the government "must show that an unusually important interest is at stake, whether that interest is denominated 'compelling.'" Second, "the government must show that granting the requested exemption will do substantial harm to that interest, whether by showing that the means adopted is the 'least restrictive' or 'essential.'" O'Connor saw no reason to jettison this two-pronged standard—as she thought the majority had done—

36. See Louis Fisher, *American Constitutional Law* (New York: McGraw-Hill, 1990), 740–746.

simply because the military was involved. In contrast, some scholars (along with a few members of the Court) did not think *Goldman* represented a significant shift in Court opinion. They argued that *Goldman* was an exceptional case: it involved the interests of the armed forces, interests to which the justices traditionally defer. Accordingly, they asserted that the Court would return to the compelling interest-least restrictive means standard, mentioned in the dissents, in future cases.

Free Exercise Claims During the Rehnquist Court, 1986–

In the first year or so of the Rehnquist Court, it appeared that those scholars who argued that *Goldman* was an anomalous ruling were correct. In *Hobbie v. Unemployment Appeals Commission of Florida* (1987) the Court returned to the compelling interest standard. The facts of *Hobbie* were similar to those of *Sherbert* and *Thomas*: a Seventh-Day Adventist was fired from her job for refusing to work certain hours, and the state denied her claim for unemployment benefits. The state claimed Hobbie had failed to meet the standard that she became "unemployed through no fault of her own." The only significant difference between *Hobbie* and *Sherbert/Thomas* was that Hobbie had converted to the Seventh-Day Adventist church after working at the company for two and a half years.

This distinction, however, was trivial to the majority, which wrote:

> We see no meaningful distinction among the situations of Sherbert, Thomas, and Hobbie. We again affirm, as we stated in *Thomas*: "Where the state conditions receipt of an important benefit upon the conduct proscribed by a religious faith, or where it denies such a benefit because of conduct mandated by a religious belief, thereby putting substantial pressure on an adherent to modify his behavior and to violate his beliefs, a burden upon religion exists."

In writing for a majority of eight, Justice Brennan also used the logic of *Sherbert* and similar cases to find for Hobbie: "Both *Sherbert* and *Thomas* held that such infringements [on the free exercise of religion] must be subjected to strict scrutiny and could be justified only by proof by the State of a compelling interest."

Hobbie seemed to indicate the willingness of most of the justices to return to the *Sherbert* standard. Whether they feared congressional retaliation (the justices knew that Congress was considering legislation to overturn *Goldman*) or because they never had really abandoned *Sherbert* is open to speculation. What is clear, however, is that one member of the Rehnquist Court—the chief justice himself—was unhappy with the *Sherbert* standard. He had written the Court's opinion in *Goldman*, in which he abstained from applying it, and he dissented in *Thomas*. Indeed, in that case, Rehnquist specifically stated his agreement with Justice Harlan's dissent in *Sherbert (see pages 91–92).* As Rehnquist put it,

> Where ... the State has enacted a general statute, the purpose and effect of which is to advance the State's secular goals, the Free Exercise Clause does not in my view require the State to conform that statute to the dictates of religious conscience of any group. As Justice Harlan recognized in his dissent in *Sherbert:* "Those situations in which the Constitution may require special treatment on account of religion are ... few and far between."

Applying this logic to *Hobbie*, Rehnquist voted in favor of Florida: the state had not discriminated against Hobbie because she was Seventh-Day Adventist.

The chief justice may not have prevailed in *Hobbie*. But in two subsequent cases, it appeared as if he won the larger war to dismantle, if not completely eradicate, the *Sherbert* standard. The first was a 1988 decision, in *Lyng v. Northwest Indian Cemetery Protective Association*, in which several Native American tribes challenged the U.S. government's road construction activities on lands the tribes used for religious activities. While the tribes argued that government construction "could have devastating effects on traditional Indian religious practices" and, therefore, constituted a major intrusion into the free exercise of their religion, the Court rejected their First Amendment claims. Here, the justices took the route they had traveled in *Goldman* and "declined to apply

Sherbert analysis" or, at the very least, "distinguished *Sherbert* on the ground that the First Amendment does not 'require the Government itself to behave in ways that the individual believes will further his or her spiritual development.'"

It was the second case, *Employment Division, Department of Human Resources of Oregon v. Smith* (1990), that raised more controversy. In *Smith* the Court seemed to turn its back on nearly three decades of free exercise cases—those from *Braunfeld* and *Sherbert* through *Hobbie*. How did the majority justify its position? Do you find its logic compelling? Keep these questions in mind as you read the facts and excerpts in this highly controversial case.

Employment Division, Department of Human Resources of Oregon v. Smith

494 U.S. 872 (1990)
Vote: 6 (Kennedy, O'Connor, Rehnquist, Scalia,
    Stevens, White)
    3 (Blackmun, Brennan, Marshall)
Opinion of the Court: Scalia
Concurring opinion: O'Connor
Dissenting opinion: Blackmun

This case centers on the use of peyote, which is a controlled substance under Oregon law. In other words, it is illegal to possess the drug unless it is prescribed by a doctor. Peyote is a hallucinogen produced by certain cactus plants found in the southwestern United States and northern Mexico. Unlike other hallucinogenic drugs (such as LSD), peyote has never been widely used or problematic. One reason is that peyote is taken by eating the buds of certain cactus plants, which are "tough, bitter, and frequently cause nausea and vomiting."[37]

There is, however, one group of citizens who regularly ingest peyote—members of a bona fide religion, the Native American church. To them "peyote is a

---

37. Douglas Laycock, "The Remnants of Free Exercise," *The Supreme Court Review* (1990): 7.

sacramental substance, an object of worship, and a source of divine protection."[38] They use the substance during religious rituals.

The spiritual nature of the church's use of peyote has been acknowledged by various governments. Although they have laws (like the one in Oregon) criminalizing the general use of peyote, twenty-three states (those with large Native American populations) and the federal government exempt the religious use of peyote from such laws. The federal government even provides licenses to grow peyote for sacramental purposes.[39]

The dispute at issue in *Smith* arose when two members of the Native American church, Alfred Smith and Galen Black, were fired from their jobs as counselors at a private drug and alcohol abuse clinic for ingesting peyote at a religious ceremony. Smith and Black applied for unemployment benefits but were turned down by the state. It found them ineligible because they had been fired for "misconduct"; under state law, workers discharged for that reason cannot obtain benefits.

Smith and Black brought suit in state court arguing that under the U.S. Supreme Court's precedents of *Sherbert* and *Thomas* (they later added *Hobbie,* which had yet to be handed down by the Court), the state could not deny them benefits. The issue for them was not that the state had criminalized peyote: they had not been charged with committing a criminal offense. Rather, they pointed to the Supreme Court's previous rulings, which indicated that states may not deny unemployment benefits because of an individual's unwillingness to forego activity mandated by religion. The state argued that it could deny the benefits—regardless of Smith and Black's free exercise claim—because the use of peyote was prohibited by a general criminal statute, which was not aimed at inhibiting religion. Oregon also noted that it—like all

38. Ibid.
39. Ibid., 8.

other government entities—has a compelling interest in regulating drug use and that the state's law represented the least intrusive means of achieving that interest.

The Oregon Supreme Court thought otherwise, however, and relied on *Sherbert* and *Thomas* to find in favor of Smith and Black. The state appealed to the U.S. Supreme Court, which heard arguments in the case in 1987. But, because the Oregon Supreme Court had not determined whether peyote use at religious ceremonies violated the state's criminal laws, the justices remanded the case back to Oregon for a decision.

That court ruled that the state law's prohibition against the use of peyote did not exempt the sacramental use of peyote, but it also said that the prohibition violated the Free Exercise Clause. The state brought its case back to the Supreme Court, where both sides assumed that the Court would use the *Sherbert* standard to resolve the dispute.

JUSTICE SCALIA delivered the opinion of the Court.

The free exercise of religion means, first and foremost, the right to believe and profess whatever religious doctrine one desires. Thus, the First Amendment obviously excludes all "governmental regulation of religious *beliefs* as such."...

But the "exercise of religion" often involves not only belief and profession but the performance of (or abstention from) physical acts: assembling with others for a worship service, participating in sacramental use of bread and wine, proselytizing, abstaining from certain foods or certain modes of transportation. It would be true, we think (though no case of ours has involved the point), that a state would be "prohibiting the free exercise [of religion]" if it sought to ban such acts or abstentions only when they are engaged in for religious reasons, or only because of the religious belief that they display. It would doubtless be unconstitutional, for example, to ban the casting of "statues that are to be used for worship purposes," or to prohibit bowing down before a golden calf.

Respondents in the present case, however, seek to carry

the meaning of "prohibiting the free exercise [of religion]" one large step further. They contend that their religious motivation for using peyote places them beyond the reach of a criminal law that is not specifically directed at their religious practice, and that is concededly constitutional as applied to those who use the drug for other reasons....

... We have never held that an individual's religious beliefs excuse him from compliance with an otherwise valid law prohibiting conduct that the State is free to regulate. On the contrary, the record of more than a century of our free exercise jurisprudence contradicts that proposition.... We first had occasion to assert that principle in *Reynolds v. United States* (1879), where we rejected the claim that criminal laws against polygamy could not be constitutionally applied to those whose religion commanded the practice....

Subsequent decisions have consistently held that the right of free exercise does not relieve an individual of the obligation to comply with a "valid and neutral law of general applicability on the ground that the law proscribes (or prescribes) conduct that his religion prescribes (or proscribes)." *United States v. Lee* (1982).... In *Prince v. Massachusetts* (1944) we held that a mother could be prosecuted under the child labor laws for using her children to dispense literature in the streets, her religious motivation notwithstanding. We found no constitutional infirmity in "excluding [these children] from doing there what no other children may do." *In Braunfeld v. Brown* (1961) (plurality opinion) we upheld Sunday-closing laws against the claim that they burdened the religious practices of persons whose religions compelled them to refrain from work on other days....

The only decisions in which we have held that the First Amendment bars application of a neutral, generally applicable law to religiously motivated action have involved not the Free Exercise Clause alone, but the Free Exercise Clause in conjunction with other constitutional protections, such as freedom of speech and of the press, see *Cantwell v. Connecticut*....

The present case does not present such a hybrid situation, but a free exercise claim unconnected with any communicative activity or parental right. Respondents urge us to hold, quite simply, that when otherwise prohibitable conduct is accompanied by religious convictions, not only the convictions but the conduct itself must be free from

governmental regulation. We have never held that, and decline to do so now. There being no contention that Oregon's drug law represents an attempt to regulate religious beliefs, the communication of religious beliefs, or the raising of one's children in those beliefs, the rule to which we have adhered ever since *Reynolds* plainly controls. "Our cases do not at their farthest reach support the proposition that a stance of conscientious opposition relieves an objector from any colliding duty fixed by a democratic government."...

Respondents argue that even though exemption from generally applicable criminal laws need not automatically be extended to religiously motivated actors, at least the claim for a religious exemption must be evaluated under the balancing test set forth in *Sherbert v. Verner* (1963). Under the *Sherbert* test, governmental actions that substantially burden a religious practice must be justified by a compelling governmental interest.... Applying that test we have, on three occasions, invalidated state unemployment compensation rules that conditioned the availability of benefits upon an applicant's willingness to work under conditions forbidden by his religion. See *Sherbert v. Verner*; *Thomas v. Review Bd. of Indiana Employment Security Div.* (1981); *Hobbie v. Unemployment Appeals Comm'n of Florida* (1987). We have never invalidated any governmental action on the basis of the *Sherbert* test except the denial of unemployment compensation. Although we have sometimes purported to apply the *Sherbert* test in contexts other than that, we have always found the test satisfied.... In recent years we have abstained from applying the *Sherbert* test (outside the unemployment compensation field) at all.... In *Goldman v. Weinberger* (1986) we rejected application of the *Sherbert* test to military dress regulations that forbade the wearing of yarmulkes....

Even if we were inclined to breathe into *Sherbert* some life beyond the unemployment compensation field, we would not apply it to require exemptions from a generally applicable criminal law. The *Sherbert* test, it must be recalled, was developed in a context that lent itself to individualized governmental assessment of the reasons for the relevant conduct....

Whether or not the decisions are that limited, they at least have nothing to do with an across-the-board criminal prohibition on a particular form of conduct. Although, as noted earlier, we have sometimes used the *Sherbert* test to analyze free exercise challenges to such laws ... we have never applied the test to invalidate one. We conclude today that the sounder approach, and the approach in accord with the vast majority of our precedents, is to hold the test inapplicable to such challenges. The government's ability to enforce generally applicable prohibitions of socially harmful conduct, like its ability to carry out other aspects of public policy, "cannot depend on measuring the effects of a governmental action on a religious objector's spiritual development."... To make an individual's obligation to obey such a law contingent upon the law's coincidence with his religious beliefs, except where the State's interest is "compelling"—permitting him, by virtue of his beliefs, "to become a law unto himself," *Reynolds v. United States*—contradicts both constitutional tradition and common sense.

The "compelling government interest" requirement seems benign, because it is familiar from other fields. But using it as the standard that must be met before the government may accord different treatment on the basis of race ... or before the government may regulate the content of speech ... is not remotely comparable to using it for the purpose asserted here. What it produces in those other fields—equality of treatment and an unrestricted flow of contending speech—are constitutional norms; what it would produce here—a private right to ignore generally applicable laws—is a constitutional anomaly.

Nor is it possible to limit the impact of respondents' proposal by requiring a "compelling state interest" only when the conduct prohibited is "central" to the individual's religion.... It is no more appropriate for judges to determine the "centrality" of religious beliefs before applying a "compelling interest" test in the free exercise field, than it would be for them to determine the "importance" of ideas before applying the "compelling interest" test in the free speech field. What principle of law or logic can be brought to bear to contradict a believer's assertion that a particular act is "central" to his personal faith? Judging the centrality of different religious practices is akin to the unacceptable "business of evaluating the relative merits of differing religious claims."... Repeatedly and in many different contexts, we have warned that courts must not presume to determine the place of a particular belief in a religion or the plausibility of a religious claim....

If the "compelling interest" test is to be applied at all, then, it must be applied across the board, to all actions thought to be religiously commanded. Moreover, if "compelling interest" really means what it says (and watering it down here would subvert its rigor in the other fields where it is applied), many laws will not meet the test. Any society adopting such a system would be courting anarchy, but that danger increases in direct proportion to the society's diversity of religious beliefs, and its determination to coerce or suppress none of them. Precisely because "we are a cosmopolitan nation made up of people of almost every conceivable religious preference," *Braunfeld v. Brown,* and precisely because we value and protect that religious divergence, we cannot afford the luxury of deeming *presumptively invalid,* as applied to the religious objector, every regulation of conduct that does not protect an interest of the highest order. The rule respondents favor would open the prospect of constitutionally required religious exemptions from civic obligations of almost every conceivable kind—ranging from compulsory military service ... to the payment of taxes ... to health and safety regulation such as manslaughter and child neglect laws ... compulsory vaccination laws ... drug laws ... and traffic laws ... to social welfare legislation such as minimum wage laws ... child labor laws ... animal cruelty laws, see, *e.g., Church of the Lukumi Babalu Aye Inc. v. City of Hialeah,* 723 F.Supp. 1467 (SD Fla. 1989) ... environmental protection laws ... and laws providing for equality of opportunity for the races.... The First Amendment's protection of religious liberty does not require this.

Values that are protected against government interference through enshrinement in the Bill of Rights are not thereby banished from the political process. Just as a society that believes in the negative protection accorded to the press by the First Amendment is likely to enact laws that affirmatively foster the dissemination of the printed word, so also a society that believes in the negative protection accorded to religious belief can be expected to be solicitous of that value in its legislation as well. It is therefore not surprising that a number of States have made an exception to their drug laws for sacramental peyote use.... But to say that a nondiscriminatory religious-practice exemption is permitted, or even that it is desirable, is not to say that it is constitutionally required, and that the appropriate occasions for its creation can be discerned by the courts. It may fairly be said that leaving accommodation to the political process will place at a relative disadvantage those religious practices that are not widely engaged in; but that unavoidable consequence of democratic government must be preferred to a system in which each conscience is a law unto itself or in which judges weigh the social importance of all laws against the centrality of all religious beliefs.

Because respondents' ingestion of peyote was prohibited under Oregon law, and because that prohibition is constitutional, Oregon may, consistent with the Free Exercise Clause, deny respondents unemployment compensation when their dismissal results from use of the drug. The decision of the Oregon Supreme Court is accordingly reversed.

It is so ordered.

JUSTICE O'CONNOR, with whom JUSTICE BRENNAN, JUSTICE MARSHALL, and JUSTICE BLACKMUN join as to Parts I and II, concurring in the judgment.*

Although I agree with the result the Court reaches in this case, I cannot join its opinion. In my view, today's holding dramatically departs from well-settled First Amendment jurisprudence, appears unnecessary to resolve the question presented, and is incompatible with our Nation's fundamental commitment to individual religious liberty.

[Part I omitted]

II

The Court today extracts from our long history of free exercise precedents the single categorical rule that "if prohibiting the exercise of religion ... is ... merely the incidental effect of a generally applicable and otherwise valid provision, the First Amendment has not been offended." Indeed, the Court holds that where the law is a generally applicable criminal prohibition, our usual free exercise jurisprudence does not even apply. To reach this sweeping result, however, the Court must not only give a strained reading of the First Amendment but must also disregard our consistent application of free exercise doctrine to cases involving generally applicable regulations that burden religious conduct.

The Free Exercise Clause of the First Amendment commands that "Congress shall make no law ... prohibiting the free exercise [of religion]." In *Cantwell v. Connecticut*

*Although JUSTICE BRENNAN, JUSTICE MARSHALL, and JUSTICE BLACKMUN join Parts I and II of this opinion, they do not concur in the judgment.

(1940) we held that this prohibition applies to the States by incorporation into the Fourteenth Amendment and that it categorically forbids government regulation of religious beliefs. As the Court recognizes, however, the "free *exercise*" of religion often, if not invariably, requires the performance of (or abstention from) certain acts.... Because the First Amendment does not distinguish between religious belief and religious conduct, conduct motivated by sincere religious belief, like the belief itself, must be at least presumptively protected by the Free Exercise Clause.

The Court today, however, interprets the Clause to permit the government to prohibit, without justification, conduct mandated by an individual's religious beliefs, so long as that prohibition is generally applicable. But a law that prohibits certain conduct—conduct that happens to be an act of worship for someone—manifestly does prohibit that person's free exercise of his religion. A person who is barred from engaging in religiously motivated conduct is barred from freely exercising his religion. Moreover, that person is barred from freely exercising his religion regardless of whether the law prohibits the conduct only when engaged in for religious reasons, only by members of that religion, or by all persons. It is difficult to deny that a law that prohibits religiously motivated conduct, even if the law is generally applicable, does not at least implicate First Amendment concerns.

The Court responds that generally applicable laws are "one large step" removed from laws aimed at specific religious practices. The First Amendment, however, does not distinguish between laws that are generally applicable and laws that target particular religious practices. Indeed, few States would be so naive as to enact a law directly prohibiting or burdening a religious practice as such. Our free exercise cases have all concerned generally applicable laws that had the effect of significantly burdening a religious practice. If the First Amendment is to have any vitality, it ought not be construed to cover only the extreme and hypothetical situation in which a State directly targets a religious practice....

To say that a person's right to free exercise has been burdened, of course, does not mean that he has an absolute right to engage in the conduct. Under our established First Amendment jurisprudence, we have recognized that the freedom to act, unlike the freedom to believe, cannot be absolute. See, *e.g., Cantwell; Reynolds v. United States* (1879).

Instead, we have respected both the First Amendment's express textual mandate and the governmental interest in regulation of conduct by requiring the government to justify any substantial burden on religiously motivated conduct by a compelling state interest and by means narrowly tailored to achieve that interest....

The Court attempts to support its narrow reading of the Clause by claiming that "[w]e have never held that an individual's religious beliefs excuse him from compliance with an otherwise valid law prohibiting conduct that the State is free to regulate." But as the Court later notes, as it must, in cases such as *Cantwell* and *Yoder* we have in fact interpreted the Free Exercise Clause to forbid application of a generally applicable prohibition to religiously motivated conduct.... Indeed, in *Yoder* we expressly rejected the interpretation the Court now adopts....

The Court endeavors to escape from our decisions in *Cantwell* and *Yoder* by labeling them "hybrid" decisions, but there is no denying that both cases expressly relied on the Free Exercise Clause ... and that we have consistently regarded those cases as part of the mainstream of our free exercise jurisprudence. Moreover, in each of the other cases cited by the Court to support its categorical rule, we rejected the particular constitutional claims before us only after carefully weighing the competing interests. See *Prince v. Massachusetts* ... *Braunfeld v. Brown*.... That we rejected the free exercise claims in those cases hardly calls into question the applicability of First Amendment doctrine in the first place. Indeed, it is surely unusual to judge the vitality of a constitutional doctrine by looking to the win-loss record of the plaintiffs who happen to come before us.

Respondents, of course, do not contend that their conduct is automatically immune from all governmental regulation simply because it is motivated by their sincere religious beliefs. The Court's rejection of that argument might therefore be regarded as merely harmless dictum. Rather, respondents invoke our traditional compelling interest test to argue that the Free Exercise Clause requires the State to grant them a limited exemption from its general criminal prohibition against the possession of peyote. The Court today, however, denies them even the opportunity to make that argument, concluding that "the sounder approach, and the approach in accord with the vast majority of our precedents, is to hold the [compelling interest] test inapplicable to" challenges to general criminal prohibitions.

In my view, however, the essence of a free exercise claim is relief from a burden imposed by government on religious practices or beliefs, whether the burden is imposed directly through laws that prohibit or compel specific religious practices, or indirectly through laws that, in effect, make abandonment of one's own religion or conformity to the religious beliefs of others the price of an equal place in the civil community.... A State that makes criminal an individual's religiously motivated conduct burdens that individual's free exercise of religion in the severest manner possible, for it "results in the choice to the individual of either abandoning his religious principle or facing criminal prosecution."... I would have thought it beyond argument that such laws implicate free exercise concerns.

Indeed, we have never distinguished between cases in which a State conditions receipt of a benefit on conduct prohibited by religious beliefs and cases in which a State affirmatively prohibits such conduct. The *Sherbert* compelling interest test applies in both kinds of cases.... I would reaffirm that principle today: a neutral criminal law prohibiting conduct that a State may legitimately regulate is, if anything, *more* burdensome than a neutral civil statute placing legitimate conditions on the award of a state benefit.

Legislatures, of course, have always been "left free to reach actions which were in violation of social duties or subversive of good order." ... Yet because of the close relationship between conduct and religious belief, "[i]n every case the power to regulate must be so exercised as not, in attaining a permissible end, unduly to infringe the protected freedom."... Once it has been shown that a government regulation or criminal prohibition burdens the free exercise of religion, we have consistently asked the Government to demonstrate that unbending application of its regulation to the religious objector "is essential to accomplish an overriding governmental interest," or represents "the least restrictive means of achieving some compelling state interest."... To me, the sounder approach—the approach more consistent with our role as judges to decide each case on its individual merits—is to apply this test in each case to determine whether the burden on the specific plaintiffs before us is constitutionally significant and whether the particular criminal interest asserted by the State before us is compelling. Even if, as an empirical matter, a government's criminal laws might usually serve a compelling interest in health, safety, or public order, the First Amendment at least requires a case-by-case determination of the question, sensitive to the facts of each particular claim.... Given the range of conduct that a State might legitimately make criminal, we cannot assume, merely because a law carries criminal sanctions and is generally applicable, that the First Amendment *never* requires the State to grant a limited exemption for religiously motivated conduct....

The Court today gives no convincing reason to depart from settled First Amendment jurisprudence. There is nothing talismanic about neutral laws of general applicability or general criminal prohibitions, for laws neutral toward religion can coerce a person to violate his religious conscience or intrude upon his religious duties just as effectively as laws aimed at religion. Although the Court suggests that the compelling interest test, as applied to generally applicable laws, would result in a "constitutional anomaly," the First Amendment unequivocally makes freedom of religion, like freedom from race discrimination and freedom of speech, a "constitutional nor[m]," not an "anomaly."... The Court's parade of horribles not only fails as a reason for discarding the compelling interest test, it instead demonstrates just the opposite: that courts have been quite capable of applying our free exercise jurisprudence to strike sensible balances between religious liberty and competing state interests.

Finally, the Court today suggests that the disfavoring of minority religions is an "unavoidable consequence" under our system of government and that accommodation of such religions must be left to the political process. In my view, however, the First Amendment was enacted precisely to protect the rights of those whose religious practices are not shared by the majority and may be viewed with hostility. The history of our free exercise doctrine amply demonstrates the harsh impact majoritarian rule has had on unpopular or emerging religious groups such as the Jehovah's Witnesses and the Amish....

III

The Court's holding today not only misreads settled First Amendment precedent; it appears to be unnecessary to this case. I would reach the same result applying our established free exercise jurisprudence.

There is no dispute that Oregon's criminal prohibition of peyote places a severe burden on the ability of re-

spondents to freely exercise their religion. Peyote is a sacrament of the Native American Church and is regarded as vital to respondents' ability to practice their religion....

There is also no dispute that Oregon has a significant interest in enforcing laws that control the possession and use of controlled substances by its citizens.... As we recently noted, drug abuse is "one of the greatest problems affecting the health and welfare of our population" and thus "one of the most serious problems confronting our society today."...

Thus, the critical question in this case is whether exempting respondents from the State's general criminal prohibition "will unduly interfere with fulfillment of the governmental interest."... Although the question is close, I would conclude that uniform application of Oregon's criminal prohibition is "essential to accomplish," ... its overriding interest in preventing the physical harm caused by the use of a ... controlled substance. Oregon's criminal prohibition represents that State's judgment that the possession and use of controlled substances, even by only one person, is inherently harmful and dangerous. Because the health effects caused by the use of controlled substances exist regardless of the motivation of the user, the use of such substances, even for religious purposes, violates the very purpose of the laws that prohibit them.... Moreover, in view of the societal interest in preventing trafficking in controlled substances, uniform application of the criminal prohibition at issue is essential to the effectiveness of Oregon's stated interest in preventing any possession of peyote....

I would therefore adhere to our established free exercise jurisprudence and hold that the State in this case has a compelling interest in regulating peyote use by its citizens and that accommodating respondents' religiously motivated conduct "will unduly interfere with fulfillment of the governmental interest."... Accordingly, I concur in the judgment of the Court.

JUSTICE BLACKMUN, with whom JUSTICE BRENNAN and JUSTICE MARSHALL join, dissenting.

This Court over the years painstakingly has developed a consistent and exacting standard to test the constitutionality of a state statute that burdens the free exercise of religion. Such a statute may stand only if the law in general, and the State's refusal to allow a religious exemption in particular, are justified by a compelling interest that cannot be served by less restrictive means.

Until today, I thought this was a settled and inviolate principle of this Court's First Amendment jurisprudence. The majority, however, perfunctorily dismisses it as a "constitutional anomaly." As carefully detailed in JUSTICE O'CONNOR's concurring opinion, the majority is able to arrive at this view only by mischaracterizing this Court's precedents. The Court discards leading free exercise cases such as *Cantwell v. Connecticut* (1940) and *Wisconsin v. Yoder* (1972), as "hybrid." The Court views traditional free exercise analysis as somehow inapplicable to criminal prohibitions (as opposed to conditions on the receipt of benefits), and to state laws of general applicability (as opposed, presumably, to laws that expressly single out religious practices). The Court cites cases in which, due to various exceptional circumstances, we found strict scrutiny inapposite, to hint that the Court has repudiated that standard altogether. In short, it effectuates a wholesale overturning of settled law concerning the Religion Clauses of our Constitution. One hopes that the Court is aware of the consequences, and that its result is not a product of overreaction to the serious problems the country's drug crisis has generated.

This distorted view of our precedents leads the majority to conclude that strict scrutiny of a state law burdening the free exercise of religion is a "luxury" that a well-ordered society cannot afford, and that the repression of minority religions is an "unavoidable consequence of democratic government." I do not believe the Founders thought their dearly bought freedom from religious persecution a "luxury," but an essential element of liberty—and they could not have thought religious intolerance "unavoidable," for they drafted the Religion Clauses precisely in order to avoid that intolerance.

For these reasons, I agree with JUSTICE O'CONNOR's analysis of the applicable free exercise doctrine, and I join parts I and II of her opinion. As she points out, "the critical question in this case is whether exempting respondents from the State's general criminal prohibition 'will unduly interfere with fulfillment of the governmental interest.'" I do disagree, however, with her specific answer to that question.

In weighing respondents' clear interest in the free exercise of their religion against Oregon's asserted interest in enforcing its drug laws, it is important to articulate in precise terms the state interest involved. It is not the State's broad interest in fighting the critical "war on drugs" that must be weighed against respondents' claim, but the State's narrow interest in refusing to make an exception for the religious, ceremonial use of peyote....

The State's interest in enforcing its prohibition, in order to be sufficiently compelling to outweigh a free exercise claim, cannot be merely abstract or symbolic. The State cannot plausibly assert that unbending application of a criminal prohibition is essential to fulfill any compelling interest, if it does not, in fact, attempt to enforce that prohibition. In this case, the State actually has not evinced any concrete interest in enforcing its drug laws against religious users of peyote. Oregon has never sought to prosecute respondents, and does not claim that it has made significant enforcement efforts against other religious users of peyote. The State's asserted interest thus amounts only to the symbolic preservation of an unenforced prohibition. But a government interest in "symbolism, even symbolism for so worthy a cause as the abolition of unlawful drugs," cannot suffice to abrogate the constitutional rights of individuals....

Similarly, this Court's prior decisions have not allowed a government to rely on mere speculation about potential harms, but have demanded evidentiary support for a refusal to allow a religious exception.... In this case, the State's justification for refusing to recognize an exception to its criminal laws for religious peyote use is entirely speculative.

The State proclaims an interest in protecting the health and safety of its citizens from the dangers of unlawful drugs. It offers, however, no evidence that the religious use of peyote has ever harmed anyone....

The State also seeks to support its refusal to make an exception for religious use of peyote by invoking its interest in abolishing drug trafficking. There is, however, practically no illegal traffic in peyote.... Also, the availability of peyote for religious use, even if Oregon were to allow an exemption from its criminal laws, would still be strictly controlled by federal regulations.... Peyote simply is not a popular drug; its distribution for use in religious rituals has nothing to do with the vast and violent traffic in illegal narcotics that plagues this country....

Finally, although I agree with JUSTICE O'CONNOR that courts should refrain from delving into questions whether, as a matter of religious doctrine, a particular practice is "central" to the religion, I do not think this means that the courts must turn a blind eye to the severe impact of a State's restrictions on the adherents of a minority religion....

For these reasons, I conclude that Oregon's interest in enforcing its drug laws against religious use of peyote is not sufficiently compelling to outweigh respondents' right to the free exercise of their religion. Since the State could not constitutionally enforce its criminal prohibition against respondents, the interests underlying the State's drug laws cannot justify its denial of unemployment benefits. Absent such justification, the State's regulatory interest in denying benefits for religiously motivated "misconduct" is indistinguishable from the state interests this Court has rejected in ... *Hobbie, Thomas,* and *Sherbert.* The State of Oregon cannot, consistently with the Free Exercise Clause, deny respondents unemployment benefits.

I dissent.

To some, *Smith* represents a change in the standards governing free exercise disputes. For the first time since it was articulated, the Court explicitly rejected the *Sherbert* test. To be sure, the justices had failed to apply it in cases such as *Goldman* and *Lyng,* but here the Court was eradicating the *Sherbert-Yoder* lineage of cases and returning to the kind of analysis it used in *Reynolds v. United States.* As Scalia wrote:

To make an individual's obligation to obey ... a law contingent upon the law's coincidence with his religious beliefs, except where the State's interest is "compelling"—permitting him, by virtue of his beliefs, "to become a law unto himself," *Reynolds v. United States*—contradicts both constitutional tradition and common sense.

In place of the *Sherbert* test, the Court would now use a standard it hinted at in *United States v. Lee:* "If prohibiting the exercise of religion ... is ... merely the incidental effect of a generally applicable and otherwise valid provision, the First Amendment has not been offended.... [T]he right of free exercise does not relieve an individual of the obligation to comply with

a 'valid and neutral law of general applicability.'"[40] In other words, under the *Smith* rule, the Court will not necessarily apply the compelling interest standard to state laws that are neutral and generally applicable. The articulation of this new standard meant, as one scholar put it, that the Court had "brought free exercise jurisprudence full circle by reaffirming the ... doctrine of *Reynolds,*" and rejecting the compelling interest approach of *Sherbert.*[41]

On what grounds did Scalia justify this alteration in Free Exercise doctrine? One of his justifications is that the precedential cases, such as *Cantwell* and *Barnette,* were "hybrids" involving "the Free Exercise Clause in conjunction with other constitutional protections, such as freedom of speech and of the press, or the right of parents ... to direct the education of their children." Therefore, it was reasonable for the Court to use a compelling interest approach. *Smith* was—at least in Scalia's view—a pure free exercise case involving a neutral and generally applicable law that the Court did not need to balance against the competing religious interests.

As you might expect, *Smith* was the subject of enormous controversy. O'Connor and Blackmun made clear their displeasure with the majority's break from precedent, asserting that the Court should stick with the compelling interest-least restrictive means approach. Yet, the two justices reached different conclusions about how *Smith* should be resolved: O'Connor would have ruled against Smith and Black, while Blackmun would have found in their favor.

Congress also voiced its disapproval. Soon after the justices handed down *Smith,* interest groups began to lobby Congress to overturn the decision. As Sen. Edward M. Kennedy, D-Mass., put it, these interests feared that, under the new standard "dry communities could ban the use of wine in communion services,

40. Ibid., 8–9.
41. Frederick Mark Gedicks, "Religion," in *The Oxford Companion to the Supreme Court,* ed. Kermit L. Hall (New York: Oxford University Press, 1992), 725.

Government meat inspectors could require changes in the preparation of kosher food and school boards could force children to attend sex education classes [contrary to their religious beliefs]."[42] With support from politicians as varied in ideological approach as Kennedy and Orrin Hatch, R-Utah, the bill—called the Religious Freedom Restoration Act—was enacted into law in 1993. It says government cannot burden religion unless it provides a compelling interest and that interest is pursued in the least restrictive manner. In other words, the Act codifies the *Sherbert* standard.

While Congress was considering the Religious Freedom Restoration Act, the Supreme Court heard yet another free exercise case. In *Church of the Lukumi Babalu Aye v. City of Hialeah* (1993) the justices considered whether city ordinances prohibiting animal sacrifice for religious purposes violate the Free Exercise Clause. Scalia had listed this dispute in his *Smith* "parade of horribles," as O'Connor called it, even though the religious sacrifice case had not yet come to the Supreme Court. Scalia used this law as one example of legislation that should be permissible but would not necessarily be so if the Court continued to use the compelling interest standard. However, he and other members of the *Smith* majority voted to strike down such laws. Why?

Church of the Lukumi Babalu Aye v. City of Hialeah

508 U.S. — (1993)

Vote: 9 (Blackmun, Kennedy, O'Connor, Rehnquist, Scalia, Souter, Stevens, Thomas, White)

0

Opinion of the Court (except as to Part II-A-2): Kennedy
Concurring opinions: Blackmun, Scalia, Souter

In 1973 the Church of the Lukumi Babalu Aye organized itself as a nonprofit corporation in the state of Florida. Church members practice the Santeria religion, which Cuban exiles brought to the United States around the time of the revolution in their country. The religion originates with the Yoruba people of West Africa, who were taken to Cuba as slaves. Santeria evolved in the 1800s as a meshing of their religion with parts of Roman Catholicism. Today, as the Supreme Court noted, "The open practice of Santeria and its rites remains infrequent" in the United States, but about 50,000 practitioners of the religion live in South Florida, with as many as 100 million worldwide.[43]

Central to the Santeria religion is animal sacrifice. Practitioners sacrifice chickens, pigeons, doves, ducks, guinea pigs, goats, sheep, and turtles at various events, including the initiations of new priests, weddings, births, and deaths, and as cures for the ailing. The animals, which are killed by cutting the carotid arteries in the neck, are cooked and eaten after some of the rituals. Santerians sacrifice as many as thirty animals during a given ritual.

In April 1987 the Church sought to establish a branch in Hialeah, Florida; by August, it had obtained the necessary approval to build a place of worship, a school, and cultural center. But, while the church was establishing itself in Hialeah, some members of the community—who apparently were less than enthusiastic about the practice of animal sacrifice—were considering ways to limit the church's exercise of its religion. They were successful, for between June 9 and September 22, the city enacted six ordinances limiting animal sacrifice, which it defined as "to unnecessarily kill, torment, or mutilate an animal in a public or private ritual or ceremony not for the primary purpose of food consumption." The ordinances did not exclude the killing of animals "on premises ... properly zoned as a slaughterhouse." Also, the law did not prohibit other types of animal killing, such as fishing or exterminating vermin, for nonreligious reasons.

---

42. Quoted by Adam Clymer in "Congress Moves to Ease Curb on Religious Acts," *New York Times*, May 10, 1993, A9.

43. Brief for the Petitioners, *Church of the Lukumi Babalu Aye.*

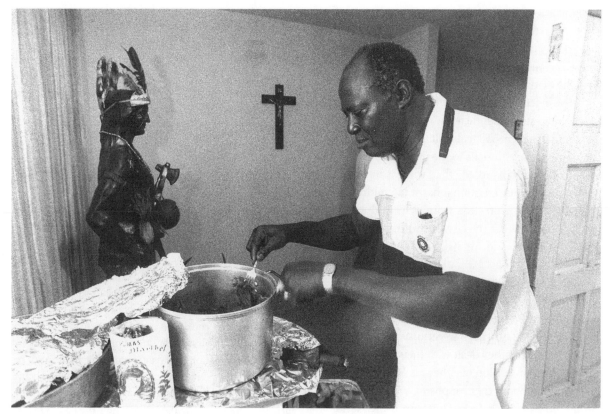

Santeria priest Rigoberto Zamora cooks the lamb and goat he sacrificed in a religious ritual the previous day. Zamora and other members of his church celebrated the Supreme Court's decision striking down city attempts to prohibit animal sacrifices in religious worship.

Before the U.S. Supreme Court issued its decision in *Smith*, the church filed suit in a U.S. district court asking it to strike down the ordinances as violations of the Free Exercise Clause. Throughout the litigation, attorneys representing the church asserted that the ordinances were aimed directly at Santeria practitioners and that they impinged on their ability to practice an important ritual of their religion. Indeed, according to the Church, "[t]he faith could not survive without animal sacrifice, because sacrifice is essential to the initiation of new priests." Using the Supreme Court's pre-*Smith* approach to free exercise claims, church attorneys also argued that the state had failed to meet the compelling interest-least restrictive means test.

The city claimed that it had good reasons for limit-

ing animal sacrifice. First was the quantity of animals being sacrificed. As the city later told the Supreme Court, the Santerians were sacrificing "thousands, indeed tens of thousands, of animals." The "specter" of such large-scale sacrificing, with "the attendant problems of keeping and feeding the animals and, later disposing of the remains," was something the city could not tolerate. Second, the city pointed to the potential health risks "because the remains of the animals attract flies, rats and other animals, which serve as vectors of serious disease." Finally, the city expressed its concern for the inhumane treatment of animals awaiting sacrifice, who, attorneys alleged, were kept in filthy and overcrowded conditions, and for the cruelty of the sacrifice procedures, which instilled "great fear and pain" in the animals. In short, as the city put it, "the slaughtering of animals on the premises other than those properly zoned as a slaughter house, is contrary to the public health, safety and welfare of the citizens of Hialeah, Florida."

The district court agreed. It found that the government's interests were sufficiently compelling to uphold the ordinances; in particular, it noted that sacrifice could present health risks to the public if the animals are not properly handled, that witnessing sacrifice might cause undue emotional harm to children, that animals deserve protection from cruel and unnecessary killing, and that the city was within its rights to restrict sacrifice to locations zoned for slaughtering animals.

After a U.S. court of appeals affirmed the district court's ruling, the church appealed to the U.S. Supreme Court. By this point, the justices had handed down *Smith*, so attorneys were unsure how to proceed. In the main, they dealt with their uncertainty by showing that invocation of either the *Sherbert* or *Smith* test would support their opposing positions. Amici curiae took a similar tack. Those from the National Jewish Commission of Law and Public Affairs, for example, urged the Court to jettison the *Smith* test, but stated that "even if the Court elected to apply ... *Smith* ... [it] should invalidate Hialeah's ordinance." People for the Ethical Treatment of Animals also asserted that both *Sherbert* and *Smith* would lead to the same conclusion: the ordinances were constitutional.

JUSTICE KENNEDY delivered the opinion of the Court, except as to Part II-A-2.

The principle that government may not enact laws that suppress religious belief or practice is so well understood that few violations are recorded in our opinions. Concerned that this fundamental nonpersecution principle of the First Amendment was implicated here, however, we granted certiorari.

Our review confirms that the laws in question were enacted by officials who did not understand, failed to per-

ceive, or chose to ignore the fact that their official actions violated the Nation's essential commitment to religious freedom. The challenged laws had an impermissible object; and in all events the principle of general applicability was violated because the secular ends asserted in defense of the laws were pursued only with respect to conduct motivated by religious beliefs. We invalidate the challenged enactments and reverse the judgment of the Court of Appeals....

II

The Free Exercise Clause of the First Amendment, which has been applied to the States through the Fourteenth Amendment, see *Cantwell v. Connecticut* (1940), provides that "Congress shall make no law respecting an establishment of religion, or *prohibiting the free exercise thereof....*" The city does not argue that Santeria is not a "religion" within the meaning of the First Amendment. Nor could it. Although the practice of animal sacrifice may seem abhorrent to some, "religious beliefs need not be acceptable, logical, consistent, or comprehensible to others in order to merit First Amendment protection." Given the historical association between animal sacrifice and religious worship, petitioners' assertion that animal sacrifice is an integral part of their religion "cannot be deemed bizarre or incredible." Neither the city nor the courts below, moreover, have questioned the sincerity of petitioners' professed desire to conduct animal sacrifices for religious reasons. We must consider petitioners' First Amendment claim.

In addressing the constitutional protection for free exercise of religion, our cases establish the general proposition that a law that is neutral and of general applicability need not be justified by a compelling governmental interest even if the law has the incidental effect of burdening a particular religious practice. *Employment Div., Dept. of Human Resources of Oregon v. Smith.* Neutrality and general applicability are interrelated, and, as becomes apparent in this case, failure to satisfy one requirement is a likely indication that the other has not been satisfied. A law failing to satisfy these requirements must be justified by a compelling governmental interest and must be narrowly tailored to advance that interest. These ordinances fail to satisfy the *Smith* requirements. We begin by discussing neutrality....

A

... At a minimum, the protections of the Free Exercise Clause pertain if the law at issue discriminates against some or all religious beliefs or regulates or prohibits conduct because it is undertaken for religious reasons. Indeed, it was "historical instances of religious persecution and intolerance that gave concern to those who drafted the Free Exercise Clause."...

1

Although a law targeting religious beliefs as such is never permissible, if the object of a law is to infringe upon or restrict practices because of their religious motivation, the law is not neutral, see *Employment Div., Dept. of Human Resources of Oregon v. Smith;* and it is invalid unless it is justified by a compelling interest and is narrowly tailored to advance that interest. There are, of course, many ways of demonstrating that the object or purpose of a law is the suppression of religion or religious conduct. To determine the object of a law, we must begin with its text, for the minimum requirement of neutrality is that a law not discriminate on its face. A law lacks facial neutrality if it refers to a religious practice without a secular meaning discernible from the language or context. Petitioners contend that three of the ordinances fail this test of facial neutrality because they use the words "sacrifice" and "ritual," words with strong religious connotations. We agree that these words are consistent with the claim of facial discrimination, but the argument is not conclusive. The words "sacrifice" and "ritual" have a religious origin, but current use admits also of secular meanings....

We reject the contention advanced by the city that our inquiry must end with the text of the laws at issue. Facial neutrality is not determinative. The Free Exercise Clause, like the Establishment Clause, extends beyond facial discrimination. The Clause "forbids subtle departures from neutrality," and "covert suppression of particular religious beliefs." Official action that targets religious conduct for distinctive treatment cannot be shielded by mere compliance with the requirement of facial neutrality. The Free Exercise Clause protects against governmental hostility which is masked, as well as overt....

The record in this case compels the conclusion that suppression of the central element of the Santeria worship service was the object of the ordinances. First, though use of the words "sacrifice" and "ritual" does not compel a finding of improper targeting of the Santeria religion, the choice of these words is support for our conclusion.... No one suggests, and on this record it cannot be maintained, that city officials had in mind a religion other than Santeria.

It becomes evident that these ordinances target Santeria sacrifice when the ordinances' operation is considered. Apart from the text, the effect of a law in its real operation is strong evidence of its object. To be sure, adverse impact will not always lead to a finding of impermissible targeting. For example, a social harm may have been a legitimate concern of government for reasons quite apart from discrimination. See, *e.g., Reynolds v. United States* (1879). The subject at hand does implicate, of course, multiple concerns unrelated to religious animosity, for example, the suffering or mistreatment visited upon the sacrificed animals, and health hazards from improper disposal. But the ordinances when considered together disclose an object remote from these legitimate concerns. The design of these laws accomplishes instead a "religious gerrymander," an impermissible attempt to target petitioners and their religious practices....

We also find significant evidence of the ordinances' improper targeting of Santeria sacrifice in the fact that they proscribe more religious conduct than is necessary to achieve their stated ends. It is not unreasonable to infer, at least when there are no persuasive indications to the contrary, that a law which visits "gratuitous restrictions" on religious conduct seeks not to effectuate the stated governmental interests, but to suppress the conduct because of its religious motivation.

The legitimate governmental interests in protecting the public health and preventing cruelty to animals could be addressed by restrictions stopping far short of a flat prohibition of all Santeria sacrificial practice. If improper disposal, not the sacrifice itself, is the harm to be prevented, the city could have imposed a general regulation on the disposal of organic garbage. It did not do so. Indeed, counsel for the city conceded at oral argument that, under the ordinances, Santeria sacrifices would be illegal even if they occurred in licensed, inspected, and zoned slaughterhouses. Thus, these broad ordinances prohibit Santeria sacrifice even when it does not threaten the city's interest in the public health....

Under similar analysis, narrower regulation would achieve the city's interest in preventing cruelty to animals. With regard to the city's interest in ensuring the adequate care of animals, regulation of conditions and treatment, regardless of why an animal is kept, is the logical response to the city's concern, not a prohibition on possession for the purpose of sacrifice. The same is true for the city's interest in prohibiting cruel methods of killing. Under federal and Florida law and [one of the] ordinance[s] which incorporates Florida law in this regard, killing an animal by the "simultaneous and instantaneous severance of the carotid arteries with a sharp instrument"—the method used in Kosher slaughter—is approved as humane.... If the city has a real concern that other methods are less humane, however, the subject of the regulation should be the method of slaughter itself, not a religious classification that is said to bear some general relation to it....

2

In determining if the object of a law is a neutral one under the Free Exercise Clause, we can also find guidance in our equal protection cases.... Here, as in equal protection cases, we may determine the city council's object from both direct and circumstantial evidence. Relevant evidence includes, among other things, the historical background of the decision under challenge, the specific series of events leading to the enactment or official policy in question, as well as the legislative or administrative history, including contemporaneous statements made by members of the decisionmaking body. These objective factors bear on the question of discriminatory object.

That the ordinances were enacted "'because of,' not merely 'in spite of,'" their suppression of Santeria religious practice, is revealed by the events preceding enactment of the ordinances. Although respondent claimed at oral argument that it had experienced significant problems resulting from the sacrifice of animals within the city before the announced opening of the Church, the city council made no attempt to address the supposed problem before its meeting in June 1987, just weeks after the Church announced plans to open. The minutes and taped excerpts of the June 9 session, both of which are in the record, evidence significant hostility exhibited by residents, members of the city council, and other city officials toward the Santeria religion and its practice of animal sacrifice. The public crowd that attended the June 9 meetings interrupted statements by council members critical of Santeria with cheers and the brief comments of [the church's leader] with taunts. When Councilman Martinez, a supporter of the ordinances, stated that in prerevolution Cuba "people were put in jail for practicing this religion," the audience applauded....

This history discloses the object of the ordinances to target animal sacrifice by Santeria worshippers because of its religious motivation.

3

In sum, the neutrality inquiry leads to one conclusion: The ordinances had as their object the suppression of religion. The pattern we have recited discloses animosity to Santeria adherents and their religious practices; the ordinances by their own terms target this religious exercise; the texts of the ordinances were gerrymandered with care to proscribe religious killings of animals but to exclude almost all secular killings; and the ordinances suppress much more religious conduct than is necessary in order to achieve the legitimate ends asserted in their defense. These ordinances are not neutral, and the court below committed clear error in failing to reach this conclusion.

B

We turn next to a second requirement of the Free Exercise Clause, the rule that laws burdening religious practice must be of general applicability. *Employment Div., Dept. of Human Resources of Oregon v. Smith.* All laws are selective to some extent, but categories of selection are of paramount concern when a law has the incidental effect of burdening religious practice. The Free Exercise Clause "protects religious observers against unequal treatment," and inequality results when a legislature decides that the governmental interests it seeks to advance are worthy of being pursued only against conduct with a religious motivation.

The principle that government, in pursuit of legitimate interests, cannot in a selective manner impose burdens only on conduct motivated by religious belief is essential to the protection of the rights guaranteed by the Free Exercise Clause.... In this case we need not define with precision the standard used to evaluate whether a prohibition is of general application, for these ordinances fall well below the minimum standard necessary to protect First Amendment rights.

Respondent claims that [the] [o]rdinances advance two interests: protecting the public health and preventing cruelty to animals. The ordinances are underinclusive for those ends. They fail to prohibit nonreligious conduct that endangers these interests in a similar or greater degree than Santeria sacrifice does. The underinclusion is substantial, not inconsequential. Despite the city's proffered interest in preventing cruelty to animals, the ordinances are drafted with care to forbid few killings but those occasioned by religious sacrifice. Many types of animal deaths or kills for nonreligious reasons are either not prohibited or approved by express provision. For example, fishing—which occurs in Hialeah—is legal. Extermination of mice and rats within a home is also permitted....

The city concedes that "neither the State of Florida nor the City has enacted a generally applicable ban on the killing of animals." It asserts, however, that animal sacrifice is "different" from the animal killings that are permitted by law. According to the city, it is "self-evident" that killing animals for food is "important"; the eradication of insects and pests is "obviously justified"; and the euthanasia of excess animals "makes sense." These *ipse dixits* do not explain why religion alone must bear the burden of the ordinances, when many of these secular killings fall within the city's interest in preventing the cruel treatment of animals.

The ordinances are also underinclusive with regard to the city's interest in public health, which is threatened by the disposal of animal carcasses in open public places and the consumption of uninspected meat. Neither interest is pursued by respondent with regard to conduct that is not motivated by religious conviction. The health risks posed by the improper disposal of animal carcasses are the same whether Santeria sacrifice or some nonreligious killing preceded it. The city does not, however, prohibit hunters from bringing their kill to their houses, nor does it regulate disposal after their activity. Despite substantial testimony at trial that the same public health hazards result from improper disposal of garbage by restaurants, restaurants are outside the scope of the ordinances. Improper disposal is a general problem that causes substantial health risks, but which respondent addresses only when it results from religious exercise....

We conclude, in sum, that each of Hialeah's ordinances pursues the city's governmental interests only against conduct motivated by religious belief. The ordinances "have every appearance of a prohibition that society is prepared to impose upon [Santeria worshippers] but not upon itself." This precise evil is what the requirement of general applicability is designed to prevent.

III

A law burdening religious practice that is not neutral or not of general application must undergo the most rigorous of scrutiny. To satisfy the commands of the First Amendment, a law restrictive of religious practice must advance "'interests of the highest order'" and must be narrowly tailored in pursuit of those interests. The compelling interest standard that we apply once a law fails to meet the *Smith* requirements is not "watered ... down" but "really means what it says." A law that targets religious conduct for distinctive treatment or advances legitimate governmental interests only against conduct with a religious motivation will survive strict scrutiny only in rare cases. It follows from what we have already said that these ordinances cannot withstand this scrutiny.

First, even were the governmental interests compelling, the ordinances are not drawn in narrow terms to accomplish those interests. As we have discussed, ... [the] ordinances are overbroad or underinclusive in substantial respects. The proffered objectives are not pursued with respect to analogous nonreligious conduct, and those interests could be achieved by narrower ordinances that burdened religion to a far lesser degree. The absence of narrow tailoring suffices to establish the invalidity of the ordinances.

Respondent has not demonstrated, moreover, that, in the context of these ordinances, its governmental interests are compelling. Where government restricts only conduct protected by the First Amendment and fails to enact feasible measures to restrict other conduct producing substantial harm or alleged harm of the same sort, the interest given in justification of the restriction is not compelling.... As we show above, the ordinances are underinclusive to a substantial extent with respect to each of the interests that respondent has asserted, and it is only conduct motivated by religious conviction that bears the weight of the governmental restrictions. There can be no serious claim that those interests justify the ordinances.

IV

The Free Exercise Clause commits government itself to religious tolerance, and upon even slight suspicion that proposals for state intervention stem from animosity to religion or distrust of its practices, all officials must pause to remember their own high duty to the Constitution and to the rights it secures. Those in office must be resolute in resisting importunate demands and must ensure that the sole reasons for imposing the burdens of law and regulation are secular. Legislators may not devise mechanisms, overt or disguised, designed to persecute or oppress a religion or its practices. The laws here in question were enacted contrary to these constitutional principles, and they are void.

Reversed.

JUSTICE SCALIA, with whom THE CHIEF JUSTICE joins, concurring in part and concurring in the judgment.

The Court analyzes the "neutrality" and the "general applicability" of the Hialeah ordinances in separate sections (Parts II-A and II-B, respectively), and allocates various invalidating factors to one or the other of those sections. If it were necessary to make a clear distinction between the two terms, I would draw a line somewhat different from the Court's. But I think it is not necessary, and would frankly acknowledge that the terms are not only "interrelated," but substantially overlap.

The terms "neutrality" and "general applicability" are not to be found within the First Amendment itself, of course, but are used in *Employment Div., Dept. of Human Resources of Oregon v. Smith* (1990) and earlier cases to describe those characteristics which cause a law that prohibits an activity a particular individual wishes to engage in for religious reasons nonetheless not to constitute a "law ... prohibiting the free exercise" of religion within the meaning of the First Amendment. In my view, the defect of lack of neutrality applies primarily to those laws that *by their terms* impose disabilities on the basis of religion ... whereas the defect of lack of general applicability applies primarily to those laws which, though neutral in their terms, through their design, construction, or enforcement target the prac-

tices of a particular religion for discriminatory treatment. But certainly a law that is not of general applicability (in the sense I have described) can be considered "nonneutral"; and certainly no law that is nonneutral (in the relevant sense) can be thought to be of general applicability. Because I agree with most of the invalidating factors set forth in Part II of the Court's opinion, and because it seems to me a matter of no consequence under which rubric ("neutrality," Part II-A, or "general applicability," Part II-B) each invalidating factor is discussed, I join the judgment of the Court and all of its opinion except section 2 of Part II-A.

I do not join that section because it departs from the opinion's general focus on the object of the *laws* at issue to consider the subjective motivation of the *lawmakers*, i.e., whether the Hialeah City Council actually *intended* to disfavor the religion of Santeria. As I have noted elsewhere, it is virtually impossible to determine the singular "motive" of a collective legislative body, and this Court has a long tradition of refraining from such inquiries.

Perhaps there are contexts in which determination of legislative motive *must* be undertaken. But I do not think that is true of analysis under the First Amendment.... The First Amendment does not refer to the purposes for which legislators enact laws, but to the effects of the laws enacted: "Congress shall make no law ... prohibiting the free exercise [of religion]...." This does not put us in the business of invalidating laws by reason of the evil motives of their authors. Had the Hialeah City Council set out resolutely to suppress the practices of Santeria, but ineptly adopted ordinances that failed to do so, I do not see how those laws could be said to "prohibit the free exercise" of religion. Nor, in my view, does it matter that a legislature consists entirely of the pure-hearted, if the law it enacts in fact singles out a religious practice for special burdens. Had the ordinances here been passed with no motive on the part of any councilman except the ardent desire to prevent cruelty to animals (as might in fact have been the case), they would nonetheless be invalid.

JUSTICE SOUTER, concurring in part and concurring in the judgment.

This case turns on a principle about which there is no disagreement, that the Free Exercise Clause bars government action aimed at suppressing religious belief or practice. The Court holds that Hialeah's animal-sacrifice laws violate that principle, and I concur in that holding without reservation.

Because prohibiting religious exercise is the object of the laws at hand, this case does not present the more difficult issue addressed in our last free-exercise case, *Employment Div., Dept. of Human Resources of Oregon v. Smith* (1990), which announced the rule that a "neutral, generally applicable" law does not run afoul of the Free Exercise Clause even when it prohibits religious exercise in effect. The Court today refers to that rule in dicta, and despite my general agreement with the Court's opinion I do not join Part II, where the dicta appear, for I have doubts about whether the *Smith* rule merits adherence. I write separately to explain why the *Smith* rule is not germane to this case and to express my view that, in a case presenting the issue, the Court should re-examine the rule *Smith* declared.

According to *Smith*, if prohibiting the exercise of religion results from enforcing a "neutral, generally applicable" law, the Free Exercise Clause has not been offended. I call this the *Smith* rule to distinguish it from the noncontroversial principle, also expressed in *Smith* though established long before, that the Free Exercise Clause is offended when prohibiting religious exercise results from a law that is not neutral or generally applicable. It is this noncontroversial principle, that the Free Exercise Clause requires neutrality and general applicability, that is at issue here. But before turning to the relationship of *Smith* to this case, it will help to get the terms in order, for the significance of the *Smith* rule is not only in its statement that the Free Exercise Clause requires no more than "neutrality" and "general applicability," but in its adoption of a particular, narrow conception of free-exercise neutrality.

That the Free Exercise Clause contains a "requirement for governmental neutrality," . . . is hardly a novel proposition; though the term does not appear in the First Amendment, our cases have used it as shorthand to describe, at least in part, what the Clause commands. . . . Nor is there anything unusual about the notion that the Free Exercise Clause requires general applicability, though the Court, until today, has not used exactly that term in stating a reason for invalidation. . . .

While general applicability is, for the most part, self-explanatory, free-exercise neutrality is not self-revealing. . . .

A law that is religion neutral on its face or in its purpose may lack neutrality in its effect by forbidding something that religion requires or requiring something that religion forbids. A secular law, applicable to all, that prohibits consumption of alcohol, for example, will affect members of religions that require the use of wine differently from members of other religions and nonbelievers, disproportionately burdening the practice of, say, Catholicism or Judaism. Without an exemption for sacramental wine, Prohibition may fail the test of religion neutrality.

It does not necessarily follow from that observation, of course, that the First Amendment requires an exemption from Prohibition; that depends on the meaning of neutrality as the Free Exercise Clause embraces it. The point here is the unremarkable one that our common notion of neutrality is broad enough to cover not merely what might be called formal neutrality, which as a free-exercise requirement would only bar laws with an object to discriminate against religion, but also what might be called substantive neutrality, which, in addition to demanding a secular object, would generally require government to accommodate religious differences by exempting religious practices from formally neutral laws. If the Free Exercise Clause secures only protection against deliberate discrimination, a formal requirement will exhaust the Clause's neutrality command; if the Free Exercise Clause, rather, safeguards a right to engage in religious activity free from unnecessary governmental interference, the Clause requires substantive, as well as formal, neutrality.

Though *Smith* used the term "neutrality" without a modifier, the rule it announced plainly assumes that free-exercise neutrality is of the formal sort. Distinguishing between laws whose "object" is to prohibit religious exercise and those that prohibit religious exercise as an "incidental effect," *Smith* placed only the former within the reaches of the Free Exercise Clause; the latter, laws that satisfy formal neutrality, *Smith* would subject to no free-exercise scrutiny at all, even when they prohibit religious exercise in application. . . .

The proposition for which the *Smith* rule stands, then, is that formal neutrality, along with general applicability, are sufficient conditions for constitutionality under the Free Exercise Clause. That proposition is not at issue in this case, however, for Hialeah's animal-sacrifice ordinances are not neutral under any definition, any more than they are generally applicable. This case, rather, involves the noncontroversial principle repeated in *Smith*, that formal neutrality and general applicability are necessary conditions for free-exercise constitutionality. It is only "this fundamental nonpersecution principle of the First Amendment [that is] implicated here," and it is to that principle that the Court adverts when it holds that Hialeah's ordinances "fail to satisfy the *Smith* requirements." In applying that principle the Court does not tread on troublesome ground. . . .

In being so readily susceptible to resolution by applying the Free Exercise Clause's "fundamental nonpersecution principle," this is far from a representative free-exercise case. While, as the Court observes, the Hialeah City Council has provided a rare example of a law actually aimed at suppressing religious exercise, *Smith* was typical of our free-exercise cases, involving as it did a formally neutral, generally applicable law. The rule *Smith* announced, however, was decidedly untypical of the cases involving the same type of law. Because *Smith* left those prior cases standing, we are left with a free-exercise jurisprudence in tension with itself, a tension that should be addressed, and that may legitimately be addressed, by reexamining the *Smith* rule in the next case that would turn upon its application. . . .

The extent to which the Free Exercise Clause requires government to refrain from impeding religious exercise defines nothing less than the respective relationships in our constitutional democracy of the individual to government and to God. "Neutral, generally applicable" laws, drafted as they are from the perspective of the nonadherent, have the unavoidable potential of putting the believer to a choice between God and government. Our cases now present competing answers to the question when government, while pursuing secular ends, may compel disobedience to what one believes religion commands. The case before us is rightly decided without resolving the existing tension, which remains for another day when it may be squarely faced.

JUSTICE BLACKMUN, with whom JUSTICE O'CONNOR joins, concurring in the judgment.

The Court holds today that the city of Hialeah violated the First and Fourteenth Amendments when it passed a set of restrictive ordinances explicitly directed at petitioners'

religious practice. With this holding I agree. I write separately to emphasize that the First Amendment's protection of religion extends beyond those rare occasions on which the government explicitly targets religion (or a particular religion) for disfavored treatment, as is done in this case. In my view, a statute that burdens the free exercise of religion "may stand only if the law in general, and the State's refusal to allow a religious exemption in particular, are justified by a compelling interest that cannot be served by less restrictive means." *Employment Div., Oregon Dept. of Human Resources v. Smith* (1990) (dissenting opinion). The Court, however, applies a different test. It applies the test announced in *Smith*, under which "a law that is neutral and of general applicability need not be justified by a compelling governmental interest even if the law has the incidental effect of burdening a particular religious practice." I continue to believe that *Smith* was wrongly decided, because it ignored the value of religious freedom as an affirmative individual liberty and treated the Free Exercise Clause as no more than an antidiscrimination principle. Thus, while I agree with the result the Court reaches in this case, I arrive at that result by a different route.

When the State enacts legislation that intentionally or unintentionally places a burden upon religiously motivated practice, it must justify that burden by "showing that it is the least restrictive means of achieving some compelling state interest." *Thomas v. Review Bd. of Indiana Employment Security Div.* (1981). . . . A State may no more create an underinclusive statute, one that fails truly to promote its purported compelling interest, than it may create an overinclusive statute, one that encompasses more protected conduct than necessary to achieve its goal. In the latter circumstance, the broad scope of the statute is unnecessary to serve the interest, and the statute fails for that reason. In the former situation, the fact that allegedly harmful conduct falls outside the statute's scope belies a governmental assertion that it has genuinely pursued an interest "of the highest order." If the State's goal is important enough to prohibit religiously motivated activity, it will not and must not stop at religiously motivated activity. . . .

In this case, the ordinances at issue are both overinclusive and underinclusive in relation to the state interests they purportedly serve. They are overinclusive, as the majority correctly explains, because the "legitimate governmental interests in protecting the public health and preventing cruelty to animals could be addressed by restrictions stopping far short of a flat prohibition of all Santeria sacrificial practice." They are underinclusive as well, because "despite the city's proffered interest in preventing cruelty to animals, the ordinances are drafted with care to forbid few killings but those occasioned by religious sacrifice." Moreover, the "ordinances are also underinclusive with regard to the city's interest in public health. . . ."

When a law discriminates against religion as such, as do the ordinances in this case, it automatically will fail strict scrutiny under *Sherbert v. Verner* (1963). . . . This is true because a law that targets religious practice for disfavored treatment both burdens the free exercise of religion and, by definition, is not precisely tailored to a compelling governmental interest.

Thus, unlike the majority, I do not believe that "[a] law burdening religious practice that is not neutral or not of general application must undergo the most rigorous of scrutiny." In my view, regulation that targets religion in this way, *ipso facto*, fails strict scrutiny. It is for this reason that a statute that explicitly restricts religious practices violates the First Amendment. Otherwise, however, "the First Amendment . . . does not distinguish between laws that are generally applicable and laws that target particular religious practices."

It is only in the rare case that a state or local legislature will enact a law directly burdening religious practice as such. Because the respondent here does single out religion in this way, the present case is an easy one to decide.

A harder case would be presented if petitioners were requesting an exemption from a generally applicable anticruelty law. The result in the case before the Court today, and the fact that every Member of the Court concurs in that result, does not necessarily reflect this Court's views of the strength of a State's interest in prohibiting cruelty to animals. This case does not present, and I therefore decline to reach, the question whether the Free Exercise Clause would require a religious exemption from a law that sincerely pursued the goal of protecting animals from cruel treatment. The number of organizations that have filed *amicus* briefs on behalf of this interest, however, demonstrates that it is not a concern to be treated lightly.

What are we to make of *Lukumi Babalu?* In particular, is it not remarkable that the Court could reach a unanimous vote? After all, the decision-making environment surrounding *Smith*—the most recent free exercise case—was far short of consensual. Moreover, the citation to the district court's opinion in *Lukumi Babalu* that appeared in Scalia's "parade of horribles," made it seem almost unthinkable that he would support the church. Why, then, did he and the rest of the *Smith* majority go along here?

Several explanations come to mind. The first is that the facts of *Smith* and *Lukumi Babalu* were different in at least one important respect. It is clear that Oregon did not pass its prohibition on peyote use to hinder the religious practice of the Native American church, while it is equally clear that Hialeah aimed its ordinance directly at the Santerians. Accordingly, as Justice Blackmun put it, "Because the respondent [Hialeah] here does single out religion in this way, the present case is an easy one to decide." A second reason is that the Court feared yet another rebuke from Congress. By the time the justices handed down *Lukumi Babalu*, Congress had overturned their decision in *Goldman* and was on its way to doing the same with *Smith*. Finally, keep in mind that *Lukumi Babalu* only gives the appearance of unanimity and that underneath the surface (presuming that the justices do not alter their views) lay some very serious disagreements, as Figure 3-1 illustrates.

What does the future hold for Free Exercise cases? With Justice White's departure and Ginsburg's ascension, the *Smith* rule may have lost a vote: as a circuit court judge Ginsburg favored Goldman's free exercise claim *(see page 100).*[44] This change in membership, especially coupled with passage of the Religious Freedom Restoration Act, may bode poorly for future application of *Smith*. But with what will the justices re-

44. On the other hand, perhaps we should not make too much of this, for Scalia joined Ginsburg's dissent and he has not proven a great champion of Free Exercise claims.

FIGURE 3-1 Free Exercise Approaches Advocated by the Justices in *Smith, Lukumi Babalu,* and Beyond

Smith	*Lukumi Babalu*	*Post Lukumi, Post-Congressional Act*
Blackmun ⟶ (*Sherbert-Yoder* standard)	Blackmun ⟶ (*Sherbert-Yoder* standard)	Breyer (?)
Brennan ⟶ (*Sherbert-Yoder* standard)	Souter ⟶ (reconsider *Smith; Smith* fails to consider substantive neutrality)	same
Kennedy ⟶ (*Smith* rule)	Kennedy ⟶ (*Smith* rule)	same
Marshall ⟶ (*Sherbert-Yoder* standard)	Thomas ⟶ (*Smith* rule)	same
O'Connor ⟶ (*Sherbert-Yoder* standard)	O'Connor ⟶ (*Sherbert-Yoder* standard)	same
Rehnquist ⟶ (*Smith* rule)	Rehnquist ⟶ (*Smith* rule, without considering legislators' motives)	same
Scalia ⟶ (*Smith* rule)	Scalia ⟶ (*Smith* rule, without considering legislators' motives)	same
Stevens ⟶ (*Smith* rule)	Stevens ⟶ (*Smith* rule)	same
White ⟶ (*Smith* rule)	White ⟶ (*Smith* rule)	Ginsburg (*Sherbert-Yoder* standard?)

place it? That issue remains unsettled, for the Court has not yet agreed to hear another Free Exercise Clause case. What is clear is that this area of the law is subject to change. Table 3-1 *(see page 127)* demonstrates the volatility here by listing the present status of Supreme Court decisions that upheld legislation challenged on free exercise grounds. Notice how many of these decisions the Court later overturned or the political branches of government sought to negate.

RELIGIOUS ESTABLISHMENT

In a letter he wrote in 1802 to the Danbury Baptist Association, Thomas Jefferson proclaimed that the First Amendment built "a wall of separation between Church and State." But what sort of wall did Jefferson conceive? Was it to be flimsy, connoting, as some suggest, that commingling between church and state is constitutional so long as government does not establish a national religion? Or was it to be a solid wall that bars all cooperative interactions between church and state? Or something in between?

Underlying the cases involving the Religious Establishment Clause is that question: What is the nature of the wall that separates church from state? To answer it, many Court opinions, as we shall see, look to the intent of the Framers, a highly elusive concept, particularly in this area of the law. As the nation's

TABLE 3-1 The Aftermath of Select Court Cases Rejecting Free Exercise Claims

Issue	Case	Status
Polygamy	*Reynolds v. United States* (1879)	Invoked as justification for *Smith* rule; remains good law
Exemption from oath "abjuring" polygamy as a condition to vote	*Davis v. Beason* (1890)	Remains good law
Exemption from naturalization pledge to "take up arms" on behalf of the United States	*United States v. Schwimmer* (1929)	Overruled by Court in *Girouard v. United States* (1946)
Exemption from naturalization pledge to "take up arms" on behalf of the United States	*United States v. MacIntosh* (1931)	Overturned by Court in *Girouard v. United States* (1946)
Exemption from compulsory classes in military science	*Hamilton v. Regents of the University of California* (1934)	Remains good law
Exemption from compulsory flag salute	*Minersville School District v. Gobitis* (1940)	Overruled by Court in *West Virginia Board of Education v. Barnette* (1943)
Exemption from license requirement for parade	*Cox v. New Hampshire* (1941)	Remains good law
Exemption from paying license taxes on book selling	*Jones v. Opelika I* (1942)	Overruled by Court in *Jones v. Opelika II* (1943)
Solicitation of religious materials by minors	*Prince v. Massachusetts* (1944)	Remains good law
Keeping stores open on Sunday	*Sunday Closing Laws* (1961)	Many states have revised blue laws to allow stores to open on Sundays
Solicitations/sales on fairgrounds	*Heffron v. International Society* (1981)	Remains good law
Exemption from Social Security taxes	*United States v. Lee* (1982)	Law changed by Congress in 1988
Racial discrimination	*Bob Jones University v. United States* (1983)	Remains good law
Exemption from minimum wage laws	*Tony and Susan Alamo Foundation v. Secretary of Labor* (1985)	Remains good law
Wearing yarmulke in military	*Goldman v. Weinberger* (1986)	Reversed by Congress in 1987
Exemption from receiving Social Security number	*Bowen v. Roy* (1986)	Remains good law
Attendance at religious services in prison	*O'Lone v. Shabazz* (1987)	Remains good law
Use of national parks for religious purposes against U.S. claims for road construction	*Lyng v. Northwest Indian Cemetery Protective Association* (1988)	Remains good law
Tax deduction for church contributions	*Hernandez v. Commissioner of Internal Revenue Service* (1989)	Remains good law
Exemption from state sales tax on religious material	*Swaggart v. Board of Equalization* (1990)	Remains good law
Attainment of unemployment benefits for loss of job due to ingestion of controlled drugs	*Employment Division v. Smith* (1990)	Reversed by Congress in 1993

SOURCE: Adapted from Henry J. Abraham, *Freedom and the Courts,* 5th ed. (New York: Oxford University Press, 1988), 308–318.

Founders were of many minds, it is possible to find evidence supporting the following interpretations of the Establishment Clause:

1. The Religious Establishment Clause erects a solid wall of separation between church and state, prohibiting most, if not all, forms of public aid for or support of religion.

2. The Religious Establishment Clause may erect a wall of separation between church and state, but that wall of separation only forbids the state to prefer one religion over another—not nondiscriminatory support or aid for all religions.

3. The Religious Establishment Clause simply prohibits the establishment of a national religion.

In a detailed analysis of the intent of the Framers, Michael J. Malbin found that the *majority* of the Founders ascribed to views 2 or 3 (*accommodationist* positions), but not view 1 (a *separationist* position), which erects the highest wall.[45]

Other scholars, however, argue that we must look to the views of Jefferson and Madison to understand the Establishment Clause because they were largely responsible for its inclusion in the Constitution. Such an examination, some analysts argue, leads to a wholly different conclusion: Madison and Jefferson agreed with view 1— government should have little or nothing to do with organized religions. Still others suggest that Madison was far more tolerant of commingling between church and state than is typically assumed and that he was more likely to have agreed with view 2 than with view 1. Box 3-2 provides some details about how Madison, Jefferson, and other Founders thought about religion.

The information in Box 3-2 will be useful because, as the cases to come indicate, the Court often refers to the views of Jefferson and Madison when it interprets the Establishment Clause. As we shall see, the Supreme Court *generally* has adhered to the position that

Jefferson and Madison advocated view 1. Accordingly, the Court has prohibited *many* forms of public support of or aid to religion. We qualify the words "generally" and "many" for the following reasons. First, while most justices have adopted Jefferson's metaphor of the wall of separation, under some circumstances (those that passed a well-entrenched test) they allow aid to religious institutions. Therefore, the Court has not subscribed to a strict version of view 1, which would eliminate *all* aid to religion. Second, several justices of the Burger and Rehnquist Courts take the position that the Framers of the First Amendment, including Madison, supported view 2, not 1. They have advocated a far different approach to Establishment Clause cases, one that would permit a good deal more public support for religion.

Do these justices now command a majority on the Court? Will they bring about a major change in the way the Court approaches religious establishment cases? What will that new policy be? These questions are on the minds of many lawyers, judges, and legal scholars. You might consider them as you read the narrative and cases that follow.

Religious Establishment Cases: Origins

One of the more interesting aspects of religious establishment is that the Supreme Court had few opportunities to rule on this clause before the 1940s. As Lucius Barker and Twiley Barker note, "Despite the potential for litigation in this area, only a few controversies over religious liberty issues reached the Supreme Court in the century following the amendment's adoption."[46] Their observation is correct for a number of reasons: the Court did not incorporate the Religious Establishment Clause until 1947, and some of its earlier decisions created procedural barriers, making it difficult for citizens to bring suit. In fact, *Bradfield v. Roberts* (1899), involving a congressional grant of $30,000 to a hospital run by Catholic nuns,

---

45. Michael J. Malbin, *Religion and Politics: The Intentions of the Authors of the First Amendment* (Washington, D.C.: American Enterprise Institute, 1978).

46. Lucius J. Barker and Twiley W. Barker, Jr., *Civil Liberties and the Constitution*, 7th ed. (Englewood Cliffs, N.J.: Prentice-Hall, 1994), 20.

BOX 3-2 WHAT DID MADISON, JEFFERSON, AND THE OTHER FOUNDERS WANT?

For many years, legal scholars have sought to throw light on Thomas Jefferson's, James Madison's, and the other Founders' views on the relationship between church and state. Why they have devoted so much time to this enterprise is not difficult to explain. From its first major decision on religious liberty, *Reynolds v. United States (see page 75)* through its more recent cases (see, for example, *Wallace v. Jaffree, page 185),* the Supreme Court has used the intent of the Founders—particularly Madison and Jefferson—as a guide to resolving religious establishment disputes. The search for original intent escalated during the Reagan administration, when members of the administration and Chief Justice Rehnquist, among others, argued that the Court's (and scholars') previous interpretations of that intent were historically incorrect. Here we summarize the positions of both sides and the major sources of support they use to justify them.

	Wall of Separation	*Nonpreferential Treatment*
Position	Jefferson and Madison advocated a wall of separation between church and state that prohibited most, if not all, forms of public aid or support of religion.	Jefferson, Madison, and the majority of the Founders merely argued that the state could not establish a national religion or give preference to one religion over another.
Notable Adherents	Constitutional law scholar Leonard W. Levy, Justice Hugo Black, political commentator Garry Wills	Constitutional law scholar Walter Berns, Chief Justice William Rehnquist, former attorney general Edwin Meese
Support (Examples)	1. In 1779 the Virginia legislature considered a bill that would have used tax dollars to support churches. At that time, Jefferson introduced a "Bill for Religious Freedom," which said that "no man shall be compelled to frequent or support any religious worship, place, or ministry whatsoever." Neither bill received majority support. Debate resumed in 1784, when Patrick Henry introduced the General Assessment Bill, which would have used tax dollars to support the "Christian religion." Jefferson was in Paris at the time this bill was introduced, but when Madison wrote him of this new attempt to use public monies Jefferson responded: "What we have to do is devoutly to pray for [Henry's] death" (Alley, 10). Madison took less drastic, but not less effective measures. Through clever political maneuvers, Madison rid the Virginia legislature of Henry (he became governor) and got the legislature to postpone the vote on the bill for one year. In the meantime, Madison distributed a pamphlet called "Memorial and Remonstrance Against Religious Assessments." It was a *tour de force* on the need for separation of church and state so that both could remain strong. Madison's arguments were so persuasive that the Assessment Bill died without consideration, while Jefferson's proposal was passed. 2. In 1802 Jefferson wrote a letter to the Danbury Baptist Association asserting that the religious Establishment Clause built a "wall of separation" between church and state. As president, Jefferson refused to proclaim Thanksgiving Day on religious establishment grounds.	1. Madison may have pushed for Virginia's Bill for Religious Freedom, but he did not advocate its incorporation into the U.S. Constitution. Indeed, he thought a Bill of Rights completely unnecessary. But, being an astute politician, Madison realized that the Constitution might not be ratified without a Bill of Rights. So he took on the task of drafting one. Madison's original version of the Establishment Clause said only that Congress shall not establish "any national religion." This, as Rehnquist wrote in *Wallace v. Jaffree,* "obviously does not conform to the 'wall of separation' between church and State idea which latter-day commentators have ascribed to him." Rather, his language and his comments during congressional debate over the amendment in 1789 make it clear that he thought it prohibited Congress from establishing a national religion and from giving preference to particular religions. There is simply no evidence that Madison attempted to get Congress to enact anything resembling Virginia's Bill for Religious Freedom. Whatever he and Jefferson did in Virginia is irrelevant to understanding his intent for the Bill of Rights. 2. Jefferson was in France when Congress passed the Bill of Rights. His letter to the Danbury Baptist Association, as Rehnquist claims, was "a short note of courtesy, written fourteen years after the Amendments were passed by Congress." It is not an "ideal source" for understanding the intent of the Framers.

(Continued on page 130)

BOX 3-2 (continued)

Wall of Separation	Nonpreferential Treatment
	Jefferson's two predecessors, Washington and Adams, issued Thanksgiving Day proclamations.
3. Madison, as Wills presents it, devoted much of his life to campaigning for separation of church and state. A partial list (Wills, 374) includes:	3. To understand the intent of the Framers, one also ought to look at the actions of early Congresses:
1774: Madison, denouncing the jailing of Baptist preachers in Virginia, concluded that "ecclesiastical establishments tend to great ignorance and corruption."	1789: On the same day Madison introduced his Amendments, the House enacted the Northwest Ordinance, which gave federal land grants to sectarian schools.
1776: At Virginia's revolutionary convention, Madison tried to amend George Mason's preamble to the new Virginia constitution, in order to remove all "emoluments or privileges" from religion. He failed at that, but substituted "free exercise of religion" for "fullest toleration in the exercise of religion." His first important legislative act, undertaken when he was only twenty-five, struck a blow for religious freedom.	1789: The day after the House passed the version of the Religious Establishment Clause that was ratified by the states, it proposed a resolution asking President Washington to issue a Thanksgiving Day proclamation.
1785: Madison published his major statement on religious freedom, "Memorial and Remonstrance against Religious Assessments."	1789: Washington issued the proclamation: "I do recommend and assign Thursday . . . to be devoted by the people of these States to the service of that great and glorious Being, who is the beneficent author of all the good that was, that is, or that will be; that we may then all unite in rendering unto Him our sincere and humble thanks."
1789: Drafting what will become the First Amendment, Madison proposed not only disestablishment at a national level but that "no *state* shall violate the equal rights of conscience." Although disestablishment at the federal level was all he could accomplish in his lifetime, he regularly referred to the First Amendment as opposing "establishments," reflecting his original intent.	1789–1823: Congress provided public land grants to the Society of the United Brethren for "propagating the Gospel among the Heathen."
	Early 1800s: Congress approved treaties with Native American tribes requiring financial support of tribes' religious education programs, churches, and clergy.

	Wall of Separation	Nonpreferential Treatment
The Bottom Line	"If Madison is any guide, our churches are not, even now, too separated from political support." "Though he is called the father of the Constitution, [Madison] has an even better claim as the father of disestablishment." (Wills, 373, 380)	"It is impossible to build sound constitutional doctrine upon a mistaken understanding of constitutional history, but unfortunately the Establishment Clause has been expressly freighted with Jefferson's misleading metaphor for nearly 40 years." (Rehnquist)
	An establishment of religion in America at the time of the framing of the Bill of Rights meant government aid and sponsorship of religion, principally by impartial tax support of the institutions of religion, the churches. (Levy, 161)	"Probably at the time of the adoption of the Constitution . . . the general if not universal sentiment in America was that Christianity ought to receive encouragement from the State so far as was not incompatible with . . . the freedom of religious worship. An attempt to level all religions, and to make it a matter of state policy to hold all in utter indifference, would have created universal disapprobation." (Story, 630–632)

WORKS CITED: Robert S. Alley, *The Supreme Court on Church and State*, (New York: Oxford University Press, 1988); Leonard W. Levy, *Constitutional Opinions* (New York: Oxford University Press, 1986); William H. Rehnquist, dissenting opinion in *Wallace v. Jaffree*, 472 U.S. 38 (1985); Joseph Story, *Commentaries on the Constitution of the United States*, vol. 2, 5th ed., 1891; Garry Wills, *Under God* (New York: Simon and Schuster, 1990).
NOTE: Material in the "Strict Separation" column draws heavily on Levy, *Constitutional Opinions*, and Levy, *The Establishment Clause* (New York: Macmillan, 1986); material in the "Nonpreferential" column comes largely from Rehnquist's dissent in *Wallace v. Jaffree* (1985).

was one of the only cases to reach the Court before the 1940s. Here, the justices agreed that the Establishment Clause did not negate the law because the hospital was not a religious institution:

Whether the individuals who compose a corporation ... happen to be all Roman Catholics, or all Methodists ... or members of any religious organization or of no organization at all is [of] the slightest consequence.... [This does] not in the least change the legal character of the hospital, or make a religious corporation out of a purely secular one.

Bradfield was important because it demonstrated from the start the Court's willingness to allow some aid, but it did not establish any legal standards by which to adjudicate future claims.

Almost fifty years elapsed between *Bradfield* and the next important religious establishment case, *Everson v. Board of Education* (1947). While reading the Court's decision in *Everson,* consider these questions: Did the Court establish any legal standards by which to determine whether state practices violate the Establishment Clause? What view of the Establishment Clause did it adopt?

Everson v. Board of Education

330 U.S. 1 (1947)
Vote: 5 *(Black, Douglas, Murphy, Reed, Vinson)*
    4 *(Burton, Frankfurter, Jackson, Rutledge)*
Opinion of the Court: Black
Dissenting opinions: Jackson, Rutledge

In 1941 New Jersey passed a law authorizing local school boards that provided "any transportation for public school children to and from school" to also supply transportation to school children living in the district who attended nonprofit private schools. At the time New Jersey enacted this legislation, at least fifteen other states had similar laws.

Ewing Township decided to use tax dollars to reimburse parents for transportation costs incurred in

sending their children to school. Because the township had no public high schools of its own, the reimbursement policy covered transportation expenses to parents sending their children to three neighboring public high schools. It also covered four private schools, all of which were affiliated with the Roman Catholic church and provided "regular religious instruction conforming to the religion's tenets and modes of worship of the Catholic faith." The average payment to parents sending their children to public or Catholic schools was $40 per student.

Arch Everson, a taxpayer living in the district, challenged the reimbursements to parents sending their children to religious private schools. He argued that they supported religion in violation of the Establishment Clause of the First Amendment.

MR. JUSTICE BLACK delivered the opinion of the Court.

The New Jersey statute is challenged as a "law respecting an establishment of religion." The First Amendment ... commands that a state "shall make no law respecting an establishment of religion, or prohibiting the free exercise thereof." These words of the First Amendment reflected in the minds of early Americans a vivid mental picture of conditions and practices which they fervently wished to stamp out in order to preserve liberty for themselves and for their posterity. Doubtless their goal has not been entirely reached; but so far has the Nation moved toward it that the expression "law respecting an establishment of religion," probably does not so vividly remind present-day Americans of the evils, fears, and political problems that caused that expression to be written into our Bill of Rights. Whether this New Jersey law is one respecting the "establishment of religion" requires an understanding of the meaning of that language, particularly with respect to the imposition of taxes. Once again, therefore, it is not inappropriate briefly to review the background and environment of the period in which that constitutional language was fashioned and adopted.

A large proportion of the early settlers of this country came here from Europe to escape the bondage of laws which compelled them to support and attend government favored churches. The centuries immediately before and contemporaneous with the colonization of America had been filled with turmoil, civil strife, and persecutions, generated in large part by established sects determined to maintain their absolute political and religious supremacy. With the power of government supporting them, at various times and places, Catholics had persecuted Protestants, Protestants had persecuted Catholics, Protestant sects had persecuted other Protestant sects, Catholics of one shade of belief had persecuted Catholics of another shade of belief, and all of these had from time to time persecuted Jews. In efforts to force loyalty to whatever religious group happened to be on top and in league with the government of a particular time and place, men and women had been fined, cast in jail, cruelly tortured, and killed....

These practices of the old world were transplanted to and began to thrive in the soil of the new America. The very charters granted by the English Crown to the individuals and companies designated to make the laws which would control the destinies of the colonials authorized these individuals and companies to erect religious establishments which all, whether believers or non-believers, would be required to support and attend. An exercise of this authority was accompanied by a repetition of many of the old world practices and persecutions. Catholics found themselves hounded and proscribed because of their faith; Quakers who followed their conscience went to jail; Baptists were peculiarly obnoxious to certain dominant Protestant sects; men and women of varied faiths who happened to be in a minority in a particular locality were persecuted because they steadfastly persisted in worshipping God only as their own consciences dictated. And all of these dissenters were compelled to pay tithes and taxes to support government-sponsored churches whose ministers preached inflammatory sermons designed to strengthen and consolidate the established faith by generating a burning hatred against dissenters.

These practices became so commonplace as to shock the freedom-loving colonials into a feeling of abhorrence. The imposition of taxes to pay ministers' salaries and to build and maintain churches and church property aroused their indignation. It was these feelings which found expression in the First Amendment. No one locality and no one group

throughout the Colonies can rightly be given entire credit for having aroused the sentiment that culminated in an adoption of the Bill of Rights' provisions embracing religious liberty. But Virginia, where the established church had achieved a dominant influence in political affairs and where many excesses attracted wide public attention, provided a great stimulus and able leadership for the movement. The people there, as elsewhere, reached the conviction that individual religious liberty could be achieved best under a government which was stripped of all power to tax, to support, or otherwise to assist any or all religions, or to interfere with the beliefs of any religious individual or group.

The movement toward this end reached its dramatic climax in Virginia in 1785-86 when the Virginia legislative body was about to renew Virginia's tax levy for the support of the established church. Thomas Jefferson and James Madison led the fight against this tax. Madison wrote his great Memorial and Remonstrance against the law. In it, he eloquently argued that a true religion did not need the support of law; that no person, either believer or non-believer, should be taxed to support a religious institution of any kind; that the best interest of a society required that the minds of men always be wholly free; and that cruel persecutions were the inevitable result of government-established religions....

The meaning and scope of the First Amendment, preventing establishment of religion or prohibiting the free exercise thereof, in the light of its history and the evils it was designed forever to suppress, have been several times elaborated by the decisions of this Court prior to the application of the First Amendment to the states by the Fourteenth. The broad meaning given the Amendment by these earlier cases has been accepted by this Court in its decisions concerning an individual's religious freedom rendered since the Fourteenth Amendment was interpreted to make the prohibitions of the First applicable to state action abridging religious freedom. There is every reason to give the same application and broad interpretation to the "establishment of religion" clause....

The "establishment of religion" clause of the First Amendment means at least this: Neither a state nor the Federal Government can set up a church. Neither can pass laws which aid one religion, aid all religions, or prefer one religion over another. Neither can force nor influence a person to go to or to remain away from church against his will or force him to profess a belief or disbelief in any religion. No person can be punished for entertaining or professing religious beliefs or disbeliefs, for church attendance or non-attendance. No tax in any amount, large or small, can be levied to support any religious activities or institutions, whatever they may be called, or whatever form they may adopt to teach or practice religion. Neither a state nor the Federal Government can, openly or secretly, participate in the affairs of any religious organizations or groups and vice versa. In the words of Jefferson, the clause against establishment of religion by law was intended to erect "a wall of separation between Church and State."

We must consider the New Jersey statute in accordance with the foregoing limitations imposed by the First Amendment. But we must not strike that state statute down if it is within the state's constitutional power even though it approaches the verge of that power. New Jersey cannot consistently with the "establishment of religion" clause of the First Amendment contribute tax-raised funds to the support of an institution which teaches the tenets and faith of any church. On the other hand, other language of the amendment commands that New Jersey cannot hamper its citizens in the free exercise of their own religion. Consequently, it cannot exclude individual Catholics, Lutherans, Mohammedans, Baptists, Jews, Methodists, Non-believers, Presbyterians, or the members of any other faith, *because of their faith, or lack of it,* from receiving the benefits of public welfare legislation. While we do not mean to intimate that a state could not provide transportation only to children attending public schools, we must be careful, in protecting the citizens of New Jersey against state-established churches, to be sure that we do not inadvertently prohibit New Jersey from extending its general State law benefits to all its citizens without regard to their religious belief.

Measured by these standards, we cannot say that the First Amendment prohibits New Jersey from spending tax-raised funds to pay the bus fares of parochial school pupils as a part of a general program under which it pays the fares of pupils attending public and other schools. It is undoubtedly true that children are helped to get to church schools. There is even a possibility that some of the children might not be sent to the church schools if the parents were compelled to pay their children's bus fares out of their own pockets when transportation to a public school would have been paid for by the State. The same possibility exists where the state requires a local transit company to provide reduced fares to school children including those attending parochial schools, or where a municipally owned transportation system undertakes to carry all school children free of charge. Moreover, state-paid policemen, detailed to protect children going to and from church schools from the very real hazards of traffic, would serve much the same purpose and accomplish much the same result as state provisions intended to guarantee free transportation of a kind which the state deems to be best for the school children's welfare. And parents might refuse to risk their children to the serious danger of traffic accidents going to and from parochial schools, the approaches to which were not protected by policemen. Similarly, parents might be reluctant to permit their children to attend schools which the state had cut off from such general government services as ordinary police and fire protection, connections for sewage disposal, public highways and sidewalks. Of course, cutting off church schools from these services, so separate and so indisputably marked off from the religious function, would make it far more difficult for the schools to operate. But such is obviously not the purpose of the First Amendment. That Amendment requires the state to be a neutral in its relations with groups of religious believers and non-believers; it does not require the state to be their adversary. State power is no more to be used so as to handicap religions, than it is to favor them.

This Court has said that parents may, in the discharge of their duty under state compulsory education laws, send their children to a religious rather than a public school if the school meets the secular educational requirements which the state has power to impose. It appears that these parochial schools meet New Jersey's requirements. The State contributes no money to the schools. It does not support them. Its legislation, as applied, does no more than provide a general program to help parents get their children, regardless of their religion, safely and expeditiously to and from accredited schools.

The First Amendment has erected a wall between church and state. That wall must be kept high and impregnable. We could not approve the slightest breach. New Jersey has not breached it here.

Affirmed.

MR. JUSTICE JACKSON, dissenting.

I find myself, contrary to first impressions, unable to join in this decision. I have a sympathy, though it is not ideological, with Catholic citizens who are compelled by law to pay taxes for public schools, and also feel constrained by conscience and discipline to support other schools for their own children. Such relief to them as this case involves is not in itself a serious burden to taxpayers and I had assumed it to be as little serious in principle. Study of this case convinces me otherwise. The Court's opinion marshals every argument in favor of state aid and puts the case in its most favorable light, but much of its reasoning confirms my conclusions that there are no good grounds upon which to support the present legislation. In fact, the undertones of the opinion, advocating complete and uncompromising separation of Church from State, seem utterly discordant with its conclusion yielding support to their commingling in educational matters. The case which irresistibly comes to mind as the most fitting precedent is that of Julia who, according to Byron's reports, "whispering 'I will ne'er consent,'—consented.''...

If we are to decide this case on the facts before us, our question is simply this: Is it constitutional to tax this complainant to pay the cost of carrying pupils to Church schools of one specified denomination?

Whether the taxpayer constitutionally can be made to contribute aid to parents of students because of their attendance at parochial schools depends upon the nature of those schools and their relation to the Church. The Constitution says nothing of education. It lays no obligation on the states to provide schools and does not undertake to regulate state systems of education if they see fit to maintain them. But they cannot, through school policy any more than through other means, invade rights secured to citizens by the Constitution of the United States.... One of our basic rights is to be free of taxation to support a transgression of the constitutional command that the authorities "shall make no law respecting an establishment of religion, or prohibiting the free exercise thereof...."...

The function of the Church school is a subject on which this record is meager. It shows only that the schools are under superintendence of a priest and that "religion is taught as part of the curriculum." But we know that such schools are parochial only in name—they, in fact, represent a world-wide and age-old policy of the Roman Catholic Church....

It is no exaggeration to say that the whole historic conflict in temporal policy between the Catholic Church and non-Catholics comes to a focus in their respective school policies. The Roman Catholic Church, counseled by experience in many ages and many lands and with all sorts and conditions of men, takes what, from the viewpoint of its own progress and the success of its mission, is a wise estimate of the importance of education to religion. It does not leave the individual to pick up religion by chance. It relies on early and indelible indoctrination in the faith and order of the Church by the word and example of persons consecrated to the task....

I should be surprised if any Catholic would deny that the parochial school is a vital, if not the most vital, part of the Roman Catholic Church. If put to the choice, that venerable institution, I should expect, would forego its whole service for mature persons before it would give up education of the young, and it would be a wise choice. Its growth and cohesion, discipline and loyalty, spring from its schools. Catholic education is the rock on which the whole structure rests, and to render tax aid to its Church school is indistinguishable to me from rendering the same aid to the Church itself....

The Court, however, compares this to other subsidies and loans to individuals and says, "Nor does it follow that a law has a private rather than a public purpose because it provides that tax-raised funds will be paid to reimburse individuals on account of money spent by them in a way which furthers a public program...." Of course, the state may pay out tax-raised funds to relieve pauperism, but it may not under our Constitution do so to induce or reward piety. It may spend funds to secure old age against want, but it may not spend funds to secure religion against skepticism. It may compensate individuals for loss of employment, but it cannot compensate them for adherence to a creed.

It seems to me that the basic fallacy in the Court's reasoning, which accounts for its failure to apply the principles it avows, is in ignoring the essentially religious test by which beneficiaries of this expenditure are selected. A policeman protects a Catholic, of course—but not because he is a Catholic; it is because he is a man and a member of our society. The fireman protects the Church school—but not because it is a Church school; it is because it is property, part of the assets of our society. Neither the fireman nor the policeman has to ask before he renders aid "Is this man or building identified with the Catholic Church?" But before these school authorities draw a check to reimburse for a student's fare they must ask just that question, and if the school is a Catholic one they may render aid because it is such, while if it is of any other faith or is run for profit, the help must be withheld. To consider the converse of the Court's reasoning will best disclose its fallacy. That there is no parallel between police and fire protection and this plan of reimbursement is apparent from the incongruity of the limitation of this Act if applied to police and fire service. Could we sustain an Act that said the police shall protect pupils on the way to or from public schools and Catholic schools but not while going to and coming from other schools, and firemen shall extinguish a blaze in public or Catholic school buildings but shall not put out a blaze in Protestant Church schools or private schools operated for profit? That is the true analogy to the case we have before us and I should think it pretty plain that such a scheme would not be valid.

The Court's holding is that this taxpayer has no grievance because the state has decided to make the reimbursement a public purpose and therefore we are bound to regard it as such. I agree that this Court has left, and always should leave to each state, great latitude in deciding for itself, in the light of its own conditions, what shall be public purposes in its scheme of things. It may socialize utilities and economic enterprises and make taxpayers' business out of what conventionally had been private business. It may make public business of individual welfare, health, education, entertainment or security. But it cannot make public business of religious worship or instruction, or of attendance at religious institutions of any character.

MR. JUSTICE FRANKFURTER joins in this opinion.

MR. JUSTICE RUTLEDGE, with whom MR. JUSTICE FRANKFURTER, MR. JUSTICE JACKSON and MR. JUSTICE BURTON agree, dissenting.

"Congress shall make no law respecting an establishment of religion, or prohibiting the free exercise thereof...." U.S. Const., Amend. I....
"We, the General Assembly, do enact, That no man shall be compelled to frequent or support any religious worship, place, or ministry whatsoever, nor shall be enforced, restrained, molested, or burthened in his body or goods, nor shall otherwise suffer, on account of his religious opinions or belief...."*

I cannot believe that the great author of those words, or the men who made them law, could have joined in this decision. Neither so high nor so impregnable today as yesterday is the wall raised between church and state by Virginia's great statute of religious freedom and the First Amendment, now made applicable to all the states by the Fourteenth....

Not simply an established church, but any law respecting an establishment of religion is forbidden. The Amendment was broadly but not loosely phrased. It is the compact and exact summation of its author's views formed during his long struggle for religious freedom....

The Amendment's purpose was not to strike merely at the official establishment of a single sect, creed or religion, outlawing only a formal relation such as had prevailed in England and some of the colonies. Necessarily it was to uproot all such relationships. But the object was broader than separating church and state in this narrow sense. It was to create a complete and permanent separation of the spheres of religious activity and civil authority by comprehensively forbidding every form of public aid or support for religion. In proof the Amendment's wording and history unite with this Court's consistent utterances whenever attention has been fixed directly upon the question....

No provision of the Constitution is more closely tied to or given content by its generating history than the religious clause of the First Amendment. It is at once the refined product and the terse summation of that history. The history includes not only Madison's authorship and the pro-

*"A Bill for Establishing Religious Freedom," enacted by the General Assembly of Virginia, January 19, 1786....

ceedings before the First Congress, but also the long and intensive struggle for religious freedom in America, more especially in Virginia, of which the Amendment was the direct culmination. In the documents of the times, particularly of Madison, who was leader in the Virginia struggle before he became the Amendment's sponsor, but also in the writings of Jefferson and others and in the issues which engendered them is to be found irrefutable confirmation of the Amendment's sweeping content. . . .

As the Remonstrance discloses throughout, Madison opposed every form and degree of official relation between religion and civil authority. For him religion was a wholly private matter beyond the scope of civil power either to restrain or to support. Denial or abridgment of religious freedom was a violation of rights both of conscience and of natural equality. State aid was no less obnoxious or destructive to freedom and to religion itself than other forms of state interference. "Establishment" and "free exercise" were correlative and coextensive ideas, representing only different facets of the single great and fundamental freedom. The Remonstrance, following the Virginia statute's example, referred to the history of religious conflicts and the effects of all sorts of establishments, current and historical, to suppress religion's free exercise. With Jefferson, Madison believed that to tolerate any fragment of establishment would be by so much to perpetuate restraint upon that freedom. Hence he sought to tear out the institution not partially but root and branch, and to bar its return forever. . . .

Does New Jersey's action furnish support for religion by use of the taxing power? Certainly it does, if the test remains undiluted as Jefferson and Madison made it, that money taken by taxation from one is not to be used or given to support another's religious training or belief, or indeed one's own. Today as then the furnishing of "contributions of money for the propagation of opinions which he disbelieves" is the forbidden exaction; and the prohibition is absolute for whatever measure brings that consequence and whatever amount may be sought or given to that end.

The funds used here were raised by taxation. The Court does not dispute, nor could it, that their use does in fact give aid and encouragement to religious instruction. It only concludes that this aid is not "support" in law. But Madison and Jefferson were concerned with aid and support in fact,

not as a legal conclusion "entangled in precedents." Here parents pay money to send their children to parochial schools and funds raised by taxation are used to reimburse them. This not only helps the children to get to school and the parents to send them. It aids them in a substantial way to get the very thing which they are sent to the particular school to secure, namely, religious training and teaching. . . .

New Jersey's action therefore exactly fits the type of exaction and the kind of evil at which Madison and Jefferson struck. Under the test they framed it cannot be said that the cost of transportation is no part of the cost of education or of the religious instruction given. That it is a substantial and a necessary element is shown most plainly by the continuing and increasing demand for the state to assume it. Nor is there pretense that it relates only to the secular instruction given in religious schools or that any attempt is or could be made toward allocating proportional shares as between the secular and the religious instruction. It is precisely because the instruction is religious and relates to a particular faith, whether one or another, that parents send their children to religious schools. . . . And the very purpose of the state's contribution is to defray the cost of conveying the pupil to the place where he will receive not simply secular, but also and primarily religious, teaching and guidance.

Indeed the view is sincerely avowed by many of various faiths, that the basic purpose of all education is or should be religious, that the secular cannot be and should not be separated from the religious phase and emphasis. Hence, the inadequacy of public or secular education and the necessity for sending the child to a school where religion is taught. But whatever may be the philosophy or its justification, there is undeniably an admixture of religious with secular teaching in all such institutions. . . .

Yet this very admixture is what was disestablished when the First Amendment forbade "an establishment of religion." Commingling the religious with the secular teaching does not divest the whole of its religious permeation and emphasis or make them of minor part, if proportion were material. Indeed, on any other view, the constitutional prohibition always could be brought to naught by adding a modicum of the secular. . . .

No one conscious of religious values can be unsympathetic toward the burden which our constitutional separation puts on parents who desire religious instruction mixed with secular for their children. They pay taxes for others' children's education, at the same time the added cost of instruction for their own. Nor can one happily see benefits denied to children which others receive, because in conscience they or their parents for them desire a different kind of training others do not demand.

But if those feelings should prevail, there would be an end to our historic constitutional policy and command. No more unjust or discriminatory in fact is it to deny attendants at religious schools the cost of their transportation than it is to deny them tuitions, sustenance for their teachers, or any other educational expense which others receive at public cost. Hardship in fact there is which none can blink. But, for assuring to those who undergo it the greater, the most comprehensive freedom, it is one written by design and firm intent into our basic law....

Two great drives are constantly in motion to abridge, in the name of education, the complete division of religion and civil authority which our forefathers made. One is to introduce religious education and observances into the public schools. The other, to obtain public funds for the aid and support of various private religious schools. In my opinion both avenues were closed by the Constitution. Neither should be opened by this Court. The matter is not one of quantity, to be measured by the amount of money expended. Now as in Madison's day it is one of principle, to keep separate the separate spheres as the First Amendment drew them; to prevent the first experiment upon our liberties; and to keep the question from becoming entangled in corrosive precedents. We should not be less strict to keep strong and untarnished the one side of the shield of religious freedom than we have been of the other.

The judgment should be reversed.

The Court's decision in *Everson* is notable for a number of reasons. First, it applied the religious establishment clause to the states, an important step because the Court had not received many cases in this area. With incorporation, the Court now opened the gates to challenges to state and local practices on establishment grounds. After nearly 150 years of dor-

mancy, the Establishment Clause would become, on average, an annual issue for the justices.

Second, Black's opinion etches into law that interpretation of Madison's and Jefferson's philosophies that suggests their desire for a strong wall of separation of church and state. Black even quoted Jefferson's comment that the clause was intended to build "a wall of separation between Church and State," thereby "constitutionalizing" the phrase.[47] Although Black's opinion does not lay down a concrete legal standard, it stresses several fundamental ideas, most notably that the aid was secular in purpose (it was going to parents, not a religious body, for a nonreligious expense); that the beneficiaries of the aid were children (not churches); and that the state was "neutral in its relations with groups of religious believers and non-believers" (public and private school children were eligible for aid). As we shall see, these themes recur in later Court opinions and foreshadow aspects of a legal standard the Court eventually formulates.

Third, *Everson* provides the first indication of the sensitive and salient nature of religious establishment questions. After the Court issued its ruling, Roman Catholic bishops in the United States mounted a public attack on it. Even though the decision supported reimbursements for costs incurred in sending children to Catholic schools, the bishops lambasted the justices for fundamentally misconstruing Jefferson's position on church and state. They argued that the Founders supported view 2 (nonpreferential treatment), and not view 1 as the Court implied. In the bishops' words: "the First Amendment means only that the Federal government may not prefer one religion over another."[48]

Finally, and perhaps most important, *Everson* indi-

47. It is interesting to note that the Court, in *Reynolds v. United States*, also quoted Jefferson on this point. Scholars and other justices, however, point to Black's opinion as etching this into law because the *Reynolds* Court was more interested in applying another part of Jefferson's passage.
48. Quoted in *Bill of Rights Reader* by Milton R. Konvitz (Ithaca, N.Y.: Cornell University Press, 1973), 31.

cates the divisive and complex nature of religious establishment questions. On the one hand, all the justices—the majority and dissenters alike—agreed with Black's portrayal of the intent of the Framers. In other words, the entire Court believed that Jefferson and Madison preferred strict separation of church and state. On the other hand—and this is the crux of the matter—the justices applied that historical framework to reach wholly disparate conclusions about the reimbursement plan. The majority, as Frank Sorauf put it, "succeeded ... in combining the strictest separationist rhetoric with an accommodationist outcome."[49] That is, Black's opinion, while adopting Jefferson's metaphor, found in favor of the township. The dissenters also advocated the same general approach, but thought it led to a disposition against the township. Indeed, they took Black to task for heading in one direction and landing in another. As Justice Jackson wrote in the opening paragraph of his dissent, the disparity between Black's rhetoric and outcome reminded him of Byron's Julia, who "whispering 'I will ne'er consent'—consented."[50]

That the adoption of a similar historical vision of religious establishment could lead to such disparate outcomes is a problem that continued to confound this area of the law at least through the Warren Court (and, as we shall see, crops up today). As Table 3-2 illustrates, between 1947 and 1968 the Court decided seven major cases involving the Establishment Clause. Three led to an accommodationist outcome (upholding a government policy challenged as a violation of the Establishment Clause), and four to a separationist outcome (striking down a government policy as a violation of the Establishment Clause). Many of these cases will be discussed in detail, but here we simply underscore several points.

The first is a reiteration: while the Court continued to adhere to Black's (and Rutledge's) historical

account of the separation between church and state, it was willing to uphold some kinds of support for religion, as it had in *Everson*, while ruling others unconstitutional. But, as Table 3-2 shows, a pattern began to emerge from the Court's rulings. The justices seemed more willing to tolerate *some* public support of private education, such as transporting children to school (*Everson*) and loaning textbooks (*Board of Education v. Allen*, 1968) than it was to legitimize the entry of religion into public education, such as prayer in school (*Abington School District v. Schempp*, 1963) and the teaching of creationism (*Epperson v. Arkansas*, 1968). Whether this trend continued during the Burger Court is a subject we consider in the next section.

Another point highlighted in Table 3-2 is this: after *Everson*, the Court began to formulate a test, flowing from Jefferson's metaphor and Black's decision in *Everson*, to determine whether government actions violated the Establishment Clause. During the Warren Court era, that test received its fullest articulation in *Abington Township*. (Near the end of this chapter, we examine in some detail all of the Court's important decisions involving prayer in school.) Writing for the majority, Justice Tom C. Clark explained that standard:

The test may be stated as follows: What are the purpose and primary effect of the enactment? If either is the advancement or inhibition of religion then the enactment exceeds the scope of legislative power as circumscribed by the Constitution. That is to say that to withstand the strictures of the Establishment Clause there must be a secular legislative purpose and a primary effect that neither advances nor inhibits religion.

With these words, Clark did what Black had failed to do in *Everson*: provide attorneys and lower court judges with a benchmark for future litigation and decisions.

Early on, some analysts argued that this standard would always lead to separationist outcomes. These scholars thought it would be difficult for government attorneys to show that their policies met the two-pronged standard reached in *Abington*: that the policy

49. Frank Sorauf, *The Wall of Separation* (Princeton: Princeton University Press, 1976), 20.
    50. Ibid.

TABLE 3-2 Major Religious Establishment Cases from *Everson* Through the Warren Court

Case	Issue	Vote (Outcome)	Rationale
Everson v. Board of Education (1947)	Reimbursement for transportation costs incurred by parents sending their children to private schools	5–4 (accommodationist)	secular purpose; child benefits; neutral
Illinois ex rel. McCollum v. Board of Education (1948)	Time-release program in which religious instructors come to public school weekly and provide religious training	8–1 (separationist)	State provides "invaluable aid" to religion
Zorach v. Clauson (1952)	Time-release program in which students are released an hour or so early each week to obtain religious instruction off school premises	6–3 (accommodationist)	State and religion need not be "hostile, suspicious, and even unfriendly"
Engel v. Vitale (1962)	Prayer, recited by public school children each morning, written by state's board of regents	8–1 (separationist)	Government cannot be in the prayer-writing business
School District of Abington Township v. Schempp (1963)	Reading of the Lord's Prayer and verses from the Bible in public schools	8–1 (separationist)	Public school prayer does not have (1) a secular legislative purpose or (2) a primary purpose that neither advances nor inhibits religion
Board of Education v. Allen (1968)	Public school loans of secular textbooks to students attending private schools	6–3 (accommodationist)	Primary purpose of the law furthers education, not religion
Epperson v. Arkansas (1968)	Barring the teaching of evolutionary theory in public schools	9–0 (separationist)	Not neutral; nonsecular purpose

has a secular legislative purpose and that its primary effect neither advances nor inhibits religion. But, as Table 3-2 shows, those commentators were wrong. In *Allen*, for example, the Court considered a New York state requirement that public schools lend, upon request, secular books to private school students in the seventh to twelfth grades. Attorneys for the American Civil Liberties Union argued that the requirement violated the Establishment Clause, but the Court disagreed. Writing for a six-person majority, Justice Byron R. White asserted:

The express purpose [of the law] was stated by the New York legislature to be furtherance of the educational opportunities available to the young. Appellants have shown us nothing about the necessary effects of the statute that is contrary to this stated purpose. The law merely makes available to all children the benefits of a general program to lend school books free of charge. Perhaps free books make it more likely that some children choose to attend a sectarian school, but that was true of the state-paid bus fare in *Everson* and does not alone demonstrate an unconstitutional degree of support for a religious institution.

In other words, White used the *Abington* "purpose" prong to reach an accommodationist outcome. Three justices, Douglas, Fortas, and Black, the author of *Everson*, dissented. Both Black and Douglas differentiated between the kind of aid at issue in *Everson* (reimbursement for transportation costs) and in *Allen* (book loans). As Douglas put it: "Whatever may be said of *Everson,* there is nothing ideological about a bus.... [But] the textbook goes to the very heart of education in a parochial school. It is the chief, although not solitary, instrumentality for propagating a particular religious creed or faith. How can we possibly approve such state aid to a religion?" Apparently there was some truth to this perspective. Several years before the Court handed down *Allen,* Professor George La Noue published a study examining books used in Catholic schools. The following are extracts he took from textbooks used to teach mathematics, presumably a secular course:

• How much money must I have to buy these four books? *Poems About the Christ Child,* $1.85; *Story of Our Lady,* $2.25; *Saint Joseph,* $1.05; *Saint Theresa,* $2.00?

• The children of St. Francis School ransomed 125 pagan babies last year. This year they hope to increase this number by 20%. If they succeed, how many babies will they ransom this year?

• David sells subscriptions to the *Catholic Digest* on a commission basis of 20%. If the subscription is $2.50 a year what is David's commission on each sale?[51]

The third point about the Warren Court's handling of religious establishment cases is that although the justices generally adopted Jefferson's "wall of separation" metaphor and agreed on the test for adjudicating Establishment Clause cases, they continued to split on case outcomes. Note the votes depicted in Table 3-2: with the exception of cases centering on prayer and teaching religious principles in schools, from *Everson* through *Allen,* the justices were divided over the resolution of cases.

Enter the Burger Court and a "New" Legal Standard

By the time Warren Burger became chief justice in 1969, observers predicted that the Court would change its approach to adjudicating Establishment

Clause cases. Although the justices generally coalesced around the *Everson* historical understanding and the *Abington* standard, they were divided over how to apply those approaches to particular disputes. What is more, organized interests were reacting to perceived inconsistencies in the Court's handling of these cases and began pressing it to apply its standards with greater coherency. Some of these interests—separationist groups, such as the American Civil Liberties Union and Americans United for Separation of Church and State—were pushing the Court to reach outcomes in line with what they perceived to be the dominant philosophical strand running through past establishment cases: a strict separation of church and state. Others—accommodationist interests—were asking the Court to move in precisely the opposite direction *(see Box 3-3).* Either way, these competing groups were unrelenting in bringing cases to the Court's attention and compounding its problems in the area.

In addition, observers expected that the new chief justice, Warren Burger, would be more inclined than his predecessor, Earl Warren, to rule with the government in many areas of the law. Analysts predicted that Burger would push for wholesale changes in the Court's approaches to cases involving liberties, rights, and justice. Most of this speculation centered on criminal law because one of the primary reasons President Nixon appointed Burger was to turn back the Warren Court's liberal rulings in this area. But, as it turned out, the new chief justice had a strong interest in taking a leadership role in religion cases. In fact, Burger was so determined to exert influence over this area of the law that during his tenure on the Court (1969–1985 terms), he wrote 69 percent (eighteen of twenty-six) of the Court's majority opinions dealing with religion, a much higher percentage than his overall rate of 20 percent in all formally decided cases.[52]

What was Burger's "understanding" of the Es-

---

51. Quoted in *Religion, State, and the Burger Court* by Leo Pfeffer (Buffalo, N.Y.: Prometheus Books, 1984), 35. The article was published in a 1962 edition of the *Harvard Education Review.*

52. Joseph F. Kobylka, "Leadership in the Supreme Court: Chief Justice Burger and Establishment Clause Litigation," *Western Political Quarterly* 42 (December 1989): 545.

BOX 3-3 CLASHING INTERESTS IN THE COURTS: SEPARATIONIST V. ACCOMMODATIONIST INTEREST GROUPS IN RELIGIOUS ESTABLISHMENT LITIGATION

Since the 1940s, but with increasing regularity in more recent decades, organized interests have sought to influence the Supreme Court's adjudication of cases involving religion. The data below well illustrate this point by depicting growth in amicus curiae participation in this area.

Terms	Percentage of Cases in Which One or More Groups Filed Amicus Curiae Briefs	Total Number of Cases
1941–1952	21.4%	42
1953–1966	44.4	18
1970–1980	62.9	35
1986–1992	100.0	21

Growth in participation is not the only interest group trend in this area. With each passing decade, it has become more likely that organized interests participate on both sides of religious establishment cases in particular. Generally speaking, these interests belong to one of two camps: separationist groups that want a strict separation of church and state and accommodationist groups that support greater intermingling between political and religious institutions. Below we provide information about the particular groups belonging to these competing coalitions.

Examples of Separationist Groups

Group	Year of Formation	Reason for Litigating Religious Establishment Clause Cases
American Civil Liberties Union	1920	Formed to defend rights and liberties generally, with religious establishment litigation representing just one of its concerns.
American Jewish Congress	1918	Dedicated to protecting civil rights and liberties of all Americans, particularly Jewish Americans, whom it views as adversely affected by intermingling between church and state.
Americans United for Separation of Church and State	1947	Formed in response to *Everson* to revitalize the principle of separation between church and state.
PEARL[a]	1968	Formed in the aftermath of *Allen,* viewing the decision as "an invitation [to legislatures] to enact laws financing parochial school operations beyond merely the cost of secular textbooks" (Pfeffer, 25).

A great deal of cooperative effort takes place among these groups. As detailed by Frank Sorauf, the first three joined forces in the early 1950s to fight what they perceived as a growing public and legal sentiment (particularly the Court decision in *McCollum* in which it upheld a released-time program) to break down the wall of separation. PEARL is a coalition representing many other groups. Cooperation among separationist groups remains high; for example, the American Jewish Congress provided supporting amicus curiae briefs for the ACLU in nearly 90 percent of its litigation efforts between 1986 and 1990 (Epstein, 670).

(Continued on page 142)

BOX 3-3 *(continued)*

Examples of Accommodationist Groups

Group	Year of Formation	Reason for Litigating Religious Establishment Clause Cases
U.S. Catholic Conference	1968	Formed to serve as the chief speaker of "American bishops on matters of social and educational policy"; litigates to bring about greater accommodation between church and state (Sorauf, 185).
Christian Legal Society	1976	Dedicated to supporting state accommodation of religious beliefs.
COLPA[b]	1965	Formed to represent the interest of Orthodox American Jews, whose interests are often divergent from those of other Jewish groups, such as the American Jewish Congress; litigates to "combat . . . separatism" (Sorauf, 189).

These are just a few of the many groups bringing an accommodationist perspective to the Court. Others, including the Rutherford Institute and the Catholic League for Religious and Civil Rights, have been very active amicus curiae participants. Like their separationist counterparts, these interests often cooperate in their litigation activities; for example, between 1986 and 1990, the Christian Legal Society filed amicus curiae briefs in 86 percent of those cases in which the Rutherford Institute also participated as an amicus (Epstein, 670).

Works cited: Lee Epstein, "Interest Group Litigation during the Rehnquist Court Era," *The Journal of Law and Politics* 4 (1993): 639–717; Frank J. Sorauf, *The Wall of Separation* (Princeton: Princeton University Press), 1976; and Leo Pfeffer, *Religion, State, and the Burger Court* (Buffalo, N.Y.: Prometheus Books, 1984).

a. PEARL stands for the New York Committee for Public Education and Religious Liberty. It is an umbrella organization for dozens of religious and community groups.

b. COLPA stands for the National Jewish Commission on Law and Public Affairs.

tablishment Clause? How did he seek to change the law? Was he successful? We can begin to address these questions by considering Burger's first two religious establishment cases, *Walz v. Tax Commission of the City of New York* (1970) and *Lemon v. Kurtzman* (1971).

Walz involved the property tax exemptions enjoyed by religious institutions. Frederick Walz bought a small, useless lot on Staten Island, New York, for the sole purpose of challenging the state's tax laws, which gave religious organizations exemptions from property taxes. Walz contended that the tax exemptions resulted in property owners making involuntary contributions to churches in violation of the Establishment Clause. After losing in the lower courts, Walz and his ACLU attorneys appealed to the U.S. Supreme Court, arguing that both the majority and dissenting opinions in *Everson* supported their position: "The

First Amendment's objective was to create a complete and permanent separation of the sphere of religious activity and civil authority by comprehensively . . . forbidding any form of . . . support for religion." New York pointed to the fact that all fifty states had property tax exemptions for religious organizations. It also asserted that "Religious property exemptions have played an integral part of public policy in New York. The role of religious organizations as charitable associations, in furthering the state, has become a fundamental concept in our society."[53]

Writing for a seven-person majority (only Justice Douglas dissented), Chief Justice Burger found in favor of the state. The outcome was not so surprising; after all, had the Court ruled the other way, the tax status of

53. For more on *Walz*, see Sorauf, *The Wall of Separation*.

every religious institution in the United States would have been dramatically altered. The startling aspect of *Walz* was that Burger, in his first writing on the Establishment Clause, sought to usher in a major change. The opinion started traditionally enough, with an examination of the "purpose" prong of *Abington:*

The legislative purpose of property tax exemptions is neither the advancement nor the inhibition of religion; it is neither sponsorship nor hostility. New York, in common with the other States, has determined that certain entities that exist in a harmonious relationship to the community at large, and that foster its "moral or mental improvement," should not be inhibited in their activities by property taxation or the hazard of loss of those properties for nonpayment of taxes.

But, instead of exploring whether the effect of the legislation inhibited or advanced religion, as the *Abington* standard specified, Burger suggested the following:

Determining that the legislative purpose of tax exemption is not aimed at establishing, sponsoring, or supporting religion does not end the inquiry, however. We must also be sure that the end result—the effect—is not *an excessive government entanglement* with religion [emphasis added].

He went on to hold that property tax exemptions did not create an excessive entanglement with religion: to the contrary, even though tax exemptions to churches "necessarily operate to afford an indirect economic benefit," involvement with religion would be far greater if the exemptions did not exist. State officials might occasionally want to examine church records, or they might need to speak with clergy about expenditures, and so forth. As Burger concluded, the tax exemption "restricts the fiscal relationship between church and state, and tends to complement and reinforce the desired separation insulating each from the other."

In the end, then, *Walz* probably raised more questions about Burger and the fate of Establishment Clause litigation than it answered. Did Burger seek to redesign the *Abington* standard—through adoption of an "excessive entanglement" criteria—as a way to

bring down the wall of separation between church and state? Would excessive entanglement now become a part of the Court's analytic toolbag for examining establishment claims? Or would the majority of the justices favor a return to a strict reading of *Abington?* Consider these questions as you read *Lemon v. Kurtzman* and its companion case, *Earley v. DiCenso.*

Lemon v. Kurtzman
Earley v. DiCenso

403 U.S. 602 (1971)
Vote in Lemon: 8 (Black, Blackmun, Brennan, Burger, Douglas, Harlan, Stewart, White)
0
Opinion of the Court: Burger
Concurring opinions: Brennan, White
Not participating: Marshall
Vote in DiCenso: 8 (Black, Blackmun, Brennan, Burger, Douglas, Harlan, Marshall, Stewart)
1 (White)
Opinion of the Court: Burger
Concurring opinion: Douglas
Dissenting opinion: White

Lemon v. Kurtzman (The Pennsylvania Program). With the assistance of numerous organized interests, including the Pennsylvania Civil Liberties Union, the American Jewish Congress, the NAACP, and the Pennsylvania Educational Association, Alton Lemon brought suit against David Kurtzman, state superintendent of schools. Lemon wanted the court to declare unconstitutional a Pennsylvania law that authorized Kurtzman to "purchase" secular educational services from nonpublic schools. Under this law, the superintendent would use state taxes levied on cigarettes to reimburse nonpublic schools for expenses incurred for teachers' salaries, textbooks, and instructional materials. The state authorized such funding with certain restrictions: it would pay for secular expenses only, that is, secular books and teachers' salaries for the same courses taught in public schools.

To receive payments, schools had to keep separate records, identifying secular and nonsecular expenses.

The act took effect in July 1968. Up to the time the Court heard the case, Pennsylvania had spent about $5 million annually. It reimbursed expenses at 1,181 nonpublic elementary and secondary schools accounting for about a half million students, around 20 percent of the school population. About 96 percent of the nonpublic school students attended religious schools, primarily Roman Catholic.

Earley v. DiCenso (The Rhode Island Program). In this case, the American Jewish Congress challenged the Rhode Island Salary Supplement Act. Aimed at improving the quality of private education, this law supplemented the salaries of teachers of secular subjects in private elementary schools up to 15 percent of their current salaries with the restriction that payments could be made only to those who agreed in writing not to teach religious subjects and salaries could not exceed the maximum salaries paid to public school instructors. The AJC challenged this law as a violation of the Establishment Clause, in part because 95 percent of the schools falling under the terms of the act were affiliated with the Roman Catholic church. Moreover, all of the 250 teachers who had applied for salary supplements worked at Roman Catholic schools. And, as evidence submitted at trial indicated, about two-thirds of them "were nuns of various religious orders."[54]

MR. CHIEF JUSTICE BURGER delivered the opinion of the Court.

These two appeals raise questions as to Pennsylvania and Rhode Island statutes providing state aid to church-related elementary and secondary schools. Both statutes are challenged as violative of the Establishment and Free Exercise Clauses of the First Amendment and the Due Process Clause of the Fourteenth Amendment....

54. See Pfeffer, *Religion, State, and the Burger Court*, 27.

In Everson v. Board of Education (1947), this Court upheld a state statute that reimbursed the parents of parochial school children for bus transportation expenses. There MR. JUSTICE BLACK, writing for the majority, suggested that the decision carried to "the verge" of forbidden territory under the Religion Clauses. Candor compels acknowledgment, moreover, that we can only dimly perceive the lines of demarcation in this extraordinarily sensitive area of constitutional law.

The language of the Religion Clauses of the First Amendment is at best opaque, particularly when compared with other portions of the Amendment. Its authors did not simply prohibit the establishment of a state church or a state religion, an area history shows they regarded as very important and fraught with great dangers. Instead they commanded that there should be "no law *respecting* an establishment of religion." A law may be one "respecting" the forbidden objective while falling short of its total realization. A law "respecting" the proscribed result, that is, the establishment of religion, is not always easily identifiable as one violative of the Clause. A given law might not establish a state religion but nevertheless be one "respecting" that end in the sense of being a step that could lead to such establishment and hence offend the First Amendment.

In the absence of precisely stated constitutional prohibitions, we must draw lines with reference to the three main evils against which the Establishment Clause was intended to afford protection: "sponsorship, financial support, and active involvement of the sovereign in religious activity." Walz v. Tax Commission (1970).

Every analysis in this area must begin with consideration of the cumulative criteria developed by the Court over many years. Three such tests may be gleaned from our cases. First, the statute must have a secular legislative purpose; second, its principal or primary effect must be one that neither advances nor inhibits religion; finally, the statute must not foster "an excessive government entanglement with religion."

Inquiry into the legislative purposes of the Pennsylvania and Rhode Island statutes affords no basis for a conclusion that the legislative intent was to advance religion. On the contrary, the statutes themselves clearly state that they are intended to enhance the quality of the secular education in all schools covered by the compulsory attendance laws.

There is no reason to believe the legislatures meant anything else. A State always has a legitimate concern for maintaining minimum standards in all schools it allows to operate. As in *Allen*, we find nothing here that undermines the stated legislative intent; it must therefore be accorded appropriate deference.

In *Allen* the Court acknowledged that secular and religious teachings were not necessarily so intertwined that secular textbooks furnished to students by the State were in fact instrumental in the teaching of religion. The legislatures of Rhode Island and Pennsylvania have concluded that secular and religious education are identifiable and separable. In the abstract we have no quarrel with this conclusion.

The two legislatures, however, have also recognized that church-related elementary and secondary schools have a significant religious mission and that a substantial portion of their activities is religiously oriented. They have therefore sought to create statutory restrictions designed to guarantee the separation between secular and religious educational functions and to ensure that State financial aid supports only the former. All these provisions are precautions taken in candid recognition that these programs approached, even if they did not intrude upon, the forbidden areas under the Religion Clauses. We need not decide whether these legislative precautions restrict the principal or primary effect of the programs to the point where they do not offend the Religion Clauses, for we conclude that the cumulative impact of the entire relationship arising under the statutes in each State involves excessive entanglement between government and religion.

In Walz v. Tax Commission, the Court upheld state tax exemptions for real property owned by religious organizations and used for religious worship. That holding, however, tended to confine rather than enlarge the area of permissible state involvement with religious institutions by calling for close scrutiny of the degree of entanglement involved in the relationship. The objective is to prevent, as far as possible, the intrusion of either into the precincts of the other....

In order to determine whether the government entanglement with religion is excessive, we must examine the character and purposes of the institutions that are benefited, the nature of the aid that the State provides, and the resulting relationship between the government and the religious authority.... Here we find that both statutes foster an impermissible degree of entanglement.

Rhode Island program

The District Court made extensive findings on the grave potential for excessive entanglement that inheres in the religious character and purpose of the Roman Catholic elementary schools of Rhode Island, to date the sole beneficiaries of the Rhode Island Salary Supplement Act.

The church schools involved in the program are located close to parish churches. This understandably permits convenient access for religious exercises since instruction in faith and morals is part of the total educational process. The school buildings contain identifying religious symbols such as crosses on the exterior and crucifixes, and religious paintings and statues either in the classrooms or hallways. Although only approximately 30 minutes a day are devoted to direct religious instruction, there are religiously oriented extracurricular activities. Approximately two-thirds of the teachers in these schools are nuns of various religious orders. Their dedicated efforts provide an atmosphere in which religious instruction and religious vocations are natural and proper parts of life in such schools. Indeed, as the District Court found, the role of teaching nuns in enhancing the religious atmosphere has led the parochial school authorities to attempt to maintain a one-to-one ratio between nuns and lay teachers in all schools rather than to permit some to be staffed almost entirely by lay teachers.

On the basis of these findings the District Court concluded that the parochial schools constituted "an integral part of the religious mission of the Catholic Church." The various characteristics of the schools make them "a powerful vehicle for transmitting the Catholic faith to the next generation." This process of inculcating religious doctrine is, of course, enhanced by the impressionable age of the pupils, in primary schools particularly. In short, parochial schools involve substantial religious activity and purpose....

The dangers and corresponding entanglements are enhanced by the particular form of aid that the Rhode Island Act provides. Our decisions from *Everson* to *Allen* have permitted the States to provide church-related schools with secular, neutral, or nonideological services, facilities, or materials. Bus transportation, school lunches, public health services, and secular textbooks supplied in common to all students were not thought to offend the Establishment Clause. We note that the dissenters in *Allen* seemed chiefly concerned with the pragmatic difficulties involved in ensuring the truly secular content of the textbooks provided at state expense....

In our view the record shows these dangers are present to a substantial degree. The Rhode Island Roman Catholic elementary schools are under the general supervision of the Bishop of Providence and his appointed representative, the Diocesan Superintendent of Schools. In most cases, each individual parish, however, assumes the ultimate financial responsibility for the school, with the parish priest authorizing the allocation of parish funds. With only two exceptions, school principals are nuns appointed either by the Superintendent or the Mother Provincial of the order whose members staff the school. By 1969 lay teachers constituted more than a third of all teachers in the parochial elementary schools, and their number is growing. They are first interviewed by the superintendent's office and then by the school principal. The contracts are signed by the parish priest, and he retains some discretion in negotiating salary levels. Religious authority necessarily pervades the school system.

The schools are governed by the standards set forth in a "Handbook of School Regulations," which has the force of synodal law in the diocese. It emphasizes the role and importance of the teacher in parochial schools: "The prime factor for the success or the failure of the school is the spirit and personality, as well as the professional competency, of the teacher...." The Handbook also states that: "Religious formation is not confined to formal courses; nor is it restricted to a single subject area." Finally, the Handbook advises teachers to stimulate interest in religious vocations and missionary work. Given the mission of the church school, these instructions are consistent and logical.

Several teachers testified, however, that they did not inject religion into their secular classes. And the District Court found that religious values did not necessarily affect the content of the secular instruction. But what has been recounted suggests the potential if not actual hazards of this form of state aid. The teacher is employed by a religious organization, subject to the direction and discipline of religious authorities, and works in a system dedicated to rearing children in a particular faith. These controls are not lessened by the fact that most of the lay teachers are of

the Catholic faith. Inevitably some of a teacher's responsibilities hover on the border between secular and religious orientation....

We do not assume, however, that parochial school teachers will be unsuccessful in their attempts to segregate their religious beliefs from their secular educational responsibilities. But the potential for impermissible fostering of religion is present. The Rhode Island Legislature has not, and could not, provide state aid on the basis of a mere assumption that secular teachers under religious discipline can avoid conflicts. The State must be certain, given the Religion Clauses, that subsidized teachers do not inculcate religion—indeed the State here has undertaken to do so. To ensure that no trespass occurs, the State has therefore carefully conditioned its aid with pervasive restrictions. An eligible recipient must teach only those courses that are offered in the public schools and use only those texts and materials that are found in the public schools. In addition the teacher must not engage in teaching any course in religion.

A comprehensive, discriminating, and continuing state surveillance will inevitably be required to ensure that these restrictions are obeyed and the First Amendment otherwise respected. Unlike a book, a teacher cannot be inspected once so as to determine the extent and intent of his or her personal beliefs and subjective acceptance of the limitations imposed by the First Amendment. These prophylactic contacts will involve excessive and enduring entanglement between state and church....

Pennsylvania program

The Pennsylvania statute also provides state aid to church-related schools for teachers' salaries. The complaint describes an educational system that is very similar to the one existing in Rhode Island. According to the allegations, the church-related elementary and secondary schools are controlled by religious organizations, have the purpose of propagating and promoting a particular religious faith, and conduct their operations to fulfill that purpose....

As we noted earlier, the very restrictions and surveillance necessary to ensure that teachers play a strictly nonideological role give rise to entanglements between church and state. The Pennsylvania statute, like that of Rhode Island, fosters this kind of relationship. Reimbursement is not only limited to courses offered in the public schools and materials approved by state officials, but the statute excludes "any subject matter expressing religious teaching, or the morals or forms of worship of any sect." In addition, schools seeking reimbursements must maintain accounting procedures that require the State to establish the cost of the secular as distinguished from the religious instruction.

The Pennsylvania statute, moreover, has the further defect of providing state financial aid directly to the church-related schools. This factor distinguishes both *Everson* and *Allen,* for in both those cases the Court was careful to point out that state aid was provided to the student and his parents—not to the church-related school.... The history of government grants of a continuing cash subsidy indicates that such programs have almost always been accompanied by varying measures of control and surveillance. The government cash grants before us now provide no basis for predicting that comprehensive measures of surveillance and controls will not follow. In particular the government's post-audit power to inspect and evaluate a church-related school's financial records and to determine which expenditures are religious and which are secular creates an intimate and continuing relationship between church and state....

The sole question is whether state aid to these schools can be squared with the dictates of the Religion Clauses. Under our system the choice has been made that government is to be entirely excluded from the area of religious instruction and churches excluded from the affairs of government. The Constitution decrees that religion must be a private matter for the individual, the family, and the institutions of private choice, and that while some involvement and entanglements are inevitable, lines must be drawn.

The judgment of the Rhode Island District Court ... is affirmed. The judgment of the Pennsylvania District Court ... is reversed, and the case is remanded for further proceedings consistent with this opinion.

The same day the Court handed down *Lemon,* it also decided *Tilton v. Richardson,* involving the constitutionality of the Higher Education Act. Passed by Congress in 1963, it provided building grants to colleges and universities so long as the facility would not be "used for sectarian instruction or a place for religious worship" for twenty years. Several taxpayers brought suit against four church-run colleges and universities, claiming that they should not have received aid because they were organized under religious authority and espoused religious doctrine. The schools countered that this point was irrelevant as they had used government funding exclusively for secular purposes; for example, Sacred Heart College had built a library, and Fairfield University, a science building.

A federal district court ruled that the schools had acted properly. After a court of appeals reversed, the colleges and universities appealed to the Supreme Court, asking this question: Does federal aid to religious universities for secular purposes violate the Religious Establishment Clause? Writing for a five-person majority, Burger held that it did not because it passed the three-pronged test. As he noted, the stated legislative purpose "expresses a legitimate secular objective to assist the nation's colleges and universities entirely appropriate for governmental action," that its "provisions ... will not advance religion," and that there are sufficiently "significant differences between religious aspects of church-related institutions of higher learning and parochial elementary and secondary schools" to nullify complaints of excessive entanglement. The Court, however, struck down the act's twenty- year provision.

What is the significance of *Lemon, DiCenso,* and *Tilton?* First, the trilogy cleared up some of the confusion created by *Walz* over legal standards governing Establishment Clause cases. It now seemed that the justices planned to adhere to a tripartite test, usually called the *Lemon* test: secular legislative purpose, primary effect, and excessive entanglement. None of these prongs is new. As Box 3-4 illustrates, they had their genesis in early Supreme Court cases. Second, because the *Lemon* test finds its roots in earlier Court decisions that were based on the belief that Madison and Jefferson envisioned a strict wall of separation be-

BOX 3-4 THE ROOTS OF THE *LEMON* TEST

Test	*Everson* (1947)	*Abington* (1963)	*Walz* (1970)	*Lemon* (1971)
Secular Purpose	The state ——————▶ has a legitimate, general interest in helping "parents get their children, regardless of their religion, safely and expeditiously to and from accredited schools."	What [is] ——————▶ the purpose . . . of the enactment? If [it] is the advancement or inhibition of religion then the enactment exceeds the scope of legislative power. . . . That is to say that to withstand the strictures of the Establishment Clause there must be secular legislative purpose."	"The ——————▶ legislative purpose of a property tax exemption is neither the advancement nor theinhibition of religion."	"The statute must have a secular legislative puposE."
Primary Effect	Governments cannot ——▶ "pass laws which aid one religion, aid all religions, or prefer one religion over another."	"What [is] . . . the primary effect of the enactment? If [it] is the advancement or inhibition of religion then the enactment exceeds the scope of legislative power. . . . That is to say that to withstand the strictures of the Establishment Clause there must be a . . . primary effect that neither advances nor inhibits religion."	——————▶	The statute's "principal or primary effect must be one that neither advances nor inhibits religion."
Excessive Entanglement			"We ——————▶ must . . . be sure that the end result—the effect—is not an excessive government entanglement with religion."	"The statute must not foster an excessive government entanglement with religion."

tween church and state, it seemed that the Court was not only following precedent but also reinforcing the historical understanding from which that precedent flowed. Yet, with the adoption of the *Lemon* test, that precedent led it to the separationist outcome it had not reached in *Everson* or *Allen,* the two major cases on aid to public schools.

If you are surprised that Chief Justice Burger, who at least in *Walz* seemed to want to lower the wall of separation, wrote these 1971 opinions, you are not alone. As separationist attorney Leo Pfeffer wrote, *Lemon* and *DiCenso* were "a shock, as if the world of aid on the elementary and secondary school levels had come to an end not with a whimper but with a great big bang; or as if a pitcher who did not allow a run through the first half of the ninth inning *(Walz v. Tax Commission)* turned around and, batting for the other side, hit the home run *(Lemon-DiCenso)* that ended the game in the bottom of the ninth." Other analysts are more critical of Burger. They point to contradictions between *Lemon* and a free exercise case, such as *Wisconsin v. Yoder,* in which Burger exempted the Amish from a compulsory state education law. As legal scholar Suzanna Sherry argues, in *Lemon* the Court read the Establishment Clause "to forbid government from preferring religion to non-religion" but, in *Yoder,* "the Court interpreted the Free Exercise Clause to require government to grant special exemptions for those who opposed general laws on religious grounds."[55] In other words, these cases illustrate a problem we mentioned at the beginning of the chapter: it is difficult to reconcile the two religion clauses of the First Amendment.

The enunciation of a legal standard by which to judge religious establishment claims raises some questions: Would the justices of the Burger Court and their successors continue to apply the *Lemon* test? Would it stand the test of time? In 1994 *Lemon* was

still good law, although many commentators would argue that its days are numbered. The three-pronged standard may continue to dominate Court adjudication of Establishment Clause claims, but this does not mean that the Court always applies *Lemon,* or that all of the justices subscribe to it and its historical underpinnings, or that different approaches have not been offered. Even when it has applied *Lemon,* the Court has not reached particularly consistent decisions.

The problem is that *Lemon* hangs on because a majority of justices have yet to coalesce behind an alternative standard, even though other standards have been proposed *(Table 3-3).* You will have further opportunities to consider these alternate standards and their proponents and *Lemon* in more detail. In the pages to come, we explore how the Court has approached four categories of religious establishment cases in the aftermath of *Lemon:* aid to religious schools, religion in public schools, holiday displays, and prayer in school. Because the Court delved into some of these areas prior to *Lemon,* you will discover trends in Court decision making in particular issues, such as prayer, over the past three decades.

Aid to Religious Schools

Questions concerning "parochiaid"—aid to religious schools—are among the most enduring of those raised in religious establishment litigation. Since *Everson,* the Court has struggled to define the parameters of government's commingling with nonpublic education.

Everson, Allen, Lemon-DiCenso, and *Tilton* provide early indications of those boundaries. But what has the Court done since 1971? At first it seemed that the Court would continue to apply the *Lemon* test, but not without dissent. For example, in *Committee for Public Education and Religious Liberty v. Nyquist* (1973), one of the first post-*Lemon* cases, separationist groups challenged a New York state law providing maintenance and repair funds for private schools on a per pupil basis and for tuition grants and tax credits. Writing

---

55. Suzanna Sherry, "Lee v. Weisman: Paradox Redux," *The Supreme Court Review,* 1990: 124.

TABLE 3-3 Religious Establishment Standards Advocated by Members of the Supreme Court, 1971–1993

Standard	Definition	Chief Supporters	Occasional Adherents
Lemon (1971)	"Every analysis in this area must begin with consideration of the cumulative criteria developed by the Court over many years. Three tests may be gleaned from our cases. First, the statute must have a secular legislative purpose; second, its principal or primary effect must be one that neither advances nor inhibits religion; finally, the statute must not foster an excessive government entanglement with religion." (Burger, majority opinion in *Lemon v. Kurtzman*)	Powell, Stewart	Burger, *Stevens, O'Connor*, Douglas, Marshall, *Blackmun*
Nonpreferentialism (1983)	"[T]he Establishment Clause . . . [forbids] establishment of a national religion, and [forbids] preference among religious sects or denominations." (Rehnquist, dissenting in *Wallace v. Jaffree*)	*Rehnquist*	*Scalia, Thomas,* White, Burger
Endorsement Approach to Lemon (1984)	"The Establishment Clause prohibits government from making adherence to a religion relevant in any person's standing in the political community. Government can run afoul of that prohibition in two principal ways. One is excessive entanglement with religious institutions. . . . The second and more direct infringement is government endorsement or disapproval of religion. . . . Under this view, *Lemon*'s inquiry as to the purpose and effect of a statute requires courts to consider whether government's purpose is to endorse religion and whether the statute actually conveys a message of endorsement." (O'Connor, concurring in *Lynch v. Donnelly* and in *Wallace v. Jaffree*)	*O'Connor*	*Blackmun, Stevens, Souter,* White
Coercion	"Our cases disclose two limiting principles: government may not coerce anyone to support or participate in any religion or its exercise; and it may not, in the guise of avoiding hostility or callous indifference, give direct benefits to a religion in such a degree that it in fact 'establishes a religion or religious faith, or tends to do so.'"	*Kennedy*	*Scalia, Thomas, Rehnquist,* White

NOTE: Justices in italic are members of the current Court. Ginsburg and Breyer are not depicted because (at the time of this writing) they had yet to write opinions in a religious establishment case. Also keep in mind that justices adhering to a particular approach do not always agree on its application in a given case. For example, Justices Scalia and Kennedy, who generally agree with the "coercion" standard, have vehemently disagreed over the kinds of coercion (such as psychological as the Founders understood it, and so forth) the Court should consider.

for the Court's majority, Justice Lewis F. Powell, Jr., struck down the law on the basis of the effect prong of *Lemon,* saying the law had "the impermissible effect of advancing the sectarian activities of religious schools." But Chief Justice Burger (along with Justices White and Rehnquist) dissented in part. Burger wrote:

> While there is no straight line running through our decisions interpreting the Establishment . . . Clause . . . our cases do, it seems . . . lay down one solid, basic principle: that the Establishment Clause does not forbid governments . . . to enact a program of general welfare . . . even though

many . . . elect to use those benefits in ways that "aid" religious instruction. . . . This fundamental principle which I see running through our prior decisions . . . is premised more on experience and history than logic.

This dissent illustrates Burger's second thoughts about the three-pronged test he helped to create and so eagerly applied in *Walz, Lemon,* and *Tilton.* What he now realized is that if the Court adhered strictly to it, as it did in *Nyquist,* his accommodationist approach to religion would not prevail. The test was too rigid to allow for many forms of intermingling between church and state, particularly in areas involving funding to elementary and secondary schools.

That Burger began to have doubts about the *Lemon* test, however, did not deter a majority of the justices from applying it, at least in the parochiaid cases coming after *Nyquist.* As Table 3-4, which lists all the important aid cases, indicates, *Lemon* dominates this category of Establishment Clause litigation. But, because of their use of the three-pronged standard, the justices have come in for much criticism from scholars who argue that they have made "distinctions that would glaze the minds of medieval scholastics."[56] Analysts also criticize the Court for its inability to achieve consensus over the application of *Lemon.* This area of the law is marked by dissenting and concurring opinions, and judgments of the Court, rather than majority opinions.

Meek v. Pittenger (1975) provides an illustration of both criticisms. Here the Court considered three kinds of support provided by the state of Pennsylvania to nonpublic schools: (1) "auxiliary services," including counseling, testing, speech and hearing therapy, and teaching services for "exceptional" and "remedial" students performed by public employees in private school facilities; (2) loans of secular instructional materials, such as periodicals, maps and charts, and equipment, such as film projectors and laboratory equipment, from public schools to private schools upon request; and (3) loans of secular textbooks from public schools to private school students. Writing for a fractured Court, Justice Potter Stewart used the *Lemon* test to find the first two kinds of support unconstitutional, while upholding the third. Justices Brennan, Marshall, and Douglas dissented from the portion of the opinion upholding the textbook loans; Burger, Rehnquist, and White dissented from those parts striking down auxiliary services and equipment/material loans. Almost all of the justices who

56. Leonard W. Levy, *The Establishment Clause* (New York: Macmillan, 1986), 128.

wrote separately—including Rehnquist and White, perhaps the most accommodationist-oriented of the Burger Court justices—used the *Lemon* standard to justify their divergent opinions. Only Chief Justice Burger, the author of *Lemon,* framed his opinion differently:

To hold, as the Court now does, that the Constitution permits the States to give special assistance to some of its children whose handicaps prevent their deriving benefit normally anticipated from the education required to be a productive member of society and, at the same time, to deny those benefits to other children *only because* they attend a Lutheran, Catholic, or other church-sponsored school does not simply tilt the Constitution against religion; it literally turns the Religion Clauses on their heads.

In concluding, Burger urged his colleagues, "at some future date," to "take a more realistic view of ... carefully limited aid to children" and to realize that such "is not a step toward establishing a state religion."

Nyquist, Meek, and many other cases, therefore, demonstrate that Chief Justice Burger grew discontent with the test he devised. They also indicate the malleable nature of *Lemon;* after all, both the majority and the dissenters used it in *Nyquist* and *Meek* to justify their conclusions. These and the other cases depicted in Table 3-4 explain why some observers call this area of the law "a mess," marred by dissensus and inconsistencies. For example, is it reasonable to allow public schools to loan books to students but not materials and equipment to schools? The Court justified this decision, in part, on the grounds that the books were going directly to the students while the equipment was going to the schools. But, to many commentators, this distinction is overly trivial and technical; after all, in both instances it is the child who ultimately benefits.

Mueller v. Allen (1983) provides yet another example. This case involved a Minnesota program similar to the New York policy addressed a decade earlier in *Nyquist:* both provided tax breaks for certain expenses incurred by parents who sent their children to

Table 3-4 Aid to Religious Schools: Major Supreme Court Cases, 1947–1994

Case	Outcome (Opinion Type)[a]	Aid Upheld	Aid Struck	Standard Used
Everson v. Board of Education (1947)	accommodation (majority, 5–4)	transportation reimbursements		neutrality, child benefit, secular purpose
Board of Education v. Allen (1968)	accommodation (majority, 6–3)	textbook loans		*Abington*
Lemon v. Kurtzman (1971)	separation (majority, 8–0)		reimbursements for teacher salaries, textbooks, instructional materials	*Lemon*
Earley v. DiCenso (1971)	separation (majority, 8–1)		teacher salary supplements	*Lemon*
Tilton v. Richardson (1971)	accommodation (judgment, 5–4)	funds for secular buildings (colleges and universities)		*Lemon*
Hunt v. McNair (1973)	accommodation (majority, 6–3)	aid for construction, financing academic buildings (colleges and universities) obtained from revenue bonds		*Lemon*
Levitt v. CPEARL (1973)	separation (majority, 8–1)		reimbursements for administering and grading tests and examinations required by state	*Lemon*
CPEARL v. Nyquist (1973)	separation (majority, 6–3)		grants for maintenance and building repair, tax benefits, tuition reimbursements	*Lemon*
Meek v. Pittenger (1975)	mixed (majority/judgment, 6–3)	textbook loans	"auxiliary services" such as counseling, testing, speech therapy loans of "instructional materials and equipment" such as maps, films, photographs, periodicals	*Lemon*
Roemer v. Maryland Public Works Board (1976)	accommodation (judgment, 5–4)	general-purpose funds to colleges and universities for secular purposes		*Lemon*
Wolman v. Walter (1977)	mixed (majority/judgment, various votes)	textbook purchases, testing services, speech and hearing diagnostic services, therapeutic, guidance, and remedial services	instructional material purchases and loans, field trip transportation	*Lemon*

Case	Outcome (Opinion Type)[a]	Aid Upheld	Aid Struck	Standard Used
New York v. Cathedral Academy (1977)	separation (majority, 6–3)		direct reimbursement for record keeping and testing	*Lemon*
CPEARL v. Regan (1980)	accommodation (majority, 5–4)	reimbursements for meeting state requirements for regents examinations, "pupil attendance reporting" and so forth		*Lemon*
Mueller v. Allen (1983)	accommodation (majority, 5–4)	tax deductions for tuition, textbooks, transportation		*Lemon*
Grand Rapids School District v. Ball (1985)	separation (majority, 7–2 and 5–4)		Community Education Program offering courses (chess, home economics, languages) at end of school day; employing private school teachers and using public and private school facilities Shared Time Program offering secular classes to private school children in private school facilities (leased by the state) during regular school hours and taught by public school teachers, many of whom had previously taught in private schools	*Lemon*
Aguilar v. Felton (1985)	separation (majority, 5–4)		teacher/counselor salaries and supplies/materials for remedial instruction to private school students in private school facilities	*Lemon*
Witters v. Washington Department for Services for the Blind (1986)	accommodation (majority, 9–0)	Disabled student at Christian college cannot be denied state vocational rehabilitation assistance		*Lemon*
Zobrest v. Catalina Foothills School District (1993)	accommodation (majority, 5–4)	Disabled student at Roman Catholic high school can be furnished with a state-funded sign-language interpreter		neutrality; child benefit
Board of Education of Kiryas Joel Village School Dist. v. Grumet (1994)	separation (majority, 6–3)		school district created to accommodate handicapped children of particular sect	neutrality

a. A judgment represents the views of a plurality, not a majority, of the Court's members. Unlike a majority opinion, a judgment lacks precedential value.

private schools. And in both cases the Court applied the *Lemon* test. The inconsistency? The Court struck down the New York program, but upheld the Minnesota plan. Rehnquist, who wrote the majority opinion in *Mueller,* justified this seeming contradiction by seizing on a difference between the New York and Minnesota schemes: New York made its tax deduction applicable only to parents of private school children, while Minnesota's was available to parents who sent their chidden to public and private schools. But, as ACLU attorney Ira Glasser wrote, "To some, the Court's reasoning seemed disingenuous. The major tax-deductible expense was tuition, which parents of public-school students didn't pay; 96 percent of Minnesota tax deductions were taken by parents sending their children to religious schools."[57]

Who is right here? Rehnquist, who claimed to be following the *Lemon* precedent, or Glasser, who believes that Rehnquist and the majority of justices twisted *Lemon* to fit their ideological inclinations toward accommodationism? No matter who you think is correct, it is clear that there are no easy solutions to the problems presented in parochiaid cases. Indeed, the Court continues to struggle with them. But among all the alleged inconsistencies and zigzag lines the Court has drawn in this area, we can locate some common themes.

First, in the area of parochiaid, rarely has the Court veered from *Lemon:* in virtually every case listed in Table 3-4, the majority used *Lemon* to reach conclusions about the specific program under challenge. This consistency, as we shall see, is not the case in other areas of establishment law (particularly prayer) where the Court has seemed on the verge of abandoning *Lemon* since the 1980s. Even in the 1993 case of *Zobrest v. Catalina Foothills School District*, the Court did not reject *Lemon;* rather, it ignored it. While James Zobrest, a hearing-impaired student, attended public school in Arizona, the school district furnished him

with a sign-language interpreter. When Zobrest enrolled in a Roman Catholic high school, the district refused to pay for the interpreter. Writing for the majority, Chief Justice Rehnquist skirted *Lemon* by relying on precedent established in *Mueller* and *Witters v. Washington Department of Services for the Blind (see Table 3-4)* to rule in Zobrest's favor. Both of those decisions used *Lemon* as their analytic framework, which may explain why the justices have not used the parochiaid cases—as they have the prayer cases, for example—as vehicles through which to criticize *Lemon:* they would have to undo years and years of established precedent.[58] Besides, with the retirement of Justice White (who joined the majority in *Zobrest*) and the ascension of Justice Ginsburg, it seems unlikely that Chief Justice Rehnquist will have the votes necessary to eradicate the use of *Lemon* in parochiaid cases or to adopt a new standard that brings a more accommodationist perspective to this line of cases *(see Table 3-3).*

Justice Ginsburg's first Supreme Court foray into the Establishment Clause area seems to bear out this sentiment. In *Board of Education of Kiryas Joel Village School Dist. v. Grumet* (1994), the Court confronted a most unusual situation, even as these cases go. The case originated in a small town forty miles north of New York City. Kiryas Joel is "a religious enclave of Satmar Hasidism," in which practitioners follow a strict form of Judaism. The residents avoid assimilation into the modern world. As Justice Souter noted, "[T]hey interpret the Torah strictly; segregate the sexes outside of the home; speak Yiddish as their primary language; eschew television, radio, and English-language publications and dress in distinctive ways that include head coverings and special garments for boys and modest dresses for girls." They send their children to private religious schools.

---

57. Ira Glasser, *Visions of Liberty* (New York: Arcade, 1991), 98.

58. On the other hand, Blackmun's dissent in *Zobrest* also relied on precedent. Blackmun made much of the fact that Rehnquist had "disregard[ed] longstanding principles" in this area, particularly those coming in cases (such as *Lemon*) that refused to provide support for teachers and other employees. Blackmun believed that interpreters, like teachers, could convey religious messages.

These religious schools, however, offered no special programs for handicapped children, who, under federal law, are entitled to such services even if they attend private school. Beginning in 1984 the religious school entered into an arrangement with the Monroe-Woodbury Central School District (the district into which the village fell) whereby those services would be provided by the public school at an annex to the private one. The handicapped children of the practitioners of Satmar received the services they required but did not have to attend a public school to obtain them. But in 1985 the Supreme Court issued two decisions, *Aguilar v. Felton* and *School District of Grand Rapids v. Ball*, which cast enough doubt on the arrangement to lead to its termination. Accordingly, children requiring special education were forced to attend public schools.

This development was troublesome. Parents withdrew their children claiming that "the panic, fear and trauma [the children] suffered in leaving their own community and being with people whose ways were so different" was simply overwhelming. By 1989 only one family from Kiryas Joel sent a child to the public school; "the village's other handicapped children received special services or went without."

It was at that point that the New York legislature intervened. It passed a law that provided that Kiryas Joel "is constituted a separate school district ... and shall have and enjoy all the powers and duties of a union free school district...." With this act in hand, the newly formed Kiryas Joel Village School District set up a special education program for handicapped children. It did not, however, create more general "public" schools; the balance of the children continued to attend private religious school.

Just when it appeared that the matter was finally settled, the New York State School Boards Association—Louis Grumet was its executive director—challenged the newly formed district as a violation of the Establishment Clause. It claimed that the district was set up to benefit a particular religion in direct contradiction to existing Court precedent. Writing for the majority (including Ginsburg), Justice Souter agreed. In his view, the creation of the school district violated a "principle at the heart of the Establishment Clause, that government should not prefer one religion to another, or religion to irreligion." New York, in this instance, had violated the "requirement of governmental neutrality by extending the benefit of a special franchise."

This ruling provoked an unusually bitter exchange between Justice Souter and Justice Scalia, who wrote a dissenting opinion for Thomas and Rehnquist. Scalia began his opinion with a sarcastic quip—"The Court today finds that the Powers That Be, up in Albany, have conspired to effect an establishment of the Satmar Hasidim"—and ended by calling it "astounding." Justice Souter's response was equally sharp: "To end on the point with which Justice Scalia begins, the license he takes in suggesting that the Court holds the Satmar sect to be New York's established church is only one symptom of his inability to accept the fact that this Court has long held that the First Amendment reaches more than classic, 18th century establishments."

For our purposes, however, the most significant aspect of the Court's decision was what it did not say: although it mentioned *Lemon*, it neither relied on *Lemon* nor overruled it. The probable reason, as journalist Linda Greenhouse observed, is that the majority of justices may not like *Lemon*, but they cannot agree on a suitable replacement. Even Justice O'Connor, who had previously offered a replacement for *Lemon*, appeared to have thrown in the towel. As she wrote in a concurring opinion, the Court would probably never be able to agree on "grand unified theory" of the Establishment Clause because these cases "cannot easily be reduced to a single test." But Justice Blackmun, in a concurring opinion, made clear that the ruling was not "a departure from the principles described in *Lemon v. Kurtzman*."

A second common theme concerns the justices' application of *Lemon* and the different results reached. These differences seem to depend of the nature of the institution receiving the support. As Table 3–4 shows, the justices have been more willing to tolerate aid to colleges and universities than to primary and secondary schools. Why? One reason offered by the Court is that "the symbolism of union between church and state is most likely to influence children of tender years, whose experience is limited and whose beliefs consequently are the function of environment as much as of free and voluntary choice."[59] Another is that religious primary and secondary schools tend to be more "pervasively sectarian" than their college counterparts.[60]

Finally, the Court has made distinctions based on the recipient of the aid. Hearkening back to *Everson*, the justices are more likely to uphold support that goes directly to parents and children rather than to the private schools, which explains why the Court usually allows public schools to lend secular textbooks: the books go to the students, not the schools. It also sheds light on Rehnquist's opinion in *Zobrest*. Supplying a sign-language interpreter to a student at a sectarian school, as he put it, "creates a neutral government program dispensing aid not to schools but to individual handicapped children." Shades of *Everson*, indeed.[61]

These are some general rules but, like all rules, there are exceptions. For example, the Court has not always upheld all forms of aid to colleges and universities. Nor, as *Zobrest* indicates, has it always applied *Lemon* to the letter. To put it somewhat differently, despite these common themes there is no denying that parochiaid remains a troubled area of Establishment case law. Even casual study of Table 3-4 attests to this.

---

59. *Grand Rapids School District v. Ball.*
60. See Tribe, *American Constitutional Law,* 1220.
61. Still, it is probably true that Justice Black, the author of *Everson,* would have dissented in *Zobrest.* He objected even to the loaning of textbooks because, unlike the buses, they convey a message. This is the point Justice Blackmun made in his dissenting opinion in *Zobrest.*

Religion in the Public Schools

While parochiaid litigation centers on public support for students and parents sending their children to religious schools or to the schools themselves, another category of cases asks the Court to assess the extent to which religion can be injected into public schools. These cases fall into three categories: (1) the use of public school facilities for religious purposes or by religious groups; (2) the teaching of ideas associated with particular religions; and (3) the recitation of prayers. In this section, we deal with the first two areas.

Use of Public School Facilities. Litigation involving the use of public facilities for religious purposes predated *Lemon* v. *Kurtzman.* In fact, the Court delved into this subject in *Illinois ex rel. McCollum v. Board of Education* (1948), just one year after it decided *Everson. McCollum* centered on so-called released-time programs, which began in the early 1900s. At that time, Catholics and Jews, who were immigrating to the United States in record numbers, expressed their displeasure with the overtly Protestant nature of America's public school systems. In response to their pressure, school boards devised programs that permitted students, with the approval of their parents, to leave school each day "for a period of time to go to their own churches or synagogues for religious instruction."[62]

By the 1940s released-time programs had sprung up across the United States, but they were not all alike. While some schools sent their students to their respective churches for religious instruction, others permitted religious instructors to come to the public schools. That kind of program was the catalyst for *McCollum.* In theory, it was supposed to work this way: the board of education arranged for Catholic, Protestant, and Jewish religious instructors to come to school once a week to teach. Those students whose

---

62. Glasser, *Visions of Liberty,* 86. This paragraph draws on material in that book, pages 86–87.

parents wanted the instruction attended the appropriate class, while the remainder continued with their secular education.

In practice, however, there were not enough Jewish students to make up a whole religion class. So the school divided the students into two groups: Protestants and Jews, who remained in their classrooms to receive religious instruction, and Catholics, who went to a different classroom. In addition to lumping Protestant and Jewish children together, the school failed to provide unbiased instruction. Consider the trial testimony of the instructor of the Protestant class:

THE TEACHER: I do not think I spoke ever of the Jews as Christ's enemies; that was several years ago and I do not remember.

ATTORNEY: Will you tell us just what you did teach with reference to who his enemies were?...

TEACHER: I think if you read the Bible you will know them.

ATTORNEY: I want to know what you teach. Don't you teach that the Jews were the enemies of Christ?

TEACHER: They were hostile to Jesus in many ways.

ATTORNEY: Did you teach the children that the Jews were afraid of Jesus?

TEACHER: Some of them were.

ATTORNEY: How about the others?

TEACHER: Some of them were not.[63]

Given this testimony, it is easy to understand why some religious groups oppose any teaching of religion in public school.[64] The U.S. Supreme Court had little trouble ruling that these on-site programs presented too much intermingling between church and state. Writing for eight members of the Court, Justice Black relied heavily on his *Everson* opinion:

Here not only are the State's tax-supported public school buildings used for the dissemination of religious doctrine.

The state also affords sectarian groups an invaluable aid in that it helps to provide pupils for their religious classes.... This is not separation of church and state.

But Black's opinion did not end the matter. Because *McCollum* proscribed a widespread, popular practice, the Court's decision generated a backlash. School boards and state legislatures were pressured to adopt released-time programs that would conform to *McCollum*. In response, school boards went back to the original programs: they let students out early to obtain instruction at various community religious schools and churches.

It was this kind of released-time program that the Court considered and upheld in *Zorach v. Clauson* (1952). Writing for the majority, Justice Douglas asserted that the new program corrected the fundamental defect of the old one; no longer would religious instruction occur on public school premises. But Douglas went further. He noted that the prohibition against religious establishment "does not say that in every and all respects there shall be separation of Church and State." If it did, according to Douglas, state and religion would be "hostile, suspicious, and even unfriendly" toward each other. This state of affairs would be out of line with the spirit of the First Amendment and the desires of the American people. For, as Douglas wrote in one of the most often quoted passages in this area of the law,

We are a religious people whose institutions presuppose a Supreme Being. We guarantee the freedom to worship as one chooses. We make room for as wide a variety of beliefs and creeds as the spiritual needs of man deem.... When the state encourages religious instruction or cooperates with religious authorities by adjusting the schedule of public events to sectarian needs, it follows the best of our traditions. For it then respects the religious nature of our people and accommodates the public service to their spiritual needs. To hold that it may not would be to find callous indifference to religious groups. That would be preferring those who believe in no religion over those who do believe.[65]

---

63. Much of the information in this paragraph, as well as the excerpts from trial, come from Pfeffer, *Religion, State, and the Burger Court,* 63–64.

64. For more on this point, ibid., chap. 3.

65. It is worth noting that this opinion was wholly uncharacteristic for Justice Douglas. During his brief tenure on the Burger Court, he was one of the leading advocates of a strict separationist position.

This logic troubled Justice Black, who, along with Frankfurter and Jackson, dissented. He believed that the Court had yielded to the public pressure resulting from *McCollum*. He wrote:

I am aware that our *McCollum* decision has been subjected to a most searching examination throughout the country. Probably few opinions from this Court in recent years have attracted more attention.... Our insistence on a "wall of separation between Church and State which must be kept high and impregnable" has seemed to some a correct exposition ... to which we should strictly adhere. With equal conviction and sincerity, others have thought the *McCollum* decision fundamentally wrong and have pledged continuous warfare against it.

And, as the author of *McCollum*, Black could find "no significant difference between the invalid Illinois program and that of New York sustained here." In his view, the *McCollum* program was unconstitutional not simply because it took place on school grounds, but because it gave "invaluable aid to religion," a characteristic of all released-time programs, as well.

With *Zorach* the Court closed the released-time issue. So long as instruction takes place off school premises, it is constitutionally permissible. But, by the 1980s, the Court was confronted with yet another set of questions in this area: May public schools deny religious groups use of their facilities for meetings or other programs? This new generation of suits was different from the early released-time cases. Now public schools were denying religious groups access to their buildings, rather than seeking to facilitate the teaching of religion on or off their premises. Keep in mind that when these cases came up the Court had a standard of law, the *Lemon* test, which it did not have at the time of *McCollum* and *Zorach*. How it would resolve this new kind of access cases was an intriguing question.

In the first of these cases, *Widmar v. Vincent* (1981), the Court provided a few answers. This dispute arose at a public institution, the University of Missouri in Kansas City, where students had organized a religious group called Cornerstone. From 1973 through 1977 Cornerstone held meetings in university facilities. In 1977 university officials, citing a 1972 school policy, denied the participants access, saying that their presence would violate the Establishment Clause. After all, officials argued, during their meetings the students prayed, sang hymns, and discussed religious experiences.

Cornerstone members challenged the closed access policy as a violation of their right to free exercise of religion and to free speech. The school countered that it could regulate religious exercise and free speech if it had a compelling reason and that the prevention of religious establishment was such a reason. If the university had an equal access policy, which would have permitted the group to continue to use school facilities, it would cross the line between church and state. The Supreme Court disagreed. Writing for the majority, Justice Powell applied the *Lemon* rule to find in favor of the students. He said that equal access policies have the secular purpose of encouraging the exchange of ideas. Further, he asserted that if the university retained its closed access policy, it would risk excessive entanglement with religion, as it would have to determine whether groups were engaging in religious speech or worship. Finally, Powell claimed that equal access policies do not have the primary effect of advancing religion; rather they encourage "all forms of discourse."

Widmar dealt exclusively with colleges and universities, asserting that "equal access" policies at these institutions would not violate the Establishment Clause. In 1984, with passage of the Equal Access Act, Congress built on *Widmar*. The act required all public secondary schools with "limited open forum" policies to give equal access to "any students who wish to conduct a meeting with that limited open forum," regardless of the "religious, political, philosophical, or content of the speech at such meetings." A "limited open forum" is in effect if a school permits "one or more non-curriculum related student groups to meet in school premises during non-instructional times."

Some observers speculated that the Court might strike down the Equal Access Act as a violation of the Religious Establishment Clause because the justices might be loath to apply a university policy to less mature secondary school students. In *Board of Education of Westside Community School v. Mergens* (1990), however, a divided Court voted to uphold the law. In a plurality opinion (fully endorsed by only four members of the Court) Justice O'Connor held that the law did not have the primary effect of advancing religion. In her argument, O'Connor adopted the logic of the endorsement test, which itself built on *Lemon (see Table 3-3):* religion was not advanced because it was private, not governmental, speech *endorsing* religion. Private endorsements of religion (such as those that might occur during a group meeting), as she noted, were protected by the Free Speech and Free Exercise Clauses of the First Amendment, but government endorsements violated the Establishment Clause.

Justices Kennedy and Scalia agreed that the act was constitutional, but they took issue with O'Connor's endorsement approach. They advocated a standard emphasizing the relative "coercive" nature of government policies *(see Table 3-3)*. Justice Kennedy wrote:

> I should think it inevitable that a public high school "endorses" a religious club, in a commonsense use of the term, if the club happens to be one of many activities that the school permits students to choose in order to further the development of their intellect and character in an extracurricular setting. But no constitutional violation occurs if the school's action is based upon a recognition of the fact that membership in a religious club is one of many permissible ways for a student to further his or her own personal enrichment. The inquiry with respect to coercion must be whether the government imposes pressure upon a student to participate in a religious activity. This inquiry, of course, must be undertaken with sensitivity to the special circumstances that exist in a secondary school where the line between voluntary and coerced participation may be difficult to draw. No such coercion ... has been shown to exist as a necessary result of this statute.

Mergens indicates the Court's willingness to uphold government policies that allow religious groups equal access to school facilities. It also shows just how divided the Court is over *the* appropriate standard by which to adjudicate religious establishment cases. That is why observers anxiously awaited the Court's decision in *Lamb's Chapel v. Center Moriches Union Free School District* (1993), a case involving use of school property by an outside religious group. Some thought that by 1993 the justices would coalesce around a particular test. Did that occur or did the justices remain divided?

Lamb's Chapel v. Center Moriches Union Free School District

508 U.S. — (1993)
*Vote: 9 (Blackmun, Kennedy, O'Connor, Rehnquist,
       Scalia, Souter, Stevens, Thomas, White)*
       0

Opinion of the Court: White
Concurring opinions: Kennedy, Scalia

A New York state law lists ten circumstances under which school property may be used by outside groups and/or used for purposes other than education. These include "social, civic, and recreational meetings, and entertainment, and other uses pertaining to the welfare of the community."

Under the law, local school boards may select from the list of ten the types of events for which they will permit use of school property. Center Moriches Union Free School District issued rules allowing only two: social, civic, or recreational uses (rule 10) and use by political organizations (rule 8). Board Rule 7 specifically states that "school premises shall not be used by a group for religious purposes." Rule 7 is consistent with the New York law, which does not include meetings for religious purposes on its list of ten, and with a New York court ruling, which stated that school boards could not allow student Bible clubs to meet on school property.

Lamb's Chapel, an evangelical church located in the Center Moriches community, twice asked the school board for permission to show a film series in school buildings. The series contained lectures by a psychologist on "the undermining influences of the media [which] could only be counterbalanced by returning to traditional, Christian family values instilled at an early age." Believing that the films were church-related, the school district denied both requests.

Lamb's Chapel took the school district to court, asserting that the denial violated the church's First Amendment guarantees of free speech and religious liberty. It presented evidence that district officials had permitted other religious groups to use school facilities, including "A New Age religious group known as the 'Mind Center,'" the Southern Harmonize Gospel Singers, and the Hampton Council of Churches. The school district countered that it could deny use of its property to a "radical" church "for the purpose of proselytizing," which might lead to violence. Just as the University of Missouri had said in *Widmar*, it claimed that it had a compelling interest in restricting the church's First Amendment rights: use of its property for religious purposes would violate the Religious Establishment Clause.

After a federal district court and a court of appeals rejected its claims, the church appealed to the U.S. Supreme Court. In his opinion for the Court, Justice White dealt first with the free speech claim. He noted that the "film ... no doubt dealt with a subject otherwise permissible under Rule 10, and its exhibition was denied solely because the film dealt with a subject from a religious standpoint." Accordingly, he held that the board's denial violated free speech principles, which forbid "the government to regulate speech in ways that favor some viewpoints or ideas at the expense of others."

He next took up the religious liberties issues. We excerpt that part of the decision.

JUSTICE WHITE delivered the opinion of the Court.

The District, as a respondent, would save its judgment below on the ground that to permit its property to be used

for religious purposes would be an establishment of religion forbidden by the First Amendment. This Court suggested in *Widmar v. Vincent* (1981) that the interest of the State in avoiding an Establishment Clause violation "may be [a] compelling" one justifying an abridgment of free speech otherwise protected by the First Amendment; but the Court went on to hold that permitting use of University property for religious purposes under the open access policy involved there would not be incompatible with the Court's Establishment Clause cases.

We have no more trouble than did the *Widmar* Court in disposing of the claimed defense on the ground that the posited fears of an Establishment Clause violation are unfounded. The showing of this film would not have been during school hours, would not have been sponsored by the school, and would have been open to the public, not just to church members. The District property had repeatedly been used by a wide variety of private organizations. Under these circumstances, as in *Widmar*, there would have been no realistic danger that the community would think that the District was endorsing religion or any particular creed, and any benefit to religion or to the Church would have been no more than incidental. As in *Widmar*, permitting District property to be used to exhibit the film involved in this case would not have been an establishment of religion under the three-part test articulated in *Lemon v. Kurtzman* (1971). The challenged governmental action has a secular purpose, does not have the principal or primary effect of advancing or inhibiting religion, and does not foster an excessive entanglement with religion.*

The District also submits that it justifiably denied use of its property to a "radical" church for the purpose of proselytizing, since to do so would lead to threats of public unrest and even violence. There is nothing in the record to support such a justification, which in any event would be difficult to defend as a reason to deny the presentation of a re-

---

* While we are somewhat diverted by JUSTICE SCALIA's evening at the cinema [see Scalia's dissent], we return to the reality that there is a proper way to inter an established decision and *Lemon*, however frightening it might be to some, has not been overruled. This case, like *Corporation of Presiding Bishop of Church of Jesus Christ of Latter-day Saints v. Amos* (1987) [concerning individuals fired from their jobs with a church-owned corporation because they did not qualify for membership in the church], presents no occasion to do so. JUSTICE SCALIA apparently was less haunted by the ghosts of the living when he joined the opinion of the Court in that case.

ligious point of view about a subject the District otherwise makes open to discussion on District property....

For the reasons stated in this opinion, the judgment of the Court of Appeals is

Reversed.

JUSTICE KENNEDY, concurring in part and concurring in the judgment.

Given the issues presented as well as the apparent unanimity of our conclusion that this overt, viewpoint-based discrimination contradicts the Speech Clause of the First Amendment and that there has been no substantial showing of a potential Establishment Clause violation, I agree with JUSTICE SCALIA that the Court's citation of *Lemon v. Kurtzman* (1971) is unsettling and unnecessary. The same can be said of the Court's use of the phrase "endorsing religion," which ... cannot suffice as a rule of decision consistent with our precedents and our traditions in this part of our jurisprudence. With these observations, I concur in part and concur in the judgment.

JUSTICE SCALIA, with whom JUSTICE THOMAS joins, concurring in the judgment.

I join the Court's conclusion that the District's refusal to allow use of school facilities for petitioners' film viewing, while generally opening the schools for community activities, violates petitioners' First Amendment free-speech rights, to the extent it compelled the District's denial. I also agree with the Court that allowing Lamb's Chapel to use school facilities poses "no realistic danger" of a violation of the Establishment Clause, but I cannot accept most of its reasoning in this regard. The Court explains that the showing of petitioners' film on school property after school hours would not cause the community to "think that the District was endorsing religion or any particular creed," and further notes that access to school property would not violate the three-part test articulated in *Lemon v. Kurtzman* (1971).

As to the Court's invocation of the *Lemon* test: Like some ghoul in a late-night horror movie that repeatedly sits up in its grave and shuffles abroad, after being repeatedly killed and buried, *Lemon* stalks our Establishment Clause jurisprudence once again, frightening the little children and

school attorneys of Center Moriches Union Free School District. Its most recent burial, only last Term, was, to be sure, not fully six-feet under: our decision in *Lee v. Weisman* (1992) conspicuously avoided using the supposed "test" but also declined the invitation to repudiate it. Over the years, however, no fewer than five of the currently sitting Justices [Scalia, O'Connor, Rehnquist, White, and Kennedy] have, in their own opinions, personally driven pencils through the creature's heart (the author of today's opinion repeatedly), and a sixth [Thomas] has joined an opinion doing so....

The secret of the *Lemon* test's survival, I think, is that it is so easy to kill. It is there to scare us (and our audience) when we wish it to do so, but we can command it to return to the tomb at will.... When we wish to strike down a practice it forbids, we invoke it, see, *e.g., Aguilar v. Felton* (1985) (striking down state remedial education program administered in part in parochial schools); when we wish to uphold a practice it forbids, we ignore it entirely, see *Marsh v. Chambers* (1983) (upholding state legislative chaplains). Sometimes, we take a middle course, calling its three prongs "no more than helpful signposts,"... Such a docile and useful monster is worth keeping around, at least in a somnolent state; one never knows when one might need him.

For my part, I agree with the long list of constitutional scholars who have criticized *Lemon* and bemoaned the strange Establishment Clause geometry of crooked lines and wavering shapes its intermittent use has produced.... I will decline to apply *Lemon*—whether it validates or invalidates the government action in question—and therefore cannot join the opinion of the Court today.*

I cannot join for yet another reason: the Court's statement that the proposed use of the school's facilities is constitutional because (among other things) it would not signal endorsement of religion in general. What a strange

---

* The Court correctly notes that I joined the opinion in *Corporation of Presiding Bishop of Church of Jesus Christ of Latter-day Saints v. Amos* (1987), which considered the *Lemon* test. Lacking a majority at that time to abandon *Lemon*, we necessarily focused on that test, which had been the exclusive basis for the lower court's judgment. Here, of course, the lower court did not mention *Lemon*, and indeed did not even address any Establishment Clause argument on behalf of respondents. Thus, the Court is ultimately correct that *Presiding Bishop* provides a useful comparison: it was as impossible to avoid *Lemon* there, as it is unnecessary to inject *Lemon* here.

notion, that a Constitution which itself gives "religion in general" preferential treatment (I refer to the Free Exercise Clause) forbids endorsement of religion in general.... That was *not* the view of those who adopted our Constitution, who believed that the public virtues inculcated by religion are a public good. It suffices to point out that during the summer of 1789, when it was in the process of drafting the First Amendment, Congress enacted the famous Northwest Territory Ordinance of 1789, Article III of which provides, "Religion, morality, and knowledge, *being necessary to good government and the happiness of mankind,* schools and the means of education shall forever be encouraged." Unsurprisingly, then, indifference to "religion in general" is not what our cases, both old and recent, demand....

For the reasons given by the Court, I agree that the Free Speech Clause of the First Amendment forbids what respondents have done here. As for the asserted Establishment Clause justification, I would hold, simply and clearly, that giving Lamb's Chapel nondiscriminatory access to school facilities cannot violate that provision because it does not signify state or local embrace of a particular religious sect.

Again, the Court had little difficulty in ruling for the religious group, but the justices were divided on the reasons. The majority's use of a combination of *Lemon* and O'Connor's endorsement approach sparked that stinging concurrence from Scalia (joined by Thomas and supported by Kennedy). In no uncertain terms, Scalia expressed his continuing displeasure with *Lemon.* But, to date, as Table 3-3 shows, no other test has garnered sufficient support. Dislike of the standard and the lack of a replacement are recurring themes in Establishment Clause decisions of the 1980s and 1990s.

Teaching Religious Principles in Public Schools. *Zorach, Lamb's Chapel,* and the other cases reviewed in the last section involve the use of public school facilities for religious purposes or by religious groups. But that is not the only way religion and public education intermingle. Another concerns the particular approach that is used to teach secular subjects.

Nonpublic schools, naturally, are free to teach secular subjects couched in religious terms. Remember the book titles that were used for a math problem? Public schools use secular books to teach subjects like math, so we would expect to find children adding up the prices of oranges, bread, and eggs rather than of religious books. However, some public schools have sought to disseminate tenets held by particular religions by slanting the curriculum to favor religious views about secular subjects. The best known and most enduring example is the way teachers address the origins of human life. Did humankind evolve, as scientists suggest (evolutionary theory), or did it come about as a result of some divine intervention, as various religions argue (creationism)?

This debate received an unusual amount of attention in 1925 when the American Civil Liberties Union—represented in court by Clarence Darrow—sponsored a legal challenge to a Tennessee law that made it a crime to teach evolutionary principles or any theory denigrating the biblical version of the creation. That case, popularized by the Scopes monkey trial, never made it to the Supreme Court *(see Box 3-5).* But two other similar challenges did reach the Court.

The first was *Epperson v. Arkansas,* a 1968 case in which the Court considered the constitutionality of a 1928 state "anti-evolution" law that was an "adaptation" of Tennessee's 1925 version. The Arkansas law made it a crime for any state university or public school instructor "to teach the theory or doctrine that mankind ascended or descended from a lower order of animals" or to "adopt or use ... a textbook that teaches" evolutionary theory. The history of the law's adoption makes it clear that its purpose was to further religious beliefs about the beginning of life. For example, an advertisement placed in an Arkansas newspaper to drum up support for the act said: "The Bible or atheism, which? All atheists favor evolution.... Shall conscientious church members be forced to pay taxes to support teachers to teach

BOX 3-5 THE SCOPES MONKEY TRIAL

"The law is a ass," observed Charles Dickens's character, Mr. Bumble, in *Oliver Twist*. In 1925 many Americans, watching with amazement the circus-like proceedings of the dramatic Scopes trial in Tennessee, found themselves echoing the same sentiments. "Isn't it difficult to realize that a trial of this kind is possible in the twentieth century in the United States of America?" demanded the lawyer for the defense, the famed Clarence Darrow. In truth, the case appeared a vestigial survival from an earlier day when people were prosecuted for witchcraft or for offenses like imagining the king's death. Headlined in the press as the Great Monkey Trial, it pitted the Biblical version of creation against the teachings of Charles Darwin, and did so in a courtroom atmosphere more closely resembling that of a revival meeting than a hall of justice.

The defendant, John T. Scopes, was a twenty-four-year-old high school teacher in Dayton, Tennessee, who was prosecuted for teaching evolution in violation of a state statute that prohibited the teaching in any public school of "any theory that denies the story of the divine creation of man as taught in the Bible, and to teach instead that man has descended from a lower order of animals." Conducted in the heat of July, the trial was a parody of all that a legal proceeding should be. Dayton was ready for what it hoped would be the Waterloo of science. "One was hard put...," an observer wrote, "to know whether Dayton was holding a camp meeting, a Chautauqua, a street fair, a carnival or a belated Fourth of July celebration. Literally, it was drunk on religious excitement."

The courtroom itself was decked with a large banner, exhorting everyone to "Read your Bible daily." Darrow finally got it removed by demanding equal space for a banner urging, "Read your Evolution." The stars of the trial were the lawyers: Clarence Darrow, perhaps the best known criminal lawyer in American history (Lincoln Steffens had called him "the attorney for the damned") representing Scopes and, indirectly, Darwin and evolution, and, against him, William Jennings Bryan, the Great Commoner, orator of the famed "Cross of Gold" speech in 1896, three-time candidate for President, and Secretary of State under Woodrow Wilson,

who had volunteered to direct the prosecution. Aging and sanctimonious, Bryan was the leading Fundamentalist of the day. "I am more interested in the Rock of Ages than in the age of rocks," he proclaimed.

At the trial's beginning, Darrow said later, "the judge ... with great solemnity and all the dignity possible announced that Brother Twitchell would invoke the Divine blessing. This was new to me. I had practiced law for more that forty years, and had never before heard God called in to referee a court trial." Darrow's objection to the blessing was overruled, and each day's session began with a prayer by a different preacher. The high point of the trial saw Darrow put Bryan himself on the stand as an expert on "religion." The *New York Times* described this as the most amazing court scene in history, and out-of-state reporters and observers like the iconoclast H. L. Mencken had a field day conveying the incongruous proceedings to the nation. Bryan stuck doggedly to his insistence on the literal truth of the Bible, refusing, in Darrow's phrase, "to choose between his crude beliefs and the common intelligence of modern times."

In the end, the local population felt it won a righteous victory when the jury found Scopes guilty. But the judge imposed only a $100 fine, and, on appeal, the Tennessee Supreme Court reversed the decision on a technicality: the court, rather than the jury, had set the fine. The case itself was more dramatic than significant—unless it deserved remembrance as an example of the law at its worst. "I think," said Darrow during the trial, "this case will be remembered because it is the first case of this sort since we stopped trying people in America for witchcraft." On another plane, Darrow's withering examination during the trial went far to discredit Fundamentalist dogma. Though anti-evolution laws remained on the books in what Mencken referred to as "the Bible Belt" of the South, they were never again enforced. And in 1968, the U.S. Supreme Court finally struck down an Arkansas anti-evolution law, though admitting that by then "the statute is presently more of a curiosity than a vital fact of life."

Source: Bernard Schwartz, *The Law in America* (New York: McGraw Hill, 1974), 224. Reprinted by permission of the author.

evolution which will undermine the faith of their children?"

Epperson began in the mid-1960s when the school system in Little Rock, Arkansas, decided to adopt a biology book that contained a chapter on evolutionary theory. Susan Epperson, a biology teacher in a Little Rock high school, wanted to use the new book but was afraid—in light of the 1928 law—that she could face criminal prosecution if she did so. She asked the Arkansas courts to nullify the law, and, when the Arkansas Supreme Court turned down her request, she appealed her case to the U.S. Supreme Court.

Writing for a unanimous Court, Justice Abe Fortas reversed the state supreme court's ruling. Relying heavily on *Everson* (the *Lemon* test had yet to be established), Fortas said, "The First Amendment mandates governmental neutrality between religion and religion, between religion and nonreligion." Under this standard the outcome was clear to the justices:

Arkansas' law cannot be defended as an act of religious neutrality. Arkansas did not seek to excise from the curricula of its schools ... all discussion of the origin of man. The law's effort was confined to an attempt to blot out a particular theory because of its supposed conflict with the Biblical account, literally read. Plainly, the law is contrary to the mandate of the First ... Amendment.

Despite the Court's clear statement about the constitutional violation posed by anti-evolutionary laws, some states devised other ways to teach creationism. In *Edwards v. Aguillard* (1987) the Court reviewed one of these attempts. This case was decided after the *Lemon* test had been established and during the chief justiceship of William Rehnquist, who—along with Antonin Scalia—sought greater accommodation between church and state. As you read this case, then, consider the difference between the Court's opinion and the dissent filed by Scalia and joined by Rehnquist.

Edwards v. Aguillard

482 U.S. 578 (1987)
Vote: 7 (Blackmun, Brennan, Marshall, O'Connor, Powell, Stevens, White)
  2 (Rehnquist, Scalia)
Opinion of the Court: Brennan
Concurring opinions: Powell, White
Dissenting opinion: Scalia

After *Epperson,* organized interests—particularly religious groups—lobbied state legislatures to pass new laws. Louisiana enacted the Balanced Treatment for Creation-Science and Evolution-Science in Public School Instruction Act in 1981. This law differed from the one struck down in *Epperson* because it did not outlaw the teaching of evolution. Rather, it prohibited schools from teaching evolutionary principles unless theories of creationism also were taught.

The state and various organizations offered two major lines of argument in support of this legislation. One is that evolutionary theory is a religion, the religion of secular humanism. If evolution is taught then so should creationism, which has its origin in a literal reading of Genesis. In other words, public school teachers must give equal time to the two primary "religious" views of the origin of humankind.[66] The second argument states that creationism is a science just like evolutionary theory and, therefore, deserves equal treatment in public school curricula.

Represented by the ACLU, Assistant Principal Don Aguillard, and several teachers, parents, and religious groups thought otherwise and challenged the act as a violation of the Establishment Clause. Attorneys and amici attacked the argument that creationism is a science. As amicus curiae National Academy of Sciences put it: "The explanatory power of a scientific hypothesis or theory is, in effect, the medium of exchange by which the value of a scientific theory is determined in

66. For more on this point, see Pfeffer, *Religion, State, and the Burger Court,* 73–75.

the market place of ideas that constitutes the scientific community. Creationists do not compete in the marketplace, and creation-science does not offer scientific value." From this base, attorneys found it easy to reject notions of academic freedom and fairness, at least as it pertained to this debate. For all the legislature had done, in the eyes of the ACLU, was to give equal time to a particular religion's view of the origins of humankind, which, the ACLU argued, violated the Establishment Clause.

JUSTICE BRENNAN delivered the opinion of the Court.

The Establishment Clause forbids the enactment of any law "respecting an establishment of religion." The Court has applied a three-pronged test to determine whether legislation comports with the Establishment Clause. First, the legislature must have adopted the law with a secular purpose. Second, the statute's principal or primary effect must be one that neither advances nor inhibits religion. Third, the statute must not result in an excessive entanglement of government with religion. State action violates the Establishment Clause if it fails to satisfy any of these prongs.

In this case, the Court must determine whether the Establishment Clause was violated in the special context of the public elementary and secondary school system. States and local school boards are generally afforded considerable discretion in operating public schools....

The Court has been particularly vigilant in monitoring compliance with the Establishment Clause in elementary and secondary schools. Families entrust public schools with the education of their children, but condition their trust on the understanding that the classroom will not purposely be used to advance religious views that may conflict with the private beliefs of the student and his or her family. Students in such institutions are impressionable and their attendance is involuntary. The State exerts great authority and coercive power through mandatory attendance requirements, and because of the students' emulation of teachers as role models and the children's susceptibility to peer pressure....

Therefore, in employing the three-pronged *Lemon* test, we must do so mindful of the particular concerns that arise in the context of public elementary and secondary

Don Aguillard, assistant principal at Acadiana High School in Scott, Louisiana, filed suit against the state's creation science law in 1981. Six years later, in *Edwards v. Aguillard*, the Supreme Court found that law to be in violation of the Establishment Clause.

schools. We now turn to the evaluation of the Act under the *Lemon* test.

Lemon's first prong focuses on the purpose that animated adoption of the Act.... If the law was enacted for the purpose of endorsing religion, "no consideration of the second or third criteria [of *Lemon*] is necessary." In this case, the petitioners have identified no clear secular purpose for the Louisiana Act.

True, the Act's stated purpose is to protect academic freedom. This phrase might, in common parlance, be understood as referring to enhancing the freedom of teachers to teach what they will. The Court of Appeals, however, correctly concluded that the Act was not designed to further that goal. We find no merit in the State's argument that the "legislature may not [have] use[d] the terms 'academic freedom' in the correct legal sense. They might have [had] in mind, instead, a basic concept of fairness; teaching all of the evidence." Even if "academic freedom" is read to mean "teaching all of the evidence" with respect to the origin of human beings, the Act does not further this purpose. The goal of providing a more comprehensive science curriculum is not furthered either by outlawing the teaching of evolution or by requiring the teaching of creation science.

While the Court is normally deferential to a State's articulation of a secular purpose, it is required that the statement of such purpose be sincere and not a sham....

It is clear from the legislative history that the purpose of the legislative sponsor, Senator Bill Keith, was to narrow the science curriculum. During the legislative hearings, Senator Keith stated: "My preference would be that neither [creationism nor evolution] be taught." Such a ban on teaching does not promote—indeed, it undermines—the provision of a comprehensive scientific education.

It is equally clear that requiring schools to teach creation science with evolution does not advance academic freedom. The Act does not grant teachers a flexibility that they did not already possess to supplant the present science curriculum with the presentation of theories, besides evolution, about the origin of life. Indeed, the Court of Appeals found that no law prohibited Louisiana public schoolteachers from teaching any scientific theory. As the president of the Louisiana Science Teachers Association testified, "[a]ny scientific concept that's based on established fact can be included in our curriculum already, and no legislation allowing this is necessary." The Act provides Louisiana schoolteachers with no new authority. Thus the stated purpose is not furthered by it....

Furthermore, the goal of basic "fairness" is hardly furthered by the Act's discriminatory preference for the teaching of creation science and against the teaching of evolution. While requiring that curriculum guides be developed for creation science, the Act says nothing of comparable guides for evolution. Similarly, research services are supplied for creation science but not for evolution. Only "creation scientists" can serve on the panel that supplies the resource services. The Act forbids school boards to discriminate against anyone who "chooses to be a creation-scientist" or to teach "creationism," but fails to protect those who choose to teach evolution or any other non-creation science theory, or who refuse to teach creation science.

If the Louisiana legislature's purpose was solely to maximize the comprehensiveness and effectiveness of science instruction, it would have encouraged the teaching of all scientific theories about the origins of humankind. But under the Act's requirements, teachers who were once free to teach any and all facets of this subject are now unable to do so. Moreover, the Act fails even to ensure that creation science will be taught, but instead requires the teaching of this theory only when the theory of evolution is taught. Thus we agree with the Court of Appeals' conclusion that the Act does not serve to protect academic freedom, but has the distinctly different purpose of discrediting "evolution by counterbalancing its teaching at every turn with the teaching of creation science."...

[W]e need not be blind in this case to the legislature's preeminent religious purpose in enacting this statute. There is a historic and contemporaneous link between the teachings of certain religious denominations and the teaching of evolution. It was this link that concerned the Court in *Epperson v. Arkansas* (1968), which also involved a facial challenge to a statute regulating the teaching of evolution. In that case, the Court reviewed an Arkansas statute that made it unlawful for an instructor to teach evolution or to use a textbook that referred to this scientific theory. Although the Arkansas anti-evolution law did not explicitly state its predominant religious purpose, the Court could not ignore that "[t]he statute was a product of the upsurge of 'fundamentalist' religious fervor" that has long viewed this particular scientific theory as contradicting the literal interpretation of the Bible. After reviewing the history of anti-evolution statutes, the Court determined that "there can be no doubt that the motivation for the [Arkansas] law was the same [as other anti-evolution statutes]: to suppress the teaching of a theory which, it was thought, 'denied' the divine creation of man." The Court found that there can be no legitimate state interest in protecting particular religions from scientific views "distasteful to them" and concluded "that the First Amendment does not permit the State to require that teaching and learning must be tailored to the principles or prohibitions of any religious sect or dogma."

These same historic and contemporaneous antagonisms between the teachings of certain religious denominations and the teaching of evolution are present in this case. The preeminent purpose of the Louisiana legislature was clearly to advance the religious viewpoint that a supernatural being created humankind. The term "creation science" was defined as embracing this particular religious doctrine by those responsible for the passage of the Creationism Act. Senator Keith's leading expert on creation science, Edward Boudreaux, testified at the legislative hearings that the theory of creation science included belief in the existence of a supernatural creator. Senator Keith also cited testimony from other experts to support the creation science view that "a creator [was] responsible for the universe and everything in it." The legislative history therefore reveals that the term "creation science," as contemplated by the legislature that adopted this Act, embodies the religious belief that a supernatural creator was responsible for the creation of humankind.

Furthermore, it is not happenstance that the legislature required the teaching of a theory that coincided with this religious view. The legislative history documents that the Act's primary purpose was to change the science curriculum of public schools in order to provide persuasive advantage to a particular religious doctrine that rejects the factual basis of evolution in its entirety. The sponsor of the Creationism Act, Senator Keith, explained during the legislative hearings that his disdain for the theory of evolution resulted from the support that evolution supplied to views contrary to his own religious beliefs.... The legislation therefore sought to alter the science curriculum to reflect endorsement of a religious view that is antagonistic to the theory of evolution.

In this case, the purpose of the Creationism Act was to restructure the science curriculum to conform with a particular religious viewpoint. Out of many possible science subjects taught in the public schools, the legislature chose to affect the teaching of the one scientific theory that historically has been opposed by certain religious sects. As in *Epperson*, the legislature passed the Act to give preference to those religious groups which have as one of their tenets the creation of humankind by a divine creator. The "overriding fact" that confronted the Court in *Epperson* was "that Arkansas' law selects from the body of knowledge a particular segment which it proscribes for the sole reason that it is deemed to conflict with ... a particular interpretation of the Book of Genesis by a particular religious group." Similarly, the Creationism Act is designed *either* to promote the

theory of creation science which embodies a particular religious tenet by requiring that creation science is taught whenever evolution is taught *or* to prohibit the teaching of a scientific theory disfavored by certain religious sects by forbidding the teaching of evolution when creation science is not also taught. The Establishment Clause, however, "forbids *alike* the preference of a religious doctrine *or* the prohibition of theory which is deemed antagonistic to a particular dogma." Because the primary purpose of the Creationism Act is to advance a particular religious belief, the Act endorses religion in violation of the First Amendment.

We do not imply that a legislature could never require that scientific critiques of prevailing scientific theories be taught.... But because the primary purpose of the Creationism Act is to endorse a particular religious doctrine, the Act furthers religion in violation of the Establishment Clause....

The Louisiana Creationism Act advances a religious doctrine by requiring either the banishment of the theory of evolution from public school classrooms or the presentation of a religious viewpoint that rejects evolution in its entirety. The Act violates the Establishment Clause of the First Amendment because it seeks to employ the symbolic and financial support of government to achieve a religious purpose. The judgment of the Court of Appeals therefore is

Affirmed.

JUSTICE SCALIA, with whom THE CHIEF JUSTICE joins, dissenting.

Even if I agreed with the questionable premise that legislation can be invalidated under the Establishment Clause on the basis of its motivation alone, without regard to its effects, I would still find no justification for today's decision. The Louisiana legislators who passed the "Balanced Treatment for Creation-Science and Evolution-Science Act" (Balanced Treatment Act), each of whom had sworn to support the Constitution, were well aware of the potential Establishment Clause problems and considered that aspect of the legislation with great care. After seven hearings and several months of study, resulting in substantial revision of the original proposal, they approved the Act overwhelmingly and specifically articulated the secular purpose they meant it to serve. Although the record contains abundant evidence of the sincerity of that purpose (the only issue pertinent to this case), the Court today holds, essentially on the basis of "its visceral knowledge regarding what must have motivated the legislators," that the members of the Louisiana Legislature knowingly violated their oaths and then lied about it. I dissent. Had requirements of the Balanced Treatment Act that are not apparent on its face been clarified by an interpretation of the Louisiana Supreme Court, or by the manner of its implementation, the Act might well be found unconstitutional; but the question of its constitutionality cannot rightly be disposed of on the gallop, by impugning the motives of its supporters. . . .

It is important to stress that the purpose forbidden by *Lemon* is the purpose to "advance religion.". . . Our cases in no way imply that the Establishment Clause forbids legislators merely to act upon their religious convictions. We surely would not strike down a law providing money to feed the hungry or shelter the homeless if it could be demonstrated that, but for the religious beliefs of the legislators, the funds would not have been approved. Notwithstanding the majority's implication to the contrary, we do not presume that the sole purpose of a law is to advance religion merely because it was supported strongly by organized religions or by adherents of particular faiths. . . . To do so would deprive religious men and women of their right to participate in the political process. Today's religious activism may give us the Balanced Treatment Act, but yesterday's resulted in the abolition of slavery, and tomorrow's may bring relief for famine victims. . . .

With the foregoing in mind, I now turn to the purposes underlying adoption of the Balanced Treatment Act.

We have relatively little information upon which to judge the motives of those who supported the Act. About the only direct evidence is the statute itself and transcripts of the seven committee hearings at which it was considered. . . . Nevertheless, there is ample evidence that the majority is wrong in holding that the Balanced Treatment Act is without secular purpose.

At the outset, it is important to note that the Balanced Treatment Act did not fly through the Louisiana Legislature on wings of fundamentalist religious fervor—which would be unlikely, in any event, since only a small minority of the State's citizens belong to fundamentalist religious denominations. The Act had its genesis (so to speak) in legislation introduced by Senator Bill Keith in June 1980. . . .

Before summarizing the testimony of Senator Keith and his supporters, I wish to make clear that I by no means intend to endorse its accuracy. But my views (and the views of this Court) about creation science and evolution are (or should be) beside the point. Our task is not to judge the debate about teaching the origins of life, but to ascertain what the members of the Louisiana Legislature believed. The vast majority of them voted to approve a bill which explicitly stated a secular purpose; what is crucial is not their *wisdom* in believing that purpose would be achieved by the bill, but their *sincerity* in believing it would be.

Most of the testimony in support of Senator Keith's bill came from the Senator himself and from scientists and educators he presented, many of whom enjoyed academic credentials that may have been regarded as quite impressive by members of the Louisiana Legislature. . . .

Senator Keith and his witnesses testified essentially as set forth in the following numbered paragraphs:

(1) There are two and only two scientific explanations for the beginning of life—evolution and creation science. . . .

(2) The body of scientific evidence supporting creation science is as strong as that supporting evolution. . . .

(3) Creation science is educationally valuable. Students exposed to it better understand the current state of scientific evidence about the origin of life. . . .

(4) Although creation science is educationally valuable and strictly scientific, it is now being censored from or misrepresented in the public schools. Evolution, in turn, is misrepresented as an absolute truth. . . .

(5) The censorship of creation science has at least two harmful effects. First, it deprives students of knowledge of one of the two scientific explanations for the origin of life and leads them to believe that evolution is proven fact; thus, their education suffers and they are wrongly taught that science has proved their religious beliefs false. Second, it violates the Establishment Clause. The United States Supreme Court has held that secular humanism is a religion. . . .

We have no way of knowing, of course, how many legislators believed the testimony of Senator Keith and his witnesses. But in the absence of evidence to the contrary, we have to assume that many of them did. Given that assumption, the Court today plainly errs in holding that the Louisiana Legislature passed the Balanced Treatment Act for exclusively religious purposes. . . .

I have to this point assumed the validity of the *Lemon* "purpose" test. In fact, however, I think the pessimistic evaluation that THE CHIEF JUSTICE made of the totality of Lemon is particularly applicable to the "purpose" prong: it is "a constitutional theory [that] has no basis in the history of the amendment it seeks to interpret, is difficult to apply and yields unprincipled results. . . . "

Our cases interpreting and applying the purpose test have made such a maze of the Establishment Clause that even the most conscientious governmental officials can only guess what motives will be held unconstitutional. We have said essentially the following: Government may not act with the purpose of advancing religion, except when forced to do so by the Free Exercise Clause (which is now and then); or when eliminating existing governmental hostility to religion (which exists sometimes); or even when merely accommodating governmentally uninhibited religious practices, except that at some point (it is unclear where) intentional accommodation results in the fostering of religion, which is of course unconstitutional.

But the difficulty of knowing what vitiating purpose one is looking for is as nothing compared with the difficulty of knowing how or where to find it. For while it is possible to discern the objective "purpose" of a statute (*i.e.,* the public good at which its provisions appear to be directed), or even the formal motivation for a statute where that is explicitly set forth (as it was, to no avail, here), discerning the subjective motivation of those enacting the statute is, to be honest, almost always an impossible task. The number of possible motivations, to begin with, is not binary, or indeed even finite. In the present case, for example, a particular legislator need not have voted for the Act either because he wanted to foster religion or because he wanted to improve education. He may have thought the bill would provide jobs for his district, or may have wanted to make amends with a faction of his party he had alienated on another vote, or he may have been a close friend of the bill's sponsor, or he may have been repaying a favor he owed the Majority Leader, or he may have hoped the Governor would appreciate his vote and make a fundraising appearance for him, or he may have been pressured to vote for a bill he disliked by a wealthy contributor . . . or, of course, he may have had (and very likely did have) a combination of some of the above and many other motivations. To look for *the sole purpose* of

even a single legislator is probably to look for something that does not exist.

Putting that problem aside, however, where ought we to look for the individual legislator's purpose? We cannot of course assume that every member present (if, as is unlikely, we know who or even how many they were) agreed with the motivation expressed in a particular legislator's pre-enactment floor or committee statement. Quite obviously, "[w]hat motivates one legislator to make a speech about a statute is not necessarily what motivates scores of others to enact it.". . . Can we assume, then, that they all agree with the motivation expressed in the staff-prepared committee reports they might have read—even though we are unwilling to assume that they agreed with the motivation expressed in the very statute that they voted for? Should we consider post-enactment floor statements? Or post-enactment testimony from legislators, obtained expressly for the lawsuit? Should we consider media reports on the realities of the legislative bargaining? All of these sources, of course, are eminently manipulable. . . .

Given the many hazards involved in assessing the subjective intent of governmental decisionmakers, the first prong of *Lemon* is defensible, I think, only if the text of the Establishment Clause demands it. That is surely not the case. The Clause states that "Congress shall make no law respecting an establishment of religion." One could argue, I suppose, that any time Congress acts with the *intent* of advancing religion, it has enacted a "law respecting an establishment of religion"; but far from being an unavoidable reading, it is quite an unnatural one. . . . It is, in short, far from an inevitable reading of the Establishment Clause that it forbids all governmental action intended to advance religion; and if not inevitable, any reading with such untoward consequences must be wrong.

In the past we have attempted to justify our embarrassing Establishment Clause jurisprudence on the ground that it "sacrifices clarity and predictability for flexibility.". . . One commentator has aptly characterized this as "a euphemism . . . for . . . the absence of any principled rationale." I think it time that we sacrifice some "flexibility" for "clarity and predictability." Abandoning *Lemon*'s purpose test—a test which exacerbates the tension between the Free Exercise and Establishment Clauses, has no basis in the language or history of the Amendment, and, as today's decision shows, has wonderfully flexible consequences— would be a good place to start.

Writing for the Court, Brennan had little trouble applying *Lemon* to rule against the state. The majority found that the law lacked a secular purpose; rather, its purpose was to "endorse a particular religious view." But Justice Scalia's dissent is a sign of things to come. Not only does Scalia adopt the state's argument that there is "ample uncontradicted testimony" to indicate that "creation science is a body of scientific knowledge rather than a revealed belief," but also he criticizes the purpose prong of *Lemon* as "indefensible" and as a main contributor to the Court's "embarrassing Establishment Clause jurisprudence." This may have been Scalia's first attack on *Lemon* but, as we know from *Lamb's Chapel*, it would not be his last. Since *Edwards v. Aguillard*, Scalia has become more adamant in his view that *Lemon* should be discarded in favor of a standard that would bring more "clarity and predictability" to this area of the law.

Government Endorsement of Religion: Holiday Displays

In *Epperson* Justice Fortas wrote, "The First Amendment mandates governmental neutrality between religion and religion, between religion and nonreligion." His statement provides a theoretical way to think about the relationship between church and state, but as citizens we are confronted with daily reminders that the United States does not follow Fortas's words. For example, all the U.S. currency in your pocket carries the words: "In God We Trust." Does that motto represent government endorsement of religion over nonreligion? What about the national Christmas tree? It stands in front of the White House, the home of the head of our secular nation. Yet the tree is a symbol associated with Christianity. Its annual appearance seems to violate Fortas's principle because it represents government endorsement of one religion over another. In fact, the presence (and general acceptance) of religious mottoes and symbols supports Justice Douglas's classic statement: "We are a religious people whose institutions presuppose a Supreme Being."

That Americans "are a religious people," the majority of whom accept "In God We Trust" on currency or even a national Christmas tree, however, should not be taken to mean that all symbolic endorsements of religion are legally acceptable. The problem is separating the permissible from the impermissible, and this issue has not been easy for the Court to resolve, as its holiday display cases indicate.

When private store owners place religious symbols in their windows, no constitutional questions arise. But when governments pay for the erection of such symbols or allow their property to be used for the placement of religious displays, questions concerning the separation of church and state abound.

The Court first considered these questions in *Lynch v. Donnelly* (1984), which involved the constitutionality of state-sponsored Christmas nativity scenes (crèches). For more than forty years, the city of Pawtucket, Rhode Island, and its Retail Merchants Association erected a Christmas display in a park owned by a nonprofit organization. The display included a Santa Claus house, reindeer, a Christmas tree, a clown, colored lights, a Season's Greetings banner, and a crèche with the Christ Child, Mary and Joseph, angels, animals, and so forth. In 1973 the city spent $1,365 for a new crèche, and it cost $20 to set it up and take it down each year. Believing that these annual expenditures for the crèche constituted a violation of the Establishment Clause, the state Civil Liberties Union brought suit against the city. City officials and area business people countered that the Christmas display had a secular purpose: to attract customers to the city's downtown shopping area.

Writing for a five-person majority, Chief Justice Burger found that the display was not an impermissible breach of the Establishment Clause. In one of his more strongly worded accommodationist opinions, he pointed to many examples indicating "an unbroken history of official acknowledgment by all three branches of government of the role of religion in American life": executive orders proclaiming Christmas and Thanksgiving as national holidays, "In God We Trust" on currency, publicly supported art galleries full of religious paintings. This examination led him to conclude that

the crèche is identified with one religious faith.... [But] to forbid the use of this one passive symbol—the crèche—at the very time people are taking note of the season with Christmas hymns and carols in public schools and other public places, and while the Congress and legislatures open session with prayers by paid chaplains, would be a stilted overreaction contrary to our history and to our holdings. If the presence of the crèche violates the Establishment Clause, a host of other forms of taking official note of Christmas, and our religious heritage, are equally offensive to the Constitution.

In short, Burger implied that Christmas was so much a part of our heritage that it came close to representing a national, nonsectarian celebration, rather than a religious holiday.

Burger's opinion is interesting because, although he applied *Lemon* to find that there was a secular purpose for the crèche, he also said, "We have repeatedly emphasized our unwillingness to be confined to any single test." This modifying statement did not go unnoticed; it was, after all, the first time a majority opinion hinted at the demise of *Lemon*. In dissent, Brennan (joined by Marshall, Blackmun, and Stevens) wrote, "The Court's less-than-vigorous application of the *Lemon* test suggests that its commitment to those standards may only be superficial." He then went on to assert that applying a more vigorous version of *Lemon* to the case leads to the conclusion that the crèche's inclusion in the display "does not reflect a clearly secular purpose."

The dissenters wanted the Court to apply *Lemon* strictly, but O'Connor, in a concurring opinion, suggested a new way to frame the three-pronged standard. She proposed to focus *Lemon*'s purpose prong on "whether the government's actual purpose is to en-

dorse or disapprove religions" and the effect prong on "whether, irrespective of government's actual purpose, the practice under review in fact conveys a message of endorsement or disapproval." Invocation of this endorsement standard led her to conclude that the city did not "intend to convey any message of endorsement of Christianity or disapproval of non-Christian religions." She based this conclusion mainly on the fact that the crèche was a small part of a larger holiday display. "Celebration of public holidays," O'Connor reasoned, "which have cultural significance even if they also have religious aspects, is a legitimate secular purpose."

As we know from our examination of *Lamb's Chapel*, this endorsement standard figured into the Court's resolution of that 1993 case. But would the Court use it in another holiday display case, *County of Allegheny v. ACLU*? Or would it simply cite Burger's majority opinion as precedent? Keep in mind that when the Court heard this case, Burger was no longer on the Court, nor was Powell, who voted with the *Lynch* majority. Did these membership changes affect the outcome of *County of Allegheny*? Also note that Blackmun's opinion was a judgment, not a statement of the majority's views. What did those who concurred and dissented advocate?

County of Allegheny v. ACLU

492 U.S. 573 (1989)
Opinion announcing the judgment of the Court: Blackmun
Concurring in part (Brennan, Kennedy, Marshall, O'Connor, Rehnquist, Scalia, Stevens, White)
Dissenting in part (Brennan, Kennedy, Marshall, Rehnquist, Scalia, Stevens, White)
Opinion concurring in part: O'Connor
Opinion concurring in part and dissenting in part: Brennan, Kennedy, Stevens

County of Allegheny concerns the constitutionality of two holiday displays erected every year in downtown

As part of its holiday decorations, Allegheny County, Pennsylvania, erected on public property a nativity scene and a combined Christmas tree and menorah display. In *County of Allegheny v. ACLU* (1989) the Supreme Court ruled that the crèche violated the separation of church and state principle, but that the combined exhibit did not.

Pittsburgh, Pennsylvania. The first is a crèche that belongs to a Roman Catholic group, the Holy Name Society. Beginning with the Christmas season of 1981, the city allowed the society to place the crèche on the grand staircase of the county courthouse, which is, by all accounts, the "main," "most beautiful," and "most public" part of the courthouse. In addition to the usual nativity scene, the display includes banner that reads *Gloria in Excelsis Deo,* a phrase from the Gospel of Luke meaning "Glory to God in the Highest." A few poinsettias and a small tree complete the display.

The second challenged display is a Hanukkah menorah located outside of the City-County Building, where the mayor and other city officials have their offices. For much of its history, the city erected only a Christmas tree outside this building, but, beginning in the 1980s, it began to include the menorah. By 1986 the entire display included a forty-five-foot Christmas tree complete with lights and ornaments; an eighteen-foot Hanukkah menorah, owned by a Jewish group, but stored and erected by the city; and a sign with the heading "Salute to Liberty" and these words: "During

this holiday season, the City of Pittsburgh salutes liberty. Let these festive lights remind us that we are the keepers of the flame of liberty and our legacy of freedom."

In 1986 the Pittsburgh chapter of the ACLU and several residents of the city filed suit, challenging the constitutionality of the crèche and the menorah. They argued that the displays violated the Religious Establishment Clause.

JUSTICE BLACKMUN announced the judgment of the Court.

In the course of adjudicating specific cases, this Court has come to understand the Establishment Clause to mean that government may not promote or affiliate itself with any religious doctrine or organization, may not discriminate among persons on the basis of their religious beliefs and practices, may not delegate a governmental power to a religious institution, and may not involve itself too deeply in such an institution's affairs. Although "the myriad, subtle ways in which Establishment Clause values can be eroded" are not susceptible to a single verbal formulation, this Court has attempted to encapsulate the essential precepts of the Establishment Clause....

In *Lemon v. Kurtzman* (1971) the Court sought to refine these principles by focusing on three "tests" for determining whether a government practice violates the Establishment Clause....

Our subsequent decisions further have refined the definition of governmental action that unconstitutionally advances religion. In recent years, we have paid particularly close attention to whether the challenged governmental practice either has the purpose or effect of "endorsing" religion, a concern that has long had a place in our Establishment Clause jurisprudence.

Of course, the word "endorsement" is not self-defining. Rather, it derives its meaning from other words that this Court has found useful over the years in interpreting the Establishment Clause. Thus, it has been noted that the prohibition against governmental endorsement of religion "preclude[s] government from conveying or attempting to convey a message that religion or a particular religious belief is *favored* or *preferred*." Moreover, the term "endorsement" is closely linked to the term "promotion," and this Court long since has held that government "may not ... promote one religion or religious theory against another or even against the militant opposite."

Whether the key word is "endorsement," "favoritism," or "promotion," the essential principle remains the same. The Establishment Clause, at the very least, prohibits government from appearing to take a position on questions of religious belief or from "making adherence to a religion relevant in any way to a person's standing in the political community."

We have had occasion in the past to apply Establishment Clause principles to the government's display of objects with religious significance.... [In] *Lynch v. Donnelly* [1984] ... we considered whether the city of Pawtucket, R.I., had violated the Establishment Clause by including a crèche in its annual Christmas display, located in a private park within the downtown shopping district....

The rationale of the majority opinion in *Lynch* is none too clear: the opinion contains two strands, neither of which provides guidance for decision in subsequent cases. First, the opinion states that the inclusion of the crèche in the display was "no more an advancement or endorsement of religion" than other "endorsements" this Court has approved in the past, but the opinion offers no discernible measure for distinguishing between permissible and impermissible endorsements. Second, the opinion observes that any benefit the government's display of the crèche gave to religion was no more than "indirect, remote, and incidental"—without saying how or why.

Although JUSTICE O'CONNOR joined the majority opinion in *Lynch*, she wrote a concurrence that differs in significant respects from the majority opinion. The main difference is that the concurrence provides a sound analytical framework for evaluating governmental use of religious symbols.

First and foremost, the concurrence squarely rejects any notion that this Court will tolerate some government endorsement of religion....

Second, the concurrence articulates a method for determining whether the government's use of an object with religious meaning has the effect of endorsing religion. The effect of the display depends upon the message that the government's practice communicates: the question is "what viewers [or "reasonable observers"] may fairly understand to be the purpose of the display." That inquiry, of necessity, turns upon the context in which the contested object appears: "a typical museum setting, though not neutralizing the religious content of a religious painting, negates any message of endorsement of that content."...

... These general principles are sound, and have been adopted by the Court in subsequent cases.... Accordingly, our present task is to determine whether the display of the crèche and the menorah, in their respective "particular physical settings," has the effect of endorsing or disapproving religious beliefs.

We turn first to the county's crèche display....

Under the Court's holding in *Lynch*, the effect of a crèche display turns on its setting. Here, unlike in *Lynch*, nothing in the context of the display detracts from the crèche's religious message. The *Lynch* display comprised a series of figures and objects, each group of which had its own focal point. Santa's house and his reindeer were objects of attention separate from the crèche, and had their specific visual story to tell.... Here, in contrast, the crèche stands alone: it is the single element of the display on the Grand Staircase....

... No viewer could reasonably think that it occupies this location without the support and approval of the government. Thus, by permitting the "display of the crèche in this particular physical setting," the county sends an unmistakable message that it supports and promotes the Christian praise to God that is the crèche's religious message....

In sum, *Lynch* teaches that government may celebrate Christmas in some manner and form, but not in a way that endorses Christian doctrine. Here, Allegheny County has transgressed this line. It has chosen to celebrate Christmas in a way that has the effect of endorsing a patently Christian message: Glory to God for the birth of Jesus Christ. Under *Lynch,* and the rest of our cases, nothing more is required to demonstrate a violation of the Establishment Clause. The display of the crèche in this context, therefore, must be permanently enjoined....

The display of the Chanukah menorah in front of the City-County Building may well present a closer constitutional question. The menorah, one must recognize, is a religious symbol: it serves to commemorate the miracle of the oil as described in the Talmud. But the menorah's message is not exclusively religious. The menorah is the primary visual symbol for a holiday that, like Christmas, has both religious and secular dimensions.

Moreover, the menorah here stands next to a Christmas tree and a sign saluting liberty. While no challenge has been made here to the display of the tree and the sign, their presence is obviously relevant in determining the effect of the menorah's display. The necessary result of placing a menorah next to a Christmas tree is to create an "overall holiday setting" that represents both Christmas and Chanukah—two holidays, not one....

Accordingly, the relevant question for Establishment Clause purposes is whether the combined display of the tree, the sign, and the menorah has the effect of endorsing both Christian and Jewish faiths, or rather simply recognizes that both Christmas and Chanukah are part of the same winter-holiday season, which has attained a secular status in our society. Of the two interpretations of this particular display, the latter seems far more plausible and is also in line with *Lynch.*

The Christmas tree, unlike the menorah, is not itself a religious symbol. Although Christmas trees once carried religious connotations, today they typify the secular celebration of Christmas. Numerous Americans place Christ-

mas trees in their homes without subscribing to Christian religious beliefs, and when the city's tree stands alone in front of the City-County Building, it is not considered an endorsement of Christian faith. Indeed, a 40-foot Christmas tree was one of the objects that validated the crèche in *Lynch.* The widely accepted view of the Christmas tree as the preeminent secular symbol of the Christmas holiday season serves to emphasize the secular component of the message communicated by other elements of an accompanying holiday display, including the Chanukah menorah.

The tree, moreover, is clearly the predominant element in the city's display. The 45-foot tree occupies the central position beneath the middle archway in front of the Grant Street entrance to the City-County Building; the 18-foot menorah is positioned to one side. Given this configuration, it is much more sensible to interpret the meaning of the menorah in light of the tree, rather than *vice versa.* In the shadow of the tree, the menorah is readily understood as simply a recognition that Christmas is not the only traditional way of observing the winter-holiday season. In these circumstances, then, the combination of the tree and the menorah communicates, not a simultaneous endorsement of both Christian and Jewish faith, but instead, a secular celebration of Christmas coupled with an acknowledgment of Chanukah as a contemporaneous alternative tradition.

Although the city has used a symbol with religious meaning as its representation of Chanukah, this is not a case in which the city has reasonable alternatives that are less religious in nature. It is difficult to imagine a predominantly secular symbol of Chanukah that the city could place next to its Christmas tree. An 18-foot dreidel would look out of place, and might be interpreted by some as mocking the celebration of Chanukah. The absence of a more secular alternative symbol is itself part of the context in which the city's actions must be judged in determining the likely effect of its use of the menorah. Where the government's secular message can be conveyed by two symbols, only one of which carries religious meaning, an observer reasonably might infer from the fact that the government has chosen to use the religious symbol that the government means to promote religious faith. But where, as here, no such choice has been made, this inference of endorsement is not present.

The Mayor's sign further diminishes the possibility that

the tree and the menorah will be interpreted as a dual endorsement of Christianity and Judaism. The sign states that during the holiday season the city salutes liberty. Moreover, the sign draws upon the theme of light, common to both Chanukah and Christmas as winter festivals, and links that theme with this Nation's legacy of freedom, which allows an American to celebrate the holiday season in whatever way he wishes, religiously or otherwise.... Here, the Mayor's sign serves to confirm what the context already reveals: that the display of the menorah is not an endorsement of religious faith but simply a recognition of cultural diversity.

Given all these considerations, it is not "sufficiently likely" that residents of Pittsburgh will perceive the combined display of the tree, the sign, and the menorah as an "endorsement" or "disapproval ... of their individual religious choices." While an adjudication of the display's effect must take into account the perspective of one who is neither Christian nor Jewish, as well as of those who adhere to either of these religions, the constitutionality of its effect must also be judged according to the standard of a "reasonable observer." When measured against this standard, the menorah need not be excluded from this particular display. The Christmas tree alone in the Pittsburgh location does not endorse Christian belief; and, on the facts before us, the addition of the menorah "cannot fairly be understood to" result in the simultaneous endorsement of Christian and Jewish faiths. On the contrary, for purposes of the Establishment Clause, the city's overall display must be understood as conveying the city's secular recognition of different traditions for celebrating the winter-holiday season....

Lynch v. Donnelly confirms, and in no way repudiates, the longstanding constitutional principle that government may not engage in a practice that has the effect of promoting or endorsing religious beliefs. The display of the crèche in the County Courthouse has this unconstitutional effect. The display of the menorah in front of the City-County Building, however, does not have this effect, given its "particular physical setting."

The judgment of the Court of Appeals is affirmed in part and reversed in part, and the cases are remanded for further proceedings.

It is so ordered.

JUSTICE KENNEDY, with whom THE CHIEF JUSTICE, JUSTICE WHITE, and JUSTICE SCALIA join, concurring in the judgment in part and dissenting in part.

The majority holds that the County of Allegheny violated the Establishment Clause by displaying a crèche in the county courthouse, because the "principal or primary effect" of the display is to advance religion within the meaning of *Lemon v. Kurtzman* (1971). This view of the Establishment Clause reflects an unjustified hostility toward religion, a hostility inconsistent with our history and our precedents, and I dissent from this holding. The crèche display is constitutional, and, for the same reasons, the display of a menorah by the city of Pittsburgh is permissible as well. On this latter point, I concur in the result, but not the reasoning ... of JUSTICE BLACKMUN'S opinion.

In keeping with the usual fashion of recent years, the majority applies the *Lemon* test to judge the constitutionality of the holiday displays here in question. I am content for present purposes to remain within the *Lemon* framework, but do not wish to be seen as advocating, let alone adopting, that test as our primary guide in this difficult area. Persuasive criticism of *Lemon* has emerged. See *Edwards v. Aguillard* (1987) (SCALIA, J., dissenting).... Substantial revision of our Establishment Clause doctrine may be in order; but it is unnecessary to undertake that task today, for even the *Lemon* test, when applied with proper sensitivity to our traditions and our case law, supports the conclusion that both the crèche and the menorah are permissible displays in the context of the holiday season....

Rather than requiring government to avoid any action that acknowledges or aids religion, the Establishment Clause permits government some latitude in recognizing and accommodating the central role religion plays in our society.... Any approach less sensitive to our heritage would border on latent hostility toward religion, as it would require government in all its multifaceted roles to acknowledge only the secular, to the exclusion and so to the detriment of the religious....

The ability of the organized community to recognize and accommodate religion in a society with a pervasive public sector requires diligent observance of the border between accommodation and establishment. Our cases disclose two limiting principles: government may not coerce anyone to support or participate in any religion or its exercise; and it may not, in the guise of avoiding hostility or callous indifference, give direct benefits to religion in such a degree that it in fact "establishes a [state] religion or religious faith, or tends to do so.". . . These two principles, while distinct, are not unrelated, for it would be difficult indeed to establish a religion without some measure of more or less subtle coercion, be it in the form of taxation to supply the substantial benefits that would sustain a state-established faith, direct compulsion to observance, or governmental exhortation to religiosity that amounts in fact to proselytizing. . . .

In determining whether there exists an establishment, or a tendency toward one, we refer to the other types of church-state contacts that have existed unchallenged throughout our history, or that have been found permissible in our case law. In *Lynch*, for example, we upheld the city of Pawtucket's holiday display of a crèche, despite the fact that "the display advance[d] religion in a sense.". . . Non-coercive government action within the realm of flexible accommodation or passive acknowledgment of existing symbols does not violate the Establishment Clause unless it benefits religion in a way more direct and more substantial than practices that are accepted in our national heritage.

These principles are not difficult to apply to the facts of the cases before us. In permitting the displays on government property of the menorah and the crèche, the city and county sought to do no more than "celebrate the season" and to acknowledge, along with many of their citizens, the historical background and the religious, as well as secular, nature of the Chanukah and Christmas holidays. This interest falls well within the tradition of government accommodation and acknowledgment of religion that has marked our history from the beginning. It cannot be disputed that government, if it chooses, may participate in sharing with its citizens the joy of the holiday season, by declaring public holidays, installing or permitting festive displays, sponsoring celebrations and parades, and providing holiday vacations for its employees. All levels of our government do precisely that. . . .

If government is to participate in its citizens' celebration of a holiday that contains both a secular and a religious component, enforced recognition of only the secular aspect would signify the callous indifference toward religious faith that our cases and traditions do not require; for by commemorating the holiday only as it is celebrated by nonadherents, the government would be refusing to acknowledge the plain fact, and the historical reality, that many of its citizens celebrate its religious aspects as well. Judicial invalidation of government's attempts to recognize the religious underpinnings of the holiday would signal not neutrality but a pervasive intent to insulate government from all things religious. The Religion Clauses do not require government to acknowledge these holidays or their religious component; but our strong tradition of government accommodation and acknowledgment permits government to do so. . . .

There is no suggestion here that the government's power to coerce has been used to further the interests of Christianity or Judaism in any way. No one was compelled to observe or participate in any religious ceremony or activity. Neither the city nor the county contributed significant amounts of tax money to serve the cause of one religious faith. The crèche and the menorah are purely passive symbols of religious holidays. Passersby who disagree with the message conveyed by these displays are free to ignore them, or even to turn their backs, just as they are free to do when they disagree with any other form of government speech. . . .

If *Lynch* is still good law—and until today it was—the judgment below cannot stand. I accept and indeed approve both the holding and the reasoning of Chief Justice Burger's opinion in *Lynch*, and so I must dissent from the judgment that the crèche display is unconstitutional. On the same reasoning, I agree that the menorah display is constitutional. . . .

Even if *Lynch* did not control, I would not commit this Court to the test applied by the majority today. The notion that cases arising under the Establishment Clause should be decided by an inquiry into whether a "'reasonable observer'" may "'fairly understand'" government action to "'sen[d] a message to nonadherents that they are outsiders, not full members of the political community,'" is a recent, and in my view most unwelcome, addition to our tangled Establishment Clause jurisprudence. . . . I submit that the endorsement test is flawed in its fundamentals and unworkable in practice. The uncritical adoption of this standard is every bit as troubling as the bizarre result it produces in the cases before us. . . .

If the endorsement test, applied without artificial exceptions for historical practice, reached results consistent with history, my objections to it would have less force. But, as I understand that test, the touchstone of an Establishment Clause violation is whether nonadherents would be made to feel like "outsiders" by government recognition or accommodation of religion. Few of our traditional practices recognizing the part religion plays in our society can withstand scrutiny under a faithful application of this formula.

Some examples suffice to make plain my concerns. Since the Founding of our Republic, American Presidents have issued Thanksgiving Proclamations establishing a national day of celebration and prayer. The first such proclamation was issued by President Washington at the request of the First Congress, and "recommend[ed] and assign[ed]" a day "to be devoted by the people of these States to the service of that great and glorious Being.". . . It requires little imagination to conclude that these proclamations would cause nonadherents to feel excluded, yet they have been a part of our national heritage from the beginning. . . .

The United States Code itself contains religious references that would be suspect under the endorsement test. Congress has directed the President to "set aside and proclaim a suitable day each year . . . as a National Day of Prayer, on which the people of the United States may turn to God in prayer and meditation at churches, in groups, and as individuals." This statute does not require anyone to pray, of course, but it is a straightforward endorsement of the concept of "turn[ing] to God in prayer.". . .

. . . Either the endorsement test must invalidate scores of traditional practices recognizing the place religion holds in our culture, or it must be twisted and stretched to avoid inconsistency with practices we know to have been permitted in the past, while condemning similar practices with no greater endorsement effect simply by reason of their lack of historical antecedent. Neither result is acceptable.

Throughout this chapter, we have noted that scholars criticize the Court for reaching inconsistent, puzzling, and even amusing decisions. *County of Allegheny* provides ammunition for these critics. Because Blackmun's judgment centers on the kinds of objects, in juxtaposition to one another, that holiday displays may or may not contain it has been the source of some ridicule. As one federal judge put it, holiday displays have come to "require scrutiny more commonly associated with interior decorators than with the judiciary."[67] Moreover, public school teachers, city officials, firefighters, and the like must now give careful consideration to the kinds of symbols they can erect. And even after careful consideration they may be unable to derive sure answers. As a 1993 newspaper article put it:

Pity the public school principal in December. Between Hanukkah, Christmas and Kwanzaa [a holiday celebrated by African Americans to honor family and community], this long last month lays a minefield of grand proportions for educators trying to acknowledge the holidays without bridging the separation of church and state. Every decoration is fraught with peril. Every lesson and every song must pass the "does not promote religion" test. Red and green cookies? Maybe. "A Christmas Carol?" Maybe. "Silent Night?" Definitely not.[68]

County of Allegheny also sends mixed signals about the appropriate legal standards to adjudicate religious establishment claims. Blackmun's judgment adopts O'Connor's endorsement standard from her concurrence in *Lynch*. But this standard does not end reliance on *Lemon;* it merely gives another way to apply parts of it *(see Table 3-3).* Kennedy (joined by Rehnquist, White, and Scalia) attacks the endorsement standard as "an unwelcome addition to our tangled Establishment Clause jurisprudence." In its (and *Lemon*'s) place, he would adopt a "coercion" standard. Under this approach, the justices would prohibit government activities only if they "coerce anyone to support or participate in any religion" or if they "give direct benefits to religion in such a degree" that it in fact "established a religion . . . or tends to do so." Applying this standard to holiday displays, Kennedy found the crèche and the menorah permissible under the Es-

---

67. Judge Easterbrook dissenting in *American Jewish Congress v. Chicago*, 827 F. 2d 120, at 129; quoted in *Lee v. Weisman* by Justice Scalia.

68. Kimberly J. McLarin, "Holiday Dilemma at Schools: Is That a Legal Decoration?" *New York Times*, December 16, 1993, 1, 15.

tablishment Clause because they do not foster even subtle coercion.[69]

Prayer in School

Throughout this section we have seen the Court change the standards by which it adjudicates religious establishment claims, reason through cases in seemingly inconsistent ways, divide over the resolution of major issues, and cause public consternation and debate. The subject of prayer magnifies all of these observations. Moreover, prayer is a topic that has occupied part of the Court's agenda since the 1960s. It therefore provides us with an excellent vehicle by which to reexamine and summarize what we have learned about how the Court, under Chief Justices Warren, Burger, and Rehnquist, has approached establishment questions.

Prayer and the Warren Court. Throughout most of the nation's history, almost all public schools engaged in religious practices of some kind: they may have held devotional services, distributed Bibles, or taught about religion. Particularly prevalent was prayer in school. Even into the 1960s, as Table 3-5 indicates, the Bible was read regularly in most public schools in the South and East; in other schools, students recited state-written prayers. Separationist groups *(see Box 3-3)* believed that these practices violated the Establishment Clause and set out to convince the Court to eradicate them. Their initial suit, *Engel v. Vitale* (1962), challenged a New York practice that each morning had public school children reciting a prayer written by the state's board of regents: "Almighty God, we acknowledge our dependence upon Thee, and we beg Thy blessings upon us, our parents, our teachers and our country." New York representatives argued that this prayer was innocuous and purposefully drafted so that it would not favor one religion over another. They also argued that recitation was voluntary: students who did not want to participate

69. See Sherry, "Lee v. Weisman: Paradox Redux," 131.

TABLE 3-5 Variations in Incidence of Bible Reading in Public School by Region, 1960 and 1966

| Region | Percentage of Schools Reporting Bible Reading | |
	1960	1966
East	67.6	4.3
Midwest	18.3	5.2
South	76.8	49.5
West	11.0	2.3

SOURCE: Frank J. Sorauf, *The Wall of Separation* (Princeton: Princeton University Press, 1976), 297.

could remain silent or leave the room. The New York Civil Liberties Union, representing parents from a Long Island school district, claimed the religious neutrality of the prayer and the voluntary aspect were irrelevant. What mattered was that the state had written it and, therefore, violated the Establishment Clause.

Writing for the Court, Justice Black adopted the separationist argument:

We think the constitutional prohibition against laws respecting the establishment of religion must at least mean that in this country it is no part of the business of government to compose official prayers for any group of the American people to recite as a part of a religious program carried out by the government.

Only Justice Stewart dissented from the Court's opinion. After citing many examples of congressional approval of religion, including the legislation adding the words "In God We Trust" on currency, he quoted Justice Douglas's statement, written a decade before in the released-time case: "We are a religious people whose institutions presuppose a Supreme Being." What New York "has done has been to recognize and to follow the deeply entrenched and highly cherished spiritual traditions of our Nation," he said.

Despite the majority's strong words, the decision was not a complete victory for separationists. The Court failed to enunciate a strict legal definition of establishment (it announced no standard), and it dealt with only one aspect of prayer in school—state-written prayers—and not the more widespread practice of Bible readings. Moreover, *Engel* generated a tremendous public backlash. Less than 20 percent of the public supported the Court's decision; Congress considered constitutional amendments to overturn it; and church leaders condemned it. Most of the justices described themselves as "surprised and pained" by the negative reaction. Chief Justice Warren later wrote: "I vividly remember one bold newspaper headline, 'Court outlaws God.' Many religious leaders in this same spirit condemned the Court." Justice Clark defended the Court's opinion in a public address: "Here was a state-written prayer circulated by the school district to state-employed teachers with instructions to have their pupils recite it. [The Constitution] provides that both state and Federal governments shall take no part respecting the establishment of religion.... 'No' means 'No.' That was all the Court decided."[70]

With all this uproar, it is no wonder that separationist groups were concerned when the Court agreed to hear arguments in a case involving the more prevalent practice of Bible readings in public schools. Would the justices cave in to public pressure and reverse their stance in *Engel?*

School District of Abington Township v. Schempp

374 U.S. 203 (1963)

Vote: 8 (Black, Brennan, Clark, Douglas, Goldberg, Harlan, Warren, White)
    1 (Stewart)

Opinion of the Court: Clark
Concurring opinions: Brennan, Douglas, Goldberg
Dissenting opinion: Stewart

Successful in convincing the Court to strike down the recitation of a state-written prayers in school, sepa-

rationist groups came back to challenge the other, more common form—readings from the Bible and the recitation of the Lord's Prayer—at the beginning of each day. Although these practices were most prevalent in the South *(see Table 3-5),* separationists decided to avoid litigating in that region, fearing a negative outcome. Instead, they found a Pennsylvania family that was willing to serve as plaintiffs.

The Schempps were not atheists; in fact, they were members of a Unitarian church, where they regularly attended services. But they did not want their children, Roger and Donna, to engage in Bible reading at their public school. To them "specific religious doctrines purveyed by a literal reading of the Bible" were discordant with their particular religious beliefs. Pennsylvania law, however, mandated that "at least ten verses from the Holy Bible shall be read, without comment, at the opening of each public school on each school day." Following the law, Roger and Donna's school, Abington High, held opening exercises each morning while the students were in their homerooms. The required number of Bible verses were read over the school's public address system, and the reading was followed by a recitation of the Lord's Prayer, during which students stood and repeated the prayer in unison. Those students whose parents did not want them to participate could, under the Pennsylvania law, leave the room.

Edward Schempp decided to challenge the practice.[71] The reasons he gave were that teachers and classmates would label Donna and Roger as "odd balls," or "atheists," a term with "very bad" connotations to Schempp; Roger and Donna would miss hearing morning announcements that were read after the religious readings; and other students, seeing Donna and Roger in the halls, would think they were being punished for "bad conduct."

---

70. Quotes from the justices come from Bernard Schwartz, *Super Chief* (New York: New York University Press, 1983), 441–442.

71. This case was decided with *Murray v. Curlett* (1963). Madalyn Murray, who would later become a leader of the atheist movement in the United States, challenged a Maryland school practice of reading a chapter in the Bible and/or the Lord's Prayer each morning.

Separationist groups presented Schempp's reasons to the trial court. They also brought in religious leaders and other religious experts to support the claim that Bible readings inherently favored some religions over others and violated principles of religious establishment. Attorneys for the school board, on the other hand, sought to frame the case in moral rather than religious terms. They also found their own expert witnesses to testify that the Bible was "nonsectarian." But, by the time it reached the Supreme Court, it was quite clear that they were asking the justices to overrule *Engel.*[72]

MR. JUSTICE CLARK delivered the opinion of the Court.

[T]his Court has rejected unequivocally the contention that the Establishment Clause forbids only governmental preference of one religion over another. Almost 20 years ago in *Everson* the Court said that "[n]either a state nor the Federal Government can set up a church. Neither can pass laws which aid one religion, aid all religions, or prefer one religion over another."...

... In short, the Court held that the Amendment

"requires the state to be a neutral in its relations with groups of religious believers and non-believers; it does not require the state to be their adversary. State power is no more to be used so as to handicap religions than it is to favor them."

... The wholesome "neutrality" of which this Court's cases speak ... stems from a recognition of the teachings of history that powerful sects or groups might bring about a fusion of governmental and religious functions or a concert or dependency of one upon the other to the end that official support of the State or Federal Government would be placed behind the tenets of one or of all orthodoxies. This the Establishment Clause prohibits. And a further reason for neutrality is found in the Free Exercise Clause, which recognizes the value of religious training, teaching and observance and, more particularly, the right of every person to freely choose his own course with reference thereto, free of any compulsion from the state. This the Free Exercise Clause

guarantees. Thus, as we have seen, the two clauses may overlap. As we have indicated, the Establishment Clause has been directly considered by this Court eight times in the past score of years and, with only one Justice dissenting on the point, it has consistently held that the clause withdrew all legislative power respecting religious belief or the expression thereof. The test may be stated as follows: what are the purpose and the primary effect of the enactment? If either is the advancement or inhibition of religion then the enactment exceeds the scope of legislative power as circumscribed by the Constitution. That is to say that to withstand the strictures of the Establishment Clause there must be a secular legislative purpose and a primary effect that neither advances nor inhibits religion. Everson v. Board of Education.... The Free Exercise Clause, likewise considered many times here, withdraws from legislative power, state and federal, the exertion of any restraint on the free exercise of religion. Its purpose is to secure religious liberty in the individual by prohibiting any invasions thereof by civil authority. Hence it is necessary in a free exercise case for one to show the coercive effect of the enactment as it operates against him in the practice of his religion. The distinction between the two clauses is apparent—a violation of the Free Exercise Clause is predicated on coercion while the Establishment Clause violation need not be so attended.

Applying the Establishment Clause principles to the cases at bar we find that the States are requiring the selection and reading at the opening of the school day of verses from the Holy Bible and the recitation of the Lord's Prayer by the students in unison. These exercises are prescribed as part of the curricular activities of students who are required by law to attend school. They are held in the school buildings under the supervision and with the participation of teachers employed in those schools. None of these factors, other than compulsory school attendance, was present in the program upheld in Zorach v. Clauson. The trial court in [Schempp] has found that such an opening exercise is a religious ceremony and was intended by the State to be so. We agree with the trial court's finding as to the religious character of the exercises. Given that finding, the exercises and the law requiring them are in violation of the Establishment Clause....

The conclusion follows that ... the [law] require[s] religious exercises and such exercises are being conducted in

---

72. See Schwartz, *Super Chief,* 466.

direct violation of the rights of the appellees and petitioners. Nor are these required exercises mitigated by the fact that individual students may absent themselves upon parental request, for that fact furnishes no defense to a claim of unconstitutionality under the Establishment Clause. Further, it is no defense to urge that the religious practices here may be relatively minor encroachments on the First Amendment. The breach of neutrality that is today a trickling stream may all too soon become a raging torrent and, in the words of Madison, "it is proper to take alarm at the first experiment on our liberties."

It is insisted that unless these religious exercises are permitted a "religion of secularism" is established in the schools. We agree of course that the State may not establish a "religion of secularism" in the sense of affirmatively opposing or showing hostility to religion, thus "preferring those who believe in no religion over those who do believe.".... We do not agree, however, that this decision in any sense has that effect. In addition, it might well be said that one's education is not complete without a study of comparative religion or the history of religion and its relationship to the advancement of civilization. It certainly may be said that the Bible is worthy of study for its literary and historic qualities. Nothing we have said here indicates that such study of the Bible or of religion, when presented objectively as part of a secular program of education, may not be effected consistently with the First Amendment. But the exercises here do not fall into those categories. They are religious exercises, required by the States in violation of the command of the First Amendment that the Government maintain strict neutrality, neither aiding nor opposing religion.

Finally, we cannot accept that the concept of neutrality, which does not permit a State to require a religious exercise even with the consent of the majority of those affected, collides with the majority's right to free exercise of religion. While the Free Exercise Clause clearly prohibits the use of state action to deny the rights of free exercise to anyone, it has never meant that a majority could use the machinery of the State to practice its beliefs....

The place of religion in our society is an exalted one, achieved through a long tradition of reliance on the home, the church and the inviolable citadel of the individual heart and mind. We have come to recognize through bitter experience that it is not within the power of government to invade that citadel, whether its purpose or effect be to aid or oppose, to advance or retard. In the relationship between man and religion, the State is firmly committed to a position of neutrality. Though the application of that rule requires interpretation of a delicate sort, the rule itself is clearly and concisely stated in the words of the First Amendment. Applying that rule to the facts of these cases, we affirm the judgment in [Schempp]....

It is so ordered.

MR. JUSTICE STEWART, dissenting.

I think the records in the two cases before us are so fundamentally deficient as to make impossible an informed or responsible determination of the constitutional issues presented. Specifically, I cannot agree that on these records we can say that the Establishment Clause has necessarily been violated. But I think there exist serious questions under both that provision and the Free Exercise Clause ... which require the remand of these cases for the taking of additional evidence....

... For there is involved in these cases a substantial free exercise claim on the part of those who affirmatively desire to have their children's school day open with the reading of passages from the Bible....

It might ... be argued that parents who want their children exposed to religious influences can adequately fulfill that wish off school property and outside school time. With all its surface persuasiveness, however, this argument seriously misconceives the basic constitutional justification for permitting the exercises at issue in these cases. For a compulsory state educational system so structures a child's life that if religious exercises are held to be an impermissible activity in schools, religion is placed at an artificial and state-created disadvantage. Viewed in this light, permission of such exercises for those who want them is necessary if the schools are truly to be neutral in the matter of religion. And a refusal to permit religious exercises thus is seen, not as the realization of state neutrality, but rather as the establishment of a religion of secularism, or at the least, as government support of the beliefs of those who think that religious exercises should be conducted only in private....

... [I]t is important to stress that, strictly speaking, what is at issue here is a privilege rather than a right. In other words, the question presented is not whether exercises such as those at issue here are constitutionally compelled, but rather whether they are constitutionally invalid. And that issue, in my view, turns on the question of coercion.

It is clear that the dangers of coercion involved in the holding of religious exercises in a schoolroom differ qualitatively from those presented by the use of similar exercises or affirmations in ceremonies attended by adults. Even as to children, however, the duty laid upon government in connection with religious exercises in the public schools is that of refraining from so structuring the school environment as to put any kind of pressure on a child to participate in those exercises; it is not that of providing an atmosphere in which children are kept scrupulously insulated from any awareness that some of their fellows may want to open the school day with prayer, or of the fact that there exist in our pluralistic society differences of religious belief....

Viewed in this light, it seems to me clear that the records in both of the cases before us are wholly inadequate to support an informed or responsible decision. Both cases involve provisions which explicitly permit any student who wishes, to be excused from participation in the exercises. There is no evidence ... as to whether there would exist any coercion of any kind upon a student who did not want to participate.... In the Schempp case the record shows no more than a subjective prophecy by a parent of what he thought would happen if a request were made to be excused from participation in the exercises under the amended statute. No such request was ever made, and there is no evidence whatever as to what might or would actually happen, nor of what administrative arrangements the school actually might or could make to free from pressure of any kind those who do not want to participate in the exercises....

What our Constitution indispensably protects is the freedom of each of us, be he Jew or Agnostic, Christian or Atheist, Buddhist or Freethinker, to believe or disbelieve, to worship or not worship, to pray or keep silent, according to his own conscience, uncoerced and unrestrained by government. It is conceivable that these school boards, or even all school boards, might eventually find it impossible to administer a system of religious exercises during school hours in such a way as to meet this constitutional standard—in such a way as completely to free from any kind of official coercion those who do not affirmatively want to partici-

pate. But I think we must not assume that school boards so lack the qualities of inventiveness and good will as to make impossible the achievement of that goal.

I would remand both cases for further hearings.

The *Schempp* decision was an important, perhaps landmark, statement. As we observed earlier, it set out a standard of law, a two-pronged test that served as the forerunner of *Lemon*. But take note of Justice Stewart's dissent: his coercion approach provided fodder for justices of the Rehnquist Court—particularly Kennedy—who would later attempt to etch some version of it into law. In 1963 it represented the position of one justice. It was the *Abington* eight-person majority that carried the day. The Court clearly indicated that it would stand behind its ruling in *Engel*, despite the public backlash.

However, if the justices thought that *Abington* would quell the prayer-in-school controversy they had ignited in *Engel*, they could not have been more wrong. Opinion polls taken after *Abington* indicated that only 24 percent of the public supported the Court's decision. As shown in Figure 3-2, that number has remained relatively stable over the past two decades; at the very least, support has never surpassed the 50 percent mark. Given public antipathy for *Abington* and *Engel*, it is not surprising to find widespread noncompliance with the Court's decisions. Several years after *Abington* came down, political scientist Robert Birkby asked school officials in Tennessee whether prayer had been eliminated from their schools.[73] One would suspect that Birkby's respondents would "overestimate compliance"[74] since the practice at issue was unconstitutional. But only 1 of the 121 respondents admitted to having totally eliminated Bible readings and the like. Note the 1966

73. Robert Birkby, "The Supreme Court in the Bible Belt: Tennessee Reaction to the *Schempp* Decision," *American Journal of Political Science* (1966) 10: 304.
74. Jeffrey A. Segal and Harold J. Spaeth, *The Supreme Court and the Attitudinal Model* (Cambridge: Cambridge University Press, 1993), 339.

FIGURE 3-2 Approval of Supreme Court Decision Preventing Organized Prayer in School

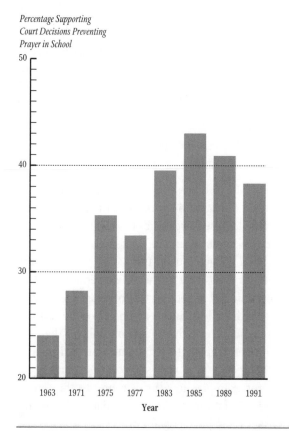

Percentage Supporting Court Decisions Preventing Prayer in School

SOURCES: 1971: Harold W. Stanley and Richard G. Niemi, *Vital Statistics on American Politics*, 3d ed. (Washington, D.C.: CQ Press, 1992), 21; all other years: Lee Epstein, Jeffrey A. Segal, Harold J. Spaeth, and Thomas G. Walker, *The Supreme Court Compendium: Data, Decisions, and Developments* (Washington, D.C.: Congressional Quarterly, 1994), Table 8-22.

NOTE: The question was: "The U.S. Supreme Court has ruled that no state or local government may require the reading of the Lord's prayer or Bible verses in public schools. What are your views on this?

data in Table 3-5: the schools in the South continued to allow Bible readings, despite the Court's decision in *Abington.*

The lack of public support for the Court's rulings in *Engel* and *Abington* also helps to explain why Congress considered nearly 150 proposals to overturn the decisions through a constitutional amendment. One introduced by Rep. Frank Becker, R-N.Y., was typical:

Nothing in this Constitution shall be deemed to prohibit the offering, reading from, or listening to prayers of Biblical Scriptures, if participation therein is on a voluntary basis, in any governmental or public school, institution or place.

In 1966 and 1971 simple majorities passed versions of a prayer-in-school amendment. But these votes were insufficient to send the amendment to the states (a two-thirds vote is required), and the proposals died in Congress.[75]

Prayer and the Burger Court. With the death of the prayer-in-school constitutional amendment in 1971, the issue moved to the back burner of American politics. But not for long. The election of Ronald Reagan, a vocal opponent of the Court's decisions, in 1980 once again brought prayer to the forefront. In one of his State of the Union addresses, Reagan proclaimed that "God should never have been expelled from America's classrooms." He also began a new movement to amend the Constitution with this proposal, introduced into Congress in 1982:

Nothing in this Constitution shall be construed to prohibit individual or group prayer in public schools or other public institutions. No person shall be required by the United States or any state to participate in prayer.

In 1984 the Republican-dominated Senate came close to approving Reagan's proposal, but the vote of 56–44 again fell short of the necessary two-thirds vote.[76]

Once the proposal was defeated, all eyes turned to the Burger Court, which gave signs of being sympathetic to the use of prayer in public places. Consider its ruling in *Marsh v. Chambers* (1983), issued while the Senate was debating Reagan's prayer-in-school amendment. Chambers, a member of the Nebraska legislature, challenged that body's use of a legislative chaplain to open each session with a prayer, a practice

75. See David G. Barnum, *The Supreme Court and American Democracy* (New York: St. Martin's, 1993), 145.

76. See Pfeffer, *Religion, State, and the Burger Court*, 99–103; and Barnum, *The Supreme Court and American Democracy*, 146.

since 1965. For his services, the chaplain, a Presbyterian minister, received $319.75 for each month the legislature was in session. Applying the three-pronged *Lemon* standard, a court of appeals held for Chambers, noting that the use of legislative chaplains violated all three parts. The legislature then appealed to the U.S. Supreme Court.

That the Court would eventually hear such a case was predicted by Justice Douglas in 1963. When Justice Black circulated his majority opinion in *Engel v. Vitale*, the first school-prayer case, Douglas wrote the following memo to Black:

As you know I have had troubles with ... *Engel v. Vitale*.... I am inclined to reverse if we are prepared to disallow public property and public funds to be used to finance religious exercise.

If, however, we would strike down a New York requirement that public school teachers open each day with a prayer, I think we could not consistently open each of our sessions with prayer. That's the kernel of my problem.[77]

Black did not adjust his opinion, and Douglas ended up filing a concurring opinion in which he stated his opposition to government funding of any religious activity, including the use of legislative chaplains.

But times had changed. Black and Douglas had long since departed the Court. They, and many other members of the Warren Court, had been replaced by jurists, such as Rehnquist and Burger, who, as we know, were far more sympathetic to accommodationist claims. It is not surprising that the Court reversed the court of appeals and upheld the use of legislative chaplains. What was surprising, however, was that Burger—writing for Justices Blackmun, O'Connor, Powell, Rehnquist, and White—ignored the *Lemon* test, substituting instead a reliance on history. He justified this substitution on the grounds that the intent of the Framers was all too clear:

[T]he first Congress, as one of its early items of business, adopted the policy of selecting a chaplain to open each session with prayer.... Clearly the men who wrote the First Amendment Religion Clauses did not view paid legislative chaplains and opening prayers as a violation of that Amendment, for the practice of opening sessions with prayer has continued without interruption ever since....

In light of the unambiguous and unbroken history of more than 200 years, there can be no doubt that the practice of opening legislative sessions with prayer has become part of the fabric of society. To invoke Divine guidance on a public body entrusted with making the laws is not, in these circumstances, an "establishment" of religion or a step toward establishment; it is simply a tolerable acknowledgment of beliefs widely held among the people of this country.

In short, *Marsh* represents the first (though, as we know from *County of Allegheny*, not the last) time the Court failed to use *Lemon* since its articulation in 1971.

The dissenters, Brennan, Marshall, and Stevens, argued that Burger's substitution of the intent of the Framers for the *Lemon* test was disingenuous, for, in their eyes, he did so because the three-pronged standard would have led him to a conclusion he did not want to reach: legislative chaplains violated the First Amendment. One might also argue that the intent of the Framers was less clear than Burger suggested. Recall, for example, how the delegates to the constitutional convention reacted to Benjamin Franklin's proposal to bring in clergy for prayer.

For the Reagan administration, Burger's opinion was cause for optimism. The chief justice had invoked originalism, an approach to adjudication Reagan and his colleagues advocated. In light of the defeat of Reagan's amendment, the decision provided some indication that the Court might be ready to reconsider prayer in school.

Would the Court take this step and overturn *Abington* and *Engel*? Would it continue its reliance on the intent of the Framers, instead of *Lemon*, to adjudicate prayer-in-school cases? These were some of the questions observers asked when the Court agreed to hear *Wallace v. Jaffree* (1985).

---

77. Memo of June 11, 1962. In *The Douglas Letters* by Melvin I. Urofsky (Bethesda, Md.: Adler and Adler, 1987), 200.

Wallace v. Jaffree

472 U.S. 38 (1985)

Vote: 6 (Blackmun, Brennan, Marshall, O'Connor,
*   Powell, Stevens)*
*   3 (Burger, Rehnquist, White)*
Opinion of the Court: Stevens
Concurring opinions: O'Connor, Powell
Dissenting opinions: Burger, Rehnquist, White

Between 1978 and 1982 the Alabama legislature passed three laws involving prayer in school.

16-1-20 (1978) authorized one minute of silence in all public schools "for meditation."

16-1-20.1 (1981) authorized a period of silence in all public schools "for meditation or voluntary prayer."

16-1-20.2 (1982) authorized teachers to lead "willing students" in prayer to "Almighty God ... the Creator and Supreme Judge of the world."

Following these laws, Chioke Jaffree's kindergarten teacher led him and the other students in a daily song: "God is Great, God is good, Let us thank Him for our food; Bow our head, we all are fed, Give us Lord our daily bread." When Chioke reported this to his father, Ishmael Jaffree, a lawyer with the Legal Services Corporation in Alabama, he was not pleased. Ishmael Jaffree had diverse religious roots, but he and his wife agreed "that their children should be raised to choose their own religious faith—or none."[78]

Jaffree first sought to stop the practice by contacting school officials. After the school board's attorney assured him that the state's laws were consistent with Court precedent, Jaffree filed suit in a U.S. district court. In his complaint, Jaffree raised the same kinds of objections that Edward Schempp had expressed two decades earlier: the state's laws and public school religious practices subjected his children to "various acts of religious indoctrination" and ostracized them

Ishmael Jaffree of Mobile, Alabama, shown with his family, challenged the constitutionality of an Alabama law that required prayer and moments of silence in public schools. In *Wallace v. Jaffree* (1985) the Supreme Court said the law was in conflict with the Establishment Clause.

"from their peer group's class members if they did not participate."

Initially, the district court found nothing defective about 16-1-20, but, based on testimony of Alabama legislator Donald Holmes, it agreed to consider the constitutionality of the other two provisions. Holmes, who had been the "prime sponsor" of 16-1-20.1, said that the purpose of that particular law was "to return voluntary prayer to our public schools"; he had "no other purpose in mind." Even so, after a four-day trial the court upheld the constitutionality of the challenged statutes. The court concluded that "the es-

---

78. See Peter Irons, *The Courage of Their Convictions*, chap. 15, for more on this case.

tablishment clause of the first amendment to the U.S. Constitution does not prohibit the state from establishing a religion." Jaffree then asked a U.S. court of appeals to overturn the district court's decision to uphold 16-1-20.1 and 16-1-20.2. It did so on the grounds that "both statutes advance and encourage religious activity" in ways that were inconsistent with Supreme Court precedent.

The state asked the U.S. Supreme Court to review the court of appeals' ruling. In 1984 the Court summarily affirmed that court's decision on 16-1-20.2. So the only remaining task for the justices was to determine whether 16-1-20.1, authorizing a period of silence in all public schools "for meditation or voluntary prayer," was constitutional. Jaffree argued that it was not: the law, at least according to its sponsor, lacked a secular purpose as required by *Lemon*. He also asserted that the previous school prayer cases, *Engel* and *Abington*, invalidated 16-1-20.2. The state countered that the law does not "in any way offend the constitution" because it "neither proscribes prayer; nor affirms religious belief; nor coerces religious exercise." The Reagan administration supported this position. In an amicus curiae brief, the solicitor general relied heavily on *Zorach v. Clauson*, upholding released-time programs for religious training, and the intent of the Framers to assert that 16-1-20.1 was "perfectly neutral with respect to religious practices. It neither favors one religion over another nor conveys endorsement of religion."

JUSTICE STEVENS delivered the opinion of the Court.

When the Court has been called upon to construe the breadth of the Establishment Clause, it has examined the criteria developed over a period of many years. Thus, in *Lemon v. Kurtzman*, we wrote:

"Every analysis in this area must begin with consideration of the cumulative criteria developed by the Court over many years. Three such tests may be gleaned from our cases. First, the statute must have a secular legislative purpose; second, its principal or primary effect must be one that neither advances nor inhibits religion ...; finally, the statute must not foster 'an excessive government entanglement with religion.'"

It is the first of these three criteria that is most plainly implicated by this case.... [N]o consideration of the second or third criteria is necessary if a statute does not have a clearly secular purpose. For even though a statute that is motivated in part by a religious purpose may satisfy the first criterion ... the First Amendment requires that a statute must be invalidated if it is entirely motivated by a purpose to advance religion.

In applying the purpose test, it is appropriate to ask "whether government's actual purpose is to endorse or disapprove of religion." In this case, the answer to that question is dispositive. For the record not only provides us with an unambiguous affirmative answer, but it also reveals that the enactment of §16-1-20.1 was not motivated by any clearly secular purpose—indeed, the statute had *no* secular purpose.

The sponsor of the bill that became §16-1-20.1, Senator Donald Holmes, inserted into the legislative record—apparently without dissent—a statement indicating that the legislation was an "effort to return voluntary prayer" to the public schools. Later Senator Holmes confirmed this purpose before the District Court. In response to the question whether he had any purpose for the legislation other than returning voluntary prayer to public schools, he stated: "No, I did not have no other purpose in mind." The State did not present evidence of *any* secular purpose....

The legislative intent to return prayer to the public schools is, of course, quite different from merely protecting every student's right to engage in voluntary prayer during an appropriate moment of silence during the school day. The 1978 statute [§16-1-20] already protected that right, containing nothing that prevented any student from engaging in voluntary prayer during a silent minute of meditation. Appellants have not identified any secular purpose that was not fully served by §16-1-20 before the enactment of §16-1-20.1. Thus, only two conclusions are consistent with the text of §16-1-20.1: (1) the statute was enacted to convey a message of state endorsement and promotion of prayer; or (2) the statute was enacted for no purpose. No one suggests that the statute was nothing but a meaningless or irrational act.

We must, therefore, conclude that the Alabama Legislature intended to change existing law and that it was motivated by the same purpose that ... Senator Holmes' testimony frankly described. The Legislature enacted §16-1-20.1, despite the existence of §16-1-20, for the sole purpose of expressing the State's endorsement of prayer activities for one minute at the beginning of each school day. The addition of "or voluntary prayer" indicates that the State intended to characterize prayer as a favored practice. Such an endorsement is not consistent with the established principle that the government must pursue a course of complete neutrality toward religion.

The importance of that principle does not permit us to treat this as an inconsequential case involving nothing more than a few words of symbolic speech on behalf of the political majority. For whenever the State itself speaks on a religious subject, one of the questions that we must ask is "whether the Government intends to convey a message of endorsement or disapproval of religion." The well-supported concurrent findings of the District Court and the Court of Appeals—that §16-1-20.1 was intended to convey a message of state approval of prayer activities in the public schools—make it unnecessary, and indeed inappropriate, to evaluate the practical significance of the addition of the words "or voluntary prayer" to the statute. Keeping in mind, as we must, "both the fundamental place held by the Establishment Clause in our constitutional scheme and the myriad, subtle ways in which Establishment Clause values can be eroded," we conclude that §16-1-20.1 violates the First Amendment.

JUSTICE POWELL, concurring.

I concur in the Court's opinion and judgment that Ala. Code §16-1-20.1 violates the Establishment Clause of the First Amendment....

I write separately to express additional views and to respond to criticism of the three-pronged *Lemon* test. *Lemon v. Kurtzman* (1971) identifies standards that have proven useful in analyzing case after case both in our decisions and in those of other courts. It is the only coherent test a majority of the Court has ever adopted. Only once since our decision in *Lemon* have we addressed an Establishment Clause issue without resort to its three-pronged test. See *Marsh v. Chambers* (1983). *Lemon* has not been overruled or

its test modified. Yet, continued criticism of it could encourage other courts to feel free to decide Establishment Clause cases on an *ad hoc* basis.

JUSTICE O'CONNOR, concurring in the judgment.

I write separately to identify the peculiar features of the Alabama law that render it invalid, and to explain why moment of silence laws in other States do not necessarily manifest the same infirmity. I also write to explain why neither history nor the Free Exercise Clause of the First Amendment validates the Alabama law struck down by the Court today....

As this case ... demonstrates, however, "it is far easier to agree on the purpose that underlies the First Amendment's Establishment and Free Exercise Clauses than to obtain agreement on the standards that should govern their application."... It once appeared that the Court had developed a workable standard by which to identify impermissible government establishments of religion. See *Lemon v. Kurtzman* (1971).... Despite its initial promise, the *Lemon* test has proven problematic.... JUSTICE REHNQUIST today suggests that we abandon *Lemon* entirely, and in the process limit the reach of the Establishment Clause to state discrimination between sects and government designation of a particular church as a "state" or "national" one.

Perhaps because I am new to the struggle, I am not ready to abandon all aspects of the *Lemon* test. I do believe, however, that the standards announced in *Lemon* should be reexamined and refined in order to make them more useful in achieving the underlying purpose of the First Amendment. We must strive to do more than erect a constitutional "signpost" ... to be followed or ignored in a particular case as our predilections may dictate. Instead, our goal should be "to frame a principle for constitutional adjudication that is not only grounded in the history and language of the first amendment, but one that is also capable of consistent application to the relevant problems." Last Term, I proposed a refinement of the *Lemon* test with this goal in mind. *Lynch v. Donnelly* (concurring opinion).

The *Lynch* concurrence suggested that the religious liberty protected by the Establishment Clause is infringed when the government makes adherence to religion relevant to a person's standing in the political community. Direct government action endorsing religion or a particular religious practice is invalid under this approach because it "sends a message to nonadherents that they are outsiders, not full members of the political community, and an accompanying message to adherents that they are insiders, favored members of the political community." Under this view, *Lemon*'s inquiry as to the purpose and effect of a statute requires courts to examine whether government's purpose is to endorse religion and whether the statute actually conveys a message of endorsement....

The endorsement test does not preclude government from acknowledging religion or from taking religion into account in making law and policy. It does preclude government from conveying or attempting to convey a message that religion or a particular religious belief is favored or preferred.... At issue today is whether state moment of silence statutes in general, and Alabama's moment of silence statute in particular, embody an impermissible endorsement of prayer in public schools.

Twenty-five states permit or require public school teachers to have students observe a moment of silence in their classrooms. A few statutes provide that the moment of silence is for the purpose of meditation alone. The typical statute, however, calls for a moment of silence at the beginning of the school day during which students may meditate, pray, or reflect on the activities of the day....

The *Engel* and *Abington* decisions are not dispositive on the constitutionality of moment of silence laws. In those cases, public school teachers and students led their classes in devotional exercises....

A state sponsored moment of silence in the public schools is different from state sponsored vocal prayer or Bible reading. First, a moment of silence is not inherently religious. Silence, unlike prayer or Bible reading, need not be associated with a religious exercise. Second, a pupil who participates in a moment of silence need not compromise his or her beliefs. During a moment of silence, a student who objects to prayer is left to his or her own thoughts, and is not compelled to listen to the prayers or thoughts of others. For these simple reasons, a moment of silence statute does not stand or fall under the Establishment Clause according to how the Court regards vocal prayer or Bible reading....

By mandating a moment of silence, a State does not necessarily endorse any activity that might occur during the period.... Even if a statute specifies that a student may choose to pray silently during a quiet moment, the State has not thereby encouraged prayer over other specified alternatives....

... The relevant issue is whether an objective observer, acquainted with the text, legislative history, and implementation of the statute, would perceive it as a state endorsement of prayer in public schools.... A moment of silence law that is clearly drafted and implemented so as to permit prayer, meditation, and reflection within the prescribed period, without endorsing one alternative over the others, should pass this test.

The analysis above suggests that moment of silence laws in many States should pass Establishment Clause scrutiny because they do not favor the child who chooses to pray during a moment of silence over the child who chooses to meditate or reflect. Alabama Code §16-1-20.1 does not stand on the same footing. However deferentially one examines its text and legislative history, however objectively one views the message attempted to be conveyed to the public, the conclusion is unavoidable that the purpose of the statute is to endorse prayer in public schools. I accordingly agree with the Court of Appeals that the Alabama statute has a purpose which is in violation of the Establishment Clause, and cannot be upheld....

The Court does not hold that the Establishment Clause is so hostile to religion that it precludes the States from affording schoolchildren an opportunity for voluntary silent prayer. To the contrary, the moment of silence statutes of many States should satisfy the Establishment Clause standard we have here applied. The Court holds only that Alabama has intentionally crossed the line between creating a quiet moment during which those so inclined may pray, and affirmatively endorsing the particular religious practice of prayer. This line may be a fine one, but our precedents and the principles of religious liberty require that we draw it.

CHIEF JUSTICE BURGER, dissenting.

Some who trouble to read the opinions in these cases will find it ironic—perhaps even bizarre—that on the very day we heard arguments in the cases, the Court's session opened with an invocation for Divine protection. Across the park a few hundred yards away, the House of Representatives and the Senate regularly open each session with a prayer. These legislative prayers are not just one minute in duration, but are extended, thoughtful invocations and prayers for Divine guidance. They are given, as they have been since 1789, by clergy appointed as official chaplains and paid from the Treasury of the United States....

Inevitably some wag is bound to say that the Court's holding today reflects a belief that the historic practice of the Congress and this Court is justified because members of the Judiciary and Congress are more in need of Divine guidance than are schoolchildren. Still others will say that all this controversy is "much ado about nothing," since no power on earth—including this Court and Congress—can stop any teacher from opening the school day with a moment of silence for pupils to meditate, to plan their day—or to pray if they voluntarily elect to do so.

I make several points about today's curious holding.

(a) It makes no sense to say that Alabama has "endorsed prayer" by merely enacting a new statute "to specify expressly that voluntary prayer is *one* of the authorized activities during a moment of silence." To suggest that a moment-of-silence statute that includes the word "prayer" unconstitutionally endorses religion, while one that simply provides for a moment of silence does not, manifests not neutrality but hostility toward religion....

(c) The Court's extended treatment of the "test" of *Lemon v. Kurtzman* suggests a naive preoccupation with an easy, bright-line approach for addressing constitutional issues. We have repeatedly cautioned that *Lemon* did not establish a rigid caliper capable of resolving every Establishment Clause issue, but that it sought only to provide "signposts."...

(d) The notion that the Alabama statute is a step toward creating an established church borders on, if it does not trespass into, the ridiculous. The statute does not remotely threaten religious liberty; it affirmatively furthers the values of religious freedom and tolerance that the Establishment Clause was designed to protect. Without pressuring those who do not wish to pray, the statute simply creates an opportunity to think, to plan, or to pray if one wishes—as Congress does by providing chaplains and chapels.... The statute "endorses" only the view that the religious obser-

vances of others should be tolerated and, where possible, accommodated. If the government may not accommodate religious needs when it does so in a wholly neutral and non-coercive manner, the "benevolent neutrality" that we have long considered the correct constitutional standard will quickly translate into the "callous indifference" that the Court has consistently held the Establishment Clause does not require.

The Court today has ignored the wise admonition of Justice Goldberg that "the measure of constitutional adjudication is the ability and willingness to distinguish between real threat and mere shadow."... The innocuous statute that the Court strikes down does not even rise to the level of "mere shadow." JUSTICE O'CONNOR paradoxically acknowledges: "It is difficult to discern a serious threat to religious liberty from a room of silent, thoughtful schoolchildren." I would add to that, "even if they choose to pray."

The mountains have labored and brought forth a mouse.

JUSTICE WHITE, dissenting.

I appreciate JUSTICE REHNQUIST's explication of the history of the Religion Clauses of the First Amendment. Against that history, it would be quite understandable if we undertook to reassess our cases dealing with these Clauses, particularly those dealing with the Establishment Clause. Of course, I have been out of step with many of the Court's decisions dealing with this subject matter, and it is thus not surprising that I would support a basic reconsideration of our precedents.

JUSTICE REHNQUIST, dissenting.

Thirty-eight years ago this Court, in *Everson v. Board of Education*, summarized its exegesis of Establishment Clause doctrine thus:

"In the words of Jefferson, the clause against establishment of religion by law was intended to erect 'a wall of separation between church and State.'" *Reynolds v. United States* (1879).

This language from *Reynolds*, a case involving the Free Exercise Clause of the First Amendment rather than the Establishment Clause, quoted from Thomas Jefferson's letter to the Danbury Baptist Association the phrase "I contemplate with sovereign reverence that act of the whole American people which declared that their legislature should 'make no law respecting an establishment of religion, or prohibiting the free exercise thereof,' thus building a wall of separation between church and State."

It is impossible to build sound constitutional doctrine upon a mistaken understanding of constitutional history, but unfortunately the Establishment Clause has been expressly freighted with Jefferson's misleading metaphor for nearly forty years. Thomas Jefferson was of course in France at the time the constitutional amendments known as the Bill of Rights were passed by Congress and ratified by the states. His letter to the Danbury Baptist Association was a short note of courtesy, written fourteen years after the amendments were passed by Congress. He would seem to any detached observer as a less than ideal source of contemporary history as to the meaning of the Religion Clauses of the First Amendment.

Jefferson's fellow Virginian, James Madison, with whom he was joined in the battle for the enactment of the Virginia Statute of Religious Liberty of 1786, did play as large a part as anyone in the drafting of the Bill of Rights. He had two advantages over Jefferson in this regard: he was present in the United States, and he was a leading Member of the First Congress. But when we turn to the record of the proceedings in the First Congress leading up to the adoption of the Establishment Clause of the Constitution, including Madison's significant contributions thereto, we see a far different picture of its purpose than the highly simplified "wall of separation between church and State."...

On the basis of the record of these proceedings in the House of Representatives, James Madison was undoubtedly the most important architect among the members of the House of the amendments which became the Bill of Rights, but it was James Madison speaking as an advocate of sensible legislative compromise.... His sponsorship of the amendments in the House was obviously not that of a zealous believer in the necessity of the Religion Clauses, but of one who felt it might do some good, could do no harm, and would satisfy those who had ratified the Constitution on the condition that Congress propose a Bill of Rights. His original language "nor shall any national religion be established" obviously does not conform to the "wall of separation" between church and State idea which latter day commentators have ascribed to him. His explanation on the floor of the meaning of his language—"that Congress

should not establish a religion, and enforce the legal observation of it by law" is of the same ilk....

It would seem ... that the Establishment Clause of the First Amendment had acquired a well-accepted meaning: it forbade establishment of a national religion, and forbade preference among religious sects or denominations. Indeed, the first American dictionary defined the word "establishment" as "the act of establishing, founding, ratifying or ordaining," such as in "[t]he episcopal form of religion, so called, in England." 1 N. Webster, American Dictionary of the English Language (1st ed. 1828). The Establishment Clause did not require government neutrality between religion and irreligion nor did it prohibit the federal government from providing nondiscriminatory aid to religion. There is simply no historical foundation for the proposition that the Framers intended to build the "wall of separation" that was constitutionalized in *Everson*.

Notwithstanding the absence of a historical basis for this theory of rigid separation, the wall idea might well have served as a useful albeit misguided analytical concept, had it led this Court to unified and principled results in Establishment Clause cases. The opposite, unfortunately, has been true; in the 38 years since *Everson* our Establishment Clause cases have been neither principled nor unified. Our recent opinions, many of them hopelessly divided pluralities, have with embarrassing candor conceded that the "wall of separation" is merely a "blurred, indistinct, and variable barrier," which "is not wholly accurate" and can only be "dimly perceived."...

But the greatest injury of the "wall" notion is its mischievous diversion of judges from the actual intentions of the drafters of the Bill of Rights.... The "wall of separation between church and State" is a metaphor based on bad history, a metaphor which has proved useless as a guide to judging. It should be frankly and explicitly abandoned.

The Court has more recently attempted to add some mortar to *Everson*'s wall through the three-part test of *Lemon v. Kurtzman* which served at first to offer a more useful test for purposes of the Establishment Clause than did the "wall" metaphor....

... [D]ifficulties [arose in applying *Lemon*] because the ... test has no more grounding in the history of the First Amendment than does the wall theory upon which it rests. The three-part test represents a determined effort to craft a workable rule from a historically faulty doctrine; but the rule can only be as sound as the doctrine it attempts to service. The three-part test has simply not provided adequate standards for deciding Establishment Clause cases, as this Court has slowly come to realize. Even worse, the *Lemon* test has caused this Court to fracture into unworkable plurality opinions, depending upon how each of the three factors applies to a certain state action. The results from our school services cases show the difficulty we have encountered in making the *Lemon* test yield principled results. . . .

If a constitutional theory has no basis in the history of the amendment it seeks to interpret, is difficult to apply and yields unprincipled results, I see little use in it. . . . We have done much straining since 1947, but still we admit that we can only "dimly perceive" the *Everson* wall. . . . Our perception has been clouded not by the Constitution but by the mists of an unnecessary metaphor.

The true meaning of the Establishment Clause can only be seen in its history. As drafters of our Bill of Rights, the Framers inscribed the principles that control today. Any deviation from their intentions frustrates the permanence of that Charter and will only lead to the type of unprincipled decision making that has plagued our Establishment Clause cases since *Everson*.

The Framers intended the Establishment Clause to prohibit the designation of any church as a "national" one. The Clause was also designed to stop the Federal Government from asserting a preference for one religious denomination or sect over others. . . . As its history abundantly shows, however, nothing in the Establishment Clause requires government to be strictly neutral between religion and irreligion, nor does that Clause prohibit Congress or the States from pursuing legitimate secular ends through nondiscriminatory sectarian means.

The Court strikes down the Alabama statute . . . because the State wished to "characterize prayer as a favored practice." It would come as much of a shock to those who drafted the Bill of Rights as it will to a large number of thoughtful Americans today to learn that the Constitution, as construed by the majority, prohibits the Alabama Legislature from "endorsing" prayer. George Washington himself, at the request of the very Congress which passed the Bill of Rights, proclaimed a day of "public thanksgiving and prayer, to be observed by acknowledging with grateful hearts the many and signal favors of Almighty God." History must judge whether it was the father of his country in 1789, or a majority of the Court today, which has strayed from the meaning of the Establishment Clause.

The State surely has a secular interest in regulating the manner in which public schools are conducted. Nothing in the Establishment Clause of the First Amendment, properly understood, prohibits any such generalized "endorsement" of prayer. I would therefore reverse the judgment of the Court of Appeals.

Wallace is an important decision, for, despite public opinion *(see Figure 3-2)* and the clear preferences of the Reagan administration, the Court did not overturn *Engel* or *Abington*. To the contrary, the Court's rejection of the Alabama law reaffirmed its commitment to those decisions. What is more, Justice Stevens's majority opinion shows that an intent of the Framers approach does not necessarily lead to the kind of accommodationist outcome the Reagan administration favored. Note how he animated the first prong of *Lemon:* by examining the intent of the legislators who wrote the law. Stevens found it easy to conclude that the law lacked a secular legislative purpose.

Finally, although the majority opinion invoked *Lemon*, the justices were not unanimous in their support for the three-pronged test. Powell expressed concern over some justices' criticism of the test, and O'Connor continued to press for her endorsement approach to *Lemon*. In dissent, Burger lamented that the majority's "extended treatment" of the *Lemon* test "suggests a naive preoccupation with an easy, bright-line approach for addressing constitutional issues." But it was Rehnquist's dissenting opinion that raised the most eyebrows because it questioned the Court's entire approach to Establishment Clause cases beginning with *Everson*. He said the Court was wrong to "concede" Jefferson's metaphor of a "wall of separation," or to etch into law such a strict separation. In other words, he asserted that for the four decades since *Everson,* the Court had operated under a misguided understanding of what the Framers meant by religious establishment. The truth, according to Rehnquist, was that the Founders, particularly Madison, intended something more in line with view 2 *(see page 128)* or the nonpreferential position that the Establishment Clause simply "forbade the establishment of a national religion and forbade preference among religious sects or denominations.... [I]t did not prohibit the federal government from providing nondiscriminatory aid to religion." Justice White, who admitted that he had "been out of step" with the Court's rulings in this area, was happy to "appreciate" Rehnquist's reexamination of history.

Whether Rehnquist was correct or whether he "flunked history," as one scholar put it,[79] is a question that is probably unresolvable. What is true, however, is that *Wallace* was the Burger Court's last major religious establishment case; a year or so after the opinion was handed down, the chief justice retired. As we noted at the beginning of this section, Burger had sought to influence this area of the law, first by establishing the *Lemon* test and, then, after realizing that *Lemon* might lead to a stronger wall of separation than he envisioned, through the adoption of a Framers' intent approach (used in *Marsh*), or of a softened version of *Lemon.* In light of *Wallace,* should we conclude that Burger failed to achieve his goals? Probably not. As political scientist Joseph Kobylka notes, "This area of the law is heavy with his legacy," even in cases Burger lost.[80] At the very least, Burger convinced many of his colleagues that *Lemon* should be applied with a soft hand or, perhaps, abandoned entirely. Note, in particular, his influence on Rehnquist, whose opinion in *Wallace* was largely devoted to an explication of the intent of the Framers, which he used as a launching pad to call for the demise of *Lemon.* This legacy is especially important because Rehnquist, who succeeded Burger, could play some

role in determining whether Burger's influence continues to be felt.

Prayer and the Rehnquist Court. It is no secret that Chief Justice Rehnquist wants the Court to move in a more accommodationist direction and to overrule *Lemon.* The problem he faces is that his colleagues do not agree on a standard of law by which to adjudicate these cases. Indeed, as shown in Table 3-3, by 1993 members of the Court had endorsed at least three different standards for Establishment Clause litigation.

When the Rehnquist Court faced its first major prayer-in-school case, *Lee v. Weisman,* a great deal of speculation arose over what the justices would do. Some observers thought the Court would overturn *Lemon,* a position advocated by President Bush's solicitor general. We know from *Lamb's Chapel* that the justices did not eradicate *Lemon.* But what did the majority in *Lee v. Weisman* advocate? Note how fractured the Court was. How did the dissenters and concurrers' positions differ from that proposed by the majority? Pay special attention to Justice David Souter's concurring opinion, as this was his first independent statement in a religious establishment case.

Lee v. Weisman

505 U.S. —- (1992)
Vote: 5 (Blackmun, Kennedy, O'Connor, Souter, Stevens)
  4 (Rehnquist, Scalia, Thomas, White)
Opinion of the Court: Kennedy
Concurring opinions: Blackmun, Souter
Dissenting opinion: Scalia

Each June the Nathan Bishop Middle School, a public school in Providence, Rhode Island, holds formal graduation exercises on school grounds. Attendance is voluntary. For years, it has been the practice of the school district to allow principals to invite local clergy to give invocations and benedictions at the

79. Levy, *The Establishment Clause,* xii.
80. Kobylka, "Leadership in the Supreme Court."

middle and high school graduation exercises. Typically, what happens is this: school principals contact members of the clergy and ask them to give an invocation/benediction; if the clergy agree, principals give them a copy of a pamphlet entitled "Guidelines for Civic Occasions." Prepared by the National Conference of Christians and Jews, the guidelines stress "inclusiveness and sensitivity" in writing nonsectarian prayers.

For the June 1989 graduation, Principal Robert E. Lee followed this procedure. He contacted Rabbi Leslie Gutterman and, once the rabbi agreed to give the invocation and benediction, Lee gave him a copy of the guidelines. Lee also advised Rabbi Gutterman that any prayers should be nonsectarian.

At the graduation the rabbi gave the following invocation:

God of the Free, Hope of the Brave:
For the legacy of America where diversity is celebrated and the rights of minorities are protected, we thank You. May these young men and women grow up to enrich it.
For the liberty of America, we thank You. May these new graduates grow up to guard it.
For the political process of America in which all its citizens may participate, for its court system where all may seek justice, we thank You. May those we honor this morning always turn to it in trust.
For the destiny of America, we thank You. May the graduates of Nathan Bishop Middle School so live that they might help to share it.
May our aspirations for our country and for these young people, who are our hope for the future, be richly fulfilled.
AMEN

In his benediction, the rabbi said:

O God, we are grateful to You for having endowed us with the capacity for learning which we have celebrated on this joyous commencement.
Happy families give thanks for seeing their children achieve an important milestone. Send Your blessings upon the teachers and administrators who helped prepare them.
The graduates now need strength and guidance for the future. Help them to understand that we are not complete with academic knowledge alone. We must each strive to fulfill what You require from all of us: To do justly, to love mercy, to walk humbly.
We give thanks to You, Lord, for keeping us alive, sustaining us and allowing us to reach this special, happy occasion.
AMEN

Daniel Weisman, whose daughter, Deborah, was in the graduating class, challenged as a violation of the First Amendment the school's allowing invocations and benedictions at graduation exercises. He asked a federal trial court to issue an order to Lee and other Providence officials prohibiting them from continuing this practice. The trial court found for Weisman, and a federal appellate court affirmed. As a result, Lee and the school board appealed to the U.S. Supreme Court. Joined by the Bush administration's solicitor general as an amicus curiae, they argued, as one justice later put it, "that these short prayers ... are of profound meaning to many students and parents throughout this country who consider that due respect and acknowledgment for divine guidance and for the deepest spiritual aspirations of our people ought to be expressed at an event as important in life as a graduation." The school board and the solicitor general also asked the Supreme Court to reconsider the *Lemon* test, which the district court had used to find against Principal Lee.

JUSTICE KENNEDY delivered the opinion of the Court.

These dominant facts mark and control the confines of our decision: State officials direct the performance of a formal religious exercise at promotional and graduation ceremonies for secondary schools. Even for those students who object to the religious exercise, their attendance and participation in the state-sponsored religious activity are in a fair and real sense obligatory, though the school district does not require attendance as a condition for receipt of the diploma.

This case does not require us to revisit the difficult questions dividing us in recent cases, questions of the definition and full scope of the principles governing the extent of permitted accommodation by the State for the religious beliefs and practices of many of its citizens. See *Allegheny County v. Greater Pittsburgh ACLU* (1989); *Wallace v. Jaffree* (1985); *Lynch v. Donnelly* (1984). For without reference to those principles in other contexts, the controlling precedents as they relate to prayer and religious exercise in primary and secondary public schools compel the holding here that the policy of the city of Providence is an unconstitutional one. We can decide the case without reconsidering the general constitutional framework by which public schools' efforts to accommodate religion are measured. Thus we do not accept the invitation of petitioners and *amicus* the United States to reconsider our decision in *Lemon v. Kurtzman.* The government involvement with religious activity in this case is pervasive, to the point of creating a state-sponsored and state-directed religious exercise in a public school. Conducting this formal religious observance conflicts with settled rules pertaining to prayer exercises for students, and that suffices to determine the question before us.

The principle that government may accommodate the free exercise of religion does not supersede the fundamental limitations imposed by the Establishment Clause. It is beyond dispute that, at a minimum, the Constitution guarantees that government may not coerce anyone to support or participate in religion or its exercise, or otherwise act in a way which "establishes a [state] religion or religious faith, or tends to do so."... The State's involvement in the school prayers challenged today violates these central principles.

That involvement is as troubling as it is undenied. A school official, the principal, decided that an invocation and a benediction should be given; this is a choice attributable to the State, and from a constitutional perspective it is as if a state statute decreed that the prayers must occur. The principal chose the religious participant, here a rabbi, and that choice is also attributable to the State. The reason for the choice of a rabbi is not disclosed by the record, but the potential for divisiveness over the choice of a particular member of the clergy to conduct the ceremony is apparent.

Divisiveness, of course, can attend any state decision respecting religions, and neither its existence nor its potential necessarily invalidates the State's attempts to accommodate religion in all cases. The potential for divisiveness

is of particular relevance here though, because it centers around an overt religious exercise in a secondary school environment where, as we discuss below, subtle coercive pressures exist and where the student had no real alternative which would have allowed her to avoid the fact or appearance of participation.

The State's role did not end with the decision to include a prayer and with the choice of clergyman. Principal Lee provided Rabbi Gutterman with a copy of the "Guidelines for Civic Occasions," and advised him that his prayers should be nonsectarian. Through these means the principal directed and controlled the content of the prayer. Even if the only sanction for ignoring the instructions were that the rabbi would not be invited back, we think no religious representative who valued his or her continued reputation and effectiveness in the community would incur the State's displeasure in this regard. It is a cornerstone principle of our Establishment Clause jurisprudence that it is "no part of the business of government to compose official prayers for any group of the American people to recite as a part of a religious program carried on by government," *Engel v. Vitale* (1962), and that is what the school officials attempted to do.

Petitioners argue, and we find nothing in the case to refute it, that the directions for the content of the prayers were a good-faith attempt by the school to ensure that the sectarianism which is so often the flashpoint for religious animosity be removed from the graduation ceremony. The concern is understandable, as a prayer which uses ideas or images identified with a particular religion may foster a different sort of sectarian rivalry than an invocation or benediction in terms more neutral. The school's explanation, however, does not resolve the dilemma caused by its participation. The question is not the good faith of the school in attempting to make the prayer acceptable to most persons, but the legitimacy of its undertaking that enterprise at all when the object is to produce a prayer to be used in a formal religious exercise which students, for all practical purposes, are obliged to attend.

We are asked to recognize the existence of a practice of nonsectarian prayer, prayer within the embrace of what is known as the Judeo-Christian tradition, prayer which is more acceptable than one which, for example, makes explicit references to the God of Israel, or to Jesus Christ, or

Daniel Weisman and his daughter, Debbie, challenged the practice of having a member of the clergy deliver invocation and benediction prayers at public junior high school graduation exercises in Providence, Rhode Island. The Supreme Court ruled in their favor in *Lee v. Weisman.*

to a patron saint. There may be some support, as an empirical observation, to the statement of the Court of Appeals for the Sixth Circuit, picked up by Judge Campbell's dissent in the Court of Appeals in this case, that there has emerged in this country a civic religion, one which is tolerated when sectarian exercises are not. If common ground can be defined which permits once conflicting faiths to express the shared conviction that there is an ethic and a morality which transcend human invention, the sense of community and purpose sought by all decent societies might be advanced. But though the First Amendment does not allow the government to stifle prayers which aspire to these ends, neither does it permit the government to undertake that task for itself. . . .

These concerns have particular application in the case of school officials, whose effort to monitor prayer will be perceived by the students as inducing a participation they might otherwise reject. Though the efforts of the school officials in this case to find common ground appear to have been a good-faith attempt to recognize the common aspects

of religions and not the divisive ones, our precedents do not permit school officials to assist in composing prayers as an incident to a formal exercise for their students. *Engel v. Vitale.* And these same precedents caution us to measure the idea of a civic religion against the central meaning of the Religion Clauses of the First Amendment, which is that all creeds must be tolerated and none favored. The suggestion that government may establish an official or civic religion as a means of avoiding the establishment of a religion with more specific creeds strikes us as a contradiction that cannot be accepted.

The degree of school involvement here made it clear that the graduation prayers bore the imprint of the State and thus put school-age children who objected in an untenable position. We turn our attention now to consider the position of the students, both those who desired the prayer and she who did not. . . .

As we have observed before, there are heightened concerns with protecting freedom of conscience from subtle coercive pressure in the elementary and secondary public schools.... Our decisions in *Engel v. Vitale* and *Abington School District* recognize, among other things, that prayer exercises in public schools carry a particular risk of indirect coercion. The concern may not be limited to the context of schools, but it is most pronounced there.... What to most believers may seem nothing more than a reasonable request that the nonbeliever respect their religious practices, in a school context may appear to the nonbeliever or dissenter to be an attempt to employ the machinery of the State to enforce a religious orthodoxy.

We need not look beyond the circumstances of this case to see the phenomenon at work. The undeniable fact is that the school district's supervision and control of a high school graduation ceremony places public pressure, as well as peer pressure, on attending students to stand as a group or, at least, maintain respectful silence during the Invocation and Benediction. This pressure, though subtle and indirect, can be as real as any overt compulsion. Of course, in our culture standing or remaining silent can signify adherence to a view or simple respect for the views of others. And no doubt some persons who have no desire to join a prayer have little objection to standing as a sign of respect for those who do. But for the dissenter of high school age, who has a reasonable perception that she is being forced by the State to pray in a manner her conscience will not allow, the injury is no less real. There can be no doubt that for many, if not most, of the students at the graduation, the act of standing or remaining silent was an expression of participation in the Rabbi's prayer. That was the very point of the religious exercise. It is of little comfort to a dissenter, then, to be told that for her the act of standing or remaining in silence signifies mere respect, rather than participation. What matters is that, given our social conventions, a reasonable dissenter in this milieu could believe that the group exercise signified her own participation or approval of it.

Finding no violation under these circumstances would place objectors in the dilemma of participating, with all that implies, or protesting. We do not address whether that choice is acceptable if the affected citizens are mature adults, but we think the State may not, consistent with the Establishment Clause, place primary and secondary school children in this position. Research in psychology supports the common assumption that adolescents are often susceptible to pressure from their peers towards conformity, and that the influence is strongest in matters of social

convention. Brittain, Adolescent Choices and Parent-Peer Cross-Pressures, 28 Am. Sociological Rev. 385 (June 1963); Clasen & Brown, The Multidimensionality of Peer Pressure in Adolescence, 14 J. of Youth and Adolescence 451 (Dec. 1985).... To recognize that the choice imposed by the State constitutes an unacceptable constraint only acknowledges that the government may no more use social pressure to enforce orthodoxy than it may use more direct means....

There was a stipulation in the District Court that attendance at graduation and promotional ceremonies is voluntary. Petitioners and the United States, as *amicus*, made this a center point of the case, arguing that the option of not attending the graduation excuses any inducement or coercion in the ceremony itself. The argument lacks all persuasion. Law reaches past formalism. And to say a teenage student has a real choice not to attend her high school graduation is formalistic in the extreme. True, Deborah could elect not to attend commencement without renouncing her diploma; but we shall not allow the case to turn on this point. Everyone knows that in our society and in our culture high school graduation is one of life's most significant occasions. A school rule which excuses attendance is beside the point. Attendance may not be required by official decree, yet it is apparent that a student is not free to absent herself from the graduation exercise in any real sense of the term "voluntary," for absence would require forfeiture of those intangible benefits which have motivated the student through youth and all her high school years. Graduation is a time for family and those closest to the student to celebrate success and express mutual wishes of gratitude and respect, all to the end of impressing upon the young person the role that it is his or her right and duty to assume in the community and all of its diverse parts.

The importance of the event is the point the school district and the United States rely upon to argue that a formal prayer ought to be permitted, but it becomes one of the principal reasons why their argument must fail. Their contention, one of considerable force were it not for the constitutional constraints applied to state action, is that the prayers are an essential part of these ceremonies because for many persons an occasion of this significance lacks meaning if there is no recognition, however brief, that human achievements cannot be understood apart from their spiritual essence. We think the Government's position that this interest suffices to force students to choose between compliance or forfeiture demonstrates fundamental inconsistency in its argumentation. It fails to acknowledge that what for many of Deborah's classmates and their parents was a spiritual imperative was for Daniel and Deborah Weisman religious conformance compelled by the State. While in some societies the wishes of the majority might prevail, the Establishment Clause of the First Amendment is addressed to this contingency and rejects the balance urged upon us. The Constitution forbids the State to exact religious conformity from a student as the price of attending her own high school graduation. This is the calculus the Constitution commands....

We do not hold that every state action implicating religion is invalid if one or a few citizens find it offensive. People may take offense at all manner of religious as well as nonreligious messages, but offense alone does not in every case show a violation. We know too that sometimes to endure social isolation or even anger may be the price of conscience or nonconformity. But, by any reading of our cases, the conformity required of the student in this case was too high an exaction to withstand the test of the Establishment Clause. The prayer exercises in this case are especially improper because the State has in every practical sense compelled attendance and participation in an explicit religious exercise at an event of singular importance to every student, one the objecting student had no real alternative to avoid....

... No holding by this Court suggests that a school can persuade or compel a student to participate in a religious exercise. That is being done here, and it is forbidden by the Establishment Clause of the First Amendment.

For the reasons we have stated, the judgment of the Court of Appeals is

Affirmed.

JUSTICE BLACKMUN, with whom JUSTICE STEVENS and JUSTICE O'CONNOR join, concurring.

In 1971, Chief Justice Burger reviewed the Court's past decisions and found: "Three ... tests may be gleaned from our cases." *Lemon v. Kurtzman....* After *Lemon*, the Court continued to rely on these basic principles in resolving Establishment Clause disputes.*

*Since 1971, the Court has decided 31 Establishment Clause cases. In only one instance, the decision of *Marsh v. Chambers* (1983), has the Court

Application of these principles to the facts of this case is straightforward. There can be "no doubt" that the "invocation of God's blessings" delivered at Nathan Bishop Middle School "is a religious activity."... The question then is whether the government has "placed its official stamp of approval" on the prayer. As the Court ably demonstrates, when the government "compose[s] official prayers," selects the member of the clergy to deliver the prayer, has the prayer delivered at a public school event that is planned, supervised and given by school officials, and pressures students to attend and participate in the prayer, there can be no doubt that the government is advancing and promoting religion. As our prior decisions teach us, it is this that the Constitution prohibits.

I join the Court's opinion today because I find nothing in it inconsistent with the essential precepts of the Establishment Clause developed in our precedents. The Court holds that the graduation prayer is unconstitutional because the State "in effect required participation in a religious exercise." Although our precedents make clear that proof of government coercion is not necessary to prove an Establishment Clause violation, it is sufficient. Government pressure to participate in a religious activity is an obvious indication that the government is endorsing or promoting religion.

But it is not enough that the government restrain from compelling religious practices: it must not engage in them either.... The Court repeatedly has recognized that a violation of the Establishment Clause is not predicated on coercion.... The Establishment Clause proscribes public schools from "conveying or attempting to convey a message that religion or a particular religious belief is favored or preferred," *County of Allegheny v. ACLU* (1989), even if the schools do not actually "impose pressure upon a student to participate in a religious activity."...

It is these understandings ... that underlie our Establishment Clause jurisprudence. We have believed that religious freedom cannot exist in the absence of a free

not rested its decision on the basic principles described in *Lemon*. For example, in the most recent Establishment Clause case, *Westside Community Bd. of Ed. v. Mergens* (1990), the Court applied the three-part *Lemon* analysis to the Equal Access Act, which made it unlawful for public secondary schools to deny equal access to any student wishing to hold religious meetings. In no case involving religious activities in public schools has the Court failed to apply vigorously the *Lemon* factors.

democratic government, and that such a government cannot endure when there is fusion between religion and the political regime. We have believed that religious freedom cannot thrive in the absence of a vibrant religious community and that such a community cannot prosper when it is bound to the secular. And we have believed that these were the animating principles behind the adoption of the Establishment Clause. To that end, our cases have prohibited government endorsement of religion, its sponsorship, and active involvement in religion, whether or not citizens were coerced to conform.

I remain convinced that our jurisprudence is not misguided, and that it requires the decision reached by the Court today. Accordingly, I join the Court in affirming the judgment of the Court of Appeals.

JUSTICE SOUTER, with whom JUSTICE STEVENS and JUSTICE O'CONNOR join, concurring.

I join the whole of the Court's opinion, and fully agree that prayers at public school graduation ceremonies indirectly coerce religious observance. I write separately nonetheless on two issues of Establishment Clause analysis that underlie my independent resolution of this case: whether the Clause applies to governmental practices that do not favor one religion or denomination over others, and whether state coercion of religious conformity, over and above state endorsement of religious exercise or belief, is a necessary element of an Establishment Clause violation.

Forty-five years ago, this Court announced a basic principle of constitutional law from which it has not strayed: the Establishment Clause forbids not only state practices that "aid one religion ... or prefer one religion over another," but also those that "aid all religions." *Everson v. Board of Education of Ewing* (1947). Today we reaffirm that principle, holding that the Establishment Clause forbids state-sponsored prayers in public school settings no matter how nondenominational the prayers may be. In barring the State from sponsoring generically Theistic prayers where it could not sponsor sectarian ones, we hold true to a line of precedent from which there is no adequate historical case to depart....

Some have challenged this precedent by reading the Establishment Clause to permit "nonpreferential" state promotion of religion. The challengers argue that, as originally

understood by the Framers, "the Establishment Clause did not require government neutrality between religion and irreligion nor did it prohibit the Federal Government from providing nondiscriminatory aid to religion." *Wallace* (REHNQUIST, J., dissenting). While a case has been made for this position, it is not so convincing as to warrant reconsideration of our settled law; indeed, I find in the history of the Clause's textual development a more powerful argument supporting the Court's jurisprudence following *Everson*....

What we ... know of the Framers' experience underscores the observation of one prominent commentator, that confining the Establishment Clause to a prohibition on preferential aid "requires a premise that the Framers were extraordinarily bad drafters—that they believed one thing but adopted language that said something substantially different, and that they did so after repeatedly attending to the choice of language."... We must presume, since there is no conclusive evidence to the contrary, that the Framers embraced the significance of their textual judgment. Thus, on balance, history neither contradicts nor warrants reconsideration of the settled principle that the Establishment Clause forbids support for religion in general no less than support for one religion or some....

Petitioners rest most of their argument on a theory that, whether or not the Establishment Clause permits extensive nonsectarian support for religion, it does not forbid the state to sponsor affirmations of religious belief that coerce neither support for religion nor participation in religious observance. I appreciate the force of some of the arguments supporting a "coercion" analysis of the Clause. See generally *Allegheny County* (opinion of KENNEDY, J.) But we could not adopt that reading without abandoning our settled law, a course that, in my view, the text of the Clause would not readily permit. Nor does the extratextual evidence of original meaning stand so unequivocally at odds with the textual premise inherent in existing precedent that we should fundamentally reconsider our course.

Over the years, this Court has declared the invalidity of many noncoercive state laws and practices conveying a message of religious endorsement. For example, in *Allegheny County* we forbade the prominent display of a nativity scene on public property; without contesting the dissent's observation that the crèche coerced no one into accepting or supporting whatever message it proclaimed, five Members of the Court found its display unconstitutional as a state endorsement of Christianity. Likewise, in *Wallace v. Jaffree* (1985), we struck down a state law requiring a moment of silence in public classrooms not because the statute coerced students to participate in prayer (for it did not), but because the manner of its enactment "conveyed a message of state approval of prayer activities in the public schools."...

Our precedents may not always have drawn perfectly straight lines. They simply cannot, however, support the position that a showing of coercion is necessary to a successful Establishment Clause claim....

Petitioners argue from the political setting in which the Establishment Clause was framed, and from the Framers' own political practices following ratification, that government may constitutionally endorse religion so long as it does not coerce religious conformity. The setting and the practices warrant canvassing, but while they yield some evidence for petitioners' argument, they do not reveal the degree of consensus in early constitutional thought that would raise a threat to *stare decisis* by challenging the presumption that the Establishment Clause adds something to the Free Exercise Clause that follows it....

Petitioners contend that because the early Presidents included religious messages in their inaugural and Thanksgiving Day addresses, the Framers could not have meant the Establishment Clause to forbid noncoercive state endorsement of religion. The argument ignores the fact, however, that Americans today find such proclamations less controversial than did the founding generation, whose published thoughts on the matter belie petitioners' claim. President Jefferson, for example, steadfastly refused to issue Thanksgiving proclamations of any kind, in part because he thought they violated the Religion Clauses....

While we may be unable to know for certain what the Framers meant by the Clause, we do know that, around the time of its ratification, a respectable body of opinion supported a considerably broader reading than petitioners urge upon us. This consistency with the textual considerations is enough to preclude fundamentally reexamining our settled law, and I am accordingly left with the task of considering whether the state practice at issue here violates our traditional understanding of the Clause's proscriptions.

While the Establishment Clause's concept of neutrality is not self-revealing, our recent cases have invested it with specific content: the state may not favor or endorse either religion generally over nonreligion or one religion over others.... This principle against favoritism and endorsement has become the foundation of Establishment Clause jurisprudence, ensuring that religious belief is irrelevant to every citizen's standing in the political community.... Our aspiration to religious liberty, embodied in the First Amendment, permits no other standard....

JUSTICE SCALIA, with whom THE CHIEF JUSTICE, JUSTICE WHITE, and JUSTICE THOMAS join, dissenting.

Three Terms ago, I joined an opinion recognizing that the Establishment Clause must be construed in light of the "[g]overnment policies of accommodation, acknowledgment, and support for religion [that] are an accepted part of our political and cultural heritage." That opinion affirmed that "the meaning of the Clause is to be determined by reference to historical practices and understandings." It said that "[a] test for implementing the protections of the Establishment Clause that, if applied with consistency, would invalidate longstanding traditions cannot be a proper reading of the Clause." *Allegheny County v. Greater Pittsburgh ACLU* (1989) (KENNEDY, J., concurring in judgment and dissenting in part).

These views of course prevent me from joining today's opinion, which is conspicuously bereft of any reference to history. In holding that the Establishment Clause prohibits invocations and benedictions at public-school graduation ceremonies, the Court—with nary a mention that it is doing so—lays waste a tradition that is as old as public-school graduation ceremonies themselves, and that is a component of an even more longstanding American tradition of nonsectarian prayer to God at public celebrations generally. As its instrument of destruction, the bulldozer of its social engineering, the Court invents a boundless, and boundlessly manipulable, test of psychological coercion.... Today's opinion shows more forcefully than volumes of argumentation why our Nation's protection, that fortress which is our Constitution, cannot possibly rest upon the changeable philosophical predilections of the Justices of this Court, but must have deep foundations in the historic practices of our people....

The history and tradition of our Nation are replete with public ceremonies featuring prayers of thanksgiving and petition.... Most recently, President Bush, continuing the tradition established by President Washington, asked those attending his inauguration to bow their heads, and made a prayer his first official act as President....

The Court presumably would separate graduation invocations and benedictions from other instances of public "preservation and transmission of religious beliefs" on the ground that they involve "psychological coercion." I find it a sufficient embarrassment that our Establishment Clause jurisprudence regarding holiday displays ... has come to "requir[e] scrutiny more commonly associated with interior decorators than with the judiciary.".... But interior decorating is a rock-hard science compared to psychology practiced by amateurs. A few citations of "[r]esearch in psychology" that have no particular bearing upon the precise issue here cannot disguise the fact that the Court has gone beyond the realm where judges know what they are doing. The Court's argument that state officials have "coerced" students to take part in the invocation and benediction at graduation ceremonies is, not to put too fine a point on it, incoherent....

The deeper flaw in the Court's opinion does not lie in its wrong answer to the question whether there was state-induced "peer-pressure" coercion; it lies, rather, in the Court's making violation of the Establishment Clause hinge on such a precious question....

... [W]hile I have no quarrel with the Court's general proposition that the Establishment Clause "guarantees that government may not coerce anyone to support or participate in religion or its exercise," I see no warrant for expanding the concept of coercion beyond acts backed by threat of penalty—a brand of coercion that, happily, is readily discernible to those of us who have made a career of reading the disciples of Blackstone rather than of Freud. The Framers were indeed opposed to coercion of religious worship by the National Government; but, as their own sponsorship of nonsectarian prayer in public events demonstrates, they understood that "speech is not coercive; the listener may do as he likes."...

Our religion-clause jurisprudence has become bedeviled (so to speak) by reliance on formulaic abstractions that are not derived from, but positively conflict with, our long-accepted constitutional traditions. Foremost among these has been the so-called *Lemon* test, see *Lemon v. Kurtzman* (1971), which has received well-earned criticism from many members of this Court.... The Court today demonstrates the irrelevance of *Lemon* by essentially ignoring it, and the interment of that case may be the one happy byproduct of the Court's otherwise lamentable decision. Unfortunately, however, the Court has replaced *Lemon* with its psycho-coercion test, which suffers the double disability of having no roots whatever in our people's historic practice, and being as infinitely expandable as the reasons for psychotherapy itself.

Another happy aspect of the case is that it is only a jurisprudential disaster and not a practical one. Given the odd basis for the Court's decision, invocations and benedictions will be able to be given at public-school graduations next June, as they have for the past century and a half, so long as school authorities make clear that anyone who abstains from screaming in protest does not necessarily participate in the prayers. All that is seemingly needed is an announcement, or perhaps a written insertion at the beginning of the graduation Program, to the effect that, while all are asked to rise for the invocation and benediction, none is compelled to join in them, nor will be assumed, by rising, to have done so. That obvious fact recited, the graduates and their parents may proceed to thank God, as Americans have always done, for the blessings He has generously bestowed on them and on their country....

For the foregoing reasons, I dissent.

Justice Kennedy may not have applied *Lemon* to resolve *Lee*, but he did not overturn it. To the contrary, he specifically declined to "revisit" *Lemon* on the grounds that the Court's previous cases on prayer in school established clear precedent for this case. Returning to the coercion standard he advocated in *County of Allegheny*, Kennedy noted that *Engel* and *Abington* recognized that "prayer exercises in public schools carry a particular risk of indirect coercion." It was this coercion, however subtle, to which Kennedy took offense. The concurrers, on the other hand, complained that coercion was insufficient: Stevens,

Blackmun, and O'Connor continued to advocate an endorsement approach to *Lemon*. Souter, joined by Stevens and O'Connor, explicitly rejected Kennedy's coercion standard and Rehnquist's nonpreferentialism in favor of the endorsement approach. Souter also stressed that the Court should not abandon precedent governing Religious Establishment cases, yet he had very little to say about *Lemon*, in particular.

Most interesting of all may be Scalia's dissent because it indicates that justices can agree over a standard of law but disagree vehemently over its application. Scalia endorsed the coercion standard in *County of Allegheny*, but here he takes issue with the way Kennedy applied it, arguing that the majority opinion is too ahistorical and psychologically grounded. Joined by Rehnquist, Thomas, and White, Scalia lambastes the Court for engaging in amateur psychology and for paying more attention to Freud than to the Framers. About the only thing the dissenters found redeemable in *Lee* was that the majority opinion seemed to "inter" *Lemon*. But they were wrong: *Lemon* re-emerged the very next year, in *Lamb's Chapel*, as a guiding standard.

Scalia and his colleagues also lost on the holding: the Court once again rejected prayer in school. With White's retirement and Ginsburg's appointment to the Court, prohibitions against prayer in school may be on even firmer ground. Throughout his career, White was one of the more accommodation-oriented justices, and it seems unlikely that Ginsburg would follow suit. But her presence does not ensure the end to litigation on this controversial subject. Indeed, given continued public support for the return of prayer in school, it is virtually assured that the Court will revisit the issue. Just a year after the decision in *Lee*, a Mississippi high school principal, Bishop Knox, became ensnared in controversy for allowing students to read a prayer over the loudspeaker. Knox defended his actions on the ground that the students had voted (490–96) to allow the prayers, but the school's superintendent fired him. That action set off a series of protests and rallies in defense of Knox, some of which were attended by the state's governor. Within three weeks, the school board overturned the superintendent's decision, and Knox was reinstated.[81]

Although the case attracted nationwide attention, the action taken by Knox was not all that unusual. Various forms of prayer in school may no longer be the norm in the United States, but they are not exceptional. The exceptional part of the Knox case was that an official fired a principal for allowing the prayers. That step is rare, especially in southern states, where noncompliance with Court decisions remains high.

What can we conclude about the Court's handling of prayer-in-school cases and religious liberty litigation in general? At the very least, we can see that this area of the law is unstable, with justices professing very different approaches to resolve the cases. As we have observed, each time the Court seems on the verge of eliminating *Lemon*, that test reappears, as Justice Scalia put it in *Lamb's Chapel*, "like some ghoul in a late-night horror movie...." Whether the Court kills off *Lemon* once and for all seems to hinge on the justices' ability to agree over a replacement and on the application of that replacement, which—as *Lee v. Weisman* illustrates—they have not been able to do.

At its most extreme, religion litigation is an area rife with contradictions and "unprincipled decisions." Professor Lawrence Rosen recently listed some of those apparent inconsistencies, many of which should be familiar to you by now:

At various times the Court has held that [prayer] in a public school classroom is impermissible but that the erection of a Nativity scene on municipal property is not; that delivery by a clergyman of an opening prayer to the state legislature is allowable but that religious headgear may not be worn if military regulations bar such attire; that the provision from public funds of books to parochial school children or released time for off-campus religious instruction is

81. See "Principal in a School Prayer Dispute is Reinstated," *New York Times*, Dec. 17, 1993, A14.

constitutional but that providing parochial students with remedial aid is not.[82]

Will the Court seek to resolve these and other inconsistencies? What standard or test will it invoke to do so? Having read about many of the significant cases, these are questions on which you might want to speculate for, as of this writing, there are still no easy answers.

READINGS

Alley, Robert S. *The Supreme Court on Church and State.* New York: Oxford University Press, 1988.

Carter, Stephen L. *The Culture of Disbelief.* New York: Basic Books, 1993.

Currey, Thomas J. *The First Amendment Freedoms: Church and State in America to the Passage of the First Amendment.* New York: Oxford University Press, 1986.

Dolbeare, Kenneth M., and Phillip E. Hammond. *The School Prayer Decision.* Chicago: University of Chicago Press, 1971.

Fellman, David. *Religion in American Public Law.* Boston: Boston University Press, 1965.

Howe, Mark Dewolfe. *The Garden and the Wilderness: Religion and Government in American Constitutional History.* Chicago: University of Chicago Press, 1965.

Kurland, Philip B., ed. *Church and State: The Supreme Court and the First Amendment.* Chicago: University of Chicago Press, 1975.

Levy, Leonard W. *The Establishment Clause.* New York: Macmillan, 1986.

Malbin, Michael J. *Religion and Politics.* Washington, D.C.: American Enterprise Institute, 1978.

Manwaring, David B. *Render unto Caesar.* Chicago: University of Chicago Press, 1962.

Morgan, Richard E. *The Politics of Religious Conflict.* New York: Pegasus, 1968.

———. *The Supreme Court and Religion.* New York: Free Press, 1972.

Pfeffer, Leo. *Church, State, and Freedom.* Boston: Beacon Press, 1967.

———. *Religion, State, and the Burger Court.* Buffalo, N.Y.: Prometheus Books, 1985.

Sorauf, Frank J. *The Wall of Separation.* Princeton, N.J.: Princeton University Press, 1976.

Stokes, Anson Phelps, and Leo Pfeffer. *Church and State in America.* New York: Harper & Row, 1964.

Wills, Garry. *Under God.* New York: Simon and Schuster, 1990.

---

82. Lawrence Rosen, "Continuing the Conversation: Creationism, the Religious Clauses, and the Politics of Culture," *Supreme Court Review* (1988): 61–62.

CHAPTER 4
FREEDOM OF SPEECH, ASSEMBLY, AND ASSOCIATION

A T ONE TIME or another, everyone has criticized someone in government. The president or a state senator has said or done something we thought was wrong. We may have been polite, simply noting our displeasure, or we may have called the official a bum, or worse. Either way, we expressed our views. Speaking our minds is a privilege we enjoy as inhabitants of the United States, but we probably have not thought very seriously about it.

The First Amendment is our most fundamental protection against government encroachment on freedom of expression. This constitutional provision was part of an original package of amendments proposed by the First Congress in 1789 and sent to the states for approval. Congress's action fulfilled a promise made during the ratification debates that one of the new government's first items of business would be the drafting of a list of guaranteed rights.

The driving force behind the Bill of Rights was James Madison, who had been elected to the House of Representatives from Virginia. While the other members of Congress were busy organizing the new government, Madison spearheaded the effort to gain approval of the Bill of Rights. His original draft of the amendments survived the legislative process largely intact. Although other members of Congress had a role in its development (future Supreme Court justices

Oliver Ellsworth and William Paterson, for example, served on the conference committee that negotiated the differences between Senate and House versions), the Bill of Rights is primarily Madison's work.

It took Congress five months to approve the Bill of Rights and an additional two years for the states to complete the ratification process. Throughout this period the freedom of expression provisions of the First Amendment received very little debate, perhaps because the Framers had a fundamental commitment to speech and press freedoms, especially as they related to the public discussion of political and social issues. After all, vigorous public oratory fueled the Revolution and helped shape the contours of the new government. In 1791 the Bill of Rights became a part of our Constitution, and its best-known provisions are those sections of the First Amendment that guarantee freedom of expression.

The First Amendment's language is very bold: "Congress shall make no law ... abridging the freedom of speech, or of the press; or the right of the people peaceably to assemble, and to petition the Government for a redress of grievances." These words seem to provide an absolute shield against government actions that would restrict any of the four components of freedom of expression: speech, press, assembly, and petition. But to what extent *does* the

Constitution protect these rights? May mischievous patrons stand up in a crowded movie theater and shout *fire* when they know there is no fire? May a publisher knowingly print lies about a member of the community in order to destroy that person's reputation? May a radical political party take actions to overthrow the government by force and violence? May a group of protesters storm onto the Senate floor to bring attention to their demands?

Despite the absolute wording of the First Amendment, the answer to each of these questions is no. The Supreme Court never has adhered to a literal interpretation of the expression guarantees; rather, it has ruled that certain expressions, whether communicated verbally, in print, or by actions, may be restricted because of the effect they may have.

This chapter is the first of three dealing with the right of expression. Here we examine the development of constitutional standards for freedom of expression and then the application of those standards to various kinds of expression. In the next two chapters we look at issues specific to the freedom of the press and discuss forms of expression that traditionally have been considered outside First Amendment protection.

THE DEVELOPMENT OF LEGAL STANDARDS: THE EMERGENCE OF LAW IN TIMES OF CRISIS

History teaches that governments tend to be more repressive in times of crisis. Such emergencies may be the result of war, economic collapse, natural catastrophes, or internal rebellion. During these times a nation's survival may be at stake, and the government may be unstable. Political dissent and opposition to the government are more likely to occur during such times. The responses of political leaders are predictable: they will place a priority on national unity and take firm action against subversive groups and opposition criticism. Often these reactions take the form of

policies that restrict the right of the people to speak, publish, and organize.

The United States is no exception to this rule. In times of peace and general prosperity there is little reason to restrict freedom of expression. The government and the nation are secure, and the people are relatively content. In times of crisis, however, the president and Congress may react harshly, contending that some forms of expression must be curtailed to protect national security. In response, political dissidents may challenge such laws, arguing that repressive government policies are unconstitutional—even in times of war or national emergency.

When such conflicts arise, the justices of the Supreme Court must ultimately decide where constitutional protections end and the government's right to restrict expression begins. These questions have come to the Court during periods of actual crisis or in the months immediately thereafter. At these times the Constitution has been most seriously tested, and the Court has been called upon to develop its most fundamental doctrines regarding freedom of expression.

To demonstrate this point, we have organized this section around times of crisis—the Revolution (1775–1781) and the Civil War (1861–1865), World War I (1917–1918), World War II (1941–1945) and resultant cold war, and the Vietnam War (1963–1973). As you read the cases associated with these times, you will be asked questions about the development of law and legal doctrine. Perhaps the most basic question is this: Had a crisis not existed, would the Court have decided this case the same way? This question should serve as a constant reminder that Supreme Court justices are as vulnerable to public pressures and to waves of patriotism as the average citizen.

The Early Crises: The Revolutionary and Civil Wars

The Founders also were vulnerable to the patriotic atmosphere that seems to permeate society following a major crisis. Not long after the Revolution, Congress passed one of the most restrictive laws in American history, the Sedition Act of 1798:

If any person shall write, print, utter or publish, or shall cause to procure to be written, printed, uttered or published, or shall knowingly and willingly assist or aid in writing, printing, uttering or publishing any false, scandalous and malicious writing or writings against the government of the United States, or either House of the Congress of the United States, or the President of the United States, with intent to defame the said government, or either House of the said Congress, or the said President, or to bring them, or either of them into contempt or disrepute; or to excite against them, or either or any of them, the hatred of the good people of the United States, done in pursuance of any such law, or of the powers in him vested by the Constitution of the United States, or to resist, oppose, or defeat any such law or act, or to aid, encourage or abet any hostile designs of any foreign nation against the United States, their people or government, then such person, being thereof convicted before any court of the United States having jurisdiction thereof, shall be punished by a fine not exceeding $2,000, and by imprisonment not exceeding two years.

The act expired in 1801, but why did our Founding Fathers, who so dearly treasured liberty, pass such a repressive law? First, Congress was dominated by the Federalist party, leading some to argue that the statute was intended to "suppress political opposition," not plain speech.[1] Indeed, Thomas Jefferson, leader of the Anti-Federalist (Democratic-Republican) party, vigorously attacked the law, claiming that it led to witch hunts. Second, it is undoubtedly true that the Framers held a view of free expression different from the present-day view. They had known only the British system, which often imposed laws that severely curtailed free expression.

For the next sixty years, the United States enjoyed relative tranquility; Congress passed no major restrictive legislation, and the Supreme Court decided no major expression cases. In the 1860s, however, peaceful times came to a crashing halt as the nation divided over the issue of slavery. As civil war broke out, President Abraham Lincoln took a number of steps to suppress "treacherous" behavior, believing "that the nation must be able to protect itself in war against utterances which actually cause insubordination."[2] Still, the Supreme Court had no opportunity to rule on the constitutionality of the president's actions, at least on First Amendment grounds.

World War I

The early decades of the twentieth century present a mixed picture of America. On one hand, as a result of efforts by Progressive groups and leaders, Congress and the states enacted legislation aimed at protecting workers and cleaning up American politics. On the other hand, as John Schmidhauser notes, "The thrust of Progressive legislative efforts ... [was] ultimately overshadowed by the channeling of national efforts into the first World War."[3] That is, as the war in Europe raged and other events ensued, most notably the Russian Revolution in 1917, the country turned its attention to defending the American system of government and away from domestic reforms.

Today, the emotional and patriotic fervor unleashed by World War I is difficult to imagine. No American was immune, not even Supreme Court justices. Consider Chief Justice Edward D. White's response to an attorney who argued that the selective draft, enacted by Congress in 1917, lacked public support: "I don't think your statement has anything to do with legal arguments and should not have been said in this Court. It is a very unpatriotic statement to make."[4] Members of Congress, too, were caught up in the patriotic fervor gripping the nation. They, like the Founders, felt it necessary to enact legislation to

1. Peter Woll, *Constitutional Law* (Englewood Cliffs, N.J.: Prentice-Hall, 1981), 581.

2. Zechariah Chafee, Jr., *Free Speech in the United States* (Cambridge: Harvard University Press, 1941), 266.
3. Cited in John R. Schmidhauser, *Constitutional Law in American Politics* (Monterey, Calif.: Brooks/Cole, 1984), 325.
4. Ibid.

Government officers and clerks loading a police ambulance with literature seized at the Communist party headquarters in Cambridge, Massachusetts, in 1919. Such activities against communist organizations were not uncommon during the Red Scare era.

ensure that Americans presented a unified front to the world. The Espionage Act of 1917 prohibited any attempt to "interfere with the operation or success of the military or naval forces of the United States … to cause insubordination … in the military or naval forces … or willfully obstruct the recruiting or enlistment service of the United States." One year later, Congress passed the Sedition Act, which prohibited the uttering of, writing, or publishing of anything dis-

loyal to the government, flag, or military forces of the United States.

Although the majority of Americans probably supported these laws, some groups and individuals thought they constituted intolerable infringements on civil liberties guarantees contained in the First Amendment. Dissenters, however, were not of one political voice: some, most notably the American Union Against Militarism (a predecessor of the American

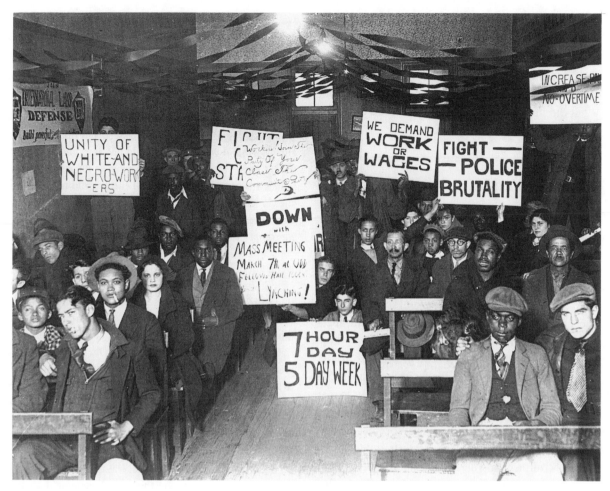

At a 1930 meeting, members of the Washington Communist Society plan a demonstration in front of the White House. The protest activities of such organizations frequently led to arrests and charges of First Amendment violations.

Civil Liberties Union), were blatantly pacifist; others, primarily leaders of the Progressive Movement, were pure civil libertarians, opposed to any government intrusion into free expressions; and, finally, there were the radicals, individuals who hoped to see the United States undergo a socialist or communist revolution. Regardless of their motivation, these individuals and groups brought legal challenges to the repressive laws and pushed the Supreme Court into freedom of expression cases for the first time. The first of the World

War I cases, *Schenck v. United States*, was decided by the Court in 1919, followed by three others the same year.

While reading *Schenck*, keep in mind the circumstances surrounding the Court's decision. The United States had just successfully completed a war effort in which more than 4 million Americans were in uniform and more than 1 million troops had been sent to fight in Europe. The number of Americans killed or seriously wounded exceeded 300,000. There had been tremendous national fervor and support for the war effort. In the face of this national unity, a socialist had engaged in active opposition to America's participation in the war. His appeal from an espionage conviction allowed the Supreme Court to make its first major doctrinal statement on freedom of expression. What did the Court decide? What standard did it develop to adjudicate future claims?

Schenck v. United States

249 U.S. 47 (1919)

Vote: 9 (Brandeis, Clarke, Day, Holmes, McKenna,
    McReynolds, Pitney, Van Devanter, White)

    0

Opinion of the Court: Holmes

In 1917 Charles Schenck, the general secretary of the Socialist party of Philadelphia, had 15,000 pamphlets printed, urging resistance to the draft. He sent these leaflets, described by the government's case as "frank, bitter, passionate appeal[s] for resistance to the Selective Service Law," to men listed in a local newspaper as eligible for service. Federal authorities charged him with violating the Espionage Act; specifically, the United States alleged that Schenck attempted to obstruct recruitment and illegally used the mail to do so.

Henry J. Gibbons, Schenck's attorney, did not dispute the government's charges; rather, he argued that the Espionage Act violated the First Amendment's Free Speech Clause because it placed a chilling effect on expression. That is, the act prohibited speech or publication before the words are uttered, and not after, as, Gibbons argued, the Constitution mandated.

MR. JUSTICE HOLMES delivered the opinion of the Court.

The document in question upon its first printed side recited the first section of the Thirteenth Amendment, said that the idea embodied in it was violated by the Conscription Act and that a conscript is little better than a convict. In impassioned language it intimated that conscription

was despotism in its worst form and a monstrous wrong against humanity in the interest of Wall Street's chosen few. It said "Do not submit to intimidation," but in form at least confined itself to peaceful measures such as a petition for the repeal of the act. The other and later printed side of the sheet was headed "Assert Your Rights." It stated reasons for alleging that any one violated the Constitution when he refused to recognize "your right to assert your opposition to the draft," and went on "If you do not assert and support your rights, you are helping to deny or disparage rights which it is the solemn duty of all citizens and residents of the United States to retain." It described the arguments on the other side as coming from cunning politicians and a mercenary capitalist press, and even silent consent to the conscription law as helping to support an infamous conspiracy. It denied the power to send our citizens away to foreign shores to shoot up the people of other lands, and added that words could not express the condemnation such cold-blooded ruthlessness deserves, &c., &c., winding up "You must do your share to maintain, support and uphold the rights of the people of this country." Of course the document would not have been sent unless it had been intended to have some effect, and we do not see what effect it could be expected to have upon persons subject to the draft except to influence them to obstruct the carrying of it out. The defendants do not deny that the jury might find against them on this point.

But it is said, suppose that that was the tendency of this circular, it is protected by the First Amendment to the Constitution. Two of the strongest expressions are said to be quoted respectively from well-known public men. It may well be that the prohibition of laws abridging the freedom of speech is not confined to previous constraints, although to prevent them may have been the main purpose. We admit that in many places and in ordinary times the defendants in saying all that was said in the circular would have been within their constitutional rights. But the character of every act depends upon the circumstances in which it is done. The most stringent protection of free speech would not protect a man in falsely shouting fire in a theatre and causing a panic. It does not even protect a man from an injunction against uttering words that may have all the effect of force. The question in every case is whether the words used are used in such circumstances and are of such a nature as to create a clear and present danger that they will bring about the substantive evils that Congress has a right to prevent. It is a question of proximity and degree. When a nation is at war many things that might be said in time of peace are such a hindrance to its effort that their utterance will not be endured so long as men fight and that no Court could regard them as protected by any constitutional right. It seems to be admitted that if an actual obstruction of the recruiting service were proved, liability for words that produced that effect might be enforced. The statute of 1917 in § 4 punishes conspiracies to obstruct as well as actual obstruction. If the act, (speaking, or circulating a paper), its tendency and the intent with which it is done are the same, we perceive no ground for saying that success alone warrants making the act a crime. Indeed that case might be said to dispose of the present contention if the precedent covers all *media concludendi* [the steps of an argument]. But as the right to free speech was not referred to specifically, we have thought fit to add a few words.

It was not argued that a conspiracy to obstruct the draft was not within the words of the Act of 1917. The words are "obstruct the recruiting or enlistment service," and it might be suggested that they refer only to making it hard to get volunteers. Recruiting heretofore usually having been accomplished by getting volunteers the word is apt to call up that method only in our minds. But recruiting is gaining fresh supplies for the forces, as well by draft as otherwise. It is put as an alternative to enlistment or voluntary enrollment in this act. . . .

Judgments affirmed.

Many scholars argue that Holmes's opinion in *Schenck* represents not only his finest work but also a most important and substantial explication of free speech. Why? First, Holmes provided the Court with a mechanism for framing such cases and a standard by which to adjudicate future claims:

The question in every case is whether the words used are used in such circumstances and are of such a nature as to create a clear and present danger that they will bring about the substantive evils that Congress has a right to prevent.

Often called the Clear and Present Danger test, the standard apparently reflected the other justices' views

on free speech as the Court's decision in *Schenck* was unanimous. Second, Holmes's opinion was politically astute. Schmidhauser notes that, given "the political context in which it arose . . . when the emphasis was on 'Americanism,'" the Court could not protect all speech.[5] Yet, in light of the First Amendment, it could not move to the opposite extreme, totally prohibiting controversial language. Seen in this way, Holmes's words created an elegant compromise and avoided a confrontation between the Court and Congress during a crisis period. Finally, that Holmes devised a test by which to adjudicate First Amendment claims provides the earliest example of the justices' willingness to recognize legitimate limits to free speech.

One week after *Schenck*, Holmes applied his Clear and Present Danger standard to two other challenges to the Espionage Act. In *Frohwerk v. United States* a newspaper editor and an editorial writer for the *Missouri Staats Zeitung* urged the Court to overturn their convictions for publishing a series of articles accusing the United States of pursuing an imperialistic policy toward Germany. In *Frohwerk*'s companion case, *Debs v. United States*, Eugene V. Debs, a leader of the Socialist party in the United States, had been convicted for a speech he delivered in Canton, Ohio. Extolling the virtues of socialism and praising the Bolshevik Revolution, Debs said:

The Socialist has a great idea. An expanding philosophy. It is spreading over the face of the earth. It is as useless to resist it as it is to resist the rising sunrise. . . . What a privilege it is to serve it. I have regretted a thousand times I can do so little for the movement that has done so much for me. . . . Do not worry over the charge of treason to your masters, but be concerned about the treason that involves yourself. This year we are going to sweep into power . . . and we are going to destroy capitalistic institutions and recreate them.

Federal authorities arrested Debs, charging him with attempting to incite insubordination, a violation of the Espionage Act. They cited as "evidence" not only his

5. Ibid., 327.

words, but the timing of his speech, right after Congress passed the Selective Service Act. Writing for the Court in both cases, Justice Holmes relied on the Clear and Present Danger test to uphold the Debs and Frohwerk convictions. In fact, his only new statement of any significance was "that the First Amendment while prohibiting legislation against free speech as such cannot have been, and obviously was not intended to give immunity for every possible use of language."

Such an assertion again underscores the Court's unwillingness to read literally and absolutely First Amendment guarantees. Moreover, because Holmes wrote for the majority in both cases, the future vitality of the Clear and Present Danger test seemed assured; the Court apparently agreed that it provided a reasonable vehicle for judging First Amendment claims. But, just eight months after the *Debs* and *Frohwerk* decisions, the majority of justices banished this test to a legal exile that would last for almost two decades. The first hint of their disaffection came in *Abrams v. United States*, the fourth of the 1919 quartet. In reading the *Abrams* decision, notice how Justice John H. Clarke's majority opinion moves away from the Clear and Present Danger language and instead emphasizes the defendants' intentions and the tendency of the expression to cause illegal actions. Holmes's dissent, on the other hand, uses the Clear and Present Danger philosophy to defend the right of political expression.

Abrams v. United States

250 U.S. 616 (1919)

Vote: 7 (Clarke, Day, McKenna, McReynolds, Pitney,
       Van Devanter, White)
     2 (Brandeis, Holmes)

Opinion of the Court: Clarke
Dissenting opinion: Holmes

In October 1918, just weeks before the end of World War I, Jacob Abrams and four others were convicted of violating the Espionage Act. The defendants, well-educated Russian immigrants, all professed revolutionary, anarchist, or socialist political views. The conspirators had published and distributed leaflets, written in English and Yiddish, criticizing President Wilson's decision to send U.S. troops into Russia and calling for a general strike to protest that policy. The leaflets were written in language characteristic of the rhetoric of the Russian Revolution: "Workers of the World! Awake! Rise! Put down your enemy and mine!" and "Yes! friends, there is only one enemy of the workers of the world and that is CAPITALISM." They described the government of the United States as a "hypocritical," "cowardly," and "capitalistic" enemy. The protesters branded Wilson a "Kaiser." The government charged Abrams and the others with intent to "cripple or hinder the United States in the prosecution of the war." The trial court sentenced the defendants to prison terms of fifteen to twenty years.

MR. JUSTICE CLARKE delivered the opinion of the Court.

It was admitted on the trial that the defendants had united to print and distribute the described circulars and that five thousand of them had been printed and distributed about the 22d day of August, 1918. The group had a meeting place in New York City, in rooms rented by defendant Abrams, under an assumed name, and there the subject of printing the circulars was discussed about two weeks before the defendants were arrested. The defendant Abrams, although not a printer, on July 27, 1918, purchased the printing outfit with which the circulars were printed and installed it in a basement room where the work was done at night. The circulars were distributed some by throwing them from a window of a building where one of the defendants was employed and others secretly, in New York City.

The defendants pleaded "not guilty," and the case of the Government consisted in showing the facts we have stated, and in introducing in evidence copies of the two printed circulars attached to the indictment, a sheet entitled "Revolutionists Unite for Action," written by the defendant Lipman, and found on him when he was arrested, and another paper, found at the headquarters of the group, and for which Abrams assumed responsibility....

The claim chiefly elaborated upon by the defendants in the oral argument and in their brief is that there is no substantial evidence in the record to support the judgment upon the verdict of guilty and that the motion of the defendants for an instructed verdict in their favor was erroneously denied. A question of law is thus presented, which calls for an examination of the record, not for the purpose of weighing conflicting testimony, but only to determine whether there was some evidence, competent and substantial, before the jury, fairly tending to sustain the verdict....

It will not do to say, as is now argued, that the only intent of these defendants was to prevent injury to the Russian cause. Men must be held to have intended, and to be accountable for, the effects which their acts were likely to produce. Even if their primary purpose and intent was to aid the cause of the Russian Revolution, the plan of action which they adopted necessarily involved, before it could be realized, defeat of the war program of the United States, for the obvious effect of this appeal, if it should become effective, as they hoped it might, would be to persuade persons of character such as those whom they regarded themselves as addressing, not to aid government loans and not to work in ammunition factories, where their work would produce "bullets, bayonets, cannon" and other munitions of war, the use of which would cause the "murder" of Germans and Russians....

This is not an attempt to bring about a change of administration by candid discussion, for no matter what may have incited the outbreak on the part of the defendant anarchists, the manifest purpose of such a publication was to create an attempt to defeat the war plans of the Government of the United States, by bringing upon the country the paralysis of a general strike, thereby arresting the production of all munitions and other things essential to the conduct of the war....

That the interpretation we have put upon these articles, circulated in the greatest port of our land, from which great numbers of soldiers were at the time taking ship daily, and in which great quantities of war supplies of every kind were at the time being manufactured for transpor-

Samuel Lipman, Hyman Lychowsky, Mollie Steimer, and Jacob Abrams, World War I era anarchists and revolutionaries, were found guilty of attempting to hinder the war effort. The Supreme Court upheld the convictions in *Abrams v. New York*.

tation overseas, is not only the fair interpretation of them, but that it is the meaning which their authors consciously intended should be conveyed by them to others is further shown by the additional writings found in the meeting place of the defendant group and on the person of one of them....

Thus was again avowed the purpose to throw the country into a state of revolution if possible and to thereby frustrate the military program of the Government....

... [T]he immediate occasion for this particular outbreak of lawlessness, on the part of the defendant alien anarchists, may have been resentment caused by our Government sending troops into Russia as a strategic operation against the Germans on the eastern battle front, yet the plain purpose of their propaganda was to excite, at the supreme crisis of the war, disaffection, sedition, riots, and, as they hoped, revolution, in this country for the purpose of embarrassing and if possible defeating the military plans of the Government in Europe. A technical distinction may perhaps be taken between disloyal and abusive language applied to the *form* of our government or language intended to bring the *form* of our government into contempt and disrepute, and language of like character and intended to produce like results directed against the President and Congress, the agencies through which that form of government must function in time of war. But it is not necessary to a decision of this case to consider whether such distinction is vital or merely formal, for the language of these circulars was obviously intended to provoke and to encourage resistance to the United States in the war, as the third count runs, and, the defendants, in terms, plainly urged and advocated a resort to a general strike of workers in ammunition factories for the purpose of curtailing the production of ordnance and munitions necessary and essential to the prosecution of the war as is charged in the fourth count. Thus it is clear not only that some evidence but that much persuasive evidence was before the jury tending to prove that the defendants were guilty as charged in both the third and fourth counts of the indictment and under the long established rule of law hereinbefore stated the judgment of the District Court must be

Affirmed.

MR. JUSTICE HOLMES, dissenting.

I never have seen any reason to doubt that the questions of law that alone were before this Court in the cases of *Schenck, Frohwerk* and *Debs* were rightly decided. I do not doubt for a moment that by the same reasoning that would justify punishing persuasion to murder, the United States constitutionally may punish speech that produces or is intended to produce a clear and imminent danger that it will bring about forthwith certain substantive evils that the United States constitutionally may seek to prevent. The power undoubtedly is greater in time of war than in time of peace because war opens dangers that do not exist at other times.

But as against dangers peculiar to war, as against others, the principle of the right to free speech is always the same. It is only the present danger of immediate evil or an intent to bring it about that warrants Congress in setting a limit to the expression of opinion where private rights are not concerned. Congress certainly cannot forbid

all effort to change the mind of the country. Now nobody can suppose that the surreptitious publishing of a silly leaflet by an unknown man, without more, would present any immediate danger that its opinions would hinder the success of the government arms or have any appreciable tendency to do so. Publishing those opinions for the very purpose of obstructing however, might indicate a greater danger and at any rate would have the quality of an attempt. So I assume that the second leaflet if published for the purposes alleged in the fourth count might be punishable. But it seems pretty clear to me that nothing less than that would bring these papers within the scope of this law. An actual intent in the sense that I have explained is necessary to constitute an attempt, where a further act of the same individual is required to complete the substantive crime.... It is necessary where the success of the attempt depends upon others because if that intent is not present the actor's aim may be accomplished without bringing about the evils sought to be checked. An intent to prevent interference with the revolution in Russia might have been satisfied without any hindrance to carrying on the war in which we were engaged.

I do not see how anyone can find the intent required by the statute in any of the defendants' words. The second leaflet is the only one that affords even a foundation for the charge, and there, without invoking the hatred of German militarism expressed in the former one, it is evident beginning to the end that the only object of the paper is to help Russia and stop American intervention there against the popular government—not to impede the United States in the war that it was carrying on. To say that two phrases taken literally might import a suggestion of conduct that would have interference with the war as an indirect and probably undesired effect seems to me by no means enough to show an attempt to produce that effect.

I return for a moment to the third count. That charges an intent to provoke resistance to the United States in its war with Germany. Taking the clause in the statute that deals with that in connection with the other elaborate provisions of the act, I think that resistance to the United States means some forcible act of opposition to some proceeding of the United States in pursuance of the war. I think the intent must be the specific intent that I have described and for the reasons that I have given I think that no such intent was proved or existed in fact. I also think that there is no hint at resistance to the United States as I construe the phrase.

In this case sentences of twenty years imprisonment have been imposed for the publishing of two leaflets that I believe the defendants had as much right to publish as the Government has to publish the Constitution of the United States now vainly invoked by them. Even if I am technically wrong and enough can be squeezed from these poor and puny anonymities to turn the color of legal litmus paper; I will add, even if what I think the necessary intent were shown; the most nominal punishment seems to me all that possibly could be inflicted, unless the defendants are to be made to suffer not for what the indictment alleges but for the creed that they avow—a creed that I believe to be the creed of ignorance and immaturity when honestly held, as I see no reason to doubt that it was held here, but which, although made the subject of examination at the trial, no one has a right even to consider in dealing with the charges before the Court.

Persecution for the expression of opinions seems to me perfectly logical. If you have no doubt of your premises or your power and want a certain result with all your heart you naturally express your wishes in law and sweep away all opposition. To allow opposition by speech seems to indicate that you think the speech impotent, as when a man says that he has squared the circle, or that you do not care whole-heartedly for the result, or that you doubt either your power or your premises. But when men have realized that time has upset many fighting faiths, they may come to believe even more than they believe the very foundations of their own conduct that the ultimate good desired is better reached by free trade in ideas—that the best test of truth is the power of the thought to get itself accepted in the competition of the market, and that truth is the only ground upon which their wishes safely can be carried out. That at any rate is the theory of our Constitution. It is an experiment, as all life is an experiment. Every year if not every day we have to wager our salvation upon some prophecy based upon imperfect knowledge. While that experiment is part of our system I think that we should be eternally vigilant against attempts to check the expression of opinions that we loathe and believe to be fraught with death, unless they so imminently threaten immediate

interference with the lawful and pressing purposes of the law that an immediate check is required to save the country. I wholly disagree with the argument of the Government that the First Amendment left the common law as to seditious libel in force. History seems to me against the notion. I had conceived that the United States through many years had shown its repentance for the Sedition Act of 1798, by repaying fines that it imposed. Only the emergency that makes it immediately dangerous to leave the correction of evil counsels to time warrants making any exception to the sweeping command, "Congress shall make no law … abridging the freedom of speech." Of course I am speaking only of expressions of opinion and exhortations, which were all that were uttered here, but I regret that I cannot put into more impressive words my belief that in their conviction upon this indictment the defendants were deprived of their rights under the Constitution of the United States.

MR. JUSTICE BRANDEIS concurs with the foregoing opinion.

That the *Abrams* decision marked a turning away from the Clear and Present Danger standard was evident to Holmes. In his dissent he tried to refine the test to show how the *Schenck* rationale could work in a variety of contexts. Many view this dissent as one of Holmes's finest, earning him the sobriquet "the Great Dissenter." *(See Box 4-1.)*

But Holmes failed to convince his colleagues in *Abrams*. Instead, Clarke's majority opinion used a standard known as the Bad Tendency Test, an approach derived from English common law. It asks, "Do the words have a *tendency* to bring about something evil?" rather than, "Do the words bring about an immediate substantive evil?" Why the majority shifted constitutional standards is a mystery. We cannot say that the Clear and Present Danger test produced results markedly different from the Bad Tendency standard. Holmes had not used it in *Schenck*, *Debs*, or *Frohwerk* to overturn convictions. Some scholars assert that the main drawback of the Holmes standard was its simplicity: it did not solve with certainty

BOX 4-1 OLIVER WENDELL HOLMES, JR. (1902–1932)

OLIVER WENDELL HOLMES, JR., was born March 8, 1841, in Boston. He was named after his father, a professor of anatomy at Harvard Medical School as well as a poet, essayist, and novelist in the New England literary circle that included Longfellow, Emerson, Lowell, and Whittier. Dr. Holmes's wife, Amelia Lee Jackson Holmes, was the third daughter of Justice Charles Jackson of the Supreme Judicial Court of Massachusetts. Young Holmes attended a private Latin school in Cambridge and received his undergraduate education at Harvard, graduating as class poet in 1861 as had his father thirty-two years before him.

Commissioned a second lieutenant in the Massachusetts Twentieth Volunteers, known as the Harvard Regiment, Holmes was wounded three times in battle. Serving three years, he was mustered out a captain in recognition of his bravery and gallant service. After the Civil War, Holmes returned to Harvard to study law despite his father's conviction that "a lawyer can't be a great man."

He was admitted to the Massachusetts bar in 1867 and practiced in Boston for fifteen years, beginning with the firm of Chandler, Shattuck, and Thayer and later forming his own partnership with Shattuck. In 1872 Holmes married Fanny Bowdich Dixwell, the daughter of his former schooolmaster and a friend since childhood. They were married fifty-seven years.

During his legal career Holmes taught constitutional law at his alma mater, edited the *American Law Review,* and lectured on common law at the Lowell Institute. His twelve lectures were compiled in a book called *The Common Law* and published shortly before his fortieth birthday. The London *Spectator* heralded Holmes's treatise as the most original work of legal speculation in decades. *The Common Law* was translated into German, Italian, and French.

IN 1882 THE GOVERNOR of Massachusetts appointed Holmes— then a full professor at the Harvard Law School in a chair established by Boston lawyer Louis D. Brandeis—

an associate justice of the Massachusetts Supreme Court. Holmes served on the state court for twenty years, the last three as chief justice, and wrote more than 1,000 opinions, many of them involving labor disputes. Holmes's progressive labor views, criticized by railroad and corporate interests, were considered favorably by President Theodore Roosevelt during his search in 1902 for someone to fill the "Massachusetts seat" on the U.S. Supreme Court, vacated by Bostonian Horace Gray. Convinced of Holmes's compatibility with the administration's national policies, Roosevelt nominated him associate justice December 2 and he was confirmed without objection two days later.

Holmes's twenty-nine years of service on the Supreme Court spanned the tenures of Chief Justices Fuller, White, Taft, and Hughes and the administrations of Presidents Roosevelt, Taft, Wilson, Harding, Coolidge, and Hoover.

For twenty-five years he never missed a session and daily walked the two and a half miles from his home to the Court. Like Justice Brandeis, Holmes voluntarily paid an income tax despite the majority's ruling that exempted federal judges. Unlike the idealistic and often moralistic Brandeis, with whom he is frequently compared, Holmes was pragmatic, approaching each case on its own set of facts without a preconceived notion of the proper result.

Although a lifelong Republican, on the Court Holmes did not fulfill Roosevelt's expectations as a loyal party man. His dissent shortly after his appointment from the Court's decision to break up the railroad trust of the Northern Securities Company surprised the nation and angered the president.

At the suggestion of Chief Justice Hughes and his colleagues on the bench, Holmes retired on January 12, 1932, at the age of ninety. A widower since 1929, he continued to spend his winters in Washington, D.C., and his summers in Beverly Farms, Massachusetts. He died at his Washington home March 6, 1935, two days before his ninety-fourth birthday.

SOURCE: Adapted from Elder Witt, *Guide to the U.S. Supreme Court,* 2d ed. (Washington, D.C.: Congressional Quarterly, 1990), 845–846.

the confusing and complicated problems of the day.[6]

Regardless of their motivation, by the early 1920s it was obvious that a majority of justices rejected the Clear and Present Danger standard in favor of more stringent constitutional interpretations, such as the Bad Tendency test. Two cases, *Gitlow v. New York* (1925) and *Whitney v. California* (1927), exemplify this shift but with a slightly different twist. *Gitlow* and *Whitney* involved state prosecutions, not Espionage Act violations. Just as the federal government wanted to foster patriotism during wartime, the states also felt the need to promulgate their own versions of nationalism. The result was the so-called state criminal syndicalism laws, which made it a crime to advocate, teach, aid, or abet in any activity designed to bring about the overthrow of the government by force or violence. The actual effect of such laws was to outlaw any association with views "abhorrent" to the interests of the United States, such as communism and socialism. Would the Court be willing to tolerate such state intrusions into free speech? That was the question with which the justices grappled in *Gitlow* and *Whitney*.

William Foster, left, and Benjamin Gitlow, presidential and vice-presidential candidates for the Workers (Communist) party, at Madison Square Garden in 1928. Gitlow's publication of a "Left Wing Manifesto" led to his arrest and conviction under New York's criminal anarchy act. The Supreme Court upheld the conviction, but ruled that states were bound by the freedom of speech provision of the First Amendment.

Gitlow v. New York

268 U.S. 652 (1925)
Vote: 7 (Butler, Reynolds, Sanford, Stone, Sutherland, Taft,
     Van Devanter)
  2 (Brandeis, Holmes)
Opinion of the Court: Sanford
Dissenting opinion: Holmes

The issues in *Gitlow* arose during the early 1900s when fear of communist subversion gripped the United States. To combat the "Red Menace," several states, including New York, created commissions to investigate subversive organizations. In 1919 and 1920 the New York Commission conducted raids on social-

ist and communist leaders and seized their materials. Among those arrested was Benjamin Gitlow, a socialist charged with distributing a pamphlet called the *Left Wing Manifesto*. The *Manifesto* called for mass action to overthrow the capitalist system in the United States. Gitlow was prosecuted in a New York trial court for violating the state's criminal anarchy law. Under the leadership of Clarence Darrow, Gitlow's defense attorneys alleged that the statute violated the First Amend-

6. Malcolm M. Feeley and Samuel Krislov, *Constitutional Law* (Boston: Little, Brown, 1985), 424.

ment's guarantee of freedom of expression. The defense was unsuccessful, and Gitlow appealed.

MR. JUSTICE SANFORD delivered the opinion of the Court.

Benjamin Gitlow was indicted in the Supreme Court of New York, with three others, for the statutory crime of criminal anarchy. He was separately tried, convicted, and sentenced to imprisonment....

The sole contention here is, essentially, that as there was no evidence of any concrete result flowing from the publication of the Manifesto or of circumstances showing the likelihood of such result, the statute as construed and applied by the trial court penalizes the mere utterance, as such, of "doctrine" having no quality of incitement, without regard either to the circumstances of its utterance or to the likelihood of unlawful sequences; and that, as the exercise of the right of free expression with relation to government is only punishable "in circumstances involving likelihood of substantive evil," the statute contravenes the due process clause of the Fourteenth Amendment. The argument in support of this contention rests primarily upon the following propositions: 1st, That the "liberty" protected by the Fourteenth Amendment includes the liberty of speech and of the press; and 2d, That while liberty of expression "is not absolute," it may be restrained "only in circumstances where its exercise bears a causal relation with some substantive evil, consummated, attempted or likely," and as the statute "takes no account of circumstances," it unduly restrains this liberty and is therefore unconstitutional.

The precise question presented, and the only question which we can consider under this writ of error, then is, whether the statute, as construed and applied in this case by the State courts, deprived the defendant of his liberty of expression in violation of the due process clause of the Fourteenth Amendment.

The statute does not penalize the utterance or publication of abstract "doctrine" or academic discussion having no quality of incitement to any concrete action. It is not aimed against mere historical or philosophical essays. It does not restrain the advocacy of changes in the form of government by constitutional and lawful means. What it prohibits is language advocating, advising or teaching the overthrow of organized government by unlawful means. These words imply urging to action. Advocacy is defined in the Century Dictionary as: "1. The act of pleading for, supporting, or recommending; active espousal." It is not the abstract "doctrine" of overthrowing organized government by unlawful means which is denounced by the statute, but the advocacy of action for the accomplishment of that purpose....

The Manifesto, plainly, is neither the statement of abstract doctrine nor, as suggested by counsel, mere prediction that industrial disturbances and revolutionary mass strikes will result spontaneously in an inevitable process of evolution in the economic system. It advocates and urges in fervent language mass action which shall progressively foment industrial disturbances and through political mass strikes and revolutionary mass action overthrow and destroy organized parliamentary government. It concludes with a call to action in these words:

"The proletariat revolution and the Communist reconstruction of society—*the struggle for these*—is now indispensable.... The Communist International calls the proletariat of the world to the final struggle!"

This is not the expression of philosophical abstraction, the mere prediction of future events; it is the language of direct incitement.

The means advocated for bringing about the destruction of organized parliamentary government, namely, mass industrial revolts usurping the functions of municipal government, political mass strikes directed against the parliamentary state, and revolutionary mass action for its final destruction, necessarily imply the use of force and violence, and in their essential nature are inherently unlawful in a constitutional government of law and order. That the jury were warranted in finding that the Manifesto advocated not merely the abstract doctrine of overthrowing organized government by force, violence and unlawful means, but action to that end, is clear.

For present purposes we may and do assume that freedom of speech and of the press—which are protected by the First Amendment from abridgment by Congress—are among the fundamental personal rights and "liberties" protected by the due process clause of the Fourteenth Amendment from impairment by the States.... It is a fundamental principle, long established, that the freedom of speech and of the press which is secured by the Constitution, does not confer an absolute right to speak or publish, without responsibility, whatever one may choose, or an unrestricted and unbridled license that gives immunity for every possible use of language and prevents the punishment of those who abuse this freedom. Reasonably limited ... this freedom is an inestimable privilege in a free government; without such limitation, it might become the scourge of the republic.

That a State in the exercise of its police power may punish those who abuse this freedom by utterances inimical to the public welfare, tending to corrupt public morals, incite to crime, or disturb the public peace, is not open to question.

And, for yet more imperative reasons, a State may punish utterances endangering the foundations of organized government and threatening its overthrow by unlawful means. These imperil its own existence as a constitutional State. Freedom of speech and press ... does not protect disturbances to the public peace or the attempt to subvert the government. It does not protect publications or teachings which tend to subvert or imperil the government or to impede or hinder it in the performance of its governmental duties. It does not protect publications prompting the overthrow of government by force; the punishment of those who publish articles which tend to destroy organized society being essential to the security of freedom and the stability of the State. And a State may penalize utterances which openly advocate the overthrow of the representative and constitutional form of government of the United States and the several States, by violence or other unlawful means. In short this freedom does not deprive a State of the primary and essential right of self preservation; which, so long as human governments endure, they cannot be denied.

By enacting the present statute the State has determined, through its legislative body, that utterances advocating the overthrow of organized government by force, violence and unlawful means, are so inimical to the general welfare and involve such danger of substantive evil that they may be penalized in the exercise of its police power. That determination must be given great weight. Every presumption is to be indulged in favor of the validity of the statute. And the case is to be considered "in the light of the prin-

ciple that the State is primarily the judge of regulations required in the interest of public safety and welfare"; and that its police "statutes may only be declared unconstitutional where they are arbitrary or unreasonable attempts to exercise authority vested in the State in the public interest." That utterances inciting to the overthrow of organized government by unlawful means, present a sufficient danger of substantive evil to bring their punishment within the range of legislative discretion, is clear. Such utterances, by their very nature, involve danger to the public peace and to the security of the State. They threaten breaches of the peace and ultimate revolution. And the immediate danger is none the less real and substantial, because the effect of a given utterance cannot be accurately foreseen. The State cannot reasonably be required to measure the danger from every such utterance in the nice balance of a jeweler's scale. A single revolutionary spark may kindle a fire that, smouldering for a time, may burst into a sweeping and destructive conflagration. It cannot be said that the State is acting arbitrarily or unreasonably when in the exercise of its judgment as to the measures necessary to protect the public peace and safety, it seeks to extinguish the spark without waiting until it has enkindled the flame or blazed into the conflagration. It cannot reasonably be required to defer the adoption of measures for its own peace and safety until the revolutionary utterances lead to actual disturbances of the public peace or imminent and immediate danger of its own destruction; but it may, in the exercise of its judgment, suppress the threatened danger in its incipiency.

We cannot hold that the present statute is an arbitrary or unreasonable exercise of the police power of the State unwarrantably infringing the freedom of speech or press; and we must and do sustain its constitutionality.

This being so it may be applied to every utterance—not too trivial to be beneath the notice of the law—which is of such a character and used with such intent and purpose as to bring it within the prohibition of the statute. In other words, when the legislative body has determined generally, in the constitutional exercise of its discretion, that utterances of a certain kind involve such danger of substantive evil that they may be punished, the question whether any specific utterance coming within the prohibited class is likely, in and of itself, to bring about the substantive evil, is not open to consideration. It is sufficient that the statute itself be constitutional and that the use of the language comes within its prohibition.

It is clear that the question in such cases is entirely different from that involved in those cases where the statute merely prohibits certain acts involving the danger of substantive evil, without any reference to language itself, and it is sought to apply its provisions to language used by the defendant for the purpose of bringing about the prohibited results. There, if it be contended that the statute cannot be applied to the language used by the defendant because of its protection by the freedom of speech or press, it must necessarily be found, as an original question, without any previous determination by the legislative body, whether the specific language used involved such likelihood of bringing about the substantive evil as to deprive it of the constitutional protection. In such case it has been held that the general provisions of the statute may be constitutionally applied to the specific utterance of the defendant if its natural tendency and probable effect was to bring about the substantive evil which the legislative body might prevent. And the general statement in the Schenck Case, that the "question in every case is whether the words used are used in such circumstances and are of such a nature as to create a clear and present danger that they will bring about the substantive evils,"—upon which great reliance is placed in the defendant's argument—was manifestly intended, as shown by the context, to apply only in cases of this class, and has no application to those like the present, where the legislative body itself has previously determined the danger of substantive evil arising from utterances of a specified character.

The defendant's brief does not separately discuss any of the rulings of the trial court. It is only necessary to say that, applying the general rules already stated, we find that none of them involved any invasion of the constitutional rights of the defendant. It was not necessary, within the meaning of the statute, that the defendant should have advocated "some definite or immediate act or acts" of force, violence or unlawfulness. It was sufficient if such acts were advocated in general terms; and it was not essential that their immediate execution should have been advocated. Nor was it necessary that the language should have been "reasonably and ordinarily calculated to incite certain persons" to acts of force, violence or unlawfulness. The advocacy need not be addressed to specific persons....

And finding, for the reasons stated, that the statute is not in itself unconstitutional, and that it has not been applied in the present case in derogation of any constitutional right, the judgment of the Court of Appeals is

Affirmed.

MR. JUSTICE HOLMES, dissenting.

MR. JUSTICE BRANDEIS and I are of opinion that this judgment should be reversed. The general principle of free speech, it seems to me, must be taken to be included in the Fourteenth Amendment, in view of the scope that has been given to the word "liberty" as there used, although perhaps it may be accepted with a somewhat larger latitude of interpretation than is allowed to Congress by the sweeping language that governs or ought to govern the laws of the United States. If I am right, then I think that the criterion sanctioned by the full Court in *Schenck v. United States* applies. "The question in every case is whether the words used are used in such circumstances and are of such a nature as to create a clear and present danger that they will bring about the substantive evils that [the State] has a right to prevent." It is true that in my opinion this criterion was departed from in *Abrams v. United States,* but the convictions that I expressed in that case are too deep for it to be possible for me as yet to believe that it and *Schaefer v. United States* [1920] have settled the law. If what I think the correct test is applied, it is manifest that there was no present danger of an attempt to overthrow the government by force on the part of the admittedly small minority who shared the defendant's views. It is said that this manifesto was more than a theory, that it was an incitement. Every idea is an incitement. It offers itself for belief and if believed it is acted on unless some other belief outweighs it or some failure of energy stifles the movement at its birth. The only difference between the expression of an opinion and an incitement in the narrower sense is the speaker's enthusiasm for the result. Eloquence may set fire to reason. But whatever may be thought of the redundant discourse before us it had no chance of starting a present conflagration. If in the long run the beliefs expressed in proletarian dictatorship are destined to be accepted by the dominant forces of the community, the only meaning of free speech is that they should be given their chance and have their way.

If the publication of this document had been laid as an attempt to induce an uprising against government at once and not at some indefinite time in the future it would have presented a different question. The object would have been one with which the law might deal, subject to the doubt whether there was any danger that the publication could produce any result, or in other words, whether it was not futile and too remote from possible consequences. But the indictment alleges the publication and nothing more.

The *Gitlow* case is important for a number of reasons, but its effect on the development of civil liberties law is somewhat mixed. Perhaps its most enduring contribution to constitutional law is its statement that for "present purposes we may and do assume that freedom of speech and of the press—which are protected by the First Amendment from abridgment by Congress—are among the fundamental personal rights and 'liberties' protected by the due process clause of the Fourteenth Amendment from impairment by the States." This sweeping incorporation vastly expanded constitutional guarantees for freedom of expression. Nevertheless, the majority held that Gitlow's rights had not been violated, that the state of New York had the authority to punish expression that might threaten the violent overthrow of the government. In dissent, Holmes continued to press his Clear and Present Danger standard, arguing that Gitlow's actions posed no obvious and immediate danger. Whatever danger Gitlow's message might pose, it was too inconsequential and too remote to justify government repression of expression rights.

Whitney v. California involved Charlotte Whitney, a well-known California heiress and a niece of former Supreme Court justice Stephen J. Field. She was a member of the Oakland branch of the Socialist party and apparently an active member because she voted for delegates sent by the chapter to a national party meeting held in 1919 in Chicago.[7] At that convention

the party ejected its more radical members, including Oakland locals, who in turn formed the Communist party of the United States. Local party chapters from California then held a state meeting in Oakland, where they created the Communist Labor party of California.

Although Whitney had opposed the radical platform "urging a revolutionary class struggle" offered at the national convention, she nevertheless served as one of her chapter's delegates to the local meeting and, in fact, became chair of the credentials committee. Based on her association with this group and its predecessor, California authorities charged Whitney with violating the state's syndicalism law. She was found guilty of organizing and associating with a party dedicated to overthrowing the U.S. government.

On appeal to the Supreme Court, her attorneys from the newly formed American Civil Liberties Union *(see Box 4-2)* argued that the California act violated the Free Speech Clause of the First Amendment. But the justices upheld her conviction. They treated her claim just as they had Gitlow's, relying on the Bad Tendency test. The majority asserted in *Whitney,*

That the freedom of speech which is secured by the Constitution does not confer an absolute right to speak ... whatever one may choose ... and that a State in the exercise of its police power may punish those who abuse this freedom by utterances inimical to the public welfare, tending to incite crime, disturb the public peace, or endanger the foundations of organized government and threaten its overthrow by unlawful means, is not open to question.

It has been noted that in *Gitlow* and *Whitney* the justices seem to be operating under "the assumption that the First Amendment ... was designed to promote the public good," rather than to provide affirmative protection for individual speech.[8]

Brandeis and Holmes filed a concurrence in *Whitney.* Clearly, they favored a return to the Clear and Present Danger standard, but with this modification: that the evil take the form of behavior. Justice Brandeis

---

7. For more on this 1927 case, see Thomas I. Emerson, *The System of Freedom of Expression* (New York: Vintage Books, 1970), 105–107.

8. Ralph A. Rossum and G. Alan Tarr, *American Constitutional Law,* 3d ed. (New York: St. Martin's Press, 1991), 346.

BOX 4-2 THE AMERICAN CIVIL LIBERTIES UNION

BY ALMOST ALL MEASURES, the American Civil Liberties Union (ACLU) is the largest and most complex organization dedicated to public interest litigation in the United States. Beyond its national organization, the ACLU maintains fifty state and local affiliates and, via its foundation, runs several specialized projects.

Given its current form, the humble origins of the ACLU may come as quite a surprise: the ACLU "was . . . very much a phenomenon of the Progressive-Populist era with its concern over government abuse." Indeed, the ACLU's roots lie in a small organization called the Henry Street Group, which was started by several leaders of the Progressive Movement to combat growing militarism. One year later, this group united with another to become the American Union Against Militarism (AUAM).

Between 1915 and 1917 the AUAM tried to lobby against any legislation designed to stimulate the U.S. "war machine." But in 1917, when Germany announced "its intention to resume unrestricted warfare," the AUAM turned its attention to the draft. The organization sought to defend those who had conscientious objections to serving in the military. This goal was handled primarily by an agency within the AUAM, the Bureau of Conscientious Objectors (BCO).

Under the leadership of the young charismatic Roger Baldwin, the BCO eventually dominated the AUAM. Baldwin's BCO doubled the size of AUAM's membership and spent more than 50 percent of its funds. Clearly, Baldwin was an effective leader, but the old-line Progressive leaders of the AUAM disliked Baldwin's strategy of providing direct assistance to conscientious objectors and threatened to resign. To save the AUAM and to show solidarity with its "greater" agenda, Baldwin changed the name of the BCO to the Civil Liberties Bureau (CLB). This last-ditch effort failed, however, and in 1917 the new National CLB split from its parent organization, which expired shortly thereafter.

Between 1917 and 1919, the NCLB continued to defend conscientious objectors. Unfortunately, it could not prevent Baldwin's imprisonment for draft violations in 1918. Ironically, during Baldwin's jail term the seed for what is now known as the American Civil Liberties Union was planted. In prison, Baldwin became acquainted with the activities of a radical labor union, the Industrial Workers of the World, an organization that made no secret of its use of violence and sabotage to achieve its policy needs.

This name alteration and reorganization forever changed the NCLB. After 1920 the newly formed ACLU would never be a single-purpose organization; by 1925 it was involved with labor, pacifists, and the "Red Scare" caused by the Palmer raids.

Defending the right of free speech eventually became the ACLU's major trademark as the organization moved into the 1930s, 1940s, and 1950s. But while cultivating such expertise, ACLU leaders realized they had to "nationalize" the growing group. Such steps included fuller recognition of the growing chain of ACLU affiliates throughout the United States and provision of more information to its membership, which increased by almost 5,000 annually.

Fortunately for the organization, its efforts to build and regroup during the 1950s were quite timely: the 1960s turned out to be critical years for the union. Not only was the decade significant in the development of law governing civil rights and liberties, but the ACLU itself seemed to embody the goals of the nation. The union's stance against the Vietnam War, President Richard Nixon, and racism, and its defense of draft dodgers and student protesters proved to be highly popular. Between 1966 and 1973, the ACLU's membership skyrocketed from 77,200 to 222,000, and its litigation activities exploded.

To deal with its increasing caseload and to focus its energies on specific areas of the law, the ACLU established the ACLU Foundation in 1967. This foundation, in turn, established special national projects, including the National Prison, Women's Rights, and Reproductive Freedom projects. Today, the union has about 250,000 members and affiliates in every state. The organization currently operates on a $12 million budget.

The ACLU has used these financial and personnel resources to build an increasingly vast and active organization. Currently, the union and its affiliates employ 225 persons and 5 to 10 student interns per year. Staff attorneys account for 38 of its 125 national employees, and 35 of the 100 affiliated workers. At the state and local levels, ACLU organizations use volunteer attorneys for 65 percent of their legal work.

SOURCE: Adapted from Karen O'Connor and Lee Epstein, *Public Interest Law Groups* (Westport, Conn.: Greenwood Press, 1989).

wrote, "No danger flowing from speech can be deemed clear and present, unless the incidence of evil apprehended is so imminent that it may befall before there is opportunity for full discussions." What is even more curious (and a matter of some scholarly interest) is why the duo concurred rather than dissented. It seems clear that Whitney's behavior did not meet the standard they articulated, making the question all the more intriguing. One reasonable hypothesis is that Brandeis wanted to demonstrate that the Clear and Present Danger test was not necessarily a vehicle created to overturn convictions, but merely a more equitable way to adjudge First Amendment claims.

Regardless of the philosophical debates triggered by the series of cases from *Schenck* to *Whitney*, one fact remains clear: the justices seemed swept away by the wave of nationalism and patriotism in the aftermath of World War I. With but one exception, they acceded to the wishes of Congress and the states, which centered around the complementary goals of promoting nationalism and suppressing radicalism.[9]

The 1930s and 1940s: A Return to Clear and Present Danger?

The United States learned many lessons from the First World War; among the most important was to appreciate the resilience of its system of government. As Sheldon Goldman notes, "America became intensely self-conscious of its civil liberties heritage in contrast to its totalitarian enemies."[10] This awareness, plus "distance in time from actual combat brought calmer voices to the debate on seditious speech."[11] In other words, as the war died down, so did the na-

tional fervor that had swept the nation over the preceding two decades.

As a microcosm of society, the Supreme Court also began to reevaluate its decisions from *Schenck* to *Whitney*. And, beginning in 1931 in *Stromberg v. California*, calmer voices began to prevail. Yetta Stromberg, a nineteen-year-old member of the Young Communist League, served as a counselor at a summer camp for children ages ten to fifteen. Stromberg regularly introduced her campers to various aspects of Marxist theory, including class consciousness and the solidarity of workers. In addition, she would raise a red banner and lead the children in reciting a workers' pledge of allegiance. State authorities prosecuted Stromberg under a California statute making it a felony to raise publicly a red flag or banner as a symbol of opposition to organized government or in support of anarchy. She was convicted over her attorneys' arguments that the California law violated the First Amendment.

Writing for a seven-justice majority, Chief Justice Charles Evans Hughes reversed the conviction. The Court found the California statute to be excessively broad because its wording applied not only to persons advocating the violent overthrow of the government but also to those engaged in orderly and peaceful opposition. Such vagueness and ambiguity do not comport with the demands of the First Amendment.

Stromberg is important because of the Court's ruling, not its reasoning. It sent a message to attorneys that the justices would be willing to listen to First Amendment claims more sympathetically now than they were during the years following World War I. But, in *Stromberg*, Hughes did not formulate a free speech standard. Such a standard did not appear until nearly six years later in *DeJonge v. Oregon* (1937). As a member of the Communist party in Portland, Oregon, Dirk De-Jonge distributed handbills throughout the city, calling for a meeting of all members and other interested parties. The purpose of the gathering was to protest police raids of members' houses. DeJonge held the

---

9. The one exception was *Fiske v. Kansas* (1927), decided on the same day as *Whitney*. The Court for the first time overturned a conviction under a state syndicalism law, the justices concluding that there was insufficient evidence to sustain Fiske's conviction.

10. Sheldon Goldman, *Constitutional Law and Supreme Court Decision Making* (New York: Harper & Row, 1982), 345.

11. Elder Witt, *The Supreme Court and Individual Rights*, 2d ed. (Washington, D.C.: Congressional Quarterly, 1988), 30.

meeting on July 27, 1934, and between 160 and 200 people attended, only a small percentage of whom belonged to the party. Although the members tried to sell copies of the party's newspaper, the *Daily Worker,* the agenda of the meeting was quite general, with all proceeding in an orderly fashion until the police raided it. They arrested DeJonge for violating Oregon's criminal syndicalism law, which prohibited the organization of the Communist party. Faced with the *Whitney* precedent, DeJonge's ACLU attorney tried to argue that his client neither created a public danger nor advocated any subversive views. State attorneys relied on an earlier Court view: "the right of free speech . . . is not an absolute one."

For a unanimous Court, Hughes wrote:

The right of peaceable assembly is a right cognate to those of free speech and free press and is equally fundamental. . . . [It] follows [that] peaceable assembly for lawful discussion cannot be made a crime. . . . The question . . . is not as to the auspices under which the meeting is held but as to its purpose; not as to the relations of the speakers, but whether their utterances transcend the bounds of the freedom of speech which the Constitution [safeguards]. . . . The state [law] as applied to the particular charge as defined by the state court is repugnant to the [Constitution].

Sound familiar? Hughes's language echoes Holmes's opinion in *Schenck,* for in *DeJonge* the majority tried to revitalize the presumably long-dead doctrine of Clear and Present Danger. Hughes overturned the convictions because the defendant did not engage in "forcible subversion." As he noted, "Legislative intervention can find constitutional justification only by dealing with the abuse."

Surely such reasoning turns the Court's decision in *Whitney* on its head. But even more dramatic was a seemingly insignificant bit of writing—a footnote contained in Justice Harlan F. Stone's opinion in *United States v. Carolene Products* (1938). This case dealt with a federal ban on the shipment of a certain kind of milk—an economic, not a First Amendment, issue. Stone wrote in Footnote Four:

There may be narrower scope for operation of the presumption of constitutionality when legislation appears on its face to be within a specific prohibition of the Constitution, such as those of the first ten Amendments, which are deemed equally specific when held to be embraced by the Fourteenth Amendment. . . .

It is unnecessary to consider now whether legislation which restricts those political processes which can ordinarily be expected to bring about repeal of undesirable legislation, is to be subjected to more exacting judicial scrutiny under the general prohibitions of the Fourteenth Amendment than are most other types of legislation. . . .

Nor need we enquire whether similar considerations enter into the review of statutes directed at particular religious, or national, or racial minorities; whether prejudice against discrete and insular minorities may be a special condition, which tends seriously to curtail the operation of those political processes ordinarily to be relied upon to protect minorities, and which may call for a correspondingly more searching judicial inquiry.

What appeared to be an obscure footnote in a relatively insignificant case took on tremendous importance for civil liberties claims, especially those based on First Amendment expression rights. As Alpheus Mason and Grier Stephenson explain, each of the footnote's three paragraphs contained powerful ideas regarding the status of constitutional rights.[12] The first paragraph holds that whenever a government regulation appears on its face to be in conflict with the Bill of Rights the usual presumption that laws are constitutional should be reduced or waived altogether. The second paragraph hints that the judiciary has a special responsibility to defend those rights essential to the effective functioning of the political process, a class of liberties that clearly includes freedom of expression rights. And finally, the third paragraph suggests a special role for the Court in protecting the rights of minorities and unpopular groups. The standard expressed in Footnote Four has become known as the Preferred Freedoms doctrine.

12. Alpheus Thomas Mason and Donald Grier Stephenson, Jr., *American Constitutional Law,* 10th ed. (Englewood Cliffs, N.J.: Prentice-Hall, 1993), 279.

This doctrine has special significance for First Amendment claims, for it means that the judiciary will proceed with a special scrutiny when faced with laws that restrict freedom of expression, especially as those laws may relate to the articulation of unpopular political views. Put another way, "Laws restricting fundamental rights ... would be regarded as suspect and potentially dangerous to the functioning of democracy."[13]

The importance of Justice Stone's footnote goes beyond its obvious declaration of a new standard for evaluating First Amendment claims. In *Carolene Products* Stone announces a modification in the fundamental role of the Court. He declares that the Court will assume a special responsibility for protecting civil rights and civil liberties and be particularly vigilant in guarding the rights of minorities and the politically unpopular. Stone's statement marked a major change in course for an institution that had, for its entire history, been tilted toward settling private economic disputes and wrestling with questions of governmental power. From this point forward the civil liberties docket began to grow, and the Court rapidly began to evolve into an institution with a primary focus on civil liberties issues.[14]

But would the majority of the justices adopt Stone's Preferred Freedoms approach to First Amendment claims? Moreover, how would such an approach square with the Clear and Present Danger standard, to which most of them seemed to want to return? Attorneys, states, and civil libertarians had to wait only a year until the Court addressed these questions in *Schneider v. Irvington* (1939). This case involved not a radical leader of the Communist party, but a member of the Jehovah's Witnesses *(see Box 3-1, page 80)*. In accordance with her religious tenets, Schneider distributed literature from house to house, leaving residents her card. Town authorities arrested her because she had failed to obtain a solicitation permit, an action Schneider claimed violated her religion, but which the city required to keep the streets uncluttered. Although this case, and three others decided with it, involved elements of religion, the Court was more interested in Schneider's claim that the permit ordinance violated her free speech guarantees. In an 8-1 decision, it struck down the municipal regulation as an unconstitutional burden on free speech. Justice Roberts stated:

We are of the opinion that the purpose to keep the streets clean [is] insufficient to justify an ordinance which prohibits a person rightfully on a public street from handing literature to one willing to receive it. Any burden imposed upon the city authorities in cleaning ... the streets ... results from the constitutional protection of the freedom of speech.

Six years later in *Thomas v. Collins* (1945) the Court moved even closer to embracing the Preferred Freedoms approach. The case arose when R. J. Thomas, president of the United Automobile, Aircraft and Agricultural Workers (UAW) and vice president of the Congress of Industrial Organizations (CIO), arrived in Houston, Texas, to deliver a speech to a group of workers a regional CIO affiliate wanted to organize. Six hours before Thomas was to speak, Texas authorities served him with a restraining order, prohibiting him from making his scheduled address. Believing that the order constituted a violation of his free speech guarantees, Thomas delivered his speech anyway to an audience of 300 people. The meeting was described as "peaceful and orderly," but authorities arrested Thomas. He was sentenced to three days in jail and a $100 fine. On appeal to the U.S. Supreme Court, Thomas's claim of a free speech infringement received reinforcement from several civil liberties organizations including the National Federation for Constitutional Liberties, which argued, "The activities of labor organizations involve the exercise of peaceful assembly, freedom of speech and freedom of the press."

13. Stanley I. Kutler, ed., *The Supreme Court and the Constitution* (New York: W. W. Norton, 1984), 429.

14. Richard L. Pacelle, *The Transformation of the Supreme Court's Agenda: From the New Deal to the Reagan Administration* (Boulder: Westview Press, 1991).

In a 6–3 opinion, the Supreme Court agreed, ruling against the state, and, most significant, the Court used a Preferred Freedoms approach to reach that conclusion. Justice Rutledge, writing for the majority, asserted:

[This] case confronts us again with the duty our system places on this Court to say where the individual's freedom ends and the State's power begins. Choice of that border, now as always delicate, is perhaps more so where the usual presumptive supporting legislation is balanced *by the preferred place given in our scheme to the great, the indispensable democratic freedoms secured by the First Amendment....* For [this] reason any attempt to restrict those liberties must be justified by clear public interest, threatened not ... remotely, but by a *clear and present danger* [emphasis added].

Constitutional experts claim that this decision represented another major breakthrough in the area of freedom of speech, but why? First, it reinforces the majority view in *Schneider* that Preferred Freedoms provides an appropriate solution to First Amendment problems. Second, Rutledge's language—"Any attempt to restrict the liberties of speech and assembly must be justified ... by a clear and present danger"—indicates that the Court, instead of abandoning Holmes's standard, had combined the Clear and Present Danger standard with the Preferred Freedoms framework. The Preferred Freedoms "concept was never a repudiation of the notion of clear and present danger, but was seen as giving its purposes a firmer base and texture—incorporating it much as Einsteinian physics incorporates Newtonian."[15]

The Aftermath of World War II: Cold War Politics and the Court

As *Thomas* indicates, by the mid-1940s it seemed as if the Court had finally settled on an approach to solve First Amendment problems. Stone's Preferred Freedoms doctrine had gained acceptance among the justices, even though it served as a vehicle by which to

15. Feeley and Krislov, *Constitutional Law,* 427.

overturn many laws restricting speech. Compare it to the Bad Tendency test of the *Gitlow* era, a test under which many restrictions on free speech could pass muster. In short, the Court had altered its position dramatically over three decades.

Like the Bad Tendency test, however, the Preferred Freedoms doctrine was short-lived. By the early 1950s, in fact, the Court turned to a modified version of the conservative Bad Tendency test—the Clear and Probable Danger standard. Between 1950 and 1956 the application of this stricter standard led the Court to uphold the vast majority of free speech convictions. What caused this sudden change in direction? Three factors may explain it.

First, several changes in Court personnel occurred between 1945 and 1952. Chief Justice Frederick M. Vinson replaced Stone, the author of Footnote Four, and two relatively conservative justices, Tom C. Clark and Sherman Minton, took the place of two liberals, Francis W. Murphy and Wiley Rutledge. As we have seen in other areas of the law, such changes can have a substantial impact on Court outcomes.

Second, by 1949 it became evident that some of the justices were not satisfied with the Preferred Freedoms framework. Keep in mind that several dissented in *Thomas*, but at the time they offered no alternative standard. This situation changed dramatically in 1949 in the case of *Kovacs v. Cooper*, which involved a challenge to a local ordinance prohibiting the use of sound and amplifying devices on city streets. Writing for the majority, Justice Stanley F. Reed argued that the law withstood the Preferred Freedoms test and was, therefore, constitutional. In a long concurring opinion Justice Frankfurter agreed with the outcome in *Kovacs*, but disagreed with Reed's reasoning. Calling Preferred Freedoms a "mischievous phrase," Frankfurter articulated a new standard by which to review First Amendment claims:

So long as a legislature does not prescribe what ideas may be ... expressed and what may not be, nor discriminate among those who would make inroads upon the public peace, it is not for us to supervise the limits the legislature may impose.

Often called the Ad Hoc Balancing test, it urges the justices to balance, on a case-by-case basis, the individual free speech claim versus the government's reason for regulating the behavior. But, in Frankfurter's judgment, these competing claims were not of equal merit; the latter should be taken more seriously as legislators had already determined that the law in question met a compelling governmental interest.

A third reason for the Court's dramatic turnaround in the 1950s was the alteration in its external environment. After World War II, the United States entered into a cold war with the Soviet Union. This period was characterized by an intense fear of communism, not unlike the time of the First World War. Some politicians, led by Sen. Joseph McCarthy, R-Wis. (1947–1957), fed the fear by alleging that Communist party sympathizers had infiltrated the upper echelon of government. Others asserted that the Communist party of the United States was growing in strength and numbers and spreading its message through motion pictures and plays.

The fear of communism manifested itself in a number of ways. Most important was congressional enactment of several pieces of legislation designed to suppress communist and other forms of subversive activity in the United States. For example, a section of the Labor-Management Relations Act of 1947 required union leaders to file affidavits proclaiming nonaffiliation with the Communist party before they could attain National Labor Relations Board recognition of their unions. Congress passed this law in recognition of Marxist-Leninist theory, which assumes that it will be the "workers" who lead the "Revolution." In *American Communication Association v. Douds* (1950) union leaders mounted a First Amendment challenge to the law. Because this was one of the earliest of the cold war cases, many eagerly awaited the Court's decision:

Would the justices, now under the leadership of Chief Justice Vinson, use the Preferred Freedoms approach or would they adopt Frankfurter's Ad Hoc Balancing test?

Apparently not immune to the pressures of the day, the Court adopted the latter. Writing for the Court, Vinson rejected the heart of the Preferred Freedoms approach, the Clear and Present Danger standard, noting, "It is the considerations that gave birth to the phrase clear and present danger, not the phrase itself, that are vital in our decisions of questions involving ... the First Amendment." In his view, the Ad Hoc Balancing approach fully encapsulated that genesis: because Congress has determined that communism constitutes harmful conduct carried on by people, then it may regulate it in the public interest.

Vinson's standard is akin to the Bad Tendency test of the 1920s. Both operate under the assumption that the First Amendment protects the public good, as defined by legislatures, rather than individual expression. In fact, just one year after *Douds*, in *Dennis v. United States*, the Court adopted the Clear and Probable Danger test. At issue in *Dennis* was the Smith Act. Enacted in 1940, this statute prohibited anyone from knowingly or willfully advocating or teaching the overthrow of any government of the United States by force, from organizing any society to teach, advocate, or encourage the overthrow of the' United States by force, or from becoming a member of any such society. By covering so many kinds of activities, the law provided authorities with a significant weapon to stop the spread of communism in the United States.

While reading *Dennis*, keep in mind the environment in which the justices operated. Remember that tremendous political pressures influenced the Court just as they did many other sectors of American life. If *Dennis* came before the Court today, would the justices reach the same conclusion?

During the anticommunist hysteria of post-World War II America, the House Un-American Activities Committee investigated alleged communist influence in the movie industry. Jack L. Warner, vice president of Warner Brothers, took the witness chair in 1947. Committee members include future president Richard Nixon *(second from right).*

Dennis v. United States

341 U.S. 494 (1951)

Vote: 6 (Burton, Frankfurter, Jackson, Minton, Reed, Vinson)
   2 (Black, Douglas)
Opinion announcing the judgment of the Court: Vinson
Concurring opinions: Frankfurter, Jackson
Dissenting opinions: Black, Douglas
Not participating: Clark

On July 20, 1948, twelve leaders of the National Board of the Communist party were indicted for con-

spiring to teach and advocate the overthrow of the government by force and violence, and to organize the Communist party for that purpose.[16] Such actions were in violation of the Smith Act. The trial was a protracted affair, lasting nine months and generating 16,000 pages of evidence. A great deal of the testimony on both sides involved Marxist-Leninist theory and the inner workings of the Communist party. The prosecutor's case read like a spy novel, full of interna-

16. The initial suit involved twelve defendants. The case against William Z. Foster, head of the party, however, was separated from the others when he became ill.

tional conspiracies, secret passwords and code books, aliases, and plots to overthrow the U.S. government. The defense was a bit more philosophical as it attempted to demonstrate that the leaders of this particular branch of the party wanted "to work for the improvement of conditions under capitalism and not for chaos and depression."

Not sympathetic to this line of reasoning, the trial court sentenced each defendant to five years in prison and a $10,000 fine. Dennis and the others appealed to the U.S. Supreme Court, requesting it to overturn their convictions and strike down the Smith Act as an unconstitutional infringement on free speech. They said, "The statute and the convictions which are here for review cannot be validated without at the same time destroying the constitutional foundations of American democracy."

MR. CHIEF JUSTICE VINSON announced the judgment of the Court.

The obvious purpose of the statute is to protect existing Government, not from change by peaceable, lawful and constitutional means, but from change by violence, revolution and terrorism. That it is within the *power* of the Congress to protect the Government of the United States from armed rebellion is a proposition which requires little discussion. Whatever theoretical merit there may be to the argument that there is a "right" to rebellion against dictatorial governments is without force where the existing structure of the government provides for peaceful and orderly change. We reject any principle of governmental helplessness in the face of preparation for revolution, which principle, carried to its logical conclusion, must lead to anarchy. No one could conceive that it is not within the power of Congress to prohibit acts intended to overthrow the Government by force and violence. The question with which we are concerned here is not whether Congress has such *power*, but whether the *means* which it has employed conflict with the First and Fifth Amendments to the Constitution....

The very language of the Smith Act negates the interpretation which petitioners would have us impose on that Act.

It is directed at advocacy, not discussion. Thus, the trial judge properly charged the jury that they could not convict if they found that petitioners did "no more than pursue peaceful studies and discussions or teaching and advocacy in the realm of ideas." He further charged that it was not unlawful "to conduct in an American college and university a course explaining the philosophical theories set forth in the books which have been placed in evidence." Such a charge is in strict accord with the statutory language, and illustrates the meaning to be placed on those words. Congress did not intend to eradicate the free discussion of political theories, to destroy the traditional rights of Americans to discuss and evaluate ideas without fear of governmental sanction. Rather Congress was concerned with the very kind of activity in which the evidence showed these petitioners engaged.

But although the statute is not directed at the hypothetical cases which petitioners have conjured, its application in this case has resulted in convictions for the teaching and advocacy of the overthrow of the Government by force and violence, which, even though coupled with the intent to accomplish that overthrow, contains an element of speech. For this reason, we must pay special heed to the demands of the First Amendment marking out the boundaries of speech.

We pointed out in Douds that the basis of the First Amendment is the hypothesis that speech can rebut speech, propaganda will answer propaganda, free debate of ideas will result in the wisest governmental policies. It is for this reason that this Court has recognized the inherent value of free discourse. An analysis of the leading cases in this Court which have involved direct limitations on speech, however, will demonstrate that both the majority of the Court and the dissenters in particular cases have recognized that this is not an unlimited, unqualified right, but that the societal value of speech must, on occasion, be subordinated to other values and considerations.

No important case involving free speech was decided by this Court prior to Schenck v. United States. Indeed, the summary treatment accorded an argument based upon an individual's claim that the First Amendment protected certain utterances indicates that the Court at earlier dates placed no unique emphasis upon that right. It was not until the classic dictum of Justice Holmes in the Schenck case that speech *per se* received that emphasis in a majority opinion.... Writing for a unanimous Court, Justice Holmes stated that the "question in every case is whether the words used are used in such circumstances and are of such a nature as to create a clear and present danger that they will bring about the substantive evils that Congress has a right to prevent." But the force of even this expression is considerably weakened by the reference at the end of the opinion to Goldman v. United States, 1918, a prosecution under the same statute. Said Justice Holmes, "Indeed Goldman might be said to dispose of the present contention if the precedent covers all *media concludendi* [the steps of an argument]. But as the right to free speech was not referred to specially, we have thought fit to add a few words." The fact is inescapable, too, that the phrase bore no connotation that the danger was to be any threat to the safety of the Republic. The charge was causing and attempting to cause insubordination in the military forces and obstruct recruiting. The objectionable document denounced conscription and its most inciting sentence was, "You must do your share to maintain, support and uphold the rights of the people of this country." Fifteen thousand copies were printed and some circulated. This insubstantial gesture toward insubordination in 1917 during war was held to be a clear and present danger of bringing about the evil of military insubordination.

In several later cases involving convictions under the Criminal Espionage Act, the nub of the evidence the Court held sufficient to meet the "clear and present danger" test enunciated in Schenck was as follows: Frohwerk v. United States—publication of twelve newspaper articles attacking the war; Debs v. United States—one speech attacking United States' participation in the war; Abrams v. United States—circulation of copies of two different socialist circulars attacking the war....

The rule we deduce from these cases is that where an offense is specified by a statute in nonspeech or nonpress terms, a conviction relying upon speech or press as evidence of violation may be sustained only when the speech or publication created a "clear and present danger" of attempting or accomplishing the prohibited crime, *e.g.*, interference with enlistment. The dissents, we repeat, in emphasizing the value of speech, were addressed to the argument of the sufficiency of the evidence.

The next important case before the Court in which free speech was the crux of the conflict was Gitlow v. People of State of New York. There New York had made it a crime to advocate "the necessity or propriety of overthrowing ... organized government by force...." The evidence of violation of the statute was that the defendant had published a Manifesto attacking the Government and capitalism. The convictions were sustained. The majority refused to apply the "clear and present danger" test to the specific utterance....

Although no case subsequent to ... Gitlow has expressly overruled the majority ... there is little doubt that subsequent opinions have inclined toward the Holmes-Brandeis rationale.... But ... neither Justice Holmes nor Justice Brandeis ever envisioned that a shorthand phrase should be crystalized into a rigid rule to be applied inflexibly without regard to the circumstances of each case. Speech is not an absolute, above and beyond control by the legislature when its judgment, subject to review here, is that certain kinds of speech are so undesirable as to warrant criminal sanction. Nothing is more certain in modern society than the principle that there are no absolutes, that a name, a phrase, a standard has meaning only when associated with the considerations which gave birth to the nomenclature. To those who would paralyze our Government in the face of impending threat by encasing it in a semantic straitjacket we must reply that all concepts are relative.

In this case we are squarely presented with the application of the "clear and present danger" test, and must decide what that phrase imports. We first note that many of the cases in which this Court has reversed convictions by use of this or similar tests have been based on the fact that the interest which the State was attempting to protect was itself too insubstantial to warrant restriction of speech. Overthrow of the Government by force and violence is certainly a substantial enough interest for the Government to limit speech. Indeed, this is the ultimate value of any society, for if a society cannot protect its very structure from armed internal attack, it must follow that no subordinate value can be protected. If, then, this interest may be protected, the literal problem which is presented is what has been meant by the use of the phrase "clear and present danger" of the utterances bringing about the evil within the power of Congress to punish.

Obviously, the words cannot mean that before the Government may act, it must wait until the *putsch* is about to be executed, the plans have been laid and the signal is awaited. If Government is aware that a group aiming at its overthrow is attempting to indoctrinate its members and to commit them to a course whereby they will strike when the leaders feel the circumstances permit, action by the Government is required. The argument that there is no need for Government to concern itself, for Government is strong, it possesses ample powers to put down a rebellion, it may defeat the revolution with ease needs no answer. For that is not the question. Certainly an attempt to overthrow the Government by force, even though doomed from the outset because of inadequate numbers or power of the revolutionists, is a sufficient evil for Congress to prevent. The damage which such attempts create both physically and politically to a nation makes it impossible to measure the validity in terms of the probability of success, or the immediacy of a successful attempt. In the instant case the trial judge charged the jury that they could not convict unless they found that petitioners intended to overthrow the Government "as speedily as circumstances would permit." This does not mean, and could not properly mean, that they would not strike until there was certainty of success. What was meant was that the revolutionists would strike when they thought the time was ripe. We must therefore reject the contention that success or probability of success is the criterion.

The situation with which Justices Holmes and Brandeis were concerned in Gitlow was a comparatively isolated event, bearing little relation in their minds to any substantial threat to the safety of the community. They were not confronted with any situation comparable to the instant one—the development of an apparatus designed and dedicated to the overthrow of the Government, in the context of world crisis after crisis.

Chief Judge Learned Hand, writing for the majority below, interpreted the phrase as follows: "In each case [courts] must ask whether the gravity of the 'evil,' discounted by its improbability, justifies such invasion of free speech as is necessary to avoid the danger." We adopt this statement of the rule. As articulated by Chief Judge Hand, it is as succinct and inclusive as any other we might devise at this time. It takes into consideration those factors which we deem relevant, and relates their significances. More we cannot expect from words....

We hold that the Smith Act, do[es] not inherently, or as construed or applied in the instant case, violate the First Amendment and other provisions of the Bill of Rights.... Petitioners intended to overthrow the Government of the United States as speedily as the circumstances would permit. Their conspiracy to organize the Communist Party and to teach and advocate the overthrow of the Government of the United States by force and violence created a "clear and present danger" of an attempt to overthrow the Government by force and violence. They were properly and constitutionally convicted for violation of the Smith Act. The judgments of conviction are affirmed.

Affirmed.

MR. JUSTICE FRANKFURTER, concurring in affirmance of the judgment.

Primary responsibility for adjusting the interests which compete in the situation before us of necessity belongs to the Congress. The nature of the power to be exercised by this Court has been delineated in decisions not charged with the emotional appeal of situations such as that now before us. We are to set aside the judgment of those whose duty it is to legislate only if there is no reasonable basis for it....

It is not for us to decide how we would adjust the clash of interests which this case presents were the primary responsibility for reconciling it ours. Congress has determined that the danger created by advocacy of overthrow justifies the ensuing restriction on freedom of speech. The determination was made after due deliberation, and the seriousness of the congressional purpose is attested by the volume of legislation passed to effectuate the same ends.

Can we then say that the judgment Congress exercised was denied it by the Constitution? Can we establish a constitutional doctrine which forbids the elected representatives of the people to make this choice? Can we hold that the First Amendment deprives Congress of what it deemed necessary for the Government's protection?

To make validity of legislation depend on judicial reading of events still in the womb of time—a forecast, that is, of the outcome of forces at best appreciated only with knowledge of the topmost secrets of nations—is to charge the judiciary with duties beyond its equipment.

MR. JUSTICE BLACK, dissenting.

[M]y basic disagreement with the Court is not as to how we should explain or reconcile what was said in prior decisions but springs from a fundamental difference in constitutional approach. Consequently, it would serve no useful purpose to state my position at length.

At the outset I want to emphasize what the crime involved in this case is, and what it is not. These petitioners were not charged with an attempt to overthrow the Government. They were not charged with overt acts of any kind designed to overthrow the Government. They were not even charged with saying anything or writing anything designed to overthrow the Government. The charge was that they agreed to assemble and to talk and publish certain ideas at a later date: The indictment is that they conspired to organize the Communist Party and to use speech or newspapers and other publications in the future to teach and advocate the forcible overthrow of the Government. No matter how it is worded, this is a virulent form of prior censorship of speech and press, which I believe the First Amendment forbids. I would hold § 3 of the Smith Act authorizing this prior restraint unconstitutional on its face and as applied.

But let us assume, contrary to all constitutional ideas of fair criminal procedure, that petitioners although not indicted for the crime of actual advocacy, may be punished for it. Even on this radical assumption, the other opinions in this case show that the only way to affirm these convictions is to repudiate directly or indirectly the established "clear and present danger" rule. This the Court does in a way which greatly restricts the protections afforded by the First Amendment. The opinions for affirmance indicate that the chief reason for jettisoning the rule is the expressed fear that advocacy of Communist doctrine endangers the safety of the Republic. Undoubtedly, a governmental policy of unfettered communication of ideas does entail dangers. To the Founders of this Nation, however, the benefits derived from free expression were worth the risk. They embodied this philosophy in the First Amendment's command that "Congress shall make no law ... abridging the freedom of speech, or of the press...." I have always believed that the First Amendment is the keystone of our Government, that the freedoms it guarantees provide the best insurance against destruction of all freedom. At least as to speech in the realm of public matters, I believe that the "clear and present danger" test does not "mark the furthermost constitutional boundaries of protected expression" but does "no more than recognize a minimum compulsion of the Bill of Rights."

So long as this Court exercises the power of judicial review of legislation, I cannot agree that the First Amendment permits us to sustain laws suppressing freedom of speech and press on the basis of Congress' or our own notions of mere "reasonableness." Such a doctrine waters down the First Amendment so that it amounts to little more than an admonition to Congress. The Amendment as so construed is not likely to protect any but those "safe" or orthodox views which rarely need its protection....

Public opinion being what it now is, few will protest the conviction of these Communist petitioners. There is hope, however, that in calmer times, when present pressures, passions and fears subside, this or some later Court will restore the First Amendment liberties to the high preferred place where they belong in a free society.

MR. JUSTICE DOUGLAS, dissenting.

Free speech has occupied an exalted position because of the high service it has given our society. Its protection is essential to the very existence of a democracy. The airing of ideas releases pressures which otherwise might become destructive. When ideas compete in the market for acceptance, full and free discussion exposes the false and they gain few adherents. Full and free discussion even of ideas we hate encourages the testing of our own prejudices and preconceptions. Full and free discussion keeps a society from becoming stagnant and unprepared for the stresses and strains that work to tear all civilizations apart.

Full and free discussion has indeed been the first article of our faith. We have founded our political system on it. It has been the safeguard of every religious, political, philosophical, economic, and racial group amongst us. We have counted on it to keep us from embracing what is cheap and false; we have trusted the common sense of our people to choose the doctrine true to our genius and to reject the rest. This has been the one single outstanding tenet that has made our institutions the symbol of freedom and equality. We have deemed it more costly to liberty to suppress a despised minority than to let them vent their spleen. We have above all else feared the political censor. We have wanted a land where our people can be exposed to all the diverse creeds and cultures of the world.

There comes a time when even speech loses its constitutional immunity. Speech innocuous one year may at another time fan such destructive flames that it must be halted in the interests of the safety of the Republic. That is the meaning of the clear and present danger test. When conditions are so critical that there will be no time to avoid the evil that the speech threatens, it is time to call a halt. Otherwise, free speech which is the strength of the Nation will be the cause of its destruction.

Yet free speech is the rule, not the exception. The restraint to be constitutional must be based on more than fear, on more than passionate opposition against the speech, on more than a revolted dislike for its contents. There must be some immediate injury to society that is likely if speech is allowed....

 Free speech—the glory of our system of government—should not be sacrificed on anything less than plain and objective proof of danger that the evil advocated is imminent. On this record no one can say that petitioners and their converts are in such a strategic position as to have even the slightest chance of achieving their aims.

The First Amendment provides that "Congress shall make no law ... abridging the freedom of speech." The Constitution provides no exception. This does not mean, however, that the Nation need hold its hand until it is in such weakened condition that there is no time to protect itself from incitement to revolution. Seditious conduct can always be punished. But the command of the First Amendment is so clear that we should not allow Congress to call a halt to free speech except in the extreme case of peril from the speech itself. The First Amendment makes confidence in the common sense of our people and in their maturity of judgment the great postulate of our democracy. Its philosophy is that violence is rarely, if ever, stopped by denying civil liberties to those advocating resort to force. The First Amendment reflects the philosophy of Jefferson "that it is time enough for the rightful purposes of civil government, for its officers to interfere when principles break out into overt acts against peace and good order." The political censor has no place in our public debates. Unless and until extreme and necessitous circumstances are shown our aim should be to keep speech unfettered and to allow the processes of law to be invoked only when the provocateurs among us move from speech to action.

Vishinsky wrote in 1938 in The Law of the Soviet State, "In our state, naturally, there is and can be no place for freedom of speech, press, and so on for the foes of socialism."

Our concern should be that we accept no such standard for the United States. Our faith should be that our people will never give support to these advocates of revolution, so long as we remain loyal to the purposes for which our Nation was founded.

Scholars consider *Dennis* a significant case for several reasons. First, a plurality of the Court accepted Vinson's Clear and Probable Danger test: "In each case courts must ask whether the gravity of the 'evil,' discounted by its improbability, justifies such invasion of free speech as is necessary to avoid the danger."[17] But is this a reasonable interpretation of the test emanating from *Schenck*; that is, would Holmes have agreed with this language? Or does it more closely resemble the Bad Tendency standard, with which Holmes disagreed? The second reason is what the dissenters, Justices Black and Douglas, had to say. As we shall see, this pair of civil libertarians remained in relative isolation during the early 1950s, but the Warren Court of the late 1950s and 1960s adopted many of their views. Based on their dissents in *Dennis*, which direction would Black and Douglas like to see the Court take? A third reason *Dennis* is significant is precedent: between 1951 and 1956 the justices used Vinson's Clear and Probable Danger standard to uphold a number of loyalty programs.[18] Moreover, *Dennis* served as a benchmark in other areas of the law in which the federal government asked the Court

17. Vinson adopted this language from Learned Hand's decision from the court below.
18. See, for example, *Adler v. Board of Education* (1952) in which the Court upheld a New York law (the so-called Feinberg Act) disqualifying from teaching positions persons affiliated with subversive groups.

for sweeping powers to investigate the Communist party, other subversive groups, and their alleged adherents.

In sum, once again we see the Supreme Court responding to perceived threats to national security. As was the case during the 1920s, when the justices moved from a Clear and Present Danger test to a Bad Tendency standard, in the 1950s they moved from a Preferred Freedoms approach to a revisionist interpretation of the Holmes standard, Clear and Probable Danger, which itself "marked a return to the 'bad tendency' views of the post-World War I period."[19]

Free Speech During the Warren Court Era

In 1956 and 1957 the Supreme Court heard back-to-back cases involving Communist party prosecutions. In the first, *Pennsylvania v. Nelson,* the justices considered a state law similar to the Smith Act. As was true during the World War I years, in the cold war period many states passed or revitalized laws that forbade the organization of subversive groups or parties and the advocacy or teaching of anarchy. Under Pennsylvania's version, the Sedition Act, authorities prosecuted Steve Nelson, a Communist party member, and a trial court sentenced him to twenty years in prison and a $10,000 fine.

On appeal to the U.S. Supreme Court, Nelson argued that the justices should uphold the decision of the Pennsylvania Supreme Court, which ruled that the federal law superseded the state's. Several states, however, filed amicus curiae briefs in support of the Pennsylvania statute. New Hampshire, for example, argued, "Neither expressly nor by implication has federal law attempted to take from the states the power to enact anti-subversive legislation." Massachusetts agreed, noting, "The state is acting to protect itself." Perhaps even more significant was an argument contained in the solicitor general's amicus curiae brief: "The Smith Act does not preclude enforcement of

19. Kutler, *The Supreme Court,* 429.

state sedition statutes." Writing for the Court, however, Chief Justice Earl Warren rejected state and federal government arguments. Rather, he asserted that federal legislation, such as the Smith Act, indicated the intent of Congress to retain sole control over subversive activity.

The following year, the Court decided another case, *Yates v. United States,* which closely resembled *Dennis.* In 1951 federal authorities alleged that fourteen second-tier leaders of the Communist party, including Oleta O'Connor Yates, engaged in subversive activities forbidden by the Smith Act. Specifically, they were party members, they organized party units in California, they helped publish the *Daily Worker,* and they conducted courses to recruit and indoctrinate potential members. At their trial, the judge explained the Smith Act to the jurors, but he did not tell them that it prohibited only the advocacy of unlawful activity, not abstract doctrines. Based on this information, the jury found the defendants guilty, and the court sentenced them to five years in prison and a $10,000 fine. On appeal, Yates's attorneys seized on this discrepancy in the judge's charge. They stated, "Lawful activities and associations not shown to be unlawful cannot by addition or multiplication be cemented into illegality." The government argued that *Dennis* should control the Court's decision.

A majority rejected the government's position. Justice Harlan wrote:

The legislative history of the Smith Act and related bills shows beyond all question that Congress was aware of the distinction between advocacy or teaching of abstract doctrine and the advocacy or teaching of action, and that it did not intend to disregard it. The statute was aimed at the advocacy and teaching of concrete action for the forcible overthrow of the Government, and not of principles divorced from action.

The government's reliance on this Court's decision is misplaced. It is true that at one point in the . . . opinion it is stated that the Smith Act "is directed at advocacy, not discussion," but it is clear that the reference was *to advocacy of action, not ideas* [emphasis added].

With the decision in *Yates*, despite some protestation to the contrary, the Court altered its position: by distinguishing between the advocacy of abstract doctrines (protected) and the advocacy of unlawful action (unprotected), the Court substantially modified the *Dennis* standard. And although *Yates* did not advocate the Preferred Freedoms or Absolutist approach favored by Black, it certainly liberalized free speech doctrine, making Smith Act prosecutions far more difficult.

Why did the Court alter its view? Some scholars point to changes in Court personnel, as shown in Table 4-1. Dramatic alterations occurred between *Dennis* and *Yates*: the more liberal Earl Warren replaced Fred Vinson as chief justice; John Marshall Harlan, grandson and namesake of another "great dissenter," stepped in for Robert H. Jackson; and President Eisenhower appointed William J. Brennan, Jr., to Sherman Minton's vacant seat.

Perhaps of equal significance was the rapidly declining fear among the American public of communist infiltration. Clearly, the year 1957 was far from the end of the cold war. In fact, certain members of Congress, still under an anticommunist influence, were less than overwhelmed by the Court's rulings and introduced a bill to overturn *Nelson*, which failed to gain approval in the Senate. By the same token, *Yates* was neither the last of the Court's cases on subversive activities nor the end of Court approval of such legislation. Four years later, in *Scales v. United States* (1961), the Court upheld the membership clause of the Smith Act. That same year, it also sustained a clause of the Subversive Activities Control Act of 1950, mandating that all Communist party-affiliated organizations register with the attorney general. Nonetheless, by 1957 the hysteria had substantially subsided. One indication was the rapid decline of Senator McCarthy's influence. As his accusations grew "ever more wild ... and arrogant," focusing on all sorts of government officials, including senators and President Eisenhower, his "conduct became too destructive for all but his

TABLE 4-1 Personnel Changes: *Dennis* to *Yates*

Dennis Court (1951)	Yates Court (1957)
Vinson, chief justice ⟶	Warren, chief justice
Black[a]	Black[b]
Reed ⟶	Whittaker
Frankfurter	Frankfurter
Douglas[a]	Douglas[b]
Jackson ⟶	Harlan
Burton	Burton
Clark	Clark[a]
Minton ⟶	Brennan

a. Dissented from majority opinion.
b. Partial dissent from majority opinion.

closest associates to tolerate."[20] In 1954 the Senate censured him by a 67–22 vote; the man who symbolized the communist witch hunt had lost his power. He died May 2, 1957, the same year as the *Yates* decision.

Once the Red Scare was over, the Supreme Court began taking positions defending freedom of expression and association against the repressive legislation passed during the McCarthy era. It handed down a series of decisions upholding the constitutional rights of communists and other so-called subversives. For example, in *Communist Party v. United States* (1963) and *Albertson v. Subversive Activities Control Board* (1965) the justices repudiated federal laws requiring communist organizations to register with the government. In *Elfbrandt v. Russell* (1966) and *Whitehill v. Elkins* (1967) loyalty oath requirements directed at subversives were found constitutionally defective. The Court also struck down laws and enforcement actions barring communists from holding office in labor unions (*United States v. Brown*, 1965), prohibiting communists from working in defense plants (*United States v. Robel*, 1967), and stripping passports from Communist party leaders (*Ap-*

20. Arthur M. Schlesinger, Jr., *The Almanac of American History* (New York: Putnam, 1983), 541.

theker v. Secretary of State, 1964). Clearly, these decisions and others handed down during more tranquil years would have been unheard of during the anticommunist hysteria.

By the end of the 1960s the Court had turned away from many of its cold war rulings. It struck down as being in violation of the freedom to speak, publish, or associate much of the federal and state anticommunist legislation still on the books. With its decision in *Brandenburg v. Ohio* (1969), one of the Warren Court's last major rulings, the justices finally closed the door on the repressive McCarthy era. Ironically, the *Brandenburg* decision had nothing to do with the Communist party or other groups dedicated to violent overthrow of the U.S. government. Instead, the dispute involved a group with a much different purpose, the racist Ku Klux Klan. As you read the Court's decision in *Brandenburg,* notice how the justices treat the right to speak and organize even when the group's message and purpose are repugnant to American values. Note also how the Court uses this Ku Klux Klan prosecution to overrule *Whitney v. California,* one of the more repressive precedents from an earlier time.

Brandenburg v. Ohio

395 U.S. 444 (1969)
Vote: 8 (Black, Brennan, Douglas, Harlan, Marshall,
*   Stewart, Warren, White)*

   0

Per curiam opinion
Concurring opinions: Black, Douglas

Clarence Brandenburg was the leader of an Ohio affiliate of the Ku Klux Klan, an organization dedicated to white supremacy. To obtain publicity for the KKK's goals, he invited a Cincinnati reporter and camera crew to attend a rally. Subsequently, local and national television stations aired some of the events that occurred at this gathering; one film "showed 12

hooded figures, some of whom carried firearms. They were gathered around a large wooden cross, which they burned." In another, Brandenburg delivered a speech to the group in which he said, "Personally I believe the nigger should be returned to Africa, the Jew returned to Israel."[21] Based on these films, Ohio authorities arrested Brandenburg for violating the Ohio Criminal Syndicalism law, which was passed in 1919 to prevent the spread of unpatriotic views. Similar to many other state laws of the sort upheld in *Gitlow,* the Ohio act prohibited the advocacy and assembly of individuals to teach criminal syndicalism.

PER CURIAM.

The appellant, a leader of a Ku Klux Klan group, was convicted under the Ohio Criminal Syndicalism statute.

The ... statute was enacted in 1919. From 1917 to 1920, identical or quite similar laws were adopted by 20 States and two territories. In 1927, this Court sustained the constitutionality of California's Criminal Syndicalism Act, the text of which is quite similar to that of the laws of Ohio. Whitney v. California (1927). The Court upheld the statute on the ground that, without more, "advocating" violent means to effect political and economic change involves such danger to the security of the State that the State may outlaw it. But *Whitney* has been thoroughly discredited by later decisions. See Dennis v. United States (1951). These later decisions have fashioned the principle that the constitutional guarantees of free speech and free press do not permit a State to forbid or proscribe advocacy of the use of force or of law violation except where such advocacy is directed to inciting or producing imminent lawless action and is likely to incite or produce such action. As we said in Noto v. United States (1961), "the mere abstract teaching ... of the moral propriety or even moral necessity for a resort to force and violence, is not the same as preparing a group for violent action and steeling it to such action." A statute which fails to draw this distinction impermissibly intrudes upon the freedoms guaranteed by the First and Fourteenth Amendments. It sweeps within its condemnation speech which our Constitution has immunized from governmental control.

21. *Brandenburg v. Ohio,* 395 U.S. 444 at 445, 447 (1969).

A Ku Klux Klan demonstration in Washington, D.C., in 1926.

Measured by this test, Ohio's Criminal Syndicalism Act cannot be sustained. The Act punishes persons who "advocate or teach the duty, necessity, or propriety" of violence "as a means of accomplishing industrial or political reform"; or who publish or circulate or display any book or paper containing such advocacy; or who "justify" the commission of violent acts "with intent to exemplify, spread or advocate the propriety of the doctrines of criminal syndicalism"; or who "voluntarily assemble" with a group formed "to teach or advocate the doctrines of criminal syndicalism." Neither the indictment nor the trial judge's instructions to the jury in any way refined the statute's bald definition of the crime in terms of mere advocacy not distinguished from incitement to imminent lawless action.

Accordingly, we are here confronted with a statute which, by its own words and as applied, purports to punish mere advocacy and to forbid, on pain of criminal punishment, assembly with others merely to advocate the described type of action. Such a statute falls within the condemnation of the First and Fourteenth Amendments. The contrary teaching of Whitney v. California cannot be supported, and that decision is therefore overruled.

Reversed.

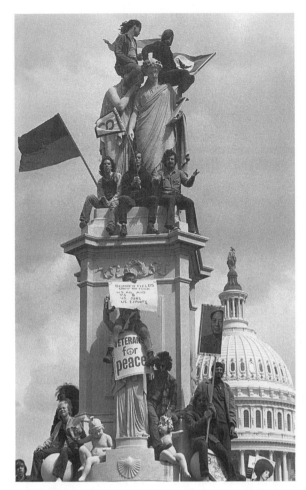

Demonstrations by civil rights and antiwar groups were common during the 1960s and early 1970s. Demonstrators protesting the Vietnam War perch atop the Peace Monument in 1971.

Vietnam, the Civil Rights Movement, and Beyond

As the nation's fear of communist infiltration ebbed, a new international crisis was brewing in Vietnam. Although our involvement in that conflict dated back to the Truman administration, it grew significantly in 1964 when President Johnson announced that the North Vietnamese had attacked American ships in the Gulf of Tonkin. Johnson launched a massive military buildup: by 1968, 541,000 U.S. troops had been sent to Vietnam.[22] Initially, many Americans approved of Johnson's pursuit of the war, but by the late 1960s, approval had turned to criticism. A peace movement, centered on college campuses, arose throughout the country. What is more, another cause was gathering strength. The civil rights movement, which in the 1950s was isolated in the South, by the 1960s had taken hold in all major urban centers. Because of these two social currents, and the resistance to them, the decade was marked by domestic upheaval and turmoil. Although Congress did not respond with any legislation like the Smith Act, these protest movements generated many free expression cases. Some involved the constitutionality of mass demonstrations, "the chief weapon of the civil rights and peace movements."[23] Others involved the issues of political expression associated with that decade—flag desecrations, draft card burnings, and so forth.

The freedom of expression cases flowing from the Vietnam War protests and civil rights movement presented the Court with a host of novel constitutional claims. The character of the Court was also undergoing change. In 1969 Warren Burger, a conservative Nixon appointee, replaced the retiring Earl Warren as chief justice. Burger would soon be followed by three additional Nixon appointees—William H. Rehnquist, Harry A. Blackmun, and Lewis F. Powell, Jr. With these appointments the Court began to take on a more conservative posture. This trend continued without interruption for the next twenty-three years as Republican presidents Ford, Reagan, and Bush filled vacancies with an eye to moving the Court to the right.

As the Court confronted new disputes over expression rights, the justices had at their disposal a half century of doctrinal development. The internal se-

22. Schlesinger, *The Almanac of American History*, 508.
23. Kutler, *The Supreme Court*, 455.

TABLE 4-2 Summary of Legal Standards Governing Free Speech

Standard	Major Proponents	Court Usage: Example
Clear and Present Danger test "Whether the words are used in such circumstances and are of such a nature as to create a clear and present danger that they will bring about substantive evils that Congress has a right to prevent."	Holmes, Brandeis	*Schenck v. United States*, 1919
Bad Tendency test Do the words have a tendency to bring about something evil?	Clarke, Sanford	*Abrams v. United States*, 1919
Preferred Freedoms "There may be a narrower scope for operation of the presumption of constitutionality when legislation appears on its face to be within a specific prohibition of the Constitution, such as those of the first ten Amendments."	Douglas, Stone, Rutledge	*United States v. Carolene Products*, 1938; *Thomas v. Collins*, 1945.
Absolutism "The First Amendment, its prohibition in terms absolute, was designed to preclude courts as well as legislatures from weighing values of speech against silence."	Black, Douglas	Never adopted. See Black's dissent in *Dennis v. United States*, 1951; Douglas's dissent in *Roth v. United States*, 1957.
Ad Hoc Balancing "So long as a legislature does not prescribe what ideas may be . . . expressed and what may not be, nor discriminate among those who would make inroads upon the public peace, it is not for us to supervise the limits the legislature may impose."	Frankfurter	Frankfurter's concurrence in *Kovacs v. Cooper*, 1949
Clear and Probable Danger "Whether the gravity of the 'evil,' discounted by its improbability, justifies such an invasion of free speech as is necessary to avoid danger."	Vinson	*Dennis v. United States*, 1951

curity cases beginning with *Schenck* and continuing into the 1960s had given birth to six major tests of how the First Amendment should be interpreted and applied *(See Table 4-2)*. In the years that followed, the justices created no significant additions to this list of competing approaches to First Amendment interpretation, but continued to debate their relative merits as applied to various expressive forms and contexts. Just as the justices before them, modern members of the Court have had to struggle with the perennial conflict between the need for an ordered society and the desire for individual liberty.

REGULATING EXPRESSION: CONTENT AND CONTEXTS

Justice Holmes noted in *Schenck* that the legitimacy of expression often depends upon the nature of the words and the conditions under which they are uttered. The major tests of the First Amendment, developed in the national security cases, provide broad guidelines for determining the boundaries of constitutional protection. Yet even if the justices could agree on a controlling philosophy of what the First Amendment means, they would still have to wrestle with the task of applying that doctrine to specific cases. In the remaining portion of this chapter, we present some of the recurring expression issues that the justices have confronted and the rules of law they developed as a response.

Guiding Principles

Before we turn our attention to specific types of expression, we set forth some of the principles the Court has deemed relevant in deciding freedom of expression issues. Keep in mind that these principles are flexible and may be applied in slightly different ways depending upon the nature of the expression and the forum in which it occurs.

When the Framers drafted the First Amendment they had specific purposes in mind. The goal was to create a society in which expression would thrive and the government could not use its power to repress individuals from expressing themselves by speech, publication, or in association with others of similar mind. The Supreme Court has accepted the duty to interpret the First Amendment with these purposes in mind: over the years the justices have referred to the goal of creating a free marketplace of ideas and a society in which a robust exchange of views occurs without government censorship.

While the vibrant exchange of thoughts and opinions might be the goal, the justices have never concluded that the First Amendment absolutely protects all forms of speech. Instead, the Court's decisions have acknowledged that freedom of expression has certain limitations. These limitations are in response to the need for an ordered society that functions well. In general, the Court has recognized that freedom of expression must be balanced against the need to safeguard the rights of others and the right of the government to carry out its legitimate functions in a reasonable fashion.

Although the First Amendment does not explicitly differentiate, the Framers approached freedom of expression with a definite hierarchy in mind. Of primary concern was the need to protect political and social speech. Other forms of expression, such as those primarily for entertainment or commercial gain, ranked lower in the hierarchy. Still others, like libel and obscenity, were viewed as illegitimate and occupied a position outside the scope of First Amendment protections. As we shall see in this section and the next two chapters, the Court has often approached freedom of expression disputes with this hierarchy in mind. It is especially vigilant in protecting political and social communication, but allows greater deference to government in regulating other forms.

Under what conditions, then, may the government regulate expression? In general, government may encroach on speech rights if the expression itself or its consequences involve matters of legitimate government concern. Holmes may have defined it best when he referred to "substantive evils that Congress has a right to prevent." The Court has applied this admittedly vague standard by designating certain conditions that justify government's authority to intervene. Although not exhaustive, the following list includes the major categories of conditions that may trigger valid government regulation of expression.

Violence. The government has authority to protect citizens from personal injury. If expression takes a violent form or incites others to violence the government may regulate it.

Property Damage. The government has the right to protect private and public property from being destroyed or damaged. Antiwar protesters, for example, who express themselves by setting fire to a National Guard armory have gone beyond their First Amendment protections and can be arrested for their conduct.

Criminal Speech. Some forms of expression are crimes by their very nature. For example, the Constitution does not protect those who might give military secrets to the enemy or engage in conspiracies to violate valid criminal laws.

Encroaching on the Rights of Others. Freedom of expression does not provide a license to infringe on the rights of others. If animal rights protesters block an entrance to a zoo or prolife groups prevent access to an abortion clinic, the government may intervene. In both cases, the protesters have curtailed the right of the public to move about without interference.

Burdens on Government Functions. Regulation is permissible if expression places a burden on a legitimate government function. If, for example, environmentalists opposed to the construction of a Corps of Engineers dam lie down in front of bulldozers, the government may arrest them.

Trespass. The freedom of expression does not include the right to speak anywhere one wishes. A campaign worker, for example, does not have the right to come into another person's home without permission to promote the candidate's cause. Similarly, some public facilities are not legitimate places for groups of demonstrators to congregate. It would be legitimate, for example, to prohibit antiwar protesters from demonstrating inside a defense facility.

Forms of Expression Considered Outside the Scope of the First Amendment. As indicated above, certain classes of expression from the very beginning have been considered unprotected by the Constitution. Chief among these are obscenity and libel. As we shall see in Chapter 6, if expression meets the Court's rather strict definitions of libel or obscenity, the First Amendment imposes no barrier to government regulation.

These various conditions of legitimate government concern have given rise to the Court's "time, place, and manner" doctrine. By this standard the Court acknowledges that government has the general authority to impose reasonable time, place, and manner restrictions on the freedom of expression. Therefore, the Court would certainly uphold the arrest of demonstrators who gathered in the middle of an expressway or of political zealots who promoted their candidate by driving a sound truck through a residential area at 2:00 a.m.

Although the Court has been sympathetic to the government's need to regulate expression under certain carefully defined conditions, the justices also have been careful to place restraints on the government to insure against abuse. The Court has constructed certain generally accepted criteria to hold the government's power within acceptable bounds. We list here some of the more frequently invoked of those standards:

Legitimate Purpose. Any government restriction on freedom of expression must have a clearly defined, legitimate government purpose. A law that makes inciting to riot a crime, for example, would rest on the legitimate government purpose of curtailing violence. A law prohibiting criticism of the president, motivated by an interest in keeping incumbents in power, would clearly fail this test.

Narrow Construction/Overbreadth. Any regulation of expression must be narrowly tailored to meet the government's objectives. If a legislature, concerned with protests that cause violence, passed a law prohibiting all public demonstrations, the statue would fail the narrow construction requirement. This regulatory scheme would be overbroad, going far beyond what is necessary to deal with the legislature's legitimate concern.

Vagueness. Legislatures must draft laws restricting freedom of expression with sufficient precision to give fair notice as to what is being regulated. If normally intelligent people have to guess what a statute means and come to different conclusions about what is prohibited by it, the statute is unconstitutionally vague.

Chilling Effect. A law intended to regulate certain forms of illegitimate expression cannot be written so as to make people fearful of engaging in legitimate activity. Often such a "chilling effect" stems from statutes that are vague or overbroad. Assume that a state legislature, concerned about sexual activities that occur in certain nightclubs, passes a statute making it illegal to serve alcoholic beverages in any establishment that also offers nude entertainment. In response to that law, museum officials may be fearful of sponsoring a gathering at which patrons would sip wine while viewing an exhibit of paintings that include some nude figures. Here a statute designed to curb obscenity creates a chilling effect on the exercise of legitimate activities.

Prior Restraint. Government may prosecute individuals who violate legitimate restrictions on expression, but, absent extraordinary circumstances, may not intervene before the fact. For example, the government may not constitutionally require a speaker to submit for review a copy of the speech before its delivery in order to make sure that nothing in it may incite the audience to riot.

Content Discrimination. Laws regulating expression should be content neutral. A local ordinance, for example, enforced in a manner that allowed a Democratic group to conduct a public rally but prohibited a Republican group to engage in the same activity would violate this principle.

As you read the cases and commentary in the remaining portion of this chapter and the two that follow, keep these principles in mind. You will observe many examples of the justices debating whether the expression in question merits regulation and whether the methods of regulation are proper. You will witness the flexibility of these standards as the Court adjusts them to different contexts. Finally, you will see how individual justices differ in the way they apply these standards based upon their own ideologies and preferences.

Symbolic Speech

The First Amendment specifically protects the freedoms of speech and press, two forms of expression with which the Framers were thoroughly familiar. In the days of the Revolution, political protest customarily took the form of eloquent addresses, sharply worded editorials, and fiery publications. Verbal expression and published communication were the methods of political debate, and the Framers unambiguously sought to protect them from government encroachment by drafting and ratifying the First Amendment.

But what if someone wishes to communicate a message by means other than word of mouth or printed copy? If a point is made by action rather than by verbal expression, does the First Amendment still grant immunity from government regulation? These questions deal with symbolic speech and whether expressive conduct qualifies as speech under the meaning of the First Amendment.

Most of the symbolic speech cases have occurred in the modern period, but the debate over expressive conduct began much earlier. Recall the discussion of *Stromberg v. California.* In that 1931 case, a camp counselor was convicted not because of anything she said, but because of an expressive act that was in conflict with California law. In reversing her conviction on First Amendment grounds, the Supreme Court acknowledged that at least some forms of symbolic speech merit constitutional protection.

In the years that followed, the Court had to decide whether the same principles applied to various forms of picketing in labor disputes. Some states sought to hinder the development and success of labor unions by passing laws prohibiting workers from carrying placards and walking picket lines to protest alleged unfair labor practices. The most significant case of this era was *Thornhill v. Alabama* (1940) in which Byron Thornhill had been arrested for violating an Alabama law that made picketing a crime. Supporters of the antipicketing statutes argued that picketing was conduct and not speech, but the Supreme Court reversed the conviction on First Amendment grounds. For the Court, Justice Frank Murphy concluded, "In the circumstances of our times the dissemination of information concerning the facts of a labor dispute must be regarded as within that area of free discussion that is guaranteed by the Constitution."

Decisions such as these established the principle that symbolic actions can qualify as speech and be accorded First Amendment protection. This principle does not mean, however, that the First Amendment shields from government regulation *any* act committed to express an idea or opinion. No one, for example, would seriously claim that assassination is a protected form of expressing political opposition. Perhaps even more than verbal expression, symbolic speech presents especially difficult questions of drawing constitutional boundaries.

The turbulence of the late 1960s brought a number of difficult symbolic expression issues before the Court. The civil rights movement and the Vietnam War protests expanded the ways of communicating political messages. Traditional forms of speech and press gave way to demonstrations, sit-ins, flag desecration, and other varieties of conduct designed to present the protesters' political messages in a graphic manner. The first of such cases was *United States v. O'Brien* (1968), in which the defendants had expressed their opposition to the war in Southeast Asia by publicly and illegally burning their draft cards. The case presents a difficult clash of values. The Warren Court had shown increasing tolerance for First Amendment expression claims, but would this trend continue? Or would the fact that thousands of American troops were engaged in combat in Asia influence the Court?

United States v. O'Brien

391 U.S. 367 (1968)
Vote: 7 (Black, Brennan, Fortas, Harlan, Stewart,
        Warren, White)
    1 (Douglas)
Opinion of the Court: Warren
Dissenting opinion: Douglas
Not participating: Marshall

On March 31, 1966, David O'Brien and three others burned their draft cards on the steps of a South Boston courthouse. A sizable crowd gathered and began attacking O'Brien and his colleagues. FBI agents took the four into the courthouse to protect them and to question them. The agents told O'Brien that he had violated a 1965 amendment to the Selective Service Act, making it illegal to "destroy or mutilate" draft cards. O'Brien replied that he understood, but had burned his card anyway because he was "a pacifist and as such [could not] kill."

After a federal court ruled that O'Brien had acted within the bounds of the Constitution, the United States asked the Supreme Court to hear the case. Solicitor General Thurgood Marshall argued that O'Brien's actions thwarted a valid business of government—to draft men into the armed forces—because his purpose was "to influence others to adopt his antiwar beliefs."[24] The solicitor general also tried to negate the chief argument made by O'Brien's ACLU attorney that his action constituted symbolic speech of the kind upheld by the Court in *Stromberg*. To this, the government argued:

Terming [O'Brien's] conduct "symbolic speech" does not transform it into activity entitled to the same kind of constitutional protection given to words and other modes of expression.

24. Solicitor General Marshall filed the petition for certiorari. After Marshall's elevation to the Supreme Court, Erwin Griswold took over the litigation, writing the major brief.

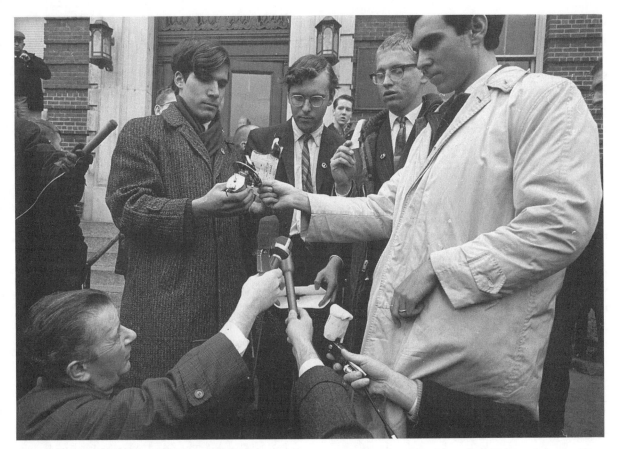

On March 31, 1966, David O'Brien and three other antiwar protestors demonstrated their opposition to U.S. military action in Vietnam by burning their draft cards on the steps of the South Boston courthouse. Their convictions for violating the Selective Service Act were affirmed in *United States v. O'Brien*.

MR. CHIEF JUSTICE WARREN delivered the opinion of the Court.

O'Brien ... argues that the 1965 Amendment is unconstitutional in its application to him, and is unconstitutional as enacted because what he calls the "purpose" of Congress was "to suppress freedom of speech." We consider these arguments separately.

O'Brien first argues that the 1965 Amendment is unconstitutional as applied to him because his act of burning his registration certificate was protected "symbolic speech" within the First Amendment. His argument is that the free-

dom of expression which the First Amendment guarantees includes all modes of "communication of ideas by conduct," and that his conduct is within this definition because he did it in "demonstration against the war and against the draft."

We cannot accept the view that an apparently limitless variety of conduct can be labeled "speech" whenever the person engaging in the conduct intends thereby to express an idea. However, even on the assumption that the alleged communicative element in O'Brien's conduct is sufficient to bring into play the First Amendment, it does not necessarily follow that the destruction of a registration certificate is constitutionally protected activity. This Court has held that when "speech" and "nonspeech" elements are combined in the same course of conduct, a sufficiently important governmental interest in regulating the nonspeech element can justify incidental limitations on First Amendment freedoms. To characterize the quality of the governmental interest which must appear, the Court has employed a variety of descriptive terms: compelling; substantial; subordinating; paramount; cogent; strong. Whatever imprecision inheres in these terms, we think it clear that a government regulation is sufficiently justified if it is within the constitutional power of the Government; if it furthers an important or substantial governmental interest; if the governmental interest is unrelated to the suppression of free expression; and if the incidental restriction on alleged First Amendment freedoms is no greater than is essential to the furtherance of that interest. We find that the 1965 Amendment to § 12(b)(3) of the Universal Military Training and Service Act meets all of these requirements, and consequently that O'Brien can be constitutionally convicted for violating it.

The constitutional power of Congress to raise and support armies and to make all laws necessary and proper to that end is broad and sweeping. The power of Congress to classify and conscript manpower for military service is "beyond question." Pursuant to this power, Congress may establish a system of registration for individuals liable for training and service, and may require such individuals within reason to cooperate in the registration system. The issuance of certificates indicating the registration and eligibility classification of individuals is a legitimate and substantial administrative aid in the functioning of this system. And legislation to insure the continuing availability of issued certificates serves a legitimate and substantial purpose in the system's administration.

O'Brien's argument to the contrary is necessarily premised upon his unrealistic characterization of Selective Service certificates. He essentially adopts the position that such certificates are so many pieces of paper designed to notify registrants of their registration or classification, to be retained or tossed in the wastebasket according to the convenience or taste of the registrant. Once the registrant has received notification, according to this view, there is no reason for him to retain the certificates. O'Brien notes that most of the information on a registration certificate serves no notification purpose at all; the registrant hardly needs to be told his address and physical characteristics. We agree that the registration certificate contains much information of which the registrant needs no notification. This circumstance, however, does not lead to the conclusion that the certificate serves no purpose, but that, like the classification certificate, it serves purposes in addition to initial notification. Many of these purposes would be defeated by the certificates' destruction or mutilation. Among these are:

1. The registration certificate serves as proof that the individual described thereon has registered for the draft. The classification certificate shows the eligibility classification of a named but undescribed individual. Voluntarily displaying the two certificates is an easy and painless way for a young man to dispel a question as to whether he might be delinquent in his Selective Service obligations.... Additionally, in a time of national crisis, reasonable availability to each registrant of the two small cards assures a rapid and uncomplicated means for determining his fitness for immediate induction, no matter how distant in our mobile society he may be from his local board.

2. The information supplied on the certificates facilitates communication between registrants and local boards, simplifying the system and benefiting all concerned. To begin with, each certificate bears the address of the registrant's local board, an item unlikely to be committed to memory. Further, each card bears the registrant's Selective Service number, and a registrant who has his number readily available so that he can communicate it to his local board can make simpler the board's task in locating his file. Finally, a registrant's inquiry, particularly through a local board other than his own, concerning his eligibility status is frequently answerable simply on the basis of his classification certificate; whereas, if the certificate were not reasonably available and the registrants were uncertain of his classification, the task of answering his questions would be considerably complicated.

3. Both certificates carry continual reminders that the registrant must notify his local board of any change of address, and other specified changes in his status. The smooth functioning of the system requires that local boards

be continually aware of the status and whereabouts of registrants, and the destruction of certificates deprives the system of a potentially useful notice device.

4. The regulatory scheme involving Selective Service certificates includes clearly valid prohibitions against the alteration, forgery, or similar deceptive misuse of certificates. The destruction or mutilation of certificates obviously increases the difficulty of detecting and tracing abuses such as these. Further, a mutilated certificate might itself be used for deceptive purposes.

The many functions performed by Selective Service certificates establish beyond doubt that Congress has a legitimate and substantial interest in preventing their wanton and unrestrained destruction and assuring their continuing availability by punishing people who knowingly and willfully destroy or mutilate them. And we are unpersuaded that the pre-existence of the non-possession regulations in any way negates this interest....

We think it apparent that the continuing availability to each registrant of his Selective Service certificates substantially furthers the smooth and proper functioning of the system that Congress has established to raise armies. We think it also apparent that the Nation has a vital interest in having a system for raising armies that functions with maximum efficiency and is capable of easily and quickly responding to continually changing circumstances. For these reasons, the Government has a substantial interest in assuring the continuing availability of issued Selective Service certificates.

It is equally clear that the 1965 Amendment specifically protects this substantial government interest. We perceive no alternative means that would more precisely and narrowly assure the continuing availability of issued Selective Service certificates than a law which prohibits their willful mutilation or destruction. The 1965 Amendment prohibits such conduct and does nothing more. In other words, both the governmental interest and the operation of the 1965 Amendment are limited to the noncommunicative aspect of O'Brien's conduct. The governmental interest and the scope of the 1965 Amendment are limited to preventing harm to the smooth and efficient functioning of the Selective Service System. When O'Brien deliberately rendered unavailable his registration certificate, he willfully frustrated this governmental interest. For this noncommunica-

tive impact of his conduct, and for nothing else, he was convicted.

The case at bar is therefore unlike one where the alleged governmental interest in regulating conduct arises in some measure because the communication allegedly integral to the conduct is itself thought to be harmful. In Stromberg v. People of State of California (1931), for example, this Court struck down a statutory phrase which punished people who expressed their "opposition to organized government" by displaying "any flag, badge, banner, or device." Since the statute there was aimed at suppressing communication it could not be sustained as a regulation of noncommunicative conduct.

In conclusion, we find that because of the Government's substantial interest in assuring the continuing availability of issued Selective Service certificates, because amended § 462(b) is an appropriately narrow means of protecting this interest and condemns only the independent noncommunicative impact of conduct within its reach, and because the noncommunicative impact of O'Brien's act of burning his registration certificate frustrated the Government's interest, a sufficient governmental interest has been shown to justify O'Brien's conviction.

O'Brien finally argues that the 1965 Amendment is unconstitutional as enacted because what he calls the "purpose" of Congress was "to suppress freedom of speech." We reject this argument because under settled principles the purpose of Congress, as O'Brien uses that term, is not a basis for declaring this legislation unconstitutional....

Warren's opinion explicitly rejects the idea that conduct used to express an idea automatically merits First Amendment protection. The Court held that whenever "speech" and "nonspeech" elements are combined, a sufficiently important government interest in regulating the nonspeech element can justify limitations on First Amendment rights. As applied in this case, the Court found that O'Brien's conduct (burning the draft card) placed a burden on a legitimate government activity (the power to raise and support armies). The government had a substantial interest in exercising its military authority, and the draft registration system was a reasonable means of achieving that end. Consequently, the government had the constitutional power to prosecute individuals who violated the Selective Service laws even if the acts in question communicated a message of political protest.

One year later the Court heard another symbolic speech case stemming from protests against the Vietnam War, *Tinker v. Des Moines* (1969). This appeal came from public school students who had been suspended for engaging in a peaceful, but prohibited, protest during the school day. As you read the excerpt of this case, ask yourself how the nature and impact of the symbolic expression in *Tinker* compare with O'Brien's draft card burning. Notice also how the justices differ on the question of First Amendment rights in the public schools.

Tinker v. Des Moines

393 U.S. 503 (1969)
Vote: 7 (Brennan, Douglas, Fortas, Marshall, Stewart,
Warren, White)
   2 (Black, Harlan)
Opinion of the Court: Fortas
Concurring opinions: Stewart, White
Dissenting opinions: Black, Harlan

In December 1965 a group of adults and secondary school students in Des Moines, Iowa, devised two strategies to demonstrate their opposition to the Vietnam War: they would fast on December 16 and New Year's Day, and they would wear black armbands every day in between. Principals of the students' schools learned of the plan and agreed to suspend any students wearing armbands. Despite the warning, the parents of five children, among them John and Mary Beth Tinker, allowed them to wear black armbands to school. All five were suspended. Representing the students, ACLU attorneys argued that the armbands constituted legitimate symbolic speech and, because the principals suppressed such expression, they engaged in illegal prior restraint.

MR. JUSTICE FORTAS delivered the opinion of the Court.

The District Court recognized that the wearing of an armband for the purpose of expressing certain views is the type of symbolic act that is within the Free Speech Clause of the First Amendment. As we shall discuss, the wearing of armbands in the circumstances of this case was entirely divorced from actually or potentially disruptive conduct by those participating in it. It was closely akin to "pure speech" which, we have repeatedly held, is entitled to comprehensive protection under the First Amendment.

First Amendment rights, applied in light of the special characteristics of the school environment, are available to teachers and students. It can hardly be argued that either students or teachers shed their constitutional rights to freedom of speech or expression at the schoolhouse gate. This has been the unmistakable holding of this Court for almost 50 years....

In West Virginia State Board of Education v. Barnette, this Court held that under the First Amendment, the student in public school may not be compelled to salute the flag.... On the other hand, the Court has repeatedly emphasized the need for affirming the comprehensive authority of the States and of school officials, consistent with fundamental constitutional safeguards, to prescribe and control conduct in the schools. Our problem lies in the area where students in the exercise of First Amendment rights collide with the rules of the school authorities.

The problem posed by the present case does not relate to regulation of the length of skirts or the type of clothing, to hair style, or deportment. It does not concern aggressive, disruptive action or even group demonstrations. Our problem involves direct, primary First Amendment rights akin to "pure speech."

The school officials banned and sought to punish petitioners for a silent, passive expression of opinion, unaccompanied by any disorder or disturbance on the part of petitioners. There is here no evidence whatever of petitioners' interference, actual or nascent, with the schools' work or of collision with the rights of other students to be secure and to be let alone. Accordingly, this case does not concern speech or action that intrudes upon the work of the schools or the rights of other students.

Mary Beth Tinker and her brother John display the black armbands that got them suspended from school in 1965. The two were protesting the Vietnam War. In *Tinker v. Des Moines* (1969) the Supreme Court held that the suspensions violated the Tinkers's right to freedom of expression.

Only a few of the 18,000 students in the school system wore the black armbands. Only five students were suspended for wearing them. There is no indication that the work of the schools or any class was disrupted. Outside the classrooms, a few students made hostile remarks to the children wearing armbands, but there were no threats or acts of violence on school premises.

... [I]n our system, undifferentiated fear or apprehension of disturbance is not enough to overcome the right to freedom of expression. Any departure from absolute regimentation may cause trouble. Any variation from the majority's opinion may inspire fear. Any word spoken, in class, in the lunchroom, or on the campus, that deviates from the views of another person may start an argument or cause a disturbance. But our Constitution says we must take this risk, and our history says that it is this sort of hazardous freedom—this kind of openness—that is the basis of our national strength and of the independence and vigor of Americans who grow up and live in this relatively permissive, often disputatious, society.

In order for the State in the person of school officials to justify prohibition of a particular expression of opinion, it must be able to show that its action was caused by something more than a mere desire to avoid the discomfort and unpleasantness that always accompany an unpopular viewpoint. Certainly where there is no finding and no showing that engaging in the forbidden conduct would "materially and substantially interfere with the requirements of appropriate discipline in the operation of the school," the prohibition cannot be sustained.

In the present case, the District Court made no such finding, and our independent examination of the record fails to yield evidence that the school authorities had reason to anticipate that the wearing of the armbands would substantially interfere with the work of the school or impinge upon the rights of other students. . . .

It is also relevant that the school authorities did not purport to prohibit the wearing of all symbols of political or controversial significance. The record shows that students in some of the schools wore buttons relating to national political campaigns, and some even wore the Iron Cross, traditionally a symbol of Nazism. The order prohibiting the wearing of armbands did not extend to these. Instead, a particular symbol—black armbands worn to exhibit opposition to this Nation's involvement in Vietnam—was singled out for prohibition. Clearly, the prohibition of expression of one particular opinion, at least without evidence that it is necessary to avoid material and substantial interference with schoolwork or discipline, is not constitutionally permissible.

In our system, state-operated schools may not be enclaves of totalitarianism. School officials do not possess absolute authority over their students. Students in school as well as out of school are "persons" under our Constitution. They are possessed of fundamental rights which the State must respect, just as they themselves must respect their obligations to the State. In our system, students may not be regarded as closed-circuit recipients of only that which the State chooses to communicate. They may not be confined to the expression of those sentiments that are officially approved. In the absence of a specific showing of constitutionally valid reasons to regulate their speech, students are entitled to freedom of expression of their views. . . .

The principal use to which the schools are dedicated is to accommodate students during prescribed hours for the purpose of certain types of activities. Among those activities is personal intercommunication among the students. This is not only an inevitable part of the process of attending school; it is also an important part of the educational process. A student's rights, therefore, do not embrace merely the classroom hours. When he is in the cafeteria, or on the playing field, or on the campus during the authorized hours, he may express his opinions, even on controversial subjects like the conflict in Vietnam, if he does so without "materially and substantially interfer[ing] with the requirements of appropriate discipline in the operation of the school" and without colliding with the rights of others. But conduct by the student, in class or out of it, which for any reason—whether it stems from time, place, or type of behavior—materially disrupts classwork or involves substantial disorder or invasion of the rights of others is, of course, not immunized by the constitutional guarantee of freedom of speech.

Under our Constitution, free speech is not a right that is given only to be so circumscribed that it exists in principle but not in fact. Freedom of expression would not truly exist if the right could be exercised only in an area that a benevolent government has provided as a safe haven for crackpots. The Constitution says that Congress (and the States) may not abridge the right to free speech. This provision means what it says. We properly read it to permit reasonable regulation of speech-connected activities in carefully restricted circumstances. But we do not confine the permissible exercise of First Amendment rights to a telephone booth or the four corners of a pamphlet, or to supervised and ordained discussion in a school classroom.

If a regulation were adopted by school officials forbidding discussion of the Vietnam conflict, or the expression by any student of opposition to it anywhere on school property except as part of a prescribed classroom exercise, it would be obvious that the regulation would violate the constitutional rights of students, at least if it could not be justified by a showing that the students' activities would materially and substantially disrupt the work and discipline of the school. . . .

As we have discussed, the record does not demonstrate any facts which might reasonably have led school authorities to forecast substantial disruption of or material interference with school activities, and no disturbances or disorders on the school premises in fact occurred. These petitioners merely went about their ordained rounds in school. Their deviation consisted only in wearing on their sleeve a band of black cloth, not more than two inches wide. They wore it to exhibit their disapproval of the Vietnam hostilities and their advocacy of a truce, to make their views known, and, by their example, to influence others to adopt them. They neither interrupted school activities nor sought to intrude in the school affairs or the lives of others. They caused discussion outside of the classrooms, but no interference with work and no disorder. In the circumstances, our Constitution does not permit officials of the State to deny their form of expression.

Reversed and remanded.

MR. JUSTICE BLACK, dissenting.

As I read the Court's opinion it relies upon the following grounds for holding unconstitutional the judgment of the Des Moines school officials and the two courts below. First, the Court concludes that the wearing of armbands is "symbolic speech" which is "akin to 'pure speech'" and therefore protected by the First and Fourteenth Amendments. Secondly, the Court decides that the public schools are an appropriate place to exercise "symbolic speech" as long as normal school functions are not "unreasonably" disrupted. Finally, the Court arrogates to itself, rather than to the State's elected officials charged with running the schools, the decision as to which school disciplinary regulations are "reasonable."

Assuming that the Court is correct in holding that the conduct of wearing armbands for the purpose of conveying political ideas is protected by the First Amendment, the crucial remaining questions are whether students and teachers may use the schools at their whim as a platform for the exercise of free speech—"symbolic" or "pure"—and whether the courts will allocate to themselves the function of deciding how the pupils' school day will be spent. While I have always believed that under the First and Fourteenth Amendments neither the State nor the Federal Government has any authority to regulate or censor the content of speech, I have never believed that any person has a right to give speeches or engage in demonstrations where he pleases and when he pleases. This Court has already rejected such a notion. In Cox v. Louisiana (1965), for example, the Court clearly stated that the rights of free speech and assembly "do not mean that everyone with opinions or beliefs to express may address a group at any public place and at any time."

While the record does not show that any of these armband students shouted, used profane language, or were violent in any manner, detailed testimony by some of them shows their armbands caused comments, warnings by other students, the poking of fun at them, and a warning by an older football player that other, nonprotesting students had better let them alone. There is also evidence that a teacher of mathematics had his lesson period practically "wrecked" chiefly by disputes with Mary Beth Tinker, who wore her armband for her "demonstration."...

I deny ... that it has been the "unmistakable holding of this Court for almost 50 years" that "students" and "teachers" take with them into the "schoolhouse gate" constitutional rights to "freedom of speech or expression." Even *Meyer* [v. Nebraska, 1923] did not hold that. It makes no reference to "symbolic speech" at all; what it did was to strike down as "unreasonable" and therefore unconstitutional a Nebraska law barring the teaching of the German language before the children reached the eighth grade. One can well agree with Mr. Justice Holmes and Mr. Justice Sutherland, as I do, that such a law was no more unreasonable than it would be to bar the teaching of Latin and Greek to pupils who have not reached the eighth grade. In fact, I think the majority's reason for invalidating the Nebraska law was that it did not like it or in legal jargon that it "shocked the Court's conscience," "offended its sense of justice," or was "contrary to fundamental concepts of the English-speaking world," as the Court has sometimes said. The truth is that a teacher of kindergarten, grammar school, or high school pupils no more carries into a school with him a complete right to freedom of speech and expression than an anti-Catholic or anti-Semite carries with him a complete freedom of speech and religion into a Catholic church or Jewish synagogue. Nor does a person carry with him into the United States Senate or House, or into the Supreme Court, or any other court, a complete constitutional right to go into those places contrary to their rules and speak his mind on any subject he pleases. It is a myth to say that any person has a constitutional right to say what he pleases, where he pleases, and when he pleases. Our Court has decided precisely the opposite....

Change has been said to be truly the law of life but sometimes the old and the tried and true are worth holding. The schools of this Nation have undoubtedly contributed to giving us tranquility and to making us a more law-abiding people. Uncontrolled and uncontrollable liberty is an enemy to domestic peace. We cannot close our eyes to the fact that some of the country's greatest problems are crimes committed by the youth, too many of school age. School discipline, like parental discipline, is an integral and important part of training our children to be good citizens—to be better citizens. Here a very small number of students have crisply and summarily refused to obey a school order designed to give pupils who want to learn the opportunity to do so. One does not need to be a prophet or the son of a prophet to know that after the Court's holding today some students in Iowa schools and indeed in all schools will be ready, able, and willing to defy their teachers on practically all orders. This is the more unfortunate for the schools since groups of students all over the land are already running loose, conducting break-ins, sit-ins, lie-ins, and smash-ins. Many of these student groups, as is all too familiar to all who read the newspapers and watch the television news programs, have already engaged in rioting, property seizures, and destruction. They have picketed schools to force students not to cross their picket lines and have too often violently attacked earnest but frightened students who wanted an education that the pickets did not want them to get. Students engaged in such activities are apparently confident that they know far more about how to operate public school systems than do their parents, teachers, and elected school officials. It is no answer to say that the particular students here have not yet reached such high points in their demands to attend class in order to exercise their political pressures. Turned loose with lawsuits for damages and injunctions against their teachers as they are here, it is nothing but wishful thinking to imagine that young, immature students will not soon believe it is their right to control the schools rather than the right of the States that collect the taxes to hire the teachers for the benefit of the pupils. This case, therefore, wholly without constitutional reasons in my judgment, subjects all the public schools in the country to the whims and caprices of their loudest-mouthed, but maybe not their brightest, students. I, for one, am not fully persuaded that school pupils are wise enough, even with this Court's expert help from Washington, to run the 23,390 public school systems in our 50 States. I wish, therefore, wholly to disclaim any purpose on my part to hold that the Federal Constitution compels the teachers, parents, and elected school officials to surrender control of the American public school system to public school students. I dissent.

The Court ruled in favor of the Tinkers, declaring that students and teachers do not "shed their constitutional rights to freedom of speech or expression at the schoolhouse gate." Important to the Court was that the protest was peaceful: there was no violence, no property damage, and no significant disruption of the school day. On this count, *Tinker* differed from *O'Brien*, in which the justices found that the burning of Selective Service documents placed a burden on a legitimate government function. In dissent, Hugo Black took issue with the majority, arguing that the freedom of speech does not extend equally to every place and circumstance. School administrators, he said, should be allowed to impose reasonable regulations to ensure conditions conducive to learning.

Among all symbolic expression issues none has given the Court greater difficulty than the flag desecration cases. As a national symbol, the American flag evokes intense emotional feelings, especially among those, like members of the Supreme Court, who have long histories of public service. Even those justices most committed to freedom of expression have indicated their discomfort in extending First Amendment protection to those who destroy the flag as a method of political expression.

During demonstrations against the Vietnam War, protesters sometimes burned American flags to symbolize their disdain for U.S. foreign policy. Many states outlawed such activity, but the question remained whether such laws were constitutional. Did flag desecration constitute symbolic speech and therefore warrant the protection of the First Amendment?

The Warren Court first grappled with this issue in *Street v. New York* (1969), a case brought to it by the ACLU. In 1966 the appellant heard on his radio that James Meredith, a civil rights activist, had been shot in Mississippi. Street took a flag he kept for display on national holidays, went outside, and burnt it. He drew attention to his action by yelling, "If they let that happen to Meredith, we don't need an American flag." The police arrested him for violating a New York law that prohibited physical and verbal desecration of the flag. A Supreme Court majority, using a Preferred Freedoms approach, agreed that the verbal part of the New York law violated free speech guarantees, but the justices divided 4–4 on whether states could prohibit the physical desecration of the flag.

It was not until 1974 that the Court, again divided, returned to this issue in *Spence v. Washington.* Harold Spence was a college student living in Washington State. To protest the deaths of antiwar demonstrators at Kent State University and the U.S. invasion of Cambodia, Spence displayed an American flag with a large peace symbol taped to both sides of it. The police informed Spence that his "desecrated" flag violated a state law, forbidding "the exhibition of a U.S. flag to which is attached or superimposed figures, symbols, or other extraneous material." Spence told the officers that he "didn't know there was anything wrong" with the flag; he fully cooperated with them when they seized it from his apartment.

At his trial, Spence explained why he had altered his flag:

I felt there had been so much killing and that this was not what America stood for. I felt that the flag stood for America and I wanted people to know that I thought America stood for peace.

Spence's testimony allowed his ACLU attorneys to frame his case differently from *Street.* Because Washington's law did not punish speech per se, the lawyers put the issue of symbolic expression squarely before the justices, arguing, "The First Amendment's protection encompasses visual symbols as well as spoken words."

In a 6–3 per curiam opinion, the justices agreed with the ACLU. In fact, they adopted the same reasoning we have seen time and time again in symbolic speech cases: as long as the action does not "incite violence or even stimulate a public demonstration," it is protected

by the First Amendment. The justices equated Spence's speech with that of the Tinkers—they were both nonviolent forms of expression. The Court also took notice of the tumultuous times during which this case arose. In a footnote, it compared Spence's activity to others occurring during that decade:

Appellant's activity occurred at a time of national turmoil.... It is difficult now, more than four years later, to recall vividly the depth of emotion that pervaded most colleges.... A spontaneous outpouring of feeling resulted in widespread action.... It was against this highly inflamed background that [Spence] chose to express his views in a manner that can fairly be described as gentle.

As the war in Vietnam abated so did the protest cases; in fact, this flag desecration series was among the last decided by the Burger Court. Now that you have read about some of the more important Warren and Burger Court cases associated with that tumultuous era, consider these questions: How do the Court's decisions of the 1960s and 1970s differ from those of the 1920s, 1930s, and 1950s? Does the thesis that the Court is more willing to suppress free speech during times of international crisis hold true for the Vietnam War era? One way of addressing this is to consider Rehnquist Court treatment of the same crisis-related issue, flag burning. Note that *Texas v. Johnson* was decided in 1989, during a period of domestic tranquility. But also keep in mind the conservative leanings of this Court.

Texas v. Johnson

491 U.S. 397 (1989)
Vote: 5 (Blackmun, Brennan, Kennedy, Marshall, Scalia)
4 (O'Connor, Rehnquist, Stevens, White)
Opinion of the Court: Brennan
Concurring opinion: Kennedy
Dissenting opinions: Rehnquist, Stevens

In the summer of 1984 the Republican party held its national convention in Dallas, Texas, and overwhelmingly supported President Ronald Reagan's re-election bid. While the party was meeting, a group of demonstrators marched through the city to protest the Reagan administration's policies. One of the demonstrators gave an American flag to Gregory Lee Johnson, who also was marching. When the march ended, Johnson "unfurled the flag, doused it with kerosene and set it on fire." As it burned, others chanted, "America, the red, white, and blue, we spit on you." Authorities arrested Johnson, charging him with violating the Texas flag desecration law. He was convicted and sentenced to a one-year prison term and a $2,000 fine.

JUSTICE BRENNAN delivered the opinion of the Court.

Johnson was convicted of flag desecration for burning the flag rather than for uttering insulting words. This fact somewhat complicates our consideration of his conviction under the First Amendment. We must first determine whether Johnson's burning of the flag constituted expressive conduct, permitting him to invoke the First Amendment in challenging his conviction. If his conduct was expressive, we next decide whether the State's regulation is related to the suppression of free expression. If the State's regulation is not related to expression, then the less stringent standard we announced in *United States v. O'Brien* for regulations of noncommunicative conduct controls. If it is, then we are outside of *O'Brien*'s test, and we must ask whether this interest justifies Johnson's conviction under a more demanding standard. A third possibility is that the State's asserted interest is simply not implicated on these facts, and in that event the interest drops out of the picture.

The First Amendment literally forbids the abridgement only of "speech," but we have long recognized that its protection does not end at the spoken or written word. While we have rejected "the view that an apparently limitless variety of conduct can be labeled 'speech' whenever the person engaging in the conduct intends thereby to express an idea," we have acknowledged that conduct may be "sufficiently imbued with elements of communication to fall within the scope of the First and Fourteenth Amendments."

In deciding whether particular conduct possesses sufficient communicative elements to bring the First Amend-

Gregory Johnson, who has a record of flag burning, holds the American flag while another protestor sets it alight. In 1989 the Supreme Court ruled that the conviction of Johnson for burning a flag during a demonstration in Dallas violated his First Amendment expression rights.

ment into play, we have asked whether "[a]n intent to convey a particularized message was present, and [whether] the likelihood was great that the message would be understood by those who viewed it." Hence, we have recognized the expressive nature of students' wearing of black armbands to protest American military involvement in Vietnam. . . .

Especially pertinent to this case are our decisions recognizing the communicative nature of conduct relating to flags. Attaching a peace sign to the flag, saluting the flag, and displaying a red flag, we have held, all may find shelter under the First Amendment. That we have had little difficulty identifying an expressive element in conduct relating to flags should not be surprising. The very purpose of a national flag is to serve as a symbol of our country; it is, one might say, "the one visible manifestation of two hundred years of nationhood."...

We have not automatically concluded, however, that any action taken with respect to our flag is expressive. Instead, in characterizing such action for First Amendment purposes, we have considered the context in which it occurred....

Johnson burned an American flag as part—indeed, as the culmination—of a political demonstration that coincided with the convening of the Republican Party and its renomination of Ronald Reagan for President. In these circumstances, Johnson's burning of the flag was conduct "sufficiently imbued with elements of communication" to implicate the First Amendment.

The Government generally has a freer hand in restricting expressive conduct than it has in restricting the written or spoken word.... "A law *directed at* the communicative nature of conduct must, like a law directed at speech itself, be justified by the substantial showing of need that the First Amendment requires." It is, in short, not simply the verbal or nonverbal nature of the expression, but the governmental interest at stake, that helps to determine whether a restriction on that expression is valid.

Thus, although we have recognized that where "'speech' and 'nonspeech' elements are combined in the same course of conduct, a sufficiently important governmental interest in regulating the nonspeech element can justify incidental limitations on First Amendment freedoms," we have limited the applicability of *O'Brien's* relatively lenient standard to those cases in which "the governmental interest is unrelated to the suppression of free expression." In stating, moreover, that *O'Brien's* test "in the last analysis is little, if any, different from the standard applied to time, place, or manner restrictions," we have highlighted the requirement that the governmental interest in question be unconnected to expression in order to come under *O'Brien's* less demanding rule.

In order to decide whether *O'Brien's* test applies here, therefore, we must decide whether Texas has asserted an

interest in support of Johnson's conviction that is unrelated to the suppression of expression. If we find that an interest asserted by the State is simply not implicated on the facts before us, we need not ask whether O'Brien's test applies. The State offers two separate interests to justify this conviction: preventing breaches of the peace, and preserving the flag as a symbol of nationhood and national unity. We hold that the first interest is not implicated on this record and that the second is related to the suppression of expression.

Texas claims that its interest in preventing breaches of the peace justifies Johnson's conviction for flag desecration. However, no disturbance of the peace actually occurred or threatened to occur because of Johnson's burning of the flag....

The State's position, therefore, amounts to a claim that an audience that takes serious offense at particular expression is necessarily likely to disturb the peace and that the expression may be prohibited on this basis. Our precedents do not countenance such a presumption. On the contrary, they recognize that a principal "function of free speech under our system of government is to invite dispute. It may indeed best serve its high purpose when it induces a condition of unrest, creates dissatisfaction with conditions as they are, or even stirs people to anger."...

Nor does Johnson's expressive conduct fall within that small class of "fighting words" that are "likely to provoke the average person to retaliation, and thereby cause a breach of the peace." No reasonable onlooker would have regarded Johnson's generalized expression of dissatisfaction with the policies of the Federal Government as a direct personal insult or an invitation to exchange fisticuffs.

We thus conclude that the State's interest in maintaining order is not implicated on these facts. The State need not worry that our holding will disable it from preserving the peace. We do not suggest that the First Amendment forbids a State to prevent "imminent lawless action."...

The State also asserts an interest in preserving the flag as a symbol of nationhood and national unity. In *Spence [v. Washington*, 1974], we acknowledged that the Government's interest in preserving the flag's special symbolic value "is directly related to expression in the context of activity" such as affixing a peace symbol to a flag. We are equally persuaded that this interest is related to expression in the case of Johnson's burning of the flag. The State, apparently, is concerned that such conduct will lead people to believe either that the flag does not stand for nationhood and national unity, but instead reflects other, less positive concepts, or that the concepts reflected in the flag do not in fact exist, that is, we do not enjoy unity as a Nation. These concerns blossom only when a person's treatment of the flag communicates some message, and thus are related "to the suppression of free expression" within the meaning of *O'Brien.* We are thus outside of *O'Brien*'s test altogether.

It remains to consider whether the State's interest in preserving the flag as a symbol of nationhood and national unity justifies Johnson's conviction....

Johnson's political expression was restricted because of the content of the message he conveyed. We must therefore subject the State's asserted interest in preserving the special symbolic character of the flag to "the most exacting scrutiny."

Texas argues that its interest in preserving the flag as a symbol of nationhood and national unity survives this close analysis. Quoting extensively from the writings of this Court chronicling the flag's historic and symbolic role in our society, the State emphasizes the "'special place'" reserved for the flag in our Nation. The State's argument is not that it has an interest simply in maintaining the flag as a symbol of *something,* no matter what it symbolizes; indeed, if that were the State's position, it would be difficult to see how that interest is endangered by highly symbolic conduct such as Johnson's. Rather, the State's claim is that it has an interest in preserving the flag as a symbol of *nationhood* and *national unity,* a symbol with a determinate range of meanings. According to Texas, if one physically treats the flag in a way that would tend to cast doubt on either the idea that nationhood and national unity are the flag's referents or that national unity actually exists, the message conveyed thereby is a harmful one and therefore may be prohibited.

If there is a bedrock principle underlying the First Amendment, it is that the Government may not prohibit the expression of an idea simply because society finds the idea itself offensive or disagreeable.

We have not recognized an exception to this principle even where our flag has been involved. In *Street v. New York* we held that a State may not criminally punish a person for uttering words critical of the flag....

In short, nothing in our precedents suggests that a State may foster its own view of the flag by prohibiting expressive conduct relating to it. To bring its argument outside our precedents, Texas attempts to convince us that even if its interest in preserving the flag's symbolic role does not allow it to prohibit words or some expressive conduct critical of the flag, it does permit it to forbid the outright destruction of the flag. The State's argument cannot depend here on the distinction between written or spoken words and nonverbal conduct. That distinction, we have shown, is of no moment where the nonverbal conduct is expressive, as it is here, and where the regulation of that conduct is related to expression, as it is here....

Texas' focus on the precise nature of Johnson's expression, moreover, misses the point of our prior decisions: their enduring lesson, that the Government may not prohibit expression simply because it disagrees with its message, is not dependent on the particular mode in which one chooses to express an idea. If we were to hold that a State may forbid flag-burning wherever it is likely to endanger the flag's symbolic role, but allow it wherever burning a flag promotes that role—as where, for example, a person ceremoniously burns a dirty flag—we would be saying that when it comes to impairing the flag's physical integrity, the flag itself may be used as a symbol—as a substitute for the written or spoken word or a "short cut from mind to mind"—only in one direction. We would be permitting a State to "prescribe what shall be orthodox" by saying that one may burn the flag to convey one's attitude toward it and its referents only if one does not endanger the flag's representation of nationhood and national unity....

There is, moreover, no indication—either in the text of the Constitution or in our cases interpreting it—that a separate juridical category exists for the American flag alone. Indeed, we would not be surprised to learn that the persons who framed our Constitution and wrote the Amendment that we now construe were not known for their reverence for the Union Jack. The First Amendment does not guarantee that other concepts virtually sacred to our Nation as a whole—such as the principle that discrimination on the basis of race is odious and destructive—will go unquestioned in the marketplace of ideas. We decline, therefore, to create for the flag an exception to the joust of principles protected by the First Amendment....

We are fortified in today's conclusion by our conviction that forbidding criminal punishment for conduct such as Johnson's will not endanger the special role played by our flag or the feelings it inspires. To paraphrase Justice Holmes, we submit that nobody can suppose that this one gesture of an unknown man will change our Nation's attitude towards its flag. See *Abrams v. United States* (1919) (Holmes, J., dissenting). Indeed, Texas' argument that the burning of an American flag "'is an act having a high likelihood to cause a breach of the peace,'" and its statute's implicit assumption that physical mistreatment of the flag will lead to "serious offense," tend to confirm that the flag's special role is not in danger; if it were, no one would riot or take offense because a flag had been burned.

We are tempted to say, in fact, that the flag's deservedly cherished place in our community will be strengthened, not weakened, by our holding today. Our decision is a reaffirmation of the principles of freedom and inclusiveness that the flag best reflects, and of the conviction that our toleration of criticism such as Johnson's is a sign and source of our strength. Indeed, one of the proudest images of our flag, the one immortalized in our own national anthem, is of the bombardment it survived at Fort McHenry. It is the Nation's resilience, not its rigidity, that Texas sees reflected in the flag—and it is that resilience that we reassert today.

The way to preserve the flag's special role is not to punish those who feel differently about these matters. It is to persuade them that they are wrong.... And, precisely because it is our flag that is involved, one's response to the flag-burner may exploit the uniquely persuasive power of the flag itself. We can imagine no more appropriate response to burning a flag than waving one's own, no better way to counter a flag-burner's message than by saluting the flag that burns, no surer means of preserving the dignity even of the flag that burned than by—as one witness here did—according its remains a respectful burial. We do not consecrate the flag by punishing its desecration, for in doing so we dilute the freedom that this cherished emblem represents.

Johnson was convicted for engaging in expressive conduct. The State's interest in preventing breaches of the peace does not support his conviction because Johnson's conduct did not threaten to disturb the peace. Nor does the State's interest in preserving the flag as a symbol of nationhood and national unity justify his criminal conviction for engaging in political expression. The judgment of the Texas Court of Criminal Appeals is therefore

Affirmed.

JUSTICE KENNEDY, concurring.

I write not to qualify the words JUSTICE BRENNAN chooses so well, for he says with power all that is necessary to explain our ruling. I join his opinion without reservation, but with a keen sense that this case, like others before us from time to time, exacts its personal toll....

The hard fact is that sometimes we must make decisions we do not like. We make them because they are right, right in the sense that the law and the Constitution, as we see them, compel the result. And so great is our commitment to the process that, except in the rare case, we do not pause to express distaste for the result, perhaps for fear of undermining a valued principle that dictates the decision. This is one of those rare cases.

Our colleagues in dissent advance powerful arguments why respondent may be convicted for his expression, reminding us that among those who will be dismayed by our holding will be some who have had the singular honor of carrying the flag in battle. And I agree that the flag holds a lonely place of honor in an age when absolutes are distrusted and simple truths are burdened by unneeded apologetics.

With all respect to those views, I do not believe the Constitution gives us the right to rule as the dissenting members of the Court urge, however painful this judgment is to announce. Though symbols often are what we ourselves make of them, the flag is constant in expressing beliefs Americans share, beliefs in law and peace and that freedom which sustains the human spirit. The case here today forces recognition of the costs to which those beliefs commit us. It is poignant but fundamental that the flag protects those who hold it in contempt.

For all the record shows, this respondent was not a philosopher and perhaps did not even possess the ability to comprehend how repellent his statements must be to the Republic itself. But whether or not he could appreciate the enormity of the offense he gave, the fact remains that his acts were speech, in both the technical and the fundamental meaning of the Constitution. So I agree with the Court that he must go free.

CHIEF JUSTICE REHNQUIST, with whom JUSTICE WHITE and JUSTICE O'CONNOR join, dissenting.

In holding this Texas statute unconstitutional, the Court ignores Justice Holmes' familiar aphorism that "a page of history is worth a volume of logic." *New York Trust Co. v. Eisner* (1921). For more than 200 years, the American flag has occupied a unique position as the symbol of our Nation, a uniqueness that justifies a governmental prohibition against flag burning in the way respondent Johnson did here....

The American flag ... has come to be the visible symbol embodying our Nation. It does not represent the views of any particular political party, and it does not represent any particular political philosophy. The flag is not simply another "idea" or "point of view" competing for recognition in the marketplace of ideas. Millions and millions of Americans regard it with an almost mystical reverence regardless of what sort of social, political, or philosophical beliefs they may have. I cannot agree that the First Amendment invalidates the Act of Congress, and the laws of 48 of the 50 States, which make criminal the public burning of the flag....

... [T]he public burning of the American flag by Johnson was no essential part of any exposition of ideas, and at the same time it had a tendency to incite a breach of the peace. Johnson was free to make any verbal denunciation of the flag that he wished; indeed, he was free to burn the flag in private. He could publicly burn other symbols of the Government or effigies of political leaders. He did lead a march through the streets of Dallas, and conducted a rally in front of the Dallas City Hall. He engaged in a "die-in" to protest nuclear weapons. He shouted out various slogans during the march, including: "Reagan, Mondale which will it be? Either one means World War III"; "Ronald Reagan, killer of the hour, Perfect example of U.S. power"; and "red, white and blue, we spit on you, you stand for plunder, you will go under." For none of these acts was he arrested or prosecuted; it was only when he proceeded to burn publicly an American flag stolen from its rightful owner that he violated the Texas statute....

... The Texas statute deprived Johnson of only one rather inarticulate symbolic form of protest—a form of protest that was profoundly offensive to many—and left him with a full panoply of other symbols and every conceivable form of verbal expression to express his deep disapproval of national policy. Thus, in no way can it be said that Texas is punishing him because his hearers—or any other group of people—were profoundly opposed to the message that he sought to convey. Such opposition is no proper basis for restricting speech or expression under the First Amendment. It was Johnson's use of this particular symbol, and not the idea that he sought to convey by it or by his many other expressions, for which he was punished....

... Uncritical extension of constitutional protection to the burning of the flag risks the frustration of the very purpose for which organized governments are instituted. The Court decides that the American flag is just another symbol, about which not only must opinions pro and con be tolerated, but for which the most minimal public respect may not be enjoined. The government may conscript men into the Armed Forces where they must fight and perhaps die for the flag, but the government may not prohibit the public burning of the banner under which they fight. I would uphold the Texas statute as applied in this case.

The Court's decision in *Johnson* is intriguing for a number of reasons. Note, for example, the rather odd alignments: two of the more conservative members of the Rehnquist Court, Antonin Scalia and Anthony M. Kennedy, voted with the majority; John Paul Stevens, usually found with the liberal wing of the Court, dissented.

Perhaps most important was the tremendous—and to some, surprising—uproar created by the Court's ruling. President George Bush immediately condemned it, and public opinion polls indicated that Americans generally favored a constitutional amendment overturning *Johnson*. But, after some politicking by civil liberties groups, senators, and representatives, Congress did not propose an amendment. Instead, it passed the Flag Protection Act of 1989, which penalized by a one-year jail sentence and a $1,000 fine anyone who "knowingly mutilates, defaces, physically defiles, burns, maintains on the floor or ground, or tramples upon any flag of the United States."

Because the federal act differed from the Texas law at issue in *Johnson*—it banned flag desecration regardless of the motivation of the burner, whereas the Texas law did so only if a jury found the activity to be offensive—some thought it would meet approval in the Supreme Court. Others saw this difference as relatively insignificant, and, as it turned out, they were correct. In *United States v. Eichman* (1990) the Court, using the same reasoning expressed in *Johnson* and by the same vote, struck down this law as a violation of the First Amendment.

Public Forums and the Preservation of Order

So far, many of the cases we have examined involve individuals who—either through verbal or symbolic conduct—have tried to relay a "message": Eugene Debs's speech, Yetta Stromberg's red flag, and David O'Brien's draft-card burning were all forms of self-expression. However, "when those seeking to exercise rights of expression choose public forums, their activities move from the realm of 'pure speech' into an arena that creates new questions of restraint."[25] Why? Shouldn't the Court treat speech occurring in a public forum the same way it deals with other forms of expression?

The answer to this question depends on the effect such speech may have rather than with its content. In short, unlike Stromberg's flag raising, an essentially private form of expression, activities conducted in open forums can threaten the public order, causing others to engage in illegal behavior.

Preserving public order and protecting citizens from injury caused by violence are among the essential duties of government. The Preamble of the Constitution includes insuring "domestic Tranquility" among the six basic purposes for which the new government

25. Jerome R. Corsi and Matthew Ross Lippman, *Constitutional Law* (Englewood Cliffs, N.J.: Prentice-Hall, 1985), 298.

was formed. Yet, in some instances free expression can threaten order. Such a breakdown of order may take the form of bodily injury, property destruction, restricting the free movement of the public, or impeding the government from carrying out its duties. In such cases a conflict arises between the nation's commitment to freedom of expression and the government's duty to maintain order. At what point is government constitutionally justified in repressing expression in order to stop or prevent violence?

To deal with such expression, the justices have promulgated legal criteria distinct from those they use to adjudicate pure speech cases. The Court began to develop these standards in 1942 with *Chaplinsky v. New Hampshire*, but the majority of public order cases did not come to it until the 1960s and 1970s. As you read Justice Murphy's opinion in *Chaplinsky*, try to ascertain the legal standard he articulates and remember it as we look at the later Court decisions in these areas. Did Murphy's approach continue to permeate Court decisions of the civil rights and Vietnam War movements, or did the Court revise it to fit changing times?

Chaplinsky v. New Hampshire

315 U.S. 568 (1942)
Vote: 9 (Black, Byrnes, Douglas, Frankfurter, Jackson, Murphy, Reed, Roberts, Stone)

0

Opinion of the Court: Murphy

On April 6, 1940, Jehovah's Witness member Walter Chaplinsky was selling biblical pamphlets and literature, including *Watchtower* and *Consolation*, on a public street in New Hampshire. While he was announcing the sale of his pamphlets, a crowd began to gather. After one person tried to attack Chaplinsky, the rest joined in. When the police arrived and handcuffed a very agitated Chaplinsky, he demanded to know why they had arrested him and not the mob. An officer replied, "Shut up, you damn bastard," and

Chaplinsky in turn called the officer a "damned fascist and a God damned racketeer." For those words, the state charged him with breaking a law prohibiting the use of "any offensive, derisive, or annoying word to any other person who is lawfully in the street."

On appeal to the Supreme Court, Chaplinsky's attorneys asked it to overturn the state statute on free speech grounds, arguing that "the fact that speech is likely to cause violence is no grounds for suppressing it." The state countered that the law constituted a valid exercise of its police powers.

MR. JUSTICE MURPHY delivered the opinion of the Court.

Allowing the broadest scope to the language and purpose of the Fourteenth Amendment, it is well understood that the right of free speech is not absolute at all times and under all circumstances. There are certain well-defined and narrowly limited classes of speech, the prevention and punishment of which have never been thought to raise any Constitutional problem. These include the lewd and obscene, the profane, the libelous, and the insulting or "fighting" words—those which by their very utterance inflict injury or tend to incite an immediate breach of the peace. It has been well observed that such utterances are no essential part of any exposition of ideas, and are of such slight social value as a step to truth that any benefit that may be derived from them is clearly outweighed by the social interest in order and morality....

The state statute here challenged comes to us authoritatively construed by the highest court of New Hampshire. It has two provisions—the first relates to words or names addressed to another in a public place; the second refers to noises and exclamations. The court said: "the two provisions are distinct. One may stand separately from the other. Assuming, without holding, that the second were unconstitutional, the first could stand if constitutional." We accept that construction of severability and limit our consideration to the first provision of the statute.

On the authority of its earlier decisions, the state court declared that the state's purpose was to preserve the public peace, no words being "forbidden except such as have a direct tendency to cause acts of violence by the persons to whom, individually, the remark is addressed." It was further said: "The word 'offensive' is not to be defined in terms of what a particular addressee thinks.... The test is what men of common intelligence would understand would be words likely to cause an average addressee to fight.... The English language has a number of words and expressions which by general consent are 'fighting words' when said without a disarming smile.... Such words, as ordinary men know, are likely to cause a fight. So are threatening, profane or obscene revilings. Derisive and annoying words can be taken as coming within the purview of the statute as heretofore interpreted only when they have this characteristic of plainly tending to excite the addressee to a breach of the peace.... The statute, as construed, does no more than prohibit the face-to-face words plainly likely to cause a breach of the peace by the addressee, words whose speaking constitutes a breach of the peace by the speaker— including 'classical fighting words,' words in current use less 'classical' but equally likely to cause violence, and other disorderly words, including profanity, obscenity and threats."

We are unable to say that the limited scope of the statute as thus construed contravenes the Constitutional right of free expression. It is a statute narrowly drawn and limited to define and punish specific conduct lying within the domain of state power, the use in a public place of words likely to cause a breach of the peace.

In unanimously affirming Chaplinsky's conviction, the Court agreed with Murphy's enunciation of the so-called Fighting Words doctrine: expressions, "as ordinary men know, which are likely to cause a fight" may be prohibited. But, would its apparent agreement over this doctrine stand the test of time? Or would it unravel, as did the unanimity surrounding *Schenck*'s Clear and Present Danger standard? Two cases, *Terminiello v. Chicago* (1949) and *Feiner v. New York* (1951) provide us with partial, but perhaps contradictory, answers to those questions. As you read about them, consider not only the Court's rationale and use of the *Chaplinsky* doctrine, but also the differences between the two cases. Why did the justices reach different conclusions in cases presenting similar situations?

Arthur Terminiello, a Catholic priest, was scheduled to give a speech in Chicago. Terminiello was widely regarded as a racist, anti-Semitic, anti-New Deal communist-hunter, who would cause turmoil wherever he spoke. At the Chicago auditorium where he was booked, Terminiello found a crowd of more than 1,000 gathered outside to oppose his views; in fact, some of the 800 individuals inside the auditorium felt the same. This hostility did not deter him. True to his reputation, Terminiello played with the angry mob by giving a particularly virulent speech. Among his statements were:

And nothing I say tonight could begin to express the contempt I have for the slimy scum that got in by mistake.... The subject I want to talk to you tonight about is the attempt that is going on outside this hall ... to destroy America by revolutions.

The tide is changing ... and if you and I turn and run ... we will all be drowned in this tidal wave of communism.

We have fifty-seven varieties of pink and reds and pastel shades in this country; and all of it can be traced to the twelve years we spent in the New Deal.

Now this danger that we face—let us call them Zionist Jews.... Do you wonder they were persecuted in other countries in the world.

As Terminiello spoke, the people outside grew increasingly hostile. They began to scream, calling him a fascist, and they threw rocks and stones, resulting in seventeen arrests. Eventually, authorities also arrested Terminiello, citing him with a violation of a city ordinance: "All persons who shall make, aid ... [in] any improper voice, riot or disturbance, breach of peace, or diversion tending to a breach of peace ... shall be deemed guilty of disorderly conduct." Terminiello appealed his conviction to the Supreme Court, arguing that such breach of peace ordinances violated his First Amendment freedom of speech guarantee. The state countered, noting that the ordinance fell squarely within the bounds of the Fighting Words doctrine.

Writing for the Court in its 5–4 decision, Justice Douglas rejected the state's position, but on a technicality. He noted:

The argument has been focused on the issue of whether the content of [Terminiello's] speech was composed of "fighting words."... We do not reach that question for there is a preliminary question that is dispositive of the case.

That question, in Douglas's view, involved the instructions the court gave to the jury. In his charge, the trial court judge defined "breach of the peace" to include speech that "stirs the public to anger, invites dispute, brings about a condition of unrest, or creates a disturbance." Douglas took issue with the charge:

Speech is often provocative and challenging. It may strike at prejudices and preconceptions and have profound unsettling effects.... That is why freedom of speech, though not absolute, is nevertheless protected against censorship ... unless shown likely to produce a clear and present danger ... that arises far above public inconvenience, annoyance, or unrest.

Douglas found that the "ordinance as construed by the trial court seriously invaded" free speech guarantees. "It permitted conviction of petitioner if his speech stirred people to anger, invited public dispute, or brought about a condition of unrest. A conviction resting on any of those grounds may not stand."

The second case, *Feiner v. New York,* began in 1949, when the City of Syracuse, New York, issued a permit to the Young Progressives, allowing O. John Rogge, a former assistant attorney general, to speak at a local auditorium. Several days later, the city canceled the permit. Protesting this development, Irving Feiner, a member of the Young Progressives, addressed a crowd of seventy-five blacks and whites outside the auditorium where Rogge was to have spoken. The police were called to investigate complaints about the noise. They found Feiner standing on top of a box and using a microphone to make "derogatory remarks concerning President Truman, the American Legion, and the Mayor of Syracuse." But police made no attempt to arrest Feiner until he began making statements concerning race; according to eye witnesses, he implied that blacks should rise up against whites. Because such comments "stirred up" the racially mixed crowd, and threats of violence were made, police arrested Feiner under a breach of peace ordinance.

Writing for the majority in the 6–3 decision, Chief Justice Vinson upheld the conviction. He noted, "It is one thing to say that police cannot be used as an instrument for the oppression of unpopular views, and another to say that, when as here the speaker passes the bounds of argument or persuasion and undertakes incitement to riot, they are powerless to prevent a breach of the peace."

Feiner and *Terminiello* raised similar issues but evoked wholly different reactions from the Court. In fact, it is somewhat ironic that the justices reversed Terminiello's conviction and upheld Feiner's, given that the former's speech actually created public disorder, while the latter's held only the "imminence of greater disorder."

At this point, the Court seemed to agree that the Fighting Words doctrine provided a reasonable framework by which to decide public order cases. What divided the justices was the appropriate interpretation of that doctrine. During the 1960s the issue took on particular urgency because, as we have seen, the convergence of the civil rights and Vietnam War protest movements produced new expression cases, many of which centered on issues of public order. Would the Court use the *Chaplinsky* doctrine to resolve cases arising out of those movements—for example, convictions resulting from mass demonstrations on college campuses and state capitols and other government buildings, sit-ins on public and private property, and protest rallies? Or, given the novelty of the times, would it seek to handle them in novel ways? These questions dominated many of the Court's expression cases, beginning in 1963 with *Edwards v. South Carolina*. While reading this case, keep in mind the Court's

decisions in *Terminiello* and *Feiner*: To which did the justices lean in *Edwards*?

Edwards v. South Carolina

372 U.S. 229 (1963)
Vote: 8 (Black, Brennan, Douglas, Goldberg, Harlan,
       Stewart, Warren, White)
    1 (Clark)
Opinion of the Court: Stewart
Dissenting opinion: Clark

On March 2, 1961, a group of black high school and college students met at a Baptist Church in Columbia, South Carolina. At noon they walked toward the state capitol building "to submit a protest to the citizens of South Carolina to show their feelings and dissatisfaction with the present condition of discriminatory actions against Negroes." By marching on the state capitol, these students used a strategy that would become symbolic of the civil rights movement. When they arrived, thirty law enforcement officers were on hand to greet them. The officers told the protesters they could go onto the capitol grounds as long as they were peaceful. For the next hour, the group walked in an orderly fashion, carrying signs with messages such as "I Am Proud to be a Negro." In time, a peaceful, nonobstructive crowd of 200 to 300 gathered. Although no violence appeared imminent, the officers told the demonstrators to disperse within five minutes or face arrest. "Instead ... they engaged in what the City Manager described as 'boisterous,' 'loud,' and 'flamboyant' conduct": they held hands and sang, "I shall not be moved." Police eventually arrested 187 of the protesters, and they were convicted under a state breach of peace law.

On appeal to the Supreme Court, attorney for the protesters, Jack Greenberg of the NAACP Legal Defense Fund, stressed the fact that no violence occurred or was ever likely to occur. The state pointed to the *Feiner* precedent.

MR. JUSTICE STEWART delivered the opinion of the Court.

It is clear to us that in arresting, convicting, and punishing the petitioners under the circumstances disclosed by this record, South Carolina infringed the petitioners' constitutionally protected rights of free speech, free assembly, and freedom to petition for redress of their grievances.

It has long been established that these First Amendment freedoms are protected by the Fourteenth Amendment from invasion by the States. The circumstances in this case reflect an exercise of these basic constitutional rights in their most pristine and classic form. The petitioners felt aggrieved by laws of South Carolina which allegedly "prohibited Negro privileges in this State." They peaceably assembled at the site of the State Government and there peaceably expressed their grievances "to the citizens of South Carolina, along with the Legislative Bodies of South Carolina." Not until they were told by police officials that they must disperse on pain of arrest did they do more. Even then, they but sang patriotic and religious songs after one of their leaders had delivered a "religious harangue." There was no violence or threat of violence on their part, or on the part of any member of the crowd watching them. Police protection was "ample."

This, therefore, was a far cry from the situation in Feiner v. New York, where two policemen were faced with a crowd which was "pushing, shoving and milling around," where at least one member of the crowd "threatened violence if the police did not act," where "the crowd was pressing closer around petitioner and the officer," and where "the speaker passes the bounds of argument or persuasion and undertakes incitement to riot." And the record is barren of any evidence of "fighting words." See Chaplinsky v. New Hampshire.

We do not review in this case criminal convictions resulting from the evenhanded application of a precise and narrowly drawn regulatory statute evincing a legislative judgment that certain specific conduct be limited or proscribed. If, for example, the petitioners had been convicted upon evidence that they had violated a law regulating traffic, or had disobeyed a law reasonably limiting the periods during which the State House grounds were open to the public, this would be a different case. These petitioners

were convicted of an offense so generalized as to be, in the words of the South Carolina Supreme Court, "not susceptible of exact definition." And they were convicted upon evidence which showed no more than that the opinions which they were peaceably expressing were sufficiently opposed to the views of the majority of the community to attract a crowd and necessitate police protection.

The Fourteenth Amendment does not permit a State to make criminal the peaceful expression of unpopular views. "[A] function of free speech under our system of government is to invite dispute. It may indeed best serve its high purpose when it induces a condition of unrest, creates dissatisfaction with conditions as they are, or even stirs people to anger. Speech is often provocative and challenging. It may strike at prejudices and preconceptions and have profound unsettling effects as it presses for acceptance of an idea. That is why freedom of speech ... is ... protected against censorship or punishment, unless shown likely to produce a clear and present danger of a serious substantive evil that rises far above public inconvenience, annoyance, or unrest.... There is no room under our Constitution for a more restrictive view. For the alternative would lead to standardization of ideas either by legislatures, courts, or dominant political or community groups." Terminiello v. Chicago. As in the Terminiello case, the courts of South Carolina have defined a criminal offense so as to permit conviction of the petitioners if their speech "stirred people to anger, invited public dispute, or brought about a condition of unrest. A conviction resting on any of those grounds may not stand."

As Chief Justice Hughes wrote in Stromberg v. California, "The maintenance of the opportunity for free political discussion to the end that government may be responsive to the will of the people and that changes may be obtained by lawful means, an opportunity essential to the security of the Republic, is a fundamental principle of our constitutional system. A statute which upon its face, and as authoritatively construed, is so vague and indefinite as to permit the punishment of the fair use of this opportunity is repugnant to the guaranty of liberty contained in the Fourteenth Amendment...."

For these reasons we conclude that these criminal convictions cannot stand.

Reversed.

In the years between *Feiner* and *Edwards*, the Court seemed to return to a *Terminiello* approach to public order issues; it overturned convictions but announced no new doctrine. Compare Douglas's opinion there with the majority view in *Edwards*, and note that Justice Stewart borrowed Douglas's words, which in turn had been influenced by Holmes's opinion in *Schenck*. In fact, only Justice Clark seemed to view *Feiner* as controlling precedent, claiming that the possibility of a "public brawl" certainly existed. Based on the Court's decision in *Edwards*, what is required for the lawful suppression of speech in public forums? One criterion clearly is the presence of real violence or a threat of violence.

Would this requirement remain viable or would the growth of the various protest movements force the Court back to its position in *Feiner*? In two 1965 cases emanating from the same event, *Cox v. Louisiana I and II*, a divided Court tried to ferret out further doctrine in this area. As you read about these cases, consider how they square with the original case in this area, *Chaplinsky v. New Hampshire*. Also, remember the social environment: by 1965 the protest movements had gained momentum and strength.

Cox I and *II* began when, as part of a general protest against racial discrimination in the South, the Congress of Racial Equality (CORE) recommended a boycott of stores with segregated lunch counters. On December 14, 1961, authorities in Baton Rouge, Louisiana, arrested twenty-three black students for picketing such stores. That same evening, B. Elton Cox, field secretary of CORE and an ordained minister, spoke at a mass meeting at Southern University, one of the country's historically black colleges. The students agreed to hold a demonstration the next day protesting segregationist policies and the arrest of the picketers.

The next morning 2,000 students, led by Cox, walked from the campus to the old State Capitol, two and a half blocks from the courthouse. As they assembled, police asked Cox why they were there, and he replied that they were protesting "the illegal arrest of some of their people who were being held in jail." Cox then led the group to the courthouse where they sang songs, but maintained order. The police questioned Cox a second time. Cox said his agenda included a peaceful protest and the singing of certain patriotic songs. An officer told Cox they could proceed as long as they stayed on the sidewalk across the street from the courthouse, approximately 125 feet away from the building. Cox complied, but a crowd of 100 to 300 curious white people, mostly court personnel, gathered to watch the activities, which included singing and the holding of signs, some of which read, "Don't buy discrimination for X-Mas."

At noon Cox obtained a microphone and made the following statement:

All right. It's lunchtime. Let's go eat. There are twelve stores we are protesting. A number of the stores have twenty counters; they accept your money from nineteen. They won't accept it from the twentieth counter. This is an act of racial discrimination. These stores are open to the public. You are members of the public.

Perceiving that Cox's speech would wreak havoc in the city, a sheriff took the microphone and said:

Now you have been allowed to demonstrate. Up until now your demonstration has been more or less peaceful, but what you are doing now is a direct violation of the law … and it has to be broken up immediately.

When the demonstrators failed to heed the warning, police exploded tear gas, which caused the group to disperse. The next day police arrested Cox for violating three state laws: disturbing the peace, obstructing public passage, and interfering with the administration of justice.

In *Cox I* the Court dealt with the validity and applicability of the first two laws; in *Cox II* it scrutinized the last. On the first, the breach of peace violation, Justice Arthur Goldberg, for the majority, compared this case to *Edwards*, saying that "the facts [were] strikingly similar." He used the *Edwards* rationale to find the statute unconstitutional:

[As] in Terminiello and Edwards the conviction under this statute must be reversed as the statute is unconstitutional in that it sweeps within its broad scope activities that are constitutionally protected free speech and assembly. Maintenance of the opportunity for free political discussion is a basic tenet of our constitutional democracy.

Goldberg also reversed Cox's conviction for obstructing public passage, but on somewhat different grounds. Although he agreed with the state that it may regulate the "time, place, duration, or manner of use" of public streets, he took issue with the way the statute was enforced. As he noted, it gave city officials far too much discretion to determine who could conduct parades or hold street meetings.

It is clearly unconstitutional to enable a public official to determine which expressions of view will be permitted and which will not or to engage in invidious discrimination among persons or groups either by use of a statute providing a system of broad discretionary licensing power or ... the equivalent of such a system by selective enforcement of an extremely broad prohibitory statute.

In *Cox II* Goldberg scrutinized the state's law on impeding the administration of justice. The statute was not constitutionally defective because "there can be no question that a state has a legitimate interest in protecting its judicial system from the pressures which picketing near a courthouse might create." But he found that its application to the circumstances here violated Cox's rights: he was "convicted for demonstrating not 'in,' but 'near' the courthouse."

In *Cox I* the majority reverted to the *Edwards* interpretation of *Chaplinsky*: no violence or threat of violence arose. Nor did Cox utter any fighting words. But Goldberg also asserts in *Cox II* that localities have a "legitimate interest in protecting" their judicial systems. And, even though several factors nullify the application of the law to the Southern University demonstrators, Goldberg is clear in holding that this does not imply that "police cannot call a halt to a meeting which originally peaceful, becomes violent. Nor does it mean that ... authorities cannot set reasonable

time limits for assemblies ... and then order them dispersed."

This ruling is important because the justices once again reiterate that political expression affecting the public order is not limitless, a point reinforced even more clearly in *Adderley v. Florida* (1966). How does the Court's holding in *Adderley* mesh with Goldberg's remarks in *Cox*? Think about Black's majority opinion and Douglas's dissenting view. This case is one of the few in which the two disagree. Why did they?

Adderley v. Florida

385 U.S. 39 (1966)
Vote: 5 (Black, Clark, Harlan, Stewart, White)
    4 (Brennan, Douglas, Fortas, Warren)
Opinion of the Court: Black
Dissenting opinion: Douglas

Protesting the arrest of several schoolmates, Harriett Adderley and some 200 other Florida A & M students marched from the university to the county jail. The group assembled outside the jailhouse door entrance and engaged in singing, clapping, and dancing to express their opposition to the county's segregationist policies. A deputy sheriff asked them to move back, claiming that they were blocking the entrance to the jail. The students partially complied by moving away from the door, but not pulling back as far as the deputy requested. In their new location the students blocked a driveway used for the delivery of goods and services and the transportation of inmates. The sheriff then told the students that because they were trespassing on jail property they would be arrested if they did not disperse within ten minutes. Some of the protesters complied, but most remained. After a second warning, the sheriff arrested 107 students for trespass. Following a jury trial the court convicted Adderley and thirty-one fellow demonstrators of "trespass with a malicious and mischievous intent."

MR. JUSTICE BLACK delivered the opinion of the Court.

Petitioners have insisted from the beginning of this case that it is controlled by and must be reversed because of our prior cases of Edwards v. South Carolina and Cox v. State of Louisiana. We cannot agree.

The *Edwards* case, like this one, did come up when a number of persons demonstrated on public property against their State's segregation policies. They also sang hymns and danced, as did the demonstrators in this case. But here the analogies to this case end. In *Edwards*, the demonstrators went to the South Carolina State Capitol grounds to protest. In this case they went to the jail. Traditionally, state capitol grounds are open to the public. Jails, built for security purposes, are not. The demonstrators at the South Carolina Capitol went in through a public driveway and as they entered they were told by state officials there that they had a right as citizens to go through the State House grounds as long as they were peaceful. Here the demonstrators entered the jail grounds through a driveway used only for jail purposes and without warning to or permission from the sheriff. More importantly, South Carolina sought to prosecute its State Capitol demonstrators by charging them with the common-law crime of breach of the peace. This Court in *Edwards* took pains to point out at length the indefinite, loose, and broad nature of this charge; indeed, this Court pointed out that the South Carolina Supreme Court had itself declared that the "breach of the peace" charge is "not susceptible of exact definition." South Carolina's power to prosecute, it was emphasized, would have been different had the State proceeded under a "precise and narrowly drawn regulatory statute evincing a legislative judgment that certain specific conduct be limited or proscribed" such as, for example, "limiting the periods during which the State House grounds were open to the public...." The South Carolina breach-of-the-peace statute was thus struck down as being so broad and all-embracing as to jeopardize speech, press, assembly and petition, under the constitutional doctrine ... of vagueness....

The Florida trespass statute under which these petitioners were charged cannot be challenged on this ground. It is aimed at conduct of one limited kind, that is, for one person or persons to trespass upon the property of another with a malicious and mischievous intent. There is no lack of notice in this law, nothing to entrap or fool the unwary.

Petitioners seem to argue that the Florida trespass law is void for vagueness because it requires a trespass to be "with a malicious and mischievous intent...." But these words do not broaden the scope of trespass so as to make it cover a multitude of types of conduct as does the common-law breach-of-the-peace charge. On the contrary, these words narrow the scope of the offense....

... Nothing in the Constitution of the United States prevents Florida from even-handed enforcement of its general trespass statute against those refusing to obey the sheriff's order to remove themselves from what amounted to the curtilage [legal term referring to the area immediately surrounding a house and regularly used by its occupants] of the jailhouse. The State, no less than a private owner of property, has power to preserve the property under its control for the use to which it is lawfully dedicated. For this reason there is no merit to the petitioners' argument that they had a constitutional right to stay on the property, over the jail custodian's objections, because this "area chosen for the peaceful civil rights demonstration was not only 'reasonable' but also particularly appropriate...." Such an argument has as its major unarticulated premise the assumption that people who want to propagandize protests or views have a constitutional right to do so whenever and however and wherever they please. That concept of constitutional law was vigorously and forthrightfully rejected in two of the cases petitioners rely on, *Cox v. Louisiana* [I and II]. We reject it again. The United States Constitution does not forbid a State to control the use of its own property for its own lawful nondiscriminatory purpose.

These judgments are

Affirmed.

MR. JUSTICE DOUGLAS, with whom THE CHIEF JUSTICE, MR. JUSTICE BRENNAN, and MR. JUSTICE FORTAS concur, dissenting.

The First Amendment, applicable to the States by reason of the Fourteenth ... provides that "Congress shall make no law ... abridging ... the right of the people peaceably to assemble, and to petition the Government for a redress of grievances."... With all respect ... the Court errs in treating the case as if it were an ordinary trespass case or an ordinary picketing case.

The jailhouse, like an executive mansion, a legislative chamber, a courthouse, or the statehouse itself (Edwards v. South Carolina) is one of the seats of governments whether it be the Tower of London, the Bastille, or a small county jail. And when it houses political prisoners or those who many think are unjustly held, it is an obvious center for protest. The right to petition for the redress of grievances has an ancient history and is not limited to writing a letter or sending a telegram to a congressman; it is not confined to appearing before the local city council, or writing letters to the President or Governor or Mayor. Conventional methods of petitioning may be, and often have been, shut off to large groups of our citizens. Legislators may turn deaf ears; normal complaints may be routed endlessly through a bureaucratic maze; courts may let the wheels of justice grind very slowly. Those who do not control television and radio, those who cannot afford to advertise in newspapers or circulate elaborate pamphlets may have only a more limited type of access to public officials. Their methods should not be condemned as tactics of obstruction and harassment as long as the assembly and petition are peaceable, as these were....

We do violence to the First Amendment when we permit this "petition for redress of grievances" to be turned into a trespass action. It does not help to analogize this problem to the problem of picketing. Picketing is a form of protest usually directed against private interests. I do not see how rules governing picketing in general are relevant to this express constitutional right to assemble and to petition for redress of grievances. In the first place the jailhouse grounds were not marked with "NO TRESPASSING!" signs, nor does respondent claim that the public was generally excluded from the grounds. Only the sheriff's fiat transformed lawful conduct into an unlawful trespass. To say that a private owner could have done the same if the rally had taken place on private property is to speak of a different case, as an assembly and a petition for redress of grievances run to government, not to private proprietors....

There may be some public places which are so clearly committed to other purposes that their use for the airing of grievances is anomalous. There may be some instances in which assemblies and petitions for redress of grievances are not consistent with other necessary purposes of public property. A noisy meeting may be out of keeping with the serenity of the statehouse or the quiet of the courthouse. No one, for example, would suggest that the Senate gallery is the proper place for a vociferous protest rally. And in other cases it may be necessary to adjust the right to petition for redress of grievances to the other interests inhering in the uses to which the public property is normally put. But this is quite different from saying that all public places are off limits to people with grievances. And it is farther yet from saying that the "custodian" of the public property in his discretion can decide when public places shall be used for the communication of ideas, especially the constitutional right to assemble and petition for redress of grievances. For to place such discretion in any public official, be he the "custodian" of the public property or the local police commissioner, is to place those who assert their First Amendment rights at his mercy. It gives him the awesome power to decide whose ideas may be expressed and who shall be denied a place to air their claims and petition their government. Such power is out of step with all our decisions prior to today where we have insisted that before a First Amendment right may be curtailed under the guise of a criminal law, any evil that may be collateral to the exercise of the right, must be isolated and defined in a "narrowly drawn" statute lest the power to control excesses of conduct be used to suppress the constitutional right itself.

That tragic consequence happens today when a trespass law is used to bludgeon those who peacefully exercise a First Amendment right to protest to government against one of the most grievous of all modern oppressions which some of our States are inflicting on our citizens....

Today a trespass law is used to penalize people for exercising a constitutional right. Tomorrow a disorderly conduct statute, a breach-of-the-peace statute, a vagrancy statute will be put to the same end. It is said that the sheriff did not make the arrests because of the views which petitioners espoused. That excuse is usually given, as we know from the many cases involving arrests of minority groups for breaches of the peace, unlawful assemblies, and parading without a permit. The charge against William Penn, who preached a nonconformist doctrine in a street in

London, was that he caused "a great concourse and tumult of people" in contempt of the King and "to the great disturbance of his peace." That was in 1670. In modern times, also, such arrests are usually sought to be justified by some legitimate function of government. Yet by allowing these orderly and civilized protests against injustice to be suppressed, we only increase the forces of frustration which the conditions of second-class citizenship are generating amongst us.

In his majority opinion Black highlighted several conditions under which government may constitutionally restrict expression. First, he emphasized the reasonable regulation of place. According to Black, the jailhouse is a facility that places a high priority on security. It is reasonable, he concluded, to enforce a trespass statute against demonstrators whose presence might compromise that security. Second, when the protesters initially crowded around the entrance, they were impeding the free movement of those who might have legitimate business at the jailhouse. Consequently, the sheriff's department acted within its authority in asking the students to move away from the doorway. Third, when the students relocated they blocked a driveway used for jailhouse business. For the majority this action placed a burden on legitimate government activity.

Douglas and the other dissenters would have no part of this thinking. For them the protest was a reasonable exercise of the right to speak and assemble. The demonstrators came to the agency of government with which they had complaints and constitutionally petitioned for a redress of those grievances. The dissenters concluded that such an exercise of political expression merits First Amendment protection.

Regardless of the interesting debate between Black and Douglas, the law emerging from *Edwards, Cox,* and *Adderley* largely governed the public order cases that were to follow. The justices generally applied the Fighting Words doctrine to adjudicate such claims unless the expressive conduct infringed on a legiti-

mate government activity. In other words, time, place, and manner considerations make a difference.

Clark v. Community for Creative Non-Violence (1984) presents another example of the time, place, and manner principle. This dispute arose when the Community for Creative Non-Violence (CCNV) sought a permit to hold a demonstration in Washington, D.C., on behalf of the homeless. They wanted to use both Lafayette Park and the Mall as locations for their activities. The park is directly across the street from the White House, and the mall stretches for two miles between the Capitol and the Lincoln Memorial, where Martin Luther King, Jr., gave his "I Have a Dream" speech. Like all other federal parks, these two are regulated by the National Park Service. Any person wishing to use the property must receive authorization from the service.

In 1982 CCNV asked the Park Service to permit it to (1) hold a demonstration on the park and Mall grounds; (2) erect two tent cities to symbolize the plight of the homeless; and (3) allow demonstrators to sleep in the sixty tents it planned to erect. When the Park Service denied the request for people to stay overnight in the parks, CCNV filed suit, claiming that the action violated its First Amendment guarantees.

Writing for the Court, Justice White upheld the Park Service's judgment:

Expression, whether oral or written or symbolized by conduct, is subject to reasonable time, place or manner restrictions. We have often noted that restrictions of this kind are valid provided that they are justified without reference to the content of the regulated speech, that they are narrowly tailored to serve a significant governmental interest, and that they leave open ample alternative channels for communication of the information.…

We have difficulty, therefore, in understanding why the prohibition against camping, with its ban on sleeping overnight, is not a reasonable time, place, or manner regulation that withstands constitutional scrutiny. Surely the regulation is not unconstitutional on its face. None of its provisions appears unrelated to the ends that it was designed to

Mass demonstrations were an important element in the civil rights movement during the 1960s. A huge crowd attended a 1963 demonstration in front of the Washington Monument.

serve. Nor is it any less valid when applied to prevent camping ... by those who wish to demonstrate and deliver a message to the public and the central Government. Damage to the parks as well as their partial inaccessibility to other members of the public can as easily result from camping by demonstrators as nondemonstrators. In neither case must the Government tolerate it.

Clark involved a clearly public arena, a federal park; even so, the Court disallowed its use for camping. It is not surprising to find the justices even less inclined to uphold speech claims occurring in more private forums. For example, unless a state, through its constitution or legislation, expands individual liberties, the First Amendment does not guarantee the right to engage in demonstrations at privately owned shopping centers.

Cases such as *Edwards, Cox, Adderley,* and *Clark* represent typical public forum disputes. Each involves large numbers of people collectively expressing their political opinions by assembling in a public place. Such gatherings are of concern to local officials who are responsible for maintaining public order and protecting public and private property. When large demonstrations also involve the communication of unpopular political views, the potential for disruption increases.

Not all public forum cases, however, involve mass demonstrations with parades, singing, and speeches.

Sometimes, a small group, or even a single individual, uses public property as a place of political protest. Occasionally such expression occurs quite silently. *Cohen v. California* (1971) is one such case. Here the justices examined the use of a county courthouse as a forum for expression. While reading *Cohen,* consider these questions: Did the justices apply previous precedents? Or was *Cohen* sufficiently different from *Edwards, Cox,* and *Adderley* that it required the Court to reexamine law governing public forum expression?

Cohen v. California

403 U.S. 15 (1971)
Vote: 5 (Brennan, Douglas, Harlan, Marshall, Stewart)
    4 (Black, Blackmun, Burger, White)
Opinion of the Court: Harlan
Dissenting opinion: Blackmun

In April 1968, at the height of the protest against the Vietnam War, Paul Cohen visited some friends in Los Angeles, his hometown.[26] While they were discussing their opposition to the war, someone scrawled on Cohen's jacket the words *Fuck the Draft* and *Stop the War.* The following morning, Cohen wore his jacket in the corridors of a Los Angeles county courthouse, knowing it bore these messages.

Although Cohen took off the jacket before entering the courtroom, a police sergeant had observed it in the corridor. The officer asked the judge to cite Cohen for contempt of court. The judge refused, but the officer arrested Cohen, charging him with "willfully and unlawfully and maliciously disturbing the peace and quiet by engaging in tumultuous and offensive conduct."

Given the nature of Cohen's alleged offense, this case could have ended where it started, in a California trial court. Clearly, it does not approach the importance of the cases we have already examined: no

26. For an in-depth account of this case, see Richard C. Cortner, *The Supreme Court and Civil Liberties Policy* (Palo Alto, Calif.: Mayfield, 1975).

violence occurred nor were large groups of people or spectators involved. But that was not to be. By the time of Cohen's trial in September, his "cause attracted rather significant support."[27] The ACLU's Southern California affiliate decided that Cohen's case presented a significant issue—that the message on his jacket represented a form of protected, albeit symbolic, expression—so significant an issue, in fact, that it offered to finance Cohen's case.

The ACLU took Cohen's case all the way to the Supreme Court. Before it arrived at the Court, however, three other judicial bodies had examined the case, reaching diverse conclusions. The trial court judge ruled that the words on Cohen's jacket constituted obscenity; a California appellate court reversed, claiming that Cohen's conduct, while "reprehensible," was "quiet and peaceful"; and a third California court ruled that Cohen's behavior constituted fighting words and as such "went beyond the permissive ambit of the First Amendment's protection."

By the time this case reached the Court, it could no longer be described as "simple." Because of the efforts of the ACLU and the diverse rulings from the California state courts, Cohen's case became a significant vehicle for testing First Amendment interpretations.[28]

MR. JUSTICE HARLAN delivered the opinion of the Court.

In order to lay hands on the precise issue which this case involves, it is useful first to canvass various matters which this record does *not* present.

The conviction quite clearly rests upon the asserted offensiveness of the *words* Cohen used to convey his message

27. Ibid., 124.
28. In addition to its significant constitutional ramifications, *Cohen* also provides a unique opportunity to view intra-organizational politics. As Cortner reports, the Southern California affiliate of the ACLU, the group sponsoring the case, always felt the "key issue ... and the one that arguments before the Court should focus on was the free expression issue." At the Supreme Court level, however, the ACLU's Northern California affiliate "urged the Court not to decide the case on the freedom of expression issue." The Southern California affiliate refused to give its consent to the filing of the brief. So the Court did it. See ibid., 128–129.

to the public. The only "conduct" which the State sought to punish is the fact of communication. Thus, we deal here with a conviction resting solely upon "speech," Stromberg v. California (1931), not upon any separately identifiable conduct which allegedly was intended by Cohen to be perceived by others as expressive of particular views but which, on its face, does not necessarily convey any message and hence arguably could be regulated without effectively repressing Cohen's ability to express himself. Further, the State certainly lacks power to punish Cohen for the underlying content of the message the inscription conveyed. At least so long as there is no showing of an intent to incite disobedience to or disruption of the draft, Cohen could not, consistently with the First and Fourteenth Amendments, be punished for asserting the evident position on the inutility or immorality of the draft his jacket reflected. Yates v. United States.

Appellant's conviction, then, rests squarely upon his exercise of the "freedom of speech" protected from arbitrary governmental interference by the Constitution and can be justified, if at all, only as a valid regulation of the manner in which he exercised that freedom, not as a permissible prohibition on the substantive message it conveys. This does not end the inquiry, of course, for the First and Fourteenth Amendments have never been thought to give absolute protection to every individual to speak whenever or wherever he pleases or to use any form of address in any circumstances that he chooses. In this vein, too, however, we think it important to note that several issues typically associated with such problems are not presented here.

In the first place, Cohen was tried under a statute applicable throughout the entire State. Any attempt to support this conviction on the ground that the statute seeks to preserve an appropriately decorous atmosphere in the courthouse where Cohen was arrested must fail in the absence of any language in the statute that would have put appellant on notice that certain kinds of otherwise permissible speech or conduct would nevertheless, under California law, not be tolerated in certain places. No fair reading of the phrase "offensive conduct" can be said sufficiently to inform the ordinary person that distinctions between certain locations are thereby created.

In the second place, as it comes to us, this case cannot be said to fall within those relatively few categories of in-

stances where prior decisions have established the power of government to deal more comprehensively with certain forms of individual expression simply upon a showing that such a form was employed. This is not, for example, an obscenity case. Whatever else may be necessary to give rise to the States' broader power to prohibit obscene expression, such expression must be, in some significant way, erotic. It cannot plausibly be maintained that this vulgar allusion to the Selective Service System would conjure up such psychic stimulation in anyone likely to be confronted with Cohen's crudely defaced jacket.

This Court has also held that the States are free to ban the simple use, without a demonstration of additional justifying circumstances, of so-called "fighting words," those personally abusive epithets which, when addressed to the ordinary citizens, are, as a matter of common knowledge, inherently likely to provoke violent reaction. Chaplinsky v. New Hampshire (1942). While the four-letter word displayed by Cohen in relation to the draft is not uncommonly employed in a personally provocative fashion, in this instance it was clearly not "directed to the person of the hearer." Cantwell v. Connecticut (1940). No individual actually or likely to be present could reasonably have regarded the words on appellant's jacket as a direct personal insult. Nor do we have here an instance of the exercise of the State's police power to prevent a speaker from intentionally provoking a given group to hostile reaction. Feiner v. New York (1951); Terminiello v. Chicago (1949). There is, as noted above, no showing that anyone who saw Cohen was in fact violently aroused or that appellant intended such a result.

Finally, in arguments before this Court much has been made of the claim that Cohen's distasteful mode of expression was thrust upon unwilling or unsuspecting viewers, and that the State might therefore legitimately act as it did in order to protect the sensitive from otherwise unavoidable exposure to appellant's crude form of protest. Of course, the mere presumed presence of unwitting listeners or viewers does not serve automatically to justify curtailing all speech capable of giving offense. While this Court has recognized that government may properly act in many situations to prohibit intrusion into the privacy of the home of unwelcome views and ideas which cannot be totally banned from the public dialogue, we have at the same time consistently stressed that "we are often 'captives' outside the sanctuary of the home and subject to objectionable speech." The ability of government, consonant with the Constitution, to shut off discourse solely to protect others from hearing it is, in other words, dependent upon a showing that substantial privacy interests are being invaded in an essentially intolerable manner. Any broader view of this authority would effectively empower a majority to silence dissidents simply as a matter of personal predilections.

In this regard, persons confronted with Cohen's jacket were in a quite different posture than, say, those subjected to the raucous emissions of sound trucks blaring outside their residences. Those in the Los Angeles courthouse could effectively avoid further bombardment of their sensibilities simply by averting their eyes. And, while it may be that one has a more substantial claim to a recognizable privacy interest when walking through a courthouse corridor than, for example, strolling through Central Park, surely it is nothing like the interest in being free from unwanted expression in the confines of one's own home. Given the subtlety and complexity of the factors involved, if Cohen's "speech" was otherwise entitled to constitutional protection, we do not think the fact that some unwilling "listeners" in a public building may have been briefly exposed to it can serve to justify this breach of the peace conviction where, as here, there was no evidence that persons powerless to avoid appellant's conduct did in fact object to it, and where that portion of the statute upon which Cohen's conviction rests evinces no concern, either on its face or as construed by the California courts, with the special plight of the captive auditor, but, instead, indiscriminately sweeps within its prohibitions all "offensive conduct" that disturbs "any neighborhood or person."

Against this background, the issue flushed by this case stands out in bold relief. It is whether California can excise, as "offensive conduct," one particular scurrilous epithet from the public discourse, either upon the theory of the court below that its use is inherently likely to cause violent reaction or upon a more general assertion that the States, acting as guardians of public morality, may properly remove this offensive word from the public vocabulary.

The rationale of the California court is plainly untenable. At most it reflects an "undifferentiated fear or apprehension of disturbance which is not enough to overcome the right to freedom of expression." We have been shown no evidence that substantial numbers of citizens are standing ready to strike out physically at whoever may assault their sensibilities with execrations like that uttered by Cohen. There may be some persons about with such lawless and violent proclivities, but that is an insufficient base upon which to erect, consistently with constitutional values, a governmental power to force persons who wish to ventilate their dissident views into avoiding particular forms of expression. The argument amounts to little more than the self-defeating proposition that to avoid physical censorship of one who has not sought to provoke such a response by a hypothetical coterie of the violent and lawless, the States may more appropriately effectuate that censorship themselves.

Admittedly, it is not so obvious that the First and Fourteenth Amendments must be taken to disable the States from punishing public utterance of this unseemly expletive in order to maintain what they regard as a suitable level of discourse within the body politic. We think, however, that examination and reflection will reveal the shortcomings of a contrary viewpoint.

At the outset, we cannot overemphasize that, in our judgment, most situations where the State has a justifiable interest in regulating speech will fall within one or more of the various established exceptions, discussed above but not applicable here, to the usual rule that governmental bodies may not prescribe the form or content of individual expression. Equally important to our conclusion is the constitutional backdrop against which our decision must be made. The constitutional right of free expression is powerful medicine in a society as diverse and populous as ours. It is designed and intended to remove governmental restraints from the arena of public discussion, putting the decision as to what views shall be voiced largely into the hands of each of us, in the hope that use of such freedom will ultimately produce a more capable citizenry and more perfect polity and in the belief that no other approach would comport with the premise of individual dignity and choice upon which our political system rests.

To many, the immediate consequence of this freedom may often appear to be only verbal tumult, discord, and even offensive utterance. These are, however, within established limits, in truth necessary side effects of the broader enduring values which the process of open debate permits us to achieve. That the air may at times seem filled with verbal cacophony is, in this sense not a sign of weakness but of strength. We cannot lose sight of the fact that, in what otherwise might seem a trifling and annoying instance of individual distasteful abuse of a privilege, these fundamental societal values are truly implicated....

Against this perception of the constitutional policies involved, we discern certain more particularized considerations that peculiarly call for reversal of this conviction. First, the principle contended for by the State seems inherently boundless. How is one to distinguish this from any other offensive word? Surely the State has no right to cleanse public debate to the point where it is grammatically palatable to the most squeamish among us. Yet no readily ascertainable general principle exists for stopping short of that result were we to affirm the judgment below. For, while the particular four-letter word being litigated here is perhaps more distasteful than most others of its genre, it is nevertheless often true that one man's vulgarity is another's lyric. Indeed, we think it is largely because governmental officials cannot make principled distinctions in this area that the Constitution leaves matters of taste and style so largely to the individual.

Additionally, we cannot overlook the fact, because it is well illustrated by the episode involved here, that much linguistic expression serves a dual communicative function: it conveys not only ideas capable of relatively precise, detached explication, but otherwise inexpressible emotions as well. In fact, words are often chosen as much for their emotive as their cognitive force. We cannot sanction the view that the Constitution, while solicitous of the cognitive content of individual speech has little or no regard for that emotive function which practically speaking, may often be the more important element of the overall message sought to be communicated....

Finally, and in the same vein, we cannot indulge the facile assumption that one can forbid particular words without also running a substantial risk of suppressing ideas in the process. Indeed, governments might soon seize upon the censorship of particular words as a convenient guise for banning the expression of unpopular views. We have been

able, as noted above, to discern little social benefit that might result from running the risk of opening the door to such grave results.

It is, in sum, our judgment that, absent a more particularized and compelling reason for its actions, the State may not, consistently with the First and Fourteenth Amendments, make the simple public display here involved of this single four-letter expletive a criminal offense. Because that is the only arguably sustainable rationale for the conviction here at issue, the judgment below must be reversed.

Reversed.

MR. JUSTICE BLACKMUN, with whom THE CHIEF JUSTICE and MR. JUSTICE BLACK join, dissenting.

Cohen's absurd and immature antic, in my view, was mainly conduct and little speech. The California Court of Appeal appears so to have described it, and I cannot characterize it otherwise. Further, the case appears to me to be well within the sphere of Chaplinsky v. New Hampshire (1942), where Justice Murphy, a known champion of First Amendment freedoms, wrote for a unanimous bench. As a consequence, this Court's agonizing over First Amendment values seems misplaced and unnecessary.

Whether you agree with Justice Harlan that "one man's vulgarity is another man's lyric" or with Justice Blackmun's view that the case presents only an "absurd and immature antic," the Court clearly extended First Amendment protection to words used in a public place that are offensive and unacceptable to many. This ruling, however, does not mean that offensive words are constitutionally protected in every context. In *Cohen* there was no evidence of disruption, violence, or other matters of legitimate concern to the state. In different situations, regulation of such vocabulary might be permissible. For example, the lower courts of several states have struggled with laws that prohibit use of obscene or offensive language on bumper stickers. States that have enacted these laws claim that such bumper stickers divert drivers' attention away from the proper operation their vehicles,

TABLE 4-3 Public Forum Cases Decided by the Rehnquist Court

Case	Facts	Outcome
Board of Airport Commissioners of the City of Los Angeles v. Jews for Jesus (1987)	Challenge to a resolution of a board of airport commissioners banning all "First Amendment activities" within the terminal.	Regardless of whether an airport is a public or nonpublic forum, the resolution is overly broad and, therefore, violative of the First Amendment.
Boos v. Barry (1988)	Challenge to a District of Columbia ordinance prohibiting the display of any sign within 500 feet of a foreign embassy that brings that foreign government into public disrepute, and prohibiting the congregation of three or more persons within 500 feet of an embassy.	The sign-display provision is an unconstitutional content-based restriction on political expression. The congregation provision is a constitutional manner and place restriction.
Frisby v. Schultz (1988)	Challenge to a city ordinance prohibiting picketing before a particular residence of an individual.	Ordinance serves a legitimate governmental interest. It does not violate the First Amendment.
Ward v. Rock Against Racism (1989)	Challenge to a city regulation requiring bands playing in a city park to use a band shell.	Government may impose reasonable restrictions on speech in public forums. This regulation was reasonable and tailored to meet a significant governmental objective. It does not violate the First Amendment.
United States v. Kokinda (1990)	Challenge to a postal service regulation prohibiting the solicitation of contributions on sidewalks outside of post office.	Sidewalk outside a post office is not a traditional public forum. The regulation does not violate the First Amendment.
International Society for Krishna Consciousness v. Lee (1992)	Challenge to a New York Port Authority regulation forbidding the repetitive solicitation of money or distribution of literature in airport terminals.	An airport terminal is not a public forum. Repetitive, face-to-face solicitation may be disruptive, impede the normal flow of the public, and be fraudulent. The regulation is reasonable. However, the ban on the distribution of literature violates the First Amendment.
Forsyth County, Georgia v. Nationalist Movement (1992)	Challenge to a county ordinance allowing an official to fix the cost of a parade permit based on the estimated cost of providing sufficient security to maintain public order during the gathering.	The ordinance is unconstitutional because it gives excessive discretion to the official and allows the fee to be fixed on the content of the message and the projected public response to it.
Bray v. Alexandria Women's Health Clinic (1993)	An abortion clinic and its supporters sued to enjoin anti-abortion protesters from demonstrating at clinics in the Washington, D.C., area, claiming that such protests are in violation of the Civil Rights Act of 1871 because they reflect an "animus" against women and restrict freedom of interstate travel.	The protests were not directed at women as a class, but were intended to protect victims of abortion, stop its practice, and reverse its legalization. Although many women travel interstate to obtain abortion services, the right to interstate travel was not the focus of the protesters' activity.
National Organization for Women v. Scheidler (1994)	Pro-choice groups sued anti-abortion groups claiming they were in violation of the Racketeer Influenced and Corrupt Organizations Act (RICO) by conspiring to engage in protests designed to shut down abortion clinics and persuade women not to have abortions.	Although the RICO law primarily targets organized crime motivated by hopes of financial gain, the statute is not restricted to crimes having economic motives. RICO laws may be applied to organized criminal activity inspired by noneconomic goals.
Madsen v. Women's Health Center, Inc. (1994)	Anti-abortion groups challenged a state court injunction prohibiting them from protesting within 36 feet of an abortion clinic, restricting noise levels during times abortion surgeries were being conducted, prohibiting protesters from physically approaching clinic clients within 300 feet of the facility, and prohibiting protests within 300 feet of the residences of clinic workers.	The injunction against protests within 36 feet of clinic is generally upheld, as are the noise level restrictions. Banning protest activity within 300 feet of clinic or private residences, however, is unconstitutional.

posing a risk to public safety. Civil libertarians, however, argue that banning these bumper stickers runs contrary to the teachings of *Cohen* and related cases. This issue illustrates the often difficult choices judges must make in balancing legitimate state concerns with individual expression.

As we move toward the end of the twentieth century, what sorts of new public forum issues will arise, and what direction will the Court take? One way to address these questions is to consider several cases decided by the Rehnquist Court that involve speech in public forums. Table 4-3 provides the facts of those disputes, their outcome, and a synopsis of the Court's reasoning. As you can see, the Court continues to face questions of how far the government may go in restricting the manner and place of protests. We also see that civil rights, religion, and foreign policy protests still dominate First Amendment litigation. But the 1990s cases include a new protest issue: abortion. These cases commonly involved a clash between pro-life advocates who protested at abortion clinics and pro-choice groups that wanted the courts to curtail the demonstrations. For the demonstrators the issue was freedom of speech. For their opponents the issue was guaranteeing free access to legal abortion services without undue interference from abortion opponents.

The decision in *Madsen v. Women's Health Center, Inc.* (1994) illustrates both the issue and the Court's reaction to it. As you read the facts and opinions in this case, compare it to the decisions of the Court on the antiwar and civil rights protest disputes of the 1960s and 1970s. Is the Court consistently applying the same standards it did in the earlier disputes? Or does the abortion controversy involve interests and concerns that distinguish it from the civil rights and antiwar protests? Finally, to what extent do you think the justices' views on abortion rights influenced their individual votes in this freedom of expression case?

Madsen v. Women's Health Center, Inc.

512 U.S. — (1994)
Vote: 6 (Blackmun, Ginsburg, O'Connor, Rehnquist, Souter,
      Stevens)
  3 (Kennedy, Scalia, Thomas)
Opinion of the Court: Rehnquist
Concurring opinion: Souter
Opinions concurring in part and dissenting in part: Stevens,
Scalia

The respondents to this suit operate abortion clinics, including one in Melbourne, Florida. In 1992 their attorneys asked a trial court judge to issue an injunction to prohibit the petitioners—Judy Madsen, other individuals, and groups, such as Operation Rescue—from blocking or interfering with public access to the clinic and from physically abusing people entering or leaving the premises. In September 1992 the trial court judge agreed to issue the injunction.

Six months later the Women's Health Center asked the judge to broaden the injunction. It argued that abortion protesters continued to block access to the clinic, approach patients, sing, and use loudspeakers. These acts, the clinic argued, were taking their toll on patients. One doctor told the judge that his patients "manifested a higher level of anxiety and hypertension causing [them] to need a higher level of sedation to undergo the surgical procedures, thereby increasing the risk associated with such procedures."

Moreover, the protesters' noise could be heard throughout the clinic "causing stress in the patients both during surgical procedures and while recuperating in the recovery rooms." Doctors and clinic workers also were targeted. Protesters picketed in front of their homes, rang neighbors' doorbells, and gave neighbors literature accusing a particular worker of being a "baby killer," among other characterizations.

With this testimony and a videotape of the protesters made by the clinic, the trial court concluded that the original injunction was not sufficient "to protect the health, safety and rights of women...." It amended the first injunction to prohibit protesters from a range of activities, including:

At all times on all days, from congregating, picketing, patrolling, demonstrating or entering that portion of public right-of-way or private property within [36] feet of the property line of the Clinic.... An exception to the 36 foot buffer zone is the area immediately adjacent to the Clinic on the east.... The [petitioners] ... must remain at least [5] feet from the Clinic's east line. Another exception to the 36 foot buffer zone relates to the record title owners of the property to the north and west of the Clinic. The prohibition against entry into the 36 foot buffer zones does not apply to such persons and their invitees. The other prohibitions contained herein do apply, if such owners and their invitees are acting in concert with the [petitioners]....

During the hours of 7:30 a.m. through noon, on Mondays through Saturdays, during surgical procedures and recovery periods, from singing, chanting, whistling, shouting, yelling, use of bullhorns, auto horns, sound amplification equipment or other sounds or images observable to or within earshot of the patients inside the Clinic.

At all times on all days, in an area within [300] feet of the Clinic, from physically approaching any person seeking the services of the Clinic unless such person indicates a desire to communicate by approaching or by inquiring of the [petitioners]....

At all times on all days, from approaching, congregating, picketing, patrolling, demonstrating or using bullhorns or other sound amplification equipment within [300] feet of the residence of any of the [respondents'] employees, staff, owners or agents, or blocking or attempting to block, barricade, or in any other manner, temporarily or otherwise, obstruct the entrances, exits or driveways of the residences of any of the [respondents'] employees, staff, owners or agents. The [petitioners] and those acting in concert with them are prohibited from inhibiting or impeding or attempting to impede, temporarily or otherwise, the free ingress or egress of persons to any street that provides the sole access to the street on which those residences are located.

The protesters challenged this injunction in both state and federal courts as a violation of the First Amendment. While the Florida Supreme Court upheld the constitutionality of the injunction, a federal court of appeals struck it down. The U.S. Supreme Court granted certiorari, according to Chief Justice Rehnquist, "to resolve the conflict between the Florida Supreme Court and the Court of Appeals over the constitutionality of the state court's injunction."

CHIEF JUSTICE REHNQUIST delivered the opinion of the Court.

Petitioners challenge the constitutionality of an injunction entered by a Florida state court which prohibits antiabortion protesters from demonstrating in certain places and in various ways outside of a health clinic that performs abortions. We hold that the establishment of a 36-foot buffer zone on a public street from which demonstrators are excluded passes muster under the First Amendment, but that several other provisions of the injunction do not....

We begin by addressing petitioners' contention that the state court's order, because it is an injunction that restricts only the speech of antiabortion protesters, is necessarily content or viewpoint based. Accordingly, they argue, we should examine the entire injunction under the strictest standard of scrutiny. We disagree. To accept petitioners' claim would be to classify virtually every injunction as content or viewpoint based. An injunction, by its very nature, applies only to a particular group (or individuals) and regulates the activities, and perhaps the speech, of that group. It does so, however, because of the group's past actions in the context of a specific dispute between real parties. The parties seeking the injunction assert a violation of their rights; the court hearing the action is charged with fashioning a remedy for a specific deprivation, not with the drafting of a statute addressed to the general public.

The fact that the injunction in the present case did not prohibit activities of those demonstrating in favor of abortion is justly attributable to the lack of any similar demonstrations by those in favor of abortion, and of any consequent request that their demonstrations be regulated by injunction. There is no suggestion in this record that Florida law would not equally restrain similar conduct directed at a target having nothing to do with abortion; none of the restrictions imposed by the court were directed at the contents of petitioner's message.

Our principal inquiry in determining content neutrality is whether the government has adopted a regulation of speech "without reference to the content of the regulated speech." *Ward v. Rock Against Racism* (1989).... We thus look to the government's purpose as the threshold consideration. Here, the state court imposed restrictions on petitioners incidental to their antiabortion message because they repeatedly violated the court's original order. That petitioners all share the same viewpoint regarding abortion does not in itself demonstrate that some invidious content- or viewpoint-based purpose motivated the issuance of the order. It suggests only that those in the group *whose conduct* violated the court's order happen to share the same opinion regarding abortions being performed at the clinic. In short, the fact that the injunction covered people with a particular viewpoint does not itself render the injunction content or viewpoint based. Accordingly, the injunction issued in this case does not demand the level of heightened scrutiny set forth in *Perry Education Assn.* [*v. Perry Local Educators' Assn.*, 1983]. And we proceed to discuss the standard which does govern.

If this were a content-neutral, generally applicable statute, instead of an injunctive order, its constitutionality would be assessed under the standard set forth in *Ward v. Rock Against Racism* and similar cases. Given that the forum around the clinic is a traditional public forum, we would determine whether the time, place, and manner regulations were "narrowly tailored to serve a significant governmental interest."

There are obvious differences, however, between an injunction and a generally applicable ordinance. Ordinances represent a legislative choice regarding the promotion of particular societal interests. Injunctions, by contrast, are remedies imposed for violations (or threatened violations) of a legislative or judicial decree. Injunctions also carry greater risks of censorship and discriminatory application than do general ordinances.... Injunctions, of course, have some advantages over generally applicable statutes in that they can be tailored by a trial judge to afford more precise relief than a statute where a violation of the law has already occurred.

We believe that these differences require a somewhat more stringent application of general First Amendment principles in this context. In past cases evaluating injunctions restricting speech, we have relied upon such general principles while also seeking to ensure that the injunction was no broader than necessary to achieve its desired goals. Our close attention to the fit between the objectives of an injunction and the restrictions it imposes on speech is consistent with the general rule, quite apart from First Amendment considerations, "that injunctive relief should be no more burdensome to the defendants than necessary to provide complete relief to the plaintiffs." Accordingly, when evaluating a content-neutral injunction, we think that our standard time, place, and manner analysis is not sufficiently rigorous. We must ask instead whether the challenged provisions of the injunction burden no more speech than necessary to serve a significant government interest....

We begin with the 36-foot buffer zone. The state court prohibited petitioners from "congregating, picketing, patrolling, demonstrating or entering" any portion of the public right-of-way or private property within 36 feet of the property line of the clinic as a way of ensuring access to the clinic.... The buffer zone also applies to private property to the north and west of the clinic property. We examine each portion of the buffer zone separately....

The 36-foot buffer zone protecting the entrances to the clinic and the parking lot is a means of protecting unfettered ingress to and egress from the clinic, and ensuring that petitioners do not block traffic....

The need for a complete buffer zone near the clinic entrances and driveway may be debatable, but some deference must be given to the state court's familiarity with the facts and the background of the dispute between the parties even under our heightened review. Moreover, one of petitioners' witnesses during the evidentiary hearing before the state court conceded that the buffer zone was narrow enough to place petitioners at a distance of no greater than 10 to 12 feet from cars approaching and leaving the clinic. Protesters standing across the narrow street from the clinic can still be seen and heard from the clinic parking lots. We also bear in mind the fact that the state court originally issued a much narrower injunction, providing no buffer zone, and that this order did not succeed in protecting access to the clinic. The failure of the first order to accomplish its purpose may be taken into consideration in evaluating the constitutionality of the broader order. On balance, we hold that the 36-foot buffer zone around the clinic entrances and driveway burdens no more speech than necessary to accomplish the governmental interest at stake.

JUSTICE SCALIA's dissent argues that a videotape made of demonstrations at the clinic represents "what one must presume to be the worst of the activity justifying the injunction." This seems to us a gratuitous assumption. The videotape was indeed introduced by respondents, presumably because they thought it supported their request for the second injunction. But witnesses also testified as to relevant facts in a 3-day evidentiary hearing, and the state court was therefore not limited to JUSTICE SCALIA's rendition of what he saw on the videotape to make its findings in support of the second injunction. Indeed, petitioners themselves studiously refrained from challenging the factual basis for the injunction both in the state courts and here. . . .

The inclusion of private property on the back and side of the clinic in the 36-foot buffer zone raises different concerns. The accepted purpose of the buffer zone is to protect access to the clinic and to facilitate the orderly flow of traffic. . . . Patients and staff wishing to reach the clinic do not have to cross the private property abutting the clinic property on the north and west, and nothing in the record indicates that petitioners' activities on the private property have obstructed access to the clinic. Nor was evidence presented that protesters located on the private property blocked vehicular traffic. . . . Absent evidence that petitioners standing on the private property have obstructed access to the clinic, blocked vehicular traffic, or otherwise unlaw-

fully interfered with the clinic's operation, this portion of the buffer zone fails to serve the significant government interests relied on by the Florida Supreme Court. We hold that on the record before us the 36-foot buffer zone as applied to the private property to the north and west of the clinic burdens more speech than necessary to protect access to the clinic.

In response to high noise levels outside the clinic, the state court restrained the petitioners from "singing, chanting, whistling, shouting, yelling, use of bullhorns, auto horns, sound amplification equipment or other sounds or images observable to or within earshot of the patients inside the [c]linic" during the hours of 7:30 a.m. through noon on Mondays through Saturdays. We must, of course, take account of the place to which the regulations apply in determining whether these restrictions burden more speech than necessary. We have upheld similar noise restrictions in the past, and as we noted in upholding a local noise ordinance around public schools, "the nature of a place, 'the pattern of its normal activities, dictate the kinds of regulations . . . that are reasonable.'" Noise control is particularly important around hospitals and medical facilities during surgery and recovery periods. . . .

We hold that the limited noise restrictions imposed by the state court order burden no more speech than necessary to ensure the health and well-being of the patients at the clinic. The First Amendment does not demand that patients at a medical facility undertake Herculean efforts to escape the cacophony of political protests. "If overamplified loudspeakers assault the citizenry, government may turn them down." That is what the state court did here, and we hold that its action was proper.

The same, however, cannot be said for the "images observable" provision of the state court's order. Clearly, threats to patients or their families, however communicated, are proscribable under the First Amendment. But rather than prohibiting the display of signs that could be interpreted as threats or veiled threats, the state court issued a blanket ban on all "images observable." This broad prohibition on all "images observable" burdens more speech than necessary to achieve the purpose of limiting threats to clinic patients or their families. Similarly, if the blanket ban on "images observable" was intended to reduce the level of anxiety and hypertension suffered by the patients inside the clinic, it would still fail. The only plausible reason a patient would be bothered by "images observable" inside the clinic would be if the patient found the expression contained in such images disagreeable. But it is much easier for the clinic to pull its curtains than for a patient to stop up her ears, and no more is required to avoid seeing placards through the windows of the clinic. This provision of the injunction violates the First Amendment.

The state court ordered that petitioners refrain from physically approaching any person seeking services of the clinic "unless such person indicates a desire to communicate" in an area within 300 feet of the clinic. The state court was attempting to prevent clinic patients and staff from being "stalked" or "shadowed" by the petitioners as they approached the clinic....

But it is difficult, indeed, to justify a prohibition on *all* uninvited approaches of persons seeking the services of the clinic, regardless of how peaceful the contact may be, without burdening more speech than necessary to prevent intimidation and to ensure access to the clinic. Absent evidence that the protesters' speech is independently proscribable (*i.e.,* "fighting words" or threats), or is so infused with violence as to be indistinguishable from a threat of physical harm, this provision cannot stand. "As a general matter, we have indicated that in public debate our own citizens must tolerate insulting, and even outrageous, speech in order to provide adequate breathing space to the freedoms protected by the First Amendment." The "consent" requirement alone invalidates this provision; it burdens more speech than is necessary to prevent intimidation and to ensure access to the clinic.

The final substantive regulation challenged by petitioners relates to a prohibition against picketing, demonstrating, or using sound amplification equipment within 300 feet of the residences of clinic staff. The prohibition also covers impeding access to streets that provide the sole access to streets on which those residences are located. The same analysis applies to the use of sound amplification equipment here as that discussed above: the government may simply demand that petitioners turn down the volume if the protests overwhelm the neighborhood.

As for the picketing, our prior decision upholding a law banning targeted residential picketing remarked on the unique nature of the home, as "'the last citadel of the tired, the weary, and the sick.'" *Frisby* [*v. Schultz,* 1988]. We stated that "'the State's interest in protecting the well-being, tranquility, and privacy of the home is certainly of the highest order in a free and civilized society.'"

But the 300-foot zone around the residences in this case is much larger than the zone provided for in the ordinance which we approved in *Frisby.* The ordinance at issue there made it "unlawful for any person to engage in picketing before or about the residence or dwelling of any individual." The prohibition was limited to "focused picketing taking place solely in front of a particular residence." By contrast, the 300-foot zone would ban "general marching through residential neighborhoods, or even walking a route in front of an entire block of houses." The record before us does not contain sufficient justification for this broad a ban on picketing; it appears that a limitation on the time, duration of picketing, and number of pickets outside a smaller zone could have accomplished the desired result....

In sum, we uphold the noise restrictions and the 36-foot buffer zone around the clinic entrances and driveway because they burden no more speech than necessary to eliminate the unlawful conduct targeted by the state court's injunction. We strike down as unconstitutional the 36-foot buffer zone as applied to the private property to the north and west of the clinic, the "images observable" provision, the 300-foot no-approach zone around the clinic, and the 300-foot buffer zone around the residences, because these provisions sweep more broadly than necessary to accomplish the permissible goals of the injunction. Accordingly, the judgment of the Florida Supreme Court is

Affirmed in part, and reversed in part.

JUSTICE SCALIA, with whom JUSTICE KENNEDY and JUSTICE THOMAS join, concurring in the judgment in part and dissenting in part.

The judgment in today's case has an appearance of moderation and Solomonic wisdom, upholding as it does some portions of the injunction while disallowing others. That appearance is deceptive. The entire injunction in this case departs so far from the established course of our jurisprudence that in any other context it would have been regarded as a candidate for summary reversal.

But the context here is abortion. A long time ago, in dissent from another abortion-related case, JUSTICE O'CONNOR, joined by then-JUSTICE REHNQUIST, wrote:

"This Court's abortion decisions have already worked a major distortion in the Court's constitutional jurisprudence. Today's decision goes further, and makes it painfully clear that no legal rule or doctrine is safe from ad hoc nullification by this Court when an occasion for its application arises in a case involving state regulation of abortion. The permissible scope of abortion regulation is not the only constitutional issue on which this Court is divided, but— except when it comes to abortion—the Court has generally refused to let such disagreements, however longstanding or deeply felt, prevent it from evenhandedly applying uncontroversial legal doctrines to cases that come before it." *Thornburgh v. American College of Obstetricians and Gynecologists* (1986).

Today the ad hoc nullification machine claims its latest, greatest, and most surprising victim: the First Amendment.

Because I believe that the judicial creation of a 36-foot zone in which only a particular group, which had broken no law, cannot exercise its rights of speech, assembly, and association, and the judicial enactment of a noise prohibition, applicable to that group and that group alone, are profoundly at odds with our First Amendment precedents and traditions, I dissent.

The record of this case contains a videotape, with running caption of time and date, displaying what one must presume to be the worst of the activity justifying the injunction issued by Judge McGregor and partially approved today by this Court. The tape was shot by employees of, or volunteers at, the ... Clinic on three Saturdays in February and March 1993....

Anyone seriously interested in what this case was about must view that tape. And anyone doing so who is familiar with run-of-the-mine labor picketing, not to mention some other social protests, will be aghast at what it shows we have today permitted an individual judge to do....

The videotape and the rest of the record, including the trial court's findings, show that a great many forms of expression and conduct occurred in the vicinity of the clinic.

These include singing, chanting, praying, shouting, the playing of music both from the clinic and from handheld boom boxes, speeches, peaceful picketing, communication of familiar political messages, handbilling, persuasive speech directed at opposing groups on the issue of abortion, efforts to persuade individuals not to have abortions, personal testimony, interviews with the press, and media efforts to report on the protest. What the videotape, the rest of the record, and the trial court's findings do not contain is any suggestion of violence near the clinic, nor do they establish any attempt to prevent entry or exit.

Under this Court's jurisprudence, there is no question that this public sidewalk area is a "public forum," where citizens generally have a First Amendment right to speak. The parties to this case invited the Court to employ one or the other of the two well established standards applied to restrictions upon this First Amendment right. Petitioners claimed the benefit of so-called "strict scrutiny," the standard applied to content-based restrictions: the restriction must be "necessary to serve a compelling state interest and ... narrowly drawn to achieve that end." *Perry Education Assn. v. Perry Local Educators' Assn.* (1983). Respondents, on the other hand, contended for what has come to be known as "intermediate scrutiny" (midway between the "strict scrutiny" demanded for content-based regulation of speech, and the "rational basis" standard that is applied— under the Equal Protection Clause—to government regulation of non-speech activities). That standard, applicable to so-called "time, place and manner regulations" of speech, provides that the regulations are permissible so long as they "are content-neutral, are narrowly tailored to serve a significant government interest, and leave open ample alternative channels of communication." The Court adopts neither of these, but creates, brand-new for this abortion-related case, an additional standard that is (supposedly) "somewhat more stringent," than intermediate scrutiny, yet not as "rigorous," as strict scrutiny. The Court does not give this new standard a name, but perhaps we could call it intermediate-intermediate scrutiny. The difference between it and intermediate scrutiny (which the Court acknowledges is inappropriate for injunctive restrictions on speech) is frankly too subtle for me to describe, so I must simply recite it: whereas intermediate scrutiny requires that the restriction be "narrowly tailored to serve a significant government interest," the new standard requires that the restriction "burden no more speech than necessary to serve a significant government interest."

... The real question in this case is not whether intermediate scrutiny, which the Court assumes to be some kind of default standard, should be supplemented because of the distinctive characteristics of injunctions; but rather whether those distinctive characteristics are not, for reasons of both policy and precedent, fully as good a reason as "content-basis" for demanding strict scrutiny. That possibility is simply not considered. Instead, the Court begins ... with the following optical illusion: "If this were a content-neutral, generally applicable statute, instead of an injunctive order, its constitutionality would be assessed under the [intermediate scrutiny] standard,"—and then proceeds to discuss whether petitioners can sustain the burden of departing from that presumed disposition.

But this is *not* a statute, and it *is* an injunctive order. The Court might just as logically (or illogically) have begun ... "If this were a content-based injunction, rather than a non-content-based injunction, its constitutionality would be assessed under the strict scrutiny standard"— and have then proceeded to discuss whether *respondents* can sustain the burden of departing from *that* presumed disposition. The question should be approached, it seems to me, without any such artificial loading of the dice. And the central element of the answer is that a restriction upon speech imposed by injunction (whether nominally content based or nominally content neutral) is *at least* as deserving of strict scrutiny as a statutory, content-based restriction.

That is so for several reasons: The danger of content-based statutory restrictions upon speech is that they may be designed and used precisely to suppress the ideas in question rather than to achieve any other proper governmental aim. But that same danger exists with injunctions. Although a speech-restricting injunction may not attack content *as content* (in the present case ... even that is not true), it lends itself just as readily to the targeted suppression of particular ideas. When a judge, on the motion of an employer, enjoins picketing at the site of a labor dispute he enjoins (and he *knows* he is enjoining) the expression of pro-union views. Such targeting of one or the other side of an ideological dispute cannot readily be achieved in speech-restricting general legislation except by making content the basis of the restriction; it is achieved in speech-restricting injunctions almost invariably. The proceedings before us here illustrate well enough what I mean. The injunction was sought against a single-issue advocacy group by persons and organizations with a business or social interest in suppressing that group's point of view.

The second reason speech-restricting injunctions are at least as deserving of strict scrutiny is obvious enough: they are the product of individual judges rather than of legislatures—and often of judges who have been chagrined by prior disobedience of their orders. The right to free speech should not lightly be placed within the control of a single man or woman. And the third reason is that the injunction is a much more powerful weapon than a statute, and so should be subjected to greater safeguards. Normally, when injunctions are enforced through contempt proceedings, only the defense of factual innocence is available. The collateral bar rule of *Walker v. Birmingham* (1967) eliminates the defense that the injunction itself was unconstitutional. Thus, persons subject to a speech-restricting injunction who have not the money or not the time to lodge an immediate appeal face a Hobson's choice: they must remain silent, since if they speak their First Amendment rights are no defense in subsequent contempt proceedings. This is good reason to require the strictest standard for issuance of such orders....

What we have decided seems to be, and will be reported by the media as, an abortion case. But it will go down in the lawbooks, it will be cited, as a free-speech injunction case— and the damage its novel principles produce will be considerable. The proposition that injunctions against speech are subject to a standard indistinguishable from (unless perhaps more lenient in its application than) the "intermediate scrutiny" standard we have used for "time, place, and manner" legislative restrictions; the notion that injunctions against speech need not be closely tied to any violation of law, but may simply implement sound social policy; and the practice of accepting trial-court conclusions permitting injunctions without considering whether those conclusions are supported by any findings of fact—these latest by-products of our abortion jurisprudence ought to give all friends of liberty great concern.

For these reasons, I dissent from that portion of the judgment upholding parts of the injunction.

Hate Speech

The cases we have discussed so far demonstrate a great diversity in the content and method of communication. Individuals in some of these cases have used conventional forms of protest, such as speeches, parades, and published documents; others have used unconventional methods that are offensive to many, such as Gregory Johnson's burning of the American flag or Paul Cohen's crude jacket. Their expressions have included a wide array of philosophies and causes—communism, socialism, civil rights, religious beliefs, and opposition to war. In spite of this diversity, however, these cases share some common elements. Each case has involved an individual or group communicating a political or social message, usually expressing dissatisfaction with certain government policies. This speech is the traditional form of political expression that the Framers sought to protect when they approved the First Amendment.

Since the mid-1970s, however, another form of communication, which differs markedly from the traditional, has come before the Court. Expression based on hatred goes well beyond offending our standards of appropriateness or good taste. It arises from hostile, discriminatory, and prejudicial attitudes toward another person's innate characteristics: sex, race, ethnicity, religion, or sexual orientation. When directed at a member of the targeted group, such expression is demeaning and hurtful. Hate speech tends to be devoid of traditional commentary on political issues or on the need for changes in public policy. Instead, its central theme is hostility toward individuals belonging to the target group. May hate speech be banned, or does the First Amendment protect it? If regulation is permissible, under what conditions? And what standard should control?

One of the first modern cases involving these issues was *National Socialist Party v. Skokie* (1977). The National Socialist party was a minor political party with no hope of gaining electoral victories. Minor parties often set their sights a bit lower, viewing activities such as public education and awareness as important tools in achieving their desired policy objectives. *Skokie* concerned the party's desire to exercise its First Amendment right to assemble. More specifically, the party wanted to "educate" the public by marching in Skokie, Illinois, suburb of Chicago.

Such marches are commonplace in America; almost daily, a political party or other group stages a demonstration or protest somewhere. But this proposed march was anything but commonplace. The National Socialist party is an American version of the Nazi party, which came into power under Adolf Hitler in Germany. A large number of Jews, including survivors of Hitler's concentration camps, live in Skokie. Together the two groups formed a potentially lethal combination. In fact, as soon as the town heard of the Nazis' plan to march in full regalia, it passed a variety of ordinances aimed specifically at stopping it. Believing that these measures abridged their First Amendment rights, party leaders turned to the ACLU for legal assistance. Many of its members objected to representing Nazi interests, but the ACLU agreed to participate because Skokie's prohibitions symbolized just the sorts of laws the organization was founded to fight—abridgements of the First Amendment. Skokie residents saw the matter in a much different light; the presence of Nazi uniforms in their town constituted fighting words.[29] Therefore, Skokie argued that it could legitimately regulate such speech to prevent a riot.

A state circuit court agreed with the town and entered an injunction prohibiting the Nazis from marching in Skokie. The ACLU asked the Illinois Supreme Court for a stay and for an expedited appeal. When

29. Many ACLU members also agreed with the town: almost half resigned in protest of its decision to defend Nazis. For an interesting account of this episode, see Aryeh Neier's *Defending My Enemy* (New York: Dutton, 1979).

both requests were denied, the matter came before the U.S. Supreme Court.

In a short per curiam opinion, five members of the Court reversed the Illinois Supreme Court's denial of the stay. The Court said:

The outstanding injunction will deprive [the Nazis] of rights protected by the First Amendment.... If a State seeks to impose a restraint of this kind, it must provide strict procedural safeguard ... including immediate appellate review.... Absent such review, the State must instead allow a stay. The order of the Illinois Supreme Court constituted a denial of that right.

The Court refused to uphold ordinances regulating speech before it occurred, claiming that such laws amounted to censorship. In the Court's eyes, governments can prohibit such expression only after it occurs, an opportunity the Town of Skokie never had, as the party chose instead to march in Chicago.

In the *Skokie* case, and in *Brandenburg* before it, the justices struck down government regulation of racially based hate speech. In both cases, however, the Court's decision rested on defects in the way the government attempted to block the unacceptable expression. In *Brandenburg* the Court found constitutional problems with Ohio's Criminal Syndicalism Act upon which the prosecution of a Ku Klux Klan leader was based. In *Skokie* the Court found that the local government was unconstitutionally attempting to repress speech before it occurred, a form of prior restraint. In neither case did the Court directly confront the question of whether the First Amendment allows government to punish expression based on hatred.

In response to an increase in hate speech incidents, many state and local governments, as well as colleges and universities, passed ordinances in the 1990s making hate speech punishable. Although most Americans consider hate-based expression reprehensible, there is a deep division of opinion over whether it can be constitutionally banned. Individuals concerned with minority rights and elimination of bigotry have argued that laws making hate speech illegal

are both necessary and constitutionally permissible. Free speech advocates, however, contend that such laws run in direct contradiction to the First Amendment. Often this issue has divided groups that have been traditional allies in the attempt to expand personal rights and liberties. *(See Box 4-3)* The issue first found its way to the Supreme Court in the case of *R.A.V. v. City of St. Paul, Minnesota* (1992).

R.A.V. v. City of St. Paul, Minnesota

505 U.S. —- (1992)
Vote: 9 (Blackmun, Kennedy, O'Connor, Rehnquist, Scalia, Souter, Stevens, Thomas, White)

0

Opinion of the Court: Scalia
Concurring opinions: Blackmun, Stevens, White

The City of St. Paul, Minnesota, alleges that between 1:00 a.m. and 3:00 a.m. on June 21, 1990, R.A.V., a seventeen-year-old high school dropout, and several other teenagers "assembled a crudely made cross by taping together broken chair legs" and then burned the cross inside the fenced back yard of a black family across the street from R.A.V's house. St. Paul could have prosecuted R.A.V. under several severe criminal laws; for example, it could have charged him with arson, which carries a maximum penalty of five years in prison and a $10,000 fine. Instead, it charged him with violating two laws, including the St. Paul Bias-Motivated Crime Ordinance. This law stated:

Whoever places on public or private property a symbol, object, appellation, characterization or graffiti, including, but not limited to, a burning cross or Nazi swastika, which one knows or has reasonable grounds to know arouses anger, alarm, or resentment in others on the basis of race, color, creed, religion, or gender commits disorderly conduct and shall be guilty of a misdemeanor.

Before R.A.V.'s trial, his attorney asked the judge to dismiss the charge, arguing that the ordinance violated the First Amendment because it was "substan-

BOX 4-3 HATE SPEECH AND THE CIVIL LIBERTIES COMMUNITY

REGULATING HATE SPEECH is an issue that divides the civil liberties community. Groups that historically have worked together to advance civil liberties and civil rights have found themselves in the uncomfortable position of fighting against each other over the hate speech controversy. Listed below are short excerpts from amicus curiae briefs submitted by traditionally liberal groups in the case of *R.A.V. v. City of St. Paul* (1992). Notice how the briefs emphasize different values. Those in favor of striking down the St. Paul ordinance stress the primacy of the First Amendment. Supporters of the law focus on the significance of equality considerations.

IN SUPPORT OF R.A.V.:

[T]he antibias ordinance cannot be defended on the ground that the State has a compelling interest in banning messages of racial and religious bigotry and intolerance. Although these messages are inconsistent with the Nation's highest aspirations, the Court has repeatedly held that the First Amendment does not permit a State to prohibit the communication of ideas simply because they are offensive or at odds with national policies.

— *Center for Individual Rights*

It is quite clear from the Court's First Amendment jurisprudence that government cannot criminalize such speech simply because it arouses anger, alarm and resentment.

— *Association of American Publishers and the Freedom to Read Foundation*

This society has rested its faith on the proposition that "the remedy [for speech] is more speech, not enforced silence." Justice Brandeis concurring in *Whitney v. California*] Accordingly, our constitutional tradition demands that even a message of racial supremacy is entitled to be heard so long as it remains in the realm of advocacy. Those who articulated this faith in public debate were not naive about the power of words or symbols. To the contrary, they believed that pernicious ideas were more dangerous when suppressed than when exposed.

— *American Civil Liberties Union, Minnesota Civil Liberties Union, and the American Jewish Congress*

IN SUPPORT OF THE ST. PAUL ORDINANCE:

Crossburnings, of which defendant R.A.V. is accused, should be recognized as a terrorist hate practice of intimidation and harassment, which, contrary to the purposes of the Fourteenth Amendment, works to institutionalize the civil inequality of protected groups.... [T]he statute in question does not violate the First Amendment because social inequality, including through expressive conduct, is a harm for which states are entitled leeway in regulation.

— *National Black Women's Health Project*

When used in a personally threatening or assaultive manner, these symbols [burning cross and NAZI swastika] are part of the marketplace of ideas of which our society is justifiably tolerant; however, when used as a form of a bias-motivated personal attack, they cease to symbolize ideas and become violent tools that inflict injury. This Court has consistently recognized that this type of "expression" should not be afforded First Amendment protection.

— *Anti-Defamation League of B'nai B'rith*

Cross burning is an especially invidious act. A burning cross is an insult and a threat; it carries with it the historical baggage of past terrorism and physical attacks. When a cross burning is targeted against an individual and his family, it is more than just expression; it is a form of violence itself—symbolic violence.

— *Asian American Legal Defense and Education Fund, the Asian Law Caucus, the Asian Pacific American Legal Center, and the National Asian Pacific American Bar Association*

In his brief, [R.A.V.] intones principles of freedom of speech with which, in the abstract, no one will disagree. But the State of Minnesota was not indulging in theory when it charged [him] with a violation of the ordinance in controversy. It was dealing with what can only fairly be described as an act of terrorism. This conduct cannot rationally be viewed as protected by the First Amendment.

— *National Association for the Advancement of Colored People and the Clarendon Foundation* tially overbroad and impermissibly content-based." The trial court judge granted the motion, and the city appealed to the Minnesota Supreme Court.

The Minnesota high court reversed the trial court's decision, holding that the ordinance did not violate freedom of expression guarantees contained in the First Amendment. The court found that the ordinance prohibits conduct equivalent to "fighting words," unprotected expression under the First Amendment. It also ruled that the ordinance was not impermissibly content-based because it was "a narrowly tailored means toward accomplishing the compelling governmental interest in protecting the community against bias-motivated threats to public safety and order."

JUSTICE SCALIA delivered the opinion of the Court.

In construing the St. Paul ordinance, we are bound by the construction given to it by the Minnesota court. Accordingly, we accept the Minnesota Supreme Court's authoritative statement that the ordinance reaches only those expressions that constitute "fighting words" within the meaning of *Chaplinsky* [*v. New Hampshire*, 1942]. Petitioner ... urge[s] us to modify the scope of the *Chaplinsky* formulation, thereby invalidating the ordinance as "substantially overbroad." We find it unnecessary to consider this issue. Assuming, *arguendo*, that all of the expression reached by the ordinance is proscribable under the "fighting words" doctrine, we nonetheless conclude that the ordinance is facially unconstitutional in that it prohibits otherwise permitted speech solely on the basis of the subjects the speech addresses.

The First Amendment generally prevents government from proscribing speech, *Cantwell v. Connecticut* (1940), or even expressive conduct, see *Texas v. Johnson* (1989), because of disapproval of the ideas expressed. Content-based regulations are presumptively invalid. *Simon & Shuster, Inc. v. Members of N.Y. State Crime Victims Bd.* (1991). From 1791 to the present, however, our society, like other free but civilized societies, has permitted restrictions upon the content of speech in a few limited areas, which are "of such slight social value as a step to truth that any benefit that

may be derived from them is clearly outweighed by the social interest in order and morality." *Chaplinsky.* We have recognized that "the freedom of speech" referred to by the First Amendment does not include a freedom to disregard these traditional limitations. See, *e.g., Roth v. United States* (1957) (obscenity); *Beauharnais v. Illinois* (1952) (defamation); *Chaplinsky v. New Hampshire* ("fighting words"). Our decisions since the 1960's have narrowed the scope of the traditional categorical exceptions for defamation and for obscenity, but a limited categorical approach has remained an important part of our First Amendment jurisprudence.

We have sometimes said that these categories of expression are "not within the area of constitutionally protected speech" or that the "protection of the First Amendment does not extend" to them. Such statements must be taken in context, however, and are no more literally true than is the occasionally repeated shorthand characterizing obscenity "as not being speech at all." What they mean is that these areas of speech can, consistently with the First Amendment, be regulated *because of their constitutionally proscribable content* (obscenity, defamation, etc.)—not that they are categories of speech entirely invisible to the Constitution, so that they may be made the vehicles for content discrimination unrelated to their distinctively proscribable content. Thus, the government may proscribe libel; but it may not make the further content discrimination of proscribing *only* libel critical of the government. We recently acknowledged this distinction in [*New York v.*] *Ferber* [1982], where, in upholding New York's child pornography law, we expressly recognized that there was no "question here of censoring a particular literary theme...."

Our cases surely do not establish the proposition that the First Amendment imposes no obstacle whatsoever to regulation of particular instances of such proscribable expression, so that the government "may regulate [them] freely." That would mean that a city council could enact an ordinance prohibiting only those legally obscene works that contain criticism of the city government or, indeed, that do not include endorsement of the city government. Such a simplistic, all-or-nothing-at-all approach to First Amendment protection is at odds with common sense and with our jurisprudence as well. It is not true that "fighting words" have at most a *"de minimis"* expressive content, or that their content is *in all respects* "worthless and undeserving of constitutional protection"; sometimes they are quite expressive indeed. We have not said that they constitute *"no* part of the expression of ideas," but only that they constitute "no *essential* part of any exposition of ideas."

The proposition that a particular instance of speech can be proscribable on the basis of one feature (*e.g.,* obscenity) but not on the basis of another (*e.g.,* opposition to the city government) is commonplace, and has found application in many contexts. We have long held, for example, that nonverbal expressive activity can be banned because of the action it entails, but not because of the ideas it expresses— so that burning a flag in violation of an ordinance against outdoor fires could be punishable, whereas burning a flag in violation of an ordinance against dishonoring the flag is not....

In other words, the exclusion of "fighting words" from the scope of the First Amendment simply means that, for purposes of that Amendment, the unprotected features of the words are, despite their verbal character, essentially a "nonspeech" element of communication. Fighting words are thus analogous to a noisy sound truck: Each is, as Justice Frankfurter recognized, a "mode of speech"; both can be used to convey an idea; but neither has, in and of itself, a claim upon the First Amendment. As with the sound truck, however, so also with fighting words: The government may not regulate use based on hostility—or favoritism—towards the underlying message expressed....

Even the prohibition against content discrimination that we assert the First Amendment requires is not absolute. It applies differently in the context of proscribable speech than in the area of fully protected speech. The rationale of the general prohibition, after all, is that content discrimination "rais[es] the specter that the Government may effectively drive certain ideas or viewpoints from the marketplace." *Simon & Schuster.* But content discrimination among various instances of a class of proscribable speech often does not pose this threat.

When the basis for the content discrimination consists entirely of the very reason the entire class of speech at issue is proscribable, no significant danger of idea or viewpoint discrimination exists. Such a reason, having been adjudged neutral enough to support exclusion of the entire class of speech from First Amendment protection, is also neutral

enough to form the basis of distinction within the class. To illustrate: A State might choose to prohibit only that obscenity which is the most patently offensive *in its prurience—* *i.e.,* that which involves the most lascivious displays of sexual activity. But it may not prohibit, for example, only that obscenity which includes offensive *political* messages....

Another valid basis for according differential treatment to even a content-defined subclass of proscribable speech is that the subclass happens to be associated with particular "secondary effects" of the speech, so that the regulation is *"justified* without reference to the content of the ... speech." A State could, for example, permit all obscene live performances except those involving minors. Moreover, since words can in some circumstances violate laws directed not against speech but against conduct (a law against treason, for example, is violated by telling the enemy the nation's defense secrets), a particular content-based subcategory of a proscribable class of speech can be swept up incidentally within the reach of a statute directed at conduct rather than speech. Thus, for example, sexually derogatory "fighting words," among other words, may produce a violation of Title VII's general prohibition against sexual discrimination in employment practices. Where the government does not target conduct on the basis of its expressive content, acts are not shielded from regulation merely because they express a discriminatory idea or philosophy....

Applying these principles to the St. Paul ordinance, we conclude that, even as narrowly construed by the Minnesota Supreme Court, the ordinance is facially unconstitutional. Although the phrase in the ordinance, "arouses anger, alarm or resentment in others," has been limited by the Minnesota Supreme Court's construction to reach only those symbols or displays that amount to "fighting words," the remaining, unmodified terms make clear that the ordinance applies only to "fighting words" that insult, or provoke violence, "on the basis of race, color, creed, religion or gender." Displays containing abusive invective, no matter how vicious or severe, are permissible unless they are addressed to one of the specified disfavored topics. Those who wish to use "fighting words" in connection with other ideas—to express hostility, for example, on the basis of political affiliation, union membership, or homosexuality— are not covered. The First Amendment does not permit St.

Paul to impose special prohibitions on those speakers who express views on disfavored subjects.

In its practical operation, moreover, the ordinance goes even beyond mere content discrimination, to actual viewpoint discrimination. Displays containing some words—odious racial epithets, for example—would be prohibited to proponents of all views. But "fighting words" that do not themselves invoke race, color, creed, religion, or gender—aspersions upon a person's mother, for example—would seemingly be usable *ad libitum* in the placards of those arguing *in favor* of racial, color, etc. tolerance and equality, but could not be used by that speaker's opponents. One could hold up a sign saying, for example, that all "anti-Catholic bigots" are misbegotten; but not that all "papists" are, for that would insult and provoke violence "on the basis of religion." St. Paul has no such authority to license one side of a debate to fight freestyle, while requiring the other to follow Marquis of Queensbury Rules.

What we have here, it must be emphasized, is not a prohibition of fighting words that are directed at certain persons or groups (which would be *facially* valid if it met the requirements of the Equal Protection Clause); but rather, a prohibition of fighting words that contain (as the Minnesota Supreme Court repeatedly emphasized) messages of "bias-motivated" hatred and in particular, as applied to this case, messages "based on virulent notions of racial supremacy." One must wholeheartedly agree with the Minnesota Supreme Court that "[i]t is the responsibility, even the obligation, of diverse communities to confront such notions in whatever form they appear," but the manner of that confrontation cannot consist of selective limitations upon speech. St. Paul's brief asserts that a general "fighting words" law would not meet the city's needs because only a content-specific measure can communicate to minority groups that the "group hatred" aspect of such speech "is not condoned by the majority." The point of the First Amendment is that majority preferences must be expressed in some fashion other than silencing speech on the basis of its content....

The content-based discrimination reflected in the St. Paul ordinance comes within neither any of the specific exceptions to the First Amendment prohibition we discussed earlier, nor within a more general exception for content discrimination that does not threaten censorship of ideas. It assuredly does not fall within the exception for content discrimination based on the very reasons why the particular class of speech at issue (here, fighting words) is proscribable. ... [T]he reason why fighting words are categorically excluded from the protection of the First Amendment is not that their content communicates any particular idea, but that their content embodies a particularly intolerable (and socially unnecessary) *mode* of expressing *whatever* idea the speaker wishes to convey. St. Paul has not singled out an especially offensive mode of expression—it has not, for example, selected for prohibition only those fighting words that communicate ideas in a threatening (as opposed to a merely obnoxious) manner. Rather, it has proscribed fighting words of whatever manner that communicate messages of racial, gender, or religious intolerance. Selectivity of this sort creates the possibility that the city is seeking to handicap the expression of particular ideas. That possibility would alone be enough to render the ordinance presumptively invalid, but St. Paul's comments and concessions in this case elevate the possibility to a certainty....

Finally, St. Paul ... defend[s] the conclusion of the Minnesota Supreme Court that, even if the ordinance regulates expression based on hostility towards its protected ideological content, this discrimination is nonetheless justified because it is narrowly tailored to serve compelling state interests. Specifically, they assert that the ordinance helps to ensure the basic human rights of members of groups that have historically been subjected to discrimination, including the right of such group members to live in peace where they wish. We do not doubt that these interests are compelling, and that the ordinance can be said to promote them. But the "danger of censorship" presented by a facially content-based statute requires that that weapon be employed only where it is *"necessary* to serve the asserted [compelling] interest."... The dispositive question in this case, therefore, is whether content discrimination is reasonably necessary to achieve St. Paul's compelling interests; it plainly is not. An ordinance not limited to the favored topics, for example, would have precisely the same beneficial effect. In fact the only interest distinctively served by the content limitation is that of displaying the city council's special hostility towards the particular biases thus singled out. That is precisely what the First Amendment forbids. The politicians of St. Paul are entitled to express that hostility—but not through the means of imposing unique limitations upon speakers who (however benightedly) disagree.

Let there be no mistake about our belief that burning a cross in someone's front yard is reprehensible. But St. Paul has sufficient means at its disposal to prevent such behavior without adding the First Amendment to the fire.

The judgment of the Minnesota Supreme Court is reversed, and the case is remanded for proceedings not inconsistent with this opinion.

It is so ordered.

The Supreme Court unanimously declared the St. Paul hate speech ordinance to be unconstitutional. The justices found the law defective because it singled out a particular kind of hate speech. The ordinance, therefore, violated the principle that laws regulating expression must not discriminate on the basis of content. The concurring justices also found the law unacceptable, but preferred to strike it down for being unconstitutionally vague.

It would be incorrect, however, to generalize from *R.A.V.* that the Court will strike down any law that imposes a penalty for hateful expression. In 1993, for example, the justices considered a Wisconsin statute that allowed judges to impose more severe sentences on defendants whose crimes were motivated by prejudicial attitudes based on race, religion, sexual orientation, national origin, and so forth. The Wisconsin law was similar to those enacted by many state and local governments in an attempt to reduce the incidence of hate crimes. Forty-nine states submitted a joint brief urging the Court to uphold Wisconsin's law. The federal government also submitted arguments in support of the constitutionality of the hate crimes provision. As you read the Court's unanimous decision in *Wisconsin v. Mitchell*, compare it to *R.A.V.* Are the two decisions compatible?

Wisconsin v. Mitchell

509 U.S. — (1993)

Vote: 9 *(Blackmun, Kennedy, O'Connor, Rehnquist, Scalia, Souter, Stevens, Thomas, White)*

0

Opinion of the Court: Rehnquist

In October 1989 Todd Mitchell and several other young black men were discussing the scene in the film *Mississippi Burning* in which a white man beats a black boy. During the conversation, Mitchell asked his companions, "Do you all feel hyped up to move on some white people?"

A little later Mitchell and his friends spotted a young white boy across the street. As the boy neared, Mitchell said, "You all want to fuck somebody up? There goes a white boy; go get him." The group then attacked the boy, beating him and stealing his sneakers. They left him unconscious, a state in which he remained for four days.

A jury found Mitchell guilty of aggravated battery, an offense that usually carries a maximum sentence of two years in prison. But, under Wisconsin's penalty-enhancement law, that maximum could reach seven years should the jury find that Mitchell had "intentionally select[ed]" his victim because of his race, religion, color, disability, sexual orientation, national origin, or ancestry. In other words, the state law enhanced the punishment for so-called "hate crimes." In Mitchell's case, the jury in fact found that he had intentionally chosen his victim on the basis of race, and he was sentenced to four years in prison.

Mitchell asked the Wisconsin courts to overturn his conviction on the ground that the state penalty-enhancement law violated freedom of expression guarantees contained in the First Amendment. Based in some measure on *R.A.V. v. St. Paul*, the Wisconsin Supreme Court ruled in favor of Mitchell, striking down the state law on constitutional grounds.

CHIEF JUSTICE REHNQUIST delivered the opinion of the Court.

Respondent Todd Mitchell's sentence for aggravated battery was enhanced because he intentionally selected his victim on account of the victim's race. The question presented in this case is whether this penalty enhancement is prohibited by the First and Fourteenth Amendments. We hold that it is not....

We granted certiorari because of the importance of the question presented and the existence of a conflict of authority among state high courts on the constitutionality of statutes similar to Wisconsin's penalty-enhancement provision.* We reverse.

Mitchell argues that we are bound by the Wisconsin Supreme Court's conclusion that the statute punishes bigoted thought and not conduct. There is no doubt that we are bound by a state court's construction of a state statute. In *Terminiello* [*v. Chicago*, 1949], for example, the Illinois courts had defined the term "'breach of the peace,'" in a city ordinance prohibiting disorderly conduct, to include "'stirs the public to anger ... or creates a disturbance.'" We held this construction to be binding on us. But here the Wisconsin Supreme Court did not, strictly speaking, construe the Wisconsin statute in the sense of defining the meaning of a particular statutory word or phrase. Rather, it merely characterized the "practical effect" of the statute for First Amendment purposes. This assessment does not bind us. Once any ambiguities as to the meaning of the statute are resolved, we may form our own judgment as to its operative effect.

The State argues that the statute does not punish bigoted thought, as the Supreme Court of Wisconsin said,

but instead punishes only conduct. While this argument is literally correct, it does not dispose of Mitchell's First Amendment challenge. To be sure, our cases reject the "view that apparently limitless variety of conduct can be labeled 'speech' whenever the person engaging in the conduct intends thereby to express an idea." Thus, a physical assault is not by any stretch of the imagination expressive conduct protected by the First Amendment.

But the fact remains that under the Wisconsin statute the same criminal conduct may be more heavily punished if the victim is selected because of his race or other protected status than if no such motive obtained. Thus, although the statute punishes criminal conduct, it enhances the maximum penalty for conduct motivated by a discriminatory point of view more severely than the same conduct engaged in for some other reason or for no reason at all. Because the only reason for the enhancement is the defendant's discriminatory motive for selecting his victim, Mitchell argues (and the Wisconsin Supreme Court held) that the statute violates the First Amendment by punishing offenders' bigoted beliefs.

Traditionally, sentencing judges have considered a wide variety of factors in addition to evidence bearing on guilt in determining what sentence to impose on a convicted defendant. The defendant's motive for committing the offense is one important factor. Thus, in many States the commission of a murder, or other capital offense, for pecuniary gain is a separate aggravating circumstance under the capital-sentencing statute.

But it is equally true that a defendant's abstract beliefs, however obnoxious to most people, may not be taken into consideration by a sentencing judge. In *Dawson* [*v. Delaware*, 1992], the State introduced evidence at a capital-sentencing hearing that the defendant was a member of a white supremacist prison gang. Because "the evidence proved nothing more than [the defendant's] abstract beliefs," we held that its admission violated the defendant's First Amendment rights. In so holding, however, we emphasized that "the Constitution does not erect a *per se* barrier to the admission of evidence concerning one's beliefs and associations at sentencing simply because those beliefs and associations are protected by the First Amendment. Thus, in *Barclay v. Florida* (1983) (plurality opinion), we allowed the sentencing judge to take into account the defendant's racial

---

*Several States have enacted penalty-enhancement provisions similar to the Wisconsin statute at issue in this case. Proposed federal legislation to the same effect passed the House of Representatives in 1992, but failed to pass the Senate (1992). The state high courts are divided over the constitutionality of penalty-enhancement statutes and analogous statutes covering bias-motivated offenses. According to *amici*, bias-motivated violence is on the rise throughout the United States.... In 1990, Congress enacted the Hate Crimes Statistics Act, directing the Attorney General to compile data "about crimes that manifest evidence of prejudice based on race, religion, sexual orientation, or ethnicity." Pursuant to the Act, the Federal Bureau of Investigation reported in January 1993, that 4,558 bias-motivated offenses were committed in 1991, including 1,614 incidents of intimidation, 1,301 incidents of vandalism, 796 simple assaults, 773 aggravated assaults, and 12 murders.

animus towards his victim. The evidence in that case showed that the defendant's membership in the Black Liberation Army and desire to provoke a "race war" were related to the murder of a white man for which he was convicted. Because "the elements of racial hatred in [the] murder" were relevant to several aggravating factors, we held that the trial judge permissibly took this evidence into account in sentencing the defendant to death.

Mitchell suggests that *Dawson* and *Barclay* are inapposite because they did not involve application of a penalty-enhancement provision. But in *Barclay* we held that it was permissible for the sentencing court to consider the defendant's racial animus in determining whether he should be sentenced to death, surely the most severe "enhancement" of all. And the fact that the Wisconsin Legislature has decided, as a general matter, that bias-motivated offenses warrant greater maximum penalties across the board does not alter the result here. For the primary responsibility for fixing criminal penalties lies with the legislature. . . .

Nothing in our decision last Term in *R.A.V.* compels a different result here. That case involved a First Amendment challenge to a municipal ordinance prohibiting the use of "'fighting words' that insult, or provoke violence, 'on the basis of race, color, creed, religion or gender.'" Because the ordinance only proscribed a class of "fighting words" deemed particularly offensive by the city—i.e., those "that contain . . . messages of 'bias-motivated' hatred," we held that it violated the rule against content-based discrimination. But whereas the ordinance struck down in *R.A.V.* was explicitly directed at expression, *i.e.,* "speech" or "messages," the statute in this case is aimed at conduct unprotected by the First Amendment.

Moreover, the Wisconsin statute singles out for enhancement bias-inspired conduct because this conduct is thought to inflict greater individual and societal harm. For example, according to the State and its *amici*, bias-motivated crimes are more likely to provoke retaliatory crimes, inflict distinct emotional harms on their victims, and incite community unrest. See, *e.g.,* Brief for Petitioner, Brief for United States as *Amicus Curiae;* Brief for Lawyers' Committee for Civil Rights Under Law as *Amicus Curiae;* Brief for the American Civil Liberties Union as *Amicus Curiae;* Brief for the Anti-Defamation League et al. as *Amici Curiae;* Brief for Congressman Charles E. Schumer et al. as *Amici Curiae.* The

State's desire to redress these perceived harms provides an adequate explanation for its penalty-enhancement provision over and above mere disagreement with offenders' beliefs or biases. . . .

Finally, there remains to be considered Mitchell's argument that the Wisconsin statute is unconstitutionally overbroad because of its "chilling effect" on free speech. Mitchell argues (and the Wisconsin Supreme Court agreed) that the statute is "overbroad" because evidence of the defendant's prior speech or associations may be used to prove that the defendant intentionally selected his victim on account of the victim's protected status. Consequently, the argument goes, the statute impermissibly chills free expression with respect to such matters by those concerned about the possibility of enhanced sentences if they should in the future commit a criminal offense covered by the statute. We find no merit in this contention.

The sort of chill envisioned here is far more attenuated and unlikely than that contemplated in traditional "overbreadth" cases. We must conjure up a vision of a Wisconsin citizen suppressing his unpopular bigoted opinions for fear that if he later commits an offense covered by the statute, these opinions will be offered at trial to establish that he selected his victim on account of the victim's protected status, thus qualifying him for penalty-enhancement. To stay within the realm of rationality, we must surely put to one side minor misdemeanor offenses covered by the statute, such as negligent operation of a motor vehicle; for it is difficult, if not impossible, to conceive of a situation where such offenses would be racially motivated. We are left, then, with the prospect of a citizen suppressing his bigoted beliefs for fear that evidence of such beliefs will be introduced against him at trial if he commits a more serious offense against person or property. This is simply too speculative a hypothesis to support Mitchell's overbreadth claim.

The First Amendment, moreover, does not prohibit the evidentiary use of speech to establish the elements of a crime or to prove motive or intent. Evidence of a defendant's previous declarations or statements is commonly admitted in criminal trials subject to evidentiary rules dealing with relevancy, reliability, and the like. Nearly half a century ago, in *Haupt v. United States* (1947), we rejected a contention similar to that advanced by Mitchell here. Haupt was tried for the offense of treason, which, as defined by the Constitution (Art. III, § 3), may depend very much on proof of motive. To prove that the acts in question were committed out of "adherence to the enemy" rather than "parental solicitude," the Government introduced evidence of conversations that had taken place long prior to the indictment, some of which consisted of statements showing Haupt's sympathy with Germany and Hitler and hostility towards the United States. We rejected Haupt's argument that this evidence was improperly admitted. While "[s]uch testimony is to be scrutinized with care to be certain the statements are not expressions of mere lawful and permissible difference of opinion with our own government or quite proper appreciation of the land of birth," we held that "these statements . . . clearly were admissible on the question of intent and adherence to the enemy."

For the foregoing reasons, we hold that Mitchell's First Amendment rights were not violated by the application of the Wisconsin penalty-enhancement provision in sentencing him. The judgment of the Supreme Court of Wisconsin is therefore reversed, and the case is remanded for further proceedings not inconsistent with this opinion.

It is so ordered.

Although the votes were unanimous in *R.A.V.* and *Mitchell*, the justices did not settle the hate speech issue, perhaps because the two rulings reached somewhat different conclusions: *Mitchell* supported government regulation, while *R.A.V.* did not. Supporters of broad First Amendment protection and those who favor restricting discriminatory expression both can find encouragement in the Court's opinions. As a result, the battle over hateful and harassing expression continues on college campuses, in the workplace, and in legislatures. The Court certainly has not seen its last dispute in this area.

The Right Not To Speak

So far we have discussed the constitutionality of government attempts to restrict or prohibit certain kinds of expression. While curtailing expression is the most common form of government regulation, there are situations in which the government requires us to speak or write. For example, we may be ordered to appear as a witness before a court, grand jury, or legislative investigating committee. The government compels us to provide information when we file our tax returns. We may be required to take an oath when we become citizens, provide court testimony, take public office, or apply for a gun permit. Americans generally consider these regulations to be reasonable requirements relevant to legitimate government functions. But what if an individual does not want to comply with a government regulation that requires expression? Other than the Fifth Amendment's protection against the government compelling self-incriminating testimony, is there any restraint on the government's authority to coerce expression? Put another way, does the First Amendment's guarantee of freedom of speech carry with it the freedom not to speak?

To understand this issue we need once again to turn our attention to the famous "flag salute" cases discussed in Chapter 3. As you recall, in 1940 the Court in *Minersville School District v. Gobitis* upheld flag salute regulations against claims that the school system was violating the children's right to free exercise of religion. Three years later, in *West Virginia Board of Education v. Barnette* (1943), the Court again considered the constitutionality of the compulsory flag salute laws, and once again the case was brought by Jehovah's Witnesses. By this time, however, some conditions had changed. First, due to American victories on the battlefield, the feverishly patriotic mood so strong at the beginning of World War II had moderated somewhat. Second, the Court had undergone some personnel changes that strengthened its civil libertarian wing. Third, the *Gobitis* decision had been roundly criticized in legal circles. These circumstances encouraged the Witnesses to be more optimistic about their chances of winning. But there was one additional factor that distinguished *Gobitis* from *Barnette*. Hayden Covington and the other lawyers supporting the challenge made a significant strategy decision to base the attack not so much on freedom of religion, but instead on the freedom of speech. As you read Justice Jackson's majority opinion in *Barnette*, notice how he weaves religion and expression rights into his explanation for striking down the flag salute laws.

West Virginia Board of Education v. Barnette

319 U.S. 624 (1943)
Vote: 6 (Black, Douglas, Jackson, Murphy, Rutledge, Stone)
   3 (Frankfurter, Reed, Roberts)
Opinion of the Court: Jackson
Concurring opinions: Black and Douglas (joint), Murphy
Dissenting opinions: Frankfurter, Reed and Roberts (joint)

Following the *Gobitis* decision, the West Virginia legislature amended its laws to require that all public schools teach courses that increased students' knowledge of the American system of government and fostered the spirit of Americanism. In support of this policy, the state board of education required that the American flag be saluted and the Pledge of Allegiance be recited each day. Students who refused to participate could be charged with insubordination and expelled. Not attending school because of such an expulsion was grounds for the child being declared delinquent. Parents of delinquent children were subject to fines and jail penalties up to thirty days. In some cases officials threatened noncomplying students with reform school.

The Jehovah's Witnesses challenged these regulations in the name of the Barnette family, church members who had been harassed by the school system for failure to participate in the flag salute ritual. One of the Barnette children, in fact, had been expelled.[30]

Despite the Supreme Court's decision in *Gobitis*, a three-judge district court sympathized with the Barnette family's plight. According to the well-respected

---

30. For more details on this case, see David Manwaring, *Render Unto Caesar: The Flag Salute Controversy* (Chicago: University of Chicago Press, 1962).

---

circuit court judge, John J. Parker: "The salute to the United States' flag is an expression of the homage of the soul. To force it upon one who has conscientious scruples against giving it is petty tyranny unworthy of the spirit of the Republic, and forbidden, we think, by the United States Constitution." After the decision, the West Virginia School Board appealed to the U.S. Supreme Court.

MR. JUSTICE JACKSON delivered the opinion of the Court.

As the present Chief Justice said in dissent in the Gobitis case, the State may "require teaching by instruction and study of all in our history and in the structure and organization of our government, including the guaranties of civil liberty which tend to inspire patriotism and love of country." Here, however, we are dealing with a compulsion of students to declare a belief. They are not merely made acquainted with the flag salute so that they may be informed as to what it is or even what it means. The issue here is whether this slow and easily neglected route to aroused loyalties constitutionally may be short-cut by substituting a compulsory salute and slogan....

There is no doubt that, in connection with the pledges, the flag salute is a form of utterance. Symbolism is a primitive but effective way of communicating ideas. The use of an emblem or flag to symbolize some system, idea, institution, or personality, is a short cut from mind to mind. Causes and nations, political parties, lodges and ecclesiastical groups seek to knit the loyalty of their following to a flag or banner, a color or design. The State announces rank, function, and authority through crowns and maces, uniforms and black robes; the church speaks through the Cross, the Crucifix, the altar and shrine, and clerical raiment. Symbols of State often convey political ideas just as religious symbols come to convey theological ones. Associated with many of these symbols are appropriate gestures of acceptance or respect: a salute, a bowed or bared head, a bended knee. A person gets from a symbol the meaning he puts into it, and what is one man's comfort and inspiration is another's jest and scorn.

Over a decade ago Chief Justice Hughes led this Court in holding that the display of a red flag as a symbol of opposition by peaceful and legal means to organized government was protected by the free speech guaranties of the Constitution. Stromberg v. California [1931]. Here it is the State that employs a flag as a symbol of adherence to government as presently organized. It requires the individual to communicate by word and sign his acceptance of the political ideas it thus bespeaks. Objection to this form of communication when coerced is an old one, well known to the framers of the Bill of Rights.

It is also to be noted that the compulsory flag salute and pledge requires affirmation of a belief and an attitude of mind. It is not clear whether the regulation contemplates that pupils forego any contrary convictions of their own and become unwilling converts to the prescribed ceremony or whether it will be acceptable if they simulate assent by words without belief and by a gesture barren of meaning. It is now a commonplace that censorship or suppression of expression of opinion is tolerated by our Constitution only when the expression presents a clear and present danger of action of a kind the State is empowered to prevent and punish. It would seem that involuntary affirmation could be commanded only on even more immediate and urgent grounds than silence. But here the power of compulsion is invoked without any allegation that remaining passive during a flag salute ritual creates a clear and present danger that would justify an effort even to muffle expression. To sustain the compulsory flag salute we are required to say that a Bill of Rights which guards the individual's right to speak his own mind, left it open to public authorities to compel him to utter what is not in his mind.

Whether the First Amendment to the Constitution will permit officials to order observance of ritual of this nature does not depend upon whether as a voluntary exercise we would think it to be good, bad or merely innocuous. Any credo of nationalism is likely to include what some disapprove or to omit what others think essential, and to give off different overtones as it takes on different accents or interpretations. If official power exists to coerce acceptance of any patriotic creed, what it shall contain cannot be decided by courts, but must be largely discretionary with the ordaining authority, whose power to prescribe would no doubt include power to amend. Hence validity of the asserted power to force an American citizen publicly to profess any statement of belief or to engage in any ceremony of assent to one presents questions of power that must be considered independently of any idea we may have as to the utility of the ceremony in question.

Nor does the issue as we see it turn on one's possession of particular religious views or the sincerity with which they are held. While religion supplies appellees' motive for enduring the discomforts of making the issue in this case, many citizens who do not share these religious views hold such a compulsory rite to infringe constitutional liberty of the individual. It is not necessary to inquire whether nonconformist beliefs will exempt from the duty to salute unless we first find power to make the salute a legal duty.

The Gobitis decision, however, *assumed*, as did the argument in that case and in this, that power exists in the State to impose the flag salute discipline upon school children in general. The Court only examined and rejected a claim based on religious beliefs of immunity from an unquestioned general rule. The question which underlies the flag salute controversy is whether such a ceremony so touching matters of opinion and political attitude may be imposed upon the individual by official authority under powers committed to any political organization under our Constitution. We examine rather than assume existence of this power and, against this broader definition of issues in this case, re-examine specific grounds assigned for the Gobitis decision.

1. It was said that the flag-salute controversy confronted the Court with "the problem which Lincoln cast in memorable dilemma: 'Must a government of necessity be too *strong* for the liberties of its people, or too *weak* to maintain its own existence?'" and that the answer must be in favor of strength. Minersville School District v. Gobitis.

We think these issues may be examined free of pressure or restraint growing out of such considerations.

It may be doubted whether Mr. Lincoln would have thought that the strength of government to maintain itself would be impressively vindicated by our confirming power of the state to expel a handful of children from school. Such oversimplification, so handy in political debate, often lacks the precision necessary to postulates of judicial reasoning. If validly applied to this problem, the utterance cited would resolve every issue of power in favor of those in authority and would require us to override every liberty thought to weaken or delay execution of their policies.

Government of limited power need not be anemic government. Assurance that rights are secure tends to diminish fear and jealousy of strong government, and by making us feel safe to live under it makes for its better support. Without promise of a limiting Bill of Rights it is doubtful if our Constitution could have mustered enough strength to enable its ratification. To enforce those rights today is not to choose weak government over strong government. It is only to adhere as a means of strength to individual freedom of mind in preference to officially disciplined uniformity for which history indicates a disappointing and disastrous end.

The subject now before us exemplifies this principle. Free public education, if faithful to the ideal of secular instruction and political neutrality, will not be partisan or enemy of any class, creed, party, or faction. If it is to impose any ideological discipline, however, each party or denomination must seek to control, or failing that, to weaken the influence of the educational system. Observance of the limitations of the Constitution will not weaken government in the field appropriate for its exercise.

2. It was also considered in the Gobitis case that functions of educational officers in states, counties and school districts were such that to interfere with their authority "would in effect make us the school board for the country."

The Fourteenth Amendment, as now applied to the States, protects the citizen against the State itself and all of its creatures—Boards of Education not excepted. These have, of course, important, delicate, and highly discretionary functions, but none that they may not perform within the limits of the Bill of Rights. That they are educating the young for citizenship is reason for scrupulous protection of Constitutional freedoms of the individual, if we are not to strangle the free mind at its source and teach youth to discount important principles of our government as mere platitudes.

Such Boards are numerous and their territorial jurisdiction often small. But small and local authority may feel less sense of responsibility to the Constitution, and agencies of publicity may be less vigilant in calling it to account. The action of Congress in making flag observance voluntary and respecting the conscience of the objector in a matter so vital as raising the Army contrasts sharply with these local

regulations in matters relatively trivial to the welfare of the nation. There are village tyrants as well as village Hampdens, but none who acts under color of law is beyond reach of the Constitution.

3. The Gobitis opinion reasoned that this is a field "where courts possess no marked and certainly no controlling competence," that it is committed to the legislatures as well as the courts to guard cherished liberties and that it is constitutionally appropriate to "fight out the wise use of legislative authority in the forum of public opinion and before legislative assemblies rather than to transfer such a contest to the judicial arena," since all the "effective means of inducing political changes are left free."

The very purpose of a Bill of Rights was to withdraw certain subjects from the vicissitudes of political controversy, to place them beyond the reach of majorities and officials and to establish them as legal principles to be applied by the courts. One's right to life, liberty, and property, to free speech, a free press, freedom of worship and assembly, and other fundamental rights may not be submitted to vote; they depend on the outcome of no elections.

In weighing arguments of the parties it is important to distinguish between the due process clause of the Fourteenth Amendment as an instrument for transmitting the principles of the First Amendment and those cases in which it is applied for its own sake. The test of legislation which collides with the Fourteenth Amendment, because it also collides with the principles of the First, is much more definite than the test when only the Fourteenth is involved. Much of the vagueness of the due process clause disappears when the specific prohibitions of the First become its standard. The right of a State to regulate, for example, a public utility may well include, so far as the due process test is concerned, power to impose all of the restrictions which a legislature may have a "rational basis" for adopting. But freedoms of speech and of press, of assembly, and of worship may not be infringed on such slender grounds. They are susceptible of restriction only to prevent grave and immediate danger to interests which the state may lawfully protect. It is important to note that while it is the Fourteenth Amendment which bears directly upon the State it is the more specific limiting principles of the First Amendment that finally govern this case....

4. Lastly, and this is the very heart of the Gobitis opin-

ion, it reasons that "National unity is the basis of national security," that the authorities have "the right to select appropriate means for its attainment," and hence reaches the conclusion that such compulsory measures toward "national unity" are constitutional. Upon the verity of this assumption depends our answer in this case.

National unity as an end which officials may foster by persuasion and example is not in question. The problem is whether under our Constitution compulsion as here employed is a permissible means for its achievement.

Struggles to coerce uniformity of sentiment in support of some end thought essential to their time and country have been waged by many good as well as by evil men. Nationalism is a relatively recent phenomenon but at other times and places the ends have been racial or territorial security, support of a dynasty or regime, and particular plans for saving souls. As first and moderate methods to attain unity have failed, those bent on its accomplishment must resort to an ever-increasing severity.... Those who begin coercive elimination of dissent soon find themselves exterminating dissenters. Compulsory unification of opinion achieves only the unanimity of the graveyard.

It seems trite but necessary to say that the First Amendment to our Constitution was designed to avoid these ends by avoiding these beginnings. There is no mysticism in the American concept of the State or of the nature or origin of its authority. We set up government by consent of the governed, and the Bill of Rights denies those in power any legal opportunity to coerce that consent. Authority here is to be controlled by public opinion, not public opinion by authority.

The case is made difficult not because the principles of its decision are obscure but because the flag involved is our own. Nevertheless, we apply the limitations of the Constitution with no fear that freedom to be intellectually and spiritually diverse or even contrary will disintegrate the social organization. To believe that patriotism will not flourish if patriotic ceremonies are voluntary and spontaneous instead of a compulsory routine is to make an unflattering estimate of the appeal of our institutions to free minds. We can have intellectual individualism and the rich cultural diversity that we owe to exceptional minds only at the price of occasional eccentricity and abnormal attitudes. When they are so harmless to others or to the State as those we deal with here, the price is not too great. But freedom to differ is not limited to things that do not matter much. That would be a mere shadow of freedom. The test of its substance is the right to differ as to things that touch the heart of the existing order.

If there is any fixed star in our constitutional constellation, it is that no official, high or petty, can prescribe what shall be orthodox in politics, nationalism, religion, or other matters of opinion or force citizens to confess by word or act their faith therein. If there are any circumstances which permit an exception, they do not now occur to us.

We think the action of the local authorities in compelling the flag salute and pledge transcends constitutional limitations on their power and invades the sphere of intellect and spirit which it is the purpose of the First Amendment to our Constitution to reserve from all official control.

The decision of this Court in Minersville School District v. Gobitis and the holdings of those few per curiam decisions which preceded and foreshadowed it are overruled, and the judgment enjoining enforcement of the West Virginia Regulation is affirmed.

Affirmed.

MR. JUSTICE FRANKFURTER, dissenting.

One who belongs to the most vilified and persecuted minority in history is not likely to be insensible to the freedoms guaranteed by our Constitution. Were my purely personal attitude relevant I should wholeheartedly associate myself with the general libertarian views in the Court's opinion, representing as they do the thought and action of a lifetime. But as judges we are neither Jew nor Gentile, neither Catholic nor agnostic. We owe equal attachment to the Constitution and are equally bound by our judicial obligations whether we derive our citizenship from the earliest or latest immigrants to these shores. As a member of this Court I am not justified in writing my private notions of policy into the Constitution, no matter how deeply I may cherish them or how mischievous I may deem their disregard. The duty of a judge who must decide which of two claims before the Court shall prevail, that of a State to enact and enforce laws within its general competence or that of an individual to refuse obedience because of the demands of his conscience, is not that of the ordinary person. It can never be emphasized too much that one's own opinion about the wisdom or evil of a law should be excluded altogether when one is doing one's duty on the bench.... [I]t would require more daring than I possess to deny that reasonable legislators could have taken the action which is before us for review. Most unwillingly, therefore, I must differ from my brethren with regard to legislation like this. I cannot bring my mind to believe that the "liberty" secured by the Due Process Clause gives this Court authority to deny to the State of West Virginia the attainment of that which we all recognize as a legitimate legislative end, namely, the promotion of good citizenship, by employment of the means here chosen....

In striking down the West Virginia compulsory flag salute law, the Court ruled that the individual has at least a qualified right to be free of government coercion to express views the individual disavows. This decision does not go so far as to hold that an individual's First Amendment right can be used to avoid obligations such as testifying in a court case or providing information on a tax return, but it precludes certain forms of coerced expression.

For another example of this principle, consider the plight of George and Maxine Maynard of Lebanon, New Hampshire. Like the Gobitas and Barnette families, the Maynards were Jehovah's Witnesses. Their entanglement with the law stemmed from a statute mandating that the state slogan appear on all vehicle license plates. The Maynards considered the slogan, "Live Free or Die," to be repugnant to their moral, religious, and political beliefs. To disassociate himself from the slogan, Maynard cut a portion of the slogan from the plates on his cars and covered the remaining words with tape, but he did not conceal the identifying letters or numbers. In November 1974 local authorities arrested Maynard for obscuring a license plate, a misdemeanor under New Hampshire law. He explained his objections to the slogan, but the court

found him guilty. The judge imposed a $25.00 fine, but agreed to suspend it if Maynard would comply with the law. The next month authorities arrested Maynard once again for the same offense. The court found him guilty and sentenced him to six months in jail and a $50.00 fine. The judge again showed leniency by permitting Maynard to avoid jail if he would pay the two fines. Maynard announced that as a matter of conscience, he would pay no fines. The judge ordered him to serve a fifteen-day jail sentence, which he did. The Maynards then sued, challenging the constitutionality of the law. They won and the state appealed.

The case of *Wooley v. Maynard* (1977) presented the justices with a classic conflict between individual and state interests. The Maynards argued that their First Amendment rights protected them from state compulsion. George Maynard filed a statement saying, "I refuse to be coerced by the State into advertising a slogan which I find morally, ethically, religiously, and politically abhorrent." The state responded by contending that its interest in promoting an appreciation of history, individualism, and state pride outweighed the narrow interests of the Maynards.

Speaking for the Court, Chief Justice Burger ruled in favor of the Maynards. He explained:

We begin with the proposition that the right of freedom of thought protected by the First Amendment against state action includes both the right to speak freely and the right to refrain from speaking at all. A system which secures the right to proselytize religious, political, and ideological causes must also guarantee the concomitant right to decline to foster such concepts. The right to speak and the right to refrain from speaking are complementary components of the broader concept of "individual freedom of mind."

The justices concluded that the countervailing interests of the state were insufficiently compelling to outweigh the First Amendment liberties at stake. The state slogan was not ideologically neutral, but proclaimed an official view of such subjects as history, state pride, and individualism. While the state may have an interest in promoting these beliefs, such an interest cannot outweigh an individual's First Amendment right to avoid becoming an unwilling spokesperson for that message.

Commercial Speech

As consumers of all sorts of goods and services, we are constantly bombarded with commercial speech—advertisements. Open a newspaper, turn on a television or radio, or take a short drive, and you are bound to find hundreds of ads, aimed at communicating all kinds of messages. Although we see ads every day, we probably do not think much about them in terms of the First Amendment. Does the First Amendment apply to this form of expression? If so, does it deserve the same constitutional protection as more traditional, equally commonplace, forms of speech?

Historically, courts have viewed commercial expression as more closely related to commerce than to speech. Government has an interest in regulating fraudulent or deceptive messages that may be found in advertisements. In addition, the subject matter of commercial expression is substantially different from the political and social speech at the heart of First Amendment protections. For these reasons, the courts have always allowed more extensive government regulation of commercial expression than of other forms of speech. In 1942, for example, the Supreme Court in *Valentine v. Chrestensen* upheld a law banning the distribution of handbills that advertised commercial goods and services. The Court concluded that the First Amendment does not protect "purely commercial advertising." Beginning in the mid-1970s, however, the justices began to reconsider the constitutional status of commercial expression. It all started with *Bigelow v. Virginia*.

Bigelow v. Virginia

421 U.S. 809 (1975)
Vote: 7 (Blackmun, Brennan, Burger, Douglas, Marshall, Stewart, Powell)
  2 (Rehnquist, White)
Opinion of the Court: Blackmun
Dissenting opinion: Rehnquist

As managing editor of the *Virginia Weekly*, a Charlottesville newspaper focusing on the University of Virginia community, Jeffrey C. Bigelow approved for publication the ad reproduced on page 295. It ran on February 8, 1971, two years before the Supreme Court's decision in *Roe v. Wade*, which legalized abortions.

Three months later, Virginia charged Bigelow with violating an 1878 state law: "if any person, by publication, lecture, advertisement ... encourage or prompt the procuring of abortion ... he shall be guilty of a misdemeanor." Bigelow was the first individual ever accused of violating the law, despite its duration.

Throughout his trial and appeals, Bigelow's attorneys (including Melvin Wulf of the ACLU) never questioned the law's applicability; clearly, by authorizing the ad, Bigelow violated the state statute. Instead, they brought a unique and broad-based argument: because the First Amendment protected commercial speech, Virginia's law was unconstitutional. Several judicial bodies, including the Supreme Court of Virginia, rejected this line of reasoning, claiming that the Free Speech Clause does not apply to paid commercial advertisements. Therefore, the U.S. Supreme Court addressed this question: Is commercial speech protected expression under the First Amendment?

MR. JUSTICE BLACKMUN delivered the opinion of the Court.

An advertisement carried in appellant's newspaper led to his conviction for a violation of a Virginia statute that made it a misdemeanor, by the sale or circulation of any publication, to encourage or prompt the procuring of an abortion. The issue here is whether the editor-appellant's First Amendment rights were unconstitutionally abridged by the statute....

The Supreme Court of Virginia ... affirmed Bigelow's conviction. The court first rejected the appellant's claim that the advertisement was purely informational and thus was not within the "encourage or prompt" language of the statute. It held, instead, that the advertisement "clearly exceeded an informational status" and "constituted an active offer to perform a service, rather than a passive statement of fact." It then rejected Bigelow's First Amendment claim. This, the court said, was a "commercial advertisement" and, as such, "may be constitutionally prohibited by the state," particularly "where, as here, the advertising relates to the medical-health field." The issue, in the court's view, was whether the statute was a valid exercise of the State's police power. It answered this question in the affirmative, noting that the statute's goal was "to ensure that pregnant women in Virginia who decided to have abortions come to their decisions without the commercial advertising pressure usually incidental to the sale of a box of soap powder."...

The central assumption made by the Supreme Court of Virginia was that the First Amendment guarantees of speech and press are inapplicable to paid commercial advertisements. Our cases, however, clearly establish that speech is not stripped of First Amendment protection merely because it appears in that form.

The fact that the particular advertisement in appellant's newspaper had commercial aspects or reflected the advertiser's commercial interests did not negate all First Amendment guarantees. The State was not free of constitutional restraint merely because the advertisement involved sales or "solicitations," or because appellant was paid for printing it, or because appellant's motive or the motive of the advertiser may have involved financial gain. The existence of "commercial activity, in itself, is no justification for narrowing the protection of expression secured by the First Amendment."

Although other categories of speech—such as fighting words, Chaplinsky v. New Hampshire (1942), or obscenity, Roth v. United States (1957), or incitement, Brandenburg v. Ohio (1969)—have been held unprotected, no contention has been made that the particular speech embraced in the

---

UNWANTED PREGNANCY
LET US HELP YOU
Abortions are now legal in New York.
There are no residency requirements.
FOR IMMEDIATE PLACEMENT IN
ACCREDITED HOSPITALS AND
CLINICS AT LOW COST
Contact
WOMEN'S PAVILION
515 Madison Avenue
New York, N. Y. 10022
or call any time
(212) 371-6670 or (212) 371-6650
AVAILABLE 7 DAYS A WEEK

STRICTLY CONFIDENTIAL. We will make all arrangements for you and help you with information and counseling.

---

advertisement in question is within any of these categories.

The appellee, as did the Supreme Court of Virginia, relies on Valentine v. Chrestensen (1942), where a unanimous Court, in a brief opinion, sustained an ordinance which had been interpreted to ban the distribution of a handbill advertising the exhibition of a submarine. The handbill solicited customers to tour the ship for a fee. The promoter-advertiser had first attempted to distribute a single-faced handbill consisting only of the advertisement, and was denied permission to do so. He then had printed, on the reverse side of the handbill, a protest against official conduct refusing him the use of wharfage facilities. The Court found that the message of asserted "public interest" was appended solely for the purpose of evading the ordinance and therefore did not constitute an "exercise of the freedom of communicating information and disseminating opinion."...

But the holding is distinctly a limited one: the ordinance

was upheld as a reasonable regulation of the manner in which commercial advertising could be distributed. The fact that it had the effect of banning a particular handbill does not mean that *Chrestensen* is authority for the proposition that all statutes regulating commercial advertising are immune from constitutional challenge. The case obviously does not support any sweeping proposition that advertising is unprotected *per se.*

This Court's cases decided since *Chrestensen* clearly demonstrate as untenable any reading of that case that would give it so broad an effect. In New York Times Co. v. Sullivan [1964], a city official instituted a civil libel action against four clergymen and the New York Times. The suit was based on an advertisement carried in the newspaper criticizing police action against members of the civil rights movement and soliciting contributions for the movement. The Court held that this advertisement, although containing factually erroneous defamatory content, was entitled to the same degree of constitutional protection as ordinary speech.... *Chrestensen* was distinguished on the ground that the handbill advertisement there did no more than propose a purely commercial transaction....

The principle that commercial advertising enjoys a degree of First Amendment protection was reaffirmed in Pittsburgh Press v. Human Rel. Comm'n (1973). There, the Court, although divided, sustained an ordinance that had been construed to forbid newspapers to carry help-wanted advertisements in sex-designated columns except where based upon a bona fide occupational exemption. The Court did describe the advertisements at issue as "classic examples of commercial speech," for each was "no more than a proposal of possible employment." But the Court indicated that the advertisements would have received some degree of First Amendment protection if the commercial proposal had been legal....

The legitimacy of appellant's First Amendment claim in the present case is demonstrated by the important differences between the advertisement presently at issue and those involved in *Chrestensen* and in *Pittsburgh Press.* The advertisement published in appellant's newspaper did more than simply propose a commercial transaction. It contained factual material of clear "public interest." Portions of its message, most prominently the lines, "Abortions are now legal in New York. There are no residency requirements," in-

volve the exercise of the freedom of communicating information and disseminating opinion.

Viewed in its entirety, the advertisement conveyed information of potential interest and value to a diverse audience—not only to readers possibly in need of the services offered, but also to those with a general curiosity about, or genuine interest in, the subject matter or the law of another State and its development, and to readers seeking reform in Virginia. The mere existence of the Women's Pavilion in New York City, with the possibility of its being typical of other organizations there, and the availability of the services offered, were not unnewsworthy. Also, the activity advertised pertained to constitutional interests. See Roe v. Wade (1973). Thus, in this case, appellant's First Amendment interests coincided with the constitutional interests of the general public.

Moreover, the placement services advertised in appellant's newspaper were legally provided in New York at that time. The Virginia Legislature could not have regulated the advertiser's activity in New York, and obviously could not have proscribed the activity in that State. Neither could Virginia prevent its residents from traveling to New York to obtain those services....

We conclude, therefore, that the Virginia courts erred in their assumptions that advertising, as such, was entitled to no First Amendment protection and that appellant Bigelow had no legitimate First Amendment interest....

Advertising, like all public expression, may be subject to reasonable regulation that serves a legitimate public interest. To the extent that commercial activity is subject to regulation, the relationship of speech to that activity may be one factor, among others, to be considered in weighing the First Amendment interest against the governmental interest alleged. Advertising is not thereby stripped of all First Amendment protection. The relationship of speech to the marketplace of products or of services does not make it valueless in the marketplace of ideas.

The Court has stated that "a State cannot foreclose the exercise of constitutional rights by mere labels." Regardless of the particular label asserted by the State—whether it calls speech "commercial" or "commercial advertising" or "solicitation"—a court may not escape the task of assessing the First Amendment interest at stake and weighing it against the public interest allegedly served by the regulation. The diverse motives, means, and messages of advertising may make speech "commercial" in widely varying degrees....

The task of balancing the interests at stake here was one that should have been undertaken by the Virginia courts before they reached their decision. We need not remand for that purpose, however, because the outcome is readily apparent from what has been said above.

In support of the statute, the appellee contends that the commercial operations of abortion referral agencies are associated with practices, such as fee splitting, that tend to diminish, or at least adversely affect, the quality of medical care, and that advertising of these operations will lead women to seek services from those who are interested only or mainly in financial gain apart from professional integrity and responsibility.

The State, of course, has a legitimate interest in maintaining the quality of medical care provided within its borders. No claim has been made, however, that this particular advertisement in any way affected the quality of medical services within Virginia. As applied to Bigelow's case, the statute was directed at the publishing of informative material relating to services offered in another State and was not directed at advertising by a referral agency or a practitioner whose activity Virginia had authority or power to regulate.

To be sure, the agency-advertiser's practices, although not then illegal, may later have proved to be at least "inimical to the public interest" in New York. But this development would not justify a Virginia statute that forbids Virginians from using in New York the then legal services of a local New York agency. Here, Virginia is really asserting an interest in regulating what Virginians may *hear* or *read* about the New York services. It is, in effect, advancing an interest in shielding its citizens from information about activities outside Virginia's borders, activities that Virginia's powers do not reach. This asserted interest, even if understandable, was entitled to little, if any, weight under the circumstances.

No claim has been made, nor could any be supported on this record, that the advertisement was deceptive or fraudulent, or that it related to a commodity or service that was then illegal in either Virginia or in New York, or that it otherwise furthered a criminal scheme in Virginia. There was no possibility that appellant's activity would invade the privacy of other citizens or infringe on other rights. Observers would not have the advertiser's message thrust upon them as a captive audience.

The strength of appellant's interest was augmented by the fact that the statute was applied against him as publisher and editor of a newspaper, not against the advertiser or a referral agency or a practitioner. The prosecution thus incurred more serious First Amendment overtones.

If application of this statute were upheld under these circumstances, Virginia might exert the power sought here over a wide variety of national publications or interstate newspapers carrying advertisements similar to the one that appeared in Bigelow's newspaper or containing articles on the general subject matter to which the advertisement referred. Other states might do the same. The burdens thereby imposed on publications would impair, perhaps severely, their proper functioning.... The policy of the First Amendment favors dissemination of information and opinion.

We conclude that Virginia could not apply Va. Code Ann. § 18.1-63 (1960), as it read in 1971, to appellant's publication of the advertisement in question without unconstitutionally infringing upon his First Amendment rights. The judgment of the Supreme Court of Virginia is therefore reversed.

Reversed.

Blackmun's majority opinion answers the question concerning the relationship between commercial speech and the First Amendment. Note his assertion: "The fact that the particular advertisement ... had commercial aspects ... did not negate all First Amendment guarantees.... The existence of 'commercial activity, in itself, is no justification for narrowing the protection of expression secured by the First Amendment.'" Yet, the Court's opinion falls a bit short; not only does it claim that constitutional protection exists only to "some degree," but also it clearly refuses to decide, as Blackmun wrote, "the precise extent to which the First Amendment permits regulation of advertisements that is related to activities the State may legitimately regulate or even prohibit." Although *Bigelow* affords First Amendment protection to commercial speech, it also implies that certain ads, under certain circumstances, may be subject to state limitations. Commercial speech does not equal political speech in the eyes of the Constitution.

It did not take long for the Court to address some of the questions left unanswered in *Bigelow*. Its first opportunity came the very next year in *Virginia State Board of Pharmacy v. Virginia Citizens Consumer Council, Inc.* (1976). This litigation centered on a constitutional challenge to a Virginia regulation making it unlawful for a pharmacy to advertise the prices of its prescription medications. A pharmacist who violated the rule risked being cited for unprofessional conduct and possible monetary fines or license suspension. The state justified its regulation as protecting the public from deceptive advertising and maintaining the professionalism of the state's pharmacists. Further, it argued that advertising prices is pure commercial expression that (unlike Bigelow's advertisement) carries no political or social information. Such advertising, the state claimed, deserves no First Amendment protection and is fully subject to state regulation. In response, the Consumer Council claimed that drug pricing information is socially relevant and the public has the right to a free flow of information without state interference.

The Court struck down the Virginia regulation as inconsistent with the First Amendment. For the Court Justice Blackmun explained that the purely economic content of the advertisement does not disqualify it from First Amendment protection. The public has the right to receive truthful information about lawful products and services. Likewise, the pharmacist has the right to communicate that information. The state could achieve its legitimate goals of promoting professionalism and protecting the public from misleading advertising by methods less severe than banning commercial expression altogether.

Taken together, the decisions in *Bigelow* and *Virginia State Board of Pharmacy* indicated that the Court was expanding constitutional protections for com-

mercial speech. In both cases only Justice Rehnquist voted to uphold the state restrictions. Yet certain factors made unclear how far the Court would go. First, Blackmun's opinion in the pharmacy decision said only that advertising is not "wholly outside" First Amendment protections. He acknowledged that "some forms of commercial speech regulation are surely permissible." Second, the justices who concurred in the pharmacy case also expressed some uneasiness. Justice Stewart's concurring opinion, for example, emphasized that the Court's opinion should not be interpreted as removing the distinction between product and price advertising on one hand and ideological expression on the other. Chief Justice Burger cautioned against applying the Court's decision to other professions. After all, he explained, today's pharmacists deal primarily in standardized products. They are not like physicians and lawyers whose services are not standardized and whose fees, therefore, cannot be directly compared.

Burger may have written his concurring opinion with one eye on the Court's docket. The very next year the justices considered *Bates v. State Bar of Arizona* (1977), a challenge to a law prohibiting lawyers from advertising the prices for their services. Does the Court back away from its trend of expanding protections for commercial expression? Or does it continue along the road it started in *Bigelow*?

Bates v. State Bar of Arizona

433 U.S. 350 (1977)
Vote: 5 (Blackmun, Brennan, Marshall, Stevens, White)
    4 (Burger, Powell, Rehnquist, Stewart)
Opinion of the Court: Blackmun
Opinions dissenting in part and concurring in part: Burger, Powell, Rehnquist

John Bates and Van O'Steen graduated from the Arizona State University College of Law in 1972 and took jobs at a state legal aid society. After two years, they developed what was then a unique idea—to open a legal clinic that would provide "legal services at modest fees to persons of moderate income who did not qualify for government aid." In March 1974 they opened such a clinic in Phoenix, Arizona, but two years later they were barely surviving. The pair decided to take a risky step: they placed an ad in an Arizona newspaper.

Why was their ad risky? Today attorney advertisements are commonplace. From the 1910s through the 1970s, however, most state bar associations explicitly prohibited such activity. Arizona's contained this provision: "A lawyer shall not ... display advertisement in the city or telephone directories or by other means of commercial publicity." And, upon seeing Bates and O'Steen's ad, the president of the state bar association initiated proceedings against them. They were found guilty and given the rather mild sentence of a one-week suspension from legal practice. Nonetheless, with the help of ACLU attorney Melvin Wulf, they decided to appeal the judgment, claiming that the ban constituted a violation of their First Amendment guarantee, under the Court's decision in *Virginia Pharmacy*.[31]

As the case moved up the judicial ladder, the debate over attorney advertisement became increasingly heated. The Arizona State Bar, backed by amicus curiae briefs from professional groups such as the American Bar Association, the American Dental Association, and the American Optometric Association, expressed its disdain for professional advertising through a number of legal and nonlegal arguments. The state bar, like the Pharmacy Board in *Virginia Pharmacy*, claimed that ads would have a negative effect on the profession, which was already held in low esteem by the public, that ads would be inherently misleading because the legal skill varies from attorney to attorney, and that ads would

have an adverse effect on the administration of justice by "stirring up" litigation. Bates and O'Steen argued that the First Amendment guaranteed them the right to place advertisements in newspapers. Their position also received legal reinforcement from several consumer groups and, significantly, from the solicitor general, who argued orally as an amicus curiae.

MR. JUSTICE BLACKMUN delivered the opinion of the Court.

Last Term, in *Virginia Pharmacy Board v. Virginia Consumer Council* (1976), the Court considered the validity under the First Amendment of a Virginia statute declaring that a pharmacist was guilty of "unprofessional conduct" if he advertised prescription drug prices.... [W]e held that commercial speech of that kind was entitled to the protection of the First Amendment....

The issue presently before us is a narrow one. First, we need not address the peculiar problems associated with advertising claims relating to the *quality* of legal services. Such claims probably are not susceptible of precise measurement or verification and, under some circumstances, might well be deceptive or misleading to the public, or even false. Appellee does not suggest, nor do we perceive, that appellants' advertisement contained claims, extravagant or otherwise, as to the quality of services. Accordingly, we leave that issue for another day. Second, we also need not resolve the problems associated with in-person solicitation of clients—at the hospital room or the accident site, or in any other situation that breeds undue influence—by attorneys or their agents or "runners." Activity of that kind might well pose dangers of overreaching and misrepresentation not encountered in newspaper announcement advertising. Hence, this issue also is not before us. Third, we note that appellee's criticism of advertising by attorneys does not apply with much force to some of the basic factual content of advertising: information as to the attorney's name, address, and telephone number, office hours, and the like. The American Bar Association itself has a provision in its current Code of Professional Responsibility that would allow the disclosure of such information, and more, in the classified section of the telephone directory. We recognize,

---

31. They also claimed that the prohibition violated the Sherman Anti-Trust Act, legislation the Court applied to the legal profession in *Goldfarb v. Virginia State Bar* (1975).

however, that an advertising diet limited to such spartan fare would provide scant nourishment.

The heart of the dispute before us today is whether lawyers also may constitutionally advertise the *prices* at which certain routine services will be performed. Numerous justifications are proffered for the restriction of such price advertising. We consider each in turn:

1. *The Adverse Effect on Professionalism.* Appellee places particular emphasis on the adverse effects that it feels price advertising will have on the legal profession. The key to professionalism, it is argued, is the sense of pride that involvement in the discipline generates. It is claimed that price advertising will bring about commercialization, which will undermine the attorney's sense of dignity and self-worth. The hustle of the marketplace will adversely affect the profession's service orientation, and irreparably damage the delicate balance between the lawyer's need to earn and his obligation selflessly to serve. Advertising is also said to erode the client's trust in his attorney: Once the client perceives that the lawyer is motivated by profit, his confidence that the attorney is acting out of a commitment to the client's welfare is jeopardized. And advertising is said to tarnish the dignified public image of the profession.

We recognize, of course, and commend the spirit of public service with which the profession of law is practiced and to which it is dedicated. The present Members of this Court, licensed attorneys all, could not feel otherwise. And we would have reason to pause if we felt that our decision today would undercut that spirit. But we find the postulated connection between advertising and the erosion of true professionalism to be severely strained. At its core, the argument presumes that attorneys must conceal from themselves and from their clients the real-life fact that lawyers earn their livelihood at the bar. We suspect that few attorneys engage in such self-deception. And rare is the client, moreover, even one of the modest means, who enlists the aid of an attorney with the expectation that his services will be rendered free of charge. In fact, the American Bar Association advises that an attorney should reach "a clear agreement with his client as to the basis of the fee charges to be made," and that this is to be done "[a]s soon as feasible after a lawyer has been employed." If the commercial basis of the relationship is to be promptly disclosed on ethical grounds, once the client is in the office, it seems inconsistent to condemn the candid revelation of the same information before he arrives at that office.

Moreover, the assertion that advertising will diminish the attorney's reputation in the community is open to question. Bankers and engineers advertise, and yet these professions are not regarded as undignified. In fact, it has been suggested that the failure of lawyers to advertise creates public disillusionment with the profession. The absence of advertising may be seen to reflect the profession's failure to reach out and serve the community: Studies reveal that many persons do not obtain counsel even when they perceive a need because of the feared price of services or because of an inability to locate a competent attorney. Indeed, cynicism with regard to the profession may be created by the fact that it long has publicly eschewed advertising, while condoning the actions of the attorney who structures his social or civic associations so as to provide contacts with potential clients.

It appears that the ban on advertising originated as a rule of etiquette and not as a rule of ethics. Early lawyers in Great Britain viewed the law as a form of public service, rather than as a means of earning a living, and they looked down on "trade" as unseemly. Eventually, the attitude toward advertising fostered by this view evolved into an aspect of the ethics of the profession. But habit and tradition are not in themselves an adequate answer to a constitutional challenge. In this day, we do not belittle the person who earns his living by the strength of his arm or the force of his mind. Since the belief that lawyers are somehow "above" trade has become an anachronism, the historical foundation for the advertising restraint has crumbled.

2. *The Inherently Misleading Nature of Attorney Advertising.* It is argued that advertising of legal services inevitably will be misleading (a) because such services are so individualized with regard to content and quality as to prevent informed comparison on the basis of an advertisement, (b) because the consumer of legal services is unable to determine in advance just what services he needs, and (c) because advertising by attorneys will highlight irrelevant factors and fail to show the relevant factor of skill.

We are not persuaded that restrained professional advertising by lawyers inevitably will be misleading. Although many services performed by attorneys are indeed unique, it is doubtful that any attorney would or could advertise fixed prices for services of that type. The only services that lend themselves to advertising are the routine ones: the uncontested divorce, the simple adoption, the uncontested personal bankruptcy, the change of name, and the like—the very services advertised by appellants. Although the precise service demanded in each task may vary slightly, and although legal services are not fungible, these facts do not make advertising misleading so long as the attorney does the necessary work at the advertised price. The argument that legal services are so unique that fixed rates cannot meaningfully be established is refuted by the record in this case: The appellee, State Bar, itself sponsors a Legal Services Program in which the participating attorneys agree to perform services like those advertised by the appellants at standardized rates....

The second component of the argument—that advertising ignores the diagnostic role—fares little better. It is unlikely that many people go to an attorney merely to ascertain if they have a clean bill of legal health. Rather, attorneys are likely to be employed to perform specific tasks. Although the client may not know the detail involved in performing the task, he no doubt is able to identify the service he desires at the level of generality to which advertising lends itself.

The third component is not without merit: Advertising does not provide a complete foundation on which to select an attorney. But it seems peculiar to deny the consumer, on the ground that the information is incomplete, at least some of the relevant information needed to reach an informed decision. The alternative—the prohibition of advertising—serves only to restrict the information that flows to consumers. Moreover, the argument assumes that the public is not sophisticated enough to realize the limitations of advertising, and that the public is better kept in ignorance than trusted with correct but incomplete information. We suspect the argument rests on an underestimation of the public. In any event, we view as dubious any justification that is based on the benefits of public ignorance. See *Virginia Pharmacy Board v. Virginia Consumer Council.* Although, of course, the bar retains the power to correct omissions that have the effect of presenting an inaccurate picture, the preferred remedy is more disclosure, rather than less. If the naivete of the public will cause advertising by attorneys to be misleading, then it is the bar's role to assure that the populace is sufficiently informed as to enable it to place advertising in its proper perspective.

3. *The Adverse Effect on the Administration of Justice.* Advertising is said to have the undesirable effect of stirring up litigation. The judicial machinery is designed to serve those who feel sufficiently aggrieved to bring forward their claims. Advertising, it is argued, serves to encourage the assertion of legal rights in the courts, thereby undesirably unsettling societal repose. There is even a suggestion of barratry.

But advertising by attorneys is not an unmitigated source of harm to the administration of justice. It may offer great benefits. Although advertising might increase the use of the judicial machinery, we cannot accept the notion that it is always better for a person to suffer a wrong silently than to redress it by legal action. As the bar acknowledges, "the middle 70% of our population is not being reached or served adequately by the legal profession." Among the reasons for this underutilization is fear of the cost, and an inability to locate a suitable lawyer. Advertising can help to solve this acknowledged problem: Advertising is the traditional mechanism in a free-market economy for a supplier to inform a potential purchaser of the availability and terms of exchange. The disciplinary rule at issue likely has served to burden access to legal services, particularly for the not-quite-poor and the unknowledgeable. A rule allowing restrained advertising would be in accord with the bar's obligation to "facilitate the process of intelligent selection of lawyers, and to assist in making legal services fully available."

4. *The Undesirable Economic Effects of Advertising.* It is claimed that advertising will increase the overhead costs of the profession, and that these costs then will be passed along to consumers in the form of increased fees. Moreover, it is claimed that the additional cost of practice will create a substantial entry barrier, deterring or preventing young attorneys from penetrating the market and entrenching the position of the bar's established members.

These two arguments seem dubious at best. Neither distinguishes lawyers from others, and neither appears relevant to the First Amendment. The ban on advertising serves to increase the difficulty of discovering the lowest cost seller of acceptable ability. As a result, to this extent attorneys are isolated from competition, and the incentive to price competitively is reduced. Although it is true that the effect of advertising on the price of services has not been demonstrated, there is revealing evidence with regard to products: where consumers have the benefit of price advertising, retail prices often are dramatically lower than they would be without advertising. It is entirely possible that advertising will serve to reduce, not advance, the cost of legal services to the consumer.

The entry-barrier argument is equally unpersuasive. In the absence of advertising, an attorney must rely on his contacts with the community to generate a flow of business. In view of the time necessary to develop such contacts, the ban in fact serves to perpetuate the market position of established attorneys. Consideration of entry-barrier problems would urge that advertising be allowed so as to aid the new competitor in penetrating the market.

5. *The Adverse Effect of Advertising on the Quality of Service.* It is argued that the attorney may advertise a given "package" of service at a set price, and will be inclined to provide, by indiscriminate use, the standard package regardless of whether it fits the client's needs.

Restraints on advertising, however, are an ineffective way of deterring shoddy work. An attorney who is inclined to cut quality will do so regardless of the rule on advertising. And the advertisement of a standardized fee does not necessarily mean that the services offered are undesirably standardized. Indeed, the assertion that an attorney who advertises a standard fee will cut quality is substantially undermined by the fixed-fee schedule of appellee's own prepaid Legal Services Program. Even if advertising leads to the creation of "legal clinics" like that of appellants'—clinics that emphasize standardized procedures for routine problems—it is possible that such clinics will improve service by reducing the likelihood of error.

6. *The Difficulties of Enforcement.* Finally, it is argued that the wholesale restriction is justified by the problems of enforcement if any other course is taken. Because the public lacks sophistication in legal matters, it may be particularly susceptible to misleading or deceptive advertising by lawyers. After-the-fact action by the consumer lured by such advertising may not provide a realistic restraint because of the inability of the layman to assess whether the service he has received meets professional standards. Thus, the vigi-

lance of a regulatory agency will be required. But because of the numerous purveyors of services, the overseeing of advertising will be burdensome.

It is at least somewhat incongruous for the opponents of advertising to extol the virtues and altruism of the legal profession at one point, and, at another, to assert that its members will seize the opportunity to mislead and distort. We suspect that, with advertising, most lawyers will behave as they always have: They will abide by their solemn oaths to uphold the integrity and honor of their profession and of the legal system. For every attorney who overreaches through advertising, there will be thousands of others who will be candid and honest and straightforward. And, of course, it will be in the latter's interest, as in other cases of misconduct at the bar, to assist in weeding out those few who abuse their trust.

In sum, we are not persuaded that any of the proffered justifications rise to the level of an acceptable reason for the suppression of all advertising by attorneys....

In holding that advertising by attorneys may not be subjected to blanket suppression, and that the advertisement at issue is protected, we, of course, do not hold that advertising by attorneys may not be regulated in any way. We mention some of the clearly permissible limitations on advertising not foreclosed by our holding.

Advertising that is false, deceptive, or misleading of course is subject to restraint. Since the advertiser knows his product and has a commercial interest in its dissemination, we have little worry that regulation to assure truthfulness will discourage protected speech. And any concern that strict requirements for truthfulness will undesirably inhibit spontaneity seems inapplicable because commercial speech generally is calculated. Indeed, the public and private benefits from commercial speech derive from confidence in its accuracy and reliability. Thus, the leeway for untruthful or misleading expression that has been allowed in other contexts has little force in the commercial arena. In fact, because the public lacks sophistication concerning legal services, misstatements that might be overlooked or deemed unimportant in other advertising may be found quite inappropriate in legal advertising. For example, advertising claims as to the quality of services—a matter we do not address today—are not susceptible of measurement or

verification; accordingly, such claims may be so likely to be misleading as to warrant restriction. Similar objections might justify restraints on in-person solicitation. We do not foreclose the possibility that some limited supplementation, by way of warning or disclaimer or the like, might be required of even an advertisement of the kind ruled upon today so as to assure that the consumer is not misled. In sum, we recognize that many of the problems in defining the boundary between deceptive and nondeceptive advertising remain to be resolved, and we expect that the bar will have a special role to play in assuring that advertising by attorneys flows both freely and cleanly.

As with other varieties of speech, it follows as well that there may be reasonable restrictions on the time, place, and manner of advertising. Advertising concerning transactions that are themselves illegal obviously may be suppressed. And the special problems of advertising on the electronic broadcast media will warrant special consideration.

The constitutional issue in this case is only whether the State may prevent the publication in a newspaper of appellants' truthful advertisement concerning the availability and terms of routine legal services. We rule simply that the flow of such information may not be restrained, and we therefore hold the present application of the disciplinary rule against appellants to be violative of the First Amendment.

The judgment of the Supreme Court of Arizona is therefore affirmed in part and reversed in part.

It is so ordered.

In *Bates* the Court provided one of its clearest statements on the issue of advertising. While refuting the bar association's arguments, Blackmun also listed the conditions under which attorneys may or may not advertise; for example, he stressed that Bates and O'Steen's ad mentioned only simple legal services, which any attorney could perform. Many have surmised from this distinction that bar associations probably could prohibit advertisements for complex legal work.

While Blackmun's opinion was reasonably specific about attorney advertising practices, it did not address some other dimensions of the problem. Consider, for example, the issue of state regulation of personal solicitation, another method some attorneys use to obtain clients. In 1977 the Court sought to resolve this issue by taking two cases that raised the subject in very different ways. One, *Ohralik v. Ohio State Bar,* was a "classic example of 'ambulance chasing'": the attorney, Albert Ohralik, followed two accident victims to the hospital, where he offered them his legal services on a contingency fee basis. The other, *In re Primus,* involved attorney Edna Primus, who was working for the ACLU for no charge. She wrote to a potential client, asking if she would be interested in serving as a plaintiff in the ACLU suit. The justices used these dissimilar facts to set clear policy regarding personal solicitation. In ruling against Ohralik, but for Primus, they found that:

1. Her solicitation had been "passive" (a letter); his had been "active" (the personal approach).

2. Her solicitation was not for financial gain (she was working for the ACLU on a voluntary basis); his was for money (he offered to work on a contingency fee basis).

3. Her solicitation was done "to advance the civil liberties objectives of the ACLU"; his was to make money.

A commercial advertising dispute involving slightly different issues was presented to the Court in *Linmark Associates v. Township of Willingboro* (1977). Here, the Court dealt with posted signs, not printed ads; but more important, it addressed a form of suppressed expression that appeared to have not economic, but social and political ends. *Linmark* arose in March 1974, when the town of Willingboro, New Jersey, passed an ordinance outlawing the posting of For Sale signs on most property. Enacted at the urging of property owners, the statute attempted to halt certain economic and social trends within the town. Located near Fort Dix, McGuire Air Force Base, and several major corporations, the town was a natural for suburban development. By the 1960s the white population of the town had increased 350 percent. But, as suburban growth stabilized during the 1970s, so did Willingboro's. By the early 1970s the town's white population had declined by 5 percent, and the black segment had grown from 11.7 percent in the 1960s to 18.2 percent. To stop what some called panic selling by whites and to maintain property values steadily dropping in the face of white flight, the town passed the ordinance banning For Sale signs.

Although the statute apparently halted white flight, a real estate agency that wanted to erect a For Sale sign challenged it as a violation of its free expression guarantees. Backed by an amicus curiae brief from the ACLU, the agency argued that For Sale signs were not distinguishable from advertisements for drugs, abortions, or attorney services. The town countered with two sets of arguments. First, the law was limited, restricting one method of communication and leaving ample alternative channels available. Second, it claimed that the statute sought to achieve a legitimate and, in fact, vital government objective—to promote racial integration. This last argument attracted the attention of the NAACP Legal Defense Fund, which filed a supporting amicus curiae brief. By the time this case appeared before the Court, the stage was set for high drama: *Linmark* was one of only a handful of occasions when two powerful allies, the ACLU and the LDF, opposed each other.

Writing for a unanimous Court, Justice Marshall, a former LDF attorney, agreed with the ACLU and struck down the town's ordinance. He acknowledged that although it had important objectives, in the final analysis the ordinance was no different from the law at issue in *Virginia Pharmacy*: it prevented "residents from obtaining certain information" without providing sufficient justification. As Marshall asserted, "If dissemination of this information can be restricted, then every locality in the country can suppress any facts that reflect poorly on it, so long as a plausible claim can be made that disclosure would cause recipients of the information to act 'irrationally.'"

The years between 1975 and 1977 were important for commercial speech. The Court's decisions in *Bigelow, Virginia Pharmacy, Bates,* and *Linmark Associates* signaled a major change by significantly elevating the degree of constitutional protection enjoyed by commercial expression. In the years that followed, the justices continued in that policy direction. For example, the Court struck down laws prohibiting the erection of advertising billboards (*Metromedia, Inc. v. San Diego,* 1981); banning the advertising of contraceptives by mail (*Bolger v. Youngs Drug Products Corporation,* 1983); and blocking a public utility from sending, along with monthly bills, statements that expressed the company's position on issues of public policy (*Consolidated Edison Company of New York, Inc. v. Public Service Commission of New York,* 1980). For the most part, the Court's decisions in the commercial expression cases were by substantial majorities, with only Justice Rehnquist consistently supporting the position of government regulators.

These decisions do not mean that the Court elevated commercial expression to the same level as political and social speech. In *Central Hudson Gas and Electric Corporation v. Public Service Commission of New York* (1980), the Court reminded us that the Constitution still accords commercial speech a lesser degree of protection than it grants other forms of guaranteed expression. At issue in *Central Hudson* was an energy conservation law prohibiting utility companies from advertising to promote the sale of their products. Justice Powell, speaking for the Court, offered a four-step analysis for deciding First Amendment challenges to government regulation of commercial expression:

At the outset, we must determine whether the expression is protected by the First Amendment. For commercial speech to come within that provision, it at least must concern lawful activity and not be misleading. Next, we ask whether the asserted governmental interest is substantial. If both inquiries yield positive answers, we must determine whether the regulation directly advances the governmental interest asserted, and whether it is not more extensive than is necessary to serve that interest.

Applying this test, the Court struck down the New York ban on advertising because the state failed to prove that a more limited intrusion on freedom of expression would not accomplish the state's objectives.

The *Central Hudson* decision provided a welcome explanation of how the Court approached commercial expression cases. However, considerable confusion arose over the meaning of the fourth prong of the *Central Hudson* test. What did Justice Powell mean when he said that the regulation cannot be more extensive than is necessary to achieve the government's interests? In *Board of Trustees of the State University of New York v. Fox* (1989), a majority lead by Justice Scalia held that the government's regulation of commercial speech need not be the "absolute least restrictive means" to achieve the desired end; rather, the Constitution requires only a "reasonable fit" between the government's ends and the means chosen to reach those ends. In applying the "reasonable fit" standard, the Court held that a university could prohibit the selling of commercial products in dormitories using a "Tupperware Party" style format. Three of the more liberal members of the Court, Blackmun, Brennan, and Marshall, dissented in *Fox*. They found the university regulation to be overbroad and hinted that they preferred a "least restrictive means" test instead of Scalia's "reasonable fit" standard.

In 1993 the Court once again turned its attention to the regulation of commercial expression by deciding how much latitude the government should have in enforcing regulations that impinge on expression rights to achieve legitimate state ends. In reading the opinions in *City of Cincinnati v. Discovery Network, Inc.* (1993), notice the three lines of argument that emerge. Justice Stevens's majority opinion stays within the line of commercial expression precedents that the Court has developed since the 1970s. Justice Blackmun's concurring opinion argues for increased protection for commercial speech. And Chief Justice Rehnquist's dissent squarely sides with the regulatory power of the state.

City of Cincinnati v. Discovery Network, Inc.

507 U.S. — (1993)
Vote: 6 (Blackmun, Kennedy, O'Connor, Scalia, Souter, Stevens)
   3 (Rehnquist, Thomas, White)
Opinion of the Court: Stevens
Concurring opinion: Blackmun
Dissenting opinion: Rehnquist

Two businesses, the Discovery Network, Inc., and Harmon Publishing Company, Inc., sought permission from Cincinnati to install newsracks on city property. Discovery Network, which provides adult educational, recreational, and social services programs, sought to erect newsracks for the purpose of distributing free magazines that advertise its programs and provide information "about current events of general interest." Harmon Publishing wanted to install racks to circulate its free real estate magazine, which contains "listings and photographs of available residential properties in the greater Cincinnati area." In 1989 the city authorized Discovery Network to install thirty-eight newsracks; it allowed Harmon to erect twenty-four racks.

A year later, in March 1990, the city notified Discovery Network and Harmon that it was revoking its permission and that it wanted the racks removed within thirty days. Cincinnati officials were relying on a city ordinance that prohibits the distribution of "commercial handbills" on public property. For purposes of the law, a commercial handbill is "any printed or written matter, dodger, circular, leaflet, pamphlet, paper, booklet or any other printed or otherwise reproduced original copies of any matter of literature: [w]hich advertises for sale any merchandise, product, commodity or thing; or [w]hich directs attention to

any business or mercantile or commercial establishment, or other activity, for the purpose of directly promoting the interest thereof by sales."

Discovery Network and Harmon believed that the city's action violated their First Amendment rights—that lawful commercial speech deserves some degree of First Amendment protection. They brought suit in a federal district court, where the city defended its order on grounds of safety and esthetics. Although the court agreed that these were "substantial interests," it asserted that the city's action had not met standards promulgated by the Supreme Court in other commercial speech cases. In particular, the district court noted that *Fox* required the city to establish a "reasonable fit" between the ordinance's ends and "the means chosen to accomplish those ends." Yet, in the district court's opinion, the "fit" here was not reasonable: the city could not justify its order on esthetic grounds because the number of newsracks erected by Discovery Network and Harmon was "minute" compared to Cincinnati's total number of dispensers (1,500–2,000). Nor did the city demonstrate a substantial safety problem. A reasonable fit could be established, the judge claimed, "by regulating the size, shape, number or placement of such devices," rather than by eliminating them altogether.

In its appeal the city argued that *Central Hudson* lent support to its position because there the Court said that the Constitution gives less protection to commercial speech than to other constitutionally guaranteed expression. This statement, coupled with the fact that it would be constitutionally impermissible for the city to prohibit traditional newspapers from using newsracks, led the city to argue that it could—in the interest of safety and esthetics—prefer newspapers over commercial publications. In a dramatic opinion the court of appeals not only rejected the city's argument but also it held, as Justice Stevens explained, that the "lesser status of commercial speech is relevant only when its regulation was designed to either prevent false or misleading advertising, or to alleviate distinctive adverse effects of the specific speech at issue." In other words, the court asserted that commercial speech should receive the same constitutional protection as traditional speech so long as it is not misleading, false, and so forth.

JUSTICE STEVENS delivered the opinion of the Court.

There is no claim in this case that there is anything unlawful or misleading about the contents of respondents' publications. Moreover, respondents do not challenge their characterization as "commercial speech." Nor do respondents question the substantiality of the city's interest in safety and esthetics. It was, therefore, proper for the District Court and the Court of Appeals to judge the validity of the city's prohibition under the standard we set forth in *Central Hudson* [*Gas & Electric Corp. v. Public Service Comm'n of New York*, 1980] and [*Board of Trustees of State Univ. of New York v.*] *Fox* [1989]. It was the city's burden to establish a "reasonable fit" between its legitimate interests in safety and esthetics and its choice of a limited and selective prohibition of newsracks as the means chosen to serve those interests.

There is ample support in the record for the conclusion that the city did not "establish the reasonable fit we require." The ordinance on which it relied was an outdated prohibition against the distribution of any commercial handbills on public property. It was enacted long before any concern about newsracks developed. Its apparent purpose was to prevent the kind of visual blight caused by littering, rather than any harm associated with permanent, freestanding dispensing devices. The fact that the city failed to address its recently developed concern about newsracks by regulating their size, shape, appearance, or number indicates that it has not "carefully calculated" the costs and benefits associated with the burden on speech imposed by its prohibition. The benefit to be derived from the removal of 62 newsracks while about 1,500–2,000 remain in place was considered "minute" by the District Court and "paltry" by the Court of Appeals. We share their evaluation of the "fit" between the city's goal and its method of achieving it.

In seeking reversal, the city argues that it is wrong to focus attention on the relatively small number of newsracks affected by its prohibition, because the city's central concern is with the overall number of newsracks on its sidewalks, rather than with the unattractive appearance of a handful of dispensing devices. It contends, first, that a categorical prohibition on the use of newsracks to disseminate commercial messages burdens no more speech than is necessary to further its interest in limiting the number of newsracks; and, second, that the prohibition is a valid "time, place, and manner" regulation because it is content-neutral and leaves open ample alternative channels of communication. We consider these arguments in turn.

The city argues that there is a close fit between its ban on newsracks dispensing "commercial handbills" and its interest in safety and esthetics because every decrease in the number of such dispensing devices necessarily effects an increase in safety and an improvement in the attractiveness of the cityscape. In the city's view, the prohibition is thus *entirely* related to its legitimate interests in safety and esthetics.

We accept the validity of the city's proposition, but consider it an insufficient justification for the discrimination against respondents' use of newsracks that are no more harmful than the permitted newsracks, and have only a minimal impact on the overall number of newsracks on the city's sidewalks. The major premise supporting the city's argument is the proposition that commercial speech has only a low value. Based on that premise, the city contends that the fact that assertedly more valuable publications are allowed to use newsracks does not undermine its judgment that its esthetic and safety interests are stronger than the interest in allowing commercial speakers to have similar access to the reading public.

We cannot agree. In our view, the city's argument attaches more importance to the distinction between commercial and noncommercial speech than our cases warrant and seriously underestimates the value of commercial speech.

This very case illustrates the difficulty of drawing bright lines that will clearly cabin commercial speech in a distinct category. For respondents' publications share important characteristics with the publications that the city classifies as "newspapers." Particularly, they are "commercial handbills" within the meaning of ... the city's Code because they contain advertising, a feature that apparently also places ordinary newspapers within the same category.

Separate provisions in the Code specifically authorize the distribution of "newspapers" on the public right of way, but that term is not defined. Presumably, respondents' publications do not qualify as newspapers because an examination of their content discloses a higher ratio of advertising to other text, such as news and feature stories, than is found in the exempted publications. Indeed, Cincinnati's City Manager has determined that publications that qualify as newspapers and therefore *can* be distributed by newsrack are those that are published daily and/or weekly and *"primarily* presen[t] coverage of, and commentary on, current events" (emphasis added).

The absence of a categorical definition of the difference between "newspapers" and "commercial handbills" in the city's Code is also a characteristic of our opinions considering the constitutionality of regulations of commercial speech. Fifty years ago, we concluded that the distribution of a commercial handbill was unprotected by the First Amendment, even though half of its content consisted of political protest. *Valentine v. Chrestensen* (1942).... Subsequent opinions, however, recognized that important commercial attributes of various forms of communication do not qualify their entitlement to constitutional protection....

In later opinions we have stated that speech proposing a commercial transaction is entitled to lesser protection than other constitutionally guaranteed expression, see *Ohralik v. Ohio State Bar Assn.* (1978). We have also suggested that such lesser protection was appropriate for a somewhat larger category of commercial speech—"that is, expression related solely to the economic interests of the speaker and its audience." *Central Hudson Gas & Elec. Corp. v. Public Service Comm'n of New York.* We did not, however, use that definition in either *Bolger v. Youngs Drug Products* (1983) or in *Board of Trustees of State Univ. of New York v. Fox* (1989).

In the *Bolger* case we held that a federal statute prohibiting the mailing of unsolicited advertisements for contraceptives could not be applied to the appellee's promotional materials.... It is noteworthy that in reaching that conclusion we did not simply apply the broader definition of commercial speech advanced in *Central Hudson*—a definition that obviously would have encompassed the mailings—but rather "examined [them] carefully to ensure that speech deserving of greater constitutional protection is not inadvert-

ently suppressed." In *Fox*, we described the category even more narrowly, by characterizing the proposal of a commercial transaction as *"the test* for identifying commercial speech" (emphasis added).

Under the *Fox* test it is clear that much of the material in ordinary newspapers is commercial speech and, conversely, that the editorial content in respondents' promotional publications is not what we have described as "core" commercial speech. There is no doubt a "common sense" basis for distinguishing between the two, but under both the city's Code and our cases the difference is a matter of degree.

... We ... agree with the Court of Appeals that Cincinnati's actions in this case run afoul of the First Amendment. Not only does Cincinnati's categorical ban on commercial newsracks place too much importance on the distinction between commercial and noncommercial speech, but in this case, the distinction bears no relationship *whatsoever* to the particular interests that the city has asserted. It is therefore an impermissible means of responding to the city's admittedly legitimate interests.

The city has asserted an interest in esthetics, but respondent publishers' newsracks are no greater an eyesore than the newsracks permitted to remain on Cincinnati's sidewalks. Each newsrack, whether containing "newspapers" or "commercial handbills," is equally unattractive.... As we have explained, the city's primary concern, as argued to us, is with the aggregate number of newsracks on its streets. On that score, however, all newsracks, regardless of whether they contain commercial or noncommercial publications, are equally at fault. In fact, the newspapers are arguably the greater culprit because of their superior number....

In the absence of some basis for distinguishing between "newspapers" and "commercial handbills" that is relevant to an interest asserted by the city, we are unwilling to recognize Cincinnati's bare assertion that the "low value" of commercial speech is a sufficient justification for its selective and categorical ban on newsracks dispensing "commercial handbills." Our holding, however, is narrow. As should be clear from the above discussion, we do not reach the question whether, given certain facts and under certain circumstances, a community might be able to justify differential treatment of commercial and noncommercial newsracks. We simply hold that on this record Cincinnati has failed to make such a showing. Because the distinction Cincinnati has drawn has absolutely no bearing on the interests it has asserted, we have no difficulty concluding, as did the two courts below, that the city has not established the "fit" between its goals and its chosen means that is required by our opinion in *Fox*. It remains to consider the city's argument that its prohibition is a permissible time, place, and manner regulation.

The Court has held that government may impose reasonable restrictions on the time, place or manner of engaging in protected speech provided that they are adequately justified "'without reference to the content of the regulated speech.'"... The city contends that its regulation of newsracks qualifies as such a restriction because the interests in safety and esthetics that it serves are entirely unrelated to the content of respondents' publications. Thus, the argument goes, the *justification* for the regulation is content neutral.

The argument is unpersuasive because the very basis for the regulation is the difference in content between ordinary newspapers and commercial speech. True, there is no evidence that the city has acted with animus toward the ideas contained within respondents' publications, but just last Term we expressly rejected the argument that "discriminatory ... treatment is suspect under the First Amendment only when the legislature intends to suppress certain ideas." *Simon & Schuster v. Members of New York State Crime Victims Bd.* Regardless of the *mens rea* of the city, it has enacted a sweeping ban on the use of newsracks that distribute "commercial handbills," but not "newspapers." Under the city's newsrack policy, whether any particular newsrack falls within the ban is determined by the content of the publication resting inside that newsrack. Thus, by any commonsense understanding of the term, the ban in this case is "content-based."...

In sum, the city's newsrack policy is neither content-neutral nor ... "narrowly tailored." Thus, regardless of whether or not it leaves open ample alternative channels of communication, it cannot be justified as a legitimate time, place, or manner restriction on protected speech.

Cincinnati has enacted a sweeping ban that bars from its sidewalks a whole class of constitutionally protected speech. As did the District Court and the Court of Appeals, we conclude that Cincinnati has failed to justify that policy.

The regulation is not a permissible regulation of commercial speech, for on this record it is clear that the interests that Cincinnati has asserted are unrelated to any distinction between "commercial handbills" and "newspapers." Moreover, because the ban is predicated on the content of the publications distributed by the subject newsracks, it is not a valid time, place, or manner restriction on protected speech. For these reasons, Cincinnati's categorical ban on the distribution, via newsrack, of "commercial handbills" cannot be squared with the dictates of the First Amendment.

The judgment of the Court of Appeals is affirmed.

JUSTICE BLACKMUN, concurring.

I agree that Cincinnati's ban on commercial newsracks cannot withstand scrutiny under *Central Hudson Gas & Electric Corp. v. Public Service Comm'n of New York* (1980) and *Board of Trustees of State University of N.Y. v. Fox* (1989), and I therefore join the Court's opinion. I write separately because I continue to believe that the analysis set forth in *Central Hudson* and refined in *Fox* affords insufficient protection for truthful, noncoercive commercial speech concerning lawful activities.... The present case demonstrates that there is no reason to treat truthful commercial speech as a class that is less "valuable" than noncommercial speech. Respondents' publications, which respectively advertise the availability of residential properties and educational opportunities, are unquestionably "valuable" to those who choose to read them, and Cincinnati's ban on commercial newsracks should be subject to the same scrutiny we would apply to a regulation burdening noncommercial speech....

The commercial publications at issue in this case illustrate the absurdity of treating all commercial speech as less valuable than all noncommercial speech. Respondent Harmon Publishing Company, Inc., publishes and distributes a free magazine containing listings and photographs of residential properties. Like the "For Sale" signs this Court, in *Linmark Associates, Inc. v. Willingboro* (1977), held could not be banned, the information contained in Harmon's publication "bear[s] on one of the most important decisions [individuals] have a right to make: where to live and raise their families." Respondent Discovery Network, Inc., advertises the availability of adult educational, recreational, and social programs. Our cases have consistently recognized the importance of education to the professional and personal development of the individual. The "value" of respondents' commercial speech, at least to those who receive it, certainly exceeds the value of the offensive, though political, slogan displayed on the petitioner's jacket in *Cohen v. California* (1971).

I think it highly unlikely that according truthful, noncoercive commercial speech the full protection of the First Amendment will erode the level of that protection. I have predicted that "the Court will never provide child pornography or cigarette advertising the level of protection customarily granted political speech." Yet I do not believe that protecting truthful advertising will test this Nation's commitment to the First Amendment to any greater extent than protecting offensive political speech. The very fact that government remains free, in my view, to ensure that commercial speech is not deceptive or coercive, to prohibit commercial speech proposing illegal activities, and to impose reasonable time, place, or manner restrictions on commercial speech greatly reduces the risk that protecting truthful commercial speech will dilute the level of First Amendment protection for speech generally.

I am heartened by the Court's decision today to reject the extreme extension of *Central Hudson*'s logic, and I hope the Court ultimately will come to abandon *Central Hudson*'s analysis entirely in favor of one that affords full protection for truthful, noncoercive commercial speech about lawful activities.

CHIEF JUSTICE REHNQUIST, with whom JUSTICE WHITE and JUSTICE THOMAS join, dissenting.

Because the city chose to address its newsrack problem by banning only those newsracks that disseminate commercial handbills, rather than regulating all newsracks (including those that disseminate traditional newspapers) alike, the Court holds that its actions violate the First Amendment to the Constitution. I believe this result is inconsistent with prior precedent.

"Our jurisprudence has emphasized that 'commercial speech [enjoys] a limited measure of protection, commensurate with its subordinate position in the scale of First Amendment values,' and is subject to 'modes of regulation that might be impermissible in the realm of noncommer-

cial expression.'" *Board of Trustees of State Univ. of New York v. Fox* (1989). We have advanced several reasons for this treatment, among which is that commercial speech is more durable than other types of speech, since it is "the offspring of economic self-interest." Commercial speech is also "less central to the interests of the First Amendment" than other types of speech, such as political expression. Finally, there is an inherent danger that conferring equal status upon commercial speech will erode the First Amendment protection accorded noncommercial speech, "simply by a leveling process of the force of the Amendment's guarantee with respect to the latter kind of speech."

... I agree with the Court that the city's prohibition against respondents' newsracks is properly analyzed under *Central Hudson*, but differ as to the result this analysis should produce.

As the Court points out, "respondents do not challenge their characterization as 'commercial speech,'" and "[t]here is no claim in this case that there is anything unlawful or misleading about the contents of respondents' publications." "Nor do respondents question the substantiality of the city's interest in safety and esthetics." This case turns, then, on the application of the last part of the *Central Hudson* analysis. Although the Court does not say so, there can be no question that Cincinnati's prohibition against respondents' newsracks "directly advances" its safety and esthetic interests because, if enforced, the city's policy will decrease the number of newsracks on its street corners. This leaves the question whether the city's prohibition is "more extensive than necessary" to serve its interests, or, as we elaborated in *Fox*, whether there is a "reasonable fit" between the city's desired ends and the means it has chosen to accomplish those ends. Because the city's "commercial handbill" ordinance was not enacted specifically to address the problems caused by newsracks, and, if enforced, the city's prohibition against respondents' newsracks would result in the removal of only 62 newsracks from its street corners, the Court finds "ample support in the record for the conclusion that the city did not establish [a] reasonable fit." I disagree.

According to the Court, the city's decision to invoke an existing ordinance "to address its recently developed concern about newsracks" indicates that "it has not 'carefully calculated' the costs and benefits associated with the burden on speech imposed by its prohibition." The implication being that, if Cincinnati had studied the problem in greater detail, it would have discovered that it could have accomplished its desired ends by regulating the "size, shape, appearance, or number" of all newsracks, rather than categorically banning only those newsracks that disseminate commercial speech. Despite its protestations to the contrary, this argument rests on the discredited notion that the availability of "less restrictive means" to accomplish the city's objectives renders its regulation of commercial speech unconstitutional. As we observed in *Fox*, "almost all of the restrictions disallowed under *Central Hudson*'s fourth prong have been substantially excessive, disregarding far less restrictive and more precise means." That there may be other—less restrictive—means by which Cincinnati could have gone about addressing its safety and esthetic concerns, then, does not render its prohibition against respondents' newsracks unconstitutional.

Nor does the fact that, if enforced, the city's prohibition would result in the removal of only 62 newsracks from its street corners. The Court attaches significance to the lower courts' findings that any benefit would be "'minute'" or "'paltry.'" The relevant inquiry, though, is not the degree to which the locality's interests are furthered in a particular case, but rather the relation that the challenged regulation of commercial speech bears to the "overall problem" the locality is seeking to alleviate. This follows from our test for reviewing the validity of "time, place, or manner" restrictions on noncommercial speech, which we have said is "substantially similar" to the *Central Hudson* analysis. Properly viewed, then, the city's prohibition against respondents' newsracks is directly related to its efforts to alleviate the problems caused by newsracks, since every newsrack that is removed from the city's sidewalks marginally enhances the safety of its streets and esthetics of its cityscape. This conclusion is not altered by the fact that the city has chosen to address its problem by banning only those newsracks that disseminate commercial speech, rather than regulating all newsracks alike....

If (as I am certain) Cincinnati may regulate newsracks that disseminate commercial speech based on the interests it has asserted, I am at a loss as to why its scheme is unconstitutional because it does not also regulate newsracks that disseminate noncommercial speech. One would have thought that the city, perhaps even following the teachings of our commercial speech jurisprudence, could have decided to place the burden of its regulatory scheme on less protected speech (i.e., commercial handbills) without running afoul of the First Amendment. Today's decision, though, places the city in the position of having to decide between restricting more speech—fully protected speech— and allowing the proliferation of newsracks on its street corners to continue unabated. It scarcely seems logical that the First Amendment compels such a result. In my view, the city may order the removal of *all* newsracks from its public right-of-ways if it so chooses. But however it decides to address its newsrack problem, it should be allowed to proceed in the manner and scope it sees fit so long as it does not violate established First Amendment principles, such as the rule against discrimination on the basis of content....

Because I believe the city has established a "reasonable fit" between its substantial safety and esthetic interests and its prohibition against respondents' newsracks, I would hold that the city's actions are permissible under *Central Hudson*.... I dissent.

City of Cincinnati v. Discovery Network was among the more anxiously awaited decisions of the 1992–1993 term. Had the majority endorsed the lower court's ruling—a position generally endorsed by Justice Blackmun—the case would have ushered in a major change in commercial speech doctrine. Yet, the balance of the Court is content with existing approaches. Or, at least, so it seems given the relatively narrow ruling in this case.

READINGS

Bollinger, Lee C. *The Tolerant Society*. New York: Oxford University Press, 1986.

Chafee, Zechariah, Jr. *Free Speech in the United States*. Cambridge, Mass.: Harvard University Press, 1941.

Cox, Archibald. *Freedom of Expression*. Cambridge, Mass.: Harvard University Press, 1981.

Emerson, Thomas I. *The System of Freedom of Expression*. New York: Vintage Books, 1970.

Fish, Stanley. *There's No Such Thing as Free Speech, and It's a Good Thing, Too.* New York: Oxford University Press, 1994.

Fortas, Abe. *Concerning Dissent and Civil Disobedience.* New York: New American Library, 1968.

Goldstein, Robert Justin. *Political Repression in Modern America.* Cambridge, Mass.: Schenkman Publishing Company, 1978.

Graber, Mark A. *Transforming Free Speech.* Berkeley: University of California Press, 1991.

Hemmer, Joseph J. *The Supreme Court and the First Amendment.* New York: Praeger, 1986.

Levy, Leonard W. *Legacy of Suppression.* Cambridge, Mass.: Harvard University Press, 1960.

MacKinnon, Catherine A. *Only Words.* Cambridge, Mass.: Harvard University Press, 1993.

Rabban, David M. "The Emergence of Modern First Amendment Doctrine." *University of Chicago Law Review* 50 (Fall 1983): 1205–1355.

Smolla, Rodney A. *Free Speech in an Open Society.* New York: Knopf, 1992.

Sunstein, Cass A. *Democracy and the Problem of Free Speech.* New York: The Free Press, 1993.

Telford, Thomas L. *Freedom of Speech in the United States.* New York: Random House, 1985.

Van Alstyne, William W. *Interpretations of the First Amendment.* Durham, N.C.: Duke University Press, 1984.

Washburn, Patrick S. *A Question of Sedition.* New York: Oxford University Press, 1986.

CHAPTER 5
FREEDOM OF THE PRESS

REEDOM OF THE PRESS is perhaps the most visible manifestation of Americans exercising their expression rights. Each day the print and broadcast media bombard the nation with news, editorials, and entertainment from almost every conceivable perspective. Newsstands and bookstores flourish by offering periodicals and books devoted to every imaginable interest. The emergence of interactive media, such as talk radio, op-ed pages, and letters to the editor, allows citizens to become participants in the press rather than merely consumers. The result is a robust exchange of information and opinion.

Much of what appears in the press is critical of government and government policies. Unlike the case in some other countries, however, those who criticize officials in the United States do so without government censorship or fear of retaliation. They enjoy protection provided by the First Amendment's stipulation that "Congress shall make no law ... abridging the freedom ... of the press."

This constitutional provision reflects the Framers' strong commitment to the rights of the press. They saw the right to publish freely not only as important for its own sake, but also as a significant protection against the government denying other political and personal liberties. The press is the watchdog that sounds a warning when other rights are threatened.

The Founders believed, for example, that the rights of speech and religion would be meaningless without a free press. Thomas Jefferson was so certain of this precept that in 1816 he proclaimed, "When the press is free, and every man is able to read, all is safe."

As British colonists, the Framers were well schooled in the values of a free press. But history also taught them that this right could not be taken for granted. They knew that England had controlled the press from the fifteenth through seventeenth centuries and that these repressive measures had become common law. One scholar noted that "shortly after the introduction of printing into England in the fifteenth century," Britain developed a licensing system under which nothing could be printed without prior approval from the government.[1] Once the licensing laws expired in 1695, however, "freedom of press [from censorship] came to be recognized as a common law or a natural right," leading Blackstone to write: "The liberty of the press consists in laying no previous restraint upon publications and not in freedom from censure for criminal matter when published."[2]

1. Thomas I. Emerson, *The System of Freedom of Expression* (New York: Vintage Books, 1970), 504.
2. *Blackstone's Commentaries on the Laws of England*, vol. 4 (London, 1765–1769), 151–152.

Blackstone's words, while not fully embraced by the Supreme Court, convey a significant message about freedom of the press, which was understood by the Framers of the Constitution. They recognized that for a society to remain free, it must allow for the emergence of divergent views and opinions, which can be formed only through the open exchange of ideas. Without a free and uncensored press, government takes away a major mechanism (indeed, *the* major one during the 1700s and 1800s) by which to accomplish that objective, and society knows only what the government wants it to know. Under such circumstances, the press becomes an extension of government, not an independent observer, a check, or even a source of information.

Why is this state of affairs so dangerous? Consider one of the most heinous regimes in the history of the world—Nazi Germany. How the Nazis came to power and carried out their deeds is still being debated, but certainly their ability to control the press and to use it as a propaganda tool provides a partial explanation. The danger of government control of the press also can be seen closer to home. The Watergate scandal involved political manipulation and illegal behavior at the highest levels of government and led to the resignation of President Richard Nixon in 1974. We should remember that it was the press that first discovered and reported the wrongdoing. If we allowed government to censor—to place prior restraints on—the press, the Watergate story never would have been published.

In the first part of this chapter, we examine the development of doctrine dealing with prior restraints. Does the Court today permit any censorship of the press, or is the press free to publish all the news it sees fit to print? Prior restraints, however, are not the only limits government has tried to place on the press. In the second part of this chapter, we explore a less obvious constraint—government control of press content. This series of cases asks the Court to determine whether the government can have any say in what the press chooses to print. We conclude with a discussion of the special privileges claimed by the media. Reporters argue that they should enjoy a unique set of guarantees to perform their jobs. How has the Court reacted to such claims?

Taken together, these issues—prior restraint, government control of press content, and the special rights of reporters—form the heart of freedom of the press questions. But the Court's decisions also distinguish the type of media in question. In general, the justices have treated printed matter (newspapers, magazines, and books) differently from the broadcast media (radio and television). Why? And how have those differences manifested themselves? Are they justified?

PRIOR RESTRAINT

No concept is more important to understanding freedom of the press than "prior restraint." Prior restraint occurs when the government reviews material to determine whether publication will be allowed. It is government censorship and antithetical to freedom of the press. If the First Amendment means anything, it means that no government has the authority to decide what may and may not be published. The government may punish press activity that violates legitimate criminal laws, but such government sanctions may take place only *after* publication, not before.

Establishing a Standard

This principle that prior restraint runs contrary to the Constitution was established in the formative case, *Near v. Minnesota* (1931). The justices took a strong stance against such censorship, but does their decision imply that the government may never block the publication of material it considers inappropriate or harmful? Are there exceptions to the constitutional prohibition against prior restraint? As you read Chief Justice Charles Evans Hughes's opinion in *Near*, pay close attention to how the justices develop the general principle against prior restraint, and look for any indication that the Court might allow exceptions to it.

Near v. Minnesota

283 U.S. 697 (1931)
Vote: 5 (Brandeis, Holmes, Hughes, Roberts, Stone)
    4 (Butler, McReynolds, Sutherland, Van Devanter)
Opinion of the Court: Hughes
Dissenting opinion: Butler

A 1925 Minnesota law provided for "the abatement, as a public nuisance, of a 'malicious, scandalous, and defamatory newspaper, magazine, or other periodical.'" In the fall of 1927, a county attorney asked a state judge to issue a restraining order banning publication of the *Saturday Press*. In the attorney's view, the newspaper, partly owned by Jay Near, was the epitome of a malicious, scandalous, and defamatory publication.[3] *The Saturday Press* committed itself to exposing corruption, bribery, gambling, and prostitution in Minneapolis. It attacked specific city officials for being in league with gangsters and chided the established press for refusing to uncover the corruption. These attacks were colored by Near's racist, anti-Semitic attitudes. In one issue, Near wrote:

I simply state a fact when I say that ninety per cent of the crimes committed against society in this city are committed by Jew gangsters.... It is Jew, Jew, Jew, as long as one cares to comb over the records. I am launching no attack against the Jewish people AS A RACE. I am merely calling attention to a FACT. And if people of that race and faith wish to rid themselves of the odium and stigma THE RODENTS OF THEIR OWN RACE HAVE BROUGHT UPON THEM, they need only to step to the front and help the decent citizens of Minneapolis rid the city of these criminal Jews.[4]

In a piece attacking establishment journalism, Near proclaimed: "Journalism today isn't prostituted so

The only known photograph of *Saturday Press* editor Jay Near appeared April 19, 1936, in the Minneapolis *Tribune*. Near's successful appeal to the Supreme Court in 1931 marked the first time the Court enforced the First Amendment's guarantee of freedom of the press to strike a state law that imposed a prior restraint on a newspaper.

much as it is disgustingly flabby. I'd rather be a louse in the cotton shirt of a nigger than be a journalistic prostitute."[5] Based on the paper's past record, a judge issued a temporary restraining order prohibiting the sale of printed and future editions of the paper.

Upset by this action, Near contacted the ACLU, which agreed to take his case. But he grew uncomfortable with the organization and instead obtained assistance from the publisher of the *Chicago Tribune*. Together, they challenged the Minnesota law as a violation of the First Amendment Freedom of Press guarantee, arguing that the law was tantamount to censorship. In their view, states could not place gag orders restraining newspapers from publishing in the future; newspapers could be punished only after publication through libel or defamation proceedings. The state's attorney thought otherwise, arguing that freedom of the press does not give publishers an unrestricted right to print anything and everything, that they must act responsibly.

---

3. For an in-depth account of this case, see Fred W. Friendly, *Minnesota Rag* (New York: Random House, 1981).
4. Ibid., 47.

5. Ibid., 43.

MR. CHIEF JUSTICE HUGHES delivered the opinion of the Court.

Chapter 285 of the Session Laws of Minnesota for the year 1925 provides for the abatement, as a public nuisance, of a "malicious, scandalous and defamatory newspaper, magazine, or other periodical."...

This statute, for the suppression as a public nuisance of a newspaper or periodical, is unusual, if not unique, and raises questions of grave importance transcending the local interests involved in the particular action. It is no longer open to doubt that the liberty of the press and of speech is within the liberty safeguarded by the due process clause of the Fourteenth Amendment from invasion by state action. It was found impossible to conclude that this essential personal liberty of the citizen was left unprotected by the general guaranty of fundamental rights of person and property. Gitlow v. New York, Whitney v. California, Fiske v. Kansas. In maintaining this guaranty, the authority of the state to enact laws to promote the health, safety, morals, and general welfare of its people is necessarily admitted. The limits of this sovereign power must always be determined with appropriate regard to the particular subject of its exercise....

It is thus important to note precisely the purpose and effect of the statute as the state court has construed it.

First. The statute is not aimed at the redress of individual or private wrongs. Remedies for libel remain available and unaffected.... It is aimed at the distribution of scandalous matter as "detrimental to public morals and to the general welfare," tending "to disturb the peace of the community" and "to provoke assaults and the commission of crime." In order to obtain an injunction to suppress the future publication of the newspaper or periodical, it is not necessary to prove the falsity of the charges that have been made in the publication condemned. In the present action there was no allegation that the matter published was not true. It is alleged, and the statute requires the allegation that the publication was "malicious." But, as in prosecutions for libel, there is no requirement of proof by the state of malice in fact as distinguished from malice inferred from the mere publication of the defamatory matter. The judgment in this case proceeded upon the mere proof of publication. The statute permits the defense, not of the truth alone, but only that the truth was published with good motives and for justifiable ends. It is apparent that under the statute the publication is to be regarded as defamatory if it injures reputation, and that it is scandalous if it circulates charges of reprehensible conduct, whether criminal or otherwise, and the publication is thus deemed to invite public reprobation and to constitute a public scandal....

Second. The statute is directed not simply at the circulation of scandalous and defamatory statements with regard to private citizens, but at the continued publication by newspapers and periodicals of charges against public officers of corruption, malfeasance in office, or serious neglect of duty. Such charges by their very nature create a public scandal. They are scandalous and defamatory within the meaning of the statute, which has its normal operation in relation to publications dealing prominently and chiefly with the alleged derelictions of public officers.

Third. The object of the statute is not punishment, in the ordinary sense, but suppression of the offending newspaper or periodical. The reason for the enactment, as the state court has said, is that prosecutions to enforce penal statutes for libel do not result in "efficient repression or suppression of the evils of scandal." Describing the business of publication as a public nuisance does not obscure the substance of the proceeding which the statute authorizes. It is the continued publication of scandalous and defamatory matter that constitutes the business and the declared nuisance. In the case of public officers, it is the reiteration of charges of official misconduct, and the fact that the newspaper or periodical is principally devoted to that purpose, that exposes it to suppression....

This suppression is accomplished by enjoining publication, and that restraint is the object and effect of the statute.

Fourth. The statute not only operates to suppress the offending newspaper or periodical, but to put the publisher under an effective censorship. When a newspaper or periodical is found to be "malicious, scandalous and defamatory," and is suppressed as such, resumption of publication is punishable as a contempt of court by fine or imprisonment. Thus, where a newspaper or periodical has been suppressed because of the circulation of charges against public officers of official misconduct, it would seem to be clear that the renewal of the publication of such charges would constitute a contempt, and that the judgment would lay a permanent restraint upon the publisher, to escape which he must satisfy the court as to the character of a new publication. Whether he would be permitted again to publish matter deemed to be derogatory to the same or other public officers would depend upon the court's ruling.…

If we cut through mere details of procedure, the operation and effect of the statute in substance is that public authorities may bring the owner or publisher of a newspaper or periodical before a judge upon a charge of conducting a business of publishing scandalous and defamatory matter—in particular that the matter consists of charges against public officers of official dereliction—and, unless the owner or publisher is able and disposed to bring competent evidence to satisfy the judge that the charges are true and are published with good motives and for justifiable ends, his newspaper or periodical is suppressed and further publication is made punishable as a contempt. This is of the essence of censorship.

The question is whether a statute authorizing such proceedings in restraint of publication is consistent with the conception of the liberty of the press as historically conceived and guaranteed. In determining the extent of the constitutional protection, it has been generally, if not universally, considered that it is the chief purpose of the guaranty to prevent previous restraints upon publication. The struggle in England, directed against the legislative power of the licenser, resulted in renunciation of the censorship of the press. The liberty deemed to be established was thus described by Blackstone: "The liberty of the press is indeed essential to the nature of a free state; but this consists in laying no *previous* restraints upon publications, and not in freedom from censure for criminal matter when published. Every freeman has an undoubted right to lay what sentiments he pleases before the public; to forbid this, is to destroy the freedom of the press; but if he publishes what is improper, mischievous or illegal, he must take the consequence of his own temerity." The distinction was early pointed out between the extent of the freedom with respect to censorship under our constitutional system and that enjoyed in England. Here, as Madison said, "the great and essential rights of the people are secured against legislative as well as against executive ambition. They are secured, not by laws paramount to prerogative, but by constitutions paramount to laws. This security of the freedom of the press requires that it should be exempt not only from previous restraint by the Executive, as in Great Britain, but from legislative restraint also.".…

The criticism upon Blackstone's statement has not been because immunity from previous restraint upon publication has not been regarded as deserving of special emphasis, but chiefly because that immunity cannot be deemed to exhaust the conception of the liberty guaranteed by State and Federal Constitutions. The point of criticism has been "that the mere exemption from previous restraints cannot be all that is secured by the constitutional provisions," and that "the liberty of the press might be rendered a mockery and a delusion, and the phrase itself a by-word, if, while every man was at liberty to publish what he pleased, the public authorities might nevertheless punish him for harmless publications." But it is recognized that punishment for the abuse of the liberty accorded to the press is essential to the protection of the public, and that the common-law rules that subject the libeler to responsibility for the public offense, as well as for the private injury, are not abolished by the protection extended in our Constitutions. The law of criminal libel rests upon that secure foundation. There is also the conceded authority of courts to punish for contempt when publications directly tend to prevent the proper discharge of judicial functions. In the present case, we have no occasion to inquire as to the permissible scope of subsequent punishment. For whatever wrong the appellant has committed or may commit, by his publications, the state appropriately affords both public and private redress by its libel laws. As has been noted, the statute in question does not deal with punishments; it provides for no punishment, except in case of contempt for violation of the court's order, but for suppression and injunction—that is, for restraint upon publication.

The objection has also been made that the principle as to immunity from previous restraint is stated too broadly, if every such restraint is deemed to be prohibited. That is undoubtedly true; the protection even as to previous restraint is not absolutely unlimited. But the limitation has been recognized only in exceptional cases. "When a nation is at war many things that might be said in time of peace are such a hindrance to its effort that their utterance will not be endured so long as men fight and that no Court could regard them as protected by any constitutional right." No one would question but that a government might prevent actual obstruction to its recruiting service or the publication of the sailing dates of transports or the number and location of troops. On similar grounds, the primary requirements of decency may be enforced against obscene publications. The security of the community life may be protected against incitements to acts of violence and the overthrow by force of orderly government. The constitutional guaranty of free speech does not "protect a man from an injunction against uttering words that may have all the effect of force." These limitations are not applicable here. Nor are we now concerned with questions as to the extent of authority to prevent publications in order to protect private rights according to the principles governing the exercise of the jurisdiction of courts of equity.

The exceptional nature of its limitations places in a strong light the general conception that liberty of the press, historically considered and taken up by the Federal Constitution, has meant, principally although not exclusively, immunity from previous restraints or censorship. The conception of the liberty of the press in this country had broadened with the exigencies of the colonial period and with the efforts to secure freedom from oppressive administration. That liberty was especially cherished for the immunity it afforded from previous restraint of the publication of censure of public officers and charges of official misconduct....

The fact that for approximately one hundred and fifty years there has been almost an entire absence of attempts to impose previous restraints upon publications relating to the malfeasance of public officers is significant of the deep-seated conviction that such restraints would violate constitutional right. Public officers, whose character and conduct remains open to debate and free discussion in the press, find their remedies for false accusations in actions under libel laws providing for redress and punishment, and not in proceedings to restrain the publication of newspapers and periodicals. The general principle that the constitutional guaranty of the liberty of the press gives immunity from previous restraints has been approved in many decisions under the provisions of state constitutions.

The importance of this immunity has not lessened. While reckless assaults upon public men, and efforts to bring obloquy upon those who are endeavoring faithfully to

discharge official duties, exert a baleful influence and deserve the severest condemnation in public opinion, it cannot be said that this abuse is greater, and it is believed to be less, than that which characterized the period in which our institutions took shape. Meanwhile, the administration of government has become more complex, the opportunities for malfeasance and corruption have multiplied, crime has grown to most serious proportions, and the danger of its protection by unfaithful officials and of the impairment of the fundamental security of life and property by criminal alliances and official neglect, emphasizes the primary need of a vigilant and courageous press, especially in great cities. The fact that the liberty of the press may be abused by miscreant purveyors of scandal does not make any the less necessary the immunity of the press from previous restraint in dealing with official misconduct. Subsequent punishment for such abuses as may exist is the appropriate remedy, consistent with constitutional privilege.

In attempted justification of the statute, it is said that it deals not with publication per se, but with the "business" of publishing defamation. If, however, the publisher has a constitutional right to publish, without previous restraint, an edition of his newspaper charging official derelictions, it cannot be denied that he may publish subsequent editions for the same purpose. He does not lose his right by exercising it. If his right exists, it may be exercised in publishing nine editions, as in this case, as well as in one edition. If previous restraint is permissible, it may be imposed at once; indeed, the wrong may be as serious in one publication as in several. Characterizing the publication as a business, and the business as a nuisance, does not permit an invasion of the constitutional immunity against restraint. Similarly, it does not matter that the newspaper or periodical is found to be "largely" or "chiefly" devoted to the publication of such derelictions. If the publisher has a right, without previous restraint, to publish them, his right cannot be deemed to be dependent upon his publishing something else, more or less, with the matter to which objection is made.

Nor can it be said that the constitutional freedom from previous restraint is lost because charges are made of derelictions which constitute crimes. With the multiplying provisions of penal codes, and of municipal charters and ordinances carrying penal sanctions, the conduct of public officers is very largely within the purview of criminal statutes.

The freedom of the press from previous restraint has never been regarded as limited to such animadversions as lay outside the range of penal enactments. Historically, there is no such limitation; it is inconsistent with the reason which underlies the privilege, as the privilege so limited would be of slight value for the purposes for which it came to be established.

The statute in question cannot be justified by reason of the fact that the publisher is permitted to show, before injunction issues, that the matter published is true and is published with good motives and for justifiable ends. If such a statute, authorizing suppression and injunction on such a basis, is constitutionally valid, it would be equally permissible for the Legislature to provide that at any time the publisher of any newspaper could be brought before a court, or even an administrative officer (as the constitutional protection may not be regarded as resting on mere procedural details), and required to produce proof of the truth of his publication, or of what he intended to publish and of his motives, or stand enjoined. If this can be done, the Legislature may provide machinery for determining in the complete exercise of its discretion what are justifiable ends and restrain publication accordingly. And it would be but a step to a complete system of censorship. The recognition of authority to impose previous restraint upon publication in order to protect the community against the circulation of charges of misconduct, and especially of official misconduct, necessarily would carry with it the admission of the authority of the censor against which the constitutional barrier was erected. The preliminary freedom, by virtue of the very reason for its existence, does not depend, as this court has said, on proof of truth.

Equally unavailing is the insistence that the statute is designed to prevent the circulation of scandal which tends to disturb the public peace and to provoke assaults and the commission of crime. Charges of reprehensible conduct, and in particular of official malfeasance, unquestionably create a public scandal, but the theory of the constitutional guaranty is that even a more serious public evil would be caused by authority to prevent publication.... There is nothing new in the fact that charges of reprehensible conduct may create resentment and the disposition to resort to violent means of redress, but this well-understood tendency did not alter the determination to protect the press against censorship and restraint upon publication. As was said in New Yorker Staats-Zeitung v. Nolan, "If the township may prevent the circulation of a newspaper for no reason other than that some of its inhabitants may violently disagree with it, and resent its circulation by resorting to physical violence, there is no limit to what may be prohibited." The danger of violent reactions becomes greater with effective organization of defiant groups resenting exposure, and, if this consideration warranted legislative interference with the initial freedom of publication, the constitutional protection would be reduced to a mere form of words.

For these reasons we hold the statute, so far as it authorized the proceedings in this action under clause (b) of section 1, to be an infringement of the liberty of the press guaranteed by the Fourteenth Amendment. We should add that this decision rests upon the operation and effect of the statute, without regard to the question of the truth of the charges contained in the particular periodical. The fact that the public officers named in this case, and those associated with the charges of official dereliction, may be deemed to be impeccable, cannot affect the conclusion that the statute imposes an unconstitutional restraint upon publication.

Judgment reversed.

Chief Justice Hughes's opinion appears definitive. Note his words: "The statute not only seeks to suppress the offending newspaper ... but to put the publisher under an effective censorship." While Hughes takes a strong position against prior censorship in *Near*, he acknowledges that the protection against "previous restraint is not absolutely unlimited." There may be exceptional circumstances under which government restraint is necessary. Hughes specifically cites three vital interests that may justify the government imposing censorship: protecting national security, regulating obscenity, and prohibiting expression that would incite acts of violence. In the preceding chapter we discussed the Court's rulings on expression and violence, and we will be examining the question of obscenity in Chapter 6. In the next section we turn our attention to national security considerations.

Prior Restraint and National Security

In *Near,* Hughes explains that the government may legitimately prohibit the publication of certain material in times of war that it might not constitutionally regulate in times of peace. For example, suppose that during World War II a major newspaper received advanced classified information about the Allied invasion of Normandy, and announced that it would publish that information so the American people would be fully informed about the war effort. The military would understandably be concerned because publication would give the enemy advance knowledge of the military operation. Could the government take action to prohibit publication, or would it be confined only to pursuing criminal charges against the paper for illegal dissemination of classified documents after publication? According to *Near,* the courts would likely rule in favor of the government.

Fortunately, the United States has rarely faced a situation in which the press threatened to publish material that would seriously jeopardize vital national security interests. However, the national security issue has come before the justices. The most notable example is the case of *New York Times v. United States* (1971). In this case, the government attempted to stop the *New York Times* and the *Washington Post* from publishing classified documents pertaining to the Vietnam War.

New York Times v. United States

403 U.S. 713 (1971)
Vote: 6 (Black, Brennan, Douglas, Marshall, Stewart, White)
    3 (Blackmun, Burger, Harlan)
Per curiam opinion
Concurring opinions: Black, Brennan, Douglas, Marshall, Stewart, White
Dissenting opinions: Blackmun, Burger, Harlan

In June 1971 the *New York Times* and the *Washington Post* began publishing articles based on two government documents: a 1965 Defense Department depiction of the Gulf of Tonkin incident and the 1968 "History of U.S. Decision-Making Process on Viet Nam Policy," a 7,000-page, forty-seven-volume study undertaken by the Pentagon. Known as the "Pentagon Papers," the documents constituted "a massive history of how the United States went to war in Indochina," a subject of acute interest in the early 1970s.

After the newspapers published several installments, the U.S. government brought action against them, requesting a district court judge to restrain them from publishing any more. The government argued that the articles would cause "irreparable injury" to the country's national security. To support this assertion, the government said that the entire 1968 study was top secret, a classification "applied only to that information or material the defense aspect of which is paramount, and the unauthorized disclosure of which could result in *exceptionally grave* damage to the Nation." The newspapers disagreed; they argued that the material was largely of historical, not current, interest, and that nothing in the documents related "to a time period subsequent to early 1968." As such, the government's attempt to enjoin publication amounted to nothing less than prior restraint.

Because the issues in this case were so important and the public controversy so intense, the judicial system responded to the dispute in a very unusual manner. The government first requested the district court to prohibit publication on June 15, 1971. The lower courts handled the case in an expedited fashion, and only nine days later the issue was before the Supreme Court. By then the justices had completed their work for the term and were about to go into their summer recess. To accommodate the case, however, the justices extended their session and heard arguments on June 26. Only four days later, the Court announced its decision. Because of its hurried consideration of the dispute, the Court issued only a short "per curiam" opinion announcing that the majority had voted to reject the government's demands. Then each of the justices submitted an opinion expressing his view. Six supported the newspapers, and three sided with the government. Seven of those opinions are presented here. From start to finish, it took the federal judiciary only two weeks to decide this major constitutional dispute.

PER CURIAM.

We granted certiorari in these cases in which the United States seeks to enjoin the New York Times and the Washington Post from publishing the contents of a classified study entitled "History of U.S. Decision-Making Process on Viet Nam Policy."

"Any system of prior restraints of expression comes to this Court bearing a heavy presumption against its constitutional validity." The Government "thus carries a heavy burden of showing justification for the imposition of such a restraint." The District Court for the Southern District of New York in the *New York Times* case held that the Government had not met that burden. We agree.

... The order of the Court of Appeals for the Second Circuit is reversed, and the case is remanded with directions to enter a judgment affirming the judgment of the District Court for the Southern District of New York. The stays entered ... by the Court are vacated. The judgments shall issue forthwith.

MR. JUSTICE BLACK, with whom MR. JUSTICE DOUGLAS joins, concurring.

I adhere to the view that the Government's case against the Washington Post should have been dismissed and that the injunction against the New York Times should have been vacated without oral argument when the cases were first presented to this Court. I believe that every moment's continuance of the injunctions against these newspapers amounts to a flagrant, indefensible, and continuing violation of the First Amendment.... In my view it is unfortunate that some of my Brethren are apparently willing to hold that the publication of news may sometimes be enjoined. Such a holding would make a shambles of the First Amendment.

Our Government was launched in 1789 with the adop-

tion of the Constitution. The Bill of Rights, including the First Amendment, followed in 1791. Now, for the first time in the 182 years since the founding of the Republic, the federal courts are asked to hold that the First Amendment does not mean what it says, but rather means that the Government can halt the publication of current news of vital importance to the people of this country.

In seeking injunctions against these newspapers and in its presentation to the Court, the Executive Branch seems to have forgotten the essential purpose and history of the First Amendment. When the Constitution was adopted, many people strongly opposed it because the document contained no Bill of Rights to safeguard certain basic freedoms. They especially feared that the new powers granted to a central government might be interpreted to permit the government to curtail freedom of religion, press, assembly, and speech. In response to an overwhelming public clamor, James Madison offered a series of amendments to satisfy citizens that these great liberties would remain safe and beyond the power of government to abridge. Madison proposed what later became the First Amendment in three parts, two of which are set out below, and one of which proclaimed: "The people shall not be deprived or abridged of their right to speak, to write, or to publish their sentiments; *and the freedom of the press, as one of the great bulwarks of liberty, shall be inviolable.*" The amendments were offered to curtail and restrict the general powers granted in the Executive, Legislative, and Judicial Branches two years before in the original Constitution. The Bill of Rights changed the original Constitution into a new charter under which no branch of government could abridge the people's freedoms of press, speech, religion, and assembly. Yet the Solicitor General argues and some members of the Court appear to agree that the general powers of the Government adopted in the original Constitution should be interpreted to limit and restrict the specific and emphatic guarantees of the Bill of Rights adopted later. I can imagine no greater perversion of history. Madison and the other Framers of the First Amendment, able men that they were, wrote in language they earnestly believed could never be misunderstood: "Congress shall make no law ... abridging the freedom ... of the press...." Both the history and language of the First Amendment support the view that the press must be left free to publish news, whatever the source, without censorship, injunctions, or prior restraints.

In the First Amendment the Founding Fathers gave the free press the protection it must have to fulfill its essential role in our democracy. The press was to serve the governed, not the governors. The Government's power to censor the press was abolished so that the press would remain forever free to censure the Government. The press was protected so that it could bare the secrets of government and inform the people. Only a free and unrestrained press can effectively expose deception in government. And paramount among the responsibilities of a free press is the duty to prevent any part of the government from deceiving the people and sending them off to distant lands to die of foreign fevers and foreign shot and shell. In my view, far from deserving condemnation for their courageous reporting, the New York Times, the Washington Post, and other newspapers should be commended for serving the purpose that the Founding Fathers saw so clearly. In revealing the workings of government that led to the Vietnam war, the newspapers nobly did precisely that which the Founders hoped and trusted they would do.

The Government's case here is based on premises entirely different from those that guided the Framers of the First Amendment....

[T]he government argues in its brief that in spite of the First Amendment, "[t]he authority of the Executive Department to protect the nation against publication of information whose disclosure would endanger the national security stems from two interrelated sources: the constitutional power of the President over the conduct of foreign affairs and his authority as Commander-in-Chief."

In other words, we are asked to hold that despite the First Amendment's emphatic command, the Executive Branch, the Congress, and the Judiciary can make laws enjoining publication of current news and abridging freedom of the press in the name of "national security." The Government does not even attempt to rely on any act of Congress. Instead, it makes the bold and dangerously far-reaching contention that the courts should take it upon themselves to "make" a law abridging freedom of the press in the name of equity, presidential power and national security, even when the representatives of the people in Congress have adhered to the command of the First Amendment and refused to make such a law. To find that the President has "inherent power" to halt the publication of news by resort to the courts would wipe out the First Amendment and destroy the fundamental liberty and security of the very people the Government hopes to make "secure." No one can read the history of the adoption of the First Amendment without being convinced beyond any doubt that it was injunctions like those sought here that Madison and his collaborators intended to outlaw in this Nation for all time.

The word "security" is a broad, vague generality whose contours should not be invoked to abrogate the fundamental law embodied in the First Amendment. The guarding of military and diplomatic secrets at the expense of informed representative government provides no real security for our Republic. The Framers of the First Amendment, fully aware of both the need to defend a new nation and the abuses of the English and Colonial Governments, sought to give this new society strength and security by providing that freedom of speech, press, religion, and assembly should not be abridged. This thought was eloquently expressed in 1937 by Mr. Chief Justice Hughes—great man and great Chief Justice that he was—when the Court held a man could not be punished for attending a meeting run by Communists.

"The greater the importance of safeguarding the community from incitements to the overthrow of our institutions by force and violence, the more imperative is the need to preserve inviolate the constitutional rights of free speech, free press and free assembly in order to maintain the opportunity for free political discussion, to the end that government may be responsive to the will of the people and that changes, if desired, may be obtained by peaceful means. Therein lies the security of the Republic, the very foundation of constitutional government."

MR. JUSTICE DOUGLAS, with whom MR. JUSTICE BLACK joins, concurring.

While I join the opinion of the Court I believe it necessary to express my views more fully.

It should be noted at the outset that the First Amendment provides that "Congress shall make no law ... abridging the freedom of speech, or of the press." That leaves, in my view, no room for governmental restraint on the press....

The dominant purpose of the First Amendment was to prohibit the widespread practice of governmental suppression of embarrassing information. It is common knowledge that the First Amendment was adopted against the widespread use of the common law of seditious libel to punish the dissemination of material that is embarrassing to the powers-that-be. The present cases will, I think, go down in history as the most dramatic illustration of that principle. A debate of large proportions goes on in the Nation over our posture in Vietnam. That debate antedated the disclosure of the contents of the present documents. The latter are highly relevant to the debate in progress.

Secrecy in government is fundamentally anti-democratic, perpetuating bureaucratic errors. Open debate and discussion of public issues are vital to our national health. On public questions there should be "uninhibited, robust, and wide-open" debate.

MR. JUSTICE BRENNAN, concurring.

I write separately in these cases only to emphasize what should be apparent, that our judgments in the present cases may not be taken to indicate the propriety, in the future, of issuing temporary stays and restraining orders to block the publication of material sought to be suppressed by the Government. So far as I can determine, never before has the United States sought to enjoin a newspaper from publishing information in its possession. The relative novelty of the questions presented, the necessary haste with which decisions were reached, the magnitude of the interests asserted, and the fact that all the parties have concentrated their arguments upon the question whether permanent restraints were proper may have justified at least some of the restraints heretofore imposed in these cases. Certainly it is difficult to fault the several courts below for seeking to assure that the issues here involved were preserved for ultimate review by this Court. But even if it be assumed that some of the interim restraints were proper in the two cases before us, that assumption has no bearing upon the propriety of similar judicial action in the future. To begin with, there has now been ample time for reflection and judgment; whatever values there may be in the preservation of novel questions for appellate review may not support any restraints in the future. More important, the First Amendment stands as an absolute bar to the imposition of judicial restraints in circumstances of the kind presented by these cases....

The entire thrust of the Government's claim throughout

these cases has been that publication of the material sought to be enjoined "could," or "might," or "may" prejudice the national interest in various ways. But the First Amendment tolerates absolutely no prior judicial restraints of the press predicated upon surmise or conjecture that untoward consequences may result. Our cases, it is true, have indicated that there is a single, extremely narrow class of cases in which the First Amendment's ban on prior judicial restraint may be overridden. Our cases have thus far indicated that such cases may arise only when the Nation "is at war," during which times "[n]o one would question but that a government might prevent actual obstruction to its recruiting service or the publication of the sailing dates of transports or the number and location of troops." Even if the present world situation were assumed to be tantamount to a time of war, or if the power of presently available armaments would justify even in peacetime the suppression of information that would set in motion a nuclear holocaust, in neither of these actions has the Government presented or even alleged that publication of items from or based upon the material at issue would cause the happening of an event of that nature. "[T]he chief purpose of [the First Amendment's] guaranty [is] to prevent previous restraints upon publication." Thus, only governmental allegation and proof that publication must inevitably, directly, and immediately cause the occurrence of an event kindred to imperiling the safety of a transport already at sea can support even the issuance of an interim restraining order. In no event may mere conclusions be sufficient: for if the Executive Branch seeks judicial aid in preventing publication, it must inevitably submit the basis upon which that aid is sought to scrutiny by the judiciary. And therefore, every restraint issued in this case, whatever its form, has violated the First Amendment—and not less so because that restraint was justified as necessary to afford the courts an opportunity to examine the claim more thoroughly. Unless and until the Government has clearly made out its case, the First Amendment commands that no injunction may issue.

MR JUSTICE STEWART, with whom MR. JUSTICE WHITE joins, concurring.

In the governmental structure created by our Constitution, the Executive is endowed with enormous power in the two related areas of national defense and international relations. This power, largely unchecked by the Legislative and Judicial branches, has been pressed to the very hilt since the advent of the nuclear missile age. For better or for worse, the simple fact is that a President of the United States possesses vastly greater constitutional independence in these two vital areas of power than does, say, a prime minister of a country with a parliamentary form of government.

In the absence of the governmental checks and balances present in other areas of our national life, the only effective restraint upon executive policy and power in the areas of national defense and international affairs may lie in an enlightened citizenry—in an informed and critical public opinion which alone can here protect the values of democratic government. For this reason, it is perhaps here that a press that is alert, aware, and free most vitally serves the basic purpose of the First Amendment. For without an informed and free press there cannot be an enlightened people.

Yet it is elementary that the successful conduct of international diplomacy and the maintenance of an effective national defense require both confidentiality and secrecy. Other nations can hardly deal with this Nation in an atmosphere of mutual trust unless they can be assured that their confidences will be kept. And within our own executive departments, the development of considered and intelligent international policies would be impossible if those charged with their formulation could not communicate with each other freely, frankly, and in confidence. In the area of basic national defense the frequent need for absolute secrecy is, of course, self-evident.

I think there can be but one answer to this dilemma, if dilemma it be. The responsibility must be where the power is. If the Constitution gives the Executive a large degree of unshared power in the conduct of foreign affairs and the maintenance of our national defense, then under the Constitution the Executive must have the largely unshared duty to determine and preserve the degree of internal security necessary to exercise that power successfully. It is an awesome responsibility, requiring judgment and wisdom of a high order. I should suppose that moral, political, and practical considerations would dictate that a very first principle of that wisdom would be an insistence upon avoiding secrecy for its own sake. For when everything is classified,

then nothing is classified, and the system becomes one to be disregarded by the cynical or the careless, and to be manipulated by those intent on self-protection or self-promotion. I should suppose, in short, that the hallmark of a truly effective internal security system would be the maximum possible disclosure, recognizing that secrecy can best be preserved only when credibility is truly maintained. But be that as it may, it is clear to me that it is the constitutional duty of the Executive—as a matter of sovereign prerogative and not as a matter of law as the courts know law—through the promulgation and enforcement of executive regulations, to protect the confidentiality necessary to carry out its responsibilities in the fields of international relations and national defense.

This is not to say that Congress and the courts have no role to play. Undoubtedly Congress has the power to enact specific and appropriate criminal laws to protect government property and preserve government secrets. Congress has passed such laws, and several of them are of very colorable relevance to the apparent circumstances of these cases. And if a criminal prosecution is instituted, it will be the responsibility of the courts to decide the applicability of the criminal law under which the charge is brought. Moreover, if Congress should pass a specific law authorizing civil proceedings in this field, the courts would likewise have the duty to decide the constitutionality of such a law as well as its applicability to the facts proved.

But in the cases before us we are asked neither to construe specific regulations nor to apply specific laws. We are asked, instead, to perform a function that the Constitution gave to the Executive, not the Judiciary. We are asked, quite simply, to prevent the publication by two newspapers of material that the Executive Branch insists should not, in the national interest, be published. I am convinced that the Executive is correct with respect to some of the documents involved. But I cannot say that disclosure of any of them will surely result in direct, immediate, and irreparable damage to our Nation or its people. That being so, there can under the First Amendment be but one judicial resolution of the issues before us. I join the judgments of the Court.

MR. JUSTICE WHITE, with whom MR. JUSTICE STEWART joins, concurring.

I concur in today's judgments, but only because of the

concededly extraordinary protection against prior restraints enjoyed by the press under our constitutional system. I do not say that in no circumstances would the First Amendment permit an injunction against publishing information about government plans or operations. Nor, after examining the materials the Government characterizes as the most sensitive and destructive, can I deny that revelation of these documents will do substantial damage to public interests. Indeed, I am confident that their disclosure will have that result. But I nevertheless agree that the United States has not satisfied the very heavy burden that it must meet to warrant an injunction against publication in these cases, at least in the absence of express and appropriately limited congressional authorization for prior restraints in circumstances such as these.

The Government's position is simply stated: The responsibility of the Executive for the conduct of the foreign affairs and for the security of the nation is so basic that the President is entitled to an injunction against publication of a newspaper story whenever he can convince a court that the information to be revealed threatens "grave and irreparable" injury to the public interest; and the injunction should issue whether or not the material to be published is classified, whether or not publication would be lawful under relevant criminal statutes enacted by Congress, and regardless of the circumstances by which the newspaper came into possession of the information.

At least in the absence of legislation by Congress, based on its own investigations and findings, I am quite unable to agree that the inherent powers of the Executive and the courts reach so far as to authorize remedies having such sweeping potential for inhibiting publications by the press. Much of the difficulty inheres in the "grave and irreparable danger" standard suggested by the United States. If the United States were to have judgment under such a standard in these cases, our decision would be of little guidance to other courts in other cases, for the material at issue here would not be available from the Court's opinion or from public records, nor would it be published by the press. Indeed, even today where we hold that the United States has not met its burden, the material remains sealed in court records and it is properly not discussed in today's opinions. Moreover, because the material poses substantial dangers to national interests and because of the hazards of criminal

sanctions, a responsible press may choose never to publish the more sensitive materials. To sustain the Government in these cases would start the courts down a long and hazardous road that I am not willing to travel, at least without congressional guidance and direction.

It is not easy to reject the proposition urged by the United States and to deny relief on its good-faith claims in these cases that publication will work serious damage to the country. But that discomfiture is considerably dispelled by the infrequency of prior-restraint cases. Normally, publication will occur and the damage be done before the Government has either opportunity or grounds for suppression. So here, publication has already begun and a substantial part of the threatened damage has already occurred. The fact of a massive breakdown in security is known, access to the documents by many unauthorized people is undeniable, and the efficacy of equitable relief against these or other newspapers to avert anticipated damage is doubtful at best.

What is more, terminating the ban on publication of the relatively few sensitive documents the Government now seeks to suppress does not mean that the law either requires or invites newspapers or others to publish them or that they will be immune from criminal action if they do. Prior restraints require an unusually heavy justification under the First Amendment; but failure by the Government to justify prior restraints does not measure its constitutional entitlement to a conviction for criminal publication. That the Government mistakenly chose to proceed by injunction does not mean that it could not successfully proceed in another way.

When the Espionage Act was under consideration in 1917, Congress eliminated from the bill a provision that would have given the President broad powers in time of war to proscribe, under threat of criminal penalty, the publication of various categories of information related to the national defense. Congress at that time was unwilling to clothe the President with such far-reaching powers to monitor the press, and those opposed to this part of the legislation assumed that a necessary concomitant of such power was the power to "filter out the news to the people through some man." However, these same members of Congress appeared to have little doubt that newspapers would be subject to criminal prosecution if they insisted on publishing information of the type Congress had itself determined should not be revealed....

The Criminal Code contains numerous provisions potentially relevant to these cases. Section 797 makes it a crime to publish certain photographs or drawings of military installations. Section 798, also in precise language, proscribes knowing and willful publication of any classified information concerning the cryptographic systems or communication intelligence activities of the United States as well as any information obtained from communication intelligence operations. If any of the material here at issue is of this nature, the newspapers are presumably now on full notice of the position of the United States and must face the consequences if they publish. I would have no difficulty in sustaining convictions under these sections on facts that would not justify the intervention of equity and the imposition of a prior restraint....

MR. CHIEF JUSTICE BURGER, dissenting.

So clear are the constitutional limitations on prior restraint against expression, that from the time of Near v. Minnesota we have had little occasion to be concerned with cases involving prior restraints against news reporting on matters of public interest. There is, therefore, little variation among the members of the Court in terms of resistance to prior restraints against publication. Adherence to this basic constitutional principle, however, does not make these cases simple ones. In these cases, the imperative of a free and unfettered press comes into collision with another imperative, the effective functioning of a complex modern government and specifically the effective exercise of certain constitutional powers of the Executive. Only those who view the First Amendment as an absolute in all circumstances—a view I respect, but reject—can find such cases as these to be simple or easy.

These cases are not simple for another and more immediate reason. We do not know the facts of the cases. No District Judge knew all the facts. No Court of Appeals Judge knew all the facts. No member of this Court knows all the facts.

Why are we in this posture, in which only those judges to whom the First Amendment is absolute and permits of no restraint in any circumstances or for any reason, are really in a position to act?

I suggest we are in this posture because these cases have been conducted in unseemly haste.... The prompt settling of these cases reflects our universal abhorrence of prior restraint. But prompt judicial action does not mean unjudicial haste.

Here, moreover, the frenetic haste is due in large part to the manner in which the Times proceeded from the date it obtained the purloined documents. It seems reasonably clear now that the haste precluded reasonable and deliberate judicial treatment of these cases and was not warranted. The precipitate action of this Court aborting trials not yet completed is not the kind of judicial conduct that ought to attend the disposition of a great issue.

The newspapers make a derivative claim under the First Amendment; they denominate this right as the public "right to know"; by implication, the Times asserts a sole trusteeship of that right by virtue of its journalistic "scoop." The right is asserted as an absolute. Of course, the First Amendment right itself is not an absolute, as Justice Holmes so long ago pointed out in his aphorism concerning the right to shout "fire" in a crowded theater if there was no fire. There are other exceptions, some of which Chief Justice Hughes mentioned by way of example in Near v. Minnesota ex rel. Olson. There are no doubt other exceptions no one has had occasion to describe or discuss. Conceivably such exceptions may be lurking in these cases and would have been flushed had they been properly considered in the trial courts, free from unwarranted deadlines and frenetic pressures. An issue of this importance should be tried and heard in a judicial atmosphere conducive to thoughtful, reflective deliberation, especially when haste, in terms of hours, is unwarranted in light of the long period the Times, by its own choice, deferred publication.

It is not disputed that the Times has had unauthorized possession of the documents for three to four months, during which it has had its expert analysts studying them, presumably digesting them and preparing the material for publication. During all of this time, the Times, presumably in its capacity as trustee of the public's "right to know," has held up publication for purposes it considered proper and thus public knowledge was delayed. No doubt this was for a good reason; the analysis of 7,000 pages of complex material drawn from a vastly greater volume of material would inevitably take time and the writing of good news stories takes time. But why should the United States Government, from whom this information was illegally acquired by someone, along with all the counsel, trial judges, and appellate judges be placed under needless pressure? After these months of deferral, the alleged "right to know" has somehow and suddenly become a right that must be vindicated instanter.

Would it have been unreasonable, since the newspaper could anticipate the Government's objections to release of secret material, to give the Government an opportunity to review the entire collection and determine whether agreement could be reached on publication? Stolen or not, if security was not in fact jeopardized, much of the material could no doubt have been declassified, since it spans a period ending in 1968. With such an approach—one that great newspapers have in the past practiced and stated editorially to be the duty of an honorable press—the newspapers and Government might well have narrowed the area of disagreement as to what was and was not publishable, leaving the remainder to be resolved in orderly litigation, if necessary. To me it is hardly believable that a newspaper long regarded as a great institution in American life would fail to perform one of the basic and simple duties of every citizen with respect to the discovery or possession of stolen property or secret government documents. That duty, I had thought—perhaps naively—was to report forthwith, to responsible public officers. This duty rests on taxi drivers, Justices, and the New York Times. The course followed by the Times, whether so calculated or not, removed any possibility of orderly litigation of the issues. If the action of the judges up to now has been correct, that result is sheer happenstance.

Our grant of the writ of certiorari before final judgment in the Times case aborted the trial in the District Court before it had made a complete record pursuant to the mandate of the Court of Appeals for the Second Circuit.

The consequence of all this melancholy series of events is that we literally do not know what we are acting on. As I see it, we have been forced to deal with litigation concerning rights of great magnitude without an adequate record, and surely without time for adequate treatment either in the prior proceedings or in this Court. It is interesting to note that counsel, on both sides, in oral argument before this Court, were frequently unable to respond to questions on factual points. Not surprisingly they pointed out that they had been working literally "around the clock" and simply were unable to review the documents that give rise to these cases and were not familiar with them. This Court is in no better posture....

We all crave speedier judicial processes but when judges are pressured as in these cases the result is a parody of the judicial function.

MR. JUSTICE HARLAN, with whom THE CHIEF JUSTICE and MR. JUSTICE BLACKMUN join, dissenting.

With all respect, I consider that the Court has been almost irresponsibly feverish in dealing with these cases.

Both the Court of Appeals for the Second Circuit and the Court of Appeals for the District of Columbia Circuit rendered judgment on June 23. The New York Times' petition for certiorari, its motion for accelerated consideration thereof, and its application for interim relief were filed in this Court on June 24 at about 11 a.m. The application of the United States for interim relief in the Post case was also filed here on June 24 at about 7:15 p.m. This Court's order setting a hearing before us on June 26 at 11 a.m., a course which I joined only to avoid the possibility of an even more peremptory action by the Court, was issued less than 24 hours before. The record in the Post case was filed with the Clerk shortly before 1 p.m. on June 25; the record in the Times case did not arrive until 7 or 8 o'clock that same night. The briefs of the parties were received less than two hours before argument on June 26.

This frenzied train of events took place in the name of the presumption against prior restraints created by the First Amendment. Due regard for the extraordinarily important and difficult questions involved in these litigations should have led the Court to shun such a precipitate timetable. In order to decide the merits of these cases properly, some or all of the following questions should have been faced:

1. Whether the Attorney General is authorized to bring these suits in the name of the United States.

2. Whether the First Amendment permits the federal courts to enjoin publication of stories which would present a serious threat to national security.

3. Whether the threat to publish highly secret docu-

ments is of itself a sufficient implication of national security to justify an injunction on the theory that regardless of the contents of the documents harm enough results simply from the demonstration of such a breach of secrecy.

4. Whether the unauthorized disclosure of any of these particular documents would seriously impair the national security.

5. What weight should be given to the opinion of high officers in the Executive Branch of the Government with respect to questions 3 and 4.

6. Whether the newspapers are entitled to retain and use the documents notwithstanding the seemingly uncontested facts that the documents, or the originals of which they are duplicates, were purloined from the Government's possession and that the newspapers received them with knowledge that they had been feloniously acquired.

7. Whether the threatened harm to the national security or the Government's possessory interest in the documents justifies the issuance of an injunction against publication in light of—

a. The strong First Amendment policy against prior restraints on publication;

b. The doctrine against enjoining conduct in violation of criminal statutes; and

c. The extent to which the materials at issue have apparently already been otherwise disseminated.

These are difficult questions of fact, of law, and of judgment; the potential consequences of erroneous decision are enormous. The time which has been available to us, to the lower courts, and to the parties has been wholly inadequate for giving these cases the kind of consideration they deserve. It is a reflection on the stability of the judicial process that these great issues—as important as any that have arisen during my time on the Court—should have been decided under the pressures engendered by the torrent of publicity that has attended these litigations from their inception.

Forced as I am to reach the merits of these cases, I dissent from the opinion and judgments of the Court. Within the severe limitations imposed by the time constraints under which I have been required to operate, I can only state my reasons in telescoped form, even though in different circumstances I would have felt constrained to deal with the cases in the fuller sweep indicated above.

It is a sufficient basis for affirming the Court of Appeals for the Second Circuit in the *Times* litigation to observe that its order must rest on the conclusion that because of the time elements the Government had not been given an adequate opportunity to present its case to the District Court. At the least this conclusion was not an abuse of discretion.

In the *Post* litigation the Government had more time to prepare; this was apparently the basis for the refusal of the Court of Appeals for the District of Columbia Circuit on rehearing to conform its judgment to that of the Second Circuit. But I think there is another and more fundamental reason why this judgment cannot stand—a reason which also furnishes an additional ground for not reinstating the judgment of the District Court in the *Times* litigation, set aside by the Court of Appeals. It is plain to me that the scope of the judicial function in passing upon the activities of the Executive Branch of the Government in the field of foreign affairs is very narrowly restricted. This view is, I think, dictated by the concept of separation of powers upon which our constitutional system rests.

In a speech on the floor of the House of Representatives, Chief Justice John Marshall, then a member of that body, stated:

"The President is the sole organ of the nation in its external relations, and its sole representative with foreign nations."

From that time, shortly after the founding of the Nation, to this, there has been no substantial challenge to this description of the scope of executive power.

From this constitutional primacy in the field of foreign affairs, it seems to me that certain conclusions necessarily follow. Some of these were stated concisely by President Washington, declining the request of the House of Representatives for the papers leading up to the negotiation of the Jay Treaty:

"The nature of foreign negotiations requires caution, and their success must often depend on secrecy; and even when brought to a conclusion, a full disclosure of all the measures, demands, or eventual concessions which may have been proposed or contemplated would be extremely impolitic; for this might have a pernicious influence on future negotiations, or produce immediate inconveniences, perhaps danger and mischief, in relation to other powers."

The power to evaluate the "pernicious influence" of premature disclosure is not, however, lodged in the Executive alone. I agree that, in performance of its duty to protect the values of the First Amendment against political pressures, the judiciary must review the initial Executive determination to the point of satisfying itself that the subject matter of the dispute does lie within the proper compass of the President's foreign relations power....

But in my judgment the judiciary may not properly go beyond these ... inquiries and redetermine for itself the probable impact of disclosure on the national security.

Even if there is some room for the judiciary to override the executive determination, it is plain that the scope of review must be exceedingly narrow. I can see no indication in the opinions of either the District Court or the Court of Appeals in the *Post* litigation that the conclusions of the Executive were given even the deference owing to an administrative agency, much less that owing to a co-equal branch of the Government operating within the field of its constitutional prerogative.

Accordingly, I would vacate the judgment of the Court of Appeals for the District of Columbia Circuit on this ground and remand the case for further proceedings in the District Court. Before the commencement of such further proceedings, due opportunity should be afforded the Government for procuring from the Secretary of State or the Secretary of Defense or both an expression of their views on the issue of national security. The ensuing review by the District Court should be in accordance with the views expressed in this opinion. And for the reasons stated above I would affirm the judgment of the Court of Appeals for the Second Circuit.

Pending further hearings in each case conducted under the appropriate ground rules, I would continue the restraints on publication. I cannot believe that the doctrine prohibiting prior restraints reaches to the point of preventing courts from maintaining the *status quo* long enough to act responsibly in matters of such national importance as those involved here.

New York Times has generated a great deal of debate among legal scholars. Some suggest that it was the Court's, or at least individual justices', strongest state-

ment to date on freedom of the press, that the justices virtually eradicated Hughes's national security exception to prior restraint. Others disagree. C. Herman Pritchett noted, "While the result in *New York Times* was clear enough, the Court's opinions do not add up to a sound defense of freedom of the press."[6] At the very least, the justices were divided in their views. Compare, for example, White's opinion with Black's; one could hardly imagine greater divergence of thought while still voting for the same outcome.

Since *New York Times* the Court has not had another important case dealing with prior restraints and national security concerns. But in 1991, during the war with Iraq, the U.S. government placed many constraints on the media. For example, most reports had to be cleared by a designated representative of the military. Although there were no serious legal challenges to these restrictions, if one had occurred, how do you think the Rehnquist Court would have ruled?

Prior Restraint and the Student Press

National security is not the only area that has given rise to cases concerning prior restraint. Any government attempt to intervene in press activities before publication can trigger a charge of prior censorship. The 1988 case of *Hazelwood School District v. Kuhlmeier* is a good example. This appeal pitted the First Amendment rights of high school journalists against the authority of administrators to impose certain standards on public school newspapers. The students claimed that the public school system had engaged in the same kind of prior censorship that the Court condemned in *Near*. As you read Justice White's opinion, ask yourself the following questions. What importance do the justices place on the fact that the newspaper was run by students? Would the outcome have been the same if the newspaper was not produced as part of a journalism class? Does the case have any implications

6. C. Herman Pritchett, *Constitutional Civil Liberties* (Englewood Cliffs, N.J.: Prentice-Hall, 1984), 65.

beyond the student press? Is the decision an isolated exception, or does it significantly dilute the prior restraint doctrine that the justices have supported since *Near*?

Hazelwood School District v. Kuhlmeier

484 U.S. 260 (1988)
Vote: 5 (O'Connor, Rehnquist, Scalia, Stevens, White)
    3 (Blackmun, Brennan, Marshall)
Opinion of the Court: White
Dissenting opinion: Brennan

In May 1983 the editors of the *Spectrum*, Hazelwood East High School's newspaper, planned to publish articles on divorce and teenage pregnancy *(see Box 5-1)*. Principal Robert E. Reynolds decided to excise two pages because, in his view, "The students and families in the articles were described in such a way that the readers could tell who they were. When it became clear that [they] were going to tread on the right of privacy of students and their parents, I stepped in to stop the process."[7]

The *Spectrum* staff objected to Reynolds's decision. Believing it amounted to censorship, they hired a lawyer and challenged it in court.

JUSTICE WHITE delivered the opinion of the Court.

This case concerns the extent to which educators may exercise editorial control over the contents of a high school newspaper produced as part of the school's journalism curriculum....

Students in the public schools do not "shed their constitutional rights to freedom of speech or expression at the schoolhouse gate." They cannot be punished merely for expressing their personal views on the school premises—whether "in the cafeteria, or on the playing field, or on the campus during the authorized hours"—unless school authorities have reason to believe that such expression will

7. Mark A. Uhlig, "From Hazelwood to the High Court," *New York Times Magazine*, September 13, 1987, 102.

"substantially interfere with the work of the school or impinge upon the rights of other students."

We have nonetheless recognized that the First Amendment rights of students in the public schools "are not automatically coextensive with the rights of adults in other settings" and must be "applied in light of the special characteristics of the school environment." A school need not tolerate student speech that is inconsistent with its "basic educational mission," even though the government could not censor similar speech outside the school. Accordingly, we held in [*Bethel School District No. 403 v.*] *Fraser* [1986] that a student could be disciplined for having delivered a speech that was "sexually explicit" but not legally obscene at an official school assembly, because the school was entitled to "disassociate itself" from the speech in a manner that would demonstrate to others that such vulgarity is "wholly inconsistent with the 'fundamental values' of public school education." We thus recognized that "[t]he determination of what manner of speech in the classroom or in school assembly is inappropriate properly rests with the school board," rather than with the federal courts. It is in this context that respondents' First Amendment claims must be considered....

The question whether the First Amendment requires a school to tolerate particular student speech—the question that we addressed in *Tinker* [*v. Des Moines,* 1969]—is different from the question whether the First Amendment requires a school affirmatively to promote particular student speech. The former question addresses educators' ability to silence a student's personal expression that happens to occur on the school premises. The latter question concerns educators' authority over school-sponsored publications, theatrical productions, and other expressive activities that students, parents, and members of the public might reasonably perceive to bear the imprimatur of the school. These activities may fairly be characterized as part of the school curriculum, whether or not they occur in a traditional classroom setting, so long as they are supervised by faculty members and designed to impart particular knowledge or skills to student participants and audiences.

Educators are entitled to exercise greater control over this second form of student expression to assure that participants learn whatever lessons the activity is designed to teach, that readers or listeners are not exposed to material

BOX 5-1 CENSORED HIGH SCHOOL NEWSPAPER ARTICLE

The uncorrected page proof of part of one of the two stories censored from the May 13, 1983, issue of the Hazelwood East High School *Spectrum*. Student editors took their objections all the way to the Supreme Court.

Divorce's impact on kids may have lifelong effect

by Shari Gordon

In the United States one marriage ends for every two that begin. The North County percentage of divorce is three marriages end out of four marriages that start.

There are more than two central characters in the painful drama of divorce. Children of divorced parents, literally million os them, are torn by the end of their parents' marriage.

> ## *"In the beginning I thought I caused the problem, but now I realize it wasn't me."*

What causes divorce? According to Mr. Ken Kerkhoff, social studies teacher some of the causes are:

- Poor dating habits that lead to marriage.
- Not enough variables in common.
- Lack f communication.
- Lack of desire or effort to make the relationship work.

Figures aren't the whole story. The fact is that divorce has a psychological and sociological change on the child.

One junior commented on how the divorce occurred, "My dad dian't make any money, so my mother divorced him."

"My father was an alcoholic and he always came home drunk and my mom really couldn't stand it any longer," said another junior.

Diana Herbert, freshman, said "My dad wasn't spending enough time with my mom, my sister and I. He was always out of town or out late playing cards with the guys. My parents always argued about everything."

"In the beginning I thought I caused the problem, but now I realize it wasn't me," added Diana.

"I was only five when my parents got divorced," said Susan Kiefer, junior. "I didn't quite understand what the divorce really meant until about the age of seven. I understood that divorce meant my mother and father wouldn't be together again."

"It stinks!" exclaimed Jill Viola, junior. "They can, afterwards, remarry and start their lives over again, but their kids will always be caught in between."

Out of the 25 students interviewe 17 f them have parents that have remarried.

The feelings of divorce affects the kids for the rest of their lives, according to Mr. Kerckhoff. The effects of divorce on the kids lead to the following:

- Higher not of absenteeism in school.
- Higher rate of trouble with school, officials and police.
- Higher rate of depression and insecurity.
- Run a higher risk of divorce themselves.

All of these are the latest findings in research on single parent homes.

that may be inappropriate for their level of maturity, and that the views of the individual speakers are not erroneously attributed to the school. Hence, a school may in its capacity as publisher of a school newspaper or producer of a school play "disassociate itself" not only from speech that would "substantially interfere with [its] work ... or impinge upon the rights of other students," but also from speech that is, for example, ungrammatical, poorly written, inadequately researched, biased or prejudiced, vulgar or profane, or unsuitable for immature audiences. A school must be able to set high standards for the student speech that is disseminated under its auspices—standards that may be higher than those demanded by some newspaper publishers or theatrical producers in the "real" world—and may refuse to disseminate student speech that does not meet those standards. In addition, a school must be able to take into account the emotional maturity of the intended audience in determining whether to disseminate student speech on potentially sensitive topics, which might range from the existence of Santa Claus in an elementary school setting to the particulars of teenage sexual activity in a high school setting. A school must also retain the authority to refuse to sponsor student speech that might reasonably be perceived to advocate drug or alcohol use, irresponsible sex, or conduct otherwise inconsistent with "the shared values of a civilized social order" or to associate the school with any position other than neutrality on matters of political controversy. Otherwise, the schools would be unduly constrained from fulfilling their role as "a principal instrument in awakening the child to cultural values, in preparing him for later professional training, and in helping him to adjust normally to his environment."

Accordingly, we conclude that the standard articulated in *Tinker* for determining when a school may punish student expression need not also be the standard for determining when a school may refuse to lend its name and resources to the dissemination of student expression. Instead, we hold that educators do not offend the First Amendment by exercising editorial control over the style and content of student speech in school-sponsored expressive activities so long as their actions are reasonably related to legitimate pedagogical concerns.

This standard is consistent with our oft-expressed view that the education of the Nation's youth is primarily the responsibility of parents, teachers, and state and local school officials, and not of federal judges. It is only when the decision to censor a school-sponsored publication, theatrical production, or other vehicle of student expression has no valid educational purpose that the First Amendment is so "directly and sharply implicate[d]" as to require judicial intervention to protect students' constitutional rights.

We also conclude that Principal Reynolds acted reasonably in requiring the deletion from the May 13 issue of Spectrum of the pregnancy article, the divorce article, and the remaining articles that were to appear on the same pages of the newspaper.

The initial paragraph of the pregnancy article declared that "[a]ll names have been changed to keep the identity of these girls a secret." The principal concluded that the students' anonymity was not adequately protected, however, given the other identifying information in the article and the small number of pregnant students at the school. Indeed, a teacher at the school credibly testified that she could positively identify at least one of the girls and possibly all three. It is likely that many students at Hazelwood East would have been at least as successful in identifying the girls. Reynolds therefore could reasonably have feared that the article violated whatever pledge of anonymity had been given to the pregnant students. In addition, he could reasonably have been concerned that the article was not sufficiently sensitive to the privacy interests of the students' boyfriends and parents, who were discussed in the article but who were given no opportunity to consent to its publication or to offer a response. The article did not contain graphic accounts of sexual activity. The girls did comment in the article, however, concerning their sexual histories and their use or nonuse of birth control. It was not unreasonable for the principal to have concluded that such frank talk was inappropriate in a school-sponsored publication distributed to 14-year-old freshmen and presumably taken home to be read by students' even younger brothers and sisters.

The student who was quoted by name in the version of the divorce article seen by Principal Reynolds made comments sharply critical of her father. The principal could reasonably have concluded that an individual publicly identified as an inattentive parent—indeed, as one who chose "playing cards with the guys" over home and family—was entitled to an opportunity to defend himself as a matter of journalistic fairness. These concerns were shared by both of Spectrum's faculty advisers for the 1982-1983 school year, who testified that they would not have allowed the article to be printed without deletion of the student's name....

In sum, we cannot reject as unreasonable Principal Reynolds' conclusion that neither the pregnancy article nor the divorce article was suitable for publication in Spectrum. Reynolds could reasonably have concluded that the students who had written and edited these articles had not sufficiently mastered those portions of the Journalism II curriculum that pertained to the treatment of controversial issues and personal attacks, the need to protect the privacy of individuals whose most intimate concerns are to be revealed in the newspaper, and "the legal, moral, and ethical restrictions imposed upon journalists within a school community" that includes adolescent subjects and readers. Finally, we conclude that the principal's decision to delete two pages of Spectrum, rather than to delete only the offending articles or to require that they be modified, was reasonable under the circumstances as he understood them. Accordingly, no violation of First Amendment rights occurred.

The judgment of the Court of Appeals for the Eighth Circuit is therefore

Reversed.

JUSTICE BRENNAN, with whom JUSTICE MARSHALL and JUSTICE BLACKMUN join, dissenting.

When the young men and women of Hazelwood East High School registered for Journalism II, they expected a civics lesson. Spectrum, the newspaper they were to publish, "was not just a class exercise in which students learned to prepare papers and hone writing skills, it was a ... forum established to give students an opportunity to express their views while gaining an appreciation of their rights and responsibilities under the First Amendment to the United States Constitution...." [T]he student journalists published a Statement of Policy—tacitly approved each year by school authorities—announcing their expectation that *"Spectrum,* as a student-press publication, accepts all rights implied by the First Amendment.... Only speech that 'materially and substantially interferes with the requirements of appropriate discipline' can be found unacceptable and

therefore prohibited." The school board itself affirmatively guaranteed the students of Journalism II an atmosphere conducive to fostering such an appreciation and exercising the full panoply of rights associated with a free student press. "School sponsored student publications," it vowed, "will not restrict free expression or diverse viewpoints within the rules of responsible journalism."

This case arose when the Hazelwood East administration breached its own promise, dashing its students' expectations. The school principal, without prior consultation or explanation, excised six articles—comprising two full pages—of the May 13, 1983, issue of Spectrum. He did so not because any of the articles would "materially and substantially interfere with the requirements of appropriate discipline," but simply because he considered two of the six "inappropriate, personal, sensitive, and unsuitable" for student consumption.

In my view the principal broke more than just a promise. He violated the First Amendment's prohibitions against censorship of any student expression that neither disrupts classwork nor invades the rights of others, and against any censorship that is not narrowly tailored to serve its purpose....

The Court opens its analysis in this case by purporting to reaffirm *Tinker's* time-tested proposition that public school students "do not 'shed their constitutional rights to freedom of speech or expression at the schoolhouse gate.'" That is an ironic introduction to an opinion that denudes high school students of much of the First Amendment protection that *Tinker* itself prescribed.... The young men and women of Hazelwood East expected a civics lesson, but not the one the Court teaches them today.

I dissent.

While deciding whether *Hazelwood* fits compatibly with *Near,* keep in mind this caveat: the Court generally has recognized more limits on the First Amendment rights of students and juveniles than adults. White sought to make this point clear in his opinion, but does he do so effectively? For example, how did he distinguish this case from *Tinker v. Des Moines?*

The discussion of prior restraint that we have seen

in the *Near, New York Times,* and *Hazelwood* cases demonstrates that the issue of censorship may be raised in many different contexts. We will revisit the prior restraint controversy in the next chapter when we take up the issue of government regulation of indecent and obscene expression.

GOVERNMENT CONTROL OF PRESS CONTENT

Prior restraints of media may constitute the most obvious way a government can control what its citizens see, hear, and read, but it is not the only one. Beyond disallowing dissemination, governments can try to control the content of the message itself. This practice may be less overt, but it is no less dangerous. In a country founded on democratic ideals, why would questions of government control of the media ever come up? After all, such practices contradict values we hold important. But, what if the government had a good reason for seeking to control the media, that it did so in the best interest of its citizens and of the democratic process? In the cases we review next, involving regulations on what the media must exclude and include, that defense was offered by states and the federal government. Does that argument convince you that government should be allowed to place controls on the freedom of the fourth estate?

Regulating the Press by Prohibiting Content

At times governments have tried to regulate the press by preventing the publication of certain information that normally would merit First Amendment protection. There may be good and humane motives behind the enactment of such prohibition, but do they square with the First Amendment?

Cox Broadcasting Corporation v. Cohn (1975) provides a good example. At issue was a Georgia statute making it a crime for "any news media" to publish or broadcast "the name or identity of any female who may have been raped or upon whom an assault with

intent to commit rape may have been made." The law was passed with the best of intentions. The victims of such brutal crimes have already suffered a great deal and to publicize their names would only add to their anguish. Because rape, unlike other crimes, often carries with it an unfortunate and undeserved stigma, the privacy of the victim should be protected.

The *Cox Broadcasting* case began in August 1971 when Cynthia Cohn, a seventeen-year-old girl, attended a party with a large number of other high school students. A great deal of drinking took place. At the party six teenage boys serially engaged in sexual relations with Cohn, and, at some point during these sexual acts, she died from suffocation. The six boys were indicted for rape and murder.

Eight months later five of the six boys pleaded guilty to the rape charge after the murder accusation was dropped. The sixth boy pleaded not guilty. In the process of covering this incident, a reporter for a television station owned by Cox Broadcasting found the name of the victim written in the indictments. Because indictments are public documents, the reporter violated no law by inspecting them, but, in a news broadcast later that day, the reporter included Cynthia Cohn's name in his story. Martin Cohn, Cynthia's father, filed suit against Cox Broadcasting claiming that the news reports containing the name of his daughter violated his right to privacy. His case was bolstered by the fact that Georgia law makes such reports unlawful. Cox Broadcasting admitted the reports, but claimed that they were protected under the First Amendment. The issue is straightforward: May a state constitutionally prohibit the press from reporting the names of rape victims?

With only Justice Rehnquist dissenting, the Court held that a state may not, consistent with the First and Fourteenth Amendments, impose sanctions on the accurate publication of the name of a rape victim obtained from judicial records that are open to public inspection. Furthermore, the Court ruled that the publication of accurate reports of judicial proceedings merits special constitutional protection. The commission of crimes and the manner in which the judiciary handles criminal prosecutions are legitimate matters of public concern and, therefore, subjects the press must cover.

In *Cox Broadcasting* the Court developed a general principle of law: it would be loath to allow states to prohibit publication, in a truthful way, of public information. Indeed, since 1975 it has clung to this general principle. In *Nebraska Press Association v. Stuart* (1976), for example, the Court refused to allow a trial court judge to place a gag order on the press coverage of pretrial proceedings, even though the order was designed to protect the defendant from prejudicial publicity. Three years later, it struck down a law prohibiting the publication of the identity of juvenile offenders (*Smith v. Daily Mail Publishing Co.*, 1979).

Governments may use methods other than outright prohibition in attempting to discourage certain kinds of publications. In *Simon & Schuster, Inc. v. Members of the New York State Crime Victims Board* (1991) the Court evaluated a state statute that attempted to control certain publications by seizing their profits and using the resulting funds for worthwhile purposes. By imposing financial sanctions the state removed the financial incentive to publish works with a particular content. Once again, the state was attempting to achieve a commendable goal, but did the law violate the constitutional right to freedom of the press?

David Berkowitz, the "Son of Sam" serial killer (center), terrorized New York for months before his arrest in August 1977. The thought of criminals, like Berkowitz, profiting from the sale of rights to their stories while their victims remained uncompensated prompted the New York legislature to pass the "Son of Sam" law challenged in *Simon & Schuster v. New York Crime Victims Board*.

Simon & Schuster, Inc. v. Members of the New York State Crime Victims Board

502 U.S. 105 (1991)
Vote: 8 (Blackmun, Kennedy, O'Connor, Rehnquist, Scalia,
        Souter, Stevens, White)
        0
Opinion of the Court: O'Connor
Concurring opinions: Blackmun, Kennedy
Not participating: Thomas

During 1977 New York was terrorized by a serial killer popularly known as the Son of Sam, but, after a long investigation, police arrested David Berkowitz for the murders. To stop individuals like Berkowitz from profiting from their crimes by participating in book or movie projects, the state of New York passed a statute that became known as the Son of Sam law. The law required any entity contracting with an accused or convicted person for a depiction of the crime to submit a copy of the contract to the state Crime Victims board. The law further stipulated that any and all income from such projects be deposited with the board. The board was to hold these funds in escrow for five years. The money eventually would be used to pay any civil damage claims filed by the victims of the crimes. If no additional civil claims were pending at the end of the five-year period, the board would turn the remaining funds over to the party who deposited it.

This case began in 1986 when the board became aware of a book contract between Simon & Schuster and organized crime figure Henry Hill. At the time Hill was under the federal witness protection program after spending some twenty-five years as a gangster and then finally testifying against his former colleagues. Hill's biography, *Wiseguy: Life in a Mafia Family,* enjoyed critical and commercial success: more than 1 million copies were printed within the first two years of publication, and a successful motion picture, *Goodfellas,* was based on the book. After examining the book and the contract, the board concluded that the project was covered by the Son of Sam law and ordered all proceeds to be turned over and held in escrow to compensate the victims of Hill's crimes. Simon & Schuster filed suit to have the Son of Sam law declared unconstitutional as a violation of the First Amendment.

JUSTICE O'CONNOR delivered the opinion of the Court.

A statute is presumptively inconsistent with the First Amendment if it imposes a financial burden on speakers because of the content of their speech. As we emphasized in invalidating a content-based magazine tax, "official scrutiny of the content of publications as the basis for imposing a tax is entirely incompatible with the First Amendment's guarantee of freedom of the press." *Arkansas Writers' Project, Inc. v. Ragland* (1987).

This is a notion so engrained in our First Amendment jurisprudence that last Term we found it so "obvious" as to not require explanation. *Leathers* [v. *Medlock,* 1991]. It is but one manifestation of a far broader principle: "Regulations which permit the Government to discriminate on the basis of the content of the message cannot be tolerated under the First Amendment." In the context of financial regulation, it bears repeating . . . that the Government's ability to impose content-based burdens on speech raises the specter that the Government may effectively drive certain ideas or viewpoints from the marketplace. The First Amendment presumptively places this sort of discrimination beyond the

power of the Government. "'The constitutional right of free expression is . . . intended to remove governmental restraints from the arena of public discussion, putting the decision as to what views shall be voiced largely into the hands of each of us . . . in the belief that no other approach would comport with the premise of individual dignity and choice upon which our political system rests.'" *Cohen v. California* (1971).

The Son of Sam law is such a content-based statute. It singles out income derived from expressive activity for a burden the State places on no other income, and it is directed only at works with a specified content. Whether the First Amendment "speaker" is considered to be Henry Hill, whose income the statute places in escrow because of the story he has told, or Simon & Schuster, which can publish books about crime with the assistance of only those criminals willing to forgo remuneration for at least five years, the statute plainly imposes a financial disincentive only on speech of a particular content.

The Board tries unsuccessfully to distinguish the Son of Sam law from the discriminatory tax at issue in *Arkansas Writers' Project.* While the Son of Sam law escrows all of the speaker's speech-derived income for at least five years, rather than taxing a percentage of it outright, this difference can hardly serve as the basis for disparate treatment under the First Amendment. Both forms of financial burden operate as disincentives to speak; indeed, in many cases it will be impossible to discern in advance which type of regulation will be more costly to the speaker.

The Board next argues that discriminatory financial treatment is suspect under the First Amendment only when the legislature intends to suppress certain ideas. This assertion is incorrect; our cases have consistently held that "[i]llicit legislative intent is not the *sine qua non* of a violation of the First Amendment." *Minneapolis Star & Tribune Co. v. Minnesota Comm'r of Revenue* (1983). Simon & Schuster need adduce "no evidence of an improper censorial motive." As we concluded in *Minneapolis Star,* "[w]e have long recognized that even regulations aimed at proper governmental concerns can restrict unduly the exercise of rights protected by the First Amendment.". . .

The Son of Sam law establishes a financial disincentive to create or publish works with a particular content. In order to justify such differential treatment, "the State must show that its regulation is necessary to serve a compelling state interest and is narrowly drawn to achieve that end."

The Board disclaims, as it must, any state interest in suppressing descriptions of crime out of solicitude for the sensibilities of readers. As we have often had occasion to repeat, "'[T]he fact that society may find speech offensive is not a sufficient reason for suppressing it. Indeed, if it is the speaker's opinion that gives offense, that consequence is a reason for according it constitutional protection.'" *Hustler Magazine, Inc. v. Falwell* (1988). "'If there is a bedrock principle underlying the First Amendment, it is that the Government may not prohibit the expression of an idea simply because society finds the idea itself offensive or disagreeable.'" *United States v. Eichman* (1990) (quoting *Texas v. Johnson* (1989)). The Board thus does not assert any interest in limiting whatever anguish Henry Hill's victims may suffer from reliving their victimization.

There can be little doubt, on the other hand, that the State has a compelling interest in ensuring that victims of crime are compensated by those who harm them. Every State has a body of tort law serving exactly this interest. The State's interest in preventing wrongdoers from dissipating their assets before victims can recover explains the existence of the State's statutory provisions for prejudgment remedies and orders of restitution....

The State likewise has an undisputed compelling interest in ensuring that criminals do not profit from their crimes....

The Board attempts to define the State's interest more narrowly, as "ensuring that criminals do not profit from storytelling about their crimes before their victims have a meaningful opportunity to be compensated for their injuries." Here the Board is on far shakier ground. The Board cannot explain why the State should have any greater interest in compensating victims from the proceeds of such "storytelling" than from any of the criminal's other assets. Nor can the Board offer any justification for a distinction between this expressive activity and any other activity in connection with its interest in transferring the fruits of crime from criminals to their victims. Thus even if the State can be said to have an interest in classifying a criminal's assets in this manner, that interest is hardly compelling.

We have rejected similar assertions of a compelling interest in the past. In ... *Minneapolis Star*, we observed that while the State certainly has an important interest in raising revenue through taxation, that interest hardly justified selective taxation of the press, as it was completely unrelated to a press/non-press distinction.... The distinction drawn by the Son of Sam law has nothing to do with the State's interest in transferring the proceeds of crime from criminals to their victims.

Like the government entities in the above cases, the Board has taken the *effect* of the statute and posited that effect as the State's interest. If accepted, this sort of circular defense can sidestep judicial review of almost any statute, because it makes all statutes look narrowly tailored. As Judge Newman pointed out in his dissent from the opinion of the Court of Appeals, such an argument "eliminates the entire inquiry concerning the validity of content-based discriminations. Every content-based discrimination could be upheld by simply observing that the state is anxious to regulate the designated category of speech."

In short, the State has a compelling interest in compensating victims from the fruits of the crime, but little if any interest in limiting such compensation to the proceeds of the wrongdoer's speech about the crime. We must therefore determine whether the Son of Sam law is narrowly tailored to advance the former, not the latter, objective.

As a means of ensuring that victims are compensated from the proceeds of crime, the Son of Sam law is significantly overinclusive. As counsel for the Board conceded at oral argument, the statute applies to works on *any* subject, provided that they express the author's thoughts or recollections about his crime, however tangentially or incidentally. In addition, the statute's broad definition of "person convicted of a crime" enables the Board to escrow the income of any author who admits in his work to having committed a crime, whether or not the author was ever actually accused or convicted.

These two provisions combine to encompass a potentially very large number of works. Had the Son of Sam law been in effect at the time and place of publication, it would have escrowed payment for such works as The Biography of Malcolm X, which describes crimes committed by the civil rights leader before he became a public figure; Civil Disobedience, in which Thoreau acknowledges his refusal to pay taxes and recalls his experience in jail; and even the

Confessions of Saint Augustine, in which the author laments "my past foulness and the carnal corruptions of my soul," one instance of which involved the theft of pears from a neighboring vineyard. *Amicus* Association of American Publishers, Inc., has submitted a sobering bibliography listing hundreds of works by American prisoners and ex-prisoners, many of which contain descriptions of the crimes for which the authors were incarcerated, including works by such authors as Emma Goldman and Martin Luther King, Jr. A list of prominent figures whose autobiographies would be subject to the statute if written is not difficult to construct: The list could include Sir Walter Raleigh, who was convicted of treason after a dubiously conducted 1603 trial; Jesse Jackson, who was arrested in 1963 for trespass and resisting arrest after attempting to be served at a lunch counter in North Carolina; and Bertrand Russell, who was jailed for seven days at the age of 89 for participating in a sit-down protest against nuclear weapons. The argument that a statute like the Son of Sam law would prevent publication of *all* of these works is hyperbole—some would have been written without compensation—but the Son of Sam law clearly reaches a wide range of literature that does not enable a criminal to profit from his crime while a victim remains uncompensated. . . .

The Federal Government and many of the States have enacted statutes designed to serve purposes similar to that served by the Son of Sam law. Some of these statutes may be quite different from New York's, and we have no occasion to determine the constitutionality of these other laws. We conclude simply that in the Son of Sam law, New York has singled out speech on a particular subject for a financial burden that it places on no other speech and no other income. The State's interest in compensating victims from the fruits of crime is a compelling one, but the Son of Sam law is not narrowly tailored to advance that objective. As a result, the statute is inconsistent with the First Amendment.

The judgment of the Court of Appeals is accordingly

Reversed.

As *Cox* and *Simon & Schuster* indicate, the Court generally has been unwilling to support laws that prohibit the press from publishing otherwise legitimate information or attempting to accomplish the same goal by the imposition of financial penalties. As a rule, content-based prohibitions run contrary to the First Amendment.

Regulating the Press by Mandating Content

Another way governments try to control the press is to require that it disseminate certain information. Totalitarian regimes in other countries have used this method to convert the press into a propaganda arm of the government. In the United States, government regulations requiring the press to carry specific information or publish particular stories have been motivated by more worthy purposes. *Miami Herald v. Tornillo* (1974) is an appropriate example. This suit challenged a Florida law that under certain circumstances compelled newspapers to publish articles by candidates for political office. The goal of the legislation was to ensure that full and fair information was available to the voters. The *Miami Herald* refused to comply, arguing that the government had no constitutional authority to order the newspaper to publish anything. How did the justices respond? Were they any more sympathetic to the government compelling the press to publish stories than they were to the government prohibiting the press from disseminating certain information?

===

Miami Herald v. Tornillo

418 U.S. 241 (1974)
Vote: 9 (*Blackmun, Brennan, Burger, Douglas, Marshall, Powell, Rehnquist, Stewart, White*)

0

Opinion of the Court: Burger
Concurring opinions: Brennan, White

In September 1972 the *Miami Herald* published a series of disparaging editorials on Pat Tornillo's candidacy for the Florida House of Representatives. One editorial said, "We cannot say it would be illegal but certainly it would be inexcusable of the voters if they sent Pat Tornillo to Tallahassee." Another asserted, "Give him public office, says Pat, and he will no doubt live by the Golden Rule. Our translation reads that as more gold and more rule."

At the time these editorials appeared, Florida had a right-to-reply law, which provided that if a candidate for nomination or election is assailed regarding his personal character or official record by any newspaper, the candidate has a right to demand that the newspaper print, free of cost to the candidate, any reply the candidate may make to the newspaper's charges. Tornillo asked the *Herald* to print his response. When the paper refused, he brought suit.

CHIEF JUSTICE BURGER delivered the opinion of the Court.

The issue in this case is whether a state statute granting a political candidate a right to equal space to reply to criticism and attacks on his record by a newspaper violates the guarantees of a free press....

The challenged statute creates a right to reply to press criticism of a candidate for nomination or election. The statute was enacted in 1913, and this is only the second recorded case decided under its provisions.

Appellant contends the statute is void on its face because it purports to regulate the content of a newspaper in violation of the First Amendment. Alternatively it is urged that the statute is void for vagueness since no editor could know exactly what words would call the statute into operation. It is also contended that the statute fails to distinguish between critical comment which is and which is not defamatory.

The appellee and supporting advocates of an enforceable right of access to the press vigorously argue that government has an obligation to ensure that a wide variety of views reach the public. The contentions of access proponents will be set out in some detail. It is urged that at the time the First Amendment to the Constitution was ratified in 1791 as part of our Bill of Rights the press was broadly representative of the people it was serving. While many of the newspapers were intensely partisan and narrow in their views, the press collectively presented a broad range of opinions to readers. Entry into publishing was inexpensive; pamphlets and books provided meaningful alternatives to the organized press for the expression of unpopular ideas

and often treated events and expressed views not covered by conventional newspapers. A true marketplace of ideas existed in which there was relatively easy access to the channels of communication.

Access advocates submit that although newspapers of the present are superficially similar to those of 1791, the press of today is in reality very different from that known in the early years of our national existence. In the past half century a communications revolution has seen the introduction of radio and television into our lives, the promise of a global community through the use of communications satellites, and the spectre of a "wired" nation by means of an expanding cable television network with two-way capabilities. The printed press, it is said, has not escaped the effects of this revolution. Newspapers have become big business and there are far fewer of them to serve a larger literate population. Chains of newspapers, national newspapers, national wire and news services, and one-newspaper towns, are the dominant features of a press that has become noncompetitive and enormously powerful and influential in its capacity to manipulate popular opinion and change the course of events. Major metropolitan newspapers have collaborated to establish news services national in scope. Such national news organizations provide syndicated "interpretive reporting" as well as syndicated features and commentary, all of which can serve as part of the new school of "advocacy journalism."

The elimination of competing newspapers in most of our large cities, and the concentration of control of media that results from the only newspaper's being owned by the same interests which own a television station and a radio station, are important components of this trend toward concentration of control of outlets to inform the public.

The result of these vast changes has been to place in a few hands the power to inform the American people and shape public opinion. Much of the editorial opinion and commentary that is printed is that of syndicated columnists distributed nationwide and, as a result, we are told, on national and world issues there tends to be a homogeneity of editorial opinion, commentary, and interpretive analysis. The abuses of bias and manipulative reportage are, likewise, said to be the result of the vast accumulations of unreviewable power in the modern media empires. In effect, it is claimed, the public has lost any ability to respond or to contribute in a meaningful way to the debate on issues. The monopoly of the means of communication allows for little or no critical analysis of the media except in professional journals of very limited readership....

The obvious solution, which was available to dissidents at an earlier time when entry into publishing was relatively inexpensive, today would be to have additional newspapers. But the same economic factors which have caused the disappearance of vast numbers of metropolitan newspapers, have made entry into the marketplace of ideas served by the print media almost impossible. It is urged that the claim of newspapers to be "surrogates for the public" carries with it a concomitant fiduciary obligation to account for that stewardship. From this premise it is reasoned that the only effective way to insure fairness and accuracy and to provide for some accountability is for government to take affirmative action. The First Amendment interest of the public in being informed is said to be in peril because the "marketplace of ideas" is today a monopoly controlled by the owners of the market.

Proponents of enforced access to the press take comfort from language in several of this Court's decisions which suggests that the First Amendment acts as a sword as well as a shield, that it imposes obligations on the owners of the press in addition to protecting the press from government regulation. In Associated Press v. United States (1945), the Court ... reject[ed] the argument that the press is immune from the antitrust laws by virtue of the First Amendment....

In New York Times Co. v. Sullivan (1964), the Court spoke of "a profound national commitment to the principle that debate on public issues should be uninhibited, robust, and wide-open." It is argued that the "uninhibited, robust" debate is not "wide-open" but open only to a monopoly in control of the press....

However much validity may be found in these arguments, at each point the implementation of a remedy such as an enforceable right of access necessarily calls for some mechanism, either governmental or consensual. If it is governmental coercion, this at once brings about a confrontation with the express provisions of the First Amendment and the judicial gloss on that Amendment developed over the years....

We see ... [that] beginning with Associated Press, the Court has expressed sensitivity as to whether a restriction

or requirement constituted the compulsion exerted by government on a newspaper to print that which it would not otherwise print. The clear implication has been that any such compulsion to publish that which "'reason' tells them should not be published" is unconstitutional. A responsible press is an undoubtedly desirable goal, but press responsibility is not mandated by the Constitution and like many other virtues it cannot be legislated.

Appellee's argument that the Florida statute does not amount to a restriction of appellant's right to speak because "the statute in question here has not prevented the *Miami Herald* from saying anything it wished" begs the core question. Compelling editors or publishers to publish that which "'reason' tells them should not be published" is what is at issue in this case. The Florida statute operates as a command in the same sense as a statute or regulation forbidding appellant to publish specified matter. Governmental restraint on publishing need not fall into familiar or traditional patterns to be subject to constitutional limitations on governmental powers. The Florida statute exacts a penalty on the basis of the content of a newspaper. The first phase of the penalty resulting from the compelled printing of a reply is exacted in terms of the cost in printing and composing time and materials and in taking up space that could be devoted to other material the newspaper may have preferred to print. It is correct, as appellee contends, that a newspaper is not subject to the finite technological limitations of time that confront a broadcaster but it is not correct to say that, as an economic reality, a newspaper can proceed to infinite expansion of its column space to accommodate the replies that a government agency determines or a statute commands the readers should have *available*.

Faced with the penalties that would accrue to any newspaper that published news or commentary arguably within the reach of the right-of-access statute, editors might well conclude that the safe course is to avoid controversy. Therefore, under the operation of the Florida statute, political and electoral coverage would be blunted or reduced. Government-enforced right of access inescapably "dampens the vigor and limits the variety of public debate."...

Even if a newspaper would face no additional costs to comply with a compulsory access law and would not be forced to forgo publication of news or opinion by the inclusion of a reply, the Florida statute fails to clear the barriers of the First Amendment because of its intrusion into the function of editors. A newspaper is more than a passive receptacle or conduit for news, comment, and advertising. The choice of material to go into a newspaper, and the decisions made as to limitations on the size and content of the paper, and treatment of public issues and public officials—whether fair or unfair—constitute the exercise of editorial control and judgment. It has yet to be demonstrated how governmental regulation of this crucial process can be exercised consistent with First Amendment guarantees of a free press as they have evolved to this time. Accordingly, the judgment of the Supreme Court of Florida is reversed.

It is so ordered.

Reversed.

Government attempts to regulate the content of the press are for good purposes. We have seen laws designed to protect or provide restitution to crime victims and to increase the fairness of campaign information. In spite of these good intentions, the Supreme Court has not been sympathetic to government regulation of press content—either by prohibiting or mandating content. This strong support for freedom of the press has been especially evident when the print media have been the target of regulation.

Regulating the Broadcast Media

The justices' strong support for the print media has not extended to the radio and television industry. While the First Amendment certainly applies to broadcast journalism, the Court has treated it much differently from newspapers, magazines, and books.

Congress regulates the broadcast industry through its power over interstate commerce. The legislature establishes general regulatory policy for the broadcast industry and has created the Federal Communications Commission (FCC) to implement those policies and carry out the day-to-day regulatory activity. The regulation is comprehensive. The federal government issues licenses to broadcast, commands that certain public interest programming be included, and prohib-

its certain kinds of language on the air. Radio and television stations must adhere to strict codes of operation and conform to regulations that are designed to promote the public interest. A station that does not conform to these rules may lose its license to broadcast, essentially putting the operation out of business.

While the degree of regulation imposed by Congress has varied over the years, the federal government has always maintained that the electronic media may be regulated in ways that would not be allowed for the print media. The broadcast industry is different because, unlike the print media, radio and television stations operate by using the public airways. Because the public airways can accommodate only a limited number of stations, the government must regulate the broadcast industry to ensure that it can operate effectively and for the public good. Does this argument have merit? The Supreme Court has had to answer this question without help from the Framers who naturally had no way to anticipate the emergence of this modern technology. The leading case in this area is *Red Lion Broadcasting v. FCC* (1969). This case involves a challenge to a federal requirement that broadcasters must give fair coverage to public issues. But the case represents much more than that. It is also a challenge to the notion that the electronic media constitutionally may be regulated far more comprehensively than can the print media. As you read *Red Lion*, compare it to the *Miami Herald* decision. Are the two compatible?

Red Lion Broadcasting v. FCC

395 U.S. 367 (1969)
Vote: 7 (Black, Brennan, Harlan, Marshall, Stewart, Warren, White)

   0

Opinion of the Court: White
Not participating: Douglas

Virtually since its creation in 1934, the FCC has "imposed on radio and television broadcasters the requirement that discussion of public issues be presented on broadcast stations, and that each side of those issues must be given fair coverage." This policy is widely known as the fairness doctrine.

Red Lion arose when Pennsylvania radio station WGCB, owned by the Red Lion Broadcasting Company, aired a program entitled the "Christian Crusade." During the show, Rev. Billy James Hargis attacked the book *Goldwater—Extremist on the Right* and its author, Fred J. Cook. Harris asserted, among other things, that Cook "was fired [from a reporting job] after he made a false charge on television against an unnamed official of New York City government," that "after losing his job, Cook went to work for [a] left-wing publication," and that he wrote this book to "smear and destroy Barry Goldwater." Believing he had been personally attacked, Cook asked WGCB to allow him to respond on the air, that the fairness doctrine mandated the right to reply. When WGCB refused, Cook took his case to the FCC, which ruled that Red Lion had failed to meet its obligation under the fairness doctrine and ordered WGCB to give Cook the air time. Rather than obeying the order, Red Lion challenged it on First Amendment grounds. Its attorneys argued that the media have a right to print and broadcast whatever they wish, free from any undue government influence.

MR. JUSTICE WHITE delivered the opinion of the Court.

The Federal Communications Commission has for many years imposed on radio and television broadcasters the requirement that discussion of public issues be presented on broadcast stations, and that each side of those issues must be given fair coverage. This is known as the fairness doctrine, which originated very early in the history of broadcasting and has maintained its present outlines for some time. It is an obligation whose content has been defined in a long series of FCC rulings in particular cases, and which is distinct from the statutory requirement of § 315 of the Communications Act that equal time be allotted all qualified candidates for public office. Two aspects of the fairness

doctrine, relating to personal attacks in the context of controversial public issues and to political editorializing, were codified more precisely in the form of FCC regulations in 1967. The . . . [case] before us now challenge[s] the constitutional and statutory bases of the doctrine and component rules. . . .

The broadcasters challenge the fairness doctrine and its specific manifestations in the personal attack and political editorial rules on conventional First Amendment grounds, alleging that the rules abridge their freedom of speech and press. Their contention is that the First Amendment protects their desire to use their allotted frequencies continuously to broadcast whatever they choose and to exclude whomever they choose from ever using that frequency. . . .

Although broadcasting is clearly a medium affected by a First Amendment interest, differences in the characteristics of new media justify differences in the First Amendment standards applied to them. For example, the ability of new technology to produce sounds more raucous than those of the human voice justifies restrictions on the sound level, and on the hours and places of use, of sound trucks so long as the restrictions are reasonable and applied without discrimination.

Just as the Government may limit the use of sound-amplifying equipment potentially so noisy that it drowns out civilized private speech, so may the Government limit the use of broadcast equipment. The right of free speech of a broadcaster, the user of a sound truck, or any other individual does not embrace a right to snuff out the free speech of others.

When two people converse face to face, both should not speak at once if either is to be clearly understood. But the range of the human voice is so limited that there could be meaningful communication if half the people in the United States were talking and the other half listening. Just as clearly, half the people might publish and the other half read. But the reach of radio signals is incomparably greater than the range of the human voice and the problem of interference is a massive reality. The lack of know-how and equipment may keep many from the air, but only a tiny fraction of those with resources and intelligence can hope to communicate by radio at the same time if intelligible communication is to be had, even if the entire radio spectrum is utilized in the present state of commercially acceptable technology.

It was this fact, and the chaos which ensued from permitting anyone to use any frequency at whatever power level he wished, which made necessary the enactment of the Radio Act of 1927 and the Communications Act of 1934. It was this reality which at the very least necessitated first the division of the radio spectrum into portions reserved respectively for public broadcasting and for other important radio uses such as amateur operation, aircraft, police, defense, and navigation; and then the subdivision of each portion, and assignment of specific frequencies to individual users or groups of users. Beyond this, however, because the frequencies reserved for public broadcasting were limited in number, it was essential for the Government to tell some applicants that they could not broadcast at all because there was room for only a few.

Where there are substantially more individuals who want to broadcast than there are frequencies to allocate, it is idle to posit an unabridgeable First Amendment right to broadcast comparable to the right of every individual to speak, write, or publish. If 100 persons want broadcast licenses but there are only 10 frequencies to allocate, all of them may have the same "right" to a license; but if there is to be any effective communication by radio, only a few can be licensed and the rest must be barred from the airwaves. It would be strange if the First Amendment, aimed at protecting and furthering communications, prevented the Government from making radio communication possible by requiring licenses to broadcast and by limiting the number of licenses so as not to overcrowd the spectrum.

This has been the consistent view of the Court. Congress unquestionably has the power to grant and deny licenses and to eliminate existing stations. No one has a First Amendment right to a license or to monopolize a radio frequency; to deny a station license because "the public interest" requires it "is not a denial of free speech."

By the same token, as far as the First Amendment is concerned those who are licensed stand no better than those to whom licenses are refused. A license permits broadcasting, but the licensee has no constitutional right to be the one who holds the license or to monopolize a radio frequency to the exclusion of his fellow citizens. There is nothing in the First Amendment which prevents the Government from re-quiring a licensee to share his frequency with others and to conduct himself as a proxy or fiduciary with obligations to present those views and voices which are representative of his community and which would otherwise, by necessity, be barred from the airwaves.

This is not to say that the First Amendment is irrelevant to public broadcasting. On the contrary, it has a major role to play as the Congress itself recognized in § 326, which forbids FCC interference with "the right of free speech by means of radio communication." Because of the scarcity of radio frequencies, the Government is permitted to put restraints on licensees in favor of others whose views should be expressed on this unique medium. But the people as a whole retain their interest in free speech by radio and their collective right to have the medium function consistently with the ends and purposes of the First Amendment. It is the right of the viewers and listeners, not the right of the broadcasters, which is paramount. It is the purpose of the First Amendment to preserve an uninhibited marketplace of ideas in which truth will ultimately prevail, rather than to countenance monopolization of that market, whether it be by the Government itself or a private licensee. It is the right of the public to receive suitable access to social, political, esthetic, moral, and other ideas and experiences which is crucial here. That right may not constitutionally be abridged either by Congress or by the FCC.

Rather than confer frequency monopolies on a relatively small number of licensees, in a nation of 200,000,000, the Government could surely have decreed that each frequency should be shared among all or some of those who wish to use it, each being assigned a portion of the broadcast day or the broadcast week. The ruling and regulations at issue here do not go quite so far. They assert that under specified circumstances, a licensee must offer to make available a reasonable amount of broadcast time to those who have a view different from that which has already been expressed on his station. The expression of a political endorsement, or of a personal attack while dealing with a controversial public issue, simply triggers this time sharing. As we have said, the First Amendment confers no right on licensees to prevent others from broadcasting on "their" frequencies and no right to an unconditional monopoly of a scarce resource which the Government has denied others the right to use.

In terms of constitutional principle, and as enforced sharing of a scarce resource, the personal attack and political editorial rules are indistinguishable from the equal-time provision of § 315, a specific enactment of Congress requiring stations to set aside reply time under specified circumstances and to which the fairness doctrine and these constituent regulations are important complements. That provision, which has been part of the law since 1927, ... has been held valid by this Court as an obligation of the licensee relieving him of any power in any way to prevent or censor the broadcast, and thus insulating him from liability for defamation. The constitutionality of the statute under the First Amendment was unquestioned.

Nor can we say that it is inconsistent with the First Amendment goal of producing an informed public capable of conducting its own affairs to require a broadcaster to permit answers to personal attacks occurring in the course of discussing controversial issues, or to require that the political opponents of those endorsed by the station be given a chance to communicate with the public. Otherwise, station owners and a few networks would have unfettered power to make time available only to the highest bidders, to communicate only their own views on public issues, people and candidates, and to permit on the air only those with whom they agreed. There is no sanctuary in the First Amendment for unlimited private censorship operating in a medium not open to all....

It is strenuously argued, however, that if political editorials or personal attacks will trigger an obligation in broadcasters to afford the opportunity for expression to speakers who need not pay for time and whose views are unpalatable to the licensees, then broadcasters will be irresistibly forced to self-censorship and their coverage of controversial public issues will be eliminated or at least rendered wholly ineffective. Such a result would indeed be a serious matter, for should licensees actually eliminate their coverage of controversial issues, the purposes of the doctrine would be stifled.

At this point, however, as the Federal Communications Commission has indicated, that possibility is at best speculative. The communications industry, and in particular the networks, have taken pains to present controversial issues in the past, and even now they do not assert that they intend to abandon their efforts in this regard. It would be better if the FCC's encouragement were never necessary to induce the broadcasters to meet their responsibility. And if experience with the administration of those doctrines indicates that they have the net effect of reducing rather than enhancing the volume and quality of coverage, there will be time enough to reconsider the constitutional implications. The fairness doctrine in the past has had no such overall effect.

That this will occur now seems unlikely, however, since if present licensees should suddenly prove timorous, the Commission is not powerless to insist that they give adequate and fair attention to public issues. It does not violate the First Amendment to treat licensees given the privilege of using scarce radio frequencies as proxies for the entire community, obligated to give suitable time and attention to matters of great public concern. To condition the granting or renewal of licenses on a willingness to present representative community views on controversial issues is consistent with the ends and purposes of those constitutional provisions forbidding the abridgment of freedom of speech and freedom of the press. Congress need not stand idly by and permit those with licenses to ignore the problems which beset the people or to exclude from the airways anything but their own views of fundamental questions....

We need not and do not now ratify every past and future decision by the FCC with regard to programming. There is no question here of the Commission's refusal to permit the broadcaster to carry a particular program or to publish his own views; of a discriminatory refusal to require the licensee to broadcast certain views which have been denied access to the airwaves; of government censorship of a particular program contrary to § 326; or of the official government view dominating public broadcasting. Such questions would raise more serious First Amendment issues. But we do hold that the Congress and the Commission do not violate the First Amendment when they require a radio or television station to give reply time to answer personal attacks and political editorials.

The degree to which the broadcast media are regulated increases and decreases as political tides change. The fairness doctrine, for example, was repealed in 1987. Yet *Red Lion* remains good law. It establishes that the First Amendment is no barrier to reasonable government control of the electronic media, and that Congress may treat broadcasting differently from the print media.

An interesting example of this difference in treatment is *Federal Communications Commission v. Pacifica Foundation* (1978). This dispute began when a radio station owned by the Pacifica Foundation one afternoon broadcast a recorded monologue by humorist George Carlin, entitled "Filthy Words." In it Carlin uses a litany of words and phrases that, while not obscene, are considered indecent and offensive by many. In response to this broadcast, a man wrote a letter of complaint to the FCC, claiming that he heard the monologue while driving with his young son. After an investigation, the FCC issued an order declaring the broadcast to have been in violation of a federal statute that prohibits the transmission of indecent language on the public airways. Pacifica appealed and was initially successful. But the Supreme Court reversed. In a 5–4 vote the justices held that of all forms of communication, broadcasting has the most limited First Amendment protection. The electronic media, the majority held, differ from the print media because they have a pervasive presence that can invade even the privacy of the home, and because it is uniquely accessible to children. Clearly, the regulation of indecent language upheld here would never be sustained by the Court if it were applied to books or magazines.[8]

THE MEDIA AND SPECIAL RIGHTS

Challenging restraints on First Amendment rights is not the only battle the media have fought. For many years, the media asked courts for "special rights" not normally accorded average citizens, but which the press considered necessary to provide "full and robust" coverage of local, national, and world events. In this section, we discuss two of those—reporters' privilege and the right of access. While reading about them, ask yourself whether, in fact, the media should enjoy a special legal status.

Reporters' Privilege

As far back as 1840 reporters asserted the need for unusual legal privileges; that year, the Senate held a secret meeting to debate a proposed treaty to end the Mexican-American War. John Nugent, a reporter for the *New York Herald*, managed to obtain a copy of the proposed draft and mailed it to his editor. The Senate subpoenaed Nugent, and, when he refused to reveal his source of information, it held him in contempt. Nugent was later sent to prison for protecting his source.[9]

Although from time to time others faced the same fate as Nugent, during the 1960s and 1970s a marked increase occurred in the frequency of claims of reporters' privilege. Some credit this increase to the trial of the Chicago Seven in which the government charged individuals with starting a riot in the streets outside of the Democratic party's 1968 convention. The United States served subpoenas on the major networks, newspapers, and magazines to obtain any information they had on the disturbances. Others suggest that it was the Nixon administration's disdain for the press that led to the increase, and still others argue that the rise in investigative reporting ushered in by Watergate led reporters to assert their right to protect sources absolutely and unconditionally.

Whatever the cause, the debate over reporters' privilege reached its climax in 1972 when the Supreme Court agreed to hear several cases involving such claims. The cases presented somewhat different

---

8. In *Turner Broadcasting System, Inc. v. FCC* (1994) the Court held that cable television systems merit a higher level of First Amendment protection than does conventially broadcast television and radio programming. The Court, however, has not yet fully defined the extent of that protection.

9. This paragraph, and that which follows, draws heavily on Mark Neubauer, "The Newsmen's Privilege after *Branzburg*," *UCLA Law Review* 24 (1976): 160–192.

issues, but the points of view were clear on both sides. The government asserted that reporters were entitled to no special rights and privileges; if ordinary citizens were forced to testify upon subpoena, then so should the media. The media responded that there were, in fact, certain privileged relationships. Doctors, for example, cannot be forced to reveal information about their patients. Reporters also argued that if they were forced to answer questions about their sources, those sources would dry up, which would have a chilling effect on their ability to do their jobs and would violate their free press guarantee.

Branzburg v. Hayes

408 U.S. 665 (1972)
Vote: 5 *(Blackmun, Burger, Powell, Rehnquist, White)*
    4 *(Brennan, Douglas, Marshall, Stewart)*
Opinion of the Court: White
Concurring opinion: Powell
Dissenting opinions: Douglas, Stewart

This case involved two articles written by Paul M. Branzburg, a reporter for the *Courier-Journal,* a Louisville, Kentucky, newspaper. In the first, he detailed his observations of two individuals, "synthesizing hashish from Marijuana, an activity which they asserted earned them about $5,000 in three weeks." The article contained this statement:

"I don't know why I am letting you do this story," [one of the individuals] said quietly. "To make the narcs mad I guess. That's the main reason." However, [the two individuals] *asked for and received a promise that their names would be changed* (emphasis added).

The second piece contained interviews Branzburg conducted with drug users in Frankfort, Kentucky.

Branzburg was subpoenaed by a grand jury. He appeared but refused to answer the following questions:

1. Who was the person or persons you observed in possession of Marijuana, about which you wrote an article?
2. Who was the person or persons you observed compounding Marijuana, producing same to a compound known as hashish?

MR. JUSTICE WHITE delivered the opinion of the Court.

The issue in these cases is whether requiring newsmen to appear and testify before state or federal grand juries abridges the freedom of speech and press guaranteed by the First Amendment. We hold that it does not....

Petitioner ... Branzburg ... press[es] First Amendment claims that may be simply put: that to gather news it is often necessary to agree either not to identify the source of information published or to publish only part of the facts revealed, or both; that if the reporter is nevertheless forced to reveal these confidences to a grand jury, the source so identified and other confidential sources of other reporters will be measurably deterred from furnishing publishable information, all to the detriment of the free flow of information protected by the First Amendment. Although the newsmen in these cases do not claim an absolute privilege against official interrogation in all circumstances, they assert that the reporter should not be forced either to appear or to testify before a grand jury or at trial until and unless sufficient grounds are shown for believing that the reporter possesses information relevant to a crime the grand jury is investigating, that the information the reporter has is unavailable from other sources, and that the need for the information is sufficiently compelling to override the claimed invasion of First Amendment interests occasioned by the disclosure. Principally relied upon are prior cases emphasizing the importance of the First Amendment guarantees to individual development and to our system of representative government, decisions requiring that official action with adverse impact on First Amendment rights be justified by a public interest that is "compelling" or "paramount," and those precedents establishing the principle that justifiable governmental goals may not be achieved by unduly broad means having an unnecessary impact on protected rights of speech, press, or association. The heart of the claim is that the burden on news gathering resulting from compelling reporters to disclose confidential information outweighs any public interest in obtaining the information.

We do not question the significance of free speech, press, or assembly to the country's welfare. Nor is it suggested that news gathering does not qualify for First Amendment protection; without some protection for seeking out the news, freedom of the press could be eviscerated. But these cases involve no intrusions upon speech or assembly, no prior restraint or restriction on what the press may publish, and no express or implied command that the press publish what it prefers to withhold. No exaction or tax for the privilege of publishing, and no penalty, civil or criminal, related to the content of published material is at issue here. The use of confidential sources by the press is not forbidden or restricted; reporters remain free to seek news from any source by means within the law. No attempt is made to require the press to publish its sources of information or indiscriminately to disclose them on request.

The sole issue before us is the obligation of reporters to respond to grand jury subpoenas as other citizens do and to answer questions relevant to an investigation into the commission of crime. Citizens generally are not constitutionally immune from grand jury subpoenas; and neither the First Amendment nor any other constitutional provision protects the average citizen from disclosing to a grand jury information that he has received in confidence. The claim is, however, that reporters are exempt from these obligations because if forced to respond to subpoenas and identify their sources or disclose other confidences, their informants will refuse or be reluctant to furnish newsworthy information in the future. This asserted burden on news gathering is said to make compelled testimony from newsmen constitutionally suspect and to require a privileged position for them. . . .

The prevailing constitutional view of the newsman's privilege is very much rooted in the ancient role of the grand jury that has the dual function of determining if there is probable cause to believe that a crime has been committed and of protecting citizens against unfounded criminal prosecutions. Grand jury proceedings are constitutionally mandated for the institution of federal criminal prosecutions for capital or other serious crimes, and "its constitutional prerogatives are rooted in long centuries of Anglo-American history." . . . Although state systems of criminal procedure differ greatly among themselves, the grand jury is similarly guaranteed by many state constitutions and plays an important role in fair and effective law enforcement in the overwhelming majority of the States. Because its task is to inquire into the existence of possible criminal conduct and to return only well-founded indictments, its investigative powers are necessarily broad. "It is a grand inquest, a body with powers of investigation and inquisition, the scope of whose inquiries is not to be limited narrowly by questions of propriety or forecasts of the probable result of the investigation, or by doubts whether any particular individual will be found properly subject to an accusation of crime." Hence the grand jury's authority to subpoena witnesses is not only historic but essential to its task. Although the powers of the grand jury are not unlimited and are subject to the supervision of a judge, the longstanding principle that "the public . . . has a right to every man's evidence," except for those persons protected by a constitutional, common-law, or statutory privilege, is particularly applicable to grand jury proceedings.

A number of States have provided newsmen a statutory privilege of varying breadth, but the majority have not done so, and none has been provided by federal statute. Until now the only testimonial privilege for unofficial witnesses that is rooted in the Federal Constitution is the Fifth Amendment privilege against compelled self-incrimination. We are asked to create another by interpreting the First Amendment to grant newsmen a testimonial privilege that other citizens do not enjoy. This we decline to do. Fair and effective law enforcement aimed at providing security for the person and property of the individual is a fundamental function of government, and the grand jury plays an important, constitutionally mandated role in this process. On the records now before us, we perceive no basis for holding that the public interest in law enforcement and in ensuring effective grand jury proceedings is insufficient to override the consequential, but uncertain, burden on news gathering that is said to result from insisting that reporters, like other citizens, respond to relevant questions put to them in the course of a valid grand jury investigation or criminal trial.

This conclusion itself involves no restraint on what newspapers may publish or on the type or quality of information reporters may seek to acquire, nor does it threaten the vast bulk of confidential relationships between reporters and their sources. Grand juries address themselves to the issues of whether crimes have been committed and who committed them. Only where news sources themselves are implicated in crime or possess information relevant to the grand jury's task need they or the reporter be concerned about grand jury subpoenas. Nothing before us indicates that a large number or percentage of *all* confidential news sources falls into either category and would in any way be deterred by our holding that the Constitution does not, as it never has, exempt the newsman from performing the citizen's normal duty of appearing and furnishing information relevant to the grand jury's task.

The preference for anonymity of those confidential informants involved in actual criminal conduct is presumably a product of their desire to escape criminal prosecution, and this preference, while understandable, is hardly deserving of constitutional protection. It would be frivolous to assert— and no one does in these cases—that the First Amendment, in the interest of securing news or otherwise, confers a license on either the reporter or his news sources to violate valid criminal laws. Although stealing documents or private wiretapping could provide newsworthy information, neither reporter nor source is immune from conviction for such conduct, whatever the impact on the flow of news. Neither is immune, on First Amendment grounds, from testifying against the other, before the grand jury or at a criminal trial. The Amendment does not reach so far as to override the interest of the public in ensuring that neither reporter nor source is invading the rights of other citizens through reprehensible conduct forbidden to all other persons. . . .

Thus, we cannot seriously entertain the notion that the First Amendment protects a newsman's agreement to conceal the criminal conduct of his source, or evidence thereof, on the theory that it is better to write about crime than to do something about it. Insofar as any reporter in these cases undertook not to reveal or testify about the crime he witnessed, his claim of privilege under the First Amendment presents no substantial question. The crimes of news sources are no less reprehensible and threatening to the public interest when witnessed by a reporter than when they are not. . . .

The argument that the flow of news will be diminished by compelling reporters to aid the grand jury in a criminal investigation is not irrational, nor are the records before us silent on the matter. But we remain unclear how often and to what extent informers are actually deterred from furnishing information when newsmen are forced to testify before

a grand jury. The available data indicate that some newsmen rely a great deal on confidential sources and that some informants are particularly sensitive to the threat of exposure and may be silenced if it is held by this Court that, ordinarily, newsmen must testify pursuant to subpoenas, but the evidence fails to demonstrate that there would be a significant constriction of the flow of news to the public if this Court reaffirms the prior common-law and constitutional rule regarding the testimonial obligations of newsmen. Estimates of the inhibiting effect of such subpoenas on the willingness of informants to make disclosures to newsmen are widely divergent and to a great extent speculative. It would be difficult to canvass the views of the informants themselves: surveys of reporters on this topic are chiefly opinions of predicted informant behavior and must be viewed in the light of the professional self-interest of the interviewees. Reliance by the press on confidential informants does not mean that all such sources will in fact dry up because of the later possible appearance of the newsman before a grand jury. The reporter may never be called and if he objects to testifying, the prosecution may not insist. Also, the relationship of many informants to the press is a symbiotic one which is unlikely to be greatly inhibited by the threat of subpoena: quite often, such informants are members of a minority political or cultural group that relies heavily on the media to propagate its views, publicize its aims, and magnify its exposure to the public. Moreover, grand juries characteristically conduct secret proceedings, and law enforcement officers are themselves experienced in dealing with informers, and have their own methods for protecting them without interference with the effective administration of justice. There is little before us indicating that informants whose interest in avoiding exposure is that it may threaten job security, personal safety, or peace of mind, would in fact be in a worse position, or would think they would be, if they risked placing their trust in public officials as well as reporters. We doubt if the informer who prefers anonymity but is sincerely interested in furnishing evidence of crime will always or very often be deterred by the prospect of dealing with those public authorities characteristically charged with the duty to protect the public interest as well as his.

Accepting the fact, however, that an undetermined number of informants not themselves implicated in crime will nevertheless, for whatever reason, refuse to talk to newsmen if they fear identification by a reporter in an official investigation, we cannot accept the argument that the public interest in possible future news about crime from undisclosed, unverified sources must take precedence over the public interest in pursuing and prosecuting those crimes reported to the press by informants and in thus deterring the commission of such crimes in the future.

We note first that the privilege claimed is that of the reporter, not the informant, and that if the authorities independently identify the informant, neither his own reluctance to testify nor the objection of the newsman would shield him from grand jury inquiry, whatever the impact on the flow of news or on his future usefulness as a secret source of information. More important, it is obvious that agreements to conceal information relevant to commission of crime have very little to recommend them from the standpoint of public policy.... It is apparent ... from our history and that of England, that concealment of crime and agreements to do so are not looked upon with favor. Such conduct deserves no encomium, and we decline now to afford it First Amendment protection by denigrating the duty of a citizen, whether reporter or informer, to respond to grand jury subpoena and answer relevant questions put to him.

Of course, the press has the right to abide by its agreement not to publish all the information it has, but the right to withhold news is not equivalent to a First Amendment exemption from the ordinary duty of all other citizens to furnish relevant information to a grand jury performing an important public function. Private restraints on the flow of information are not so favored by the First Amendment that they override all other public interests....

We are admonished that refusal to provide a First Amendment reporter's privilege will undermine the freedom of the press to collect and disseminate news. But this is not the lesson history teaches us. As noted previously, the common law recognized no such privilege, and the constitutional argument was not even asserted until 1958. From the beginning of our country the press has operated without constitutional protection for press informants, and the press has flourished. The existing constitutional rules have not been a serious obstacle to either the development or retention of confidential news sources by the press.

It is said that currently press subpoenas have multiplied, that mutual distrust and tension between press and officialdom have increased, that reporting styles have changed, and that there is now more need for confidential sources, particularly where the press seeks news about minority cultural and political groups or dissident organizations suspicious of the law and public officials. These developments, even if true, are treacherous grounds for a far-reaching interpretation of the First Amendment fastening a nationwide rule on courts, grand juries, and prosecuting officials everywhere. The obligation to testify in response to grand jury subpoenas will not threaten these sources not involved with criminal conduct and without information relevant to grand jury investigations, and we cannot hold that the Constitution places the sources in these two categories either above the law or beyond its reach.

The argument for such a constitutional privilege rests heavily on those cases holding that the infringement of protected First Amendment rights must be no broader than necessary to achieve a permissible governmental purpose. We do not deal, however, with a governmental institution that has abused its proper function, as a legislative committee does when it "expose[s] for the sake of exposure." Nothing in the record indicates that these grand juries were "prob[ing] at will and without relation to existing need." Nor did the grand juries attempt to invade protected First Amendment rights by forcing wholesale disclosure of names and organizational affiliations for a purpose that was not germane to the determination of whether crime has been committed, and the characteristic secrecy of grand jury proceedings is a further protection against the undue invasion of such rights. The investigative power of the grand jury is necessarily broad if its public responsibility is to be adequately discharged....

At the federal level, Congress has freedom to determine whether a statutory newsman's privilege is necessary and desirable and to fashion standards and rules as narrow or broad as deemed necessary to deal with the evil discerned and, equally important, to refashion those rules as experience from time to time may dictate. There is also merit in leaving state legislatures free, within First Amendment limits, to fashion their own standards in light of the conditions and problems with respect to the relations between law enforcement officials and press in their own areas. It goes without saying, of course, that we are powerless to bar state courts from responding in their own way and construing their own constitutions so as to recognize a newsman's privilege, either qualified or absolute.

In addition, there is much force in the pragmatic view that the press has at its disposal powerful mechanisms of communication and is far from helpless to protect itself from harassment or substantial harm. Furthermore, if what the newsman urged in these cases is true—that law enforcement cannot hope to gain and may suffer from subpoenaing newsmen before grand juries—prosecutors will be loath to risk so much for so little. Thus, at the federal level the Attorney General has already fashioned a set of rules for federal officials in connection with subpoenaing members of the press to testify before grand juries or at criminal trials. These rules are a major step in the direction the reporters herein desire to move. They may prove wholly sufficient to resolve the bulk of disagreements and controversies between press and federal officials.

Finally, as we have earlier indicated, news gathering is not without its First Amendment protections, and grand jury investigations if instituted or conducted other than in good faith, would pose wholly different issues for resolution under the First Amendment. Official harassment of the press undertaken not for the purposes of law enforcement but to disrupt a reporter's relationship with his news sources would have no justification. Grand juries are subject to judicial control and subpoenas to motions to quash. We do not expect courts will forget that grand juries must operate within the limits of the First Amendment as well as the Fifth.

The decision ... in Branzburg v. Hayes ... must be affirmed. Here, petitioner refused to answer questions that directly related to criminal conduct that he had observed and written about. The Kentucky Court of Appeals noted that marijuana is defined as a narcotic drug by statute and that unlicensed possession or compounding of it is a felony punishable by both fine and imprisonment. It held that petitioner "saw the commission of the statutory felonies of unlawful possession of marijuana and the unlawful conversion of it into hashish."... [I]f what the petitioner wrote was true, he had direct information to provide the grand jury concerning the commission of serious crimes.

Affirmed.

In *Branzburg* the majority emphatically denied the existence of reporters' privilege. The dissenters were distraught; Justice Stewart, who had worked in his youth as a reporter for a Cincinnati newspaper and also edited the *Yale Daily News* while in college, wrote, "The Court's crabbed view of the First Amendment reflects a disturbing insensitivity to the critical role of an independent press in our society." The reaction of the media was even more vehement, with an outpouring of condemnation of *Branzburg* and calls for federal and state statutes that would shield reporters from revealing their sources. As a result of this pressure, some twenty-six states (but not Congress) enacted reporters' privilege laws, which allowed reporters to refuse to divulge information about certain newsgathering activities. Pritchett noted that the laws are "not necessarily effective" because courts have ruled "that the law must yield when it conflicted with fair-trial" rights.[10] Moreover, such laws often limit protections to specific circumstances. Kentucky already had a shield law on the books at the time of Branzburg's grand jury proceedings. Unfortunately for the reporter, it covered only sources of information and not personal observation. Journalists still face the threat of imprisonment if they refuse to answer questions pertaining to their stories.

Immunity from testifying was not the only privilege for which reporters pressed. In *Zurcher v. Stanford Daily* (1978) they also asserted a need for special treatment under the Fourth Amendment. In April 1971 the *Stanford Daily*, a Stanford University student newspaper, published a special edition devoted to an incident at the university's hospital. A group of demonstrators had seized the hospital's administrative offices and barricaded the doors. When police forced their way in, a riot broke out, which resulted in injuries to the officers. They could not identify their assailants, but one claimed to have seen a photographer in the building. In fact, the *Daily* published several pic-

10. Pritchett, *Constitutional Civil Liberties*, 70.

tures of the incident, none of which fully revealed the identity of the demonstrators. But, because it was reasonable to think that the photographer had more pictures, the day after the special edition, police obtained a warrant to search the *Daily*'s office for the pictures. They found no pictures.

The *Daily* initiated a civil action against all those involved in issuing and executing the warrant. Its lawyers argued that the First Amendment forbade such searches:

Petitioners view this case as if only the Fourth Amendment is implemented. But the search of a newspaper must be judged by the more restrictive standards that apply where First and Fourteenth Amendment interests coalesce.

The attorneys suggested that searches of newspapers were not necessarily unconstitutional, but that they should be based on a subpoena rather than a warrant. This distinction, in their view, would eliminate "police scrutiny [of] unrelated material, which may be highly confidential and sensitive, retained in the newspaper's files." The government responded that the warrant had been properly obtained and executed and that newspapers were undeserving of special Fourth Amendment protection.

Writing for a divided Court, Justice White agreed with the government. He relied on the intent of the Framers, noting that they "did not forbid warrants where the press was involved." He also suggested there was no reason to believe that those authorizing search warrants could not "guard against searches of the type, scope, and intrusiveness that would actually interfere with the timely publication of a newspaper." The Court dismissed the *Stanford Daily*'s claim, and here the alignments were almost identical to those in *Branzburg*. White reiterated the *Branzburg* position that the press is not above the law; and Stewart reasserted his dissenting view in no uncertain terms: "It seems to me self-evident that police searches of newspapers burden the freedom of the press." But the two cases differ in that *Branzburg* led to no federal legislative response, while *Zurcher* caused Congress to enact the Privacy

Protection Act, which prohibits federal agents from conducting search and seizures on "work-product materials unless the reporter or writer is suspected of committing a crime or there is some life-threatening situation."[11] That law does not prohibit state police from obtaining warrants to conduct newsroom searches, so *Zurcher* remains a controlling precedent.

The Right of Access

Several months after *Zurcher* the Court decided *Houchins v. KQED* (1978), which raised another issue involving the press. Of concern in *Houchins* was the right of reporters to have access to inmates in a county jail, which ordinarily would be denied to other individuals. Although this case is different from *Zurcher*, it poses a similar question: Should the justices accord the press rights and privileges beyond those enjoyed by average citizens?

A divided Court ruled that it should not. As Chief Justice Burger explained for the majority:

The media are not a substitute for or an adjunct of the government, and like the courts, are "ill equipped" to deal with the problems of prison administration. We must not confuse the role of the media with that of government; each has special, crucial functions, each complementing—and sometimes conflicting with—the other.

Burger said that the Court would be no more amenable to special access claims than it was to newsmen's privilege; indeed, relying on past decisions such as *Branzburg*, Burger called the media's arguments "flawed." He held that the First Amendment did not mandate "a right of access to government information or sources of information within the government's control." This was strong language, which could be understood to limit press access to a wide range of state and federal proceedings.

In cases following *Houchins*, however, the Court has not gone so far as Burger's words suggested. In *Richmond Newspapers v. Virginia* (1980) *(see Chapter 9)*, for

11. Ibid., 72.

example, it overruled a trial court judge who had denied the press access to a highly publicized murder trial. Burger wrote, "The right to attend criminal trials is implicit within the guarantees of the First Amendment," and, if such access were denied, "important aspects of freedom of speech and of the press could be eviscerated."

READINGS

Anderson, David A. "The Origins of the Press Clause." *UCLA Law Review* 30 (1983): 456–541.

Daly, John Charles. *The Press and the Courts.* Washington, D.C.: American Enterprise Institute, 1978.

Friendly, Fred. *Minnesota Rag.* New York: Random House, 1981.

Lahav. Pnina. *Press Law in Modern Democracies.* New York: Longman, 1984.

Levy, Leonard W. *Emergence of a Free Press.* New York: Oxford University Press, 1985.

Lichtenberg, Judith. *Democracy and the Mass Media.* New York: Cambridge University Press, 1990.

Kelly, Sean. *Access Denied: The Politics of Press Censorship.* Beverly Hills, Calif.: Sage Publications, 1978.

Neubauer, Mark. "The Newsmen's Privilege after *Branzburg.*" *UCLA Law Review* 24 (1976): 160–192.

Shapiro, Martin. *The Pentagon Papers and the Courts.* San Francisco: Chandler, 1972.

CHAPTER 6
THE BOUNDARIES OF FREE EXPRESSION: OBSCENITY AND LIBEL

T HE SUPREME COURT consistently has
taught us that the First Amendment is not absolute. This lesson began in *Schenck v. United
States* (1919) when Justice Holmes noted that the First
Amendment would not protect a person who falsely
yelled "fire" in a crowded theater. Periodically, other
justices have reminded us of the limits of First
Amendment protection as the Court has developed its
freedom of expression doctrines.

First Amendment protection does not mean that
people are shielded from government regulation of
anything published or expressed verbally. Some varieties of expression are illegitimate and may be punished. Several examples immediately come to mind.
One may not communicate military secrets to the
enemy or make terrorist threats. One may not provide
fraudulent information in commercial transactions or
engage in discussions that amount to criminal conspiracies. One may not tell falsehoods under oath, or
exchange "insider information" in securities transactions. In each of these cases the expression falls outside the boundaries of First Amendment protection.

This chapter explores the limits of First Amendment protection by examining two varieties of expression, obscenity and libel, that have presented the
justices with perplexing constitutional questions.
There is almost universal agreement that the Framers
considered neither to be legitimate expression and
did not intend the First Amendment to protect them
from government regulation. Accepting this proposition, however, does not settle the matter: other questions remain. How do we define obscenity and libel?
What distinguishes obscene and libelous expression
from protected speech and press? What standards of
evidence should be imposed? How can government
regulate obscenity and libel without imposing a "chilling effect" on protected expression?

OBSCENITY

According to Justice Harlan, "The subject of obscenity has produced a variety of views among the
members of the Court unmatched in any other course
of constitutional interpretation."[1] Justice Brennan, the
member of the Court most associated with the subject, was even more candid *(see Box 6-1)*. Discussing
service on the Court, Brennan noted, "It takes a while
before you can become even calm about approaching
a job like this. Which is not to say you do not make
mistakes. In my case, there has been the obscenity
area."[2]

1. *Interstate Circuit v. Dallas*, 390 U.S. 676 (1968).
2. Nat Hentoff, "Profiles—The Constitutionalists," *New Yorker*, March
12, 1990, 54.

BOX 6-1   WILLIAM JOSEPH BRENNAN, JR. (1956–1990)

William J. Brennan, Jr., was born April 25, 1906, in Newark, New Jersey. He was the second of eight children of Irish parents who immigrated to the United States in 1890. Brennan displayed impressive academic abilities early in life. He was an outstanding student in high school, an honors student at the University of Pennsylvania's Wharton School of Finance, and in the top 10 percent of his Harvard Law School class in 1931.

Brennan married Marjorie Leonard, May 5, 1928, and they had two sons and one daughter. (Marjorie Brennan died in 1982, and Brennan married Mary Fowler, March 9, 1983.) After law school Brennan returned to Newark, where he joined a prominent law firm. Following passage of the Wagner Labor Act in 1935, Brennan began to specialize in labor law.

With the outbreak of World War II, Brennan entered the Army, serving as a manpower trouble-shooter on the staff of the undersecretary of war, Robert B. Patterson. At the conclusion of the war, Brennan returned to his old law firm. But as his practice swelled, Brennan, a dedicated family man, began to resent the demands it placed on his time.

A desire to temper the pace of his work was one of the reasons Brennan accepted an appointment to the newly created New Jersey Superior Court in 1949. Brennan had been a leader in the movement to establish the court as part of a large program of judicial reform. It came as no surprise when Republican governor Alfred E. Driscoll named Brennan, a registered but inactive Democrat, to the court.

During his tenure on the superior court, Brennan's use of pretrial procedures to speed up the disposition of cases brought him to the attention of New Jersey Supreme Court justice Arthur T. Vanderbilt. It was reportedly at Vanderbilt's suggestion that Brennan was moved first in 1950 to the appellate division of the superior court and then in 1952 to the state supreme court.

Late in 1956, when President Eisenhower was looking for a justice to replace Sherman Minton, Vanderbilt and others strongly recommended Brennan for the post, and Eisenhower gave him a recess appointment in October. There was some criticism that Eisenhower was currying favor with voters by nominating a Roman Catholic Democrat to the bench so close to the election, but Brennan's established integrity and nonpolitical background minimized the impact of the charges. He was confirmed by the Senate March 19, 1957. Brennan retired from the Court July 20, 1990.

SOURCE: Adapted from Elder Witt, *Guide to the U.S. Supreme Court*, 2d ed. (Washington, D.C.: Congressional Quarterly, 1990), 871.

What is it about obscenity that has produced such extraordinary statements from these justices? After all, the Court uniformly has held that obscenity is not entitled to First Amendment protection. The problem is determining what makes a work obscene. In other words, how should we define the term? The answer is important because how we differentiate protected from unprotected expression has broad implications for what we see, read, and hear. Consider the movie industry: in the not-so-distant past, strict definitions of obscenity required an actor to keep one foot on the floor when performing a bedroom scene. Imagine the number of contemporary movies the courts would ban under such a standard! Today, the issues are no less important: groups throughout the country try to bar certain books from public schools, to prohibit the sale of particular records to minors, and to stop libraries from subscribing to certain magazines—all on obscenity grounds.

Given the task involved, one might think the Court has set definitive policy in this area, but nothing could be farther from reality. For more than four decades the Court has grappled with the issue, particularly with fashioning a definition of obscenity. Why has this issue caused such problems? Is there a reasonable solution? Or will the Court continue to flounder among competing schools of thought?

Obscenity in Perspective: The Origins

The adjudication of obscenity claims is a modern phenomenon. Before the 1950s the Court generally avoided the issue by adopting the British definition of obscenity. In *Regina v. Hicklin* (1868), which involved a pamphlet questioning the morals of Catholic priests, a British court promulgated the following test:

whether the tendency of the matter charged as obscenity is to deprave and corrupt those whose minds are open to such immoral influences and into whose hands a publication of this sort might fall.

Under this standard, commonly referred to as the *Hicklin* test, the British court found the pamphlet obscene. That it did so is not surprising: three aspects of the *Hicklin* test make it particularly difficult to overcome. First, the test targets "those whose minds are open to such immoral influences and into whose hands a publication of this sort might fall." Although this standard is vague, in practice, prosecutors often asked, "What if this material would fall into the hands of a child?" In other words, the *Hicklin* test used a stringent level of acceptability—whether the material could be seen by a child. Second, the *Hicklin* test did not require that the publication be considered as a whole. Instead, a work could be declared obscene based upon one of its parts. Third, the *Hicklin* test did

not direct the courts to consider the social value of the work; rather, it only provided that impact of the offensive sections be examined. As a result, the *Hicklin* standard left a wide range of expression unprotected.

The U.S. Supreme Court not only adopted the standard; it also strengthened it. In *Ex parte Jackson* (1878) the Court upheld the Comstock Act, which made it a crime to send obscene materials, including information on abortion and birth control, through the U.S. mail. The justices applied the *Hicklin* test and extended its coverage to reproduction.

While the Supreme Court clung to *Hicklin,* some lower courts were attempting to liberalize it or even reject it. Among the examples cited most often is *United States v. One Book Called Ulysses* (1933) in which Judge Augustus Hand argued that the proper standard should be whether the author *intended* to produce obscenity. The promulgations of diverse rulings from the lower courts, coupled with the Supreme Court's silence on the issue, started to have an effect. By the 1950s the pornography business was flourishing in this country. "There was a steady increase in the volume and sale of obscene material,"[3] with little restriction on who could buy or view such material. This situation led to a backlash, with irate citizens clamoring for tighter controls. Others, particularly the ACLU, pressured courts to move in precisely the opposite direction—to rule that the First Amendment covers all materials, including those previously adjudged obscene. By the late 1950s these interests, however diverse, were sending the same signal to the justices: the time had come to deal with the issue.

The Court responded in *Butler v. Michigan* (1957), an appeal challenging a state statute that defined obscenity along *Hicklin* test lines. Specifically, the law made it a crime to distribute material "found to have a potentially deleterious influence on youth." The justices struck down the statute, finding fault with the

3. Lucius J. Barker and Twiley W. Barker, Jr., *Freedom, Courts and Politics* (Englewood Cliffs, N.J.: Prentice-Hall, 1965), 65.

child standard. It is incompatible with the First Amendment, the justices said, to reduce the reading material available to adults to that which is fit for children. To do so, according to Justice Frankfurter's opinion, is "to burn the house to roast the pig."

The *Butler* decision mortally wounded the *Hicklin* test, but the justices failed to provide an alternative. Later that year, however, the Court took its first stab at creating a contemporary American obscenity standard. The case was *Roth v. United States* (1957), decided with a companion case, *Alberts v. California*. While reading *Roth*, consider the critical issue of standards: Justice Brennan continued to find fault with *Hicklin*, but what did he propose as a replacement?

Roth v. United States

354 U.S. 476 (1957)
Vote: 6 (Brennan, Burton, Clark, Frankfurter, Warren,
        Whittaker)
    3 (Black, Douglas, Harlan)
Opinion of the Court: Brennan
Concurring opinion: Warren
Dissenting opinions: Douglas, Harlan[4]

In 1955 the U.S. government obtained a twenty-six-count indictment against Samuel Roth for violating a federal obscenity law. The government alleged that Roth had sent "obscene, indecent, and filthy matter" through the mail. Among those materials was a circular advertising *Photo and Body, Good Times,* and *American Aphrodite Number Thirteen*.

At Roth's trial the judge instructed the jury with this definition of obscenity: the material "must be calculated to debauch the minds and morals of those into whose hands it may fall and that the test in each case is the effect of the book, picture or publication considered as a whole, not upon any particular class,

4. Harlan dissented in *Roth*, but concurred in the companion case, *Alberts v. California*.

but upon all those whom it is likely to reach. In other words, you determine its impact upon the average person in the community." The jury found Roth guilty on four of the counts, and the judge sentenced him to the maximum punishment: five years in prison and a $5,000 fine.

MR. JUSTICE BRENNAN delivered the opinion of the Court.

In Roth, the primary constitutional question is whether the federal obscenity statute violates the provision of the First Amendment that "Congress shall make no law ... abridging the freedom of speech, or of the press...."

The dispositive question is whether obscenity is utterance within the area of protected speech and press. Although this is the first time the question has been squarely presented to this Court, either under the First Amendment or under the Fourteenth Amendment, expressions found in numerous opinions indicate that this Court has always assumed that obscenity is not protected by the freedom of speech and press.

The guaranties of freedom of expression in effect in 10 of the 14 States which by 1792 had ratified the Constitution, gave no absolute protection for every utterance. Thirteen of the 14 States provided for the prosecution of libel, and all of those States made either blasphemy or profanity, or both, statutory crimes. As early as 1712, Massachusetts made it criminal to publish "any filthy, obscene, or profane song, pamphlet, libel or mock sermon" in imitation or mimicking of religious services. Thus, profanity and obscenity were related offenses.

In light of this history, it is apparent that the unconditional phrasing of the First Amendment was not intended to protect every utterance. This phrasing did not prevent this Court from concluding that libelous utterances are not within the area of constitutionally protected speech. At the time of the adoption of the First Amendment, obscenity law was not as fully developed as libel law, but there is sufficiently contemporaneous evidence to show that obscenity, too, was outside the protection intended for speech and press.

The protection given speech and press was fashioned to assure unfettered interchange of ideas for the bringing about of political and social changes desired by the people....

All ideas having even the slightest redeeming social importance—unorthodox ideas, controversial ideas, even ideas hateful to the prevailing climate of opinion—have the full protection of the guaranties, unless excludable because they encroach upon the limited area of more important interests. But implicit in the history of the First Amendment is the rejection of obscenity as utterly without redeeming social importance. This rejection for that reason is mirrored in the universal judgment that obscenity should be restrained, reflected in the international agreement of over 50 nations, in the obscenity laws of all of the 48 States, and in the 20 obscenity laws enacted by the Congress from 1842 to 1956. This is the same judgment expressed by this Court in Chaplinsky v. New Hampshire.... We hold that obscenity is not within the area of constitutionally protected speech or press.

It is strenuously urged that these obscenity statutes offend the constitutional guaranties because they punish incitation to impure sexual *thoughts*, not shown to be related to any overt antisocial conduct which is or may be incited in the persons stimulated to such *thoughts*. In Roth, the trial judge instructed the jury: "The words 'obscene, lewd and lascivious' as used in the law, signify that form of immorality which has relation to sexual impurity and has a tendency to excite lustful *thoughts.*" It is insisted that the constitutional guaranties are violated because convictions may be had without proof either that obscene material will perceptibly create a clear and present danger of antisocial conduct, or will probably induce its recipients to such conduct. But, in light of our holding that obscenity is not protected speech, the complete answer to this argument is in the holding of this Court in Beauharnais v. People of State of Illinois [1952].

"Libelous utterances not being within the area of constitutionally protected speech, it is unnecessary, either for us or for the State courts, to consider the issues behind the phrase 'clear and present danger.' Certainly no one would contend that obscene speech, for example, may be punished only upon a showing of such circumstances. Libel, as we have seen, is in the same class."

However, sex and obscenity are not synonymous. Obscene material is material which deals with sex in a manner appealing to prurient interest. The portrayal of sex, *e. g.*, in art, literature and scientific works, is not itself sufficient reason to deny material the constitutional protection of freedom of speech and press. Sex, a great and mysterious motive force in human life, has indisputably been a subject of absorbing interest to mankind through the ages; it is one of the vital problems of human interest and public concern....

The fundamental freedoms of speech and press have contributed greatly to the development and well-being of our free society and are indispensable to its continued growth. Ceaseless vigilance is the watchword to prevent their erosion by Congress or by the States. The door barring federal and state intrusion into this area cannot be left ajar; it must be kept tightly closed and opened only the slightest crack necessary to prevent encroachment upon more important interests. It is therefore vital that the standards for judging obscenity safeguard the protection of freedom of speech and press for material which does not treat sex in a manner appealing to prurient interest.

The early leading standard of obscenity allowed material to be judged merely by the effect of an isolated excerpt upon particularly susceptible persons. Regina v. Hicklin. Some American courts adopted this standard but later decisions have rejected it and substituted this test: whether to the average person, applying contemporary community standards, the dominant theme of the material taken as a whole appeals to prurient interest. The Hicklin test, judging obscenity by the effect of isolated passages upon the most susceptible persons, might well encompass material legitimately treating with sex, and so it must be rejected as unconstitutionally restrictive of the freedoms of speech and press. On the other hand, the substituted standard provides safeguards adequate to withstand the charge of constitutional infirmity.

Both trial courts below sufficiently followed the proper standard. Both courts used the proper definition of obscenity.... [I]n Roth, the trial judge instructed the jury as follows:

"... The test is not whether it would arouse sexual desires or sexual impure thoughts in those comprising a particular segment of the community, the young, the immature or the highly prudish or would leave another segment, the scientific or highly educated or the so-called worldly-wise and sophisticated indifferent and unmoved...."

"The test in each case is the effect of the book, picture or publication considered as a whole, not upon any particular class, but upon all those whom it is likely to reach. In other words, you determine its impact upon the average person in the community. The books, pictures and circulars must be judged as a whole, in their entire context, and you are not to consider detached or separate portions in reaching a conclusion. You judge the circulars, pictures and publications which have been put in evidence by present-day standards of the community. You may ask yourselves does it offend the common conscience of the community by present-day standards.

"In this case, ladies and gentlemen of the jury, you and you alone are the exclusive judges of what the common conscience of the community is, and in determining that conscience you are to consider the community as a whole, young and old, educated and uneducated, the religious and the irreligious—men, women and children."...

In summary, then, we hold that these statutes, applied according to the proper standard for judging obscenity, do not offend constitutional safeguards against convictions based upon protected material, or fail to give men in acting adequate notice of what is prohibited.

At first glance, Brennan's opinion seems to forge a compromise between competing views. On one hand, he appeased pro-decency forces by rejecting the view that nothing is obscene; on the other, he set a new standard of obscenity that was far less restrictive than *Hicklin*: "whether to the average person, applying contemporary community standards, the dominant theme of the material taken as a whole appeals to prurient interests."

This new *Roth* test was a significant departure from the *Hicklin* standard. First, *Roth* imposed an "average person" test, replacing *Hicklin*'s child standard with that of an adult. Second, the "contemporary community standards" criterion recognized the evolving nature of society's views of sexual morality. Third, the "dominant theme of the material taken as a whole" approach rejected *Hicklin*'s notion that a work can be declared obscene based on the content of a single part. And finally, the "prurient interests" ele-

ment ensured that only material with sexual content would potentially fall under the obscenity rubric.

The Court may have thought this a workable standard, but experience with it revealed several glaring gaps. First, what did the Court mean by "contemporary community standards"? Was it referring to the nation or a state or a town? The values of citizens living in a rural area may be somewhat different from those living in a big city. Second, what is the meaning of the phrase "dominant theme"? How much social value need a book or movie have to offset portions of the work that might appeal to prurient interests? And, finally, how could police and prosecutors enforce this standard?

The Court tried to fill in these gaps. As you read the cases and narrative, consider not only the answers the Court gave, but also the increasing difficulty the Court had in reaching them. *Roth* created divisions among the justices, and the Court remained divided as it tried to refine Brennan's test.

Contemporary Community Standards. A major question emerging from *Roth* was whether the new standard left it to states and localities to differentiate obscenity based on their own norms, or whether they had to base their distinctions on those found nationwide. In *Jacobellis v. Ohio* (1964) the Court sought to address this issue. Ohio charged Nico Jacobellis, the manager of a movie theater, with showing an obscene film. Called *Les Amants* (The Lovers), the movie depicts the love affair of an archaeologist and a woman who leaves her husband and children. *Les Amants* contains one "explicit love scene" at the end.

Brennan's opinion in *Jacobellis* is noteworthy for several reasons. First, and most important, Brennan refined his *Roth* test: he stated that contemporary community standards were those of the nation, not of a local community. In doing so, he not only held the film to be protected speech, but also substantially liberalized *Roth*. It is bound to be the case that communities seeking to ban obscenity have stricter standards than those of the country at large. Under Brennan's refinement, Tulsa, Oklahoma, would be bound by the same obscenity standards as New York City. Second, Brennan's opinion gave the legal community some insight into the inner workings of the Court. He noted that the Court had viewed the film and not found it obscene. Would the justices now be watching every movie coming to their doorstep? According to *The Brethren*, that is precisely what they did, going so far as to have movie days.[5] Third, we begin to see the intractable problem of obscenity take its toll. Brennan's may have been the opinion of the Court, but the other eight justices filed concurrences or dissents. Among the most famous was Justice Potter Stewart's: he was becoming so disgruntled with the issue that he almost gave up, writing "I shall not today attempt further to define [hard-core pornography].... But I know it when I see it."

The Dominant Theme. In *Jacobellis* Brennan also provided some insight into what the phrase *dominant theme* meant. He suggested that only work "utterly without redeeming social value," perhaps hard-core pornography, would represent unprotected expression.

Even with that admonition, prosecutors were uncertain about what Brennan was attempting to do. Could they ban books and movies that were generally obscene, but had some element of artistry or social value? Or were they limited to banning those works totally devoid of merit? The Court tried to address these questions in *Memoirs v. Massachusetts* (1966) in which the state urged it to find obscene *Memoirs of a Woman of Pleasure*, popularly known as *Fanny Hill*, written by John Cleland in 1749. A concededly erotic novel, *Memoirs* traces the escapades of a London prostitute. The Massachusetts Supreme Court held that a book need not be "unqualifiedly worthless before it could be deemed obscene"; that is, just because *Mem-*

---

5. Bob Woodward and Scott Armstrong, *The Brethren* (New York: Avon Books, 1979), 233–235.

> ### BOX 6-2 *ROTH*, *JACOBELLIS*, AND *MEMOIRS*, COMPARED
>
> *ROTH:* "whether to the average person applying contemporary community standards, the dominant theme of the material, taken as a whole, appeals to prurient interests."
>
> *ROTH* and *JACOBELLIS:* "whether to the average person applying" standards of "the society at large," the material is "utterly without redeeming social importance."
>
> *ROTH*, *JACOBELLIS*, and *MEMOIRS:* "whether to the average person applying standards of the society at large, the material is utterly without redeeming social importance," possessing not "a modicum of social value."

oirs contained some nonerotic passages did not mean that it had redeeming value. Although divided, the U.S. Supreme Court disagreed. In his judgment for the Court, Brennan expanded the parameters of *Roth*. If a work had a "modicum of social value" it could not be adjudged obscene.

By 1966, then, a divided Court had radically altered *Roth*, as shown in Box 6-2, which compares the test in 1957 to that articulated in 1966. Would anything be defined as obscene under the *Roth-Jacobellis-Memoirs* test? We might think that hard-core pornography would fall outside of it, but could not a clever movie maker, author, or publisher circumvent it? If a short passage of some merit appears in the middle of an erotic book or pornographic movie, does the product have redeeming value?

Enforcing Roth. Even though the Court's decisions were far from unanimous, they had the combined effect of eliminating most works from the obscene category. This "doctrinal liberalization" generally continued when it came to issues of enforcement of state laws.[6] One of the earliest indications of the Court's direction came in *Bantam Books v. Sullivan* (1963), which tested the constitutionality of a Rhode Island law. That state created a commission to review materials and, if they were found obscene, to declare them "objectionable for sale, distribution, or display to youths under 18." The commission had no enforcement power—it could not ban books—but it could make recommendations to the state attorney general to prosecute "purveyors of obscenity," sufficient "intimidation" for the justices to strike down the law. Writing for the Court, Brennan claimed,

[T]hough the Commission is limited to informal sanction—the threat of invoking legal sanctions and other means of coercion ... the record amply demonstrates that the Commission definitely set about to achieve the suppression of publications deemed objectionable.

He further asserted that the commission was usurping judicial functions—for example, declaring material obscene—without providing any of the safeguards, such as notices or hearings. This practice, according to the Court, was censorship.

Two years later, the Court handed prosecutors a rare victory when it upheld a federal conviction against a panderer of obscene material. In *Ginzburg v. United States* (1965) the justices ruled that anyone who deliberately portrays material for sale in an "erotically arousing" way can be convicted of a crime. By doing so, they acknowledged that prosecutors could obtain obscenity convictions, not just against books, authors, and so forth, but against those engaged in "the business of purveying textual or graphic matter openly advertised to appeal to the erotic interests of their customers."

Ginzburg raised the hopes of prosecutors, but the Court dimmed them again in *Redrup v. New York* (1967). At issue here were the actions of a plainclothes police officer who approached a newsstand in New York, where Redrup worked as a clerk. The officer spotted two books, *Lust Pool* and *Shame Agent*, he thought were obscene. He bought the books and arrested Redrup for pandering. In a per curiam opinion, the Court reversed Redrup's conviction. But its decision smacked of resignation; apparently some of the justices gave up on the issue, and the rest were fractionalized. The Court said,

Whichever of [the] constitutional views [used to adjudge obscenity] is brought to bear upon the cases before us, it is clear the judgments cannot stand.

The *Redrup* opinion, according to Joseph Kobylka, "admitted that the Justices could not agree on a specific definition of obscenity but that under their various tests the material . . . was not obscene."[7] By 1967 the members of the Court had adopted many different views of obscenity *(see Box 6-3)*.[8] The result was that state prosecutors and legislators had no firm guidelines to fashion specific definitions of obscenity. Should they adopt the principles set forth in *Roth* when a majority of the justices now rejected that standard? If not, what could they substitute for it?

The justices' inability to define obscenity in turn crippled enforcement efforts. If *Redrup* did not meet *Ginzburg*'s pandering standard, what would? Apparently, very little. After 1967 the Court "summarily reversed 32 cases simply by citing *Redrup*."[9] This move led many scholars to suggest that by the end of the 1960s obscenity prosecutions were almost impossible to obtain. In other words, after *Redrup*, it appeared that the Court was protecting almost any kind of expression. The country was, in short, approaching the "end of obscenity."

The Political Environment and the "Nixon" Court

As the Court puzzled over obscenity, Congress took matters into its own hands. In July 1968 it created the Federal Commission on Obscenity and Pornography

6. See Joseph F. Kobylka, *The Politics of Obscenity* (Westport, Conn.: Greenwood Press, 1991).

7. Ibid., 6.
8. C. Peter Magrath, "The Obscenity Cases: The Grapes of *Roth*," *Supreme Court Review* (1966): 7–77.
9. Kobylka, *The Politics of Obscenity*, 6.

BOX 6-3   WHAT IS OBSCENE?

CASE	STANDARD
Roth v. United States, 1957	BRENNAN (for Frankfurter, Burton, Clark, Whittaker): "whether to the average person applying contemporary community standards, the dominant theme of the material, taken as a whole, appeals to prurient interests."
	WARREN: engaging in "the business of purveying textual or graphic matter openly advertised to appeal to erotic interests of customers."
	HARLAN: materials that have the "tendency to deprave or corrupt its readers by exciting lascivious thoughts or arousing lustful desires."
	BLACK/DOUGLAS: "The First Amendment puts speech in a preferred position.... As a people, we cannot afford to relax that standard. For the test that suppresses a cheap tract today can suppress a literary gem tomorrow."
Jacobellis v. Ohio, 1964	BRENNAN (for Goldberg): "whether to the average person applying" standards of "the society at large," the material is "utterly without redeeming social importance."
	STEWART: "I shall not today attempt further to define [hard-core pornography].... But I know it when I see it."
	WARREN/CLARK: "contemporary community standards" should not mean a "national standard."
	HARLAN: "the states are constitutionally permitted greater latitude in determining what is bannable."
Redrup v. New York, 1967	PER CURIAM: "Whichever of [the] constitutional standards is brought to bear ... it is clear that [the conviction] cannot stand."
	HARLAN/CLARK: this decision does "not reflect well on the process of the Court."

"to investigate the effect of pornography on social behavior, to determine the need for new laws and to report on the constitutionality of such laws." Composed mainly of Lyndon Johnson appointees—most of whom were sympathetic to the civil liberties posture—the commission issued its first report in 1970. Its conclusion seemed to parallel that of the Court's: it said "federal, state, and local legislation prohibiting the sale, exhibition, or distribution of sexual material to consenting adults should be repealed."[10]

By the time the commission handed in its report, however, the nation had a new president, who firmly and emphatically rejected these conclusions. This turn

10. President's Commission on Obscenity and Pornography, *Report* (New York: Bantam Books, 1970), 57.

of events was not surprising; after all, during his campaign Richard Nixon had criticized the Court's rulings and vowed to work for their reversal. His opportunity came with the appointment of four new justices to the Court. But the question remained whether the so-called Nixon Court, led by Warren Burger, could handle the issue any better than its predecessor.

The first indication that the Burger Court's approach to obscenity would be more conservative than that used by the Warren justices came with the 1972 decision of *California v. LaRue.* Upset by sexually oriented performances and activities in some California bars and nightclubs, state authorities amended the alcoholic beverage code to ban various forms of nude entertainment in any establishment holding a liquor license. Violation of the regulations could lead to a revocation of the business's alcoholic beverage permit. Robert LaRue and other holders of state liquor licenses challenged the constitutionality of the new regulations on First Amendment grounds. They argued that the state was attempting to use the power to regulate alcohol as a means of restricting expression rights. The state countered by showing that investigations of the entertainment establishments under review revealed "topless" and "bottomless" waitresses and dancers, sexual contact between customers and entertainers, prostitution, and other activities of concern to the state occurring on the premises. Over the objections of liberal justices Brennan, Marshall, and Douglas, the Court upheld the regulations.[11] The majority skirted the First Amendment issue, and based its decision on the power to regulate alcohol granted to the states by the Twenty-first Amendment. While the ruling was restricted to alcoholic beverage situations, *LaRue* was a clear prediction that obscenity law was about to change.

The Burger justices next turned their attention to revamping the definition of obscenity and, therefore,

the whole approach to the topic. This reformulation came in *Miller v. California,* handed down June 21, 1973.

Miller v. California

413 U.S. 15 (1973)
Vote: 5 (Blackmun, Burger, Powell, Rehnquist, White)
  4 (Brennan, Douglas, Marshall, Stewart)
Opinion of the Court: Burger
Dissenting opinions: Douglas, Brennan

Marvin Miller, a vendor of so-called adult material, conducted a mass-mail campaign to drum up sales for his books. The pamphlets were fairly explicit: some contained pictures of "men and women in groups of two or more engaging in a variety of sexual activities, with genitals often prominently displayed."[12]

Had Miller sent the brochures to interested individuals only, he might not have been caught. But because he did a mass mailing, some pamphlets ended up in the hands of people who did not want them. Indeed, Miller's arrest came when the manager of a restaurant and his mother opened one of the envelopes and complained to the police.

MR. CHIEF JUSTICE BURGER delivered the opinion of the Court.

This is one of a group of "obscenity-pornography" cases being reviewed by the Court in a re-examination of standards enunciated in earlier cases involving what Mr. Justice Harlan called "the intractable obscenity problem."...

This case involves the application of a State's criminal obscenity statute to a situation in which sexually explicit materials have been thrust by aggressive sales action upon unwilling recipients who had in no way indicated any desire to receive such materials. This Court has recognized that the States have a legitimate interest in prohibiting dissemination or exhibition of obscene material when the mode of dissemination carries with it a significant danger

---

11. The Court handed down similar rulings in *New York State Liquor Authority v. Bellanca* (1981) and *City of Newport, Kentucky v. Iacobucci* (1986).

12. *Miller v. California,* 413 U.S. 15 (1973).

of offending the sensibilities of unwilling recipients or of exposure to juveniles. It is in this context that we are called on to define the standards which must be used to identify obscene material that a State may regulate without infringing on the First Amendment as applicable to the States through the Fourteenth Amendment.

The dissent of Mr. Justice BRENNAN reviews the background of the obscenity problem, but since the Court now undertakes to formulate standards more concrete than those in the past, it is useful for us to focus on two of the landmark cases in the somewhat tortured history of the Court's obscenity decisions. In Roth v. United States (1957) the Court sustained a conviction under a federal statute punishing the mailing of "obscene, lewd, lascivious or filthy ..." materials. The key to that holding was the Court's rejection of the claim that obscene materials were protected by the First Amendment. Five Justices joined in the opinion stating:

"All ideas having even the slightest redeeming social importance—unorthodox ideas, controversial ideas, even ideas hateful to the prevailing climate of opinion—have the full protection of the [First Amendment] guaranties, unless excludable because they encroach upon the limited area of more important interests. But implicit in the history of the First Amendment is the rejection of obscenity as utterly without redeeming social importance....

"'... There are certain well-defined and narrowly limited classes of speech, the prevention and punishment of which have never been thought to raise any Constitutional problem. *These include the lewd and obscene.... It has been well observed that such utterances are no essential part of any exposition of ideas, and are of such slight social value as a step to truth that any benefit that may be derived from them is clearly outweighed by the social interest in order and morality ....*'" [Emphasis by Court in *Roth* opinion.]

Nine years later, in Memoirs v. Massachusetts (1966), the Court veered sharply away from the *Roth* concept and, with only three Justices in the plurality opinion, articulated a new test of obscenity. The plurality held that under the *Roth* definition

"as elaborated in subsequent cases, three elements must coalesce: it must be established that (a) the dominant theme of the material taken as a whole appeals to a prurient interest in sex; (b) the material is patently offensive because it af-

fronts contemporary community standards relating to the description or representation of sexual matters; and (c) the material is utterly without redeeming social value."

The sharpness of the break with *Roth*, represented by the third element of the *Memoirs* test, ... was further underscored when the *Memoirs* plurality went on to state:

"The Supreme Judicial Court erred in holding that a book need not be 'unqualifiedly worthless before it can be deemed obscene.' A book cannot be proscribed unless it is found to be *utterly* without redeeming social value."

While *Roth* presumed "obscenity" to be "utterly without redeeming social importance," *Memoirs* required that to prove obscenity it must be affirmatively established that the material is "*utterly* without redeeming social value." Thus, even as they repeated the words of *Roth*, the *Memoirs* plurality produced a drastically altered test that called on the prosecution to prove a negative, *i.e.*, that the material was "*utterly* without redeeming social value"—a burden virtually impossible to discharge under our criminal standards of proof. Such considerations caused Mr. Justice Harlan to wonder if the "*utterly* without redeeming social value" test had any meaning at all.

Apart from the initial formulation in the *Roth* case, no majority of the Court has at any given time been able to agree on a standard to determine what constitutes obscene, pornographic material subject to regulation under the States' police power. We have seen "a variety of views among the members of the Court unmatched in any other course of constitutional adjudication." This is not remarkable, for in the area of freedom of speech and press the courts must always remain sensitive to any infringement on genuinely serious literary, artistic, political, or scientific expression. This is an area in which there are few eternal verities.

The case we now review was tried on the theory that the California Penal Code § 311 approximately incorporates the three-stage *Memoirs* test. But now the *Memoirs* test has been abandoned as unworkable by its author, and no Member of the Court today supports the *Memoirs* formulation.

This much has been categorically settled by the Court, that obscene material is unprotected by the First Amendment. We acknowledge, however, the inherent dangers of undertaking to regulate any form of expression. State statutes designed to regulate obscene materials must be carefully limited. As a result, we now confine the permissible scope of such regulation to works which depict or describe sexual conduct. That conduct must be specifically defined by the applicable state law, as written or authoritatively construed. A state offense must also be limited to works which, taken as a whole, appeal to the prurient interest in sex, which portray sexual conduct in a patently offensive way, and which, taken as a whole, do not have serious literary, artistic, political, or scientific value.

The basic guidelines for the trier of fact must be: (a) whether "the average person, applying contemporary community standards" would find that the work, taken as a whole, appeals to the prurient interest; (b) whether the work depicts or describes, in a patently offensive way, sexual conduct specifically defined by the applicable state law; and (c) whether the work, taken as a whole, lacks serious literary, artistic, political, or scientific value. We do not adopt as a constitutional standard the "*utterly* without redeeming social value" test of Memoirs v. Massachusetts; that concept has never commanded the adherence of more than three Justices at one time. If a state law that regulates obscene material is thus limited, as written or construed, the First Amendment values applicable to the States through the Fourteenth Amendment are adequately protected by the ultimate power of appellate courts to conduct an independent review of constitutional claims when necessary.

We emphasize that it is not our function to propose regulatory schemes for the States. That must await their concrete legislative efforts. It is possible, however, to give a few plain examples of what a state statute could define for regulation under part (b) of the standard announced in this opinion.

(a) Patently offensive representations or descriptions of ultimate sexual acts, normal or perverted, actual or simulated.

(b) Patently offensive representation or descriptions of masturbation, excretory functions, and lewd exhibition of the genitals.

Sex and nudity may not be exploited without limit by films or pictures exhibited or sold in places of public accommodation any more than live sex and nudity can be exhibited or sold without limit in such public places. At a minimum, prurient, patently offensive depiction or de-

scription of sexual conduct must have serious literary, artistic, political, or scientific value to merit First Amendment protection. . . .

Under the holdings announced today, no one will be subject to prosecution for the sale or exposure of obscene materials unless these materials depict or describe patently offensive "hard core" sexual conduct specifically defined by the regulating state law, as written or construed. We are satisfied that these specific prerequisites will provide fair notice to a dealer in such materials that his public and commercial activities may bring prosecution. If the inability to define regulated materials with ultimate, god-like precision altogether removes the power of the States or the Congress to regulate, then "hard core" pornography may be exposed without limit to the juvenile, the passerby, and the consenting adult alike. . . .

It is certainly true that the absence, since *Roth*, of a single majority view of this Court as to proper standards for testing obscenity has placed a strain on both state and federal courts. But today, for the first time since *Roth* was decided in 1957, a majority of this Court has agreed on concrete guidelines to isolate "hard core" pornography from expression protected by the First Amendment. Now we . . . attempt to provide positive guidance to federal and state courts alike.

This may not be an easy road, free from difficulty. But no amount of "fatigue" should lead us to adopt a convenient "institutional" rationale—an absolutist, "anything goes" view of the First Amendment—because it will lighten our burdens. "Such an abnegation of judicial supervision in this field would be inconsistent with our duty to uphold the constitutional guarantees." Nor should we remedy "tension between state and federal courts" by arbitrarily depriving the States of a power reserved to them under the Constitution, a power which they have enjoyed and exercised continuously from before the adoption of the First Amendment to this day. "Our duty admits of no 'substitute for facing up to the tough individual problems of constitutional judgment involved in every obscenity case.'"

Under a National Constitution, fundamental First Amendment limitations on the powers of the States do not vary from community to community, but this does not mean that there are, or should or can be, fixed, uniform national standards of precisely what appeals to the "prurient interest" or is "patently offensive." These are essentially questions of fact, and our Nation is simply too big and too diverse for this Court to reasonably expect that such standards could be articulated for all 50 States in a single formulation, even assuming the prerequisite consensus exists. When triers of fact are asked to decide whether "the average person, applying contemporary community standards" would consider certain materials "prurient," it would be unrealistic to require that the answer be based on some abstract formulation. The adversary system, with lay jurors as the usual ultimate fact-finders in criminal prosecutions, has historically permitted triers of fact to draw on the standards of their community, guided always by limiting instructions on the law. To require a State to structure obscenity proceedings around evidence of a *national* "community standard" would be an exercise in futility.

As noted before, this case was tried on the theory that the California obscenity statute sought to incorporate the tripartite test of *Memoirs.* This, a "national" standard of First Amendment protection enumerated by a plurality of this Court, was correctly regarded at the time of trial as limiting state prosecution under the controlling case law. The jury, however, was explicitly instructed that, in determining whether the "dominant theme of the material as a whole ... appeals to the prurient interest" and in determining whether the material "goes substantially beyond customary limits of candor and affronts contemporary community standards of decency," it was to apply "contemporary community standards of the State of California."

During the trial, both the prosecution and the defense assumed that the relevant "community standards" in making the factual determination of obscenity were those of the State of California, not some hypothetical standard of the entire United States of America. Defense counsel at trial never objected to the testimony of the State's expert on community standards or to the instructions of the trial judge on "statewide" standards. On appeal to the Appellate Department, Superior Court of California, County of Orange, appellant for the first time contended that application of state, rather than national, standards violated the First and Fourteenth Amendments.

We conclude that neither the State's alleged failure to offer evidence of "national standards," nor the trial court's

charge that the jury consider state community standards, were constitutional errors. Nothing in the First Amendment requires that a jury must consider hypothetical and unascertainable "national standards" when attempting to determine whether certain materials are obscene as a matter of fact.... It is neither realistic nor constitutionally sound to read the First Amendment as requiring that the people of Maine or Mississippi accept public depiction of conduct found tolerable in Las Vegas, or New York City. People in different States vary in their tastes and attitudes, and this diversity is not to be strangled by the absolutism of imposed uniformity.... We hold that the requirement that the jury evaluate the materials with reference to "contemporary standards of the State of California" serves this protective purpose and is constitutionally adequate.

The dissenting Justices sound the alarm of repression. But, in our view, to equate the free and robust exchange of ideas and political debate with commercial exploitation of obscene material demeans the grand conception of the First Amendment and its high purposes in the historic struggle for freedom. It is a "misuse of the great guarantees of free speech and free press...." The First Amendment protects works which, taken as a whole, have serious literary, artistic, political, or scientific value, regardless of whether the government or a majority of the people approve of the ideas these works represent.... But the public portrayal of hard-core sexual conduct for its own sake, and for the ensuing commercial gain, is a different matter....

In sum, we (a) reaffirm the *Roth* holding that obscene material is not protected by the First Amendment; (b) hold that such material can be regulated by the States, subject to the specific safeguards enunciated above, without a showing that the material is "*utterly* without redeeming social value"; and (c) hold that obscenity is to be determined by applying "contemporary community standards," not "national standards."...

Vacated and remanded.

The same day, the Court also handed down a decision in *Paris Adult Theatre I v. Slaton,* which involved a 1970 complaint filed by Atlanta, Georgia, against the Paris Adult Theatre, asserting that the theater was showing obscene films. During the trial, the judge

TABLE 6-1 *Roth* and *Miller*, Compared

	Warren Court	Burger Court
Relevant audience:	Average person	Average person
Scope of consideration:	Work taken as a whole	Work taken as a whole
Standard:	Sexual material found patently offensive by the national standards of society at large	Sexual conduct found patently offensive by contemporary community standards as specifically defined by applicable state law
Value of the work:	Utterly without redeeming social importance	Lacks serious literary, artistic, political, or scientific value

viewed two of the offending films, which depicted simulated fellatio, cunnilingus, and group sexual intercourse. The judge ruled in favor of the theater, mainly because the owners did not admit anyone under age twenty-one. After the Georgia Supreme Court reversed, the owners appealed to the U.S. Supreme Court. The justices, however, affirmed the ruling, refusing to extend the theater First Amendment protection, even though only consenting adults would be exposed to the films.

Some have suggested that *Miller* (and *Paris Adult Theatre I*) did not substantially alter *Roth* et al., but we see significant changes. In Table 6-1 we compare the *Roth* test (and its expansions) with the new *Miller* standard. Although the Court retained three important elements of the *Roth* test (the adult standard, the work taken as a whole, and the restriction of obscenity to sexually oriented materials), two major changes stand out. First, the *Miller* test specifically gives the states the authority to define what is obscene. The Court, therefore, emphasized local values rather than the national standard articulated in *Roth*. Second, the Court did away with the notion that a work merited protection as long as it did not meet the "utterly without redeeming social value" criterion. Instead, the justices held that to receive First Amend-

ment protection, sexually oriented materials had to have serious literary, artistic, political, or scientific value. As a consequence, the new *Miller* test permitted much greater regulation of sexually explicit materials than did the *Roth* standard.

In addition to the significant change in obscenity law ushered in by *Miller* and its companion case, *Paris Adult Theatre I*, liberals from the Warren Court era also expressed a change in approach. Justice Brennan wrote in his dissenting opinion in *Paris Adult Theatre I*,

Our experience since *Roth* requires us not only to abandon the effort to pick out obscene materials on a case-by-case basis, but also to reconsider a fundamental postulate of *Roth*: that there exists a definable class of sexually oriented expression that may be totally suppressed by the Federal and State Governments. Assuming that such a class of expression does in fact exist, I am forced to conclude that the concept of "obscenity" cannot be defined with sufficient specificity and clarity to provide fair notice to persons who create and distribute sexually oriented materials, to prevent substantial erosion of protected speech as a byproduct of the attempt to suppress unprotected speech, and to avoid very costly institutional harms. Given these inevitable side effects of state efforts to suppress what is assumed to be *unprotected* speech, we must scrutinize with care the state interest that is asserted to justify the suppression. For in the absence of some very substantial interest in suppressing such speech, we can hardly condone the ill effects that seem to flow inevitably from the effort. . . .

In short, while I cannot say that the interests of the State—apart from the question of juveniles and unconsenting adults—are trivial or nonexistent, I am compelled to conclude that these interests cannot justify the substantial damage to constitutional rights and to this Nation's judicial machinery that inevitably results from state efforts to bar the distribution even of unprotected material to consenting adults. . . . I would hold, therefore, that at least in the absence of distribution to juveniles or obtrusive exposure to unconsenting adults, the First and Fourteenth Amendments prohibit the State and Federal Governments from attempting wholly to suppress sexually oriented materials on the basis of their allegedly "obscene" contents.

Brennan's opinion, joined by Justices Marshall and Stewart, is remarkable for three reasons. First, after almost two decades of leading the Court in attempts to define obscenity, the author of *Roth* decided finally that it could not be done. Second, the three liberals argued that efforts to regulate "obscene" material inevitably led to unacceptable restrictions on protected expression. Third, Brennan and the others concluded that, except for protecting juveniles and unconsenting adults, state and federal authorities should be banned from regulating sexually oriented expression altogether.

While it would be hard to imagine two more different positions than those taken by the majority and the dissenters in these obscenity cases, they are remarkably alike in one respect: both sides wanted to extricate the Court from the obscenity business. Brennan and the other dissenters advocated an almost total end to government regulation of obscenity. The *Miller* majority wanted to put an end to federal obscenity cases by shifting authority to the states.

The Warren Court's message to prosecutors had been that obscenity convictions would not stand, but the Nixon justices signaled encouragement. Law enforcement officials, state legislators, and prosecutors now recognized that they could enforce obscenity laws with some hope of obtaining solid convictions.

Miller in Action

Surely, the most significant change wrought by *Miller* was the shift from a national to a local focus on obscenity. As a result, towns felt relatively free to enact laws that fit their own community's values. As the justices anticipated, the number of cases heard by the Court did go down, but *Miller* did not free the justices entirely. Indeed, between 1974 and 1988, the Court decided more than thirty cases involving many different issues. Three examples follow:

1. Could a city prohibit the performance of the play *Hair* on the basis of reports that it was obscene? (Maybe. Refusal to rent an auditorium for the production of a show that some think obscene constitutes prior restraint, and the city could prohibit the performance only if it took proper procedural steps. See *Southeastern Promotions, Ltd. v. Conrad*, 1975).

2. Could a city ban the showing of movies containing nudity, but which are not necessarily obscene, at drive-in theaters? (No. Such statutes violate the First Amendment rights of film exhibitors. See *Erznoznik v. City of Jacksonville*, 1975).

3. Does a community have free reign to define obscenity in a more stringent way than that specified in *Miller*? (Not necessarily. Local juries do not have "unbridled discretion" to determine what is obscene; they are to follow the *Miller* standard. See *Jenkins v. Georgia*, 1974).

That this Court answered these and other questions in diverse ways lends credence to the view that its "path on obscenity material proved almost as serpentine as that of its predecessor."[13] The observation is true to the extent that *Miller* did not end the Court's involvement with the issue, but the Burger Court treated the subject in a way very different from the Warren Court. Between 1957 and 1969—the heyday of the *Roth* test—the justices supported First Amendment claims in 78 percent of their decisions; that number dropped to 22

13. Melvin I. Urofsky, *A March of Liberty* (New York: Knopf, 1988), 913.

percent after *Miller*.[14] Clearly, the Burger Court did not side with government in every obscenity case it heard, but, as those percentages indicate, the shift in jurisprudence from *Roth* to *Miller* was significant.

The evolution of the Court's philosophy can best be seen, not through aggregated statistics, but in its handling of one issue, child pornography. We do not suggest that the case, *New York v. Ferber* (1982), is typical of obscenity cases; on the contrary, the justices have treated child pornography differently from other forms of obscenity. But it indicates the Court's increased willingness to leave the issue to state authorities and thereby to encourage prosecutions.

New York v. Ferber

458 U.S. 747 (1982)

Vote: 9 (Blackmun, Brennan, Burger, Marshall, O'Connor,
     Powell, Rehnquist, Stevens, White)

          0

Opinion of the Court: White
Concurring opinions: Brennan, O'Connor, Stevens

New York and nineteen other states prohibited the "dissemination of material depicting children [under the age of sixteen] engaged in sexual conduct regardless of whether the material is obscene." Bookstore owner Paul Ferber was charged with violating this law when he sold two movies to an undercover police officer. The films were "devoted almost exclusively to depicting two young boys masturbating." In his defense, Ferber argued that the law "works serious and substantial violation of the First Amendment by measures and means unnecessary to accomplish its legislative objectives." State attorneys acknowledged the potential ramifications of closing an entire area to constitutional protection, but they suggested that the state had a compelling and overriding interest "in protecting children from sexual abuse."

14. Kobylka, *The Politics of Obscenity.*

JUSTICE WHITE delivered the opinion of the Court.

At issue in this case is the constitutionality of a New York criminal statute which prohibits persons from knowingly promoting sexual performances by children under the age of 16 by distributing material which depicts such performances.

In recent years, the exploitative use of children in the production of pornography has become a serious national problem. The Federal Government and 47 States have sought to combat the problem with statutes specifically directed at the production of child pornography. At least half of such statutes do not require that the materials produced be legally obscene. Thirty-five States and the United States Congress have also passed legislation prohibiting the distribution of such materials; 20 States prohibit the distribution of material depicting children engaged in sexual conduct without requiring that the material be legally obscene.

New York is one of the 20. In 1977, the New York Legislature enacted Article 263 of its Penal Law. Section 263.05 criminalizes as a class C felony the use of a child in a sexual performance:

"A person is guilty of the use of a child in a sexual performance if knowing the character and content thereof he employs, authorizes or induces a child less than sixteen years of age to engage in a sexual performance or being a parent, legal guardian or custodian of such child, he consents to the participation by such child in a sexual performance."...

In *Chaplinsky v. New Hampshire* (1942), the Court laid the foundation for the excision of obscenity from the realm of constitutionally protected expression:

"There are certain well-defined and narrowly limited classes of speech, the prevention and punishment of which have never been thought to raise any Constitutional problem. These include the lewd and obscene.... It has been well observed that such utterances are no essential part of any exposition of ideas, and are of such slight social value as a step to truth that any benefit that may be derived from them is clearly outweighed by the social interest in order and morality."

Embracing this judgment, the Court squarely held in *Roth v. United States* (1957) that "obscenity is not within the area of constitutionally protected speech or press." The

Court recognized that "rejection of obscenity as utterly without redeeming social importance" was implicit in the history of the First Amendment: The original States provided for the prosecution of libel, blasphemy, and profanity, and the "universal judgment that obscenity should be restrained [is] reflected in the international agreement of over 50 nations, in the obscenity laws of all of the 48 states, and in the 20 obscenity laws enacted by Congress from 1842 to 1956."

Roth was followed by 15 years during which this Court struggled with "the intractable obscenity problem." Despite considerable vacillation over the proper definition of obscenity, a majority of the Members of the Court remained firm in the position that "the States have a legitimate interest in prohibiting dissemination or exhibition of obscene material when the mode of dissemination carries with it a significant danger of offending the sensibilities of unwilling recipients or of exposure to juveniles."

Throughout this period, we recognized "the inherent dangers of undertaking to regulate any form of expression." Consequently, our difficulty was not only to assure that statutes designed to regulate obscene materials sufficiently defined what was prohibited, but also to devise substantial limits on what fell within the permissible scope of regulation. In *Miller v. California* a majority of the Court agreed that a "state offense must also be limited to works which, taken as a whole, appeal to the prurient interest in sex, which portray sexual conduct in a patently offensive way, and which, taken as a whole, do not have serious literary, artistic, political, or scientific value." Over the past decade, we have adhered to the guidelines expressed in *Miller,* which subsequently has been followed in the regulatory schemes of most States.

The *Miller* standard, like its predecessors, was an accommodation between the State's interests in protecting the "sensibilities of unwilling recipients" from exposure to pornographic material and the dangers of censorship inherent in unabashedly content-based laws. Like obscenity statutes, laws directed at the dissemination of child pornography run the risk of suppressing protected expression by allowing the hand of the censor to become unduly heavy. For the following reasons, however, we are persuaded that the States are entitled to greater leeway in the regulation of pornographic depictions of children.

First. It is evident beyond the need for elaboration that a State's interest in "safeguarding the physical and psychological well-being of a minor" is "compelling."...

The prevention of sexual exploitation and abuse of children constitutes a government objective of surpassing importance. The legislative findings accompanying passage of the New York laws reflect this concern:

"[T]here has been a proliferation of exploitation of children as subjects in sexual performances. The care of children is a sacred trust and should not be abused by those who seek to profit through a commercial network based upon the exploitation of children. The public policy of the state demands the protection of children from exploitation through sexual performances."

We shall not second-guess this legislative judgment. Respondent has not intimated that we do so. Suffice it to say that virtually all of the States and the United States have passed legislation proscribing the production of or otherwise combating "child pornography." The legislative judgment, as well as the judgment found in the relevant literature, is that the use of children as subjects of pornographic materials is harmful to the physiological, emotional, and mental health of the child. That judgment, we think, easily passes muster under the First Amendment.

Second. The distribution of photographs and films depicting sexual activity by juveniles is intrinsically related to the sexual abuse of children in at least two ways. First, the materials produced are a permanent record of the children's participation and the harm to the child is exacerbated by their circulation. Second, the distribution network for child pornography must be closed if the production of material which requires the sexual exploitation of children is to be effectively controlled. Indeed, there is no serious contention that the legislature was unjustified in believing that it is difficult, if not impossible, to halt the exploitation of children by pursuing only those who produce the photographs and movies. While the production of pornographic materials is a low-profile, clandestine industry, the need to market the resulting products requires a visible apparatus of distribution. The most expeditious if not the only practical method of law enforcement may be to dry up the market for this material by imposing severe criminal penalties on persons selling, advertising, or otherwise promoting the product. Thirty-five States and Congress have concluded that restraints on the distribution of pornographic materials are required in order to effectively combat the problem, and there is a body of literature and testimony to support these legislative conclusions.

Respondent does not contend that the State is unjustified in pursuing those who distribute child pornography. Rather, he argues that it is enough for the State to prohibit the distribution of materials that are legally obscene under the *Miller* test. While some States may find that this approach properly accommodates its interests, it does not follow that the First Amendment prohibits a State from going further. The *Miller* standard, like all general definitions of what may be banned as obscene, does not reflect the State's particular and more compelling interest in prosecuting those who promote the sexual exploitation of children. Thus, the question under the *Miller* test of whether a work, taken as a whole, appeals to the prurient interest of the average person bears no connection to the issue of whether a child has been physically or psychologically harmed in the production of the work. Similarly, a sexually explicit depiction need not be "patently offensive" in order to have required the sexual exploitation of a child for its production. In addition, a work which, taken on the whole, contains serious literary, artistic, political, or scientific value may nevertheless embody the hardest core of child pornography. "It is irrelevant to the child [who has been abused] whether or not the material … has a literary, artistic, political, or social value." We therefore cannot conclude that the *Miller* standard is a satisfactory solution to the child pornography problem.

Third. The advertising and selling of child pornography provide an economic motive for and are thus an integral part of the production of such materials, an activity illegal throughout the Nation. "It rarely has been suggested that the constitutional freedom for speech and press extends its immunity to speech or writing used as an integral part of conduct in violation of a valid criminal statute." We note that were the statutes outlawing the employment of children in these films and photographs fully effective, and the constitutionality of these laws has not been questioned, the First Amendment implications would be no greater than that presented by laws against distribution: enforce-

able production laws would leave no child pornography to be marketed.

Fourth. The value of permitting live performances and photographic reproductions of children engaged in lewd sexual conduct is exceedingly modest, if not *de minimis*. We consider it unlikely that visual depictions of children performing sexual acts or lewdly exhibiting their genitals would often constitute an important and necessary part of a literary performance or scientific or educational work. As a state judge in this case observed, if it were necessary for literary or artistic value, a person over the statutory age who perhaps looked younger could be utilized. Simulation outside of the prohibition of the statute could provide another alternative. Nor is there any question here of censoring a particular literary theme or portrayal of sexual activity. The First Amendment interest is limited to that of rendering the portrayal somewhat more "realistic" by utilizing or photographing children.

Fifth. Recognizing and classifying child pornography as a category of material outside the protection of the First Amendment is not incompatible with our earlier decisions. …

There are, of course, limits on the category of child pornography which, like obscenity, is unprotected by the First Amendment. As with all legislation in this sensitive area, the conduct to be prohibited must be adequately defined by the applicable state law, as written or authoritatively construed. Here the nature of the harm to be combated requires that the state offense be limited to works that *visually* depict sexual conduct by children below a specified age. The category of "sexual conduct" proscribed must also be suitably limited and described.

The test for child pornography is separate from the obscenity standard enunciated in *Miller,* but may be compared to it for the purpose of clarity. The *Miller* formulation is adjusted in the following respects: A trier of fact need not find that the material appeals to the prurient interest of the average person; it is not required that sexual conduct portrayed be done so in a patently offensive manner; and the material at issue need not be considered as a whole. We note that the distribution of descriptions or other depictions of sexual conduct, not otherwise obscene, which do not involve live performance or photographic or other visual reproduction of live performances, retains First Amendment protection. As with obscenity laws, criminal responsibility may not be imposed without some element of scienter on the part of the defendant.

The Future of Obscenity: The Rehnquist Court

Child pornography hit a nerve with the justices; even the most liberal members agreed with the *Ferber* resolution. The Rehnquist Court showed similar distaste in *Osborne v. Ohio* (1990). Based on a tip from a postal inspector, Ohio police obtained a warrant to search Clyde Osborne's home. They found sexually explicit pictures of a fourteen-year-old boy. Osborne was arrested and convicted under a state law that outlawed possession of child pornography. He appealed his conviction on the basis of *Stanley v. Georgia* (1969), a decision based on First Amendment and privacy guarantees that upheld the right of an individual to possess pornographic films in the home for personal, noncommercial viewing. Ohio countered that its law was legitimate in light of *Ferber* and that nineteen other states had similar prohibitions.

Once again, the Court sided with the state. Writing for a six-person majority, Justice White asserted:

Stanley should not be read too broadly.... [W]e ... find this case distinct from *Stanley* because the interests underlying child pornography prohibitions far exceed the interests justifying the Georgia law at issue in *Stanley*....

Given the importance of the State's interest in protecting the victims of child pornography, we cannot fault Ohio for attempting to stamp out this vice at all levels in the distribution chain.... [S]ince ... our decision in *Ferber*, much of the child pornography market has been driven underground; as a result, it is now difficult, if not impossible, to solve the child pornography problem by only attacking production and distribution.

Does *Osborne* tell us much about the future of obscenity litigation? The *Roth* standard clearly had become unworkable, making it almost impossible to find anything obscene, but has the Court moved too far in the other direction? Will it eventually be forced to reformulate the *Miller* test, as moral values and standards change?

Barnes v. Glen Theatre, Inc. (1991) offers additional insights to the Rehnquist Court and may help us answer some of these questions. The Kitty Kat Lounge and Glen Theatre, Inc., sued to have the Indiana public indecency statute declared unconstitutional as an infringement on the First Amendment. The law bans total nudity in public places. The businesses involved in this case wished to offer their customers the opportunity to watch totally nude dancing. Because such entertainment would be illegal under the public nudity statute, the dancers were required to wear "pasties" and "G-strings." According to the businesses and some of their female entertainers, the public nudity law infringed on the right to engage in expressive conduct. The case did not present a question of obscenity, but rather whether the state could prohibit public nudity—obscene or not.

A fractured Court upheld the Indiana public nudity law in a judgment announced by Chief Justice Rehnquist. Although acknowledging that "nude dancing may involve only the barest minimum of protected expression," Rehnquist argued that the Indiana law was not directed at expressive conduct. Instead, the law controlled public nudity generally, whether it occurred in the streets, on the beaches, or in any other public area—including nightclubs. The majority concluded that the state had a legitimate interest in regulating the evil of public nudity. The fact that the law applied to nude dancers whose conduct may have expressive content is not controlling. Citing *United States v. O'Brien* (the draft card burning case discussed in Chapter 4), Rehnquist's plurality opinion argued that in pursuing a substantial government interest the state may regulate conduct even if it results in an incidental limitation on some expressive activity. Regulating public nudity is just such a substantial government interest. The application of the law does not prohibit the dancers from expressing themselves, but only blunts how graphic those dances may be.

Adding to the controversy over sexually explicit materials has been a recent call by some feminist scholars to frame the obscenity question in different terms.[15] The issue of obscenity, they argue, should not focus on the rights of the author, producer, or distributor. Instead, society should place emphasis on the negative impact pornographic materials have on women. Sexually explicit material does not merit First Amendment protection because it demeans and subjugates women. It is discriminatory on the basis of sex. Under this argument the courts should view obscenity as a sexual equality issue and not a freedom of expression question. Adopting this view would allow government to regulate sexually oriented materials as part of an effort to bring about greater equality between the sexes. Support for this position has divided the liberal community, which traditionally has fought to defeat conservative efforts to restrict freedom of expression. So far, the Supreme Court has treated obscenity as a First Amendment issue, refraining from framing the question on sexual equality grounds. The feminist attack on pornography as an equality issue, however, continues to build in strength *(see Box 6-4, pages 373–374)*.

Clearly, the efforts by the Burger and Rehnquist justices to remove the Court from the obscenity fray have not been a complete success. The questions of what constitutes obscenity and to what degree the dissemination of sexually explicit materials merits constitutional protection have proven stubbornly persistent. Conservative, liberal, and feminist groups have vastly different positions on these matters. With such diverse and conflicting views on such a sensitive subject, there is little doubt that the courts will have to settle the inevitable disputes that will arise. Will the Supreme Court continue to rely on *Miller,* or will the justices need to reformulate obscenity standards as such issues move to the forefront? As society continues to debate the limits of tolerable behavior, these questions become more important.

Enforcing Obscenity Statutes

While the major pornography controversies have involved questions of defining what is obscene, simultaneous legal battles have been fought over methods of enforcing anti-obscenity statutes. If material is legally obscene, what weapons does government have to combat it? How can the government enforce such restrictions without unduly impinging on legitimate expression?

Controlling Distribution. A major strategy in controlling obscenity is to attack its distribution channels. The federal effort relies on three types of laws. The first prohibits the importation of pornography. Customs officials may intercept shipments of obscene films and publications produced abroad and intended for domestic distribution. The second prohibits the interstate shipment of obscene materials and allows federal officials to take legal action against individuals who commercially transport materials across state lines. The third prohibits use of the U.S. mail to distribute obscene goods and brings federal postal officials into the fight against obscenity. If a book, magazine, or film meets the legal definition of obscenity, the federal government may use any of these laws to block its distribution.

State authorities regulate essentially local activities such as pornographic book stores and adult movie theaters. Under the *Miller* test, states and localities have broad authority to define what is patently offensive and to enforce laws against selling obscene materials or commercially showing obscene films. Individuals who knowingly sell or otherwise distribute legally obscene materials may be prosecuted under state criminal laws or be subject to other state legal action.[16]

Prior Restraint. You may recall from Chapter 5 that Chief Justice Hughes in *Near v. Minnesota* (1931) ruled that prior restraint generally was incompatible with First Amendment freedoms. But he also said that

---

15. See, for example, Catharine MacKinnon, *Only Words* (Cambridge, Mass.: Harvard University Press, 1993).

16. *Smith v. California* (1959).

BOX 6-4 OBSCENITY AND FEMINISM

The liberal community traditionally has supported the position that the First Amendment provides broad protection for those who produce and distribute sexually explicit materials. Recently, however, that solidly pro-expression position has been broken by some members of the feminist movement who argue that because of pornography's negative impact on women, government should be allowed to regulate it. Presented here is the transcript of a discussion between Professor Catharine MacKinnon, an active proponent of legally restricting pornography, and Floyd Abrams, a prominent advocate of the traditional freedom of expression position. *New York Times* columnist Anthony Lewis moderated the discussion.

MacKinnon: What about the film, "Deep Throat," which Linda "Lovelace" was coerced into making? Is that what you call the expression of ideas I disagree with?

Abrams: Well, I think first of all it is the expression of ideas—

MacKinnon: So is the rape of women.

Abrams: The rape of women is handled by rape laws.

MacKinnon: And "Deep Throat"—how should that be handled?

Abrams: Judged by obscenity laws.

MacKinnon: It's been judged obscene in some places and not in others. You think Linda "Lovelace" should have no equality rights in relation to that film? How does that film give rise to a speech interest you want to protect?

Abrams: I don't even know what you mean in this case about equality rights. She has a perfect right not to be raped.

MacKinnon: I mean that, as a woman, Linda was sexually subordinated to make it and that—as she puts it—"every time someone watches that film they are watching me be raped." She has an equality right not to have that done. And to stop the film that is doing it, and whose profit is an incentive to keep doing it.

Lewis: Am I right in thinking that coercion as you would define it in the law you drafted with Andrea Dworkin—that is, graphic, sexually explicit materials that subordinate women through pictures and words—disallows voluntarily engaging in a pornographic film since it says that a written consent shall not be proof that there was no coercion?

MacKinnon: No, you're not. If you can

force a woman to have sex with a dog, you can force her to sign a contract. The mere fact of a contract being signed doesn't in itself negate a finding of coercion. The coercion itself would have to be proven under our ordinance.

Abrams: Look, your statute provides in part that graphic, sexually explicit subordination of women in which women are presented as sexual objects for domination, conquest, violation, exploitation, possession or use, etc., can give rise to a private cause of action. The Court of Appeals in holding the statute unconstitutional—a decision affirmed by the Supreme Court—indicated that books like Joyce's "Ulysses," Homer's "Iliad," poems by Yeats, novels by D. H. Lawrence and the like could all be subject to a finding of violation of the statute that you have drafted.

MacKinnon: And that's just simply false.

Abrams: Well, I don't think it *is* false.

MacKinnon: Those materials are not even sexually explicit. They don't even get in the door.

Lewis: Why don't you just repeat your definition of pornography?

MacKinnon: Professor Abrams just quoted the definition. Andrea Dworkin's and my approach to pornography is to define it in terms of what it does, not in terms of what it says, not by whether somebody doesn't like it. None of that has anything to do with our definition. Our definition, and our legal causes of action, all have to do with what it does to the women in it, to the children in it and to the other people who can prove that as a direct result of these materi-

als they were assaulted or made second-class citizens on the basis of sex.

Abrams: You mean because people will think less of women on account of how they're portrayed?

MacKinnon: No, because people will *do* things to them like not hiring them, like sexualizing them and not taking them seriously as students, the entire array of violent and nonviolent civil subordination, when they can prove it comes from pornography.

Abrams: That is why your legislation is so frontal an attack on the First Amendment. When the Court of Appeals said that the impact of your statute is such that it could apply to everything from hard-core films to the collected works of James Joyce, D. H. Lawrence and John Cleland, it was entirely correct. It is correct because what you have drafted as a definition of actionable pornography is "graphic sexual explicit subordination of women, in which women are presented as sexual objects for domination." Lots of great art as well as cheap and vile productions have depicted women in just that way—"The Rape of the Sabine Women," for example. And my point is not that your definition is vague, but that it is clear. It includes any art, whether it is good or bad, art or nonart, that you have concluded may do harm. That's an unacceptable basis and it should be.

MacKinnon: O.K., there are several things wrong with this. No. 1, those materials are not sexually explicit. The court was told exactly what sexually explicit means in law and in ordinary use, and it should have known better. No. 2, these materials have never yet been shown in any study to have produced any of the effects that pornography produces. So no one could prove that women are subordinated as a result of them. This statute does not cover those materials, period. It is false as a matter of statutory construction. The statute could potentially cover something like a film in which somebody was actually killed but claims are made that it has artistic value—an artistic snuff film—or in which someone is raped but the film has interesting camera angles. That does raise a conflict between existing law and our statute. The examples you cite do not.

Lewis: Professor MacKinnon, we do have a concrete example of what your view of the law might result in. The Canadian Supreme Court adopted your view. Since then, there has been an intensification of gay and lesbian books' being intercepted at the border. That seems to be the result of a country actually adopting your standard.

MacKinnon: That's disinformation. Canada customs has singled out those materials for years, and customs laws were not involved in the case I was part of in Canada. What happened was, the Supreme Court of Canada rejected its morality-based standard for obscenity and held that when pornography hurts equality it can be stopped. Customs has not reviewed its standards since. I think that if Canada customs is still stopping materials because they are gay or lesbian, on a moral ground not a harm ground, they have lost their constitutional authority to do it under this ruling. If the materials hurt women or men or their equality, they can still stop them. But Andrea Dworkin and I do not favor addressing pornography through criminal law, especially obscenity law, so in that way Canada has not adopted our approach.

Lewis: Professor MacKinnon, there's an assumption explicitly stated in your book that pornography as you define it results in antisocial, abusive activity by the customers.

MacKinnon: There's overwhelming documentation of it.

Lewis: But it is a fact that in countries in which pornography is lawful and there are no legal restraints whatever on sexually explicit materials the incidence of sexual crimes is much lower than in this country.

MacKinnon: Actually, that isn't true. It's urban legend.

Lewis: In Denmark, in Germany, in Japan—

MacKinnon: In Denmark, data on reported rape after liberalization is inconclusive. It did not drop, though. Also, the definitions and categories of sexual offenses were changed at the same time that pornography was decriminalized. Also, reporting may well have dropped. If your government supports pornography, reporting sexual abuse seems totally pointless to women. So, too, Germany and Sweden. Once pornography is legitimized throughout society, you get an explosion in sexual abuse, but women don't report it anymore because they know that nothing will be done about it. Feminists and sex educators in Denmark are beginning to say that selling 12-year-old children on street corners is not what they mean by sexual liberation. What's happened in Japan and other places is that much of sexual abuse is just part of the way women are normally treated. If you're still essentially chattel, what is it to rape you? In Sweden there aren't any rape-crisis centers. All there are is battered-women shelters. So the battered-women's movement has been pushing the government to look at the reality of rape there, which is massive.

Abrams: But those countries that are harshest on what you would call pornography are also harshest on women. In China promulgation of pornography leads to capital punishment. In Iran it leads to the harshest and most outrageous physical torture. These are not good countries for women to live in. If you look at countries like Sweden and Japan and Holland and Germany, which have allowed more rather than less free expression in this area of sexually explicit speech, you'll find that these are the countries in which sexual abuse of women is not particularly prevalent. It's one thing for you to advocate a statute such as you have proposed in Sweden, but I daresay it has not been seriously suggested that Swedish women as a group have been victimized by their free-press and free-speech laws.

MacKinnon: Swedish women have seriously supported our law, against the legalized victimization of pornography. But it's hard to know what the reality is. It's wrong to base how much rape there is on reported rape. It's also very hard to know how much pornography is actually available. You could look at the United States laws and get the impression that pornography was being taken seriously as a problem in this country.

Abrams: But when you cite, for example, the Balkans as a place where there's been a vast amount of rape and infer that it has something to do with the existence of sexually explicit materials, you don't tell us that in 1913 there was an orgy of rapes at a time when such material didn't exist at all. It puts into question the validity of the whole thesis.

MacKinnon: It is not an exclusive thesis. There are lots of ways of sexualizing subordination—religion, veiling, clitoridectomies. Pornography is one way, and some of the abuses it is connected to we can do something about. In countries where women have recently got more voice, like the United States and Sweden, women are becoming more able to identify the sources of our subordination. The United States is a mass culture, media-saturated and capitalistic. In asking how women are subordinated in the United States, it would be wrong to eliminate the capitalistic mass media of the pornography industry. At other times and places, the ways in which women are subordinated are different. But now, the United States is exporting this form of subordination to the rest of the world.

SOURCE: "The First Amendment, Under Fire From the Left," *New York Times Magazine*, March 13, 1994, 57ff.

there were certain exceptions to this principle. One of the exceptions pertained to publications "that threatened public decency." This cited exception has encouraged governments to impose certain forms of prior censorship as part of the battle against obscenity. These restrictions, however, have not gone without legal challenge.

The first battle over such regulations occurred in *Kingsley Books v. Brown* (1957). This dispute began when the state of New York charged Kingsley Books with selling obscene materials, compiled under the title *Nights of Horror.* Under New York law, the state could request a temporary injunction blocking the sale of such materials after publication, but before a trial judge determined whether the material was legally obscene. The statute further required that such a determination be made promptly. New York obtained such an injunction against Kingsley Books, and the company appealed, arguing that the law amounted to prior restraint. The Supreme Court, however, upheld the statute. Writing for a majority of five, Justice Frankfurter declared,

[O]ver a long stretch of this Court's history, it has been accepted as a postulate that "the primary requirement of decency may be enforced against obscene publication...." Unlike *Near* [the law here] is concerned solely with obscenity and, as authoritatively construed, it studiously withholds restraint upon matters not already published and not yet found to be offensive.

This ruling constituted the Court's first application of the prior restraint doctrine in the field of obscenity. The majority seemed to agree with Hughes that public decency considerations provided an exception to the constitutional prohibition against prior restraint. However, the majority also made clear that prior censorship would be tolerated only if proper safeguards (temporary injunctions imposed only after publication and speedy judicial determinations) were included.

Similar questions regarding prior restraint have been raised with respect to motion pictures, although films have proven to be a more difficult issue for the Court than has printed material. In *Mutual Film Corporation v. Industrial Commission* (1915), its earliest ruling on motion pictures, the Court even ruled that movies were undeserving of First Amendment protection because they were "business pure and simple." The justices, therefore, allowed the states to censor films that might corrupt the morals of their citizens.

The Court abandoned its position that motion pictures were qualitatively unlike printed matter with its decision in *Burstyn v. Wilson* (1953). Although acknowledging that films might possess a greater potential for evil than books, newspapers, or magazines, the justices held that movies deserved a degree of First Amendment protection that precluded unbridled censorship. In so ruling, however, the Court did not disallow all community control over the showing of motion pictures.

As the film industry produced more movies with content that many found morally objectionable, cities and states developed comprehensive regulatory measures. One of the most controversial was the requirement that movie distributors submit a copy of their films to local authorities prior to showing them to the public. The authorities would examine the content of the films for possible obscenity violations and then decide whether to issue a license permitting a theater showing. These laws appeared to be flagrant examples of prior restraint, but because they were imposed to combat obscenity and promote public decency, there was reason to believe that the Court might approve them.

In two decisions, *Times Film Corporation v. Chicago* (1961) and *Freedman v. Maryland* (1965), the justices settled the issue of prior submission of films. Consistent with the public decency exception articulated by Chief Justice Hughes, the Court held that nothing in the Constitution necessarily prohibited state or local governments from requiring film exhibitors to submit films before showing them commercially. However, the Court demanded that such plans meet exacting procedural safeguards. First, the government must initiate any procedures to determine whether the film is obscene, and the government must also bear the burden of proof. Second, only a judicial body, and not an administrative agency, has the authority officially to declare a work obscene. Third, prior to a judicial determination, any restraint against the showing of the film must be temporary. Fourth, if a temporary restraint is imposed, the state must have procedures for a prompt judicial resolution of the obscenity question.

The *Times Film* and *Freedman* decisions pleased neither local governments nor the film industry. State and local governments were satisfied that the Court upheld their authority to impose prior submission laws, but did not like the cumbersome procedural safeguards the justices demanded. The film industry did not like any prior restraint, but was comforted by the fact that the Court was not granting unfettered

regulatory authority to the states. In response, three years after *Freedman* the Motion Picture Association of America and the International Film Importers and Distributors of America devised a system for rating and labeling movies. The industry informs the public of the "general suitability" of a film by assigning it one of the following ratings:

G: suitable for all audiences

PG: parental guidance suggested

PG-13: parental guidance strongly suggested for children under 13

R: restricted to those 17 or older unless accompanied by a guardian

NC-17: no one under 17 admitted[17]

This system of voluntary ratings has been successful. Although the Court has stuck with its *Times*

---

17. Originally, NC-17 was the X-rating.

Film and *Freedman* decisions, state and local governments have been happy to defer to the ratings system and cease their prior submission programs. The film industry is much more comfortable with self-regulation rather than with the scrutiny of state and local censorship boards. The system has worked so well that the recording industry, under rising criticism from various parent groups for explicit lyrics, developed a voluntary labeling system to avoid government regulation *(see Box 6-5)*.

Zoning. To combat the effects of adult theaters, nightclubs, and bookstores, local governments frequently rely on their zoning powers. The Court examined the question of zoning restrictions on such establishments in *Young v. American Mini Theatres, Inc.* (1976). At issue were amendments to Detroit's "anti–Skid Row ordinance," which targeted theaters exhibiting sexually explicit films. The law prohibited the location of an "adult" theater within 500 feet of a residential area or within 1,000 feet of two or more other such theaters, bars, pool halls, dance halls, pawn shops, or other specified establishments. The goal of the legislation was to avoid a concentration of businesses considered undesirable. American Mini Theatres owned adult entertainment businesses. The company converted a corner gas station into a mini-theater, called the "Pussy Cat," at which it hoped to show sexually explicit films. The city, however, denied the company's request for a license to operate on the grounds that the theater's location was in violation of the anti–Skid Row amendments. The company challenged the denial on First Amendment grounds. The Supreme Court upheld the denial by a 5–4 vote, but the justices were unable to issue an opinion endorsed by a majority of the justices.

The zoning issue was revisited in *City of Renton v. Playtime Theatres, Inc.* (1986). In this case Renton, Washington, passed a zoning ordinance similar to the Detroit law upheld in *American Mini Theatres*. The city prohibited adult theaters within 1,000 feet of any resi-

dential area, church, school, or park. In a majority opinion written by Justice Rehnquist, the Court upheld the ordinance in spite of arguments by the theater company that it constituted content-based discrimination. Because the ordinance did not prohibit adult theaters, but only regulated their placement, the Court treated the law as a "time, place or manner" restriction. Over the dissents of Justices Brennan and Marshall, the majority found that the law was not aimed at the content of the expression, but designed to control the secondary effects of such establishments on the surrounding community. Taken together, the rulings in *American Mini Theatres* and *Playtime Theatres* strongly reinforced the authority of local governments to use their zoning powers to regulate for public decency.

Racketeering Statutes. As part of a strategy to combat obscenity some jurisdictions have employed RICO (Racketeer Influenced and Corrupt Organizations) laws. RICO statutes commonly are used to prosecute organized crime. They are applicable when a party engages in a demonstrable pattern of repeated criminal violations. RICO statutes apply severe procedures and penalties, including seizures of property that may have been acquired with the profits from criminal acts, and, as such, they can be a powerful weapon against crime. But are RICO laws appropriate for use in obscenity cases? Or, are they so severe as to place an unconstitutional burden on freedom of expression? The Rehnquist Court provided answers to these questions in *Fort Wayne Books, Inc. v. Indiana* (1989).

To bolster its enforcement efforts, Indiana amended its state RICO law to include obscenity violations. The law allowed the state to seize all allegedly obscene materials and to padlock adult book stores, prior to any judicial determination of whether the books, films, and so forth were obscene. The penalties were steep: violators could spend substantial time in prison, be forced to pay large fines, and forfeit all property, real and personal, used in or derived from the criminal activity. Normally, obscenity violations were misdemeanors; prosecuted under the RICO statute, they became felonies.

In March 1984 Indiana attempted to apply its RICO statute to a number of bookstores, including Fort Wayne Books, Inc. The bookstores had long histories of obscenity violations, which established the pattern of criminal behavior required under the RICO laws. Prosecutors asked the local court to allow police to seize all property contained in the stores and to authorize the sheriff to padlock the buildings. The judge agreed, even though the material at issue had yet to be judged obscene. The bookstores countered that the judge's order amounted to a prior restraint, that it had a "chilling effect" on First Amendment rights by making booksellers so fearful of prosecution that they would significantly reduce the range of materials offered for sale. They also argued that the use of RICO laws against obscenity was draconian.

The Supreme Court, through an opinion by Justice White, generally upheld the authority of the state to use RICO laws to combat obscenity. The Court concluded that the "deterrence of the sale of obscene materials is a legitimate end of state anti-obscenity laws," and that there was no constitutional bar to enhancing obscenity penalties through the use of a RICO statute. It also rejected the bookstores' "chilling effect" argument, holding that, "The mere assertion of some possible self-censorship resulting from a statute is not enough to render an anti-obscenity law unconstitutional under our precedents." The justices ruled in favor of the bookstores on the prior restraint question, holding that the *pretrial* seizure of the bookstores and their contents was constitutionally improper.

The decision in *Fort Wayne Books* is representative of the Court's rulings on questions of obscenity law enforcement. The justices are generally sympathetic to government attempts to combat legally obscene material, and are willing to provide state and local authorities the necessary constitutional leeway to prosecute the distributors of obscenity.

LIBEL

On any given day in America, we can buy a newspaper or turn on the television and find information on the activities of public officials, well-known figures, and even private citizens who, for various reasons, have made news. Sometimes the reports imply criticism—for instance, a newspaper article about a public official accused of wrongdoing. In other cases, the reports are blatantly false. To see this phenomenon we need go no farther than a supermarket checkout and read the tabloid headlines about the doings of celebrities.

As we know from our readings on freedom of the press, individuals or even governments generally cannot prohibit the media from disseminating such information—true or false. But once the story is published or televised, do people have any recourse? Under U.S. law they do: they can bring a *libel* action against the offender. That is, if individuals believe that falsehoods contained in an article resulted in the defamation of their character, they can attempt to have a court hold the media responsible for their actions.[18] The reason is that, like obscenity, libelous statements remain outside of the reach of the First Amendment.[19]

Public Officials and Libel

The lack of First Amendment protection does not mean that libel is a simple area of law. As we shall see, the Supreme Court has had a difficult time developing standards for the application of libel. Why? One reason is that before 1964 libel was an undeveloped area of law. Recall that in 1798, the Federalist Congress enacted the Sedition Act, which outlawed seditious libel—criticism of the government

---

18. C. Herman Pritchett, *Constitutional Civil Liberties* (Englewood Cliffs, N.J.: Prentice-Hall, 1984), 99.

19. See *Chaplinsky v. New Hampshire*, 315 U.S. 568 (1942).

and of government officials. Under this act, the government could bring criminal charges against those who made "false, scandalous, and malicious" statements that brought the United States or its representatives into "contempt or disrepute." Because President Thomas Jefferson later pardoned all those who had been convicted under it, the Supreme Court never had an opportunity to rule on the law's constitutionality. For most of our nation's history, therefore, it was unclear whether seditious libel was protected or unprotected speech. Indeed, some scholars argued that the purpose of the First Amendment was to "abolish seditious libel," while others contended the contrary.[20]

What is clear, however, is that until 1964 states were free to determine their own standards for the more typical version of libel: civil actions brought by individuals against other individuals, for example, those running a newspaper. Some variation existed among state laws, but most allowed defamed individuals to seek two kinds of damages: compensatory, which provide money for actual financial loss (an individual loses his or her job because of the story), and punitive, which punish the offender. To collect such monies, all the plaintiff generally had to demonstrate was that the story was false—truth is always a defense against claims of libel—and damaging.

These criteria might sound like simple standards for plaintiffs to meet. In fact, the simplicity further compounded the Court's problems. Many newspapers, television stations, and other media argued that the traditional standard had a chilling effect on their First Amendment guarantee of a free press. They feared printing anything critical of government or public officials, in particular, because if the story contained even the smallest factual error, they could

face a costly lawsuit. Therefore, they felt constrained in their reporting of news.

Until 1964 the Supreme Court ignored this complaint and allowed states to formulate their own libel laws. In the seminal case of *New York Times v. Sullivan*, however, the Court radically departed from this position. What standard did the Court articulate? How did it alter existing libel law?

New York Times v. Sullivan

376 U.S. 254 (1964)

Vote: 9 (Black, Brennan, Clark, Douglas, Goldberg, Harlan, Stewart, Warren, White)

0

Opinion of the Court: Brennan
Concurring opinions: Black, Goldberg

The March 29, 1960, edition of the *New York Times* ran an advertisement to publicize the struggle for civil rights and to raise money for the cause. L. B. Sullivan, an elected commissioner of the City of Montgomery, Alabama, took offense at the ad. It did not mention his name, but it gave an account of a racial incident that had occurred in the city. The ad suggested that the police, of whom Sullivan was in charge, participated in some wrongdoing.

Sullivan brought a libel action against the paper, alleging that the ad contained falsehoods, which, in fact, it did. For example, it claimed that demonstrating students sang "My Country, 'Tis of Thee," when they actually sang the "Star-Spangled Banner," and so forth. In his charge to the jury, the judge said that the ad was "libelous per se," meaning that because it contained lies, it was unprotected speech, and, that if the jury found that the statements were made "of and concerning" Sullivan, it could hold the *Times* liable. Taking these words to heart, the jury awarded Sullivan $500,000 in damages.

The Supreme Court of Alabama affirmed this judgment. In doing so, it specified that words are libelous

---

20. See Zechariah Chafee, Jr., *Free Speech in the United States* (Cambridge, Mass.: Harvard University Press, 1941); and Leonard W. Levy, *Legacy of Suppression* (Cambridge, Mass.: Harvard University Press, 1960). See also Levy's revised and enlarged edition, *Emergence of a Free Press* (New York: Oxford University Press, 1985). See also Pritchett, *Constitutional Civil Liberties*, for an interesting review of these debates.

❝ *The growing movement of peaceful mass demonstrations by Negroes is something new in the South, something understandable. . . . Let Congress heed their rising voices, for they will be heard.*❞

—*New York Times editorial*
Saturday, March 19, 1960

Heed Their Rising Voices

As the whole world knows by now, thousands of Southern Negro students are engaged in widespread non-violent demonstrations in positive affirmation of the right to live in human dignity as guaranteed by the U.S. Constitution and the Bill of Rights. In their efforts to uphold these guarantees, they are being met by an unprecedented wave of terror by those who would deny and negate that document which the whole world looks upon as setting the pattern for modern freedom . . .

In Orangeburg, South Carolina, when 400 students peacefully sought to buy doughnuts and coffee at lunch counters in the business district, they were forcibly ejected, tear-gassed, soaked to the skin in freezing weather with fire hoses, arrested en masse and herded into an open barbed-wire stockade to stand for hours in bitter cold.

In Montgomery, Alabama, after students sang "My Country 'Tis of Thee" on the State Capitol steps, their leaders were expelled from school, and truckloads of police armed with shotguns and tear-gas ringed the Alabama State College Campus. When the entire student body protested to state authorities by refusing to re-register, their dining hall was padlocked in an attempt to starve them into submission.

In Tallahassee, Atlanta, Nashville, Savannah, Greensboro, Memphis, Richmond, Charlotte, and a host of other cities in the South, young American teenagers, in face of the entire weight of official state apparatus and police power, have boldly stepped forth as protagonists of democracy. Their courage and amazing restraint have inspired millions and given a new dignity to the cause of freedom.

Small wonder that the Southern violators of the Constitution fear this new, non-violent brand of freedom fighter . . . even as they fear the upswelling right-to-vote movement. Small wonder that they are determined to destroy the one man who, more than any other, symbolizes the new spirit now sweeping the South—the Rev. Dr. Martin Luther King, Jr., world-famous leader of the Montgomery Bus Protest. For it is his doctrine of non-violence which has inspired and guided the students in their widening wave of sit-ins; and it is this same Dr. King who founded and is president of the Southern Christian Leadership Conference—the organization which is spearheading the surging right-to-vote movement. Under Dr. King's direction the Leadership Conference conducts Student Workshops and Seminars in the philosophy and techniques of non-violent resistance.

Again and again the Southern violators have answered Dr. King's peaceful protests with intimidation and violence. They have bombed his home almost killing his wife and child. They have assaulted his person. They have arrested him seven times—for "speeding," "loitering" and similar "offenses." And now they have charged him with "perjury"—a felony under which they could imprison him for ten years. Obviously, their real purpose is to remove him physically as the leader to whom the students and millions of others—look for guidance and support, and thereby to intimidate all leaders who may rise in the South. Their strategy is to behead this affirmative movement, and thus to demoralize Negro Americans and weaken their will to struggle. The defense of Martin Luther King, spiritual leader of the student sit-in movement, clearly, therefore, is an integral part of the total struggle for freedom in the South.

Decent-minded Americans cannot help but applaud the creative daring of the students and the quiet heroism of Dr. King. But this is one of those moments in the stormy history of Freedom when men and women of good will must do more than applaud the rising-to-glory of others. The America whose good name hangs in the balance before a watchful world, the America whose heritage of Liberty these Southern Upholders of the Constitution are defending, is *our* America as well as theirs . . .

We must heed their rising voices—yes—but we must add our own.

We must extend ourselves above and beyond moral support and render the material help so urgently needed by those who are taking the risks, facing jail, and even death in a glorious re-affirmation of our Constitution and its Bill of Rights.

We urge you to join hands with our fellow Americans in the South by supporting, with your dollars, this combined appeal for all three needs—the defense of Martin Luther King—the support of the embattled students—and the struggle for the right-to-vote.

Stella Adler	Dr. Alan Knight Chalmers	Anthony Franciosa	John Killens	L. Joseph Overton	Maureen Stapleton
Raymond Pace Alexander	Richard Coe	Lorraine Hansbury	Eartha Kitt	Clarence Pickett	Frank Silvera
Harry Van Arsdale	Nat King Cole	Rev. Donald Harrington	Rabbi Edward Klein	Shad Polier	Hope Stevens
Harry Belafonte	Cheryl Crawford	Nat Hentoff	Hope Lange	Sidney Poitier	George Tabor
Julie Belafonte	Dorothy Dandridge	James Hicks	John Lewis	A. Philip Randolph	Rev. Gardner C.
Dr. Algernon Black	Ossie Davis	Mary Hinkson	Viveca Lindfors	John Raitt	Taylor
Marc Blitztein	Sammy Davis, Jr.	Van Heflin	Carl Murphy	Elmer Rice	Norman Thomas
William Branch	Ruby Dee	Langston Hughes	Don Murray	Jackie Robinson	Kenneth Tynan
Marlon Brando	Dr. Philip Ellliott	Morris Iushewitz	John Murray	Mrs. Eleanor Roosevelt	Charles White
Mrs. Ralph Bunche	Dr. Harry Emerson	Mahalia Jackson	A. J. Muste	Bayard Rustin	Shelley Winters
Diahann Carroll	Fosdick	Mordecai Johnson	Frederick O'Neal	Robert Ryan	Max Youngstein

We in the south who are struggling daily for dignity and freedom warmly endorse this appeal

Rev. Ralph D. Abernathy
(*Montgomery, Ala.*)

Rev. Fred L. Shuttlesworth
(*Birmingham, Ala.*)

Rev. Kelly Miller Smith
(*Nashville, Tenn.*)

Rev. W. A. Dennis
(*Chattanooga, Tenn.*)

Rev. C. K. Steele
(*Tallahassee, Fla.*)

Rev. Matthew D. McCollom
(*Orangeburg, S.C.*)

Rev. William Holmes Borders
(*Atlanta, Ga.*)

Rev. Douglas Moore
(*Durham, N.C.*)

Rev. Wyatt Tee Walker
(*Parkersburg, Va.*)

Rev. Walter L. Hamilton
(*Norfolk, Va.*)

I. S. Levy
(*Columbia, S.C.*)

Rev. Martin Luther King, Sr.
(*Atlanta, Ga.*)

Rev. Henry C. Bunton
(*Memphis, Tenn.*)

Rev. S. S. Seay, Sr.
(*Montgomery, Ala.*)

Rev. Samuel W. Williams
(*Atlanta, Ga.*)

Rev. A. L. Davis
(*New Orleans, La.*)

Mrs. Katie E. Whickham
(*New Orleans, La.*)

Rev. W. H. Hall
(*Hattiesburg, Miss.*)

Rev. J. E. Lowery
(*Mobile, Ala.*)

Rev. T. J. Jemison
(*Baton Rouge, La.*)

Please mail this coupon TODAY!

Committee To Defend Martin Luther King
and
The Struggle For Freedom in The South
312 West 125th Street, New York 27, N.Y.
UNiversity 6-1700

I am enclosing my contribution of $_____ for the work of the Committee.

Name _____
Address _____
City _____ Zone _____ State _____

☐ I want to help   ☐ Please send further information

Please make checks payable to:
Committee to Defend Martin Luther King

COMMITTEE TO DEFEND MARTIN LUTHER KING AND THE STRUGGLE FOR FREEDOM IN THE SOUTH
312 West 125th Street, New York 27, N.Y. UNiversity 6-1700

Chairmen: A. Philip Randolph, Dr. Gardner C. Taylor; *Chairmen of Cultural Division:* Harry Belafonte, Sidney Poitier; *Treasurer:* Nat King Cole; *Executive Director:* Bayard Rustin; *Chairmen of Church Division:* Father George B. Ford, Rev. Harry Emerson Fosdick, Rev. Thomas Kilgore, Jr., Rabbi Edward E. Klein; *Chairman of Labor Division:* Morris Iushewitz per se when they "tend to injure a person labeled by them in his reputation, profession, trade or business, or charge him with an indictable offense, or tend to bring the individual into public contempt." This definition was fairly typical. The *New York Times* challenged the decision, arguing that the libel standard "presumes malice and falsity.... Such a rule of liability works an abridgment of the free press." Its attorneys added, "It is implicit in this Court's decisions that speech which is critical of governmental action may not be repressed upon the ground that it diminishes the reputation of those officers whose conduct it deplores."

MR. JUSTICE BRENNAN delivered the opinion of the Court.

We are required in this case to determine for the first time the extent to which the constitutional protections for speech and press limit a State's power to award damages in a libel action brought by a public official against critics of his official conduct....

Because of the importance of the constitutional issues involved, we granted the separate petitions for certiorari of the individual petitioners and of the Times. We reverse the judgment. We hold that the rule of law applied by the Alabama courts is constitutionally deficient for failure to provide the safeguards for freedom of speech and of the press that are required by the First and Fourteenth Amendments in a libel action brought by a public official against critics of his official conduct. We further hold that under the proper safeguards the evidence presented in this case is constitutionally insufficient to support the judgment for respondent.

We may dispose at the outset of [t]he ... contention ... that the constitutional guarantees of freedom of speech and of the press are inapplicable here, at least so far as the Times is concerned, because the allegedly libelous statements were published as part of a paid, "commercial" advertisement....

The publication here was not a "commercial" advertisement in the sense in which the word was used in Chrestensen. It communicated information, expressed opinion, re-

cited grievances, protested claimed abuses, and sought financial support on behalf of a movement whose existence and objectives are matters of the highest public interest and concern. That the Times was paid for publishing the advertisement is as immaterial in this connection as is the fact that newspapers and books are sold. Any other conclusion would discourage newspapers from carrying "editorial advertisements" of this type, and so might shut off an important outlet for the promulgation of information and ideas by persons who do not themselves have access to publishing facilities—who wish to exercise their freedom of speech even though they are not members of the press. The effect would be to shackle the First Amendment in its attempt to secure "the widest possible dissemination of information from diverse and antagonistic sources." To avoid placing such a handicap upon the freedoms of expression, we hold that if the allegedly libelous statements would otherwise be constitutionally protected from the present judgment, they do not forfeit that protection because they were published in the form of a paid advertisement.

Under Alabama law as applied in this case, a publication is "libelous per se" if the words "tend to injure a person ... in his reputation" or to "bring [him] into public contempt"; the trial court stated that the standard was met if the words are such as to "injure him in his public office, or impute misconduct to him in his office, or want of official integrity, or want of fidelity to a public trust...." The jury must find that the words were published "of and concerning" the plaintiff, but where the plaintiff is a public official his place in the governmental hierarchy is sufficient evidence to support a finding that his reputation has been affected by statements that reflect upon the agency of which he is in charge. Once "libel per se" has been established, the defendant has no defense as to stated facts unless he can persuade the jury that they were true in all their particulars. His privilege of "fair comment" for expressions of opinion depends on the truth of the facts upon which the comment is based. Unless he can discharge the burden of proving truth, general damages are presumed, and may be awarded without proof of pecuniary injury. A showing of actual malice is apparently a prerequisite to recovery of punitive damages, and the defendant may in any event forestall a punitive award by a retraction meeting the statutory requirements. Good motives and belief in truth do not negate an inference of malice, but are relevant only in mitigation of punitive damages if the jury chooses to accord them weight.

The question before us is whether this rule of liability, as applied to an action brought by a public official against critics of his official conduct, abridges the freedom of speech and of the press that is guaranteed by the First and Fourteenth Amendments.

Respondent relies heavily, as did the Alabama courts, on statements of this Court to the effect that the Constitution does not protect libelous publications. Those statements do not foreclose our inquiry here. None of the cases sustained the use of libel laws to impose sanctions upon expression critical of the official conduct of public officials.... In deciding the question now, we are compelled by neither precedent nor policy to give any more weight to the epithet "libel" than we have to other "mere labels" of state law. Like insurrection, contempt, advocacy of unlawful acts, breach of the peace, obscenity, solicitation of legal business, and the various other formulae for the repression of expression that have been challenged in this Court, libel can claim no talismanic immunity from constitutional limitations. It must be measured by standards that satisfy the First Amendment.

The general proposition that freedom of expression upon public questions is secured by the First Amendment has long been settled by our decisions. The constitutional safeguard, we have said, "was fashioned to assure unfettered interchange of ideas for the bringing about of political and social changes desired by the people." The First Amendment, said Judge Learned Hand, "presupposes that right conclusions are more likely to be gathered out of a multitude of tongues, than through any kind of authoritative selection. To many this is, and always will be, folly; but we have staked upon it our all." Mr. Justice Brandeis, in his concurring opinion in Whitney v. California, gave the principle its classic formulation:

"Those who won our independence believed ... that public discussion is a political duty; and that this should be a fundamental principle of the American government. They recognized the risks to which all human institutions are subject. But they knew that order cannot be secured merely through fear of punishment for its infraction; that it is hazardous to discourage thought, hope and imagination; that fear breeds repression; that repression breeds hate; that

hate menaces stable government; that the path of safety lies in the opportunity to discuss freely supposed grievances and proposed remedies; and that the fitting remedy for evil counsels is good ones. Believing in the power of reason as applied through public discussion, they eschewed silence coerced by law—the argument of force in its worst form. Recognizing the occasional tyrannies of governing majorities, they amended the Constitution so that free speech and assembly should be guaranteed."

Thus we consider this case against the background of a profound national commitment to the principle that debate on public issues should be uninhibited, robust, and wide-open, and that it may well include vehement, caustic, and sometimes unpleasantly sharp attacks on government and public officials. The present advertisement, as an expression of grievance and protest on one of the major public issues of our time, would seem clearly to qualify for the constitutional protection. The question is whether it forfeits that protection by the falsity of some of its factual statements and by its alleged defamation of respondent.

Authoritative interpretations of the First Amendment guarantees have consistently refused to recognize an exception for any test of truth—whether administered by judges, juries, or administrative officials—and especially one that puts the burden of proving truth on the speaker. The constitutional protection does not turn upon "the truth, popularity, or social utility of the ideas and beliefs which are offered."... That erroneous statement is inevitable in free debate, and that it must be protected if the freedoms of expression are to have the "breathing space" that they "need ... to survive," was ... recognized by the Court of Appeals for the District of Columbia Circuit in Sweeney v. Patterson....

Injury to official reputation error affords no more warrant for repressing speech that would otherwise be free than does factual error. Where judicial officers are involved, this Court has held that concern for the dignity and reputation of the courts does not justify the punishment as criminal contempt of criticism of the judge or his decision. This is true even though the utterance contains "half-truths" and "misinformation." Such repression can be justified, if at all, only by a clear and present danger of the obstruction of justice. If judges are to be treated as "men of fortitude, able to thrive in a hardy climate," surely the same must be true of other government officials, such as elected city commissioners. Criticism of their official conduct does not lose its constitutional protection merely because it is effective criticism and hence diminishes their official reputations.

If neither factual error nor defamatory content suffices to remove the constitutional shield from criticism of official conduct, the combination of the two elements is no less inadequate. This is the lesson to be drawn from the great controversy over the Sedition Act of 1798, which first crystallized a national awareness of the central meaning of the First Amendment. That statute made it a crime, punishable by a $5,000 fine and five years in prison, "if any person shall write, print, utter or publish ... any false, scandalous and malicious writing or writings against the government of the United States, or either House of the Congress ... or the President ..., with intent to defame ... or to bring them, or either of them, into contempt or disrepute; or to excite against them, or either or any of them, the hatred of the good people of the United States."...

Although the Sedition Act was never tested in this Court, the attack upon its validity has carried the day in the court of history. Fines levied in its prosecution were repaid by Act of Congress on the ground that it was unconstitutional. Calhoun, reporting to the Senate on February 4, 1836, assumed that its invalidity was a matter "which no one now doubts." Jefferson, as President, pardoned those who had been convicted and sentenced under the Act and remitted their fines, stating: "I discharged every person under punishment or prosecution under the sedition law, because I considered, and now consider, that law to be a nullity, as absolute and as palpable as if Congress had ordered us to fall down and worship a golden image." [This view reflects] a broad consensus that the Act, because of the restraint it imposed upon criticism of government and public officials, was inconsistent with the First Amendment.

There is no force in respondent's argument that the constitutional limitations implicit in the history of the Sedition Act apply only to Congress and not to the States. It is true that the First Amendment was originally addressed only to action by the Federal Government, and that Jefferson, for one, while denying the power of Congress "to controul the freedom of the press," recognized such a power in the States. But this distinction was eliminated with the adoption of the Fourteenth Amendment and the application to the States of the First Amendment's restrictions.

What a State may not constitutionally bring about by means of a criminal statute is likewise beyond the reach of its civil law of libel. The fear of damage awards under a rule such as that invoked by the Alabama courts here may be markedly more inhibiting than the fear of prosecution under a criminal statute. Alabama, for example, has a criminal libel law which subjects to prosecution "any person who speaks, writes, or prints of and concerning another any accusation falsely and maliciously importing the commission by such person of a felony, or any other indictable offense involving moral turpitude," and which allows as punishment upon conviction a fine not exceeding $500 and a prison sentence of six months. Presumably a person charged with violation of this statute enjoys ordinary criminal-law safeguards such as the requirements of an indictment and of proof beyond a reasonable doubt. These safeguards are not available to the defendant in a civil action. The judgment awarded in this case—without the need for any proof of actual pecuniary loss—was one thousand times greater than the maximum fine provided by the Alabama criminal statute, and one hundred times greater than that provided by the Sedition Act. And since there is no double-jeopardy limitation applicable to civil lawsuits, this is not the only judgment that may be awarded against petitioners for the same publication. Whether or not a newspaper can survive a succession of such judgments, the pall of fear and timidity imposed upon those who would give voice to public criticism is an atmosphere in which the First Amendment freedoms cannot survive. Plainly the Alabama law of civil libel is "a form of regulation that creates hazards to protected freedoms markedly greater than those that attend reliance upon the criminal law."

The state rule of law is not saved by its allowance of the defense of truth. A defense for erroneous statements honestly made is no less essential here than was the requirement of proof of guilty knowledge which we held indispensable to a valid conviction of a bookseller for possessing obscene writings for sale.... A rule compelling the critic of official conduct to guarantee the truth of all his factual assertions—and to do so on pain of libel judgments virtually unlimited in amount—leads to a comparable "self-censorship." Allowance of the defense of truth, with the burden of proving it on the defendant, does not mean that only false speech will be deterred. Even courts accepting this defense as an adequate safeguard have recognized the difficulties of adducing legal proofs that the alleged libel was true in all its factual particulars. Under such a rule, would-be critics of official conduct may be deterred from voicing their criticism, even though it is believed to be true and even though it is in fact true, because of doubt whether it can be proved in court or fear of the expense of having to do so. They tend to make only statements which "steer far wider of the unlawful zone." The rule thus dampens the vigor and limits the variety of public debate. It is inconsistent with the First and Fourteenth Amendments.

The constitutional guarantees require, we think, a federal rule that prohibits a public official from recovering damages for a defamatory falsehood relating to his official conduct unless he proves that the statement was made with "actual malice"—that is, with knowledge that it was false or with reckless disregard of whether it was false or not....

... [A] privilege for criticism of official conduct is appropriately analogous to the protection accorded a public official when *he* is sued for libel by a private citizen.... The reason for the official privilege is said to be that the threat of damage suits would otherwise "inhibit the fearless, vigorous, and effective administration of policies of government" and "dampen the ardor of all but the most resolute, or the most irresponsible, in the unflinching discharge of their duties." Analogous considerations support the privilege for the citizen-critic of government. It is as much his duty to criticize as it is the official's duty to administer. As Madison said, "the censorial power is in the people over the Government, and not in the Government over the people." It would give public servants an unjustified preference over the public they serve, if critics of official conduct did not have a fair equivalent of the immunity granted to the officials themselves.

We conclude that such a privilege is required by the First and Fourteenth Amendments.

We hold today that the Constitution delimits a State's power to award damages for libel in actions brought by public officials against critics of their official conduct. Since this is such an action, the rule requiring proof of actual malice is applicable. While Alabama law apparently requires proof of actual malice for an award of punitive damages, where general damages are concerned malice is "pre-

sumed." Such a presumption is inconsistent with the federal rule.... Since the trial judge did not instruct the jury to differentiate between general and punitive damages, it may be that the verdict was wholly an award of one or the other. But it is impossible to know, in view of the general verdict returned. Because of this uncertainty, the judgment must be reversed and the case remanded.

Since respondent may seek a new trial, we deem that considerations of effective judicial administration require us to review the evidence in the present record to determine whether it could constitutionally support a judgment for respondent. This Court's duty is not limited to the elaboration of constitutional principles; we must also in proper cases review the evidence to make certain that those principles have been constitutionally applied. This is such a case, particularly since the question is one of alleged trespass across "the line between speech unconditionally guaranteed and speech which may legitimately be regulated." In cases where that line must be drawn, the rule is that we "examine for ourselves the statements in issue and the circumstances under which they were made to see ... whether they are of a character which the principles of the First Amendment, as adopted by the Due Process Clause of the Fourteenth Amendment, protect." We must "make an independent examination of the whole record," so as to assure ourselves that the judgment does not constitute a forbidden intrusion on the field of free expression.

Applying these standards, we consider that the proof presented to show actual malice lacks the convincing clarity which the constitutional standard demands, and hence that it would not constitutionally sustain the judgment for respondent under the proper rule of law. The case of the individual petitioners requires little discussion. Even assuming that they could constitutionally be found to have authorized the use of their names on the advertisement, there was no evidence whatever that they were aware of any erroneous statements or were in any way reckless in that regard. The judgment against them is thus without constitutional support.

As to the Times, we similarly conclude that the facts do not support a finding of actual malice. The statement by the Times' Secretary that ... he thought the advertisement was "substantially correct," affords no constitutional warrant for the Alabama Supreme Court's conclusion that it was a "cavalier ignoring of the falsity of the advertisement from which, the jury could not have but been impressed with the bad faith of The Times, and its maliciousness inferable therefrom." The statement does not indicate malice at the time of the publication; even if the advertisement was not "substantially correct"—although respondent's own proofs tend to show that it was—that opinion was at least a reasonable one, and there was no evidence to impeach the witness' good faith in holding it. The Times' failure to retract upon respondent's demand, although it later retracted upon the demand of Governor Patterson, is likewise not adequate evidence of malice for constitutional purposes. Whether or not a failure to retract may ever constitute such evidence, there are two reasons why it does not here. *First,* the letter written by the Times reflected a reasonable doubt on its part as to whether the advertisement could reasonably be taken to refer to respondent at all. *Second,* it was not a final refusal, since it asked for an explanation on this point—a request that respondent chose to ignore. Nor does the retraction upon the demand of the Governor supply the necessary proof. It may be doubted that a failure to retract which is not itself evidence of malice can retroactively become such by virtue of a retraction subsequently made to another party. But in any event that did not happen here, since the explanation given by the Times' Secretary for the distinction drawn between respondent and the Governor was a reasonable one, the good faith of which was not impeached.

Finally, there is evidence that the Times published the advertisement without checking its accuracy against the news stories in the Times' own files. The mere presence of the stories in the files does not, of course, establish that the Times "knew" the advertisement was false, since the state of mind required for actual malice would have to be brought home to the persons in the Times' organization having responsibility for the publication of the advertisement. With respect to the failure of those persons to make the check, the record shows that they relied upon their knowledge of the good reputation of many of those whose names were listed as sponsors of the advertisement, and upon the letter from A. Philip Randolph, known to them as a responsible individual, certifying that the use of the names was authorized. There was testimony that the persons handling the advertisement saw nothing in it that would render it unacceptable under the Times' policy of rejecting advertisements containing "attacks of a personal character"; their failure to reject it on this ground was not unreasonable. We think the evidence against the Times supports at most a finding of negligence in failing to discover the misstatements, and is constitutionally insufficient to show the recklessness that is required for a finding of actual malice.

We also think the evidence was constitutionally defective in another respect: it was incapable of supporting the jury's finding that the allegedly libelous statements were made "of and concerning" respondent. Respondent relies on the words of the advertisement and the testimony of six witnesses to establish a connection between it and himself.... There was no reference to respondent in the advertisement, either by name or official position. A number of the allegedly libelous statements—the charges that the dining hall was padlocked and that Dr. King's home was bombed, his person assaulted, and a perjury prosecution instituted against him—did not even concern the police; despite the ingenuity of the arguments which would attach this significance to the word "They," it is plain that these statements could not reasonably be read as accusing respondent of personal involvement in the acts in question. The statements upon which respondent principally relies as referring to him are the two allegations that did concern the police or police functions: that "truckloads of police ... ringed the Alabama State College Campus" after the demonstration on the State Capitol steps, and that Dr. King had been "arrested ... seven times." These statements were false only in that the police had been "deployed near" the campus but had not actually "ringed" it and had not gone there in connection with the State Capitol demonstration, and in that Dr. King had been arrested only four times. The ruling that these discrepancies between what was true and what was asserted were sufficient to injure respondent's reputation may itself raise constitutional problems, but we need not consider them here. Although the statements may be taken as referring to the police, they did not on their face make even an oblique reference to respondent as an individual. Support for the asserted reference must, therefore, be sought in the testimony of respondent's witnesses. But none of them suggested any basis for the belief that respondent himself was attacked in the advertisement beyond the bare fact that he was in overall charge of the Police Department and thus bore official responsibility for police conduct; to the extent that some of the witnesses thought respondent to have been charged with ordering or approving the conduct or otherwise being personally involved in it, they based this notion not on any statements in the advertisement, and not on any evidence that he had in fact been so involved, but solely on the unsupported assumption that, because of his official position, he must have been. This reliance on the bare fact of respondent's official position was made explicit by the Supreme Court of Alabama. That court, in holding that the trial court "did not err in overruling the demurrer [of the Times] in the aspect that the libelous matter was not of and concerning the [plaintiff,]" based its ruling on the proposition that:

"We think it common knowledge that the average person knows that municipal agents, such as police and firemen, and others, are under the control and direction of the city governing body, and more particularly under the direction and control of a single commissioner. In measuring the performance or deficiencies of such groups, praise or criticism is usually attached to the official in complete control of the body."

This proposition has disquieting implications for criticism of governmental conduct. For good reason, "no court of last resort in this country has ever held, or even suggested, that prosecutions for libel on government have any place in the American system of jurisprudence." The present proposition would side-step this obstacle by transmuting criticism of government, however impersonal it may seem on its face, into personal criticism, and hence potential libel, of the officials of whom the government is composed. There is no legal alchemy by which a State may thus create the cause of action that would otherwise be denied for a publication which, as respondent himself said of the advertisement, "reflects not only on me but on the other Commissioners and the community." Raising as it does the possibility that a good-faith critic of government will be penalized for his criticism, the proposition relied on by the Alabama courts strikes at the very center of the constitutionally protected area of free expression. We hold that such a proposition may not constitutionally be utilized to establish that an otherwise impersonal attack on governmental operations was a libel of an official responsible for those operations. Since it was relied on exclusively here, and there was no other evidence to connect the statements with respondent, the evidence was constitutionally insufficient to support a finding that the statements referred to respondent.

The judgment of the Supreme Court of Alabama is reversed and the case is remanded to that court for further proceedings not inconsistent with this opinion.

Reversed and remanded.

Many consider Brennan's opinion a tour de force on the subject of libel. By holding the Sedition Act of 1798 unconstitutional, however belatedly, Brennan said that the First Amendment protects seditious libel, that the government cannot criminally punish individuals who speak out, in a true or false manner, against it. But more important was the part of the opinion that dealt with civil actions. The concurrers argued that the press had an absolute and unconditional right to criticize government officials, that states could not permit civil actions in such cases. Brennan and the majority did not go that far, but they radically altered the standards that public officials acting in a public capacity had to meet before they could prove libel and receive damages. Calling previous rules of falsehood and defamation "constitutionally deficient," Brennan asserted that if plaintiffs were public officials, they had to demonstrate that the statement was false, damaging, and "made with 'actual malice'—that is, with knowledge that it was false or with reckless disregard of whether it was false or not." In his view, such an exacting standard—now called the *New York Times* test—was necessary because of a "profound national commitment to the principle that debate on public issues should be uninhibited, robust, and wide-open."

Expanding the New York Times *Test*

Brennan's opinion significantly altered the course of libel law, making it more difficult for public offi-

L. B. Sullivan, second from right, poses with his attorneys after winning his libel suit against the *New York Times*. The Supreme Court overturned the decision in 1964. Justice Brennan's opinion stated that public officials are held to a higher standard than private citizens when proving libel.

cials to bring actions against the media. But the decision had some gaps. First, who constitutes a public official? In note 23 Brennan wrote, "We have no occasion here to determine how far down into lower ranks of government employees the 'public official' designation would extend." Obviously, such an occasion would present itself shortly, and the Court would have to draw some distinctions. How it did so would have significant ramifications because, under the *New York Times* test, only public officials had to prove actual malice; other plaintiffs were bound only to the traditional standards that the statements were false and damaging. Second, how could a public official prove actual malice? What did that term encompass?

In 1967 the Supreme Court decided two cases, *Curtis Publishing Company v. Butts* and *Associated Press v. Walker*, in hopes of clarifying its *New York Times* ruling. At issue in Curtis was an article entitled "The Story of a College Football Fix," published by the *Saturday Evening Post*. The author asserted that Wally Butts, the athletic director of the University of Georgia's sports program, had given Paul Bryant, the football coach at the University of Alabama, "the plays, defensive patterns, and all the significant secrets Georgia's football team possessed." He did so, according to the article, to fix a 1962 game between the two schools. The author claimed he had obtained this information from an Atlanta insurance salesman, who accidentally overheard the conversation between Butts and Bryant. Butts initiated a libel suit against the publishing company, arguing that the article was false and damaging.[21] And, although the Court had yet to hand down the *New York Times* decision, Butts's suit also alleged that actual malice had occurred because the *Saturday Evening Post* "had departed greatly from the standards of good investigation and reporting." The magazine's attorneys "were aware of the progress" of the *New York Times* case, but offered only a defense of truth. A jury awarded Butts $3,060,000, which was later reduced by an appeals court. The *Post* asked for a new trial on *New York Times* grounds—that Butts was a public figure and should have to prove malice. The judge refused, asserting that Butts was not a public official and, even if he were, the magazine had demonstrated a "reckless disregard for the truth."

Associated Press v. Walker concerned a 1962 AP story, an eyewitness account of the riots at the University of Mississippi over the government-ordered admission of James Meredith, a black student. According to the story, retired army general Edwin Walker "took command of the violent crowd and … led a charge against federal marshals," who were in Mississippi to oversee the desegregation process. It also alleged that Walker gave the segregationists "lessons" on the use of tear gas. Walker sued the Associated Press for $2,000,000 in compensatory and punitive damages, arguing that the article was false and damaging. The jury awarded $500,000 in compensation and $300,000 in punishment, but the judge set aside the latter on the ground that Walker, while not a public official, was a public figure—his views on integration were well known and, as such, he had to prove actual malice under the *New York Times* standard.

Writing for the Court, Justice Harlan ruled in favor of Butts's claim and against Walker's. In reaching those conclusions, Harlan used the differences between the two cases to clarify *New York Times.* On one hand, he made it somewhat less burdensome for public officials to demonstrate malice: if the media engaged in "highly unreasonable conduct constituting an extreme departure from the standards of investigation and reporting," they could be held liable for their actions. On the other, the Court expanded the coverage of the *New York Times* test to include public figures. That is, even though Walker and Butts were not officials of the government, they would have to meet the *New York Times* test to win their suits because they were individuals in the public eye. Butts met this burden—he demonstrated that the magazine had abandoned professional standards and exhibited a reckless disregard for the truth. Walker failed to prove such press improprieties.

Adding to the rapidly changing interpretations of press freedoms was another 1967 decision, *Time, Inc. v. Hill.* This case involved not public figures but private individuals who became the victims of false media reports. The dispute began in 1952 when three escaped convicts held the Hill family hostage for nineteen hours. The incident received national press attention and later became the subject of a novel and subsequently a play entitled *The Desperate Hours.* As the story evolved from news-to-novel-to-play it became more fictionalized. The most significant departure from reality concerned the play's description of violence against the Hills. In fact, the convicts had treated the Hills relatively well and no violence whatever took place. *Life Magazine,* owned by Time, Inc., published a pictorial essay on the play's opening, but failed to point out that the play was not an accurate representation of what had occurred. The Hill family successfully sued for invasion of privacy, receiving a judgment of $30,000 on the basis of a New York law that allowed compensation for the victims of stories containing "substantial falsification."

Time appealed this decision, asking the Supreme Court to apply the *New York Times* test. It argued that

---

21. Up to this point, Butts had been a respected figure in coaching ranks and in fact had been negotiating for a coaching position with a professional team. After the *Saturday Evening Post* published the story, he resigned from the University of Georgia for "health" reasons.

the opening of the play was a newsworthy event and the press should be given latitude in covering such matters of public interest. The Hills countered that they were private individuals and that they should only have to show that Time invaded their privacy by publishing false information about them. The Supreme Court, in an opinion written by Justice Brennan, extended the *New York Times* test to press coverage of such matters of public interest. Although the Hills were private individuals, the First Amendment must provide sufficient protection so that the press can responsibly cover newsworthy events without an unreasonable fear of damage awards. Consequently, the Hills would have to prove not only that the story's description of them was false, but also that it was published with knowledge of the falsity or reckless disregard for the truth.

Butts and *Associated Press* helped clarify some aspects of *New York Times,* but they opened a new set of questions concerning public figures. For purposes of libel law, how far does the "public figure" definition stretch? The *Time, Inc. v. Hill* invasion of privacy case further complicated matters. Did the Court totally blur the distinction between public figures and private citizens? What constituted a matter of public interest? In the 1971 case of *Rosenbloom v. Metromedia,* the Court attempted to provide some answers.

At issue in *Rosenbloom* were the actions of a Philadelphia police captain. In an attempt to enforce his city's obscenity laws, the captain purchased magazines from more than twenty city newsstands. Concluding that the material was obscene, he directed officers to arrest the vendors. As police were doing so, they happened upon George Rosenbloom, who was delivering adult magazines to one of the stands. They also arrested him and obtained a warrant to search his home and warehouse. That search resulted in the seizure of a high volume of allegedly obscene matter, which the police captain reported to several radio sta-

tions and newspapers. Station WIP broadcast the following story:

City Cracks Down on Smut Merchants

The Special Investigations Squad raided the home of George Rosenbloom in the 1800 block of Vesta Street this afternoon. Police confiscated 1,000 allegedly obscene books at Rosenbloom's home and arrested him on charges of possession of obscene literature. The Special Investigations Squad also raided a barn in the 20 Hundred block of Welsh Road near Bustleton Avenue and confiscated 3,000 obscene books. Capt. Ferguson says he believes they have hit the supply of a main distributor of obscene material in Philadelphia.

Rosenbloom initiated a libel action against the station, arguing that his books were not obscene, that, in fact, a jury had acquitted him on those charges. WIP offered a defense of truth, but the jury found for Rosenbloom, awarding him $750,000 in damages.

In a 5–3 decision, the Court reversed.[22] Writing for the majority, Justice Brennan altered the primary emphasis of the *New York Times* test: it "derives not so much from whether the plaintiff is a 'public official,' 'public figure,'" or "'private individual' as it derives from the question whether the allegedly defamatory publication concerns a matter of public or general interest." In writing these words, Brennan claimed that the *New York Times* test applied to all stories of public interest regardless of the public status of the individual.

The Court Retrenches

The reaction to *Rosenbloom* was mixed. The media were delighted: it would now be extremely difficult for any individual mentioned in a story of public interest to prove libel. Others were quick to criticize: Justice Marshall, usually an ally of Brennan's, thought the opinion went way too far, that Rosenbloom was "just one of the millions of Americans who live their lives

22. Douglas did not participate.

in obscurity"; others argued that it put a heavy burden on lower court judges to determine what is in the public's interest.

Given the complaints, it comes as no surprise that the Court largely abandoned the *Rosenbloom* framework. While reading *Gertz v. Welch* (1974), consider the following: With what did the Court replace the *Rosenbloom* standard? Did it substantially alter the entire *New York Times* test or just that portion at issue in *Rosenbloom?*

Gertz v. Welch

418 U.S. 323 (1974)
Vote: 5 (Blackmun, Marshall, Powell, Rehnquist, Stewart)
    4 (Brennan, Burger, Douglas, White)
Opinion of the Court: Powell
Concurring opinion: Blackmun
Dissenting opinions: Brennan, Burger, Douglas, White

After a jury had convicted a police officer for murder, the victim's family retained Elmer Gertz, a Chicago attorney, to bring a civil action against the officer. Robert Welch published a story in *American Opinion,* an "outlet for the views of the John Birch Society," that suggested that Gertz was a "Communist-fronter," engaged in a plot to disgrace and frame the police. Gertz sued Welch for libel. He argued that the story was false and damaging to his career.

MR. JUSTICE POWELL delivered the opinion of the Court.

This court has struggled for nearly a decade to define the proper accommodation between the law of defamation and the freedoms of speech and press protected by the First Amendment. With this decision we return to that effort. We granted certiorari to reconsider the extent of a publisher's constitutional privilege against liability for defamation of a private citizen. . . .

The principal issue in this case is whether a newspaper or broadcaster that publishes defamatory falsehoods about

an individual who is neither a public official nor a public figure may claim a constitutional privilege against liability for the injury inflicted by those statements. The Court considered this question on the rather different set of facts presented in Rosenbloom v. Metromedia, Inc. . . .

This Court affirmed the decision below, but no majority could agree on a controlling rationale. The eight Justices who participated in *Rosenbloom* announced their views in five separate opinions, none of which commanded more than three votes. The several statements not only reveal disagreement about the appropriate result in that case, they also reflect divergent traditions of thought about the general problem of reconciling the law of defamation with the First Amendment. One approach has been to extend the *New York Times* test to an expanding variety of situations. Another has been to vary the level of constitutional privilege for defamatory falsehood with the status of the person defamed. And a third view would grant to the press and broadcast media absolute immunity from liability for defamation. . . .

We begin with the common ground. Under the First Amendment there is no such thing as a false idea. However pernicious an opinion may seem, we depend for its correction not on the conscience of judges and juries but on the competition of other ideas. But there is no constitutional value in false statements of fact. Neither the intentional lie nor the careless error materially advances society's interest in "uninhibited, robust, and wide-open" debate on public issues. New York Times Co. v. Sullivan. They belong to that category of utterances which "are no essential part of any exposition of ideas, and are of such slight social value as a step to truth that any benefit that may be derived from them is clearly outweighed by the social interest in order and morality." Chaplinsky v. New Hampshire (1942).

. . . The First Amendment requires that we protect some falsehood in order to protect speech that matters.

The need to avoid self-censorship by the news media is, however, not the only societal value at issue. If it were, this Court would have embraced long ago the view that publishers and broadcasters enjoy an unconditional and indefeasible immunity from liability for defamation. Such a rule would, indeed, obviate the fear that the prospect of civil liability for injurious falsehood might dissuade a timorous press from the effective exercise of First Amendment freedoms. Yet absolute protection for the communications media requires a total sacrifice of the competing value served by the law of defamation.

The legitimate state interest underlying the law of libel is the compensation of individuals for the harm inflicted on them by defamatory falsehood. We would not lightly require the State to abandon this purpose, ... the individual's right to the protection of his own good name....

Some tension necessarily exists between the need for a vigorous and uninhibited press and the legitimate interest in redressing wrongful injury.... In our continuing effort to define the proper accommodation between these competing concerns, we have been especially anxious to assure to the freedoms of speech and press that "breathing space" essential to their fruitful exercise. To that end this Court has extended a measure of strategic protection to defamatory falsehood.

The *New York Times* standard defines the level of constitutional protection appropriate to the context of defamation of a public person. Those who, by reason of the notoriety of their achievements or the vigor and success with which they seek the public's attention, are properly classed as public figures and those who hold governmental office may recover for injury to reputation only on clear and convincing proof that the defamatory falsehood was made with knowledge of its falsity or with reckless disregard for the truth. This standard administers an extremely powerful antidote to the inducement to media self-censorship of the common-law rule of strict liability for libel and slander. And it exacts a correspondingly high price from the victims of defamatory falsehood. Plainly many deserving plaintiffs, including some intentionally subjected to injury, will be unable to surmount the barrier of the *New York Times* test. Despite this substantial abridgment of the state law right to compensation for wrongful hurt to one's reputation, the Court has concluded that the protection of the *New York Times* privilege should be available to publishers and broadcasters of defamatory falsehood concerning public officials and public figures. New York Times Co. v. Sullivan; Curtis Publishing Co. v. Butts. We think that these decisions are correct, but we do not find their holdings justified solely by reference to the interest of the press and broadcast media in immunity from liability. Rather, we believe that the *New York Times* rule states an accommo-

dation between this concern and the limited state interest present in the context of libel actions brought by public persons. For the reasons stated below, we conclude that the state interest in compensating injury to the reputation of private individuals requires that a different rule should obtain with respect to them.

Theoretically, of course, the balance between the needs of the press and the individual's claim to compensation for wrongful injury might be struck on a case-by-case basis. As Mr. Justice Harlan hypothesized, "it might seem, purely as an abstract matter, that the most utilitarian approach would be to scrutinize carefully every jury verdict in every libel case, in order to ascertain whether the final judgment leaves fully protected whatever First Amendment values transcend the legitimate state interest in protecting the particular plaintiff who prevailed." But this approach would lead to unpredictable results and uncertain expectations, and it could render our duty to supervise the lower courts unmanageable. Because an *ad hoc* resolution of the competing interests at stake in each particular case is not feasible, we must lay down broad rules of general application. Such rules necessarily treat alike various cases involving differences as well as similarities. Thus it is often true that not all of the considerations which justify adoption of a given rule will obtain in each particular case decided under its authority.

With that caveat we have no difficulty in distinguishing among defamation plaintiffs. The first remedy of any victim of defamation is self-help—using available opportunities to contradict the lie or correct the error and thereby to minimize its adverse impact on reputation. Public officials and public figures usually enjoy significantly greater access to the channels of effective communication and hence have a more realistic opportunity to counteract false statements than private individuals normally enjoy. Private individuals are therefore more vulnerable to injury, and the state interest in protecting them is correspondingly greater.

More important than the likelihood that private individuals will lack effective opportunities for rebuttal, there is a compelling normative consideration underlying the distinction between public and private defamation plaintiffs. An individual who decides to seek governmental office must accept certain necessary consequences of that involvement in public affairs. He runs the risk of closer public scrutiny than might otherwise be the case. And society's interest in the officers of government is not strictly limited to the formal discharge of official duties....

Those classed as public figures stand in a similar position. Hypothetically, it may be possible for someone to become a public figure through no purposeful action of his own, but the instances of truly involuntary public figures must be exceedingly rare. For the most part those who attain this status have assumed roles of especial prominence in the affairs of society. Some occupy positions of such persuasive power and influence that they are deemed public figures for all purposes. More commonly, those classed as public figures have thrust themselves to the forefront of particular public controversies in order to influence the resolution of the issues involved. In either event, they invite attention and comment.

Even if the foregoing generalities do not obtain in every instance, the communications media are entitled to act on the assumption that public officials and public figures have voluntarily exposed themselves to increased risk of injury from defamatory falsehood concerning them. No such assumption is justified with respect to a private individual. He has not accepted public office or assumed an "influential role in ordering society." He has relinquished no part of his interest in the protection of his own good name, and consequently he has a more compelling call on the courts for redress of injury inflicted by defamatory falsehood. Thus, private individuals are not only more vulnerable to injury than public officials and public figures; they are also more deserving of recovery.

For these reasons we conclude that the States should retain substantial latitude in their efforts to enforce a legal remedy for defamatory falsehood injurious to the reputation of a private individual. The extension of the *New York Times* test proposed by the *Rosenbloom* plurality would abridge this legitimate state interest to a degree that we find unacceptable. And it would occasion the additional difficulty of forcing state and federal judges to decide on an *ad hoc* basis which publications address issues of "general or public interest" and which do not—to determine, in the words of MR. JUSTICE MARSHALL, "what information is relevant to self-government." Rosenbloom v. Metromedia, Inc. We doubt the wisdom of committing this task to the conscience of judges. Nor does the Constitution require us

to draw so thin a line between the drastic alternatives of the *New York Times* privilege and the common law of strict liability for defamatory error. The "public or general interest" test for determining the applicability of the *New York Times* standard to private defamation actions inadequately serves both of the competing values at stake. On the one hand, a private individual whose reputation is injured by defamatory falsehood that does concern an issue of public or general interest has no recourse unless he can meet the rigorous requirements of *New York Times.* This is true despite the factors that distinguish the state interest in compensating private individuals from the analogous interest involved in the context of public persons. On the other hand, a publisher or broadcaster of a defamatory error which a court deems unrelated to an issue of public or general interest may be held liable in damages even if it took every reasonable precaution to ensure the accuracy of its assertions. And liability may far exceed compensation for any actual injury to the plaintiff, for the jury may be permitted to presume damages without proof of loss and even to award punitive damages.

We hold that, so long as they do not impose liability without fault, the States may define for themselves the appropriate standard of liability for a publisher or broadcaster of defamatory falsehood injurious to a private individual. This approach provides a more equitable boundary between the competing concerns involved here. It recognizes the strength of the legitimate state interest in compensating private individuals for wrongful injury to reputation, yet shields the press and broadcast media from the rigors of strict liability for defamation. At least this conclusion obtains where, as here, the substance of the defamatory statement "makes substantial danger to reputation apparent." This phrase places in perspective the conclusion we announce today. Our inquiry would involve considerations somewhat different from those discussed above if a State purported to condition civil liability on a factual misstatement whose content did not warn a reasonably prudent editor or broadcaster of its defamatory potential. Such a case is not now before us, and we intimate no view as to its proper resolution.

Our accommodation of the competing values at stake in defamation suits by private individuals allows the States to impose liability on the publisher or broadcaster of defamatory falsehood on a less demanding showing than that required by *New York Times.* This conclusion is not based on a belief that the considerations which prompted the adoption of the *New York Times* privilege for defamation of public officials and its extension to public figures are wholly inapplicable to the context of private individuals. Rather, we endorse this approach in recognition of the strong and legitimate state interest in compensating private individuals for injury to reputation. But this countervailing state interest extends no further than compensation for actual injury.... [W]e hold that the States may not permit recovery of presumed or punitive damages, at least when liability is not based on a showing of knowledge of falsity or reckless disregard for the truth....

Notwithstanding our refusal to extend the *New York Times* privilege to defamation of private individuals, respondent contends that we should affirm the judgment below on the ground that petitioner is either a public official or a public figure. There is little basis for the former assertion. Several years prior to the present incident, petitioner had served briefly on housing committees appointed by the mayor of Chicago, but at the time of publication he had never held any remunerative governmental position. Respondent admits this but argues that petitioner's appearance at the coroner's inquest rendered him a "de facto public official." Our cases recognized no such concept. Respondent's suggestion would sweep all lawyers under the *New York Times* rule as officers of the court and distort the plain meaning of the "public official" category beyond all recognition. We decline to follow it.

Respondent's characterization of petitioner as a public figure ... may rest on either of two alternative bases. In some instances an individual may achieve such pervasive fame or notoriety that he becomes a public figure for all purposes and in all contexts. More commonly, an individual voluntarily injects himself or is drawn into a particular public controversy and thereby becomes a public figure for a limited range of issues. In either case such persons assume special prominence in the resolution of public questions.

Petitioner has long been active in community and professional affairs. He has served as an officer of local civic groups and of various professional organizations, and he has published several books and articles on legal subjects.

Although petitioner was consequently well known in some circles, he had achieved no general fame or notoriety in the community. None of the prospective jurors called at the trial had ever heard of petitioner prior to this litigation, and respondent offered no proof that this response was atypical of the local population. We would not lightly assume that a citizen's participation in community and professional affairs rendered him a public figure for all purposes. Absent clear evidence of general fame or notoriety in the community, and pervasive involvement in the affairs of society, an individual should not be deemed a public personality for all aspects of his life. It is preferable to reduce the public-figure question to a more meaningful context by looking to the nature and extent of an individual's participation in the particular controversy giving rise to the defamation.

In this context it is plain that petitioner was not a public figure. He played a minimal role at the coroner's inquest, and his participation related solely to his representation of a private client. He took no part in the criminal prosecution of Officer Nuccio. Moreover, he never discussed either the criminal or civil litigation with the press and was never quoted as having done so. He plainly did not thrust himself into the vortex of this public issue, nor did he engage the public's attention in an attempt to influence its outcome. We are persuaded that the trial court did not err in refusing to characterize petitioner as a public figure for the purpose of this litigation.

We therefore conclude that the *New York Times* standard is inapplicable to this case and that the trial court erred in entering judgment for respondent. Because the jury was allowed to impose liability without fault and was permitted to presume damages without proof of injury, a new trial is necessary. We reverse and remand for further proceedings in accordance with this opinion.

It is so ordered.

Reversed and remanded.

Two years later, in *Time, Inc. v. Firestone,* the Court dealt with a similar issue. In 1961 Mary Alice Sullivan married Russell Firestone, heir to the tire fortune. Three years later she filed for separation, and he countered with a plea for a divorce. The trial was a

protracted, well-publicized affair, owing to the notoriety of the Firestones and the details of their relationship. In granting the divorce, the trial judge
wrote:

According to certain testimony in behalf of the defendant,
extramarital escapades of the plaintiff were bizarre and of
an amatory nature which would have made Dr. Freud's hair
curl. Other testimony, in plaintiff's behalf, would indicate
that defendant was guilty of bounding from one bed partner to another with the erotic zest of a satyr. The court is
inclined to discount much of this testimony as unreliable.
Nevertheless, it is the conclusion and finding of the court
that neither party is domesticated, within the meaning of
that term as used by the Supreme Court of Florida.…

In the present case, it is abundantly clear from the evidence of marital discord that neither of the parties has
shown the least susceptibility to domestication, and that
the marriage should be dissolved.

Then *Time* magazine ran the following story in its
"Milestones" section:

DIVORCED. By Russell A. Firestone Jr., 41, heir to the tire
fortune: Mary Alice Sullivan Firestone, 32, his third wife; a
onetime Palm Beach schoolteacher; on grounds of extreme
cruelty and adultery; after six years of marriage, one son; in
West Palm Beach, Fla. The 17-month intermittent trial produced enough testimony of extramarital adventures on both
sides, said the judge, "to make Dr. Freud's hair curl."

Because the magazine reported as true material the
judge explicitly discounted as unreliable, Ms. Firestone
requested a printed retraction. When *Time* refused,
she sued on the ground that the story was "false, malicious, and defamatory." *Time* argued that she was a
public figure and, therefore, had to prove "actual
malice."

Relying on its ruling in *Gertz,* the Court disagreed.
As it suggested,

[Firestone] did not assume any role of especial prominence
in the affairs of society, other than perhaps Palm Beach society, and did not thrust herself to the forefront of any particular public controversy in order to influence the resolution of the issues involved in it.

As we can see, the Court excised *Rosenbloom* to
the point of virtually overruling it. Under *Gertz*
and *Firestone* the focus moved back to the individual's status and away from the nature of the story
or event. In the eyes of the majority, both *Gertz*
and *Firestone* were essentially private figures who
came into public view only because of the defamation itself. Under these circumstances, the *New York
Times* test is not applicable; in other words, private
citizens need not prove actual malice to win a libel
case.

Why did the majority reject the *Rosenbloom* approach? For one thing, it led to a situation in which
trial court judges had to determine "on an ad hoc basis
which publication addresses issues of 'general or
public interest' and which do not." Further, the Court
reasoned that while public figures and officials often
have access to the media, which would enable them to
repudiate articles, private citizens do not enjoy such a
privilege, and, therefore, they deserve more legal
leeway than those in the public eye.

Have *Gertz* and *Firestone* made it easier for plaintiffs
to prove libel? Certainly they eased the burden carried
by private citizens, but, because the *New York Times*
test remains, it can be quite difficult for public officials
and figures to meet the legal standards. Some have
gone even further, suggesting that the *Times* test
makes it virtually impossible for public figures to win
libel judgments against the press, even when stories
contain falsehoods.

Libel in the 1980s and Beyond

Court treatment of claims raised in *Gertz* and *Firestone* led many commentators to suggest that it would
further narrow the scope of *New York Times.* Indeed,
when the justices agreed to hear arguments in *Hustler
Magazine v. Falwell,* some looked for a decision that
would run counter to, if not overrule, *New York Times.*
Did the Court do so?

Hustler Magazine v. Falwell

485 U.S. 46 (1988)

Vote: 8 (Blackmun, Brennan, Marshall, O'Connor,
Rehnquist, Scalia, Stevens, White)

0

Opinion of the Court: Rehnquist
Concurring opinion: White
Not participating: Kennedy

In the March 1984 issue of *Hustler* magazine publisher Larry Flynt printed a parody of an advertisement for Campari Liqueur. The advertisement mimicked a Campari promotional campaign based on interviews with various celebrities in which they described their "first time." While these interviews were laced with sexual double entendres, it became clear by the end of the ads that the celebrities were actually referring to the first time they tasted Campari Liqueur.

The *Hustler* magazine advertisement used the same format and layout as the real Campari ads. It was entitled, "Jerry Falwell talks about his first time." Falwell was a nationally prominent Protestant minister, a leading political conservative, and head of the now defunct Moral Majority organization. In the interview portion of the advertisement, Falwell discussed his "first time"—an incestuous sexual encounter with his mother in an outhouse while both were intoxicated from drinking Campari. The advertisement portrayed Falwell as drunk, immoral, and hypocritical. At the bottom of the ad the following words appeared in small print: "Ad parody—not to be taken seriously." The magazine's table of contents listed the item as "Fiction: Ad and Personality Parody."

Shortly after the issue was available for public purchase, Falwell sued the magazine and its publisher for libel, invasion of privacy, and intentional infliction of emotional distress. The trial judge dismissed the privacy claim before sending the case to the jury. The jury decided in favor of the magazine on the libel

issue, concluding that the advertisement could not reasonably be understood as describing actual facts about Falwell or actual events in which he participated. However, the jury awarded Falwell $150,000 on the claim that the publisher of *Hustler* intentionally inflicted emotional distress.

At the Supreme Court level, there was no question as to whether Falwell was a public figure—he clearly was and, as such, had to prove malicious intent. Rather, the issue was whether Falwell could even bring a suit against a cartoon that did not purport to be factually accurate.

CHIEF JUSTICE REHNQUIST delivered the opinion of the Court.

Petitioner Hustler Magazine, Inc., is a magazine of nationwide circulation. Respondent Jerry Falwell, a nationally known minister who has been active as a commentator on politics and public affairs, sued petitioner and its publisher, petitioner Larry Flynt, to recover damages for invasion of privacy, libel, and intentional infliction of emotional distress. The District Court directed a verdict against respondent on the privacy claim, and submitted the other two claims to a jury. The jury found for petitioners on the defamation claim, but found for respondent on the claim for intentional infliction of emotional distress and awarded damages. We now consider whether this award is consistent with the First and Fourteenth Amendments of the United States Constitution....

This case presents us with a novel question involving First Amendment limitations upon a State's authority to protect its citizens from the intentional infliction of emotional distress. We must decide whether a public figure may recover damages for emotional harm caused by the publication of an ad parody offensive to him, and doubtless gross and repugnant in the eyes of most. Respondent would have us find that a State's interest in protecting public figures from emotional distress is sufficient to deny First Amendment protection to speech that is patently offensive and is intended to inflict emotional injury, even when that speech could not reasonably have been interpreted as stating actual facts about the public figure involved. This we decline to do.

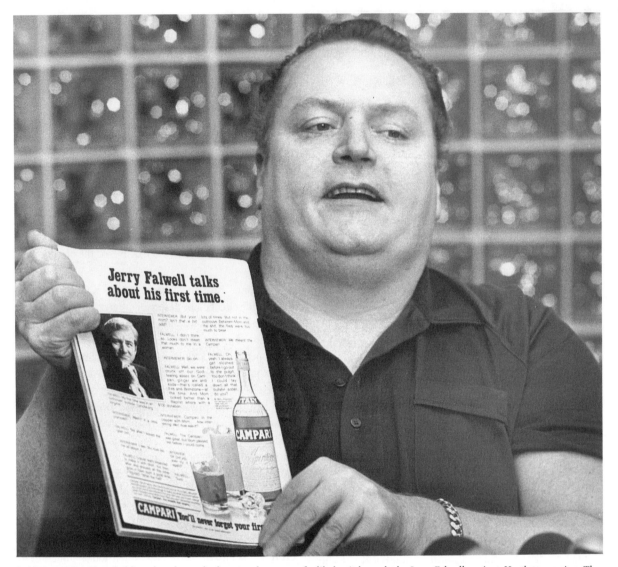

Publisher Larry Flynt holding the ad parody that was the cause of a libel suit brought by Jerry Falwell against *Hustler* magazine. The Supreme Court ruled in 1988 that Falwell was not entitled to damages because parody is a protected form of speech.

At the heart of the First Amendment is the recognition of the fundamental importance of the free flow of ideas and opinions on matters of public interest and concern.... We have therefore been particularly vigilant to ensure that individual expressions of ideas remain free from governmentally imposed sanctions. The First Amendment recognizes no such thing as a "false" idea....

The sort of robust political debate encouraged by the First Amendment is bound to produce speech that is critical of those who hold public office or those public figures who are "intimately involved in the resolution of important public questions or, by reason of their fame, shape events in areas of concern to society at large." Such criticism, inevitably, will not always be reasoned or moderate; public figures as well as public officials will be subject to "vehement, caustic, and sometimes unpleasantly sharp attacks.". . .

Of course, this does not mean that any speech about a public figure is immune from sanction in the form of damages. Since *New York Times v. Sullivan*, we have consistently ruled that a public figure may hold a speaker liable for the damage to reputation caused by publication of a defamatory falsehood, but only if the statement was made "with knowledge that it was false or with reckless disregard of whether it was false or not." False statements of fact are particularly valueless; they interfere with the truth-seeking function of the marketplace of ideas, and they cause damage to an individual's reputation that cannot easily be repaired by counterspeech, however persuasive or effective. But even though falsehoods have little value in and of themselves, they are "nevertheless inevitable in free debate," and a rule that would impose strict liability on a publisher for false factual assertions would have an undoubted "chilling" effect on speech relating to public figures that does have constitutional value. "Freedoms of expression require 'breathing space.'" This breathing space is provided by a constitutional rule that allows public figures to recover for libel or defamation only when they can prove *both* that the statement was false and that the statement was made with the requisite level of culpability.

Respondent argues, however, that a different standard should apply in this case because here the State seeks to prevent not reputational damage, but the severe emotional distress suffered by the person who is the subject of an offensive publication. In respondent's view, and in the view of the Court of Appeals, so long as the utterance was intended to inflict emotional distress, was outrageous, and did in fact inflict serious emotional distress, it is of no constitutional import whether the statement was a fact or an opinion, or whether it was true or false. It is the intent to cause injury that is the gravamen of the tort, and the State's interest in preventing emotional harm simply outweighs whatever interest a speaker may have in speech of this type.

Generally speaking the law does not regard the intent to inflict emotional distress as one which should receive much solicitude, and it is quite understandable that most if not all jurisdictions have chosen to make it civilly culpable where the conduct in question is sufficiently "outrageous." But in the world of debate about public affairs, many

things done with motives that are less than admirable are protected by the First Amendment. In *Garrison v. Louisiana* (1964) we held that even when a speaker or writer is motivated by hatred or ill-will his expression was protected by the First Amendment:

"Debate on public issues will not be uninhibited if the speaker must run the risk that it will be proved in court that he spoke out of hatred; even if he did speak out of hatred, utterances honestly believed contribute to the free interchange of ideas and the ascertainment of truth."

Thus while such a bad motive may be deemed controlling for purposes of tort liability in other areas of the law, we think the First Amendment prohibits such a result in the area of public debate about public figures.

Were we to hold otherwise, there can be little doubt that political cartoonists and satirists would be subjected to damages awards without any showing that their work falsely defamed its subject. Webster's defines a caricature as "the deliberately distorted picturing or imitating of a person, literary style, etc. by exaggerating features or mannerisms for satirical effect." The appeal of the political cartoon or caricature is often based on exploration of unfortunate physical traits or politically embarrassing events—an exploration often calculated to injure the feelings of the subject of the portrayal. The art of the cartoonist is often not reasoned or evenhanded, but slashing and one-sided. One cartoonist expressed the nature of the art in these words:

"The political cartoon is a weapon of attack, of scorn and ridicule and satire; it is least effective when it tries to pat some politician on the back. It is usually as welcome as a bee sting and is always controversial in some quarters."

Several famous examples of this type of intentionally injurious speech were drawn by Thomas Nast, probably the greatest American cartoonist to date, who was associated for many years during the post–Civil War era with Harper's Weekly. In the pages of that publication Nast conducted a graphic vendetta against William M. "Boss" Tweed and his corrupt associates in New York City's "Tweed Ring." It has been described by one historian of the subject as "a sustained attack which in its passion and effectiveness stands alone in the history of American graphic art." Another writer explains that the success of the Nast cartoon was

Thomas Nast's 1871 cartoon depicting "Boss" Tweed and his cronies was typical of the artist's hardhitting depictions of public figures. In *Hustler Magazine v. Falwell*, Chief Justice Rehnquist refers directly to Nast's work as well as to several other examples of satirical political cartoons and caricatures.

achieved "because of the emotional impact of its presentation. It continuously goes beyond the bounds of good taste and conventional manners."

Despite their sometimes caustic nature, from the early cartoon portraying George Washington as an ass down to the present day, graphic depictions and satirical cartoons have played a prominent role in public and political debate. Nast's castigation of the Tweed Ring, Walt McDougall's characterization of presidential candidate James G. Blaine's banquet with the millionaires at Delmonico's as "The Royal Feast of Belshazzar," and numerous other efforts have un-

doubtedly had an effect on the course and outcome of contemporaneous debate. Lincoln's tall, gangling posture, Teddy Roosevelt's glasses and teeth, and Franklin D. Roosevelt's jutting jaw and cigarette holder have been memorialized by political cartoons with an effect that could not have been obtained by the photographer or the portrait artist. From the viewpoint of history it is clear that our political discourse would have been considerably poorer without them.

Respondent contends, however, that the caricature in question here was so "outrageous" as to distinguish it from more traditional political cartoons. There is no doubt that the caricature of respondent and his mother published in Hustler is at best a distant cousin of the political cartoons described above, and a rather poor relation at that. If it were possible by laying down a principled standard to separate the one from the other, public discourse would probably suffer little or no harm. But we doubt that there is any such standard, and we are quite sure that the pejorative description "outrageous" does not supply one. "Outrageousness" in the area of political and social discourse has an inherent subjectiveness about it which would allow a jury to impose liability on the basis of the jurors' tastes or views, or perhaps on the basis of their dislike of a particular expression. An "outrageousness" standard thus runs afoul of our longstanding refusal to allow damages to be awarded because the speech in question may have an adverse emotional impact on the audience....

Admittedly ... First Amendment principles, like other principles, are subject to limitations. We recognized that speech that is "'vulgar,' 'offensive,' and 'shocking'" is "not entitled to absolute constitutional protection under all circumstances." In *Chaplinsky v. New Hampshire* (1942), we held that a state could lawfully punish an individual for the use of insulting "'fighting' words—those which by their very utterance inflict injury or tend to incite an immediate breach of the peace." These limitations are but recognition ... that this Court has "long recognized that not all speech is of equal First Amendment importance." But the sort of expression involved in this case does not seem to us to be governed by any exception to the general First Amendment principles stated above.

We conclude that public figures and public officials may not recover for the tort of intentional infliction of emotional distress by reason of publications such as the one here at issue without showing in addition that the publication contains a false statement of fact which was made with "actual malice," *i.e.*, with knowledge that the statement was false or with reckless disregard as to whether or not it was true. This is not merely a "blind application" of the *New York Times* standard; it reflects our considered judgment that such a standard is necessary to give adequate "breathing space" to the freedoms protected by the First Amendment.

Here it is clear that respondent Falwell is a "public figure" for purposes of First Amendment law. The jury found against respondent on his libel claim when it decided that the Hustler ad parody could not "reasonably be understood as describing actual facts about [respondent] or actual events in which [he] participated." The Court of Appeals interpreted the jury's finding to be that the ad parody "was not reasonably believable," and in accordance with our custom we accept this finding. Respondent is thus relegated to his claim for damages awarded by the jury for the intentional infliction of emotional distress by "outrageous" conduct. But for reasons heretofore stated this claim cannot, consistently with the First Amendment, form a basis for the award of damages when the conduct in question is the publication of a caricature such as the ad parody involved here. The judgment of the Court of Appeals is accordingly

Reversed.

The opinion surprised some Court observers; after all, it was written by Chief Justice Rehnquist, who is not particularly well known for supporting free press claims, and it was unanimous, a rarity in libel law. The media applauded the opinion, while Falwell fumed that "the Supreme Court has given the green light to Larry Flynt and his ilk to print what they wish about any public figure at any time with no fear of reprisal."[23]

The *Hustler Magazine* decision continued the trend set by the Court in *New York Times* to extend First Amendment protections to the press when it covers public officials and public figures. To sue successfully for damages, persons of such notoriety must prove

actual malice as well as falsity. But what kinds of actions on the part of the press might qualify as proof of reckless disregard for the truth? How much leeway should the press be given in the interpretation and presentation of factual material? In *Masson v. New Yorker Magazine, Inc.* (1991) the justices faced these questions. In this particular dispute, does the intentional distortion of quoted material establish actual malice?

Masson v. New Yorker Magazine, Inc.

501 U.S. 496 (1991)
*Vote: 7 (Blackmun, Kennedy, Marshall, O'Connor,
            Rehnquist, Souter, Stevens)
        2 (Scalia, White)*
Opinion of the Court: Kennedy
Opinion concurring in part and dissenting in part: White

In 1980 Jeffrey Masson, a prominent psychoanalyst, was appointed Projects Director of the Sigmund Freud Archives outside London. During his short tenure in that position, Masson became disillusioned with Freudian psychology. In 1981 he delivered a lecture to the Western New England Psychoanalytical Society in New Haven, Connecticut, in which he advanced his own theories of Freud. Soon after, the board of directors at the archives dismissed him. In 1982 Janet Malcolm, a contributor to the *New Yorker* magazine, contacted Masson regarding the possibility of an article about his relationship with the archives, and he agreed to be interviewed. The two engaged in a series of discussions both in person and by telephone. Most, but not all, of the interview sessions were tape recorded by Malcolm. As a result of the interviews and other research, Malcolm wrote a long article that was published in two parts by the *New Yorker* in December 1983. The material subsequently appeared in book form published by Alfred A. Knopf.

Malcolm's journalist style includes heavy usage of long block quotations. Prior to the article's publication, a researcher for the magazine telephoned Masson to confirm the accuracy of the quotations to be printed. Masson expressed alarm about a number of errors. He claimed that he demanded to review quoted material prior to publication, but that claim was disputed by the magazine. Some of the quoted material dealt with Masson's evaluation of his own ability, his ethnic origins, his sexual activities, and his relationships with others at the archives.

Malcolm's article received a great deal of attention and critical praise. It was devastatingly critical of Masson. A reviewer for the *Boston Globe* described it this way:

Masson the promising psychoanalytic scholar emerges gradually, as a grandiose egotist—mean-spirited, self-serving, full of braggadocio, impossibly arrogant and, in the end, a self-destructive fool. But it is not Janet Malcolm who calls him such: his own words reveal this psychological profile.

Masson brought a libel suit against the *New Yorker*, Malcolm, and Knopf in federal district court in California. He based his case on quotations attributed to him that he claimed were fabrications. During pretrial discovery the printed quotations were compared to the more than forty hours of taped interviews. In a number of instances the quotations were substantially correct; however, in at least five cases it appeared that the long quotations published in the magazine had little or no relation to the taped conversations, although they dealt with some subjects the two had discussed. Malcolm explained that not all of the interviews were taped and that some of the quotations were based on her memory from the nontaped sessions.

The parties agreed that Masson was a public figure, requiring him to show that the falsehoods contained in the article were printed with actual malice. The trial court entered a summary judgment (a ruling without a full trial) for the magazine, finding that the alleged fabricated quotations were either substantially true or one of a number of rational interpretations from the conversations that took place during the

interview. The court of appeals affirmed. The majority generally assumed that many of the contested quotations were altered deliberately by Malcolm, but that actual malice had not been proven. A dissenting appeals court judge agreed with Masson's contention that an intentional or reckless alteration in quoted material was proof of malice. Masson appealed, arguing that the distorted quotations provided sufficient evidence to justify a full jury trial on his suit.

JUSTICE KENNEDY delivered the opinion of the Court.

In this libel case, a public figure claims he was defamed by an author who, with full knowledge of the inaccuracy, used quotation marks to attribute to him comments he had not made. The First Amendment protects authors and journalists who write about public figures by requiring a plaintiff to prove that the defamatory statements were made with what we have called "actual malice," a term of art denoting deliberate or reckless falsification. We consider in this opinion whether the attributed quotations had the degree of falsity required to prove this state of mind, so that the public figure can defeat a motion for summary judgment and proceed to a trial on the merits of the defamation claim....

Under California law, "[l]ibel is a false and unprivileged publication by writing ... which exposes any person to hatred, contempt, ridicule, or obloquy, or which causes him to be shunned or avoided, or which has a tendency to injure him in his occupation." False attribution of statements to a person may constitute libel, if the falsity exposes that person to an injury comprehended by the statute. It matters not under California law that petitioner alleges only part of the work at issue to be false. "[T]he test of libel is not quantitative; a single sentence may be the basis for an action in libel even though buried in a much longer text," though the California courts recognize that "[w]hile a drop of poison may be lethal, weaker poisons are sometimes diluted to the point of impotency."

The First Amendment limits California's libel law in various respects. When, as here, the plaintiff is a public figure, he cannot recover unless he proves by clear and convincing evidence that the defendant published the defamatory statement with actual malice, *i.e.*, with "knowledge that it was false or with reckless disregard of whether it was false or not." *New York Times Co. v. Sullivan* (1964). Mere negligence does not suffice. Rather, the plaintiff must demonstrate that the author "in fact entertained serious doubts as to the truth of his publication," or acted with a "high degree of awareness of ... probable falsity."

Actual malice under the *New York Times* standard should not be confused with the concept of malice as an evil intent or a motive arising from spite or ill will. We have used the term actual malice as a shorthand to describe the First Amendment protections for speech injurious to reputation and we continue to do so here. But the term can confuse as well as enlighten. In this respect, the phrase may be an unfortunate one. In place of the term actual malice, it is better practice that jury instructions refer to publication of a statement with knowledge of falsity or reckless disregard as to truth or falsity. This definitional principle must be remembered in the case before us.

In general, quotation marks around a passage indicate to the reader that the passage reproduces the speaker's words verbatim. They inform the reader that he or she is reading the statement of the speaker, not a paraphrase or other indirect interpretation by an author. By providing this information, quotations add authority to the statement and credibility to the author's work. Quotations allow the reader to form his or her own conclusions, and to assess the conclusions of the author, instead of relying entirely upon the author's characterization of her subject.

A fabricated quotation may injure reputation in at least two senses, either giving rise to a conceivable claim of defamation. First, the quotation might injure because it attributes an untrue factual assertion to the speaker. An example would be a fabricated quotation of a public official admitting he had been convicted of a serious crime when in fact he had not.

Second, regardless of the truth or falsity of the factual matters asserted within the quoted statement, the attribution may result in injury to reputation because the manner of expression or even the fact that the statement was made indicates a negative personal trait or an attitude the speaker does not hold. John Lennon once was quoted as saying of the Beatles, "We're more popular than Jesus Christ now." Supposing the quotation had been a fabrication, it appears California law could permit recovery for defamation because, even without regard to the truth of the underlying assertion, false attribution of the statement could have injured his reputation. Here, in like manner, one need not determine whether petitioner is or is not the greatest analyst who ever lived in order to determine that it might have injured his reputation to be reported as having so proclaimed.

A self-condemnatory quotation may carry more force than criticism by another. It is against self-interest to admit one's own criminal liability, arrogance, or lack of integrity, and so all the more easy to credit when it happens. This principle underlies the elemental rule of evidence which permits the introduction of admissions, despite their hearsay character, because we assume "that persons do not make statements which are damaging to themselves unless satisfied for good reason that they are true."

Of course, quotations do not always convey that the speaker actually said or wrote the quoted material. . . .

The work at issue here, however, as with much journalistic writing, provides the reader no clue that the quotations are being used as a rhetorical device or to paraphrase the speaker's actual statements. To the contrary, the work purports to be nonfiction, the result of numerous interviews. At least a trier of fact could so conclude. The work contains lengthy quotations attributed to petitioner, and neither Malcolm nor her publishers indicate to the reader that the quotations are anything but the reproduction of actual conversations. Further, the work was published in The New Yorker, a magazine which at the relevant time seemed to enjoy a reputation for scrupulous factual accuracy. These factors would, or at least could, lead a reader to take the quotations at face value. A defendant may be able to argue to the jury that quotations should be viewed by the reader as nonliteral or reconstructions, but we conclude that a trier of fact in this case could find that the reasonable reader would understand the quotations to be nearly verbatim reports of statements made by the subject.

The constitutional question we must consider here is whether, in the framework of a summary judgment motion, the evidence suffices to show that respondents acted with the requisite knowledge of falsity or reckless disregard as to truth or falsity. This inquiry in turn requires us to consider the concept of falsity; for we cannot discuss the standards for knowledge or reckless disregard without some understanding of the acts required for liability. We must consider whether the requisite falsity inheres in the attribution of words to the petitioner which he did not speak.

In some sense, any alteration of a verbatim quotation is false. But writers and reporters by necessity alter what people say, at the very least to eliminate grammatical and syntactical infelicities. If every alteration constituted the falsity required to prove actual malice, the practice of journalism, which the First Amendment standard is designed to protect, would require a radical change, one inconsistent with our precedents and First Amendment principles. Petitioner concedes this absolute definition of falsity in the quotation context is too stringent, and acknowledges that "minor changes to correct for grammar or syntax" do not amount to falsity for purposes of proving actual malice. We agree, and must determine what, in addition to this technical falsity, proves falsity for purposes of the actual malice inquiry.

Petitioner argues that, excepting correction of grammar or syntax, publication of a quotation with knowledge that it does not contain the words the public figure used demonstrates actual malice. The author will have published the quotation with knowledge of falsity, and no more need be shown. Petitioner suggests that by invoking more forgiving standards the Court of Appeals would permit and encourage the publication of falsehoods. Petitioner believes that the intentional manufacture of quotations does not "represen[t] the sort of inaccuracy that is commonplace in the forum of robust debate to which the *New York Times* rule applies," and that protection of deliberate falsehoods would hinder the First Amendment values of robust and well-informed public debate by reducing the reliability of information available to the public.

We reject the idea that any alteration beyond correction of grammar or syntax by itself proves falsity in the sense relevant to determining actual malice under the First Amendment. An interviewer who writes from notes often will engage in the task of attempting a reconstruction of the speaker's statement. That author would, we may assume, act with knowledge that at times she has attributed to her subject words other than those actually used. Under petitioner's proposed standard, an author in this situation would lack First Amendment protection if she reported as quotations the substance of a subject's derogatory statements about himself.

Even if a journalist has tape recorded the spoken statement of a public figure, the full and exact statement will be reported in only rare circumstances. The existence of both a speaker and a reporter; the translation between two media, speech and the printed word; the addition of punctuation; and the practical necessity to edit and make intelligible a speaker's perhaps rambling comments, all make it misleading to suggest that a quotation will be reconstructed with complete accuracy. The use or absence of punctuation may distort a speaker's meaning, for example, where that meaning turns upon a speaker's emphasis of a particular word. In other cases, if a speaker makes an obvious misstatement, for example by unconscious substitution of one name for another, a journalist might alter the speaker's words but preserve his intended meaning. And conversely, an exact quotation out of context can distort meaning, although the speaker did use each reported word.

In all events, technical distinctions between correcting grammar and syntax and some greater level of alteration do not appear workable, for we can think of no method by which courts or juries would draw the line between cleaning up and other changes, except by reference to the meaning a statement conveys to a reasonable reader. To attempt narrow distinctions of this type would be an unnecessary departure from First Amendment principles of general applicability, and, just as important, a departure from the underlying purposes of the tort of libel as understood since the latter half of the 16th century.... If an author alters a speaker's words but effects no material change in meaning, including any meaning conveyed by the manner or fact of expression, the speaker suffers no injury to reputation that is compensable as a defamation.

These essential principles of defamation law accommodate the special case of inaccurate quotations without the necessity for a discrete body of jurisprudence directed to this subject alone. Last Term, in *Milkovich v. Lorain Journal Co.*, we refused "to create a wholesale defamation exemption for anything that might be labeled 'opinion.'" We recognized that "expressions of 'opinion' may often imply an assertion of objective fact." We allowed the defamation action to go forward in that case, holding that a reasonable trier of fact could find that the so-called expressions of opinion could be interpreted as including false assertions as to factual matters. So too in the case before us, we reject any special test of falsity for quotations, including one which would draw the line at correction of grammar or syntax. We conclude, rather, that the exceptions suggested by petitioner for grammatical or syntactical corrections serve to illuminate a broader principle....

We conclude that a deliberate alteration of the words uttered by a plaintiff does not equate with knowledge of falsity for purposes of *New York Times Co. v. Sullivan* and *Gertz v. Robert Welch, Inc.* unless the alteration results in a material change in the meaning conveyed by the statement. The use of quotations to attribute words not in fact spoken bears in a most important way on that inquiry, but it is not dispositive in every case.

Deliberate or reckless falsification that comprises actual malice turns upon words and punctuation only because words and punctuation express meaning. Meaning is the life of language. And, for the reasons we have given, quotations may be a devastating instrument for conveying false meaning. In the case under consideration, readers of In the Freud Archives may have found Malcolm's portrait of petitioner especially damning because so much of it appeared to be a self-portrait, told by petitioner in his own words. And if the alterations of petitioner's words gave a different meaning to the statements, bearing upon their defamatory character, then the device of quotations might well be critical in finding the words actionable.

The Court of Appeals applied a test of substantial truth which, in exposition if not in application, comports with much of the above discussion. The Court of Appeals, however, went one step beyond protection of quotations that convey the meaning of a speaker's statement with substantial accuracy and concluded that an altered quotation is protected so long as it is a "rational interpretation" of an actual statement, drawing this standard from our decisions in *Time, Inc. v. Pape* (1971) and *Bose Corp. v. Consumers Union of United States, Inc.* (1984). Application of our protection for rational interpretation in this context finds no support in general principles of defamation law or in our First Amendment jurisprudence. Neither *Time, Inc. v. Pape,* nor *Bose Corp.,* involved the fabrication of quotations, or any analogous claim, and because many of the quotations at issue might reasonably be construed to state or imply factual assertions that are both false and defamatory, we cannot accept the reasoning of the Court of Appeals on this point....

The protection for rational interpretation serves First Amendment principles by allowing an author the interpretive license that is necessary when relying upon ambiguous sources. Where, however, a writer uses a quotation, and where a reasonable reader would conclude that the quotation purports to be a verbatim repetition of a statement by the speaker, the quotation marks indicate that the author is not involved in an interpretation of the speaker's ambiguous statement, but attempting to convey what the speaker said. This orthodox use of a quotation is the quintessential "direct account of events that speak for themselves." *Time, Inc. v. Pape.* More accurately, the quotation allows the subject to speak for himself.

The significance of the quotations at issue, absent any qualification, is to inform us that we are reading the statement of petitioner, not Malcolm's rational interpretation of what petitioner has said or thought. Were we to assess quotations under a rational interpretation standard, we would give journalists the freedom to place statements in their subjects' mouths without fear of liability. By eliminating any method of distinguishing between the statements of the subject and the interpretation of the author, we would diminish to a great degree the trustworthiness of the printed word, and eliminate the real meaning of quotations. Not only public figures but the press doubtless would suffer under such a rule. Newsworthy figures might become more wary of journalists, knowing that any comment could be transmuted and attributed to the subject, so long as some bounds of rational interpretation were not exceeded. We would ill serve the values of the First Amendment if we were to grant near absolute, constitutional protection for such a practice. We doubt the suggestion that as a general rule readers will assume that direct quotations are but a rational interpretation of the speaker's words, and we decline to adopt any such presumption in determining the permissible interpretations of the quotations in question here.

We apply these principles to the case before us. On summary judgment, we must draw all justifiable inferences in favor of the nonmoving party, including questions of credibility and of the weight to be accorded particular evidence. So we must assume, except where otherwise evidenced by the transcripts of the tape recordings, that petitioner is correct in denying that he made the statements attributed to him by Malcolm, and that Malcolm reported with knowledge or reckless disregard of the differences between what petitioner said and what was quoted.

Respondents argue that, in determining whether petitioner has shown sufficient falsification to survive summary judgment, we should consider not only the tape-recorded statements but also Malcolm's typewritten notes. We must decline that suggestion. To begin with, petitioner affirms in an affidavit that he did not make the complained of statements. The record contains substantial additional evidence, moreover, evidence which, in a light most favorable to petitioner, would support a jury determination under a clear and convincing standard that Malcolm deliberately or recklessly altered the quotations.

First, many of the challenged passages resemble quotations that appear on the tapes, except for the addition or alteration of certain phrases, giving rise to a reasonable inference that the statements have been altered. Second, Malcolm had the tapes in her possession and was not working under a tight deadline. Unlike a case involving hot news, Malcolm cannot complain that she lacked the practical ability to compare the tapes with her work in progress. Third, Malcolm represented to the editor-in-chief of The New Yorker that all the quotations were from the tape recordings. Fourth, Malcolm's explanations of the time and place of unrecorded conversations during which petitioner allegedly made some of the quoted statements have not been consistent in all respects. Fifth, petitioner suggests that the progression from typewritten notes, to manuscript, then to galleys provides further evidence of intentional alteration. Malcolm contests petitioner's allegations, and only a trial on the merits will resolve the factual dispute. But at this stage, the evidence creates a jury question whether Malcolm published the statements with knowledge or reckless disregard of the alterations....

The judgment of the Court of Appeals is reversed, and the case is remanded for further proceedings consistent with this opinion.

It is so ordered.

The Court's decision in *Masson* attempts to walk a fine line between the realities of journalistic practice and the integrity of factual reporting. The justices held that writers who alter a subject's words or even totally fabricate quotations attributed to public figures do not necessarily act with actual malice. The actual malice standard requires proof that the reporter knowingly published altered quotations that materially changed the meaning conveyed by the subject. There was sufficient evidence that Malcolm may have offended this standard to compel the Court to reverse the lower court's summary judgment for the magazine and order a jury trial on Masson's lawsuit. The *Masson* case reveals that even though the Court has steadfastly adhered to the *New York Times* test for public figures, additional constitutional questions continue to plague the justices in their effort to balance the individual's right not to be defamed falsely and the First Amendment rights of a free press.

READINGS

Adler, Renata. *Reckless Disregard.* New York: Vintage Books, 1986.

Berger, Ronald. *Feminism and Pornography.* New York: Praeger, 1991.

Downs, Donald Alexander. *The New Politics of Pornography.* Chicago: University of Chicago Press, 1989.

Forer, Lois G. *A Chilling Effect.* New York: W. W. Norton, 1987.

Gillmor, Donald M. *Power, Publicity, and the Abuse of Libel Law.* New York: Oxford University Press, 1992.

Gubar, Susan. *For Adult Use Only: The Dilemmas of Violent Pornography.* Bloomington: Indiana University Press, 1989.

Hopkins, W. Wat. *Actual Malice.* New York: Praeger, 1989.

Kane, Peter E. *Errors, Lies and Libel.* Carbondale: Southern Illinois University Press, 1992.

Kirby, James. *Fumble: Bear Bryant, Wally Butts and the Great College Football Scandal.* San Diego: Harcourt Brace Jovanovich, 1986.

Kobylka, Joseph F. *The Politics of Obscenity: Group Litigation in a Time of Legal Change.* New York: Greenwood Press, 1991.

Lewis, Anthony. *Make No Law: The Sullivan Case and the First Amendment.* New York: Random House, 1991.

Randall, Richard S. *Freedom and Taboo.* Berkeley: University of California Press, 1989.

Rembar, Charles. *The End of Obscenity.* New York: Bantam Books, 1968.

CHAPTER 7
THE RIGHT TO PRIVACY

L ET US SUPPOSE that the semester is drawing to a close, with final examinations only a week away. Two roommates plan to spend the week studying in their dorm room. For many, studying is an activity they do by themselves, behind closed doors. Assume the roommates went to their room, closed the door, and placed a Do Not Disturb sign outside. Would they not expect that others would leave them alone and respect their privacy?

But is that expectation reasonable? The answer seems obvious: of course, people have a right to be let alone. To many Americans, it is a basic and fundamental part of civil liberties and rights. But the issue is far more complicated than that, primarily because the Constitution makes no explicit mention of this right. The word *privacy* appears neither in the text of the charter nor in the Bill of Rights. This omission has led to questions about this presumed guarantee, questions the Supreme Court has had difficulty answering.

First, do Americans have a constitutional right to privacy and, if so, where does this right originate? Justices of recent Courts have responded affirmatively to the first part of the query, but offered different answers to the second. As we shall see, some assert that the right emanates from several specific constitutional guarantees, most notably,

1. The First Amendment's right of association
2. The Third Amendment's prohibition against quartering soldiers
3. The Fourth Amendment's Search and Seizure Clause
4. The Fifth Amendment guarantees against self-incrimination
5. The Ninth Amendment

Other justices argue they need look only at the Ninth Amendment, which says that the "enumeration ... of certain rights shall not be construed to deny or disparage others retained by the people." Finally, some find that the Fourteenth Amendment's Due Process Clause prohibits government intrusion in ways that infringe upon liberties of citizens.

Second, to what areas does the right extend? Today, many Americans equate the right to privacy with reproductive freedom, and, in fact, the Court has used privacy as a basis for legalizing birth control and abortion. But, consider a twist on the studying scenario we described. Suppose the two roommates, in the privacy of their room, decide to use some cocaine. If possession of this substance is illegal, does someone have the right to use it—engage in criminal activity—in the privacy of his or her home? Or does the government have the right to invade that privacy? In short, where do we draw the line? To what extent should the state limit the right to privacy so that it may act in the best interests of its citizens?

In the end, we are left with many questions concerning the amorphous right to privacy. But, while reading this chapter, also consider these. Have approaches to privacy and those rights encompassed in privacy, such as abortion, changed substantially over the years? If so, why? Do alterations in the membership of the Court generate changes in the reach of the right to privacy? Or has the Court succumbed to pressure from the larger political environment?

RIGHT TO PRIVACY: FOUNDATIONS

In today's legal and political context, the right to privacy has become more or less synonymous with reproductive freedom, particularly abortion. The reason may be that the case in which the Court articulated a constitutional right to privacy, *Griswold v. Connecticut* (1965), involved birth control, and a decision that depended on *Griswold*, *Roe v. Wade* (1973), legalized abortion.

Prior to these decisions, however, members of the Court had contemplated privacy in somewhat different contexts. Following the common law dictates that "a man's home is his castle" and all "have the right to be left alone," future Supreme Court justice Louis Brandeis co-authored an 1890 *Harvard Law Review* article, asserting that privacy rights should be applied to civil law cases of libel.[1] The influence of the article was enormous. As one scholar wrote, "Out of a few fragments of common law, [they] invented a brand new tort, the invasion of privacy ... [doing] nothing less than [to] add a chapter to the law."[2]

After Brandeis ascended to the bench, he continued his quest to see a right to privacy etched into law.

Among his most famous attempts was a dissent in *Olmstead v. United States* (1928), which involved the ability of federal agents to place wiretaps on telephones without warrants. The majority of the justices ruled that neither the Fifth Amendment's protection against self-incrimination nor the Fourth Amendment's search and seizure provision protected individuals against wiretaps. Brandeis, however, thought that the Fourth and Fifth Amendments prohibited such activity. He noted:

The makers of our Constitution undertook to secure conditions favorable to the pursuit of happiness. They recognized the significance of man's spiritual nature, of his feelings and of his intellect. They knew that only a part of the pain, pleasure and satisfactions of life are to be found in material things. They sought to protect Americans in their beliefs, their thoughts, their emotions and their sensations. They conferred, as against the Government, the right to be let alone—the most comprehensive of rights and the right most valued by civilized men. To protect that right, every unjustifiable intrusion by the Government upon the privacy of the individual, whatever the means employed, must be deemed a violation of the Fourth Amendment. And the use, as evidence in a criminal proceeding, of facts ascertained by such intrusion must be deemed a violation of the Fifth.

However persuasive Brandeis's logic might appear, it stood for nearly thirty years as the only serious mention of a right to privacy. Court after Court ignored his dissent in *Olmstead*. However, Courts of earlier eras did pay attention to a concept that would later become associated with privacy—the concept of liberty. The word *liberty* appears in the Due Process Clauses of the Fifth and Fourteenth Amendments. The Fifth Amendment states that Congress shall not deprive any person of "life, *liberty*, or property, without due process of law," while the Fourteenth Amendment uses the same wording to apply to the states. In the early 1900s, the Supreme Court created a doctrine, called substantive due process, to guide its interpretation of some government policies challenged as violations of the guarantees contained in the Due Process Clauses.

---

1. Louis Brandeis and Samuel Warren, "The Right of Privacy," *Harvard Law Review* 4 (1890): 193. William L. Prosser notes that they wrote this piece in response to the yellow journalism of the day. See "Privacy," *California Law Review* 48 (1960): 383–423.

2. M. Glenn Abernathy, *Civil Liberties Under the Constitution*, 4th ed. (Columbia: University of South Carolina Press, 1985), 578.

Under the doctrine of substantive due process, the Court stressed the word *liberty* in the Due Process Clauses to prevent governments from enacting certain kinds of laws, particularly those that regulated business practices. *Lochner v. New York* (1905) illustrates the point. In this case, the Court reviewed an 1897 New York law that prohibited employees of bakeries from working more than ten hours per day and sixty hours per week. Joseph Lochner, the owner of a New York bakery who was convicted of violating the law, challenged it on Fourteenth Amendment due process grounds. He argued that the Due Process Clause gives employers and employees the liberty to enter into contracts specifying the number of hours employees could work. By interfering with that contractual arrangement with no valid reason, the New York law, in his view, violated this guarantee. The justices agreed. They struck down the law on the ground that it was a "meddlesome" and "unreasonable interference with an employer's right of contract protected in the liberty guarantee of the 14th Amendment."[3]

The Court also applied the doctrine of substantive due process to regulations outside of business. In *Meyer v. Nebraska* (1923) the justices considered a state law, enacted after World War I, that forbade schools to teach German and other foreign languages to students below the eighth grade. They invoked a substantive due process approach to strike down the law, reasoning that the word *liberty* in the Fourteenth Amendment protects more than the right to contract. It also covers "the right of the individual ... to engage in any of the common occupations of life, to acquire useful knowledge, to marry, establish a home and bring up children, to worship God according to the dictates of his own conscience, and generally to enjoy those privileges long recognized at common law as essential to the orderly pursuit of happiness by free men." According to the Court, government cannot interfere with these liberties, "under the guise of protecting the public interest, by legislative action which is arbitrary or without reasonable relation to some purpose within the competency of the State to that effect." *Meyer* and *Lochner* provide examples of substantive due process in action: under this approach, the Court is free to strike down legislation interfering with liberty unless governments can demonstrate that they are seeking to achieve an end that is not "arbitrary," "capricious," or "unreasonable." To some analysts, this doctrine was the epitome of judicial activism because it allowed the Court to function "as a self-appointed czar over social and economic legislation."[4]

Through the 1930s the Court used the doctrine of substantive due process to strike down many laws, particularly those—as in *Lochner*—that sought to regulate businesses. The members of the Court were laissez-faire-oriented justices, who did not believe that the government should interfere with the business of business. During the New Deal, however, substantive due process fell into disrepute because the public demanded government involvement to straighten out the economy. As a result, the Court changed its approach: states would be "free to adopt whatever economic policy" they wanted so long as it "may reasonably be deemed to promote public welfare."[5] If such a policy is reasonably related to a legitimate government interest, the Court would not strike it down. This reasoning is called the *rational basis* approach to the Fourteenth Amendment. It differs significantly from substantive due process because, under it, courts generally defer to governments and presume the validity of their policies.

Application of the rational basis test led the Court to uphold legislation such as maximum hour and minimum wage laws, which it had previously struck down on liberty grounds, even if the laws did not necessarily seem reasonable to the justices. In one case,

3. See Louis Fisher and Neal Devins, *Political Dynamics of Constitutional Law* (St. Paul: West Publishing, 1992), 199.

4. Ibid.
5. *Nebbia v. New York* (1934).

in fact, the justices characterized a particular state's economic policy as "needless" and "wasteful." They upheld the law anyway, proclaiming that "[t]he day is gone when this Court uses the Due Process Clause of the Fourteenth Amendment to strike down state laws, regulatory of business and industrial conditions, because they may be unwise, improvident, or out of harmony with a particular school of thought."[6] The majority added that if the people did not like the legislation their governments passed they should "resort to the polls, not to the courts." With this declaration, the Court seemed to strike the death knell for substantive due process. It would no longer substitute its "social and economic beliefs for the judgment of legislative bodies, who are elected to pass laws."[7]

What, then, does the discredited doctrine of substantive due process have to do with the right to privacy? It was Justice Harlan who tied these two concepts together. Neither an activist nor a liberal, he took great offense at the Court's handling of a 1961 case, *Poe v. Ullman*. At issue in *Poe* was the constitutionality of an 1879 Connecticut law prohibiting the use of birth control, even by married couples. A physician challenged the act on behalf of two women who wanted to use contraceptives for health reasons.

The majority of the Court voted to dismiss the case on procedural grounds.[8] Several other justices disagreed with the Court, but Harlan's dissent was memorable. He argued that the Fourteenth Amendment's Due Process Clause could be used to strike the law:

I consider that this Connecticut legislation ... violates the Fourteenth Amendment.... [It] involves what, by common understanding throughout the English-speaking world, must be granted to be the fundamental aspect of "liberty," the privacy of the home in its most basic sense, and it is this which requires that the statute be subjected to "strict scrutiny."

In making this claim, Harlan sought to demonstrate that the concepts of liberty and privacy were constitutionally bound together, that the word *liberty*, as used in the Due Process Clauses, "embraced" a right to privacy. And, because that right was fundamental, laws that touched on liberty/privacy interests, such as the one at issue in *Poe*, must be subjected to "strict scrutiny," meaning that the Court should presume that laws infringing on liberty/privacy were unconstitutional unless the state could show that the policies were the least restrictive means to accomplish a *compelling* interest.

Harlan's opinion was extraordinary in two ways.[9] First, some scholars have pointed out that it resurrected the long-dead (and discredited) doctrine of substantive due process, which the Court had buried in the 1930s. Now Harlan wanted to reinject some substance into the word *liberty*, but with a twist. Rather than protecting economic rights, in his view, due process protects fundamental rights, those the Court believes to be important in the concept of ordered liberty.

It is one of these fundamental liberties—privacy— that provides the second novel aspect of Harlan's opinion. As we have indicated, he was not writing on a blank slate; Brandeis had written about a right to privacy in the contexts of libel and search and seizure. In fact, Harlan cited—with approval—Brandeis's dissent in *Olmstead*. Still, Harlan's application of the doctrine to marital sexual relations was bold. As he (and Justice Douglas) wrote, "it is difficult to imagine what

---

6. The case was *Williamson v. Lee Optical Company* (1955). The law at issue prohibited persons other than ophthalmologists and optometrists from fitting, adjusting, adapting, or applying lenses and frames.

7. *Ferguson v. Skrupa* (1963).

8. For an interesting account of this case, see Bernard Schwartz, *Super Chief* (New York: New York University Press, 1983), 378–379.

9. As was Douglas's, which read: "Though I believe that 'due process' as used in the Fourteenth Amendment includes all of the first eight Amendments, I do not think it is restricted ... to them. The right 'to marry, establish a home and bring up children' was said in *Meyer v. State of Nebraska*, to come within the 'liberty' of the person protected by the Due Process Clause of the Fourteenth Amendment ... 'liberty' within the purview of the Fifth Amendment includes the right of 'privacy.'... This notion of privacy is not drawn from the blue. It emanates from the totality of the constitutional scheme under which we live."

is more private or more intimate than a husband and wife's relations."

Harlan and Douglas's assertion of a constitutional right to privacy proved too much, too soon for the Court; the majority was not yet willing to adopt it. But just four years later in *Griswold v. Connecticut*, a dramatic change took place. Why did the justices suddenly alter their views? More important is what the Court said about the right to privacy: the majority agreed that it existed, but disagreed over where it resided in the Constitution.

Griswold v. Connecticut

381 U.S. 479 (1965)

Vote: 7 (*Brennan, Clark, Douglas, Goldberg, Harlan, Warren, White*)

2 (*Black, Stewart*)

Opinion of the Court: Douglas
Concurring opinions: Goldberg, Harlan, White
Dissenting opinions: Black, Stewart

Griswold was virtually a carbon copy of *Poe v. Ullman*, with but a few alterations designed to meet some of the shortcomings of the earlier case.[10] Estelle Griswold, the executive director of the Planned Parenthood League of Connecticut, and Dr. C. Lee Buxton (the same physician involved in *Poe*) opened a birth control clinic in 1961 with the intent of being arrested for violating the same Connecticut law at issue in *Poe*. Three days later, Griswold was arrested for dispensing contraceptives to a married couple.

In the U.S. Supreme Court, Griswold's attorney, Yale Law School professor Thomas Emerson, challenged the Connecticut law on some of the same grounds set forth in the *Poe* dissent. Emerson took a substantive due process approach to the Fourteenth Amendment, arguing that the law infringed on individual liberty. He strengthened the privacy argument

Estelle Griswold opened a birth control clinic in New Haven in violation of an 1879 Connecticut law prohibiting the use of contraceptives. She challenged the constitutionality of the statute, and in *Griswold v. Connecticut* (1965) the Supreme Court struck down the law and established a constitutionally protected right to privacy.

by asserting that it could be found in five amendments: the First, Third, Fourth, Ninth, and Fourteenth.

10. For an interesting account of *Griswold*, see Fred W. Friendly and Martha J. H. Elliot, *The Constitution—That Delicate Balance* (New York: Random House, 1984).

MR. JUSTICE DOUGLAS delivered the opinion of the Court.

[W]e are met with a wide range of questions that implicate the Due Process Clause of the Fourteenth Amendment.... We do not sit as a super-legislature to determine the wisdom, need, and propriety of laws that touch economic problems, business affairs, or social conditions. This law, however, operates directly on an intimate relation of husband and wife and their physician's role in one aspect of that relation.

The association of people is not mentioned in the Constitution nor in the Bill of Rights. The right to educate a child in a school of the parents' choice—whether public or private or parochial—is also not mentioned. Nor is the right to study any particular subject or any foreign language. Yet the First Amendment has been construed to include certain of those rights....

Without those peripheral rights the specific rights would be less secure....

... [Previous] cases suggest that specific guarantees in the Bill of Rights have penumbras, formed by emanations from those guarantees that help give them life and substance. Various guarantees create zones of privacy. The right of association contained in the penumbra of the First Amendment is one.... The Third Amendment in its prohibition against the quartering of soldiers "in any house" in time of peace without the consent of the owner is another facet of that privacy. The Fourth Amendment explicitly affirms the "right of the people to be secure in their persons, houses, papers, and effects, against unreasonable searches and seizures." The Fifth Amendment in its Self-Incrimination Clause enables the citizen to create a zone of privacy which government may not force him to surrender to his detriment. The Ninth Amendment provides: "The enumeration in the Constitution, of certain rights, shall not be construed to deny or disparage others retained by the people."

The Fourth and Fifth Amendments were described in Boyd v. United States as protection against all governmental invasions "of the sanctity of a man's home and the privacies of life." We recently referred to the Fourth Amendment as creating a "right to privacy, no less important than any other right carefully and particularly reserved to the people."

We have had many controversies over these penumbral rights of "privacy and repose." These cases bear witness that the right of privacy which presses for recognition here is a legitimate one.

The present case, then, concerns a relationship lying within the zone of privacy created by several fundamental constitutional guarantees. And it concerns a law which, in forbidding the *use* of contraceptives rather than regulating their manufacture or sale, seeks to achieve its goals by means having a maximum destructive impact upon that relationship. Such a law cannot stand in light of the familiar principle, so often applied by this Court, that a "governmental purpose to control or prevent activities constitutionally subject to state regulation may not be achieved by means which sweep unnecessarily broadly and thereby invade the area of protected freedoms." Would we allow the police to search the sacred precincts of marital bedrooms for telltale signs of the use of contraceptives? The very idea is repulsive to the notions of privacy surrounding the marriage relationship.

We deal with a right of privacy older than the Bill of Rights—older than our political parties, older than our school system. Marriage is a coming together for better or for worse, hopefully enduring, and intimate to the degree of being sacred. It is an association that promotes a way of life, not causes; harmony in living, not political faiths; bilateral loyalty, not commercial or social projects. Yet it is an association for as noble a purpose as any involved in our prior decisions.

Reversed.

MR. JUSTICE GOLDBERG, whom THE CHIEF JUSTICE and MR. JUSTICE BRENNAN join, concurring.

I agree with the Court that Connecticut's birth-control law unconstitutionally intrudes upon the right of marital privacy, and I join in its opinion and judgment. Although I have not accepted the view that "due process" as used in the Fourteenth Amendment includes all of the first eight Amendments, I do agree that the concept of liberty protects those personal rights that are fundamental, and is not confined to the specific terms of the Bill of Rights. My conclusion that the concept of liberty is not so restricted and that it embraces the right of marital privacy though that right is not mentioned explicitly in the Constitution is supported both by numerous decisions of this Court, referred to in the Court's opinion, and by the language and history of the Ninth Amendment. In reaching the conclusion that the right of marital privacy is protected, as being within the protected penumbra of specific guarantees of the Bill of Rights, the Court refers to the Ninth Amendment....

The language and history of the Ninth Amendment reveal that the Framers of the Constitution believed that there are additional fundamental rights, protected from governmental infringement, which exist alongside those fundamental rights specifically mentioned in the first eight constitutional amendments.

The Ninth Amendment reads, "The enumeration in the Constitution, of certain rights, shall not be construed to deny or disparage others retained by the people." The Amendment is almost entirely the work of James Madison. It was introduced in Congress by him and passed the House and Senate with little or no debate and virtually no change in language. It was proffered to quiet expressed fears that a bill of specifically enumerated rights could not be sufficiently broad to cover all essential rights and that the specific mention of certain rights would be interpreted as a denial that others were protected....

While this Court has had little occasion to interpret the Ninth Amendment, "it cannot be presumed that any clause in the constitution is intended to be without effect." The Ninth Amendment to the Constitution may be regarded by some as a recent discovery and may be forgotten by others, but since 1791 it has been a basic part of the Constitution which we are sworn to uphold. To hold that a right so basic and fundamental and so deep-rooted in our society as the right of privacy in marriage may be infringed because that right is not guaranteed in so many words by the first eight amendments to the Constitution is to ignore the Ninth Amendment and to give it no effect whatsoever. Moreover, a judicial construction that this fundamental right is not protected by the Constitution because it is not mentioned in explicit terms by one of the first eight amendments or elsewhere in the Constitution would violate the Ninth Amendment, which specifically states that "the enumeration in the Constitution, of certain rights shall not be *construed* to deny or disparage others retained by the people." (Emphasis added.)...

In sum, I believe that the right of privacy in the marital relation is fundamental and basic—a personal right "retained by the people" within the meaning of the Ninth Amendment. Connecticut cannot constitutionally abridge

this fundamental right, which is protected by the Fourteenth Amendment from infringement by the States. I agree with the Court that petitioners' convictions must therefore be reversed.

MR. JUSTICE HARLAN, concurring in the judgment.

I fully agree with the judgment of reversal, but find myself unable to join the Court's opinion....

In my view, the proper constitutional inquiry in this case is whether this Connecticut statute infringes the Due Process Clause of the Fourteenth Amendment because the enactment violates basic values "implicit in the concept of ordered liberty." For reasons stated at length in my dissenting opinion in Poe v. Ullman, I believe that it does. While the relevant inquiry may be aided by resort to one or more of the provisions of the Bill of Rights, it is not dependent on them or any of their radiations. The Due Process Clause of the Fourteenth Amendment stands, in my opinion, on its own bottom.

MR. JUSTICE BLACK, with whom MR. JUSTICE STEWART joins, dissenting.

The Court talks about a constitutional "right of privacy" as though there is some constitutional provision or provisions forbidding any law ever to be passed which might abridge the "privacy" of individuals. But there is not. There are, of course, guarantees in certain specific constitutional provisions which are designed in part to protect privacy at certain times and places with respect to certain activities. Such, for example, is the Fourth Amendment's guarantee against "unreasonable searches and seizures." But I think it belittles that Amendment to talk about it as though it protects nothing but "privacy." To treat it that way is to give it a niggardly interpretation, not the kind of liberal reading I think any Bill of Rights provision should be given. The average man would very likely not have his feelings soothed any more by having his property seized openly than by having it seized privately and by stealth. He simply wants his property left alone. And a person can be just as much, if not more, irritated, annoyed and injured by an unceremonious public arrest by a policeman as he is by a seizure in the privacy of his office or home.

One of the most effective ways of diluting or expanding a constitutionally guaranteed right is to substitute for the crucial word or words of a constitutional guarantee another word or words, more or less flexible and more or less restricted in meaning. This fact is well illustrated by the use of the term "right of privacy" as a comprehensive substitute for the Fourth Amendment's guarantee against "unreasonable searches and seizures." "Privacy" is a broad, abstract and ambiguous concept which can easily be shrunken in meaning but which can also, on the other hand, easily be interpreted as a constitutional ban against many things other than searches and seizures. I have expressed the view many times that First Amendment freedoms, for example, have suffered from a failure of the courts to stick to the simple language of the First Amendment in construing it, instead of invoking multitudes of words substituted for those the Framers used.... For these reasons I get nowhere in this case by talk about a constitutional "right of privacy" as an emanation from one or more constitutional provisions. I like my privacy as well as the next one, but I am nevertheless compelled to admit that government has a right to invade it unless prohibited by some specific constitutional provision. For these reasons I cannot agree with the Court's judgment and the reasons it gives for holding this Connecticut law unconstitutional.

This brings me to the arguments made by my Brothers HARLAN, WHITE and GOLDBERG for invalidating the Connecticut law. Brothers HARLAN and WHITE would invalidate it by reliance on the Due Process Clause of the Fourteenth Amendment, but Brother GOLDBERG, while agreeing with Brother HARLAN, relies also on the Ninth Amendment. I have no doubt that the Connecticut law could be applied in such a way as to abridge freedom of speech and press and therefore violate the First and Fourteenth Amendments. My disagreement with the Court's opinion holding that there is such a violation here is a narrow one, relating to the application of the First Amendment to the facts and circumstances of this particular case. But my disagreement with Brothers HARLAN, WHITE and GOLDBERG is more basic. I think that if properly construed neither the Due Process Clause nor the Ninth Amendment, nor both together, could under any circumstances be a proper basis for invalidating the Connecticut law. I discuss the due process and Ninth Amendment arguments together because on analysis they turn out to be the same thing—merely using different words to claim for this Court and the federal judiciary power to invalidate any legislative act which the judges find irrational, unreasonable or offensive.

The due process argument which my Brothers HARLAN and WHITE adopt here is based, as their opinions indicate, on the premise that this Court is vested with power to invalidate all state laws that it considers to be arbitrary, capricious, unreasonable, or oppressive, or on this Court's belief that a particular state law under scrutiny has no "rational or justifying" purpose, or is offensive to a "sense of fairness and justice." If these formulas based on "natural justice," or others which mean the same thing, are to prevail, they require judges to determine what is or is not constitutional on the basis of their own appraisal of what laws are unwise or unnecessary. The power to make such decisions is of course that of a legislative body. Surely it has to be admitted that no provision of the Constitution specifically gives such blanket power to courts to exercise such a supervisory veto over the wisdom and value of legislative policies and to hold unconstitutional those laws which they believe unwise or dangerous. I readily admit that no legislative body, state or national, should pass laws that can justly be given any of the invidious labels invoked as constitutional excuses to strike down state laws. But perhaps it is not too much to say that no legislative body ever does pass laws without believing that they will accomplish a sane, rational, wise and justifiable purpose. While ... our Court has constitutional power to strike down statutes, state or federal, that violate commands of the Federal Constitution, I do not believe that we are granted power by the Due Process Clause or any other constitutional provision or provisions to measure constitutionality by our belief that legislation is arbitrary, capricious or unreasonable, or accomplishes no justifiable purpose, or is offensive to our own notions of "civilized standards of conduct." Such an appraisal of the wisdom of legislation is an attribute of the power to make laws, not of the power to interpret them. The use by federal courts of such a formula or doctrine or whatnot to veto federal or state laws simply takes away from Congress and States the power to make laws based on their own judgment of fairness and wisdom and transfers that power to this Court for ultimate determination—a power which was specifically denied to federal courts by the convention that framed the Constitution....

My Brother GOLDBERG has adopted the recent discovery that the Ninth Amendment as well as the Due Process Clause can be used by this Court as authority to strike down all state legislation which this Court thinks violates "fundamental principles of liberty and justice," or is contrary to the "traditions and [collective] conscience of our people." He also states, without proof satisfactory to me, that in making decisions on this basis judges will not consider "their personal and private notions." One may ask how they can avoid considering them. Our Court certainly has no machinery with which to take a Gallup Poll. And the scientific miracles of this age have not yet produced a gadget which the Court can use to determine what traditions are rooted in the "[collective] conscience of our people." Moreover, one would certainly have to look far beyond the language of the Ninth Amendment to find that the Framers vested in this Court any such awesome veto powers over lawmaking, either by the States or by the Congress. Nor does anything in the history of the Amendment offer any support for such a shocking doctrine. The whole history of the adoption of the Constitution and Bill of Rights points the other way.... That Amendment was passed, not to broaden the powers of this Court or any other department of "the General Government," but, as every student of history knows, to assure the people that the Constitution in all its provisions was intended to limit the Federal Government to the powers granted expressly or by necessary implication.... [F]or a period of a century and a half no serious suggestion was ever made that the Ninth Amendment, enacted to protect state powers against federal invasion, could be used as a weapon of federal power to prevent state legislatures from passing laws they consider appropriate to govern local affairs. Use of any such broad, unbounded judicial authority would make of this Court's members a day-to-day constitutional convention....

I realize that many good and able men have eloquently spoken and written, sometimes in rhapsodical strains, about the duty of this Court to keep the Constitution in tune with the times. The idea is that the Constitution must be changed from time to time and that this Court is charged with a duty to make those changes. For myself, I must with all deference reject that philosophy. The Constitution makers knew the need for change and provided for it. Amendments suggested by the people's elected representatives can be submitted to the people or their selected agents for ratification. That method of change was good for our Fathers, and being somewhat old-fashioned I must add it is good enough for me. And so, I cannot rely on the Due Process Clause or the Ninth Amendment or any mysterious and uncertain natural law concept as a reason for striking down this state law. The Due Process Clause with an "arbitrary and capricious" ... formula was liberally used by this Court to strike down economic legislation in the early decades of this century, threatening, many people thought, the tranquility and stability of the Nation. See, e.g., Lochner v. New York. That formula, based on subjective considerations of "natural justice," is no less dangerous when used to enforce this Court's views about personal rights than those about economic rights. I had thought that we had laid that formula, as a means for striking down state legislation, to rest once and for all.

MR. JUSTICE STEWART, whom MR. JUSTICE BLACK joins, dissenting.

Since 1879 Connecticut has had on its books a law which forbids the use of contraceptives by anyone. I think this is an uncommonly silly law. As a practical matter, the law is obviously unenforceable, except in the oblique context of the present case. As a philosophical matter, I believe the use of contraceptives in the relationship of marriage should be left to personal and private choice, based upon each individual's moral, ethical, and religious beliefs. As a matter of social policy, I think professional counsel about methods of birth control should be available to all, so that each individual's choice can be meaningfully made. But we are not asked in this case to say whether we think this law is unwise, or even asinine. We are asked to hold that it violates the United States Constitution. And that I cannot do.

In the course of its opinion the Court refers to no less than six Amendments to the Constitution: the First, the Third, the Fourth, the Fifth, the Ninth, and the Fourteenth. But the Court does not say which of these Amendments, if any, it thinks is infringed by this Connecticut law.

We *are* told that the Due Process Clause of the Fourteenth Amendment is not, as such, the "guide" in this case. With that much I agree. There is no claim that this law, duly enacted by the Connecticut Legislature, is unconstitutionally vague. There is no claim that the appellants were denied any of the elements of procedural due process at their trial, so as to make their convictions constitutionally invalid. And, as the Court says, the day has long passed since the Due Process Clause was regarded as a proper instrument for determining "the wisdom, need, and propriety" of state laws....

The Court also quotes the Ninth Amendment, and my Brother GOLDBERG's concurring opinion relies heavily upon it. But to say that the Ninth Amendment has anything to do with this case is to turn somersaults with history. The Ninth Amendment, like its companion the Tenth, which this Court held "states but a truism that all is retained which has not been surrendered," was framed by James Madison and adopted by the States simply to make clear that the adoption of the Bill of Rights did not alter the plan that the *Federal* Government was to be a government of express and limited powers, and that all rights and powers not delegated to it were retained by the people and the individual States. Until today no member of this Court has ever suggested that the Ninth Amendment meant anything else, and the idea that a federal court could ever use the Ninth Amendment to annul a law passed by the elected representatives of the people of the State of Connecticut would have caused James Madison no little wonder.

What provision of the Constitution, then, does make this state law invalid? The Court says it is the right of privacy "created by several fundamental constitutional guarantees." With all deference, I can find no such general right of privacy in the Bill of Rights, in any other part of the Constitution, or in any case ever before decided by this Court.

At the oral argument in this case we were told that the Connecticut law does not "conform to current community standards." But it is not the function of this Court to decide cases on the basis of community standards. We are here to decide cases "agreeably to the Constitution and laws of the United States." It is the essence of judicial duty to subordinate our own personal views, our own ideas of what legislation is wise and what is not. If, as I should surely hope, the law before us does not reflect the standards of the people of Connecticut, the people of Connecticut can freely exercise their true Ninth and Tenth Amendment rights to persuade their elected representatives to repeal it. That is the constitutional way to take this law off the books.

Griswold was a landmark decision because it created a constitutional right to privacy and deemed that right fundamental. To put it another way, under *Griswold* governments may place limits on the right to privacy only if those limits survive "strict" constitutional scrutiny, which means that the government must demonstrate that its restrictions are necessary and narrowly tailored to serve a compelling government interest. However, the justices disagreed about where that right existed within the Constitution *(see Table 7-1)*. Douglas's opinion for the Court asserted that specific guarantees in the Bill of Rights have penumbras, formed by emanations from First, Third, Fourth, Fifth, and Ninth Amendment guarantees "that help give them life and substance." In other words, Douglas claimed that even though the Constitution failed to mention privacy, clauses within the document created zones that gave rise to the right. Note that in making this argument, Douglas avoided reliance on the Fourteenth Amendment's Due Process Clause. He apparently believed that grounding privacy in that clause would hark back to the days of *Lochner* and substantive due process, a doctrine he explicitly rejected.[11]

Justice Goldberg, writing for Earl Warren and William Brennan, did not dispute Douglas's penum-

TABLE 7-1 The *Griswold* Splits

Location of the Privacy Right	Justices
First, Third, Fourth, Fifth, and Ninth Amendments	Douglas, Clark
Ninth Amendment	Goldberg, Brennan, Warren
Fourteenth Amendment (Due Process Clause)	Harlan, White
No general right to privacy in the Constitution	Black, Stewart

11. For an interesting and inside view of the Court's decision-making process in *Griswold*, see Bernard Schwartz, *The Unpublished Opinions of the Warren Court* (New York: Oxford University Press, 1985).

bra theory, but chose to emphasize the relevance of the Ninth Amendment. In Goldberg's view that amendment, which states, "The enumeration in the Constitution, of certain rights, shall not be construed to deny or disparage others retained by the people," could be read to contain a right to privacy. His logic was simple: the wording of the amendment, coupled with its history, suggested that it was "proffered to quiet expressed fears that a bill of specifically enumerated rights could not be sufficiently broad to cover all essential rights," including the right to privacy. Harlan took the opportunity to reiterate his stance in *Poe* that the Due Process Clause of the Fourteenth Amendment prohibits such legislation. In holding to his *Poe* opinion, however, Harlan went one step beyond the Goldberg concurrers; he rejected the Douglas penumbra theory, asserting, "While the relevant inquiry may be aided by resort to one or more of the provisions of the Bill of Rights, it is not dependent on them or any of their radiations." Justice White also filed a concurring opinion lending support to Harlan's due process view of privacy.

As important as *Griswold* was and still is, it is clear that the justices did not speak with one voice. Seven agreed, more or less, that a right to privacy existed, but they located that right in three distinct constitutional spheres. The other two—Black and Stewart—argued that the Constitution did not contain a general right to privacy, but they did more than that. They took their colleagues to task for, in their view, reverting back to the days of *Lochner* and substantive due process. From Black and Stewart's vantage point, it should be the people, not the courts, that pressure legislatures to change "unwise" laws.

Whether a right to privacy existed and where the right was located, however, were not the only questions raised by *Griswold*. Another important issue concerned the areas covered by this newly found right. Clearly, it protected "notions of privacy surrounding the marriage relationship," but beyond that observers could only speculate.

In this chapter we examine the other areas where the Court has applied *Griswold*. We look first at its extensions into private activities and then at its role in the more controversial issue of abortion. Keep the *Griswold* precedent in mind. To which interpretation of the right to privacy has the Court subscribed in the cases that follow? Has the Court's approach changed with its increasing conservatism? Or do the majority of justices continue to adopt its basic tenets?

PRIVATE ACTIVITIES AND THE APPLICATION OF *GRISWOLD*

Many Americans now equate *Griswold*'s right to privacy with reproductive freedom, especially the right to abortion, but one of the first important applications came in a criminal procedure case, *Katz v. United States* (1967).[12] FBI agents suspected Charles Katz of engaging in illegal bookmaking activity; in particular, they thought he was "transmitting wagering information by telephone from Los Angeles to Miami and Boston." To gather evidence, they placed listening and recording devices outside the telephone booth Katz used to make his calls and used the transcripts of his conversations to obtain an eight-count indictment.

Katz challenged the use of the transcripts as evidence against him, asserting that his conversations were private and that the government had violated his rights under the Fourth Amendment. The government argued that in previous Fourth Amendment search and seizure cases, the justices permitted the use of bugs and mikes so long as agents did not "physically penetrate" an individual's space. Here, the FBI had attached listening devices to the *outside* of the booth; it claimed that did not invade Katz's space.

The Court disagreed. In his majority opinion, Justice Stewart dealt primarily with existing precedent governing searches and seizures, a topic covered in Chapter 8. But Stewart touched on the privacy issue,

12. An excerpt of *Katz* appears in Chapter 8.

asserting that "What a person knowingly exposes to the public, even in his own home or office, is not a subject of Fourth Amendment protection. But what he seeks to preserve as private, even in an area accessible to the public, may be constitutionally protected." Justice Harlan, in a concurring opinion, put it in these terms: if a person has "exhibited an actual (subjective) expectation of privacy," and "the expectation ... [is] one that society is prepared to recognize as 'reasonable,'" then he or she comes under the protection of the Fourth Amendment. In other words, the justices—even Stewart, who dissented in *Griswold*—were willing to apply the right to privacy to searches and seizures. If citizens expect privacy, as Charles Katz did when he entered the telephone booth, then they are entitled to it. This position was not wholly different from what Justice Brandeis had advocated in *Olmstead v. United States* about forty years before *Katz!*

Two years later, the Court had another occasion to examine the privacy doctrine and its relationship to searches and seizures. While reading *Stanley v. Georgia*, think about the Court's application of it. Did the Court's decision here go beyond *Katz?*

Stanley v. Georgia

394 U.S. 557 (1969)
Vote: 9 (Black, Brennan, Douglas, Fortas, Harlan, Marshall,
        Stewart, Warren, White)
    0

Opinion of the Court: Marshall
Concurring opinions: Black, Stewart

In the course of investigating Robert Stanley for illegal bookmaking, police obtained a warrant to search his home. The police found little evidence of gambling activity, but they did find three reels of film. They watched the movies and arrested Stanley for possessing obscene material. Stanley's attorney challenged the seizure and arrest on the ground that the law should not "punish mere private possession of ob-

scene material"—that his client had a right of privacy to view whatever he wished in his own home. The state argued that it had the right to seize obscene materials because they are illegal to possess. Indeed, in previous decisions, the Court had said that states could regulate the dissemination of obscene movies, magazines, and so forth.

MR. JUSTICE MARSHALL delivered the opinion of the Court.

For reasons set forth below, we agree that the mere private possession of obscene matter cannot constitutionally be made a crime....

It is now well established that the Constitution protects the right to receive information and ideas. This right to receive information and ideas, regardless of their social worth, is fundamental to our free society. Moreover, in the context of this case—a prosecution for mere possession of printed or filmed matter in the privacy of a person's own home—that right takes on an added dimension. For also fundamental is the right to be free, except in very limited circumstances, from unwanted governmental intrusions into one's privacy.... (See Griswold v. Connecticut.)

These are the rights that appellant is asserting in the case before us. He is asserting the right to read or observe what he pleases—the right to satisfy his intellectual and emotional needs in the privacy of his own home. He is asserting the right to be free from state inquiry into the contents of his library. Georgia contends that appellant does not have these rights, that there are certain types of materials that the individual may not read or even possess. Georgia justifies this assertion by arguing that the films in the present case are obscene. But we think that mere categorization of these films as "obscene" is insufficient justification for such a drastic invasion of personal liberties guaranteed by the First and Fourteenth Amendments. Whatever may be the justifications for other statutes regulating obscenity, we do not think they reach into the privacy of one's own home. If the First Amendment means anything, it means that a State has no business telling a man, sitting alone in his own house, what books he may read or what films he may watch. Our whole constitutional heritage rebels at the thought of giving government the power to control men's minds.

And yet, in the face of these traditional notions of individual liberty, Georgia asserts the right to protect the individual's mind from the effects of obscenity. We are not certain that this argument amounts to anything more than the assertion that the State has the right to control the moral content of a person's thoughts. To some, this may be a noble purpose, but it is wholly inconsistent with the philosophy of the First Amendment.... Nor is it relevant that obscene materials in general, or the particular films before the Court, are arguably devoid of any ideological content. The line between transmission of ideas and mere entertainment is much too elusive for this Court to draw, if indeed such a line can be drawn at all. Whatever the power of the state to control public dissemination of ideas inimical to the public morality, it cannot constitutionally premise legislation on the desirability of controlling a person's private thoughts....

Finally, we are faced with the argument that prohibition of possession of obscene materials is a necessary incident to statutory schemes prohibiting distribution. That argument is based on alleged difficulties of proving an intent to distribute or in producing evidence of actual distribution. We are not convinced that such difficulties exist, but even if they did we do not think that they would justify infringement of the individual's right to read or observe what he pleases. Because that right is so fundamental to our scheme of individual liberty, its restriction may not be justified by the need to ease the administration of otherwise valid criminal laws.

We hold that the First and Fourteenth Amendments prohibit making mere private possession of obscene material a crime.*... As we have said, the States retain broad power to regulate obscenity; that power simply does not extend to mere possession by the individual in the privacy of his own home. Accordingly, the judgment of the court below is reversed and the case is remanded for proceedings not inconsistent with this opinion.

It is so ordered.

Judgment reversed and case remanded.

*What we have said in no way infringes upon the power of the State or Federal Government to make possession of other items, such as narcotics, firearms, or stolen goods, a crime. Our holding in the present case turns upon the Georgia statute's infringement of fundamental liberties protected by the First Amendment. No First Amendment rights are involved in most statutes making mere possession a crime.

The Court's acceptance of Stanley's argument was unanimous: "If the First Amendment means anything, it means that a State has no business telling a man, sitting alone in his house, what books he may read or films he may watch." Put somewhat differently, states can regulate obscenity, but cannot prohibit such activity inside someone's house. The First Amendment and privacy rights simply prohibit this kind of intrusion into the home.

This point is important: as Marshall's footnote indicated, *Stanley* hinged on an infringement of a fundamental liberty—in this instance, the First Amendment. But would the Court apply *Stanley* to activities forbidden by the state that did not fall under the First Amendment? In *Bowers v. Hardwick* (1986) the Court considered the constitutionality of a man's conviction for engaging in sodomy. As you read *Bowers* think about how the Court applied *Stanley* to the dispute. Some scholars allege that the Court virtually gutted the underpinnings of *Stanley*. Is this assertion accurate? Or did the Court merely seek to limit its application and that of the *Griswold* right to privacy, more generally?

Bowers v. Hardwick

478 U.S. 186 (1986)
Vote: 5 (Burger, O'Connor, Powell, Rehnquist, White)
    4 (Blackmun, Brennan, Marshall, Stevens)
Opinion of the Court: White
Concurring opinions: Burger, Powell
Dissenting opinions: Blackmun, Stevens

In August 1982 a police officer appeared at Michael Hardwick's residence to serve him with an arrest warrant for failure to keep a court date. According to the officer, one of Hardwick's housemates let him in and he then observed Hardwick engaged in sodomy with another man.[13] The officer arrested Hardwick for vio-

13. For more on this case, see Peter Irons, *The Courage of Their Convictions* (New York: Free Press, 1988).

Michael Hardwick was arrested for violating the Georgia sodomy statute in 1982. With help from the American Civil Liberties Union, Hardwick sued the state, claiming the law violated his constitutional rights. In *Bowers v. Hardwick* (1986) the Supreme Court rejected Hardwick's privacy argument and upheld the Georgia law.

lating a Georgia law that prohibited the practice of oral or anal sex.[14] The district attorney decided not to pursue the matter, but Hardwick and his ACLU attorneys challenged the law, asserting that it violated the fundamental right to privacy as articulated in *Griswold* and should be subject to strict constitutional scrutiny.

JUSTICE WHITE delivered the opinion of the Court.

The issue presented is whether the Federal Constitution confers a fundamental right upon homosexuals to engage in sodomy and hence invalidates the laws of the many States that still make such conduct illegal and have done so for a very long time. The case also calls for some judgment about the limits of the Court's role in carrying out its constitutional mandate.

14. The majority opinion dealt exclusively with "consensual homosexual sodomy," expressing "no opinion ... on other acts of sodomy."

We first register our disagreement ... with respondent that the Court's prior cases have construed the Constitution to confer a right of privacy that extends to homosexual sodomy and for all intents and purposes have decided this case....

... [N]one of the rights announced in ... [past] cases bears any resemblance to the claimed constitutional right of homosexuals to engage in acts of sodomy....

Precedent aside, however, respondent would have us announce ... a fundamental right to engage in homosexual sodomy. This we are quite unwilling to do. It is true that despite the language of the Due Process Clauses of the Fifth and Fourteenth Amendments, which appears to focus only on the processes by which life, liberty, or property is taken, the cases are legion in which those Clauses have been interpreted to have substantive content, subsuming rights that to a great extent are immune from federal or state regulation or proscription. Among such cases are those recognizing rights that have little or no textual support in the constitutional language....

Striving to assure itself and the public that announcing rights not readily identifiable in the Constitution's text involves much more than the imposition of the Justices' own choice of values on the States and the Federal Government, the Court has sought to identify the nature of the rights qualifying for heightened judicial protection. ... [I]t was said that this category includes those fundamental liberties that are "implicit in the concept of ordered liberty," such that "neither liberty nor justice would exist if [they] were sacrificed." ... [F]undamental liberties ... are characterized as those ... that are "deeply rooted in this Nation's history and tradition."

It is obvious to us that neither of these formulations would extend a fundamental right to homosexuals to engage in acts of consensual sodomy. Proscriptions against that conduct have ancient roots. Sodomy was a criminal offense at common law and was forbidden by the laws of the original thirteen States when they ratified the Bill of Rights.... In fact, until 1961, all 50 States outlawed sodomy, and today 24 States and the District of Columbia continue to provide criminal penalties for sodomy performed in private and between consenting adults. Against this background, to claim that a right to engage in such conduct is "deeply rooted in this Nation's history and tradition" or "implicit in the concept of ordered liberty" is, at best, facetious.

Nor are we inclined to take a more expansive view of our authority to discover new fundamental rights imbedded in the Due Process Clause. The Court is most vulnerable and comes nearest to illegitimacy when it deals with judge-made constitutional law having little or no cognizable roots in the language or design of the Constitution. That this is so was painfully demonstrated by the face-off between the Executive and the Court in the 1930's, which resulted in the repudiation of much of the substantive gloss that the Court had placed on the Due Process Clause of the Fifth and Fourteenth Amendments. There should be, therefore, great resistance to expand the substantive reach of those Clauses, particularly if it requires redefining the category of rights deemed to be fundamental. Otherwise, the Judiciary necessarily takes to itself further authority to govern the country without express constitutional authority. The claimed right pressed on us today falls far short of overcoming this resistance.

Respondent, however, asserts that the result should be different where the homosexual conduct occurs in the privacy of the home. He relies on *Stanley v. Georgia* (1969), where the Court held that the First Amendment prevents conviction for possessing and reading obscene material in the privacy of his home....

Stanley did protect conduct that would not have been protected outside the home, and it partially prevented the enforcement of state obscenity laws; but the decision was firmly grounded in the First Amendment. The right pressed upon us here has no similar support in the text of the Constitution, and it does not qualify for recognition under the prevailing principles for construing the Fourteenth Amendment. Its limits are also difficult to discern. Plainly enough, otherwise illegal conduct is not always immunized whenever it occurs in the home. Victimless crimes, such as the possession and use of illegal drugs, do not escape the law where they are committed at home. *Stanley* itself recognized that its holding offered no protection for the possession in the home of drugs, firearms, or stolen goods. And if respondent's submission is limited to the voluntary sexual conduct between consenting adults, it would be difficult, except by fiat, to limit the claimed right to homosexual conduct while leaving exposed to prosecution

adultery, incest, and other sexual crimes even though they are committed in the home. We are unwilling to start down that road....

Accordingly, the judgment of the Court of Appeals is

Reversed.

JUSTICE BLACKMUN, with whom JUSTICE BRENNAN, JUSTICE MARSHALL, and JUSTICE STEVENS join, dissenting.

This case is no more about "a fundamental right to engage in homosexual sodomy," as the Court purports to declare, than *Stanley v. Georgia* (1969), was about a fundamental right to watch obscene movies, or *Katz v. United States* (1967), was about a fundamental right to place interstate bets from a telephone booth. Rather, this case is about "the most comprehensive of rights and the right most valued by civilized men," namely, "the right to be let alone." *Olmstead v. United States* (1928) (Brandeis, J., dissenting)....

In its haste to reverse the Court of Appeals and hold that the Constitution does not "confe[r] a fundamental right upon homosexuals to engage in sodomy," the Court relegates the actual statute being challenged to a footnote and ignores the procedural posture of the case before it. A fair reading of the statute and of the complaint clearly reveals that the majority has distorted the question this case presents.

First, the Court's almost obsessive focus on homosexual activity is particularly hard to justify in light of the broad language Georgia has used. Unlike the Court, the Georgia Legislature has not proceeded on the assumption that homosexuals are so different from other citizens that their lives may be controlled in a way that would not be tolerated if it limited the choices of those other citizens.... The sex or status of the persons who engage in the act is irrelevant as a matter of state law.... Michael Hardwick's standing may rest in significant part on Georgia's apparent willingness to enforce against homosexuals a law it seems not to have any desire to enforce against heterosexuals. But his claim that ... [the law] involves an unconstitutional intrusion into his privacy and his right of intimate association does not depend in any way on his sexual orientation.

Second, I disagree with the Court's refusal to consider whether ... [the law] runs afoul of the ... Ninth Amendment.... Respondent's complaint expressly invoked the Ninth Amendment and he relied heavily before this Court on *Griswold v. Connecticut* (1965), which identifies that Amendment as one of the specific constitutional provisions giving "life and substance" to our understanding of privacy.... I believe that Hardwick has stated a cognizable claim that ... [the law] interferes with constitutionally protected interests in privacy and freedom of intimate association.....

The Court concludes today that none of our prior cases dealing with various decisions that individuals are entitled to make free of governmental interference "bears any resemblance to the claimed constitutional right of homosexuals to engage in acts of sodomy that is asserted in this case."...

In a variety of circumstances we have recognized that a necessary corollary of giving individuals freedom to choose how to conduct their lives is acceptance of the fact that different individuals will make different choices. For example, in holding that the clearly important state interest in public education should give way to a competing claim by the Amish to the effect that extended formal schooling threatened their way of life, the Court declared: "There can be no assumption that today's majority is 'right' and the Amish and others like them are 'wrong.' A way of life that is odd or even erratic but interferes with no rights or interests of others is not to be condemned because it is different." *Wisconsin v. Yoder* (1972). The Court claims that its decision today merely refuses to recognize a fundamental right to engage in homosexual sodomy; what the Court really has refused to recognize is the fundamental interest all individuals have in controlling the nature of their intimate associations with others.

The behavior for which Hardwick faces prosecution occurred in his own home, a place to which the Fourth Amendment attaches special significance. The Court's treatment of this aspect of the case is symptomatic of its overall refusal to consider the broad principles that have informed our treatment of privacy in specific cases. Just as the right to privacy is more than the mere aggregation of a number of entitlements to engage in specific behavior, so too, protecting the physical integrity of the home is more than merely a means of protecting specific activities that often take place there....

The Court's interpretation of the pivotal case of *Stanley v. Georgia* (1969) is entirely unconvincing. *Stanley* held that Georgia's undoubted power to punish the public distribution of constitutionally unprotected, obscene material did not permit the State to punish the private possession of such material. According to the majority here, *Stanley* relied entirely on the First Amendment, and thus, it is claimed, sheds no light on cases not involving printed materials. But that is not what *Stanley* said. Rather, the *Stanley* Court anchored its holding in the Fourth Amendment's special protection for the individual in his home....

The central place that *Stanley* gives Justice Brandeis' dissent in *Olmstead*, a case raising no First Amendment claim, shows that *Stanley* rested as much on the Court's understanding of the Fourth Amendment as it did on the First.... [T]hus I cannot agree with the Court's statement that "[t]he right pressed upon us here has no ... support in the text of the Constitution." Indeed, the right of an individual to conduct intimate relationships in the intimacy of his or her own home seems to me to be the heart of the Constitution's protection of privacy.

The Court's failure to comprehend the magnitude of the liberty interests at stake in this case leads it to slight the question whether petitioner, on behalf of the State, has justified Georgia's infringement of these interests. I believe that neither of the two general justifications for ... [the law] that petitioner has advanced warrants dismissing respondent's challenge for failure to state a claim.

First, petitioner asserts that the acts made criminal by the statute may have serious adverse consequences for "the general public health and welfare," such as spreading communicable diseases or fostering other criminal activity. Inasmuch as this case was dismissed by the District Court on the pleadings, it is not surprising that the record before us is barren of any evidence to support petitioner's claim.... Nothing in the record before the Court provides any justification for finding the activity forbidden by ... [the law] to be physically dangerous, either to the persons engaged in it or to others.

The core of petitioner's defense of ... [the law], however, is that respondent and others who engage in the conduct prohibited by ... [it] interfere with Georgia's exercise of the "'right of the Nation and of the States to maintain a decent society.'"... Essentially, petitioner argues, and the

Court agrees, that the fact that the acts described in ... [the law] "for hundreds of years, if not thousands, have been uniformly condemned as immoral" is a sufficient reason to permit a State to ban them today.

I cannot agree that either the length of time a majority has held its convictions or the passions with which it defends them can withdraw legislation from this Court's scrutiny.... As Justice Jackson wrote so eloquently for the Court in *West Virginia Board of Education v. Barnette* (1943), "we apply the limitations of the Constitution with no fear that freedom to be intellectually and spiritually diverse or even contrary will disintegrate the social organization.... [F]reedom to differ is not limited to things that do not matter much. That would be a mere shadow of freedom. The test of its substance is the right to differ as to things that touch the heart of the existing order." It is precisely because the issue raised by this case touches the heart of what makes individuals what they are that we should be especially sensitive to the rights of those whose choices upset the majority....

This case involves no real interference with the rights of others, for the mere knowledge that other individuals do not adhere to one's value system cannot be a legally cognizable interest, let alone an interest that can justify invading the houses, hearts, and minds of citizens who choose to live their lives differently.

It took but three years for the Court to see the error in its analysis in *Minersville School District v. Gobitis* and to recognize that the threat to national cohesion posed by a refusal to salute the flag was vastly outweighed by the threat to those same values posed by compelling such a salute. See *West Virginia Board of Education v. Barnette* (1943). I can only hope that here, too, the Court soon will reconsider its analysis and conclude that depriving individuals of the right to choose for themselves how to conduct their intimate relationships poses a far greater threat to the values most deeply rooted in our Nation's history than tolerance of nonconformity could ever do. Because I think the Court today betrays those values, I dissent.

Both the majority and dissenting opinions in *Bowers* dealt with privacy concerns. White's opinion found fault with a due process approach to privacy or, at the very least, of using it to "discover" a new "fundamental right to engage in homosexual sodomy." Nor was he interested in using *Stanley* to find in favor of Hardwick. He read *Stanley* narrowly: it protected the activity of some otherwise illegal activity only if the First Amendment was implicated. Hence, because Hardwick did not raise a First Amendment objection to sodomy laws, *Stanley* was inapplicable. The dissenters (including Marshall, the author of *Stanley*) called this interpretation "unconvincing." In their view, *Stanley* took its cues from Brandeis's dissent in *Olmstead* and, accordingly, rested as much on the Fourth Amendment as on the First.

We leave it to you to consider whether the Burger Court, in *Bowers*, began to dismantle the Warren Court's rulings in *Stanley* and *Griswold* or if it merely drew sensible limits around them. For most Americans, the latter would be true. In surveys conducted during the 1980s and 1990s, about 75 percent of respondents said they believed "sexual relations between two adults of the same sex" is wrong. The justices showed less consensus than the public: the case was decided by a one-vote margin, and, since his retirement, Justice Powell has stated he "probably made a mistake" in voting to uphold the Georgia laws.

Powell's remark provides some indication of the difficulty involved in resolving disputes touching on the amorphous right to privacy. The disputes have become even more difficult over time. In *Cruzan v. Director, Missouri Department of Health* (1990), the Court—under the leadership of William Rehnquist—took an initial look at one of the most troublesome of all privacy issues—the right to die.

Right-to-die cases present two levels of questions. The first concerns whether and under what circumstances individuals can make the decision to refuse medical treatment necessary to sustain their lives. Most of the state courts resolving right-to-die cases in the 1970s—well before the Supreme Court's ruling in *Cruzan*—agreed that the rights of privacy/liberty

FIGURE 7-1 Percentage of Respondents Supporting an Individual's Right to Die

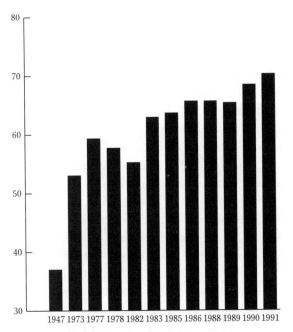

1947 1973 1977 1978 1982 1983 1985 1986 1988 1989 1990 1991

SOURCE: Lee Epstein, Jeffrey A. Segal, Harold J. Spaeth, and Thomas G. Walker, *The Supreme Court Compendium: Data, Decisions, and Developments* (Washington, D.C.: Congressional Quarterly, 1994), Table 8-23.

NOTE: The question was: Do you believe that doctors should be allowed by law to end an incurable patient's life if the patient and his family request it?

act in the "best interest" of the patient.[15] A frequently cited example of the use of "substituted judgment" is the New Jersey Supreme Court's ruling in *In re Quinlan* (1976). As their twenty-two-year-old daughter Karen lay in a coma, her parents sought to have the respirator, which was sustaining her life, removed. When Karen's doctors refused their request, the Quinlans went to court. The state supreme court decided that the right to privacy is broad enough to allow a patient to "decline medical treatment under certain circumstances." And, because Karen could not make that decision for herself, the "only practical way to prevent the destruction of the right [to privacy] is to permit the guardian and family of Karen to render their best judgment as to whether she would exercise it in these circumstances."

Under this decision, the Quinlans could (and did) have Karen's respirator removed without intervention from the state and its courts. Although most state courts endorsed *Quinlan*, the Missouri Supreme Court took a different stance.[16] Viewing the state's interest in preserving life as controlling,[17] it asserted that the family must provide "clear and convincing" evidence that the patient would have wanted medical care terminated. This kind of standard is often difficult for families to meet because they must provide direct evidence about the patient's desires.

In any event, rules that permit patients and the families to end treatment have garnered public support. As Figure 7-1 shows, in the 1940s only about 37 percent of the citizenry agreed that doctors should be allowed to end a terminal patient's life if that pa-

were broad enough to permit competent individuals to refuse medical treatment. But the issue becomes far more complicated when individuals seek to commit suicide or seek assistance in ending their life ("assisted suicides") when they have terminal illnesses.

A second right-to-die question centers on whether and under what circumstances the family or guardian of an incapacitated individual can make that decision. This question has proven the more problematic of the two. In the 1970s and 1980s, most state courts allowed various forms of what are called "substituted judgments," that is, they permitted relatives or guardians to "surmise" what the patient would have wanted or to

15. See Laurence Tribe, *American Constitutional Law* (Mineola, N.Y.: Foundation Press, 1988), 1368.

16. In "Policy Making and State Supreme Courts" (*The American Courts: A Critical Assessment*, ed. John B. Gates and Charles A. Johnson, Washington, D.C.: CQ Press, 1990, 108–110), Henry R. Glick provides a list of state right-to-die cases that predate *Cruzan*.

17. Preserving life is only one of several state interests. In *Belchertown v. Saikewicz* (1977), the Massachusetts Supreme Judicial Court offered three others: the maintenance of "ethical integrity of the medical profession," "the prevention of suicide," and the "protection of the interests of innocent third parties." See Tribe, *American Constitutional Law*, 1365.

tient or the family request it. By 1991 that number had grown to 70.2 percent.

Would the Supreme Court agree with the public? Would it allow even competent patients to end their medical treatment? If so, would it permit families to make these decisions? What kind of proof would it require? These were the questions the Court with which the Court dealt in its first right-to-die case, *Cruzan v. Director, Missouri Health Department.*

Cruzan v. Director, Missouri Department of Health

497 U.S. 261 (1990)
Vote: 5 (Kennedy, O'Connor, Rehnquist, Scalia, White)
    4 (Blackmun, Brennan, Marshall, Stevens)
Opinion of the Court: Rehnquist
Concurring opinions: O'Connor, Scalia
Dissenting opinions: Brennan, Stevens

In January 1983 Nancy Beth Cruzan was in a serious car accident. When paramedics found her, she was "lying face down in a ditch without detectable respiratory or cardiac function." Although they were able to restore her breathing and heartbeat, Cruzan remained unconscious and was taken to a hospital. Both short- and long-term medical efforts failed, and, as a result, Cruzan degenerated to a persistent vegetative state, "a condition in which a person exhibits motor reflexes but evinces no indications of significant cognitive function." She required feeding and hydration tubes to stay alive. In short, when her case was before the Court, Nancy Cruzan was not dead, and some experts suggested that she could live another thirty years, but no one predicted any improvement in her condition.

Her parents, Lester and Joyce Cruzan, asked doctors to remove her feeding tubes, a step that would lead to Nancy's death. The hospital staff refused, and the Cruzans sought permission from a state court. They argued that "a person in Nancy's condition had a fundamental right to refuse or direct the withdrawal

of 'death prolonging procedures.'" The Cruzans presented as evidence that when Nancy was twenty-five, she had told a friend that "she would not wish to continue her life unless she could live it at least halfway normally."

The trial court ruled in their favor, but the state supreme court reversed. It found no support in common law for a right to die, and it refused to apply privacy doctrines to the Cruzan situation. It also held that because the state had a strong interest in preserving life, the Cruzans would have to provide "clear and convincing evidence" that Nancy would have wanted her feeding tubes withdrawn.

CHIEF JUSTICE REHNQUIST delivered the opinion of the Court.

We granted certiorari to consider the question of whether Cruzan has a right under the United States Constitution which would require the hospital to withdraw life-sustaining treatment from her under these circumstances. . . .

The Fourteenth Amendment provides that no state shall "deprive any person of life, liberty, or property, without due process of law." The principle that a competent person has a constitutionally protected liberty interest in refusing unwanted medical treatment may be inferred from our prior decisions. . . .

But determining that a person has a "liberty interest" under the Due Process Clause does not end the inquiry; "whether respondent's constitutional rights have been violated must be determined by balancing his liberty interests against the relevant state interests."

Petitioners insist that under the general holdings of our cases, the forced administration of life-sustaining medical treatment, and even of artificially-delivered food and water essential to life, would implicate a competent person's liberty interest. Although we think the logic of the cases . . . would embrace such a liberty interest, the dramatic consequences involved in refusal of such treatment would inform the inquiry as to whether the deprivation of that interest is constitutionally permissible. But for purposes of this case, we assume that the United States Constitution would grant a competent person a constitutionally protected right to refuse lifesaving hydration and nutrition.

Petitioners go on to assert that an incompetent person should possess the same right in this respect as is possessed by a competent person. . . .

The difficulty with petitioners' claim is that in a sense it begs the question: an incompetent person is not able to make an informed and voluntary choice to exercise a hypothetical right to refuse treatment or any other right. Such a "right" must be exercised for her, if at all, by some sort of surrogate. Here, Missouri has in effect recognized that under certain circumstances a surrogate may act for the patient in electing to have hydration and nutrition withdrawn in such a way as to cause death, but it has established a procedural safeguard to assure that the action of the surrogate conforms as best it may to the wishes expressed by the patient while competent. Missouri requires that evidence of the incompetent's wishes as to the withdrawal of treatment be proved by clear and convincing evidence. The question, then, is whether the United States Constitution forbids the establishment of this procedural requirement by the State. We hold that it does not.

Whether or not Missouri's clear and convincing evidence requirement comports with the United States Constitution depends in part on what interests the State may properly seek to protect in this situation. Missouri relies on its interest in the protection and preservation of human life, and there can be no gainsaying this interest. As a general matter, the States—indeed, all civilized nations—demonstrate their commitment to life by treating homicide as a serious crime. Moreover, the majority of States in this country have laws imposing criminal penalties on one who assists another to commit suicide. We do not think a State is required to remain neutral in the face of an informed and voluntary decision by a physically-able adult to starve to death.

But in the context presented here, a State has more particular interests at stake. The choice between life and death is a deeply personal decision of obvious and overwhelming finality. We believe Missouri may legitimately seek to safeguard the personal element of this choice through the imposition of heightened evidentiary requirements. It cannot be disputed that the Due Process Clause protects an interest in life as well as an interest in refusing life-sustaining medical treatment. Not all incompetent patients will have loved ones available to serve as surrogate decision-makers. And even where family members are present, "there will, of course, be some unfortunate situations in which family members will not act to protect a patient." A State is entitled to guard against potential abuses in such situations. Similarly, a State is entitled to consider that a judicial proceeding to make a determination regarding an incompetent's wishes may very well not be an adversarial one, with the added guarantee of accurate factfinding that the adversary process brings with it. Finally, we think a State may properly decline to make judgments about the "quality" of life that a particular individual may enjoy, and simply assert an unqualified interest in the preservation of human life to be weighed against the constitutionally protected interests of the individual.

In our view, Missouri has permissibly sought to advance these interests through the adoption of . . . "an intermediate standard of proof—'clear and convincing evidence'—when the individual interests at stake in a state proceeding are both 'particularly important' and 'more substantial than mere loss of money.'"

We think it self-evident that the interests at stake in the instant proceedings are more substantial, both on an individual and societal level, than those involved in a run-of-the-mine civil dispute. But not only does the standard of proof reflect the importance of a particular adjudication, it also serves as "a societal judgment about how the risk of error should be distributed between the litigants." The more stringent the burden of proof a party must bear, the more that party bears the risk of an erroneous decision. We believe that Missouri may permissibly place an increased risk of an erroneous decision on those seeking to terminate an incompetent individual's life-sustaining treatment. An erroneous decision not to terminate results in a maintenance of the status quo; the possibility of subsequent developments such as advancements in medical science, the discovery of new evidence regarding the patient's intent, changes in the law, or simply the unexpected death of the patient despite the administration of life-sustaining treatment, at least create the potential that a wrong decision will eventually be corrected or its impact mitigated. An erroneous decision to withdraw life-sustaining treatment, however, is not susceptible of correction. . . .

It is also worth noting that most, if not all, States simply forbid oral testimony entirely in determining the wishes of parties in transactions which, while important, simply do not have the consequences that a decision to terminate a person's life does. At common law and by statute in most States, the parole evidence rule prevents the variations of the terms of a written contract by oral testimony. The statute of frauds makes unenforceable oral contracts to leave property by will, and statutes regulating the making of wills universally require that those instruments be in writing. There is no doubt that statutes requiring wills to be in writing, and statutes of frauds which require that a contract to make a will be in writing, on occasion frustrate the effectuation of the intent of a particular decedent, just as Missouri's requirement of proof in this case may have frustrated the effectuation of the not-fully-expressed desires of Nancy Cruzan. But the Constitution does not require general rules to work faultlessly; no general rule can.

In sum, we conclude that a State may apply a clear and convincing evidence standard in proceedings where a guardian seeks to discontinue nutrition and hydration of a person diagnosed to be in a persistent vegetative state. . . .

The Supreme Court of Missouri held that in this case the testimony adduced at trial did not amount to clear and convincing proof of the patient's desire to have hydration and nutrition withdrawn. In so doing, it reversed a decision of the Missouri trial court which had found that the evidence "suggest[ed]" Nancy Cruzan would not have desired to continue such measures, but which had not adopted the standard of "clear and convincing evidence" enunciated by the Supreme Court. The testimony adduced at trial consisted primarily of Nancy Cruzan's statements made to a housemate about a year before her accident that she would not want to live should she face life as a "vegetable," and other observations to the same effect. The observations did not deal in terms with withdrawal of medical treatment or of hydration and nutrition. We cannot say that the Supreme Court of Missouri committed constitutional error in reaching the conclusion that it did.

Petitioners alternatively contend that Missouri must accept the "substituted judgment" of close family members even in the absence of substantial proof that their views reflect the views of the patient. . . . Here again petitioners would seek to turn a decision which allowed a State to rely on family decisionmaking into a constitutional requirement that the State recognize such decisionmaking. But constitutional law does not work that way.

No doubt is engendered by anything in this record but that Nancy Cruzan's mother and father are loving and caring parents. If the State were required by the United States Constitution to repose a right of "substituted judgment" with anyone, the Cruzans would surely qualify. But we do not think the Due Process Clause requires the State to repose judgment on these matters with anyone but the patient herself. Close family members may have a strong feeling—a feeling not at all ignoble or unworthy, but not entirely disinterested, either—that they do not wish to witness the continuation of the life of a loved one which they regard as hopeless, meaningless, and even degrading. But there is no automatic assurance that the view of close family members will necessarily be the same as the patient's would have been had she been confronted with the prospect of her situation while competent. All of the reasons previously discussed for allowing Missouri to require clear and convincing evidence of the patient's wishes lead us to conclude that the State may choose to defer only to those wishes, rather than confide the decision to close family members.

The judgment of the Supreme Court of Missouri is

Affirmed.

JUSTICE O'CONNOR, concurring.

I agree that a protected liberty interest in refusing unwanted medical treatment may be inferred from our prior decisions . . . and that the refusal of artificially delivered food and water is encompassed within that liberty interest. . . .

I . . . write separately to emphasize that the Court does not today decide the issue whether a State must also give effect to the decisions of a surrogate decisionmaker. In my view, such a duty may well be constitutionally required to protect the patient's liberty interest in refusing medical treatment. Few individuals provide explicit oral or written instructions regarding their intent to refuse medical treatment should they become incompetent. States which decline to consider any evidence other than such instructions may frequently fail to honor a patient's intent. Such failures might be avoided if the State considered an equally probative source of evidence: the patient's appointment of a proxy to make health care decisions on her behalf. Delegating the authority to make medical decisions to a family member or friend is becoming a common method of planning for the future. Several States have recognized the practical wisdom of such a procedure by enacting durable power of attorney statutes that specifically authorize an individual to appoint a surrogate to make medical treatment decisions. Some state courts have suggested that an agent appointed pursuant to a general durable power of attorney statute would also be empowered to make health care decisions on behalf of the patient. Other States allow an individual to designate a proxy to carry out the intent of a living will. These procedures for surrogate decisionmaking, which appear to be rapidly gaining in acceptance, may be a valuable additional safeguard of the patient's interest in directing his medical care. Moreover, as patients are likely to select a family member as a surrogate, giving effect to a proxy's decisions may also protect the "freedom of personal choice in matters of . . . family life."

Today's decision, holding only that the Constitution permits a State to require clear and convincing evidence of Nancy Cruzan's desire to have artificial hydration and nutrition withdrawn, does not preclude a future determination that the Constitution requires the States to implement the decisions of a patient's duly appointed surrogate. Nor does it prevent States from developing other approaches for protecting an incompetent individual's liberty interest in refusing medical treatment. . . . [N]o national consensus has yet emerged on the best solution for this difficult and sensitive problem. Today we decide only that one State's practice does not violate the Constitution; the more challenging task of crafting appropriate procedures for safeguarding incompetents' liberty interests is entrusted to the "laboratory" of the States.

JUSTICE SCALIA, concurring.

The various opinions in this case portray quite clearly the difficult, indeed agonizing, questions that are presented by the constantly increasing power of science to keep the human body alive for longer than any reasonable person would want to inhabit it. The States have begun to grapple with these problems through legislation. I am concerned, from the tenor of today's opinions, that we are poised to

confuse that enterprise as successfully as we have confused the enterprise of legislating concerning abortion—requiring it to be conducted against a background of federal constitutional imperatives that are unknown because they are being newly crafted from Term to Term. That would be a great misfortune.

While I agree with the Court's analysis today, and therefore join in its opinion, I would have preferred that we announce, clearly and promptly, that the federal courts have no business in this field; that American law has always accorded the State the power to prevent, by force if necessary, suicide—including suicide by refusing to take appropriate measures necessary to preserve one's life; that the point at which life becomes "worthless," and the point at which the means necessary to preserve it become "extraordinary" or "inappropriate," are neither set forth in the Constitution nor known to the nine Justices of this Court any better than they are known to nine people picked at random from the Kansas City telephone directory; and hence, that even when it *is* demonstrated by clear and convincing evidence that a patient no longer wishes certain measures to be taken to preserve her life, it is up to the citizens of Missouri to decide, through their elected representatives, whether that wish will be honored. It is quite impossible (because the Constitution says nothing about the matter) that those citizens will decide upon a line less lawful than the one we would choose; and it is unlikely (because we know no more about "life-and-death" than they do) that they will decide upon a line less reasonable.

The text of the Due Process Clause does not protect individuals against deprivations of liberty *simpliciter*. It protects them against deprivations of liberty "without due process of law." To determine that such a deprivation would not occur if Nancy Cruzan were forced to take nourishment against her will, it is unnecessary to reopen the historically recurrent debate over whether "due process" includes substantive restrictions. It is at least true that no "substantive due process" claim can be maintained unless the claimant demonstrates that the State has deprived him of a right historically and traditionally protected against State interference. That cannot possibly be established here.

At common law in England, a suicide—defined as one who "deliberately puts an end to his own existence, or commits any unlawful malicious act, the consequence of which is his own death"—was criminally liable. Although the States abolished the penalties imposed by the common law (*i.e.,* forfeiture and ignominious burial), they did so to spare the innocent family, and not to legitimize the act. Case law at the time of the Fourteenth Amendment generally held that assisting suicide was a criminal offense....

Petitioners rely on three distinctions to separate Nancy Cruzan's case from ordinary suicide: (1) that she is permanently incapacitated and in pain; (2) that she would bring on her death not by any affirmative act but by merely declining treatment that provides nourishment; and (3) that preventing her from effectuating her presumed wish to die requires violation of her bodily integrity. None of these suffices....

[An] asserted distinction—suggested by the recent cases canvassed by the Court concerning the right to refuse treatment—relies on the dichotomy between action and inaction. Suicide, it is said, consists of an affirmative act to end one's life; refusing treatment is not an affirmative act "causing" death, but merely a passive acceptance of the natural process of dying. I readily acknowledge that the distinction between action and inaction has some bearing upon the legislative judgment of what ought to be prevented as suicide—though even there it would seem to me unreasonable to draw the line precisely between action and inaction, rather than between various forms of inaction. It would not make much sense to say that one may not kill oneself by walking into the sea, but may sit on the beach until submerged by the incoming tide; or that one may not intentionally lock oneself into a cold storage locker, but may refrain from coming indoors when the temperature drops below freezing. Even as a legislative matter, in other words, the intelligent line does not fall between action and inaction but between those forms of inaction that consist of abstaining from "ordinary" care and those that consist of abstaining from "excessive" or "heroic" measures. Unlike action vs. inaction, that is not a line to be discerned by logic or legal analysis, and we should not pretend that it is.

But to return to the principal point for present purposes: the irrelevance of the action-inaction distinction. Starving oneself to death is no different from putting a gun to one's temple as far as the common-law definition of suicide is concerned; the cause of death in both cases is the

suicide's conscious decision to "pu[t] an end to his own existence."...

It is not surprising, therefore, that the early cases considering the claimed right to refuse medical treatment dismissed as specious the nice distinction between "passively submitting to death and actively seeking it. The distinction may be merely verbal, as it would be if an adult sought death by starvation instead of a drug. If the State may interrupt one mode of self-destruction, it may with equal authority interfere with the other."

The third asserted basis of distinction—that frustrating Nancy Cruzan's wish to die in the present case requires interference with her bodily integrity—is likewise inadequate, because such interference is impermissible only if one begs the question whether her refusal to undergo the treatment on her own is suicide. It has always been lawful not only for the State, but even for private citizens, to interfere with bodily integrity to prevent a felony. It is not even reasonable, much less required by the Constitution, to maintain that although the State has the right to prevent a person from slashing his wrists it does not have the power to apply physical force to prevent him from doing so, nor the power, should he succeed, to apply, coercively if necessary, medical measures to stop the flow of blood....

What I have said above is not meant to suggest that I would think it desirable, if we were sure that Nancy Cruzan wanted to die, to keep her alive by the means at issue here. I assert only that the Constitution has nothing to say about the subject. To raise up a constitutional right here we would have to create out of nothing (for it exists neither in text nor tradition) some constitutional principle whereby, although the State may insist that an individual come in out of the cold and eat food, it may not insist that he take medicine; and although it may pump his stomach empty of poison he has ingested, it may not fill his stomach with food he has failed to ingest. Are there, then, no reasonable and humane limits that ought not to be exceeded in requiring an individual to preserve his own life? There obviously are, but they are not set forth in the Due Process Clause. What assures us that those limits will not be exceeded is the same constitutional guarantee that is the source of most of our protection—what protects us, for example, from being assessed a tax of 100% of our income above the subsistence level, from being forbidden to drive cars, or from being required to send our children to school for 10 hours a day, none of which horribles is categorically prohibited by the Constitution. Our salvation is the Equal Protection Clause, which requires the democratic majority to accept for themselves and their loved ones what they impose on you and me. This Court need not, and has no authority to, inject itself into every field of human activity where irrationality and oppression may theoretically occur, and if it tries to do so it will destroy itself.

JUSTICE BRENNAN, with whom JUSTICE MARSHALL and JUSTICE BLACKMUN join, dissenting.

"Medical technology has effectively created a twilight zone of suspended animation where death commences while life, in some form, continues. Some patients, however, want no part of a life sustained only by medical technology. Instead, they prefer a plan of medical treatment that allows nature to take its course and permits them to die with dignity."

Nancy Cruzan has dwelt in that twilight zone for six years. She is oblivious to her surroundings and will remain so....

Today the Court, while tentatively accepting that there is some degree of constitutionally protected liberty interest in avoiding unwanted medical treatment, including life-sustaining medical treatment such as artificial nutrition and hydration, affirms the decision of the Missouri Supreme Court. The majority opinion, as I read it, would affirm that decision on the ground that a State may require "clear and convincing" evidence of Nancy Cruzan's prior decision to forgo life-sustaining treatment under circumstances such as hers in order to ensure that her actual wishes are honored. Because I believe that Nancy Cruzan has a fundamental right to be free of unwanted artificial nutrition and hydration, which right is not outweighed by any interests of the State, and because I find that the improperly biased procedural obstacles imposed by the Missouri Supreme Court impermissibly burden that right, I respectfully dissent. Nancy Cruzan is entitled to choose to die with dignity.

"[T]he timing of death—once a matter of fate—is now a matter of human choice." Of the approximately two million people who die each year, 80% die in hospitals and long-term care institutions, and perhaps 70% of those after a de-cision to forgo life-sustaining treatment has been made. Nearly every death involves a decision whether to undertake some medical procedure that could prolong the process of dying. Such decisions are difficult and personal. They must be made on the basis of individual values, informed by medical realities, yet within a framework governed by law. The role of the courts is confined to defining that framework, delineating the ways in which government may and may not participate in such decisions.

The question before this Court is a relatively narrow one: whether the Due Process Clause allows Missouri to require a now-incompetent patient in an irreversible persistent vegetative state to remain on life-support absent rigorously clear and convincing evidence that avoiding the treatment represents the patient's prior, express choice....

Although the right to be free of unwanted medical intervention, like other constitutionally protected interests, may not be absolute, no State interest could outweigh the rights of an individual in Nancy Cruzan's position. Whatever a State's possible interests in mandating life-support treatment under other circumstances, there is no good to be obtained here by Missouri's insistence that Nancy Cruzan remain on life-support systems if it is indeed her wish not to do so. Missouri does not claim, nor could it, that society as a whole will be benefited by Nancy's receiving medical treatment. No third party's situation will be improved and no harm to others will be averted.

The only state interest asserted here is a general interest in the preservation of life. But the State has no legitimate general interest in someone's life, completely abstracted from the interest of the person living that life, that could outweigh the person's choice to avoid medical treatment.... Thus, the State's general interest in life must accede to Nancy Cruzan's particularized and intense interest in self-determination in her choice of medical treatment. There is simply nothing legitimately within the State's purview to be gained by superseding her decision....

I do not suggest that States must sit by helplessly if the choices of incompetent patients are in danger of being ignored. Even if the Court had ruled that Missouri's rule of decision is unconstitutional, as I believe it should have, States would nevertheless remain free to fashion procedural protections to safeguard the interests of incompetents under these circumstances. The Constitution provides merely a framework here: protections must be genuinely aimed at ensuring decisions commensurate with the will of the patient, and must be reliable as instruments to that end. Of the many States which have instituted such protections, Missouri is virtually the only one to have fashioned a rule that lessens the likelihood of accurate determinations. In contrast, nothing in the Constitution prevents States from reviewing the advisability of a family decision, by requiring a court proceeding or by appointing an impartial guardian ad litem.

There are various approaches to determining an incompetent patient's treatment choice in use by the several States today and there may be advantages and disadvantages to each and other approaches not yet envisioned. The choice, in largest part, is and should be left to the States, so long as each State is seeking, in a reliable manner, to discover what the patient would want. But with such momentous interests in the balance, States must avoid procedures that will prejudice the decision....

Finally, I cannot agree with the majority that where it is not possible to determine what choice an incompetent patient would make, a State's role as *parens patriae* permits the State automatically to make that choice itself. Under fair rules of evidence, it is improbable that a court could not determine what the patient's choice would be. Under the rule of decision adopted by Missouri and upheld today by this Court, such occasions might be numerous. But in neither case does it follow that it is constitutionally acceptable for the State invariably to assume the role of deciding for the patient. A State's legitimate interest in safeguarding a patient's choice cannot be furthered by simply appropriating it.

The majority justifies its position by arguing that, while close family members may have a strong feeling about the question, "there is no automatic assurance that the view of close family members will necessarily be the same as the patient's would have been had she been confronted with the prospect of her situation while competent." I cannot quarrel with this observation. But it leads only to another question: Is there any reason to suppose that a State is *more* likely to make the choice that the patient would have made than someone who knew the patient intimately? To ask this is to answer it....

A State's inability to discern an incompetent patient's choice still need not mean that a State is rendered power-less to protect that choice. But I would find that the Due Process Clause prohibits a State from doing more than that. A State may ensure that the person who makes the decision on the patient's behalf is the one whom the patient himself would have selected to make that choice for him. And a State may exclude from consideration anyone having improper motives. But a State generally must either repose the choice with the person whom the patient himself would most likely have chosen as proxy or leave the decision to the patient's family.

As many as 10,000 patients are being maintained in persistent vegetative states in the United States, and the number is expected to increase significantly in the near future. Medical technology, developed over the past 20 or so years, is often capable of resuscitating people after they have stopped breathing or their hearts have stopped beating. Some of those people are brought fully back to life. Two decades ago, those who were not and could not swallow and digest food, died. Intravenous solutions could not provide sufficient calories to maintain people for more than a short time. Today, various forms of artificial feeding have been developed that are able to keep people metabolically alive for years, even decades. In addition, in this century, chronic or degenerative ailments have replaced communicable diseases as the primary causes of death. The 80% of Americans who die in hospitals are "likely to meet their end ... 'in a sedated or comatose state; betubed nasally, abdominally and intravenously; and far more like manipulated objects than like moral subjects.'" A fifth of all adults surviving to age 80 will suffer a progressive dementing disorder prior to death.

... The new medical technology can reclaim those who would have been irretrievably lost a few decades ago and restore them to active lives. For Nancy Cruzan, it failed, and for others with wasting incurable disease it may be doomed to failure. In these unfortunate situations, the bodies and preferences and memories of the victims do not escheat to the State; nor does our Constitution permit the State or any other government to commandeer them. No singularity of feeling exists upon which such a government might confidently rely as *parens patriae*.... Missouri and this Court have displaced Nancy's own assessment of the processes associated with dying. They have discarded evidence of her will, ignored her values, and deprived her of the right to a

BOX 7-1 LIVING WILLS

In 1976 California became the first state to adopt living will legislation. Since then almost all the other states have followed suit. Living wills permit individuals various types of control over the use of heroic, life-sustaining medical treatment in the event of a terminal illness. Demand for living will laws is a product of increased social concern with the ability and tendency of modern medicine to keep elderly, terminally ill, and permanently comatose patients alive beyond the natural course of death from age or infirmity. Respirators, cardiac resuscitation, artificial feeding and hydration, drug treatment, and other procedures all have surpassed a natural and easy death, often from pneumonia, known widely in the past as the "old man's friend." Living will laws—and the broader issue of the right to die—affect all age and social groups, although the growing elderly population is disproportionately affected. The issue is similar to abortion because it concerns the preservation of life, but at the opposite end of the life cycle.

NATURAL DEATH ACT DECLARATION
("LIVING WILL")

Virginia's Natural Death Act was enacted in 1983 to permit Virginians to record their wishes regarding extraordinary care in the event of terminal illness. The declaration below is the suggested form developed by the state legislators to implement the Act. Fill out this form and give it to your physician and any relatives and friends you would like to have a copy. You must sign in the presence of two witnesses, and both witnesses must sign in your presence. Blood relatives or spouse may not be witnesses.

DECLARATION

In accordance with the Virginia Natural Death Act, this Declaration was made on _____.
Month/Day/Year

I, _____, willfully and voluntarily make known my desire and do here-
Name of person making declaration

by declare:

You must choose between the following two paragraphs. PARAGRAPH ONE designates a person to make a decision for you. In PARAGRAPH TWO, you make the decision. Cross through the paragraph you do NOT want.

PARAGRAPH ONE:

If at any time I should have a terminal condition and I am comatose, incompetent or otherwise mentally or physically incapable of communication, I designate _____
to make a decision on my behalf as to whether life-prolonging procedures shall be withheld or withdrawn. In the event that my designee decides that such procedures should be withheld or withdrawn, I wish to be permitted to die naturally with only the administration of medication or the performance of any medical procedure deemed necessary to provide me with comfort care or to alleviate pain. (OPTION: I specifically direct that the following procedures or treatments be provided to me:

OR

PARAGRAPH TWO:

If at any time I should have a terminal condition where the application of life-prolonging procedures would serve only to artificially prolong the dying process, I direct that such procedures be withheld or withdrawn, and that I be permitted to die naturally with only the administration of medication or the performance of any medical procedure deemed necessary to provide me with comfort care or to alleviate pain. (OPTION: I specifically direct that the following procedures or treatments be provided to me:

_____

_____

decision as closely approximating her own choice as humanly possible. They have done so disingenuously in her name, and openly in Missouri's own. That Missouri and this Court may truly be motivated only by concern for incompetent patients makes no matter. . . .

I respectfully dissent.

In August 1990, two months after the Court's decision, the Cruzans petitioned a Missouri court for a new hearing. Three of Nancy's former co-workers testified that she had said she would not want to live "like a vegetable." Despite protests from right-to-life groups, a state court judge ruled December 14 that the Cruzans could have Nancy's feeding tube removed. She died December 26.

For the Cruzans the battle was over. But there are approximately 10,000 "Nancy Cruzans" in the United States, a figure that may increase tenfold as medical technology advances. Does the Court's opinion provide guidance for them and their families? Yes and no. On the one hand, the Court clearly ruled that the Fourteenth Amendment's Due Process Clause permits a competent individual to terminate medical treatment. As to incompetent patients, the majority of the justices suggested that states may fashion their own standards, including those that require "clear and convincing evidence" of the patient's interests. Living wills, as Justice O'Connor's concurrence suggests, may be the best form of such evidence *(see Box 7-1)*.

On the other hand, the case did not call for the Court to address squarely another dimension of the right-to-die question, suicides or "assisted suicides" for the terminally ill. May a person take his own life or arrange an assisted suicide when suffering from an illness that will surely result in death? In the 1990s this question has taken on unusual importance: the media are full of accounts of people in the advanced stages of AIDS seeking to end their lives and of the assisted suicides conducted by Dr. Jack Kevorkian and others. Some of the justices (see Scalia's opinion) pro-

vided indications of how they would rule on "mercy killings," assisted suicides, and so forth. But, for the most part, the Court has yet to decide whether the right to privacy or "liberty interest" is broad enough to encompass these practices. While we might speculate on the Court's response, it does seem inevitable that it will have to address this issue within the not-too-distant future.

REPRODUCTIVE FREEDOM AND THE RIGHT TO PRIVACY: ABORTION

Cruzan's treatment of the right-to-die issue and *Griswold*'s assertion of a right to privacy, more generally, continue to be hotly debated, but those discussions are mild compared to the controversy stirred up by the Court's use of the right-to-privacy doctrine to legalize abortion in *Roe v. Wade* (1973). Since this decision, virtually no other issue has come close to abortion on any political, legal, or emotional scale. It has affected the outcome of many political races; occupied preeminent places on legislative, executive, and judicial agendas; and played a role in the nomination proceedings for Supreme Court and lower federal court judges.

What is particularly intriguing about the issue is that the Court generated the furor. Prior to the 1973 decision in *Roe v. Wade*, abortion was not a significant political issue. As Figure 7-2 shows, many states had on their books laws enacted in the late 1800s that permitted abortion only to save the life of the mother. Other states had reformed their legislation in the 1960s to include legal abortion for pregnancies resulting from incest or those in which there was a high likelihood of a deformed baby. The majority of states defined performing or obtaining an abortion, under all other circumstances, as criminal offenses. These conditions do not mean that states were under no pressure to change their laws. During the 1960s a growing pro-choice movement, consisting of groups such as the ACLU and NARAL, which at that time

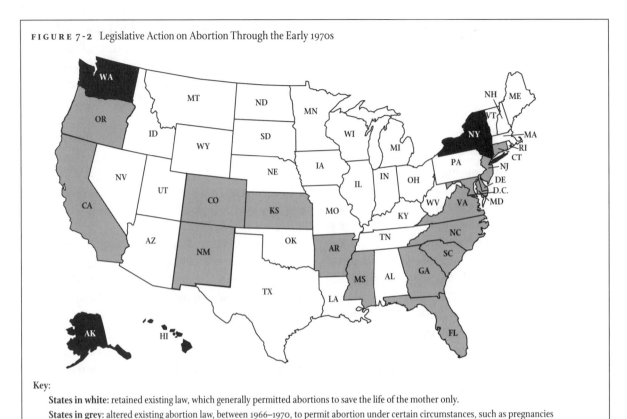

FIGURE 7-2   Legislative Action on Abortion Through the Early 1970s

Key:

States in white: retained existing law, which generally permitted abortions to save the life of the mother only.

States in grey: altered existing abortion law, between 1966–1970, to permit abortion under certain circumstances, such as pregnancies resulting from rape or incest.

States in black: repealed existing abortion law in 1970 to allow for some form of "abortion on demand."

stood for the National Association for Repeal of Abortion Laws, sought to convince states to legalize fully the procedure, that is, allow abortion on demand.

When only a handful of states even considered taking such action, attorneys and leaders of the pro-choice movement supplemented their legislative lobbying with litigation, initiating dozens of suits in federal and state courts. These cases challenged restrictive abortion laws on a number of grounds, including the First Amendment's freedoms of association and speech for doctors (and patients) and the Fourteenth Amendment's Equal Protection Clause (discrimination against women). But the most commonly invoked legal ground was *Griswold*'s right to privacy. Because it was unclear to attorneys which

clause of the Constitution generated the right to privacy *(see Table 7-1)*, in many cases, pro-choice lawyers covered their bases by arguing on all three specific grounds. But their larger point was clear: the right to privacy was broad enough to encompass the right to obtain an abortion. And, because the right to privacy was "fundamental," logic would hold that the right to obtain an abortion was also fundamental, meaning that states could proscribe the procedure only with a compelling interest. Such an interest, pro-choice attorneys asserted, did not exist.

The result of this legal activity was an "avalanche" of litigation. Pro-choice groups had flooded the U.S. courts with lawsuits—some on behalf of doctors, some for women—challenging both major kinds of abortion laws: those that permitted abortion only to save the life of the mother and those that allowed abortion in cases of rape or incest or to save the life of the mother. They were hoping that the Supreme Court would hear at least one.

Their wish was granted when the Court agreed to hear arguments in December of 1971 in two cases, *Roe v. Wade*, a challenge to a Texas law, representing the most restrictive kinds of abortion laws, and *Doe v. Bolton*, a challenge to a Georgia law, representing the newer, less restrictive laws. But, as Box 7-2 describes, the Court faced problems in resolving these cases and asked the attorneys to reargue them at the beginning of the next term.

In the meantime, the justices handed down a decision that had some bearing on the debate. The Court struck down a Massachusetts law that prohibited the sale of contraceptives to unmarried people. Writing for a six-person majority (with only Burger dissenting) in *Eisenstadt v. Baird* (1972), Justice Brennan asserted that the law violated the "rights of single people" under the Fourteenth Amendment's Equal Protection Clause. But, in dicta, he went much further:

If under *Griswold* the distribution of contraceptives to married persons cannot be prohibited, a ban on distribution to unmarried persons would be equally impermissible. It is true that in *Griswold* the right of privacy in question inhered in the marital relationship. Yet the marital couple is not an independent entity with a mind and heart of its own, but an association of two individuals each with separate intellectual and emotional makeup. If the right of privacy means anything, it is the right of the *individual,* married or single, to be free from unwarranted governmental intrusion into matters so fundamentally affecting a person as the decision whether to bear or beget a child.

Whether he wrote this with *Roe* and *Doe* in mind we do not know, but clearly *Eisenstadt* heartened prochoice forces. Their optimism was not misplaced, for, on January 22, 1973, when the Court handed down its decisions in *Roe* and *Doe*, they had won. As you read *Roe*, pay particular attention to the Court's logic: On what grounds did it strike the Texas law?

Roe v. Wade

410 U.S. 113 (1973)
Vote: 7 (Blackmun, Brennan, Burger, Douglas, Marshall,
     Powell, Stewart)
  2 (Rehnquist, White)
Opinion of the Court: Blackmun
Concurring opinions: Burger, Douglas, Stewart
Dissenting opinions: Rehnquist, White

In August 1969, twenty-one-year-old Norma McCorvey claimed to have been raped and, as a result, was pregnant.[18] Her doctor refused to give her an abortion, citing an 1857 Texas law, revised in 1879, that made it a crime to "procure an abortion" unless it was necessary to save the life of a mother. He provided her with the name of a lawyer who handled adoptions. The lawyer, in turn, sent her to two other attorneys, Linda Coffee and Sarah Weddington, who he knew were interested in challenging the Texas law.

Coffee and Weddington went after the Texas law with a vengeance, challenging it on all possible grounds: privacy, women's rights, due process, and so forth. Their efforts paid off; a three-judge district court ruled in their favor, mostly on Ninth Amendment privacy grounds. But because it would not issue an injunction to the state law, McCorvey, using the pseudonym Jane Roe, and her attorneys appealed to the U.S. Supreme Court.

Once the Supreme Court agreed to hear the case, pro-choice and pro-life sides mobilized their forces. On the pro-choice side, the ACLU and other groups helped Weddington and Coffee, who had never appeared before the Court, prepare their briefs and arguments. These groups also lined up numerous

---

18. We draw some of this discussion from Marion Faux, *Roe v. Wade* (New York: Macmillan, 1988); and Lee Epstein and Joseph F. Kobylka, *The Supreme Court and Legal Change* (Chapel Hill: University of North Carolina Press, 1992). For other accounts, see Eva Rubin, *Abortion, Politics, and the Courts* (Westport, Conn.: Greenwood Press, 1987); and Richard C. Cortner, *The Supreme Court and Civil Liberties Policy* (Palo Alto, Calif.: Mayfield, 1975).

BOX 7-2 WHY WERE *ROE* AND *DOE* REARGUED?

On December 13, 1971, the Supreme Court heard oral arguments in *Roe v. Wade* and *Doe v. Bolton*, but it did not decide those cases until January 22, 1973. What took the Court so long to issue its opinion?

Three days after the oral arguments, the Court met in conference to decide the cases. Only seven justices were present because President Nixon's newest appointees, Lewis F. Powell, Jr., and William H. Rehnquist, had not participated in the cases' oral arguments. Of the seven participating justices, a four-person majority (Douglas, Brennan, Marshall, and Stewart) thought the abortion laws should be stricken, although for somewhat different reasons. Moreover, they were unsure about the "time problem"—whether a woman could obtain an abortion any time during her pregnancy or over a more limited period, such as the first six months. The remaining three justices were more fragmented. White came down most definitively in favor of the pro-life position. Burger and Blackmun, who had joined the Court in 1969 and 1970, respectively, were less decisive; the chief justice leaned toward upholding laws prohibiting abortion, and Blackmun leaned toward the pro-choice camp. Therefore—although there was disagreement over the reason why the laws were unconstitutional and over the time frame for abortions—the result was clear: the pro-choice side would win by a vote of 5–2 or 4–3, depending on how Blackmun voted.

Despite the fact that Blackmun's vote was unclear, Chief Justice Burger assigned the opinion to him. Burger may have assumed that Blackmun, as the weakest link in the Brennan-Douglas-Stewart-Marshall chain (if he was indeed part of that chain), would write the narrowest possible opinion. This (mis)assignment triggered a series of events, the first of which was an irate letter from Douglas to Burger. He had two bones to pick: first, that as the senior member of the majority, he should have assigned the opinion; and second, Blackmun should not have received the assignment in any event because he was in the minority or, at best, ambivalent. Douglas wrote, "I would think, therefore, that to save time and trouble, one of the four [in the majority], rather than

one of the three [in the minority], should write the opinion." Burger responded two days later: "At the close of discussion of this case, I remarked to the Conference that there were, literally, not enough columns to mark up an accurate reflection of the voting in either the Georgia or the Texas cases. I therefore marked down no votes and said this was a case that would have to stand or fall on the writing, when it was done." Burger concluded, "That is still my view of how to handle these two ... sensitive cases, which, I might add, *are quite probable candidates for reargument*" (emphasis added).

On the heels of this dispute, some of the justices began preparing draft opinions. It took Douglas only four days to write a "dissenting" opinion, which he gave to Brennan. In it, he asserted that the right to an abortion could be found in the word "liberty" in the Due Process Clause. Brennan responded ten days later with some suggestions for revision and with the admonition that Douglas hold off sending the draft to Blackmun until he circulated his. Douglas heeded this advice, redrafting the opinion to center on a woman's right to obtain abortion services. By late February, however, his patience exhausted, Douglas sent his revised opinion to Blackmun.

It was not until mid-May 1972 that Blackmun circulated his draft of the *Roe* opinion. While he stressed in his cover memo that this was a "first and tentative draft," Douglas and Brennan were deeply disappointed. Blackmun struck down the Texas law on the narrowest possible grounds and did not deal with the "core constitutional questions," such as whether the right to privacy encapsulated the abortion right.

Several days after both Brennan and Douglas urged him to recast his draft, Blackmun circulated his *Doe* opinion. This opinion was far more to the their liking because it adopted much of what Douglas's second draft had to say about privacy and women's rights. Where they thought Blackmun went astray was in exploring the state's interest in protecting life. In this version, he stressed the point that somewhere around quickening a woman's right to privacy is no longer "unlimited. It must be balanced against the state. [Thus] we cannot automatically strike down ... features of the Georgia statute simply because they restrict any right on the part of the woman to have an abortion at will." Despite the qualms Brennan and Douglas had over such a balancing approach, they planned to sign the opinion; it led Blackmun to the "right" result.

Just when it appeared as if a five-person majority would coalesce around Blackmun's opinion, Burger re-initiated efforts to have the case reargued. Ostensibly, his reason was that "These cases ... are not as simple for me as they appear for the others." He also "complained that part of his problem ... resulted from the poor quality of oral argument." Brennan, Douglas, Stewart, and Marshall disagreed. In their view, Burger pushed for reargument because he was displeased with Blackmun's opinion in *Doe* and thought his side would stand a better chance of victory next term when two more Nixon appointees—Powell and Rehnquist—would participate in orals. Douglas later suggested that Burger believed the *Doe* opinion would prove embarrassing to President Nixon's reelection campaign, and sought to minimize the damage. On the same day, May 31, Blackmun also suggested that the cases be reargued. In a memo to conference, he wrote: "Although it would prove costly to me personally, in the light of energy and hours expended, I have now concluded, somewhat reluctantly, that reargument in *both* cases at an early date in the next term, would perhaps be advisable." Despite Brennan's and Douglas's attempts to thwart this action,* after White and the two new appointees voted with Burger, on the last day of the 1971 term the Court ordered rearguments in both *Roe* and *Doe.*

SOURCE: Lee Epstein and Joseph F. Kobylka, *The Supreme Court and Legal Change: Abortion and the Death Penalty* (Chapel Hill: University of North Carolina Press, 1992), 182–186.

* Both Brennan and Douglas wrote letters to Blackmun attempting to convince him that the cases should not be reargued. When they failed to convince Blackmun, Douglas warned Burger, saying, "If the vote of Conference is to reargue, then I will file a statement telling what is happening to us and the tragedy it entails." He also accused Burger, in a memo to conference, of trying "to bend the Court to his will" and imperiling "the integrity of the institution." Douglas never carried through on his threat to take the matter public, but the *Washington Post* carried a story about it.

amici, ranging from the American College of Obstetricians and Gynecologists to the Planned Parenthood Federation to the American Association of University Women. In general, the pro-choice side wanted to convince the Court that abortion was a fundamental right under the *Griswold* doctrine. So unless the state could provide a compelling and narrowly drawn interest, the Texas law should fall. It also presented a mass of data indicating that physical and mental health risks are associated with restrictive abortion laws.

The state countered with arguments concerning the rights of fetuses. In its brief, it devoted twenty-four pages, along with nine photographs of fetuses at various stages of development, to depict the "humanness" of the unborn and to support its argument that a state has a compelling interest in protecting human life. The state's position was supported by several pro-life organizations (including the National Right to Life Committee and the League for Infants, Fetuses, and the Elderly) and groups of doctors and nurses.

MR. JUSTICE BLACKMUN delivered the opinion of the Court.

We forthwith acknowledge our awareness of the sensitive and emotional nature of the abortion controversy, of the vigorous opposing views, even among physicians, and of the deep and seemingly absolute convictions that the subject inspires. One's philosophy, one's experiences, one's exposure to the raw edges of human existence, one's religious training, one's attitudes toward life and family and their values, and the moral standards one establishes and seeks to observe, are all likely to influence and to color one's thinking and conclusions about abortion.

In addition, population growth, pollution, poverty, and racial overtones tend to complicate and not to simplify the problem.

Our task, of course, is to resolve the issue by constitutional measurement, free of emotion and of predilection. We seek earnestly to do this, and, because we do, we have inquired into, and in this opinion place some emphasis

Norma McCorvey (shown here in 1989) was the real "Jane Roe." She challenged the constitutionality of the Texas anti-abortion statute. The suit was resolved in 1973 when the Supreme Court handed down its decision in *Roe v. Wade*, declaring that the right to privacy protected a woman's freedom to terminate a pregnancy.

upon, medical and medical-legal history and what that history reveals about man's attitudes toward the abortion procedure over the centuries....

The principal thrust of appellant's attack on the Texas statutes is that they improperly invade a right, said to be possessed by the pregnant woman, to choose to terminate her pregnancy. Appellant would discover this right in the concept of personal "liberty" embodied in the Fourteenth Amendment's Due Process Clause in personal, marital, familial, and sexual privacy said to be protected by the Bill of Rights or its penumbras, see Griswold v. Connecticut (1965), or among those rights reserved to the people by the Ninth Amendment, Griswold v. Connecticut. Before addressing this claim, we feel it desirable briefly to survey, in several aspects, the history of abortion, for such insight as that history may afford us, and then to examine the state purposes and interests behind the criminal abortion laws.

It perhaps is not generally appreciated that the restrictive criminal abortion laws in effect in a majority of

States today are of relatively recent vintage. Those laws, generally proscribing abortion or its attempt at any time during pregnancy except when necessary to preserve the pregnant woman's life, are not of ancient or even of common-law origin. Instead, they derive from statutory changes effected, for the most part, in the latter half of the 19th century.

1. *Ancient attitudes.* These are not capable of precise determination. We are told that at the time of the Persian Empire abortifacients were known and that criminal abortions were severely punished. We are also told, however, that abortion was practiced in Greek times as well as in the Roman Era, and that "it was resorted to without scruple."... Greek and Roman law afforded little protection to the unborn. If abortion was prosecuted in some places, it seems to have been based on a concept of a violation of the father's right to his offspring. Ancient religion did not bar abortion....

[2 omitted]

3. *The common law.* It is undisputed that at common law, abortion performed *before* "quickening"—the first recognizable movement of the fetus *in utero,* appearing usually from the 16th to the 18th week of pregnancy—was not an indictable offense. The absence of a common-law crime for pre-quickening abortion appears to have developed from a confluence of earlier philosophical, theological, and civil and canon law concepts of when life begins.... There was agreement ... that prior to this point the fetus was to be regarded as part of the mother, and its destruction, therefore, was not homicide.... The significance of quickening was echoed by later common-law scholars and found its way into the received common law in this country.

Whether abortion of a *quick* fetus was a felony at common law, or even a lesser crime, is still disputed.... In a frequently cited passage, Coke[19] took the position that abortion of a woman "quick with childe" is "a great misprision, and no murder."... A recent review of the common-law precedents argues, however, that those precedents contradict Coke and that even post-quickening abortion was never established as a common-law crime. This is of some importance because while most American courts ruled, in holding or dictum, that abortion of an unquickened fetus was not criminal under their received common law, others followed Coke in stating that abortion of a quick fetus was a "misprision," a term they translated to mean "misdemeanor." That their reliance on Coke on this aspect of the law was uncritical and, apparently in all the reported cases, dictum (due probably to the paucity of common-law prosecutions for post-quickening abortion), makes it now appear doubtful that abortion was ever firmly established as a common-law crime even with respect to the destruction of a quick fetus.

4. *The English statutory law.* England's first criminal abortion statute, Lord Ellenborough's Act, came in 1803. It made abortion of a quick fetus a capital crime, but in § 2 it provided lesser penalties for the felony of abortion before quickening, and thus preserved the "quickening" distinction. This contrast was continued in the general revision of 1828. It disappeared, however, together with the

death penalty, in 1837 and did not reappear in the Offenses Against the Person Act of 1861 that formed the core of English anti-abortion law until the liberalizing reforms of 1967. In 1929, the Infant Life (Preservation) Act came into being. Its emphasis was upon the destruction of "the life of a child capable of being born alive." It made a willful act performed with the necessary intent a felony....

Recently, Parliament enacted a new abortion law. This is the Abortion Act of 1967. The Act permits a licensed physician to perform an abortion where two other licensed physicians agree (a) "that the continuance of the pregnancy would involve risk to the life of the pregnant woman, or of injury to the physical or mental health of the pregnant woman or any existing children of her family, greater than if the pregnancy were terminated," or (b) "that there is a substantial risk that if the child were born it would suffer from such physical or mental abnormalities as to be seriously handicapped."...

5. *The American law.* In this country, the law in effect in all but a few States until mid-19th century was the pre-existing English common law. Connecticut, the first State to enact abortion legislation, adopted in 1821 that part of Lord Ellenborough's Act that related to a woman "quick with child." The death penalty was not imposed. Abortion before quickening was made a crime in that State only in 1860. In 1828, New York enacted legislation that, in two respects, was to serve as a model for early anti-abortion statutes. First, while barring destruction of a quickened fetus as well as a quick fetus, it made the former only a misdemeanor, but the latter second-degree manslaughter. Second, it incorporated a concept of therapeutic abortion by providing that an abortion was excused if it "shall have been necessary to preserve the life of such mother, or shall have been advised by two physicians to be necessary for such purpose." By 1840, when Texas had received the common law, only eight American States had statutes dealing with abortion. It was not until after the War Between the States that legislation began generally to replace the common law. Most of these initial statutes dealt severely with abortion after quickening but were lenient with it before quickening. Most punished attempts equally with completed abortions. While many statutes included the exception for an abortion thought by one or more physicians to be necessary to save the mother's life, that provision

19. [Authors' note.] Sir Edward Coke (1552–1634) was chief justice of the British Court of Common Pleas. He is known as a great, if not the greatest, authority on common law.

soon disappeared and the typical law required that the procedure actually be necessary for that purpose.

Gradually, in the middle and late 19th century the quickening distinction disappeared from the statutory law of most States and the degree of the offense and the penalties were increased. By the end of the 1950's a large majority of the jurisdictions banned abortion, however and whenever performed, unless done to save or preserve the life of the mother.... In the past several years, however, a trend toward liberalization of abortion statutes has resulted in adoption, by about one-third of the States, of less stringent laws.

It is thus apparent that at common law, at the time of the adoption of our Constitution, and throughout the major portion of the 19th century, abortion was viewed with less disfavor than under most American statutes currently in effect. Phrasing it another way, a woman enjoyed a substantially broader right to terminate a pregnancy than she does in most States today. At least with respect to the early stage of pregnancy, and very possibly without such a limitation, the opportunity to make this choice was present in this country well into the 19th century. Even later, the law continued for some time to treat less punitively an abortion procured in early pregnancy.

6. *The position of the American Medical Association.* The anti-abortion mood prevalent in this country in the late 19th century was shared by the medical profession. Indeed, the attitude of the profession may have played a significant role in the enactment of stringent criminal abortion legislation during that period.

An AMA Committee on Criminal Abortion was appointed in May 1857. It presented its report (1859) to the Twelfth Annual Meeting. That report observed that the Committee had been appointed to investigate criminal abortion "with a view to its general suppression." It deplored abortion and its frequency....

In 1970, after the introduction of a variety of proposed resolutions, and of a report from its Board of Trustees, a reference committee noted "polarization of the medical profession on this controversial issue"; division among those who had testified; a difference of opinion among AMA councils and committees; "the remarkable shift in testimony" in six months, felt to be influenced "by the rapid changes in state laws and by the judicial decisions which tend to make abortion more freely available"; and a feeling "that this trend will continue." On June 25, 1970, the House of Delegates adopted preambles and most of the resolutions proposed by the reference committee. The preambles emphasized "the best interests of the patient," "sound clinical judgment," and "informed patient consent," in contrast to "mere acquiescence to the patient's demand." The resolutions asserted that abortion is a medical procedure that should be performed by a licensed physician in an accredited hospital only after consultation with two other physicians and in conformity with state law, and that no party to the procedure should be required to violate personally held moral principles. The AMA Judicial Council rendered a complementary opinion....

Three reasons have been advanced to explain historically the enactment of criminal abortion laws in the 19th century and to justify their continued existence.

It has been argued occasionally that these laws were the product of a Victorian social concern to discourage illicit sexual conduct. Texas, however, does not advance this justification in the present case, and it appears that no court or commentator has taken the argument seriously....

A second reason is concerned with abortion as a medical procedure. When most criminal abortion laws were first enacted, the procedure was a hazardous one for the woman. This was particularly true prior to the development of antisepsis.... Thus, it has been argued that a State's real concern in enacting a criminal abortion law was to protect the pregnant woman, that is, to restrain her from submitting to a procedure that placed her life in serious jeopardy.

The modern medical techniques have altered this situation.... Consequently, any interest of the State in protecting the woman from an inherently hazardous procedure, except when it would be equally dangerous for her to forgo it, has largely disappeared. Of course, important state interests in the areas of health and medical standards do remain. The State has a legitimate interest in seeing to it that abortion, like any other medical procedure, is performed under circumstances that insure maximum safety for the patient.... Moreover, the risk to the woman increases as her pregnancy continues. Thus, the State retains a definite interest in protecting the woman's own health and safety when an abortion is proposed at a late stage of pregnancy.

The third reason is the State's interest—some phrase it in terms of duty—in protecting prenatal life. Some of the argument for this justification rests on the theory that a new human life is present from the moment of conception. The State's interest and general obligation to protect life then extends, it is argued, to prenatal life. Only when the life of the pregnant mother herself is at stake, balanced against the life she carries within her, should the interest of the embryo or fetus not prevail. Logically, of course, a legitimate state interest in this area need not stand or fall on acceptance of the belief that life begins at conception or at some other point prior to live birth. In assessing the State's interest, recognition may be given to the less rigid claim that as long as at least *potential* life is involved, the State may assert interests beyond the protection of the pregnant woman alone....

It is with these interests, and the weight to be attached to them, that this case is concerned.

The Constitution does not explicitly mention any right of privacy. In a line of decisions, however, the Court has recognized that a right of personal privacy, or a guarantee of certain areas or zones of privacy, does exist under the Constitution. In varying contexts, the Court or individual Justices have, indeed, found at least the roots of that right in the First Amendment, in the Fourth and Fifth Amendments, in the penumbras of the Bill of Rights, in the Ninth Amendment, or in the concept of liberty guaranteed by the first section of the Fourteenth Amendment. These decisions make it clear that only personal rights that can be deemed "fundamental" or "implicit in the concept of ordered liberty" are included in this guarantee of personal privacy. They also make it clear that the right has some extension to activities relating to marriage, procreation, family relationships, and child rearing and education.

This right of privacy, whether it be founded in the Fourteenth Amendment's concept of personal liberty and restrictions upon state action, as we feel it is, or, as the District Court determined, in the Ninth Amendment's reservation of rights to the people, is broad enough to encompass a woman's decision whether or not to terminate her pregnancy. The detriment that the State would impose upon the pregnant woman by denying this choice altogether is apparent. Specific and direct harm medically diagnosable even in early pregnancy may be involved. Maternity, or additional offspring, may force upon the woman a distressful life and future. Psychological harm may be imminent. Mental and physical health may be taxed by child care. There is also the distress, for all concerned, associated with the unwanted child, and there is the problem of bringing a child into a family already unable, psychologically and otherwise, to care for it. In other cases, as in this one, the additional difficulties and continuing stigma of unwed motherhood may be involved. All these are factors the woman and her responsible physician necessarily will consider in consultation.

On the basis of elements such as these, appellant and some *amici* argue that the woman's right is absolute and that she is entitled to terminate her pregnancy at whatever time, in whatever way, and for whatever reason she alone chooses. With this we do not agree. Appellant's arguments that Texas either has no valid interest at all in regulating the abortion decision, or no interest strong enough to support any limitation upon the woman's sole determination, are unpersuasive. The Court's decisions recognizing a right of privacy also acknowledge that some state regulation in areas protected by that right is appropriate. As noted above, a State may properly assert important interests in safeguarding health, in maintaining medical standards, and in protecting potential life. At some point in pregnancy, these respective interests become sufficiently compelling to sustain regulation of the factors that govern the abortion decision. The privacy right involved, therefore, cannot be said to be absolute....

We, therefore, conclude that the right of personal privacy includes the abortion decision, but that this right is not unqualified and must be considered against important state interests in regulation....

The District Court held that the appellee failed to meet his burden of demonstrating that the Texas statute's infringement upon Roe's rights was necessary to support a compelling state interest, and that, although the appellee presented "several compelling justifications for state presence in the area of abortions," the statutes outstripped these justifications and swept "far beyond any areas of compelling state interest." Appellant and appellee both contest that holding. Appellant, as has been indicated, claims an absolute right that bars any state imposition of criminal penalties in the area. Appellee argues that the State's determination to recognize and protect prenatal life from and after conception constitutes a compelling state interest. As noted above, we do not agree fully with either formulation.

A. The appellee and certain *amici* argue that the fetus is a "person" within the language and meaning of the Fourteenth Amendment....

The Constitution does not define "person" in so many words. Section 1 of the Fourteenth Amendment contains three references to "person." The first, in defining "citizens," speaks of "persons born or naturalized in the United States." The word also appears both in the Due Process Clause and in the Equal Protection Clause. "Person" is used in other places in the Constitution: in the listing of qualifications for Representatives and Senators, Art. I, § 2, cl. 2, and § 3, cl. 3; in the Apportionment Clause, Art. I, § 2, § 3.... But in nearly all these instances, the use of the word is such that it has application only postnatally. None indicates, with any assurance, that it has any possible prenatal application.

All this, together with our observation that throughout the major portion of the 19th century prevailing legal abortion practices were far freer than they are today, persuades us that the word "person," as used in the Fourteenth Amendment, does not include the unborn....

This conclusion, however, does not of itself fully answer the contentions raised by Texas, and we pass on to other considerations.

B. The pregnant woman cannot be isolated in her privacy. She carries an embryo and, later, a fetus, if one accepts the medical definitions of the developing young in the human uterus. The situation therefore is inherently different from marital intimacy, or bedroom possession of obscene material, or marriage, or procreation.... As we have intimated above, it is reasonable and appropriate for a State to decide that at some point in time another interest, that of health of the mother or that of potential human life, becomes significantly involved. The woman's privacy is no longer sole and any right of privacy she possesses must be measured accordingly.

Texas urges that, apart from the Fourteenth Amendment, life begins at conception and is present throughout pregnancy, and that, therefore, the State has a compelling interest in protecting that life from and after conception. We need not resolve the difficult question of when life

begins. When those trained in the respective disciplines of medicine, philosophy, and theology are unable to arrive at any consensus, the judiciary, at this point in the development of man's knowledge, is not in a position to speculate as to the answer....

In view of all this, we do not agree that, by adopting one theory of life, Texas may override the rights of the pregnant woman that are at stake. We repeat, however, that the State does have an important and legitimate interest in preserving and protecting the health of the pregnant woman, whether she be a resident of the State or a non-resident who seeks medical consultation and treatment there, and that it has still another important and legitimate interest in protecting the potentiality of human life. These interests are separate and distinct. Each grows in substantiality as the woman approaches term and, at a point during pregnancy, each becomes "compelling."

With respect to the State's important and legitimate interest in the health of the mother, the "compelling" point, in the light of present medical knowledge, is at approximately the end of the first trimester. This is so because of the now-established medical fact ... that until the end of the first trimester mortality in abortion may be less than mortality in normal childbirth. It follows that, from and after this point, a State may regulate the abortion procedure to the extent that the regulation reasonably relates to the preservation and protection of maternal health. Examples of permissible state regulation in this area are requirements as to the qualifications of the person who is to perform the abortion; as to the licensure of that person; as to the facility in which the procedure is to be performed, that is, whether it must be a hospital or may be a clinic or some other place of less-than-hospital status; as to the licensing of the facility; and the like.

This means, on the other hand, that, for the period of pregnancy prior to this "compelling" point, the attending physician, in consultation with his patient, is free to determine, without regulation by the State, that, in his medical judgment, the patient's pregnancy should be terminated. If that decision is reached, the judgment may be effectuated by an abortion free of interference by the State.

With respect to the State's important and legitimate interest in potential life, the "compelling" point is at viability. This is so because the fetus then presumably has the capability of meaningful life outside the mother's womb. State regulation protective of fetal life after viability thus has both logical and biological justifications. If the State is interested in protecting fetal life after viability, it may go so far as to proscribe abortion during that period, except when it is necessary to preserve the life or health of the mother.

Measured against these standards, ... the Texas [law] ..., in restricting legal abortions to those "procured or attempted by medical advice for the purpose of saving the life of the mother," sweeps too broadly. The statute makes no distinction between abortions performed early in pregnancy and those performed later, and it limits to a single reason, "saving" the mother's life, the legal justification for the procedure. The statute, therefore, cannot survive the constitutional attack made upon it here....

To summarize and to repeat:

1. A state criminal abortion statute of the current Texas type, that excepts from criminality only a *life-saving* procedure on behalf of the mother, without regard to pregnancy stage and without recognition of the other interests involved, is violative of the Due Process Clause of the Fourteenth Amendment.

(a) For the stage prior to approximately the end of the first trimester, the abortion decision and its effectuation must be left to the medical judgment of the pregnant woman's attending physician.

(b) For the stage subsequent to approximately the end of the first trimester, the State, in promoting its interest in the health of the mother, may, if it chooses, regulate the abortion procedure in ways that are reasonably related to maternal health.

(c) For the stage subsequent to viability, the State in promoting its interest in the potentiality of human life may, if it chooses, regulate, and even proscribe, abortion except where it is necessary, in appropriate medical judgment, for the preservation of the life or health of the mother....

This holding, we feel, is consistent with the relative weights of the respective interests involved, with the lessons and examples of medical and legal history, with the lenity of the common law, and with the demands of the profound problems of the present day. The decision leaves the State free to place increasing restrictions on abortion as the period of pregnancy lengthens, so long as those re-

strictions are tailored to the recognized state interests. The decision vindicates the right of the physician to administer medical treatment according to his professional judgment up to the points where important state interests provide compelling justifications for intervention. Up to those points, the abortion decision in all its aspects is inherently, and primarily, a medical decision, and basic responsibility for it must rest with the physician. If an individual practitioner abuses the privilege of exercising proper medical judgment, the usual remedies, judicial and intra-professional, are available.[20]

MR. JUSTICE REHNQUIST, dissenting.

The Court's opinion brings to the decision of this troubling question both extensive historical fact and a wealth of legal scholarship. While the opinion thus commands my respect, I find myself nonetheless in fundamental disagreement with those parts of it that invalidate the Texas statute in question, and therefore dissent....

... I have difficulty in concluding, as the Court does, that the right of "privacy" is involved in this case. Texas, by the statute here challenged, bars the performance of a medical abortion by a licensed physician on a plaintiff such as Roe. A transaction resulting in an operation such as this is not "private" in the ordinary usage of that word. Nor is the "privacy" that the Court finds here even a distant relative of the freedom from searches and seizures protected by the Fourth Amendment to the Constitution, which the Court has referred to as embodying a right to privacy. Katz v. United States (1967).

If the Court means by the term "privacy" no more than that the claim of a person to be free from unwanted state regulation of consensual transactions may be a form of

20. [Authors' note.] In *Doe*, decided the same day as *Roe*, the Court reviewed a challenge to the newer abortion laws, enacted by some states in the 1960s. While Texas permitted abortions only to save a mother's life, Georgia allowed them under the following circumstances: (1) when a "duly licensed Georgia physician" determines in "his best clinical judgment" that carrying the baby to term would injure the mother's life or health; (2) when a high likelihood existed that the fetus would be born with a serious deformity; and (3) when the pregnancy was the result of rape. The law contained other requirements, the most stringent of which was that two other doctors agree with the judgment of the one performing the abortion. Reiterating his opinion in *Roe*, Blackmun struck down the Georgia law as a violation of Fourteenth Amendment guarantees. Once again, six other members of the Court agreed with his conclusion.

"liberty" protected by the Fourteenth Amendment, there is no doubt that similar claims have been upheld in our earlier decisions on the basis of that liberty. I agree ... that the "liberty," against deprivation of which without due process the Fourteenth Amendment protects, embraces more than the rights found in the Bill of Rights. But that liberty is not guaranteed absolutely against deprivation, only against deprivation without due process of law. The test traditionally applied in the area of social and economic legislation is whether or not a law such as that challenged has a rational relation to a valid state objective.... The Due Process Clause of the Fourteenth Amendment undoubtedly does place a limit, albeit a broad one, on legislative power to enact laws such as this. If the Texas statute were to prohibit an abortion even where the mother's life is in jeopardy, I have little doubt that such a statute would lack a rational relation to a valid state objective.... But the Court's sweeping invalidation of any restrictions on abortion during the first trimester is impossible to justify under that standard, and the conscious weighing of competing factors that the Court's opinion apparently substitutes for the established test is far more appropriate to a legislative judgment than to a judicial one.

The Court eschews the history of the Fourteenth Amendment in its reliance on the "compelling state interest" test.... But the Court adds a new wrinkle to this test by transposing it from the legal considerations associated with the Equal Protection Clause of the Fourteenth Amendment to this case arising under the Due Process Clause of the Fourteenth Amendment. Unless I misapprehend the consequences of this transplanting of the "compelling state interest test," the Court's opinion will accomplish the seemingly impossible feat of leaving this area of the law more confused than it found it.

While the Court's opinion quotes from the dissent of Mr. Justice Holmes in Lochner v. New York (1905), the result it reaches is more closely attuned to the majority opinion ... in that case. As in *Lochner* and similar cases applying substantive due process standards to economic and social welfare legislation, the adoption of the compelling state interest standard will inevitably require this Court to examine the legislative policies and pass on the wisdom of these policies in the very process of deciding whether a particular state interest put forward may or may not be "com-

pelling." The decision here to break pregnancy into three distinct terms and to outline the permissible restrictions the State may impose in each one, for example, partakes more of judicial legislation than it does of a determination of the intent of the drafters of the Fourteenth Amendment.

The fact that a majority of the States reflecting, after all, the majority sentiment in those States, have had restrictions on abortions for at least a century is a strong indication, it seems to me, that the asserted right to an abortion is not "so rooted in the traditions and conscience of our people as to be ranked as fundamental."... Even today, when society's views on abortion are changing, the very existence of the debate is evidence that the "right" to an abortion is not so universally accepted as the appellant would have us believe.

To reach its result, the Court necessarily has had to find within the scope of the Fourteenth Amendment a right that was apparently completely unknown to the drafters of the Amendment. As early as 1821, the first state law dealing directly with abortion was enacted by the Connecticut Legislature. By the time of the adoption of the Fourteenth Amendment in 1868, there were at least 36 laws enacted by state or territorial legislatures limiting abortion. While many States have amended or updated their laws, 21 of the laws on the books in 1868 remain in effect today. Indeed, the Texas statute struck down today was, as the majority notes, first enacted in 1857 and "has remained substantially unchanged to the present time."

There apparently was no question concerning the validity of this provision or of any of the other state statutes when the Fourteenth Amendment was adopted. The only conclusion possible from this history is that the drafters did not intend to have the Fourteenth Amendment withdraw from the States the power to legislate with respect to this matter....

For all of the foregoing reasons, I respectfully dissent.

MR. JUSTICE WHITE, with whom MR. JUSTICE REHNQUIST joins, dissenting.

The Court for the most part sustains this position: During the period prior to the time the fetus becomes viable, the Constitution of the United States values the convenience, whim, or caprice of the putative mother more than the life or potential life of the fetus; the Constitution, therefore, guarantees the right to an abortion as against any state law or policy seeking to protect the fetus from an abortion not prompted by more compelling reasons of the mother.

With all due respect, I dissent. I find nothing in the language or history of the Constitution to support the Court's judgment. The Court simply fashions and announces a new constitutional right for pregnant women and, with scarcely any reason or authority for its action, invests that right with sufficient substance to override most existing state abortion statutes. The upshot is that the people and the legislatures of the 50 States are constitutionally disentitled to weigh the relative importance of the continued existence and development of the fetus, on the one hand, against a spectrum of possible impacts on the mother, on the other hand. As an exercise of raw judicial power, the Court perhaps has authority to do what it does today; but in my view its judgment is an improvident and extravagant exercise of the power of judicial review that the Constitution extends to this Court.

The Court apparently values the convenience of the pregnant mother more than the continued existence and development of the life or potential life that she carries. Whether or not I might agree with that marshaling of values, I can in no event join the Court's judgment because I find no constitutional warrant for imposing such an order of priorities on the people and legislatures of the States. In a sensitive area such as this, involving as it does issues over which reasonable men may easily and heatedly differ, I cannot accept the Court's exercise of its clear power of choice by interposing a constitutional barrier to state efforts to protect human life and by investing mothers and doctors with the constitutionally protected right to exterminate it. This issue, for the most part, should be left with the people and to the political processes the people have devised to govern their affairs.

Justice Blackmun's decisions in *Roe* and *Doe* were a *tour de force* on the subject of abortion. They provided a comprehensive history of government regulation of abortion and reviewed in some detail arguments for and against the procedure. Most important was his conclusion: the right to privacy "is broad enough to encompass a woman's decision whether or not to terminate a pregnancy." Behind this assertion are several important ideas. First, the Court, while not rejecting a Ninth Amendment theory of privacy, preferred to locate the right in the Fourteenth Amendment's Due Process Clause, an approach suggested by Justices Harlan and White in their concurring opinions in *Griswold (see Table 7-1)*. Second, the Court found the abortion right fundamental and, therefore, would use a compelling state interest test to assess the constitutionality of restrictions on that right—but with something of a twist. For the reasons Blackmun gave in his opinion, the state's interests in protecting the woman's health and in protecting the "potentiality of human life" grow "in substantiality as the woman approaches term and, at a point during pregnancy … become compelling." This point led the majority to adopt the trimester scheme *(see Table 7-2)*. Under this scheme, the state's compelling interest arises at the point of viability. It may, however, regulate second trimester abortions in ways that "are reasonably related to the mother's health."

In their dissents, Justices White and Rehnquist lambasted the trimester scheme, as well as almost every other aspect of the opinion. They thought it relied on "raw judicial power" to reach an "extravagant" and "improvident" decision. Rehnquist found that the Court's use of a compelling state interest test to assess statutes under the Fourteenth Amendment's Due Process Clause represented a return to the discredited doctrine of substantive due process as expressed in *Lochner v. New York* (1905), a complaint that echoed Black's dissent in *Griswold*. Rehnquist would have preferred that the Court had adopted a "rational basis" approach to the abortion right as it had to regulations challenged on due process grounds after the fall of substantive due process. Under this approach, the Court would have to decide only whether the government had acted reasonably to achieve a legitimate government objective. Using a rational basis approach, as you can imagine, the Court generally

TABLE 7-2   The *Roe v. Wade* Trimester Scheme

Stage of Pregnancy	Degree of Permissible State Regulation of the Decision to Terminate Pregnancy
Prior to the end of the first trimester (approximately months 1–3)	Almost None: "the abortion and its effectuation must be left to [the woman and] the medical judgment of the pregnant woman's attending physician."
The end of the first trimester through "viability" (approximately months 4–6)	Some: "the state, in promoting its interest in the health of the mother, may, if it chooses, regulate the abortion procedure in ways that are reasonably related to maternal health." But it may not prohibit abortions.
Subsequent to viability (approximately months 7–9)	High: "the state, in promoting its interest in the potentiality of human life, may, if it chooses, regulate, and even proscribe, abortion except where necessary, in appropriate medical judgment, for the preservation of the life or health of the mother."

defers to the government and presumes the validity of the government's action. Had the Court adopted this approach to the abortion right, it would have upheld the Texas and Georgia restrictions. White, joined by Rehnquist, thought the Court had gone well beyond the scope of its powers and of the text and history of the Constitution to generate a policy statement that smacked of judicial activism. To White, it was up to the people and their elected officials to determine the fate of abortion, not the Court.

As Blackmun's opinion was nearly two years in the making, the other justices knew that, if nothing else, it would be a comprehensive statement. Outsiders, however, were shocked; few expected such an opinion from a Nixon appointee and Warren Burger's childhood friend *(see Box 7-3)*. But Blackmun's opinion was not the only surprise; Burger's decision to go along with the majority startled many observers. Moreover, White and Stewart cast rather puzzling votes given their opinions in *Griswold*. Stewart dissented in *Griswold*, asserting that the Constitution did not guarantee a general right to privacy. If he believed that to be so, then how could he agree to the creation of the right to obtain legal abortions, a right that

rested on privacy? White, on the other hand, had been in the majority in *Griswold*. But, for him, apparently the right to privacy was not broad enough to cover abortion.

The factors that explain the justices' position in *Roe* and *Doe* are matters of speculation, for, as Justice Blackmun once noted, it is always hard to predict how a new justice will come down on the abortion issue. What is not a matter of speculation is that the responses to *Roe*—both positive and negative—were (and still are) perhaps the strongest in the Court's history.

Reaction came from all quarters of American life. Some legal scholars applauded the *Roe* opinion, asserting that it indicated the Court's sensitivity to changing times. Others ripped it to shreds. They called the trimester scheme unworkable and said that, as medical technology advanced, viability would come increasingly earlier in pregnancy. Others attacked the decision's use of the Fourteenth Amendment, agreeing with Justice Rehnquist that it was a retreat to pre-New Deal days. Still others claimed it usurped the intention of *Griswold*. John Hart Ely wrote that a right to privacy against "governmental

BOX 7-3   HARRY ANDREW BLACKMUN
(1970-1994)

Harry A. Blackmun was born November 12, 1908, in Nashville, Illinois. He spent most of his early life in the Minneapolis- St. Paul area, where his father was an official of the Twin Cities Savings and Loan Company. In grade school Blackmun began a friendship with Warren Burger, with whom he was later to serve on the Supreme Court.

Showing an early aptitude for mathematics, Blackmun attended Harvard University on a scholarship. He majored in mathematics and thought briefly of becoming a physician, but chose the law instead. He graduated Phi Beta Kappa from Harvard in 1929 and entered Harvard Law School, graduating in 1932. During his law school years, Blackmun supported himself with a variety of odd jobs, including tutoring in math and driving the launch for the college crew team.

After law school, Blackmun returned to St. Paul, where he served for a year and a half as a law clerk to Judge John B. Sanborn, whom Blackmun was to succeed on the U.S. Circuit Court twenty-six years later. He left the clerkship in 1933 to enter private practice with a Minneapolis law firm, where he remained for sixteen years. During that time he also taught at the Mitchell College of Law in St. Paul, Chief Justice Burger's alma mater, and at the University of Minnesota Law School.

Blackmun married Dorothy E. Clark, June 21, 1941, and they have three daughters.

In 1950 he accepted a post as "house counsel" for the world-famous Mayo Clinic in Rochester, Minnesota. There, Blackmun quickly developed a reputation among his colleagues as a serious man totally engrossed in his profession.

His reputation followed him to the bench of the Eighth Circuit Court of Appeals, to which Blackmun was appointed by President Dwight D. Eisenhower in 1959. As an appeals court judge, Blackmun became known for his scholarly and thorough opinions.

Blackmun's nomination to the Supreme Court was President Richard Nixon's third try to fill the seat vacated by Justice Abe Fortas's resignation. The Senate had refused to confirm Nixon's first two nominees—Clement F. Haynesworth, Jr., of South Carolina and G. Harrold Carswell of Florida. Nixon remarked that he had concluded from the rejection of his first two nominees that the Senate "as it is presently constituted" would not confirm a southern nominee who was also a judicial conservative.

Nixon then turned to Blackmun, who was confirmed without opposition. During his first years on the Court, Blackmun was frequently linked with Burger as the "Minnesota Twins," who thought and voted alike, but, beginning with his authorship of the Court's 1973 ruling in *Roe v. Wade*, which legalized abortion, Blackmun moved in a steadily more liberal direction, leaving Burger behind in the Court's conservative wing.

In April 1994 Blackmun announced his retirement from the Court.

SOURCE: Adapted from Elder Witt, *Guide to the U.S. Supreme Court*, 2d ed. (Washington, D.C.: Congressional Quarterly, 1990), 876–877.

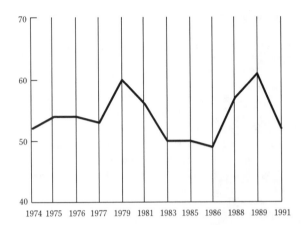

SOURCE: Lee Epstein, Jeffrey A. Segal, Harold J. Spaeth, and Thomas G. Walker, *The Supreme Court Compendium: Data, Decisions, and Developments* (Washington, D.C.: Congressional Quarterly, 1994), Table 8-19.

snooping" is legitimate, but a general freedom of "autonomy"—"to live one's life without governmental interference"—goes beyond the scope of *Griswold*.[21]

Roe also divided the political community. Some legislators were pleased that the Court, and not they, had handled a political hot potato. Others were outraged on moral grounds ("abortion is murder") and on constitutional grounds (this is a matter of public policy for legislators, not judges, to determine).

As Figure 7-3 shows, the public was (and remains) split over its support for the Court's ruling. But divisions over the abortion right did not come about as a result of *Roe*. Since the first public opinion polls taken on abortion in the 1960s, citizens have been of many different minds on abortion. For example, in the 1990s nearly 80 percent of survey respondents indicate that a pregnant woman should be able to obtain an abortion if there is a chance of "serious defect" in

the baby, while only 41 percent say that a woman should be able to terminate a pregnancy because she "is not married and does not want to marry the man." In the final analysis, all *Roe* did, as political scientists Charles Franklin and Liane Kosaki show, was to intensify basic divisions over abortion: if one was pro-choice before the decision, one became even more so; the same held true for those favoring the pro-life side.[22]

Although *Roe* may not have changed public opinion on abortion, it had the important effect of mobilizing the pro-life movement. Before 1973 groups opposed to legalized abortion had lobbied successfully against efforts to liberalize state laws. When *Roe* nullified these legislative victories, these groups vowed to see the decision overturned; in short, *Roe* and *Doe* fanned the fire, rather than quenched it.

The Aftermath of Roe: *Attempts to Limit the Decision*

Pro-life groups are dedicated to the eradication of *Roe v. Wade*, a goal that they can accomplish in one of two ways: they can convince Congress to propose an amendment to the Constitution or convince the Court to overrule its decision. In the immediate aftermath of *Roe*, neither of these options was likely. Despite the public's mixed view of abortion, during the 1970s only about a third of Americans supported a constitutional amendment to proscribe it. The lack of support may explain why Congress, ever cognizant of the polls, did not pass any of the "human life" amendments it considered in the 1970s. And, given the 7–2 vote in *Roe*, wholesale changes in the Court's membership would be required before the Court would reconsider its stance on abortion.

Faced with this situation, pro-life groups determined that their best course of action was to seek limitations on the right to choice. They lobbied legis-

21. John Hart Ely, "The Wages of Crying Wolf: A Comment on *Roe v. Wade*," *Yale Law Journal* 82 (1973): 920.

22. Charles H. Franklin and Liane C. Kosaki, "The Republican Schoolmaster: The Supreme Court, Public Opinion, and Abortion," *American Political Science Review* 83 (1989): 751–772.

latures to enact restrictions on *Roe*. Two types of restrictions predominated—those that required *consent* and those that limited government *funding* for abortion services. These efforts were quite successful. During the 1970s, eighteen states required some form of consent and thirty (along with the federal government) restricted funding. To put it another way, by 1978 only about fifteen states had not enacted laws requiring consent or restricting funding.

Consent. As pro-life forces convinced states to enact these laws, pro-choice forces just as quickly challenged them in court. The first major post-*Roe* battle, *Planned Parenthood v. Danforth* (1976) involved consent, a subject the Court had not considered in *Roe*. The state of Missouri passed legislation that required the written consent of a pregnant woman and her spouse or parents (in the case of an unmarried minor) before an abortion could be performed.

While the Court found no constitutional violation in requiring a woman to give her own consent to the procedure, it struck down parental and spousal consent provisions as violative of the Constitution and inconsistent with *Roe*. However, Justice Blackmun's majority opinion gave pro-life movements a little hope. It struck down Missouri's parental consent requirement, but it also stated:

We emphasize that our holding that parental consent is invalid does not suggest that every minor, regardless of age or maturity, may give effective consent for the termination of her pregnancy.

With these words, Blackmun opened the door to the possibility of some form of required parental consent.

As illustrated in Table 7-3, pro-life forces took advantage of Blackmun's statement, convincing states to enact various parental and other consent requirements, many of which were tested by the Court. And, although the Court has continued to strike down laws forcing a woman to obtain the consent of or to notify her spouse prior to obtaining an abortion, it has been much more willing to permit forms of parental consent or notification. By the time of *Planned Parenthood of Southeastern Pennsylvania v. Casey* in 1992 *(see Table 7-3)*, the Court simply indicated that it had been "over most of this ground before. Our cases establish, and we reaffirm today, that a State may require a minor seeking an abortion to obtain the consent of a parent or guardian, provided that there is an adequate judicial bypass procedure," which means that states that have consent laws for minors must also provide them with an alternative route to obtain abortion if they do not want to notify a parent. Typically, this alternative route, called a judicial bypass, is through the courts; that is, minors can seek authorization for an abortion procedure from a judge.

Funding. Consent laws were not the only way pro-life forces sought to restrict the abortion right in the wake of *Roe*. They also sought to convince states and the federal government to restrict government funding for abortions.[23] To pro-life organizations, this type of restriction was another step toward the eradication of *Roe*. Funding was inextricably bound to implementation: if women could not afford abortions and the government could not pay for them, then either doctors would not perform them or women would be deterred from having them. Pro-choice groups viewed these laws as backdoor attempts to gut *Roe*. From their perspective, *Roe* was a victory not just for doctors or even middle-class women, but for those women who could not afford to travel to other countries or states to obtain abortions. Logically, they assumed, that once the Court established the right to choose, governments had an obligation to protect that right, even if meant funding for the poor through government health insurance programs.

Few governments, however, shared this pro-choice vision, at least in the immediate aftermath of *Roe*. In

---

23. Material in the next two paragraphs draws heavily on Epstein and Kobylka, *The Supreme Court and Legal Change,* 220–221.

TABLE 7-3 Cases Involving Consent to Abortions, 1976–1993

Case	Consent Provision at Issue	Court Holding
Planned Parenthood v. Danforth (1976)	Written consent required of the (1) pregnant woman, (2) her spouse, or (3) her parents.	The Court struck spousal and parental requirements. It upheld the provision requiring the woman's consent.
Bellotti v. Baird II (1979)	Parental consent required prior to abortions performed on unmarried women under eighteen. If one or both parents refuse, the "abortion may be obtained by order of a judge . . . for good cause shown."	The Court struck the law, but claimed that it was not "persuaded as a general rule" that parental consent "unconstitutionally burdens a minor's right to seek an abortion."
H. L. v. Matheson (1981)	Doctors should "notify, if possible" a minor's parents prior to performing an abortion.	The Court upheld the law on the ground that "the Constitution does not compel a state to fine-tune its statutes as to encourage or facilitate abortions."
Akron v. Akron Center for Reproductive Health (1983)	Parental notification and consent required prior to abortions performed on unmarried minors under fifteen. Doctors must make "certain specified statements" to ensure that consent for all those seeking abortions is "truly informed." Requires a twenty-four-hour waiting period "between the time a woman signs a consent form and the time the abortion is performed."	The Court invalidated all three provisions.
Planned Parenthood v. Ashcroft (1983)	Parental or judicial consent required prior to abortions performed on unmarried minors.	The Court upheld the provision, asserting that judges may give their consent to abortions.
Hodgson v. Minnesota (1990)	Requirement that both parents be notified prior to the performance of an abortion (unless a court orders otherwise). Abortions cannot be performed on minors until forty-eight hours after both parents have been notified.	The Court upheld the two-parent requirement with an exemption option. It upheld the forty-eight hour waiting period.
Ohio v. Akron Center for Reproductive Health (1990)	Requirement that one parent be notified prior to the performance of an abortion on an unmarried, unemancipated minor (unless a court authorizes it).	The Court upheld the law.
Planned Parenthood of Southeastern Pennsylvania v. Casey (1992)	Required three kinds of consent: (1) informed consent of the woman; (2) statement from woman indicating that she has notified her spouse; (3) in the case of minors, informed consent of one parent.	The Court upheld informed consent, struck spousal notifications, and upheld parental consent.

September 1976, after several years of prodding by pro-life forces, Congress passed the Hyde Amendment (named after its sponsor, Henry Hyde). In its original form, it stated that no federal funds "shall be used to perform abortions except where the life of the mother would be endangered if the fetus were carried to full term." In 1977 and 1978 Congress altered the language to expand the circumstances under which funding could be obtained but, even so, under the Hyde Amendment federal funds paid for only about 10 percent of all abortion services for women.[24] Following the lead of the federal government, more than half the states passed legislation restricting the use of Medicaid funds for abortion procedures. The states were particularly easy targets for pro-life groups: all these organizations needed to do was to point out that funding limits constituted fiscally prudent measures. Before the limitations went into effect, 25 percent of all abortions were funded by state monies.[25]

In response to these pro-life legislative victories, pro-choice groups challenged the funding laws as violations of the fundamental right to obtain an abortion, as articulated in *Roe*. The courts again became battlefields, and the Supreme Court reentered the fray in 1977. As Table 7-4 shows, the Court decided three cases that year, *Maher v. Roe*, *Beal v. Doe*, and *Poelker v. Doe*—all of which involved state or local restrictions on abortion funding. The Court upheld all of these various restrictions. In the eyes of the justices, the regulations did not infringe significantly on abortion rights and, as Justice Powell wrote in *Maher*, "The State unquestionably has 'a strong and legitimate interest in encouraging normal childbirth.'" In short, the justices found that there is a right to abortion, but states have no obligation to fund it. It is worth em-

phasizing that these rulings did not *prohibit* states from funding abortions; rather, they held that, because the Constitution does not mandate such funding, states could enact restrictions.

As Table 7-4 indicates, pro-choice groups also failed in their challenge to the Hyde Amendment. Immediately after the amendment was passed, a coalition of pro-choice advocates, including the ACLU, Planned Parenthood, and the Center for Constitutional Rights, challenged its constitutionality. In bringing *Harris v. McCrae* (1980) they marshaled an array of legal arguments and sociological evidence suggesting that poor women might resort to self-abortion or other unsafe procedures if the Hyde Amendment remained law. In a 5–4 decision the Court rejected their arguments, asserting that it "cannot overturn duly enacted statutes simply because they may be unwise, improvident or out of harmony with a particular school of thought." More important, however, was its legal rationale:

[R]egardless of whether the freedom of a woman to choose to terminate her pregnancy for health reasons lies at the core or the periphery of the due process liberty recognized in [*Roe v. Wade*], it simply does not follow that a woman's freedom of choice carries with it a constitutional entitlement to the financial resources to avail herself of the full range of protected choices.... [A]lthough government may not place obstacles in the path of a woman's exercise of her freedom of choice, it need not remove those not of its own creation. Indigency falls in the latter category.

Justice Marshall, a dissenter in the case along with Harry Blackmun, *Roe*'s author, summarized accurately the greatest fears of the pro-choice movement when he wrote:

The denial of Medicaid benefits to individuals who meet all the statutory criteria for eligibility, solely because the treatment that is medically necessary involves the exercise of the fundamental right to choose abortion, is a form of discrimination repugnant to [equal protection]. The Court's decision today marks a retreat from *Roe v. Wade* and represents a cruel blow to the most powerless members of our society.

---

24. At one point, the Hyde Amendment provided Medicaid funding if two doctors certified that carrying a pregnancy to full term would result in "severe and long lasting physical health damages" or the pregnancy was the result of incest or rape.

25. See Epstein and Kobylka, *The Supreme Court and Legal Change*, 220.

TABLE 7-4 Cases Involving Restrictions on Abortions

Case	Funding Restriction at Issue	Court Holding
Beal v. Doe (1977)	Pennsylvania law limiting Medicaid funding "to those abortions that are certified by physicians as medically necessary."	The Court upheld the restriction against constitutional claims that the law interfered with the fundamental right to obtain an abortion as articulated in *Roe* and that it discriminated on the basis of socioeconomic status and against those choosing abortion over childbirth.
Maher v. Roe (1977)	Connecticut Welfare Department regulation limiting state Medicaid "benefits for first trimester abortions ... that are 'medically necessary.'"	The Court upheld the restriction against various constitutional claims (see above).
Poelker v. Doe (1977)	St. Louis policy directive that barred city-owned hospitals from performing abortions.	The Court upheld the restriction against various constitutional claims (see above).
Harris v. McCrae (1980)	Federal government regulation (the Hyde Amendment) limiting Medicaid funding of abortions to those "where the life of the mother would be endangered if the fetus were carried to term."	The Court upheld the restrictions against claims that the law violated due process (impinges on a fundamental right), equal protection (discriminates against women, especially poor women), and First Amendment (burdens religious exercise and constitutes religious establishment) guarantees.

Challenges to Roe v. Wade: *The Burger Court in the 1980s*

Harris v. McCrae was a major victory for pro-life forces, which saw it as an indication of the Court's willingness to allow some incursions into the abortion right. Still, this decision only cut into the right to abortion; it did not eradicate it. After *Harris* and the elections of 1980, however, pro-life groups thought that the time might be right to achieve their goal. The elections of 1980 saw the victory of Ronald Reagan, the first presidential contender ever to support, unequivocally, the goals of the pro-life movement, as well as the Republican capture of the Senate.

In this environment the pro-life groups thought they could finally eliminate legalized abortion. They continued to lobby states and localities to pass laws that cut into the heart of *Roe*. And, when pro-choice groups challenged these laws, the pro-life groups

began asking the courts to adopt legal standards that would make it more difficult to obtain abortions. The first of these cases to reach the Supreme Court was *Akron v. Akron Center for Reproductive Health* (1983).

As you read *Akron* keep in mind that two Court membership changes had occurred since *Roe*. John Paul Stevens replaced the pro-choice Justice Douglas, and Sandra Day O'Connor had taken the place of another *Roe* majority member, Justice Stewart. Based on his vote in *Planned Parenthood v. Danforth* (1976) it seemed clear that Stevens was pro-choice. O'Connor's position, however, was far from clear, and *Akron* was her first vote in an abortion case. Before her appointment to the Court, some pro-life groups alleged that O'Connor supported the pro-choice side because of votes she had cast in the Arizona state legislature. But during her confirmation proceedings, she refused to answer pointed questions on abortion, saying only that it was "a practice in which [she] would not have engaged," but that she was "over the hill" and "not going to be pregnant any more ... so perhaps it's easy for me to speak." How would O'Connor come down on the abortion issue? This question was very much on the minds of Court watchers as they waited for the decision in *Akron Center for Reproductive Health*.

═══════════════════════════════

Akron v. Akron Center for Reproductive Health

462 U.S. 416 (1983)
Vote: 6 (Blackmun, Brennan, Burger, Marshall,
    Powell, Stevens)
   3 (O'Connor, Rehnquist, White)
Opinion of the Court: Powell
Dissenting opinion: O'Connor

After studying the Supreme Court's post-*Roe* decisions (such as *Planned Parenthood v. Danforth*, 1976), pro-life groups formulated "national model legislation," which would restrict the right to choice, while simultaneously fitting within the contours of existing doctrine.[26] One of their first successes came in 1978 in Akron, Ohio, where the city council voted to adopt a version of this model law. The new Akron ordinance contained the following provisions:

Hospital requirement. All post–first trimester abortions must be performed in a hospital (§ 1870.03).

Consent for minors. If a minor is under the age of fifteen, she must obtain the informed written consent of a parent or a court before a physician can perform an abortion (§ 1870.05(B)).

Informed consent. A woman's consent to abortion services must be informed. That is, a physician must tell her (1) the number of weeks she is pregnant; (2) that the "unborn child is a human life form from the moment of conception"; (3) about the "anatomical

and physiological characteristics of the particular unborn child" at the gestational point of development at which time the abortion is to be performed; (4) that the "unborn child" may be viable if "more than 22 weeks have elapsed from the time of conception"; and (5) about public and private adoption agencies (§ 1870.06).

A twenty-four-hour waiting period. A physician cannot perform an abortion until twenty-four hours after the pregnant woman signs a consent form (§ 1870.07).

Disposal of remains. Doctors who perform abortion "shall insure that the remains of the unborn child are disposed of in a humane and sanitary manner" (§ 1870.16).

A month before the ordinance was to take effect, ACLU attorneys brought suit on behalf of an abortion clinic, the Akron Center for Reproductive Health. They argued that the provisions interfered with a woman's right to obtain an abortion without sufficiently compelling reasons. After a federal district court and court of appeals struck down most of the ordinance's provisions (the only one upheld by the court of appeals was the hospitalization requirement), the city appealed to the U.S. Supreme Court.

In its appeal, the city was joined by the Reagan administration's solicitor general, Rex E. Lee. According to one source, some members of the administration "hounded" Lee into asking the justices to use the Akron case to overrule *Roe*.[27] Lee did not go quite that far. In his amicus curiae brief, Lee advanced two arguments. First, on abortion, he articulated a constitutional standard that he said derived from previous Court decisions. His reading of *Roe*'s progeny led him to conclude that the justices had never really "applied" *Roe*'s "sweeping" language regarding first-trimester abortions: from *Danforth* on, they had made ex-

---

26. We adopt these facts and the discussion following the *Akron* excerpt from Epstein and Kobylka, *The Supreme Court and Legal Change*, 236–247.

27. Lincoln Caplan, *The Tenth Justice* (New York: Vintage Books, 1987), 107.

ceptions. Instead, he argued that the Court *"has repeatedly adopted an 'unduly burdensome' analysis...."* That is, the Court had permitted state regulations of abortion as long as they did not "unduly burden" that decision. Second, Lee proposed a way to distinguish an *unduly burdensome* regulation from a regulation that was *simply* burdensome. In his view, the justices should defer to legislatures:

Whether or not a particular regulation "unduly burdens" the abortion decision is far from self-evident. In light of the breadth and the ambiguity of the "unduly burdensome" standard—and in the interest of preserving the difference between what courts do and what legislatures do—this Court should clarify that in applying that standard on a case-by-case basis courts should be mindful that (1) at their root, the issues to which the "unduly burdensome" test is applied are policy issues, and different segments of our society have strong competing views concerning them; (2) the legislature has already considered the competing arguments, made the necessary factual inquiries, and reached a decision; and (3) the net effect of holding the legislative product unconstitutional is that those who succeeded in persuading the legislature of the soundness of their policy viewpoint are deprived of their legislative victory, whereas the legislative losers become the winners. These realities counsel that, in deciding which legislative policy choices are "unduly burdensome" and which are not, the Court should accord heavy deference to the legislative judgment.

JUSTICE POWELL delivered the opinion of the Court.

[*Akron Center* comes] to us a decade after we held in *Roe v. Wade* (1973) that the right of privacy, grounded in the concept of personal liberty guaranteed by the Constitution, encompasses a woman's right to decide whether to terminate her pregnancy. Legislative responses to the Court's decision have required us on several occasions, and again today, to define the limits of a State's authority to regulate the performance of abortions. And arguments continue to be made, in these cases as well, that we erred in interpreting the Constitution. Nonetheless, the doctrine of *stare decisis*, while perhaps never entirely persuasive on a constitutional question, is a doctrine that demands respect in a society governed by the rule of law.* We respect it today, and reaffirm *Roe v. Wade*....

In *Roe v. Wade* the Court held that after the end of the first trimester of pregnancy the State's interest becomes compelling, and it may "regulate the abortion procedure to the extent that the regulation reasonably relates to the preservation and protection of maternal health."...

We reaffirm today that a State's interest in health regulation becomes compelling at approximately the end of the first trimester. The existence of a compelling state interest in health, however, is only the beginning of the inquiry. The State's regulation may be upheld only if it is reasonably designed to further that state interest. And the Court in *Roe* did not hold that it always is reasonable for a State to adopt an abortion regulation that applies to the entire second trimester. A State necessarily must have latitude in adopting regulations of general applicability in this sensitive area.

---

*There are especially compelling reasons for adhering to *stare decisis* in applying the principles of *Roe v. Wade*. That case was considered with special care. It was first argued during the 1971 Term, and reargued—with extensive briefing—the following Term. The decision was joined by the Chief Justice and six other Justices. Since *Roe* was decided in January 1973, the Court repeatedly and consistently has accepted and applied the basic principle that a woman has a fundamental right to make the highly personal choice whether or not to terminate her pregnancy.... Today, however, the dissenting opinion rejects the basic premise of *Roe* and its progeny. The dissent stops short of arguing flatly that *Roe* should be overruled. Rather, it adopts reasoning that, for all practical purposes, would accomplish precisely that result. The dissent states that "[e]ven assuming that there is a fundamental right to terminate pregnancy in some situations," the State's compelling interests in maternal health and potential human life "are present *throughout* pregnancy." The existence of these compelling interests turns out to be largely unnecessary, however, for the dissent does not think that even one of the numerous abortion regulations at issue imposes a sufficient burden on the "limited" fundamental right to require heightened scrutiny. Indeed, the dissent asserts that, regardless of cost, "[a] health regulation, such as the hospitalization requirement, simply does not rise to the level of 'official interference' with the abortion decision." The dissent therefore would hold that a requirement that all abortions be performed in an acute-care, general hospital does not impose an unacceptable burden on the abortion decision. It requires no great familiarity with the cost and limited availability of such hospitals to appreciate that the effect of the dissent's views would be to drive the performance of many abortions back underground free of effective regulation and often without the attendance of a physician.

In sum, it appears that the dissent would uphold virtually any abortion regulation under a rational-basis test. It also appears that even where heightened scrutiny is deemed appropriate, the dissent would uphold virtually any abortion-inhibiting regulation because of the State's interest in preserving potential human life.... This analysis is wholly incompatible with the existence of the fundamental right recognized in *Roe v. Wade*.

But if it appears that during a substantial portion of the second trimester the State's regulation "depart[s] from accepted medical practice," the regulation may not be upheld simply because it may be reasonable for the remaining portion of the trimester. Rather, the State is obligated to make a reasonable effort to limit the effect of its regulations to the period in the trimester during which its health interest will be furthered.

There can be no doubt that § 1870.03's second-trimester hospitalization requirement places a significant obstacle in the path of women seeking an abortion. A primary burden created by the requirement is additional cost to the woman. The Court of Appeals noted that there was testimony that a second-trimester abortion costs more than twice as much in a hospital as in a clinic. ([I]n-hospital abortion costs $850–$900, whereas a dilatation-and-evacuation (D&E) abortion performed in a clinic costs $350–$400.) Moreover, the court indicated that second-trimester abortions were rarely performed in Akron hospitals. ([O]nly nine second-trimester abortions were performed in Akron hospitals in the year before trial.) Thus, a second-trimester hospitalization requirement may force women to travel to find available facilities, resulting in both financial expense and additional health risk. It therefore is apparent that a second-trimester hospitalization requirement may significantly limit a woman's ability to obtain an abortion.

Akron does not contend that §1870.03 imposes only an insignificant burden on women's access to abortion, but rather defends it as a reasonable health regulation. This position had strong support at the time of Roe v. Wade, as hospitalization for second-trimester abortions was recommended by the American Public Health Association (APHA) and the American College of Obstetricians and Gynecologists (ACOG). Since then, however, the safety of second-trimester abortions has increased dramatically. The principal reason is that the D&E procedure is now widely and successfully used for second-trimester abortions. The Court of Appeals found that there was "an abundance of evidence that D&E is the safest method of performing post–first trimester abortions today.". . .

These developments, and the professional commentary supporting them, constitute impressive evidence that—at least during the early weeks of the second trimester—D&E abortions may be performed as safely in an outpatient clinic as in a full-service hospital. We conclude, therefore, that "present medical knowledge," convincingly undercuts Akron's justification for requiring that *all* second-trimester abortions be performed in a hospital. . . .

We turn next to § 1870.05(B), the provision prohibiting a physician from performing an abortion on a minor pregnant woman under the age of 15 unless he obtains "the informed written consent of one of her parents or her legal guardian" or unless the minor obtains "an order from a court having jurisdiction over her that the abortion be performed or induced.". . .

The relevant legal standards are not in dispute. The Court has held that "the State may not impose a blanket provision . . . requiring the consent of a parent or person *in loco parentis* as a condition for abortion of an unmarried minor." In *Bellotti v. Baird* (1979) (*Bellotti II*), a majority of the Court indicated that a State's interest in protecting immature minors will sustain a requirement of a consent substitute, either parental or judicial. The *Bellotti II* plurality cautioned, however, that the State must provide an alternative procedure whereby a pregnant minor may demonstrate that she is sufficiently mature to make the abortion decision herself or that, despite her immaturity, an abortion would be in her best interests. Under these decisions, it is clear that Akron may not make a blanket determination that *all* minors under the age of 15 are too immature to make this decision or that an abortion never may be in the minor's best interests without parental approval. . . .

. . . We therefore affirm the Court of Appeals' judgment that § 1870.05(B) is unconstitutional.

The Akron ordinance provides that no abortion shall be performed except "with the informed written consent of the pregnant woman, . . . given freely and without coercion."

The validity of an informed consent requirement thus rests on the State's interest in protecting the health of the pregnant woman. The decision to have an abortion has "implications far broader than those associated with most other kinds of medical treatment," and thus the State legitimately may seek to ensure that it has been made "in the light of all attendant circumstances—psychological and emotional as well as physical—that might be relevant to the well-being of the patient.". . . This does not mean, however, that a State has unreviewable authority to decide what information a woman must be given before she chooses to have an abortion. It remains primarily the responsibility of the physician to ensure that appropriate information is conveyed to his patient, depending on her particular circumstances. *Danforth*'s recognition of the State's interest in ensuring that this information be given will not justify abortion regulations designed to influence the woman's informed choice between abortion or childbirth.

Viewing the city's regulations in this light, we believe that § 1870.06(B) attempts to extend the State's interest in ensuring "informed consent" beyond permissible limits. First, it is fair to say that much of the information required is designed not to inform the woman's consent but rather to persuade her to withhold it altogether. Subsection (3) requires the physician to inform his patient that "the unborn child is a human life from the moment of conception," a requirement inconsistent with the Court's holding in *Roe v. Wade* that a State may not adopt one theory of when life begins to justify its regulation of abortions. Moreover, much of the detailed description of "the anatomical and physiological characteristics of the particular unborn child" required by subsection (3) would involve at best speculation by the physician....

The Akron ordinance prohibits a physician from performing an abortion until 24 hours after the pregnant woman signs a consent form. § 1870.07. The District Court upheld this provision on the ground that it furthered Akron's interest in ensuring "that a woman's abortion decision is made after careful consideration of all the facts applicable to her particular situation." The Court of Appeals reversed, finding that the inflexible waiting period had "no medical basis," and that careful consideration of the abortion decision by the woman "is beyond the state's power to require." We affirm the Court of Appeals' judgment....

We find that Akron has failed to demonstrate that any legitimate state interest is furthered by an arbitrary and inflexible waiting period. There is no evidence suggesting that the abortion procedure will be performed more safely. Nor are we convinced that the State's legitimate concern that the woman's decision be informed is reasonably served by requiring a 24-hour delay as a matter of course.

The decision whether to proceed with an abortion is one as to which it is important to "affor[d] the physician adequate discretion in the exercise of his medical judgment."... In accordance with the ethical standards of the profession, a physician will advise the patient to defer the abortion when he thinks this will be beneficial to her. But if a woman, after appropriate counseling, is prepared to give her written informed consent and proceed with the abortion, a State may not demand that she delay the effectuation of that decision.

Section 1870.16 of the Akron ordinance requires physicians performing abortions to "insure that the remains of the unborn child are disposed of in a humane and sanitary manner." The Court of Appeals found that the word "humane" was impermissibly vague as a definition of conduct subject to criminal prosecution. The court invalidated the entire provision, declining to sever the word "humane" in order to uphold the requirement that disposal be "sanitary." We affirm this judgment.

Akron contends that the purpose of § 1870.16 is simply "'to preclude the mindless dumping of aborted fetuses on garbage piles.'" It is far from clear, however, that this provision has such a limited intent. The phrase "humane and sanitary" does, as the Court of Appeals noted, suggest a possible intent to "mandate some sort of 'decent burial' of an embryo at the earliest stages of formation." This level of uncertainty is fatal where criminal liability is imposed. Because § 1870.16 fails to give a physician "fair notice that his contemplated conduct is forbidden," we agree that it violates the Due Process Clause.

We affirm the judgment of the Court of Appeals invalidating those sections of Akron's "Regulations of Abortions" ordinance that deal with parental consent, informed consent, a 24-hour waiting period, and the disposal of fetal remains. The remaining portion of the judgment, sustaining Akron's requirement that all second-trimester abortions be performed in a hospital, is reversed.

It is so ordered.

JUSTICE O'CONNOR, with whom JUSTICE WHITE and JUSTICE REHNQUIST join, dissenting.

In *Roe v. Wade* (1973) the Court held that the "right of privacy ... founded in the Fourteenth Amendment's concept of personal liberty and restrictions upon state action ... is broad enough to encompass a woman's decision whether or not to terminate her pregnancy." The parties in these cases have not asked the Court to re-examine the validity of that holding and the court below did not address it. Accordingly, the Court does not re-examine its previous holding. Nonetheless, it is apparent from the Court's opinion that neither sound constitutional theory nor our need to decide cases based on the application of neutral principles can accommodate an analytical framework that varies according to the "stages" of pregnancy, where those stages, and their concomitant standards of review, differ according to the level of medical technology available when a particular challenge to state regulation occurs. The Court's analysis of the Akron regulations is inconsistent both with the methods of analysis employed in previous cases dealing with abortion, and with the Court's approach to fundamental rights in other areas.

Our recent cases indicate that a regulation imposed on "a lawful abortion 'is not unconstitutional unless it unduly burdens the right to seek an abortion.'" *Maher v. Roe* (1977). See also *Harris v. McRae* (1980). In my view, this "unduly burdensome" standard should be applied to the challenged regulations throughout the entire pregnancy without reference to the particular "stage" of pregnancy involved. If the particular regulation does not "unduly burden" the fundamental right, then our evaluation of that regulation is limited to our determination that the regulation rationally relates to a legitimate state purpose. Irrespective of what we may believe is wise or prudent policy in this difficult area, "the Constitution does not constitute us as 'Platonic Guardians' nor does it vest in this Court the authority to strike down laws because they do not meet our standards of desirable social policy, 'wisdom,' or 'common sense.'"...

The trimester or "three-stage" approach adopted by the Court in *Roe* and, in a modified form, employed by the Court to analyze the regulations in these cases, cannot be supported as a legitimate or useful framework for accommodating the woman's right and the State's interests. The decision of the Court today graphically illustrates why the trimester approach is a completely unworkable method of accommodating the conflicting personal rights and compelling state interests that are involved in the abortion context.

As the Court indicates today, the State's compelling interest in maternal health changes as medical technology changes, and any health regulation must not "depart from accepted medical practice." In applying this standard, the Court holds that "the safety of second-trimester abortions has increased dramatically" since 1973, when *Roe* was decided. Although a regulation such as one requiring that all second-trimester abortions be performed in hospitals "had strong support" in 1973 "as a reasonable health regulation," this regulation can no longer stand because, according to the Court's diligent research into medical and scientific literature, the dilation and evacuation (D&E) procedure used in 1973 only for first-trimester abortions, "is now widely and successfully used for second-trimester abortions." Further, the medical literature relied on by the Court indicates that the D&E procedure may be performed in an appropriate nonhospital setting for "at least ... the early weeks of the second trimester...." The Court then chooses the period of 16 weeks of gestation as that point at which D&E procedures may be performed safely in a nonhospital setting, and thereby invalidates the Akron hospitalization regulation.

It is not difficult to see that despite the Court's purported adherence to the trimester approach adopted in *Roe*, the lines drawn in that decision have now been "blurred" because of what the Court accepts as technological advancement in the safety of abortion procedure. The State may no longer rely on a "bright line" that separates permissible from impermissible regulation, and it is no longer free to consider the second trimester as a unit and weigh the risks posed by all abortion procedures throughout that trimester. Rather, the State must continuously and conscientiously study contemporary medical and scientific literature in order to determine whether the effect of a particular regulation is to "depart from accepted medical practice" insofar as particular procedures and particular periods within the trimester are concerned. Assuming that legislative bodies are able to engage in this exacting task, it is difficult to believe that our Constitution requires that they do it as a prelude to protecting the health of their citizens. It is even more difficult to believe that this Court, without the resources available to those bodies entrusted with making legislative choices, believes itself competent to make these inquiries and to revise these standards every time the American College of Obstetricians and Gynecologists (ACOG) or similar group revises its views about what is and what is not appropriate medical procedure in this area. Indeed, the ACOG Standards on which the Court relies were changed in 1982 after trial in the present cases. Before ACOG changed its Standards in 1982, it recommended that all mid-trimester abortions be performed in a hospital.... As today's decision indicates, medical technology is changing, and this change will necessitate our continued functioning as the nation's *"ex officio* medical board with powers to approve or disapprove medical and operative practices and standards throughout the United States."...

Just as improvements in medical technology inevitably will move *forward* the point at which the State may regulate for reasons of maternal health, different technological improvements will move *backward* the point of viability at which the State may proscribe abortions except when necessary to preserve the life and health of the mother.

In 1973, viability before 28 weeks was considered unusual.... However, recent studies have demonstrated increasingly earlier fetal viability. It is certainly reasonable to believe that fetal viability in the first trimester of pregnancy may be possible in the not too distant future. Indeed, the Court has explicitly acknowledged that *Roe* left the point of viability "flexible for anticipated advancements in medical skill."...

The *Roe* framework, then, is clearly on a collision course with itself. As the medical risks of various abortion procedures decrease, the point at which the State may regulate for reasons of maternal health is moved further forward to actual childbirth. As medical science becomes better able to provide for the separate existence of the fetus, the point of viability is moved further back toward conception.... The *Roe* framework is inherently tied to the state of medical technology that exists whenever particular litigation ensues. Although legislatures are better suited to make the necessary factual judgments in this area, the Court's framework forces legislatures, as a matter of constitutional law, to speculate about what constitutes "accepted medical practice" at any given time. Without the necessary expertise or ability, courts must then pretend to act as science review boards and examine those legislative judgments.

The Court adheres to the *Roe* framework because the doctrine of *stare decisis* "demands respect in a society governed by the rule of law." Although respect for *stare decisis* cannot be challenged, "this Court's considered practice [is] not to apply *stare decisis* as rigidly in constitutional as in nonconstitutional cases."... Although we must be mindful of the "desirability of continuity of decision in constitutional questions ... when convinced of former error, this Court has never felt constrained to follow precedent. In constitutional questions, where correction depends upon amendment and not upon legislative action this Court throughout its history has freely exercised its power to reexamine the basis of its constitutional decisions."

Even assuming that there is a fundamental right to terminate pregnancy in some situations, there is no justification in law or logic for the trimester framework adopted in *Roe* and employed by the Court today on the basis of *stare decisis.* For the reasons stated above, that framework is clearly an unworkable means of balancing the fundamental right and the compelling state interests that are indisputably implicated....

The fallacy inherent in the *Roe* framework is apparent: just because the State has a compelling interest in ensuring maternal safety once an abortion may be more dangerous than childbirth, it simply does not follow that the State has no interest before that point that justifies state regulation to ensure that first-trimester abortions are performed as safely as possible.

The state interest in potential human life is likewise extant throughout pregnancy. In *Roe,* the Court held that although the State had an important and legitimate interest in protecting potential life, that interest could not become compelling until the point at which the fetus was viable. The difficulty with this analysis is clear: *potential* life is no less potential in the first weeks of pregnancy than it is at viability or afterward. At any stage in pregnancy, there is the *potential* for human life. Although the Court refused to "resolve the difficult question of when life begins," the Court chose the point of viability—when the fetus is capable of life independent of its mother—to permit the complete proscription of abortion. The choice of viability as the point at which the state interest in potential life becomes compelling is no less arbitrary than choosing any point before viability or any point afterward. Accordingly, I believe that the State's interest in protecting potential human life exists throughout the pregnancy.

Although the State possesses compelling interests in the protection of potential human life and in maternal health throughout pregnancy, not every regulation that the State imposes must be measured against the State's compelling interests and examined with strict scrutiny. This Court has acknowledged that "the right in *Roe v. Wade* can be understood only by considering both the woman's interest and the nature of the State's interference with it. *Roe* did not declare an unqualified 'constitutional right to an abortion,'... Rather, the right protects the woman from unduly burdensome interference with her freedom to decide whether to terminate her pregnancy."... The Court and its individual Justices have repeatedly utilized the "unduly burdensome" standard in abortion cases....

The "unduly burdensome" standard is particularly appropriate in the abortion context because of the *nature* and *scope* of the right that is involved. The privacy right involved in the abortion context "cannot be said to be absolute."... Rather, the *Roe* right is intended to protect against state action "drastically limiting the availability and safety of the desired service," against the imposition of an "absolute obstacle" on the abortion decision, or against "official interference" and "coercive restraint" imposed on the abortion decision. That a state regulation may "inhibit" abortions to some degree does not require that we find that the regulation is invalid....

In determining whether the State imposes an "undue burden," we must keep in mind that when we are concerned with extremely sensitive issues, such as the one involved here, "the appropriate forum for their resolution in a democracy is the legislature. We should not forget that 'legislatures are ultimate guardians of the liberties and welfare of the people in quite as great a degree as the courts.'..." This does not mean that in determining whether a regulation imposes an "undue burden" on the *Roe* right we defer to the judgments made by state legislatures. "The point is, rather, that when we face a complex problem with many hard questions and few easy answers we do well to pay careful atten-

tion to how the other branches of Government have addressed the same problem."*...

Section 1870.03 of the Akron ordinance requires that second-trimester abortions be performed in hospitals. The Court holds that this requirement imposes a "significant obstacle" in the form of increased costs and decreased availability of abortions, and the Court rejects the argument offered by the State that the requirement is a reasonable health regulation under *Roe*.

For the reasons stated above, I find no justification for the trimester approach used by the Court to analyze this restriction. I would apply the "unduly burdensome" test and find that the hospitalization requirement does not impose an undue burden on that decision.

The Court's reliance on increased abortion costs and decreased availability is misplaced. As the city of Akron points out, there is no evidence in this case to show that the two Akron hospitals that performed second-trimester abortions denied an abortion to any woman, or that they would not permit abortion by the D&E procedure. In addition, there was no evidence presented that other hospitals in nearby areas did not provide second-trimester abortions. Further, almost *any* state regulation, including the licensing requirements that the Court *would* allow, inevitably and necessarily entails increased costs for *any* abortion....

The hospitalization requirement does not impose an undue burden, and it is not necessary to apply an exacting standard of review. Further, the regulation has a "rational relation" to a valid state objective of ensuring the health and welfare of its citizens....

Section 1870.05 of the Akron ordinance provides that no physician shall perform an abortion on a minor under 15 years of age unless the minor gives written consent, and the physician first obtains the informed written consent of

---

*In his *amicus curiae* brief in support of the city of Akron, the Solicitor General of the United States argues that we should adopt the "unduly burdensome" standard and in doing so, we should "accord heavy deference to the legislative judgment" in determining what constitutes an "undue burden." The "unduly burdensome" standard is appropriate *not* because it incorporates deference to legislative judgment at the threshold stage of analysis, but rather because of the limited *nature* of the fundamental right that has been recognized in the abortion cases. Although our cases do require that we "pay careful attention" to the legislative judgment before we invoke strict scrutiny, ... it is not appropriate to *weigh* the state interests at the threshold stage.

a parent or guardian, or unless the minor first obtains "an order from a court having jurisdiction over her that the abortion be performed or induced." Despite the fact that this regulation has yet to be construed in the state courts, the Court holds that the regulation is unconstitutional because it is not "reasonably susceptible of being construed to create an 'opportunity for case-by-case evaluations of the maturity of pregnant minors.'" I believe that the Court should have abstained from declaring the ordinance unconstitutional. . . .

The Court invalidates the informed-consent provisions of § 1870.06(B) and § 1870.06(C) of the Akron ordinance. . . .

We have approved informed-consent provisions in the past even though the physician was required to deliver certain information to the patient. In *Danforth*, the Court upheld a state informed-consent requirement because "[t]he decision to abort, indeed, is an important, and often a stressful one, and it is desirable and imperative that it be made with full knowledge of its nature and consequences.". . .

The remainder of § 1870.06(B) and § 1870.06(C) impose no undue burden or drastic limitation on the abortion decision. The city of Akron is merely attempting to ensure that the decision to abort is made in light of that knowledge that the city deems relevant to informed choice. As such, these regulations do not impermissibly affect any privacy right under the Fourteenth Amendment.

Section 1870.07 of the Akron ordinance requires a 24-hour waiting period between the signing of a consent form and the actual performance of the abortion, except in cases of emergency. . . . The Court accepts the arguments made by Akron Center that the waiting period increases the costs of obtaining an abortion by requiring the pregnant woman to make two trips to the clinic, and increases the risks of abortion through delay and scheduling difficulties. The decision whether to proceed should be left to the physician's "'discretion in the exercise of his medical judgment.'"

It is certainly difficult to understand how the Court believes that the physician-patient relationship is able to accommodate any interest that the State has in maternal physical and mental well-being in light of the fact that the record in this case shows that the relationship is nonexistent. . . .

Assuming, *arguendo*, that any additional costs are such as to impose an undue burden on the abortion decision,

the State's compelling interests in maternal physical and mental health and protection of fetal life clearly justify the waiting period. . . . The decision also has grave consequences for the fetus, whose life the State has a compelling interest to protect and preserve. . . .

Finally, § 1870.16 of the Akron ordinance requires that "[a]ny physician who shall perform or induce an abortion upon a pregnant woman shall insure that the remains of the unborn child are disposed of in a humane and sanitary manner." The Court finds this provision void for vagueness. I disagree.

. . . In light of the fact that the city of Akron indicates no intent to require that physicians provide "decent burials" for fetuses, and that "humane" is no more vague than the term "sanitary," the vagueness of which Akron Center does not question, I cannot conclude that the statute is void for vagueness.

For the reasons set forth above, I dissent from the judgment of the Court in these cases.

In *Akron Center* the Supreme Court handed the pro-choice side its biggest victory since *Roe*. In a 6-3 ruling, the justices reaffirmed their commitment to the 1973 decision and even showed how *Roe* could be updated to apply to conditions in 1983. Consider, for example, the Court's treatment of the city's hospitalization requirement, which was the only provision of the ordinance that the court of appeals had upheld. Akron defended this requirement on the grounds that it was a "reasonable health regulation," a position that, as Powell noted, "had strong support at the time of *Roe* . . . as hospitalization was recommended by the American Public Health Association and the American College of Obstetricians and Gynecologists (ACOG)." But times had changed. Medical advances increased the "safety" of second-trimester abortions to the point that the ACOG no longer recommended hospitalization. This development led Powell to conclude that "present medical knowledge . . . undercuts Akron's justification for requiring that *all* second trimester abortions be performed in hospitals." By combining precedent and the current state of medical knowledge, Powell proceeded to strike down all sections of the Akron ordinance as being out of kilter with the 1973 framework viewed from the perspective of 1983.

Despite this resounding affirmation of *Roe*, the pro-choice side had apparently lost a vote. In a dissent, signed by *Roe*'s two dissenters (Rehnquist and White)—O'Connor provided a scathing critique of *Roe*. Her initial argument was straightforward:

1. Because of medical advances, the lines separating "permissible from impermissible" regulation are blurred.

2. As a result, legislatures and, then, courts must "continuously and conscientiously study contemporary medical and scientific literature" to determine what they can and cannot do.

3. This task is difficult for legislatures and inappropriate for courts.

Even if *Roe* requires courts and legislatures to conduct such inquiries, this, in O'Connor's view, did not necessarily mean that courts should always strike legislation. Why? Because medical advances cut both ways: "Just as improvements in medical technology will move *forward* at the point at which the State may regulate for reasons of maternal health, different technological improvements will move *backward* the point of viability at which the State may proscribe abortions."

In other words, while Powell used medical advances to strike down parts of the Akron ordinance, those same "advances" could be used to move back the line of viability, giving states more leeway. At the time of *Roe*, viability "before 28 weeks was considered unusual," but O'Connor cited newer studies showing viability as early as 25 weeks, which led her to two conclusions. First, because it is "inherently" tied to ever-changing medical technology, "the Roe framework . . . is clearly on a collision course with itself." Second, in part because the lines separating viability from nonviability are fading, "compelling state interests" exist throughout the pregnancy.

This kind of analysis paralleled that which appeared in Solicitor General Lee's amicus brief. So it is hardly surprising that O'Connor agreed to the standard he had proposed: she urged the Court to abandon the trimester framework in favor of one that "protects the woman from unduly burdensome interference with her freedom to decide whether to terminate her pregnancy." O'Connor did, however, part company with Lee on how the Court should determine whether a law "imposes an undue burden." She explicitly rejected Lee's assertion that it simply requires courts to defer to legislatures: "The 'unduly burdensome' standard is appropriate *not* because it incorporates deference to legislative judgment at the threshold stage of analysis, but rather because of the limited *nature* of the fundamental right that has been recognized in the abortion cases. . . . [I]t is not appropriate to *weigh* the state interests at the threshold stage." What, then, would O'Connor count as "unduly burdensome" regulation? Powell claimed that "the dissent would uphold virtually any abortion regulation under a rational-basis test," meaning that it would find constitutional any regulation that was reasonably related to a governmental interest. Such a standard, Powell noted, would gut *Roe*. O'Connor did not go that far. Rather, she suggested that if the law in question "unduly burdened" the fundamental right to seek an abortion, the Court should apply strict scrutiny; if the law does not "unduly burden" the abortion right, then the Court should apply a rational basis test.

Thus, as displayed in Box 7-4, by 1983, the justices had proposed three different approaches to restrictive abortion laws. While the majority of the justices continued to support *Roe*'s strict scrutiny standard, O'Connor's dissent raised questions. Would she stick with her "undue burden" standard? If so, would she be able to convince other justices to adopt it? And what exactly did she mean by an "undue burden." These questions were on the minds of observers when the Court agreed to decide *Thornburgh v. American College of Obstetricians and Gynecologists* (1986) be-

---

BOX 7-4   PROPOSED APPROACHES TO RESTRICTIVE ABORTION LAWS

APPROACH	EXEMPLARY OPINIONS	DEFINITION
Strict scrutiny	Blackmun in *Roe;* Powell in *Akron*	The right to abortion is fundamental. So laws restricting that right must be the least restrictive means available to achieve a compelling state interest. In the abortion context, a state's interest grows more compelling as the pregnancy passes from the first to second to third trimesters.
Undue burden	O'Connor in *Akron Center*	The right to decide whether to terminate a pregnancy is fundamental. So laws placing an undue burden on the women's decision to terminate her pregnancy may be subject to strict scrutiny; other kinds of laws need only be rationally related to a legitimate state interest (rational basis test).
Rational basis	Rehnquist in *Roe*	The right to abortion is no different from economic rights claimed under the Fourteenth Amendment Due Process Clause. So the law must be a reasonable measure designed to achieve a legitimate state interest.

---

cause, in this case, the Reagan administration had now decided to deemphasize the undue burden approach and to ask the Court to overrule *Roe.*

In many important ways the Pennsylvania law at issue in *Thornburgh* was similar to that struck in *Akron.* The legislation contained several provisions regulating abortion:

Informed consent. Requires women to give their "voluntary and informed" consent for abortions.

Printed information. Requires a pregnant woman's physician to present her with seven kinds of "explicit" information twenty-four hours prior to abortions: the name of the doctor performing the abortion; the "fact" that "there may be" psychological and physical damage; the medical risks associated with abortion; the gestational age; the medical risks associated with carrying a child to term; availability of prenatal and postnatal care; "the fact that the father is liable" to help support the child.

Determination of viability. Requires doctors "to report the basis for [their] determination 'that a child is not viable.'"

Report. Specifies the sort of report required for a finding of nonviability.

Degree of care for postviability abortions. Mandates that doctors seek to preserve "the life and health of any unborn child."

Second physician. Requires that a "second physician be present during an abortion performed when viability is possible."

The only real difference between this law and the one struck in *Akron* was that Pennsylvania sought to regulate postviability abortions; the informed consent provisions were virtually indistinguishable. Not surprisingly, various pro-choice groups joined forces, on behalf of the American College of Obstetricians and Gynecologists, to challenge the act. This challenge was countered by the state of Pennsylvania, various pro-life groups, and the Reagan Justice Department, now under the command of Attorney General Edwin Meese, an avowed opponent of abortion.

Meese instructed Charles Fried, the acting solicitor general, to ask the Court to overrule *Roe*. Fried mounted a two-pronged assault: *Roe* was a source of "instability" in law and, in the measure of "history," it belied the Framers' intent. After attacking Powell's *Akron* opinion as a significant departure from *Roe*, Fried suggested that it "is a symptom, not the source, of the problem." That distinction belonged to *Roe*, which mandated "an inquiry not easy for courts to follow in a principled fashion. The key factors in the equation—viability, trimesters...—are inherently unworkable." Using O'Connor's dissent in *Akron* and other legal arguments, Fried sought to demonstrate that the trimester scheme and viability represented arbitrary schema that change with medical advances. As such, *Roe* would always lead courts to differing conclusions over the constitutionality of specific state regulations. The brief then launched into one of Meese's favored approaches to constitutional interpretation, the intent of the Framers: "Constitutional interpretation retains the fullest measure of legitimacy when it is disciplined by fidelity to the framers' intent as revealed by history." On that score, in Fried and Meese's view, *Roe* could not be justified.

Writing for a five-person majority, the Court completely refuted Fried's position. Justice Blackmun's majority opinion blasted legislation designed to undermine *Roe* ("The States are not free, under the guise of protecting maternal health or potential life, to intimidate women into continuing pregnancies"); chastised Pennsylvania for its repeated efforts to circumvent *Roe* (this "was not the Commonwealth's first attempt ... after ... *Roe* ... to impose abortion restraints"); and implicitly refuted the solicitor general's position ("Again today, we reaffirm the general principles laid down in *Roe*.... As judges ... we are sworn to uphold the law even when its content gives rise to bitter dispute").

But the pro-life side had picked up another vote. After thirteen years of generally supporting the abortion right, Chief Justice Burger joined *Roe*'s opponents. In his *Thornburgh* dissent, he wrote:

I based my concurring statements in Roe and Maher on the principle expressed in the Court's opinion in Roe that the right to an abortion "is not unqualified and must be considered against important state interests in regulation." In short, every Member of the Roe Court rejected the idea of abortion on demand. The Court's opinion today, however, plainly undermines that important principle, and I regretfully conclude that some of the concerns of the dissenting Justices in Roe, as well as the concerns I expressed in my separate opinion, have now been realized.

Less surprising were dissents registered by White, O'Connor, and Rehnquist. White, joined by Rehnquist, lambasted the Court's "venture" into abortion as "fundamentally misguided since its conception." Although he rejected a jurisprudence of original intent, he agreed with Meese and Fried's "bottom line" on *Roe*: it should be overruled. O'Connor's dissent, also signed by Rehnquist, refrained from arguing that the Court should overrule *Roe*. She continued to press her *Akron* position: the justices should move to an "unduly burdensome" standard. She remained critical of *Roe*: "This Court's abortion decisions have already worked a major distortion in the Court's constitutional jurisprudence"; the justices were not dealing with abortion "evenhandedly."

The Reversal of Roe v. Wade? *The Rehnquist Court and the Abortion Right*

Although pro-choice advocates won the 1980s cases, they were steadily losing ground. As Table 7-5 shows, the *Roe* majority of seven became six in 1983 and was down to five in 1986. Indeed, diminishing support for *Roe* was widely acknowledged in the popular press and noted by legislative bodies. And it was evident in 1987 when pro-choice forces (among many others) rallied to oppose President Reagan's nomination of Robert Bork, an avowed *Roe* opponent,

TABLE 7-5 Diminishing Support for *Roe v. Wade:* The Supreme Court at the time of *Webster v. Reproductive Health Services*

Roe v. Wade (1973)	Akron v. Akron Center (1983)	Thornburgh v. ACOG (1986)	Webster v. Reproductive Health Services (1989)
Blackmun	Blackmun	Blackmun	Blackmun
Brennan	Brennan	Brennan	Brennan
Burger	Burger	*Burger*	*Rehnquist*
Douglas	Stevens	Stevens	Stevens
Marshall	Marshall	Marshall	Marshall
Powell	Powell	Powell	Kennedy
Rehnquist	*Rehnquist*	*Rehnquist*	Scalia
Stewart	*O'Connor*	*O'Connor*	*O'Connor*
White	*White*	*White*	*White*

Key: justices in boldface support *Roe;* justices in italics oppose *Roe;* justices in regular type had not participated in an abortion case prior to *Webster.*

to replace Justice Powell. Pro-choice advocates, along with the members of the Senate, realized that Bork's appointment to the Court could tip the balance between maintaining *Roe* and overruling it. Undoubtedly Bork's position on abortion, coupled with many of his other controversial stances, contributed to his defeat.[28]

Even with Bork's rejection, pro-choice forces were concerned when the Rehnquist Court agreed to hear *Webster v. Reproductive Health Services,* a new challenge to *Roe.* By that time, the Senate had confirmed Powell's replacement, Anthony Kennedy, whose views on abortion were not known. Moreover, Justice Rehnquist, a persistent critic, had been elevated to chief justice, with Reagan appointee Antonin Scalia taking his place. These changes led many observers to conclude that *Webster* would be a major ruling on abortion. As Table 7-5 shows, if the two new Reagan

appointees, Scalia and Kennedy, opposed *Roe,* the Court would overrule the 1973 decision. Even *Roe's* author thought it was doomed. In a speech given before the start of the 1988 term, during which the Court would decide *Webster,* Justice Blackmun wondered aloud: "Will *Roe v. Wade* go down the drain? I think there's a very distinct possibility that it will, this term. You can count the votes."[29]

The possibility that *Webster* would reverse *Roe* was not lost on pro-choice and pro-life forces, who filed seventy-eight amicus curiae briefs (the largest number ever submitted to the Court in a single case), representing more than 5,000 individual groups and interests. The Bush administration's solicitor general not only filed a brief supporting state regulation of abortions but also participated in oral argument, again requesting the Court to overrule *Roe.* Would the newly configured Rehnquist Court accept this invitation? Was the ruling as much of a landmark as many Court watchers expected? Consider these questions as you read the opinions in *Webster.*

28. There were many reasons for Bork's defeat. Numerous civil rights and liberties groups opposed him for his stances on women's rights and homosexual conduct. Moreover, public opinion was squarely against him. By September 1987, only 29 percent of Americans supported his appointment to the Court.

29. "Justice Fears for *Roe* Ruling," *New York Times,* September 14, 1988.

Webster v. Reproductive Health Services

492 U.S. 490 (1989)

Vote: 5 (Kennedy, O'Connor, Rehnquist, Scalia, White)

  4 (Blackmun, Brennan, Marshall, Stevens)

Opinion announcing the judgment of the Court and the opinion of the Court: Rehnquist

Concurring opinions: O'Connor, Scalia

Opinions concurring in part and dissenting in part: Blackmun, Stevens

With legal assistance from Planned Parenthood and the ACLU, Reproductive Health Services, an abortion counseling facility, challenged numerous provisions of a 1986 Missouri law regulating abortions. They were:

1. The law's preamble, which stated that "the life of each human being begins at the moment of conception" and "unborn children have protectable interests in life, health, and well being."

2. A prohibition on the ability of public employees to "perform or assist in abortion, not necessary to save the life of the mother" (§ 188.210). Nor can "any public facility . . . be used to perform an abortion not necessary to save the life of the mother," even if no public monies are expended.

3. Prohibitions relating to "encouraging or counseling a woman to have an abortion not necessary to save her life." Section 188.210 prohibits public employees in engaging in such speech; § 188.215 bars such speech in public facilities; and § 188.205 disallows the use of public funds for such speech.

4. The requirement that "before a physician performs an abortion on a woman he has reason to believe is carrying an unborn child of twenty or more weeks gestational age, the physician first determine if the unborn child is viable. . . . In making this determination, the physician shall perform or cause to be performed such medical examinations and [viability] tests as are necessary to make a finding of the gesta-

tional age, weight, and lung maturity of the unborn child." (§ 188.029).

A U.S. district court struck down most of the act's provisions as violative of *Roe*, and the court of appeals affirmed. Missouri appealed to the U.S. Supreme Court, and, in its briefs, asserted that *Roe*'s trimester scheme is "inherently flawed" because the "State has a compelling interest in protecting life through all stages of the pregnancy." Relying on dissents by O'Connor, Rehnquist, and White in earlier abortion cases, the intent of the Framers of the Constitution, and medical evidence, Missouri asked the Court to "abandon" *Roe*, a position the solicitor general also pressed. Alternatively, should the Court not be ready to overrule *Roe*, the state argued that it should adopt O'Connor's unduly burdensome approach.

Attorneys for Reproductive Health Services took precisely the opposite position, asking the Court to apply *Roe* to find against the law. In their view, Missouri was attempting to regulate abortions prior to viability, when *Roe* said that the state lacks a compelling interest in regulating abortions prior to that time. If the Court adopts Missouri's argument, they maintained, there will be no legal distinction between a "freshly fertilized egg" and a nine-month-old fetus. In other words, the state will be free to regulate abortions at any stage of the pregnancy in direct contradiction to the precepts of *Roe*.

Oral arguments in *Webster* were dramatic. Outside the Court, demonstrators chanted their various battle cries. Police arrested some pro-choice supporters who would not remain behind the barricades. Inside, the courtroom was packed, with the press and pro-choice/pro-life advocates taking most of the available seats. One of the most electric moments came immediately after the solicitor general's arguments. In his opening comments, Fried tried to respond to concerns that overruling *Roe* (that is, subjecting abortion laws to a rational basis test) would infringe on the more general right to privacy created in *Griswold*:

Anti-abortion protesters mark the January 22 anniversary of *Roe v. Wade* with a march in front of the Supreme Court January 21, 1994.

Today the United States asks this Court to reconsider and overrule its decision in *Roe v. Wade*. At the outset, I would like to make it quite clear how limited that submission is.... We are not asking the Court to unravel the fabric of unenumerated and privacy rights which this Court has woven in cases like ... *Griswold*. Rather, we are asking the Court to pull one thread [because] abortion is different.

As soon as Fried had finished his argument, pro-choice attorney Frank Susan responded:

I think the Solicitor General's submission is somewhat disingenuous when he suggests to this Court that he does not seek to unravel the whole cloth of procreation rights, but merely to pull a thread. It has always been my personal experience that, when I pull a thread, my sleeve falls off. There is no stopping. It is not a thread he is after. It is the full range of procreation rights and choices that constitute the fundamental right that has been recognized by this Court.

CHIEF JUSTICE REHNQUIST announced the judgment of the Court and delivered the opinion of the Court with respect to Parts I, II-A, II-B, and II-C, and an opinion with respect to Parts II-D and III in which JUSTICE WHITE and JUSTICE KENNEDY join.

[I omitted]

II

... In our view, the Court of Appeals misconceived the meaning of the *Akron* dictum, which was only that a State could not "justify" an abortion regulation otherwise invalid under *Roe v. Wade* on the ground that it embodied the State's view about when life begins. Certainly the preamble does not by its terms regulate abortion or any other aspect of appellee's medical practice. The Court has emphasized that *Roe v. Wade* "implies no limitation on the authority of a State to make a value judgment favoring childbirth over abortion."... The preamble can be read simply to express that sort of value judgment.

We think the extent to which the preamble's language might be used to interpret other state statutes or regulations is something that only the courts of Missouri can definitively decide.... It will be time enough for federal courts to address the meaning of the preamble should it be applied to restrict the activities of appellee in some concrete way. Until then, this Court "is not empowered to decide ... abstract propositions, or to declare, for the government of future cases, principles or rules of law which cannot affect the result as to the thing in issue in the case before it."... We therefore need not pass on the constitutionality of the Act's preamble.

B

Section 188.210 provides that "[i]t shall be unlawful for any public employee within the scope of his employment to perform or assist an abortion, not necessary to save the life of the mother," while § 188.215 makes it "unlawful for any public facility to be used for the purpose of performing or assisting an abortion not necessary to save the life of the mother." The Court of Appeals held that these provisions contravened this Court's abortion decisions. We take the contrary view....

Maher [*v. Roe*, 1977], *Poelker* [*v. Doe*, 1977], and [*Harris v.*] *McRae* [1980] all support the view that the State need not commit any resources to facilitating abortions, even if it can turn a profit by doing so. In *Poelker*, the suit was filed by an indigent who could not afford to pay for an abortion, but the ban on the performance of nontherapeutic abortions in city-owned hospitals applied whether or not the pregnant woman could pay. The Court emphasized that the Mayor's decision to prohibit abortions in city hospitals was "subject to public debate and approval or disapproval at the polls," and that "the Constitution does not forbid a State or city, pursuant to democratic processes, from expressing a preference for normal childbirth as St. Louis has done." Thus we uphold the Act's restrictions on the use of public employees and facilities for the performance or assistance of nontherapeutic abortions.

C

[In this section, Rehnquist discusses Missouri's prohibitions relating to "encouraging or counseling a woman to have an abortion not necessary to save her life." The State chose not to appeal § 188.210 (prohibiting public employees in engaging in such speech) or § 188.215 (barring such speech in public facilities).

Using the same logic he applied to the state's bans on the use of public facilities or employees to perform abortions, he upheld the one section it did appeal (§ 188.205 disallowing the use of public funds for such speech).]

D

... The viability-testing provision of the Missouri Act is concerned with promoting the State's interest in potential human life rather than in maternal health. Section 188.029 creates what is essentially a presumption of viability at 20 weeks, which the physician must rebut with tests indicating that the fetus is not viable prior to performing an abortion. It also directs the physician's determination as to viability by specifying consideration, if feasible, of gestational age, fetal weight, and lung capacity....

In *Roe v. Wade*, the Court recognized that the State has "important and legitimate" interests in protecting maternal health and in the potentiality of human life. During the second trimester, the State "may, if it chooses, regulate the abortion procedure in ways that are reasonably related to maternal health." After viability, when the State's interest in potential human life was held to become compelling, the State "may, if it chooses, regulate, and even proscribe, abortion except where it is necessary, in appropriate medical judgment, for the preservation of the life or health of the mother."

... To the extent that § 188.029 regulates the method for determining viability, it undoubtedly does superimpose state regulation on the medical determination of whether a particular fetus is viable. The Court of Appeals and the District Court thought it unconstitutional for this reason. To the extent that the viability tests increase the cost of what are in fact second-trimester abortions, their validity may also be questioned....

We think that the doubt cast upon the Missouri statute by these cases is not so much a flaw in the statute as it is a reflection of the fact that the rigid trimester analysis of the course of a pregnancy enunciated in *Roe* has resulted in subsequent cases like *Colautti* [*v. Franklin*, 1979] ... making constitutional law in this area a virtual Procrustean bed....

Stare decisis is a cornerstone of our legal system, but it has less power in constitutional cases, where, save for constitutional amendments, this Court is the only body able to make needed changes. We have not refrained from reconsideration of a prior construction of the Constitution that has proved "unsound in principle and unworkable in practice.". . . We think the *Roe* trimester framework falls into that category.

In the first place, the rigid *Roe* framework is hardly consistent with the notion of a Constitution cast in general terms, as ours is, and usually speaking in general principles, as ours does. The key elements of the *Roe* framework—trimesters and viability—are not found in the text of the Constitution or in any place else one would expect to find a constitutional principle. Since the bounds of the inquiry are essentially indeterminate, the result has been a web of legal rules that have become increasingly intricate, resembling a code of regulations rather than a body of constitutional doctrine. As JUSTICE WHITE has put it, the trimester framework has left this Court to serve as the country's *"ex officio* medical board with powers to approve or disapprove medical and operative practices and standards throughout the United States.". . .

In the second place, we do not see why the State's interest in protecting potential human life should come into existence only at the point of viability, and that there should therefore be a rigid line allowing state regulation after viability but prohibiting it before viability. The dissenters in *Thornburgh,* writing in the context of the *Roe* trimester analysis, would have recognized this fact by positing against the "fundamental right" recognized in *Roe* the State's "compelling interest" in protecting potential human life throughout pregnancy. . . .

The tests that § 188.029 requires the physician to perform are designed to determine viability. The State here has chosen viability as the point at which its interest in potential human life must be safeguarded. It is true that the tests in question increase the expense of abortion, and regulate the discretion of the physician in determining the viability of the fetus. Since the tests will undoubtedly show in many cases that the fetus is not viable, the tests will have been performed for what were in fact second-trimester abortions. But we are satisfied that the requirement of these tests permissibly furthers the State's interest in protecting potential human life, and we therefore believe § 188.029 to be constitutional.

The dissent takes us to task for our failure to join in a "great issues" debate as to whether the Constitution includes an "unenumerated" general right to privacy as recognized in cases such as *Griswold v. Connecticut* (1965) and *Roe.* But *Griswold v. Connecticut,* unlike *Roe,* did not purport to adopt a whole framework, complete with detailed rules and distinctions, to govern the cases in which the asserted liberty interest would apply. As such, it was far different from the opinion, if not the holding, of *Roe v. Wade,* which sought to establish a constitutional framework for judging state regulation of abortion during the entire term of pregnancy. That framework sought to deal with areas of medical practice traditionally subject to state regulation, and it sought to balance once and for all by reference only to the calendar the claims of the State to protect the fetus as a form of human life against the claims of a woman to decide for herself whether or not to abort a fetus she was carrying. The experience of the Court in applying *Roe v. Wade* in later cases suggests to us that there is wisdom in not unnecessarily attempting to elaborate the abstract differences between a "fundamental right" to abortion, . . . a "limited fundamental constitutional right," which JUSTICE BLACKMUN's dissent today treats *Roe* as having established, or a liberty interest protected by the Due Process Clause, which we believe it to be. The Missouri testing requirement here is reasonably designed to ensure that abortions are not performed where the fetus is viable—an end which all concede is legitimate—and that is sufficient to sustain its constitutionality.

The dissent also accuses us . . . of cowardice and illegitimacy in dealing with "the most politically divisive domestic legal issue of our time." There is no doubt that our holding today will allow some governmental regulation of abortion that would have been prohibited. . . . But the goal of constitutional adjudication is surely not to remove inexorably "politically divisive" issues from the ambit of the legislative process, whereby the people through their elected representatives deal with matters of concern to them. The goal of constitutional adjudication is to hold true the balance between that which the Constitution puts beyond the reach of the democratic process and that which it does not. We think we have done that today. The dissent's suggestion that legislative bodies, in a Nation where more than half of our population is women, will treat our decision today as an invitation to enact abortion regulation reminiscent of the dark ages not only misreads our views but does scant justice to those who serve in such bodies and the people who elect them.

III

Both appellants and the United States as *Amicus Curiae* have urged that we overrule our decision in *Roe v. Wade.* The facts of the present case, however, differ from those at issue in *Roe.* Here, Missouri has determined that viability is the point at which its interest in potential human life must be safeguarded. In *Roe,* on the other hand, the Texas statute criminalized the performance of *all* abortions, except when the mother's life was at stake. This case therefore affords us no occasion to revisit the holding of *Roe,* which was that the Texas statute unconstitutionally infringed the right to an abortion derived from the Due Process Clause, and we leave it undisturbed. To the extent indicated in our opinion, we would modify and narrow *Roe* and succeeding cases.

Because none of the challenged provisions of the Missouri Act properly before us conflict with the Constitution, the judgment of the Court of Appeals is

Reversed.

JUSTICE O'CONNOR, concurring in part and concurring in the judgment.

I concur in Parts I, II-A, II-B, and II-C of the Court's opinion.

[I omitted]

II

... Unlike the plurality, I do not understand [the] viability testing requirements to conflict with any of the Court's past decisions concerning state regulation of abortion. Therefore, there is no necessity to accept the State's invitation to reexamine the constitutional validity of *Roe v. Wade* (1973). Where there is no need to decide a constitutional question, it is a venerable principle of this Court's adjudicatory processes not to do so for "[t]he Court will not 'anticipate a question of constitutional law in advance of the necessity of deciding it.'"... Neither will it generally "formulate a rule of constitutional law broader than is required by the precise facts to which it is to be applied." Quite simply, "[i]t is not the habit of the court to decide questions of a constitutional nature unless absolutely

necessary to a decision of the case."... The Court today has accepted the State's every interpretation of its abortion statute and has upheld, under our existing precedents, every provision of that statute which is properly before us. Precisely for this reason reconsideration of *Roe* falls not into any "good-cause exception" to this "fundamental rule of judicial restraint...."... When the constitutional invalidity of a State's abortion statute actually turns on the constitutional validity of *Roe v. Wade,* there will be time enough to reexamine *Roe.* And to do so carefully....

... I dissented from the Court's opinion in *Akron* because it was my view that, even apart from *Roe*'s trimester framework which I continue to consider problematic, the *Akron* majority had distorted and misapplied its own standard for evaluating state regulation of abortion which the Court had applied with fair consistency in the past: that, previability, "a regulation imposed on a lawful abortion is not unconstitutional unless it unduly burdens the right to seek an abortion."

It is clear to me that requiring the performance of examinations and tests useful to determining whether a fetus is viable, when viability is possible, and when it would not be medically imprudent to do so, does not impose an undue burden on a woman's abortion decision. On this ground alone I would reject the suggestion that § 188.029 as interpreted is unconstitutional.... [T]he cost of examinations and tests that could usefully and prudently be performed when a woman is 20–24 weeks pregnant to determine whether the fetus is viable would only marginally, if at all, increase the cost of an abortion....

JUSTICE SCALIA, concurring in part and concurring in the judgment.

I join Parts I, II-A, II-B, and II-C of the opinion of THE CHIEF JUSTICE. As to Part II-D, I share JUSTICE BLACKMUN's view that it effectively would overrule *Roe v. Wade* (1973). I think that should be done, but would do it more explicitly. Since today we contrive to avoid doing it, and indeed to avoid almost any decision of national import, I need not set forth my reasons, some of which have been well recited in dissents of my colleagues in other cases....

The outcome of today's case will doubtless be heralded as a triumph of judicial statesmanship. It is not that, unless it is statesmanlike needlessly to prolong this Court's self-awarded sovereignty over a field where it has little proper business since the answers to most of the cruel questions posed are political and not juridical—a sovereignty which therefore quite properly, but to the great damage of the Court, makes it the object of the sort of organized public pressure that political institutions in a democracy ought to receive.

JUSTICE O'CONNOR'S assertion that a "'fundamental rule of judicial restraint'" requires us to avoid reconsidering *Roe* cannot be taken seriously. By finessing *Roe* we do not, as she suggests, adhere to the strict and venerable rule that we should avoid "'decid[ing] questions of a constitutional nature.'" We have not disposed of this case on some statutory or procedural ground, but have decided, and could not avoid deciding, whether the Missouri statute meets the requirements of the United States Constitution. The only choice available is whether, in deciding that constitutional question, we should use *Roe v. Wade* as the benchmark, or something else. What is involved, therefore, is not the rule of avoiding constitutional issues where possible, but the quite separate principle that we will not "'formulate a rule of constitutional law broader than is required by the precise facts to which it is to be applied.'" ...

The real question, then, is whether there are valid reasons to go beyond the most stingy possible holding today. It seems to me there are not only valid but compelling ones. Ordinarily, speaking no more broadly than is absolutely required avoids throwing settled law into confusion; doing so today preserves a chaos that is evident to anyone who can read and count. Alone sufficient to justify a broad holding is the fact that our retaining control, through *Roe*, of what I believe to be, and many of our citizens recognize to be, a political issue, continuously distorts the public perception of the role of this Court. We can now look forward to at least another Term with carts full of mail from the public, and streets full of demonstrators, urging us—their unelected and life-tenured judges who have been awarded those extraordinary, undemocratic characteristics precisely in order that we might follow the law despite the popular will—to follow the popular will. Indeed, I expect we can look forward to even more of that than before, given our indecisive decision today....

... The result of our vote today is that we will not reconsider ... [*Roe*], even if most of the Justices think it is wrong, unless we have before us a statute that in fact contradicts it—and even then (under our newly discovered "no-broader-than-necessary" requirement) only minor problematical aspects of *Roe* will be reconsidered, unless one expects State legislatures to adopt provisions whose compliance with *Roe* cannot even be argued with a straight face. It thus appears that the mansion of constitutionalized abortion-law, constructed overnight in *Roe v. Wade*, must be disassembled door-jamb by door-jamb, and never entirely brought down, no matter how wrong it may be.

Of the four courses we might have chosen today—to reaffirm *Roe*, to overrule it explicitly, to overrule it *sub silentio*, or to avoid the question—the last is the least responsible.... I concur in the judgment of the Court and strongly dissent from the manner in which it has been reached.

JUSTICE BLACKMUN, with whom JUSTICE BRENNAN and JUSTICE MARSHALL join, concurring in part and dissenting in part.

Today, *Roe v. Wade* (1973) and the fundamental constitutional right of women to decide whether to terminate a pregnancy, survive but are not secure. Although the Court extricates itself from this case without making a single, even incremental, change in the law of abortion, the plurality and JUSTICE SCALIA would overrule *Roe* (the first silently, the other explicitly) and would return to the States virtually unfettered authority to control the quintessentially intimate, personal, and life-directing decision whether to carry a fetus to term. Although today, no less than yesterday, the Constitution and the decisions of this Court prohibit a State from enacting laws that inhibit women from the meaningful exercise of that right, a plurality of this Court implicitly invites every state legislature to enact more and more restrictive abortion regulations in order to provoke more and more test cases, in the hope that sometime down the line the Court will return the law of procreative freedom to the severe limitations that generally prevailed in this country before January 22, 1973. Never in my memory has a plurality announced a judgment of this Court that so foments disregard for the law and for our standing decisions.

Nor in my memory has a plurality gone about its business in such a deceptive fashion. At every level of its review, from its effort to read the real meaning out of the Missouri statute, to its intended evisceration of precedents and its deafening silence about the constitutional protections that it would jettison, the plurality obscures the portent of its analysis. With feigned restraint, the plurality announces that its analysis leaves *Roe* "undisturbed," albeit "modif[ied] and narrowed." But this disclaimer is totally meaningless. The plurality opinion is filled with winks, and nods, and knowing glances to those who would do away with *Roe* explicitly, but turns a stone face to anyone in search of what the plurality conceives as the scope of a woman's right under the Due Process Clause to terminate a pregnancy free from the coercive and brooding influence of the State. The simple truth is that *Roe* would not survive the plurality's analysis, and that the plurality provides no substitute for *Roe*'s protective umbrella.

I fear for the future. I fear for the liberty and equality of the millions of women who have lived and come of age in the 16 years since *Roe* was decided. I fear for the integrity of, and public esteem for, this Court.

I dissent.

[I-A omitted]

B

Having set up the conflict between § 188.029 and the *Roe* trimester framework, the plurality summarily discards *Roe*'s analytic core as "'unsound in principle and unworkable in practice.'" This is so, the plurality claims, because the key elements of the framework do not appear in the text of the Constitution, because the framework more closely resembles a regulatory code than a body of constitutional doctrine, and because under the framework the State's interest in potential human life is considered compelling only after viability, when, in fact, that interest is equally compelling throughout pregnancy. The plurality does not bother to explain these alleged flaws in *Roe*. Bald assertion masquerades as reasoning. The object, quite clearly, is not to persuade, but to prevail. . . .

C

Having contrived an opportunity to reconsider the *Roe* framework, and then having discarded that framework, the plurality finds the testing provision unobjectionable because it "permissibly furthers the State's interest in protect-

ing potential human life." This newly minted standard is circular and totally meaningless. Whether a challenged abortion regulation "permissibly furthers" a legitimate state interest is the *question* that courts must answer in abortion cases, not the standard for courts to apply. In keeping with the rest of its opinion, the plurality makes no attempt to explain or to justify its new standard, either in the abstract or as applied in this case. Nor could it. The "permissibly furthers" standard has no independent meaning, and consists of nothing other than what a majority of this Court may believe at any given moment in any given case. The plurality's novel test appears to be nothing more than a dressed-up version of rational-basis review, this Court's most lenient level of scrutiny. One thing is clear, however: were the plurality's "permissibly furthers" standard adopted by the Court, for all practical purposes, *Roe* would be overruled.

The "permissibly furthers" standard completely disregards the irreducible minimum of *Roe*: the Court's recognition that a woman has a limited fundamental constitutional right to decide whether to terminate a pregnancy. That right receives no meaningful recognition in the plurality's written opinion. Since, in the plurality's view, the State's interest in potential life is compelling as of the moment of conception, and is therefore served only if abortion is abolished, every hindrance to a woman's ability to obtain an abortion must be "permissible." Indeed, the more severe the hindrance, the more effectively (and permissibly) the State's interest would be furthered. A tax on abortions or a criminal prohibition would both satisfy the plurality's standard. So, for that matter, would a requirement that a pregnant woman memorize and recite today's plurality opinion before seeking an abortion.

The plurality pretends that *Roe* survives, explaining that the facts of this case differ from those in *Roe*: here, Missouri has chosen to assert its interest in potential life only at the point of viability, whereas, in *Roe,* Texas had asserted that interest from the point of conception, criminalizing all abortions, except where the life of the mother was at stake. This, of course, is a distinction without a difference. The plurality repudiates every principle for which *Roe* stands; in good conscience, it cannot possibly believe that *Roe* lies "undisturbed" merely because this case does not call upon the Court to reconsider the Texas statute, or one like it. If the Constitution permits a State to enact any statute that reasonably furthers its interest in potential life, and if that interest arises as of conception, why would the Texas statute fail to pass muster? One suspects that the plurality agrees. It is impossible to read the plurality opinion and especially its final paragraph, without recognizing its implicit invitation to every State to enact more and more restrictive abortion laws, and to assert their interest in potential life as of the moment of conception. All these laws will satisfy the plurality's non-scrutiny, until sometime, a new regime of old dissenters and new appointees will declare what the plurality intends: that *Roe* is no longer good law.

D

Thus, "not with a bang, but a whimper," the plurality discards a landmark case of the last generation, and casts into darkness the hopes and visions of every woman in this country who had come to believe that the Constitution guaranteed her the right to exercise some control over her unique ability to bear children. The plurality does so either oblivious or insensitive to the fact that millions of women, and their families, have ordered their lives around the right to reproductive choice, and that this right has become vital to the full participation of women in the economic and political walks of American life. The plurality would clear the way once again for government to force upon women the physical labor and specific and direct medical and psychological harms that may accompany carrying a fetus to term. The plurality would clear the way again for the State to conscript a woman's body and to force upon her a "distressful life and future."

The result, as we know from experience, would be that every year hundreds of thousands of women, in desperation, would defy the law, and place their health and safety in the unclean and unsympathetic hands of back-alley abortionists, or they would attempt to perform abortions upon themselves, with disastrous results. Every year, many women, especially poor and minority women, would die or suffer debilitating physical trauma, all in the name of enforced morality or religious dictates or lack of compassion, as it may be.

Of the aspirations and settled understandings of American women, of the inevitable and brutal consequences of what it is doing, the tough-approach plurality utters not a word. This silence is callous. It is also profoundly destructive of this Court as an institution. To overturn a constitutional decision is a rare and grave undertaking. To overturn a constitutional decision that secured a fundamental personal liberty to millions of persons would be unprecedented in our 200 years of constitutional history....

This comes at a cost. The doctrine of *stare decisis* "permits society to presume that bedrock principles are founded in the law rather than in the proclivities of individuals, and thereby contributes to the integrity of our constitutional system of government, both in appearance and in fact." Today's decision involves the most politically divisive domestic legal issue of our time. By refusing to explain or to justify its proposed revolutionary revision in the law of abortion, and by refusing to abide not only by our precedents, but also by our canons for reconsidering those precedents, the plurality invites charges of cowardice and illegitimacy to our door. I cannot say that these would be undeserved.

II

For today, at least, the law of abortion stands undisturbed. For today, the women of this Nation still retain the liberty to control their destinies. But the signs are evident and very ominous, and a chill wind blows.

I dissent.

In *Webster* the Court came within one vote of overturning *Roe*: Justice O'Connor's "unduly burdensome" approach kept it alive, at least for the moment. But, in the eyes of many observers, *Roe* was operating on borrowed time because President George Bush eventually would have the opportunity to appoint justices who could tip the balance against *Roe*.

It was not long before this view was tested. By the time the Court agreed to hear arguments in another abortion case, *Planned Parenthood of Southeastern Pennsylvania v. Casey*, Bush had appointed two justices. David Souter and Clarence Thomas replaced the pro-choice justices Brennan and Marshall, respectively. These membership changes seemed to confirm the greatest hope and fear of the pro-life and pro-choice movements: *Roe* would finally go. Or would it?

Planned Parenthood of Southeastern Pennsylvania v. Casey

505 U.S. — (1992)

Opinion announcing the judgment of the Court and delivering the opinion of the Court: Kennedy, O'Connor, Souter
Concurring in part: Blackmun, Rehnquist, Scalia, Stevens, Thomas, White
Dissenting in part: Blackmun, Rehnquist, Scalia, Stevens, Thomas, White
Opinions concurring in part and dissenting in part: Blackmun, Rehnquist, Scalia, Stevens

After the Court's decision in *Webster v. Reproductive Health Services,* Pennsylvania revised its Abortion Control Act, which the Court had, by a 5–4 vote, struck down in *Thornburgh v. American College of Obstetricians and Gynecologists* (1986). Given membership changes on the Court and the *Webster* decision, the state thought the Court would now uphold the amended law, which contained the following provisions:

Informed consent/twenty-four-hour waiting period. At least twenty-four hours before a physician performs an abortion, physicians must inform women of "the nature of the procedure, the health risks of the abortion and of childbirth, and the 'probable gestational age of the unborn child.'" The physician also must provide women with a list of adoption agencies. Abortions may not be performed unless the woman "certifies in writing" that she has given her informed consent. Twenty-four hours must elapse between the time women give their consent and the abortion procedure is performed (§ 3205).

Spousal notice. Before performing an abortion on a married woman, a physician must receive a statement from her stating that she has notified her spouse that she "is about to undergo an abortion." Alternatively, the woman may "provide a statement certifying that her husband is not the man who impregnated her; that her husband could not be located; that the pregnancy is the result of spousal sexual assault which she has reported; or that the women believes that notifying her husband will cause him or someone else to inflict bodily injury upon her" (§ 3209).

Parental consent. Unless she exercises a judicial bypass option, a woman under the age of eighteen must obtain the informed consent of one parent prior to obtaining an abortion (§ 3206).

Reporting and recordkeeping. All facilities performing abortions must file reports containing information about the procedure, including: the physician, the woman's age, the number of prior pregnancies or abortions she has had, "pre-existing medical conditions that would complicate the pregnancy," the weight and age of the aborted fetus, whether or not the woman was married, and, if relevant, the reason(s) the woman has failed to notify her spouse. If the abortion is performed in a facility funded by the state, the information becomes public (§ 3207).

Before these provisions went into effect, five abortion clinics challenged their constitutionality.[30] A federal district court generally agreed with the clinics, but the Court of Appeals for the Third Circuit reversed, using O'Connor's "undue burden" standard, which—based on its reading of *Webster*— was "the law of the land." In the appeals court's opinion, the provisions, with the exception of spousal consent, did not place an undue burden on the decision of whether to terminate a pregnancy. The court applied a rational basis test under which the three provisions easily passed constitutional muster. The spousal consent provision, in the court's view, placed an undue burden on the abortion decision by exposing women to spousal abuse and violence. It, therefore, applied the strict scrutiny test and concluded that the provision could not stand.

---

30. We adopt the discussion that follows from Barbara Hinkson Craig and David M. O'Brien, *Abortion and American Politics* (Chatham, N.J.: Chatham House, 1993), 330–333.

As a result of this mixed opinion, the state and the clinics appealed to the Supreme Court. In a move designed to intensify "the abortion debate before the 1992 presidential election," Planned Parenthood asked the justices to issue a nonambiguous decision: either affirm or overturn *Roe*.[31] The state, joined by the Bush administration's solicitor general, also asked the Court "to end the current uncertainty" surrounding the abortion issue. The solicitor general's position was particularly clear: once again the administration suggested that *"Roe v. Wade* was wrongly decided and should be overruled." The state and the federal government wanted the Court to adopt a rational basis approach to abortion and to use that standard to uphold all of Pennsylvania's laws. Given the membership changes on the Court, many observers predicted the Court would do precisely that.

JUSTICE O'CONNOR, JUSTICE KENNEDY, and JUSTICE SOUTER announced the judgment of the Court and delivered the opinion of the Court with respect to Parts I, II, III, V-A, V-C, and VI, an opinion with respect to Part V-E, in which JUSTICE STEVENS joins, and an opinion with respect to Parts IV, V-B, and V-D.

I

Liberty finds no refuge in a jurisprudence of doubt. Yet 19 years after our holding that the Constitution protects a woman's right to terminate her pregnancy in its early stages, *Roe v. Wade* (1973), that definition of liberty is still questioned. Joining the respondents as *amicus curiae,* the United States, as it has done in five other cases in the last decade, again asks us to overrule *Roe*.

... And at oral argument in this Court, the attorney for the parties challenging the statute took the position that none of the enactments can be upheld without overruling *Roe v. Wade*. We disagree with that analysis; but we acknowledge that our decisions after *Roe* cast doubt upon the meaning and reach of its holding. Further, the CHIEF JUSTICE admits that he would overrule the central holding of *Roe* and adopt the rational relationship test as the sole cri-

31. Ibid., 333.

terion of constitutionality. State and federal courts as well as legislatures throughout the Union must have guidance as they seek to address this subject in conformance with the Constitution. Given these premises, we find it imperative to review once more the principles that define the rights of the woman and the legitimate authority of the State respecting the termination of pregnancies by abortion procedures.

After considering the fundamental constitutional questions resolved by *Roe*, principles of institutional integrity, and the rule of *stare decisis,* we are led to conclude this: the essential holding of *Roe v. Wade* should be retained and once again reaffirmed.

It must be stated at the outset and with clarity that *Roe*'s essential holding, the holding we reaffirm, has three parts. First is a recognition of the right of the woman to choose to have an abortion before viability and to obtain it without undue interference from the State. Before viability, the State's interests are not strong enough to support a prohibition of abortion or the imposition of a substantial obstacle to the woman's effective right to elect the procedure. Second is a confirmation of the State's power to restrict abortions after fetal viability, if the law contains exceptions for pregnancies which endanger a woman's life or health. And third is the principle that the State has legitimate interests from the outset of the pregnancy in protecting the health of the woman and the life of the fetus that may become a child. These principles do not contradict one another; and we adhere to each.

II

... These considerations begin our analysis of the woman's interest in terminating her pregnancy but cannot end it, for this reason: though the abortion decision may originate within the zone of conscience and belief, it is more than a philosophic exercise. Abortion is a unique act. It is an act fraught with consequences for others: for the woman who must live with the implications of her decision; for the persons who perform and assist in the procedure; for the spouse, family, and society which must confront the knowledge that these procedures exist, procedures some deem nothing short of an act of violence against innocent human life; and, depending on one's beliefs, for the life or potential life that is aborted. Though abortion is conduct, it does not follow that the State is entitled to proscribe it in all instances. That is because the liberty of the woman is at stake in a sense unique to the human condition and so unique to the law. The mother who carries a child to full term is subject to anxieties, to physical constraints, to pain that only she must bear. That these sacrifices have from the beginning of the human race been endured by woman with a pride that ennobles her in the eyes of others and gives to the infant a bond of love cannot alone be grounds for the State to insist she make the sacrifice. Her suffering is too intimate and personal for the State to insist, without more, upon its own vision of the woman's role, however dominant that vision has been in the course of our history and our culture. The destiny of the woman must be shaped to a large extent on her own conception of her spiritual imperatives and her place in society. . . .

While we appreciate the weight of the arguments made on behalf of the State in the case before us, arguments which in their ultimate formulation conclude that *Roe* should be overruled, the reservations any of us may have in reaffirming the central holding of *Roe* are outweighed by the explication of individual liberty we have given combined with the force of *stare decisis*. We turn now to that doctrine.

III

A

. . . The sum of . . . precedential inquiry . . . shows *Roe*'s underpinnings unweakened in any way affecting its central holding. While it has engendered disapproval, it has not been unworkable. An entire generation has come of age free to assume *Roe*'s concept of liberty in defining the capacity of women to act in society, and to make reproductive decisions; no erosion of principle going to liberty or personal autonomy has left *Roe*'s central holding a doctrinal remnant; *Roe* portends no developments at odds with other precedent for the analysis of personal liberty; and no changes of fact have rendered viability more or less appropriate as the point at which the balance of interests tips. Within the bounds of normal *stare decisis* analysis, then, and subject to the considerations on which it customarily turns, the stronger argument is for affirming *Roe*'s central holding, with whatever degree of personal reluctance any of us may have, not for overruling it.

B

In a less significant case, *stare decisis* analysis could, and would, stop at the point we have reached. . .

C

. . . Our analysis would not be complete, however, without explaining why overruling *Roe*'s central holding would not only reach an unjustifiable result under principles of *stare decisis*, but would seriously weaken the Court's capacity to exercise the judicial power and to function as the Supreme Court of a Nation dedicated to the rule of law. To understand why this would be so it is necessary to understand the source of this Court's authority, the conditions necessary for its preservation, and its relationship to the country's understanding of itself as a constitutional Republic.

The root of American governmental power is revealed most clearly in the instance of the power conferred by the Constitution upon the Judiciary of the United States and specifically upon this Court. As Americans of each succeeding generation are rightly told, the Court cannot buy support for its decisions by spending money and, except to a minor degree, it cannot independently coerce obedience to its decrees. The Court's power lies, rather, in its legitimacy, a product of substance and perception that shows itself in the people's acceptance of the Judiciary as fit to determine what the Nation's law means and to declare what it demands.

The underlying substance of this legitimacy is of course the warrant for the Court's decisions in the Constitution and the lesser sources of legal principle on which the Court draws. That substance is expressed in the Court's opinions, and our contemporary understanding is such that a decision without principled justification would be no judicial act at all. But even when justification is furnished by apposite legal principle, something more is required. Because not every conscientious claim of principled justification will be accepted as such, the justification claimed must be beyond dispute. The Court must take care to speak and act in ways that allow people to accept its decisions on the terms the Court claims for them, as grounded truly in principle, not as compromises with social and political pressures having, as such, no bearing on the principled choices that the Court is obliged to make. Thus, the Court's legitimacy depends on making legally principled decisions under circumstances in which their principled character is sufficiently plausible to be accepted by the Nation.

The need for principled action to be perceived as such is implicated to some degree whenever this, or any other appellate court, overrules a prior case. This is not to say, of course, that this Court cannot give a perfectly satisfactory explanation in most cases. People understand that some of the Constitution's language is hard to fathom and that the Court's Justices are sometimes able to perceive significant facts or to understand principles of law that eluded their predecessors and that justify departures from existing decisions. However upsetting it may be to those most directly affected when one judicially derived rule replaces another, the country can accept some correction of error without necessarily questioning the legitimacy of the Court.

In two circumstances, however, the Court would almost certainly fail to receive the benefit of the doubt in overruling prior cases. There is, first, a point beyond which frequent overruling would overtax the country's belief in the Court's good faith. Despite the variety of reasons that may inform and justify a decision to overrule, we cannot forget that such a decision is usually perceived (and perceived correctly) as, at the least, a statement that a prior decision was wrong. There is a limit to the amount of error that can plausibly be imputed to prior courts. If that limit should be exceeded, disturbance of prior rulings would be taken as evidence that justifiable reexamination of principle had given way to drives for particular results in the short term. The legitimacy of the Court would fade with the frequency of its vacillation.

That first circumstance can be described as hypothetical; the second is to the point here and now. Where, in the performance of its judicial duties, the Court decides a case in such a way as to resolve the sort of intensely divisive controversy reflected in *Roe* and those rare, comparable cases, its decision has a dimension that the resolution of the normal case does not carry. It is the dimension present whenever the Court's interpretation of the Constitution calls the contending sides of a national controversy to end their national division by accepting a common mandate rooted in the Constitution.

The Court is not asked to do this very often, having thus addressed the Nation only twice in our lifetime, in the decisions of *Brown* [*v. Board of Education*] and *Roe*. But when the Court does act in this way, its decision requires an equally rare precedential force to counter the inevitable efforts to overturn it and to thwart its implementation. Some of those efforts may be mere unprincipled emotional reactions; others may proceed from principles worthy of profound respect. But whatever the premises of opposition may be, only the most convincing justification under accepted standards of precedent could suffice to demonstrate that a later decision overruling the first was anything but a surrender to political pressure, and an unjustified repudiation of the principle on which the Court staked its authority in the first instance. So to overrule under fire in the absence of the most compelling reason to reexamine a watershed decision would subvert the Court's legitimacy beyond any serious question. . . .

The Court's duty in the present case is clear. In 1973, it confronted the already-divisive issue of governmental power to limit personal choice to undergo abortion, for which it provided a new resolution based on the due process guaranteed by the Fourteenth Amendment. Whether or not a new social consensus is developing on that issue, its divisiveness is no less today than in 1973, and pressure to overrule the decision, like pressure to retain it, has grown only more intense. A decision to overrule *Roe*'s essential holding under the existing circumstances would address error, if error there was, at the cost of both profound and unnecessary damage to the Court's legitimacy, and to the Nation's commitment to the rule of law. It is therefore imperative to adhere to the essence of *Roe*'s original decision, and we do so today.

IV

. . . The woman's right to terminate her pregnancy before viability is the most central principle of *Roe v. Wade*. It is a rule of law and a component of liberty we cannot renounce. . . .

Yet it must be remembered that *Roe v. Wade* speaks with clarity in establishing not only the woman's liberty but also the State's "important and legitimate interest in potential life." That portion of the decision in *Roe* has been given too little acknowledgment and implementation by the Court in its subsequent cases. Those cases decided that any regulation touching upon the abortion decision must survive strict scrutiny, to be sustained only if drawn in narrow terms to further a compelling state interest. Not all of the cases decided under that formulation can be reconciled with the holding in *Roe* itself that the State has legitimate interests in the health of the woman and in protecting the potential life within her. In resolving this tension, we choose to rely upon *Roe,* as against the later cases.

Roe established a trimester framework to govern abortion regulations. Under this elaborate but rigid construct, almost no regulation at all is permitted during the first trimester of pregnancy; regulations designed to protect the woman's health, but not to further the State's interest in potential life, are permitted during the second trimester; and during the third trimester, when the fetus is viable, prohibitions are permitted provided the life or health of the mother is not at stake. Most of our cases since *Roe* have involved the application of rules derived from the trimester framework. See, *e.g., Thornburgh v. American College of Obstetricians and Gynecologists; Akron [v. Akron Center].* . . .

We reject the trimester framework, which we do not consider to be part of the essential holding of *Roe.* . . . Measures aimed at ensuring that a woman's choice contemplates the consequences for the fetus do not necessarily interfere with the right recognized in *Roe,* although those measures have been found to be inconsistent with the rigid trimester framework announced in that case. A logical reading of the central holding in *Roe* itself, and a necessary reconciliation of the liberty of the woman and the interest of the State in promoting prenatal life, require, in our view, that we abandon the trimester framework as a rigid prohibition on all previability regulation aimed at the protection of fetal life. The trimester framework suffers from these basic flaws: in its formulation it misconceives the nature of the pregnant woman's interest; and in practice it undervalues the State's interest in potential life, as recognized in *Roe.*

As our jurisprudence relating to all liberties save perhaps abortion has recognized, not every law which makes a right more difficult to exercise is, *ipso facto,* an infringement of that right. An example clarifies the point. We have held that not every ballot access limitation amounts to an infringement of the right to vote. Rather, the States are granted substantial flexibility in establishing the framework within which voters choose the candidates for whom they wish to vote.

The abortion right is similar. Numerous forms of state regulation might have the incidental effect of increasing the cost or decreasing the availability of medical care, whether for abortion or any other medical procedure. The fact that a law which serves a valid purpose, one not designed to strike at the right itself, has the incidental effect of making it more difficult or more expensive to procure an abortion cannot be enough to invalidate it. Only where state regulation imposes an undue burden on a woman's ability to make this decision does the power of the State reach into the heart of the liberty protected by the Due Process Clause. . . .

The concept of an undue burden has been utilized by the Court as well as individual members of the Court, including two of us, in ways that could be considered inconsistent. . . . Because we set forth a standard of general application to which we intend to adhere, it is important to clarify what is meant by an undue burden.

A finding of an undue burden is a shorthand for the conclusion that a state regulation has the purpose or effect of placing a substantial obstacle in the path of a woman seeking an abortion of a nonviable fetus. A statute with this purpose is invalid because the means chosen by the State to further the interest in potential life must be calculated to inform the woman's free choice, not hinder it. And a statute which, while furthering the interest in potential life or some other valid state interest, has the effect of placing a substantial obstacle in the path of a woman's choice cannot be considered a permissible means of serving its legitimate ends. To the extent that the opinions of the Court or of individual Justices use the undue burden standard in a manner that is inconsistent with this analysis, we set out what in our view should be the controlling standard. . . . Understood another way, we answer the question, left open in previous opinions discussing the undue burden formulation, whether a law designed to further the State's interest in fetal life which imposes an undue burden on the woman's decision before fetal viability could be constitutional. See, *e.g., Akron I* (O'CONNOR, J., dissenting). The answer is no.

Some guiding principles should emerge. What is at stake is the woman's right to make the ultimate decision, not a right to be insulated from all others in doing so. Regulations which do no more than create a structural mechanism by which the State, or the parent or guardian of a minor, may express profound respect for the life of the unborn are permitted, if they are not a substantial obstacle to the woman's exercise of the right to choose. Unless it has that effect on her right of choice, a state measure designed to persuade her to choose childbirth over abortion will be upheld if reasonably related to that goal. Regulations designed to foster the health of a woman seeking an abortion are valid if they do not constitute an undue burden.

Even when jurists reason from shared premises, some disagreement is inevitable. That is to be expected in the application of any legal standard which must accommodate life's complexity. We do not expect it to be otherwise with respect to the undue burden standard. We give this summary:

(a) To protect the central right recognized by *Roe v. Wade* while at the same time accommodating the State's profound interest in potential life, we will employ the undue burden analysis as explained in this opinion. An undue burden exists, and therefore a provision of law is invalid, if its purpose or effect is to place a substantial obstacle in the path of a woman seeking an abortion before the fetus attains viability.

(b) We reject the rigid trimester framework of *Roe v. Wade.* To promote the State's profound interest in potential life, throughout pregnancy the State may take measures to ensure that the woman's choice is informed, and measures designed to advance this interest will not be invalidated as long as their purpose is to persuade the woman to choose childbirth over abortion. These measures must not be an undue burden on the right.

(c) As with any medical procedure, the State may enact regulations to further the health or safety of a woman seeking an abortion. Unnecessary health regulations that have the purpose or effect of presenting a substantial obstacle to a woman seeking an abortion impose an undue burden on the right.

(d) Our adoption of the undue burden analysis does not disturb the central holding of *Roe v. Wade,* and we reaffirm that holding. Regardless of whether exceptions are made for particular circumstances, a State may not prohibit any woman from making the ultimate decision to terminate her pregnancy before viability.

(e) We also reaffirm *Roe's* holding that "subsequent to viability, the State in promoting its interest in the potential-ity of human life may, if it chooses, regulate, and even proscribe, abortion except where it is necessary, in appropriate medical judgment, for the preservation of the life or health of the mother." *Roe v. Wade.*

These principles control our assessment of the Pennsylvania statute, and we now turn to the issue of the validity of its challenged provisions.

V

The Court of Appeals applied what it believed to be the undue burden standard and upheld each of the provisions except for the husband notification requirement. We agree generally with this conclusion, but refine the undue burden analysis in accordance with the principles articulated above. We now consider the separate statutory sections at issue.

[A omitted]

B [Informed Consent]

... Our prior decisions establish that as with any medical procedure, the State may require a woman to give her written informed consent to an abortion.... In this respect, the statute is unexceptional. Petitioners challenge the statute's definition of informed consent because it includes the provision of specific information by the doctors and the mandatory 24-hour waiting period. The conclusions reached by a majority of the Justices in separate opinions filed today and the undue burden standard adopted in this opinion require us to overrule in part some of the Court's past decisions, decisions driven by the trimester framework's prohibition of all previablity regulation designed to further the State's interest in fetal life.

In *Akron I* (1983), we invalidated an ordinance which required that a woman seeking an abortion be provided by her physician with specific information "designed to influence the woman's informed choice between abortion or childbirth." As we later described the *Akron I* holding in *Thornburgh v. American College of Obstetricians and Gynecologists,* there were two purported flaws in the Akron ordinance: the information was designed to dissuade the woman from having an abortion and the ordinance imposed "a rigid requirement that a specific body of information be given in all cases, irrespective of the particular needs of the patient...."

To the extent *Akron I* and *Thornburgh* find a constitutional violation when the government requires, as it does here, the giving of truthful, nonmisleading information about the nature of the procedure, the attendant health risks and those of childbirth, and the "probable gestational age" of the fetus, those cases go too far, are inconsistent with *Roe*'s acknowledgment of an important interest in potential life, and are overruled....

... Even the broadest reading of *Roe* ... has not suggested that there is a constitutional right to abortion on demand.... Rather, the right protected by *Roe* is a right to decide to terminate a pregnancy free of undue interference by the State. Because the informed consent requirement facilitates the wise exercise of that right it cannot be classified as an interference with the right *Roe* protects. The informed consent requirement is not an undue burden on that right.

C [Spousal Notification]

... The limited research that has been conducted with respect to notifying one's husband about an abortion, although involving samples too small to be representative ... [suggests that] [t]he vast majority of women notify their male partners of their decision to obtain an abortion. In many cases in which married women do not notify their husbands, the pregnancy is the result of an extramarital affair. Where the husband is the father, the primary reason women do not notify their husbands is that the husband and wife are experiencing marital difficulties, often accompanied by incidents of violence.

This information ... reinforce[s] what common sense would suggest. In well-functioning marriages, spouses discuss important intimate decisions such as whether to bear a child. But there are millions of women in this country who are the victims of regular physical and psychological abuse at the hands of their husbands. Should these women become pregnant, they may have very good reasons for not wishing to inform their husbands of their decision to obtain an abortion. Many may have justifiable fears of physical abuse, but may be no less fearful of the consequences of reporting prior abuse to the Commonwealth of Pennsylvania. Many may have a reasonable fear that notifying their husbands will provoke further instances of child abuse....

The spousal notification requirement is thus likely to prevent a significant number of women from obtaining an abortion. It does not merely make abortions a little more difficult or expensive to obtain; for many women, it will impose a substantial obstacle. We must not blind ourselves to the fact that the significant number of women who fear for their safety and the safety of their children are likely to be deterred from procuring an abortion as surely as if the Commonwealth had outlawed abortion in all cases....

Section 3209 embodies a view of marriage consonant with the common-law status of married women but repugnant to our present understanding of marriage and of the nature of the rights secured by the Constitution. Women do not lose their constitutionally protected liberty when they marry. The Constitution protects all individuals, male or female, married or unmarried, from the abuse of governmental power, even where that power is employed for the supposed benefit of a member of the individual's family. These considerations confirm our conclusion that § 3209 is invalid.

D [Parental Consent]

We next consider the parental consent provision....

We have been over most of this ground before. Our cases establish, and we reaffirm today, that a State may require a minor seeking an abortion to obtain the consent of a parent or guardian, provided that there is an adequate judicial bypass procedure....

E [Recordkeeping and Reporting]

... In [*Planned Parenthood v.*] *Danforth*, we held that recordkeeping and reporting provisions "that are reasonably directed to the preservation of maternal health and that properly respect a patient's confidentiality and privacy are permissible." We think that under this standard, all the provisions at issue here except that relating to spousal notice are constitutional. Although they do not relate to the State's interest in informing the woman's choice, they do relate to health. The collection of information with respect to actual patients is a vital element of medical research, and so it cannot be said that the requirements serve no purpose other than to make abortions more difficult. Nor do we find that the requirements impose a substantial obstacle to a woman's choice. At most they might increase the cost of some abortions by a slight amount. While at some point increased cost could become a substantial obstacle, there is no such showing on the record before us.

Subsection (12) of the reporting provision requires the reporting of, among other things, a married woman's "reason for failure to provide notice" to her husband. This provision in effect requires women, as a condition of obtaining an abortion, to provide the Commonwealth with the precise information we have already recognized that many women have pressing reasons not to reveal. Like the spousal notice requirement itself, this provision places an undue burden on a woman's choice, and must be invalidated for that reason.

VI

Our Constitution is a covenant running from the first generation of Americans to us and then to future generations. It is a coherent succession. Each generation must learn anew that the Constitution's written terms embody ideas and aspirations that must survive more ages than one. We accept our responsibility not to retreat from interpreting the full meaning of the covenant in light of all of our precedents. We invoke it once again to define the freedom guaranteed by the Constitution's own promise, the promise of liberty.

JUSTICE STEVENS, concurring in part and dissenting in part.

[I omitted]

II

My disagreement with the joint opinion begins with its understanding of the trimester framework established in *Roe.* Contrary to the suggestion of the joint opinion, it is not a "contradiction" to recognize that the State may have a legitimate interest in potential human life and, at the same time, to conclude that interest does not justify the regulation of abortion before viability (although other interests, such as maternal health, may). The fact that the State's interest is legitimate does not tell us when, if ever, that interest outweighs the pregnant woman's interest in personal liberty....

In my opinion, the principles established in this long line of cases and the wisdom reflected in Justice Powell's opinion for the Court in *Akron* (and followed by the Court just six years ago in *Thornburgh*) should govern our decision today. Under these principles, §§ 3205(a)(2)(i)-(iii) of the Pennsylvania statute are unconstitutional. Those sections require a physician or counselor to provide the woman with a range of materials clearly designed to persuade her to choose not to undergo the abortion. While the State is free ... to produce and disseminate such material, the State may not inject such information into the woman's deliberations just as she is weighing such an important choice.

Under this same analysis, §§ 3205(a)(1)(i) and (iii) of the Pennsylvania statute are constitutional. Those sections, which require the physician to inform a woman of the nature and risks of the abortion procedure and the medical risks of carrying to term, are neutral requirements comparable to those imposed in other medical procedures. Those sections indicate no effort by the State to influence the woman's choice in any way. If anything, such requirements enhance, rather than skew, the woman's decisionmaking.

III

The 24-hour waiting period ... raises even more serious concerns. Such a requirement arguably furthers the State's interests in two ways, neither of which is constitutionally permissible.

First, it may be argued that the 24-hour delay is justified by the mere fact that it is likely to reduce the number of abortions, thus furthering the State's interest in potential life. But such an argument would justify any form of coercion that placed an obstacle in the woman's path. The State cannot further its interests by simply wearing down the ability of the pregnant woman to exercise her constitutional right.

Second, it can more reasonably be argued that the 24-hour delay furthers the State's interest in ensuring that the woman's decision is informed and thoughtful. But there is no evidence that the mandated delay benefits women or that it is necessary to enable the physician to convey any relevant information to the patient. The mandatory delay thus appears to rest on outmoded and unacceptable assumptions about the decisionmaking capacity of women. While there are well-established and consistently maintained reasons for the State to view with skepticism the ability of minors to make decisions, none of those reasons applies to an adult woman's decisionmaking ability. Just as we have left behind the belief that a woman must consult her husband before undertaking serious matters, so we must reject the notion that a woman is less capable of deciding matters of gravity....

IV

In my opinion, a correct application of the "undue burden" standard leads to the same conclusion concerning the constitutionality of these requirements. A state-imposed burden on the exercise of a constitutional right is measured both by its effects and by its character: A burden may be "undue" either because the burden is too severe or because it lacks a legitimate, rational justification.

The 24-hour delay requirement fails both parts of this test. The findings of the District Court establish the severity of the burden that the 24-hour delay imposes on many pregnant women. Yet even in those cases in which the delay is not especially onerous, it is, in my opinion, "undue" because there is no evidence that such a delay serves a useful and legitimate purpose. As indicated above, there is no legitimate reason to require a woman who has agonized over her decision to leave the clinic or hospital and return again another day. While a general requirement that a physician notify her patients about the risks of a proposed medical procedure is appropriate, a rigid requirement that all patients wait 24 hours or (what is true in practice) much longer to evaluate the significance of information that is either common knowledge or irrelevant is an irrational and, therefore, "undue" burden....

Accordingly, while I disagree with Parts IV, V-B, and V-D of the joint opinion, I join the remainder of the Court's opinion.

JUSTICE BLACKMUN, concurring in part, concurring in the judgment in part, and dissenting in part.

I join parts I, II, III, V-A, V-C, and VI of the joint opinion of JUSTICES O'CONNOR, KENNEDY, and SOUTER.

Three years ago, in *Webster v. Reproductive Health Serv.*, four Members of this Court appeared poised to "cas[t] into darkness the hopes and visions of every woman in this country" who had come to believe that the Constitution guaranteed her the right to reproductive choice. All that remained between the promise of *Roe* and the darkness of the plurality was a single, flickering flame.... But now, just

when so many expected the darkness to fall, the flame has grown bright.

I do not underestimate the significance of today's joint opinion. Yet I remain steadfast in my belief that the right to reproductive choice is entitled to the full protection afforded by this Court before *Webster*. And I fear for the darkness as four Justices anxiously await the single vote necessary to extinguish the light.

I

Make no mistake, the joint opinion of JUSTICES O'CONNOR, KENNEDY, and SOUTER is an act of personal courage and constitutional principle. In contrast to previous decisions in which JUSTICES O'CONNOR and KENNEDY postponed reconsideration of *Roe v. Wade* (1973), the authors of the joint opinion today join JUSTICE STEVENS and me in concluding that "the essential holding of *Roe* should be retained and once again reaffirmed." In brief, five Members of this Court today recognize that "the Constitution protects a woman's right to terminate her pregnancy in its early stages."...

In striking down the Pennsylvania statute's spousal notification requirement, the Court has established a framework for evaluating abortion regulations that responds to the social context of women facing issues of reproductive choice.* In determining the burden imposed by the challenged regulation, the Court inquires whether the regulation's *"purpose or effect* is to place a substantial obstacle in the path of a woman seeking an abortion before the fetus attains viability."...

... [W]hile I believe that the joint opinion errs in failing to invalidate the other regulations, I am pleased that the joint opinion has not ruled out the possibility that these regulations may be shown to impose an unconstitutional burden. The joint opinion makes clear that its specific holdings are based on the insufficiency of the record before it. I am confident that in the future evidence will be produced to show that "in a large fraction of the cases in which [these regulations are] relevant, [they] will operate as a substantial obstacle to a woman's choice to undergo an abortion."....

---

*... [T]he joint opinion and I disagree on the appropriate standard of review for abortion regulations. I do agree, however, that the reasons advanced by the joint opinion suffice to invalidate the spousal notification requirement under a strict scrutiny standard.

II

... *Roe*'s requirement of strict scrutiny as implemented through a trimester framework should not be disturbed. No other approach has gained a majority, and no other is more protective of the woman's fundamental right. Lastly, no other approach properly accommodates the woman's constitutional right with the State's legitimate interests....

Application of the strict scrutiny standard results in the invalidation of all the challenged provisions. Indeed, as this Court has invalidated virtually identical provisions in prior cases, *stare decisis* requires that we again strike them down....

III

At long last, THE CHIEF JUSTICE admits it. Gone are the contentions that the issue need not be (or has not been) considered. There, on the first page, for all to see, is what was expected: "We believe that *Roe* was wrongly decided, and that it can and should be overruled consistently with our traditional approach to *stare decisis* in constitutional cases." If there is much reason to applaud the advances made by the joint opinion today, there is far more to fear from THE CHIEF JUSTICE's opinion....

IV

In one sense, the Court's approach is worlds apart from that of THE CHIEF JUSTICE and JUSTICE SCALIA. And yet, in another sense, the distance between the two approaches is short—the distance is but a single vote.

I am 83 years old. I cannot remain on this Court forever, and when I do step down, the confirmation process for my successor well may focus on the issue before us today. That, I regret, may be exactly where the choice between the two worlds will be made.

CHIEF JUSTICE REHNQUIST, with whom JUSTICE WHITE, JUSTICE SCALIA, and JUSTICE THOMAS join, concurring in the judgment in part and dissenting in part.

The joint opinion, following its newly-minted variation on *stare decisis*, retains the outer shell of *Roe v. Wade* (1973), but beats a wholesale retreat from the substance of that case. We believe that *Roe* was wrongly decided, and that it can and should be overruled consistently with our traditional approach to *stare decisis* in constitutional cases.

We would adopt the approach of the plurality in *Webster v. Reproductive Health Services* (1989), and uphold the challenged provisions of the Pennsylvania statute in their entirety.

I

... We think ... both in view of this history and of our decided cases dealing with substantive liberty under the Due Process Clause, that the Court was mistaken in *Roe* when it classified a woman's decision to terminate her pregnancy as a "fundamental right" that could be abridged only in a manner which withstood "strict scrutiny."...

We believe that the sort of constitutionally imposed abortion code of the type illustrated by our decisions following *Roe* is inconsistent "with the notion of a Constitution cast in general terms, as ours is, and usually speaking in general principles, as ours does." *Webster v. Reproductive Health Services* (plurality opinion). The Court in *Roe* reached too far when it analogized the right to abort a fetus to the right ... involved in ... *Griswold*, and thereby deemed the right to abortion fundamental....

II

... [T]he joint opinion ... state[s] that when the Court "resolve[s] the sort of intensely divisive controversy reflected in *Roe* and those rare, comparable cases," its decision is exempt from reconsideration under established principles of *stare decisis* in constitutional cases. This is so, the joint opinion contends, because in those "intensely divisive" cases the Court has "call[ed] the contending sides of a national controversy to end their national division by accepting a common mandate rooted in the Constitution," and must therefore take special care not to be perceived as "surrender[ing] to political pressure" and continued opposition. This is a truly novel principle, one which is contrary to both the Court's historical practice and to the Court's traditional willingness to tolerate criticism of its opinions. Under this principle, when the Court has ruled on a divisive issue, it is apparently prevented from overruling that decision for the sole reason that it was incorrect, *unless opposition to the original decision has died away.*

The ... difficulty with this principle lies in its assumption that cases which are "intensely divisive" can be readily distinguished from those that are not. The question of whether a particular issue is "intensely divisive" enough to qualify for special protection is entirely subjective and dependent on the individual assumptions of the members of this Court. In addition, because the Court's duty is to ignore public opinion and criticism on issues that come before it, its members are in perhaps the worst position to judge whether a decision divides the Nation deeply enough to justify such uncommon protection. Although many of the Court's decisions divide the populace to a large degree, we have not previously on that account shied away from applying normal rules of *stare decisis* when urged to reconsider earlier decisions. Over the past 21 years, for example, the Court has overruled in whole or in part 34 of its previous constitutional decisions....

The end result of the joint opinion's paeans of praise for legitimacy is the enunciation of a brand new standard for evaluating state regulation of a woman's right to abortion—the "undue burden" standard. As indicated above, *Roe v. Wade* adopted a "fundamental right" standard under which state regulations could survive only if they met the requirement of "strict scrutiny." While we disagree with that standard, it at least had a recognized basis in constitutional law at the time *Roe* was decided. The same cannot be said for the "undue burden" standard, which is created largely out of whole cloth by the authors of the joint opinion. It is a standard which even today does not command the support of a majority of this Court. And it will not, we believe, result in the sort of "simple limitation," easily applied, which the joint opinion anticipates. In sum, it is a standard which is not built to last.

... Accordingly, we think that the correct analysis is that set forth by the plurality opinion in *Webster*. A woman's interest in having an abortion is a form of liberty protected by the Due Process Clause, but States may regulate abortion procedures in ways rationally related to a legitimate state interest....

[III omitted]

IV

[Using this standard] we ... would hold that each of the challenged provisions of the Pennsylvania statute is consistent with the Constitution. It bears emphasis that our conclusion in this regard does not carry with it any neces-

sary approval of these regulations. Our task is, as always, to decide only whether the challenged provisions of a law comport with the United States Constitution. If, as we believe, these do, their wisdom as a matter of public policy is for the people of Pennsylvania to decide.

JUSTICE SCALIA, with whom THE CHIEF JUSTICE, JUSTICE WHITE, and JUSTICE THOMAS join, concurring in the judgment in part and dissenting in part.

My views on this matter are unchanged from those I set forth in my separate opinion ... in *Webster v. Reproductive Health Services* (1989) (SCALIA, J., concurring in part and concurring in judgment).... The States may, if they wish, permit abortion-on-demand, but the Constitution does not *require* them to do so. The permissibility of abortion, and the limitations upon it, are to be resolved like most important questions in our democracy: by citizens trying to persuade one another and then voting....

Beyond that brief summary of the essence of my position, I will not swell the United States Reports with repetition of what I have said before; and applying the rational basis test, I would uphold the Pennsylvania statute in its entirety. I must, however, respond to a few of the more outrageous arguments in today's opinion, which it is beyond human nature to leave unanswered. I shall discuss each of them under a quotation from the Court's opinion to which they pertain....

"Liberty finds no refuge in a jurisprudence of doubt."

One might have feared to encounter this august and sonorous phrase in an opinion defending the real *Roe v. Wade,* rather than the revised version fabricated today by the authors of the joint opinion. The shortcomings of *Roe* did not include lack of clarity: Virtually all regulation of abortion before the third trimester was invalid. But to come across this phrase in the joint opinion—which calls upon federal district judges to apply an "undue burden" standard as doubtful in application as it is unprincipled in origin—is really more than one should have to bear.

The joint opinion frankly concedes that the amorphous concept of "undue burden" has been inconsistently applied by the Members of this Court in the few brief years since that "test" was first explicitly propounded by JUSTICE o'connor in her dissent in *Akron I*. Because the three Justices now wish to "set forth a standard of general application," the joint opinion announces that "it is important to clarify what is meant by an undue burden." I certainly agree with that, but I do not agree that the joint opinion succeeds in the announced endeavor. To the contrary, its efforts at clarification make clear only that the standard is inherently manipulable and will prove hopelessly unworkable in practice.

The joint opinion explains that a state regulation imposes an "undue burden" if it "has the purpose or effect of placing a substantial obstacle in the path of a woman seeking an abortion of a nonviable fetus." An obstacle is "substantial," we are told, if it is "calculated, [not] to inform the woman's free choice, [but to] hinder it." This latter statement cannot possibly mean what it says. *Any* regulation of abortion that is intended to advance what the joint opinion concedes is the State's "substantial" interest in protecting unborn life will be "calculated [to] hinder" a decision to have an abortion. It thus seems more accurate to say that the joint opinion would uphold abortion regulations only if they do not *unduly* hinder the woman's decision. That, of course, brings us right back to square one: Defining an "undue burden" as an "undue hindrance" (or a "substantial obstacle") hardly "clarifies" the test. Consciously or not, the joint opinion's verbal shell game will conceal raw judicial policy choices concerning what is "appropriate" abortion legislation....

"While we appreciate the weight of the arguments ... that *Roe* should be overruled, the reservations any of us may have in reaffirming the central holding of *Roe* are outweighed by the explication of individual liberty we have given combined with the force of *stare decisis*."

The Court's reliance upon *stare decisis* can best be described as contrived. It insists upon the necessity of adhering not to all of *Roe*, but only to what it calls the "central holding."...

I am certainly not in a good position to dispute that the Court *has saved* the "central holding" of *Roe*, since to do that effectively I would have to know what the Court has saved, which in turn would require me to understand (as I do not) what the "undue burden" test means. I must confess, however, that I have always thought, and I think a lot

of other people have always thought, that the arbitrary trimester framework, which the Court today discards, was quite as central to *Roe* as the arbitrary viability test, which the Court today retains. It seems particularly ungrateful to carve the trimester framework out of the core of *Roe*, since its very rigidity (in sharp contrast to the utter indeterminability of the "undue burden" test) is probably the only reason the Court is able to say, in urging *stare decisis*, that *Roe* "has in no sense proven 'unworkable.'" I suppose the Court is entitled to call a "central holding" whatever it wants to call a "central holding"—which is, come to think of it, perhaps one of the difficulties with this modified version of *stare decisis*. I thought I might note, however, that the following portions of *Roe* have not been saved:

• Under *Roe*, requiring that a woman seeking an abortion be provided truthful information about abortion before giving informed written consent is unconstitutional, if the information is designed to influence her choice, *Thornburgh*; *Akron I*. Under the joint opinion's "undue burden" regime (as applied today, at least) such a requirement is constitutional.

• Under *Roe*, requiring that information be provided by a doctor, rather than by nonphysician counselors, is unconstitutional, *Akron I*. Under the "undue burden" regime (as applied today, at least) it is not.

• Under *Roe*, requiring a 24-hour waiting period between the time the woman gives her informed consent and the time of the abortion is unconstitutional, *Akron I*. Under the "undue burden" regime (as applied today, at least) it is not.

• Under *Roe*, requiring detailed reports that include demographic data about each woman who seeks an abortion and various information about each abortion is unconstitutional, *Thornburgh*. Under the "undue burden" regime (as applied today, at least) it generally is not....

The Imperial Judiciary lives....

We should get out of this area, where we have no right to be, and where we do neither ourselves nor the country any good by remaining.

What are we to make of *Casey*? On the one hand, reports of *Roe*'s demise were greatly exaggerated. The

Court did not overrule *Roe*: to the contrary, it reaffirmed the "central holding" of the 1973 decision that a woman should have "some" freedom to terminate a pregnancy. On the other hand, the "joint opinion" gutted the core of *Roe*. The trimester framework was gone. Under *Casey,* states may now enact laws—regulating the entire pregnancy—that further their interest in potential life so long as those laws are rationally related to that end and do not put an undue burden on the right to terminate a pregnancy. Laws that do not meet this standard will be subject to strict scrutiny, such as the spousal notification provision at issue in *Casey.*

In general, this undue burden approach, which Justice O'Connor originally proposed in 1983 in her *Akron Center* dissent, *could* lead to very different outcomes in abortion cases. Justice Scalia's dissent indicates that many of the provisions at issue in *Casey* that the Court upheld under the undue burden standard would have been struck down under the *Roe*'s strict scrutiny approach. Yet, Justice Blackmun's opinion holds out hope that the undue burden standard could be applied, in the future, to strike down restrictive laws. Moreover, as Justice Stevens's writing illustrates, a different treatment of the undue burden would have led the Court to strike down the twenty-four-hour waiting period.

Is *Casey* the Court's final word on abortion? Will undue burden now be the standard the justices use to assess regulations on abortion? Perhaps not. As Table 7-6 indicates, in 1993 the justices were truly divided over legal approaches to abortion. Moreover, we cannot forget that a justice can have a change of heart: Burger went from a *Roe* supporter to an opponent; Kennedy signed Rehnquist's opinion in *Webster,* yet provided crucial support for O'Connor's undue burden approach in *Casey.* Justice Ginsburg's ascension to the bench—she replaced White, a *Roe* critic—only complicates the picture. Although Ginsburg supports a woman's right to choose, she has been critical of the *Roe* framework. In a 1985 law review article, she

TABLE 7-6 Approaches to Abortion: The 1994–1995 Supreme Court

Justice	Favored Approach
Breyer	Unknown
Ginsburg	equal protection analysis[a]
Kennedy	undue burden
O'Connor	undue burden
Rehnquist	rational basis
Scalia	rational basis
Souter	undue burden
Stevens	*Roe*'s strict scrutiny
Thomas	rational basis

[a] In a 1985 law review article, Judge Ginsburg urged courts to acknowledge a "women's equality aspect" to the abortion issue. See Ruth Bader Ginsburg, "Some Thoughts on Autonomy and Equality in Relation to *Roe v. Wade*," *North Carolina Law Review* 63 (1985): 375–386.

argued that abortion rights should be framed in equal protection terms; that is, the Court should consider whether laws restricting the right discriminate against women. Had the Court adopted this approach, Ginsburg asserted, it would have struck down many state laws, including those that restricted funding for abortions. As she put it, "If the Court had acknowledged a woman's equality aspect [and] not simply a patient-physician autonomy constitutional dimension to the abortion issue, a majority perhaps might have seen the public assistance cases as instances in which ... the [government] had violated its duty to govern impartially."[32]

Whether Justice Ginsburg will press this position on her colleagues is something on which we can only speculate. What is true is that the political and legal environment surrounding abortion has changed even since *Casey.* With Bill Clinton's election, it is doubtful that we will see a solicitor general, at least in the imme-

32. Ruth Bader Ginsburg, "Some Thoughts on Autonomy and Equality in Relation to *Roe v. Wade*," *University of North Carolina Law Review* 63 (1985): 382.

diate future, ask the Court to overturn *Roe*; if anything, the Clinton administration might adopt Ginsburg's approach or even request a return to *Roe*. Moreover, pro-choice advocates, discouraged by the Supreme Court, have begun to bring their cases into state courts and asking those judiciaries to protect the abortion right under state constitutional guarantees. This strategy has its advantages. For example, many commentators note that several state courts have held that their constitutions, unlike the federal document, require public funding of abortions. In addition, some state courts have shown a willingness to rule for pro-choice forces. An oft-cited example is *In re T. W.* (1989), a decision of the Florida Supreme Court striking down a parental consent law.[33] Yet, use of state courts to secure abortion rights has an obvious drawback: some states will go along with the wishes of pro-choice advocates, while others will not. Thus, rights will differ on a state-by-state basis, resembling the situation in the United States before *Roe* (with the caveat that under *Casey* states may not proscribe abortion).

In all of these changes, there is one constant, which may be decisive, at least as abortion plays in political branches and in the states: public opinion. In the twenty-year period since *Roe*, the public remains ambivalent about the scope of the abortion right. Polls taken immediately after *Casey* indicate that the public—like the Court—overwhelmingly (82 percent) favors legalized abortion but—just as they have since *Roe*—48 percent of Americans support some restrictions on that right.[34] It seems inevitable that Americans (and the Court) will continue to debate the abortion issue, with no easy answers apparent.

READINGS

Craig, Barbara Hinkson, and David M. O'Brien. *Abortion and American Politics*. Chatham, N.J.: Chatham House, 1993.

Ely, John Hart. "The Wages of Crying Wolf: A Comment on Roe v. Wade." *Yale Law Journal* 82 (1973): 920–949.

Emerson, Thomas I. "Nine Justices in Search of a Doctrine." *Michigan Law Review* 64 (1965): 219–234.

Epstein, Lee, and Joseph F. Kobylka. *The Supreme Court and Legal Change: Abortion and the Death Penalty*. Chapel Hill: University of North Carolina Press, 1992.

Epstein, Richard A. "Substantive Due Process by Any Other Name." *Supreme Court Review* (1973): 159–186.

Faux, Marian. *Roe v. Wade*. New York: Macmillan, 1988.

Glick, Henry R. *The Right to Die: Policy Innovation and Its Consequences*. New York: Columbia University Press, 1992.

Johnson, Charles A., and Bradley C. Canon. *Judicial Policies: Implementation and Impact*. Washington, D.C.: CQ Press, 1984.

Lader, Lawrence. *Abortion*. Indianapolis: Bobbs-Merrill, 1966.

———. *Abortion II*. Boston: Beacon Press, 1973.

Luker, Kristen. *Abortion and the Politics of Motherhood*. Berkeley: University of California Press, 1984.

Mohr, James C. *Abortion in America*. New York: Oxford University Press, 1978.

Rubin, Eva R. *Abortion, Politics, and the Courts*. Westport, Conn.: Greenwood Press, 1987.

Tribe, Laurence H. *Abortion: The Clash of Absolutes*. New York: W. W. Norton, 1990.

Wardle, Lynn D., and Mary A. Wood. *A Lawyer Looks at Abortion*. Provo, Utah: Brigham Young University Press, 1982.

---

33. See Fisher and Devins, *Political Dynamics of Constitutional Law*, 238.

34. Polls cited in Craig and O'Brien, *Abortion and American Politics*, 327.

PART III
THE CRIMINAL JUSTICE SYSTEM AND CONSTITUTIONAL RIGHTS

W E AMERICANS regard the Bill of Rights as an enumeration of our most cherished freedoms. The right to speak freely and to practice our religions without undue interference from government are the guarantees to which politicians and citizens refer most often when they describe the unique character of the United States. We may need to be reminded, therefore, that four of the first eight amendments explicitly guarantee rights for the *criminally accused*. The Framers of the Constitution placed great emphasis on criminal rights because they had grown to despise the abusive practices of British criminal procedure. The Founders believed that agents of government should not enter private homes and search personal property without proper justification and that the accused should not be tried without the benefit of public scrutiny.

Consequently, the Fourth Amendment protects us from unreasonable searches and prescribes the procedures by which law enforcement officials can obtain warrants. The Fifth Amendment prohibits self-incrimination and double jeopardy and provides for grand juries and due process of law. The Sixth Amendment governs criminal proceedings. It calls for speedy and public jury trials during which defendants can call witnesses and face their accusers. It also

provides for the assistance of counsel. The Eighth Amendment prohibits excessive bail and monetary fines and any punishments that are cruel and unusual. The Framers insisted on constitutional guarantees that would protect the guilty as well as the innocent against the potentially abusive prosecutorial powers of the government.

Just because these rights are not the first that come to mind when we think about the Bill of Rights does not mean that they are any less important or less relevant to society. At least once during your life, you are likely to be a participant in the criminal justice system. You may be the victim of a crime. You may serve as a juror in a criminal trial or become involved as a witness. You may even be accused of a crime. As citizens we should understand the rights the Founders accorded us and the procedures that invoke such guarantees.

The two chapters that follow explore the constitutional rights of the criminally accused and the Supreme Court's interpretation of them. To appreciate their importance, however, we first take a brief look at the stages of the criminal justice process. Following that discussion, we describe trends in Supreme Court decision making in this area.

FIGURE III-1 The American Criminal Justice System

Stage	Governing Amendment[a]
Reported or suspected crime ↓	
Investigation by law enforcement officials ↓	Fourth Amendment search and seizure rights Fifth Amendment self-incrimination clause
Arrest ↓	Sixth Amendment right to counsel clause
Booking ↓	
Decision to prosecute ↓	
Pretrial hearings (initial appearance, bail hearing, preliminary hearing, arraignment) ↓	Fifth Amendment grand jury clause Sixth Amendment notification clause Eighth Amendment bail clause
Trial ↓	Fifth Amendment self-incrimination clause Sixth Amendment speedy and public trial, jury, confrontation, and compulsory process clauses
Sentencing ↓	Eighth Amendment cruel and unusual punishment clause
Appeals, postconviction stages	Fifth Amendment double jeopardy clause

[a]The right to due process of law is in effect throughout the process.

OVERVIEW OF THE CRIMINAL JUSTICE SYSTEM

Figure III-1 provides a general overview of the criminal justice system and the constitutional rights effective at each stage. Two points should be kept in mind. First, because the states are given a degree of latitude in developing their criminal justice systems, these procedures vary from jurisdiction to jurisdiction. Second, fewer than 5 percent of all criminal cases actually proceed through every stage of the system. At some point during the process, most criminal defendants plead guilty, thereby waiving their right to a jury trial, and proceed directly to sentencing. Most of these guilty pleas are the result of plea-bargaining arrangements in which the accused agrees to admit guilt in exchange for reduced charges or a lenient sentence.

This qualification noted, the process normally begins with an alleged or suspected violation of a state or federal criminal law. However, the first step in the criminal justice system is the response of law enforcement officials to the reporting of the offense. Many scholars and lawyers consider this part of the process to be of the utmost importance. The way police conduct their investigation and gather evidence affects all subsequent decisions made by lawyers, judges, and juries. The police are also significant actors because of the conflicting roles society asks them to play. We expect police officers to act lawfully, within the confines of the Constitution. We do not want them to break down our doors and search our houses without proper cause. But society also expects effective law enforcement, with the police using reasonable discretion to make arrests and apply the laws. We do not want a heinous crime to go unpunished because constitutional guarantees have unreasonably tied the hands of police. Law enforcement officers must understand the rules well enough to act without violating them because, when they make mistakes, the consequences can be enormous.

Once police make an arrest and take an individual into custody, the prosecuting attorney joins the process. The prosecutor of state crimes, commonly known as the district attorney, is an elected official having jurisdiction over criminal matters in a given local jurisdiction, usually a county. The prosecutor of federal offenses is called a United States attorney. U.S. attorneys are appointed by the president and confirmed by the Senate. Their assignments correspond to the geographical jurisdiction of the federal district courts, and they serve at the president's pleasure. State and federal prosecutors decide whether the government will bring charges against the accused. Prosecutors consider, among other factors, whether police acted properly in gathering evidence and making the arrest. If the prosecutor decides not to press charges, the police must release the suspect, and the process ends. If prosecution is indicated, the government brings the individual before a judge, who ensures that the accused has legal representation and understands the charges. The judge also must verify that police had adequate initial justification for holding the accused. Further, the judge also sets bail, a monetary guarantee that the accused will appear for trial.

The system next provides a step to ensure that the prosecutor is not abusing the power to charge persons with crimes. This check on prosecutorial discretion takes place in one of two ways. Individuals accused of committing federal offenses or of violating the laws of some states will receive grand jury hearings in accordance with the Fifth Amendment. Composed of lay persons, grand juries, without the accused being pres-

ent, examine the strength of the prosecutor's case to determine whether the government's evidence is strong enough to support formal charges. If the grand jury decides that the prosecutor has satisfied the legal requirements, it will issue a formal document, known as an *indictment*, ordering the accused to stand trial on specified charges. If the grand jury concludes that the prosecutor's case is insufficient, the defendant is released.

The right to a grand jury hearing is not one of the incorporated provisions of the Bill of Rights. Accordingly, the states are free to develop other methods of checking the prosecutor. As an alternative to the grand jury, several states use preliminary hearings. Such proceedings more closely resemble trials than does the grand jury process. Both prosecution and defense may present their cases to a judge, who evaluates the adequacy of the government's evidence. If the judge agrees that the prosecutor's case justifies a trial, an *information* is issued. The information is a formal document, roughly the equivalent of an indictment, that orders the accused to stand trial on certain specified violations of the criminal code. If the prosecutor's case is found inadequate to justify a trial, the judge may order the release of the defendant.

After being formally charged, the defendant proceeds to the arraignment stage. At arraignment, a judge reads the indictment or information to ensure that the defendant understands the charges and the applicable constitutional rights. The judge also asks if the defendant is represented by counsel. Because the specific criminal accusations may have changed in seriousness or number of counts since the defendant's initial appearance, the judge reviews and perhaps modifies the bail amount. Finally, the judge accepts the defendant's plea: guilty, *nolo contendere* (no contest), or not guilty. Should the defendant plead either of the first two, a trial is not necessary, and the accused proceeds to sentencing.

A plea of not guilty normally leads to a full trial governed by constitutional provisions found in the

Fifth and Sixth Amendments. The accused is entitled to a fair, public, and speedy trial by jury. The judge presides over the trial, and the two opposing lawyers question witnesses and summarize case facts. When both sides have presented their cases, the jury deliberates to reach a verdict. If the individual is found guilty, the judge issues a sentence, which under Eighth Amendment protections cannot be cruel and unusual.

If the defendant is found not guilty, the process ends. Fifth Amendment prohibition against double jeopardy bars the government from putting an acquitted defendant on trial a second time for the same offense. The prosecution has no right to appeal an acquittal verdict reached by the trial court. Should the verdict be guilty, however, the defendant has the right to appeal the conviction to a higher court. The appeals court reviews the trial procedures to determine if any significant errors in law or procedure occurred. If dissatisfied with the findings of the appeals court, either side—the government or the defense—may try for a review by an even higher court. These requests may be denied because the system generally provides for only one appeal as a matter of right. Subsequent appeals are left to the discretion of the appellate courts.

TRENDS IN COURT DECISION MAKING

In what follows, we examine each stage in the criminal justice system vis-à-vis the constitutional rights of the criminally accused. While reading the narrative and cases, keep in mind that the four amendments governing criminal proceedings do not work in isolation. Rather, they fit into a larger scheme that includes law, politics, local custom, and the practical necessities of coping with crime in a contemporary society.

The rights accorded the criminally accused in the four amendments set limits that, in tandem with the legal system, define the criminal justice process.

The system depends heavily upon Supreme Court interpretation of the several clauses contained in those amendments. As we have seen in other legal areas, however, the way the Court interprets constitutional rights is not determined exclusively by traditional legal factors such as precedent, the plain language of the law, or the intent of the Framers. Historical circumstances, ideological stances, and pressure from other institutions and private groups also affect the course of law, which explains why jurisprudence varies from one Court era to the next or even from term to term.

Perhaps no issue illustrates this intersection of law and politics better than criminal rights. In the 1960s the Warren Court revolutionized criminal law by expanding the protections accorded those charged with crimes. The extent to which the Warren Court altered existing law will become clear when you read the cases to come. For now, note the high percentage of decisions favoring the criminally accused during the 1960s, as depicted in Figure III-2.

This liberal trend did not go unnoticed. President Richard Nixon was among the first to recognize that expanded rights for the criminally accused touched the nerves of a majority of Americans. During his presidential campaign of 1968 (and after his election), Nixon emphasized the law and order theme, proclaiming to the voters that the liberal Warren Court had gone too far.

In a 1968 speech, for example, Nixon said, "And tonight it's time for some honest talk about the problem of order in the United States. Let us always respect, as I do, our courts and those who serve on them, but let us also recognize that some of our courts in their decisions have gone too far in weakening the peace forces as against the criminal forces in this country." All of those who heard these words knew Nixon was referring only to the Warren Court. Apparently, many voters agreed with the future president. Public opinion polls taken in 1968 show that nearly two-thirds of Americans believed that the courts were not dealing with criminals harshly

BOX III-1 WARRREN EARL BURGER
(1969–1986)

Warren Burger was born September 17, 1907, in St. Paul, Minnesota. He was the fourth of seven children of Swiss and German parents. Financially unable to attend college full time, Burger spent the years following his 1925 graduation from high school attending college and law school evening classes—two at the University of Minnesota and four at St. Paul College of Law. To support himself, Burger sold life insurance.

He graduated magna cum laude from law school in 1931 and joined a respected law firm in Minnesota, where he practiced until 1953. He also taught part time at his alma mater, Mitchell College of Law, from 1931 to 1948.

Burger married Elvera Stromberg, November 8, 1933. They have one son and one daughter.

Burger developed a deep interest in art and is an accomplished sculptor; as chief justice, he served as chairman of the board of the National Gallery of Art. He is also an antiques buff and a connoisseur of fine wines. He also served as chancellor of the Smithsonian Institution.

Soon after beginning his law career in Minnesota, Burger became involved in Republican state politics. In 1938 he helped in Harold E. Stassen's successful campaign for governor of Minnesota.

During Stassen's unsuccessful bid for the Republican presidential nomination ten years later, Burger met a man who was to figure prominently in his future—Herbert Brownell, then campaign manager for GOP presidential nominee Thomas E. Dewey. Brownell, who became attorney general during the Eisenhower administration, brought Burger to Washington in 1953 to serve as assistant attorney general in charge of the Justice Department's Civil Division.

Burger's stint as assistant attorney general from 1953 to 1956 was not without controversy. His decision to defend the government's action in the dismissal of John F. Peters, a part-time federal employee, on grounds of disloyalty—after Solicitor General Simon E. Sobeloff had refused to do so on grounds of conscience—won Burger the enmity of many liberals.

But Burger's overall record as assistant attorney general apparently met with President Dwight D. Eisenhower's approval, and in 1956 Burger was appointed to the U.S. Court of Appeals for the District of Columbia circuit. As an appeals court judge, Burger developed a reputation as a conservative, especially in criminal justice cases.

Off the bench, Burger became increasingly outspoken in his support of major administrative reform of the judicial system—a cause he continued to advocate as chief justice. During Burger's years as chief justice, Congress approved a number of measures to modernize the operations of the federal judiciary.

President Richard Nixon's appointment of Burger as chief justice on May 21, 1969, caught most observers by surprise. Despite Burger's years of service in the Justice Department and the court of appeals, he was little known outside the legal community. But Nixon apparently was impressed by Burger's consistent argument as an appeals judge that the Constitution should be read narrowly—a belief Nixon shared. Burger was confirmed by the Senate, 74–3, June 9, 1969.

Burger served for seventeen years as chief justice, retiring in 1986 to devote full time to the chairmanship of the commission that planned the Constitution's bicentennial celebration in 1987.

SOURCE: Adapted from Elder Witt, *Guide to the U.S. Supreme Court*, 2d ed. (Washington, D.C.: Congressional Quarterly, 1990), 875–876.

FIGURE III-2. Percentage of Supreme Court Criminal Rights Cases Decided in Favor of the Accused, 1953–1991

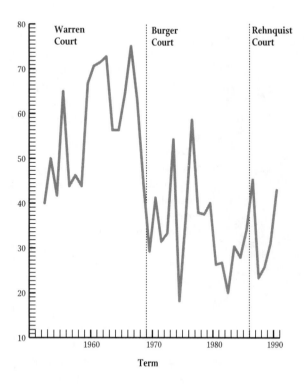

SOURCE: Lee Epstein, Jeffrey A. Segal, Harold J. Spaeth, and Thomas G. Walker, *The Supreme Court Compendium: Data, Decisions, and Developments* (Washington, D.C.: Congressional Quarterly, 1994), Table 3–8.

enough, compared with about 50 percent just three years earlier.[1] In short, Nixon had hit a nerve with U.S. citizens; he placed crime on the public agenda, where it remains.

Nixon also had the opportunity to keep his promise to restore law and order to American communities by changing the composition of the Supreme Court. One year before Nixon took office Earl Warren had resigned to give President Lyndon Johnson the chance

1. Harold W. Stanley and Richard G. Niemi, *Vital Statistics on American Politics*, 4th ed. (Washington, D.C.: CQ Press, 1994), 409.

to appoint his successor. When Johnson's choice for that position, Associate Justice Abe Fortas, failed to obtain Senate confirmation, the chief justiceship remained vacant for Nixon to fill. His choice was Warren Burger, a court of appeals judge who agreed with Nixon's stance on criminal law *(see Box III-1)*.

During the 1970s those who sympathized with the liberal decisions of the Warren Court watched in horror as Nixon appointed three more justices to the Court. The American Civil Liberties Union and various legal aid societies predicted that this new Court not only would stop any expansion of criminal rights, but also would begin to overturn Warren Court precedents. Figure III-2 shows there may be some truth to this view. The justices were far less supportive of criminal rights under Burger's leadership than they were under Warren's.

But the data depicted in the figure present only an aggregated view of Court behavior. To understand whether, in fact, the Burger and Rehnquist Courts managed to alter existing precedent, we must examine the changes in particular areas of criminal law and procedure. As you read the chapters, note the date of each decision. Cases decided between 1953 and 1969 are Warren Court decisions, those between 1970 and 1986, Burger Court opinions, and all subsequent cases belong to the Rehnquist Court. Are there identifiable differences in interpretation? Did the Burger Court act as many civil libertarians predicted? These questions take on added significance in the 1990s. The Rehnquist Court, with several Burger Court holdovers and Reagan/Bush appointees, may attempt to limit the rulings of the Warren Court even more. Whether the more law-and-order-minded justices of the current Court will be able to accomplish this may depend on President Clinton's appointees, Ruth Bader Ginsburg and Stephen Breyer. Will these Democrats go along with their Republican colleagues to limit further liberal Warren Court precedents? Or will they attempt to block the conservative counterrevolution?

CHAPTER 8
INVESTIGATIONS AND EVIDENCE

O NE AFTERNOON Amtrak railroad officials in San Diego observed Gregory Machado and Bridget Leary loading a heavy brown footlocker, which was leaking a white powder, onto a train heading to Boston. Because talcum powder is often used to mask the odor of marijuana and because Machado matched a profile used to spot drug traffickers, the railroad officials believed the couple was transporting illegal substances. They reported what they had seen to federal agents in San Diego who then contacted their counterparts in Boston.

Federal agents in Boston did not obtain a warrant to search the locker; rather, they came to the Boston train station with a police dog trained to sniff out marijuana. Agents watched as Machado and Leary got off the train and lifted the footlocker from the baggage area. At that point, they released the dog. Without arousing the couple's suspicions, the dog signaled that illegal drugs were present in the footlocker. At this point, agents followed Machado and Leary out of the station and watched as they loaded the footlocker into the trunk of a car owned by Joseph Chadwick. While the trunk of the car was still open, the agents arrested the couple and the driver; they also searched all three. They found no weapons, but took the keys to the footlocker.

Agents took the suspects and the footlocker to a federal building, where, an hour and half later, they opened the locker, even though they did not have a search warrant or the consent of the couple. As they suspected, the locker contained large quantities of marijuana. With this evidence in hand, the government tried to prosecute Machado, Leary, and Chadwick for possession of marijuana with intent to distribute. But the three courts that heard the case of *United States v. Chadwick* (1977)—including the U.S. Supreme Court—rejected the government's case, and the couple and the driver were set free.

How is it possible that our judicial system could release these three? After all, there was no doubt that they were carrying controlled substances and, therefore, seemed guilty of violating the law. The answer is quite simple: proof that a crime was committed is a necessary but insufficient condition for a successful prosecution. The government must also show that the proof (or evidence) was gathered in a way that respected the rights of the accused. At the time this case was decided, the courts believed that the government had impinged on those rights because it did not obtain a warrant to search the locker.[1]

In broader terms, when police seek to gather physical evidence, they are bound to respect the guarantees

---

1. As we shall see, nearly fifteen years after the Supreme Court decided this case, it overruled it in *California v. Acevedo* (1991).

accorded to the criminally accused in the two clauses of the Fourth Amendment:

[1] The right of the people to be secure in their persons, houses, papers, and effects, against unreasonable searches and seizures, shall not be violated, and

[2] no Warrants shall issue, but upon probable cause, supported by Oath or affirmation, and particularly describing the place to be searched, and the persons or things to be seized.

In short, clause one requires that searches be reasonable; clause two prescribes the procedures by which warrants can be obtained.

At first glance, these clauses seem to suggest that police may not conduct searches and seizures without warrants and that is why the courts turned down the government's case against Machado, Leary, and Chadwick. That interpretation is not correct. The Supreme Court, as we shall see, has said the Fourth Amendment does not always require that searches and seizures be authorized by a warrant to be valid. In the case of our drug dealers, for example, the Court may have allowed the government to open the footlocker—without a warrant—had the agents provided a reasonable justification, for example, that they had reason to believe the locker contained explosives and needed to be opened immediately or that Machado and Leary had consented to the search.

Physical evidence, such as illegal drugs, is not the only kind presented in court: there is also verbal evidence. Indeed, from the perspective of the government, the best form of proof that an accused person in fact committed the crime is a confession—a form of verbal evidence. Yet, once again, law enforcement officials are not free to obtain confessions, or other kinds of verbal evidence, in just any fashion. They are bound to respect the privilege against self-incrimination contained in the Fifth Amendment: "No person ... shall be compelled in any criminal case to be a witness against himself."

In this chapter we shall have a good deal to say about the Court's interpretation of the Fifth Amendment's self-incrimination provision, along with its decisions regarding the Fourth Amendment. For now, it is enough to note that these guarantees, just like most provisions of the Constitution, permit various interpretations. To see why, we have only to remember that the Fourth Amendment was written in 1789, long before the need for dogs trained to sniff out drugs! Moreover, the terms used in the Fourth and Fifth Amendments, like many others in the Constitution, are vague and require interpretation. For example, in Clause 1 of the Fourth Amendment, what does the word *unreasonable* mean? What separates a reasonable search from an "unreasonable" search? In Clause 2 what is the meaning of *probable cause*? Clearly, the answers to these questions are of critical importance if the Fourth Amendment is to have any force. As you read the cases, then, keep in mind the material we reviewed in the Part III essay and consider how different Courts and justices have approached the rights of the criminally accused.

THE FOURTH AMENDMENT: HISTORICAL NOTES

Like many of the constitutional guarantees accorded the criminally accused, the Fourth Amendment has its genesis in the Framers' resentment of an English institution, the writs of assistance. These writs were general search warrants that did not specify the places or things to be searched. They were authorized by the crown in England beginning in the mid-1600s; by the early 1700s they were used in the colonies primarily to allow customs officials to conduct unrestricted searches. By authorizing these searches, Britain hoped to discourage smuggling by colonial merchants and to enforce existing restrictions on colonial trade.[2]

2. For more on this, see Melvin I. Urofsky, *A March on Liberty* (New York: Knopf, 1988), 36–42.

As general searches became increasingly common, some colonists began to express their distaste for what they felt were major intrusions on their personal privacy and political liberty.[3] James Otis, a Massachusetts lawyer, summed up the situation in a now famous statement. In 1761, when customs officials asked a Massachusetts court for writs of assistance to enforce the "hated Stamp Act," Otis mounted a legal challenge.[4] He argued that the writs went "against the fundamental principles of law," not because the government lacked the power to conduct searches but because it should not be permitted to conduct the open-ended searches—those that did not specify the places and things to be searched—authorized by writs of assistance. In his view, a "man's house is his castle; and whilst he is quiet, he is well guarded as a prince in his castle." He thought the general warrants, to put it in modern-day terms, intruded on personal privacy.

The Massachusetts court ignored Otis's plea and issued the writs. But his concerns were echoed in England by William Pitt. In a speech delivered in the House of Commons, Pitt uttered these equally famous words:

The poorest may, in his cottage, bid defiance to all the forces of the Crown. It may be frail; its roof may shake; the wind may blow through it; the storm may enter; the rain may enter; but the King of England may not enter.

Unlike Otis, Pitt was successful: in 1766 the House of Commons invalidated general warrants.

Still the damage had been done. Right before the Declaration of Independence was issued, Samuel Adams said that opposition over the general searches was the "Commencement of the Controversy between Great Britain and America."[5] And, by the time Madison proposed the Bill of Rights to Congress, it was clear that most Americans agreed with the position

Otis had advocated: almost all of the newly adopted state constitutions restricted government searches and seizures. In other words, they outlawed use of general warrants in favor of those that provided for limited searches. It is not surprising that such restrictions in the federal Constitution met with little opposition.

THE SUPREME COURT AND THE FOURTH AMENDMENT

Madison's version of the Fourth Amendment may have caused little public or political controversy, but that does not mean that the Supreme Court has had an easy time interpreting it. To the contrary, throughout the twentieth century the justices have struggled with developing rules to govern searches and seizures. To be sure, the Court has wanted to be true to the spirit of the Fourth Amendment, providing protection for all citizens against abusive intrusions by the government, but not restricting police so as to render effective law enforcement impossible.

In grappling with these often conflicting goals, the Court has reached decisions that appear contradictory. But it has been guided by one important principle: the Fourth Amendment requires that searches be *reasonable.* Over the years the justices have designated eight types of searches and seizures as reasonable. The first, and most obvious, is the search based on a warrant, which we discuss in the next section. The other seven are exceptions to the need for a warrant but considered by the Court to be reasonable. For each of the eight types, the Court has drafted procedures that must be followed for the police procedure to be valid.

Searches with Warrants

The warrant procedure is the only search authorization method that is mentioned in the Constitution. Clause 2 of the Fourth Amendment outlines the steps to be followed. A police officer must go before a judge or magistrate and swear under oath that reason exists

---

3. See Marvin Zalman and Larry Siegel, *Criminal Procedure* (St. Paul, Minn.: West Publishing, 1991), 99.
4. Ibid.
5. Ira Glasser, *Visions of Liberty* (New York: Arcade, 1991), 166.

to believe that a crime has been committed and that evidence of the crime is located in a particular place. This information often is a sworn written statement called an affidavit. The judge then must determine whether probable cause exists to issue the warrant. If such cause is present, the judge authorizes a search by issuing a warrant that carefully describes the area to be searched and the items that may be seized.

Probable Cause. Although obtaining a search warrant sounds like a straightforward procedure, searches conducted with warrants occur less frequently than we might expect, and the elusive nature of probable cause is the primary reason. The rationale behind the probable cause requirement is easy to understand: individuals are deserving of security in their private lives, and government intrusion should not be allowed unless there is substantial reason for it. But defining probable cause presents a more difficult problem. What is probable cause, and how do police know when they have it?

In *Brinegar v. United States* (1949) the Supreme Court explained that when police, or even judges, deal "with probable cause ... as the very name implies, [they] deal with probabilities. These are not technical; they are the factual and practical considerations of everyday life on which reasonable and prudent men, not legal technicians, act." But does this statement provide police with any guidance? For example, assume that a number of credible witnesses inform police that a certain man is operating as a fence, buying and reselling stolen goods out of a particular apartment. One of these witnesses then provides police with a stolen wristwatch the witness claims to have purchased at the apartment. Under these conditions police clearly have probable cause to believe that crimes have been committed and a sufficient factual basis to convince a judge to issue a warrant to search the apartment. Much police work, however, is not so simple. Officers frequently are forced to investigate on the basis of informants' tips, anonymous letters, and

the like. Do these items constitute sufficient probable cause to allow a judge to issue a search warrant?

In *Aguilar v. Texas* (1964) the Supreme Court, under Earl Warren's leadership, articulated a stringent two-pronged test to determine whether informants' tips or letters could be used as probable cause to obtain search warrants. First, the tip had to "reveal adequately" the informant's "basis of knowledge." How did the individual come to possess the information given to the police? Second, the tip "had to provide facts sufficiently establishing either the veracity of the affiant's informant, or, alternatively, the 'reliability' of the informant's report." The Court later developed the test more fully in *Spinelli v. United States* (1969), and thereafter referred to it as the *Aguilar-Spinelli* test.

In the years following *Aguilar,* police and law enforcement organizations complained that this test made it almost impossible for them to use any letter or tip as the basis for probable cause. These criticisms, coupled with changes in Supreme Court personnel, created an atmosphere in which the Court would reevaluate *Aguilar-Spinelli.* The opportunity came in *Illinois v. Gates* (1983). Pay careful attention to Justice Rehnquist's opinion. It not only analyzes the concept of probable cause, but also provides an interesting example of how the Court deals with precedent it no longer feels to be prudent policy.

Illinois v. Gates

462 U.S. 213 (1983)
Vote: 6 (Blackmun, Burger, O'Connor, Powell,
        Rehnquist, White)
    3 (Brennan, Marshall, Stevens)
Opinion of the Court: Rehnquist
Concurring opinion: White
Dissenting opinions: Brennan, Stevens

On May 3, 1978, police in a Chicago suburb received the following anonymous letter:

This letter is to inform you that you have a couple in your town who strictly make their living on selling drugs. They are Sue and Lance Gates, they live on Greenway, off Bloomingdale Rd. in the condominiums. Most of their buys are done in Florida. Sue his wife drives their car to Florida, where she leaves it to be loaded up with drugs, then Lance flies down and drives it back. Sue flies back after she drops the car off in Florida. May 3 she is driving down there again and Lance will be flying down in a few days to drive it back. At the time Lance drives the car back he has the trunk loaded with over $100,000.00 in drugs. Presently they have over $100,000.00 worth of drugs in their basement.

They brag about the fact they never have to work, and make their entire living on pushers.

I guarantee if you watch them carefully you will make a big catch. They are friends with some big drug dealers, who visit their house often.

A precinct detective verified all the information in the note and went to a judge to obtain a search warrant based on probable cause. Warrant in hand, the police waited for the couple to return from Florida to search their car. The search turned up 350 pounds of marijuana.

The Gateses' attorney argued that the judge should exclude this evidence from trial because police, under the *Aguilar* test, lacked sufficient probable cause. Specifically, the letter failed to state how the writer came upon the information, a requirement mandated by *Aguilar-Spinelli.* The lower state courts ruled that the evidence should be suppressed, and the Illinois Supreme Court affirmed that conclusion.

The state, along with several amicus curiae, asked the Supreme Court to review the decision. Illinois argued, "Probable cause to justify issuance of a search warrant exists when the facts and circumstances presented to the magistrate are sufficient to warrant a prudent person to believe that the described items are in the indicated locale." The U.S. Supreme Court, therefore, addressed this question: May a judge issue a search warrant on the basis of a "partially corroborated anonymous informant's tip"?

JUSTICE REHNQUIST delivered the opinion of the Court.

We granted certiorari to consider the application of the Fourth Amendment to a magistrate's issuance of a search warrant on the basis of a partially corroborated anonymous informant's tip....

The Illinois Supreme Court concluded—and we are inclined to agree—that standing alone, the anonymous letter sent to the Bloomingdale Police Department would not provide the basis for a magistrate's determination that there was probable cause to believe contraband would be found in the Gateses' car and home. The letter provides virtually nothing from which one might conclude that its author is either honest or his information reliable; likewise, the letter gives absolutely no indication of the basis for the writer's predictions regarding the Gateses' criminal activities. Something more was required, then, before a magistrate could conclude that there was probable cause to believe that contraband would be found in the Gateses' home and car.

The Illinois Supreme Court also properly recognized that Detective Mader's affidavit might be capable of supplementing the anonymous letter with information sufficient to permit a determination of probable cause. In holding that the affidavit in fact did not contain sufficient additional information to sustain a determination of probable cause, the Illinois court applied a "two-pronged test," derived from our decision in *Spinelli v. United States* (1969). The Illinois Supreme Court, like some others, apparently understood *Spinelli* as requiring that the anonymous letter satisfy each of two independent requirements before it could be relied on. According to this view, the letter, as supplemented by Mader's affidavit, first had to adequately reveal the "basis of knowledge" of the letterwriter—the particular means by which he came by the information given in his report. Second, it had to provide facts sufficiently establishing either the "veracity" of the affiant's informant, or, alternatively, the "reliability" of the informant's report in this particular case. The Illinois court, alluding to an elaborate set of legal rules that have developed among various lower courts to enforce the "two-pronged test," found that the test had not been satisfied. First, the "veracity" prong was not satisfied because, "[t]here was simply no basis [for] concluding that the anonymous person [who wrote the letter to the

Bloomingdale Police Department] was credible." The court indicated that corroboration by police of details contained in the letter might never satisfy the "veracity" prong, and in any event, could not do so if, as in the present case, only "innocent" details are corroborated. In addition, the letter gave no indication of the basis of its writer's knowledge of the Gateses' activities. The Illinois court understood *Spinelli* as permitting the detail contained in a tip to be used to infer that the informant had a reliable basis for his statements, but it thought that the anonymous letter failed to provide sufficient detail to permit such an inference. Thus, it concluded that no showing of probable cause had been made.

We agree with the Illinois Supreme Court that an informant's "veracity," "reliability," and "basis of knowledge" are all highly relevant in determining the value of his report. We do not agree, however, that these elements should be understood as entirely separate and independent requirements to be rigidly exacted in every case, which the opinion of the Supreme Court of Illinois would imply. Rather, as detailed below, they should be understood simply as closely intertwined issues that may usefully illuminate the commonsense, practical question whether there is "probable cause" to believe that contraband or evidence is located in a particular place.

This totality-of-the-circumstances approach is far more consistent with our prior treatment of probable cause than is any rigid demand that specific "tests" be satisfied by every informant's tip. Perhaps the central teaching of our decisions bearing on the probable-cause standard is that it is a "practical, nontechnical conception." "In dealing with probable cause, . . . as the very name implies, we deal with probabilities. These are not technical; they are the factual and practical considerations of everyday life on which reasonable and prudent men, not legal technicians, act.". . .

As these comments illustrate, probable cause is a fluid concept—turning on the assessment of probabilities in particular factual contexts—not readily, or even usefully, reduced to a neat set of legal rules. Informants' tips doubtless come in many shapes and sizes from many different types of persons. . . .

Moreover, the "two-pronged test" directs analysis into two largely independent channels—the informant's "veracity" or "reliability" and his "basis of knowledge." There are persuasive arguments against according these two elements such independent status. Instead, they are better understood as relevant considerations in the totality-of-the-circumstances analysis that traditionally has guided probable-cause determinations: a deficiency in one may be compensated for, in determining the overall reliability of a tip, by a strong showing as to the other, or by some other indicia of reliability. . . .

We . . . have recognized that affidavits "are normally drafted by nonlawyers in the midst and haste of a criminal investigation. Technical requirements of elaborate specificity once exacted under common law pleadings have no proper place in this area." Likewise, search and arrest warrants long have been issued by persons who are neither lawyers nor judges, and who certainly do not remain abreast of each judicial refinement of the nature of "probable cause." The rigorous inquiry into the *Spinelli* prongs and the complex superstructure of evidentiary and analytical rules that some have seen implicit in our *Spinelli* decision, cannot be reconciled with the fact that many warrants are—quite properly, issued on the basis of nontechnical, commonsense judgments of laymen applying a standard less demanding than those used in more formal legal proceedings. Likewise, given the informal, often hurried context in which it must be applied, the "built-in subtleties" of the "two-pronged test" are particularly unlikely to assist magistrates in determining probable cause.

Similarly, we have repeatedly said that after-the-fact scrutiny by courts of the sufficiency of an affidavit should not take the form of *de novo* review. . . .

If the affidavits submitted by police officers are subjected to the type of scrutiny some courts have deemed appropriate, police might well resort to warrantless searches, with the hope of relying on consent or some other exception to the Warrant Clause that might develop at the time of the search. . . .

Finally, the direction taken by decisions following *Spinelli* poorly serves "the most basic function of any government": "to provide for the security of the individual and of his property." The strictures that inevitably accompany the "two-pronged test" cannot avoid seriously impeding the task of law enforcement. . . .

For all these reasons, we conclude that it is wiser to abandon the "two-pronged test" established by our decisions in *Aguilar* and *Spinelli*. In its place we reaffirm the totality-of-the-circumstances analysis that traditionally has informed probable-cause determinations. The task of the issuing magistrate is simply to make a practical, common-sense decision whether, given all the circumstances set forth in the affidavit before him, including the "veracity" and "basis of knowledge" of persons supplying hearsay information, there is a fair probability that contraband or evidence of a crime will be found in a particular place. And the duty of a reviewing court is simply to ensure that the magistrate had a "substantial basis for . . . concluding" that probable cause existed. We are convinced that this flexible, easily applied standard will better achieve the accommodation of public and private interests that the Fourth Amendment requires than does the approach that has developed from *Aguilar* and *Spinelli*. . . .

The showing of probable cause in the present case . . . [is] compelling. . . . Even standing alone, the facts obtained through the independent investigation of Mader and the DEA at least suggested that the Gateses were involved in drug trafficking. In addition to being a popular vacation site, Florida is well-known as a source of narcotics and other illegal drugs. Lance Gates' flight to West Palm Beach, his brief, overnight stay in a motel, and apparent immediate return north to Chicago in the family car, conveniently awaiting him in West Palm Beach, is as suggestive of a pre-arranged drug run, as it is of an ordinary vacation trip.

In addition, the judge could rely on the anonymous letter, which had been corroborated in major part. . . . The corroboration of the letter's predictions that the Gateses' car would be in Florida, that Lance Gates would fly to Florida in the next day or so, and that he would drive the car north toward Bloomingdale all indicated, albeit not with certainty, that the informant's other assertions also were true. . . .

Finally, the anonymous letter contained a range of details relating not just to easily obtained facts and conditions existing at the time of the tip, but to future actions of third parties ordinarily not easily predicted. The letterwriter's accurate information as to the travel plans of each of the Gateses was of a character likely obtained only from the Gateses themselves, or from someone familiar with their not entirely ordinary travel plans. If the informant had access to accurate information of this type, a magistrate could properly conclude that it was not unlikely that he also had access to reliable information of the Gateses' alleged il-

legal activities. Of course, the Gateses' travel plans might have been learned from a talkative neighbor or travel agent; under the "two-pronged test" developed from *Spinelli*, the character of the details in the anonymous letter might well not permit a sufficiently clear inference regarding the letterwriter's "basis of knowledge." But, as discussed previously, probable cause does not demand the certainty we associate with formal trials. It is enough that there was a fair probability that the writer of the anonymous letter had obtained his entire story either from the Gateses or someone they trusted. And corroboration of major portions of the letter's predictions provides just this probability. It is apparent, therefore, that the judge issuing the warrant had a "substantial basis for . . . concluding" that probable cause to search the Gateses' home and car existed. The judgment of the Supreme Court of Illinois therefore must be

Reversed.

The "totality-of-the-circumstances" standard established in *Illinois v. Gates* clearly facilitates police efforts to obtain search warrants. But, in addition to establishing probable cause, police must (1) specify the area to be searched and the things to be seized; (2) execute the warrant in an orderly and timely fashion; and (3) seize only things specifically listed in the warrant unless they find items whose very possession is a crime, for example, contraband.

Warrants and Electronic Surveillance. As you can see, police face several legal and political obstacles in obtaining search warrants. Perhaps no other area of law illustrates this point as well as that involving wiretapping and electronic eavesdropping, where "special, statutory warrant requirements" have been developed.[6] Careful study of this line of cases also provides us with some insight into the myriad problems the Court has faced more generally in its Fourth Amendment jurisprudence.

As is typical in Fourth Amendment cases, the Court's initial forays involved situations in which law enforcement officials failed to obtain warrants to

6. See Zalman and Siegel, *Criminal Procedure*, 152.

eavesdrop on conversations. For example, *Olmstead v. United States* (1928) centered on the ability of federal agents to place wiretaps on outside telephone lines without warrants. Olmstead, who was accused of importing and selling alcohol in violation of the National Prohibition Act, alleged that even though agents had not entered his home or office, they had, through the wiretaps, "seized" his conversations in violation of the Fourth Amendment. The government maintained that wiretapping was not a search and seizure within the meaning of the Fourth Amendment.

The Court ruled in favor of the government. After reviewing the general history of the amendment, the Court concluded that the Fourth Amendment did not protect Olmstead's conversations because it only covers searches of "material things—the person, the house, his papers or his effects." Therefore, "[t]he Amendment does not forbid what was done here. There was no searching. There was no seizure. The evidence was secured by the use of the sense of hearing and that only. There was no entry of the houses or offices of the defendants." Certainly, the majority stated, Congress may "protect the secrecy of telephone messages by making them, when intercepted, inadmissible in evidence in federal criminal trials, by direct legislation.... But the courts may not adopt such a policy by attributing an enlarged and unusual meaning to the Fourth Amendment."

The Court's logic was lost on four justices, who wrote dissenting opinions. Perhaps the one best remembered was by Justice Brandeis. He echoed the words of Otis, Pitt, and the others who had fought against the general warrants when he wrote:

The makers of our Constitution undertook to secure conditions favorable to the pursuit of happiness.... They conferred, as against the Government, the right to be left alone—the most comprehensive of rights and the right most valued by civilized men. To protect that right, every unjustifiable intrusion by the Government upon the privacy of the individual, whatever the means employed, must be deemed a violation of the Fourth Amendment.

To Brandeis, it was "immaterial" that agents had not needed to enter Olmstead's home or office to place the wiretaps; it was equally unimportant that "the intrusion was in aid of law enforcement." He declared, "The greatest dangers to liberty lurk in insidious encroachment by men of zeal, well-meaning but without understanding."

Brandeis's position did not garner support from the majority of justices but apparently reflected the wishes of the people. The reaction to *Olmstead* was highly unfavorable. Newspaper editorials criticized it as an infringement on privacy, and more than half the states enacted legislation outlawing wiretapping.[7] Finally, with passage of the Federal Communications Act of 1934, Congress took up the Court's invitation to constrain wiretapping efforts. A section of the act specified that "no person not authorized by the sender shall intercept any communication to any person."

This act may have impinged on the holding in *Olmstead*, but it did little to eliminate the concerns Brandeis raised. Nor did it anticipate that changing technology would give law enforcement officials a host of new ways to "snoop" on suspects. *Goldman v. United States* (1942) makes both points clear. In this case, the Court considered an evolved version of wiretaps, the dectaphone, a device similar to a stethoscope wired to a recording device.[8] Federal agents, who suspected that two lawyers, Goldman and Shulman, were engaged in illegal business practices, placed dectaphones on a wall adjoining Shulman's office, without obtaining a warrant. Through this device, the agents overheard conversations between Shulman, Goldman, and others, which they used as evidence against them.

Goldman and Shulman tried to convince the Court to distinguish *Olmstead* and find in their favor. In particular, they argued that *Olmstead* dealt "with the tapping of telephone wires, and [that] in using a telephone, the speaker projects his voice beyond the confines of his home or office, and therefore, assumes the risk that his message may be intercepted." In this case,

7. Ibid., 179.   8. Ibid., 180.

however, Shulman and Goldman argued that their conversations took place in an office; they did not intend for them "to go beyond those walls." But the Court found the distinction "too nice for practical application" of the Fourth Amendment's constitutional guarantee. Instead, relying on the logic of *Olmstead*, it created what has become known as the physical penetration rule: so long as agents do not physically penetrate the space of individuals, they need not obtain warrants to record their conversations.

From the perspective of the accused, this test suffered from a fundamental flaw. Given modern technology, there was never really any need for agents to enter spaces to obtain recordings of conversations. They could use dectaphones, microphones, and so forth to pick up conversations from afar. In other words, the physical penetration test supported not just the rationale of *Olmstead*, but also it would lead to the same kind of antidefendant holdings. Agents could freely and without warrants gather evidence against the criminally suspect.

With no serious congressional attempts to soften this decision, "bugging by the FBI and local police became extensive."[9] It was a tool that law enforcement officials found particularly useful in the war against organized crime. As Figure 8-1 shows, following *Goldman* (and today) Americans supported general efforts to fight crime, with most believing that the courts were not sufficiently hard on criminals. However, Americans were not then, nor are they now, supportive of electronic surveillance. A Gallup Poll taken in 1949 indicated that only 22 percent of the citizenry approved of wiretapping; in the 1990s the vast majority continued to disapprove of the practice. Only 24.1 percent thought it was "right ... to get evidence for use in a court trial by means of wiretapping."

By the time the Supreme Court decided its most important snooping case, *Katz v. United States* (1967), the political environment was murky. Americans

9. Ibid.

FIGURE 8-1 Public Opinion on Court Treatment of Criminals and on Wiretapping

Percentage

Think Courts Are Not Harsh Enough

Support Wiretapping

SOURCES: For court data: Harold W. Stanley and Richard G. Niemi, *Vital Statistics on American Politics*, 4th ed. (Washington, D.C.: CQ Press, 1994), 409; for wiretap data: Lee Epstein, Jeffrey A. Segal, Harold J. Spaeth, and Thomas G. Walker, *The Supreme Court Compendium: Data, Decisions, and Developments* (Washington, D.C.: Congressional Quarterly, 1994), Table 8-8.

NOTE: The questions were: "In general, do you think the courts in this area deal too harshly or not harshly enough with criminals?" (The figure shows the percentage of respondents believing that the courts are not harsh enough); "Everything considered, would you say that, in general, you approve or disapprove of wiretapping?" (The figure shows the percentage of respondents approving).

wanted less crime but disapproved of a major enforcement weapon—electronic surveillance. How would the generally liberal Warren Court deal with these mixed signals? Would it merely apply the precedents established in *Olmstead* and *Goldman?* Or would it devise a new approach? Keep these questions in mind as you read *Katz*.

Katz v. United States

389 U.S. 347 (1967)

Vote: 7 (Brennan, Douglas, Fortas, Harlan, Stewart,
      Warren, White)
   1 (Black)

Opinion of the Court: Stewart
Concurring opinions: Douglas, Harlan, White
Dissenting opinion: Black
Not participating: Marshall

FBI agents suspected Charles Katz of engaging in illegal bookmaking activity; in particular, they thought he was placing bets and other wagering information by telephone from Los Angeles to Miami and Boston. To gather evidence, they placed listening and recording devices outside the telephone booth Katz used to make his calls. (Keep in mind that back then public telephones were often housed in glass booths.) Despite the fact that law enforcement officials had listened in on Katz's conversations without a warrant, federal attorneys used the transcripts of those conversations to obtain an eight-count indictment.

Both sides believed that the Court would use *Goldman*'s physical penetration test; therefore, Katz and the government centered their arguments on the nature of the place where the conversations took place. Katz challenged the use of the transcripts as evidence against him on the ground that the telephone booth was a "constitutionally protected area." In making this argument, which was not so different from Olmstead's

nearly forty years earlier, Katz may have been on somewhat stronger ground. In the 1965 case of *Griswold v. Connecticut (see Chapter 7)*, the Supreme Court had created a constitutional right to privacy. Although the *Griswold* decision came in a case involving birth control, some observers believed it was applicable to Katz's situation, as well. In other words, police could not invade his privacy unless they obtained a search warrant.

The government argued that Supreme Court cases covered its evidence-gathering procedures, and it pointed out that, in previous Fourth Amendment cases (such as *Goldman*), the justices permitted the warrantless use of bugs and mikes so long as agents did not "physically penetrate" an individual's space. Here, the FBI attached the listening device to the *outside* of the booth; it never invaded Katz's space.

Should the Court be unwilling to follow this precedent—and, given the general liberal inclination of this Court, there were good reasons to suspect that it would not—then the government urged a back-up position: that the justices create an exception to the warrant rule to cover this case. The government noted that the Court had already ruled that police need not obtain a warrant to conduct searches if they were incident to a lawful arrest *(pages 506–512)* or if they were in "hot pursuit" of a suspect *(pages 527–528)*. To this list, it urged the Court to rule that "surveillance of a telephone booth ... be exempted from the usual requirement" that a search warrant be obtained.

MR. JUSTICE STEWART delivered the opinion of the Court.

We granted certiorari in order to consider the constitutional questions thus presented.

The petitioner has phrased those questions as follows:

"A. Whether a public telephone booth is a constitutionally protected area so that evidence obtained by attaching an electronic listening recording device to the top of such a booth is obtained in violation of the right to privacy of the user of the booth.

"B. Whether physical penetration of a constitutionally protected area is necessary before a search and seizure can be said to be violative of the Fourth Amendment to the United States Constitution."

We decline to adopt this formulation of the issues. In the first place, the correct solution of Fourth Amendment problems is not necessarily promoted by incantation of the phrase "constitutionally protected area." Secondly, the Fourth Amendment cannot be translated into a general constitutional "right to privacy." That Amendment protects individual privacy against certain kinds of governmental intrusion, but its protections go further, and often have nothing to do with privacy at all. Other provisions of the Constitution protect personal privacy from other forms of governmental invasion. But the protection of a person's *general* right to privacy—his right to be let alone by other people—is, like the protection of his property and of his very life, left largely to the law of the individual States.

Because of the misleading way the issues have been formulated, the parties have attached great significance to the characterization of the telephone booth from which the petitioner placed his calls. The petitioner has strenuously argued that the booth was a "constitutionally protected area." The Government has maintained with equal vigor that it was not. But this effort to decide whether or not a given "area," viewed in the abstract, is "constitutionally protected" deflects attention from the problem presented by this case. For the Fourth Amendment protects people, not places. What a person knowingly exposes to the public, even in his own home or office, is not a subject of Fourth Amendment protection. But what he seeks to preserve as private, even in an area accessible to the public, may be constitutionally protected.

The Government stresses the fact that the telephone booth from which the petitioner made his calls was constructed partly of glass, so that he was as visible after he entered it as he would have been if he had remained outside. But what he sought to exclude when he entered the booth was not the intruding eye—it was the uninvited ear. He did not shed his right to do so simply because he made his calls from a place where he might be seen. No less than an individual in a business office, in a friend's apartment, or in a

taxicab, a person in a telephone booth may rely upon the protection of the Fourth Amendment. One who occupies it, shuts the door behind him, and pays the toll that permits him to place a call is surely entitled to assume that the words he utters into the mouthpiece will not be broadcast to the world. To read the Constitution more narrowly is to ignore the vital role that the public telephone has come to play in private communication.

The Government contends, however, that the activities of its agents in this case should not be tested by Fourth Amendment requirements, for the surveillance technique they employed involved no physical penetration of the telephone booth from which the petitioner placed his calls. It is true that the absence of such penetration was at one time thought to foreclose further Fourth Amendment inquiry, Olmstead v. United States; Goldman v. United States, for that Amendment was thought to limit only searches and seizures of tangible property. But "the premise that property interests control the right of the Government to search and seize has been discredited.". . . Indeed, we have expressly held that the Fourth Amendment governs not only the seizure of tangible items, but extends as well to the recording of oral statements, overheard without any "technical trespass under . . . local property law." Once this much is acknowledged, and once it is recognized that the Fourth Amendment protects people—and not simply "areas"—against unreasonable searches and seizures, it becomes clear that the reach of that Amendment cannot turn upon the presence or absence of a physical intrusion into any given enclosure.

We conclude that the underpinnings of Olmstead and Goldman have been so eroded . . . [that they] can no longer be regarded as controlling. The Government's activities in electronically listening to and recording the petitioner's words violated the privacy upon which he justifiably relied while using the telephone booth and thus constituted a "search and seizure" within the meaning of the Fourth Amendment. The fact that the electronic device employed to achieve that end did not happen to penetrate the wall of the booth can have no constitutional significance.

The question remaining for decision, then, is whether the search and seizure conducted in this case complied with constitutional standards. In that regard, the Government's position is that its agents acted in an entirely defensible manner: They did not begin their electronic surveillance until investigation of the petitioner's activities had established a strong probability that he was using the telephone in question to transmit gambling information to persons in other States, in violation of federal law. Moreover, the surveillance was limited, both in scope and in duration, to the specific purpose of establishing the contents of the petitioner's unlawful telephonic communications. The agents confined their surveillance to the brief periods during which he used the telephone booth, and they took great care to overhear only the conversations of the petitioner himself.

Accepting this account of the Government's actions as accurate, it is clear that this surveillance was so narrowly circumscribed that a duly authorized magistrate, properly notified of the need for such investigation, specifically informed of the basis on which it was to proceed, and clearly apprised of the precise intrusion it would entail, could constitutionally have authorized, with appropriate safeguards, the very limited search and seizure that the Government asserts in fact took place. Only last Term we sustained the validity of such an authorization, holding that, under sufficiently "precise and discriminate circumstances," a federal court may empower government agents to employ a concealed electronic device "for the narrow and particularized purpose of ascertaining the truth of the ... allegations" of a "detailed factual affidavit alleging the commission of a specific criminal offense."... Here, too, a similar judicial order could have accommodated "the legitimate needs of law enforcement" by authorizing the carefully limited use of electronic surveillance.

The Government urges that, because its agents relied upon the decisions in Olmstead and Goldman, and because they did no more here than they might properly have done with prior judicial sanction, we should retroactively validate their conduct. That we cannot do. It is apparent that the agents in this case acted with restraint. Yet the inescapable fact is that this restraint was imposed by the agents themselves, not by a judicial officer. They were not required, before commencing the search, to present their estimate of probable cause for detached scrutiny by a neutral magistrate. They were not compelled, during the conduct of the search itself, to observe precise limits established in advance by a specific court order. Nor were they directed, after the search had been completed, to notify the authorizing

magistrate in detail of all that had been seized. In the absence of such safeguards, this Court has never sustained a search upon the sole ground that officers reasonably expected to find evidence of a particular crime and voluntarily confined their activities to the least intrusive means consistent with that end. Searches conducted without warrants have been held unlawful "notwithstanding facts unquestionably showing probable cause," for the Constitution requires "that the deliberate, impartial judgment of a judicial officer ... be interposed between the citizen and the police ...." "Over and again this Court has emphasized that the mandate of the [Fourth] Amendment requires adherence to judicial processes," and that searches conducted outside the judicial process, without prior approval by judge or magistrate, are per se unreasonable under the Fourth Amendment—subject only to a few specifically established and well-delineated exceptions.

It is difficult to imagine how any of those exceptions could ever apply to the sort of search and seizure involved in this case. Even electronic surveillance substantially contemporaneous with an individual's arrest could hardly be deemed an "incident" of that arrest.... And, of course, the very nature of electronic surveillance precludes its use pursuant to the suspect's consent.

The Government does not question these basic principles. Rather, it urges the creation of a new exception to cover this case. It argues that surveillance of a telephone booth should be exempted from the usual requirement of advance authorization by a magistrate upon a showing of probable cause. We cannot agree. Omission of such authorization "bypasses the safeguards provided by an objective predetermination of probable cause, and substitutes instead the far less reliable procedure of an after-the-event justification for the ... search, too likely to be subtly influenced by the familiar shortcomings of hindsight judgment." And bypassing a neutral predetermination of the scope of a search leaves individuals secure from Fourth Amendment violations "only in the discretion of the police."

These considerations do not vanish when the search in question is transferred from the setting of a home, an office, or a hotel room to that of a telephone booth. Wherever a man may be, he is entitled to know that he will remain free from unreasonable searches and seizures. The government agents here ignored "the procedure of antecedent justification ... that is central to the Fourth Amendment," a procedure that we hold to be a constitutional precondition of the kind of electronic surveillance involved in this case. Because the surveillance here failed to meet that condition, and because it led to the petitioner's conviction, the judgment must be reversed.

MR. JUSTICE HARLAN, concurring.

I join the opinion of the Court, which I read to hold only (a) that an enclosed telephone booth is an area where, like a home ... a person has a constitutionally protected reasonable expectation of privacy; (b) that electronic as well as physical intrusion into a place that is in this sense private may constitute a violation of the Fourth Amendment; and (c) that the invasion of a constitutionally protected area by federal authorities is, as the Court has long held, presumptively unreasonable in the absence of a search warrant.

As the Court's opinion states, "the Fourth Amendment protects people, not places." The question, however, is what protection it affords to those people. Generally, as here, the answer to that question requires reference to a "place." My understanding of the rule that has emerged from prior decisions is that there is a twofold requirement, first that a person have exhibited an actual (subjective) expectation of privacy and, second, that the expectation be one that society is prepared to recognize as "reasonable." Thus a man's home is, for most purposes, a place where he expects privacy, but objects, activities, or statements that he exposes to the "plain view" of outsiders are not "protected" because no intention to keep them to himself has been exhibited. On the other hand, conversations in the open would not be protected against being overheard, for the expectation of privacy under the circumstances would be unreasonable.

The critical fact in this case is that "[o]ne who occupies it, [a telephone booth] shuts the door behind him, and pays the toll that permits him to place a call is surely entitled to assume" that his conversation is not being intercepted. The point is not that the booth is "accessible to the public" at other times, but that it is a temporarily private place whose momentary occupants' expectations of freedom from intrusion are recognized as reasonable....

This case requires us to reconsider Goldman, and I agree that it should now be overruled. Its limitation on Fourth Amendment protection is, in the present day, bad physics as well as bad law, for reasonable expectations of privacy may be defeated by electronic as well as physical invasion.

Finally, I do not read the Court's opinion to declare that no interception of a conversation one-half of which occurs in a public telephone booth can be reasonable in the absence of a warrant. As elsewhere under the Fourth Amendment, warrants are the general rule, to which the legitimate needs of law enforcement may demand specific exceptions. It will be time enough to consider any such exceptions when an appropriate occasion presents itself, and I agree with the Court that this is not one.

Katz is an important, perhaps landmark, ruling for the following reasons. First, the Court applied the right of privacy to searches and seizures. If citizens have a reasonable "expectation of privacy," as Justice Harlan's concurrence noted, then they are entitled to it. It is not the place that is protected but the person occupying that place. This position is what Brandeis had advocated in his *Olmstead* dissent. It took a mere forty years for a majority of the justices to adopt it!

Second, and most relevant here, is the Court's statement about the Fourth Amendment's warrant requirement. While the justices noted their preference for searches conducted pursuant to warrants, they acknowledged that they had created exceptions—special circumstances under which police did not need to obtain warrants to conduct searches. They found, however, that electronic surveillance did not fall under any of those exceptions, and they declined to create a new one. The clear holding of *Katz*, then, is if police want to engage in electronic surveillance, they must obtain search warrants.

Although, as Figure 8-1 shows, most Americans agree with this position, it was seen in some circles as a hindrance to state and federal law enforcement efforts. In 1968 Congress responded to these divergent concerns with legislation designed to "retain eavesdropping while maintaining the Constitution."[10] Under Title III of the Federal Omnibus Crime Control and Safe Streets Act, agents may "intercept a wire, oral, or electronic communication" without a warrant if one of the parties to the conversation has consented. The act also spells out the procedures by which agents can obtain warrants to intercept conversations.

The Warren Court's decision in *Katz* may have precipitated the need for Title III, but resolving cases that emanated from it fell to more conservative Courts. Generally, the Court under Burger and Rehnquist interpreted "the statute broadly, typically upholding law enforcement agents when they are challenged on appeal."[11] In *United States v. White* (1971), for example, the Court found no constitutional defect in permitting agents to wear body mikes to record conversations with the criminally suspect. The majority ruled that when people make incriminating statements during the course of open conversations, they have no reasonable expectation of privacy under *Katz*. Moreover, the Court noted that Title III allowed agents to tape conversations if one party had given consent. To the majority, this provision meant that an undercover police officer wearing a wire could be the consenting party.

Do *White* and related cases, coupled with police practices, erode *Katz*'s concern with the Fourth Amendment's warrant requirement? On the one hand, the Court continues to express its belief that police generally should obtain a warrant to conduct searches. Officials know that searches and seizures based on valid search warrants are the most authoritative of all Fourth Amendment justifications. Evidence gathered in this way is most likely to stand up in court. On the other hand, as we have seen, police face many legal and practical obstacles in obtaining warrants. Accordingly, governments have pushed the Court to uphold warrantless searches by creating more and more exceptions to the warrant rule.

Despite the Court's firm position in *Katz*, the justices—particularly those serving under Burger and Rehnquist—have been open to these arguments. So far, the justices have created seven exceptions to the warrant requirement: (1) searches incident to valid arrests; (2) searches to ensure that evidence is not lost; (3) searches based on consent; (4) searches to ensure the safety of law enforcement officials; (5) searches conducted under the plain view doctrine; (6) searches done in "hot pursuit"; and (7) searches conducted in specified places that merit low levels of protection. The Court has designated each of these searches, in addition to those conducted with warrants, as "reasonable" under the Fourth Amendment. However, the justices have placed constraints on each: they are limited in scope based on the initial justification the Court used to create them.

As you read the material to come, ask yourself these questions: Why did the Court create the exception to the warrant requirement? What are the limits placed on the exception? Keep in mind the ideological propensities of the various Courts. Have the justices of the Burger and Rehnquist Courts eradicated the constitutional protections for the criminally accused devised by the Warren Court? If so, have they gone too far? Or have they merely sought to rebalance the scales of justice?

Searches Incident to a Valid Arrest

As a general principle of law, police may conduct a search when placing a suspect under a valid arrest. For example, if a law enforcement official checks an apprehended suspect for weapons, the officer is engaging in a search incident to a valid arrest. The Supreme Court has allowed such searches for three reasons: to protect the safety of the police officer in case the suspect is armed, to remove any means of escape, and to prevent the suspect from disposing of evidence.

The Court also has imposed two types of limits—temporal and spatial—on searches incident to a valid arrest. The temporal limit means that police can conduct such a search only at the time of the arrest. If the

---

10. Ibid., 182.   11. Ibid., 184.

arresting officers forget to check something or someone, they cannot later return to conduct a search unless they have some other justification. This rule makes sense in light of the original purposes for allowing searches incident to arrest: an individual can place a police officer in jeopardy or attempt escape at the time of an arrest, but no danger exists once police remove the individual from the scene. The spatial limitation means that searches made incident to a valid arrest may go no farther than searching the arrested suspect and the area under the suspect's immediate control. Such searches are allowed so that police can respond to any immediate threats to safety and security. They are not designed to be full, evidentiary searches such as those authorized by a warrant.

Chimel v. California (1969) is a clear example of the spatial limitation rule in practice; the justices specifically addressed the question of how far arrest searches may extend. In addition to the contribution this case makes to the development of search and seizure law, it provides an opportunity to examine the thinking of Justice Potter Stewart. Students of the judicial process label judges *liberal* or *conservative,* but Stewart often took a middle course. In his majority opinion in this case, he steers the law between those on the left who wanted to restrict police authority and those on the right who favored broad police discretion.

Chimel v. California

395 U.S. 752 (1969)
Vote: 6 (Brennan, Douglas, Harlan, Marshall,
　　　　Stewart, Warren)
　　　2 (Black, White)
Opinion of the Court: Stewart
Concurring opinion: Harlan
Dissenting opinion: White

On September 13, 1965, police appeared at the Chimel home with a warrant for Ted Steven Chimel's arrest in connection with the burglary of a coin shop. *(See Box 8-1.)* Chimel's wife let police enter the house, where they waited for her husband to return from work. When Chimel arrived, police presented him with the arrest warrant and asked if they could search the house. Chimel objected because the officers did

---

BOX 8-1　ARREST AND ARREST WARRANTS

Most Court cases centering on warrants deal with searches and seizures, not arrests. Still, in many of the opinions excerpted in this chapter you will come across the terms *arrest* and *arrest warrant.* Here we answer some questions associated with these terms.

What is an arrest? Although many citizens think of an arrest as police taking a person into custody, it is—for legal purposes—something less. An arrest takes place when a legal authority deprives an individual of his or her freedom of movement and rights of personal privacy for some period of time.

What is required for police to make an arrest? An arrest, which is a seizure of a person, is subject to constitutional strictures under the Fourth Amendment. In particular, before they can make an arrest, police must have probable cause to show that a crime has been committed and that the individual they wish to arrest is the perpetrator.

Under what circumstances may police make an arrest? Police may make an arrest with or without an arrest warrant. In both instances, they must meet the probable cause requirement.

For an arrest with a warrant, police appear before a magistrate and present sworn evidence in support of probable cause. If such evidence exists, the magistrate will issue the warrant.

For a warrantless arrest, police can establish probable cause on the basis of things they observe, smell, hear, taste, or touch. Police can also establish probable cause on the basis of reliable hearsay—second-hand evidence or what persons say they have heard other persons say.

SOURCE: Marvin Zalman and Larry Siegel, *Criminal Procedure* (St. Paul, Minn.: West Publishing, 1991), 305–306.

not have a search warrant, but they went ahead anyway. After searching the entire three-bedroom house, including attic, garage, and workshop, for almost an hour, police seized some items (including coins), which the state used to prosecute Chimel.

In a California trial court, Chimel's attorney argued that goods seized by police should not be introduced as evidence because their search, justified only by the arrest, extended well beyond the area directly under Chimel's immediate control. The trial judge and the appellate courts, however, adopted the state's position that the police had acted in good faith. If sufficient probable cause existed to make the arrest, then there was sufficient cause to search the entire house. Chimel appealed to the Supreme Court.[12]

MR. JUSTICE STEWART delivered the opinion of the Court.

This case raises basic questions concerning the permissible scope under the Fourth Amendment of a search incident to a lawful arrest. . . .

The decisions of this Court bearing upon that question have been far from consistent, as even the most cursory review makes evident.

Approval of a warrantless search incident to a lawful arrest seems first to have been articulated by the Court in 1914 as dictum in Weeks v. United States. . . . Eleven years later the case of Carroll v. United States brought the following embellishment of . . . Weeks . . . :

"When a man is legally arrested for an offense, whatever is found upon his person *or in his control* which it is unlawful for him to have and which may be used to prove the offense may be seized and held as evidence in the prosecution."

Still, that assertion too was far from a claim that the "place" where one is arrested may be searched so long as the arrest is valid. Without explanation, however, the principle emerged in expanded form a few months later in

Agnello v. United States—although still by way of dictum:

"The right without a search warrant contemporaneously to search persons lawfully arrested while committing crime and to search the place where the arrest is made in order to find and seize things connected with the crime as its fruits or as the means by which it was committed, as well as weapons and other things to effect and escape from custody, is not to be doubted."

And in Marron v. United States, two years later, the dictum of *Agnello* appeared to be the foundation of the Court's decision. In that case federal agents had secured a search warrant authorizing the seizure of liquor and certain articles used in its manufacture. When they arrived at the premises to be searched, they saw "that the place was used for retailing and drinking intoxicating liquors." They proceeded to arrest the person in charge and to execute the warrant. In searching a closet for the items listed in the warrant they came across an incriminating ledger, concededly not covered by the warrant, which they also seized. The Court upheld the seizure of the ledger by holding that since the agents had made a lawful arrest, "[t]hey had a right without a warrant contemporaneously to search the place in order to find and seize the things used to carry on the criminal enterprise."

That the *Marron* opinion did not mean all that it seemed to say became evident, however, a few years later in Go-Bart Importing Co. v. United States and United States v. Lefkowitz. In each of those cases the opinion of the Court was written by Mr. Justice Butler, the author of the opinion in *Marron*. In *Go-Bart*, agents had searched the office of persons whom they had lawfully arrested, and had taken several papers from a desk, a safe, and other parts of the office. The Court noted that no crime had been committed in the agents' presence, and that although the agent in charge "had an abundance of information and time to swear out a valid search warrant, he failed to do so." In holding the search and seizure unlawful, the Court stated:

"Plainly the case before us is essentially different from Marron v. United States. There, officers executing a valid search warrant for intoxicating liquors found and arrested one Birdsall who in pursuance of a conspiracy was actually engaged in running a saloon. As an incident to the arrest they seized a ledger in a closet where the liquor or some of it was kept and some bills beside the cash register. These things were visible and accessible and in the offender's immediate custody. There was no threat of force or general search or rummaging of the place."

This limited characterization of *Marron* was reiterated in *Lefkowitz*, a case in which the Court held unlawful a search of desk drawers and a cabinet despite the fact that the search had accompanied a lawful arrest.

The limiting views expressed in *Go-Bart* and *Lefkowitz* were thrown to the winds, however, in Harris v. United States, decided in 1947. In that case, officers had obtained a warrant for Harris' arrest on the basis of his alleged involvement with the cashing and interstate transportation of a forged check. He was arrested in the living room of his four-room apartment, and in an attempt to recover two canceled checks thought to have been used in effecting the forgery, the officers undertook a thorough search of the entire apartment. Inside a desk drawer they found a sealed enveloped marked "George Harris, personal papers." The envelope, which was then torn open, was found to contain altered Selective Service documents, and those documents were used to secure Harris' conviction for violating the Selective Training and Service Act of 1940. The Court rejected Harris' Fourth Amendment claim, sustaining the search as "incident to arrest."

Only a year after *Harris*, however, the pendulum swung again. In Trupiano v. United States, agents raided the site of an illicit distillery, saw one of several conspirators operating the still, and arrested him, contemporaneously "seiz[ing] the illicit distillery." The Court held that the arrest and others made subsequently had been valid, but that the unexplained failure of the agents to procure a search warrant—in spite of the fact that they had had more than enough time before the raid to do so—rendered the search unlawful. The opinion stated:

"It is a cardinal rule that, in seizing goods and articles, law enforcement agents must secure and use search warrants wherever reasonably practicable.... This rule rests upon the desirability of having magistrates rather than police officers determine when searches and seizures are permissible and what limitations should be placed upon such activities.... To provide the necessary security against unreasonable intrusions upon the private lives of individuals, the framers of the Fourth Amendment required ad-

herence to judicial processes wherever possible. And subsequent history has confirmed the wisdom of that requirement....

"A search or seizure without a warrant as an incident to a lawful arrest has always been considered to be a strictly limited right. It grows out of the inherent necessities of the situation at the time of the arrest. But there must be something more in the way of necessity than merely a lawful arrest."

In 1950, two years after *Trupiano*, came United States v. Rabinowitz, the decision upon which California primarily relies in the case now before us. In *Rabinowitz*, federal authorities had been informed that the defendant was dealing in stamps bearing forged overprints. On the basis of that information they secured a warrant for his arrest, which they executed at his one-room business office. At the time of the arrest, the officers "searched the desk, safe, and file cabinets in the office for about an hour and a half" and seized 573 stamps with forged overprints. The stamps were admitted into evidence at the defendant's trial, and this Court affirmed his conviction, rejecting the contention that the warrantless search had been unlawful. The Court held that the search in its entirety fell within the principle giving law enforcement authorities "[t]he right 'to search the place where the arrest is made in order to find and seize things connected with the crime....'" *Harris* was regarded as "ample authority" for that conclusion. The opinion rejected the rule of *Trupiano* that "in seizing goods and articles, law enforcement agents must secure and use search warrants wherever reasonably practicable." The test, said the Court, "is not whether it is reasonable to procure a search warrant, but whether the search was reasonable."

Rabinowitz has come to stand for the proposition, *inter alia*, that a warrantless search "incident to a lawful arrest" may generally extend to the area that is considered to be in the "possession" or under the "control" of the person arrested. And it was on the basis of that proposition that the California courts upheld the search of the petitioner's entire house in this case. That doctrine, however, at least in the broad sense in which it was applied by the California courts in this case, can withstand neither historical nor rational analysis.

Even limited to its own facts, the *Rabinowitz* decision

was, as we have seen, hardly founded on an unimpeachable line of authority.... The approach taken in cases such as *Go-Bart*, *Lefkowitz*, and *Trupiano* was essentially disregarded by the *Rabinowitz* Court.

Nor is the rationale by which the State seeks here to sustain the search of the petitioner's house supported by a reasoned view of the background and purpose of the Fourth Amendment.... The Amendment was in large part a reaction to the general warrants and warrantless searches that had so alienated the colonists and had helped speed the movement for independence. In the scheme of the Amendment, therefore, the requirement that "no Warrants shall issue, but upon probable cause," plays a crucial part....

Only last Term in Terry v. Ohio, we emphasized that "the police must, whenever practicable, obtain advance judicial approval of searches and seizures through the warrant procedure," that "[t]he scope of a search must be 'strictly tied to and justified by' the circumstances which rendered its initiation permissible." The search undertaken by the officer in that "stop and frisk" case was sustained under that test, because it was no more than a "protective ... search for weapons."

A similar analysis underlies the "search incident to arrest" principle, and marks its proper extent. When an arrest is made, it is reasonable for the arresting officer to search the person arrested in order to remove any weapons that the latter might seek to use in order to resist arrest or effect his escape. Otherwise, the officer's safety might well be endangered, and the arrest itself frustrated. In addition, it is entirely reasonable for the arresting officer to search for and seize any evidence on the arrestee's person in order to prevent its concealment or destruction. And the area into which an arrestee might reach in order to grab a weapon or evidentiary items must, of course, be governed by a like rule. A gun on a table or in a drawer in front of one who is arrested can be as dangerous to the arresting officer as one concealed in the clothing of the person arrested. There is ample justification, therefore, for a search of the arrestee's person and the area "within his immediate control"—construing that phrase to mean the area from within which he might gain possession of a weapon or destructible evidence.

There is no comparable justification, however, for routinely searching any room other than that in which an arrest occurs—or, for that matter, for searching through all the desk drawers or other closed or concealed areas in that room itself. Such searches, in the absence of well-recognized exceptions, may be made only under the authority of a search warrant. The "adherence to judicial processes" mandated by the Fourth Amendment requires no less....

It is argued in the present case that it is "reasonable" to search a man's house when he is arrested in it. But that argument is founded on little more than a subjective view regarding the acceptability of certain sorts of police conduct, and not on considerations relevant to Fourth Amendment interests. Under such an unconfined analysis, Fourth Amendment protection in this area would approach the evaporation point. It is not easy to explain why, for instance, it is less subjectively "reasonable" to search a man's house when he is arrested on his front lawn—or just down the street—than it is when he happens to be in the house at the time of arrest....

It would be possible, of course, to draw a line between *Rabinowitz* and *Harris* on the one hand, and this case on the other. For *Rabinowitz* involved a single room, and *Harris* a four-room apartment, while in the case before us an entire house was searched. But such a distinction would be highly artificial. The rationale that allowed the searches and seizures in *Rabinowitz* and *Harris* would allow the searches and seizures in this case. No consideration relevant to the Fourth Amendment suggests any point of rational limitation, once the search is allowed to go beyond the area from which the person arrested might obtain weapons or evidentiary items. The only reasoned distinction is one between a search of the person arrested and the area within his reach on the one hand, and more extensive searches on the other.

The petitioner correctly points out that one result of decisions such as *Rabinowitz* and *Harris* is to give law enforcement officials the opportunity to engage in searches not justified by probable cause, by the simple expedient of arranging to arrest suspects at home rather than elsewhere. We do not suggest that the petitioner is necessarily correct in his assertion that such a strategy was utilized here, but the fact remains that had he been arrested earlier in the day, at his place of employment rather than at home, no search of his house could have been made without a search warrant....

Rabinowitz and *Harris* have been the subject of critical commentary for many years, and have been relied upon less and less in our own decisions. It is time, for the reasons we have stated, to hold that on their own facts, and insofar as the principles they stand for are inconsistent with those that we have endorsed today, they are no longer to be followed.

Application of sound Fourth Amendment principles to the facts of this case produces a clear result. The search here went far beyond the petitioner's person and the area from within which he might have obtained either a weapon or something that could have been used as evidence against him. There was no constitutional justification, in the absence of a search warrant, for extending the search beyond that area. The scope of the search was, therefore, "unreasonable" under the Fourth and Fourteenth Amendments and the petitioner's conviction cannot stand.

Reversed.

MR. JUSTICE WHITE, with whom MR. JUSTICE BLACK joins, dissenting.

Few areas of the law have been as subject to shifting constitutional standards over the last 50 years as that of the search "incident to an arrest." There has been a remarkable instability in this whole area, which has seen at least four major shifts in emphasis. Today's opinion makes an untimely fifth. In my view, the Court should not now abandon the old rule....

The rule which has prevailed, but for very brief or doubtful periods of aberration, is that a search incident to an arrest may extend to those areas under the control of the defendant and where items subject to constitutional seizure may be found. The justification for this rule must, under the language of the Fourth Amendment, lie in the reasonableness of the rule. The Amendment provides:

"The right of the people to be secure in their persons, houses, papers, and effects, against unreasonable searches and seizures, shall not be violated, and no Warrants shall issue, but upon probable cause, supported by Oath or affirmation, and particularly describing the place to be searched, and the persons or things to be seized."

In terms, then, the Court must decide whether a given search is reasonable. The Amendment does not proscribe "warrantless searches" but instead it proscribes "unreasonable searches" and this Court has never held nor does the majority today assert that warrantless searches are necessarily unreasonable.

Applying this reasonableness test to the area of searches incident to arrests, one thing is clear at the outset. Search of an arrested man and of the items within his immediate reach must in almost every case be reasonable. There is always a danger that the suspect will try to escape, seizing concealed weapons with which to overpower and injure the arresting officers, and there is a danger that he may destroy evidence vital to the prosecution. Circumstances in which these justifications would not apply are sufficiently rare that inquiry is not made into searches of this scope, which have been considered reasonable throughout.

The justifications which make such a search reasonable obviously do not apply to the search of areas to which the accused does not have ready physical access. This is not enough, however, to prove such searches unconstitutional. The Court has always held, and does not today deny, that when there is probable cause to search and it is "impracticable" for one reason or another to get a search warrant, then a warrantless search may be reasonable.... This is the case whether an arrest was made at the time of the search or not.

This is not to say that a search can be reasonable without regard to the probable cause to believe that seizable items are on the premises. But when there are exigent circumstances, and probable cause, then the search may be made without a warrant, reasonably. An arrest itself may often create an emergency situation making it impracticable to obtain a warrant before embarking on a related search. Again assuming that there is probable cause to search premises at the spot where a suspect is arrested, it seems to me unreasonable to require the police to leave the scene in order to obtain a search warrant when they are already legally there to make a valid arrest, and when there must almost always be a strong possibility that confederates of the arrested man will in the meanwhile remove the items for which the police have probable cause to search. This must so often be the case that it seems to me as unreasonable to require a warrant for a search of the premises as to require a warrant for search of the person and his very immediate surroundings.

This case provides a good illustration of my point that it is unreasonable to require police to leave the scene of an arrest in order to obtain a search warrant when they already have probable cause to search and there is a clear danger that the items for which they may reasonably search will be removed before they return with a warrant. Petitioner was arrested in his home after an arrest whose validity will be explored below, but which I will now assume was valid. There was doubtless probable cause not only to arrest petitioner, but also to search his house. He had obliquely admitted, both to a neighbor and to the owner of the burglarized store, that he had committed the burglary. In light of this, and the fact that the neighbor had seen other admittedly stolen property in petitioner's house, there was surely probable cause on which a warrant could have issued to search the house for the stolen coins. Moreover, had the police simply arrested petitioner, taken him off to the station house, and later returned with a warrant, it seems very likely that petitioner's wife, who in view of petitioner's generally garrulous nature must have known of the robbery, would have removed the coins. For the police to search the house while the evidence they had probable cause to search out and seize was still there cannot be considered unreasonable.

This line of analysis, supported by the precedents of this Court, hinges on two assumptions. One is that the arrest of petitioner without a valid warrant was constitutional as the majority assumes; the other is that the police were not required to obtain a search warrant in advance, even though they knew that the effect of the arrest might well be to alert petitioner's wife that the coins had better be removed soon. Thus it is necessary to examine the constitutionality of the arrest since if it was illegal, the exigent circumstances which it created may not, as the consequences of a lawless act, be used to justify the contemporaneous warrantless search. But for the arrest, the warrantless search may not be justified. And if circumstances can justify the warrantless arrest, it would be strange to say that the Fourth Amendment bars the warrantless search, regardless of the circumstances, since the invasion and disruption of a man's life and privacy which stem from his arrest are ordinarily far greater than the relatively minor intrusions attending a search of his premises. . . .

If circumstances so often require the warrantless arrest that the law generally permits it, the typical situation will find the arresting officers lawfully on the premises without arrest or search warrant. Like the majority, I would permit the police to search the person of a suspect and the area under his immediate control either to assure the safety of the officers or to prevent the destruction of evidence. And like the majority, I see nothing in the arrest alone furnishing probable cause for a search of any broader scope. However, where as here the existence of probable cause is independently established and would justify a warrant for a broader search for evidence, I would follow past cases and permit such a search to be carried out without a warrant, since the fact of arrest supplies an exigent circumstance justifying police action before the evidence can be removed, and also alerts the suspect to the fact of the search so that he can immediately seek judicial determination of probable cause in an adversary proceeding, and appropriate redress.

Justice Stewart's rationale for spatial limits corresponded to the Court's temporal limits; the search must match the justification. As searches incident to arrest could be conducted only to protect police, to remove means of escape, and to deter the loss of evidence, spatial limits as well as temporal limits were justified.

Loss of Evidence Searches

As a general principle of law, police can conduct warrantless searches and seizures to prevent the loss of evidence. Frequently officers come upon situations in which they must act quickly to preserve evidence that is in danger of being destroyed by, for example, a drug dealer about to flush narcotics down the toilet or an armed robber intent on throwing the weapon into the river. It would not be reasonable to require an officer faced with such a situation to find a judge to issue a search warrant. By the time the law enforcement official complied with this requirement, the evidence would be gone. Therefore, the Supreme Court has allowed police considerable latitude in acting without a warrant under such circumstances. But like other searches and seizures, evidence-loss searches are limited; the search and seizure may extend no farther than necessary to preserve the evidence from loss or destruction. Searches justified under evidence-loss conditions, therefore, may not be full evidence-seeking procedures, but must focus exclusively on the evidence at risk.

Cupp v. Murphy provides an example of such a search and seizure. In this case, the police, without any other justification, acted quickly to secure possible evidence of a murder, fearing that any delay would allow the suspect to dispose of the material.

Cupp v. Murphy

412 U.S. 291 (1973)

Vote: 7 *(Blackmun, Burger, Marshall, Powell, Rehnquist, Stewart, White)*

  2 *(Brennan, Douglas)*

Opinion of the Court: Stewart

Concurring opinions: Blackmun, Marshall, Powell

Opinions dissenting in part: Brennan, Douglas

The dead body of Daniel Murphy's wife was discovered in her Portland, Oregon, home. The cause of death was strangulation, and abrasions and lacerations were found on her neck and throat. There was no evidence of a break-in or robbery. When word of the murder reached Murphy, who was not living with his wife, he telephoned Portland police and volunteered to come to the police station for questioning. He was met by his attorney. A police officer noticed a dark spot on Murphy's finger, which he thought might be dried blood. Because evidence of violent acts can be found under fingernails, the officer asked Murphy if he would allow police to take scrapings from his nails. Murphy refused. In spite of Murphy's protests and without a warrant, police took the scrapings, which turned out to include traces of blood and skin cells from the victim and fibers from her nightgown. On the basis of this and other evidence, Murphy was convicted of second-degree murder. He challenged the evidence as a violation of his Fourth Amendment rights.

When the court of appeals agreed with Murphy, the state appealed to the Supreme Court.

MR. JUSTICE STEWART delivered the opinion of the Court.

The trial court, the Oregon Court of Appeals, and the Federal District Court all agreed that the police had probable cause to arrest the respondent at the time they detained him and scraped his fingernails. As the Oregon Court of Appeals said,

"At the time the detectives took these scrapings they knew:

"The bedroom in which the wife was found dead showed no signs of disturbance, which fact tended to indicate a killer known to the victim rather than to a burglar or other stranger.

"The decedent's son, the only other person in the house that night, did not have fingernails which could have made the lacerations observed on the victim's throat.

"The defendant and his deceased wife had had a stormy marriage and did not get along well.

"The defendant had, in fact, been at his home on the night of the murder. He left and drove back to central Oregon claiming that he did not enter the house or see his wife. He volunteered a great deal of information without being asked, yet expressed no concern or curiosity about his wife's fate."

The Court of Appeals for the Ninth Circuit did not disagree with the conclusion that the police had probable cause to make an arrest, nor do we.

It is also undisputed that the police did not obtain an arrest warrant or formally "arrest" the respondent, as that term is understood under Oregon law. The respondent was detained only long enough to take the fingernail scrapings, and was not formally "arrested" until approximately one month later. Nevertheless, the detention of the respondent against his will constituted a seizure of his person, and the Fourth Amendment guarantee of freedom from "unreasonable searches and seizures" is clearly implicated. "Nothing is more clear than that the Fourth Amendment was meant to prevent wholesale intrusions upon the personal security of our citizenry, whether these intrusions be termed 'arrests' or 'investigatory detentions.'"...

We believe this search was constitutionally permissible under the principles of Chimel v. California. *Chimel* stands in a long line of cases recognizing an exception to the warrant requirement when a search is incident to a valid arrest. The basis for this exception is that when an arrest is made, it is reasonable for a police officer to expect the arrestee to use any weapons he may have and to attempt to destroy any incriminating evidence then in his possession. The Court recognized in *Chimel* that the scope of a warrantless search must be commensurate with the rationale that excepts the search from the warrant requirement. Thus, a warrantless search incident to arrest, the Court held in *Chimel,* must be limited to the area "into which an arrestee might reach."

Where there is no formal arrest, as in the case before us, a person might well be less hostile to the police and less likely to take conspicuous, immediate steps to destroy incriminating evidence on his person. Since he knows he is going to be released, he might be likely instead to be concerned with diverting attention away from himself. Accordingly, we do not hold that a full *Chimel* search would have been justified in this case without a formal arrest and without a warrant. But the respondent was not subjected to such a search.

At the time Murphy was being detained at the station house, he was obviously aware of the detectives' suspicions. Though he did not have the full warning of official suspicion that a formal arrest provides, Murphy was sufficiently apprised of his suspected role in the crime to motivate him to attempt to destroy what evidence he could without attracting further attention. Testimony at trial indicated that after he refused to consent to the taking of fingernail samples, he put his hands behind his back and appeared to rub them together. He then put his hands in his pockets, and a "metallic sound, such as keys or change rattling" was heard. The rationale of *Chimel*, in these circumstances, justified the police in subjecting him to the very limited search necessary to preserve the highly evanescent evidence they found under his fingernails.

On the facts of this case, considering the existence of probable cause, the very limited intrusion undertaken incident to the station house detention, and the ready destructibility of the evidence, we cannot say that this search violated the Fourth and Fourteenth Amendments. Accordingly, the judgment of the Court of Appeals is reversed.

Reversed.

A more complicated set of issues is involved when the evidence about to be destroyed has been ingested, which can happen when the offense is related to drug possession or alcohol consumption. As it is inevitable that the body's natural processes will, with time, eliminate all traces of the drugs or alcohol, may the police act quickly without judicial authorization to retrieve such evidence? Intrusions into the human body are certainly more invasive than those into a home or office, and the privacy concerns discussed in Chapter 7 also come into play, but the government does have an interest in obtaining evidence for the prosecution of crime.

Rochin v. California, decided by the Supreme Court in 1952, provided a foundation for many cases in this area. With information that Rochin was selling drugs, three police officers went to his house, where he lived with his common-law wife, mother, and siblings. The officers, finding the front door ajar, went in, walked upstairs to Rochin's bedroom, and forced open the closed door. Rochin was sitting, partly dressed, on his bed where his wife was reclining. Noticing two capsules on the nightstand, the police asked Rochin about them, but, instead of answering, Rochin stuffed the capsules into his mouth. The officers jumped on him, trying to remove the capsules from his throat. When that failed, they handcuffed him and took him to a hospital, where doctors pumped his stomach. The doctors found the capsules, which contained a controlled substance, morphine.

Was this an appropriate way for police to obtain evidence? Grounding their decision in principles of due process of law, the justices expressed obvious disgust with the police procedures used here. This sense of outrage was so overwhelming that it led to the formulation of the shocked-conscience rule, the legal test used by the Court to judge the validity of investigatory procedures. Simply stated, if the way police obtain evidence shocks civilized people or causes unreasonable pain and discomfort, the principles of due process of law are violated. While *Rochin* articulated the standard to be used in such cases, it provided little guidance for assessing the constitutionality of intrusions into the human body that are less shocking and violent than stomach pumping.

Schmerber v. California (1966) asked the Court to consider whether police can force an individual to submit to a blood test administered in a hospital. Attorneys representing Schmerber asserted two major claims. First, they argued that blood tests violate the shocked-conscience rule because they are major intrusions into the body. Second, they claimed that the blood test constituted an illegal search and seizure of the body.[13]

Writing for the 5-4 Court, the generally liberal William J. Brennan, Jr., dismissed the first argument, noting that the procedure did not violate the *Rochin* doctrine because Schmerber's blood test was a routine, minor intrusion, conducted in the safety of a hospital by trained medical staff. Justice Brennan, however, expended some effort in dismissing Schmerber's Fourth Amendment argument. He began by raising the following fundamental question: Was the search—the blood test—reasonable? Based on two factors, he concluded that it was. Police had probable cause because they had observed that Schmerber exhibited symptoms of drunkenness, and the loss-of-evidence exception was in effect. If police had taken the time to obtain a warrant to sample Schmerber's blood, the evidence would have vanished.

Together, *Schmerber* and *Rochin* hold that law enforcement officials may, with good cause but without a warrant, order minor and safe intrusions into the human body to obtain evidence that would otherwise be destroyed. But in attempting to follow this mandate, police faced a problem: besides forced

stomach pumps, what constitutes a major intrusion?

The Court addressed this question in *Winston v. Lee* (1985), which stemmed from a shoot-out in a robbery attempt in which both the store owner and the perpetrator were wounded. Rudolph Lee had a gunshot wound in the chest when he was apprehended. Prosecutors sought a court order to have Lee undergo surgery to have the bullet removed, as it would prove he was the man shot by the store owner. Lee's x-rays showed that the bullet could not be removed except by an operation under general anesthesia, to which his attorneys objected. On appeal to the Supreme Court, the justices unanimously concluded that the compulsory surgery (even with a court order) would constitute an unreasonable search and seizure in violation of the Fourth Amendment. They had several reasons. First, the operation would be a severe intrusion on Lee's privacy interests. Second, the uncertain dangers of an operation under general anesthesia made the procedure presumptively unreasonable. Third, the state, while able to show that obtaining the bullet would be helpful to a prosecution, was unable to demonstrate that it was absolutely necessary. Still, the Court made clear that it would not always strike down such warrantless incursions into the body; it was just that it did not find the procedure at issue here to be reasonable.

Despite the differences of the degree of intrusion into the body, *Rochin, Schmerber,* and *Lee* have two features in common. First, they pertained to searches that the *government* wanted to conduct. Second, these cases involved suspects who police had reason to believe had committed crimes the evidence of which would be lost if action were not taken. In 1989 the Court considered a kind of bodily search that did not meet either of these criteria: drug screening or testing programs for job applicants or employees. Under some of these programs, employees must have their urine checked for the presence of drugs, even though the employer has no reason to suspect illegal drug use on the part of particular individuals.

13. As we saw in *Rochin,* the gathering of evidence from the body also is regulated by the Fifth Amendment's Due Process Clause. In *Schmerber,* attorneys made this additional claim: that blood tests violate the Fifth Amendment's Self-Incrimination Clause because prosecutors used Schmerber's blood, which contained traces of alcohol, against him. Brennan dismissed the self-incrimination claim, noting that the Fifth Amendment covers only "testimony," not physical items.

Would the Court uphold these programs? The *Schmerber* ruling provides some ammunition for employers as it allows minor incursions into the body, a category into which urine tests probably fall. Mitigating against this position, however, are two important ideas. One, as we have already indicated, is that employers lack cause to believe a crime has been committed by specific employees. Second, under *Katz*, employers may be intruding into a reasonable privacy expectation held by their employees. That argument is put forward by those who object to drug-testing programs. Consider these competing positions as you read *National Treasury Employees Union v. Von Raab*, one of two 1989 cases in which the Rehnquist Court addressed the constitutionality of drug-testing programs.

National Treasury Employees Union v. Von Raab

489 U.S. 656 (1989)
Vote: 5 (Blackmun, Kennedy, O'Connor, Rehnquist, White)
  4 (Brennan, Marshall, Scalia, Stevens)
Opinion of the Court: Kennedy
Dissenting opinions: Marshall, Scalia

The U.S. Customs Service is a bureau of the Department of the Treasury. Among its responsibilities is "the interdiction and seizure of contraband, including illegal drugs." Around the time this case was initiated, customs agents were annually seizing about $9 billion in illegal drugs. Because the job is dangerous, many customs operatives are required to carry guns.

In December 1985, with the illegal drug trade growing larger and more violent, the commissioner of the Customs Service created a task force to consider the possibility of creating a drug-screening program for service employees. Although the commissioner believed that his bureau was "largely drug-free," he noted that "unfortunately no segment of society is immune from the threat of illegal drug use." He further stated that "there is no room in the Customs Service for those who break the laws prohibiting the possession and use of illegal drugs."

The task force recommended creation of a drug-screening program through urinalysis. In 1986 the commissioner announced the establishment of a drug-screening program for all job applicants. He also noted that drug tests would be made a condition of employment for positions that met the following criteria: (1) the position involved direct drug "interdiction" or enforcement of federal laws; (2) the position required the employee to carry weapons; and (3) the position required the employee to handle "classified" material, which the commissioner thought could "fall into the hands of smugglers if accessible to employees who, by reason of their illegal drug use, are susceptible to bribery or blackmail."

The government believed that this drug-testing and -screening program was a reasonable and minor intrusion into the bodies of its employees. A union representing some federal employees thought otherwise. It challenged the programs as an unreasonable search and seizure, infringing on the right to privacy and conducted without sufficient probable and individualized cause.

The same day the Court heard arguments in this case, it also heard *Skinner v. Railway Labor Executives' Association*. While *Skinner* involved a drug-testing program, it was distinct from that implemented by the Customs Service. The Federal Railroad Administration required that employees take a breath or urine test if they were involved in a train accident or other serious incident. In a 7–2 decision, the Court upheld this program in part because of the government's interest in preventing train accidents, some of which had been caused by drug and alcohol use by employees. But would the Court uphold the program at issue in *Von Raab*, a "suspicionless" program that authorized drug testing in the absence of any evidence that a crime had been committed?

JUSTICE KENNEDY delivered the opinion of the Court.

We granted certiorari to decide whether it violates the Fourth Amendment for the United States Customs Service to require a urinalysis test from employees who seek transfer or promotion to certain positions....

In *Skinner v. Railway Labor Executives Assn.,* decided today, we hold that federal regulations requiring employees of private railroads to produce urine samples for chemical testing implicate the Fourth Amendment, as those tests invade reasonable expectations of privacy. Our earlier cases have settled that the Fourth Amendment protects individuals from unreasonable searches conducted by the Government, even when the Government acts as an employer, and, in view of our holding in *Railway Labor Executives* that urine tests are searches, it follows that the Customs Service's drug-testing program must meet the reasonableness requirement of the Fourth Amendment.

While we have often emphasized, and reiterate today, that a search must be supported, as a general matter, by a warrant issued upon probable cause, our decision in *Railway Labor Executives* reaffirms the longstanding principle that neither a warrant nor probable cause, nor, indeed, any measure of individualized suspicion, is an indispensable component of reasonableness in every circumstance. As we note in *Railway Labor Executives,* our cases establish that where a Fourth Amendment intrusion serves special governmental needs, beyond the normal need for law enforcement, it is necessary to balance the individual's privacy expectations against the Government's interests to determine whether it is impractical to require a warrant or some level of individualized suspicion in the particular context.

It is clear that the Customs Service's drug-testing program is not designed to serve the ordinary needs of law enforcement. Test results may not be used in a criminal prosecution of the employee without the employee's consent. The purposes of the program are to deter drug use among those eligible for promotion to sensitive positions within the Service and to prevent the promotion of drug users to those positions. These substantial interests, no less than the Government's concern for safe rail transportation at issue in *Railway Labor Executives,* present a special need that may justify departure from the ordinary warrant and probable cause requirements.

Petitioners do not contend that a warrant is required by the balance of privacy and governmental interests in this context, nor could any such contention withstand scrutiny. We have recognized before that requiring the Government to procure a warrant for every work-related intrusion "would conflict with 'the common-sense realization that government offices could not function if every employment decision became a constitutional matter.'"... Even if Customs Service employees are more likely to be familiar with the procedures required to obtain a warrant than most other Government workers, requiring a warrant in this context would serve only to divert valuable agency resources from the Service's primary mission. The Customs Service has been entrusted with pressing responsibilities, and its mission would be compromised if it were required to seek search warrants in connection with routine, yet sensitive, employment decisions.

Furthermore, a warrant would provide little or nothing in the way of additional protection of personal privacy. A warrant serves primarily to advise the citizen that an intrusion is authorized by law and limited in its permissible scope and to interpose a neutral magistrate between the citizen and the law enforcement officer "engaged in the often competitive enterprise of ferreting out crime."... But in the present context, "the circumstances justifying toxicological testing and the permissible limits of such intrusions are defined narrowly and specifically ..., and doubtless are well known to covered employees." Under the Customs program, every employee who seeks a transfer to a covered position knows that he must take a drug test, and is likewise aware of the procedures the Service must follow in administering the test. A covered employee is simply not subject "to the discretion of the official in the field."... The process becomes automatic when the employee elects to apply for, and thereafter pursue, a covered position. Because the Service does not make a discretionary determination to search based on a judgment that certain conditions are present, there are simply "no special facts for a neutral magistrate to evaluate."...

Even where it is reasonable to dispense with the warrant requirement in the particular circumstances, a search ordinarily must be based on probable cause. Our cases teach, however, that the probable-cause standard "'is peculiarly related to criminal investigations.'"... In particular, the traditional probable-cause standard may be unhelpful in ana-lyzing the reasonableness of routine administrative func-tions, especially where the government seeks to prevent the development of hazardous conditions or to detect vio-lations that rarely generate articulable grounds for searching any particular place or person.... Our precedents have set-tled that, in certain limited circumstances, the Govern-ment's need to discover such latent or hidden conditions, or to prevent their development, is sufficiently compelling to justify the intrusion on privacy entailed by conducting such searches without any measure of individualized suspicion. We think the Government's need to conduct the suspicion-less searches required by the Customs program outweighs the privacy interests of employees engaged directly in drug interdiction, and of those who otherwise are required to carry firearms.

The Customs Service is our Nation's first line of defense against one of the greatest problems affecting the health and welfare of our population....

Many of the Service's employees are often exposed to this criminal element and to the controlled substances it seeks to smuggle into the country. The physical safety of these employees may be threatened, and many may be tempted not only by bribes from the traffickers with whom they deal, but also by their own access to vast sources of valuable contraband seized and controlled by the Service. The Commissioner indicated below that "Customs [o]f-ficers have been shot, stabbed, run over, dragged by auto-mobiles, and assaulted with blunt objects while performing their duties." At least nine officers have died in the line of duty since 1974. He also noted that Customs officers have been the targets of bribery by drug smugglers on numer-ous occasions, and several have been removed from the Service for accepting bribes and for other integrity vio-lations....

It is readily apparent that the Government has a com-pelling interest in ensuring that front-line interdiction per-sonnel are physically fit, and have unimpeachable integrity and judgment.... This national interest in self-protection could be irreparably damaged if those charged with safe-guarding it were, because of their own drug use, unsympa-thetic to their mission of interdicting narcotics....

Against these valid public interests we must weigh the interference with individual liberty that results from re-

quiring these classes of employees to undergo a urine test. The interference with individual privacy that results from the collection of a urine sample for subsequent chemical analysis could be substantial in some circumstances. We have recognized, however, that the "operational realities of the workplace" may render entirely reasonable certain work-related intrusions by supervisors and co-workers that might be viewed as unreasonable in other contexts. While these operational realities will rarely affect an employee's expectations of privacy with respect to searches of his person, or of personal effects that the employee may bring to the workplace, it is plain that certain forms of public em-ployment may diminish privacy expectations even with re-spect to such personal searches....

We think Customs employees who are directly involved in the interdiction of illegal drugs or who are required to carry firearms in the line of duty likewise have a diminished expectation of privacy in respect to the intrusions occa-sioned by a urine test. Unlike most private citizens or government employees in general, employees involved in drug interdiction reasonably should expect effective in-quiry into their fitness and probity. Much the same is true of employees who are required to carry firearms. Because successful performance of their duties depends uniquely on their judgment and dexterity, these employees cannot rea-sonably expect to keep from the Service personal infor-mation that bears directly on their fitness. While reason-able tests designed to elicit this information doubtless in-fringe some privacy expectations, we do not believe these expectations outweigh the Government's compelling inter-ests in safety and in the integrity of our borders....

In sum, we believe the Government has demonstrated that its compelling interests in safeguarding our borders and the public safety outweigh the privacy expectations of employees who seek to be promoted to positions that di-rectly involve the interdiction of illegal drugs or that re-quire the incumbent to carry a firearm....

We hold that the suspicionless testing of employees who apply for promotion to positions directly involving the interdiction of illegal drugs, or to positions that require the incumbent to carry a firearm, is reasonable. The Govern-ment's compelling interests in preventing the promotion of drug users to positions where they might endanger the in-tegrity of our Nation's borders or the life of the citizenry outweigh the privacy interests of those who seek promotion to these positions, who enjoy a diminished expectation of privacy by virtue of the special, and obvious, physical and ethical demands of those positions....

JUSTICE SCALIA, with whom JUSTICE STEVENS joins, dissenting.

Until today this Court had upheld a bodily search separate from arrest and without individualized suspicion of wrongdoing only with respect to prison inmates, relying upon the uniquely dangerous nature of that environment. Today, in *Skinner*, we allow a less intrusive bodily search of railroad employees involved in train accidents. I joined the Court's opinion there because the demonstrated frequency of drug and alcohol use by the targeted class of employees, and the demonstrated connection between such use and grave harm, rendered the search a reasonable means of protecting society. I decline to join the Court's opinion in the present case because neither frequency of use nor connection to harm is demonstrated or even likely. In my view the Customs Service rules are a kind of immolation of privacy and human dignity in symbolic opposition to drug use.

... [T]he substantive analysis of our opinion today in *Skinner* begins, "[t]he problem of alcohol use on American railroads is as old as the industry itself," and goes on to cite statistics concerning that problem and the accidents it causes, including a 1979 study finding that "23% of the operating personnel were 'problem drinkers.'"

The Court's opinion in the present case, however, will be searched in vain for real evidence of a real problem that will be solved by urine testing of Customs Service employees. Instead, there are assurances that "[t]he Customs Service is our Nation's first line of defense against one of the greatest problems affecting the health and welfare of our population"; that "[m]any of the Service's employees are often exposed to [drug smugglers] and to the controlled substances [they seek] to smuggle into the country"; that "Customs officers have been the targets of bribery by drug smugglers on numerous occasions, and several have been removed from the Service for accepting bribes and other integrity violations."... To paraphrase Churchill, all this contains much that is obviously true, and much that is rele-

vant; unfortunately, what is obviously true is not relevant, and what is relevant is not obviously true. The only pertinent points, it seems to me, are supported by nothing but speculation, and not very plausible speculation at that. It is not apparent to me that a Customs Service employee who uses drugs is significantly more likely to be bribed by a drug smuggler, any more than a Customs Service employee who wears diamonds is significantly more likely to be bribed by a diamond smuggler—unless, perhaps, the addiction to drugs is so severe, and requires so much money to maintain, that it would be detectable even without benefit of a urine test....

What is absent in the Government's justifications—notably absent, revealingly absent, and as far as I am concerned dispositively absent—is the recitation of *even a single instance* in which any of the speculated horribles actually occurred: an instance, that is, in which the cause of bribetaking, or of poor aim, or of unsympathetic law enforcement, or of compromise of classified information, was drug use. Although the Court points out that several employees have in the past been removed from the Service for accepting bribes and other integrity violations, and that at least nine officers have died in the line of duty since 1974, there is no indication whatever that these incidents were related to drug use by Service employees....

The Court's response to this lack of evidence is that "[t]here is little reason to believe that American workplaces are immune from [the] pervasive social problem" of drug abuse. Perhaps such a generalization would suffice if the workplace at issue could produce such catastrophic social harm that no risk whatever is tolerable—the secured areas of a nuclear power plant, for example. But if such a generalization suffices to justify demeaning bodily searches, without particularized suspicion, to guard against the bribing or blackmailing of a law enforcement agent, or the careless use of a firearm, then the Fourth Amendment has become frail protection indeed....

There is only one apparent basis that sets the testing at issue here apart from all these other situations—but it is not a basis upon which the Court is willing to rely. I do not believe for a minute that the driving force behind these drug-testing rules was any of the feeble justifications put forward by counsel here and accepted by the Court. The only plausible explanation, in my view, is what the Commissioner himself offered in the concluding sentence of his memorandum to Customs Service employees announcing the program: "Implementation of the drug screening program would set an important example in our country's struggle with this most serious threat to our national health and security."... What better way to show that the Government is serious about its "war on drugs" than to subject its employees on the front line of that war to this invasion of their privacy and affront to their dignity? To be sure, there is only a slight chance that it will prevent some serious public harm resulting from Service employee drug use, but it will show to the world that the Service is "clean," and—most important of all—will demonstrate the determination of the Government to eliminate this scourge of our society! I think it obvious that this justification is unacceptable; that the impairment of individual liberties cannot be the means of making a point; that symbolism, even symbolism for so worthy a cause as the abolition of unlawful drugs, cannot validate an otherwise unreasonable search.

There is irony in the Government's citation, in support of its position, of Justice Brandeis' statement in *Olmstead v. United States* (1928) that "[f]or good or for ill, [our Government] teaches the whole people by its example." Brandeis was there *dissenting* from the Court's admission of evidence obtained through an unlawful Government wiretap. He was not praising the Government's example of vigor and enthusiasm in combating crime, but condemning its example that "the end justifies the means." An even more apt quotation from that famous Brandeis dissent would have been the following:

"[I]t is ... immaterial that the intrusion was in aid of law enforcement. Experience should teach us to be most on our guard to protect liberty when the Government's purposes are beneficent. Men born to freedom are naturally alert to repel invasion of their liberty by evil-minded rulers. The greatest dangers to liberty lurk in insidious encroachment by men of zeal, well-meaning but without understanding."

Those who lose because of the lack of understanding that begot the present exercise in symbolism are not just the Customs Service employees, whose dignity is thus offended, but all of us—who suffer a coarsening of our national manners that ultimately give the Fourth Amendment its content, and who become subject to the administration of federal officials whose respect for our privacy can hardly be greater than the small respect they have been taught to have for their own.

At first glance, the Rehnquist Court's logic in *Von Raab* and *Skinner* appears not so different from the Warren Court's in *Schmerber*: the intrusion was minor, and the interest of the government was compelling enough to outweigh the privacy claim. But the dissents point to important distinctions in these cases. Justices Brennan (who wrote the majority opinion in *Schmerber*) and Marshall refused to join the majority in either *Von Raab* or *Skinner*. In their view, *both* testing programs involved suspicionless intrusions into the body; unlike *Schmerber*, officials did not have to show probable cause to believe that a particular *individual* committed a crime. Justices Scalia and Stevens joined the majority opinion in *Skinner* but not in *Von Raab*. To them, the drug-testing program in *Skinner* at least rested on some notion of cause: drug tests were to be performed only in the event of suspicion or an accident. But, as Scalia's dissent indicates, he believed that the *Von Raab* program was defective because it lacked even a general element of cause. He wrote, "What is absent in the Government's justifications ... is the recitation of *even a single instance* in which any of the speculated horribles actually occurred."

Consent Searches

As a rule, law enforcement officials can conduct searches upon consent. Like most general principles of law, however, the Court has placed constraints on such searches. To be considered valid, consent searches must satisfy two criteria. First, permission must be freely and voluntarily granted. Second, the individual granting consent must have the authority to do so.

The required voluntary nature of the consent means that permission cannot be granted as a result of coercion. If police extract consent by actual or threatened physical force or by means of trickery, the permission is invalid and so is the resulting search.

For example, *Bumper v. North Carolina* (1968) involved investigation of a rape in which Bumper was the primary suspect. Police went to his house and told his grandmother, with whom he lived, that they had a search warrant when in fact they did not. Believing the police, Bumper's grandmother granted her permission for the search, which yielded a .22-caliber rifle used in the rape. At the trial the state asserted that the search and seizure were valid because permission was granted. Bumper's attorney argued otherwise, noting that police tricked and, in essence, coerced the grandmother to give consent. The U.S. Supreme Court agreed with Bumper's counsel. The justices found the grant of consent coercive and therefore not voluntary.

The second requirement is that only an authorized person can give permission to search. Clearly, the person who owns or leases a house or apartment has the proper authority to grant police permission to search. But who else may rightfully give permission? What about a third party: a hotel clerk, a chambermaid, or a roommate? Can these individuals give their consent to search another's property?

In two cases, decided ten years apart, the Supreme Court attempted to deal with these questions. In *Stoner v. California* (1964), the justices considered a disputed police search of a hotel room. The case involved a grocery store robbery. At the scene of the crime police found a checkbook belonging to Joey Stoner. The checkbook showed payments made to a local hotel. The desk clerk there told police that Stoner was not in his room. Police then asked and received permission from the clerk to search the room, where they found substantial evidence of Stoner's participation in the robbery.

Was the search of Stoner's hotel room valid? According to the Supreme Court it was not because the desk clerk did not have the proper authority to grant police permission to enter the room. In the absence of any waiver of that right, a person who rents or leases property is the only one who may grant permission to enter it.[14] The hotel room was an area in which Stoner had an expectation of privacy, and a warrantless intrusion into that room could not be authorized by anyone but Stoner.

Here the Court clearly stated that only an owner, or renter, or leaser—not a cleaner, landlord, or clerk—can give permission for a search. But what about the other occupants of the rooms or houses? Can they give (or withhold) consent? In *United States v. Matlock* (1974), Justice White concluded that a co-occupant of a room could give (or refuse) police consent to search the area.[15] Writing for the Court, he stated:

When the prosecution seeks to justify a warrantless search by proof of voluntary consent, it is not limited to proof that consent was given by the defendant, but may show that permission to search was obtained from a third party who possessed common authority over or other sufficient relationship to the premises or effects sought to be inspected.[16]

In general, then, police may search when they have obtained permission to do so and they apply two tests: permission must be truly voluntary, and the individual from whom police obtain consent must have authority over the premises.

Safety Searches

As the Warren Court expanded the rights of the criminally accused during the 1960s, police throughout the United States complained not only that the justices hampered their ability to conduct investigations, but also that the new rules placed their lives in jeopardy—they could no longer conduct full searches unless they made an arrest. To comply with existing law while ensuring their own safety,

14. Several exceptions to this general rule exist; for example, some tenant-landlord agreements contain clauses that allow superintendents to search residences or give permission to police to do so.

15. Generally minors do not have this authority.

16. This position was further broadened by the Court in *Illinois v. Rodriguez* (1990). The Court ruled that consent searches may be valid when police reasonably believe the person granting consent has common authority over the premises, but in fact does not.

police began using "stop and frisk" searches. Rather than doing a full search, police "patted down" individuals they thought to be dangerous. Did such activity fall beyond the purview of the Fourth Amendment? In *Terry v. Ohio* the Warren Court addressed this issue.

Terry v. Ohio

392 U.S. 1 (1968)

Vote: 8 (Black, Brennan, Fortas, Harlan, Marshall, Stewart, Warren, White)

1 (Douglas)

Opinion of the Court: Warren

Concurring opinions: Black, Harlan, White

Dissenting opinion: Douglas

While Officer-Detective Martin McFadden, a thirty-nine-year veteran of the police force, patrolled in plainclothes in downtown Cleveland one afternoon, he observed two men he had never seen before. As he watched, the two paced along the street, "pausing to stare in the same store window roughly 24 times." McFadden also observed a third man join the two briefly. Acting on his suspicion that the men were casing the store for a robbery, McFadden approached the trio and identified himself as a police officer, at which point they began whispering to each other. McFadden then frisked Terry, and, feeling a pistol in his pocket, had him remove his coat. McFadden also found a gun on another man and arrested them on concealed weapons charges.

In trial court, the prosecuting attorney argued that McFadden's warrantless search was incident to arrest. While the judge rejected that plea, noting that no probable cause existed, he held for the state, ruling that officers have the right to stop and frisk when they believe their lives are in jeopardy.

MR. CHIEF JUSTICE WARREN delivered the opinion of the Court.

This case presents serious questions concerning the role of the Fourth Amendment in the confrontation on the street between the citizen and the policeman investigating suspicious circumstances. . . .

. . . We have recently held that "the Fourth Amendment protects people, not places," and wherever an individual may harbor a reasonable "expectation of privacy," he is entitled to be free from unreasonable governmental intrusion. . . . Unquestionably petitioner was entitled to the protection of the Fourth Amendment as he walked down the street in Cleveland. The question is whether in all the circumstances of this on-the-street encounter, his right to personal security was violated by an unreasonable search and seizure.

We would be less than candid if we did not acknowledge that this question thrusts to the fore difficult and troublesome issues regarding a sensitive area of police activity—issues which have never before been squarely presented to this Court. Reflective of the tensions involved are the practical and constitutional arguments pressed with great vigor on both sides of the public debate over the power of the police to "stop and frisk"—as it is sometimes euphemistically termed—suspicious persons.

On the one hand, it is frequently argued that in dealing with the rapidly unfolding and often dangerous situations on city streets the police are in need of an escalating set of flexible responses, graduated in relation to the amount of information they possess. For this purpose it is urged that distinctions should be made between a "stop" and an "arrest" (or a "seizure" of a person), and between a "frisk" and a "search." Thus, it is argued, the police should be allowed to "stop" a person and detain him briefly for questioning upon suspicion that he may be connected with criminal activity. Upon suspicion that the person may be armed, the police should have the power to "frisk" him for weapons. If the "stop" and the "frisk" give rise to probable cause to believe that the suspect has committed a crime, then the police should be empowered to make a formal "arrest," and a full incident "search" of the person. This scheme is justified in part upon the notion that a "stop" and a "frisk" amount to a mere "minor inconvenience and petty indignity," which can properly be imposed upon the citizen in the interest of effective law enforcement on the basis of a police officer's suspicion.

On the other side the argument is made that the authority of the police must be strictly circumscribed by the law of arrest and search as it has developed to date in the traditional jurisprudence of the Fourth Amendment. It is contended with some force that there is not—and cannot be—a variety of police activity which does not depend solely upon the voluntary cooperation of the citizen and yet which stops short of an arrest based upon probable cause to make such an arrest. The heart of the Fourth Amendment, the argument runs, is a severe requirement of specific justification for any intrusion upon protected personal security, coupled with a highly developed system of judicial controls to enforce upon the agents of the State the commands of the Constitution. Acquiescence by the courts in the compulsion inherent in the field interrogation practices at issue here, it is urged, would constitute an abdication of judicial control over, and indeed an encouragement of, substantial interference with liberty and personal security by police officers whose judgment is necessarily colored by their primary involvement in "the often competitive enterprise of ferreting out crime." This, it is argued, can only serve to exacerbate police-community tensions in the crowded centers of our Nation's cities. . . .

Having thus roughly sketched the perimeters of the constitutional debate over the limits on police investigative conduct in general and the background against which this case presents itself, we turn our attention to the quite narrow question posed by the facts before us: whether it is always unreasonable for a policeman to seize a person and subject him to a limited search for weapons unless there is probable cause for an arrest. Given the narrowness of this question, we have no occasion to canvass in detail the constitutional limitations upon the scope of a policeman's power when he confronts a citizen without probable cause to arrest him.

Our first task is to establish at what point in this encounter the Fourth Amendment becomes relevant. That is, we must decide whether and when Officer McFadden "seized" Terry and whether and when he conducted a "search." There is some suggestion in the use of such terms as "stop" and "frisk" that such police conduct is outside the purview of the Fourth Amendment because neither action rises to the level of a "search" or "seizure" within the meaning of the Constitution. We emphatically reject this notion. It is quite plain that the Fourth Amendment governs "seizures" of the person which do not eventuate in a trip to the station house and prosecution for crime—"arrests" in traditional terminology. It must be recognized that whenever a police officer accosts an individual and restrains his freedom to walk away, he has "seized" that person. And it is nothing less than sheer torture of the English language to suggest that a careful exploration of the outer surfaces of a person's clothing all over his or her body in an attempt to find weapons is not a "search." Moreover, it is simply fantastic to urge that such a procedure performed in public by a policeman while the citizen stands helpless, perhaps facing a wall with his hands raised, is a "petty indignity." It is a serious intrusion upon the sanctity of the person, which may inflict great indignity and arouse strong resentment, and it is not to be undertaken lightly.

The danger in the logic which proceeds upon distinctions between a "stop" and an "arrest," or "seizure" of the person, and between a "frisk" and a "search" is twofold. It seeks to isolate from constitutional scrutiny the initial stages of the contact between the policeman and the citizen. And by suggesting a rigid all-or-nothing model of justification and regulation under the Amendment, it obscures the utility of limitations upon the scope, as well as the initiation, of police action as a means of constitutional regulation. This Court has held in the past that a search which is reasonable at its inception may violate the Fourth Amendment by virtue of its intolerable intensity and scope. . . .

The distinctions of classical "stop-and-frisk" theory thus serve to divert attention from the central inquiry under the Fourth Amendment—the reasonableness in all the circumstances of the particular governmental invasion of a citizen's personal security. "Search" and "seizure" are not talismans. We therefore reject the notions that the Fourth Amendment does not come into play at all as a limitation upon police conduct if the officers stop short of something called a "technical arrest" or a "full-blown search."

In this case there can be no question, then, that Officer McFadden "seized" petitioner and subjected him to a "search" when he took hold of him and patted down the outer surfaces of his clothing. We must decide whether at that point it was reasonable for Officer McFadden to have interfered with petitioner's personal security as he did. . . .

. . . In order to assess the reasonableness of Officer McFadden's conduct as a general proposition, it is necessary "first to focus upon the governmental interest which allegedly justifies official intrusion upon the constitutionally protected interests of the private citizen," for there is "no ready test for determining reasonableness other than by balancing the need to search or seize against the invasion which the search or seizure entails." And in justifying the particular intrusion the police officer must be able to point to specific and articulable facts which, taken together with rational inferences from those facts, reasonably warrant that intrusion. The scheme of the Fourth Amendment becomes meaningful only when it is assured that at some point the conduct of those charged with enforcing the laws can be subjected to the more detached, neutral scrutiny of a judge who must evaluate the reasonableness of a particular search or seizure in light of the particular circumstances. And in making that assessment it is imperative that the facts be judged against an objective standard: would the facts available to the officer at the moment of the seizure or the search "warrant a man of reasonable caution in the belief" that the action taken was appropriate? . . .

Applying these principles to this case, we consider first the nature and extent of the governmental interests involved. One general interest is of course that of effective crime prevention and detection; it is this interest which underlies the recognition that a police officer may in appropriate circumstances and in an appropriate manner approach a person for purposes of investigating possibly criminal behavior even though there is no probable cause to make an arrest. It was this legitimate investigative function Officer McFadden was discharging when he decided to approach petitioner and his companions. He had observed Terry, Chilton, and Katz go through a series of acts, each of them perhaps innocent in itself, but which taken together warranted further investigation. There is nothing unusual in two men standing together on a street corner, perhaps waiting for someone. Nor is there anything suspicious about people in such circumstances strolling up and down the street, singly or in pairs. Store windows, moreover, are

made to be looked in. But the story is quite different where, as here, two men hover about a street corner for an extended period of time, at the end of which it becomes apparent that they are not waiting for anyone or anything; where these men pace alternately along an identical route, pausing to stare in the same store window roughly 24 times; where each completion of this route is followed immediately by a conference between the two men on the corner; where they are joined in one of these conferences by a third man who leaves swiftly; and where the two men finally follow the third and rejoin him a couple of blocks away. It would have been poor police work indeed for an officer of 30 years' experience in the detection of thievery from stores in this same neighborhood to have failed to investigate this behavior further.

The crux of this case, however, is not the propriety of Officer McFadden's taking steps to investigate petitioner's suspicious behavior, but rather, whether there was justification for McFadden's invasion of Terry's personal security by searching him for weapons in the course of that investigation. We are now concerned with more than the governmental interest in investigating crime; in addition, there is the more immediate interest of the police officer in taking steps to assure himself that the person with whom he is dealing is not armed with a weapon that could unexpectedly and fatally be used against him. Certainly it would be unreasonable to require that police officers take unnecessary risks in the performance of their duties. American criminals have a long tradition of armed violence, and every year in this country many law enforcement officers are killed in the line of duty, and thousands more are wounded. . . .

In view of these facts, we cannot blind ourselves to the need for law enforcement officers to protect themselves and other prospective victims of violence in situations where they may lack probable cause for an arrest. When an officer is justified in believing that the individual whose suspicious behavior he is investigating at close range is armed and presently dangerous to the officer or to others, it would appear to be clearly unreasonable to deny the officer the power to take necessary measures to determine whether the person is in fact carrying a weapon and to neutralize the threat of physical harm. . . .

We conclude that the revolver seized from Terry was

properly admitted in evidence against him. At the time he seized petitioner and searched him for weapons, Officer McFadden had reasonable grounds to believe that petitioner was armed and dangerous, and it was necessary for the protection of himself and others to take swift measures to discover the true facts and neutralize the threat of harm if it materialized. The policeman carefully restricted his search to what was appropriate to the discovery of the particular items which he sought. Each case of this sort will, of course, have to be decided on its own facts. We merely hold today that where a police officer observes unusual conduct which leads him reasonably to conclude in light of his experience that criminal activity may be afoot and that the persons with whom he is dealing may be armed and presently dangerous, where in the course of investigating this behavior he identifies himself as a policeman and makes reasonable inquiries, and where nothing in the initial stages of the encounter serves to dispel his reasonable fear for his own or others' safety, he is entitled for the protection of himself and others in the area to conduct a carefully limited search of the outer clothing of such persons in an attempt to discover weapons which might be used to assault him.

Such a search is a reasonable search under the Fourth Amendment, and any weapons seized may properly be introduced in evidence against the person from whom they were taken.

Affirmed.

Scholars, lawyers, judges, and others concerned with the process of criminal justice regard *Terry v. Ohio* as one of the Supreme Court's more significant decisions. Now that you have had an opportunity to read the facts of the case and Warren's opinion, can you explain *Terry*'s value?[17]

In *Terry* the Court rather begrudgingly added stop and frisks to the growing list of exceptions to searches conducted without a warrant. Seven of the justices

17. It is interesting to note that *Terry* was decided by the Warren Court, and, as such, represents one of its few significant departures from its generally liberal stances.

agreed with Warren's opinion that something short of probable cause allows police to conduct stop searches, but Justice Douglas vehemently dissented:

The infringement on personal liberty of any "seizure" of a person can only be "reasonable" under the Fourth Amendment if we require police to possess "probable cause" before they seize him. Only that line draws a meaningful distinction between an officer's mere inkling and the presence of facts ... which could convince a reasonable man that the person seized has committed, is committing, or is about to commit a particular crime.

Despite Douglas's words, the majority in *Terry* agreed that safety searches should be an exception to the warrant requirement of the Fourth Amendment. As with other exceptions, the Court has limited stop and frisks to their justification: police may employ them only when they have some reason to suspect a threat to their lives, and not merely to gather evidence. Furthermore, the search is limited to the area in which the officer suspects the presence of weapons.

Even the more conservative Rehnquist Court has generally subscribed to these limits on safety searches, with *Minnesota v. Dickerson* (1993) providing a good example. Minneapolis police observed Timothy Dickerson leave an apartment building they thought was a "crack house." When Dickerson entered a nearby alley, the officers followed him. Eventually, they stopped and frisked him. Although the officer conducting the search did not find a weapon, he did feel a "lump" in Dickerson's jacket. He removed the lump, which turned out to be a plastic bag containing a small amount of crack cocaine.

Dickerson's attorney asserted that the officer's "stop and frisk" went beyond the bounds of *Terry*. Writing for six members of the Supreme Court, Justice White—a member of the *Terry* majority— agreed. He pointed to the Minnesota Supreme Court's decision, which held that the officer had overstepped the bounds of the "strictly circumscribed" search for weapons permitted under *Terry*. In Justice White's words "Here, the officer's continued exploration of respondent's pocket after having concluded that it contained no weapon was unrelated to 'the sole justification of *Terry* searches': the protection of the police officers and others nearby." To the majority, this search "amounted to the sort of evidentiary search that *Terry* expressly refused to authorize."

Plain View Doctrine

Our discussion so far has described circumstances under which police may search and the guidelines the Court has established to determine reasonableness. Under each justification for a search there are limitations: searches based on a warrant must be confined to the place specified in the document; consent searches may go no farther than the grant of permission stipulates; and safety searches can extend only far enough to discover or remove the possible danger. But what if, while conducting a valid search, police come upon seizable articles that are outside the scope of the search authorization? For example, suppose law enforcement officials have a valid warrant to search a house for stolen goods and, in the course of their investigation, come across illegal narcotics. What should they do? Must they ignore such items? Or may they seize the drugs? These questions are addressed by the plain view doctrine, a controversial rule that expands the powers of police to gather evidence. This doctrine holds that if police officers are lawfully present and items subject to seizure come into plain view, the officers may take possession of those articles without any additional authorization.

Some analysts refer to the plain view doctrine as yet another exception to the Fourth Amendment's warrant requirement. This interpretation is reasonable because the doctrine provides officers with some freedom to seize contraband and other evidence of a crime, without necessarily having a warrant. Still, it is important to understand that, at the heart of the doctrine, is the requirement that police must be acting

lawfully when seizable items come into plain view. Accordingly, the plain view doctrine often supplements other searches. Suppose, for example, that two officers came to a student's apartment and the student allowed them to enter. Walking into the apartment, police spot marijuana on a table. Under the plain view doctrine, the officers could seize the marijuana because the student *consented* to the search. Had the student denied the officers permission and they entered anyway, the plain view doctrine would not apply unless the officers had some other legitimate reason for conducting a search or they had a search warrant.

This hypothetical case brings to light yet another important aspect of the doctrine or exception: to qualify, the items must clearly be in plain view. In *Arizona v. Hicks* (1987), for example, police lawfully entered an apartment looking for weapons thought to have been used in a shooting. The officers found some very expensive stereo equipment in the otherwise squalid apartment. Suspecting that the stereo equipment had been stolen, one of the officers moved some of the components to get the serial numbers. A check against police records confirmed that the items had been reported stolen, and the occupant of the apartment was convicted of robbery. On appeal to the Supreme Court, however, the actions of the officers were found to be in violation of the Fourth Amendment. The justices reasoned that, although the officers had a legitimate reason for entering the apartment, they had violated the plain view doctrine when the officer moved the stereo components to find the serial number. Unlike the marijuana in our hypothetical case, those serial numbers were not in plain view, and moving the components was not part of the legitimate search for weapons.

The plain view doctrine clearly expands the opportunities of police to seize evidence. But, as *Hicks* demonstrates, there are important conditions that must be met before such seizures are considered valid. Particularly important is that the plain view doctrine, like the exceptions to the warrant requirement we have examined, is limited to the justification the Court originally invoked to create it: people have reasonable expectations of privacy for items not in the plain view of police officers. Unless officers have a legitimate reason to take goods beyond their plain view (such as specification in a warrant), they cannot use the plain view doctrine to justify their seizures.

Hot Pursuit

Suppose a police officer witnesses a mugging on a city street and chases the perpetrators.[18] The muggers run into an apartment building and close the door. Must the police officer obtain a warrant to enter the building? As a general rule of law, the answer is no, and the reason is that the Supreme Court has carved out yet another exception to the Fourth Amendment's warrant requirement: "hot pursuit." In other words, the Court has said that it would be reasonable for the police officer to enter the apartment, without a search warrant, because evidence could be destroyed and lives could be endangered. And, if the officer found evidence of a crime—for example, the wallet of the person the officer saw being mugged—under the hot pursuit exception, the evidence could be used against the defendant.

As with all other exceptions to the warrant requirement, the Court has placed limits on the hot pursuit exception—limits that, as always, reflect the original justifications for permitting the exception. These limits were laid out by the justices in *Warden v. Hayden* (1967), a Warren Court case that provides an important example of the hot pursuit exception. Hayden robbed a taxi company and fled on foot. Hearing yells of "Holdup!" from company employees, two cab drivers followed Hayden and saw him enter a house. One of the drivers radioed the cab dispatcher with a description of Hayden and where he was hiding. The police arrived immediately, entered the house, and found Hayden in a bedroom pretending to be asleep. In the

18. We adopt this discussion from Zalman and Siegel, *Criminal Procedure,* 258–259.

meantime, another officer found—in an adjoining bathroom—two guns and the clothing that witnesses had said the robber was wearing. These and other items were introduced as evidence against Hayden.

Even though police officers had entered the house without a warrant, the Supreme Court ruled that the search was constitutional on the grounds that they were in hot pursuit of a suspect. It is reasonable to allow warrantless searches in such circumstances, as Justice Brennan put it for the majority, because the "Fourth Amendment does not require police officers to delay in the course of an investigation if to do so would gravely endanger their lives or the lives of others. Speed here was essential, and only a thorough search of the house for persons and weapons could have ensured that Hayden was the only man present and the police had control of all weapons which could be used against them or to effect an escape." The "exigencies of the situation"—the fact that lives were in danger, that evidence could have been lost, and so forth—made the warrantless entry into Hayden's house "imperative."

The Court was careful to note that the hot pursuit exception was limited to those circumstances that warranted its creation in the first place. Police may not, for example, conduct a warrantless search and expect courts to admit seized evidence under the hot pursuit exception unless the officers have probable cause to believe that the individual they are pursuing committed a crime or is likely to endanger lives—both of which existed in the Hayden search. In general, the Court is willing to tolerate only a short delay between the observed crime and the warrantless search, a limitation that makes sense given the reason for creating the exception—that police must act quickly.

Even the more conservative Burger Court stressed the importance of these limits. In *Welsh v. Wisconsin* (1984) the justices considered whether the Fourth Amendment "prohibits the police from making a warrantless night entry of a person's home in order to arrest him for a violation of a nonjailable traffic offense." One rainy night an apparently drunk Welsh drove his car off the road. Another driver pulled over, blocked Welsh's car with his truck, and had someone call the police. He also suggested to Welsh that he wait in the car, but Welsh walked off. The police arrived at Welsh's house at about 9:00 p.m. Welsh's step-daughter answered the door and, without gaining her consent, police entered the house. They found Welsh in bed and arrested him. At the police station, Welsh would not submit to a breath analysis. This refusal led authorities to revoke his license.

The state tried to use the hot pursuit exception to justify the officers' warrantless entry into Welsh's home. It suggested that police need to act with speed to prevent the loss of evidence and to prevent the threat to public safety posed by drunk drivers. But the Supreme Court did not agree. Writing for the majority, Justice Brennan found the hot pursuit claim "unconvincing because there was no immediate or continuous pursuit of the petitioner from the scene of the crime. Moreover, because the petitioner had already arrived home, and had abandoned his car at the scene of the accident, there was little remaining threat to the public safety." As for the state's claim that the hot pursuit exception was activated by the need to test Welsh for the presence of alcohol before the substance left his body, Brennan had this to say: "A warrantless home arrest cannot be upheld simply because evidence of the petitioner's blood-alcohol level might have dissipated while police obtained a warrant. To allow [it] on these facts would be to approve unreasonable police behavior that the principles of the Fourth Amendment will not sanction."

Welsh reinforced existing limits on the hot pursuit exception, but it also created yet another restriction, the gravity of the offense. As the majority noted, "We ... hold that an important factor to be considered when determining whether any exigency exits is the gravity of the underlying offense for which the arrest is being made." In short, the Court is unwilling to apply the hot pursuit exception "when there is probable cause to believe that only a minor offense ... has been committed," as was the case in *Welsh*. Although the Court has yet to define what it means by a "minor offense," its intent is clear: it desires to limit the hot pursuit exception to situations in which a grave emergency exists.

Place Searches

All the cases (and exceptions) we have examined so far have dealt with police procedure, addressing the questions of when and under what circumstances police could conduct searches and seizures. The Court, under the leadership of Warren Burger, examined a number of cases that asked different questions: Where can law enforcement officials search and seize without a warrant? Do certain places require special consideration? These questions assume that not all places deserve equal levels of Fourth Amendment protection. In some places we have a higher expectation of privacy than in others. The home, for example, merits the highest degree of protection. Other places, such as automobiles, open fields, and prisons, have not fared as well in the decisions of the Court.

Cars. The issue of place search exceptions originates in modern jurisprudence with automobile searches. With the appearance of automobiles on the American scene in the early 1900s, the Supreme Court has been forced to address the following question: Should the law treat cars the same as houses, in which case traditional search and seizure rules would apply, or as something special? Since its first car search case in 1925, *Carroll v. United States*, the Court has always decided that cars do not deserve the same degree of protection as people, houses, papers, and the like. In general, the Court has given the police broad latitude in searching cars without warrants because (1) cars are mobile and, as such, can quickly leave the jurisdiction of the police; (2) automobile windows allow outsiders to look in, and drivers have a lower expectation of privacy inside a car than they do in their homes; and (3) the government has a pervasive interest in regulating cars.

Although the doctrine that automobiles deserve little constitutional protection from warrantless searches was well established, the Court was confronted with many car search questions during the 1970s and 1980s. How far may such searches extend? May police search only the area where driver and passengers sit? What about glove compartments and trunks? Are baggage or boxes in a car fair game? What degree of justification or cause does a law enforcement official need before a warrantless search can be conducted? If an automobile is impounded, may police search and inventory the contents?

The answers to these questions often were confusing and contradictory. The Court began to draw some very unusual lines; for example, officers could search clear (see-through) bags, but they could not examine opaque containers in an automobile. Likewise, officers could search the open areas of cars, but not locked glove compartments.

Conservative and liberal organizations alike chastised Court doctrine emanating from these cases. Americans for Effective Law Enforcement, for example, suggested that the Court make a "clear cut pronouncement . . . that once there is probable cause to search a car, the police may search any container within any part of the car."[19] Liberal groups had different ideas—they wanted the Court to give car searches full Fourth Amendment protection. In *United States v. Ross* (1982) the Supreme Court had the opportunity to settle the issue. The facts of this case forced the Court to confront and sort out the confusion that had developed on the question of automobile searches.

19. Americans for Effective Law Enforcement, Amicus curiae brief filed in *United States v. Ross*, No. 2209, 3.

Based on Justice Stevens's opinion, what are the grounds for legitimate automobile searches? May police stop and search a car merely because they suspect unlawful behavior or must they have more concrete reasons?

United States v. Ross

456 U.S. 798 (1982)
Vote: 6 (Blackmun, Burger, O'Connor, Powell,
        Rehnquist, Stevens)
    3 (Brennan, Marshall, White)
Opinion of the Court: Stevens
Concurring opinions: Blackmun, Powell
Dissenting opinions: Marshall, White

On November 27, 1978, Detective Marcum of the Washington, D.C., Metropolitan Police received a phone call from a reliable informant, who said that he had observed a man, known on the streets as "Bandit," selling narcotics at 439 Ridge Street. He also gave the detective a description of the man and reported that drugs were in the trunk of Bandit's car. Marcum, accompanied by Detective Cassidy and Sergeant Gonzales, found the car, and a check of the tag numbers revealed that it was registered to Albert Ross. The officers stopped the car, identified themselves, and asked Ross to step out. As Marcum and Cassidy searched Ross, Gonzales saw a bullet on the front seat of Ross's car. He picked up the bullet and searched inside the car for weapons, finding a pistol in the glove compartment. He placed Ross under arrest for firearms violations and handcuffed him. Cassidy then unlocked the trunk, where he found a closed but unsealed lunch bag and a small zippered pouch made of leather. In the bag Cassidy found several clear plastic envelopes containing white powder. Leaving the bag and leather pouch in the trunk, Cassidy drove the car to the police station, where it was impounded. Cassidy reopened the bag and determined that it contained thirty envelopes of what later proved to be heroin. Cassidy also opened the leather pouch and found $3,200 in currency. At no point did the officers seek a search warrant.

JUSTICE STEVENS delivered the opinion of the Court.

In *Carroll v. United States,* the Court held that a warrantless search of an automobile stopped by police officers who had probable cause to believe the vehicle contained contraband was not unreasonable within the meaning of the Fourth Amendment. The Court in *Carroll* did not explicitly address the scope of the search that is permissible. In this case, we consider the extent to which police officers—who have legitimately stopped an automobile and who have probable cause to believe that contraband is concealed somewhere within it—may conduct a probing search of compartments and containers within the vehicle whose contents are not in plain view. We hold that they may conduct a search of the vehicle that is as thorough as a magistrate could authorize in a warrant "particularly describing the place to be searched.". . .

We begin with a review of the decision in *Carroll* itself. In the fall of 1921, federal prohibition agents obtained evidence that George Carroll and John Kiro were "bootleggers" who frequently traveled between Grand Rapids and Detroit in an Oldsmobile Roadster. On December 15, 1921, the agents unexpectedly encountered Carroll and Kiro driving west on that route in that car. The officers gave pursuit, stopped the roadster on the highway, and directed Carroll and Kiro to get out of the car.

No contraband was visible in the front seat of the Oldsmobile and the rear portion of the roadster was closed. One of the agents raised the rumble seat but found no liquor. He raised the seat cushion and again found nothing. The officer then struck at the "lazyback" of the seat and noticed that it was "harder than upholstery ordinarily is in those backs." He tore open the seat cushion and discovered 68 bottles of gin and whiskey concealed inside. No warrant had been obtained for the search.

Carroll and Kiro were convicted of transporting intoxicating liquor in violation of the National Prohibition Act. On review of those convictions, this Court ruled that the warrantless search of the roadster was reasonable within the meaning of the Fourth Amendment. In an extensive opinion written by Chief Justice Taft, the Court held:

"On reason and authority the true rule is that if the search and seizure without a warrant are made upon probable cause, that is, upon a belief, reasonably arising out of circumstances known to the seizing officer, that an automobile or other vehicle contains that which by law is subject to seizure and destruction, the search and seizure are valid. The Fourth Amendment is to be construed in the light of what was deemed an unreasonable search and seizure when it was adopted, and in a manner which will conserve public interests as well as the interests and rights of individual citizens."

The Court explained at length the basis for this rule. The Court noted that historically warrantless searches of vessels, wagons, and carriages—as opposed to fixed premises such as a home or other building—had been considered reasonable by Congress. . . .

[The Court] again noted that "the guaranty of freedom from unreasonable searches and seizures by the Fourth Amendment has been construed, practically since the beginning of the Government, as recognizing a necessary difference between a search of a store, dwelling house or other structure in respect of which a proper official warrant readily may be obtained, and a search of a ship, motor boat, wagon or automobile, for contraband goods, where it is not practicable to secure a warrant because the vehicle can be quickly moved out of the locality or jurisdiction in which the warrant must be sought."

Thus, since its earliest days Congress had recognized the impracticability of securing a warrant in cases involving the transportation of contraband goods. It is this impracticability, viewed in historical perspective, that provided the basis for the *Carroll* decision. Given the nature of an automobile in transit, the Court recognized that an immediate intrusion is necessary if police officers are to secure the illicit substance. In this class of cases, the Court held that a warrantless search of an automobile is not unreasonable.

In defining the nature of this "exception" to the general rule that "[i]n cases where the securing of a warrant is reasonably practicable, it must be used," the Court in *Carroll* emphasized the importance of the requirement that officers have probable cause to believe that the vehicle contains contraband. . . . Moreover, the probable-cause determination must be based on objective facts that could justify the issuance of a warrant by a magistrate and not merely on the subjective good faith of the police officers....

In short, the exception to the warrant requirement established in *Carroll*—the scope of which we consider in this case—applies only to searches of vehicles that are supported by probable cause. In this class of cases, a search is not unreasonable if based on facts that would justify the issuance of a warrant, even though a warrant has not actually been obtained....

[I]n this case police officers had probable cause to search respondent's entire vehicle.... [I]n this case the parties have squarely addressed the question whether, in the course of a legitimate warrantless search of an automobile, police are entitled to open containers found within the vehicle. We now address that question. Its answer is determined by the scope of the search that is authorized by the exception to the warrant requirement set forth in *Carroll*....

As we have stated, the decision in *Carroll* was based on the Court's appraisal of practical considerations viewed in the perspective of history. It is therefore significant that the practical consequences of the *Carroll* decision would be largely nullified if the permissible scope of a warrantless search of an automobile did not include containers and packages found inside the vehicle. Contraband goods rarely are strewn across the trunk or floor of a car; since by their very nature such goods must be withheld from public view, they rarely can be placed in an automobile unless they are enclosed within some form of container....

A lawful search of fixed premises generally extends to the entire area in which the object of the search may be found and is not limited by the possibility that separate acts of entry or opening may be required to complete the search. Thus, a warrant that authorizes an officer to search a home for illegal weapons also provides authority to open closets, chests, drawers, and containers in which the weapon might be found. A warrant to open a footlocker to search for marihuana would also authorize the opening of packages found inside. A warrant to search a vehicle would support a search of every part of the vehicle that might contain the object of the search. When a legitimate search is under way, and when its purpose and its limits have been precisely defined, nice distinctions between closets, drawers, and containers, in the case of a home, or between glove compartments, up-

holstered seats, trunks, and wrapped packages, in the case of a vehicle, must give way to the interest in the prompt and efficient completion of the task at hand.

This rule applies equally to all containers, as indeed we believe it must. One point on which the Court was in virtually unanimous agreement ... was that a constitutional distinction between "worthy" and "unworthy" containers would be improper. Even though such a distinction perhaps could evolve in a series of cases in which paper bags, locked trunks, lunch buckets, and orange crates were placed on one side of the line or the other, the central purpose of the Fourth Amendment forecloses such a distinction. For just as the most frail cottage in the kingdom is absolutely entitled to the same guarantees of privacy as the most majestic mansion, so also may a traveler who carries a toothbrush and a few articles of clothing in a paper bag or knotted scarf claim an equal right to conceal his possessions from official inspection as the sophisticated executive with the locked attachée case.

As Justice Stewart stated ... the Fourth Amendment provides protection to the owner of every container that conceals its contents from plain view. But the protection afforded by the Amendment varies in different settings. The luggage carried by a traveler entering the country may be searched at random by a customs officer; the luggage may be searched no matter how great the traveler's desire to conceal the contents may be. A container carried at the time of arrest often may be searched without a warrant and even without any specific suspicion concerning its contents. A container that may conceal the object of a search authorized by a warrant may be opened immediately; the individual's interest in privacy must give way to the magistrate's official determination of probable cause.

In the same manner, an individual's expectation of privacy in a vehicle and its contents may not survive if probable cause is given to believe that the vehicle is transporting contraband. Certainly the privacy interests in a car's trunk or glove compartment may be no less than those in a movable container. An individual undoubtedly has a significant interest that the upholstery of his automobile will not be ripped or a hidden compartment within it opened. These interests must yield to the authority of a search, however, which—in light of *Carroll*—does not itself require the prior approval of a magistrate. The scope of a warrantless search based on probable cause is no narrower—and no broader—than the scope of a search authorized by a warrant supported by probable cause. Only the prior approval of the magistrate is waived; the search otherwise is as the magistrate could authorize.

The scope of a warrantless search of an automobile thus is not defined by the nature of the container in which the contraband is secreted. Rather, it is defined by the object of the search and the places in which there is probable cause to believe that it may be found. Just as probable cause to believe that a stolen lawnmower may be found in a garage will not support a warrant to search an upstairs bedroom, probable cause to believe that undocumented aliens are being transported in a van will not justify a warrantless search of a suitcase. Probable cause to believe that a container placed in the trunk of a taxi contains contraband or evidence does not justify a search of the entire cab.

Our decision today is inconsistent with the disposition in . . . [other cases]. Nevertheless, the doctrine of *stare decisis* does not preclude this action. . . . [I]t is clear that no legitimate reliance interest can be frustrated by our decision today. Of greatest importance, we are convinced that the rule we apply in this case is faithful to the interpretation of the Fourth Amendment that the Court has followed with substantial consistency throughout our history.

. . . The exception recognized in *Carroll* is unquestionably one that is "specifically established and well delineated." We hold that the scope of the warrantless search authorized by that exception is no broader and no narrower than a magistrate could legitimately authorize by warrant. If probable cause justifies the search of a lawfully stopped vehicle, it justifies the search of every part of the vehicle and its contents that may conceal the object of the search.

The judgment of the Court of Appeals is reversed. The case is remanded for further proceedings consistent with this opinion.

It is so ordered.

JUSTICE MARSHALL, with whom JUSTICE BRENNAN joins, dissenting.

The majority today not only repeals all realistic limits on warrantless automobile searches, it repeals the Fourth Amendment warrant requirement itself. By equating a police officer's estimation of probable cause with a magis-

trate's, the Court utterly disregards the value of a neutral and detached magistrate. For as we recently, and unanimously, reaffirmed:

"The warrant traditionally has represented an independent assurance that a search and arrest will not proceed without probable cause to believe that a crime has been committed and that the person or place named in the warrant is involved in the crime. Thus, an issuing magistrate must meet two tests. He must be neutral and detached, and he must be capable of determining whether probable cause exists for the requested arrest or search. This Court long has insisted that inferences of probable cause be drawn by 'a neutral and detached magistrate instead of being judged by the officer engaged in the often competitive enterprise of ferreting out crime.'" *Shadwick v. City of Tampa* (1972), quoting *Johnson v. United States* (1948).

A police officer on the beat hardly satisfies these standards. In adopting today's new rule, the majority opinion shows contempt for these Fourth Amendment values, ignores this Court's precedents, is internally inconsistent, and produces anomalous and unjust consequences. I therefore dissent. . . .

"[I]t is a cardinal principle that 'searches conducted outside the judicial process, without prior approval by judge or magistrate, are *per se* unreasonable under the Fourth Amendment—subject only to a few specifically established and well-delineated exceptions.'". . . The warrant requirement is crucial to protecting Fourth Amendment rights because of the importance of having the probable cause determination made in the first instance by a neutral and detached magistrate. Time and again, we have emphasized that the warrant requirement provides a number of protections that a post-hoc judicial evaluation of a policeman's probable cause does not. . . .

Our cases do recognize a narrow exception to the warrant requirement for certain automobile searches. Throughout our decisions, two major considerations have been advanced to justify the automobile exception to the warrant requirement. We have upheld only those searches that are actually justified by those considerations.

First, these searches have been justified on the basis of the exigency of the mobility of the automobile. This "mobility" rationale is something of a misnomer, since the police ordinarily can remove the car's occupants and secure the vehicle on the spot. However, the inherent mobility of the vehicle often creates situations in which the police's only alternative to an immediate search may be to release the automobile from their possession. This alternative creates an unacceptably high risk of losing the contents of the vehicle, and is a principal basis for the Court's automobile exception to the warrant requirement. . . .

[Second,] because an automobile presents much of its contents in open view to police officers who legitimately stop it on a public way, is used for travel, and is subject to significant government regulation, this Court has determined that the intrusion of a warrantless search of an automobile is constitutionally less significant than a warrantless search of more private areas. This justification has been invoked for warrantless automobile searches in circumstances where the exigency of mobility was clearly not present. By focusing on the defendant's reasonable expectation of privacy, this Court has refused to require a warrant in situations where the process of obtaining such a warrant would be more intrusive than the actual search itself. A defendant may consider the seizure of the car a greater intrusion than an immediate search. Therefore, even where police *can* bring both the defendant and the automobile to the station safely and can house the car while they seek a warrant, the police are permitted to decide whether instead to conduct an immediate search of the car. In effect, the warrantless search is permissible because a warrant requirement would not provide significant protection of the defendant's Fourth Amendment interests.

. . . Today, the majority makes no attempt to base its decision on these justifications. This failure is not surprising, since the traditional rationales for the automobile exception plainly do not support extending it to the search of a container found inside a vehicle.

The practical mobility problem—deciding what to do with both the car and the occupants if an immediate search is not conducted—is simply not present in the case of movable containers, which can easily be seized and brought to the magistrate. The lesser expectation of privacy rationale also has little force. A container, as opposed to the car itself, does not reflect diminished privacy interests. Moreover, the practical corollary that this Court has recognized—that depriving occupants of the use of a car may be a greater intrusion than an immediate search—is of doubtful relevance here, since the owner of a container will rarely suffer significant inconvenience by being deprived of its use while a warrant is being obtained.

Ultimately, the majority, unable to rely on the justifications underlying the automobile exception, simply creates a new "probable cause" exception to the warrant requirement for automobiles. We have soundly rejected attempts to create such an exception in the past, and we should do so again today. . . .

The only convincing explanation I discern for the majority's broad rule is expediency: it assists police in conducting automobile searches, ensuring that the private containers into which criminal suspects often place goods will no longer be a Fourth Amendment shield. "When a legitimate search is under way," the Court instructs us, "nice distinctions between . . . glove compartments, upholstered seats, trunks, and wrapped packages . . . must give way to the interest in the prompt and efficient completion of the task at hand." No "nice distinctions" are necessary, however, to comprehend the well-recognized differences between movable containers (which, even after today's decision, would be subject to the warrant requirement if located outside an automobile), and the automobile itself, together with its integral parts. Nor can I pass by the majority's glib assertion that the "prompt and efficient completion of the task at hand" is paramount to the Fourth Amendment interests of our citizens. I had thought it well established that "the mere fact that law enforcement may be made more efficient can never by itself justify disregard of the Fourth Amendment.". . .

This case will have profound implications for the privacy of citizens traveling in automobiles, as the Court well understands. "For countless vehicles are stopped on highways and public streets every day and our cases demonstrate that it is not uncommon for police officers to have probable cause to believe that contraband may be found in a stopped vehicle." A closed paper bag, a toolbox, a knapsack, a suitcase, and an attachée case can alike be searched without the protection of the judgment of a neutral magistrate, based only on the rarely disturbed decision of a police officer that he has probable cause to search for contraband in the vehicle. The Court derives satisfaction from the fact that its rule does not exalt the rights of the wealthy over the rights of the poor. A rule so broad that all citizens lose vital Fourth Amendment protection is no cause for celebration.

I dissent.

Ross is an important case because it *appeared* to clarify existing car search doctrine. Many observers thought that police would no longer have to puzzle over what they could and could not open during an automobile search because the Court seemed to state the policy clearly. "If probable cause justifies the search of a lawfully stopped vehicle, it justifies the search of every part of the vehicle and its contents that may conceal the object of the search." In other words, *Ross* permits police to conduct "probing" searches of compartments and containers of a car "so long as the search is supported by probable cause."

But *Ross* left open an important question: What if police lack probable cause to search an entire car but had sufficient probable cause to obtain a warrant to open a container in that car? Under the automobile exception, might they still open a container within that car? Or do they need to obtain a warrant? Based on *United States v. Chadwick,* the case with which we began this chapter, the answer to the last question appeared to be yes; that is, if police lacked probable cause to search the entire car, then they could not open a container within it.

Ross did not specifically address this question; nor did it overrule *Chadwick.* And so the scope of the car search exception remained a source of confusion for lower courts and police until the Supreme Court handed down *California v. Acevedo* (1991). Police observed Charles Steven Acevedo enter the apartment of J. R. Daza, a man whom they had good reason to suspect was dealing drugs. About ten minutes later Acevedo left the apartment carrying a bag about the size of a package of marijuana police knew Daza possessed. Acevedo walked to a car in a parking lot and placed the bag in the trunk. As he started to drive away police pulled him over and opened the trunk

and the bag, which contained marijuana. Basing his argument in part on *Chadwick,* Acevedo challenged the search; he maintained that police should have obtained a warrant to open the bag. A California court agreed with him. In the court's view, police might have had probable cause to believe that the bag contained drugs, but they lacked probable cause to "suspect that Acevedo's car, itself, otherwise contained contraband." Because probable cause centered on the bag, the ruling in *Chadwick* applied. In other words, Acevedo's bag was analogous to Chadwick's footlocker.

The Rehnquist Court disagreed. In his opinion, Justice Blackmun wrote that the Fourth Amendment does not require police to obtain a warrant to open a container in a car simply because they lack probable cause to search the entire car. If police have probable cause to suspect that a container—in this case, a bag—in a car contains contraband, they may open it without obtaining a warrant. Why? The majority offered several justifications for its decision, which, in essence, overruled *Chadwick.* First, because the automobile exceptions were based, in part, on the need to prevent the loss of evidence, the Court could not justify a different rule for searches in which the police lacked probable cause to search the entire car and those in which they had sufficient probable cause to obtain a warrant to open a container in that car. As Blackmun put it, "A container found after a general search of the automobile and a container found in a car after a limited search for the container are equally easy for the police to store and for the suspect to hide or destroy." Second, the Court could find "no principled distinction in terms of . . . the privacy expectation . . . between the paper bag found in *Ross* and the paper bag found by police here." Finally, and more pragmatically, the Court reasoned that the gap between *Chadwick* and *Ross* had "confused courts and police officers and impeded effective law enforcement."

As *Acevedo* indicates, in the years following *Ross* the Court continued to support the position that automobiles constitute a special case in search and seizure law. As a general rule, police have received from the Burger and Rehnquist Courts broad discretion to conduct warrantless car searches. The degree of Fourth Amendment protection accorded to individuals in their automobiles is minimal.

Fields. Automobiles are not the only place exceptions to the Fourth Amendment. Ever since *Hester v. United States* (1924), the Supreme Court had adhered to an open fields doctrine that allowed police to enter and search a field without a warrant. The status of the open field doctrine, however, was brought into question following the Court's ruling in *Katz v. United States.* Katz held that Fourth Amendment requirements apply whenever an individual has a reasonable expectation of privacy. Some civil libertarians argued that the open field exception to the Fourth Amendment would be nullified if the owner of the field took steps to declare an expectation of privacy, perhaps by installing a fence or posting No Trespassing signs.

The issue was settled in *Oliver v. United States* (1984). In this case, Oliver cultivated a marijuana crop in a remote field on his property. The field, posted against trespassers, was bounded on all sides by trees, an earthen embankment, and a chicken wire fence. By doing so, his attorneys argued, Oliver was clearly declaring the field to be a private area. Nevertheless, drug enforcement officers entered the field without a warrant and collected evidence of drug violations. Was this intrusion valid under the *Hester* open fields doctrine, or unconstitutional under the *Katz* expectation of privacy rule?

In a 6–3 decision, the Court ruled in favor of the federal government. Writing for the majority, Justice Powell concluded that *Hester*, not *Katz*, controlled the open field search. He drew upon the intent of the Framers of the Fourth Amendment, noting that James Madison's original wording of the Search and Seizure Clause included the words "other property," but this term was later stricken. He dismissed the applicability of *Katz*, arguing that open fields inherently do not provide privacy even if owners post No Trespassing signs. According to Powell:

It is true, of course, that petitioner Oliver . . . in order to conceal . . . criminal activities, planted the marijuana upon secluded land and erected fences and "No Trespassing" signs around the property. And it may be that because of such precautions, few members of the public stumbled upon the marijuana crops seized by the police. Neither of these suppositions demonstrates, however, that the expectation of privacy was legitimate in the sense required by the Fourth Amendment.

Has the Rehnquist Court continued to narrow privacy expectations in the open field context? Its decision in *Florida v. Riley* (1988) indicates that it may be giving police even greater latitude than did the Burger Court. At issue in *Riley* was the validity of a warrantless aerial observation. From a helicopter flying 400 feet above ground, law enforcement officials viewed marijuana growing in a greenhouse. Quoting from an earlier decision, Justice White asserted, "In an age where private and commercial flight in the public airways is routine, it is unreasonable for [Riley] to expect that his marijuana plants were constitutionally protected from being observed with the naked eye. . . ."

Prisons. In addition to automobiles and open fields, police and other officials may conduct warrantless searches of prisoners and, subject to some constraints, those in police custody. In *Hudson v. Palmer* (1984) the Court ruled that, although some constitutional guarantees apply to prisoners, others do not because imprisonment by its very nature necessitates the loss of rights, among them the guarantees contained in the Fourth Amendment. If the law accorded prisoners such rights, Chief Justice Burger's opinion for the majority reasoned, then it would "undermine the effectiveness of prison operations," an important element of which involves "surprise searches" for contraband. Burger argued that prisons are "volatile communities," lacking any expectations of privacy, and therefore lie beyond Fourth Amendment protection.

The Court has applied similar reasoning to warrantless searches by law enforcement officials of individuals in custody. *Illinois v. Lafayette* (1983) concerned a warrantless search of Ralph Lafayette, whom police had arrested for disturbing the peace. While booking him, an officer searched him and a cigarette pack in his shoulder bag. The pack contained amphetamines. Illinois state courts ruled against the officer's claim that standard police procedure dictated inventory searches of arrested persons; the courts said that expectation of privacy standards exempted shoulder bags from custodial searches. A unanimous Supreme Court dismissed this reasoning. Once again writing for the Court, Burger argued that inventory searches were a well-established aspect of police procedure. As long as the police conduct such searches in a reasonable fashion, they are legally entitled to do so.

ENFORCING THE FOURTH AMENDMENT: THE EXCLUSIONARY RULE

So far, our discussion has focused on the constitutional rules governing searches and seizures. We learned that the Court has carved out numerous exceptions to the general principle that police should obtain warrants to conduct searches. At the same time, we saw that the Court has placed limits on those exceptions. For example, if police use the "incident to arrest" exception to conduct the warrantless search of an individual, then they must conduct that search *at the time* the individual is arrested. As we discussed, the Court justified this exception on the grounds that the suspect may be carrying weapons that could endanger the lives of police officers. If police returned to the crime scene after the suspect was removed and conducted a warrantless search, the Court would not allow them to use the "incident to arrest" exception to justify their search. After all, police could not be harmed by an individual who was no longer there.

But suppose that is precisely what police did? They went back to the scene of the crime a day later, found evidence, and tried to justify the search under the incident to arrest exception. We know that this would be an illegal search, but what is to prevent police from doing it anyway? In England, if police conduct an illegal search and seizure, the evidence they obtain *may* be used in court against the accused, but the person whose privacy rights have been violated can sue the police for damages. This system of police liability enables the British to enforce search and seizure rights.

The United States imposes a different remedy for police infractions.[20] We enforce the Fourth Amendment through the application of the exclusionary rule, a judicially created principle that removes any incentive police might otherwise have for violating search and seizure rights. The exclusionary rule holds that evidence gathered illegally may not be admitted into court. It is excluded from use by prosecutors in attempting to establish the suspect's guilt. The rationale behind the rule is straightforward: if police know that evidence produced by an illegal search will be of no use, they have no motive for violating the Constitution.

Development of the Exclusionary Rule

At one time, law enforcement officials faced no federal punitive measures for conducting illegal searches and seizures. Unless individual state laws imposed some form of redress, the police were not held liable for their activities, nor was evidence obtained unconstitutionally excluded from trials. In 1914, however, the Supreme Court decided *Weeks v. United States,* a

---

20. It is true, however, that in the United States civil suits can be initiated against officers for violations of Fourth Amendment rights. The discussion that follows focuses on the exclusionary rule, the major remedy used in criminal proceedings.

case arising from a federal investigation into the business practices of Freemont Weeks. Police officers went to Weeks's office, placed him under arrest, and conducted a search. Later, the police and a U.S. marshal went to Weeks's house and, without a warrant, carried off boxes of his papers and documents, a clear violation of search and seizure rules. In addition, the materials seized were not narrowly selected for their relevance, but were voluminous business records on which authorities could conduct a fishing expedition in search of possible incriminating evidence.

Should the documents be used as evidence against *Weeks*, even though police and the marshal had gathered the materials in an illegal manner? Writing for the Court, Justice William R. Day proclaimed:

If letters and private documents can thus be seized and held and used as evidence against a citizen accused of an offense, the protection of the Fourth Amendment declaring his right to be secure against such searches and seizures is of no value, and, so far as those thus placed are concerned, might as well be stricken from the Constitution.

With this conclusion, the Court, through Justice Day, created the exclusionary rule: judges must exclude from trial any evidence gathered in violation of the Fourth Amendment.

Although *Weeks* constituted a major decision, it was limited in scope, applying only to *federal* agents and *federal* judges in *federal* criminal cases. It was clear, however, that eventually the Court would be asked to apply the exclusionary rule to the states because that is where most criminal prosecutions take place. But it was also the case that many states or their judges resisted adopting an exclusionary rule. *People v. Defore* (1926) provides perhaps the most famous example. In that case, Benjamin Cardozo, then a judge on the New York Court of Appeals, rejected adoption of *Weeks* to New York. In this opinion he wrote the now famous lines disparaging the exclusionary rule: "The criminal is to go free because the constable has blundered.... A room is searched against the law, and the body of a murdered man is found.... The privacy

of the home has been infringed, and the murderer goes free."

The issue first reached the Supreme Court in 1949 in *Wolf v. Colorado*. This case involved a Colorado physician who was suspected of performing illegal abortions. Because the police were unable to obtain any solid evidence against him, a deputy sheriff surreptitiously took Dr. Wolf's appointment book and followed up on the names in it. The police gathered enough evidence to convict him. Wolf's attorney argued that because the case against his client rested on illegally obtained evidence, the Court should dismiss it. To implement his arguments, however, the justices would have to apply or incorporate the Fourth Amendment and impose the exclusionary rule on the states (*see Chapter 2*).

Writing for the Court, Justice Frankfurter agreed to incorporate the Fourth Amendment. The right to be secure against unreasonable searches and seizures was deemed a fundamental right, "basic to a free society," and the provisions of the amendment applied to the states through the Due Process Clause of the Fourteenth Amendment. However, the Court refused to hold that the exclusionary rule was a necessary part of the Fourth Amendment. The rule was one method of enforcing search and seizure rights, but not the only one. In other words, although state law enforcement officials must abide by the guarantees contained in the Fourth Amendment, judges need not use a particular mechanism, such as the exclusionary rule, to ensure compliance. Frankfurter noted that the law in England, where there was no exclusionary rule, and in the states, the majority of which rejected the rule, proved that justice could be served without this check on police behavior. States were left free to adopt whatever procedures they wished to enforce search and seizure rights. The exclusionary rule was not mandatory.

Growing conflicts between state and federal search and seizure rules, coupled with changes in Court personnel, caused the Court to reconsider the applicability of the exclusionary rule to states in *Mapp v.*

Ohio (1961).[21] As you read *Mapp*, can you discern why it is such a significant, yet controversial, opinion? Does Justice Clark's majority opinion leave any room for exceptions? This question arose during the 1980s and continues into the current Supreme Court era.

Mapp v. Ohio

367 U.S. 643 (1961)
Vote: 6 (Black, Brennan, Clark, Douglas, Stewart, Warren)
    3 (Frankfurter, Harlan, Whittaker)
Opinion of the Court: Clark
Concurring opinions: Black, Douglas, Stewart
Dissenting opinion: Harlan

Dollree Mapp, a woman in her early twenties, was involved in myriad illegal activities, ranging from gambling to prostitution, which she carried on in her Cleveland home. For several months the police had attempted to shut down her operations, but apparently Mapp was tipped off because, each time police planned a raid, she managed to elude them.

On May 23, 1957, police officers, led by Sgt. Carl Delau, tried to enter Mapp's house, this time on the grounds that she was harboring a fugitive from justice. (The fugitive was suspected of bombing the house of an alleged Cleveland numbers racketeer, Don King, who was later to become a prominent boxing promoter.[22]) When the police arrived, Mapp refused to let them in because they did not have a search warrant. Delau returned to his car, radioed for a search warrant, and kept the house under surveillance. Three hours later, and with additional police officers, Delau again tried to enter. This time Mapp did not come to the door, so police forced it open.

At this point several events occurred almost simultaneously. Mapp's attorney, whom she had called when police first appeared, arrived and tried to see her. Police would not let him in. Hearing the police break in, Mapp came downstairs and began arguing with them. Delau held up a piece of a paper, which he claimed was a search warrant. Mapp grabbed it and stuffed it down her blouse. A fight broke out, during which police handcuffed Mapp, retrieved the paper, and searched the house. The police seized some allegedly obscene pictures, which were illegal to possess under Ohio law. The existence of a valid search warrant was never established by the state. Mapp was found guilty of possession of obscene materials and sentenced to prison. Her attorney appealed to the U.S. Supreme Court, asking the justices to review Mapp's claim on First Amendment grounds, but the justices were more interested in exploring the search and seizure issue.[23]

MR. JUSTICE CLARK delivered the opinion of the Court.

Seventy-five years ago, in Boyd v. United States ... [t]he Court noted that

"constitutional provisions for the security of person and property should be liberally construed.... It is the duty of courts to be watchful for the constitutional rights of the citizen, and against any stealthy encroachments thereon."

In this jealous regard for maintaining the integrity of individual rights, the Court gave life to Madison's prediction that "independent tribunals of justice ... will be naturally led to resist every encroachment upon rights expressly stipulated for in the Constitution by the declaration of rights."...

---

21. See *Elkins v. United States* (1960) for an example of the jurisdictional problems inherent in conflicting search and seizure rules. In this decision the Court struck down the infamous "silver platter doctrine" in which federal courts would admit evidence gathered illegally by state law enforcement officials.

22. See Fred W. Friendly and Martha J. H. Elliott, *The Constitution—That Delicate Balance* (New York: Random House, 1984), 128–133.

23. Indeed, both Mapp's and the state's attorneys argued this case on First Amendment grounds because she was convicted for possessing obscene material. The ACLU, in an amicus curiae brief, raised the Fourth Amendment issue on which the Court ultimately decided. *Mapp*, therefore, presents an excellent illustration of the effect amicus curiae briefs can have on the justices. It also is used as an example of the uneven quality of state attorneys general. During oral argument, a justice asked Ohio's attorney about the applicability of *Wolf* to *Mapp*. The attorney responded that he did not know anything about *Wolf*, even though it was the leading case in the area.

In 1957 Dollree Mapp was arrested for possession of obscene materials. The police seized vital evidence against her during an unconstitutional search. In *Mapp v. Ohio* (1961) the Supreme Court reversed her conviction holding that evidence obtained through an illegal search could not be admitted in court.

Less than 30 years after Boyd, this Court, in Weeks v. United States, 1914, ... stated that use of the seized evidence involved "a denial of the constitutional rights of the accused." Thus, in the year 1914, in the Weeks case, this Court "for the first time" held that "in a federal prosecution the Fourth Amendment barred the use of evidence secured through an illegal search and seizure." This Court has ever since required of federal law officers a strict adherence to that command which this Court has held to be a clear, specific, and constitutionally required—even if judicially implied—deterrent safeguard without insistence upon which the Fourth Amendment would have been reduced to "a form of words." It meant, quite simply, that "conviction by means of unlawful seizures and enforced confessions ... should find no sanction in the judgments of the courts ... ," that such evidence "shall not be used at all."

There are in the cases of this Court some passing references to the Weeks rule as being one of evidence. But the plain and unequivocal language of Weeks—and its later paraphrase in Wolf—to the effect that the Weeks rule is of constitutional origin, remains entirely undisturbed....

In 1949, 35 years after Weeks was announced, this Court, in Wolf v. People of State of Colorado, again for the first time, discussed the effect of the Fourth Amendment upon the states through the operation of the Due Process Clause of the Fourteenth Amendment. It said:

"[W]e have no hesitation in saying that were a State affirmatively to sanction such police incursion into privacy it would run counter to the guaranty of the Fourteenth Amendment."

Nevertheless, after declaring that the "security of one's privacy against arbitrary intrusion by the police" is "implicit in 'the concept of ordered liberty' and as such enforceable against the States through the Due Process Clause," and announcing that it "stoutly adhere[d]" to the Weeks decision, the Court decided that the Weeks exclusionary rule would not then be imposed upon the States as "an essential ingredient of the right." The Court's reasons for not considering essential to the right to privacy, as a curb imposed upon the States by the Due Process Clause, that which decades before had been posited as part and parcel of the Fourth Amendment's limitation upon federal encroachment of individual privacy, were bottomed on factual considerations.

While they are not basically relevant to a decision that the exclusionary rule is an essential ingredient of the Fourth Amendment as the right it embodies is vouchsafed against the States by the Due Process Clause, we will consider the current validity of the factual grounds upon which Wolf was based.

The Court in Wolf first stated that "[t]he contrariety of views of the States" on the adoption of the exclusionary rule of Weeks was "particularly impressive" and, in this connection that it could not "brush aside the experience of States which deem the incidence of such conduct by the police too slight to call for a deterrent remedy ... by overriding the [States'] relevant rules of evidence." While in 1949, prior to the Wolf case, almost two-thirds of the States were opposed to the use of the exclusionary rule, now, despite the Wolf case, more than half of those since passing upon it, by their own legislative or judicial decision, have wholly or partly adopted or adhered to the Weeks rule. Significantly, among those now following the rule is California, which, according to its highest court, was "compelled to reach that conclusion because other remedies have completely failed to secure compliance with the constitutional provisions...." In connection with this California case, we note that the second basis elaborated in Wolf in support of its failure to enforce the exclusionary doctrine against the States was that "other means of protection" have been afforded "the right to privacy." The experience of California that such other remedies have been worthless and futile is buttressed by the experience of other States....

Likewise, time has set its face against ... Wolf.... [T]he force of that reasoning has been largely vitiated by later decisions of this Court. These include the recent discarding of the "silver platter" doctrine which allowed federal judicial use of evidence seized in violation of the Constitution by state agents; the relaxation of the formerly strict requirements as to standing to challenge the use of evidence thus seized, so that now the procedure of exclusion, "ultimately referable to constitutional safeguards," is available to anyone even "legitimately on [the] premises" unlawfully searched; and finally, the formulation of a method to prevent state use of evidence unconstitutionally seized by federal agents. Because there can be no fixed formula, we are admittedly met with "recurring questions of the [r]easonableness of searches," but less is not to be expected when dealing with a Constitution, and, at any rate, "reasonableness is in the first instance for the [trial court] to determine."

It, therefore, plainly appears that the factual considerations supporting the failure of the Wolf Court to include the Weeks exclusionary rule when it recognized the enforceability of the right to privacy against the States in 1949, while not basically relevant to the constitutional consideration, could not, in any analysis, now be deemed controlling.

Some five years after Wolf, in answer to a plea made here Term after Term that we overturn its doctrine on applicability of the Weeks exclusionary rule, this Court indicated that such should not be done until the States had "adequate opportunity to adopt or reject the [Weeks] rule."... Today we once again examine Wolf's constitutional documentation of the right to privacy free from unreasonable state intrusion, and, after its dozen years on our books, are led by it to close the only courtroom door remaining open to evidence secured by official lawlessness in flagrant abuse of that basic right, reserved to all persons as a specific guarantee against that very same unlawful conduct. We hold that all evidence obtained by searches and seizures in violation of the Constitution is, by that same authority, inadmissible in a state court.

Since the Fourth Amendment's right of privacy has been declared enforceable against the States through the Due Process Clause of the Fourteenth, it is enforceable against them by the same sanction of exclusion as is used against the Federal Government. Were it otherwise, then just as without the Weeks rule the assurance against unreasonable federal searches and seizures would be "a form of words," valueless and undeserving of mention in a perpetual charter of inestimable human liberties, so too, without that rule the freedom from state invasions of privacy would be so ephemeral and so neatly severed from its conceptual nexus with the freedom from all brutish means of coercing evidence as not to merit this Court's high regard as a freedom "implicit in 'the concept of ordered liberty.'" At the time that the Court held in Wolf that the Amendment was applicable to the States through the Due Process Clause, the cases of this Court, as we have seen, had steadfastly held that as to federal officers the Fourth Amendment included the exclusion of the evidence seized in violation of its provisions. Even Wolf "stoutly adhered" to that proposition. The right to privacy, when conceded operatively enforceable against the States, was not susceptible of destruction by avulsion of the sanction upon which its protection and enjoyment had always been deemed dependent.... Therefore, in extending the substantive protections of due process to all constitutionally unreasonable searches—state or federal—it was logically and constitutionally necessary that the exclusion doctrine—an essential part of the right to privacy—be also insisted upon as an essential ingredient of the right newly recognized by the Wolf case. In short, the admission of the new constitutional right by Wolf could not consistently tolerate denial of its most important constitutional privilege, namely, the exclusion of the evidence which an accused had been forced to give by reason of the unlawful seizure. To hold otherwise is to grant the right but in reality to withhold its privilege and enjoyment. Only last year the Court itself recognized that the purpose of the exclusionary rule "is to deter—to compel respect for the constitutional guaranty in the only effectively available way—by removing the incentive to disregard it."

Indeed, we are aware of no restraint, similar to that rejected today, conditioning the enforcement of any other basic constitutional right. The right to privacy, no less important than any other right carefully and particularly reserved to the people, would stand in marked contrast to all other rights declared as "basic to a free society." This Court has not hesitated to enforce as strictly against the States as it does against the Federal Government the rights of free speech and of a free press, the rights to notice and to a fair, public trial, including, as it does, the right not to be convicted by use of a coerced confession, however logically relevant it be, and without regard to its reliability. And

nothing could be more certain than that when a coerced confession is involved, "the relevant rules of evidence" are overridden without regard to "the incidence of such conduct by the police," slight or frequent. Why should not the same rule apply to what is tantamount to coerced testimony by way of unconstitutional seizure of goods, papers, effects, documents, etc.? We find that, as to the Federal Government, the Fourth and Fifth Amendments and, as to the States, the freedom from unconscionable invasions of privacy and the freedom from convictions based upon coerced confessions do enjoy an "intimate relation" in their perpetuation of "principles of humanity and civil liberty [secured] ... only after years of struggle." The philosophy of each Amendment and of each freedom is complementary to, although not dependent upon, that of the other in its sphere of influence—the very least that together they assure in either sphere is that no man is to be convicted on unconstitutional evidence.

Moreover, our holding that the exclusionary rule is an essential part of both the Fourth and Fourteenth Amendments is not only the logical dictate of prior cases, but it also makes very good sense. There is no war between the Constitution and common sense. Presently, a federal prosecutor may make no use of evidence illegally seized, but a State's attorney across the street may, although he supposedly is operating under the enforceable prohibitions of the same Amendment. Thus the State, by admitting evidence unlawfully seized, serves to encourage disobedience to the Federal Constitution which it is bound to uphold. Moreover, "[t]he very essence of a healthy federalism depends upon the avoidance of needless conflict between state and federal courts." Such a conflict, hereafter needless, arose this very Term, in Wilson v. Schnettler, in which ... we gave full recognition to our practice in this regard by refusing to restrain a federal officer from testifying in a state court as to evidence unconstitutionally seized by him in the performance of his duties. Yet the double standard recognized until today hardly put such a thesis into practice. In non-exclusionary States, federal officers, being human, were by it invited to and did, as our cases indicate, step across the street to the State's attorney with their unconstitutionally seized evidence. Prosecution on the basis of that evidence was then had in a state court in utter disregard of the enforceable Fourth Amendment. If the fruits of an unconstitutional search had been inadmissible in both state and federal courts, this inducement to evasion would have been sooner eliminated. There would be no need to reconcile such cases as ... Schnettler, pointing up the hazardous uncertainties of our heretofore ambivalent approach....

There are those who say, as did Justice (then Judge) Cardozo, that under our constitutional exclusionary doctrine "[t]he criminal is to go free because the constable has blundered." *People v. Defore.* In some cases this will undoubtedly be the result. But ... "there is another consideration—the imperative of judicial integrity." The criminal goes free, if he must, but it is the law that sets him free. Nothing can destroy a government more quickly than its failure to observe its own laws, or worse, its disregard of the character of its own existence. Nor can it lightly be assumed that, as a practical matter, adoption of the exclusionary rule fetters law enforcement. Only last year this Court expressly considered that contention and found that "pragmatic evidence of a sort" to the contrary was not wanting.... Moreover, the experience of the states is impressive.... The movement towards the rule of exclusion has been halting but seemingly inexorable.

The ignoble shortcut to conviction left open to the State tends to destroy the entire system of constitutional restraints on which the liberties of the people rest. Having once recognized that the right to privacy embodied in the Fourth Amendment is enforceable against the States, and that the right to be secure against rude invasions of privacy by state officers is, therefore, constitutional in origin, we can no longer permit that right to remain an empty promise. Because it is enforceable in the same manner and to like effect as other basic rights secured by the Due Process Clause, we can no longer permit it to be revocable at the whim of any police officer who, in the name of law enforcement itself, chooses to suspend its enjoyment. Our decision, founded on reason and truth, gives to the individual no more than that which the Constitution guarantees him, to the police officer no less than that to which honest law enforcement is entitled, and, to the courts, that judicial integrity so necessary in the true administration of justice.

The judgment of the Supreme Court of Ohio is reversed and the cause remanded for further proceedings not inconsistent with this opinion.

Reversed and remanded.

MR. JUSTICE HARLAN, whom MR. JUSTICE FRANKFURTER and MR. JUSTICE WHITTAKER join, dissenting.

In overruling the Wolf case the Court, in my opinion, has forgotten the sense of judicial restraint which, with due regard for *stare decisis,* is one element that should enter into deciding whether a past decision of this Court should be overruled. Apart from that I also believe that the Wolf rule represents sounder Constitutional doctrine than the new rule which now replaces it.

From the Court's statement of the case one would gather that the central, if not controlling, issue on this appeal is whether illegally state-seized evidence is Constitutionally admissible in a state prosecution, an issue which would of course face us with the need for re-examining Wolf. However, such is not the situation. For, although that question was indeed raised here and below among appellant's subordinate points, the new and pivotal issue brought to the Court by this appeal is whether ... [the Ohio law] making criminal the *mere* knowing possession or control of obscene material, and under which appellant has been convicted, is consistent with the rights of free thought and expression assured against state action by the Fourteenth Amendment. That was the principal issue which was decided by the Ohio Supreme Court, which was tendered by appellant's Jurisdictional Statement, and which was briefed* and argued in this Court.

In this posture of things, I think it fair to say that five members of this Court have simply "reached out" to overrule Wolf. With all respect for the views of the majority, and recognizing that *stare decisis* carries different weight in Constitutional adjudication than it does in nonconstitutional decision, I can perceive no justification for regarding this case as an appropriate occasion for re-examining Wolf....

Since the demands of the case before us do not require

*The appellant's brief did not urge the overruling of Wolf. Indeed it did not even cite the case. The brief of the appellee merely relied on Wolf in support of the State's contention that appellant's conviction was not vitiated by the admission in evidence of the fruits of the alleged unlawful search and seizure by the police. The brief of the American and Ohio Civil Liberties Unions, as *amici,* did in one short concluding paragraph of its argument "request" the Court to re-examine and overrule Wolf, but without argumentation....

us to reach the question of the validity of Wolf, I think this case furnishes a singularly inappropriate occasion for consideration of that decision, if reconsideration is indeed warranted. Even the most cursory examination will reveal that the doctrine of the Wolf case has been of continuing importance in the administration of state criminal law. Indeed, certainly as regards its "nonexclusionary" aspect, Wolf did no more than articulate the then existing assumption among the States that the federal cases enforcing the exclusionary rule "do not bind [the States], for they construe provisions of the Federal Constitution, the Fourth and Fifth Amendments, not applicable to the States." People v. Defore. Though, of course, not reflecting the full measure of this continuing reliance, I find that during the last three Terms, for instance, the issue of the inadmissibility of illegally state-obtained evidence appears on an average of about fifteen times per Term just in the *in forma pauperis* cases summarily disposed of by us. This would indicate both that the issue which is now being decided may well have untoward practical ramifications respecting state cases long since disposed of in reliance on Wolf, and that were we determined to re-examine that doctrine we would not lack future opportunity....

Thus, if the Court were bent on reconsidering Wolf, I think that there would soon have presented itself an appropriate opportunity in which we could have had the benefit of full briefing and argument. In any event, at the very least, the present case should have been set down for reargument, in view of the inadequate briefing and argument we have received on the Wolf point. To all intents and purposes the Court's present action amounts to a summary reversal of Wolf, without argument.

I am bound to say that what has been done is not likely to promote respect either for the Court's adjudicatory process or for the stability of its decisions. Having been unable, however, to persuade any of the majority to a different procedural course, I now turn to the merits of the present decision....

I would not impose upon the States this federal exclusionary remedy. The reasons given by the majority for now suddenly turning its back on Wolf seem to me notably unconvincing.

First, it is said that "the factual grounds upon which Wolf was based" have since changed, in that more States now follow the Weeks exclusionary rule than was so at the time Wolf was decided. While that is true, a recent survey indicates that at present one-half of the States still adhere to the common-law non-exclusionary rule, and one, Maryland, retains the rule as to felonies. But in any case surely all this is beside the point, as the majority itself indeed seems to recognize. Our concern here, as it was in Wolf, is not with the desirability of that rule but only with the question whether the States are Constitutionally free to follow it or not as they may themselves determine, and the relevance of the disparity of views among the States on this point lies simply in the fact that the judgment involved is a debatable one. Moreover, the very fact on which the majority relies, instead of lending support to what is now being done, points away from the need of replacing voluntary state action with federal compulsion.

The preservation of a proper balance between state and federal responsibility in the administration of criminal justice demands patience on the part of those who might like to see things move faster among the States in this respect. Problems of criminal law enforcement vary widely from State to State. One State, in considering the totality of its legal picture, may conclude that the need for embracing the Weeks rule is pressing because other remedies are unavailable or inadequate to secure compliance with the substantive Constitutional principle involved. Another, though equally solicitous of Constitutional rights, may choose to pursue one purpose at a time, allowing all evidence relevant to guilt to be brought into a criminal trial, and dealing with Constitutional infractions by other means. Still another may consider the exclusionary rule too rough-and-ready a remedy, in that it reaches only unconstitutional intrusions which eventuate in criminal prosecution of the victims. Further, a State after experimenting with the Weeks rule for a time may, because of unsatisfactory experience with it, decide to revert to a non-exclusionary rule. And so on. From the standpoint of Constitutional permissibility in pointing a State in one direction or another, I do not see at all why "time has set its face against" the considerations which led Mr. Justice Cardozo, then chief judge of the New York Court of Appeals, to reject for New York in People v. Defore, the Weeks exclusionary rule. For us the question remains, as it has always been, one of state power, not one of passing judgment on the wisdom of one state course or another. In my view this Court should continue to forbear from fettering the States with an adamant rule which may embarrass them in coping with their own peculiar problems in criminal law enforcement.

Further, we are told that imposition of the Weeks rule on the States makes "very good sense," in that it will promote recognition by state and federal officials of their "mutual obligation to respect the same fundamental criteria" in their approach to law enforcement, and will avoid "'needless conflict between state and federal courts.'"...

An approach which regards the issue as one of achieving procedural symmetry or of serving administrative convenience surely disfigures the boundaries of this Court's functions in relation to the state and federal courts. Our role in promulgating the Weeks rule ... was quite a different one than it is here. There, in implementing the Fourth Amendment, we occupied the position of a tribunal having the ultimate responsibility for developing the standards and procedures of judicial administration within the judicial system over which it presides. Here we review state procedures whose measure is to be taken not against the specific substantive commands of the Fourth Amendment but under the flexible contours of the Due Process Clause. I do not believe that the Fourteenth Amendment empowers this Court to mould state remedies effectuating the right to freedom from "arbitrary intrusion by the police" to suit its own notions of how things should be done....

In conclusion, it should be noted that the majority opinion in this case is in fact an opinion only for the *judgment* overruling Wolf, and not for the basic rationale by which four members of the majority have reached that result. For my Brother BLACK is unwilling to subscribe to their view that the Weeks exclusionary rule derives from the Fourth Amendment itself....

I regret that I find so unwise in principle and so inexpedient in policy a decision motivated by the high purpose of increasing respect for Constitutional rights. But in the last analysis I think this Court can increase respect for the Constitution only if it rigidly respects the limitations which the Constitution places upon it, and respects as well the principles inherent in its own processes. In the present case I think we exceed both, and that our voice becomes only a voice of power, not of reason.

The application of the exclusionary rule provides yet another example of the Warren Court's revolutionary treatment of the rights of the criminally accused. It also illustrates the highly politicized nature of criminal law. Since 1961, when the Court informed states that they must adopt it, the rule has been attacked and defended by scholars, lawyers, and judges. Opponents of the rule argue that letting a guilty person go free is too great a price for society to pay just because a police officer violated search and seizure guidelines. Supporters fear that if the exclusionary rule is eliminated, police will have no incentive to respect the law. *(See Box 8-2 for the major points of the debate.)*

Exceptions to the Exclusionary Rule

Disagreement over the exclusionary rule, expressed in academic circles and the public, also was evident among the justices. Six voted to overturn Mapp's conviction, but only five expressed full support for the exclusionary rule. Stewart, who voted with the majority, explicitly did so on other grounds. When Chief Justice Warren left the Court and was replaced by the law-and-order-minded Warren Burger in 1969, legal scholars predicted that the Court might well overrule *Mapp.* With each additional Court appointment by Richard Nixon and then by Ronald Reagan, speculation on the end of the exclusionary rule increased.

At first, predictions of the reversal of *Mapp* were proven unfounded. Between 1969 and 1974, the justices made no significant move to alter the applicability of the exclusionary rule. Even so, Burger made no attempts to hide his disdain for it. As early as 1971, in a dissenting opinion in *Bivens v. Six Unknown Named Agents of Federal Bureau of Narcotics,* he provided a clear indication of his views about the exclusionary rule. He began by rejecting part of the Court's rationale for creating the rule—the so-called "sporting thesis" under which the government must "play the game fairly" and cannot be permitted to "profit from its own illegal acts." Instead, he claimed that the only reasonable justification for the rule was that it might

BOX 8-2   DEBATE OVER THE EXCLUSIONARY RULE

Following are excerpts from an article by Judge Malcolm Richard Wilkey of the U.S. Court of Appeals arguing that the exclusionary rule should be abolished and a response by Professor Yale Kamisar asserting that it is necessary.

Malcolm Richard Wilkey: "Why Suppress Valid Evidence?"

No matter what rationale we consider, the rule in its indiscriminate workings does far more harm than good and, in many respects, it actually prevents us from dealing with the real problems of Fourth Amendment violations in the course of criminal investigations.

In the eyes of the Supreme Court, the first and primary rationale of the exclusionary rule is deterrence. I submit that all available facts and logic show that excluding the most reliable evidence does absolutely nothing to punish and thus deter the official wrongdoer, but the inevitable and certain result is that the guilty criminal defendant goes free.

The second—now rather distant second—rationale in the eyes of the Court has been protection of privacy. I submit a policy of excluding incriminating evidence can never protect an innocent victim of an illegal search against whom no incriminating evidence is discovered. The only persons protected by the rule are the guilty against whom the most serious reliable evidence should be offered. It cannot be separately argued that the innocent person is protected *in the future* by excluding evidence against the criminal *now*, for this is only the deterrent argument all over again.

The third rationale found in the past opinions of the Court is that the use of illegally obtained evidence brings our court system into disrepute. I submit that the exclusion of valid, probative, undeniably truthful evidence undermines the reputation of and destroys the respect for the entire judicial system.

Ask any group of laymen if they can understand why a pistol found on a man when he is searched by an officer should not be received in evidence when the man is charged with illegal possession of a weapon, or why a heroin package found under similar circumstances should be not always received in evidence when he is prosecuted for a narcotics possession, and I believe you will receive a lecture that these are outrageous technicalities of law which the American people should not tolerate. If you put the same issue to a representative group of lawyers and judges, I predict you would receive a strong preponderance of opinions supporting the lay view, although from those heavily imbued with a mystique of the exclusionary rule as of almost divine origin you would doubtless hear some support.

Yale Kamisar: "The Struggle to Make the Fourth Amendment More than an Empty Promise"

Over the years, I have written about the impact of ... *Mapp* and other decisions on crime rates and police-prosecution efficiency. I will not restate my findings again.... I would, however, like to summarize a few points:

•Long before the exclusionary rule became law in the states—indeed, long before any of the procedural safeguards in the federal Constitution was held applicable to the states—invidious comparisons were made between the rate of crime in our nation and the incidence of crime in others.

Thus, in 1911, the distinguished ex-president of Cornell University, Andrew D. White, pointed out that, although London's population was two million larger than New York's, there were ten times more murders in New York. And in 1920, Edwin W. Sims, the first head of the Chicago Crime Commission, pointed out that "[d]uring 1919 there were more murders in Chicago (with a population of three million) than in the entire British Isles (with a population of forty million)." This history ought to raise some doubts about the alleged causal link between the high rate of crime in America and the exclusionary rule.

•England and Wales have not experienced anything like the "revolution" in American criminal procedure which began at least as early as the 1961 *Mapp* case. Nevertheless, from 1955–65 (a decade which happened to be subjected to a most intensive study), the number of indictable offenses against the person in England and Wales increased 162 percent. How do opponents of the exclusionary rule explain such increases in countries which did not suffer from the wounds the Warren Court supposedly inflicted upon America? ...

The predictions and descriptions of near-disaster in California law enforcement which greeted the 1955 *Cahan* decision [applying the exclusionary rule to California] find precious little empirical support. The percentage of narcotics convictions did drop almost 10 points (to 77 percent), but only possession cases were significantly affected. Meanwhile, both the rate of arrests and felony complaints filed for narcotics offenses actually increased! ...

The overall felony conviction rate was 84.5 percent for three years before *Cahan*, 85.4 percent for the *Cahan* year and 86.4 percent in the three years after *Cahan* (even including the low narcotic percentages). Conviction rates for murder, manslaughter, felony assault, rape, robbery and burglary remained almost the same, though the number of convicted felons rose steadily.

The exclusionary rule, to be sure, does free some "guilty criminals" (as would an effective tort remedy that inhibited the police from making illegal searches and seizures in the first place), but very rarely are they robbers or murderers. Rather they are "offenders caught in the everyday world of police initiated vice and narcotics enforcement...."

SOURCE: M. Ethan Katsh, *Taking Sides* (Guilford, Conn.: Dushkin, 1991), 288, 292–293, 303–304.

deter "law enforcement authorities from using improper methods to obtain evidence." Yet he questioned whether, in fact, the exclusionary rule had accomplished this objective:

> Although I would hesitate to abandon it until some meaningful substitute is developed, the history of the [exclusionary rule] demonstrates that it is both conceptually sterile and practically ineffective in accomplishing its stated objective....
>
> Some clear demonstration of the benefits and effectiveness of the exclusionary rule is required to justify it in view of the high price it extracts from society—the release of countless guilty criminals. But there is no empirical evidence to support the claim that the rule actually deters illegal conduct of law enforcement officials.

To some scholars, Burger's opinion was disingenuous. They reasoned that Burger selected the deterrence rationale on which to rest the exclusionary rule because he knew that it would provide the greatest leeway to narrow it and eventually abolish it; after all, it is very hard to demonstrate that any particular measure—including the exclusionary rule—deters crime, while it is always true that the exclusionary rule makes the government, or should make the government, "play the game fairly." If this was Burger's plan, would he succeed? This question was present in many minds when, in 1974, much to the elation of law enforcement interests and the horror of civil libertarians, the Court decided to hear oral arguments in *United States v. Calandra*, a case involving the applicability of the exclusionary rule to grand jury proceedings. Many observers expected the Court to use this case to overrule *Mapp*; instead, the Court ruled solely on the issue of grand jury hearings, stating that *Mapp* did not apply to such proceedings. Civil libertarians breathed a sigh of relief after *Calandra*. After all, the Court had not overruled *Mapp*.

However, it did narrow *Mapp*'s reach—the exclusionary rule would not apply to grand jury hearings—and it moved a step closer to embracing Burger's deterrence theory as the sole rationale for the exclusionary rule. As Justice Powell wrote for the majority,

> In deciding whether to extend the exclusionary rule to grand jury proceedings, we must weigh the potential injury to the historic role and functions of the grand jury against the potential benefits of the rule as applied in this context. It is evident that this extension of the exclusionary rule would seriously impede the grand jury.... Permitting witnesses to invoke the exclusionary rule before a grand jury would precipitate adjudication of issues hitherto reserved for the trial on the merits and would delay and disrupt grand jury proceedings....
>
> Against this potential damage to the role and functions of the grand jury, we must weight the benefits to be derived from this proposed extension of the exclusionary rule.... Any incremental deterrent effect which might be achieved by extending the rule to grand jury proceedings is uncertain at best. Whatever deterrence of police misconduct may result from the exclusion of illegally seized evidence from criminal trials, it is unrealistic to assume that application of the rule to grand jury proceedings would significantly further that goal.

Can you see how reliance solely on a deterrence theory can lead to the narrowing of the exclusionary rule? Think about it this way: What if the Court had adopted the sporting thesis? Would it have decided this case the same way?

As the Court continued to rely on the deterrence rationale and to neglect other justifications, such as the sporting approach, some scholars remained convinced that the exclusionary rule's days were numbered. But, with the passage of time, other analysts began to believe that the Court would let *Mapp* stand. That prediction has turned out to be the more accurate; the Court still has not overruled *Mapp*. During the 1980s, however, it created certain exceptions to the use of the rule, exceptions that, according to some justices, are so pervasive as to undermine its usefulness.

The most important of these is called the good faith exception, which the Court created in *United States v. Leon* (1984). While reading the opinion, think about why the Court authorized this exception to *Mapp*. Also consider Justice Brennan's dissent. By the time this case was decided, Brennan was the sole remaining member of the five-person majority that agreed to Clark's opinion in *Mapp* applying the exclusionary rule to the states. Why did he object to the Court's decision? Note that he points to *Calandra* and its adoption of the deterrence rationale as the beginning of the demise of the rule.

United States v. Leon

468 U.S. 897 (1984)

Vote: 6 (Blackmun, Burger, O'Connor, Powell,
    Rehnquist, White)
    3 (Brennan, Marshall, Stevens)
Opinion of the Court: White
Concurring opinion: Blackmun
Dissenting opinions: Brennan, Stevens

In 1981 Burbank police received a tip from a person of disputed credibility, identifying two individuals, Patsy and Armando, as drug dealers. Apparently, the pair kept small quantities of drugs in their house and the remainder at another residence in Burbank. Police began a surveillance of the Burbank residence, where they spotted a car belonging to Ricardo Del Castillo, whose records led police to Alberto Leon, a known drug dealer. Based on observation, continued surveillance of the residences, and information from a second informant, a veteran detective drew up an affidavit to obtain a search warrant, which a judge issued. With the warrant, police searched the residences and seized illegal substances at both.

At the trial stage, Leon's attorney argued that the warrant was invalid because the detective lacked sufficient probable cause to sign an affidavit, and the judge, to issue it. The defect was the lack of established credibility of the original tip. The government's lawyers admitted that Leon had a valid point, but argued that the courts should decline to throw out the entire case because of a defective warrant. They claimed that the officers had acted in "good faith"; the police believed they had a legitimate warrant and acted accordingly.

JUSTICE WHITE delivered the opinion of the Court.

This case presents the question whether the Fourth Amendment exclusionary rule should be modified so as not to bar the use in the prosecution's case-in-chief of evidence obtained by officers acting in reasonable reliance on a search warrant issued by a detached and neutral magistrate but ultimately found to be unsupported by probable cause. To resolve this question, we must consider once again the tension between the sometimes competing goals of, on the one hand, deterring official misconduct and removing inducements to unreasonable invasions of privacy and, on the other, establishing procedures under which criminal defendants are "acquitted or convicted on the basis of all the evidence which exposes the truth."...

The Fourth Amendment contains no provision expressly precluding the use of evidence obtained in violation of its commands, and an examination of its origin and purposes makes clear that the use of fruits of a past unlawful search or seizure "work[s] no new Fourth Amendment wrong." The wrong condemned by the Amendment is "fully accomplished" by the unlawful search or seizure itself, and the exclusionary rule is neither intended nor able to "cure the invasion of the defendant's rights which he has already suffered." The rule thus operates as "a judicially created remedy designed to safeguard Fourth Amendment rights generally through its deterrent effect, rather than a personal constitutional right of the person aggrieved."

Whether the exclusionary sanction is appropriately imposed in a particular case, our decisions make clear, is "an issue separate from the question whether the Fourth Amendment rights of the party seeking to invoke the rule were violated by police conduct." Only the former question is currently before us, and it must be resolved by weighing the costs and benefits of preventing the use in the prosecution's case-in-chief of inherently trustworthy tangible evidence obtained in reliance on a search warrant issued by a detached and neutral magistrate that ultimately is found to be defective.

The substantial social costs exacted by the exclusionary rule for the vindication of Fourth Amendment rights have long been a source of concern. "Our cases have consistently recognized that unbending application of the exclusionary sanction to enforce ideals of governmental rectitude would impede unacceptably the truth-finding functions of judge and jury." Particularly when law enforcement officers have acted in objective good faith or their transgressions have been minor, the magnitude of the benefit conferred on such guilty defendants offends basic concepts of the criminal justice system. Indiscriminate application of the exclusionary rule, therefore, may well "generat[e] disrespect for the law and the administration of justice." Accordingly, "[a]s with any remedial device, the application of the rule has been restricted to those areas where its remedial objectives are thought most efficaciously served."

Close attention to those remedial objectives has characterized our recent decisions concerning the scope of the Fourth Amendment exclusionary rule. The Court has, to be sure, not seriously questioned, "in the absence of a more efficacious sanction, the continued application of the rule to suppress evidence from the [prosecution's] case where a Fourth Amendment violation has been substantial and deliberate.... " Nevertheless, the balancing approach that has evolved in various contexts—including criminal trials—"forcefully suggest[s] that the exclusionary rule be more generally modified to permit the introduction of evidence obtained in the reasonable good-faith belief that a search or seizure was in accord with the Fourth Amendment."...

The same attention to the purposes underlying the exclusionary rule also has characterized decisions not involving the scope of the rule itself. We have not required suppression of the fruits of a search incident to an arrest made in good-faith reliance on a substantive criminal statute that subsequently is declared unconstitutional. Similarly, although the Court has been unwilling to conclude that new Fourth Amendment principles are always to have only prospective effect, no Fourth Amendment decision marking a "clear break with the past" has been applied retroactively....

As yet, we have not recognized any form of good-faith exception to the Fourth Amendment exclusionary rule. But the balancing approach that has evolved during the years of experience with the rule provides strong support for the modification currently urged upon us. As we discuss below, our evaluation of the costs and benefits of suppressing reliable physical evidence seized by officers reasonably relying on a warrant issued by a detached and neutral magistrate

leads to the conclusion that such evidence should be admissible in the prosecution's case-in-chief.

Because a search warrant "provides the detached scrutiny of a neutral magistrate, which is a more reliable safeguard against improper searches than the hurried judgment of a law enforcement officer 'engaged in the often competitive enterprise of ferreting out crime,'" we have expressed a strong preference for warrants and declared that "in a doubtful or marginal case a search under a warrant may be sustainable where without one it would fail." Reasonable minds frequently may differ on the question whether a particular affidavit establishes probable cause, and we have thus concluded that the preference for warrants is most appropriately effectuated by according "great deference" to a magistrate's determination.

Deference to the magistrate, however, is not boundless. It is clear, first, that the deference accorded to a magistrate's finding of probable cause does not preclude inquiry into the knowing or reckless falsity of the affidavit on which that determination was based. Second, the courts must also insist that the magistrate purport to "perform his 'neutral and detached' function and not serve merely as a rubber stamp for the police."...

Third, reviewing courts will not defer to a warrant based on an affidavit that does not "provide the magistrate with a substantial basis for determining the existence of probable cause."... Even if the warrant application was supported by more than a "bare bones" affidavit, a reviewing court may properly conclude that, notwithstanding the deference that magistrates deserve, the warrant was invalid because the magistrate's probable-cause determination reflected an improper analysis of the totality of the circumstances.

Only in the first of these three situations, however, has the Court set forth a rationale for suppressing evidence obtained pursuant to a search warrant; in the other areas, it has simply excluded such evidence without considering whether Fourth Amendment interests will be advanced. To the extent that proponents of exclusion rely on its behavioral effects on judges and magistrates in these areas, their reliance is misplaced. First, the exclusionary rule is designed to deter police misconduct rather than to punish the errors of judges and magistrates. Second, there exists no evidence suggesting that judges and magistrates are inclined to ignore or subvert the Fourth Amendment or that lawlessness among these actors requires application of the extreme sanction of exclusion.

Third, and most important, we discern no basis, and are offered none, for believing that exclusion of evidence seized pursuant to a warrant will have a significant deterrent effect on the issuing judge or magistrate. Many of the factors that indicate that the exclusionary rule cannot provide an effective "special" or "general" deterrent for individual offending law enforcement officers apply as well to judges or magistrates. And, to the extent that the rule is thought to operate as a "systemic" deterrent on a wider audience, it clearly can have no such effect on individuals empowered to issue search warrants. Judges and magistrates are not adjuncts to the law enforcement team; as neutral judicial officers, they have no stake in the outcome of particular criminal prosecutions. The threat of exclusion thus cannot be expected significantly to deter them. Imposition of the exclusionary sanction is not necessary meaningfully to inform judicial officers of their errors, and we cannot conclude that admitting evidence obtained pursuant to a warrant while at the same time declaring that the warrant was somehow defective will in any way reduce judicial officers' professional incentives to comply with the Fourth Amendment, encourage them to repeat their mistakes, or lead to the granting of all colorable warrant requests.

If exclusion of evidence obtained pursuant to a subsequently invalidated warrant is to have any deterrent effect, therefore, it must alter the behavior of individual law enforcement officers or the policies of their departments. One could argue that applying the exclusionary rule in cases where the police failed to demonstrate probable cause in the warrant application deters future inadequate presentations or "magistrate shopping" and thus promotes the ends of the Fourth Amendment. Suppressing evidence obtained pursuant to a technically defective warrant supported by probable cause also might encourage officers to scrutinize more closely the form of the warrant and to point out suspected judicial errors. We find such arguments speculative and conclude that suppression of evidence obtained pursuant to a warrant should be ordered only on a case-by-case basis and only in those unusual cases in which exclusion will further the purposes of the exclusionary rule.

We have frequently questioned whether the exclusionary rule can have any deterrent effect when the offending officers acted in the objectively reasonable belief that their conduct did not violate the Fourth Amendment.... But even assuming that the rule effectively deters some police misconduct and provides incentives for the law enforcement profession as a whole to conduct itself in accord with the Fourth Amendment, it cannot be expected, and should not be applied, to deter objectively reasonable law enforcement activity....

We conclude that the marginal or nonexistent benefits produced by suppressing evidence obtained in objectively reasonable reliance on a subsequently invalidated search warrant cannot justify the substantial costs of exclusion. We do not suggest, however, that exclusion is always inappropriate in cases where an officer has obtained a warrant and abided by its terms. "[S]earches pursuant to a warrant will rarely require any deep inquiry into reasonableness," for "a warrant issued by a magistrate normally suffices to establish" that a law enforcement officer has "acted in good faith in conducting the search." Nevertheless, the officer's reliance on the magistrate's probable-cause determination and on the technical sufficiency of the warrant he issues must be objectively reasonable, and it is clear that in some circumstances the officer will have no reasonable grounds for believing that the warrant was properly issued.

Suppression therefore remains an appropriate remedy if the magistrate or judge in issuing a warrant was misled by information in an affidavit that the affiant knew was false or would have known was false except for his reckless disregard of the truth. The exception we recognize today will also not apply in cases where the issuing magistrate wholly abandoned his judicial role.... [I]n such circumstances, no reasonably well-trained officer should rely on the warrant. Nor would an officer manifest objective good faith in relying on a warrant based on an affidavit "so lacking in indicia of probable cause as to render official belief in its existence entirely unreasonable." Finally, depending on the circumstances of the particular case, a warrant may be so facially deficient—*i.e.*, in failing to particularize the place to be searched or the things to be seized—that the executing officers cannot reasonably presume it to be valid.

In so limiting the suppression remedy, we leave untouched the probable-cause standard and the various requirements for a valid warrant. Other objections to the modification of the Fourth Amendment exclusionary rule we consider to be insubstantial. The good-faith exception for searches conducted pursuant to warrants is not intended to signal our unwillingness strictly to enforce the requirements of the Fourth Amendment, and we do not believe that it will have this effect. As we have already suggested, the good-faith exception, turning as it does on objective reasonableness, should not be difficult to apply in practice. . . .

When the principles we have enunciated today are applied to the facts of this case, it is apparent that the judgment of the Court of Appeals cannot stand. The Court of Appeals applied the prevailing legal standards to Officer Rombach's warrant application and concluded that the application could not support the magistrate's probable-cause determination. In so doing, the court clearly informed the magistrate that he had erred in issuing the challenged warrant. This aspect of the court's judgment is not under attack in this proceeding.

Having determined that the warrant should not have issued, the Court of Appeals understandably declined to adopt a modification of the Fourth Amendment exclusionary rule that this Court had not previously sanctioned. Although the modification finds strong support in our previous cases, the Court of Appeals' commendable self-restraint is not to be criticized. We have now re-examined the purposes of the exclusionary rule and the propriety of its application in cases where officers have relied on a subsequently invalidated search warrant. Our conclusion is that the rule's purposes will only rarely be served by applying it in such circumstances.

In the absence of an allegation that the magistrate abandoned his detached and neutral role, suppression is appropriate only if the officers were dishonest or reckless in preparing their affidavit or could not have harbored an objectively reasonable belief in the existence of probable cause. Only respondent Leon has contended that no reasonably well-trained police officer could have believed that there existed probable cause to search his house; significantly, the other respondents advance no comparable argument. Officer Rombach's application for a warrant clearly was supported by much more than a "bare bones" affidavit. The affidavit related the results of an extensive investigation and, as the opinions of the divided panel of the

Court of Appeals make clear, provided evidence sufficient to create disagreement among thoughtful and competent judges as to the existence of probable cause. Under these circumstances, the officers' reliance on the magistrate's determination of probable cause was objectively reasonable, and application of the extreme sanction of exclusion is inappropriate.

Accordingly, the judgment of the Court of Appeals is

Reversed.

JUSTICE BRENNAN, with whom JUSTICE MARSHALL joins, dissenting.

Ten years ago in *United States v. Calandra* (1974), I expressed the fear that the Court's decision "may signal that a majority of my colleagues have positioned themselves to reopen the door [to evidence secured by official lawlessness] still further and abandon altogether the exclusionary rule in search-and-seizure cases." (BRENNAN, J., dissenting.) Since then, in case after case, I have witnessed the Court's gradual but determined strangulation of the rule. It now appears that the Court's victory over the Fourth Amendment is complete. That today's decision represents the *pièce de resistance* of the Court's past efforts cannot be doubted, for today the Court sanctions the use in the prosecution's case-in-chief of illegally obtained evidence against the individual whose rights have been violated—a result that had previously been thought to be foreclosed.

The Court seeks to justify this result on the ground that the "costs" of adhering to the exclusionary rule in cases like those before us exceed the "benefits." But the language of deterrence and of cost/benefit analysis, if used indiscriminately, can have a narcotic effect. It creates an illusion of technical precision and ineluctability. It suggests that not only constitutional principle but also empirical data support the majority's result. When the Court's analysis is examined carefully, however, it is clear that we have not been treated to an honest assessment of the merits of the exclusionary rule, but have instead been drawn into a curious world where the "costs" of excluding illegally obtained evidence loom to exaggerated heights and where the "benefits" of such exclusion are made to disappear with a mere wave of the hand.

The majority ignores the fundamental constitutional importance of what is at stake here. While the machinery of law enforcement and indeed the nature of crime itself have changed dramatically since the Fourth Amendment became part of the Nation's fundamental law in 1791, what the Framers understood then remains true today—that the task of combating crime and convicting the guilty will in every era seem of such critical and pressing concern that we may be lured by the temptations of expediency into forsaking our commitment to protecting individual liberty and privacy. It was for that very reason that the Framers of the Bill of Rights insisted that law enforcement efforts be permanently and unambiguously restricted in order to preserve personal freedoms. In the constitutional scheme they ordained, the sometimes unpopular task of ensuring that the government's enforcement efforts remain within the strict boundaries fixed by the Fourth Amendment was entrusted to the courts.... If those independent tribunals lose their resolve, however, as the Court has done today, and give way to the seductive call of expediency, the vital guarantees of the Fourth Amendment are reduced to nothing more than a "form of words."...

A proper understanding of the broad purposes sought to be served by the Fourth Amendment demonstrates that the principles embodied in the exclusionary rule rest upon a far firmer constitutional foundation than the shifting sands of the Court's deterrence rationale. But even if I were to accept the Court's chosen method of analyzing the question posed by these cases, I would still conclude that the Court's decision cannot be justified....

At bottom, the Court's decision turns on the proposition that the exclusionary rule is merely a "'judicially created remedy designed to safeguard Fourth Amendment rights generally through its deterrent effect, rather than a personal constitutional right.'"... The germ of that idea is found in *Wolf v. Colorado* (1949), and although I had thought that such a narrow conception of the rule had been forever put to rest by our decision in *Mapp v. Ohio* (1961), it has been revived by the present Court and reaches full flower with today's decision. The essence of this view, as expressed initially in the *Calandra* opinion and as reiterated today, is that the sole "purpose of the Fourth Amendment is to prevent unreasonable governmental intrusions into the privacy of one's person, house, papers, or effects. The wrong condemned is the unjustified governmental invasion of these areas of an individual's life. That wrong ... is *fully*

accomplished by the original search without probable cause." (Emphasis added.) This reading of the Amendment implies that its proscriptions are directed solely at those government agents who may actually invade an individual's constitutionally protected privacy. The courts are not subject to any direct constitutional duty to exclude illegally obtained evidence, because the question of the admissibility of such evidence is not addressed by the Amendment. This view of the scope of the Amendment relegates the judiciary to the periphery. Because the only constitutionally cognizable injury has already been "fully accomplished" by the police by the time a case comes before the courts, the Constitution is not itself violated if the judge decides to admit the tainted evidence. Indeed, the most the judge *can* do is wring his hands and hope that perhaps by excluding such evidence he can deter future transgressions by the police.

Such a reading appears plausible, because, as critics of the exclusionary rule never tire of repeating, the Fourth Amendment makes no express provision for the exclusion of evidence secured in violation of its commands. A short answer to this claim, of course, is that many of the Constitution's most vital imperatives are stated in general terms and the task of giving meaning to these precepts is therefore left to subsequent judicial decisionmaking in the context of concrete cases....

A more direct answer may be supplied by recognizing that the Amendment, like other provisions of the Bill of Rights, restrains the power of the government as a whole; it does not specify only a particular agency and exempt all others. The judiciary is responsible, no less than the executive, for ensuring that constitutional rights are respected.

When that fact is kept in mind, the role of the courts and their possible involvement in the concerns of the Fourth Amendment comes into sharper focus. Because seizures are executed principally to secure evidence, and because such evidence generally has utility in our legal system only in the context of a trial supervised by a judge, it is apparent that the admission of illegally obtained evidence implicates the same constitutional concerns as the initial seizure of that evidence. Indeed, by admitting unlawfully seized evidence, the judiciary becomes a part of what is in fact a single governmental action prohibited by the terms of the Amendment. Once that connection between the evidence-gathering role of the police and the evidence-admitting function of the courts is acknowledged, the plausibility of the Court's interpretation becomes more suspect. Certainly nothing in the language or history of the Fourth Amendment suggests that a recognition of this evidentiary link between the police and the courts was meant to be foreclosed. It is difficult to give any meaning at all to the limitations imposed by the Amendment if they are read to proscribe only certain conduct by the police but to allow other agents of the same government to take advantage of evidence secured by the police in violation of its requirements. The Amendment therefore must be read to condemn not only the initial unconstitutional invasion of privacy—which is done, after all, for the purpose of securing evidence—but also the subsequent use of any evidence so obtained.

The Court evades this principle by drawing an artificial line between the constitutional rights and responsibilities that are engaged by actions of the police and those that are engaged when a defendant appears before the courts. According to the Court, the substantive protections of the Fourth Amendment are wholly exhausted at the moment when police unlawfully invade an individual's privacy and thus no substantive force remains to those protections at the time of trial when the government seeks to use evidence obtained by the police.

I submit that such a crabbed reading of the Fourth Amendment casts aside the teaching of those Justices who first formulated the exclusionary rule, and rests ultimately on an impoverished understanding of judicial responsibility in our constitutional scheme. For my part, "[t]he right of the people to be secure in their persons, houses, papers, and effects, against unreasonable searches and seizures" comprises a personal right to exclude all evidence secured by means of unreasonable searches and seizures. The right to be free from the initial invasion of privacy and the right of exclusion are coordinate components of the central embracing right to be free from unreasonable searches and seizures.

. . . [I]t is clear why the question whether the exclusion of evidence would deter future police misconduct was never considered a relevant concern in the early cases from *Weeks* to *Olmstead.* In those formative decisions, the Court plainly understood that the exclusion of illegally obtained evidence was compelled not by judicially fashioned remedial purposes, but rather by a direct constitutional command. . . .

. . . [T]he Court since *Calandra* has gradually pressed the deterrence rationale for the rule back to center stage. The various arguments advanced by the Court in this campaign have only strengthened my conviction that the deterrence theory is both misguided and unworkable. First, the Court has frequently bewailed the "cost" of excluding reliable evidence. In large part, this criticism rests upon a refusal to acknowledge the function of the Fourth Amendment itself. If nothing else, the Amendment plainly operates to disable the government from gathering information and securing evidence in certain ways. In practical terms, of course, this restriction of official power means that some incriminating evidence inevitably will go undetected if the government obeys these constitutional restraints. It is the loss of that evidence that is the "price" our society pays for enjoying the freedom and privacy safeguarded by the Fourth Amendment. Thus, some criminals will go free *not*, in Justice (then Judge) Cardozo's misleading epigram, "because the constable has blundered," *People v. Defore* (1926), but rather because official compliance with Fourth Amendment requirements makes it more difficult to catch criminals. Understood in this way, the Amendment directly contemplates that some reliable and incriminating evidence will be lost to the government; therefore, it is not the exclusionary rule, but the Amendment itself that has imposed this cost.

In addition, the Court's decisions over the past decade have made plain that the entire enterprise of attempting to assess the benefits and costs of the exclusionary rule in various contexts is a virtually impossible task for the judiciary to perform honestly or accurately. Although the Court's language in those cases suggests that some specific empirical basis may support its analyses, the reality is that the Court's opinions represent inherently unstable compounds of intuition, hunches, and occasional pieces of partial and often inconclusive data. In *Calandra,* for example, the Court, in considering whether the exclusionary rule should apply in grand jury proceedings, had before it no concrete evidence whatever concerning the impact that application of the rule in such proceedings would have either in terms of the long-term costs or the expected benefits. To the extent empirical data are available regarding the general costs and benefits of the exclusionary rule, such data have shown, on the one hand, as the Court acknowledges today, that the costs are not as substantial as critics have asserted in the past, and, on the other hand, that while the exclusionary rule may well have certain deterrent effects, it is extremely difficult to determine with any degree of precision whether the incidence of unlawful conduct by police is now lower than it was prior to *Mapp*. . . .

By remaining within its redoubt of empiricism and by basing the rule solely on the deterrence rationale, the Court has robbed the rule of legitimacy. A doctrine that is explained as if it were an empirical proposition but for which there is only limited empirical support is both inherently unstable and an easy mark for critics. The extent of this Court's fidelity to Fourth Amendment requirements, however, should not turn on such statistical uncertainties. . . . Rather than seeking to give effect to the liberties secured by the Fourth Amendment through guesswork about deterrence, the Court should restore to its proper place the principle framed 70 years ago in *Weeks* that an individual whose privacy has been invaded in violation of the Fourth Amendment has a right grounded in that Amendment to prevent the government from subsequently making use of any evidence so obtained. . . .

Even if I were to accept the Court's general approach to the exclusionary rule, I could not agree with today's result. . . .

If the overall educational effect of the exclusionary rule is considered, application of the rule to even those situations in which individual police officers have acted on the basis of a reasonable but mistaken belief that their conduct was authorized can still be expected to have a considerable long-term deterrent effect. If evidence is consistently excluded in these circumstances, police departments will surely be prompted to instruct their officers to devote greater care and attention to providing sufficient information to establish probable cause when applying for a warrant, and to review with some attention the form of the warrant that they have been issued, rather than automatically assuming that whatever document the magistrate has signed will necessarily comport with Fourth Amendment requirements.

After today's decisions, however, that institutional incentive will be lost. Indeed, the Court's "reasonable mistake" exception to the exclusionary rule will tend to put a premium on police ignorance of the law. Armed with the assurance provided by today's decisions that evidence will always be admissible whenever an officer has "reasonably" relied upon a warrant, police departments will be encouraged to train officers that if a warrant has simply been signed, it is reasonable, without more, to rely on it. Since in close cases there will no longer be any incentive to err on the side of constitutional behavior, police would have every reason to adopt a "let's-wait-until-it's-decided" approach in situations in which there is a question about a warrant's validity or the basis for its issuance.

Although the Court brushes these concerns aside, a host of grave consequences can be expected to result from its decision to carve this new exception out of the exclusionary rule. A chief consequence of today's decisions will be to convey a clear and unambiguous message to magistrates that their decisions to issue warrants are now insulated from subsequent judicial review. Creation of this new exception for good-faith reliance upon a warrant implicitly tells magistrates that they need not take much care in reviewing warrant applications, since their mistakes will from now on have virtually no consequence: If their decision to issue a warrant was correct, the evidence will be admitted; if their decision was incorrect but the police relied in good faith on the warrant, the evidence will also be admitted. Inevitably, the care and attention devoted to such an inconsequential chore will dwindle. Although the Court is correct to note that magistrates do not share the same stake in the outcome of a criminal case as the police, they nevertheless need to appreciate that their role is of some moment in order to continue performing the important task of carefully reviewing warrant applications. Today's decisions effectively remove that incentive. . . .

When the public, as it quite properly has done in the past as well as in the present, demands that those in government increase their efforts to combat crime, it is all too easy for those government officials to seek expedient solutions. . . . In the long run, however, we as a society pay a heavy price for such expediency, because as Justice Jackson observed, the rights guaranteed in the Fourth Amendment "are not mere second-class rights but belong in the catalog of indispensable freedoms." Once lost, such rights are difficult to recover. There is hope, however, that in time this or some later Court will restore these precious freedoms to their rightful place as a primary protection for our citizens against overreaching officialdom.

I dissent.

As you can see, Justice White's opinion rests on the view that the exclusionary rule is not a constitutionally protected right, but serves as a deterrent against corrupt police behavior. When police act in good faith, as they did in this case, the punitive aspect of the exclusionary rule becomes irrelevant.

In his dissent, Justice Brennan called *Leon* the *pièce de resistance* for those opposed to the rule. Unlike White, he believed that *Leon* erodes the rule's deterrent function because it can lead to all sorts of illegal police behavior. For example, he predicted that police would attempt to secure warrants on only minimal information, knowing full well that if they can obtain one, whatever evidence seized will stand up in court.

Brennan was expressing his fear that the Supreme Court would blunt the effectiveness of the exclusionary rule by creating exceptions to it. To him, the Court, while stating its allegiance to *Mapp,* weakened the precedent in decisions such as *Leon* and another 1984 case, *Nix v. Williams.* In *Nix* the Court established an additional exception to the exclusionary rule, the inevitable discovery exception. This ruling holds that evidence discovered as the result of an illegal search can still be introduced in court if it can be shown that the evidence would have been found anyway. Was Brennan correct in fearing that the Court is effectively overruling *Mapp* without doing so explicitly?

Finally, note that the evolution of the exclusionary rule has been closely tied to personnel changes on the Court. Table 8-1 illustrates the division among the justices on the three major exclusionary rule decisions—*Wolf, Mapp,* and *Leon.* Given the appointments to the Court since *Leon,* would you predict any additional changes in the Court's interpretation of the exclusionary rule? On the one hand, Brennan's and Marshall's departures surely have weakened support for the exclusionary rule or, at least, a broad application of it. On the other hand, it is possible that Justice Ginsburg, who replaced White, and Justice Breyer, who holds Blackmun's seat, will take a position similar to that advocated by Brennan and Marshall. If so, the status quo will prevail, for there does not seem to be strong support among the current justices for the elimination of the exclusionary rule. The Warren Court's decision in *Mapp* remains good law, but, according to Justice Brennan's dissent in *Leon,* in a much watered-down form.

THE FIFTH AMENDMENT AND SELF-INCRIMINATION

As we now know, the Fourth Amendment governs the procedures by which police obtain evidence—generally physical evidence. But evidence used to make an arrest is not always physical or material. Very often arrests, and ultimately convictions, hinge on verbal evidence—testimony, confessions, and the like—the gathering of which is governed by the Fifth Amendment's Self-Incrimination Clause: "No person . . . shall be compelled in any criminal case to be a witness against himself." Taken together, the Fourth (physical) and Fifth (verbal) Amendments dictate the procedures police use to gather most evidence against individuals.

The Self-Incrimination Clause is violated by the presence of two elements. First, there must be some form of testimonial evidence that incriminates the person who provides it, and, second, the testimonial evidence must somehow be compelled by the government. Given these standards, self-incrimination violations occur most commonly during police interrogations and government hearings. Of the two, the police interrogations have presented the more difficult questions of constitutional interpretation.

TABLE 8-1 Court Coalitions in Three Exclusionary Rule Cases

Case	For Broad Application	For Limited Application
Wolf v. Colorado, 1949	Murphy[a] Rutledge[a] Douglas	Frankfurter Black[b] Vinson[a] Jackson[a] Burton[a] Reed[a]
Mapp v. Ohio, 1961	Clark[a] Black[ab] Douglas[ab] Warren[a] Brennan	Harlan[a] Frankfurter[a] Whittaker[a]
United States v. Leon, 1984	Brennan Marshall Stevens	White Blackmun[b] O'Connor Powell Rehnquist Burger

NOTE: *In Mapp* Stewart refused to issue or sign an opinion on the Fourth Amendment aspect.
   a. Retired or died before next case.
   b. Concurred.

The Self-Incrimination Clause and Police Interrogations

Even before the 1960s when the courts became the most sensitive to defendants' rights, the Supreme Court had established certain guidelines for police interrogations. For the most part, these guidelines dealt with the concept of coercion. Principles of self-incrimination and due process of law are violated, the Court held, when confessions are coerced from a suspect. Such illegal coercion may be either physical or psychological.

The issue of the use of physical force to obtain confessions was first raised at the Supreme Court in *Brown v. Mississippi* (1936).[24] Law officers, with the as-

24. For more details, see Richard C. Cortner, *A Scottsboro Case in Mississippi: The Supreme Court and Brown v. Mississippi* (Jackson: University of Mississippi Press, 1986).

sistance of other racist citizens, stripped, whipped, hanged until near death, and otherwise physically tortured black suspects to force them into confessing to a murder. Writing for the Court, Chief Justice Charles Evans Hughes claimed, "It would be difficult to conceive of methods more revolting to the sense of justice than those taken to procure the confessions of these petitioners."

More than twenty years later, in *Spano v. New York* (1959), the Court outlawed the use of psychological coercion. Vincent Joseph Spano, an Italian immigrant with a negligible command of English, was drinking in a bar one night when another man, a former professional boxer, took some of his money. Spano followed him out of the bar, and a fight ensued. The boxer left Spano on the street with severe head lacerations. Spano went to his apartment for a gun and, in a candy store the boxer was known to patronize, Spano shot and killed him in front of an eyewitness. After the shooting Spano disappeared. A grand jury returned an indictment and a warrant was issued for his arrest. Several days later, Spano telephoned a close friend, Gaspar Bruno, who was in the police academy. Bruno agreed with Spano that he should hire a lawyer and turn himself in. Spano gave himself up, and Bruno told the whole story to his superiors.

Spano's attorney told him not to answer any questions, and, following this advice, Spano refused to explain to the police his fight with the boxer. Frustrated by Spano's refusal to talk, police called Bruno and asked him to lie to Spano by telling him that his job with the police was in danger if Spano did not confess. After repeated pleas from Bruno, Spano gave in. Using this confession as a primary piece of evidence, the prosecutor convinced the jury to sentence Spano to death.

But may police use psychological coercion to obtain confessions? The justices unanimously agreed that police behavior in *Spano* violated the accused's rights: psychological torture has no place in a modern criminal justice system. Three members of the Court felt that Chief Justice Warren's majority opinion did not go far enough toward protecting the privilege against self-incrimination. In their concurring opinion, Justices Brennan, Douglas, and Black argued that attorneys should be present to protect unsuspecting and naive defendants against unscrupulous police behavior.

As the concurring justices predicted, suspects continued to be subjected to manipulative police practices even though *Spano* prohibited such activity. In 1964 and again in 1966 the Supreme Court was asked two new questions based on *Spano*. First, in *Escobedo v. Illinois,* the justices grappled with the issue raised by the concurring opinions in *Spano:* If a person under arrest wants an attorney to be present during police questioning, must that request be honored? And, because the Court answered this question affirmatively, how should this right be enforced? The Court answered in *Miranda v. Arizona.*

Escobedo and *Miranda* are two of the most important decisions in criminal law. Consider the following questions as you read these decisions: first, and most critical, what does the Court argue about the privilege against self-incrimination? Second, how does the Court safeguard that right? And, finally, why do scholars and lawyers consider these decisions and the cases that follow them to be so significant and so controversial?

Escobedo v. Illinois

378 U.S. 478 (1964)

Vote: 5 (Black, Brennan, Douglas, Goldberg, Warren)
     4 (Clark, Harlan, Stewart, White)
Opinion of the Court: Goldberg
Dissenting opinions: Harlan, Stewart, White

At 2:30 a.m. on January 20, 1960, police arrested Danny Escobedo for the murder of his brother-in-law. They attempted to interrogate him, but, on the advice of his counsel, Escobedo refused to make any state-

ments and was released. A week or so later, Benedict DiGerlando, who was in police custody and considered another suspect, told police that Escobedo indeed had shot his brother-in-law because he had mistreated his sister. Based on DiGerlando's story, police again arrested Escobedo, as well as his sister.

As police transported the pair to the station they explained that DiGerlando had told them the whole story so they might as well confess. Escobedo again declined. At the station, Escobedo asked to see his attorney, but the police refused. Instead, they questioned him for fourteen and a half hours until he admitted knowledge of the crime. Found guilty of murder, Escobedo appealed, claiming that he was denied his right to counsel and that counsel should have been present during the interrogation.

MR. JUSTICE GOLDBERG delivered the opinion of the Court.

The critical question in this case is whether, under the circumstances, the refusal by the police to honor petitioner's request to consult with his lawyer during the course of an interrogation constitutes a denial of "the Assistance of Counsel" in violation of the Sixth Amendment to the Constitution as "made obligatory upon the States by the Fourteenth Amendment," and thereby renders inadmissible in a state criminal trial any incriminating statement elicited by the police during the interrogation....

We granted a writ of certiorari to consider whether the petitioner's statement was constitutionally admissible at his trial. We conclude, for the reasons stated below, that it was not and, accordingly, we reverse the judgment of conviction....

The interrogation here was conducted before petitioner was formally indicted. But in the context of this case, that fact should make no difference. When petitioner requested, and was denied, an opportunity to consult with his lawyer, the investigation had ceased to be a general investigation of "an unsolved crime." Petitioner had become the accused, and the purpose of the interrogation was to "get him" to confess his guilt despite his constitutional right not to do so. At the time of his arrest and throughout the course of the interrogation, the police told petitioner that they had convincing evidence that he had fired the fatal shots. Without informing him of his absolute right to remain silent in the face of this accusation, the police urged him to make a statement.... Petitioner, a layman, was undoubtedly unaware that under Illinois law an admission of "mere" complicity in the murder plot was legally as damaging as an admission of firing of the fatal shots. The "guiding hand of counsel" was essential to advise petitioner of his rights in this delicate situation. This was the "stage when legal aid and advice" were most critical to petitioner. [I]t was a stage surely as critical as ... arraignment and preliminary hearing. What happened at this interrogation could certainly "affect the whole trial," since rights "may be as irretrievably lost, if not then and there asserted, as they are when an accused represented by counsel waives a right for strategic purposes." It would exalt form over substance to make the right to counsel, under these circumstances, depend on whether at the time of the interrogation, the authorities had secured a formal indictment. Petitioner had, for all practical purposes, already been charged with murder....

In Gideon v. Wainwright we held that every person accused of a crime, whether state or federal, is entitled to a lawyer at trial....

It is argued that if the right to counsel is afforded prior to indictment, the number of confessions obtained by the police will diminish significantly, because most confessions are obtained during the period between arrest and indictment, and "any lawyer worth his salt will tell the suspect in no uncertain terms to make no statement to police under any circumstances." This argument, of course, cuts two ways. The fact that many confessions are obtained during this period points up its critical nature as a "stage when legal aid and advice" are surely needed. The right to counsel would indeed be hollow if it began at a period when few confessions were obtained. There is necessarily a direct relationship between the importance of a stage to the police in their quest for a confession and the criticalness of that stage to the accused in his need for legal advice. Our Constitution, unlike some others, strikes the balance in favor of the right of the accused to be advised by his lawyer of his privilege against self-incrimination.

We have learned the lesson of history, ancient and

Danny Escobedo's 1960 arrest and conviction for the murder of his brother-in-law led to a Supreme Court decision that expanded constitutional protections for criminal defendants during police interrogations. This photograph of Escobedo was taken as he awaited processing on charges of burglarizing a hot dog stand not long after the Supreme Court issued its landmark ruling in *Escobedo v. Illinois* in 1964.

modern, that a system of criminal law enforcement which comes to depend on the "confession" will, in the long run, be less reliable and more subject to abuses than a system which depends on extrinsic evidence independently secured through skillful investigation.... This Court also has recognized that "history amply shows that confessions have often been extorted to save law enforcement officials the trouble and effort of obtaining valid and independent evidence...."

We have also learned the companion lesson of history that no system of criminal justice can, or should, survive if it comes to depend for its continued effectiveness on the citizens' abdication through unawareness of their constitutional rights. No system worth preserving should have to fear that if an accused is permitted to consult with a lawyer, he will become aware of, and exercise, these rights. If the exercise of constitutional rights will thwart the effectiveness of a system of law enforcement, then there is something very wrong with that system.

We hold, therefore, that where, as here, the investigation is no longer a general inquiry into an unsolved crime but has begun to focus on a particular suspect, the suspect has been taken into police custody, the police carry out a process of interrogations that lends itself to eliciting incriminating statements, the suspect has requested and been denied an opportunity to consult with his lawyer, and the police have not effectively warned him of his absolute constitutional right to remain silent, the accused has been denied "the Assistance of Counsel" in violation of the Sixth Amendment to the Constitution as "made obligatory upon the States by the Fourteenth Amendment," and that no statement elicited by the police during the interrogation may be used against him at a criminal trial....

Nothing we have said today affects the powers of the police to investigate "an unsolved crime" by gathering information from witnesses and by other "proper investigative efforts." We hold only that when the process shifts from investigatory to accusatory—when its focus is on the accused and its purpose is to elicit a confession—our adversary system begins to operate, and, under the circumstances here, the accused must be permitted to consult with his lawyer.

The judgment of the Illinois Supreme Court is reversed and the case remanded for proceedings not inconsistent with this opinion.

Reversed and remanded.

Danny Escobedo had been denied his right to counsel, and the majority found this right to be a primary defense against violations of the Self-Incrimination Clause. If an attorney is present, it is not likely that police will employ even subtle methods to coerce confessions from suspects. The *Escobedo* majority held that the right to counsel begins at the accusatory stage of the process, defined as the point at which the investigation ceases to be general and focuses on a specific individual. The right is in effect for every critical stage of the process, which includes all interrogations. But once the Court ruled this way, it was faced, in *Miranda v. Arizona*, with a more difficult and far-reaching question. How should this new right be enforced?

Miranda v. Arizona

384 U.S. 436 (1966)
Vote: 5 (Black, Brennan, Douglas, Fortas, Warren)
*   4 (Clark, Harlan, Stewart, White)*
Opinion of the Court: Warren
Opinion dissenting in part: Clark
Dissenting opinions: Harlan, White

Ernesto Miranda, a twenty-three-year-old indigent, nearly illiterate truck driver, allegedly kidnapped and raped a young woman outside of Phoenix, Arizona. Ten days after the incident, police arrested him, took him to the station, and interrogated him. Within two hours of questioning, Miranda confessed. There was no evidence of any police misbehavior during the interrogation, and at no point during questioning did Miranda request an attorney. Because of the decision in *Gideon v. Wainwright* (1963) *(see Chapter 9)*, which mandated that all indigent criminal defendants receive a defense attorney at government expense, the trial judge appointed a lawyer to defend Miranda against the charges. Unfortunately, that attorney provided an inadequate defense—he hoped to prove Miranda insane or mentally defective—and Miranda received a twenty- to thirty-year sentence. The conviction was based not only on the confession but also on the basis of other evidence including the victim's positive identification of Miranda as her assailant.

Miranda obtained new attorneys, who presented

Ernesto Miranda, right, pictured with his defense attorney, John L. Flynn, was convicted of kidnapping and rape after he confessed to the crimes while in police custody. In a landmark ruling, *Miranda v. Arizona* (1966), the Supreme Court reversed the conviction because Miranda had not been told he had the right to remain silent and to have an attorney present during questioning.

wholly different arguments to the Supreme Court, where Miranda's appeal was combined with three others presenting similar issues. The attorneys claimed that because the entire interrogation process is so inherently coercive that any individual will eventually break down, the Court should affirmatively protect the right against self-incrimination by adding to those protections already extended in *Escobedo*.

MR. CHIEF JUSTICE WARREN delivered the opinion of the Court.

The cases* before us raise questions which go to the roots of our concepts of American criminal jurisprudence: the restraints society must observe consistent with the Federal Constitution in prosecuting individuals for crime. More specifically, we deal with the admissibility of statements obtained from an individual who is subjected to custodial police interrogation and the necessity for procedures which assure that the individual is accorded his privilege under the Fifth Amendment to the Constitution not to be compelled to incriminate himself.

*Authors' note: Along with *Miranda*, the Court decided *Vignera v. New York*, *Westover v. United States*, and *California v. Stewart*.

We dealt with certain phases of this problem recently in Escobedo v. State of Illinois (1964). . . .

This case has been the subject of judicial interpretation and spirited legal debate since it was decided two years ago. Both state and federal courts, in assessing its implications, have arrived at varying conclusions. A wealth of scholarly material has been written tracing its ramifications and underpinnings. Police and prosecutor have speculated on its range and desirability. We granted certiorari in these cases in order further to explore some facets of the problems, thus exposed, of applying the privilege against self-incrimination to in-custody interrogation, and to give concrete constitutional guidelines for law enforcement agencies and courts to follow.

We start here, as we did in *Escobedo*, with the premise that our holding is not an innovation in our jurisprudence, but is an application of principles long recognized and applied in other settings. We have undertaken a thorough reexamination of the *Escobedo* decision and the principles it announced, and we reaffirm it. That case was but an explication of basic rights that are enshrined in our Constitution—that "No person . . . shall be compelled in any criminal case to be a witness against himself," and that "the accused shall . . . have the Assistance of Counsel"—rights which were put in jeopardy in that case through official overbearing. . . .

It was necessary in *Escobedo*, as here, to insure that what was proclaimed in the Constitution had not become but a "form of words" in the hands of government officials. And it is in this spirit, consistent with our role as judges, that we adhere to the principles of *Escobedo* today.

Our holding will be spelled out with some specificity in the pages which follow but briefly stated it is this: the prosecution may not use statements, whether exculpatory or inculpatory, stemming from custodial interrogation of the defendant unless it demonstrates the use of procedural safeguards effective to secure the privilege against self-incrimination. By custodial interrogation, we mean questioning initiated by law enforcement officers after a person has been taken into custody or otherwise deprived of his freedom of action in any significant way. As for the procedural safeguards to be employed, unless other fully effective means are devised to inform accused persons of their right of silence and to assure a continuous opportunity to exercise it, the following measures are required. Prior to any questioning, the person must be warned that he has a right to remain silent, that any statement he does make may be used as evidence against him, and that he has a right to the presence of an attorney, either retained or appointed. The defendant may waive effectuation of these rights, provided the waiver is made voluntarily, knowingly and intelligently. If, however, he indicates in any manner and at any stage of the process that he wishes to consult with an attorney before speaking there can be no questioning. Likewise, if the individual is alone and indicates in any manner that he does not wish to be interrogated, the police may not question him. The mere fact that he may have answered some questions or volunteered some statements on his own does not deprive him of the right to refrain from answering any further inquiries until he has consulted with an attorney and thereafter consents to be questioned.

The constitutional issue we decide in each of these cases is the admissibility of statements obtained from a defendant questioned while in custody or otherwise deprived of his freedom of action in any significant way....

An understanding of the nature and setting of this in-custody interrogation is essential to our decisions today. The difficulty in depicting what transpires at such interrogations stems from the fact that in this country they have largely taken place incommunicado. From extensive factual studies undertaken in the early 1930's, including the famous Wickersham Report to Congress by a Presidential Commission, it is clear that police violence and the "third degree" flourished at that time. In a series of cases decided by this Court long after these studies, the police resorted to physical brutality—beatings, hanging, whipping—and to sustained and protracted questioning incommunicado in order to extort confessions. The Commission on Civil Rights in 1961 found much evidence to indicate that "some policemen still resort to physical force to obtain confessions...." Only recently in Kings County, New York, the police brutally beat, kicked and placed lighted cigarette butts on the back of a potential witness under interrogation for the purpose of securing a statement incriminating a third party.

The examples given above are undoubtedly the exception now, but they are sufficiently widespread to be the object of concern. Unless a proper limitation upon custodial interrogation is achieved—such as these decisions will advance—there can be no assurance that practices of this nature will be eradicated in the foreseeable future....

Again we stress that the modern practice of in-custody interrogation is psychologically rather than physically oriented. As we have stated before, "[T]his Court has recognized that coercion can be mental as well as physical, and that the blood of the accused is not the only hallmark of an unconstitutional inquisition." *Blackburn v. State of Alabama* (1960). Interrogation still takes place in privacy. Privacy results in secrecy and this in turn results in a gap in our knowledge as to what in fact goes on in the interrogation rooms. A valuable source of information about present police practices, however, may be found in various police manuals and texts which document procedures employed with success in the past, and which recommend various other effective tactics. These texts are used by law enforcement agencies themselves as guides. It should be noted that these texts professedly present the most enlightened and effective means presently used to obtain statements through custodial interrogation. By considering these texts and other data, it is possible to describe the procedures observed and noted around the country.

The officers are told by the manuals that the "principal psychological factor contributing to a successful interrogation is privacy—being alone with the person under interrogation."...

To highlight the isolation and unfamiliar surroundings,

the manuals instruct the police to display an air of confidence in the suspect's guilt and from outward appearance to maintain only an interest in confirming certain details. The guilt of the subject is to be posited as a fact. The interrogator should direct his comments toward the reasons why the subject committed the act, rather than court failure by asking the subject whether he did it. Like other men, perhaps the subject has had a bad family life, had an unhappy childhood, had too much to drink, had an unrequited desire for women. The officers are instructed to minimize the moral seriousness of the offense, to cast blame on the victim or on society. These tactics are designed to put the subject in a psychological state where his story is but an elaboration of what the police purport to know already—that he is guilty. Explanations to the contrary are dismissed and discouraged.

The texts thus stress that the major qualities an interrogator should possess are patience and perseverance....

The manuals suggest that the suspect be offered legal excuses for his actions in order to obtain an initial admission of guilt....

When the techniques described above prove unavailing, the texts recommend they be alternated with a show of some hostility....

The interrogators sometimes are instructed to induce a confession out of trickery....

Even without employing brutality, the "third degree" or the specific stratagems described above, the very fact of custodial interrogation exacts a heavy toll on individual liberty and trades on the weakness of individuals....

In the cases before us today, given this background, we concern ourselves primarily with this interrogation atmosphere and the evils it can bring. In No. 759, Miranda v. Arizona, the police arrested the defendant and took him to a special interrogation room where they secured a confession....

In these cases, we might not find the defendants' statements to have been involuntary in traditional terms. Our concern for adequate safeguards to protect precious Fifth Amendment rights is, of course, not lessened in the slightest. In each of the cases, the defendant was thrust into an unfamiliar atmosphere and run through menacing police interrogation procedures. The potentiality for compulsion is forcefully apparent, for example, in *Miranda*, where the indigent Mexican defendant was a seriously disturbed individual with pronounced sexual fantasies.... To be sure, the records do not evince overt physical coercion or patent psychological ploys. The fact remains that in none of these cases did the officers undertake to afford appropriate safeguards at the outset of the interrogation to insure that the statements were truly the product of free choice.

It is obvious that such an interrogation environment is created for no purpose other than to subjugate the individual to the will of his examiner. This atmosphere carries its own badge of intimidation. To be sure, this is not physical intimidation, but it is equally destructive of human dignity. The current practice of incommunicado interrogation is at odds with one of our Nation's most cherished principles—that the individual may not be compelled to incriminate himself. Unless adequate protective devices are employed to dispel the compulsion inherent in custodial surroundings, no statement obtained from the defendant can truly be the product of his free choice.

From the foregoing, we can readily perceive an intimate connection between the privilege against self-incrimination and police custodial questioning....

Today, then, there can be no doubt that the Fifth Amendment privilege is available outside of criminal court proceedings and serves to protect persons in all settings in which their freedom of action is curtailed in any significant way from being compelled to incriminate themselves. We have concluded that without proper safeguards the process of in-custody interrogation of persons suspected or accused of crime contains inherently compelling pressures which work to undermine the individual's will to resist and to compel him to speak where he would not otherwise do so freely. In order to combat these pressures and to permit a full opportunity to exercise the privilege against self-incrimination, the accused must be adequately and effectively apprised of his rights and the exercise of those rights must be fully honored....

At the outset, if a person in custody is to be subjected to interrogation, he must first be informed in clear and unequivocal terms that he has the right to remain silent. For those unaware of the privilege, the warning is needed simply to make them aware of it—the threshold requirement for an intelligent decision as to its exercise. More important, such a warning is an absolute prerequisite in overcoming the inherent pressures of the interrogation atmosphere.... Further, the warning will show the individual that his interrogators are prepared to recognize his privilege should he choose to exercise it.

The Fifth Amendment privilege is so fundamental to our system of constitutional rule and the expedient of giving an adequate warning as to the availability of the privilege so simple, we will not pause to inquire in individual cases whether the defendant was aware of his rights without a warning being given. Assessments of the knowledge the defendant possessed, based on information as to his age, education, intelligence, or prior contact with authorities, can never be more than speculation; a warning is a clearcut fact. More important, whatever the background of the person interrogated, a warning at the time of the interrogation is indispensable to overcome its pressures and to insure that the individual knows he is free to exercise the privilege at that point in time.

The warning of the right to remain silent must be accompanied by the explanation that anything said can and will be used against the individual in court. This warning is needed in order to make him aware not only of the privilege, but also of the consequences of forgoing it. It is only through an awareness of these consequences that there can be any assurance of real understanding and intelligent exercise of the privilege. Moreover, this warning may serve to make the individual more acutely aware that he is faced with a phase of the adversary system—that he is not in the presence of persons acting solely in his interest.

The circumstances surrounding in-custody interrogation can operate very quickly to overbear the will of one merely made aware of his privilege by his interrogators. Therefore, the right to have counsel present at the interrogation is indispensable to the protection of the Fifth Amendment privilege under the system we delineate today. Our aim is to assure that the individual's right to choose between silence and speech remains unfettered throughout the interrogation process. A once-stated warning, delivered by those who will conduct the interrogation, cannot itself suffice to that end among those who most require knowledge of their rights. A mere warning given by the interrogators is not alone sufficient to accomplish that end. Prosecutors themselves claim that the admonishment of the right to remain silent without more "will benefit only the recidivist and the professional." Even preliminary advice given to the accused by his own attorney can be swiftly overcome by the secret interrogation process. Thus, the need for counsel to protect the Fifth Amendment privilege comprehends not merely a right to consult with counsel prior to questioning, but also to have counsel present during any questioning if the defendant so desires.

The presence of counsel at the interrogation may serve several significant subsidiary functions as well. If the accused decides to talk to his interrogators, the assistance of counsel can mitigate the dangers of untrustworthiness. With a lawyer present the likelihood that the police will practice coercion is reduced, and if coercion is nevertheless exercised the lawyer can testify to it in court. The presence of a lawyer can also help to guarantee that the accused gives a fully accurate statement to the police and that the statement is rightly reported by the prosecution at trial.

An individual need not make a pre-interrogation request for a lawyer. While such request affirmatively secures his right to have one, his failure to ask for a lawyer does not constitute a waiver. No effective waiver of the right to counsel during interrogation can be recognized unless specifically made after the warnings we here delineate have been given. The accused who does not know his rights and therefore does not make a request may be the person who most needs counsel. . . .

Accordingly we hold that an individual held for interrogation must be clearly informed that he has the right to consult with a lawyer and to have the lawyer with him during interrogation under the system for protecting the privilege we delineate today. As with the warnings of the right to remain silent and that anything stated can be used in evidence against him, this warning is an absolute prerequisite to interrogation. No amount of circumstantial evidence that the person may have been aware of this right will suffice to stand in its stead. Only through such a warning is there ascertainable assurance that the accused was aware of this right.

If an individual indicates that he wishes the assistance of counsel before any interrogation occurs, the authorities cannot rationally ignore or deny his request on the basis that the individual does not have or cannot afford a retained attorney. The financial ability of the individual has no relationship to the scope of the rights involved here. The privilege against self-incrimination secured by the Constitution applies to all individuals. The need for counsel in order to protect the privilege exists for the indigent as well as the affluent. In fact, were we to limit these constitutional rights to those who can retain an attorney, our decisions today would be of little significance. The cases before us as well as the vast majority of confession cases with which we have dealt in the past involve those unable to retain counsel. While authorities are not required to relieve the accused of his poverty, they have the obligation not to take advantage of indigence in the administration of justice. Denial of counsel to the indigent at the time of interrogation while allowing an attorney to those who can afford one would be no more supportable by reason or logic than the similar situation at trial and on appeal struck down in Gideon v. Wainwright (1963).

In order fully to apprise a person interrogated of the extent of his rights under this system then, it is necessary to warn him not only that he has the right to consult with an attorney, but also that if he is indigent a lawyer will be appointed to represent him. Without this additional warning, the admonition of the right to consult with counsel would often be understood as meaning only that he can consult with a lawyer if he has one or has the funds to obtain one. The warning of a right to counsel would be hollow if not couched in terms that would convey to the indigent—the person most often subjected to interrogation—the knowledge that he too has a right to have counsel present. As with the warnings of the right to remain silent and of the general right to counsel, only by effective and express explanation to the indigent of this right can there be assurance that he was truly in a position to exercise it.

Once warnings have been given, the subsequent procedure is clear. If the individual indicates in any manner, at any time prior to or during questioning, that he wishes to remain silent, the interrogation must cease. At this point he has shown that he intends to exercise his Fifth Amendment privilege; any statement taken after the person invokes his privilege cannot be other than the product of compulsion, subtle or otherwise. Without the right to cut off questioning, the setting of in-custody interrogation operates on the individual to overcome free choice in producing a statement after the privilege has been once invoked. If the individual states that he wants an attorney, the interrogation must cease until an attorney is present.

At that time, the individual must have an opportunity to confer with the attorney and to have him present during any subsequent questioning. If the individual cannot obtain an attorney and he indicates that he wants one before speaking to police, they must respect his decision to remain silent....

If the interrogation continues without the presence of an attorney and a statement is taken, a heavy burden rests on the government to demonstrate that the defendant knowingly and intelligently waived his privilege against self-incrimination and his right to retained or appointed counsel....

The warnings required and the waiver necessary in accordance with our opinion today are, in the absence of a fully effective equivalent, prerequisites to the admissibility of any statement made by a defendant. No distinction can be drawn between statements which are direct confessions and statements which amount to "admissions" of part or all of an offense. The privilege against self-incrimination protects the individual from being compelled to incriminate himself in any manner; it does not distinguish degrees of incrimination....

To summarize, we hold that when an individual is taken into custody or otherwise deprived of his freedom by the authorities in any significant way and is subjected to questioning, the privilege against self-incrimination is jeopardized. Procedural safeguards must be employed to protect the privilege and unless other fully effective means are adopted to notify the person of his right of silence and to assure that the exercise of the right will be scrupulously honored, the following measures are required. He must be warned prior to any questioning that he has the right to remain silent, that anything he says can be used against him in a court of law, that he has the right to the presence of an attorney, and that if he cannot afford an attorney one will be appointed for him prior to any questioning if he so desires. Opportunity to exercise these rights must be afforded to him throughout the interrogation. After such warnings have been given, and such opportunity afforded him, the individual may knowingly and intelligently waive these rights and agree to answer questions or make a statement. But unless and until such warnings and waiver are demonstrated by the prosecution at trial, no evidence obtained as a result of interrogation can be used against him.

A recurrent argument made in these cases is that society's need for interrogation outweighs the privilege. This argument is not unfamiliar to this Court. The whole thrust of our foregoing discussion demonstrates that the Constitution has prescribed the rights of the individual when confronted with the power of government when it provided in the Fifth Amendment that an individual cannot be compelled to be a witness against himself. That right cannot be abridged. . . .

In announcing these principles, we are not unmindful of the burdens which law enforcement officials must bear, often under trying circumstances. We also fully recognize the obligation of all citizens to aid in enforcing the criminal laws. This Court, while protecting individual rights, has always given ample latitude to law enforcement agencies in the legitimate exercise of their duties. The limits we have placed on the interrogation process should not constitute an undue interference with a proper system of law enforcement. . . . [O]ur decision does not in any way preclude police from carrying out their traditional investigatory functions. Although confessions may play an important role in some convictions, the cases before us present graphic examples of the overstatement of the "need" for confessions. . . .

Over the years the Federal Bureau of Investigation has compiled an exemplary record of effective law enforcement while advising any suspect or arrested person, at the outset of an interview, that he is not required to make a statement, that any statement may be used against him in court, that the individual may obtain the services of an attorney of his own choice and, more recently, that he has a right to free counsel if he is unable to pay. . . .

The practice of the FBI can readily be emulated by state and local enforcement agencies. The argument that the FBI deals with different crimes than are dealt with by state authorities does not mitigate the significance of the FBI experience. . . .

Judicial solutions to problems of constitutional dimension have evolved decade by decade. As courts have been presented with the need to enforce constitutional rights, they have found means of doing so. That was our responsibility when *Escobedo* was before us and it is our responsibility today. Where rights secured by the Constitution are involved, there can be no rule making or legislation which would abrogate them.

Reversed.

MR. JUSTICE WHITE, with whom MR. JUSTICE HARLAN and MR. JUSTICE STEWART join, dissenting.

That the Court's holding today is neither compelled nor even strongly suggested by the language of the Fifth Amendment, is at odds with American and English legal history, and involves a departure from a long line of precedent does not prove either that the Court has exceeded its powers or that the Court is wrong or unwise in its present reinterpretation of the Fifth Amendment. It does, however, underscore the obvious—that the Court has not discovered or found the law in making today's decision, nor has it derived it from some irrefutable sources; what it has done is to make new law and new public policy in much the same way that it has in the course of interpreting other great clauses of the Constitution. This is what the Court historically has done. Indeed, it is what it must do and will continue to do until and unless there is some fundamental change in the constitutional distribution of governmental powers.

But if the Court is here and now to announce new and fundamental policy to govern certain aspects of our affairs, it is wholly legitimate to examine the mode of this or any other constitutional decision in this Court and to inquire into the advisability of its end product in terms of the long-range interest of the country. At the very least the Court's text and reasoning should withstand analysis and be a fair exposition of the constitutional provision which its opinion interprets. Decisions like these cannot rest alone on syllogism, metaphysics or some ill-defined notions of natural justice, although each will perhaps play its part. In proceeding to such constructions as it now announces, the Court should also duly consider all the factors and interests bearing upon the cases, at least insofar as the relevant materials are available; and if the necessary considerations are not treated in the record or obtainable from some other reliable source, the Court should not proceed to formulate fundamental policies based on speculation alone.

First, we may inquire what are the textual and factual bases of this new fundamental rule. To reach the result announced on the grounds it does, the Court must stay within the confines of the Fifth Amendment, which forbids self-incrimination only if *compelled*. Hence the core of the Court's opinion is that because of the "compulsion inherent in custodial surroundings, no statement obtained from [a] defendant [in custody] can truly be the product of his free choice," absent the use of adequate protective devices as described by the Court. However, the Court does not point to any sudden inrush of new knowledge requiring the rejection of 70 years' experience. Nor does it assert that its novel conclusion reflects a changing consensus among state courts, see Mapp v. Ohio, or that a succession of cases had steadily eroded the old rule and proved it unworkable. Rather than asserting new knowledge, the Court concedes that it cannot truly know what occurs during custodial questioning, because of the innate secrecy of such proceedings. It extrapolates a picture of what it conceives to be the norm from police investigatorial manuals, published in 1959 and 1962 or earlier, without any attempt to allow for adjustments in police practices that may have occurred in the wake of more recent decisions of state appellate tribunals or this Court. But even if the relentless application of the described procedures could lead to involuntary confessions, it most assuredly does not follow that each and every case will disclose this kind of interrogation or this kind of consequence. Insofar as appears from the Court's opinion, it has not examined a single transcript of any police interrogation, let alone the interrogation that took place in any one of these cases which it decides today. Judged by any of the standards for empirical investigation utilized in the social sciences the factual basis for the Court's premise is patently inadequate.

Although in the Court's view in-custody interrogation is inherently coercive, the Court says that the spontaneous product of the coercion of arrest and detention is still to be deemed voluntary. An accused, arrested on probable cause, may blurt out a confession which will be admissible despite the fact that he is alone and in custody, without any showing that he had any notion of his right to remain silent or of the consequences of his admission. Yet, under the Court's rule, if the police ask him a single question such as "Do you have anything to say?" or "Did you kill your wife?" his response, if there is one, has somehow been compelled, even if the accused has been clearly warned of his right to remain silent. Common sense informs us to the contrary. While one may say that the response was "involuntary" in the sense the question provoked or was the occasion for the response and thus the defendant was induced to speak out when he might have remained silent if not arrested and not questioned, it is patently unsound to say the response is compelled....

If the rule announced today were truly based on a conclusion that all confessions resulting from custodial interrogation are coerced, then it would simply have no rational foundation.... A fortiori that would be true of the extension of the rule to exculpatory statements, which the Court effects after a brief discussion of why, in the Court's view, they must be deemed incriminatory but without any discussion of why they must be deemed coerced. Even if one were to postulate that the Court's concern is not that all confessions induced by police interrogation are coerced but rather that some such confessions are coerced and present judicial procedures are believed to be inadequate to identify the confessions that are coerced and those that are not, it would still not be essential to impose the rule that the Court has now fashioned. Transcripts or observers could be required, specific time limits, tailored to fit the cause, could be imposed, or other devices could be utilized to reduce the chances that otherwise indiscernible coercion will produce an inadmissible confession.

On the other hand, even if one assumed that there was an adequate factual basis for the conclusion that all confessions obtained during in-custody interrogation are the product of compulsion, the rule propounded by the Court would still be irrational, for, apparently, it is only if the accused is also warned of his right to counsel and waives both that right and the right against self-incrimination that the inherent compulsiveness of interrogation disappears. But if the defendant may not answer without a warning a question such as "Where were you last night?" without having his answer be a compelled one, how can the Court ever accept his negative answer to the question of whether he wants to consult his retained counsel or counsel whom the court will appoint? And why if counsel is present and the accused nevertheless confesses, or counsel tells the accused to tell the truth, and that is what the accused does, is the situation any less coercive insofar as the accused is concerned? The Court apparently realizes its dilemma of foreclosing questioning without the necessary warnings but at the same time permitting the accused, sitting in the same chair in front of the same policemen, to waive his right to consult an attorney. It expects, however, that the accused will not often waive the right; and if it is claimed that he has, the State faces a severe, if not impossible burden of proof.

All of this makes very little sense in terms of the compulsion which the Fifth Amendment proscribes. That amendment deals with compelling the accused himself. It is his free will that is involved. Confessions and incriminating admissions, as such, are not forbidden evidence; only those which are compelled are banned. I doubt that the Court observes these distinctions today. By considering any answers to any interrogation to be compelled regardless of the content and course of examination and by escalating the requirements to prove waiver, the Court not only prevents the use of compelled confessions but for all practical purposes forbids interrogation except in the presence of counsel. That is, instead of confining itself to protection of the right against compelled self-incrimination the Court has created a limited Fifth Amendment right to counsel—or, as the Court expresses it, a "need for counsel to protect the Fifth Amendment privilege...." The focus then is not on the will of the accused but on the will of counsel and how much influence he can have on the accused. Obviously there is no warrant in the Fifth Amendment for thus installing counsel as the arbiter of the privilege.

In sum, for all the Court's expounding on the menacing atmosphere of police interrogation procedures, it has failed to supply any foundation for the conclusions it draws or the measures it adopts.

Criticism of the Court's opinion, however, cannot stop with a demonstration that the factual and textual bases for the rule it propounds are, at best, less than compelling. Equally relevant is an assessment of the rule's consequences measured against community values. The Court's duty to assess the consequences of its action is not satisfied by the utterance of the truth that a value of our system of criminal justice is "to respect the inviolability of the human personality" and to require government to produce the evidence against the accused by its own independent labors. More than the human dignity of the accused is involved; the human personality of others in the society must also be preserved. Thus the values reflected by the privilege are not the sole desideratum; society's interest in the general security is of equal weight.

The obvious underpinning of the Court's decision is a deep-seated distrust of all confessions. As the Court declares that the accused may not be interrogated without counsel present, absent a waiver of the right to counsel, and as the Court all but admonishes the lawyer to advise the accused to remain silent, the result adds up to a judicial judgment that evidence from the accused should not be used against him in any way, whether compelled or not. This is the not so subtle overtone of the opinion—that it is inherently wrong for the police to gather evidence from the accused himself. And this is precisely the nub of this dissent. I see nothing wrong or immoral, and certainly nothing unconstitutional, in the police's asking a suspect whom they have reasonable cause to arrest whether or not he killed his wife or in confronting him with the evidence on which the arrest was based, at least where he has been plainly advised that he may remain completely silent. Until today, "the admissions or confessions of the prisoner, when voluntarily and freely made, have always ranked high in the scale of incriminating evidence." Particularly when corroborated, as where the police have confirmed the accused's disclosure of the hiding place of implements or fruits of the crime, such confessions have the highest reliability and significantly contribute to the certitude with which we may believe the accused is guilty. Moreover, it is by no means certain that the process of confessing is injurious to the accused. To the contrary it may provide psychological relief and enhance the prospects for rehabilitation.

This is not to say that the value of respect for the inviolability of the accused's individual personality should be accorded no weight or that all confessions should be indiscriminately admitted. This Court has long read the Constitution to proscribe compelled confessions, a salutary rule from which there should be no retreat. But I see no sound basis, factual or otherwise, and the Court gives none, for concluding that the present rule against the receipt of coerced confessions is inadequate for the task of sorting out inadmissible evidence and must be replaced by the per se rule which is now imposed. Even if the new concept can be said to have advantages of some sort over the present law, they are far outweighed by its likely undesirable impact on other very relevant and important interests.

The most basic function of any government is to provide for the security of the individual and of his property. These ends of society are served by the criminal laws which for the most part are aimed at the prevention of crime. Without the reasonably effective performance of the task of preventing private violence and retaliation, it is idle to talk about human dignity and civilized values.

The modes by which the criminal laws serve the interest

in general security are many. First the murderer who has taken the life of another is removed from the streets, deprived of his liberty and thereby prevented from repeating his offense. In view of the statistics on recidivism in this country and of the number of instances in which apprehension occurs only after repeated offenses, no one can sensibly claim that this aspect of the criminal law does not prevent crime or contribute significantly to the personal security of the ordinary citizen.

Secondly, the swift and sure apprehension of those who refuse to respect the personal security and dignity of their neighbor unquestionably has its impact on others who might be similarly tempted. That the criminal law is wholly or partly ineffective with a segment of the population or with many of those who have been apprehended and convicted is a very faulty basis for concluding that it is not effective with respect to the great bulk of our citizens or for thinking that without the criminal laws, or in the absence of their enforcement, there would be no increase in crime. Arguments of this nature are not borne out by any kind of reliable evidence that I have seen to this date.

Thirdly, the law concerns itself with those whom it has confined. The hope and aim of modern penology, fortunately, is as soon as possible to return the convict to society a better and more law-abiding man than when he left. Sometimes there is success, sometimes failure. But at least the effort is made, and it should be made to the very maximum extent of our present and future capabilities.

The rule announced today will measurably weaken the ability of the criminal law to perform these tasks. It is a deliberate calculus to prevent interrogations, to reduce the incidence of confessions and pleas of guilty and to increase the number of trials. Criminal trials, no matter how efficient the police are, are not sure bets for the prosecution, nor should they be if the evidence is not forthcoming. Under the present law, the prosecution fails to prove its case in about 30% of the criminal cases actually tried in the federal courts. But it is something else again to remove from the ordinary criminal case all those confessions which heretofore have been held to be free and voluntary acts of the accused and to thus establish a new constitutional barrier to the ascertainment of truth by the judicial process. There is, in my view, every reason to believe that a good many criminal defendants who otherwise would have been convicted on what this Court has previously thought to be the most satisfactory kind of evidence will now, under this new version of the Fifth Amendment, either not be tried at all or will be acquitted if the State's evidence, minus the confession, is put to the test of litigation.

I have no desire whatsoever to share the responsibility for any such impact on the present criminal process.

Chief Justice Warren's majority opinion in *Miranda* is a *tour de force* on self-incrimination, creating the so-called *Miranda* warnings that police must read to suspects before any custodial interrogation. But the opinion left open a number of questions. In fact, the majority of self-incrimination cases after 1966 are the fallout from *Miranda*, seeking to fill three gaps it left open: (1) What is custody? (2) What constitutes interrogation? (3) Must statements made in absence of *Miranda* warnings be excluded from evidence?

The first two questions are of the utmost importance for police. The *Miranda* ruling provided little guidance to police questioning individuals outside of the traditional interrogation room setting. Nor did the decision discuss situations in which police question individuals in a nonaccusatory fashion. Under such circumstances, must police advise individuals of their rights?

As you read the Court's answers to these questions, keep another point in mind: immediately after *Miranda*, law enforcement officials condemned the decision. They—as did the dissenters—thought it would seriously hamper their ability to investigate and solve crimes. Given his general propensity to support the government in criminal cases, some analysts thought Chief Justice Burger—whose Court was largely responsible for filling *Miranda*'s gaps—would be sympathetic to the concerns of law enforcement officials. Was he? Moreover, has *Miranda* created the burden some suspected?

What Is Custody? The first post-*Miranda* case heard by the justices dealt with the issue of custody.

PD 47
Rev. 8/73

METROPOLITAN POLICE DEPARTMENT
WARNING AS TO YOUR RIGHTS

You are under arrest. Before we ask you any questions, you must understand what your rights are.

You have the right to remain silent. You are not required to say anything to us at any time or to answer any questions. Anything you say can be used against you in court.

You have the right to talk to a lawyer for advice before we question you and to have him with you during questioning.

If you cannot afford a lawyer and want one, a lawyer will be provided for you.

If you want to answer questions now without a lawyer present you will still have the right to stop answering at any time. You also have the right to stop answering at any time until you talk to a lawyer.

WAIVER

1. Have you read or had read to you the warning as to your rights? _____

2. Do you understand these rights? _____

3. Do you wish to answer any questions? _____

4. Are you willing to answer questions without having an attorney present? _____

5. Signature of defendant on line below.

_____

6. Time _____   Date _____

7. Signature of Officer _____

8. Signature of Witness _____

In *Orozco v. Texas* (1969) the Court determined that "custodial interrogations," regardless of where they occur, require *Miranda* warnings. In this instance, police questioned an alleged murderer in his boardinghouse room at four o'clock in the morning, while he was in bed. They did not read him his rights, believing that they must do so only when they take individuals out of their environment, that is, into police headquarters. But as Justice Black noted,

> The State has argued here that since *Orozco* was interrogated on his own bed, in familiar surroundings, our *Miranda* holding should not apply.... But the opinion iterated and reiterated the absolute necessity for officers interrogating people "in custody" to give the described warnings. According to the officers' testimony, petitioner was under arrest and not free to leave.... The *Miranda* opinion declared that the warnings were required when the person being interrogated was in custody at the station *or otherwise deprived of his freedom of action in any significant way.*

Orozco was the Warren Court's only major post-*Miranda* decision on the subject of custody. Although it sent a clear signal to law enforcement officials that they must provide the required warnings to all individuals deprived of their freedom, regardless of where that deprivation occurs, it created more gaps for the Burger Court to fill in. For example, must police warn an individual who voluntarily accedes to police questioning? Is interrogation of a person suspected of certain kinds of crimes exempt from *Miranda?*

In several cases the more conservative Burger Court moved away from the rather definitive *Orozco* decision. In *Oregon v. Mathiason* (1977), for example, the Court held that a noncoercive custodial interrogation, in which an individual voluntarily appears at a police station for questioning, does not require *Miranda* warnings. In *Beckwith v. United States* (1976) the Court held that *Miranda* warnings were not required when IRS agents questioned a man in a congenial and noncoercive manner at the man's residence, even though the investigation could lead to criminal tax fraud violations. As the Burger Court gradually narrowed the circumstances under which police had to inform suspects of their rights, many thought that the Court would overrule *Miranda*. *Berkemer v. McCarty* (1984) seemed the perfect vehicle. Justice Thurgood

Marshall wrote the majority opinion. He did not over-rule *Miranda*, but did he provide the police with definitive guidelines for its execution?

Berkemer v. McCarty

468 U.S. 420 (1984)

Vote: 9 (Blackmun, Brennan, Burger, Marshall, O'Connor,
     Powell, Rehnquist, Stevens, White)
          0

Opinion of the Court: Marshall
Concurring opinion: Stevens

In 1980 an Ohio patrolman spotted Richard McCarty's car weaving in and out of highway lanes. The officer signaled McCarty to pull over and asked him to get out of the car, but McCarty could not stand up. The officer asked him if he had taken anything, and McCarty said that he had drunk two beers and smoked two joints of marijuana. The officer arrested McCarty, and at the police station he was given a blood test, which showed no alcohol. But McCarty was further interrogated, and he made additional incriminating statements. McCarty was charged with driving while intoxicated, a misdemeanor, for which he received ten days in jail and a fine.

On appeal the Supreme Court confronted two important questions. First, does the *Miranda* rule apply to minor infractions such as misdemeanor traffic offenses or only to more serious crimes? And second, if *Miranda* does apply to such minor crimes, at what point should McCarty have been advised of his rights—at the initial roadside stop or later when he was arrested and taken to the station?

JUSTICE MARSHALL delivered the opinion of the Court.

This case presents two related questions: First, does our decision in *Miranda v. Arizona* govern the admissibility of statements made during custodial interrogation by a suspect accused of a misdemeanor traffic offense? Second, does the roadside questioning of a motorist detained pursuant to a traffic stop constitute custodial interrogation for the purposes of the doctrine enunciated in *Miranda*?...

In *Miranda v. Arizona* (1966) the Court addressed the problem of how the privilege against compelled self-incrimination guaranteed by the Fifth Amendment could be protected from the coercive pressures that can be brought to bear upon a suspect in the context of custodial interrogation....

In the years since the decision in *Miranda*, we have frequently reaffirmed the central principle established by that case: if the police take a suspect into custody and then ask him questions without informing him of [his] rights ... his responses cannot be introduced into evidence to establish his guilt.

Petitioner asks us to carve an exception out of the foregoing principle. When the police arrest a person for allegedly committing a misdemeanor traffic offense and then ask him questions without telling him his constitutional rights, petitioner argues, his responses should be admissible against him. We cannot agree.

One of the principal advantages of the doctrine that suspects must be given warnings before being interrogated while in custody is the clarity of that rule....

The exception to *Miranda* proposed by petitioner would substantially undermine this crucial advantage of the doctrine. The police often are unaware when they arrest a person whether he may have committed a misdemeanor or a felony. Consider, for example, the reasonably common situation in which the driver of a car involved in an accident is taken into custody. Under Ohio law, both driving while under the influence of intoxicants and negligent vehicular homicide are misdemeanors, while reckless vehicular homicide is a felony. When arresting a person for causing a collision, the police may not know which of these offenses he may have committed. Indeed, the nature of his offense may depend upon circumstances unknowable to the police, such as whether the suspect has previously committed a similar offense or has a criminal record of some other kind. It may even turn upon events yet to happen, such as whether a victim of the accident dies. It would be unreasonable to expect the police to make guesses as to the nature of the criminal conduct at issue before deciding how they may interrogate the suspect.

Equally important, the doctrinal complexities that would confront the courts if we accepted petitioner's proposal would be byzantine. Difficult questions quickly spring to mind: For instance, investigations into seemingly minor offenses sometimes escalate gradually into investigations into more serious matters; at what point in the evolution of an affair of this sort would the police be obliged to give *Miranda* warnings to a suspect in custody?...

We hold therefore that a person subjected to custodial interrogation is entitled to the benefit of the procedural safeguards enunciated in *Miranda*, regardless of the nature or severity of the offense of which he is suspected or for which he was arrested.

The implication of this holding is that the Court of Appeals was correct in ruling that the statements made by respondent at the County Jail were inadmissible. There can be no question that respondent was "in custody" at least as of the moment he was formally placed under arrest and instructed to get into the police car. Because he was not informed of his constitutional rights at that juncture, respondent's subsequent admissions should not have been used against him.

To assess the admissibility of the self-incriminating statements made by respondent prior to his formal arrest, we are obliged to address a second issue concerning the scope of our decision in *Miranda*: whether the roadside questioning of a motorist detained pursuant to a routine traffic stop should be considered "custodial interrogation." Respondent urges that it should, on the ground that *Miranda* by its terms applies whenever "a person has been taken into custody *or otherwise deprived of his freedom of action in any significant way.*" Petitioner contends that a holding that every detained motorist must be advised of his rights before being questioned would constitute an unwarranted extension of the *Miranda* doctrine.

It must be acknowledged at the outset that a traffic stop significantly curtails the "freedom of action" of the driver and the passengers, if any, of the detained vehicle. Under the law of most States, it is a crime either to ignore a policeman's signal to stop one's car or, once having stopped, to drive away without permission. Certainly few motorists would feel free either to disobey a directive to pull over or to leave the scene of a traffic stop without being told they might do so....

However, we decline to accord talismanic power to the phrase in the *Miranda* opinion emphasized by respondent. Fidelity to the doctrine announced in *Miranda* requires that it be enforced strictly, but only in those types of situations in which the concerns that powered the decision are implicated. Thus, we must decide whether a traffic stop exerts upon a detained person pressures that sufficiently impair his free exercise of his privilege against self-incrimination to require that he be warned of his constitutional rights.

Two features of an ordinary traffic stop mitigate the danger that a person questioned will be induced "to speak where he would not otherwise do so freely." First, detention of a motorist pursuant to a traffic stop is presumptively temporary and brief. The vast majority of roadside detentions last only a few minutes. A motorist's expectations, when he sees a policeman's light flashing behind him, are that he will be obliged to spend a short period of time answering questions and waiting while the officer checks his license and registration, that he may then be given a citation, but that in the end he most likely will be allowed to continue on his way. In this respect, questioning incident to an ordinary traffic stop is quite different from stationhouse interrogation, which frequently is prolonged, and in which the detainee often is aware that questioning will continue until he provides his interrogators the answers they seek.

Second, circumstances associated with the typical traffic stop are not such that the motorist feels completely at the mercy of the police. To be sure, the aura of authority surrounding an armed, uniformed officer and the knowledge that the officer has some discretion in deciding whether to issue a citation, in combination, exert some pressure on the detainee to respond to questions. But other aspects of the situation substantially offset these forces. Perhaps most importantly, the typical traffic stop is public, at least to some degree. Passersby, on foot or in other cars, witness the interaction of officer and motorist. This exposure to public view both reduces the ability of an unscrupulous policeman to use illegitimate means to elicit self-incriminating statements and diminishes the motorist's fear that, if he does not cooperate, he will be subjected to abuse. The fact that the detained motorist typically is confronted by only one or at most two policemen further mutes his sense of vulnerability. In short, the atmosphere surrounding an ordinary traffic stop is substantially less "police dominated" than that surrounding the kinds of interrogation at issue in *Miranda* itself.

In both of these respects, the usual traffic stop is more analogous to a so-called *"Terry* stop" than to a formal arrest. Under the Fourth Amendment, we have held, a policeman who lacks probable cause but whose "observations lead him reasonably to suspect" that a particular person has committed, is committing, or is about to commit a crime, may detain that person briefly in order to "investigate the circumstances that provoke suspicion." "[T]he stop and inquiry must be 'reasonably related in scope to the justification for their initiation.'" Typically, this means that the officer may ask the detainee a moderate number of questions to determine his identity and to try to obtain information confirming or dispelling the officer's suspicions. But the detainee is not obliged to respond. And, unless the detainee's answers provide the officer with probable cause to arrest him, he must then be released. The comparatively nonthreatening character of detentions of this sort explains the absence of any suggestion in our opinions that *Terry* stops are subject to the dictates of *Miranda.* The similarly noncoercive aspect of ordinary traffic stops prompts us to hold that persons temporarily detained pursuant to such stops are not "in custody" for the purposes of *Miranda.*

Respondent contends that to "exempt" traffic stops from the coverage of *Miranda* will open the way to widespread abuse. Policemen will simply delay formally arresting detained motorists, and will subject them to sustained and intimidating interrogation at the scene of their initial detention. The net result, respondent contends, will be a serious threat to the rights that the *Miranda* doctrine is designed to protect.

We are confident that the state of affairs projected by respondent will not come to pass. It is settled that the safeguards prescribed by *Miranda* become applicable as soon as a suspect's freedom of action is curtailed to a "degree associated with formal arrest." If a motorist who has been detained pursuant to a traffic stop thereafter is subjected to treatment that renders him "in custody" for practical purposes, he will be entitled to the full panoply of protections prescribed by *Miranda.* . . .

Turning to the case before us, we find nothing in the record that indicates that respondent should have been given *Miranda* warnings at any point prior to the time Trooper Williams placed him under arrest. For the reasons indicated above, we reject the contention that the initial stop of respondent's car, by itself, rendered him "in custody." And respondent has failed to demonstrate that, at any time between the initial stop and the arrest, he was subjected to restraints comparable to those associated with a formal arrest. Only a short period of time elapsed between the stop and the arrest. At no point during that interval was respondent informed that his detention would not be temporary. Although Trooper Williams apparently decided as soon as respondent stepped out of his car that respondent would be taken into custody and charged with a traffic offense, Williams never communicated his intention to respondent. A policeman's unarticulated plan has no bearing on the question whether a suspect was "in custody" at a particular time; the only relevant inquiry is how a reasonable man in the suspect's position would have understood his situation. Nor do other aspects of the interaction of Williams and respondent support the contention that respondent was exposed to "custodial interrogation" at the scene of the stop. From aught that appears in the stipulation of facts, a single police officer asked respondent a modest number of questions and requested him to perform a simple balancing test at a location visible to passing motorists. Treatment of this sort cannot fairly be characterized as the functional equivalent of formal arrest.

We conclude, in short, that respondent was not taken into custody for the purposes of *Miranda* until Williams arrested him. Consequently, the statements respondent made prior to that point were admissible against him. . . .

Accordingly, the judgment of the Court of Appeals is

Affirmed.

Marshall's opinion in *Berkemer* continues to provide the definitive guidelines on the issue of custody and *Miranda*: police must read *Miranda* warnings only when some element of coercion exists during custodial questioning. If an individual is interrogated in a noncoercive atmosphere, such as in a routine roadside stop, the possibility for police abuse is dramatically diminished.

Although Marshall's ruling may have ended police confusion over the issue of custody, we must consider its compatibility with the Warren Court's mandate in *Miranda* and *Orozco*. Did *Berkemer* merely clarify those opinions, as some have suggested, or did it undermine their intent? If you believe the latter, how else could Marshall have ruled? Would the reading of *Miranda* rights at all roadside stops, even for relatively minor offenses such as speeding, have been a viable alternative?

What Constitutes Interrogation? Based on *Escobedo* and *Miranda* police must inform individuals of their rights before they question them in an accusatory fashion. But both of these decisions dealt with traditional interrogations, occurring within the confines of a police station. What about less traditional questioning in the guise of conversation? That is, must police read *Miranda* warnings before they engage in any dialogue with a suspect?

The Burger Court grappled with this question in *Brewer v. Williams* (1977). This case involved Robert Williams, a deeply religious man with severe psychological problems, who allegedly kidnapped and killed a ten-year-old girl in Des Moines, Iowa, on Christmas Eve, in 1968. Two days later Williams turned himself in to police in Davenport, some miles away, after apparently dumping the girl's body somewhere along the way. Williams telephoned an attorney in Des Moines, who told him to remain silent, talking neither to the Davenport police nor to the Des Moines detectives who were to take him back.

As the detectives drove Williams to Des Moines, they engaged the suspect in a wide-ranging conversation. At one point they began reciting what has become known as the Christian burial speech. Recognizing Williams's religious convictions, one of the detectives addressed him as Reverend, and said:

I want to give you something to think about while we're traveling down the road.... Number one, I want you to observe the weather conditions, it's raining, it's sleeting, it's freezing, driving is very treacherous, visibility is poor, it's going to be dark early this evening. They are predicting several inches of snow for tonight, and I feel that you yourself are the only person that knows where this little girl's body is, that you yourself have only been there once, and if you get a snow on top of it you yourself may be unable to find it. And, since we will be going right past the area on the way into Des Moines, I feel that we could stop and locate the body, that the parents of this little girl should be entitled to a Christian burial for the little girl who was snatched away from them on Christmas Eve and murdered. And I feel we should stop and locate it on the way in rather than waiting until morning and trying to come back out after a snow storm and possibly not being able to find it at all.... I do not want you to answer me. I don't want to discuss it any further. Just think about it as we're riding down the road.

This speech proved effective; Williams promptly directed police to the girl's body.

At his trial, Williams's attorney argued that the statements made by him in the car should be excluded as evidence, as should any evidence—the body—resulting from those statements. The statements, the attorney argued, were inadmissible because they had been obtained by illegal means. By playing off of Williams's weaknesses, police had tricked him. Their conversation, therefore, amounted to an interrogation, prior to which Williams should have been advised of his rights.

In a 5–4 vote the U.S. Supreme Court agreed. Writing for the majority, Justice Stewart said:

There can be no serious doubt ... that [the detective] deliberately and designedly set out to elicit information from Williams just as surely as ... if he had formally interrogated him. [He] was fully aware before departing ... that Williams was being represented [by counsel]. Yet, he purposely sought during Williams' isolation from his lawyers to obtain as much incriminating evidence as possible.

In 1977 the majority of the justices agreed that police need to advise suspects of their rights before nontraditional interrogations. If they fail to do so, judges must discard the evidence obtained from such conversations even when that material may be crucial to a prosecutor's case, as it was in *Brewer*.

Three years later, in *Rhode Island v. Innis* (1980) the Court reevaluated its *Brewer* position. The facts in *Innis* bear a strong resemblance to those in *Brewer*, but the Court took the opportunity to enunciate a standard that law enforcement officials could use to define an interrogation for *Miranda* purposes. Justice Stewart claimed that the *Innis* test flowed from the *Miranda* and *Brewer* precedents. Does it? Is this interrogation test compatible with those decisions or was it carefully worded to avoid overruling them?

Rhode Island v. Innis

446 U.S. 291 (1980)
Vote: 6 (Blackmun, Burger, Powell, Rehnquist, Stewart, White)
    3 (Brennan, Marshall, Stevens)
Opinion of the Court: Stewart
Concurring opinions: Burger, White
Dissenting opinions: Marshall, Stevens

On January 12, 1975, a cabdriver disappeared on his way to pick up a passenger; his body was later discovered with a shotgun blast to the back of the head. On January 17, police received a report from another cabdriver that he had been robbed by a man with a sawed-off shotgun. From a picture of Thomas Innis, the cabdriver identified him as his assailant. A Rhode Island patrolman spotted Innis walking down a street, arrested him, and advised him of his rights. Innis was unarmed. A sergeant and then a captain arrived on the scene, and they both read Innis his rights, which he said he understood. Innis also stated that he wanted an attorney before making any statement. Two patrolmen, joined by a third, put Innis into a caged wagon, a four-door car with a wire screen between the front and rear seats. Their superior officer told them not to speak to Innis or coerce him in any way.

While en route to the central station, one of the officers, Patrolman Gleckman, initiated a conversation with one of his colleagues, Patrolman McKenna, con-

cerning the missing gun. As Patrolman Gleckman later testified:

At this point, I was talking back and forth with Patrolman McKenna stating that I frequent this area while on patrol and [that because a school for handicapped children is located nearby,] there's a lot of handicapped children running around in this area, and God forbid one of them might find a weapon with shells and they might hurt themselves.

Patrolman McKenna apparently shared his fellow officer's concern:

I more or less concurred with him [Gleckman] that it was a safety factor and that we should, you know, continue to search for the weapon and try to find it.

While the third officer, Patrolman Williams, said nothing, he overheard the conversation between the two officers:

He [Gleckman] said it would be too bad if the little—I believe he said a girl—would pick up the gun, maybe kill herself.

At this point, Innis interrupted the officers and told them that he would show them where he had discarded the gun because he wanted no harm to come to any children. The gun Innis turned over to the police matched the one used to kill the first cabdriver, and a trial court convicted Innis of murder. He appealed, claiming that police had tricked him into showing them the gun. In essence, his claim matched Brewer's: the police conversation was a nontraditional form of interrogation to which *Miranda* applied.

JUSTICE STEWART delivered the opinion of the Court.

The issue ... is whether the respondent was "interrogated" by the police officers in violation of the respondent's undisputed right under *Miranda* to remain silent until he had consulted with a lawyer. In resolving this issue, we first define the term "interrogation" under *Miranda* before turning to a consideration of the facts of this case. The starting point for defining "interrogation" in this context is, of course, the Court's *Miranda* opinion. There the Court observed that "[b]y custodial interrogation, we mean questioning initiated by law enforcement officers after a person has been taken into custody or otherwise deprived of his freedom of action in any significant way." This passage and other references throughout the opinion to "questioning" might suggest that the *Miranda* rules were to apply only to those police interrogation practices that involve express questioning of a defendant while in custody.

We do not, however, construe the *Miranda* opinion so narrowly....

This is not to say, however, that all statements obtained by the police after a person has been taken into custody are to be considered the product of interrogation. As the Court in *Miranda* noted:

"Confessions remain a proper element in law enforcement. Any statement given freely and voluntarily without any compelling influences is, of course, admissible in evidence. *The fundamental import of the privilege while an individual is in custody is not whether he is allowed to talk to the police without the benefit of warnings and counsel, but whether he can be interrogated....* Volunteered statements of any kind are not barred by the Fifth Amendment and their admissibility is not affected by our holding today."

It is clear therefore that the special procedural safeguards outlined in *Miranda* are required not where a suspect is simply taken into custody, but rather where a suspect in custody is subjected to interrogation. "Interrogation," as conceptualized in the *Miranda* opinion, must reflect a measure of compulsion above and beyond that inherent in custody itself.

We conclude that the *Miranda* safeguards come into play whenever a person in custody is subjected to either express questioning or its functional equivalent. That is to say, the term "interrogation" under *Miranda* refers not only to express questioning, but also to any words or actions on the part of the police (other than those normally attendant to arrest and custody) that the police should know are reasonably likely to elicit an incriminating response from the suspect. The latter portion of this definition focuses primarily upon the perceptions of the suspect, rather than the intent of the police. This focus reflects the fact that the *Miranda* safeguards were designed to vest a suspect in custody with an added measure of protection against coercive police practices, without regard to objective proof of the underlying intent of the police. A practice that the police should know is reasonably likely to evoke an incriminating response from a suspect thus amounts to interrogation. But, since the police surely cannot be held accountable for the unforeseeable results of their words or actions, the definition of interrogation can extend only to words or actions on the part of police officers that they should have known were reasonably likely to elicit an incriminating response.

Turning to the facts of the present case, we conclude that the respondent was not "interrogated" within the meaning of *Miranda*. It is undisputed that the first prong of the definition of "interrogation" was not satisfied, for the conversation between Patrolmen Gleckman and McKenna included no express questioning of the respondent. Rather, that conversation was, at least in form, nothing more than a dialogue between the two officers to which no response from the respondent was invited.

Moreover, it cannot be fairly concluded that the respondent was subjected to the "functional equivalent" of questioning. It cannot be said, in short, that Patrolmen Gleckman and McKenna should have known that their conversation was reasonably likely to elicit an incriminating response from the respondent. There is nothing in the record to suggest that the officers were aware that the respondent was peculiarly susceptible to an appeal to his conscience concerning the safety of handicapped children. Nor is there anything in the record to suggest that the police knew that the respondent was unusually disoriented or upset at the time of his arrest.

The case thus boils down to whether, in the context of a brief conversation, the officers should have known that the respondent would suddenly be moved to make a self-incriminating response. Given the fact that the entire conversation appears to have consisted of no more than a few offhand remarks, we cannot say that the officers should have known that it was reasonably likely that Innis would so respond. This is not a case where the police carried on a lengthy harangue in the presence of the suspect. Nor does the record support the respondent's contention that, under the circumstances, the officers' comments were particularly "evocative." It is our view, therefore, that the respondent was not subjected by the police to words or actions that the police should have known were reasonably likely to elicit an incriminating response from him.

The Rhode Island Supreme Court erred, in short, in equating "subtle compulsion" with interrogation. That the officers' comments struck a responsive chord is readily apparent. Thus, it may be said, as the Rhode Island Supreme Court did say, that the respondent was subjected to "subtle compulsion." But that is not the end of the inquiry. It must also be established that a suspect's incriminating response was the product of words or actions on the part of the police that they should have known were reasonably likely to elicit an incriminating response. This was not established in the present case.

For the reasons stated, the judgment of the Supreme Court of Rhode Island is vacated, and the case is remanded to that court for further proceedings not inconsistent with this opinion.

It is so ordered.

Stewart's interrogation test draws a fine distinction between *Brewer* and *Innis*. The *Brewer* burial speech fails to meet the standard because police had a specific aim in reciting the speech and knew that Williams would be responsive. The *Innis* conversation required no *Miranda* warnings as it was not expressed questioning, and police did not know that the suspect was susceptible to the child-based argument. Is Justice Stewart convincing? Does this test provide a reasonable way to determine interrogations for purposes of *Miranda*? Or is it merely an artifact, created to alleviate obstacles created by *Brewer*?

The Uses of Incriminating Statements Made in the Absence of* Miranda *Warnings. The Warren Court premised its decision in *Miranda* on the inevitable inequities between the accused and police during custodial interrogations. In 1966 the justices thought the likelihood that individuals would forgo their privilege against self-incrimination under intense and ultimately coercive police questioning was too high to ignore. Arguably, the justices operated under the implicit assumption that incriminating statements made in the absence of *Miranda* warnings would automatically violate the Fifth Amendment and that judges

and/or juries should exclude them from consideration.

Beginning in 1971 and continuing into the 1990s, however, the Burger Court and the Rehnquist Court began to create exceptions to this rule. In *Harris v. New York* (1971), for instance, the Court held that incriminating statements made in the absence of *Miranda* warnings could be used by prosecutors to impeach the testimony of witnesses or the accused. Chief Justice Burger noted in his first major post-*Miranda* decision: "The shield of *Miranda* cannot be perverted into a license to use perjury by way of defense." Three years later the Court added another exception. In *Michigan v. Tucker* (1974) the majority buttressed police investigation efforts, holding that leads from statements made without the benefit of *Miranda* warnings could be used to assist officials in developing their cases.

After *Tucker* the Court waited a decade until it carved out any new exception to the Miranda ruling. But when it did, in *New York v. Quarles* (1984) and *Oregon v. Elstad* (1985), it went well beyond the limits previously established. In the first case, the justices scrutinized the following facts: in 1980 a woman approached two Queens, New York, police officers and reported that she had been raped by a tall black man, who was armed. The officers drove to the site, where they spotted the alleged assailant, Benjamin Quarles, who had entered a grocery store. One officer pursued Quarles, ordered him to stop, and frisked him. Quarles was wearing an empty gun holster, so the officer asked him where his gun was. Quarles answered, "The gun is over there." He nodded toward empty cartons where he had thrown the weapon while temporarily out of the officer's view. At this point the officer placed Quarles under arrest and read him his *Miranda* warnings.

A trial judge excluded Quarles's statement concerning the gun on the grounds that he made it prior to hearing his rights. The Supreme Court reversed. Writing for the Court, Justice Rehnquist established a public safety exception to *Miranda*, holding that, the need for answers to questions in a situation posing a threat to public safety outweighs the need for the prophylactic rule protecting the Fifth Amendment privilege.... We decline to place officers ... in the untenable position of having to consider ... whether it best serves society for them to ask the necessary question without *Miranda* ... or for them to give the warnings in order to preserve the admissibility of evidence ... but possibly damage or destroy their ability to obtain that evidence and neutralize the volatile situation confronting them.

One year later the majority agreed that additional limits on *Miranda* were needed. The case was *Oregon v. Elstad*, which originated from a 1981 burglary investigation. Police were told that eighteen-year-old Michael Elstad was involved in the crime. Two police officers went to Elstad's house with a warrant for his arrest, and his mother let them in. One officer went into the kitchen with Elstad's mother, and the other sat down in the living room with the suspect. The officer told Elstad that he was investigating a burglary and that he felt Elstad was involved. Elstad said, "Yes, I was there." *Miranda* warnings had not been given at this time.

Elstad was arrested and, at the police station approximately one hour later, he was advised of his rights. He said he understood his rights, waived them, and signed a confession. He was convicted based in part on the confession. At no time during the investigation did police engage in any overt actions to coerce a confession.

On appeal, Elstad's attorneys argued that the confession should not have been admitted into evidence. They claimed that the first incriminating statements made at Elstad's house were obtained in violation of *Miranda*. Because he had let the "cat out of the bag" in this initial questioning, Elstad felt psychological pressure not to disclaim his incriminating statements. According to this argument, the *Miranda* warnings administered prior to the second round of questioning were insufficient to immunize Elstad against being compelled to give a formal confession. The damage had already been done.

The Supreme Court did not agree, finding that the formal confession was not tainted by the failure of police to advise Elstad of his rights during the first interview. According to Justice Sandra Day O'Connor's opinion for the Court, the initial violation of the *Miranda* warning procedure was largely technical. There was no evidence of coercion. Elstad's statement that he was a participant in the crime was voluntarily given. Nonetheless, because he had not been advised of his rights, that initial statement was constitutionally flawed and could not be admitted. However, the Court held "that a suspect who has once responded to unwarned yet uncoercive questioning is not thereby disabled from waiving his rights and confessing after he has been given the requisite *Miranda* warnings." The formal, signed confession, therefore, was admissible. O'Connor's opinion in *Elstad* imposed a major limitation on the meaning of *Miranda*. Although her opinion did not overrule *Miranda* and, in fact, proclaimed its continuing viability, the Court had narrowed its applicability.[25]

As the Court entered the 1990s the justices gave additional indications that they might weaken *Miranda* even further. The warning came in *Arizona v. Fulminante* (1991). Oreste Fulminante was suspected of murdering his stepdaughter, who went missing while her mother was in the hospital. He left Arizona but was later arrested in New York on firearms violations and incarcerated in a federal prison. Fulminante was subjected to rough treatment by his fellow inmates, who had heard rumors that he might be a child murderer. But then he was befriended by another inmate, Anthony Sarivola, who promised to protect him in return for the truth. Fulminante confessed to Sarivola in great detail. Unknown to Fulminante, Sarivola was a paid FBI informant. After his release, Fulminante also confessed to Sarivola's wife.

25. In *Moran v. Burbine* (1986) the Court further narrowed *Miranda*'s scope, ruling that a confession need not be suppressed even though police failed to inform a suspect of his attorney's attempts to reach him by telephone.

Based on these confessions, Arizona indicted Fulminante for murder, and over his attorney's objections, the trial court allowed both confessions to be introduced as evidence. He was convicted and sentenced to death, but the Arizona Supreme Court reversed the conviction, holding that the confession to Sarivola was coerced.

The Supreme Court affirmed the decision of the Arizona high court. The justices ruled that the prison confession was obtained only because the informant promised to protect Fulminante from physical violence. Naturally, no *Miranda* warnings had been given before the informant obtained the confession. The majority concluded that the coerced confession had been a significant factor in the prosecution's case and, therefore, the conviction could not stand. However, five justices, led by Chief Justice Rehnquist, held that if there had been sufficient evidence to convict Fulminante independent of the tainted confession, a reversal of the conviction would not have been necessary. Under such circumstances the unconstitutional confession would have been considered a "harmless error." *Fulminante* was the first time a majority had applied the harmless error principle in a coerced confession case.

Now that you have a good understanding of how the Fifth Amendment Self-Incrimination Clause governs out-of-court "testimony," let's return to the question we posed earlier in this section: Why is *Miranda* so controversial? Some continue to argue that the decision binds the hands of police to an intolerable degree. Moreover, they point to cases like *Fulminante*, in which a confessed murderer and other criminals go free simply because their confessions were the product of coercion. That Fulminante's conviction was overturned, even though he confessed to a murder, is precisely what concerned Justice White and the others who dissented in *Miranda*. Yet supporters of *Miranda* make equally strong arguments. As Marvin Zalman and Larry Siegel point out, *Miranda* has not, in fact, made it more difficult for police to obtain incriminating statements. Empirical investigations of the ef-

fect of *Miranda* in cities—both large and small—indicate that "equivalent proportions of confessions were obtained in the post-*Miranda* period as before and that police effectiveness did not appear to suffer." Why this is the case is a matter of speculation, but the answer, in part, lies with the pervasiveness of *Miranda* in our society, as anyone who watches the current "cop" shows on television can confirm. Police and suspects alike have come to view *Miranda* as part and parcel of the criminal justice system. In light of the cases you have read, particularly recent Supreme Court opinions, on which side of the debate do you come down?

Before answering, read Box 8-3, the African Queen story, which details the procedures New York detectives used to obtain evidence against a murder suspect. The officers said their tactics were perfectly legitimate under Supreme Court precedent. Their view may have received some general support from Justice Kennedy, who, writing for the majority in *Illinois v. Perkins* (1990), stated: "*Miranda* forbids coercion, not mere strategic deception." The point is that *Miranda* in its most unadulterated form may have unduly hampered police efforts, but haven't recent decisions served to loosen some of the chains? Perhaps that is why many officers have come to accept *Miranda*; it no longer seriously constrains their efforts.

The Self-Incrimination Clause and Testimony

In addition to governing custodial interrogations, the Fifth Amendment's Self-Incrimination Clause covers testimony in all government hearings. Individuals called to testify in a court of law or before a congressional committee can refuse to answer any questions on the grounds that the answers may incriminate or implicate them in some unlawful activity. Journalists and other observers call this "taking the Fifth."

History is full of important investigations during which witnesses refused to cooperate by asserting their Fifth Amendment privilege. During the Red Scare of the 1950s, many called before Sen. Joseph R. McCarthy's committee investigating communist ac-

BOX 8-3   AFRICAN QUEEN STORY

The following was told to a reporter by two New York police officers:

Powerful as the internal pressure is, the *Miranda* rule and other constraints on questioning suspects have placed some limits on a detective's ability to exploit it. Nonetheless, there's one ancient technique that still has a place in the modern detective's repertory: trickery.

"We can still deceive them," Weidenbaum tells me. "We can use trickery as long as it doesn't violate their rights."

He then proceeds to give me a classic instance of what he called permissible deception in a case he and Cachie worked on, a case they called "the African Queen."

"She cut her husband's head off," Weidenbaum begins. "What happened was, this man was, well. . . ."

"Retarded," says Cachie.

"He was a veteran from World War II with 100 percent disability. She was an immigrant from. . . ."

"The Cameroons," supplies Cachie.

"In any case, she met him and decided she's going to get his Government insurance. And one day she calls the police and says, 'Look what happened to my husband.' And the police come there, and there he is, a bloody mess on the floor, the only thing holding his head onto the body is maybe a little piece of skin. You lift him, the head's going to roll right off. And so how do we investigate this? We start talking with her, and she thinks she's smart enough to fool everybody. Every day she comes to the precinct to talk to us."

The more she talked to them, the more suspicious they became. The blackberry brandy story was the last straw for the two detectives.

She had set the table in the apartment as if to show there were four people up there drinking the night of the murder, a night she claimed she was "away." She had put out an empty bottle of blackberry brandy and four glasses.

The problem was, the glasses in which the four people were supposed to have downed the blackberry brandy "were sparkling clean," says Weidenbaum. "She hadn't thought through her deception very thoroughly."

Convinced now that she'd murdered her husband, but handicapped by the lack of any witnesses or conclusive evidence, the detectives decided to use some deception of their own.

"I explain to her that when a person is murdered the last thing a person sees is the person who killed them. And this image remains on the lens of their eyes after they die, and with all this modern technology that we have, at the time of the autopsy we have the eyes removed and they are sent to a special lab, and in this lab they develop them like you would develop film, and we get a picture back of the murderer."

"That isn't true, is it?" I say, almost gulled by his deceptively sincere recitation.

"No, this is what I'm telling her," Weidenbaum clarifies for my benefit. "And she's sitting there listening to the story, and then she says to me, 'I guess you're going to find my picture.' The next day she goes back to the morgue and asks somebody at the morgue, 'Can you do this with the eyes?' And they thought she was crazy. She insisted on having the body immediately cremated with the eyes in it."

Her guilty reaction to the detectives' ruse helped convince a grand jury to indict the woman, Weidenbaum says. She subsequently pleaded guilty.

SOURCE: Ron Rosenbaum, "Crack Murder," *New York Times Magazine*, February 15, 1987. Copyright © 1987 by the New York Times Company. Reprinted by permission.

tivities refused to testify on those grounds. In 1987 the Fifth Amendment was invoked when Congress investigated the sale of arms to Iran in exchange for hostages. Several of those directly involved in the scandal refused to testify on the grounds that their statements would implicate them.

If a witness refuses to answer questions on Fifth Amendment grounds, no inference of guilt may be made. Judges may not instruct jurors to consider a defendant's refusal to take the witness stand and deny guilt under oath; nor may prosecutors argue that a defendant's decision not to testify is evidence of wrongdoing. Such actions by prosecutors or judges would be clear violations of the Fifth Amendment. An individual's decision to invoke the Fifth Amendment privilege and not answer questions can be interpreted as nothing more than a decision to remain silent.

Furthermore, individuals must be free to exercise their Fifth Amendment rights. Governments may not coerce a person to testify. A prosecutor, for example, may not threaten a defendant that if he or she does not take the witness stand, the government will ask for a more severe sentence. Nor may the government use economic pressure to coerce an individual to waive the Fifth Amendment privilege. In *Garrity v. New Jersey* (1967) and *Gardner v. Broderick* (1968) the Supreme Court ruled that public employees could not be threatened with the loss of their jobs if they did not testify in government investigations of corruption and wrongdoing. Citizens must be given the choice of exercising their rights against self-incrimination.

Although taking the Fifth is rarely challenged (only those asserting their right can know with certainty whether their statements would be incriminating), the right is not absolute. There are situations in which individuals may be forced to testify and provide answers that may link them to criminal activities. Under a grant of immunity, the prosecution agrees that it will not use any of the testimony against the witness.

In return, the witness provides information that the prosecution believes will result in the convictions of other criminals, more dangerous or more important than the immune witness. Because a grant of immunity means that nothing the witness says may be used against him or her, it is a direct substitute for the Fifth Amendment, and the witness may not take the Fifth Amendment.

There are two types of immunity. Transactional immunity provides witnesses with complete protection from all prosecutions related to the subject of their testimony. This arrangement is usually involuntary. The prosecutor awards a grant of transactional immunity, and the witness must testify or face penalties for contempt of court. The second kind, use/derivative use immunity, provides only partial security to defendants. Prosecutors promise not to use the testimony of the witness or anything derived from it, but the individual may be prosecuted on evidence gathered completely independent of the testimony.

Because the coverage of use/derivative use immunity is less comprehensive than transactional immunity, some thought that it was not sufficiently protective to replace the guarantees provided by the Fifth Amendment. Others argued that potential witnesses should be allowed to turn down such immunity offers. The position of the federal government was that this limited form of immunity was as protective as transactional immunity and that witnesses should have no choice if the prosecution awarded it. In 1972, in *Kastigar v. United States*, the Supreme Court examined the issue. After reviewing the history of immunity, the Court agreed with the government. For the majority, Justice Powell wrote that use/derivative use immunity "leaves the witness and the prosecutorial authorities in substantially the same position as if the witness had claimed the Fifth Amendment privilege. The immunity therefore is coextensive with the privilege and suffices to supplant it."

READINGS

Baker, Liva. *Miranda: Crime, Law, and Politics.* New York: Atheneum, 1983.

Canon, Bradley. "Testing the Effectiveness of Civil Liberties Policies at the State and Federal Levels: The Case of the Exclusionary Rule." *American Politics Quarterly* 5 (1977): 57–82.

Casper, Jonathan D. *American Criminal Justice: The Defendant's Perspective.* Englewood Cliffs, N.J.: Prentice-Hall, 1972.

Creamer, J. Shane. *The Law of Arrest, Search and Seizure.* New York: Holt, Rinehart & Winston, 1980.

Eisenstein, James, Roy B. Fleming, and Peter F. Nardulli. *The Contours of Justice: Communities and Their Courts.* Boston: Little, Brown, 1988.

Jacob, Herbert. *Law and Politics in the United States.* Boston: Little, Brown, 1988.

Kamisar, Yale. "The Warren Court (Was it Really so Defense-Minded?), the Burger Court (Was it Really so Prosecution-Oriented?) and Police Investigatory Procedures." In *The Burger Court,* ed. Vincent Blasi. New Haven: Yale University Press, 1983.

Landynski, Jacob W. *Search and Seizure and the Supreme Court.* Baltimore: Johns Hopkins University Press, 1966.

Levy, Leonard W. *Against the Law: The Nixon Court and Criminal Justice.* New York: Harper & Row, 1974.

Medalie, Richard J. *From Escobedo to Miranda.* Washington, D.C.: Lerner Law Books, 1966.

Myren, Richard A. *Law and Justice.* Pacific Grove, Calif.: Brooks/Cole, 1987.

Neubauer, David W. *America's Courts and the Criminal Justice System.* 3d ed. Pacific Grove, Calif.: Brooks/Cole, 1988.

Scheingold, Stuart. *The Politics of Law and Order.* New York: Longman, 1984.

CHAPTER 9
ATTORNEYS, TRIALS, AND PUNISHMENTS

T HE FRAMERS clearly understood the importance of fairness in evidence gathering, but
they also realized the need to protect the integrity of the more formal stages of the criminal
process. Consequently, the Bill of Rights included
specific guarantees to prohibit the government from
abusing prosecuted defendants. These rights are
among those we hold most dear, such as the right to
be represented by counsel, to be tried by an impartial
jury of our peers, and to be protected against punishments that are cruel and unusual. Other guarantees,
less well known but no less important, also enjoy constitutional status—the right to a speedy and public
trial, to confront our accusers in open court, to have
access to evidence favorable to our defense, and to
have reasonable opportunity for bail. Taken as a
whole, these rights were designed to help achieve a
universally valued goal—fundamentally fair criminal
trials. In this chapter we discuss what the Constitution says about these important procedural guarantees and how they have evolved through Supreme
Court interpretations over the years.

THE RIGHT TO COUNSEL

The Sixth Amendment guarantees that "In all
criminal prosecutions, the accused shall enjoy the
right . . . to have the Assistance of Counsel for his defence." At the time these words were written, the law
was relatively uncomplicated, and lawyers in the new
nation were scarce. Some individuals charged with
crimes sought the advice of counsel, but most handled their own cases. Still, the Framers understood
the importance of legal representation enough to include the right to counsel in the Bill of Rights.

Today, probably no other right guaranteed to the
criminally accused is more important than the right
to counsel. Until recently, a lawyer representing a
criminal client could do the job by appearing at trial
and dealing with well-established principles of evidence and procedure. Appearing at the trial is now
only a small part of what a criminal defense attorney
must do. As the Supreme Court emphasized repeatedly in the Fifth Amendment cases we reviewed in
Chapter 8, the role of the defense attorney begins
when police first interrogate a suspect. From arrest
through appeal, there are critical and complicated
stages during which a defendant's rights might be violated. It is the responsibility of counsel to ensure that
the interests of the defendant are not jeopardized.
The defense attorney, therefore, is the primary guarantee that all of the other rights of criminal due
process will be observed.

The provisions of the Sixth Amendment are sufficiently clear that there has been little controversy over the right of an individual to have legal representation throughout the various stages of the criminal process. Historically, however, it has always been the responsibility of the individual to secure a lawyer and to pay for the services. The most prolonged controversy over legal representation in criminal matters has centered on the rights of those who do not have the money to pay for legal assistance.

Indigents and the Right to Counsel: Foundations

As the U.S. system of justice became increasingly complex, more people retained lawyers to handle their cases. But as soon as this practice took hold, complaints of economic discrimination were heard. Civil libertarians and reformers throughout the country argued that only those who could afford it were guaranteed the right to counsel; indigent defendants were denied their constitutional guarantee. Reformers claimed that the only way to eliminate this injustice was a Supreme Court decision that would force governments to appoint free counsel for poor defendants.

In *Powell v. Alabama* (1932) the Supreme Court scrutinized this claim for the first time. Justice George Sutherland's opinion for the majority does not adopt the view that states must assign counsel to indigents in *all* cases. But does he completely shut the door on such an interpretation of the Constitution?

Powell v. Alabama
(The Scottsboro Boys Case)

287 U.S. 45 (1932)
Vote: 7 *(Brandeis, Cardozo, Hughes, Roberts, Stone,
        Sutherland, Van Devanter)*
    2 *(Butler, McReynolds)*
Opinion of the Court: Sutherland
Dissenting opinion: Butler

Riding in an open car on a freight train traveling from Chattanooga through Alabama March 25, 1931,

were nine young black males, seven white males, and two white females. During the journey, the white and black youths got into a fight, which ended with the white males being thrown off the train and the females claiming they had been raped by the blacks.[1] Word of the alleged rape spread, and, when the train reached Paint Rock, a sheriff's posse arrested the blacks, who ranged in age from twelve to twenty, and jailed them in the county seat of Scottsboro. A hostile, racist crowd gathered to harass the alleged assailants, and extra security personnel were needed to prevent a lynching.

When the youths appeared at the courthouse, it was obvious they were scared. They were young, uneducated, and away from home, with no friends or family to help them. At their initial hearing, the judge showed no sympathy for them. Under Alabama law, he was supposed to appoint counsel to assist them because they were charged with a capital offense; instead, he assigned all the town's members of the bar to represent them. [2] No single lawyer took responsibility for their defense. Moreover, the judge set the trial date for April 6, just six days after they had been indicted.

On the morning of April 6, an out-of-town lawyer, Stephen R. Roddy, appeared to represent the youths. The first thing he did was to ask the judge for more time to prepare his defense, but the judge refused, and the trial began. Given the hostile environment in which they were tried, it should come as no surprise that the "Scottsboro boys" were found guilty and sentenced to death.

The main question emerging from this case was: Do indigents have the right to counsel at government expense?

---

1. For more on this case, see Dan T. Carter, *Scottsboro—A Tragedy of the American South* (New York: Oxford University Press, 1969).

2. Many states had laws mandating the appointment of counsel for capital crimes such as rape. We should note, however, that in *Coker v. Georgia* (1977) the Supreme Court outlawed the use of the death penalty in rape cases.

The plight of the nine "Scottsboro boys," arrested in rural Alabama in 1931 for raping two white females, spawned numerous legal actions including *Powell v. Alabama* (1932), which expanded the rights of indigents to legal representation. Samuel Leibowitz, a prominent attorney and later a judge, handled the defendants' cases after their original conviction. He is shown here conferring with his clients.

MR. JUSTICE SUTHERLAND delivered the opinion of the Court.

It is hardly necessary to say that the right to counsel being conceded, a defendant should be afforded a fair opportunity to secure counsel of his own choice. Not only was that not done here, but such designation of counsel as was attempted was either so indefinite or so close upon the trial as to amount to a denial of effective and substantial aid in that regard....

... [U]ntil the very morning of the trial no lawyer had been named or definitely designated to represent the defendants. Prior to that time, the trial judge had "appointed all the members of the bar" for the limited "purpose of arraigning the defendants." Whether they would represent the defendants thereafter, if no counsel appeared in their behalf, was a matter of speculation only, or, as the judge indicated, of mere anticipation on the part of the court. Such a designation, even if made for all purposes, would, in our opinion, have fallen far short of meeting, in any proper sense, a requirement for the appointment of counsel. How many lawyers were members of the bar does not appear; but, in the very nature of things, whether many or few, they would not, thus collectively named, have been given that clear appreciation of responsibility or impressed with that individual sense of duty which should and naturally would accompany the appointment of a selected member of the bar, specifically named and assigned.

That this action of the trial judge in respect of appointment of counsel was little more than an expansive gesture, imposing no substantial or definite obligation upon any one, is borne out by the fact that prior to the calling of the case for trial on April 6, a leading member of the local bar accepted employment on the side of the prosecution and actively participated in the trial.... This lawyer in question, of his own accord, frankly stated to the court; and no doubt he acted with the utmost good faith. Probably other members of the bar had a like understanding. In any event, the circumstance lends emphasis to the conclusion that during perhaps the most critical period of the proceedings against these defendants, that is to say, from the time of their arraignment until the beginning of their trial, when consultation, thoroughgoing investigation and preparation were vitally important, the defendants did not have the aid of counsel in any real sense, although they were as much entitled to such aid during that period as at the trial itself....

The defendants, young, ignorant, illiterate, surrounded by hostile sentiment, haled back and forth under guard of soldiers, charged with an atrocious crime regarded with especial horror in the community where they were to be tried, were thus put in peril of their lives within a few moments after counsel for the first time charged with any degree of responsibility began to represent them.

It is not enough to assume that counsel thus precipitated into the case thought there was no defense, and exercised their best judgment in proceeding to trial without preparation. Neither they nor the court could say what a prompt and thoroughgoing investigation might disclose as to the facts. No attempt was made to investigate. No opportunity to do so was given....

... [W]e think the failure of the trial court to give them reasonable time and opportunity to secure counsel was a clear denial of due process.

But passing that, and assuming their inability, even if opportunity had been given, to employ counsel, as the trial court evidently did assume, we are of opinion that, under the circumstances just stated, the necessity of counsel was so vital and imperative that the failure of the trial court to make an effective appointment of counsel was likewise a denial of due process within the meaning of the Fourteenth Amendment. Whether this would be so in other criminal prosecutions, or under other circumstances, we need not determine. All that is necessary now to decide, as we do decide, is that in a capital case, where the defendant is unable to employ counsel, and is incapable adequately of making his own defense because of ignorance, feeblemindedness, illiteracy, or the like, it is the duty of the court, whether requested or not, to assign counsel for him as a necessary requisite of due process of law; and that duty is not discharged by an assignment at such a time or under such circumstances as to preclude the giving of effective aid in the preparation and trial of the case. To hold otherwise would be to ignore the fundamental postulate, already adverted to, "that there are certain immutable principles of justice which inhere in the very idea of free government which no member of the Union may disregard." In a case such as this, whatever may be the rule in other cases, the right to have counsel appointed, when necessary, is a logical corollary from the constitutional right to be heard by counsel....

Judgments reversed.

The Court declined to decide if the Sixth Amendment guarantees the right to counsel for every defendant. But, writing for the majority, Justice Sutherland recognized that cases involving unusual situations (capital offenses, intense public pressure, or young, uneducated, and inexperienced defendants) would necessitate a lawyer's participation to secure fundamental fairness for defendants. Although the Court in *Powell* made no sweeping statements about the Sixth Amendment, it did for the first time mandate the appointment of counsel.

Just six years after *Powell*, the Court went one step further. In *Johnson v. Zerbst* it ruled that indigent defendants involved in federal criminal prosecutions must be represented by counsel. Although *Johnson* was a major ruling, like *Powell*, it was limited. As we saw with the series of cases leading to the universal application of the exclusionary rule, decisions applying only to the federal government affect an insignificant number of defendants because most prosecutions occur in the states. Criminal defense attorneys, therefore, pushed the Court to apply *Johnson* to the states in the same way they argued, in *Wolf v. Colorado* (1949), that *Weeks v. United States* (1914), establishing the exclusionary rule, ought to govern state investigations. But just as the *Wolf* attempt failed to convince a majority of the Court to apply certain Fourth Amendment guarantees to the states, so too did *Betts v. Brady* (1942), the first attempt after *Johnson*.

Indicted for robbery in Maryland, Betts—a poor, uneducated, but literate, white man—wanted an attorney at government expense. Like many states, Maryland provided indigents with counsel only in rape and murder cases. Betts conducted his own defense and was convicted. On appeal he asked the Supreme Court to apply *Johnson* to the states, thereby incorporating the Sixth Amendment guarantee. The Court refused, 6–3. Writing for the majority, Justice Roberts claimed that the Framers never intended that the right to counsel be defined as a fundamental guarantee, just that it apply to extreme situations as in *Powell*. When Roberts compared Betts's claim to that of the Scottsboro defendants, he found that it came up short because Betts was not helpless or illiterate, and he could not have received the death penalty for his offense.

Justice Black dissented. He wrote:

Denial to the poor of the request for counsel in proceedings based on charges of serious crime has been long regarded as shocking to the "universal sense of justice" throughout this country.... Most ... states have shown their agreement [and] assure that no man shall be deprived of counsel merely because of his poverty. Any other practice seems to me to defeat the promise of our democratic society to provide equal justice under law.

More than twenty years later, a Court more sympathetic to the rights of the criminally accused reevaluated the wisdom of *Betts v. Brady*. As you read the famous case of *Gideon v. Wainwright*, think about these questions: Why did the Court extend the right to government-provided attorneys to indigents accused of state crimes? Did something distinguish *Gideon* from *Betts*, or did other factors come into play?

Gideon v. Wainwright

372 U.S. 355 (1963)
Vote: 9 (Black, Brennan, Clark, Douglas, Goldberg, Harlan,
　　　Stewart, Warren, White)
　　　0
Opinion of the Court: Black
Concurring opinions: Clark, Douglas, Harlan

Florida officials charged Clarence Earl Gideon with breaking and entering a poolroom. The trial court refused to appoint counsel for him because Florida did not provide free lawyers to those charged with less than a capital offense. Gideon (like Betts, a poor, uneducated white man) tried to defend himself, but failed. After studying the law in a prison library and attempting a number of lower court actions, Gideon filed a petition for a writ of certiorari with the U.S. Supreme Court.[3] The petition was handwritten on prison notepaper, but the justices granted it a review.

Because Gideon was without counsel, the Court appointed Abe Fortas, a well-known attorney (and future Supreme Court justice) to represent him. Twenty-two states filed an amicus curiae brief, which was written by Walter Mondale (then the attorney general of Minnesota and later vice president of the United States), supporting Gideon's argument. Clarence Gideon went from being a poor convict facing a lonely court battle to a man represented by some of the country's finest legal minds.

MR. JUSTICE BLACK delivered the opinion of the Court.

Since 1942, when Betts v. Brady was decided by a divided Court, the problem of a defendant's federal constitutional right to counsel in a state court has been a continuing source of controversy and litigation in both state and federal courts. To give this problem another review here, we granted certiorari. Since Gideon was proceeding *in forma pauperis*, we appointed counsel to represent him and requested both sides to discuss in their briefs and oral arguments the following: "Should this Court's holding in Betts v. Brady be reconsidered?"

The facts upon which Betts claimed that he had been unconstitutionally denied the right to have counsel appointed to assist him are strikingly like the facts upon which Gideon here bases his federal constitutional claim. ... Since the facts and circumstances of the two cases are so nearly indistinguishable, we think the Betts v. Brady holding if left standing would require us to reject Gideon's claim

that the Constitution guarantees him the assistance of counsel. Upon full reconsideration we conclude that Betts v. Brady should be overruled.

The Sixth Amendment provides, "In all criminal prosecutions, the accused shall enjoy the right ... to have the Assistance of Counsel for his defence." We have construed this to mean that in federal courts counsel must be provided for defendants unable to employ counsel unless the right is competently and intelligently waived. Betts argued that this right is extended to indigent defendants in state courts by the Fourteenth Amendment. In response the Court stated that, while the Sixth Amendment laid down "no rule for the conduct of the states, the question recurs whether the constraint laid by the amendment upon the national courts expresses a rule so fundamental and essential to a fair trial, and so, to due process of law, that it is made obligatory upon the states by the Fourteenth Amendment." In order to decide whether the Sixth Amendment's guarantee of counsel is of this fundamental nature, the Court in Betts set out and considered "[r]elevant data on the subject ... afforded by constitutional and statutory provisions subsisting in the colonies and the states prior to the inclusion of the Bill of Rights in the national Constitution, and in the constitutional, legislative, and judicial history of the states to the present date." On the basis of this historical data the Court concluded that "appointment of counsel is not a fundamental right, essential to a fair trial.". . .

We accept Betts v. Brady's assumption, based as it was on our prior cases, that a provision of the Bill of Rights which is "fundamental and essential to a fair trial" is made obligatory upon the States by the Fourteenth Amendment. We think the Court in Betts was wrong, however, in concluding that the Sixth Amendment's guarantee of counsel is not one of these fundamental rights. Ten years before Betts v. Brady, this Court, after full consideration of all the historical data examined in Betts, had unequivocally declared that "the right to the aid of counsel is of this fundamental character." Powell v. Alabama (1932). While the Court at the close of its Powell opinion did by its language, as this Court frequently does, limit its holding to the particular facts and circumstances of that case, its conclusions about the fundamental nature of the right to counsel are unmistakable. Several years later, in 1936, the Court reempha-

---

3. See Anthony Lewis, *Gideon's Trumpet* (New York: Vintage Books, 1964).

(left) Clarence Earl Gideon's handwritten petition to the Supreme Court. The Court ruled unanimously that indigent defendants must be provided counsel in state trials.

(above) Clarence Earl Gideon

sized what it had said about the fundamental nature of the right to counsel in this language:

"We concluded that certain fundamental rights, safeguarded by the first eight amendments against federal action, were also safeguarded against state action by the due process of law clause of the Fourteenth Amendment, and among them the fundamental right of the accused to the aid of counsel in a criminal prosecution." Grosjean v. American Press Co. (1936)....

In light of these and many other prior decisions of the Court, it is not surprising that the Betts Court, when faced with the contention that "one charged with crime, who is unable to obtain counsel, must be furnished counsel by the state," conceded that "[e]xpressions in the opinions of this court lend color to the argument...." The fact is that in deciding as it did—that "appointment of counsel is not a fundamental right, essential to a fair trial"—the Court in Betts v. Brady made an abrupt break with its own well-considered precedents. In returning to these old precedents, sounder we believe than the new, we but restore constitutional principles established to achieve a fair system of justice. Not only these precedents but also reason and reflection require us to recognize that in our adversary system of criminal justice, any person haled into court, who is too poor to hire a lawyer, cannot be assured a fair trial unless counsel is provided for him. This seems to us to be an obvious truth. Governments, both state and federal, quite properly spend vast sums of money to establish machinery to try defendants accused of crime. Lawyers to prosecute are everywhere deemed essential to protect the public's interest in an orderly society. Similarly, there are few defendants charged with crime, few indeed, who fail to hire the best lawyers they can get to prepare and present their defenses. That government hires lawyers to prosecute and defendants who have the money hire lawyers to defend are the strongest indications of the widespread belief that lawyers in criminal courts are necessities, not luxuries. The right of one charged with crime to counsel may not be deemed fundamental and essential to fair trials in some countries, but it is in ours. From the very beginning, our state and national constitutions and laws have laid great emphasis on procedural and substantive safeguards designed to assure fair trials before impartial tribunals in which every defendant stands equal before the law. This noble ideal cannot be realized if the poor man charged with crime has to face his accusers without a lawyer to assist him. A defendant's need for a lawyer is nowhere better stated than in the moving words of Mr. Justice Sutherland in Powell v. Alabama:

"The right to be heard would be, in many cases, of little avail if it did not comprehend the right to be heard by counsel. Even the intelligent and educated layman has small and sometimes no skill in the science of law. If charged with crime, he is incapable, generally, of determining for himself whether the indictment is good or bad. He is unfamiliar with the rules of evidence. Left without the aid of counsel he may be put on trial without a proper charge, and convicted upon incompetent evidence, or evidence irrelevant to the issue or otherwise inadmissible. He lacks both the skill and knowledge adequately to prepare his defense, even though he have a perfect one. He requires the guiding hand of counsel at every step in the proceedings against him. Without it, though he be not guilty, he faces the danger of conviction because he does not know how to establish his innocence."

The Court in Betts v. Brady departed from the sound wisdom upon which the Court's holding in Powell v. Alabama rested. Florida, supported by two other States, has asked that Betts v. Brady be left intact. Twenty-two States, as friends of the Court, argue that Betts was "an anachronism when handed down" and that it should now be overruled. We agree. The judgment is reversed and the cause is remanded to the Supreme Court of Florida for further action not inconsistent with this opinion.

Reversed.

Beyond the legal significance of *Gideon*, the case is interesting for several reasons. First, *Gideon* provides another example of the Warren Court's revolution in criminal rights. The Court of 1963 took a carbon copy of *Betts* and came up with a radically different solution. *Gideon* completed a process of constitutional evolution in which the Court first applied a rule of law to the federal government, refused to extend that rule to the states, and then reversed its position and brought the states under the rule's applicability. As indicated in Table 9-1, this historical pattern is the same as in the battle over applicability of the exclusionary rule, a subject considered in Chapter 8.

Second, *Gideon* is a classic example of the importance of dissents. In considering cases applying the Bill of Rights to the states, we saw how Justice Harlan's minority views in the incorporation cases were adopted by later justices. Here, however, we see an even more unusual event: Justice Black, who wrote the dissenting opinion in *Betts*, wrote the majority opinion for the Supreme Court twenty-one years later in *Gideon*.

Finally, *Gideon v. Wainwright* has had a tremendous impact on the U.S. criminal justice system, in which 75 percent of the criminally accused are indigent. To comply with the Court's ruling, states had to alter their defender systems, creating mechanisms to provide lawyers for the accused. Today, indigent criminals may receive one of two kinds of legal services, depending on where they are being tried.[4] Many locali-

---

4. For more information on counsel for indigents, see David W. Neubauer, *America's Courts and the Criminal Justice System* (Monterey, Calif.: Brooks/Cole, 1984); Herbert Jacob, ed., *The Potential for Reform of*

TABLE 9-1 Comparison of the Development of the Exclusionary Rule and the Right to Counsel for Indigents

Doctrine	Exclusionary Rule	Right to Counsel for Indigents
Establishment of right for federal prosecutions	*Weeks v. United States* (1918)	*Johnson v. Zerbst* (1938)
Refusal to apply to states	*Wolf v. Colorado* (1949)	*Betts v. Brady* (1942)
Application to states	*Mapp v. Ohio* (1961)	*Gideon v. Wainwright* (1963)

ties have created a public defender office that mirrors the prosecuting attorney's office. In other words, the state hires lawyers to represent indigents. Other areas use court-appointed attorney systems in which judges assign members of the legal community to represent the underprivileged.

For all its importance, however, *Gideon* left several questions unanswered. First, what crimes does the ruling cover? Does it apply only to felonies, as in Gideon's case, or to lesser crimes as well? Second, through what stages in the criminal system does *Gideon* apply? That is, when does the right to counsel end? After trial? After the first appeal?

For the most part, these fallout questions were left to the Burger Court justices to answer. As you read further, think again about whether the Burger Court followed the Warren Court's mandate or if it tried to blunt the impact of the Warren era decisions.

The Application of Gideon: *The Nature of the Offense*

The applicability of *Gideon* to offenses less serious than Gideon's breaking and entering conviction was addressed in *Argersinger v. Hamlin* (1972), an appeal from a man sentenced to serve ninety days in jail for weapons violations. Writing for the majority, Justice

Douglas developed a rule known as the loss of liberty rule: whoever is deprived of liberty even for one day is entitled to an attorney. By articulating such a standard, the Court rejected the argument of several states (including Florida once again) that only indigents facing jail sentences of more than six months are entitled to a lawyer at public expense.

Although *Argersinger* seemed to be the final statement on the question, the state of Illinois found a gap in this ruling. In *Scott v. Illinois* (1979) it argued that the loss of liberty standard should apply only when individuals receive a jail sentence, not when just the potential for imprisonment exists.[5]

The case arose when Illinois charged Aubrey Scott with theft, a crime carrying a maximum sentence of a $500 fine and/or one year in prison. Prior to trial the prosecutor announced that he had no intention of asking for a jail sentence if Scott was convicted. Without the assistance of counsel, Scott was tried, convicted, and fined $50. He appealed, claiming that he should have had a lawyer.

When the case reached the Supreme Court, the justices were presented with this question: Should the loss of liberty rule apply to those crimes for which the potential for imprisonment exists, but the accused does not receive it? Writing for the Court, Justice

---

Criminal Justice (Beverly Hills, Calif.: Sage, 1974); Lee Silverstein, *Defense of the Poor* (Chicago: American Bar Association, 1965). For an informative firsthand account of "what a criminal lawyer does and what it does to him," see Seymour Wishman, *Confessions of a Criminal Lawyer* (New York: Penguin Books, 1982).

5. The justices were aware that this argument would likely arise. In *Argersinger* Justice Lewis Powell's concurring opinion pressed the point that Douglas's "loss of liberty" analysis failed to consider the serious consequences resulting from some misdemeanor convictions even if a jail sentence is not imposed.

Rehnquist read *Argersinger* to answer this question negatively. As he noted:

Although the intentions of the *Argersinger* Court are not unmistakably clear from its opinion, we conclude today that *Argersinger* did indeed delimit the constitutional right to appointed counsel in state criminal proceedings. Even were the matter *res nova* [a new issue], we believe that the central premise of *Argersinger* that actual imprisonment is a penalty different in kind from fines or the mere threat of imprisonment—is eminently sound and warrants adoption of actual imprisonment as the line defining the constitutional right to appointment of counsel. *Argersinger* has proved reasonably workable, whereas any extension would create confusion and impose unpredictable, but necessarily substantial, costs on 50 quite diverse States. We therefore hold that the Sixth and Fourteenth Amendments to the United States Constitution require only that no indigent criminal defendant be sentenced to a term of imprisonment unless the State has afforded him the right to assistance of appointed counsel in his defense.

Justice Rehnquist draws a clear line for states to follow: they are constitutionally required to appoint counsel only when actual imprisonment is a reality. Did this decision undermine the spirit of *Gideon* and *Argersinger?* According to the dissenters (including Justice Brennan, who had been in the *Gideon* majority), it did. Brennan wrote in a dissenting opinion in *Scott*:

Earlier precedents had recognized that the assistance of appointed counsel was critical not only to equalize the sides in an adversary criminal process, but also to give substance to other constitutional and procedural protections afforded criminal defendants. *Gideon* established the right to appointed counsel for indigent accuseds as a categorical requirement.... [It] involved a felony prosecution, but that fact was not crucial to the decision; its reasoning extended, in the words of the Sixth Amendment, to *"all* criminal prosecutions."

He also had some unkind words for Rehnquist's interpretation of *Argersinger:*

The Court's opinion turns the reasoning of *Argersinger* on its head.... The abstract pretext that "constitutional line drawing becomes more difficult as the reach of the Constitution is extended further" ... cannot camouflage the anomalous result the Court reaches. Today's decision reminds one of Mr. Justice Black's description of *Betts v. Brady:* "an anachronism when handed down" that "ma[kes] an abrupt break with its own well-considered precedents."

What do you think? Does Brennan or Rehnquist make the better case?

Gideon *and the Appellate Stage*

Justice Black's decision in *Gideon* said that an indigent accused of a criminal offense must be represented by counsel at trial. What Black did not address was whether that right extended through the appellate process. And if so, did such a right apply only to obligatory appeals (usually the first appeal after a trial) or also to discretionary appeals (subsequent appeals that the appellate court may or may not agree to hear)?

In *Douglas v. California* (1963) the Court answered part of this question, holding that the right indeed extended through the first obligatory appeal. Writing for the Court, Justice Douglas proclaimed:

[W]here the merits of *the one and only appeal* an indigent has as of right are decided without benefit of counsel, we think an unconstitutional line has been drawn between rich and poor.... There is lacking that equality demanded by the Fourteenth Amendment where the rich man, who appeals as of right, enjoys the benefit of the counsel's examination into the record, research of the law, and marshaling of arguments on his behalf, while the indigent ... is forced to shift for himself.

Justice Douglas's opinion, however, left open the question of whether the Sixth Amendment right extends to the discretionary review stages, an issue the Burger Court took up in *Ross v. Moffitt* (1974).

Moffitt involved two separate cases from two counties in North Carolina for forgery offenses. In both, Moffitt, an indigent, pleaded not guilty, receive court-appointed counsel, and was convicted. An intermediate state appellate court affirmed both convictions. Moffitt then sought review in the North Carolina Supreme Court and asked that his attorney represent him at government expense. The court denied this request. Moffitt also sought the same objective in the federal courts. Here, he was more successful: the Fourth Circuit Court of Appeals ordered the state to appoint him counsel to prepare an appeal to the U.S. Supreme Court. By accepting this case, the Court could address the following question for both state and federal courts: Does *Douglas v. California* require the appointment of counsel at discretionary review stages?

Writing for the Court, Justice Rehnquist concluded that it did not. He stated:

We do not believe ... that a defendant in respondent's circumstances is denied meaningful access to the North Carolina Supreme Court simply because the State does not appoint counsel to aid him in seeking review. At that stage he will have, at the very least, a transcript or other record of the trial proceedings, a brief on his behalf in the Court of Appeals setting forth his error, and in many cases an opinion by the court of appeals disposing of his case....

We do not mean by this opinion to in any way discourage those States which have, as a matter of legislative choice, made counsel available ... at all stages of judicial review.... Our reading [of the Constitution] leaves these choices to the State.

The justices of the Burger Court failed to overrule revolutionary Warren Court decisions, but, as *Ross* shows, they shut the door on any further expansions of rights.

THE PRETRIAL PERIOD AND THE RIGHT TO BAIL

The defense attorney must protect the accused's rights during every stage of the criminal process, starting with interrogation and investigation and the formal stages of the pretrial period. If already retained or appointed, counsel represents the accused at the initial appearance and is present at the preliminary hearing and arraignment. The defense attorney negotiates with the prosecuting attorney over the exact crimes to be charged. Pretrial motions may be made for judicial rulings on questions of evidence and procedure. The defense attorney also begins preparing the case to be presented in court should the defendant go to trial.

Of all the pretrial stages, the setting of bail is perhaps the most important to the defendant. Bail is a monetary guarantee ensuring that the accused will show up for the trial. Defendants who are not eligible for bail and those who cannot raise the money must wait in jail until their trial date. Defendants who can "make bail" are released, pending their trial.

How does a judge decide who is eligible for release? How is the bail amount determined? Individuals charged with misdemeanors are automatically eligible for bail, and the amount is usually set according to a specific fee schedule. For those charged with felonies, a judge sets bail on a case-by-case basis. Among the factors the judge considers are the seriousness of the offense, the trustworthiness of the individual, and the Eighth Amendment's prohibition against excessive bail. Until 1987 the Supreme Court had not decided a major dispute over what factors a judge may appropriately consider in making bail determinations; that year, *United States v. Salerno* challenged the Bail Reform Act of 1984.

United States v. Salerno

481 U.S. 739 (1987)
Vote: 6 (Blackmun, O'Connor, Powell, Rehnquist,
        Scalia, White)
    3 (Brennan, Marshall, Stevens)
Opinion of the Court: Rehnquist
Dissenting opinions: Marshall, Stevens

In 1986 the Justice Department brought racketeering charges against Anthony Salerno, the boss of the Genovese crime family. At Salerno's bail hearing, U.S. attorneys urged the judge to deny bail on the grounds that the accused would continue to engage in criminal activity if released. Before 1984 judges probably would not have considered such a factor in their decision-making processes because bail had always been used only to ensure a defendant's presence at trial. But in 1984 Congress passed the Bail Reform Act, authorizing judges to deny bail to defendants to "assure . . . the safety of any other person and the community." After federal prosecutors presented evidence suggesting that Salerno would commit murder if let out, the judge denied bail. Salerno successfully appealed to the U.S. court of appeals, which declared the 1984 act unconstitutional. The federal government then asked the Supreme Court to reverse.

CHIEF JUSTICE REHNQUIST delivered the opinion of the Court.

The Bail Reform Act of 1984 allows a federal court to detain an arrestee pending trial if the government demonstrates by clear and convincing evidence after an adversary hearing that no release conditions "will reasonably assure . . . the safety of any other person and the community." The United States Court of Appeals for the Second Circuit struck down this provision of the Act as facially unconstitutional, because, in that court's words, this type of pretrial detention violates "substantive due process." We granted certiorari because of a conflict among the Courts of Appeals regarding the validity of the Act. We hold that, as against the facial attack mounted by these respondents, the Act fully comports with constitutional requirements. We therefore reverse.

Responding to "the alarming problem of crimes committed by persons on release," Congress formulated the Bail Reform Act of 1984 as the solution to the bail crisis in the federal courts. The Act represents the National Legislature's considered response to numerous perceived deficiencies in the federal bail process. By providing for sweeping changes in both the way federal courts consider bail applications and the circumstances under which bail is granted, Congress hoped to "give the courts adequate authority to make release decisions that give appropriate recognition to the danger a person may pose to others if released." . . .

A facial challenge to a legislative Act is, of course, the most difficult challenge to mount successfully, since the challenger must establish that no set of circumstances exists under which the Act would be valid. . . . We think respondents have failed to shoulder their heavy burden to demonstrate that the Act is "facially" unconstitutional.

Respondents present two grounds for invalidating the Bail Reform Act's provisions permitting pretrial detention on the basis of future dangerousness. First, they rely upon the Court of Appeals' conclusion that the Act exceeds the limitations placed upon the Federal Government by the Due Process Clause of the Fifth Amendment. Second, they contend that the Act contravenes the Eighth Amendment's proscription against excessive bail. We treat these contentions in turn.

The Due Process Clause of the Fifth Amendment provides that "No person shall . . . be deprived of life, liberty, or property, without due process of law. . . ." This Court has held that the Due Process Clause protects individuals against two types of government action. So-called "substantive due process" prevents the government from engaging in conduct that "shocks the conscience" or interferes with rights "implicit in the concept of ordered liberty." When government action depriving a person of life, liberty, or property survives substantive due process scrutiny, it must still be implemented in a fair manner. This requirement has traditionally been referred to as "procedural" due process.

Respondents first argue that the Act violates substantive due process because the pretrial detention it authorizes constitutes impermissible punishment before trial. The Government, however, has never argued that pretrial detention could be upheld if it were "punishment." The Court of Appeals assumed that pretrial detention under the Bail Reform Act is regulatory, not penal, and we agree that it is.

As an initial matter, the mere fact that a person is detained does not inexorably lead to the conclusion that the government has imposed punishment. To determine whether a restriction on liberty constitutes impermissible punishment or permissible regulation, we first look to legislative intent. Unless Congress expressly intended to impose punitive restrictions, the punitive/regulatory distinction turns on "'whether an alternative purpose to which the restriction may rationally be connected is assignable for it, and whether it appears excessive in relation to the alternative purpose assigned [to it].'"

We conclude that the detention imposed by the Act falls on the regulatory side of the dichotomy. The legislative history of the Bail Reform Act clearly indicates that Congress did not formulate the pretrial detention provisions as punishment for dangerous individuals. Congress instead perceived pretrial detention as a potential solution to a pressing societal problem. There is no doubt that preventing danger to the community is a legitimate regulatory goal.

Nor are the incidents of pretrial detention excessive in relation to the regulatory goal Congress sought to achieve. The Bail Reform Act carefully limits the circumstances under which detention may be sought to the most serious of crimes. The arrestee is entitled to a prompt detention hearing, and the maximum length of pretrial detention is limited by the stringent time limitations of the Speedy Trial Act. Moreover, ... the conditions of confinement envisioned by the Act "appear to reflect the regulatory purposes relied upon by the" government.... We conclude, therefore, that the pretrial detention contemplated by the Bail Reform Act is regulatory in nature, and does not constitute punishment before trial in violation of the Due Process Clause.

The Court of Appeals nevertheless concluded that "the Due Process Clause prohibits pretrial detention on the ground of danger to the community as a regulatory measure, without regard to the duration of the detention." Respondents characterize the Due Process Clause as erecting an impenetrable "wall" in this area that "no governmental interest—rational, important, compelling or otherwise— may surmount."

We do not think the Clause lays down any such categorical imperative. We have repeatedly held that the government's regulatory interest in community safety can, in appropriate circumstances, outweigh an individual's liberty interest. For example, in times of war or insurrection, when society's interest is at its peak, the government may detain individuals whom the government believes to be dangerous. Even outside the exigencies of war, we have found that sufficiently compelling governmental interests can justify detention of dangerous persons. Thus, we have found no absolute constitutional barrier to detention of potentially dangerous resident aliens pending deportation proceedings. We have also held that the government may detain mentally unstable individuals who present a danger to the public and dangerous defendants who become incompetent to stand trial. We have approved of post-arrest regulatory detention of juveniles when they present a continuing danger to the community....

Respondents characterize all of these cases as exceptions to the "general rule" of substantive due process that the government may not detain a person prior to a judgment of guilt in a criminal trial. Such a "general rule" may freely be conceded, but we think that these cases show a sufficient number of exceptions to the rule that the congressional action challenged here can hardly be characterized as totally novel. Given the well-established authority of the government, in special circumstances, to restrain individuals' liberty prior to or even without criminal trial and conviction, we think that the present statute providing for pretrial detention on the basis of dangerousness must be evaluated in precisely the same manner that we evaluated the laws in the cases discussed above.

The government's interest in preventing crime by arrestees is both legitimate and compelling.... The Bail Reform Act ... narrowly focuses on a particularly acute problem in which the government interests are overwhelming. The Act operates only on individuals who have been arrested for a specific category of extremely serious offenses. Congress specifically found that these individuals are far more likely to be responsible for dangerous acts in the community after arrest....

On the other side of the scale, of course, is the individual's strong interest in liberty. We do not minimize the importance and fundamental nature of this right. But, as our cases hold, this right may, in circumstances where the government's interest is sufficiently weighty, be subordinated to the greater needs of society. We think that Congress' careful delineation of the circumstances under which detention will be permitted satisfies this standard. When the government proves by clear and convincing evidence that an arrestee presents an identified and articulable threat to an individual or the community, we believe that, consistent with the Due Process Clause, a court may disable the arrestee from executing that threat. Under these circumstances, we cannot categorically state that pretrial detention "offends some principle of justice so rooted in the traditions and conscience of our people as to be ranked as fundamental."...

Respondents also contend that the Bail Reform Act violates the Excessive Bail Clause of the Eighth Amendment. The Court of Appeals did not address this issue because it found that the Act violates the Due Process Clause. We think that the Act survives a challenge founded upon the Eighth Amendment.

The Eighth Amendment addresses pretrial release by providing merely that "Excessive bail shall not be required." This Clause, of course, says nothing about whether bail shall be available at all. Respondents nevertheless contend that this Clause grants them a right to bail calculated solely upon considerations of flight. They rely on *Stack v. Boyle* (1951) in which the Court stated that "Bail set at a figure higher than an amount reasonably calculated [to ensure the defendant's presence at trial] is 'excessive' under the Eighth Amendment." In respondents' view, since the Bail Reform Act allows a court essentially to set bail at an infinite amount for reasons not related to the risk of flight, it violates the Excessive Bail Clause. Respondents concede that the right to bail they have discovered in the Eighth Amendment is not absolute. A court may, for example, refuse bail in capital cases. And, as the Court of Appeals noted and respondents admit, a court may refuse bail when the defendant presents a threat to the judicial process by intimidating witnesses. Respondents characterize these exceptions as consistent with what they claim to be the sole purpose of bail—to ensure integrity of the judicial process.

While we agree that a primary function of bail is to safeguard the courts' role in adjudicating the guilt or innocence of defendants, we reject the proposition that the Eighth Amendment categorically prohibits the government from pursuing other admittedly compelling interests through regulation of pretrial release. The above-quoted *dicta* in *Stack v. Boyle* is far too slender a reed on which to rest this argument. The Court in *Stack* had no occasion to consider whether the Excessive Bail Clause requires courts to admit all defendants to bail, because the statute before the Court in that case in fact allowed the defendants to be bailed. Thus, the Court had to determine only whether bail, admittedly available in that case, was excessive if set at a sum greater than that necessary to ensure the arrestees' presence at trial....

Nothing in the text of the Bail Clause limits permissible government considerations solely to questions of flight.

The only arguable substantive limitation of the Bail Clause is that the government's proposed conditions of release or detention not be "excessive" in light of the perceived evil. Of course, to determine whether the government's response is excessive, we must compare that response against the interest the government seeks to protect by means of that response. Thus, when the government has admitted that its only interest is in preventing flight, bail must be set by a court at a sum designed to ensure that goal, and no more. We believe that when Congress has mandated detention on the basis of a compelling interest other than prevention of flight, as it has here, the Eighth Amendment does not require release on bail.

In our society liberty is the norm, and detention prior to trial or without trial is the carefully limited exception. We hold that the provisions for pretrial detention in the Bail Reform Act of 1984 fall within that carefully limited exception. The Act authorizes the detention prior to trial of arrestees charged with serious felonies who are found after an adversary hearing to pose a threat to the safety of individuals or to the community which no condition of release can dispel. The numerous procedural safeguards detailed above must attend this adversary hearing. We are unwilling to say that this congressional determination, based as it is upon that primary concern of every government—a concern for the safety and indeed the lives of its citizens—on its face violates either the Due Process Clause of the Fifth Amendment or the Excessive Bail Clause of the Eighth Amendment.

The judgment of the Court of Appeals is therefore

Reversed.

By upholding this federal law, the Supreme Court gave implicit assent to the statutes of twenty-four states that allowed the denial of bail on similar bases.

Unlike Salerno, the majority of defendants will be eligible for bail. The job of their attorneys is to convince the judges to set bail at affordable levels. Most criminal defendants cannot put up the entire bail amount, even if set at modest levels. Many seek the services of a bail bondsman, who, for a significant and nonrefundable fee, files a bail bond with the court.

The bond substitutes for cash bail and allows the defendant to be free, pending trial.

Because the bail procedure discriminates against the poor and the bail bonding industry has often been linked to unsavory practices, many criminal justice experts regard the bail stage as one of the weakest links in the system.[6] There has been, however, little support for bail reform, as most citizens lack sympathy for those accused of crimes. Many law-and-order-minded Americans believe that the criminally accused should not be released. As a result, the bail system operates today much as it did 100 years ago.

THE SIXTH AMENDMENT AND FAIR TRIALS

From a quantitative perspective, trials are insignificant; only about 5 percent of all criminal prosecutions go to trial. In the other 95 percent, the defendant pleads guilty, usually after arriving at a plea-bargaining agreement with the prosecutor. In such arrangements, the defendant waives the right to a jury trial and agrees to plead guilty in return for certain concessions made by the prosecutor. These concessions normally involve a reduction in the seriousness of the crimes charged, a reduction in the number of counts, or a recommendation for a lenient sentence. Although many citizens look at such arrangements unfavorably, the Supreme Court has sanctioned the practice, and it remains the most common way criminal prosecutions are settled.[7]

Qualitatively, however, trials are significant; the most serious crimes go to trial. In addition, trials serve a symbolic function and educate the public about crime and justice in the community. And they embody what Americans treasure so much—fundamental, objective, and open fairness.

The Framers of the Constitution clearly intended American trials to be the epitome of justice. They drafted the Sixth Amendment to correct the weaknesses they had observed in the English justice system, weaknesses that included closed proceedings, long delays, and few safeguards for defendants. Specifically, Sixth Amendment provisions governing trials state that:

In all criminal prosecutions, the accused shall enjoy the right to a speedy and public trial, by an impartial jury of the State and district wherein the crime shall have been committed, ... to be confronted with the witnesses against him; to have compulsory process for obtaining witnesses in his favor.

In short, the Sixth Amendment provides strict guidelines for trial proceedings. The next pages examine how the Supreme Court has interpreted each right and the overall impact of its decisions on the trial process.

Speedy Trials

Before the late 1960s the speedy trial provision of the Sixth Amendment was seldom invoked. Most cases proceeded from arrest to trial in a timely fashion. Then backlogs of cases began to build up at the trial court level.[8] The Supreme Court was asked to interpret the Speedy Trial Clause, and, because very little legal doctrine existed, the cases coming to the Court raised basic issues about its meaning. In one of the first, *United States v. Marion* (1971), the justices were asked to determine what stages of the criminal process the Speedy Trial Clause governed. Some lawyers argued that the constitutional ban against unreasonable delays covered the period from the commission of the crime to the beginning of the trial. Others held the provision governed only the period

---

6. See Neubauer, *America's Courts*, 213; and George F. Cole, *The American System of Criminal Justice*, 6th ed. (Monterey, Calif.: Brooks/Cole, 1992), 402–408.

7. See, for example, *North Carolina v. Alford* (1970).

8. For discussions of caseloads and workloads of trial courts, see Peter Nardulli, "The Caseload Controversy and the Study of Criminal Courts," *Journal of Criminal Law and Criminology* 70 (1979): 101; and Laurence Friedman and Robert Percival, "A Tale of Two Courts: Litigation in Alameda and San Benito Counties," *Law and Society Review* 4 (1970): 331.

from formal charges (arrest, indictment, or information) to the beginning of the trial.

Marion originated with a series of articles published in the *Washington Post* in October 1967. The pieces alleged fraudulent practices by home improvement firms, including a company called Allied Enterprises. One of the articles quoted a U.S. attorney as saying that indictments against some unnamed business would be forthcoming. Sure enough, during the summer of 1968, federal prosecutors conducted interviews with Allied officials. In the fall of 1969 a grand jury was impaneled, and in April 1970 it handed down indictments against Allied officials.

Before their trial, Allied employees argued that their Sixth Amendment right to a speedy trial had been violated because of the three-year lapse between the commission of the alleged offense and the grand jury indictment. During this prolonged period, they claimed, witnesses had forgotten certain events, and bias against them had grown. They asked the Court to rule that the delay between the commission of the crime and arrest or indictment was unreasonable.

In a unanimous decision, the Court refused to do so, but not on the grounds that the delay had been too long. Rather, Justice White's opinion said that the Speedy Trial Clause does not apply to the time before the formal charges are issued. The intent of the provision was to keep those publicly charged with a criminal offense from suffering unreasonable delays before they had their day in court. Several facts, he claimed, supported this view:

1. The Framers of the Sixth Amendment could hardly have selected less appropriate language if they intended the speedy trial provision to protect against pre-accusation delay.

2. Legislative efforts to implement the speedy trial provision also plainly reveal the view that these guarantees are applicable only after a person has been accused of a crime.

3. The law has provided other mechanisms, such as statutes of limitation, to guard against possible prejudice resulting from the passage of time between crime and arrest or charge.

Clearly, *Marion* instructed defense attorneys that the Court would be unwilling to find violations of the Speedy Trial Clause unless unreasonable delays occurred after arrest or formal charges had been made.

The next year, in *Barker v. Wingo* (1972), the Court confronted the question left unanswered in *Marion:* What criteria are to be used to determine if there has been unreasonable postindictment delay? In this case, two individuals, Barker and Manning, were charged with beating an elderly Kentucky couple to death with a tire iron. The prosecutor had a strong case against Manning, but not against Barker. To convict Barker, the prosecutor needed Manning to testify, but Manning refused on Fifth Amendment grounds. The prosecutor devised the following strategy: he would put Manning on trial first, and, after obtaining a conviction against Manning, he would try Barker and call Manning as a major witness. Manning would no longer be able to refuse to testify on Fifth Amendment grounds because, having already been convicted of murder, further incrimination would be impossible.

While this strategy was theoretically sound, it ran into difficulties. Getting Manning convicted took longer than the prosecutor had anticipated. In fact, because of hung juries, successful appeals, and subsequent retrials, it took several years. During this time, prosecutors had to ask the court to postpone Barker's trial sixteen times. Beginning with the twelfth continuance request, Barker's attorneys started asserting that the speedy trial provision of the Sixth Amendment was being violated. Finally, five years after he was indicted for murder, Barker went on trial. He was found guilty and sentenced to life in prison.

Barker's attorneys appealed the conviction on the grounds that the five-year delay was a violation of the

Sixth Amendment. A unanimous Supreme Court, through an opinion by Justice Powell, refused to designate a specific length of time that would constitute unreasonable delay. Instead, the justices recognized that this period could vary from case to case. However, the Court established four criteria that should be considered in deciding questions of unreasonable delay:

1. The length of the delay
2. The reason for the delay
3. The point at which the defendant begins asserting a Sixth Amendment violation
4. Whether the delay prejudiced the defendant's case

As applied to Barker, the Court found no constitutional violation. While the five-year delay was admittedly long, the reason for the delay—the unavailability of an important witness—was sound. Furthermore, the defendant did not even register objections to the delay until well into the process. Finally, the Court was unable to see any prejudice suffered by the defendant due to the delay. Under Justice Powell's balancing test, defendants have a great deal to prove before the Court finds a violation of the speedy trial provision.[9]

Jury Trials

Like many other aspects of law and procedure, the Framers incorporated the British jury system into the U.S. Constitution. The Sixth Amendment states in part, "In all criminal prosecutions, the accused shall enjoy the right to a . . . trial, by an impartial jury." But what did the term *jury* mean to the Framers? We can speculate that they had in mind at least three aspects

of the British system: that a jury be composed of the defendant's peers, that it consist of twelve persons, and that it reach unanimous verdicts. Today, none of these three guarantees is fully operative in criminal proceedings.

Jury Members. Presumably, in England being tried by a jury of one's peers meant that one would face members of one's social class. In other words, a commoner would be tried by a jury of commoners and a nobleman by a jury of noblemen. In the United States such class distinctions are not recognized; rather, a jury of one's peers means a jury that represents a cross-section of the community. To put together representative panels, most jurisdictions follow a procedure that works this way:

1. Individuals living within a specified geographical area are called for jury duty. Most localities use voter registration, property tax, or driver's license lists from which to select names.

2. Those selected form the jury pool or venire, the group from which attorneys choose the actual jury.

3. The judge may conduct initial interviews excusing certain classes of people (felons, illiterates, the mentally ill) and certain occupational groups, as allowed under the laws of the particular jurisdiction.

4. The remaining individuals are available to be chosen to serve on a trial (petit) jury. In the final selection phase, the opposing attorneys interview the prospective jurors. This process is called *voir dire.* During *voir dire* attorneys can dismiss those individuals they believe would not vote in the best interests of their clients. The attorneys, therefore, select the jury.

During *voir dire,* attorneys use two mechanisms or challenges to eliminate potential jurors. When a prospective juror appears to be unqualified to carry out the obligations of service, attorneys can *challenge for cause.* To do so they must explain to the judge their reason for eliminating that individual (for example,

9. After *Barker,* as Neubauer notes, "There was considerable interest in putting some teeth into the guarantee of a speedy trial." In 1974 Congress passed the Speedy Trial Act, requiring indictment within thirty days of arrest, arraignment ten days after indictment, and trial sixty days after arraignment. Moreover, every state has enacted speedy trial laws of various sorts. See Neubauer, *America's Courts,* 394–395.

conflict of interest or expressions of extreme prejudice), and the judge must agree. Challenges for cause
are unlimited. Attorneys also have a fixed number of
peremptory challenges, which they may use to excuse
jurors without stating a reason.

The objective of this longstanding process is to
form a petit jury representing a cross-section of the
community. Does the process work? This question
has been the center of numerous scholarly analyses,
and is still debated. Many argue that the system is the
best among myriad inferior alternatives. Others claim
that it is plagued with problems from beginning to
end, resulting in unacceptable biases. For example,
because most localities now draw their jury pools
from voter registration lists, juries reflect the average
voter—white, middle-aged, and middle class.

Another serious concern is that attorneys, specifically prosecutors, use their peremptory challenges
systematically to excuse blacks from juries. This
action is based on the belief that black jurors are reluctant to convict black defendants. Although trial
court judges have long recognized that prosecutors
engaged in this practice, they could do little about it
because peremptory challenges do not require the approval of the judge. Most courts refused to interfere
with the traditional privilege of attorneys to excuse
jurors for no specific reason, viewing it as part of a litigation strategy. The Supreme Court, in *Swain v. Alabama* (1965), generally rejected an argument that
prosecutors should be prohibited from using the
peremptory challenge to remove prospective jurors
for reasons of race.

In *Batson v. Kentucky* (1986), however, the Court
reevaluated *Swain* and startled the legal community
by holding that even peremptory challenges are subject to court scrutiny. As you read this case, note that
all but two of the Burger Court justices agreed with a
ruling that clearly flew in the face of well-established
custom and precedent. *Batson* is an interesting (and
unusual) example of a decision in which the Burger
Court modified a Warren Court precedent and re-

placed it with a decision more favorable to the rights
of the criminally accused.

Batson v. Kentucky

476 U.S. 79 (1986)
Vote: 7 *(Blackmun, Brennan, Marshall, O'Connor, Powell,*
Stevens, White)
  2 *(Burger, Rehnquist)*
Opinion of the Court: Powell
Concurring opinions: Marshall, O'Connor, Stevens, White
Dissenting opinions: Burger, Rehnquist

James Batson, a black, was indicted for second
degree burglary. Although his venire had four blacks,
the prosecutor used his peremptory challenges to
eliminate them, leaving Batson with an all-white jury.
Batson's attorney challenged this outcome, claiming
that it denied his client equal protection of the laws
and his Sixth Amendment right to an impartial jury
representing a cross-section of the community. The
trial court (and later the Kentucky Supreme Court)
denied this claim in part on the basis of the sanctity of
peremptory challenges.

The U.S. Supreme Court was asked to address this
question: May prosecutors use their peremptory challenges to eliminate prospective jurors of a specific
racial group? Naturally, such an issue drew many
opinions, in the form of amicus curiae briefs, from organized interest groups. The NAACP Legal Defense
Fund, for instance, argued, "The exclusion of Blacks
from juries not only stigmatizes them and deprives
them of their right ... to participate in the criminal
justice system. It destroys the appearance of justice."
The National Legal Aid and Defender Association,
representing the public defender offices and legal
aid societies, framed its argument a bit differently:
"No significant state interest exists in allowing unrestricted use of the peremptory challenge ... because it
is not essential to the ability of the prosecutor to
select fair and impartial jurors."

JUSTICE POWELL delivered the opinion of the Court.

This case requires us to reexamine that portion of *Swain v. Alabama* concerning the evidentiary burden placed on a criminal defendant who claims that he has been denied equal protection through the State's use of peremptory challenges to exclude members of his race from the petit jury....

In *Swain v. Alabama*, this Court recognized that a "State's purposeful or deliberate denial to Negroes on account of race of participation as jurors in the administration of justice violates the Equal Protection Clause." This principle has been "consistently and repeatedly" reaffirmed, in numerous decisions of this Court both preceding and following *Swain.* We reaffirm the principle today.

More than a century ago, the Court decided that the State denies a black defendant equal protection of the laws when it puts him on trial before a jury from which members of his race have been purposefully excluded. *Strauder v. West Virginia* (1880). That decision laid the foundation for the Court's unceasing efforts to eradicate racial discrimination in the procedures used to select the venire from which individual jurors are drawn. In *Strauder,* the Court explained that the central concern of the recently ratified Fourteenth Amendment was to put an end to governmental discrimination on account of race. Exclusion of black citizens from service as jurors constitutes a primary example of the evil the Fourteenth Amendment was designed to cure.

In holding that racial discrimination in jury selection offends the Equal Protection Clause, the Court in *Strauder* recognized, however, that a defendant has no right to a "petit jury composed in whole or in part of persons of his own race." But the defendant does have the right to be tried by a jury whose members are selected pursuant to nondiscriminatory criteria. The Equal Protection Clause guarantees the defendant that the State will not exclude members of his race from the jury venire on account of race or on the false assumption that members of his race as a group are not qualified to serve as jurors.

Purposeful racial discrimination in selection of the venire violates a defendant's right to equal protection because it denies him the protection that a trial by jury is intended to secure. "The very idea of a jury is a body ... composed of the peers or equals of the person whose rights it is selected or summoned to determine; that is, of his neighbors, fellows, associates, persons having the same legal status in society as that which he holds."...

Racial discrimination in selection of jurors harms not only the accused whose life or liberty they are summoned to try. Competence to serve as a juror ultimately depends on an assessment of individual qualifications and ability impartially to consider evidence presented at a trial. A person's race simply "is unrelated to his fitness as a juror." As long ago as *Strauder,* therefore, the Court recognized that by denying a person participation in jury service on account of his race, the State unconstitutionally discriminated against the excluded juror....

In *Strauder,* the Court invalidated a state statute that provided that only white men could serve as jurors. We can be confident that no state now has such a law. The Constitution requires, however, that we look beyond the face of the statute defining juror qualifications and also consider challenged selection practices to afford "protection against action of the State through its administrative officers in effecting the prohibited discrimination."...

Accordingly, the component of the jury selection process at issue here, the State's privilege to strike individual jurors through peremptory challenges, is subject to the commands of the Equal Protection Clause. Although a prosecutor ordinarily is entitled to exercise permitted peremptory challenges "for any reason at all, as long as that reason is related to his view concerning the outcome" of the case to be tried, the Equal Protection Clause forbids the prosecutor to challenge potential jurors solely on account of their race or on the assumption that black jurors as a group will be unable impartially to consider the State's case against a black defendant.

The principles announced in *Strauder* never have been questioned in any subsequent decision of this Court. Rather, the Court has been called upon repeatedly to review the application of those principles to particular facts. A recurring question in these cases, as in any case alleging a violation of the Equal Protection Clause, was whether the defendant had met his burden of proving purposeful discrimination on the part of the State. That question also was at the heart of the portion of *Swain v. Alabama* we reexamine today.

Swain required the Court to decide, among other issues, whether a black defendant was denied equal protection by the State's exercise of peremptory challenges to exclude members of his race from the petit jury. The record in *Swain* showed that the prosecutor had used the State's peremptory challenges to strike the six black persons included on the petit jury venire. While rejecting the defendant's claim for failure to prove purposeful discrimination, the Court nonetheless indicated that the Equal Protection Clause placed some limits on the State's exercise of peremptory challenges.

The Court sought to accommodate the prosecutor's historical privilege of peremptory challenge free of judicial control, and the constitutional prohibition on exclusion of persons from jury service on account of race. While the Constitution does not confer a right to peremptory challenges, those challenges traditionally have been viewed as one means of assuring the selection of a qualified and unbiased jury. To preserve the peremptory nature of the prosecutor's challenge, the Court in Swain declined to scrutinize his actions in a particular case by relying on a presumption that he properly exercised the State's challenges.

The Court went on to observe, however, that a state may not exercise its challenges in contravention of the Equal Protection Clause. It was impermissible for a prosecutor to use his challenges to exclude blacks from the jury "for reasons wholly unrelated to the outcome of the particular case on trial" or to deny to blacks "the same right and opportunity to participate in the administration of justice enjoyed by the white population." Accordingly, a black defendant could make out a prima facie case of purposeful discrimination on proof that the peremptory challenge system was "being perverted" in that manner. For example, an inference of purposeful discrimination would be raised on evidence that a prosecutor, "in case after case, whatever the circumstances, whatever the crime and whoever the defendant or the victim may be, is responsible for the removal of Negroes who have been selected as qualified jurors by the jury commissioners and who have survived challenges for cause, with the result that no Negroes ever serve on petit juries." Evidence offered by the defendant in *Swain* did not meet that standard. While the defendant showed that prosecutors in the jurisdiction had exercised their strikes to exclude blacks from the jury, he offered no proof of the circumstances under which prosecutors were responsible for striking black jurors beyond the facts of his own case.

A number of lower courts following the teaching of *Swain* reasoned that proof of repeated striking of blacks over a number of cases was necessary to establish a violation of the Equal Protection Clause. Since this interpretation of *Swain* has placed on defendants a crippling burden of proof, prosecutors' peremptory challenges are now largely immune from constitutional scrutiny.... [We] reject this evidentiary formulation as inconsistent with standards that have been developed since *Swain* for assessing a prima facie case under the Equal Protection Clause....

The standards for assessing a prima facie case in the context of discriminatory selection of the venire have been fully articulated since *Swain.* These principles support our conclusion that a defendant may establish a prima facie case of purposeful discrimination in selection of the petit jury solely on evidence concerning the prosecutor's exercise of peremptory challenges at the defendant's trial. To establish such a case, the defendant first must show that he is a member of a cognizable racial group and that the prosecutor has exercised peremptory challenges to remove from the venire members of the defendant's race. Second, the defendant is entitled to rely on the fact, as to which there can be no dispute, that peremptory challenges constitute a jury selection practice that permits "those to discriminate who are of a mind to discriminate." Finally, the defendant must show that these facts and any other relevant circumstances raise an inference that the prosecutor used that practice to exclude the veniremen from the petit jury on account of their race. This combination of factors in the empanelling of the petit jury, as in the selection of the venire, raises the necessary inference of purposeful discrimination.

In deciding whether the defendant has made the requisite showing, the trial court should consider all relevant circumstances. For example, a "pattern" of strikes against black jurors included in the particular venire might give rise to an inference of discrimination. Similarly, the prosecutor's questions and statements during *voir dire* examination and in exercising his challenges may support or refute an inference of discriminatory purpose. These examples are merely illustrative. We have confidence that trial judges, experienced in supervising *voir dire*, will be able to decide if the circumstances concerning the prosecutor's use of peremptory challenges creates a prima facie case of discrimination against black jurors.

Once the defendant makes a prima facie showing, the burden shifts to the State to come forward with a neutral explanation for challenging black jurors. Though this requirement imposes a limitation in some cases on the full peremptory character of the historic challenge, we emphasize that the prosecutor's explanation need not rise to the level justifying exercise of a challenge for cause. But the prosecutor may not rebut the defendant's prima facie case of discrimination by stating merely that he challenged jurors of the defendant's race on the assumption—or his intuitive judgment—that they would be partial to the defendant because of their shared race. Just as the Equal Protection Clause forbids the States to exclude black persons from the venire on the assumption that blacks as a group are unqualified to serve as jurors, so it forbids the States to strike black veniremen on the assumption that they will be biased in a particular case simply because the defendant is black. The core guarantee of equal protection, ensuring citizens that their State will not discriminate on account of race, would be meaningless were we to approve the exclusion of jurors on the basis of such assumptions, which arise solely from the jurors' race. Nor may the prosecutor rebut the defendant's case merely by denying that he had a discriminatory motive or "affirming his good faith in individual selections." If these general assertions were accepted as rebutting a defendant's prima facie case, the Equal Protection Clause "would be but a vain and illusory requirement." The prosecutor therefore must articulate a neutral explanation related to the particular case to be tried. The trial court then will have the duty to determine if the defendant has established purposeful discrimination.

The State contends that our holding will eviscerate the fair trial values served by the peremptory challenge. Conceding that the Constitution does not guarantee a right to peremptory challenges and that *Swain* did state that their use ultimately is subject to the strictures of equal protection, the State argues that the privilege of unfettered exercise of the challenge is of vital importance to the criminal justice system.

While we recognize, of course, that the peremptory challenge occupies an important position in our trial procedures, we do not agree that our decision today will under-mine the contribution the challenge generally makes to the administration of justice. The reality of practice, amply reflected in many state and federal court opinions, shows that the challenge may be, and unfortunately at times has been, used to discriminate against black jurors. By requiring trial courts to be sensitive to the racially discriminatory use of peremptory challenges, our decision enforces the mandate of equal protection and furthers the ends of justice. In view of the heterogeneous population of our nation, public respect for our criminal justice system and the rule of law will be strengthened if we ensure that no citizen is disqualified from jury service because of his race. . . .

In this case, petitioner made a timely objection to the prosecutor's removal of all black persons on the venire. Because the trial court flatly rejected the objection without requiring the prosecutor to give an explanation for his action, we remand this case for further proceedings. If the trial court decides that the facts establish, prima facie, purposeful discrimination and the prosecutor does not come forward with a neutral explanation for his action, our precedents require that petitioner's conviction be reversed.

It is so ordered.

JUSTICE MARSHALL, concurring.

I join JUSTICE POWELL's eloquent opinion for the Court, which takes a historic step toward eliminating the shameful practice of racial discrimination in the selection of juries. The Court's opinion cogently explains the pernicious nature of the racially discriminatory use of peremptory challenges, and the repugnancy of such discrimination to the Equal Protection Clause. The Court's opinion also ably demonstrates the inadequacy of any burden of proof for racially discriminatory use of peremptories that requires that "justice . . . sit supinely by" and be flouted in case after case before a remedy is available. I nonetheless write separately to express my views. The decision today will not end the racial discrimination that peremptories inject into the jury-selection process. That goal can be accomplished only by eliminating peremptory challenges entirely. . . .

Misuse of the peremptory challenge to exclude black jurors has become both common and flagrant. Black defendants rarely have been able to compile statistics showing the extent of that practice, but the few cases setting out such figures are instructive. See *United States v. Carter* (CA8 [Court of Appeals] 1975) (in 15 criminal cases in 1974 in the Western District of Missouri involving black defendants, prosecutors peremptorily challenged 81% of black jurors), cert. denied (1976); *United States v. McDaniels* (ED [Eastern District] La. 1974) (in 53 criminal cases in 1972–1974 in the Eastern District of Louisiana involving black defendants, federal prosecutors used 68.9% of their peremptory challenges against black jurors, who made up less than one-quarter of the venire).... An instruction book used by the prosecutor's office in Dallas County, Texas, explicitly advised prosecutors that they conduct jury selection so as to eliminate "'any member of a minority group.'" In 100 felony trials in Dallas County in 1983–1984, prosecutors peremptorily struck 405 out of 467 eligible black jurors; the chance of a qualified black sitting on a jury was one-in-ten, compared to one-in-two for a white....

Much ink has been spilled regarding the historic importance of defendants' peremptory challenges.... [T]he *Swain* Court emphasized the "very old credentials" of the peremptory challenge and cited the "long and widely held belief that peremptory challenge is a necessary part of trial by jury." But this Court has also repeatedly stated that the right of peremptory challenge is not of constitutional magnitude, and may be withheld altogether without impairing the constitutional guarantee of impartial jury and fair trial. The potential for racial prejudice, further, inheres in the defendant's challenge as well. If the prosecutor's peremptory challenge could be eliminated only at the cost of eliminating the defendant's challenge as well, I do not think that would be too great a price to pay.

I applaud the Court's holding that the racially discriminatory use of peremptory challenges violates the Equal Protection Clause, and I join the Court's opinion. However, only by banning peremptories entirely can such discrimination be ended.

JUSTICE REHNQUIST, with whom THE CHIEF JUSTICE joins, dissenting.

I cannot subscribe to the Court's unprecedented use of the Equal Protection Clause to restrict the historic scope of the peremptory challenge, which has been described as "a necessary part of trial by jury." *Swain.* In my view, there is simply nothing "unequal" about the State's using its peremptory challenges to strike blacks from the jury in cases involving black defendants, so long as such challenges are also used to exclude whites in cases involving white defendants, Hispanics in cases involving Hispanic defendants, Asians in cases involving Asian defendants, and so on. This case-specific use of peremptory challenges by the State does not single out blacks, or members of any other race for that matter, for discriminatory treatment. Such use of peremptories is at best based upon seat-of-the-pants instincts, which are undoubtedly crudely stereotypical and may in many cases be hopelessly mistaken. But as long as they are applied across the board to jurors of all races and nationalities, I do not see—and the Court most certainly has not explained—how their use violates the Equal Protection Clause.

Nor does such use of peremptory challenges by the State infringe upon any other constitutional interests. The Court does not suggest that exclusion of blacks from the jury through the State's use of peremptory challenges results in a violation of either the fair cross-section or impartiality component of the Sixth Amendment. And because the case-specific use of peremptory challenges by the State does not deny blacks the right to serve as jurors in cases involving nonblack defendants, it harms neither the excluded jurors nor the remainder of the community.

The use of group affiliations, such as age, race, or occupation, as a "proxy" for potential juror partiality, based on the assumption or belief that members of one group are more likely to favor defendants who belong to the same group, has long been accepted as a legitimate basis for the State's exercise of peremptory challenges. See *Swain.* Indeed, given the need for reasonable limitations on the time devoted to *voir dire,* the use of such "proxies" by both the State and the defendant may be extremely useful in eliminating from the jury persons who might be biased in one way or another. The Court today holds that the State may not use its peremptory challenges to strike black prospective jurors on this basis without violating the Constitution. But I do not believe there is anything in the Equal Protection Clause, or any other constitutional provision, that justifies such a departure from the substantive holding contained in Part II of *Swain.* Petitioner in the instant case failed to make a sufficient showing to overcome the presumption announced in *Swain* that the State's use of peremptory challenges was related to the context of the case. I would therefore affirm the judgment of the court below.

Batson represents an important turn in Supreme Court doctrine governing jury selection. Prior to this case, the justices *generally* refused to interfere with attorney exercise of peremptory challenges, even in the face of evidence that prosecutors often used them to exclude blacks from juries. In *Batson* the justices reevaluated their approach and established a framework by which defendants could challenge prosecutors who appeared to be using their peremptory challenges in a racially discriminatory way.

Batson, however, was just the beginning of the Court's reevaluation of the peremptory challenge system. In *Powers v. Ohio* (1991) it ruled that in criminal trials involving white defendants, prosecutors may not exclude blacks from a jury on the basis of race. The same term, in *Edmonson v. Leesville Concrete Co.,* it also applied the *Batson* framework to civil cases, holding that private litigants may not use their peremptory challenges in a racially biased manner.

Subsequent terms have seen further extensions of the *Batson* decision. In *Georgia v. McCollum* (1992), the Court considered the converse of *Batson:* whether the *prosecution* can stop the *defense* from exercising its peremptories to eliminate blacks from a jury. This case had its origins in Dougherty County, Georgia, where the population is 43 percent black. In August 1990 a grand jury there indicted Thomas, William, and Ella McCollum, who are white, for assaulting and beating Jerry and Myra Collins, who are black. After the McCollums were indicted, "a leaflet was widely distributed in the local African-American community reporting the assault and urging community residents not to patronize" the McCollums' business. Naturally, the defense thought the broad distribution of the pamphlet would generate community hostility

toward the McCollums, making it difficult to find impartial blacks to serve as jurors.

Before jury selection began, the prosecution asked the judge to prohibit the defense from using its peremptory challenges to eliminate blacks from the jury. The prosecution asserted that it was mathematically possible for the defense to eliminate all potential jurors who were black and this was precisely what the defense planned to do. The trial judge refused to grant the prosecutor's motion, and Georgia's highest court affirmed. The decision was based on U.S. Supreme Court precedent: challenges to peremptory challenges apply only to the prosecution, not the defense.

The Supreme Court reversed. In a 7–2 decision, the justices held the "Constitution prohibits a criminal defendant from engaging in purposeful discrimination on the ground of race in the exercise of peremptory challenges." In other words, they ruled that the *Batson* framework applies to both sides of criminal cases, the prosecution *and the defense.* Why? Justice Blackmun addressed this question in an opinion for the majority:

> Be it at the hands of the State or the defense, if a court allows jurors to be excluded because of group bias, it is a willing participant in a scheme that could only undermine the very foundation of our system of justice—our citizens' confidence in it. Just as public confidence in criminal justice is undermined by a conviction in a trial where racial discrimination has occurred in jury selection, so is public confidence undermined where a defendant, assisted by racially discriminatory peremptory strikes, obtains an acquittal.

Even Chief Justice Rehnquist—a dissenter in *Batson* and in other cases extending its reach—concurred in *McCollum*. In explaining his vote, Rehnquist noted:

I was in dissent in *Edmonson v. Leesville Concrete Co.* (1991) and continue to believe that case to have been wrongly decided. But so long as it remains the law, I believe that it controls the disposition of this case.... I therefore join the opinion of the Court.

Two years after *McCollum,* in *J.E.B. v. T.B.* (1994), the Court considered whether to extend *Batson* beyond racial discrimination to sex discrimination. At issue in *J.E.B.* was the use of peremptory challenges by an Alabama prosecutor who filed—on behalf of the mother of a minor child—a complaint for paternity and child support against James E. Bowman. Of the thirty-six potential jurors assembled to hear the case, twelve were men and twenty-four were women. The judge dismissed three of the jurors for cause, and only ten men remained. The prosecution used nine of its ten peremptories to remove male jurors, and the defense used all but one to remove female jurors. The result: an all-female jury.

The jury found Bowman to be the child's father. He appealed, arguing that the prosecution had intentionally eliminated men from the jury. In other words, it had engaged in sex discrimination. In a 6–3 decision, the Supreme Court agreed. Writing for the majority, Justice Blackmun used the same kind of rationale he developed in *McCollum* to apply *Batson* to discrimination based on sex. He noted:

Since *Batson,* we have reaffirmed repeatedly our commitment to jury selection procedures that are fair and nondiscriminatory. We have recognized that whether the trial is criminal or civil, potential jurors, as well as litigants, have an equal protection right to jury selection procedures that are free from state-sponsored group stereotypes rooted in, and reflective of, historical prejudice.

Blackmun went on to review important constitutional cases involving gender-based discrimination, many of which had been argued by his new colleague, Justice Ruth Bader Ginsburg *(see Chapter 10).* His conclusion was straightforward:

Today we reaffirm what, by now, should be axiomatic: Intentional discrimination on the basis of gender by state actors violates the [Equal Protection Clause], particularly where, as here, the discrimination serves to ratify and perpetuate invidious, archaic, and overbroad stereotypes about the relative abilities of men and women.

In something of an about-face from his position in *McCollum,* Chief Justice Rehnquist wrote a dissenting opinion. He, along with Justice Thomas, also joined a dissent written by Justice Scalia, which poked fun at the majority:

Today's opinion is an inspiring demonstration of how thoroughly up-to-date and right-thinking we Justices are in matters pertaining to the sexes (or as the Court would have it, the genders), and how sternly we disapprove the male chauvinist attitudes of our predecessors.

According to some observers, the decisions in *McCollum* and *J.E.B.* were not unexpected; rather, they represent logical extensions of *Batson* and related Court decisions that opened up to judicial scrutiny the exercise of peremptory challenges. But others argue that the Court has gone too far, that it has moved perilously close to the position advocated by Justice Marshall in his *Batson* concurrence: the eradication of peremptory challenges altogether. As Justice Scalia, a critic of Court doctrine in this area, put it in his *McCollum* dissent:

Today's decision gives the lie once again to the belief that an activist, "evolutionary" constitutional jurisprudence always evolves in the direction of greater individual rights. In the interest of promoting the supposedly greater good of race relations in the society as a whole (make no mistake that that is what underlies all of this), we use the Constitution to destroy the ages-old right of criminal defendants to exercise peremptory challenges as they wish, to secure a jury that they consider fair.

Do you agree? Or do you think the Court has taken appropriate steps to ensure fairness in the jury selection process?

Jury Size. Another longstanding tradition Americans adopted from the British is jury size. Since the fourteenth century all English juries had twelve people, a number of disputed origin. Some suggest that it represents the twelve apostles; others claim it emanates from the twelve tribes of Israel. A point on which all agree is that the Framers accepted twelve as the proper number for a jury.

Beginning in the mid-1960s, however, many states began to abandon this practice, substituting six-person juries in noncapital cases. These states reasoned that six-person juries would be more economical, faster, and more likely to reach a verdict. Was the use of less than twelve people consistent with the demands of the Sixth Amendment? The Court answered this question in *Williams v. Florida,* a 1970 appeal from a robbery conviction. For the Court, Justice White explained that the number twelve had no special constitutional significance. The traditional twelve-person jury was basically the result of historical accident. All the Constitution requires, according to the Court, is a jury sufficiently large to allow actual deliberation and to represent a cross-section of the community. The six-person jury used to convict Williams was sufficiently large to meet these standards.

White's reasoning has been closely scrutinized by legal scholars. In addition, numerous empirical investigations have tried to determine whether six-person juries reach conclusions significantly different from their twelve-person counterparts. Although the scholarly verdict is far from unanimous, many now agree that "research on the effects of panel size on jury performance indicates that the use of six-member juries does not result in significant differences in either trial outcome or deliberation quality."[10] A number of states have followed Florida's lead and now regularly use six-person juries at least in some cases.

Jury Verdicts. Following the English tradition the Framers thought juries should reach unanimous verdicts or none at all. In the event of the latter, judges declared the jury hung, and the prosecutor could schedule a retrial or release the defendant. For the sake of efficient justice, some states altered the unanimity rule for twelve-person juries, requiring instead the agreement of nine or ten of the twelve.

Two cases, *Johnson v. Louisiana* and *Apodaca v.*

Oregon, decided together in 1972, tested the constitutionality of non-unanimous juries. The side in support of non-unanimity claimed that the alternative was excessive and obsolete in modern society, that because hung juries occurred more frequently, it often led to miscarriages of justice. The other side pointed out that the very essence of jury decision making is that verdicts are based on doubt. If no reasonable doubt exists about a person's guilt, the jury is supposed to reach a guilty verdict; if doubt is present, the jury should come to the opposite conclusion. But if a jury is split 9–3 or 10–2, does that not indicate a reasonable doubt? According to Justice White, writing for the Court, less than unanimous verdicts do not violate the Sixth Amendment. A lack of unanimity is not the equivalent of doubt. He concluded:

[T]he fact of three dissenting votes to acquit raises no question of institutional substance about either the integrity or the accuracy of the majority vote of guilt.... [By obtaining] nine [votes] to convict, the State satisfied its burden of proving guilt beyond any reasonable doubt.

Impartial Juries

As we have seen, Supreme Court decisions have led to jury practices that differ substantially from the vision of the Framers. These decisions have been controversial, but they pale in comparison to the furor over the notion of impartial juries.[11] Given the constitutional guarantees of a public trial and freedom of the press, how can judges see to it that defendants receive fair, impartial jury trials? This question has major constitutional importance because it forces courts to deal with conflicting rights. The Sixth Amendment requires judges to regulate trials, ensuring, among other things, that the jury is impartial. In a highly publicized case, the judge's task can become arduous. The judge must deal with the media exercising their constitutional guarantee of a free press. How can judges keep trials fair without interfering with the rights of the press and the public?

---

10. Reid Hastie et al., *Inside the Jury* (Cambridge, Mass.: Harvard University Press, 1983), 38. Other scholars have found differences between large and small juries, but agree that "regardless of which jury type is chosen some desirable features of the unchosen type are lost." Michael J. Saks, *Jury Verdicts* (Lexington, Mass.: Lexington Books, 1977), 107.

One study, however, has indicated that twelve-person juries are more likely to support plaintiffs in civil trials. See Hans Zeisel et al., "Convincing Empirical Evidence on the Six Member Jury," *University of Chicago Law Review* 41 (1974): 281–295.

11. See *Patton v. Yount* (1984).

The cases that follow deal with the controversies surrounding impartial juries. Has the Court struck a reasonable balance between competing constitutional rights? Is such a balance even possible?

Press v. Jury: The Warren Court. Before the mid-1960s no balance existed between freedom of the press and the right to an impartial jury—the former far outweighed the latter. In cases involving well-known individuals or otherwise of interest to the public, the press descended on courtrooms. Because there were no well-defined rules, reporters, accompanied by crews carrying bulky, noisy equipment, simply showed up and interviewed and photographed witnesses and other participants at will.

Not surprisingly, the Warren Court placed limitations on the media. Although this issue is not necessarily one that can be placed on an ideological continuum, the Warren Court clearly favored the rights of the criminally accused. *Sheppard v. Maxwell* (1966) is the Warren Court's strongest statement on this clash of rights. This case provided an excellent vehicle for the Court as it was the most widely publicized case of its day, and clearly illustrates the ill effects media pressure can produce.[12]

Sheppard v. Maxwell

384 U.S. 333 (1966)

Vote: 8 (Brennan, Clark, Douglas, Fortas, Harlan, Stewart, Warren, White)
    1 (Black)

Opinion of the Court: Clark

On July 4, 1954, Marilyn Sheppard, the pregnant wife of Dr. Sam Sheppard, a well-known osteopath, was murdered. According to Dr. Sheppard, he and his wife had entertained friends and watched television in

---

12. Several movies were made from this case, including *The Lawyer* and *The Fugitive* as well as a television series with the same name.

their lakefront home the night before. He fell asleep on the couch, and Marilyn went upstairs to bed. In the early morning, he awoke to her screams. He ran upstairs where he struggled with a "form," who knocked him unconscious. Returning to consciousness, he heard noises outside, ran to the lake's edge, and unsuccessfully wrestled with this "form" on the beach. Then he went back into the house, found his wife dead, and called his neighbor, the village mayor. The events following the arrival of the neighbor, police, and coroner form the heart of the case as Justice Clark explains in his majority opinion.

MR. JUSTICE CLARK delivered the opinion of the Court.

This federal habeas corpus application involves the question whether Sheppard was deprived of a fair trial in his state conviction for the second-degree murder of his wife because of the trial judge's failure to protect Sheppard sufficiently from the massive, pervasive and prejudicial publicity that attended his prosecution. The United States District Court held that he was not afforded a fair trial and granted the writ subject to the State's right to put Sheppard to trial again. The Court of Appeals for the Sixth Circuit reversed by a divided vote. We granted certiorari. We have concluded that Sheppard did not receive a fair trial consistent with the Due Process Clause of the Fourteenth Amendment and, therefore, reverse the judgment.

Marilyn Sheppard, petitioner's pregnant wife, was bludgeoned to death in the upstairs bedroom of their lakeshore home....

From the outset officials focused suspicion on Sheppard. After a search of the house and premises on the morning of the tragedy, Dr. Gerber, the Coroner, is reported—and it is undenied—to have told his men, "Well, it is evident the doctor did this, so let's go get the confession out of him." He proceeded to interrogate and examine Sheppard while the latter was under sedation in his hospital room. On the same occasion, the Coroner was given the clothes Sheppard wore at the time of the tragedy together with the personal items in them. Later that afternoon Chief Eaton and two Cleveland police officers interrogated Sheppard at some length, confronting him with evidence and demanding explanations. Asked by Officer Shotke to take a lie detector test,

Sheppard said he would if it were reliable. Shotke replied that it was "infallible" and "you might as well tell us all about it now." At the end of the interrogation Shotke told Sheppard: "I think you killed your wife." Still later in the same afternoon a physician sent by the Coroner was permitted to make a detailed examination of Sheppard. Until the Coroner's inquest on July 22, at which time he was subpoenaed, Sheppard made himself available for frequent and extended questioning without the presence of an attorney.

On July 7, the day of Marilyn Sheppard's funeral, a newspaper story appeared in which Assistant County Attorney Mahon—later the chief prosecutor of Sheppard—sharply criticized the refusal of the Sheppard family to permit his immediate questioning. From there on headline stories repeatedly stressed Sheppard's lack of cooperation with the police and other officials. Under the headline "Testify Now In Death, Bay Doctor Is Ordered," one story described a visit by Coroner Gerber and four police officers to the hospital on July 8. When Sheppard insisted that his lawyer be present, the Coroner wrote out a subpoena and served it on him. Sheppard then agreed to submit to questioning without counsel and the subpoena was torn up. The officers questioned him for several hours. On July 9, Sheppard, at the request of the Coroner, re-enacted the tragedy at his home before the Coroner, police officers, and a group of newsmen, who apparently were invited by the Coroner. The home was locked so that Sheppard was obliged to wait outside until the Coroner arrived. Sheppard's performance was reported in detail by the news media along with photographs. The newspapers also played up Sheppard's refusal to take a lie detector test and "the protective ring" thrown up by his family. Front-page newspaper headlines announced on the same day that "Doctor Balks At Lie Test; Retells Story." A column opposite that story contained an "exclusive" interview with Sheppard headlined: " 'Loved My Wife, She Loved Me,' Sheppard Tells News Reporter."...

On the 20th, the "editorial artillery" opened fire with a front-page charge that somebody is "getting away with murder." The editorial attributed the ineptness of the investigation to "friendships, relationships, hired lawyers, a husband who ought to have been subjected instantly to the same third-degree to which any other person under similar circumstances is subjected...." The following day, July 21, another page-one editorial was headed: "Why No Inquest?

Do It Now, Dr. Gerber." The Coroner called an inquest the same day and subpoenaed Sheppard. It was staged the next day in a school gymnasium; the Coroner presided with the County Prosecutor as his advisor and two detectives as bailiffs. In the front of the room was a long table occupied by reporters, television and radio personnel, and broadcasting equipment. The hearing was broadcast with live microphones placed at the Coroner's seat and the witness stand. A swarm of reporters and photographers attended. Sheppard was brought into the room by police who searched him in full view of several hundred spectators. Sheppard's counsel were present during the three-day inquest but were not permitted to participate. When Sheppard's chief counsel attempted to place some documents in the record, he was forcibly ejected from the room by the Coroner, who received cheers, hugs, and kisses from ladies in the audience. Sheppard was questioned for five and one-half hours about his actions on the night of the murder, his married life, and a love affair with Susan Hayes. At the end of the hearing the Coroner announced that he "could" order Sheppard held for the grand jury, but did not do so.

Throughout this period the newspapers emphasized evidence that tended to incriminate Sheppard and pointed out discrepancies in his statements to authorities.... The newspapers also delved into Sheppard's personal life. Articles stressed his extramarital love affairs as a motive for the crime. The newspapers portrayed Sheppard as a Lothario, fully explored his relationship with Susan Hayes, and named a number of other women who were allegedly involved with him. The testimony at trial never showed that Sheppard had any illicit relationships besides the one with Susan Hayes.

On July 28, an editorial entitled "Why Don't Police Quiz Top Suspect" demanded that Sheppard be taken to police headquarters. It described him in the following language:

"Now proved under oath to be a liar, still free to go about his business, shielded by his family, protected by a smart lawyer who has made monkeys of the police and authorities, carrying a gun part of the time, left free to do whatever he pleases...."

A front-page editorial on July 30 asked: "Why Isn't Sam Sheppard in Jail?" It was later titled "Quit Stalling—Bring Him In." After calling Sheppard "the most unusual murder suspect ever seen around these parts" the article said that "[e]xcept for some superficial questioning during Coroner Sam Gerber's inquest he has been scot-free of any official grilling...." It asserted that he was "surrounded by an iron curtain of protection [and] concealment."

That night at 10 o'clock Sheppard was arrested at his father's home on a charge of murder. He was taken to the Bay Village City Hall where hundreds of people, newscasters, photographers and reporters were awaiting his arrival. He was immediately arraigned—having been denied a temporary delay to secure the presence of counsel—and bound over to the grand jury.

The publicity then grew in intensity until his indictment on August 17. Typical of the coverage during this period is a front-page interview entitled: "DR. SAM: 'I Wish There Was Something I Could Get Off My Chest—but There Isn't.'" Unfavorable publicity included items such as a cartoon of the body of a sphinx with Sheppard's head and the legend below: "'I Will Do Everything In My Power to Help Solve This Terrible Murder.' Dr. Sam Sheppard."... We do not detail the coverage further. There are five volumes filled with similar clippings from each of the three Cleveland newspapers covering the period from the murder until Sheppard's conviction in December 1954. The record includes no excerpts from newscasts on radio and television but since space was reserved in the courtroom for these media we assume that their coverage was equally large.

With this background the case came on for trial two weeks before the November general election at which the chief prosecutor was a candidate for common pleas judge and the trial judge, Judge Blythin, was a candidate to succeed himself. Twenty-five days before the case was set, 75 veniremen were called as prospective jurors. All three Cleveland newspapers published the names and addresses of the veniremen. As a consequence, anonymous letters and telephone calls, as well as calls from friends, regarding the impending prosecution were received by all of the prospective jurors. The selection of the jury began on October 18, 1954.

The courtroom in which the trial was held measured 26 by 48 feet. A long temporary table was set up inside the bar, in back of the single counsel table. It ran the width of the courtroom, parallel to the bar railing, with one end less than three feet from the jury box. Approximately 20 representatives of newspapers and wire services were assigned seats at this table by the court. Behind the bar railing there were four rows of benches. These seats were likewise assigned by the court for the entire trial. The first row was occupied by representatives of television and radio stations, and the second and third rows by reporters from out-of-town newspapers and magazines. One side of the last row, which accommodated 14 people, was assigned to Sheppard's family and the other to Marilyn's. The public was permitted to fill vacancies in this row on special passes only. Representatives of the news media also used all the rooms on the courtroom floor, including the room where cases were ordinarily called and assigned for trial. Private telephone lines and telegraphic equipment were installed in these rooms so that reports from the trial could be speeded to the papers....

On the sidewalk and steps in front of the courthouse, television and newsreel cameras were occasionally used to take motion pictures of the participants in the trial, including the jury and the judge. Indeed, one television broadcast carried a staged interview of the judge as he entered the courthouse. In the corridors outside the courtroom there was a host of photographers and television personnel with flash cameras, portable lights and motion picture cameras. This group photographed the prospective jurors during selection of the jury. After the trial opened, the witnesses, counsel, and jurors were photographed and televised whenever they entered or left the courtroom. Sheppard was brought to the courtroom about 10 minutes before each session began; he was surrounded by reporters and extensively photographed for the newspapers and television. A rule of court prohibited picture-taking in the courtroom during the actual sessions of the court, but no restraints were put on photographers during recesses, which were taken once each morning and afternoon, with a longer period for lunch.

All of these arrangements with the news media and their massive coverage of the trial continued during the entire nine weeks of the trial. The courtroom remained crowded to capacity with representatives of news media. Their movement in and out of the courtroom often caused so much confusion that, despite the loud-speaker system installed in the courtroom, it was difficult for the witnesses and counsel to be heard. Furthermore, the reporters clustered within the bar of the small courtroom made confidential talk among Sheppard and his counsel almost impossible during the proceedings. They frequently had to leave the courtroom to obtain privacy. And many times when counsel wished to raise a point with the judge out of the hearing of the jury it was necessary to move to the judge's chambers. Even then, news media representatives so packed the judge's anteroom that counsel could hardly return from the chambers to the courtroom. The reporters vied with each other to find out what counsel and the judge had discussed, and often these matters later appeared in newspapers accessible to the jury.

The daily record of the proceedings was made available to the newspapers and the testimony of each witness was printed verbatim in the local editions, along with objections of counsel, and rulings by the judge. Pictures of Sheppard, the judge, counsel, pertinent witnesses, and the jury often accompanied the daily newspaper and television accounts. At times the newspapers published photographs of exhibits introduced at the trial, and the rooms of Sheppard's house were featured along with relevant testimony.

The jurors themselves were constantly exposed to the news media. Every juror, except one, testified at *voir dire* to reading about the case in the Cleveland papers or to having heard broadcasts about it. Seven of the 12 jurors who rendered the verdict had one or more Cleveland papers delivered in their home; the remaining jurors were not interrogated on the point. Nor were there questions as to radios or television sets in the jurors' homes, but we must assume that most of them owned such conveniences. As the selection of the jury progressed, individual pictures of prospective members appeared daily. During the trial, pictures of the jury appeared over 40 times in the Cleveland papers alone. The court permitted photographers to take pictures of the jury in the box, and individual pictures of the members in the jury room. One newspaper ran pictures of the jurors at the Sheppard home when they went there to view the scene of the murder. Another paper featured the home life of an alternate juror. The day before the verdict was rendered—while the jurors were at lunch and sequestered by two bailiffs—the jury was separated into two groups to pose for photographs which appeared in the newspapers.

We now reach the conduct of the trial. While the intense publicity continued unabated, it is sufficient to relate only the more flagrant episodes:

1. On October 9, 1954, nine days before the case went to trial, an editorial in one of the newspapers criticized defense counsel's random poll of people on the streets as to their opinion of Sheppard's guilt or innocence in an effort to use the resulting statistics to show the necessity for change of venue. The article said the survey "smacks of mass jury tampering," called on defense counsel to drop it, and stated that the bar association should do something about it. . . .

2. On the second day of *voir dire* examination a debate was staged and broadcast live over WHK radio. The participants, newspaper reporters, accused Sheppard's counsel of throwing roadblocks in the way of the prosecution and asserted that Sheppard conceded his guilt by hiring a prominent criminal lawyer. Sheppard's counsel objected to this broadcast and requested a continuance, but the judge denied the motion. . . .

3. While the jury was being selected, a two-inch headline asked: "But Who Will Speak for Marilyn?" The front-page story spoke of the "perfect face" of the accused. "Study that face as long as you want. Never will you get from it a hint of what might be the answer.". . . The author then noted Marilyn Sheppard was "still off stage," and that she was an only child whose mother died when she was very young and whose father had no interest in the case. But the author— through quotes from Detective Chief James McArthur—assured readers that the prosecution's exhibits would speak for Marilyn. "Her story," McArthur stated, "will come into this courtroom through our witnesses.". . .

4. As has been mentioned, the jury viewed the scene of the murder on the first day of the trial. Hundreds of reporters, cameramen and onlookers were there, and one representative of the news media was permitted to accompany the jury while it inspected the Sheppard home. The time of the jury's visit was revealed so far in advance that one of the newspapers was able to rent a helicopter and fly over the house taking pictures of the jurors on their tour. . . .

[5, 6, and 7 Omitted]

8. After the case was submitted to the jury, it was sequestered for its deliberations, which took five days and four nights. After the verdict, defense counsel ascertained that the jurors had been allowed to make telephone calls to their homes every day while they were sequestered at the hotel. Although the telephones had been removed from the jurors' rooms, the jurors were permitted to use the phones in the bailiffs' rooms. The calls were placed by the jurors

themselves; no record was kept of the jurors who made calls, the telephone numbers or the parties called. The bailiffs sat in the room where they could hear only the jurors' end of the conversation. The court had not instructed the bailiffs to prevent such calls. By a subsequent motion, defense counsel urged that this ground alone warranted a new trial, but the motion was overruled and no evidence was taken on the question.

The principle that justice cannot survive behind walls of silence has long been reflected in the "Anglo-American distrust for secret trials." A responsible press has always been regarded as the handmaiden of effective judicial administration, especially in the criminal field. Its function in this regard is documented by an impressive record of service over several centuries. The press does not simply publish information about trials but guards against the miscarriage of justice by subjecting the police, prosecutors, and judicial processes to extensive public scrutiny and criticism. This Court has, therefore, been unwilling to place any direct limitations on the freedom traditionally exercised by the news media for "[w]hat transpires in the court room is public property."...

But the Court has also pointed out that "[l]egal trials are not like elections, to be won through the use of the meeting-hall, the radio, and the newspaper." And the Court has insisted that no one be punished for a crime without "a charge fairly made and fairly tried in a public tribunal free of prejudice, passion, excitement, and tyrannical power."...

Only last Term in Estes v. State of Texas (1965) we set aside a conviction despite the absence of any showing of prejudice. We said there:

"It is true that in most cases involving claims of due process deprivations we require a showing of identifiable prejudice to the accused. Nevertheless, at times a procedure employed by the State involves such a probability that prejudice will result that it is deemed inherently lacking in due process."

And we cited with approval the language of Mr. Justice Black ... that "our system of law has always endeavored to prevent even the probability of unfairness."

It is clear that the totality of circumstances in this case also warrants such an approach. Unlike Estes, Sheppard was not granted a change of venue to a locale away from where the publicity originated; nor was his jury sequestered.... [T]he Sheppard jurors were subjected to newspaper, radio and television coverage of the trial while not taking part in the proceedings. They were allowed to go their separate ways outside of the courtroom, without adequate directions not to read or listen to anything concerning the case.... At intervals during the trial, the judge simply repeated his "suggestions" and "requests" that the jurors not expose themselves to comment upon the case. Moreover, the jurors were thrust into the role of celebrities by the judge's failure to insulate them from reporters and photographers. The numerous pictures of the jurors, with their addresses, which appeared in the newspapers before and during the trial itself, exposed them to expressions of opinion from both cranks and friends. The fact that anonymous letters had been received by prospective jurors should have made the judge aware that this publicity seriously threatened the jurors' privacy.

The press coverage of the Estes trial was not nearly as massive and pervasive as the attention given by the Cleveland newspapers and broadcasting stations to Sheppard's prosecution. Sheppard stood indicted for the murder of his wife; the State was demanding the death penalty. For months the virulent publicity about Sheppard and the murder had made the case notorious. Charges and countercharges were aired in the news media besides those for which Sheppard was called to trial. In addition, only three months before trial, Sheppard was examined for more than five hours without counsel during a three-day inquest which ended in a public brawl. The inquest was televised live from a high school gymnasium seating hundreds of people. Furthermore, the trial began two weeks before a hotly contested election at which both Chief Prosecutor Mahon and Judge Blythin were candidates for judgeships.

While we cannot say that Sheppard was denied due process by the judge's refusal to take precautions against the influence of pretrial publicity alone, the court's later rulings must be considered against the setting in which the trial was held. In light of this background, we believe that the arrangements made by the judge with the news media caused Sheppard to be deprived of that "judicial serenity and calm to which [he] was entitled." The fact is that bedlam reigned at the courthouse during the trial and newsmen took over practically the entire courtroom, hounding most of the participants in the trial, especially Sheppard....

There can be no question about the nature of the publicity which surrounded Sheppard's trial.... Indeed, every court that has considered this case, save the court that tried it, has deplored the manner in which the news media inflamed and prejudiced the public....

Nor is there doubt that this deluge of publicity reached at least some of the jury. On the only occasion that the jury was queried, two jurors admitted in open court to hearing the highly inflammatory charge that a prison inmate claimed Sheppard as the father of her illegitimate child. Despite the extent and nature of the publicity to which the jury was exposed during trial, the judge refused defense counsel's other requests that the jurors be asked whether they had read or heard specific prejudicial comment about the case, including the incidents we have previously summarized. In these circumstances, we can assume that some of this material reached members of the jury.

The court's fundamental error is compounded by the holding that it lacked power to control the publicity about the trial. From the very inception of the proceedings the judge announced that neither he nor anyone else could restrict prejudicial news accounts. And he reiterated this view on numerous occasions. Since he viewed the news media as his target, the judge never considered other means that are often utilized to reduce the appearance of prejudicial material and to protect the jury from outside influence. We conclude that these procedures would have been sufficient to guarantee Sheppard a fair trial and so do not consider what sanctions might be available against a recalcitrant press nor the charges of bias now made against the state trial judge.

The carnival atmosphere at trial could easily have been avoided since the courtroom and courthouse premises are subject to the control of the court.... [T]he presence of the press at judicial proceedings must be limited when it is apparent that the accused might otherwise be prejudiced or disadvantaged. Bearing in mind the massive pretrial publicity, the judge should have adopted stricter rules governing the use of the courtroom by newsmen, as Sheppard's counsel requested. The number of reporters in the courtroom itself could have been limited at the first sign that their presence would disrupt the trial. They certainly should not have been placed inside the bar. Furthermore,

the judge should have more closely regulated the conduct of newsmen in the courtroom. For instance, the judge belatedly asked them not to handle and photograph trial exhibits lying on the counsel table during recesses.

Secondly, the court should have insulated the witnesses. All of the newspapers and radio stations apparently interviewed prospective witnesses at will, and in many instances disclosed their testimony....

Thirdly, the court should have made some effort to control the release of leads, information, and gossip to the press by police officers, witnesses, and the counsel for both sides. Much of the information thus disclosed was inaccurate, leading to groundless rumors and confusion....

The fact that many of the prejudicial news items can be traced to the prosecution, as well as the defense, aggravates the judge's failure to take any action. Effective control of these sources—concededly within the court's power—might well have prevented the divulgence of inaccurate information, rumors, and accusations that made up much of the inflammatory publicity, at least after Sheppard's indictment.

More specifically, the trial court might well have proscribed extrajudicial statements by any lawyer, party, witness, or court official which divulged prejudicial matters, such as the refusal of Sheppard to submit to interrogation or take any lie detector tests; any statement made by Sheppard to officials; the identity of prospective witnesses or their probable testimony; any belief in guilt or innocence; or like statements concerning the merits of the case....

From the cases coming here we note that unfair and prejudicial news comment on pending trials has become increasingly prevalent. Due process requires that the accused receive a trial by an impartial jury free from outside influences. Given the pervasiveness of modern communications and the difficulty of effacing prejudicial publicity from the minds of the jurors, the trial courts must take strong measures to ensure that the balance is never weighed against the accused. And appellate tribunals have the duty to make an independent evaluation of the circumstances. Of course, there is nothing that proscribes the press from reporting events that transpire in the courtroom. But where there is a reasonable likelihood that prejudicial news prior to trial will prevent a fair trial, the judge should continue the case until the threat abates, or transfer it to another county not so permeated with publicity. In addition, sequestration of the jury was something the judge should have raised *sua sponte* with counsel. If publicity during the proceedings threatens the fairness of the trial, a new trial should be ordered. But we must remember that reversals are but palliatives; the cure lies in those remedial measures that will prevent the prejudice at its inception. The courts must take such steps by rule and regulation that will protect their processes from prejudicial outside interferences. Neither prosecutors, counsel for defense, the accused, witnesses, court staff nor enforcement officers coming under the jurisdiction of the court should be permitted to frustrate its function. Collaboration between counsel and the press as to information affecting the fairness of a criminal trial is not only subject to regulation, but is highly censurable and worthy of disciplinary measures.

Since the state trial judge did not fulfill his duty to protect Sheppard from the inherently prejudicial publicity which saturated the community and to control disruptive influences in the courtroom, we must reverse the denial of the habeas petition. The case is remanded to the District Court with instructions to issue a writ and order that Sheppard be released from custody unless the State puts him to its charges again within a reasonable time.

It is so ordered.

Sheppard provides lower court judges with real ammunition to combat the dangers of an overzealous press. In Clark's view, judges can take a variety of actions to prevent trials from becoming carnivals, mockeries of justice, as the Sheppard trial did.[13]

Press v. Juries: The 1980s and Beyond. As trial court judges continued to limit the role and presence of the media at criminal proceedings, critics began to question the new balance between rights. This time the criticism was that the courts were excessively favoring the rights of the defendant. In a 1979 case, *Gannett Company v. DePasquale,* the Burger Court had the opportunity to "rebalance" the scales. A newspaper company asked the Court to prohibit a judge from closing

13. F. Lee Bailey, a well-known defense attorney, represented Dr. Sheppard and, in fact, credits this case with launching his career. See F. Lee Bailey, *The Defense Never Rests* (New York: Signet, 1971), chap. 2.

the pretrial hearings for a highly publicized case. Writing for a majority of the Court, however, Justice Stewart declined to do so. Adopting the Warren Court's reasoning in *Sheppard,* he claimed that adverse publicity can endanger proceedings, a problem particularly acute at the pretrial stages. Stewart wrote,

This Court has long recognized that adverse publicity can endanger the ability of a defendant to receive a fair trial.... To safeguard the due process rights of the accused, a trial judge has an affirmative constitutional duty to minimize the effects of prejudicial pretrial publicity.... And because of the Constitution's pervasive concern for these due process rights, a trial judge may surely take protective measures even when they are not strictly and inescapably necessary.

He also dealt with the company's assertion of a First Amendment right by stating that "any denial of access in this case was not absolute but only temporary."

But a year later, in *Richmond Newspapers v. Virginia,* the Court ruled in favor of a First Amendment claim over a Sixth Amendment claim, thereby modifying the balance between these rights. In this case, the justices addressed what some consider the bottom-line issue in this kind of dispute: May a judge completely close a trial? The justices ruled against such a practice, but why? What distinguishes trials from pretrial hearings?

===

Richmond Newspapers v. Virginia

448 U.S. 555 (1980)

Vote: 7 (Blackmun, Brennan, Burger, Marshall, Stevens, Stewart, White)

1 (Rehnquist)

Opinion announcing the judgment of the Court: Burger
Concurring opinions: Blackmun, Brennan, Stevens, Stewart, White
Dissenting opinion: Rehnquist
Not participating: Powell

In July 1976 a Virginia court convicted a man named Stevenson for stabbing a hotel manager to death. An appellate court reversed the conviction on a procedural error, and a new trial occurred before the same court. But that proceeding and one other ended in mistrials. By the time the fourth trial date was set for 1978, the case had garnered a great deal of public and media interest. Because such attention could interfere with jury selection, Stevenson's attorney asked the judge to close the trial to the public. When the prosecutor voiced no objection, the judge granted the request, a privilege judges had under Virginia law.

Reporters covering the case brought suit against the state, arguing that its law violated the First Amendment. This claim received legal support from numerous civil liberties and media organizations. They not only agreed with the appellants, but also asked the Court to overrule *Gannett*. The Reporters Committee for Freedom of the Press, on behalf of several media associations, said, "Great confusion has arisen as to what *Gannett* means, and the case is being used as grounds for closing all types of criminal proceedings." The ACLU stated, "The public and press have a constitutionally protected right of access to criminal pretrial and trial proceedings."

MR. CHIEF JUSTICE BURGER announced the judgment of the Court.

The narrow question presented in this case is whether the right of the public and press to attend criminal trials is guaranteed under the United States Constitution....

We begin consideration of this case by noting that the precise issue presented here has not previously been before this Court for decision. In *Gannett Co. v. DePasquale* [1979], the Court was not required to decide whether a right of access to *trials*, as distinguished from hearings on *pre*trial motions, was constitutionally guaranteed. The Court held that the Sixth Amendment's guarantee to the accused of a public trial gave neither the public nor the press an enforceable right of access to a *pre*trial suppression hearing....

In prior cases the Court has treated questions involving conflicts between publicity and a defendant's right to a fair

trial. But here for the first time the Court is asked to decide whether a criminal trial itself may be closed to the public upon the unopposed request of a defendant, without any demonstration that closure is required to protect the defendant's superior right to a fair trial, or that some other overriding consideration requires closure.

The origins of the proceeding which has become the modern criminal trial in Anglo-American justice can be traced back beyond reliable historical records.... What is significant for present purposes is that throughout its evolution, the trial has been open to all who care to observe....

... [T]he historical evidence demonstrates conclusively that at the time when our organic laws were adopted, criminal trials both here and in England had long been presumptively open. This is no quirk of history; rather, it has long been recognized as an indispensable attribute to an Anglo-American trial....

From this unbroken, uncontradicted history, supported by reasons as valid today as in centuries past, we are bound to conclude that a presumption of openness inheres in the very nature of a criminal trial under our system of justice. This conclusion is hardly novel; without a direct holding on the issue, the Court has voiced its recognition of it in a variety of contexts over the years....

Despite the history of criminal trials being presumptively open since long before the Constitution, the State presses its contention that neither the Constitution nor the Bill of Rights contains any provision which by its terms guarantees to the public the right to attend criminal trials. Standing alone, this is correct, but there remains the question whether, absent an explicit provision, the Constitution affords protection against exclusion of the public from criminal trials.

The First Amendment, in conjunction with the Fourteenth, prohibits governments from "abridging the freedom of speech, or of the press; or the right of the people peaceably to assemble, and to petition the Government for a redress of grievances." These expressly guaranteed freedoms share a common core purpose of assuring freedom of communication on matters relating to the functioning of government. Plainly it would be difficult to single out any aspect of government of higher concern and importance to the people than the manner in which criminal trials are conducted;... recognition of this pervades the centuries-old history of open trials and the opinions of this Court.

The Bill of Rights was enacted against the backdrop of the long history of trials being presumptively open. Public access to trials was then regarded as an important aspect of the process itself; the conduct of trials "before as many of the people as chuse to attend" was regarded as one of "the inestimable advantages of a free English constitution of government." In guaranteeing freedoms such as those of speech and press, the First Amendment can be read as protecting the right of everyone to attend trials so as to give meaning to those explicit guarantees.... What this means in the context of trials is that the First Amendment guarantees of speech and press, standing alone, prohibit government from summarily closing courtroom doors which had long been open to the public at the time that Amendment was adopted....

It is not crucial whether we describe this right to attend criminal trials to hear, see, and communicate observations concerning them as a "right of access" or a "right to gather information," for we have recognized that "without some protection for seeking out the news, freedom of the press could be eviscerated." The explicit, guaranteed rights to speak and to publish concerning what takes place at a trial would lose much meaning if access to observe the trial could, as it was here, be foreclosed arbitrarily....

The State argues that the Constitution nowhere spells out a guarantee for the right of the public to attend trials, and that accordingly no such right is protected. The possibility that such a contention could be made did not escape the notice of the Constitution's draftsmen; they were concerned that some important rights might be thought disparaged because not specifically guaranteed. It was even argued that because of this danger no Bill of Rights should be adopted....

But arguments such as the State makes have not precluded recognition of important rights not enumerated. Notwithstanding the appropriate caution against reading into the Constitution rights not explicitly defined, the Court has acknowledged that certain unarticulated rights are implicit in enumerated guarantees. For example, the rights of association and of privacy, the right to be presumed innocent, and the right to be judged by a standard of proof beyond a reasonable doubt in a criminal trial, as well as the right to travel, appear nowhere in the Constitution or Bill of Rights. Yet these important but unarticulated rights have nonetheless been found to share constitutional protection in common with explicit guarantees....

We hold that the right to attend criminal trials is implicit in the guarantees of the First Amendment; without the freedom to attend such trials, which people have exercised for centuries, important aspects of freedom of speech and "of the press could be eviscerated."

Having concluded there was a guaranteed right of the public under the First and Fourteenth Amendments to attend the trial of Stevenson's case, we return to the closure order challenged by appellants. The Court in *Gannett* made clear that although the Sixth Amendment guarantees the accused a right to a public trial, it does not give a right to a private trial. Despite the fact that this was the fourth trial of the accused, the trial judge made no findings to support closure; no inquiry was made as to whether alternative solutions would have met the need to ensure fairness; there was no recognition of any right under the Constitution for the public or press to attend the trial. In contrast to the pretrial proceeding dealt with in *Gannett,* there exist in the context of the trial itself various tested alternatives to satisfy the constitutional demands of fairness. There was no suggestion that any problems with witnesses could not have been dealt with by their exclusion from the courtroom or their sequestration during the trial. Nor is there anything to indicate that sequestration of the jurors would not have guarded against their being subjected to any improper information. All of the alternatives admittedly present difficulties for trial courts, but none of the factors relied on here was beyond the realm of the manageable. Absent an overriding interest articulated in findings, the trial of a criminal case must be open to the public. Accordingly, the judgment under review is

Reversed.

Given the decisions of the Warren and Burger Courts, a balance generally exists between defendants' rights and those of the press. Judges can pursue a variety of strategies to protect the accused, but they cannot completely close trial proceedings to the public and press.

TRIAL PROCEEDINGS

Once attorneys complete the *voir dire* and select the petit jury, the trial begins. Almost all trials follow the same format. First, attorneys make opening statements. Each side, beginning with the prosecution because it must prove guilt beyond a reasonable doubt, presents an opening argument, explaining the crime and what it must prove to obtain a guilty or not guilty verdict.

Next, each side presents its case, again beginning with the prosecution. At this point, attorneys call witnesses who testify for their side and then are cross-examined by the opposing attorney. This stage is the heart of the trial, and here, as in all other important parts of the criminal justice system, the Constitution affords defendants a great many rights. For example, a Sixth Amendment clause states that the accused shall "be confronted with the witnesses against him." This provision, often called the Confrontation Clause, means that defendants have the right to be present during their own trials and to cross-examine prosecution witnesses, who must appear in court to testify.

The right to confrontation generally prohibits trials *in absentia*, but there are limits to this right. In *Illinois v. Allen* (1970) for example, the Supreme Court considered the actions of a trial judge in response to a defendant's misbehavior in the courtroom. Allen, on trial for armed robbery, verbally abused the judge and others in the courtroom, threw papers, continually talked loudly, and interrupted witnesses. After ample warning, the judge ordered Allen removed, and the trial continued in his absence. Allen was convicted, and he appealed on the grounds that he was not allowed to be present during his trial. A unanimous Supreme Court rejected his appeal. Writing for the Court, Justice Black explained that the right to confrontation can be waived by the defendant's own abusive behavior. As a response to such disruptive action, a trial court judge may find the accused in contempt of court or remove him, as the judge did with Allen.

Black indicated that in extreme cases a judge may order the defendant to be bound and gagged.

In *Coy v. Iowa* (1988), however, the justices faced the difficult and controversial issue of the defendant's right to confront prosecution witnesses face to face. In recognition of the emotional trauma children may undergo when forced to testify in open court against those accused of abusing them, Iowa passed a law limiting visual contact. The state allowed judges to place a screen between the accused and a child so that the child could not see an alleged abuser; the defendant, however, could dimly perceive and fully hear the child. John Coy was accused of molesting two thirteen-year-old girls while they were camping in the backyard of the house next door to his. He objected to the use of a screen, arguing that it violated his right to confront witnesses against him.

In a 6–2 decision, the Supreme Court ruled that Coy's constitutional rights had been violated. Writing for the Court, Justice Scalia said the Confrontation Clause guaranteed the defendant a face-to-face meeting with witnesses appearing against him. The screen procedure, while imposed with good intentions, violated that constitutional right. Scalia acknowledged that the *Coy* decision did not finally settle this sensitive issue, but he left "for another day, however, whether any exceptions exist."

Scalia and the other justices did not have to wait long for the issue to return to the Court's doorstep. *Maryland v. Craig* (1990) presented the same conflict between the Constitution's guarantee of confrontation and the state's desire to protect children. This time the Court allowed the special protective procedures for children and rejected the Confrontation Clause claim.

Justice O'Connor wrote for the majority. Justice Scalia, who had expressed the majority's views in *Coy*, wrote for the dissenters. It is noteworthy that the opinion of the very conservative Scalia was endorsed by three of the Court's most liberal justices, Brennan, Marshall, and Stevens. Is the majority position in

Craig an acceptable balance of the interests involved? If the Framers had envisioned the technological advances used here, would they have agreed that it is an acceptable substitute for face-to-face confrontation?

Maryland v. Craig

497 U.S. 836 (1990)
Vote: 5 (Blackmun, Kennedy, O'Connor, Rehnquist, White)
    4 (Brennan, Marshall, Scalia, Stevens)
Opinion of the Court: O'Connor
Dissenting opinion: Scalia

Sandra Ann Craig was charged by Maryland authorities with child abuse, sexual offenses, perverted sexual practice, assault, and battery. The alleged victim was a six-year-old girl who was enrolled for two years in a preschool that Craig owned and operated.

Maryland law allowed a special procedure to be invoked if the trial court judge determined that testifying in open court would cause a child serious emotional distress and reduce the child's ability to communicate. This procedure permitted the child to be questioned and cross-examined by the prosecutor and defense attorney in a room separate from the trial courtroom. Closed-circuit television transmitted the testimony to the courtroom, where the accused, the judge, and the jury would view it. This procedure was used at Craig's trial over her objections, and she was found guilty.

JUSTICE O'CONNOR delivered the opinion of the Court.

The Confrontation Clause of the Sixth Amendment, made applicable to the States through the Fourteenth Amendment, provides: "In all criminal prosecutions, the accused shall enjoy the right ... to be confronted with the witnesses against him."

We observed in *Coy v. Iowa* that "the Confrontation Clause guarantees the defendant a face-to-face meeting with witnesses appearing before the trier of fact.". . .

We have never held, however, that the Confrontation Clause guarantees criminal defendants the absolute right to a face-to-face meeting with witnesses against them at trial. Indeed, in *Coy v. Iowa*, we expressly "le[ft] for another day ... the question whether any exceptions exist" to the "irreducible literal meaning of the Clause: 'a right to meet face to face all those who appear and give evidence at trial.'". . .

The central concern of the Confrontation Clause is to ensure the reliability of the evidence against a criminal defendant by subjecting it to rigorous testing in the context of an adversary proceeding before the trier of fact. The word "confront," after all, also means a clashing of forces or ideas, thus carrying with it the notion of adversariness. . . . [T]he right guaranteed by the Confrontation Clause includes not only a "personal examination," but also "(1) insures that the witness will give his statements under oath— thus impressing him with the seriousness of the matter and guarding against the lie by the possibility of a penalty for perjury; (2) forces the witness to submit to cross-examination, the 'greatest legal engine ever invented for the discovery of truth'; [and] (3) permits the jury that is to decide the defendant's fate to observe the demeanor of the witness in making his statement, thus aiding the jury in assessing his credibility."

The combined effect of these elements of confrontation—physical presence, oath, cross-examination, and observation of demeanor by the trier of fact—serves the purposes of the Confrontation Clause by ensuring that evidence admitted against an accused is reliable and subject to the rigorous adversarial testing that is the norm of Anglo-American criminal proceedings. . . .

We have recognized, for example, that face-to-face confrontation enhances the accuracy of factfinding by reducing the risk that a witness will wrongfully implicate an innocent person. . . .

Although face-to-face confrontation forms "the core of the values furthered by the Confrontation Clause," we have nevertheless recognized that it is not the *sine qua non* of the confrontation right. . . .

For this reason, we have never insisted on an actual face-to-face encounter at trial in *every* instance in which testimony is admitted against a defendant. . . .

[O]ur precedents establish that "the Confrontation Clause reflects a *preference* for face-to-face confrontation at trial," a preference that "must occasionally give way to considerations of public policy and the necessities of the case."... Thus, though we reaffirm the importance of face-to-face confrontation with witnesses appearing at trial, we cannot say that such confrontation is an indispensable element of the Sixth Amendment's guarantee of the right to confront one's accusers....

This interpretation of the Confrontation Clause is consistent with our cases holding that other Sixth Amendment rights must also be interpreted in the context of the necessities of trial and the adversary process....

That the face-to-face confrontation requirement is not absolute does not, of course, mean that it may easily be dispensed with. As we suggested in *Coy,* our precedents confirm that a defendant's right to confront accusatory witnesses may be satisfied absent a physical, face-to-face confrontation at trial only where denial of such confrontation is necessary to further an important public policy and only where the reliability of the testimony is otherwise assured.

Maryland's statutory procedure, when invoked, prevents a child witness from seeing the defendant as he or she testifies against the defendant at trial. We find it significant, however, that Maryland's procedure preserves all of the other elements of the confrontation right: the child witness must be competent to testify and must testify under oath; the defendant retains full opportunity for contemporaneous cross-examination; and the judge, jury, and defendant are able to view (albeit by video monitor) the demeanor (and body) of the witness as he or she testifies. Although we are mindful of the many subtle effects face-to-face confrontation may have on an adversary criminal proceeding, the presence of these other elements of confrontation—oath, cross-examination, and observation of the witness' demeanor—adequately ensures that the testimony is both reliable and subject to rigorous adversarial testing in a manner functionally equivalent to that accorded live, in-person testimony. These safeguards of reliability and adversariness render the use of such a procedure a far cry from the undisputed prohibition of the Confrontation Clause: trial by *ex parte,* affidavit, or inquisition.... We are therefore confident that use of the one-way closed-circuit television procedure, where necessary to further an im-

portant state interest, does not impinge upon the truth-seeking or symbolic purposes of the Confrontation Clause.

The critical inquiry in this case, therefore, is whether use of the procedure is necessary to further an important state interest. The State contends that it has a substantial interest in protecting children who are allegedly victims of child abuse from the trauma of testifying against the alleged perpetrator and that its statutory procedure for receiving testimony from such witnesses is necessary to further that interest.

We have of course recognized that a State's interest in "the protection of minor victims of sex crimes from further trauma and embarrassment" is a "compelling" one....

We likewise conclude today that a State's interest in the physical and psychological well-being of child abuse victims may be sufficiently important to outweigh, at least in some cases, a defendant's right to face his or her accusers in court....

... Given the State's traditional and "'transcendent interest in protecting the welfare of children,'" buttressed by the growing body of academic literature documenting the psychological trauma suffered by child abuse victims who must testify in court, we will not second-guess the considered judgment of the Maryland Legislature regarding the importance of its interest in protecting child abuse victims from the emotional trauma of testifying. Accordingly, we hold that, if the State makes an adequate showing of necessity, the state interest in protecting child witnesses from the trauma of testifying in a child abuse case is sufficiently important to justify the use of a special procedure that permits a child witness in such cases to testify at trial against a defendant in the absence of face-to-face confrontation with the defendant.

The requisite finding of necessity must of course be a case-specific one: the trial court must hear evidence and determine whether use of the one-way closed-circuit television procedure is necessary to protect the welfare of the particular child witness who seeks to testify. The trial court must also find that the child witness would be traumatized, not by the courtroom generally, but by the presence of the defendant. Denial of face-to-face confrontation is not needed to further the state interest in protecting the child witness from trauma unless it is the presence of the defendant that causes the trauma. In other words, if the state interest were merely the interest in protecting child witnesses from courtroom trauma generally, denial of face-to-face confrontation would be unnecessary because the child could be permitted to testify in less intimidating surroundings, albeit with the defendant present. Finally, the trial court must find that the emotional distress suffered by the child witness in the presence of the defendant is more than *de minimis, i.e.*, more than "mere nervousness or excitement or some reluctance to testify.". . .

In sum, we conclude that where necessary to protect a child witness from trauma that would be caused by testifying in the physical presence of the defendant, at least where such trauma would impair the child's ability to communicate, the Confrontation Clause does not prohibit use of a procedure that, despite the absence of face-to-face confrontation, ensures the reliability of the evidence by subjecting it to rigorous adversarial testing and thereby preserves the essence of effective confrontation. Because there is no dispute that the child witnesses in this case testified under oath, were subject to full cross-examination, and were able to be observed by the judge, jury, and defendant as they testified, we conclude that, to the extent that a proper finding of necessity has been made, the admission of such testimony would be consonant with the Confrontation Clause. . . .

. . . We therefore vacate the judgment of the Court of Appeals of Maryland and remand the case for further proceedings not inconsistent with this opinion.

JUSTICE SCALIA . . . dissenting.

Seldom has this Court failed so conspicuously to sustain a categorical guarantee of the Constitution against the tide of prevailing current opinion. The Sixth Amendment provides, with unmistakable clarity, that "[i]n all criminal prosecutions, the accused shall enjoy the right . . . to be confronted with the witnesses against him." The purpose of enshrining this protection in the Constitution was to assure that none of the many policy interests from time to time pursued by statutory law could overcome a defendant's right to face his or her accusers in court. The Court, however, says:

"We . . . conclude today that a State's interest in the physical and psychological well-being of child abuse victims may be sufficiently important to outweigh, at least in some cases, a defendant's right to face his or her accusers in court. That a significant majority of States has enacted statutes to protect child witnesses from the trauma of giving testimony in child abuse cases attests to the widespread belief in the importance of such a public policy."

Because of this subordination of explicit constitutional text to currently favored public policy, the following scene can be played out in an American courtroom for the first time in two centuries: A father whose young daughter has been given over to the exclusive custody of his estranged wife, or a mother whose young son has been taken into custody by the State's child welfare department, is sentenced to prison for sexual abuse on the basis of testimony by a child the parent has not seen or spoken to for many months; and the guilty verdict is rendered without giving the parent so much as the opportunity to sit in the presence of the child, and to ask, personally or through counsel, "it is really not true, is it, that I—your father (or mother) whom you see before you—did these terrible things?" Perhaps that is a procedure today's society desires; perhaps (though I doubt it) it is even a fair procedure; but it is assuredly not a procedure permitted by the Constitution.

Because the text of the Sixth Amendment is clear, and because the Constitution is meant to protect against, rather than conform to, current "widespread belief," I respectfully dissent. . . .

In the last analysis, however, this debate is not an appropriate one. I have no need to defend the value of confrontation, because the Court has no authority to question it. It is not within our charge to speculate that, "where face-to-face confrontation causes significant emotional distress in a child witness," confrontation might "in fact *disserve* the Confrontation Clause's truth-seeking goal." If so, that is a defect in the Constitution—which should be amended by the procedures provided for such an eventuality, but cannot be corrected by judicial pronouncement that it is archaic, contrary to "widespread belief" and thus null and void. For good or bad, the Sixth Amendment requires confrontation, and we are not at liberty to ignore it. To quote the document one last time (for it plainly says all that need be said): "In *all* criminal prosecutions, the accused shall enjoy the right . . . to be confronted with the witnesses against him" (emphasis added).

The Court today has applied "interest-balancing" analysis where the text of the Constitution simply does not permit it. We are not free to conduct a cost-benefit analysis of clear and explicit constitutional guarantees, and then to adjust their meaning to comport with our findings. The Court has convincingly proved that the Maryland procedure serves a valid interest, and gives the defendant virtually everything the Confrontation Clause guarantees (everything, that is, except confrontation). I am persuaded, therefore, that the Maryland procedure is virtually constitutional. Since it is not, however, actually constitutional, I would affirm the judgment of the Maryland Court of Appeals reversing the judgment of conviction.

In addition to specific Sixth Amendment guarantees, defendants also have the right to a fair trial, generally guaranteed by the Due Process Clauses of the Fifth and Fourteenth Amendments. As we have seen, this rather vague term—*due process*—has been used to ensure that police obtain evidence by fair means and as a way to apply constitutional guarantees to the states. The Court also has used it to guarantee that defendants receive fair treatment from prosecutors and courts.

One of the most important manifestations of due process in criminal proceedings is what is known in civil cases as discovery. This long-standing legal tradition allows both sides of a civil dispute to have access to each other's cases. Until 1963 *mandated* discovery was not a part of most criminal proceedings. Instead, each side prepared its case in relative isolation, knowing little of the evidence the other side had. That year, however, the Supreme Court in *Brady v. Maryland* radically changed criminal procedure by creating the so-called Brady request.[14] That is, upon the request of the defense, prosecutors must divulge all relevant information about the case. The defense, however, does not have to provide any information to the prosecutor

unless specifically mandated under state law. The Supreme Court viewed the Brady request as a necessary mechanism to preserve the fundamental fairness of the trial process. "We now hold that the suppression by the prosecution of evidence favorable to an accused upon request violates due process where the evidence is material either to guilt or to punishment, irrespective of the good faith or bad faith of the prosecution," the Court said.

In 1976 the Court greatly expanded the Brady request procedure. The case, *United States v. Agurs*, evolved from charges against Linda Agurs for stabbing to death James Sewell after a brief interlude in a motel room. Agurs claimed self-defense, but the jury returned a guilty verdict after less than twenty-five minutes of deliberation. Agurs's defense attorney later discovered that Sewell had a history of violent behavior, a fact the attorney believed could have been used to establish self-defense. The prosecutor knew Sewell's history, but had not told it to the defense because the defense had made no Brady request. Agurs's attorney claimed that this information should have been disclosed even without a specific request. The Supreme Court held that the Constitution requires the prosecutor to disclose everything relevant to the case that might establish a reasonable doubt of the defendant's guilt that would not otherwise exist. This obligation rests on the prosecutor even when the defense makes no request for information. With respect to Agurs, however, the Court held that Sewell's violent history would not have created a reasonable doubt that was not already apparent from information at the disposal of the defendant, and, therefore, the prosecutor had not committed a constitutional violation for failing to volunteer the information.

FINAL TRIAL STAGE: AN OVERVIEW OF SENTENCING

Judges run trials in fairly standardized ways and in accordance with an established set of rules based on

14. *Escobedo, Gideon,* and *Brady* all were decided in 1963, leading some observers to call them the great triumvirate of criminal rights.

constitutional guarantees. The closing stages are no exception. Once both sides have presented their cases, the attorneys make their closing arguments; they summarize their cases and try to convince the jury that they have proved them. Next, the judge makes a charge to the jury, providing the jurors with instructions and guidelines upon which to base a decision of guilt or innocence. The jury then deliberates to reach a verdict. What goes on in the jury room is private and known only to the jurors. Once the jury reaches a verdict, it announces its decision in open court. If it finds the defendant not guilty, the accused goes free. If it finds the defendant guilty, the judge pronounces sentence.[15]

In general, sentencing is a highly discretionary process. Within limits for various crimes, judges—particularly those in state courts—enjoy wide latitude in selecting an appropriate penalty. On any given day in the United States, defendants convicted of the same crime in different localities may receive vastly different sentences. Why do disparities exist? A partial explanation is that a judge considers all kinds of information before pronouncing sentence, including the nature of the crime committed; the individual's job prospects, family situation, prior criminal record, history of alcohol or drug abuse; and any presentencing reports supplied by social workers or other state agents. And now, under the Supreme Court's decision in *Wisconsin v. Mitchell* (1993) *(see pages 285–288)*, judges may "enhance" sentences for racially motivated crimes. Mitchell was convicted of battery—a crime carrying a maximum sentence of two years. When it was determined that Mitchell "intentionally" selected his victim because of his race, his sentence was "enhanced" to four years.

As Lawrence Baum notes, most judges and attorneys prefer wide latitude in sentencing "as a means to

---

BOX 9-1   A SUMMARY OF THE FEDERAL SENTENCING GUIDELINES

1. In imposing a sentence, a district judge must consider the guidelines of the Sentencing Commission, a body established by the statute. Under these guidelines, the possible sentence ranges are based on 43 offense level categories (determined from the offense, adjusted for factors such as the type of victim and the defendant's role in the offense) and six criminal history categories (determined primarily from the number and characteristics of past convictions). For each combination of offense and criminal history categories, a range of possible imprisonment lengths (for instance, 57 to 71 months) is indicated. Other guidelines indicate when probation may be substituted for a prison sentence and the amounts of monetary fines appropriate for each offense level.

2. In each case the judge must impose a sentence within the range established by the Sentencing Commission unless the judge finds a relevant aggravating or mitigating circumstance that the Commission did not adequately take into account. Not ordinarily relevant are such personal characteristics as age, education, employment record, and family and community ties; never relevant are race, sex, religion, and socio-economic status. A judge can depart from the guidelines if the prosecution states that the defendant has provided substantial assistance in the investigation or prosecution of another offender.

3. If the sentence is above the range established by the Sentencing Commission, the defendant may appeal the sentence; if it is below the range, the prosecution may appeal. If the court of appeals finds that the sentence is unreasonable, it may return the case to the district judge for resentencing or amend the sentence itself.

SOURCE: Lawrence Baum, *American Courts*, 3d ed. (Boston: Houghton Mifflin, 1994).

---

15. In only six states do juries sentence defendants. However, in cases involving the death penalty juries often determine whether the convicted should be executed. See Lawrence Baum, *American Courts*, 3d ed. (Boston: Houghton Mifflin, 1994), 20.

achieve what they regard as good results."[16] By considering various kinds of information about convicted defendants, judges assert that they can form a more complete picture of them and, in turn, hand down appropriate sentences. Discretionary sentencing has its share of detractors. Some scholars argue that inappropriate factors enter the process; for example, one study indicates that federal judges appointed by Democratic presidents are much more supportive of criminal defendants than those appointed by Republicans.[17] Just as partisanship and ideology seem to play a role in Supreme Court decision making, they also may influence the sentences lower court judges reach. Another serious charge is that discrimination pervades sentencing decisions, with some research suggesting that white judges are likely to deal more harshly with blacks who are convicted of crimes than with whites.[18]

Given these complaints, it is not surprising that Congress has tried to limit judges' discretion by changing the sentencing system.[19] First, for about sixty federal crimes, Congress set mandatory minimum sentences, which compel judges to reach sentences that are no more lenient than the law permits. Second, Congress created the U.S. Sentencing Commission to formulate rules to limit judicial sentencing latitude (see Box 9-1).

THE EIGHTH AMENDMENT

In addition to these kinds of statutory attempts to limit judicial discretion in sentencing is an important constitutional limit: the clause in the Eighth Amendment that bans cruel and unusual punishments. But the meaning of this clause has plagued a generation of justices, with no issue more perplexing than the constitutionality of the death penalty.

The justices' opinions in the death penalty cases tell us a great deal about what cruel and unusual punishment means and what it does not. Since 1947 the Court has held that the death penalty is inherently neither cruel nor unusual.[20] Never has a *majority* of the justices agreed that it is, but why not? The answer lies with the intent of the Framers (at the time of ratification, death penalties were in use) and with the Due Process Clauses of the Fifth and Fourteenth Amendments, which state that no person can be deprived of life without due process of law. Presumably, if due process is observed, life *can* be deprived.

The majority of Americans also support use of the death penalty *(see page 631)*, but there are many interest groups working to eliminate it. These groups believe that the death penalty constitutes cruel and unusual punishment, but, recognizing the Court's unwillingness to agree, they have tried to convince the justices that the way the death penalty is applied violates due process norms.

One of the first attempts to implement a due process strategy was undertaken by the NAACP Legal Defense and Educational Fund in *Furman v. Georgia* (1972). This case involved William Furman, a black man accused of murdering a white man, the father of five children. Under Georgia law, it was completely up to the jury to determine whether a convicted murderer should be put to death. This system, the LDF argued, led to unacceptable disparities in sentencing; specifically, blacks convicted of murdering whites were far more likely to receive the death penalty than whites convicted of the same crime.

A divided Supreme Court agreed with the LDF. In a short per curiam opinion, deciding *Furman* and two companion cases, the justices said, "The Court holds

16. Ibid.

17. C. K. Rowland, Donald R. Songer, and Robert A. Carp, "Presidential Effects on Criminal Justice in the Lower Federal Courts," *Law and Society* 22 (1988): 191–200.

18. See Susan Welch, Michael Combs, and John Gruhl, "Do Black Judges Make a Difference?" *American Journal of Political Science* 32 (1988): 126–136. Other studies, however, have not found much evidence of racially based sentencing. In general, a reasonable conclusion is that "[d]iscrimination appears to exist in some places, for some types of crimes, and for some judges, but not universally." Baum, *American Courts,* 209.

19. We draw this paragraph from Baum, *American Courts,* 213.

20. See *Louisiana ex rel. Frances v. Resweber* (1947).

that the imposition and carrying out of the death penalty in these cases constitutes cruel and unusual punishment." Following this terse statement, however, were nine separate opinions (five for the LDF and four against), running 243 pages (50,000 words)—the longest in Court history.[21]

The views presented in the opinions of the five-member majority varied considerably— three justices (White, Stewart, and Douglas) thought capital punishment, *as currently imposed,* violated the Constitution, and two (Brennan and Marshall) said it is unconstitutional under all circumstances. Beyond these general groupings, the five justices agreed on only one major point of law: that those states using capital punishment do so in an arbitrary manner, particularly with regard to race. However, they framed even this statement in divergent terms. Douglas said arbitrariness led to discriminatory sentencing. Brennan used arbitrariness as part of a four-part test designed to determine whether the death penalty is acceptable punishment. He found that it was (1) degrading, (2) arbitrary, (3) unacceptable to contemporary society, and (4) excessive. Marshall adopted a similar approach, but explained that arbitrariness was but one reason why capital punishment was cruel and unusual and "morally unacceptable." To Stewart, arbitrariness in sentencing meant that the death penalty was imposed in a "wanton" and "freak[ish] manner," akin to being struck by lightening. For White, arbitrariness led to the infrequency of imposition, which in turn made death a less than credible deterrent.

The dissenters, Blackmun, Burger, Rehnquist, and Powell (the four Nixon appointees), were more uniform in their critiques. To a lesser or greater extent, all expressed the view that the Court was encroaching on legislative turf and that Americans had not "repudiated" the death penalty. Justice Blackmun also lambasted the majority for expressing views wholly inconsistent with past precedent. In particular, he noted that Stewart and White had previously found that it would be virtually impossible to create sentencing standards, but now they were striking laws in part because of the absence of such standards.

Chief Justice Burger's opinion raised a unique issue: he noted that the plurality (Douglas, Stewart, and White) had not ruled that capital punishment under all circumstances was unconstitutional and that it may be possible for states to rewrite their laws to meet their objections. As he asserted: "It is clear that if state legislatures and the Congress wish to maintain the availability of capital punishment, significant statutory changes will have to be made.... [L]egislative bodies may seek to bring their laws into compliance with the Court's ruling by providing standards for juries and judges to follow ... or by more narrowly defining crimes for which the penalty is imposed." Privately, however, Burger thought his suggestion futile, lamenting later that "There will never be another execution in this country."[22]

This view was echoed in many quarters. A University of Washington law professor wrote, "My hunch is that *Furman* spells the complete end of capital punishment in this country."[23] LDF attorneys, predictably, were ecstatic. One called it "the biggest step forward criminal justice has taken in 1,000 years."[24]

As it turned out, the abolitionist celebration was a bit premature, for the Supreme Court was not finished with the death penalty. Just three years after *Furman,* the Court agreed to hear *Gregg v. Georgia* to consider the constitutionality of a new breed of death penalty laws written to overcome the defects of the old laws. Did these new laws reduce the chance for "wanton and freakish" punishment of the sort the Court found so distasteful in *Furman?* Consider this

21. We adopt this discussion from Lee Epstein and Joseph F. Kobylka, *The Supreme Court and Legal Change* (Chapel Hill: University of North Carolina Press, 1992), 78–80.

22. Bob Woodward and Scott Armstrong, *The Brethren* (New York: Simon and Schuster, 1979), 219.

23. John M. Junker, "The Death Penalty Cases: A Preliminary Comment," *Washington Law Review* 48 (1972): 109.

24. Quoted in Frederick Mann, "Anthony Amsterdam," *Juris Doctor* 3 (1973): 31–32.

question as you read the facts and opinions in *Gregg v. Georgia*.

Gregg v. Georgia

428 U.S. 153 (1976)

Vote: 7 *(Blackmun, Burger, Powell, Rehnquist, Stevens,
      Stewart, White)*
  2 *(Brennan, Marshall)*

Opinion announcing the judgment of the Court: Stewart
Concurring opinions: Blackmun, Burger and Rehnquist, White
Dissenting opinions: Brennan, Marshall

Taking cues from the justices' opinions in *Furman*, many states set out to revise their death penalty laws. Among the new plans was one proposed by Georgia (and other states). At the heart of this law was the "bifurcated trial," which consisted of two stages—the trial and the sentencing phase. The trial would proceed as usual, with a jury finding the defendant guilty or innocent. If the verdict was guilty, the prosecution could seek the death penalty at the sentencing stage, in which the defense attorney presents the mitigating facts and the prosecution presents the aggravating facts. Mitigating facts include the individual's age,[25] record, family responsibility, psychiatric reports, and chances for rehabilitation. Such data are not specified in law. The prosecution, on the other hand, has to demonstrate that at least one codified aggravating factor exists.

The Georgia law specified ten, including: murders committed "while the offender was engaged in the commission of another capital offense," the murder of "a judicial officer ... or ... district attorney because of the exercise of his official duty," and murders that are

---

25. In 1982 in *Eddings v. Oklahoma* the Court agreed that age constituted a mitigating factor, which does not mean that minors cannot receive the death penalty—just that juries/judges may consider age during the sentencing stage. In fact, the Court has held that those sixteen and older (at the time the crime was committed) can be executed. See *Thompson v. Oklahoma* (1988) and *Sanford v. Kentucky* (1989).

"outrageously or wantonly vile, horrible, or inhumane." After hearing arguments in mitigation and aggravation, the jury determines whether the individual receives the death penalty. By spelling out the conditions that must be present before a death penalty can be imposed, the law sought to reduce the jury's discretion and eliminate the arbitrary application of the death penalty that the Court in *Furman* found unacceptable. As a further safeguard, the Georgia Supreme Court was to review all jury determinations of death. This new law was applied to Troy Gregg and quickly challenged by abolitionist interests.

Gregg and a friend were hitchhiking north in Florida. Two men picked them up, and later the foursome was joined by another passenger who rode with them as far as Atlanta. The four then continued to a rest stop on the highway. The next day, the bodies of the two drivers were found in a nearby ditch. The individual let off in Atlanta identified Gregg and his friend as possible assailants. Gregg was tried under Georgia's new death penalty system. He was convicted of murder and sentenced to death, a penalty the state's highest court upheld.

Judgment of the Court, and opinions of MR. JUSTICE STEWART, MR. JUSTICE POWELL, and MR. JUSTICE STEVENS announced by MR. JUSTICE STEWART.

The issue in this case is whether the imposition of the sentence of death for the crime of murder under the law of Georgia violates the Eighth and Fourteenth Amendments....

We address initially the basic contention that the punishment of death for the crime of murder is, under all circumstances, "cruel and unusual" in violation of the Eighth and Fourteenth Amendments of the Constitution.... [W]e will consider the sentence of death imposed under the Georgia statutes at issue in this case.

The Court on a number of occasions has both assumed and asserted the constitutionality of capital punishment. In several cases that assumption provided a necessary foundation for the decision, as the Court was asked to decide whether a particular method of carrying out a capital sentence would be allowed to stand under the Eighth Amendment. But until *Furman v. Georgia* (1972), the Court never confronted squarely the fundamental claim that the punishment of death always, regardless of the enormity of the offense or the procedure followed in imposing the sentence, is cruel and unusual punishment in violation of the Constitution. Although this issue was presented and addressed in *Furman*, it was not resolved by the Court. Four Justices would have held that capital punishment is not unconstitutional *per se*; two Justices would have reached the opposite conclusion; and three Justices, while agreeing that the statutes then before the Court were invalid as applied, left open the question whether such punishment may ever be imposed. We now hold that the punishment of death does not invariably violate the Constitution.

The history of the prohibition of "cruel and unusual" punishment already has been reviewed at length. The phrase first appeared in the English Bill of Rights of 1689, which was drafted by Parliament at the accession of William and Mary. The English version appears to have been directed against punishments unauthorized by statute and beyond the jurisdiction of the sentencing court, as well as those disproportionate to the offense involved. The American draftsmen, who adopted the English phrasing in drafting the Eighth Amendment, were primarily concerned, however, with proscribing "tortures" and other "barbarous" methods of punishment.

In the earliest cases raising Eighth Amendment claims, the Court focused on particular methods of execution to determine whether they were too cruel to pass constitutional muster. The constitutionality of the sentence of death itself was not at issue, and the criterion used to evaluate the mode of execution was its similarity to "torture" and other "barbarous" methods.

But the Court has not confined the prohibition embodied in the Eighth Amendment to "barbarous" methods that were generally outlawed in the 18th century. Instead, the Amendment has been interpreted in a flexible and dynamic manner. The Court early recognized that "a principle to be vital, must be capable of wider application than the mischief which gave it birth." *Weems v. United States* (1910). Thus the Clause forbidding "cruel and unusual" punishments "is not fastened to the obsolete but may acquire meaning as public opinion becomes enlightened by a humane justice.". . .

It is clear from . . . these precedents that the Eighth Amendment has not been regarded as a static concept. As Mr. Chief Justice Warren said, in an oft-quoted phrase, "[t]he Amendment must draw its meaning from the evolving standards of decency that mark the progress of a maturing society." Thus, an assessment of contemporary values concerning the infliction of a challenged sanction is relevant to the application of the Eighth Amendment. As we develop below more fully, this assessment does not call for a subjective judgment. It requires, rather, that we look to objective indicia that reflect the public attitude toward a given sanction.

But our cases also make clear that public perceptions of standards of decency with respect to criminal sanctions are not conclusive. A penalty also must accord with "the dignity of man," which is the "basic concept underlying the Eighth Amendment." This means, at least, that the punishment not be "excessive." When a form of punishment in the abstract (in this case, whether capital punishment may ever be imposed as a sanction for murder) rather than in the particular (the propriety of death as a penalty to be applied to a specific defendant for a specific crime) is under consideration, the inquiry into "excessiveness" has two aspects. First, the punishment must not involve the unnecessary and wanton infliction of pain. Second, the punishment must not be grossly out of proportion to the severity of the crime.

Of course, the requirements of the Eighth Amendment must be applied with an awareness of the limited role to be played by the courts. This does not mean that judges have no role to play, for the Eighth Amendment is a restraint upon the exercise of legislative power. . . .

But, while we have an obligation to insure that constitutional bounds are not overreached, we may not act as judges as we might as legislators. . . .

Therefore, in assessing a punishment selected by a democratically elected legislature against the constitutional measure, we presume its validity. We may not require the legislature to select the least severe penalty possible so long as the penalty selected is not cruelly inhumane or disproportionate to the crime involved. And a heavy burden rests on those who would attack the judgment of the representatives of the people. . . .

In the discussion to this point we have sought to identify the principles and considerations that guide a court in addressing an Eighth Amendment claim. We now consider specifically whether the sentence of death for the crime of murder is a *per se* violation of the Eighth and Fourteenth Amendments to the Constitution. We note first that history and precedent strongly support a negative answer to this question.

The imposition of the death penalty for the crime of murder has a long history of acceptance both in the United States and in England....

It is apparent from the text of the Constitution itself that the existence of capital punishment was accepted by the Framers. At the time the Eighth Amendment was ratified, capital punishment was a common sanction in every State.... The Fifth Amendment, adopted at the same time as the Eighth, contemplated the continued existence of the capital sanction by imposing certain limits on the prosecution of capital cases:

"No person shall be held to answer for a capital, or otherwise infamous crime, unless on a presentment or indictment of a Grand Jury ...; nor shall any person be subject for the same offense to be twice put in jeopardy of life or limb; ... nor be deprived of life, liberty, or property, without due process of law...."

And the Fourteenth Amendment, adopted over three quarters of a century later, similarly contemplates the existence of the capital sanction in providing that no State shall deprive any person of "life, liberty, or property" without due process of law.

For nearly two centuries, this Court, repeatedly and often expressly, has recognized that capital punishment is not invalid *per se*....

Four years ago, the petitioners in *Furman* and its companion cases predicated their argument primarily upon the asserted proposition that standards of decency had evolved to the point where capital punishment no longer could be tolerated. The petitioners in those cases said, in effect, that the evolutionary process had come to an end, and that standards of decency required that the Eighth Amendment be construed finally as prohibiting capital punishment for any crime regardless of its depravity and impact on society. This view was accepted by two Justices. Three other Justices were unwilling to go so far; focusing on the procedures by which convicted defendants were selected for the death penalty rather than on the actual punishment inflicted, they joined in the conclusion that the statutes before the Court were constitutionally invalid.

The petitioners in the capital cases before the Court today renew the "standards of decency" argument, but developments during the four years since *Furman* have undercut substantially the assumptions upon which their argument rested. Despite the continuing debate, dating back to the 19th century, over the morality and utility of capital punishment, it is now evident that a large proportion of American society continues to regard it as an appropriate and necessary criminal sanction.

The most marked indication of society's endorsement of the death penalty for murder is the legislative response to *Furman.* The legislatures of at least 35 States have enacted new statutes that provide for the death penalty for at least some crimes that result in the death of another person. And the Congress of the United States, in 1974, enacted a statute providing the death penalty for aircraft piracy that results in death. These recently adopted statutes have attempted to address the concerns expressed by the Court in *Furman* primarily (i) by specifying the factors to be weighed and the procedures to be followed in deciding when to impose a capital sentence, or (ii) by making the death penalty mandatory for specified crimes. But all of the post-*Furman* statutes make clear that capital punishment itself has not been rejected by the elected representatives of the people.

In the only statewide referendum occurring since *Furman* and brought to our attention, the people of California adopted a constitutional amendment that authorized capital punishment, in effect negating a prior ruling by the Supreme Court of California that the death penalty violated the California Constitution.

The jury also is a significant and reliable objective index of contemporary values because it is so directly involved.... It may be true that evolving standards have influenced juries in recent decades to be more discriminating in imposing the sentence of death. But the relative infrequency of jury verdicts imposing the death sentence does not indicate rejection of capital punishment *per se.* Rather, the reluctance of juries in many cases to impose the sentence may well reflect the humane feeling that this most irrevocable of sanctions should be reserved for a small number of extreme cases. Indeed, the actions of juries in many States since *Furman* are fully compatible with the legislative judgments, reflected in the new statutes, as to the continued utility and necessity of capital punishment in appropriate cases. At the close of 1974 at least 254 persons had been sentenced to death since Furman, and by the end of March 1976, more than 460 persons were subject to death sentences.

As we have seen, however, the Eighth Amendment demands more than that a challenged punishment be acceptable to contemporary society. The Court also must ask whether it comports with the basic concept of human dignity at the core of the Amendment. Although we cannot "invalidate a category of penalties because we deem less severe penalties adequate to serve the ends of penology," the sanction imposed cannot be so totally without penological justification that it results in the gratuitous infliction of suffering.

The death penalty is said to serve two principal social purposes: retribution and deterrence of capital crimes by prospective offenders.

In part, capital punishment is an expression of society's moral outrage at particularly offensive conduct. This function may be unappealing to many, but it is essential in an ordered society that asks its citizens to rely on legal processes rather than self-help to vindicate their wrongs.... "Retribution is no longer the dominant objective of the criminal law," but neither is it a forbidden objective nor one inconsistent with our respect for the dignity of men....

Statistical attempts to evaluate the worth of the death penalty as a deterrent to crimes by potential offenders have occasioned a great deal of debate. The results simply have been inconclusive....

Although some of the studies suggest that the death penalty may not function as a significantly greater deterrent than lesser penalties, there is no convincing empirical evidence either supporting or refuting this view. We may nevertheless assume safely that there are murderers, such as those who act in passion, for whom the threat of death has little or no deterrent effect. But for many others, the death penalty undoubtedly is a significant deterrent. There are carefully contemplated murders, such as murder for hire, where the possible penalty of death may well enter into the cold calculus that precedes the decision to act. And there are some categories of murder, such as murder by a life prisoner, where other sanctions may not be adequate.

The value of capital punishment as a deterrent of crime is a complex factual issue the resolution of which properly rests with the legislatures, which can evaluate the results of statistical studies in terms of their own local conditions and with a flexibility of approach that is not available to the courts. Indeed, many of the post-*Furman* statutes reflect just such a responsible effort to define those crimes and those criminals for which capital punishment is most probably an effective deterrent.

In sum, we cannot say that the judgment of the Georgia Legislature that capital punishment may be necessary in some cases is clearly wrong. Considerations of federalism, as well as respect for the ability of a legislature to evaluate, in terms of its particular State, the moral consensus concerning the death penalty and its social utility as a sanction, require us to conclude, in the absence of more convincing evidence, that the infliction of death as a punishment for murder is not without justification and thus is not unconstitutionally severe.

Finally, we must consider whether the punishment of death is disproportionate in relation to the crime for which it is imposed. There is no question that death as a punishment is unique in its severity and irrevocability. When a defendant's life is at stake, the Court has been particularly sensitive to insure that every safeguard is observed. But we are concerned here only with the imposition of capital punishment for the crime of murder, and when a life has been taken deliberately by the offender, we cannot say that the punishment is invariably disproportionate to the crime. It is an extreme sanction, suitable to the most extreme of crimes.

We hold that the death penalty is not a form of punishment that may never be imposed, regardless of the circumstances of the offense, regardless of the character of the offender, and regardless of the procedure followed in reaching the decision to impose it.

We now consider whether Georgia may impose the death penalty on the petitioner in this case.

While *Furman* did not hold that the infliction of the death penalty *per se* violates the Constitution's ban on cruel and unusual punishments, it did recognize that the penalty of death is different in kind from any other punishment imposed under our system of criminal justice. Because of the uniqueness of the death penalty, *Furman* held that it could not be imposed under sentencing procedures that created a substantial risk that it would be inflicted in an arbitrary and capricious manner....

Furman mandates that where discretion is afforded a sentencing body on a matter so grave as the determination of whether a human life should be taken or spared, that discretion must be suitably directed and limited so as to minimize the risk of wholly arbitrary and capricious action....

Jury sentencing has been considered desirable in capital cases in order "to maintain a link between contemporary community values and the penal system—a link without which the determination of punishment could hardly reflect 'the evolving standards of decency that mark the progress of a maturing society.'" But it creates special problems. Much of the information that is relevant to the sentencing decision may have no relevance to the question of guilt, or may even be extremely prejudicial to a fair determination of that question. This problem, however, is scarcely insurmountable. Those who have studied the question suggest that a bifurcated procedure—one in which the question of sentence is not considered until the determination of guilt has been made—is the best answer.... When a human life is at stake and when the jury must have information prejudicial to the question of guilt but relevant to the question of penalty in order to impose a rational sentence, a bifurcated system is more likely to ensure elimination of the constitutional deficiencies identified in *Furman*.

But the provision of relevant information under fair procedural rules is not alone sufficient to guarantee that the information will be properly used in the imposition of punishment, especially if sentencing is performed by a jury. Since the members of a jury will have had little, if any, previous experience in sentencing, they are unlikely to be skilled in dealing with the information they are given. To the extent that this problem is inherent in jury sentencing, it may not be totally correctible. It seems clear, however, that the problem will be alleviated if the jury is given guidance regarding the factors about the crime and the defendant that the State, representing organized society, deems particularly relevant to the sentencing decision.

The idea that a jury should be given guidance in its decisionmaking is also hardly a novel proposition. Juries are invariably given careful instructions on the law and how to apply it before they are authorized to decide the merits of a lawsuit. It would be virtually unthinkable to follow any other course in a legal system that has traditionally operated by following prior precedents and fixed rules of law. When erroneous instructions are given, retrial is often required. It is quite simply a hallmark of our legal system that juries be carefully and adequately guided in their deliberations.

While some have suggested that standards to guide a capital jury's sentencing deliberations are impossible to formulate, the fact is that such standards have been developed.... While such standards are by necessity somewhat general, they do provide guidance to the sentencing authority and thereby reduce the likelihood that it will impose a sentence that fairly can be called capricious or arbitrary. Where the sentencing authority is required to specify the factors it relied upon in reaching its decision, the further safeguard of meaningful appellate review is available to ensure that death sentences are not imposed capriciously or in a freakish manner.

In summary, the concerns expressed in *Furman* that the penalty of death not be imposed in an arbitrary or capricious manner can be met by a carefully drafted statute that ensures that the sentencing authority is given adequate information and guidance. As a general proposition these concerns are best met by a system that provides for a bifurcated proceeding at which the sentencing authority is apprised of the information relevant to the imposition of sentence and provided with standards to guide its use of the information.

We do not intend to suggest that only the above-described procedures would be permissible under *Furman* or that any sentencing system constructed along these general lines would inevitably satisfy the concerns of *Furman*, for each distinct system must be examined on an individual basis. Rather, we have embarked upon this general exposition to make clear that it is possible to construct capital-sentencing systems capable of meeting *Furman*'s constitutional concerns.

We now turn to consideration of the constitutionality of Georgia's capital-sentencing procedures. In the wake of *Furman*, Georgia amended its capital punishment statute, but chose not to narrow the scope of its murder provisions. Thus, now as before *Furman*, in Georgia "[a] person commits murder when he unlawfully and with malice aforethought, either express or implied, causes the death of another human being." All persons convicted of murder "shall be punished by death or by imprisonment for life."

Georgia did act, however, to narrow the class of murderers subject to capital punishment by specifying 10 statutory aggravating circumstances, one of which must be found by the jury to exist beyond a reasonable doubt before a death sentence can ever be imposed. In addition, the jury is authorized to consider any other appropriate aggravating or mitigating circumstances. The jury is not required to find any mitigating circumstance in order to make a recommendation of mercy that is binding on the trial court, but it must find a *statutory* aggravating circumstance before recommending a sentence of death.

These procedures require the jury to consider the circumstances of the crime and the criminal before it recommends sentence. No longer can a Georgia jury do as *Furman*'s jury did: reach a finding of the defendant's guilt and then, without guidance or direction, decide whether he should live or die. Instead, the jury's attention is directed to the specific circumstances of the crime.... In addition, the jury's attention is focused on the characteristics of the person who committed the crime.... As a result, while some jury discretion still exists, "the discretion to be exercised is controlled by clear and objective standards so as to produce nondiscriminatory application."

As an important additional safeguard against arbitrariness and caprice, the Georgia statutory scheme provides for automatic appeal of all death sentences to the State's Supreme Court. That court is required by statute to review each sentence of death and determine whether it was imposed under the influence of passion or prejudice, whether the evidence supports the jury's finding of a statutory aggravating circumstance, and whether the sentence is disproportionate compared to those sentences imposed in similar cases.

In short, Georgia's new sentencing procedures require as a prerequisite to the imposition of the death penalty, specific jury findings as to the circumstances of the crime or the character of the defendant. Moreover, to guard further against a situation comparable to that presented in

Furman, the Supreme Court of Georgia compares each death sentence with the sentences imposed on similarly situated defendants to ensure that the sentence of death in a particular case is not disproportionate. On their face these procedures seem to satisfy the concerns of *Furman*. No longer should there be "no meaningful basis for distinguishing the few cases in which [the death penalty] is imposed from the many cases in which it is not."...

The basic concern of *Furman* centered on those defendants who were being condemned to death capriciously and arbitrarily. Under the procedures before the Court in that case, sentencing authorities were not directed to give attention to the nature or circumstances of the crime committed or to the character or record of the defendant. Left unguided, juries imposed the death sentence in a way that could only be called freakish. The new Georgia sentencing procedures, by contrast, focus the jury's attention on the particularized nature of the crime and the particularized characteristics of the individual defendant. While the jury is permitted to consider any aggravating or mitigating circumstances, it must find and identify at least one statutory aggravating factor before it may impose a penalty of death. In this way the jury's discretion is channeled. No longer can a jury wantonly and freakishly impose the death sentence; it is always circumscribed by the legislative guidelines. In addition, the review function of the Supreme Court of Georgia affords additional assurance that the concerns that prompted our decision in *Furman* are not present to any significant degree in the Georgia procedure applied here.

For the reasons expressed in this opinion, we hold that the statutory system under which Gregg was sentenced to death does not violate the Constitution. Accordingly, the judgment of the Georgia Supreme Court is affirmed.

MR. JUSTICE WHITE, with whom THE CHIEF JUSTICE and MR. JUSTICE REHNQUIST join, concurring in the judgment.

In *Furman v. Georgia* (1972), this Court held the death penalty as then administered in Georgia to be unconstitutional. That same year the Georgia Legislature enacted a new statutory scheme under which the death penalty may be imposed for several offenses, including murder. The issue in this case is whether the death penalty imposed for murder on petitioner Gregg under the new Georgia statutory scheme may constitutionally be carried out. I agree that it may. . . .

The threshold question in this case is whether the death penalty may be carried out for murder under the Georgia legislative scheme consistent with the decision in *Furman v. Georgia.* In *Furman,* this Court held that as a result of giving the sentencer unguided discretion to impose or not to impose the death penalty for murder, the penalty was being imposed discriminatorily, wantonly and freakishly, and so infrequently that any given death sentence was cruel and unusual. Petitioner argues that, as in *Furman,* the jury is still the sentencer; that the statutory criteria to be considered by the jury on the issue of sentence under Georgia's new statutory scheme are vague and do not purport to be all-inclusive; and that, in any event, there are *no* circumstances under which the jury is required to impose the death penalty. Consequently, the petitioner argues that the death penalty will inexorably be imposed in as discriminatory, standardless, and rare a manner as it was imposed under the scheme declared invalid in *Furman.*

The argument is considerably overstated. . . . The Georgia Legislature has plainly made an effort to guide the jury in the exercise of its discretion, while at the same time permitting the jury to dispense mercy on the basis of factors too intangible to write into a statute, and I cannot accept the naked assertion that the effort is bound to fail. As the types of murders for which the death penalty may be imposed become more narrowly defined and are limited to those which are particularly serious or for which the death penalty is peculiarly appropriate as they are in Georgia by reason of the aggravating-circumstance requirement, it becomes reasonable to expect that juries—even given discretion *not* to impose the death penalty—will impose the death penalty in a substantial portion of the cases so defined. If they do, it can no longer be said that the penalty is being imposed wantonly and freakishly or so infrequently that it loses its usefulness as a sentencing device. There is, therefore, reason to expect that Georgia's current system would escape the infirmities which invalidated its previous system under *Furman.* However, the Georgia Legislature was not satisfied with a system which might, but also might not, turn out in practice to result in death sentences being imposed with reasonable consistency for certain serious murders. Instead, it gave the Georgia Supreme

Court the power and the obligation to perform precisely the task which three Justices of this Court, whose opinions were necessary to the result, performed in *Furman*: namely, the task of deciding whether in fact the death penalty was being administered for any given class of crime in a discriminatory, standardless, or rare fashion.

. . . Indeed, if the Georgia Supreme Court properly performs the task assigned to it under the Georgia statutes, death sentences imposed for discriminatory reasons or wantonly or freakishly for any given category of crime will be set aside. Petitioner has wholly failed to establish, and has not even attempted to establish, that the Georgia Supreme Court failed properly to perform its task in this case or that it is incapable of performing its task adequately in all cases; and this Court should not assume that it did not do so.

MR. JUSTICE BRENNAN, dissenting.

My opinion in *Furman v. Georgia* concluded that . . . the punishment of death, for whatever crime and under all circumstances, is "cruel and unusual" in violation of the Eighth and Fourteenth Amendments of the Constitution. I shall not again canvass the reasons that led to that conclusion. I emphasize only that foremost among the "moral concepts" recognized in our cases and inherent in the Clause is the primary moral principle that the State, even as it punishes, must treat its citizens in a manner consistent with their intrinsic worth as human beings—a punishment must not be so severe as to be degrading to human dignity. A judicial determination whether the punishment of death comports with human dignity is therefore not only permitted but compelled by the Clause.

I do not understand that the Court disagrees that "[i]n comparison to all other punishments today . . . the deliberate extinguishment of human life by the State is uniquely degrading to human dignity." For three of my Brethren hold today that mandatory infliction of the death penalty constitutes the penalty cruel and unusual punishment. I perceive no principled basis for this limitation. Death for whatever crime and under all circumstances "is truly an awesome punishment. The calculated killing of a human being by the State involves, by its very nature, a denial of the executed person's humanity. . . . An executed person has indeed 'lost the right to have rights.'" Death is not only an unusually severe punishment, unusual in its pain, in its finality, and in its enormity, but it serves no penal purpose more effectively than a less severe punishment; therefore the principle inherent in the Clause that prohibits pointless infliction of excessive punishment when less severe punishment can adequately achieve the same purposes invalidates the punishment.

The fatal constitutional infirmity in the punishment of death is that it treats "members of the human race as non-humans, as objects to be toyed with and discarded. [It is] thus inconsistent with the fundamental premise of the Clause that even the vilest criminal remains a human being possessed of common human dignity." As such it is a penalty that "subjects the individual to a fate forbidden by the principle of civilized treatment guaranteed by the [Clause]." I therefore would hold, on that ground alone, that death is today a cruel and unusual punishment prohibited by the Clause.

MR. JUSTICE MARSHALL, dissenting.

In *Furman v. Georgia* (1972) (concurring opinion), I set forth at some length my views on the basic issue presented to the Court in these cases. The death penalty, I concluded, is a cruel and unusual punishment prohibited by the Eighth and Fourteenth Amendments. That continues to be my view.

I have no intention of retracing the "long and tedious journey," that led to my conclusion in *Furman.* My sole purposes here are to consider the suggestion that my conclusion in *Furman* has been undercut by developments since then, and briefly to evaluate the basis for my Brethren's holding that the extinction of life is a permissible form of punishment under the Cruel and Unusual Punishments Clause.

In *Furman* I concluded that the death penalty is constitutionally invalid for two reasons. First, the death penalty is excessive. And second, the American people, fully informed as to the purposes of the death penalty and its liabilities, would in my view reject it as morally unacceptable.

Since the decision in *Furman,* the legislatures of 35 States have enacted new statutes authorizing the imposition of the death sentence for certain crimes, and Congress has enacted a law providing the death penalty for air piracy

resulting in death. I would be less than candid if I did not acknowledge that these developments have a significant bearing on a realistic assessment of the moral acceptability of the death penalty to the American people. But if the constitutionality of the death penalty turns, as I have urged, on the opinion of an informed citizenry, then even the enactment of new death statutes cannot be viewed as conclusive. In *Furman,* I observed that the American people are largely unaware of the information critical to a judgment on the morality of the death penalty, and concluded that if they were better informed they would consider it shocking, unjust, and unacceptable. A recent study, conducted after the enactment of the post-*Furman* statutes, has confirmed that the American people know little about the death penalty, and that the opinions of an informed public would differ significantly from those of a public unaware of the consequences and effects of the death penalty.

Even assuming, however, that the post-*Furman* enactment of statutes authorizing the death penalty renders the prediction of the views of an informed citizenry an uncertain basis for a constitutional decision, the enactment of those statutes has no bearing whatsoever on the conclusion that the death penalty is unconstitutional because it is excessive. An excessive penalty is invalid under the Cruel and Unusual Punishments Clause "even though popular sentiment may favor." The inquiry here, then, is simply whether the death penalty is necessary to accomplish the legitimate legislative purposes in punishment, or whether a less severe penalty—life imprisonment—would do as well.

The two purposes that sustain the death penalty as nonexcessive in the Court's view are general deterrence and retribution. In *Furman,* I canvassed the relevant data on the deterrent effect of capital punishment.... The available evidence, I concluded in *Furman,* was convincing that "capital punishment is not necessary as a deterrent to crime in our society."...

The evidence I reviewed in *Furman* remains convincing, in my view, that "capital punishment is not necessary as a deterrent to crime in our society." The justification for the death penalty must be found elsewhere.

The other principal purpose said to be served by the death penalty is retribution. The notion that retribution can serve as a moral justification for the sanction of death finds credence in the opinion of my Brothers STEWART, POWELL, and STEVENS, and that of my Brother WHITE....

See also *Furman v. Georgia* (BURGER, C.J., dissenting). It is this notion that I find to be the most disturbing aspect of today's unfortunate decisions.

The concept of retribution is a multifaceted one, and any discussion of its role in the criminal law must be undertaken with caution. On one level, it can be said that the notion of retribution or reprobation is the basis of our insistence that only those who have broken the law be punished, and in this sense the notion is quite obviously central to a just system of criminal sanctions. But our recognition that retribution plays a crucial role in determining who may be punished by no means requires approval of retribution as a general justification for punishment. It is the question whether retribution can provide a moral justification for punishment—in particular, capital punishment—that we must consider.

My Brothers STEWART, POWELL, and STEVENS offer the following explanation of the retributive justification for capital punishment:

"'The instinct for retribution is part of the nature of man, and channeling that instinct in the administration of criminal justice serves an important purpose in promoting the stability of a society governed by law. When people begin to believe that organized society is unwilling or unable to impose upon criminal offenders the punishment they "deserve," then there are sown the seeds of anarchy— of self-help, vigilante justice, and lynch law.'"

This statement is wholly inadequate to justify the death penalty. As my Brother BRENNAN stated in *Furman*, "[t]here is no evidence whatever that utilization of imprisonment rather than death encourages private blood feuds and other disorders." It simply defies belief to suggest that the death penalty is necessary to prevent the American people from taking the law into their own hands....

The death penalty, unnecessary to promote the goal of deterrence or to further any legitimate notion of retribution, is an excessive penalty forbidden by the Eighth and Fourteenth Amendments. I respectfully dissent from the Court's judgment upholding the sentences of death imposed upon the petitioners in these cases.

Despite the plethora of opinions in *Gregg*, the majority of justices agreed that the Georgia law was constitutional; indeed, some members of the Court re-

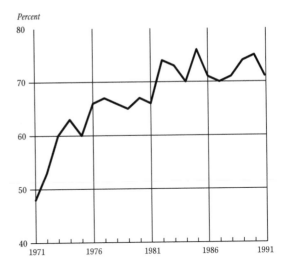

FIGURE 9-1 Support for Capital Punishment, 1971–1991

Percent

DATA SOURCES: Harold W. Stanley and Richard G. Niemi, *Vital Statistics on American Politics*, 4th ed. (Washington, D.C.: CQ Press, 1994), 33; Lee Epstein, Jeffrey A. Segal, Harold J. Spaeth, and Thomas G. Walker, *The Supreme Court Compendium: Data, Decisions, and Developments* (Washington, D.C.: Congressional Quarterly, 1994), Table 8-6.

ferred to it as a model death penalty scheme. But what accounts for the abrupt change in the law between *Furman* and *Gregg*? Given that some scholars and even justices thought that *Furman* had brought an end to capital punishment, this about-face is all the more puzzling. [26] Analysts offer several explanations. Some point to the membership change on the Court that occurred between the two cases: William Douglas, who had voted with the five-person *Furman* majority, had been replaced by John Paul Stevens, who voted with the seven-person *Gregg* majority.

Another set of explanations center on the turn in the political environment between 1972 and 1976. As Figure 9-1 shows, public opinion became more supportive of capital punishment. Around the time of the *Furman* decision, Americans were relatively divided on the issue. By November 1972, those in favor of capital punishment had jumped by seven percentage points;

26. We derive this discussion from Epstein and Kobylka, *The Supreme Court and Legal Change*, chap. 4.

TABLE 9-2 Capital Punishment in the United States

State	Method	Death Row Population, 1992	Executions 1990–1992
Alabama	Electrocution	113	2
Alaska	No death penalty	—	—
Arizona	Lethal gas	102	1
Arkansas	Lethal injection	33	4
California	Lethal gas	331	1
Colorado	Lethal injection	3	0
Connecticut	Electrocution	4	0
Delaware	Lethal injection	6	1
District of Columbia	No death penalty	—	—
Florida	Electrocution	319	6
Georgia	Electrocution	110	0
Hawaii	No death penalty	—	—
Idaho	Lethal injection	23	0
Illinois	Lethal injection	146	1
Indiana	Electrocution	55	0
Iowa	No death penalty	—	—
Kansas	No death penalty	—	—
Kentucky	Electrocution	26	0
Louisiana	Electrocution	39	1
Maine	No death penalty	—	—
Maryland	Lethal gas	15	0
Massachusetts	No death penalty	—	—
Michigan	No death penalty	—	—
Minnesota	No death penalty	—	—
Mississippi	Lethal injection	53	0
Missouri	Lethal injection	82	5
Montana	Hanging or lethal injection	8	0
Nebraska	Electrocution	13	0
Nevada	Lethal injection	61	1
New Hampshire	Lethal injection	0	0
New Jersey	Lethal injection	7	0
New Mexico	Lethal injection	1	0
New York	No death penalty	—	—
North Carolina	Lethal gas or injection	110	1
North Dakota	No death penalty	—	—
Ohio	Electrocution	118	0
Oklahoma	Lethal injection	120	3
Oregon	Lethal injection	15	0
Pennsylvania	Electrocution	143	0
Rhode Island	No death penalty	—	—
South Carolina	Electrocution	45	1
South Dakota	Lethal injection	0	0
Tennessee	Electrocution	104	0
Texas	Lethal injection	356	14
Utah	Firing squad or lethal injection	12	1
Vermont	No death penalty	—	—
Virginia	Electrocution	51	6
Washington	Hanging or lethal injection	9	0
West Virginia	No death penalty	—	—
Wisconsin	No death penalty	—	—
Wyoming	Lethal injection	1	0
TOTAL		2,632[a]	50

sources: Lee Epstein, Jeffrey A. Segal, Harold J. Spaeth, and Thomas G. Walker, *The Supreme Court Compendium: Data, Decisions, and Developments* (Washington, D.C.: Congressional Quarterly, 1994), Table 9-3; Harold W. Stanley and Richard G. Niemi, *Vital Statistics on American Politics*, 3d ed. (Washington, D.C.: CQ Press, 1992), 30–32.

[a]Number of inmates; some are multiply sentenced and are listed in more than one state.

by 1974, roughly two-thirds of Americans supported legal executions. Given this trend in public opinion, state legislators could barely wait to reconvene after *Furman* and pass new laws designed to limit arbitrariness in sentencing. Indeed, almost every state that had a death penalty prior to *Furman* had reinstated it prior to 1976. And the national government even got into the act. The day after *Furman* came down, President Nixon seized on Burger's dissent in noting that the Court had not completely ruled out capital punishment. He subsequently sent to Congress a bill calling for the death penalty in certain federal crimes.

It is not surprising that some scholars suggest that the Court merely succumbed to public pressure in this area: Americans wanted the death penalty and the justices caved in, or so the argument goes. Even Justice Marshall, in his *Gregg* dissent, acknowledged that post-*Furman* "developments have a significant bearing on a realistic assessment of the moral acceptability of the death penalty to the American people." (But recall that he also maintained that "the American people are largely unaware of the information critical to a judgment on the morality of the death penalty, and ... if they were better informed they would consider it shocking, unjust, and unacceptable.")

Yet another set of explanations centers on the new laws themselves and the way attorneys tried to challenge them. To put it simply, abolitionist lawyers may have overestimated the degree of their victory in *Furman*. In their arguments to the Court, they asserted that "death is different." But this view was held only by two justices in *Furman*—Brennan and Marshall. Remember that the others, especially White and Stewart, were more concerned with the arbitrariness of death penalty sentencing and not with the constitutionality of the death penalty. In the end, as Justice White's concurrence in *Gregg* indicates, abolitionist attorneys were unable to convince the majority that the new laws—which explicitly sought to eliminate arbitrariness in sentencing by limiting jury discretion—were unconstitutional.

Whatever the explanation for the Court's change of heart, the results were clear. Many states adopted Georgia's death penalty law, and executions increased accordingly. During the 1970s, only three people were legally executed in the United States; between 1990 and 1992, that figure was fifty. As Table 9-2 shows, states in the South and Southwest have been responsible for a disproportionate share of the nation's death row inmates and executions.

In the Aftermath of Gregg

In some ways, *Gregg* settled the death penalty issue: the Court asserted that capital punishment did not violate the Constitution, a position to which it still adheres. But opponents of the death penalty have not given up. They have continued to bring lawsuits, many of which were aimed at narrowing the application of capital punishment. In other words, this litigation challenged procedural practices adopted by the states, and not the constitutionality of the death penalty.

A good number of these procedural cases involved this question: What factors should sentencers consider in their deliberations? Occasionally, the Court has ruled for defendants in these disputes; in *Eddings v. Oklahoma* (1982) it held that a trial court judge could not refuse to hear mitigating evidence pointing to the defendant's youth, troubled childhood, and history of mental problems. But the Court, especially in the late 1980s, generally has taken a pro–death penalty posture in post-*Gregg* disputes. A prime example is *McCleskey v. Kemp* (1987), which some observers consider the most significant capital punishment case since *Gregg*. Why was *McCleskey* so important? Can you square the Court's opinion in this case with the logic of *Furman*?

McCleskey v. Kemp

481 U.S. 279 (1987)
Vote: 5 *(O'Connor, Powell, Rehnquist, Scalia, White)*
    4 *(Blackmun, Brennan, Marshall, Stevens)*
Opinion of the Court: Powell
Dissenting opinions: Blackmun, Brennan, Stevens

On May 13, 1978, Warren McCleskey, a black man, and three accomplices attempted to rob a furniture store in Atlanta, Georgia. One of the employees hit a silent alarm button, which was answered by a white, thirty-one-year-old police officer. As the officer entered the store, he was shot and killed. Several weeks later, when police arrested him on another charge, McCleskey confessed to the robbery. At his trial, McCleskey was identified by one of the accomplices as the individual who killed the officer. The prosecution also entered evidence indicating that McCleskey had bragged about the shooting.

Three months after the robbery, a jury of eleven whites and one black convicted McCleskey and sentenced him to death. At that point, the NAACP LDF took over his defense. The LDF based its appeal in the federal courts on a 1986 study showing that blacks convicted of murdering whites received death sentences at disproportionately high rates. The study centered on a statistical examination by several professors of the application of Georgia's death penalty.[27] Called the Baldus study after one of the researchers, Professor David Baldus, the data consisted of 2,484 Georgia murder cases from 1973 to 1979, coded for some 230 variables. To analyze this mammoth amount of data, Baldus used a multivariate technique, which allows researchers to demonstrate the effects of possible explanatory variables (such as the race of the defendant or victim) on outcomes (such as the decision to sentence to death).[28]

27. We adopt this discussion from ibid., 123–125.
28. For more on this study, see David Baldus, George G. Woodworth, and Charles Pulaski, *Equal Justice and the Death Penalty* (Boston: Northeastern University Press, 1990).

Warren McCleskey based the appeal of his death sentence on a study showing that someone convicted for killing a white person was four times more likely to receive the death penalty than someone convicted for killing a black person. His appeal was rejected in *McCleskey v. Kemp* (1987), and he was executed in 1991.

Baldus's conclusions were dramatic. Among the most noteworthy were the following:

The chances of receiving a death sentence were 4.3 times greater for defendants whose victims were white than for defendants whose victims were black.

Of the 128 cases in which death was imposed, 87 percent (108) involved white victims.

Prosecutors sought the death penalty in 70 percent of cases involving black defendants and white victims, but in only 32 percent in which both the defendant and victim were white.

Black defendants were 1.1 times more likely than other defendants to receive death sentences.

Armed with this study the LDF tried to convince the justices once and for all that the disparate application of death penalty laws led to unacceptable violations of the Equal Protection and Due Process Clauses.

JUSTICE POWELL delivered the opinion of the Court.

This case presents the question whether a complex statistical study that indicates a risk that racial considerations enter into capital sentencing determinations proves that petitioner McCleskey's capital sentence is unconstitutional under the Eighth or Fourteenth Amendment....

Our analysis begins with the basic principle that a defendant who alleges an equal protection violation has the burden of proving "the existence of purposeful discrimination." A corollary to this principle is that a criminal defendant must prove that the purposeful discrimination "had a discriminatory effect" on him. Thus, to prevail under the Equal Protection Clause, McCleskey must prove that the decisionmakers in *his* case acted with discriminatory purpose. He offers no evidence specific to his own case that would support an inference that racial considerations played a part in his sentence. Instead, he relies solely on the Baldus study. McCleskey argues that the Baldus study compels an inference that his sentence rests on purposeful discrimination. McCleskey's claim that these statistics are sufficient proof of discrimination, without regard to the facts of a particular case, would extend to all capital cases in Georgia, at least where the victim was white and the defendant is black.

The Court has accepted statistics as proof of intent to discriminate in certain limited contexts. First, this Court has accepted statistical disparities as proof of an equal protection violation in the selection of the jury venire in a particular district. Although statistical proof normally must present a "stark" pattern to be accepted as the sole proof of discriminatory intent under the Constitution, "[b]ecause of the nature of the jury-selection task, ... we have permitted a finding of constitutional violation even when the statistical pattern does not approach [such] extremes." Second, this Court has accepted statistics in the form of multiple regression analysis to prove statutory violations under Title VII.

But the nature of the capital sentencing decision, and the relationship of the statistics to that decision, are fundamentally different from the corresponding elements in the venire-selection or Title VII cases. Most importantly, each particular decision to impose the death penalty is made by a petit jury selected from a properly constituted venire. Each jury is unique in its composition, and the Constitution requires that its decision rest on consideration of innumerable factors that vary according to the characteristics of the individual defendant and the facts of the particular capital offense. Thus, the application of an inference drawn from the general statistics to a specific decision in a trial and sentencing simply is not comparable to the application of an inference drawn from general statistics to a specific venire-selection or Title VII case. In those cases, the statistics relate to fewer entities, and fewer variables are relevant to the challenged decisions.

Another important difference between the cases in which we have accepted statistics as proof of discriminatory intent and this case is that, in the venire-selection and Title VII contexts, the decisionmaker has an opportunity to explain the statistical disparity. Here, the State has no practical opportunity to rebut the Baldus study....

Finally, McCleskey's statistical proffer must be viewed in the context of his challenge. McCleskey challenges decisions at the heart of the State's criminal justice system. "[O]ne of society's most basic tasks is that of protecting the lives of its citizens and one of the most basic ways in which it achieves the task is through criminal laws against murder." Implementation of these laws necessarily requires discretionary judgments. Because discretion is essential to the criminal justice process, we would demand exceptionally clear proof before we would infer that the discretion has been abused. The unique nature of the decisions at issue in this case also counsel against adopting such an inference from the disparities indicated by the Baldus study. Accordingly, we hold that the Baldus study is clearly insufficient to support an inference that any of the decisionmakers in McCleskey's case acted with discriminatory purpose....

McCleskey also argues that the Baldus study demonstrates that the Georgia capital sentencing system violates the Eighth Amendment....

Two principal decisions guide our resolution of McCleskey's Eighth Amendment claim. In *Furman v. Georgia* (1972), the Court concluded that the death penalty was so irrationally imposed that any particular death sentence could be presumed excessive....

In *Gregg*, the Court specifically addressed the question left open in *Furman*—whether the punishment of death for murder is "under all circumstances, 'cruel and unusual' in violation of the Eighth and Fourteenth Amendments of the Constitution.". . . We noted that any punishment might be unconstitutionally severe if inflicted without penological justification, but concluded:

"Considerations of federalism, as well as respect for the ability of a legislature to evaluate, in terms of its particular State, the moral consensus concerning the death penalty and its social utility as a sanction, require us to conclude, in the absence of more convincing evidence, that the infliction of death as a punishment for murder is not without justification and thus is not unconstitutionally severe.". . .

In light of our precedents under the Eighth Amendment, McCleskey cannot argue successfully that his sentence is "disproportionate to the crime in the traditional sense." He does not deny that he committed a murder in the course of a planned robbery, a crime for which this Court has determined that the death penalty constitutionally may be imposed. His disproportionality claim "is of a different sort." McCleskey argues that the sentence in his case is disproportionate to the sentences in other murder cases.

On the one hand, he cannot base a constitutional claim on an argument that his case differs from other cases in which defendants did receive the death penalty. On automatic appeal, the Georgia Supreme Court found that McCleskey's death sentence was not disproportionate to other death sentences imposed in the State. . . .

On the other hand, absent a showing that the Georgia capital punishment system operates in an arbitrary and capricious manner, McCleskey cannot prove a constitutional violation by demonstrating that other defendants who may be similarly situated did not receive the death penalty. In *Gregg*, the Court confronted the argument that "the opportunities for discretionary action that are inherent in the processing of any murder case under Georgia law," specifically, the opportunities for discretionary leniency, rendered the capital sentences imposed arbitrary and capricious. We rejected this contention. . . .

Because McCleskey's sentence was imposed under Georgia's sentencing procedures that focus discretion "on the particularized nature of the crime and the particularized characteristics of the individual defendant," we lawfully may presume that McCleskey's death sentence was not "wantonly and freakishly" imposed, and thus that the sentence is not disproportionate within any recognized meaning under the Eighth Amendment.

Although our decision in *Gregg* as to the facial validity of the Georgia capital punishment statute appears to foreclose McCleskey's disproportionality argument, he further contends that the Georgia capital punishment system is arbitrary and capricious in *application*, and therefore his sentence is excessive, because racial considerations may influence capital sentencing decisions in Georgia. We now address this claim.

To evaluate McCleskey's challenge, we must examine exactly what the Baldus study may show. Even Professor Baldus does not contend that his statistics prove that race enters into any capital sentencing decisions or that race was a factor in McCleskey's particular case. Statistics at most may show only a likelihood that a particular factor entered into some decisions. There is, of course, some risk of racial prejudice influencing a jury's decision in a criminal case. There are similar risks that other kinds of prejudice will influence other criminal trials. The question "is at what point that risk becomes constitutionally unacceptable." McCleskey asks us to accept the likelihood allegedly shown by the Baldus study as the constitutional measure of an unacceptable risk of racial prejudice influencing capital sentencing decisions. This we decline to do.

Because of the risk that the factor of race may enter the criminal justice process, we have engaged in "unceasing efforts" to eradicate racial prejudice from our criminal justice system. Our efforts have been guided by our recognition that "the inestimable privilege of trial by jury . . . is a vital principle, underlying the whole administration of criminal justice." Specifically, a capital sentencing jury representative of a criminal defendant's community assures a " 'diffused impartiality' " in the jury's task of "express[ing] the conscience of the community on the ultimate question of life or death."

Individual jurors bring to their deliberations "qualities of human nature and varieties of human experience, the range of which is unknown and perhaps unknowable." The capital sentencing decision requires the individual jurors to focus their collective judgment on the unique characteristics of a particular criminal defendant. It is not surprising that such collective judgments often are difficult to explain. But the inherent lack of predictability of jury decisions does not justify their condemnation....

McCleskey's argument that the Constitution condemns the discretion allowed decisionmakers in the Georgia capital sentencing system is antithetical to the fundamental role of discretion in our criminal justice system. Discretion in the criminal justice system offers substantial benefits to the criminal defendant. Not only can a jury decline to impose the death sentence, it can decline to convict, or choose to convict of a lesser offense. Whereas decisions against a defendant's interest may be reversed by the trial judge or on appeal, these discretionary exercises of leniency are final and unreviewable. Similarly, the capacity of prosecutorial discretion to provide individualized justice is "firmly entrenched in American law." As we have noted, a prosecutor can decline to charge, offer a plea bargain, or decline to seek a death sentence in any particular case. Of course, "the power to be lenient [also] is the power to discriminate," but a capital-punishment system that did not allow for discretionary acts of leniency "would be totally alien to our notions of criminal justice."

At most, the Baldus study indicates a discrepancy that appears to correlate with race. Apparent disparities in sentencing are an inevitable part of our criminal justice system.... Despite these imperfections, our consistent rule has been that constitutional guarantees are met when "the mode [for determining guilt or punishment] itself has been surrounded with safeguards to make it as fair as possible." Where the discretion that is fundamental to our criminal process is involved, we decline to assume that what is unexplained is invidious. In light of the safeguards designed to minimize racial bias in the process, the fundamental value of jury trial in our criminal justice system, and the benefits that discretion provides to criminal defendants, we hold that the Baldus study does not demonstrate a constitutionally significant risk of racial bias affecting the Georgia capital-sentencing process.

Two additional concerns inform our decision in this case. First, McCleskey's claim, taken to its logical conclusion, throws into serious question the principles that underlie our entire criminal justice system. The Eighth Amendment is not limited in application to capital punishment, but applies to all penalties. Thus, if we accepted McCleskey's claim that racial bias has impermissibly tainted the capital sentencing decision, we could soon be faced with similar claims as to other types of penalty. Moreover, the claim that his sentence rests on the irrelevant factor of race easily could be extended to apply to claims based on unexplained discrepancies that correlate to membership in other minority groups, and even to gender. Similarly, since McCleskey's claim relates to the race of his victim, other claims could apply with equally logical force to statistical disparities that correlate with the race or sex of other actors in the criminal justice system, such as defense attorneys, or judges. Also, there is no logical reason that such a claim need be limited to racial or sexual bias. If arbitrary and capricious punishment is the touchstone under the Eighth Amendment, such a claim could—at least in theory—be based upon any arbitrary variable, such as the defendant's facial characteristics, or the physical attractiveness of the defendant or the victim, that some statistical study indicates may be influential in jury decisionmaking. As these examples illustrate, there is no limiting principle to the type of challenge brought by McCleskey. The Constitution does not require that a State eliminate any demonstrable disparity that correlates with a potentially irrelevant factor in order to operate a criminal justice system that includes capital punishment. As we have stated specifically in the context of capital punishment, the Constitution does not "plac[e] totally unrealistic conditions on its use." Second, McCleskey's arguments are best presented to the legislative bodies. It is not the responsibility—or indeed even the right—of this Court to determine the appropriate punishment for particular crimes.... Legislatures also are better qualified to weigh and "evaluate the results of statistical studies in terms of their own local conditions and with a flexibility of approach that is not available to the courts." Capital punishment is now the law in more than two thirds of our States. It is the ultimate duty of courts to determine on a case-by-case basis whether these laws are applied consistently with the Constitution. Despite McCleskey's wide ranging arguments that basically challenge the validity of capital punishment in our multiracial society, the only question before us is whether in his case the law of Georgia was properly applied. We agree with the District Court and the Court of Appeals for the Eleventh Circuit that this was carefully and correctly done in this case.

Accordingly, we affirm the judgment of the Court of Appeals for the Eleventh Circuit.

It is so ordered.

The Current State of the Death Penalty

Before the Court handed down *McCleskey*, some observers speculated that if the justices agreed with the LDF, they might have found that capital punishment was an inherently arbitrary form of punishment, which could never be imposed fairly. Such a decision would have, in effect, resurrected *Furman*. But it was not to be. Although *McCleskey* caused great division among the justices, the majority of the Court upheld the constitutionality of the death penalty. In short, the LDF's ace in the hole, the Baldus study, failed.

For abolitionists, Court decisions in the wake of *McCleskey* generally have not been encouraging. If anything, the Court grew less tolerant of the long procedural delays and appeals processes often involved in capital punishment cases. For example, in 1991 the justices restricted the use of habeas corpus petitions by state prisoners, making it difficult for lower federal court judges to accept second petitions in all but the rarest of circumstances. By coincidence, this ruling came in a case brought by attorneys representing Warren McCleskey (*McCleskey v. Zant*). In this particular petition (McCleskey filed many over the years, including the one that led to the ruling in *McCleskey v. Kemp*), McCleskey alleged that police had violated his rights when they used a prison informant to "coerce" a confession from him.

This case was a significant setback for death penalty opponents because most death-row inmates, like McCleskey, "typically file several successive writ of *habeas corpus* petitions, raising different constitutional claims, in their efforts to overturn their convictions and sentences.... By limiting lower courts' consideration of successive petitions ... [the ruling] en-

ables states to carry out death sentences more quickly."[29] This was obviously the case for Warren McCleskey. Shortly after the Court's decision in *Zant*, in September 1991 the State of Georgia finally executed him—thirteen years after he allegedly shot a police officer.

Should we conclude from these decisions that opponents of the death penalty have lost their cause? After all, public support for capital punishment remains strong *(see Figure 9-1)*; politicians rarely take public stances against it (in fact, the most recent presidents—Reagan, Bush, and Clinton—all support the death penalty); and the Court has made its position quite clear. Yet the future may not be completely devoid of hope for abolitionists. Early in 1994 Justice Blackmun—a member of the minority in *Furman* and of the majority in *Gregg*—expressed a change of heart on the death penalty. In a dissent from the Court's refusal to hear a Texas death penalty appeal *(see Box 9-2, page 640)*, he stated that he now thought "no sentence of death may be constitutionally imposed." Blackmun's dissent provoked an interesting response from Justice Scalia, a capital punishment supporter. Blackmun is not the only justice to have changed his mind on the death penalty. In 1994 the press reported that Lewis Powell, the author of the original *McKleskey* opinion and an important vote in capital punishment cases of the 1980s, expressed regret over supporting Georgia's claims in the 1987 case.

While Blackmun's and Powell's new positions on the death penalty are interesting, they hold little promise for the abolitionist cause. These two justices have retired from the Court and cannot influence future decisions. But what of the current justices? Are there any Powells or Blackmuns among them? Justices Souter, Stevens, and Ginsburg, while not explicitly advocating the abolition of capital punishment, have

---

29. David M. O'Brien, *Supreme Court Watch—1993* (New York: Norton, 1993), 220.

taken more moderate stances than Justices Scalia, Thomas, and the other members of the pro–death penalty wing of the Court. Justice Breyer has little first-hand experience in this area; before joining the Supreme Court he served on the U.S. Court of Appeals for the First Circuit, which hears virtually no death penalty cases.[30] During his confirmation hearings Breyer was asked his views on the death penalty in light of Blackmun's dissent. Breyer replied, "[T]hat there are some circumstances in which the death penalty is consistent with the Cruel and Unusual Punishment Clause ... is, in my opinion, settled law. At this point it is settled."

Still, as the Court confronts the results of decisions limiting access to federal courts, perhaps it will have a change of heart. Journalist Linda Greenhouse had this to say about oral arguments in a 1993 term death penalty case, *McFarland v. Scott.*

In a death penalty argument marked by tense exchanges and an unusual display of anger from the bench, the Supreme Court came face to face today with the implications of its recent rulings sharply limiting the access of state death-row inmates to Federal court.

The question was whether Federal judges have the power to grant stays of execution to inmates who have exhausted their state appeals but have not found lawyers to help them file an initial petition for Federal court review. A majority of the Justices were visibly disturbed when the lawyer for the State of Texas argued that Federal judges did not have such power.[31]

The Eighth Amendment and Non-Capital Cases

In the future, opponents of the death penalty may win their war. Perhaps, as Justice Brennan wrote in 1986, "a majority of the Supreme Court will one day accept that when the state punishes with death, it denies the humanity and dignity of the victim and transgresses the prohibition against cruel and unusual punishment."[32] For now, the Court remains committed to the position that the Cruel and Unusual Punishments Clause of the Eighth Amendment does not prohibit the death penalty.

But are there other kinds of punishments that may be "cruel and unusual"? Has the Court provided us with any definition of that concept? Indeed, in *Solem v. Helm* (1983), it attempted to do just that.

By 1979 South Dakota courts had convicted Jerry Helm for the commission of six nonviolent felonies. That year he was charged with yet another offense— writing bad checks. Normally, that crime carries with it a maximum sentence of five years in prison and/or a $5,000 fine. But because of Helm's previous record, a South Dakota judge invoked a state recidivism law: if an individual is convicted of three felonies, the sentence can be that imposed for a Class 1 felony, which includes a life prison sentence (with no parole) and/or a $25,000 fine. Believing that Helm was beyond rehabilitation, the judge sentenced him to life imprisonment. After two years of trying to get the governor to commute his sentence, Helm appealed to the Supreme Court, claiming that his punishment was cruel and unusual.

By a 5–4 vote, the justices found the life sentence violated the Cruel and Unusual Punishments Clause. Justice Powell's majority opinion held that the Eighth Amendment proscribes not only barbaric punishments, but also sentences that are disproportionate to the crime committed. The justices held that this concept of proportionality could be traced back to the earliest development of English law. As applied in this case, life in prison was out of proportion to the bad check charges. Finally, after years of death penalty litigation, the Court provided attorneys with a working definition of cruel and unusual, ironically using a non-

---

30. With the exception of New Hampshire, none of the states in the First Circuit permit capital punishment, and New Hampshire has not had an inmate on death row since the 1930s.

31. Linda Greenhouse, "Supreme Court Confronts Results of Limiting Death-Row Appeals," *New York Times*, March 30, 1994, 1.

32. William J. Brennan, Jr., "Constitutional Adjudication and the Death Penalty: A View from the Court," *Harvard Law Review* 100 (1986): 331.

BOX 9-2 JUSTICES BLACKMUN AND SCALIA ON THE
DEATH PENALTY

Below are excerpts from Justice Blackmun's dissent from the Court's denial of review in *Callins v. Collins* (1994) and Justice Scalia's response.

JUSTICE BLACKMUN

On February 23, 1994, at approximately 1:00 A.M., Bruce Edwin Callins will be executed by the State of Texas. Intravenous tubes attached to his arms will carry the instrument of death, a toxic fluid designed specifically for the purpose of killing human beings. The witnesses, standing a few feet away, will behold Callins, no longer a defendant, an appellant or a petitioner, but a man, strapped to a gurney, and seconds away from extinction.

Within days, or perhaps hours, the memory of Callins will begin to fade. The wheels of justice will churn again, and somewhere, another jury or another judge will have the unenviable task of determining whether some human being is to live or die. We hope, of course, that the defendant whose life is at risk will be represented by competent counsel—someone who is inspired by the awareness that a less-than-vigorous defense truly could have fatal consequences for the defendant. We hope that the attorney will investigate all aspects of the case, follow all evidentiary and procedural rules, and appear before a judge who is still committed to the protection of defendants' rights—even now, as the prospect of meaningful judicial oversight has diminished. In the same vein, we hope that the prosecution, in urging the penalty of death, will have exercised its discretion wisely, free from bias, prejudice, or political motive, and will be humbled, rather than emboldened, by the awesome authority conferred by the State.

But even if we can feel confident that these actors will fulfill their roles to the best of their human ability, our collective conscience will remain uneasy. Twenty years have passed since this Court declared that the death penalty must be imposed fairly, and with reasonable consistency, or not at all, see *Furman v. Georgia* (1972), and, despite the effort of the States and courts to devise legal formulas and procedural rules to meet this daunting challenge, the death penalty remains fraught with arbitrariness, discrimination, caprice, and mistake....

... Having virtually conceded that both fairness and rationality cannot be achieved in the administration of the death penalty, see *McCleskey v. Kemp* (1987), the Court has chosen to deregulate the entire enterprise, replacing, it would seem, substantive constitutional requirements with mere aesthetics, and abdicating its statutorily and constitutionally imposed duty to provide meaningful judicial oversight to the administration of death by the States.

From this day forward, I no longer shall tinker with the machinery of death. For more than 20 years I have endeavored—indeed, I have struggled—along with a majority of this Court, to develop procedural and substantive rules that would lend more than the mere appearance of fairness to the death penalty endeavor. Rather than continue to coddle the Court's delusion that the desired level of fairness has been achieved and the need for regulation eviscerated, I feel morally and intellectually obligated simply to concede that the death penalty experiment has failed. It is virtually self-evident to me now that no combination of procedural rules or substantive regulations ever can save the death penalty from its inherent constitutional deficiencies. The basic question—does the system accurately and consistently determine which defendants "deserve" to die?—cannot be answered in the affirmative.... The problem is that the inevitability of factual, legal, and moral error gives us a system that we know must wrongly kill some defendants, a system that fails to deliver the fair, consistent, and reliable sentences of death required by the Constitution....

There is little doubt now that Furman's essential holding was correct. Although most of the public seems to desire, and the Constitution appears to permit, the penalty of death, it surely is beyond dispute that if the death penalty cannot be administered consistently and rationally, it may not be administered at all....

Delivering on the Furman promise, however, has proved to be another matter. Furman aspired to eliminate the vestiges of racism and the effects of poverty in capital sentencing; it deplored the "wanton" and "random" infliction of death by a government with constitutionally limited power. Furman demanded that the sentencer's discretion be directed and limited by procedural rules and objective standards in order to minimize the risk of arbitrary and capricious sentences of death.

In the years following Furman, serious efforts were made to comply with its mandate. State legislatures and appellate courts struggled to provide judges and juries with sensible and objective guidelines for determining who should live and who should die . . .

Unfortunately, all this experimentation and ingenuity yielded little of what Furman demanded. It soon became apparent that discretion could not be eliminated from capital sentencing without threatening the fundamental fairness due a defendant when life is at stake. . . .

Perhaps one day this Court will develop procedural rules or verbal formulas that actually will provide consistency, fairness, and reliability in a capital-sentencing scheme. I am not optimistic that such a day will come. I am more optimistic, though, that this Court eventually will conclude that the effort to eliminate arbitrariness while preserving fairness "in the infliction of (death) is so plainly doomed to failure that it and the death penalty must be abandoned altogether." I may not live to see that day, but I have faith that eventually it will arrive. The path the Court has chosen lessens us all. I dissent.

JUSTICE SCALIA

Convictions in opposition to the death penalty are often passionate and deeply held. That would be no excuse for reading them into a Constitution that does not contain them, even if they represented the convictions of a majority of Americans. Much less is there any excuse for using that course to thrust a minority's views upon the people. JUSTICE BLACKMUN begins his statement by describing with poignancy the death of a convicted murderer by lethal injection. He chooses, as the case in which to make that statement, one of the less brutal of the murders that regularly come before us—the murder of a man ripped by a bullet suddenly and unexpectedly, with no opportunity to prepare himself and his affairs, and left to bleed to death on the floor of a tavern. The death-by-injection which JUSTICE BLACKMUN describes looks pretty desirable next to that. It looks even better next to some of the other cases currently before us, which JUSTICE BLACKMUN did not select as the vehicle for his announcement that the death penalty is always unconstitutional—for example, the case of the 11-year-old girl raped by four men and then killed by stuffing her panties down her throat. . . . How enviable a quiet death by lethal injection compared with that! If the people conclude that such more brutal deaths may be deterred by capital punishment; indeed, if they merely conclude that justice requires such brutal deaths to be avenged by capital punishment; the creation of false, untextual and unhistorical contradictions within "the Court's Eighth Amendment jurisprudence" should not prevent them.

capital case to do so. The Court seemed to abide by the old adage—let the punishment fit the crime.

POST-TRIAL STAGES

Individuals convicted of crimes can appeal their convictions in the hope that appellate judges will find errors in the trial court's handling of the case. Under the American concept of due process, someone convicted of a criminal offense is entitled to at least one appeal. A new trial might be granted if new evidence is discovered that brings into serious question the guilt of the defendant, although such instances are rare.

What about those individuals whom juries and judges acquit? Is there any way that the government can reinitiate proceedings against them? The answer lies in the Court's interpretation of a much misunderstood provision of the Fifth Amendment, the Double Jeopardy Clause, which states, "nor shall any person be subject for the same offence to be twice put in jeopardy of life or limb."

A great deal of the confusion surrounding this clause stems from the words "same offence." If a man sets fire to an apartment building killing five residents, has he committed one homicide or five? If a man spends an evening robbing a series of liquor stores, has he committed a single offense or several?

What does the Double Jeopardy Clause mean when it prohibits trying a person more than once for the same offense? We find a partial answer in *Ashe v. Swenson* (1970).

Ashe v. Swenson

397 U.S. 436 (1970)
Vote: 7 *(Black, Brennan, Douglas, Harlan, Marshall,*
        Stewart, White)
    1 *(Burger)*
Opinion of the Court: Stewart
Concurring opinions: Black, Brennan, Harlan
Dissenting opinion: Burger

In January 1960 three or four masked and armed individuals broke into John Gladson's house and robbed him and five of his companions with whom he was playing poker. The robbers also stole one of the players' cars to make their getaway. Police found the car abandoned and three of the alleged robbers nearby. They located a fourth suspect "some distance away."

Several months later, the state brought one of the suspects, Ashe, to trial for robbing one of the poker players, Knight. The jury found Ashe not guilty due to insufficient evidence. Six weeks later, the state brought Ashe to trial again, charging him with the same crime, but against Roberts, another poker player. This time the state succeeded—the jury found Ashe guilty as charged. Among other claims, Ashe argued that this second trial violated his double jeopardy guarantee.

MR. JUSTICE STEWART delivered the opinion of the Court.

In Benton v. Maryland [1969] the Court held that the Fifth Amendment guarantee against double jeopardy is enforceable against the States through the Fourteenth Amendment. The question in this case is whether the State of Missouri violated that guarantee when it prosecuted the petitioner a second time for armed robbery....

The question is ... whether collateral estoppel is a requirement ... of the Fifth Amendment's guarantee against double jeopardy. And if collateral estoppel is embodied in that guarantee, then its applicability in a particular case is no longer a matter to be left for state court determination within the broad bounds of "fundamental fairness," but a matter of constitutional fact we must decide through an examination of the entire record.

"Collateral estoppel" is an awkward phrase, but it stands for an extremely important principle in our adversary system of justice. It means simply that when an issue of ultimate fact has once been determined by a valid and final judgment, that issue cannot again be litigated between the same parties in any future lawsuit. Although first developed in civil litigation, collateral estoppel has been an established rule of federal criminal law at least since this Court's decision more than 50 years ago in United States v. Oppenheimer.

The federal decisions have made clear that the rule of collateral estoppel in criminal cases is not to be applied with the hypertechnical and archaic approach of a 19th century pleading book, but with realism and rationality. Where a previous judgment of acquittal was based upon a general verdict, as is usually the case, this approach requires a court to "examine the record of a prior proceeding, taking into account the pleadings, evidence, charge, and other relevant matter, and conclude whether a rational jury could have grounded its verdict upon an issue other than that which the defendant seeks to foreclose from consideration." The inquiry "must be set in a practical frame and viewed with an eye to all circumstances of the proceedings." Any test more technically restrictive would, of course, simply amount to a rejection of the rule of collateral estoppel in criminal proceedings, at least in every case where the first judgment was based upon a general verdict of acquittal.

Straightforward application of the federal rule to the present case can lead to but one conclusion. For the record is utterly devoid of any indication that the first jury could rationally have found that an armed robbery had not occurred, or that Knight had not been a victim of that robbery. The single rationally conceivable issue in dispute before the jury was whether the petitioner had been one of the robbers. And the jury by its verdict found that he had not. The federal rule of law, therefore, would make a second prosecution for the robbery of Roberts wholly impermissible.

The ultimate question to be determined, then, in the light of Benton v. Maryland, is whether this established rule of federal law is embodied in the Fifth Amendment guarantee against double jeopardy. We do not hesitate to hold that it is. For whatever else that constitutional guarantee may embrace, it surely protects a man who has been acquitted from having to "run the gauntlet" a second time.

The question is not whether Missouri could validly charge the petitioner with six separate offenses for the robbery of the six poker players. It is not whether he could have received a total of six punishments if he had been convicted in a single trial of robbing the six victims. It is simply whether, after a jury determined by its verdict that the petitioner was not one of the robbers, the State could constitutionally hale him before a new jury to litigate that issue again.

After the first jury had acquitted the petitioner of robbing Knight, Missouri could certainly not have brought him to trial again upon that charge. Once a jury had determined upon conflicting testimony that there was at least a reasonable doubt that the petitioner was one of the robbers, the State could not present the same or different identification evidence in a second prosecution for the robbery of Knight in the hope that a different jury might find that evidence more convincing. The situation is constitutionally no different here, even though the second trial related to another victim of the same robbery. For the name of the victim, in the circumstances of this case, had no bearing whatever upon the issue of whether the petitioner was one of the robbers.

In this case the State in its brief has frankly conceded that following the petitioner's acquittal, it treated the first trial as no more than a dry run for the second prosecution: "No doubt the prosecutor felt the state had a provable case on the first charge and, when he lost, he did what every good attorney would do—he refined his presentation in light of the turn of events at the first trial." But this is precisely what the constitutional guarantee forbids.

The judgment is reversed, and the case is remanded to the Court of Appeals for the Eighth Circuit for further proceedings consistent with this opinion.

It is so ordered.

Reversed and remanded.

As you can see, the Court adopted Ashe's arguments. In Stewart's words, the Fifth Amendment "surely protects a man who has been acquitted from having to 'run the gauntlet' a second time." But does the Double Jeopardy Clause apply to individuals who have not quite run the gauntlet? That is, must a case have been completed, with a jury or judge reaching a verdict, before the privilege is involved? Or is a case ending in a mistrial or hung jury sufficient to prevent the initiation of new proceedings? In general, the Court historically has allowed a second trial when the first did not reach a conclusion. For example, as early as 1824, in *United States v. Perez*, the justices held that the Double Jeopardy Clause did not bar retrial following a hung jury. In *United States v. Ball* (1896) the Court ruled that convictions overturned on appeal for reasons other than a lack of evidence were subject to retrial. The justices also have held that when trials are terminated on certain mistrial grounds, the defendant may be retried (*Wade v. Hunter*, 1949, and *Illinois v. Sommerville*, 1973).

Cases like *Ashe v. Swenson* and *United States v. Ball* confront the Court with a fundamental question that concerns the Double Jeopardy Clause: When may the government reinitiate proceedings against a defendant? In *Department of Revenue, Montana v. Kurth Ranch* (1994) the justices dealt with a novel variation on that question, namely, do states violate the Double Jeopardy Clause when they follow up a narcotics conviction with a "drug tax" imposed on the illegal substances? This case began in 1987, when police arrested members of the Kurth family for growing marijuana on their Montana ranch. The Kurths pled guilty, and two members of the family received prison sentences.

Ordinarily, a criminal case would end at this point,

but two weeks before the Kurths were arrested, the Drug Tax Act went into effect in Montana. It provided that the state could impose a "dangerous drug tax" against individuals charged with or convicted of illegal drug offenses. For marijuana, the tax was $100 an ounce or eight times the drug's street value.[33]

Under the new law, Montana began additional proceedings against the Kurths, seeking to impose on them a drug tax of almost $900,000. The Kurths fought back. In their view, the tax was a violation of the Double Jeopardy Clause because, among other things, it punished them twice for the same criminal conduct. The state asserted that the tax was not a form of punishment; rather, like most taxes, its purpose was to raise revenue.

The Supreme Court disagreed by a 5–4 vote. Writing for the majority, Justice Stevens asserted that the "proceeding Montana initiated to collect a tax on the possession of drugs was the functional equivalent of a successive criminal prosecution that placed the Kurths in jeopardy a second time 'for the same offence.'" In his opinion Stevens detailed the factors that made Montana's tax punitive in nature: it is extremely high; it is aimed at deterring crime; it "hinges on the commission of a crime"; and it "is exacted only after the taxpayer has been arrested for the precise conduct that gives rise to the tax obligation in the first place."

Four justices—Rehnquist, Scalia, O'Connor, and Thomas—in three separate opinions disagreed with this logic. Their reasons differed slightly, but almost all concurred with the state: because the tax was not punitive in nature, it did not constitute a violation of the Double Jeopardy Clause. For that and other rea-

sons, O'Connor went so far as to conclude that the majority's opinion represented "an unwarranted expansion of our double jeopardy clause jurisprudence." Do you agree? Or was *Kurth* a reasonable application of existing precedent? The answer depends, as the Court's opinions reveal, on whether you think the tax is punitive in nature.

READINGS

"Bail: An Ancient Practice Reexamined." *Yale Law Journal* (1961): 966.

Baldus, David C., George G. Woodworth, and Charles A. Pulaski, Jr. *Equal Justice and the Death Penalty.* Boston: Northeastern University Press, 1990.

Eisenstein, James, and Herbert Jacob. *Felony Justice.* Boston: Little, Brown, 1977.

Epstein, Lee, and Joseph F. Kobylka. *The Supreme Court and Legal Change.* Chapel Hill: University of North Carolina Press, 1992.

Goldfarb, Ronald. *Ransom: A Critique of the American Bail System.* New York: Harper & Row, 1965.

Hastie, Reid, Steven D. Penrod, and Nancy Pennington. *Inside the Jury.* Cambridge: Harvard University Press, 1983.

Heumann, Milton. *Plea Bargaining.* Chicago: University of Chicago Press, 1978.

Kalven, Harry, Jr., and Hans Zeisel. *The American Jury.* Boston: Little, Brown, 1966.

Lewis, Anthony. *Gideon's Trumpet.* New York: Vintage Books, 1964.

Meltsner, Michael. *Cruel and Unusual: The Supreme Court and Capital Punishment.* New York: Random House, 1973.

Sigler, Jay A. *Double Jeopardy: The Development of Legal and Social Policy.* Ithaca, N.Y.: Cornell University Press, 1969.

Simon, Rita James. *The Jury: Its Role in American Society.* Lexington, Mass.: Lexington Books, 1980.

Way, Frank H. *Criminal Justice and the American Constitution.* North Scituate, Mass.: Duxbury Press, 1980.

Wishman, Seymour. *Confessions of a Criminal Lawyer.* New York: Penguin Books, 1982.

---

33. Montana was not alone in enacting such a tax; twenty-six other states had adopted similar laws mostly intended to wage war on illegal drugs. See Linda Greenhouse, "Supreme Court Says Tax in Drug Cases Is Unconstitutional," *New York Times*, June 7, 1994, 1.

PART IV
CIVIL RIGHTS AND THE CONSTITUTION

IN MARKED CONTRAST to the colonial period, in which most Americans were from British roots, today the citizens of the United States are from many different backgrounds. Immigration has diversified the population, and this trend is expected to continue. Americans are a people of wide-ranging religions, races, ethnic backgrounds, and levels of wealth. The slogan, "e pluribus unum" or "one from many," often appears to be more of a challenge than a statement of fact. In spite of the differences, however, the nation has pledged itself to fairness and equality. All Americans are to be free from unconstitutional discrimination, to have equal opportunity, and to participate fully in the political process.

Many times people feel they have been mistreated by their government, not because of what they have done but because of who they are. They claim that discrimination has occurred because of race, creed, national origin, sex, economic status, or some other characteristic that government should not use as a basis for policy. When disputes over such charges arise, the court system provides a venue for their resolution. In this part, we discuss the civil rights of Americans and how the Supreme Court has interpreted them. By civil rights we mean those legal provisions emanating from the concept of equality. Unlike civil liberties issues, which focus on personal freedoms protected by the Bill of Rights, civil rights issues involve the status of persons with shared characteristics who historically have been disadvantaged in some way. Civil rights laws attempt to guarantee full and equal citizenship for such persons and to protect them from arbitrary and capricious treatment. Chapter 10 examines discrimination, and Chapter 11 the rights of political participation. Before we confront those subjects, however, a review of some basic concepts of history and law might be useful.

THE CONSTITUTION AND THE CONCEPT OF EQUALITY

Today, we have become accustomed to hearing not only about charges of discrimination, but also Supreme Court rulings on the proper meaning of the Constitution governing such issues. These phenomena are comparatively recent. Although "equality" in the United States was relatively advanced for those times, colonial Americans discriminated in a number of ways that we now consider abhorrent. The most significant breach of fundamental equality was the institution of slavery. In spite of the Declaration of Independence, which proclaimed all men to be created equal, the enslavement of Africans brought to North America against their will was politically accepted, although not universally supported. The Constitution recognized this form of inequality, stipulating in Article I that a slave would be counted as three-fifths of a person for representation purposes; it also gave slavery a degree of protection by prohibiting any federal restrictions on the importation of slaves until 1808. Other forms of discrimination also were common. Voting qualifications, for example, were quite restrictive: only men could vote, and in some states only men who owned property could vote.

Guarantees of equality did not officially become part of the Constitution until after the Civil War. When the Radical Republicans took control of the legislative branch, three constitutional amendments were proposed and ratified that would change dramatically the concept of civil rights in the United States. These amendments, the Thirteenth, Fourteenth, and Fifteenth, are generally referred to as the Civil War Amendments (*see Box IV–1*). They incorporated into the Constitution what had been won on the battlefield.

The Thirteenth Amendment was ratified in 1865. The language of the amendment unambiguously ended the institution of slavery. Although there have been some disputes over the involuntary servitude prohibition (in relation, for example, to the military draft), the slavery issue, over which the nation had been divided since the Constitutional Convention, was finally put to rest.

The Fourteenth Amendment is unlike the other two because of its length and complexity. The first section is the most significant. In that passage, United States citizenship is accorded superior status to state citizenship, constitutionally reinforcing the Civil War outcome of national superiority over states' rights. This idea was a dramatic change from the pre–Civil War concept that national citizenship was dependent upon state citizenship. The first section also includes the Due Process and Privileges and Im-

munities Clauses we have discussed in earlier chapters, as well as the Equal Protection Clause, which forms the basis of constitutional protections against discrimination. The remaining sections of the Fourteenth Amendment require the former slaves to be fully counted for representational purposes, impose universal adult male suffrage, restrict the civil rights of certain participants in the rebellion, and guarantee the public debt resulting from the war. The amendment was ratified in 1868.

The Fifteenth Amendment removed race as a condition by which the right to vote could be denied. Unlike the Thirteenth Amendment, which was almost self-executing, the policy expressed so clearly in the Fifteenth Amendment in 1870 did not become a reality until almost a century later. Stubborn resistance by the southern states denied black citizens full participatory rights. It was not until the 1960s, when the nation renewed its commitment to civil rights, that equality in voting rights was substantially achieved.

The long delay in implementing the principles of the Fifteenth Amendment was not unique. The nation's leaders seemed unshakably committed to equality right after the Civil War, but they turned their attention to other matters. Issues ranging from political corruption to the nation's industrialization moved to the top of the political agenda. At the same time, the white power structure of the prewar South began to reassert itself. Although forced to accept the Civil War Amendments as a condition of rejoining the union, the southern states survived Reconstruction and, once freed from the direct supervision of their victors, began to reinstitute discriminatory laws. Slavery was never again seriously considered, but, in its place, racial segregation became the official policy. For years the federal legislative and executive branches showed little interest in pursuing civil rights issues, and the Supreme Court dealt with such matters only on occasion. It was not until the civil rights movement gained momentum in the 1960s that the

BOX IV-1   THE CIVIL WAR AMENDMENTS

AMENDMENT 13
(Ratified December 6, 1865)

SECTION 1. Neither slavery nor involuntary servitude, except as a punishment for crime whereof the party shall have been duly convicted, shall exist within the United States, or any place subject to their jurisdiction.

SECTION 2. Congress shall have power to enforce this article by appropriate legislation.

AMENDMENT 14
(Ratified July 9, 1868)

SECTION 1. All persons born or naturalized in the United States, and subject to the jurisdiction thereof, are citizens of the United States and of the State wherein they reside. No State shall make or enforce any law which shall abridge the privileges or immunities of citizens of the United States; nor shall any State deprive any person of life, liberty, or property, without due process of law; nor deny to any person within its jurisdiction the equal protection of the laws.

SECTION 2. Representatives shall be apportioned among the several States according to their respective numbers, counting the whole number of persons in each State, excluding Indians not taxed. But when the right to vote at any election for the choice of electors for President and Vice President of the United States, Representatives in Congress, the Executive and Judicial officers of a State, or the members of the Legislature thereof, is denied to any of the male inhabitants of such State, being twenty-one years of age, and citizens of the United States, or in any way abridged, except for participation in rebellion, or other crime, the basis of representation therein shall be reduced in the proportion which the number of such male citizens shall bear to the whole number of male citizens twenty-one years of age in such State.

SECTION 3. No person shall be a Senator or Representative in Congress, or elector of President or Vice President, or hold any office, civil or military, under the United States, or under any State, who, having previously taken an oath, as a member of Congress, or as an officer of the United States, or as a member of any State legislature, or as an executive or judicial officer to any State, to support the Constitution of the United States, shall have engaged in insurrection or rebellion against the same, or given aid or comfort to the enemies thereof. But Congress may by a vote of two-thirds of each House, remove such disability.

SECTION 4. The validity of the public debt of the United States, authorized by law, including debts incurred for payment of pensions and bounties for services in suppressing insurrection or rebellion, shall not be questioned. But neither the United States nor any State shall assume or pay any debt or obligation incurred in aid of insurrection or rebellion against the United States, or claim for the loss or emancipation of any slave; but all such debts, obligations and claims shall be held illegal and void.

SECTION 5. The Congress shall have power to enforce, by appropriate legislation, the provisions of this article.

AMENDMENT 15
(Ratified February 3, 1870)

SECTION 1. The rights of the citizens of the United States to vote shall not be denied or abridged by the United States or by any State on account of race, color, or previous condition of servitude.

SECTION 2. The Congress shall have power to enforce this article by appropriate legislation.

nation again turned its attention to freedom from discrimination and full participatory rights for all.

THE SUPREME COURT AND EQUAL PROTECTION OF THE LAWS

The Equal Protection Clause of the Fourteenth Amendment is the Constitution's most important passage with respect to issues of discrimination. An analysis of the wording of this brief provision will help us understand what it covers and what its limitations are. It says, "[N]or shall any State ... deny to any person within its jurisdiction the equal protection of the laws."

The first significant element of the clause is the

word *state.* The members of Congress who drafted the Fourteenth Amendment were concerned primarily with the danger of the states (especially those in the South) imposing discriminatory laws. With the Radical Republicans, who were deeply committed to an abolition ideology, in full control of Congress and the White House, the legislators had little fear that the federal government would impose discriminatory policies. Consequently, the prohibitions of the clause apply only to the states and their political subdivisions, such as counties and cities.

Second, the amendment protects all persons within a state's jurisdiction. Although the authors of the amendment were primarily interested in the treatment of the former slaves, the wording of the amendment is not restricted to them. Quite early in the history of disputes over the amendment, the Supreme Court acknowledged its broad applicability. In *Yick Wo v. Hopkins* (1886), a dispute over the enforcement of fire safety regulations in San Francisco, the Court held that the Equal Protection Clause applies to persons other than black Americans, also protecting noncitizens who are the target of discrimination by the state.

Finally, the clause outlaws a denial of equal protection of the laws; in other words, it prohibits discrimination. Any person within a state's jurisdiction is constitutionally entitled to be treated equitably, to be free from arbitrary and unreasonable treatment at the hands of the state government.

The wording of the Equal Protection Clause means that before an individual can legitimately assert a claim of its violation, two important elements must be demonstrated. First, the aggrieved party must prove some form of unequal treatment or discrimination. Second, there must be state action; that is, the discrimination must have been initiated or supported by the state or its local governments. These two requirements have undergone substantial interpretation by the justices of the Supreme Court, and we need to understand what is included in each requirement.

Discrimination

Discrimination simply means to distinguish between people or things. It occurs in many forms, not all of which are prohibited by the Constitution. For example, in administering an admissions program, a state university must discriminate among its applicants. It admits some, rejects others. Decisions usually are based on an applicant's high school grades, standardized test scores, and letters of recommendation. The university admits those who, based on valid predictors of performance, have the best chance to succeed. Those who are rejected usually accept the decision because the university's admissions criteria appear reasonable. But the reaction would be quite different if an applicant received a letter that said, "In spite of your demonstrated potential for college studies, we cannot admit you because of our policy not to accept students of your ethnic background." In this case, the rejected applicant would rightly feel victimized by unreasonable discrimination.

What rule of law distinguishes acceptable discrimination from that which is in violation of the Constitution? The Supreme Court answered this question by declaring that the Equal Protection Clause goes no further than prohibiting "invidious discrimination."[1] By invidious discrimination, the Court means discrimination that is arbitrary and capricious, unequal treatment that has no rational basis. Reasonable discrimination, on the other hand, is not unconstitutional. When the state treats two individuals differently, we need to ask upon what criteria the state is distinguishing them. If two surgeons perform heart operations on patients and one is thrown in jail and the other is not, we might feel that the imprisoned person has not been treated fairly. Our opinion would change, however, if we learned that this "surgeon" had never been to medical school and was not licensed. Here the state would be discriminating on the basis of legitimate, reasonable criteria. The Equal Pro-

---

1. See *Williamson v. Lee Optical* (1955).

tection Clause demands that similarly situated persons be treated equally. The two surgeons, because of their vastly different qualifications, are not similarly situated, and consequently the Constitution does not require that they be treated the same.

Almost every government action involves some form of discrimination. Most are perfectly legitimate, although all those affected might not agree. For example, when a state government passes an income tax law that imposes a higher rate on the wealthy than it does on the poor, the rich may feel they are the target of unconstitutional discrimination. When individuals believe they have been denied equal protection at the hands of the state, the courts must decide if the government's discrimination runs afoul of the Fourteenth Amendment. For taxes, the courts have ruled that progressive rate structures are not invidious, but reasonable.

To assist the judiciary in deciding such disputes, the Supreme Court has developed three basic tests of the Equal Protection Clause. Which test is applied in any given case is determined by the alleged discrimination and the government interests at stake.

The traditional test used to decide discrimination cases is the "rational basis" test. When using this approach to the Constitution, the justices ask: Is the challenged discrimination rational? Or is it arbitrary and capricious? If a state passes a law that says a person must be at least eighteen years old to enter a legally binding contract, it is imposing an age-based discrimination. Individuals under eighteen are not granted the right to consummate legal agreements; those over eighteen are. If a dispute over the validity of this law were brought to court, the judge would have to decide whether the state had acted reasonably to achieve a legitimate government objective.[2] Using the rational basis test, the Court generally defers to the state and presumes the validity of the government's action. The burden of proof rests with the party challenging the law to establish that the statute is irrational. Unless the Court has determined otherwise, discrimination claims proceed according to the rules of the rational basis test.

The second test is called the "suspect class" or "strict scrutiny" test. This test is used when the state discriminates on the basis of a criterion that the Supreme Court has declared to be inherently suspect or when there is a claim that a fundamental right has been violated. A suspect classification is based on characteristics assumed to be irrational. The Supreme Court has ruled, for example, that race is a suspect class. Laws that discriminate on racial grounds are given strict scrutiny by the courts. The reason for moving racial discrimination from the rational basis test to the suspect class test is that the Supreme Court has concluded that racial criteria are inherently arbitrary, that compelling state interests are rarely (if ever) served by treating people differently according to race. For a law to be valid under strict scrutiny, it must be found to advance a compelling state interest by the least restrictive means available. When the suspect class test is used, the Court presumes that the state action is unconstitutional, and the burden of proof is on the government to demonstrate that the law is rational.

Given the rules associated with these two tests, it should be obvious that it is much easier to establish that a violation of the Constitution has occurred if the suspect class test is used. Therefore, many cases before the Supreme Court have been filed by attorneys representing groups seeking that classification. The Court has ruled that suspect class status should be accorded only to those groups that constitute discrete and insular minorities that have experienced a history of unequal treatment and a lack of political power.[3] Applying such criteria is difficult and has given rise to sharp divisions of opinion among the justices.

---

2. See *McGowan v. Maryland*, 366 U.S. 420 (1961).

3. See *United States v. Carolene Products* (1938); *San Antonio Independent School District v. Rodriguez* (1973).

TABLE IV-1 Equal Protection Tests

Test	Examples of Applicability	Validity Standard
Rational basis test	General discrimination claims	The law must be a *reasonable* measure designed to achieve a *legitimate* government purpose.
Intermediate ("heightened") scrutiny test	Sex discrimination	The law must be *substantially related* to the achievement of an *important* objective.
Suspect class (strict scrutiny) test	Racial discrimination; cases involving fundamental rights (e.g., voting)	The law must be the *least restrictive* means available to achieve a *compelling* state interest.

Legal battles over what rules should apply to sex discrimination cases were particularly difficult for the Court to resolve.[4] A majority could not agree to elevate sex to suspect class status, but there was substantial opinion that the rational basis test was also inappropriate for dealing with sex discrimination. This conflict gave rise to a third test of the Equal Protection Clause, the "intermediate (or heightened) scrutiny" test. This test holds that to be valid the unequal treatment must serve important government objectives and must be substantially related to the achievement of those objectives.[5] As such, this test falls squarely between the rational basis test and the suspect class test (*see Table IV-1*).

To be sure, this three-tiered approach can be confusing, and the Supreme Court has been neither clear nor consistent in applying the principles. Justice Marshall in *Dunn v. Blumstein* (1972) acknowledged that the tests do not have the "precision of mathematical formulas." Justice White hinted that in reality the Court may be using a spectrum of tests rather than three separate tests. Frustration over the status of the Equal Protection Clause tests prompted Justice Stevens to claim in his concurring opinion in *Cleburne v. Cleburne Living Center* (1985) that a continuum of

standards was being used. Not persuaded of the wisdom of the Court's approach, Stevens has argued that a single test should be adopted for all equal protection claims. In spite of these criticisms, the Court has stuck to the three-tiered approach, which reflects the belief that the more historically disadvantaged and politically powerless a class of people has been, the greater justification government must provide for any state action that discriminates against the members of that class.

State Action

As we have noted, the Equal Protection Clause specifically prohibits discrimination by any state. The Supreme Court has interpreted this concept to include a wide array of state actions—statutes, their enforcement and administration, and the actions of state officials. For example, in *Yick Wo v. Hopkins* the Court struck down a fire safety regulation that was racially neutral as written but enforced in a discriminatory manner against Chinese laundry operators. State action includes the policies of political subdivisions such as towns, cities, counties, or special purpose agencies. The states are prohibited from engaging in invidious discrimination either directly or indirectly. A city, for instance, may not run its municipal swimming pools in a racially segregated manner, nor may it donate the

4. See, for example, *Frontiero v. Richardson* (1973).
5. *Craig v. Boren* (1976).

pools to a private organization that will restrict pool use to a particular racial group. In whatever form, however, some element of state action supporting invidious discrimination must be shown before a violation of the Equal Protection Clause occurs.

This requirement means that discrimination by purely private individuals or organizations is not prohibited by the Equal Protection Clause. A white apartment house owner who refuses to rent to a black family is not in violation of the Constitution; neither is a restaurant manager who will not serve Hispanics, a private club that will not admit women, nor an employer who will not hire applicants over forty years of age. In each of these cases there is ample evidence of irrational discrimination, but no state action. The discrimination is conducted by private individuals or organizations. These forms of discrimination may well be in violation of any number of state or federal statutes, but they do not offend the Equal Protection Clause of the Fourteenth Amendment.

Moreover, because it is restricted to the states, the Equal Protection Clause does not prohibit the federal government from engaging in discrimination. The Supreme Court, therefore, faced a difficult situation in 1954 in the school desegregation cases. The best-known case is *Brown v. Board of Education of Topeka, Kansas,* but *Brown* was only one of several cases involving the same basic issue. In *Bolling v. Sharpe* the Court faced the thorny issue of racial segregation in the Washington, D.C., public schools. The District of Columbia is not a state. In the 1950s, as now, Congress was the ultimate authority over Washington. The Equal Protection Clause was not applicable there. Given the political situation at the time, the Court had to find a way to declare *all* segregated schools unconstitutional.

The justices found a solution in the Due Process Clause of the Fifth Amendment, which states, "No person shall ... be deprived of life, liberty, or property, without due process of law." This guarantee of essential fairness applies to the federal government

and was used by the justices in *Bolling* as a bar against racial discrimination. Chief Justice Warren explained for a unanimous Court:

The Fifth Amendment, which is applicable in the District of Columbia, does not contain an equal protection clause as does the Fourteenth Amendment which applies only to the states. But the concepts of equal protection and due process, both stemming from our American ideal of fairness, are not mutually exclusive. The "equal protection of the laws" is a more explicit safeguard of prohibited unfairness than "due process of law," and, therefore, we do not imply that the two are always interchangeable phrases. But, as this Court has recognized, discrimination may be so unjustifiable as to be violative of due process.

While Warren cautioned that the Due Process Clause and the Equal Protection Clause could not be used interchangeably, the Court has consistently ruled that both provisions stand for the same general principles. In most areas of discrimination law (but not all), the justices have applied the same standards to both state and federal governments by using these two constitutional provisions. As a rule, any discriminatory action by a state found to be in violation of the Equal Protection Clause would also be a violation of the Fifth Amendment if engaged in by the federal government. However, we should understand which provision of the Constitution is offended when invidious discrimination is practiced by either state governments or the federal government. If the U.S. National Park Service were to require racially segregated camp grounds at Yellowstone, it would violate the Due Process Clause of the Fifth Amendment; if a state imposed the same restriction at a state park, it would violate the Equal Protection Clause of the Fourteenth Amendment.

CONGRESSIONAL ENFORCEMENT OF CIVIL RIGHTS

The civil rights of Americans are defined and protected by more than just the Constitution. Over the years Congress has passed laws designed to enforce and extend constitutional guarantees *(see Box IV-2)*. These laws expand prohibitions against discriminatory behavior, give the federal executive branch authority to enforce civil rights protections, and enlarge the opportunities for aggrieved parties to seek redress in the courts. The rules of evidence and procedure in some of these laws make it easier for litigants to prevail by proving a violation of a civil rights statute rather than a constitutional violation.

The authority for Congress to pass such laws can be found in several constitutional provisions. The Civil War Amendments each contain a section granting Congress the power to enforce the amendment with appropriate legislation. Consequently, these amendments have had considerable impact not only because of their basic substantive content, but also because they give Congress new legislative power. Immediately following the Civil War, Congress used this authority to pass laws intended to give the new amendments teeth. For example, the Civil Rights Act of 1866, passed over the veto of President Andrew Johnson, guaranteed blacks the right to purchase, lease, and use real property. The Supreme Court upheld the law, ruling that the Thirteenth Amendment's enforcement section gave Congress the power not only to outlaw slavery but also to legislate against the "badges and incidents of slavery."[6] Much of the federal regulation on fair housing is based on this authority.

Congress learned by trial and error to ground legislation in the correct Civil War Amendment. In 1883 the Supreme Court handed down its decisions in *The Civil Rights Cases,* which involved challenges to the Civil Rights Act of 1875, a statute based on the Fourteenth Amendment that made discrimination in public accommodations unlawful. Because the law covered privately owned businesses, the owners of hotels, entertainment facilities, and transportation companies claimed that Congress had exceeded the authority granted to it by the amendment. The Court, with only one justice dissenting, struck down the statute, holding that any legislation based on the Fourteenth Amendment could regulate only discrimination promoted by state action. Discrimination by private individuals was not covered by the amendment and, therefore, Congress could not prohibit it through an enforcement statute.

Congress eventually was able to pierce the private discrimination veil by finding a different constitutional grant of power upon which to base the Civil Rights Act of 1964. The most comprehensive civil rights statute ever, the law regulated discrimination in employment, education, and public accommodations. It placed restrictions on federal appropriations and programs to ensure that nondiscrimination principles were followed in any activity supported by the U.S. government. The act outlawed discrimination based not only on race but also on other factors as well, such as sex, national origin, and religion. Much of what was regulated by the statute was private behavior, including prohibitions of discrimination by restaurants, hotels, and other privately run public accommodations. Rather than the Fourteenth Amendment, Congress used the Commerce Clause of Article I. That clause gives the national legislature the power to regulate interstate commerce, and the provisions of the 1964 Civil Rights Act apply to all activities in interstate commerce. The Supreme Court upheld the constitutionality of the law and gave it increased effectiveness by broadly defining what is considered to be within interstate commerce.[7] The same commerce power has allowed Congress to pass additional statutes that extend civil rights protection beyond what was intended by the Civil War Amendments.

The Fifteenth Amendment, prohibiting states from denying the right to vote on the basis of race, also has extended significant powers to the federal government to preserve fairness and equality in the political

---

6. *Jones v. Alfred H. Mayer, Inc.* (1968).

7. See *Heart of Atlanta Motel v. United States* (1964); *Katzenbach v. McClung* (1964).

BOX IV-2   MAJOR CIVIL RIGHTS ACTS

CIVIL RIGHTS ACTS OF 1866, 1870, 1871, AND 1875.

Laws passed by Congress after the Civil War to guarantee the rights of blacks. The public accommodation provisions of the 1875 law were declared unconstitutional by the Supreme Court in the Civil Rights Cases (1883), as a federal invasion of private rights. Other provisions of these laws were struck down by the courts or repealed by Congress. Today, a few major provisions remain from the acts of 1866 and 1871. One makes it a federal crime for any person acting under the authority of a state law to deprive another of any rights protected by the Constitution or by laws of the United States. Another authorizes suits for civil damages against state or local officials by persons whose rights are abridged. Others permit actions against persons who conspire to deprive people of their rights.

CIVIL RIGHTS ACT OF 1957.

The first civil rights law passed by Congress since Reconstruction, designed to secure the right to vote for blacks. Its major feature empowers the Department of Justice to seek court injunctions against any deprivation of voting rights, and authorizes criminal prosecutions for violations of an injunction. In addition, the act established a Civil Rights Division, headed by an Assistant Attorney General in the Department of Justice, and created a bipartisan Civil Rights Commission to investigate civil rights violations and to recommend legislation.

CIVIL RIGHTS ACT OF 1960.

A law designed to further secure the right to vote for blacks and to meet the problems arising from racial upheavals in the South in the late 1950s. The major provision authorizes federal courts to appoint referees who will help blacks to register after a voter-denial conviction is obtained under the 1957 Civil Rights Act, and after a court finding of a "pattern or practice" of discrimination against qualified voters. Other provisions: (1) authorize punishment for persons who obstruct any federal court order, such as a school desegregation order, by threats or force; (2) authorize criminal penalties for transportation of explosives for the purpose of bombing a building; (3) require preservation of voting records for twenty-two months, and authorize the Attorney General to inspect the records; (4) provide for schooling of children of armed forces personnel in the event that a school closes because of an integration dispute.

CIVIL RIGHTS ACT OF 1964.

A major enactment designed to erase racial discrimination in most areas of American life. Major provisions of the act: (1) outlaw arbitrary discrimination in voter registration and expedite voting rights suits; (2) bar discrimination in public accommodations, such as hotels and restaurants, that have a substantial relation to interstate commerce; (3) authorize the national government to bring suits to desegregate public facilities and schools; (4) extend the life and expand the power of the Civil Rights Commission; (5) provide for the withholding of federal funds from programs administered in a discriminatory manner; (6) establish the right to equality in employment opportunities; and (7) establish a Community Relations Service to help resolve civil rights problems. The act forbids discrimination based on race, color, religion, national origin, and, in the case of employment, sex. Techniques for gaining voluntary compliance are stressed in the act, and the resolution of civil rights problems through state and local action is encouraged. Discrimination in housing is not covered by the law, but is prohibited by the Civil Rights Act of 1968.

Significance. The Civil Rights Act of 1964 is the most far-reaching civil rights legislation since Reconstruction. It was passed after the longest debate in Senate history (eighty-three days) and only after cloture was invoked for the first time to cut off a civil rights filibuster. Compliance with the act's controversial provisions on public accommodations and equal employment opportunities has been widespread. Title VI of the act, which authorizes the cutoff of federal funds to state and local programs practicing discrimination, proved to be the most effective provision of the act. For example, a dramatic jump in southern school integration took place when the national government threatened to withhold federal funds from schools failing to comply with desegregation orders. All agencies receiving federal funds are required to submit assurance of compliance with the 1964 act. Hundreds of grant-in-aid programs are involved, amounting to 20 percent of all state and local revenues.

CIVIL RIGHTS ACT OF 1968.

A law which prohibits discrimination on the advertising, financing, sale, or rental of housing, based on race, religion, or national origin and, as of 1974, sex, but provided limited and ineffective enforcement powers. A major amendment to the act in 1988 extended coverage to the handicapped and to families with children and added enforcement machinery through either administrative enforcement by the Department of Housing and Urban Development (HUD) or by

BOX IV-2   MAJOR CIVIL RIGHTS ACTS *(continued)*

suits filed in federal court, with the choice of forums left to either party in the dispute. The law covers about 80 percent of all housing. Major exclusions are owner-occupied dwellings of four units or less and those selling without services of a broker.

VOTING RIGHTS ACT

A major law enacted by Congress in 1965 and renewed and expanded in 1970, 1975, and 1982 that has sought to eliminate restrictions on voting that have been used to discriminate against blacks and other minority groups. A major provision of the 1965 act suspended the use of literacy and other tests used to discriminate. The act also authorized registration by federal registrars in any state or county where such tests had been used and where less than 50 percent of eligible voters were registered. Seven southern states were mainly affected by these provisions. The act also authorized a legal test of poll taxes in state elections, and the Supreme Court in 1966 declared payment of poll taxes as a condition of voting to be unconstitutional. Major provisions of the 1965 act were upheld by the Court as a valid exercise of power under the Fifteenth Amendment. The Voting Rights Act of 1970: (1) extended the 1965 act for five years; (2) lowered the minimum age for all elections from twenty-one to eighteen; (3) prohibited the states from disqualifying voters in presidential elections because of their failure to meet state residence requirements beyond thirty days; and (4) provided for uniform national rules for absentee registration and voting in presidential elections. In 1970 the Court upheld the eighteen-year-old vote for national elections but found its application to state and local elections unconstitutional. In 1975 the act was continued for seven years. Federal voting protection was extended to all parts of ten additional states, bilingual ballots were required, election law changes in states covered by the act were required to be approved by either a United States attorney or a federal court, and legal protection of voting rights was extended to Spanish-Americans, Alaskan natives, American Indians, and Asian-Americans. The 1982 act extends the law for twenty-five years, authorizes a "bailout" for covered states showing a clear record for ten years, and provides the intent to discriminate need not be proven if the results demonstrate otherwise.

CIVIL RIGHTS ACT OF 1991.

A reaffirmation and expansion of protection against discrimination in employment. The main purpose of the legislation was to overturn several 1989 Supreme Court decisions that made it harder for employees to challenge or prove discrimination, that narrowly interpreted the scope of civil rights laws, and that limited access to the courts.

SOURCE: Jack C. Plano and Milton Greenberg, *The American Political Dictionary* (Fort Worth, Texas: Harcourt Brace Jovanovich, 1993).

process. So too have the Nineteenth, Twenty-fourth, and Twenty-sixth Amendments, which expanded the electorate by limiting state discrimination based on sex, the ability to pay a tax, and age. From the enforcement provisions of these four voting rights amendments, Congress has passed a number of statutes ensuring the integrity of the election process. The most important of these is the Voting Rights Act of 1965, which has been strengthened by amendment over the years. This statute provided the machinery for federal enforcement and prosecution of voting rights violations. Its provisions have been the catalyst for significant growth in voter registration rates among segments of the population where political participation historically has been depressed.

Because this volume deals with constitutional law, our discussion of the various forms of discrimination focuses on the civil rights guarantees provided by our nation's fundamental law. It should be kept in mind, however, that in many areas Congress has passed statutes that extend those constitutional provisions to create various legal rights that go well beyond protections included in the Constitution itself.

CHAPTER 10
DISCRIMINATION

D ISCRIMINATION has been a difficult and persistent problem for the United States since its beginnings. Although our Founders were considered the vanguard of enlightened politics, different treatment based on race, economic status, religious affiliation, and sex was the rule in the colonies. Since those early years of nationhood, issues of discrimination have been prominent on the country's political agenda. During the first half of our history, slavery eroded national unity. Although officially settled by the Civil War and the constitutional amendments that followed, racial inequity did not disappear. Rather, it continued through the Jim Crow era, the organized civil rights struggle that followed, and it persists, in some degree, today.

The twentieth century also has seen the national spotlight turn to claims of unfair treatment by women, the poor, aliens, ethnic minorities, the handicapped, and other disadvantaged segments of society. Attempts to address these claims have given rise to arguments against an expansive government response by those who fear that a government overly sensitive to the needs of minorities will deprive the majority of its rights. With each new claim and counterclaim, the issues become more complex. This chapter explores how the justices of the Supreme Court have interpreted the Constitution in response to these conflicting claims.

RACIAL DISCRIMINATION

The institution of slavery is a blight on the record of a nation that otherwise has led the way in protecting individual rights. From 1619, when the first slaves were brought to Jamestown, to the ratification of the Civil War Amendments 250 years later, people of African ancestry were considered an inferior race; they could be bought, sold, and used as personal property. Although some states extended various civil and political rights to emancipated slaves and their descendants, the national Constitution did not recognize black Americans as full citizens. In *Scott v. Sandford* (1857), Chief Justice Taney, delivering the opinion of the Court, described the prevailing view of blacks at the time the Constitution was written:

They had for more than a century before been regarded as beings of an inferior order, and altogether unfit to associate with the white race, either in social or political relations; and so far inferior, that they had no rights which the white man was bound to respect; and that the negro might justly and lawfully be reduced to slavery for his benefit. He was bought and sold, and treated as an ordinary article of merchandise and traffic, whenever a profit could be made by it. This opinion was at that time fixed and universal in the civilized portion of the white race.

The Court's decision in *Scott v. Sanford* interpreted the Constitution consistent with this view and helped set the stage for the Civil War. The ruling, which held that a black slave could not become a full member of the political community and be entitled to all of the constitutional privileges of citizens, undermined the legitimacy of the Court and forever damaged Taney's reputation. It was only because of the Union victories on the battlefield that the Constitution was later amended to end slavery and confer full national citizenship on black Americans.

Congress moved with dispatch to give force to the new amendments, but the Supreme Court did not act with the same level of zeal. Although the justices supported the claims of newly emancipated black Americans in some cases, they did not construe the new amendments broadly, nor did they enthusiastically support new legislation designed to enforce them. In the *Slaughterhouse Cases* (1873) for example, the Court interpreted the Fourteenth Amendment's Privileges and Immunities Clause quite narrowly. In *United States v. Harris* (1883) and the *Civil Rights Cases* (1883), the justices nullified major provisions of the Ku Klux Klan Act of 1871 and the Civil Rights Act of 1875 for failure to confine statutory provisions to discriminatory actions by the state. It was clear that the battle for legal equality of the races was not over.

Equality

By the end of the nineteenth century, the Supreme Court still had not answered what was perhaps the most important question arising from the Fourteenth Amendment: What is equal protection? As the vitality of the Reconstruction Acts and federal efforts to enforce them gradually waned, the political forces of the old order began to reassert control in the South. During this period, known as the Jim Crow era, what progress had been made to achieve racial equality not only came to a halt but also began to run in reverse. The South, where 90 percent of the minority population lived, began to enact laws that reimposed an inferior legal status on blacks and commanded a strict separation of the races. Northern liberals were of little

help. With the battle against slavery won, they turned their attention to other issues.

While the Constitution made it clear that slavery was dead and the right to vote could not be denied on the basis of race, the validity of many other racially based state actions remained unresolved. With more conservative political forces gaining power in Congress, it was left to the Court, still smarting from the *Scott* debacle, to give meaning to the constitutional guarantee of equal protection of the laws.

The most important case of this period was *Plessy v. Ferguson*, in which the justices were forced to confront directly the meaning of equality under the Constitution. At odds were the Equal Protection Clause of the Fourteenth Amendment and a host of segregation statutes by then in force in the southern and border states. While reading the *Plessy* decision, note that the Court uses the reasonableness standard (rational basis test) to interpret the Equal Protection Clause. Ironically, the majority opinion upholding the separation standards of the South was written by Justice Henry B. Brown, a Lincoln Republican, who had grown up in New England and supported the abolitionist movement. The lone dissent was registered by Justice Harlan, an aristocratic Kentuckian, whose family had owned slaves. Harlan's dissent is considered a classic and one of the most prophetic ever registered.

Plessy v. Ferguson

163 U.S. 537 (1896)
Vote: 7 (Brown, Field, Fuller, Gray, Peckham, Shiras, White)
    1 (Harlan)
Opinion of the Court: Brown
Dissenting opinion: Harlan
Not participating: Brewer

In 1890 Louisiana, following the lead of Florida, Mississippi, and Texas, passed a statute commanding the separation of the races on all railroads. The act was opposed by an organized group of New Orleans residents of black and mixed-race heritage, with the support of the railroads. Attempts to have the judiciary invalidate the statute were partially successful when the Louisiana Supreme Court struck down the law as applied to passengers crossing state lines for placing an unconstitutional burden on interstate commerce. This decision, however, left unanswered the question of segregated travel wholly within the state's borders.

On June 7, 1892, as part of the litigation strategy, Homer Adolph Plessy, who described himself as "of seven-eighths Caucasian and one-eighth African blood," bought a first-class rail ticket from New Orleans to Covington, Louisiana. He took a seat in a car reserved for white passengers. The conductor demanded that Plessy, under pain of ejection and imprisonment, move to a car for black passengers. Plessy refused. With the help of a police officer, Plessy was taken off the train and held in a New Orleans jail to await trial.

His lawyer moved to block the trial on the grounds that the segregation law was in violation of the U.S. Constitution. Judge John Ferguson denied the motion, and appeal was taken to the Louisiana Supreme Court. The state high court, under the leadership of Chief Justice Francis Tillou Nicholls, who, as governor two years earlier, had signed the segregation statute into law, denied Plessy's petition, and the case moved to the U.S. Supreme Court.

MR. JUSTICE BROWN delivered the opinion of the Court.

This case turns upon the constitutionality of an act of the General Assembly of the State of Louisiana, passed in 1890, providing for separate railway carriages for the white and colored races....

By the Fourteenth Amendment, all persons born or naturalized in the United States, and subject to the jurisdiction thereof, are made citizens of the United States and of the State wherein they reside; and the States are forbidden from making or enforcing any law which shall abridge the privileges or immunities of citizens of the United States, or

shall deprive any person of life, liberty or property without due process of law, or deny to any person within their jurisdiction the equal protection of the laws....

The object of the amendment was undoubtedly to enforce the absolute equality of the two races before the law, but in the nature of things it could not have been intended to abolish distinctions based upon color, or to enforce social, as distinguished from political equality, or a commingling of the two races upon terms unsatisfactory to either. Laws permitting, and even requiring, their separation in places where they are liable to be brought into contact do not necessarily imply the inferiority of either race to the other, and have been generally, if not universally, recognized as within the competency of the state legislatures in the exercise of their police power. The most common instance of this is connected with the establishment of separate schools for white and colored children, which has been held to be a valid exercise of the legislative power even by courts of States where the political rights of the colored race have been longest and most earnestly enforced.

One of the earliest of these cases is that of *Roberts v. City of Boston*, in which the Supreme Judicial Court of Massachusetts held that the general school committee of Boston had power to make provision for the instruction of colored children in separate schools established exclusively for them, and to prohibit their attendance upon the other schools....

Laws forbidding the intermarriage of the two races may be said in a technical sense to interfere with the freedom of contract, and yet have been universally recognized as within the police power of the State.

The distinction between laws interfering with the political equality of the negro and those requiring the separation of the two races in schools, theatres and railway carriages has been frequently drawn by this court. Thus in *Strauder v. West Virginia* [1880] it was held that a law of West Virginia limiting to white male persons, 21 years of age and citizens of the State, the right to sit upon juries, was a discrimination which implied a legal inferiority in civil society, which lessened the security of the right of the colored race, and was a step toward reducing them to a condition of servility. Indeed, the right of a colored man that, in the selection of jurors to pass upon his life, liberty, and property, there shall be no exclusion of his race, and no discrimination against them because of color, has been asserted in a number of cases....

So far, then, as a conflict with the Fourteenth Amendment is concerned, the case reduces itself to the question whether the statute of Louisiana is a reasonable regulation, and with respect to this there must necessarily be a large discretion on the part of the legislature. In determining the question of reasonableness it is at liberty to act with reference to the established usages, customs and traditions of the people, and with a view to the promotion of their comfort, and the preservation of the public peace and good order. Gauged by this standard, we cannot say that a law which authorizes or even requires the separation of the two races in public conveyances is unreasonable, or more obnoxious to the Fourteenth Amendment than the acts of Congress requiring separate schools for colored children in the District of Columbia, the constitutionality of which does not seem to have been questioned, or the corresponding acts of state legislatures.

We consider the underlying fallacy of the plaintiff's argument to consist in the assumption that the enforced separation of the two races stamps the colored race with a badge of inferiority. If this be so, it is not by reason of anything found in the act, but solely because the colored race chooses to put that construction upon it. The argument necessarily assumes that if, as has been more than once the case, and is not unlikely to be so again, the colored race should become the dominant power in the state legislature, and should enact a law in precisely similar terms, it would thereby relegate the white race to an inferior position. We imagine that the white race, at least, would not acquiesce in this assumption. The argument also assumes that social prejudices may be overcome by legislation, and that equal rights cannot be secured to the negro except by an enforced commingling of the two races. We cannot accept this proposition. If the two races are to meet upon terms of social equality, it must be the result of natural affinities, a mutual appreciation of each other's merits and a voluntary consent of individuals.... Legislation is powerless to eradicate racial instincts or to abolish distinctions based upon physical differences, and the attempt to do so can only result in accentuating the difficulties of the present situation. If the civil and political rights of both races be equal one cannot be inferior to the other civilly or politically. If one race be inferior to the other socially, the Constitution of the United States cannot put them upon the same plane....

The judgment of the court below is, therefore,

Affirmed.

MR. JUSTICE HARLAN dissenting.

In respect of civil rights, common to all citizens, the Constitution of the United States does not, I think, permit any public authority to know the race of those entitled to be protected in the enjoyment of such rights. Every true man has pride of race, and under appropriate circumstances when the rights of others, his equals before the law, are not to be affected, it is his privilege to express such pride and to take such action based upon it as to him seems proper. But I deny that any legislative body or judicial tribunal may have regard to the race of citizens when the civil rights of those citizens are involved. Indeed, such legislation, as that here in question, is inconsistent not only with that equality of rights which pertains to citizenship, National and State, but with the personal liberty enjoyed by every one within the United States.

The Thirteenth Amendment does not permit the withholding or the deprivation of any right necessarily inhering in freedom. It not only struck down the institution of slavery as previously existing in the United States, but it prevents the imposition of any burdens or disabilities that constitute badges of slavery or servitude. It decreed universal civil freedom in this country. This court has so adjudged. But that amendment having been found inadequate to the protection of the rights of those who had been in slavery, it was followed by the Fourteenth Amendment, which added greatly to the dignity and glory of American citizenship, and to the security of personal liberty.... These two amendments, if enforced according to their true intent and meaning, will protect all the civil rights that pertain to freedom and citizenship. Finally, and to the end that no citizen should be denied, on account of his race, the privilege of participating in the political control of his country, it was declared by the Fifteenth Amendment that "the right of citizens of the United States to vote shall not be denied or abridged by the United States or by any State on account of race, color or previous condition of servitude."

These notable additions to the fundamental law were welcomed by the friends of liberty throughout the world. They removed the race line from our governmental systems. They had, as this court has said, a common purpose, namely, to secure "to a race recently emancipated, a race that through many generations have been held in slavery, all the civil rights that the superior race enjoy."...

If a State can prescribe, as a rule of civil conduct, that whites and blacks shall not travel as passengers in the same railroad coach, why may it not so regulate the use of the streets of its cities and towns as to compel white citizens to keep on one side of a street and black citizens to keep on the other? Why may it not, upon like grounds, punish whites and blacks who ride together in street cars or in open vehicles on a public road or street? Why may it not require sheriffs to assign whites to one side of a court-room and blacks to the other? And why may it not also prohibit the commingling of the two races in the galleries of legislative halls or in public assemblages convened for the consideration of the political questions of the day? Further, if this statute of Louisiana is consistent with the personal liberty of citizens, why may not the State require the separation in railroad coaches of native and naturalized citizens of the United States, or of Protestants and Roman Catholics?...

The white race deems itself to be the dominant race in this country. And so it is, in prestige, in achievements, in education, in wealth and in power. So, I doubt not, it will continue to be for all time, if it remains true to its great heritage and holds fast to the principles of constitutional liberty. But in view of the Constitution, in the eye of the law, there is in this country no superior, dominant, ruling class of citizens. There is no caste here. Our Constitution is color-blind, and neither knows nor tolerates classes among citizens. In respect of civil rights, all citizens are equal before the law. The humblest is the peer of the most powerful. The law regards man as man, and takes no account of his surroundings or of his color when his civil rights as guaranteed by the supreme law of the land are involved. It is, therefore, to be regretted that this high tribunal, the final expositor of the fundamental law of the land, has reached the conclusion that it is competent for a State to regulate the enjoyment by citizens of their civil rights solely upon the basis of race.

In my opinion, the judgment this day rendered will, in time, prove to be quite as pernicious as the decision made by this tribunal in the *Dred Scott case*....

I am of opinion that the statute of Louisiana is inconsistent with the personal liberty of citizens, white and black, in that State, and hostile to both the spirit and letter of the Constitution of the United States. If laws of like character should be enacted in the several States of the Union, the effect would be in the highest degree mischievous. Slavery, as an institution tolerated by law would, it is true, have disappeared from our country, but there would remain a power in the States, by sinister legislation, to interfere with the full enjoyment of the blessings of freedom; to regulate civil rights, common to all citizens, upon the basis of race; and to place in a condition of legal inferiority a large body of American citizens, now constituting a part of the political community called the People of the United States, for whom, and by whom through representatives, our government is administered. Such a system is inconsistent with the guarantee given by the Constitution to each State of a republican form of government, and may be stricken down by Congressional action, or by the courts in the discharge of their solemn duty to maintain the supreme law of the land, anything in the constitution or laws of any State to the contrary notwithstanding.

For the reasons stated, I am constrained to withhold my assent from the opinion and judgment of the majority.

The *Plessy* decision's separate but equal doctrine ushered in full-scale segregation in the southern and border states. According to the Court, separation did not constitute inequality under the Fourteenth Amendment; as long as facilities and opportunities were somewhat similar, the Equal Protection Clause permitted the separation of the races. Encouraged by the ruling, the legislatures of the South passed a wide variety of statutes to keep blacks segregated from the white population. The segregation laws affected transportation, schools, hospitals, parks, public rest rooms and water fountains, libraries, cemeteries, recreational facilities, hotels, restaurants, and almost every other public and commercial facility. These laws, coupled with segregated private lives, inevitably resulted in two separate societies.

During the first half of the twentieth century, the separate but equal doctrine dominated race relations law. The southern states continued to pass and enforce segregationist laws, largely insulated from legal attack. Over the years, however, it became clear that the "equality" part of the separate but equal doctrine was being ignored.

Segregated public facilities became increasingly unequal, and the blacks became more and more disadvantaged. Although this disparity extended to almost every area of life, education became the center of attention. Whites and blacks were given access to public schools, but the black schools, at all levels, received support and funding far inferior to that of white institutions.

These conditions spurred the growth of civil rights groups dedicated to eradicating segregation. None was more prominent than the National Association for the Advancement of Colored People and its affiliate, the Legal Defense and Educational Fund (LDF). Thurgood Marshall, who had been associated with the NAACP since he graduated first in his class at Howard University Law School, became the head of the Legal Defense Fund in 1940 and initiated a twenty-year campaign in the courts to win equal rights for black Americans. During those years, Marshall and his staff won substantial victories in the Supreme Court in housing, voting rights, public education, employment, and public accommodations. Marshall also served as a judge on the court of appeals and as U.S. solicitor general before being appointed in 1967 to the Supreme Court, the first black to serve on the Court *(see Box 10-1)*.

When Marshall took over leadership of the Legal Defense Fund, the rule set in *Plessy* was already on less than firm ground. In 1938 the Court had handed segregationist forces a significant defeat in *Missouri ex rel. Gaines v. Canada*. Lloyd Gaines, a Missouri resident,

who had graduated from the all-black Lincoln University, applied for admission to the University of Missouri's law school. He was denied admission because of his race. Although Missouri did not have a law school for its black citizens, the state offered to finance the education of qualified black students who would attend law school in a neighboring state that did not have segregationist policies. The Supreme Court, 7–2, concluded that the Missouri plan to provide opportunities out of state did not meet the obligations imposed by the Equal Protection Clause. The state then moved to establish a law school for blacks at Lincoln. Although this ruling imposed little substantive change, it served notice that segregation policies were about to undergo close evaluation. The Supreme Court's message was reinforced in 1948 when in two cases, *Sipuel v. Board of Regents* and *Fisher v. Hurst*, the justices unanimously demanded that states provide equal facilities for blacks pursuing a legal education.

By the late 1940s a substantial movement had developed to challenge the conditions of racial inequality. Much of the impetus for social change stemmed from the nation's experiences during World War II. With the support and approval of Presidents Roosevelt and Truman, strict separation in the armed forces was reduced, and black and white soldiers fought together on the battlefields. At home, workers of both races joined to produce the arms and equipment necessary to support the war effort.

When the war was over, black soldiers returned to the United States intent on pursuing a better life for themselves and their families. Once they had experienced something different, there was little likelihood that blacks would be satisfied with a segregated society. Many whites, having had their first substantial contacts with blacks during the war, began questioning the wisdom of segregation.

In this political climate, the Supreme Court was asked to reevaluate the validity of the separate but equal doctrine. Civil rights advocates hoped that the

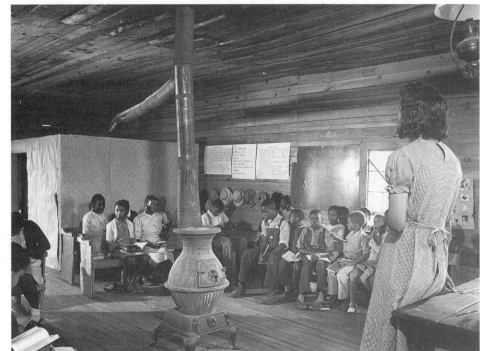

Under the rule of law established in *Plessy v. Ferguson* (1896), states could require racial separation if facilities for blacks and whites were of equal quality. In public education black schools were not always equal to those reserved for whites.

Pictured on the steps of the U.S. Supreme Court are the NAACP Legal Defense Fund lawyers who argued the school segregation cases that resulted in the May 17, 1954, *Brown v. Board of Education* precedent. Left to right: Howard Jenkins, James M. Nabrit, Jr., Spottswood W. Robinson III, Frank Reeves, Jack Greenberg, Special Counsel Thurgood Marshall, Louis Redding, U. Simpson Tate, and George E. C. Hayes. Missing from the photograph is Robert L. Carter, who argued the Topeka, Kansas, case.

BOX 10-1   THURGOOD MARSHALL
(1967–1991)

Thurgood Marshall was born July 2, 1908, in Baltimore, Maryland. He was the son of a primary teacher and a club steward. In 1926 he left Baltimore to attend the all-black Lincoln University in Chester, Pennsylvania, where he developed a reputation as an outstanding debater. After graduating cum laude in 1930, Marshall decided to study law and entered Howard University in Washington, D. C.

During his law school years, Marshall developed an interest in civil rights. After graduating first in his class in 1933, he began a long and historic involvement with the National Association for the Advancement of Colored People (NAACP). In 1940 he became the head of the newly formed NAACP Legal Defense and Educational Fund, a position he held for more than twenty years.

Over those two decades, Marshall coordinated the fund's attack on segregation in voting, housing, public accommodations, and education. The culmination of his career as a civil rights attorney came in 1954 as chief counsel in a series of cases grouped under the title *Brown v. Board of Education*. In that historic case, civil rights advocates convinced the Supreme Court to declare segregation in public schools unconstitutional.

Marshall married Vivian Burey, September 4, 1929. They had two sons. Vivian Marshall died in February 1955, and Marshall married Cecilia Suyat, December 17, 1955.

In 1961 Marshall was appointed by President John F. Kennedy to the Second Circuit Court of Appeals, but because of heated opposition from southern Democratic senators, he was not confirmed for a year.

Four years after he was named to the appeals court, Marshall was chosen by President Lyndon B. Johnson to be solicitor general. Marshall was the first black to serve in that capacity. During his years as the government's chief advocate before the Supreme Court, Marshall scored impressive victories in the areas of civil and constitutional rights. He won Supreme Court approval of the 1965 Voting Rights Act, voluntarily informed the Court that the government had used eavesdropping devices in two cases, and joined a suit that successfully overturned a California constitutional amendment that prohibited open housing legislation.

On June 13, 1967, President Johnson nominated Marshall to the seat vacated by Justice Tom C. Clark, who retired. Marshall was confirmed by the Senate, 69–11, August 30, 1967. Marshall, the first black justice of the Supreme Court, retired on October 1, 1991. He died January 24, 1993 at the age of 84.

SOURCE: Adapted from Elder Witt, *Guide to the U.S. Supreme Court*, 2d ed. (Washington, D.C.: Congressional Quarterly, 1990), 875.

Court would do away with the precedent that legitimized racial segregation, but at a minimum they demanded that the justices ensure that facilities and opportunities were truly equal.

In *Sweatt v. Painter* (1950) the Legal Defense Fund launched a frontal attack on the separate but equal doctrine. Although the Court's decision was not everything civil rights advocates had hoped, it marked another significant step in the development of race relations law. As you read Chief Justice Vinson's opinion for the Court, note the emphasis he places on the importance of equal facilities for black and white students.

Sweatt v. Painter

339 U.S. 629 (1950)

Vote: 9 (Black, Burton, Clark, Douglas, Frankfurter, Jackson, Minton, Reed, Vinson)

0

Opinion of the Court: Vinson

In 1946 H. M. Sweatt, a Texas postal worker, applied for admission to the racially segregated University of Texas law school. His application was rejected on the exclusive ground that he was black. Because there was no Texas law school that admitted blacks, Sweatt filed suit demanding that the University of Texas admit him. Given the *Gaines* precedent, the trial court judge was aware that Sweatt had a strong case. Rather than grant Sweatt's motion, however, he continued the case for six months to allow the state time to address the problem. The state hastily established an interim law school for blacks in Austin that was to open in February 1947. A permanent black law school, part of the Texas State University for Negroes, was later to open in Houston.

When the six-month period ended in December 1946, the judge dismissed Sweatt's complaint on the grounds that the state was meeting its obligations under the Equal Protection Clause. Sweatt served notice of appeal, refusing to attend the new school. Supported by the NAACP and Thurgood Marshall's Legal Defense Fund, Sweatt challenged the school as substantially inferior to the University of Texas law school. The Texas courts concluded that the two schools were "substantially equivalent," and appeal was taken to the U.S. Supreme Court, where Sweatt asked the Court to reconsider the *Plessy* separate but equal principle. Sweatt's appeal was supported by amicus curiae briefs submitted by the U.S. government as well as a number of organizations such as the American Federation of Teachers and the American Jewish Committee. Eleven southern and border states filed briefs supporting Texas.

MR. CHIEF JUSTICE VINSON delivered the opinion of the Court.

The University of Texas Law School, from which petitioner was excluded, was staffed by a faculty of sixteen full-time and three part-time professors, some of whom are nationally recognized authorities in their field. Its student body numbered 850. The library contained over 65,000 volumes. Among the other facilities available to the students were a law review, moot court facilities, scholarship funds, and Order of the Coif affiliation. The school's alumni occupy the most distinguished positions in the private practice of the law and in the public life of the State. It may properly be considered one of the nation's ranking law schools.

The law school for Negroes which was to have opened in February, 1947, would have had no independent faculty or library. The teaching was to be carried on by four members of the University of Texas Law School faculty, who were to maintain their offices at the University of Texas while teaching at both institutions. Few of the 10,000 volumes ordered for the library had arrived; nor was there any full-time librarian. The school lacked accreditation.

Since the trial of this case, respondents report the opening of a law school at the Texas State University for Negroes. It is apparently on the road to full accreditation. It has a faculty of five full-time professors; a student body of 23; a library of some 16,500 volumes serviced by a full-time staff; a practice court and legal aid association; and one alumnus who has become a member of the Texas Bar.

Whether the University of Texas Law School is compared with the original or the new law school for Negroes, we cannot find substantial equality in the educational opportunities offered white and Negro law students by the State. In terms of number of the faculty, variety of courses and opportunity for specialization, size of student body, scope of the library, availability of law review and similar activities, the University of Texas Law School is superior. What is more important, the University of Texas Law School possesses to a far greater degree those qualities which are incapable of objective measurement but which make for greatness in a law school. Such qualities, to name but a few, include reputation of the faculty, experience of the administration, position and influence of the alumni, standing in the community, traditions and prestige. It is difficult to believe that one who had a free choice between these law schools would consider the question close.

Moreover, although the law is a highly learned profession, we are well aware that it is an intensely practical one. The law school, the proving ground for legal learning and practice, cannot be effective in isolation from the individuals and institutions with which the law interacts. Few students and no one who has practiced law would choose to study in an academic vacuum, removed from the interplay of ideas and the exchange of views with which the law is concerned. The law school to which Texas is willing to admit petitioner excludes from its student body members of the racial groups which number 85% of the population of the State and include most of the lawyers, witnesses, jurors, judges and other officials with whom petitioner will inevitably be dealing when he becomes a member of the Texas Bar. With such a substantial and significant segment of society excluded, we cannot conclude that the education offered petitioner is substantially equal to that which he would receive if admitted to the University of Texas Law School.

It may be argued that excluding petitioner from that school is no different from excluding white students from the new law school. This contention overlooks realities. It is unlikely that a member of a group so decisively in the majority, attending a school with rich traditions and prestige which only a history of consistently maintained excellence could command, would claim that the opportunities afforded him for legal education were unequal to those held open to petitioner. That such a claim, if made, would be dishonored by the State, is no answer. "Equal protection of the laws is not achieved through indiscriminate imposition of inequalities." *Shelley v. Kraemer* (1948).

It is fundamental that these cases concern rights which are personal and present. This Court has stated unanimously that "The State must provide [legal education] for [petitioner] in conformity with the equal protection clause of the Fourteenth Amendment and provide it as soon as it does for applicants of any other group." *Sipuel v. Board of Regents* (1948).... In *Missouri ex rel. Gaines v. Canada* (1938), the Court, speaking through Chief Justice Hughes, declared that "petitioner's right was a personal one. It was as an individual that he was entitled to the equal protection of the laws, and the State was bound to furnish him within its borders facilities for legal education substantially equal to those which the State there afforded for persons of the white race, whether or not other negroes sought the same opportunity." These are the only cases in this Court which present the issue of the constitutional validity of race distinctions in state-supported graduate and professional education.

In accordance with these cases, petitioner may claim his full constitutional right: legal education equivalent to that offered by the State to students of other races. Such education is not available to him in a separate law school as offered by the State. We cannot, therefore, agree with respondents that the doctrine of *Plessy v. Ferguson* (1896) requires affirmance of the judgment below. Nor need we reach petitioner's contention that *Plessy v. Ferguson* should be reexamined in the light of contemporary knowledge respecting the purposes of the Fourteenth Amendment and the effects of racial segregation.

We hold that the Equal Protection Clause of the Fourteenth Amendment requires that petitioner be admitted to the University of Texas Law School. The judgment is reversed and the cause is remanded for proceedings not inconsistent with this opinion.

Reversed.

The same day the Court decided *Sweatt*, it also issued a ruling in *McLaurin v. Oklahoma State Regents* (1950), which took another step toward racial equality in higher education. *McLaurin* highlights an interesting aspect of the desegregation battle; many segregationists feared that if blacks and whites attended the same schools, such intermingling would inevitably lead to interracial dating and marriage.[1] To comply with judicial decisions, the University of Oklahoma admitted black graduate students when these students could not obtain the desired degrees at minority schools. However, to protect against the possibilities of interracial marriage, the university restricted blacks

1. For a discussion of this issue, see Richard Kluger, *Simple Justice* (New York: Random House, 1975), especially chap. 12.

to segregated areas of classrooms, libraries, and dining halls. Fraternization between the races was almost impossible.

To neutralize this fear of interracial marriage, the Legal Defense Fund chose George W. McLaurin to challenge the segregationist policies of the University of Oklahoma. McLaurin was a black graduate student, already holding a master's degree, who was pursuing a doctorate in education. What made him perfect to challenge the separatist regulations was that McLaurin was sixty-eight years old and unlikely to marry. Although McLaurin's suit was unsuccessful in the lower courts, the Supreme Court unanimously found Oklahoma's system in violation of the Equal Protection Clause.

As the nation entered the 1950s, the conditions were ripe for a final assault on the half-century-old separate but equal doctrine. Civil rights groups continued to marshal legal arguments and political support to eliminate segregation. Legal challenges to a wide array of discriminatory laws were filed throughout the country, and the Justice Department under President Truman supported these efforts. The Supreme Court, through its unanimous rulings in favor of racial equality in higher education, appeared on the verge of seriously considering an end to *Plessy*. In addition, there had been an important leadership change on the Court. Chief Justice Vinson died September 8, 1953, and was replaced by Earl Warren, a former governor of California, who was much more comfortable with activist judicial policies than was his predecessor *(see Box 10-2)*.

All of these factors combined to produce *Brown v. Board of Education of Topeka, Kansas* (1954), considered by many to be the Supreme Court's most significant decision of the twentieth century. Unlike earlier civil rights cases that involved relatively small professional and graduate education programs, the *Brown* case challenged official racial segregation in the nation's primary and secondary public schools. The decision affected thousands of school districts concen-

This photograph of Linda Brown, plaintiff in *Brown v. Board of Education*, was taken in 1952 when she was nine years old.

trated primarily in southern and border states. In addition, it was apparent to all that the precedent to be set for public education would be extended to other areas as well.

As you read Warren's opinion for a unanimous Court, note how the concept of equality has changed. No longer does the Court examine only physical facilities and tangible items such as buildings, libraries, teacher qualifications, and funding levels; instead it emphasizes the intangible negative impact of racial segregation on children. Warren's opinion includes a footnote listing social science references as authorities for his arguments. This opinion was criticized for citing sociological and psychological studies to sup-

BOX 10-2 EARL WARREN
(1953–1969)

Earl Warren, the son of Scandinavian immigrant parents, was born on March 19, 1891, in Los Angeles, California. Soon after his birth, the family moved to Bakersfield, where his father worked as a railroad car repairman.

Warren worked his way through college and law school at the University of California. After graduating in 1914, he worked in law offices in San Francisco and Oakland, the only time in his career that he engaged in private practice.

Warren married Nina P. Meyers, October 14, 1925. They had three daughters and three sons.

In 1938, after Warren had become active in politics, his father was bludgeoned to death in a crime that was never solved.

From 1919 until his resignation from the Supreme Court in 1969, Warren served without interruption in public office. His first post was deputy city attorney for Oakland. Then he was named a deputy district attorney for Alameda County, which embraces the cities of Oakland, Alameda, and Berkeley.

In 1925 Warren was appointed district attorney when the incumbent resigned. He won election to the post in his own right in 1926, 1930, and 1934. During his fourteen years as district attorney, Warren developed a reputation as a crime fighter, sending a city manager and several councilmen to jail on graft charges and smashing a crooked deal on garbage collection.

A Republican, Warren decided in 1938 to run for state attorney general. He cross-filed and won three primaries—his own party's as well as the Democratic and Progressive party contests.

In 1942 Warren ran for governor of California. Although he was an underdog, he wound up defeating incumbent Democratic governor Culbert Olson by a margin of 342,000, winning 57.1 percent of the total votes cast. He was twice reelected, winning the Democratic as well as the Republican nomination in 1946 and defeating Democrat James Roosevelt, son of President Franklin D. Roosevelt, by an almost two-to-one margin in 1950.

At first viewed as a conservative governor—he denounced "communist radicals" and supported the wartime federal order to move all persons of Japanese ancestry away from the West Coast—Warren developed a progressive image after the war. In 1945 he proposed a state program of prepaid medical insurance and later championed liberal pension and welfare benefits.

Warren made two bids for national political office. In 1948 he ran for Vice President on the Republican ticket with Gov. Thomas E. Dewey of New York. In 1952 he sought the Republican presidential nomination. But with little chance to win he threw his support at a crucial moment behind Gen. Dwight D. Eisenhower, helping him win the battle with Sen. Robert A. Taft of Ohio for the nomination.

That support resulted in Eisenhower's political indebtedness to Warren, which the president repaid in 1953 with a recess appointment to the Supreme Court. Warren replaced Chief Justice Fred M. Vinson, who had died. Warren was confirmed by the Senate March 1, 1954 by a voice vote. Eisenhower, reflecting on his choice years later in the light of the Warren Court's liberal record, called the appointment "the biggest damn-fool mistake I ever made."

In addition to his work on the Court, Warren headed the commission that investigated the assassination of President John F. Kennedy.

In 1968 Warren submitted his resignation, conditional on confirmation of a successor. But the Senate got bogged down in the fight to confirm President Lyndon B. Johnson's nomination of Justice Abe Fortas to succeed Warren, so Warren agreed to serve another year. In 1969, when Richard Nixon assumed office, he chose Warren E. Burger as the new chief justice, and Warren stepped down. He died July 9, 1974.

SOURCE: Adapted from Elder Witt, *Guide to the U.S. Supreme Court,* 2d ed. (Washington, D.C.: Congressional Quarterly, 1990), 869–870.

port the Court's conclusions rather than confining the analysis to legal arguments. Are these criticisms valid? Should the Court take social science evidence into account in arriving at constitutional decisions? Consider how similar Warren's opinion is to Justice Harlan's lone dissent in the *Plessy* decision.

Brown v. Board of Education

347 U.S. 483 (1954)

Vote: 9 (Black, Burton, Clark, Douglas, Frankfurter, Jackson, Minton, Reed, Warren)

0

Opinion of the Court: Warren

Brown v. Board of Education was one of five cases involving similar issues consolidated by the Court for consideration at the same time. Part of the desegregation litigation strategy orchestrated by Thurgood Marshall and funded by the NAACP, these cases challenged the segregated public schools of Delaware, Virginia, South Carolina, and the District of Columbia, in addition to Topeka, Kansas. The most prominent lawyers in the civil rights movement, Spottswood Robinson III, Louis Redding, Jack Greenberg, Constance Baker Motley, Robert Carter, and James Nabrit, Jr., prepared them. As Marshall had expected, the suits were unsuccessful at the trial level, with the lower courts relying on *Plessy* as precedent. The leading lawyer for the states was John W. Davis, a prominent constitutional lawyer who had been a Democratic candidate for president in 1924. (Davis had reportedly once been offered a nomination to the Court by President Warren G. Harding.)

Linda Carol Brown was an eight-year-old black girl, whose father, Oliver, was an assistant pastor of a Topeka church. The Browns lived in a predominantly white neighborhood only a short distance from the local elementary school. Under state law, cities with populations over 15,000 were permitted to administer racially segregated schools. The Board of Education in Topeka required its elementary schools to be racially divided. The Browns did not want their daughter to be sent to the school reserved for black students. It was far from home, and they considered the trip dangerous. In addition, their neighborhood school was a good one, and the Browns wanted their daughter to receive an integrated education. They filed suit challenging the segregated school system as violating their daughter's rights under the Equal Protection Clause of the Fourteenth Amendment.

The *Brown* appeal was joined by those from the other four suits. The cases were originally argued in December 1952, but the following June the Court issued an order for the cases to be reargued in December 1953 with special emphasis to be placed on a series of questions dealing with the history and meaning of the Fourteenth Amendment. This delay also allowed the newly appointed Earl Warren to participate fully in the decision. Six months later, on May 17, 1954, the Court issued its ruling.

MR. CHIEF JUSTICE WARREN delivered the opinion of the Court.

In each of the cases, minors of the Negro race, through their legal representatives, seek the aid of the courts in obtaining admission to the public schools of their community on a nonsegregated basis. In each instance, they had been denied admission to schools attended by white children under laws requiring or permitting segregation according to race. This segregation was alleged to deprive the plaintiffs of the equal protection of the laws under the Fourteenth Amendment....

The plaintiffs contend that segregated public schools are not "equal" and cannot be made "equal," and that hence they are deprived of the equal protection of the laws. Because of the obvious importance of the question presented, the Court took jurisdiction. Argument was heard in the 1952 Term, and reargument was heard this Term on certain questions propounded by the Court.

Reargument was largely devoted to the circumstances surrounding the adoption of the Fourteenth Amendment in 1868. It covered exhaustively consideration of the Amendment in Congress, ratification by the states, then existing practices in racial segregation, and the views of proponents and opponents of the Amendment. This discussion and our own investigation convince us that, although these sources cast some light, it is not enough to resolve the problem with which we are faced. At best, they are inconclusive....

An additional reason for the inconclusive nature of the Amendment's history, with respect to segregated schools, is the status of public education at that time. In the South, the movement toward free common schools, supported by general taxation, had not yet taken hold. Education of white children was largely in the hands of private groups. Education of Negroes was almost nonexistent, and practically all of the race were illiterate. In fact, any education of Negroes was forbidden by law in some states. Today, in contrast, many Negroes have achieved outstanding success in the arts and sciences as well as in the business and professional world. It is true that public school education at the time of the Amendment had advanced further in the North, but the effect of the Amendment on Northern States was generally ignored in the congressional debates. Even in the North, the conditions of public education did not approximate those existing today. The curriculum was usually rudimentary; ungraded schools were common in rural areas; the school term was but three months a year in many states; and compulsory school attendance was virtually unknown. As a consequence, it is not surprising that there should be so little in the history of the Fourteenth Amendment relating to its intended effect on public education.

In the first cases in this Court construing the Fourteenth Amendment, decided shortly after its adoption, the Court interpreted it as proscribing all state-imposed discriminations against the Negro race. The doctrine of "separate but equal" did not make its appearance in this Court until 1896 in the case of *Plessy v. Ferguson,* involving not education but transportation. American courts have since labored with the doctrine for over half a century....

Here, unlike *Sweatt v. Painter,* there are findings below that the Negro and white schools involved have been equalized, or are being equalized, with respect to buildings, curricula, qualifications and salaries of teachers, and other "tangible" factors. Our decision, therefore, cannot turn on merely a comparison of these tangible factors in the Negro and white schools involved in each of the cases. We must look instead to the effect of segregation itself on public education.

In approaching this problem, we cannot turn the clock back to 1868 when the Amendment was adopted, or even to 1896 when *Plessy v. Ferguson* was written. We must consider public education in the light of its full development and its present place in American life throughout the Nation. Only in this way can it be determined if segregation in public schools deprives these plaintiffs of the equal protection of the laws.

Today, education is perhaps the most important function of state and local governments. Compulsory school attendance laws and the great expenditures for education both demonstrate our recognition of the importance of education to our democratic society. It is required in the performance of our most basic public responsibilities, even service in the armed forces. It is the very foundation of good citizenship. Today it is a principal instrument in awakening the child to cultural values, in preparing him for later professional training, and in helping him to adjust normally to his environment. In these days, it is doubtful that any child may reasonably be expected to succeed in life if he is denied the opportunity of an education. Such an opportunity, where the state has undertaken to provide it, is a right which must be made available to all on equal terms.

We come then to the question presented: Does segregation of children in public schools solely on the basis of race, even though the physical facilities and other "tangible" factors may be equal, deprive the children of the minority group of equal educational opportunities? We believe that it does.

In *Sweatt v. Painter*, in finding that a segregated law school of Negroes could not provide them equal educational opportunities, this Court relied in large part on "those qualities which are incapable of objective measurement but which make for greatness in a law school." In *McLaurin v. Oklahoma State Regents*, the Court, in requiring that a Negro admitted to a white graduate school be treated like all other students, again resorted to intangible considerations: ". . . his ability to study, to engage in discussions and exchange views with other students, and, in general, to learn his profession." Such considerations apply with added force to children in grade and high schools. To separate them from others of similar age and qualifications solely because of their race generates a feeling of inferiority as to their status in the community that may affect their hearts and minds in a way unlikely ever to be undone. The effect of this separation on their educational opportunities was well stated by a finding in the Kansas case by a court which nevertheless felt compelled to rule against the Negro plaintiffs:

"Segregation of white and colored children in public schools has a detrimental effect upon the colored children. The impact is greater when it has the sanction of the law; for the policy of separating the races is usually interpreted as denoting the inferiority of the negro group. A sense of inferiority affects the motivation of a child to learn. Segregation with the sanction of law, therefore, has a tendency to [retard] the educational and mental development of negro children and to deprive them of some of the benefits they would receive in a racial[ly] integrated school system."

Whatever may have been the extent of psychological knowledge at the time of *Plessy v. Ferguson*, this finding is amply supported by modern authority.* Any language in *Plessy v. Ferguson* contrary to this finding is rejected.

We conclude that in the field of public education the doctrine of "separate but equal" has no place. Separate educational facilities are inherently unequal. Therefore, we hold that the plaintiffs and others similarly situated for whom the actions have been brought are, by reason of the segregation complained of, deprived of the equal protection of the laws guaranteed by the Fourteenth Amendment. . . .

It is so ordered.

Of obvious importance to the Court in *Brown* was public acceptance of the ruling. The Court has no formal enforcement powers, and the justices expected resistance, especially in the South. Chief Justice Warren went to great pains to obtain a unanimous vote and to unite the Court in a single opinion, written by him, demonstrating that the justices wanted to speak with all the authority they could muster in the hopes of encouraging voluntary compliance.

In the years following *Brown*, the Supreme Court

* K. B. Clark, Effect of Prejudice and Discrimination on Personality Development (Midcentury White House Conference on Children and Youth, 1950); Witmer and Kotinsky, Personality in the Making (1952), c. VI; Deutscher and Chein, The Psychological Effects of Enforced Segregation: A Survey of Social Science Opinion, 26 J. Psychol. 259 (1948); Chein, What Are the Psychological Effects of Segregation Under Conditions of Equal Facilities?, 3 Int. J. Opinion and Attitude Res. 229 (1949); Brameld, Educational Costs, in Discrimination and National Welfare (MacIver, ed., 1949), 44–48; Frazier, The Negro in the United States (1949), 674–681. And see generally Myrdal, An American Dilemma (1944).

regularly confronted questions of racial discrimination. The death of the separate but equal doctrine had widespread ramifications for American society because a number of states and local governments had laws that mandated segregated facilities. Other rules and restrictions, while not segregating the races, discriminated directly or indirectly against blacks. Civil rights groups launched attacks on many of these discriminatory policies, as did the Justice Department, especially during the Kennedy and Johnson administrations.

As such challenges were brought before the Supreme Court, the justices faithfully applied the *Brown* precedent. The Court presumed that racial classifications used to discriminate against black Americans violated the Equal Protection Clause, and states attempting to justify such actions faced a heavy burden of proof. As members of a suspect class, black litigants enjoyed the advantages of the strict scrutiny test. These factors made it difficult for the states to withstand the attacks made against discriminatory policies and practices. One by one the legal barriers between the races fell.

An illustration of the Warren Court's approach to racial equality is the ruling in *Loving v. Virginia* (1967), which concerned the part of life segregationist forces least wanted to see integrated: marriage. When *Loving* came to the Court, sixteen states, all of them southern or border, had miscegenation statutes that made interracial marriages unlawful. However, other states, including California, Colorado, Indiana, Arizona, and Oregon, only recently had repealed similar laws. The *Loving* case presents an interesting twist to the equality issue. Virginia argued that the Equal Protection Clause was not violated because whites and blacks were treated with absolute equality. Members of both races were equally prohibited from marrying outside their own race. If violations occurred, both whites and blacks were subject to the same criminal penalties. How does Chief Justice Warren's opinion respond to this argument? Note the Court's discussion of the

heavy burden carried by a state attempting to justify any racial classification.

Loving v. Virginia

388 U.S. 1 (1967)
Vote: 9 *(Black, Brennan, Clark, Douglas, Fortas, Harlan, Stewart, Warren, White)*

0

Opinion of the Court: Warren
Concurring opinion: Stewart

In June 1958 two Virginia residents, Mildred Jeter, a black woman, and Richard Loving, a white man, were married in Washington, D.C. They returned to Virginia to live, and later that year they were charged with violating Virginia's miscegenation law, an offense punishable by up to five years in the state penitentiary. They pleaded guilty to the charge and were sentenced to one year in jail. The judge, however, suspended the sentence on condition that the Lovings leave Virginia and not return for twenty-five years. In handing down the sentence, the judge said, "Almighty God created the races white, black, yellow, malay and red, and he placed them on separate continents. And but for the interference with his arrangement there would be no cause for such marriages. The fact that he separated the races shows that he did not intend for the races to mix."

The Lovings moved to Washington. In 1963 they initiated a suit to have the sentence set aside on the grounds that it violated their rights under the Equal Protection Clause of the Fourteenth Amendment. The Virginia Supreme Court upheld the constitutionality of the law and affirmed the original convictions.

MR. CHIEF JUSTICE WARREN delivered the opinion of the Court.

This case presents a constitutional question never addressed by this Court: whether a statutory scheme adopted by the State of Virginia to prevent marriages between persons solely on the basis of racial classifications violates the Equal Protection and Due Process Clauses of the Fourteenth Amendment. For reasons which seem to us to reflect the central meaning of those constitutional commands, we conclude that these statutes cannot stand consistently with the Fourteenth Amendment....

While the state court is no doubt correct in asserting that marriage is a social relation subject to the State's police power, the State does not contend in its argument before this Court that its powers to regulate marriage are unlimited notwithstanding the commands of the Fourteenth Amendment. Instead, the State argues that the meaning of the Equal Protection Clause, as illuminated by the statements of the Framers, is only that state penal laws containing an interracial element as part of the definition of the offense must apply equally to whites and Negroes in the sense that members of each race are punished to the same degree. Thus, the State contends that, because its miscegenation statutes punish equally both the white and the Negro participants in an interracial marriage, these statutes, despite their reliance on racial classifications do not constitute an invidious discrimination based upon race. The second argument advanced by the State assumes the validity of its equal application theory. The argument is that, if the Equal Protection Clause does not outlaw miscegenation statutes because of their reliance on racial classifications, the question of constitutionality would thus become whether there was any rational basis for a State to treat interracial marriages differently from other marriages. On this question, the State argues, the scientific evidence is substantially in doubt and, consequently, this Court should defer to the wisdom of the state legislature in adopting its policy of discouraging interracial marriages.

Because we reject the notion that the mere "equal application" of a statute containing racial classifications is enough to remove the classifications from the Fourteenth Amendment's proscription of all invidious racial discriminations, we do not accept the State's contention that these statutes should be upheld if there is any possible basis for concluding that they serve a rational purpose.... In the case at bar, we deal with statutes containing racial classifications, and the fact of equal application does not immunize the statute from the very heavy burden of justification

which the Fourteenth Amendment has traditionally required of state statutes drawn according to race....

The State finds support for its "equal application" theory in the decision of the Court in Pace v. State of Alabama (1883). In that case, the Court upheld a conviction under an Alabama statute forbidding adultery or fornication between a white person and a Negro which imposed a greater penalty than that of a statute proscribing similar conduct by members of the same race. The Court reasoned that the statute could not be said to discriminate against Negroes because the punishment for each participant in the offense was the same. However, as recently as the 1964 Term, in rejecting the reasoning of that case, we stated "Pace represents a limited view of the Equal Protection Clause which has not withstood analysis in the subsequent decisions of this Court." As we there demonstrated, the Equal Protection Clause requires the consideration of whether the classifications drawn by any statute constitute an arbitrary and invidious discrimination. The clear and central purpose of the Fourteenth Amendment was to eliminate all official state sources of invidious racial discrimination in the States.

There can be no question but that Virginia's miscegenation statutes rest solely upon distinctions drawn according to race. The statutes proscribe generally accepted conduct if engaged in by members of different races. Over the years, this Court has consistently repudiated "[d]istinctions between citizens solely because of their ancestry" as being "odious to a free people whose institutions are founded upon the doctrine of equality." Hirabayashi v. United States (1943). At the very least, the Equal Protection Clause demands that racial classifications, especially suspect in criminal statutes, be subjected to the "most rigid scrutiny," Korematsu v. United States (1944), and, if they are ever to be upheld, they must be shown to be necessary to the accomplishment of some permissible state objective, independent of the racial discrimination which it was the object of the Fourteenth Amendment to eliminate....

There is patently no legitimate overriding purpose independent of invidious racial discrimination which justifies this classification. The fact that Virginia prohibits only interracial marriages involving white persons demonstrates that the racial classifications must stand on their own justification, as measures designed to maintain White Supremacy. We have consistently denied the constitutionality of measures which restrict the rights of citizens on account of race. There can be no doubt that restricting the freedom to marry solely because of racial classifications violates the central meaning of the Equal Protection Clause.

These statutes also deprive the Lovings of liberty without due process of law in violation of the Due Process Clause of the Fourteenth Amendment. The freedom to marry has long been recognized as one of the vital personal rights essential to the orderly pursuit of happiness by free men.

Marriage is one of the "basic civil rights of man," fundamental to our very existence and survival. To deny this fundamental freedom on so unsupportable a basis as the racial classifications embodied in these statutes, classifications so directly subversive of the principle of equality at the heart of the Fourteenth Amendment, is surely to deprive all the State's citizens of liberty without due process of law. The Fourteenth Amendment requires that the freedom of choice to marry not be restricted by invidious racial discriminations. Under our Constitution, the freedom to marry or not marry a person of another race resides with the individual and cannot be infringed by the State.

These convictions must be reversed. It is so ordered.

Reversed.

The *Loving* decision illustrates the Warren Court's rejection of discriminatory racial classifications. Government policies that allocated benefits or imposed penalties exclusively on the basis of race rarely survived Supreme Court scrutiny, especially when such laws or programs placed minorities at a disadvantage or were based on racial stereotypes. While the Burger and Rehnquist Court justices were generally conservative on civil rights issues, they were no more willing to accept blatant racial discrimination by the government than were their more liberal predecessors. Consider, for example, the Court's decision in *Palmore v. Sidoti* (1984). Here the Court confronts racial discrimination by the state in the sensitive area of parent-child relationships. Chief Justice Burger's opinion for the Court is short, direct, and endorsed unanimously by the other justices.

Palmore v. Sidoti

466 U.S. 429 (1984)

Vote: 9 (Blackmun, Brennan, Burger, Marshall, O'Connor, Powell, Rehnquist, Stevens, White)

0

Opinion of the Court: Burger

A Florida couple, Linda and Anthony J. Sidoti, both Caucasian, divorced in May 1980. The court awarded custody of the couple's three-year-old daughter, Melanie, to the mother. In September 1981, Anthony Sidoti filed a petition requesting a change in the custody arrangement because of new conditions. He objected to his former wife cohabiting with a black man, Clarence Palmore, Jr., whom she married two months after the court action was initiated. Sidoti also made several allegations of improper child care.

A court counselor investigated the child care situation. While there was no evidence of serious neglect, the counselor recommended a change in custody on the grounds that the child would be forced to suffer significant environmental pressures flowing from the mother's choice of a life style "unacceptable to the father and to society." The judge agreed, concluding that the best interests of the child would be served by awarding custody to the father. He gave the following reason for his decision:

The father's evident resentment of the mother's choice of a black partner is not sufficient to wrest custody from the mother. It is of some significance, however, that the mother did see fit to bring a man into her home and carry on a sexual relationship with him without being married to him. Such action tended to place gratification of her own desires ahead of her concern for the child's future welfare. This Court feels that despite the strides that have been made in bettering relations between the races in this country, it is inevitable that Melanie will, if allowed to remain in her present situation and attains school age and [is] thus more vulnerable to peer pressures, suffer from the social stigmatization that is sure to come.

A Florida appellate court upheld the judge's custody ruling, and Linda Palmore requested review by the Supreme Court.

CHIEF JUSTICE BURGER delivered the opinion of the Court:

The judgment of a state court determining or reviewing a child custody decision is not ordinarily a likely candidate for review by this Court. However, the court's opinion, after stating that the "father's evident resentment of the mother's choice of a black partner is not sufficient" to deprive her of custody, then turns to what it regarded as the damaging impact on the child from remaining in a racially mixed household. This raises important federal concerns arising from the Constitution's commitment to eradicating discrimination based on race.

The Florida court did not focus directly on the parental qualifications of the natural mother or her present husband, or indeed on the father's qualifications to have custody of the child. The court found that "there is no issue as to either party's devotion to the child, adequacy of housing facilities, or respectability of the new spouse of either parent." This, taken with the absence of any negative finding as to the quality of the care provided by the mother, constitutes a rejection of any claim of petitioner's unfitness to continue the custody of her child.

The court correctly stated that the child's welfare was the controlling factor. But that court was entirely candid and made no effort to place its holding on any ground other than race. Taking the court's findings and rationale at face value, it is clear that the outcome would have been different had petitioner married a Caucasian male of similar respectability.

A core purpose of the Fourteenth Amendment was to do away with all governmentally imposed discrimination based on race. See *Strauder v. West Virginia* (1880). Classifying persons according to their race is more likely to reflect racial prejudice than legitimate public concerns; the race, not the person, dictates the category. Such classifications are subject to the most exacting scrutiny; to pass constitutional muster, they must be justified by a compelling governmental interest and must be "necessary . . . to the ac-

complishment" of their legitimate purpose, *McLaughlin v. Florida* (1964). See *Loving v. Virginia* (1967).

The State, of course, has a duty of the highest order to protect the interests of minor children, particularly those of tender years. In common with most states, Florida law mandates that custody determinations be made in the best interests of the children involved. The goal of granting custody based on the best interests of the child is indisputably a substantial governmental interest for purposes of the Equal Protection Clause.

It would ignore reality to suggest that racial and ethnic prejudices do not exist or that all manifestations of those prejudices have been eliminated. There is a risk that a child living with a stepparent of a different race may be subject to a variety of pressures and stresses not present if the child were living with parents of the same racial or ethnic origin.

The question, however, is whether the reality of private biases and the possible injury they might inflict are permissible considerations for removal of an infant child from the custody of its natural mother. We have little difficulty concluding that they are not. The Constitution cannot control such prejudices but neither can it tolerate them. Private biases may be outside the reach of the law, but the law cannot, directly or indirectly, give them effect. "Public officials sworn to uphold the Constitution may not avoid a constitutional duty by bowing to the hypothetical effects of private racial prejudice that they assume to be both widely and deeply held." *Palmer v. Thompson* (1971) (WHITE, J., dissenting).

This is by no means the first time that acknowledged racial prejudice has been invoked to justify racial classifications. In *Buchanan v. Warley* (1917), for example, this Court invalidated a Kentucky law forbidding Negroes to buy homes in white neighborhoods.

"It is urged that this proposed segregation will promote the public peace by preventing race conflicts. Desirable as this is, and important as is the preservation of the public peace, this aim cannot be accomplished by laws or ordinances which deny rights created or protected by the Federal Constitution."

Whatever problems racially mixed households may pose for children in 1984 can no more support a denial of constitutional rights than could the stresses that residential integration was thought to entail in 1917. The effects of racial prejudice, however real, cannot justify a racial classification removing an infant child from the custody of its natural mother found to be an appropriate person to have such custody.

The judgment of the District Court of Appeal is reversed.

It is so ordered.

The cases we have examined so far involve challenges to laws or regulations in which racial bias is evident in their wording or in their application. The Court had little trouble finding a violation of the Constitution in *Brown, Loving,* and *Palmore* and, in each, unanimously struck down the discriminatory policies.

The intent to discriminate, however, is not always so evident. Some laws are written in language that is racially neutral, but the impact of the statute disproportionately disadvantages a particular racial group. Suppose such a law were passed to accomplish a legitimate government objective, and those who drafted the law had no racially discriminatory intent whatever. Are such laws unconstitutional? The Court was presented with this question in *Washington v. Davis.* Pay close attention to the interpretation of the Fourteenth and Fifth amendments by Justice Byron R. White in explaining the Court's decision.

Washington v. Davis

426 U.S. 229 (1976)

Vote: 7 (Blackmun, Burger, Powell, Rehnquist, Stevens,
　　　Stewart, White)
　　2 (Brennan, Marshall)

Opinion of the Court: White
Concurring opinion: Stevens
Dissenting opinion: Brennan

Applicants to the police force in Washington, D.C., were required to fulfill a number of criteria before being admitted into an intensive seventeen-week training program. In addition to meeting standards for physical abilities, character, and education, successful applicants had to receive a grade of at least forty out of eighty on Test 21, an examination used throughout the federal service to test verbal ability, vocabulary, reading, and comprehension. The test was developed by the Civil Service Commission, not the Washington Police Department.

The Test 21 requirement was challenged by unsuccessful black applicants. The federal district court upheld the use of the test, but the court of appeals reversed, finding that the test violated the Due Process Clause of the Fifth Amendment. The critical factor, according to the court of appeals, was that black applicants were disproportionately disadvantaged by the test requirement. In fact, four times as many blacks as whites failed. This disproportionate impact, standing alone and without regard to proof of discriminatory intent, was sufficient to invalidate the examination on constitutional grounds. The city appealed to the Supreme Court.

MR. JUSTICE WHITE delivered the opinion
of the Court.

The central purpose of the Equal Protection Clause of the Fourteenth Amendment is the prevention of official conduct discriminating on the basis of race. It is also true that the Due Process Clause of the Fifth Amendment contains an equal protection component prohibiting the United States from invidiously discriminating between individuals or groups. *Bolling v. Sharpe* (1954). But our cases have not embraced the proposition that a law or other official act, without regard to whether it reflects a racially discriminatory purpose, is unconstitutional solely because it has a racially disproportionate impact.

Almost 100 years ago, *Strauder v. West Virginia* (1880) established that the exclusion of Negroes from grand and petit juries in criminal proceedings violated the Equal Protection Clause, but the fact that a particular jury or a series of juries does not statistically reflect the racial composition of the community does not in itself make out an invidious discrimination forbidden by the Clause. "A purpose to discriminate must be present which may be proven by systematic exclusion of eligible jurymen of the proscribed race or by unequal application of the law to such an extent as to show intentional discrimination." *Akins v. Texas* (1945). . . .

The rule is the same in other contexts. *Wright v. Rockefeller* (1964) upheld a New York congressional apportionment statute against claims that district lines had been racially gerrymandered. The challenged districts were made up predominantly of whites or of minority races, and their boundaries were irregularly drawn. The challengers did not prevail because they failed to prove that the New York Legislature "was either motivated by racial considerations or in fact drew the districts on racial lines"; the plaintiffs had not shown that the statute "was the product of a state contrivance to segregate on the basis of race or place of origin.". . .

The school desegregation cases have also adhered to the basic equal protection principle that the invidious quality of a law claimed to be racially discriminatory must ultimately be traced to a racially discriminatory purpose. That there are both predominantly black and predominantly white schools in a community is not alone violative of the Equal Protection Clause. The essential element of *de jure* segregation is "a current condition of segregation resulting from intentional state action. *Keyes v. School Dist. No. 1* (1973). The differentiating factor between *de jure* segregation and so-called *de facto* segregation . . . is purpose or intent to segregate." The Court has also recently rejected allegations of racial discrimination based solely on the statistically disproportionate racial impact of various provisions of the Social Security Act because "[t]he acceptance of appellants' constitutional theory would render suspect each difference in treatment among the grant classes, however lacking in racial motivation and however otherwise rational the treatment might be." *Jefferson v. Hackney* (1972).

This is not to say that the necessary discriminatory racial purpose must be express or appear on the face of the statute, or that a law's disproportionate impact is irrelevant in cases involving Constitution-based claims of racial discrimination. A statute, otherwise neutral on its face, must not be applied so as invidiously to discriminate on the basis of race. *Yick Wo v. Hopkins* (1886). . . .

Necessarily, an invidious discriminatory purpose may often be inferred from the totality of the relevant facts, including the fact, if it is true, that the law bears more heavily on one race than another. It is also not infrequently true that the discriminatory impact—in the jury cases for example, the total or seriously disproportionate exclusion of Negroes from jury venires—may for all practical purposes demonstrate unconstitutionality because in various circumstances the discrimination is very difficult to explain on nonracial grounds. Nevertheless, we have not held that a law, neutral on its face and serving ends otherwise within the power of government to pursue, is invalid under the Equal Protection Clause simply because it may affect a greater proportion of one race than of another. Disproportionate impact is not irrelevant, but it is not the sole touchstone of an invidious racial discrimination forbidden by the Constitution. Standing alone, it does not trigger the rule that racial classifications are to be subjected to the strictest scrutiny and are justifiable only by the weightiest of considerations. . . .

As an initial matter, we have difficulty understanding how a law establishing a racially neutral qualification for employment is nevertheless racially discriminatory and denies "any person . . . equal protection of the laws" simply because a greater proportion of Negroes fail to qualify than members of other racial or ethnic groups. Had respondents, along with all others who had failed Test 21, whether white or black, brought an action claiming that the test denied each of them equal protection of the laws as compared with those who had passed with high enough scores to qualify them as police recruits, it is most unlikely that their challenge would have been sustained. Test 21, which is administered generally to prospective Government employees, concededly seeks to ascertain whether those who take it have acquired a particular level of verbal skill; and it is untenable that the Constitution prevents the Government from seeking modestly to upgrade the communicative abilities of its employees rather than to be satisfied with some lower level of competence, particularly where the job requires special ability to communicate orally and in writing. Respondents, as Negroes, could no more successfully claim that the test denied them equal protection than could white applicants who also failed. The conclusion would not be different in the face of proof that more

Negroes than whites had been disqualified by Test 21. That other Negroes also failed to score well would, alone, not demonstrate that respondents individually were being denied equal protection of the laws by the application of an otherwise valid qualifying test being administered to prospective police recruits.

Nor on the facts of the case before us would the disproportionate impact of Test 21 warrant the conclusion that it is a purposeful device to discriminate against Negroes and hence an infringement of the constitutional rights of respondents as well as other black applicants. As we have said, the test is neutral on its face and rationally may be said to serve a purpose the Government is constitutionally empowered to pursue. Even agreeing with the District Court that the differential racial effect of Test 21 called for further inquiry, we think the District Court correctly held that the affirmative efforts of the Metropolitan Police Department to recruit black officers, the changing racial composition of the recruit classes and of the force in general, and the relationship of the test to the training program negated any inference that the Department discriminated on the basis of race or that "a police officer qualifies on the color of his skin rather than ability."

Under Title VII [of the 1964 Civil Rights Act], Congress provided that when hiring and promotion practices disqualifying substantially disproportionate numbers of blacks are challenged, discriminatory purpose need not be proved, and that it is an insufficient response to demonstrate some rational basis for the challenged practices. It is necessary, in addition, that they be "validated" in terms of job performance in any one of several ways, perhaps by ascertaining the minimum skill, ability, or potential necessary for the position at issue and determining whether the qualifying tests are appropriate for the selection of qualified applicants for the job in question. However this process proceeds, it involves a more probing judicial review of, and less deference to, the seemingly reasonable acts of administrators and executives than is appropriate under the Constitution where special racial impact, without discriminatory purpose, is claimed. We are not disposed to adopt this more rigorous standard for the purposes of applying the Fifth and the Fourteenth Amendments in cases such as this.

A rule that a statute designed to serve neutral ends is nevertheless invalid, absent compelling justification, if in practice it benefits or burdens one race more than another would be far-reaching and would raise serious questions about, and perhaps invalidate, a whole range of tax, welfare, public service, regulatory, and licensing statutes that may be more burdensome to the poor and to the average black than to the more affluent white....

The District Court's accompanying conclusion that Test 21 was in fact directly related to the requirements of the police training program was supported by a validation study, as well as by other evidence of record; and we are not convinced that this conclusion was erroneous....

The judgment of the Court of Appeals accordingly is reversed.

So ordered.

The Court's opinion in *Washington v. Davis* was a blow to civil rights groups. The requirement that racially discriminatory intent must be shown to demonstrate a constitutional violation can be a difficult if not insurmountable obstacle. Certainly, disproportionate impact is much easier to establish using statistical analyses and other studies. Justice White's opinion, however, reminds us that under some federal civil rights statutes disproportionate impact is enough to trigger a violation of the law. Therefore, it may be easier for civil rights advocates to win suits under congressional statutes than to claim a violation of the Constitution.

Since 1954 the Court has developed constitutional doctrine in many areas related to race. Some of these, such as the expression liberties of civil rights protesters, we have already discussed, and others, such as affirmative action and voting rights, will be covered in this chapter and the next. The justices have not always agreed, especially on how to eliminate the effects of past discrimination. But throughout the Court's post-*Brown* history, the justices have said consistently that the Constitution does not permit government classifications that penalize historically disadvantaged racial minorities or impose distinctions that imply the racial inferiority of any group.

State Action

The wording of the Equal Protection Clause is clear: the constitutional provisions against discrimination were intended to provide protection against actions taken by the government. The Framers expressed no desire to use the Constitution to prohibit discrimination by private individuals. As early as 1883, in the *Civil Rights Cases*, the Supreme Court affirmed that the provisions of the Fourteenth Amendment do not extend beyond actions by the state. Consequently, establishing a violation of the Fourteenth Amendment requires more than just proving invidious discrimination. It also requires proof that the discrimination was initiated, sponsored, or supported by a state government. Violations of the Due Process Clause of the Fifth Amendment demand a showing that the federal government was somehow involved in the discriminatory action.

In many instances, this state action requirement posed no obstacle for civil rights litigants; the most onerous forms of discrimination, such as the forced segregation of the races, were imposed by state laws or local ordinances. In other areas, the discriminatory treatment was due to the actions of state agencies, law enforcement departments, or public officials, and the state's involvement in discrimination was both blatant and purposeful. When these conditions were present, court victories for civil rights advocates were almost certain.

However, much of the discrimination that most affected black Americans was private in nature.[2] Important areas of life such as access to housing and public accommodations fell into this category. Blacks often found they could not buy or rent the housing of their choice because of racial barriers. They were barred from certain restaurants and hotels. In all these cases, the private individuals who owned properties and businesses simply refused to do business with blacks. Such discrimination, without any government involvement, was beyond the reach of the Constitution.

Lawyers representing the victims of discrimination often used imaginative arguments to convince judges that state action was present, and the Supreme Court has been quite receptive to such approaches. The justices have held that any government involvement in racial discrimination, even the most indirect involvement, is sufficient to trigger the applicability of the Equal Protection and Due Process Clauses. *Shelley v. Kraemer* (1948) is a good example. In this suit, the Supreme Court found the presence of state action in an essentially private matter, the purchase of a house. Some have criticized the *Shelley* case for adopting an inappropriately broad definition of what constitutes state action. Those who drafted and ratified the Equal Protection Clause, it is argued, had no intention of prohibiting such indirect government involvement. Did the justices wrongfully interpret the concept of state action? Or did the Court appropriately condemn a form of discrimination that could not have existed without state support?

Shelley v. Kraemer

334 U.S. 1 (1948)

Vote: 6 *(Black, Burton, Douglas, Frankfurter, Murphy, Vinson)*

0

Opinion of the Court: Vinson
Not participating: Jackson, Reed, Rutledge

J. D. and Ethel Lee Shelley, a black couple, moved from Mississippi to Missouri just before World War II. When their family grew to six children, the Shelleys decided to move from their poor, predominantly black neighborhood to a more desirable location. On August 11, 1945, the Shelleys bought a house in the Grand Prairie neighborhood of St. Louis, a white resi-

---

2. Such discrimination could be regulated only by the legislature passing civil rights statutes based on some grant of authority other than the Fifth and Fourteenth Amendments. The most successful of such legislation, for example, was the Civil Rights Act of 1964, enacted by Congress pursuant to its power to regulate interstate commerce.

In 1948 the Supreme Court held that the state of Missouri had engaged in unconstitutional discrimination when it enforced a restrictive covenant that prevented J. D. and Ethel Lee Shelley and their six children from retaining ownership of their newly purchased home in St. Louis.

dential area, with only a few houses occupied by blacks.

Two months later, on October 9, Louis and Fern Kraemer, along with other property owners in the neighborhood, filed suit asking the court to divest the Shelleys of their property. Their suit was based on a violation of a restrictive covenant signed in 1911. This covenant was a legal contract signed by thirty neighborhood property owners who agreed that for fifty years they would not allow their respective properties to be occupied by any person not of the Caucasian race. This restriction was binding upon subsequent owners of the properties as well as the original parties. The Shelley house was covered by the agreement, and the white property owners demanded that it be enforced.

Restrictive covenants were not uncommon during this period. They were a response to increasing black migration into northern cities. Because a 1917

Supreme Court decision, *Buchanan v. Warley*, struck down state laws that mandated racial segregation in housing, whites opposing residential integration took private actions to keep blacks from moving into their neighborhoods. Restrictive covenants were so effective that the NAACP considered their elimination a top priority.

The Missouri Supreme Court ruled that the covenant should be enforced. The Shelleys, represented by Thurgood Marshall and the staff of the Legal Defense Fund, appealed to the U.S. Supreme Court. The appeal was combined with a similar case from Michigan. There was no doubt that such restrictive covenants constituted invidious discrimination, but they were essentially private agreements not regulated by the Equal Protection Clause. Marshall argued, however, that when the courts of Missouri enforced the agreement the state became party to the discrimination. The Justice Department and a host of civil rights organizations submitted briefs supporting Marshall's position.

MR. CHIEF JUSTICE VINSON delivered the opinion of the Court.

Whether the equal protection clause of the Fourteenth Amendment inhibits judicial enforcement by state courts of restrictive covenants based on race or color is a question which this Court has not heretofore been called upon to consider.... Here the particular patterns of discrimination and the areas in which the restrictions are to operate, are determined, in the first instance, by the terms of agreements among private individuals. Participation of the State consists in the enforcement of the restrictions so defined. The crucial issue with which we are here confronted is whether this distinction removes these cases from the operation of the prohibitory provisions of the Fourteenth Amendment.

Since the decision of this Court in the *Civil Rights Cases* (1883), the principle has become firmly embedded in our constitutional law that the action inhibited by the first section of the Fourteenth Amendment is only such action as may fairly be said to be that of the States. That Amendment erects no shield against merely private conduct, however discriminatory or wrongful.

We conclude, therefore, that the restrictive agreements standing alone cannot be regarded as violative of any rights guaranteed to petitioners by the Fourteenth Amendment. So long as the purposes of those agreements are effectuated by voluntary adherence to their terms, it would appear clear that there has been no action by the State and the provisions of the Amendment have not been violated.

But here there was more. These are cases in which the purposes of the agreements were secured only by judicial enforcement by state courts of the restrictive terms of the agreements. The respondents urge that judicial enforcement of private agreements does not amount to state action; or, in any event, the participation of the State is so attenuated in character as not to amount to state action within the meaning of the Fourteenth Amendment....

That the action of state courts and judicial officers in their official capacities is to be regarded as action of the State within the meaning of the Fourteenth Amendment, is a proposition which has long been established by decisions of this Court. That principle was given expression in the earliest cases involving the construction of the terms of the Fourteenth Amendment....

The short of the matter is that from the time of the adoption of the Fourteenth Amendment until the present, it has been the consistent ruling of this Court that the action of the States to which the Amendment has reference includes action of state courts and state judicial officials. Although, in construing the terms of the Fourteenth Amendment, differences have from time to time been expressed as to whether particular types of state action may be said to offend the Amendment's prohibitory provisions, it has never been suggested that state court action is immunized from the operation of those provisions simply because the act is that of the judicial branch of the state government.

Against this background of judicial construction, extending over a period of some three-quarters of a century, we are called upon to consider whether enforcement by state courts of the restrictive agreements in these cases may be deemed to be the acts of those States; and, if so, whether that action has denied these petitioners the equal protection of the laws which the Amendment was intended to insure.

We have no doubt that there has been state action in these cases in the full and complete sense of the phrase. The undisputed facts disclose that petitioners were willing purchasers of properties upon which they desired to establish homes. The owners of the properties were willing sellers; and contracts of sale were accordingly consummated. It is clear that but for the active intervention of the state courts, supported by the full panoply of state power, petitioners would have been free to occupy the properties in question without restraint.

These are not cases, as has been suggested, in which the States have merely abstained from action, leaving private individuals free to impose such discriminations as they see fit. Rather, these are cases in which the States have made available to such individuals the full coercive power of government to deny to petitioners, on the grounds of race or color, the enjoyment of property rights in premises which petitioners are willing and financially able to acquire and which the grantors are willing to sell. The difference between judicial enforcement and nonenforcement of the restrictive covenants is the difference to petitioners between being denied rights of property available to other members of the community and being accorded full enjoyment of those rights on an equal footing....

State action, as that phrase is understood for the purposes of the Fourteenth Amendment, refers to exertions of state power in all forms. And when the effect of that action is to deny rights subject to the protection of the Fourteenth Amendment, it is the obligation of this Court to enforce the constitutional commands.

We hold that in granting judicial enforcement of the restrictive agreements in these cases, the States have denied petitioners the equal protection of the laws and that, therefore, the action of the state courts cannot stand. We have noted that freedom from discrimination by the States in the enjoyment of property rights was among the basic objectives sought to be effectuated by the framers of the Fourteenth Amendment. That such discrimination has occurred in these cases is clear. Because of the race or color of these petitioners they have been denied rights of ownership or occupancy enjoyed as a matter of course by other citizens of different race or color....

The problem of defining the scope of the restrictions which the Federal Constitution imposes upon exertions of power by the States has given rise to many of the most persistent and fundamental issues which this Court has been called upon to consider. That problem was foremost in the minds of the framers of the Constitution, and, since that early day, has arisen in a multitude of forms. The task of determining whether the action of a State offends constitutional provisions is one which may not be undertaken lightly. Where, however, it is clear that the action of the State violates the terms of the fundamental charter, it is the obligation of this Court so to declare.

The historical context in which the Fourteenth Amendment became a part of the Constitution should not be forgotten. Whatever else the framers sought to achieve, it is clear that the matter of primary concern was the establishment of equality in the enjoyment of basic civil and political rights and the preservation of those rights from discriminatory action on the part of the States based on considerations of race or color. Seventy-five years ago this Court announced that the provisions of the Amendment

are to be construed with this fundamental purpose in mind. Upon full consideration, we have concluded that in these cases the States have acted to deny petitioners the equal protection of the laws guaranteed by the Fourteenth Amendment....

Reversed.

Another example of the Court's rather broad posture on the state action requirement is its ruling in *Burton v. Wilmington Parking Authority* (1961). In this case a black man was discriminated against by a privately owned and operated business, and, therefore, the Equal Protection Clause did not seem to apply. But the attorneys representing Burton argued that the state was indeed a participant in the discrimination. Was the Court correct in concluding that state action was involved here? Or was the involvement of the state government too remote to warrant an application of the Fourteenth Amendment?

Burton v. Wilmington Parking Authority

365 U.S. 715 (1961)
Vote: 6 (Black, Brennan, Clark, Douglas, Stewart, Warren)
    3 (Frankfurter, Harlan, Whittaker)
Opinion of the Court: Clark
Concurring opinion: Stewart
Dissenting opinions: Frankfurter, Harlan

In August 1958 William Burton parked his car in a downtown parking garage in Wilmington, Delaware, and went to the Eagle Coffee Shoppe, a restaurant located within the parking structure. Burton was denied service in the restaurant because he was black.

The parking garage was built, owned, and operated by the Wilmington Parking Authority, a municipally created public agency. Before the structure was completed, it had become clear that parking revenues alone would be insufficient to service the loans and bonds that financed the construction. To increase revenues, the parking authority leased space in the building to private business ventures, including the Eagle Coffee Shoppe, which had a thirty-year lease to operate a restaurant in the garage. The Eagle Corporation invested some $220,000 of its own money to convert the space for restaurant use. The parking authority, under the terms of the lease, provided certain materials and services for the operation, and the city collected more than $28,000 in annual rent from Eagle.

Burton filed suit claiming that his rights under the Equal Protection Clause had been violated. The parking authority disagreed, arguing that the discrimination was purely private with the state having no substantive involvement. The trial court ruled in favor of Burton, finding that the lease arrangement did not insulate the parking authority from the discrimination of its tenant. The Delaware Supreme Court, however, reversed, holding that Eagle was operating in a purely private capacity.

MR. JUSTICE CLARK delivered the opinion of the Court.

It is clear, as it always has been since the *Civil Rights Cases* [1883], that "Individual invasion of individual rights is not the subject-matter of the [Fourteenth] amendment," and that private conduct abridging individual rights does no violence to the Equal Protection Clause unless to some significant extent the State in any of its manifestations has been found to have become involved in it. Because the virtue of the right to equal protection of the laws could lie only in the breadth of its application, its constitutional assurance was reserved in terms whose imprecision was necessary if the right were to be enjoyed in the variety of individual-state relationships which the Amendment was designed to embrace. For the same reason, to fashion and apply a precise formula for recognition of state responsibility under the Equal Protection Clause is an "impossible task" which "This Court has never attempted."

The trial court's disposal of the issues on summary judgment has resulted in a rather incomplete record, but the opinion of the Supreme Court as well as that of the Chancellor presents the facts in sufficient detail for us to determine the degree of state participation in Eagle's refusal to serve petitioner. In this connection the Delaware Supreme Court seems to have placed controlling emphasis on its conclusion, as to the accuracy of which there is doubt, that only some 15% of the total cost of the facility was "advanced" from public funds; that the cost of the entire facility was allocated three-fifths to the space for commercial leasing and two-fifths to parking space; that anticipated revenue from parking was only some 30.5% of the total income, the balance of which was expected to be earned by the leasing; that the Authority had no original intent to place a restaurant in the building, it being only a happenstance resulting from the bidding; that Eagle expended considerable moneys on furnishings; that the restaurant's main and marked public entrance is on Ninth Street without any public entrance direct from the parking area; and that "the only connection Eagle has with the public facility ... is the furnishing of the sum of $28,700 annually in the form of rent which is used by the Authority to defray a portion of the operating expense of an otherwise unprofitable enterprise." While these factual considerations are indeed validly accountable aspects of the enterprise upon which the State has embarked, we cannot say that they lead inescapably to the conclusion that state action is not present. Their persuasiveness is diminished when evaluated in the context of other factors which must be acknowledged.

The land and building were publicly owned. As an entity, the building was dedicated to "public uses" in performance of the Authority's "essential governmental functions." The costs of land acquisition, construction, and maintenance are defrayed entirely from donations by the City of Wilmington, from loans and revenue bonds and from the proceeds of rentals and parking services out of which the loans and bonds were payable. Assuming that the distinction would be significant, the commercially leased areas were not surplus state property, but constituted a physically and financially integral and, indeed, indispensable part of the State's plan to operate its project as a self-sustaining unit. Upkeep and maintenance of the building, including necessary repairs, were responsibilities of the Authority and were payable out of public funds. It cannot be doubted that the peculiar relationship of the restaurant to the parking facility in which it is located confers on each an incidental variety of mutual benefits. Guests of the restaurant are afforded a convenient place to park their automobiles, even if they cannot enter the restaurant directly from the parking area. Similarly, its convenience for diners may well provide additional demand for the Authority's parking facilities. Should any improvements effected in the leasehold by Eagle become part of the realty, there is no possibility of increased taxes being passed on to it since the fee is held by a tax-exempt government agency. Neither can it be ignored, especially in view of Eagle's affirmative allegation that for it to serve Negroes would injure its business, that profits earned by discrimination not only contribute to, but also are indispensable elements in, the financial success of a governmental agency.

Addition of all these activities, obligations and responsibilities of the Authority, the benefits mutually conferred, together with the obvious fact that the restaurant is operated as an integral part of a public building devoted to a public parking service, indicates that degree of state participation and involvement in discriminatory action which it was the design of the Fourteenth Amendment to condemn. It is irony amounting to grave injustice that in one part of a single building, erected and maintained with public funds by an agency of the State to serve a public purpose, all persons have equal rights, while in another portion, also serving the public, a Negro is a second-class citizen, offensive because of his race, without rights and unentitled to service, but at the same time fully enjoys equal access to nearby restaurants in wholly privately owned buildings. As the Chancellor pointed out, in its lease with Eagle the Authority could have affirmatively required Eagle to discharge the responsibilities under the Fourteenth Amendment imposed upon the private enterprise as a consequence of state participation. But no State may effectively abdicate its responsibilities by either ignoring them or by merely failing to discharge them whatever the motive may be. It is of no consolation to an individual denied the equal protection of the laws that it was done in good faith.... By its inaction, the Authority, and through it the State, has not only made itself a party to the refusal of service, but has elected to place its power, property and prestige behind the admitted discrimination. The State has so far insinuated itself into a position of interdependence with Eagle that it must be recognized as a joint participant in the challenged activity, which, on that account, cannot be considered to have been so "purely private" as to fall without the scope of the Fourteenth Amendment.

Because readily applicable formulae may not be fashioned, the conclusions drawn from the facts and circumstances of this record are by no means declared as universal truths on the basis of which every state leasing agreement is to be tested. Owing to the very "largeness" of government, a multitude of relationships might appear to some to fall within the Amendment's embrace, but that, it must be remembered, can be determined only in the framework of the peculiar facts or circumstances present. Therefore respondents' prophecy of nigh universal application of a constitutional precept so peculiarly dependent for its invocation upon appropriate facts fails to take into account "Differences in circumstances which beget appropriate differences in law." Specifically defining the limits of our inquiry, what we hold today is that when a State leases public property in the manner and for the purpose shown to have been the case here, the proscriptions of the Fourteenth Amendment must be complied with by the lessee as certainly as though they were binding covenants written into the agreement itself....

Reversed and remanded.

Shelley and *Burton* demonstrate the Court's willingness to impose an expansive view of state action. But these decisions did not eliminate the public/private distinction. The Court's decision in *Moose Lodge #107 v. Irvis* (1972) serves as a reminder that the definition of state action has its limits. Note how Justice Rehnquist distinguishes the state's involvement here from Delaware's relationship with the Eagle Coffee Shoppe. Is he convincing in his argument that the *Burton* precedent is inapplicable? Would finding state action in this case blur any meaningful state/private distinction? Or is Justice Brennan more persuasive when he argues that the state was involved in racial discrimination? If the Court had taken the dissenters' position, what implications would it have had for other private organizations, such as country clubs or fraternal organizations?

Moose Lodge #107 v. Irvis

407 U.S. 163 (1972)

Vote: 6 (Blackmun, Burger, Powell, Rehnquist, Stewart, White)
    3 (Brennan, Douglas, Marshall)
Opinion of the Court: Rehnquist
Dissenting opinions: Brennan, Douglas

A white member in good standing of the Harrisburg, Pennsylvania, Moose Lodge, accompanied by a guest, entered the lodge's dining room and bar and requested service. The lodge employees refused to serve him because his guest, K. Leroy Irvis, was black. He was also a member of the Pennsylvania state legislature. Lodge #107, part of the national Moose organization, was subject to the rules of its Supreme Lodge, which limited membership to Caucasians and permitted members to entertain only Caucasian guests at the lodge. Irvis sued the lodge, claiming that he had been denied his rights under the Equal Protection Clause of the Fourteenth Amendment. His suit was based on the theory that in granting the Moose Lodge a liquor license the state of Pennsylvania was approving the organization's racially discriminatory policies. A federal court ruled in favor of Irvis, declaring that the lodge's liquor license would be invalid until such time as the discriminatory practices ceased. The lodge appealed.

MR. JUSTICE REHNQUIST delivered the opinion of the Court.

Moose Lodge is a private club in the ordinary meaning of that term. It is a local chapter of a national fraternal organization having well-defined requirements for membership. It conducts all of its activities in a building that is owned by it. It is not publicly funded. Only members and guests are permitted in any lodge of the order; one may become a guest only by invitation of a member or upon invitation of the house committee.

Appellee, while conceding the right of private clubs to choose members upon a discriminatory basis, asserts that the licensing of Moose Lodge to serve liquor by the Pennsylvania Liquor Control Board amounts to such state involvement with the club's activities as to make its discriminatory practices forbidden by the Equal Protection Clause of the Fourteenth Amendment.... We conclude that Moose Lodge's refusal to serve food and beverages to a guest by reason of the fact that he was a Negro does not, under the circumstances here presented, violate the Fourteenth Amendment.

In 1883, this Court in *The Civil Rights Cases* set forth the essential dichotomy between discriminatory action by the State, which is prohibited by the Equal Protection Clause, and private conduct, "however discriminatory or wrongful," against which that clause "erects no shield." That dichotomy has been subsequently reaffirmed in *Shelley v. Kraemer* and in *Burton v. Wilmington Parking Authority*.

While the principle is easily stated, the question of whether particular discriminatory conduct is private, on the one hand, or amounts to "state action," on the other hand, frequently admits of no easy answer. "Only by sifting facts and weighing circumstances can the nonobvious involvement of the State in private conduct be attributed its true significance."

Our cases make clear that the impetus for the forbidden discrimination need not originate with the State if it is state action that enforces privately originated discrimination. Shelley v. Kraemer. The Court held in Burton v. Wilmington Parking Authority that a private restaurant owner who refused service because of a customer's race violated the Fourteenth Amendment, where the restaurant was located in a building owned by a state-created parking authority and leased from the authority. The Court, after a comprehensive review of the relationship between the lessee and the parking authority concluded that the latter had "so far insinuated itself into a position of interdependence with Eagle [the restaurant owner] that it must be recognized as a joint participant in the challenged activity, which, on that account, cannot be considered to have been so 'purely private' as to fall without the scope of the Fourteenth Amendment."

The Court has never held, of course, that discrimination by an otherwise private entity would be violative of the Equal Protection Clause if the private entity receives any sort of benefit or service at all from the State, or if it is subject to state regulation in any degree whatever. Since state-furnished services include such necessities of life as electricity, water, and police and fire protection, such a holding would utterly emasculate the distinction between private as distinguished from state conduct set forth in *The Civil Rights Cases* and adhered to in subsequent decisions. Our holdings indicate that where the impetus for the discrimination is private, the State must have "significantly involved itself with invidious discriminations" in order for the discriminatory action to fall within the ambit of the constitutional prohibition....

Here there is nothing approaching the symbiotic relationship between lessor and lessee that was present in *Burton*, where the private lessee obtained the benefit of locating in a building owned by the state-created parking authority, and the parking authority was enabled to carry out its primary public purpose of furnishing parking space by advantageously leasing portions of the building constructed for that purpose to commercial lessees such as the owner of the Eagle Restaurant. Unlike *Burton*, the Moose Lodge building is located on land owned by it, not by any public authority. Far from apparently holding itself out as a place of public accommodation, Moose Lodge quite ostentatiously proclaims the fact that it is not open to the public at large. Nor is it located and operated in such surroundings that although private in name, it discharges a function or performs a service that would otherwise in all likelihood be performed by the State. In short, while Eagle was a public restaurant in a public building, Moose Lodge is a private social club in a private building.

With the exception hereafter noted, the Pennsylvania Liquor Control Board plays absolutely no part in establishing or enforcing the membership or guest policies of the club that it licenses to serve liquor. There is no suggestion in this record that Pennsylvania law, either as written or as applied, discriminates against minority groups either in their right to apply for club licenses themselves or in their right to purchase and be served liquor in places of public accommodation. The only effect that the state licensing of Moose Lodge to serve liquor can be said to have on the right of any other Pennsylvanian to buy or be served liquor on premises other than those of Moose Lodge is that for some purposes club licenses are counted in the maximum number of licenses that may be issued in a given municipality....

The District Court was at pains to point out in its opinion what it considered to be the "pervasive" nature of the regulation of private clubs by the Pennsylvania Liquor Control Board. As that court noted, an applicant for a club license must make such physical alterations in its premises as the board may require, must file a list of the names and addresses of its members and employees, and must keep extensive financial records. The board is granted the right to inspect the licensed premises at any time when patrons, guests, or members are present.

However detailed this type of regulation may be in some particulars, it cannot be said to in any way foster or encourage racial discrimination. Nor can it be said to make the State in any realistic sense a partner or even a joint venturer in the club's enterprise. The limited effect of the prohibition against obtaining additional club licenses when the maximum number of retail licenses allotted to a municipality has been issued, when considered together with the availability of liquor from hotel, restaurant, and retail licensees, falls far short of conferring upon club licensees a monopoly in the dispensing of liquor in any given municipality or in the State as a whole. We therefore hold that ... the operation of the regulatory scheme enforced by the Pennsylvania Liquor Control Board does not sufficiently implicate the State in the discriminatory guest policies of Moose Lodge to make the latter "state action" within the ambit of the Equal Protection Clause of the Fourteenth Amendment.

Reversed.

MR. JUSTICE BRENNAN ... dissenting.

When Moose Lodge obtained its liquor license, the State of Pennsylvania became an active participant in the operation of the Lodge bar. Liquor licensing laws are only incidentally revenue measures; they are primarily pervasive regulatory schemes under which the State dictates and continually supervises virtually every detail of the operation of the licensee's business. Very few, if any, other licensed businesses experience such complete state involvement. Yet the Court holds that such involvement does not constitute "state action" making the Lodge's refusal to serve a guest liquor solely because of his race a violation of the Fourteenth Amendment. The vital flaw in the Court's reasoning is its complete disregard of the fundamental value underlying the "state action" concept....

Plainly, the State of Pennsylvania's liquor regulations intertwine the State with the operation of the Lodge bar in a "significant way [and] lend [the State's] authority to the sordid business of racial discrimination." The opinion of the late Circuit Judge Freedman, for the three-judge District Court, most persuasively demonstrates the "state action" present in this case:

"We believe the decisive factor is the uniqueness and the all-pervasiveness of the regulation by the Commonwealth of Pennsylvania of the dispensing of liquor under licenses granted by the state. The regulation inherent in the grant of a state liquor license is so different in nature and extent from the ordinary licenses issued by the state that it is different in quality."…

This is thus a case requiring application of the principle that until today has governed our determinations of the existence of "state action": "Our prior decisions leave no doubt that the mere existence of efforts by the State, through legislation or otherwise, to authorize, encourage, or otherwise support racial discrimination in a particular facet of life constitutes illegal state involvement in those pertinent private acts of discrimination that subsequently occur."

I therefore dissent and would affirm the final decree entered by the District Court.

This ruling demonstrates that the Burger Court was less likely than the Warren Court to use expansive definitions in reaching decisions. The three dissenters in *Moose Lodge #107*—Brennan, Marshall, and Douglas—had been members of the Warren Court's liberal majority responsible for expanding the rights of racial minorities.

When state action is not present or is difficult to prove, victims of invidious discrimination may find recourse in federal or state statutes that outlaw private forms of discrimination. Governments enjoy a number of powers, especially those over commercial activities, that permit regulating certain forms of private discriminatory behavior. Although the Supreme Court ruled in *Moose Lodge #107* that state action had not contributed to the discrimination, several states have used the power to regulate alcoholic beverages as a means of combating racial bias. For example, in 1973 the Supreme Court upheld a Maine regulation that made the granting of a liquor license contingent on nondiscriminatory service policies.[3]

The Supreme Court consistently has held that invidious discrimination and state action must be demonstrated before a violation of the Constitution is established. These principles, first fully developed in race relations law, have been extended to other claims of unconstitutional bias as well.

SEX DISCRIMINATION

Lawsuits based on claims of sex discrimination have increased dramatically since the 1970s. Before, such cases were rare, and those that reached the Supreme Court ended in decisions that reinforced traditional views of sex roles. In *Bradwell v. Illinois* (1873), for example, the Court heard a challenge to an action by the Illinois Supreme Court denying Myra Bradwell a license to practice law solely because of her sex. The Court, with only Chief Justice Salmon P. Chase dissenting, upheld the state action. Justice Joseph P. Bradley's concurring opinion, which Justices Noah H. Swayne and Stephen J. Field joined, illustrates the attitude of the legal community toward women. Bradley said that he gave his "heartiest concurrence" to contemporary society's "multiplication of avenues for women's advancement," but he added, "The natural and proper timidity and delicacy which belongs to the female sex evidently unfits it for many of the occupations of civil life." This condition, according to Bradley, was the product of divine ordinance.

Similar decisions followed. In 1875 the Court in *Minor v. Happersett* upheld Missouri's denial of voting rights to women, a precedent in effect until ratification of the Nineteenth Amendment in 1920. As late as

3. *B.P.O.E. Lodge #2043 v. Ingraham* (1973).

1948, the Court upheld the right of the state to ban women from certain occupations. In *Goesaert v. Cleary,* decided that year, the justices declared valid a Michigan law that barred women from becoming bartenders unless they belonged to the immediate family of the bar owner. In explaining the ruling, Justice Frankfurter wrote, "The fact that women may now have achieved the virtues that men have long claimed as their prerogatives and now indulge in vices that men have long practiced, does not preclude the States from drawing a sharp line between the sexes, certainly in such matters as the regulation of the liquor traffic." In a comparatively modern case, *Hoyt v. Florida* (1961), the justices upheld a Florida law that automatically exempted women from jury duty unless they asked to serve.

During the first half of this century, the Court upheld a number of state laws enacted to protect women in the workplace. These laws dealt with matters such as hours, working conditions, physical demands, and compensation. At the time of their implementation these statutes were seen as a progressive response to the increasing numbers of women working outside the home. Today, these protective laws are considered paternalistic, based on an assumption of the inferiority of women.

Social change in the 1950s and 1960s, and the growing strength of the women's movement, prompted major alterations in the law. Congress passed a number of federal statutes extending equal rights to women, among them the Equal Pay Act of 1963 and various amendments to the 1964 Civil Rights Act. Many states have passed similar laws to eliminate discriminatory conditions in the marketplace and in state legal codes. In addition to these legislative actions, in 1972 Congress proposed an amendment to the Constitution. Known as the Equal Rights Amendment, it declared, "Equality of rights under the law shall not be denied or abridged by the United States or by any State on account of sex." The amendment failed to be approved by the required number of

Myra Bradwell studied law with her husband, a judge, and edited and published the *Chicago Legal News,* the most important legal publication in the Midwest. Although she passed the bar exam, the Illinois Supreme Court refused to admit her to the state bar because of her sex. She appealed to the U.S. Supreme Court, but lost.

states, even though Congress extended the deadline for ratification.

In addition to working for changes in the Constitution and laws, women turned to the courts for redress of their grievances. Like the advocates for black Americans, many in the women's movement believed that the Due Process and Equal Protection Clauses held the same potential for ensuring women's rights, and they began organizing to assert their claims in court.

Standard of Scrutiny

The Supreme Court issued its first major sex discrimination decision of the contemporary period in

BOX 10-4 RUTH BADER GINSBURG
(1993-)

When President Bill Clinton nominated Ruth Bader Ginsburg in 1993 to fill the vacancy left by retiring justice Byron White, the president was enjoying the first such opportunity for a Democrat in more than a quarter century. Ginsburg became the second woman to sit on the Court and the first Jewish justice since the resignation of Abe Fortas in 1969. She brought to the Court a sterling record as a law professor, advocate, and federal judge. She earned a reputation as the "Thurgood Marshall of sex discrimination law" for her pioneering work in that field.

Ginsburg was born in Brooklyn, New York, in 1933 to Nathan and Celia

Bader. In 1950 she began her undergraduate studies at Cornell University, where she met her future husband, Martin Ginsburg. After her graduation in 1954, the Ginsburgs lived briefly in Oklahoma where Martin was stationed in the army and Ruth worked for the Social Security Administration. In 1956 they moved to Cambridge, Massachusetts, to attend Harvard Law School. After graduation Martin accepted a job in New York City and Ruth transferred to Columbia Law School to finish her legal training. She graduated from Columbia in 1959, tied for first in her class and having the distinction of serving on the law review staffs at both Harvard and Columbia.

In spite of her academic credentials, Ginsburg's attempts to obtain employment in a major law firm were unsuccessful. She later explained these rejections by noting: "To be a woman, a Jew and a mother to boot, that combination was a bit much." She secured a clerkship with federal district judge Edmund Palmieri, where she worked from 1959 to 1961. She then joined a Columbia University research project on civil law procedures in other countries and became an expert on the Swedish legal system. Ginsburg joined the law

faculty at Rutgers University where she worked up the ranks from assistant professor to full professor. In 1972 she returned to Columbia University as professor of law and became the first woman to be awarded tenure at that school.

While on the faculty at Columbia, Ginsburg served as general counsel for the American Civil Liberties Union, heading the Women's Rights Project. In that capacity she was in the vanguard of sex discrimination cases of the 1970s. Her legal arguments before the Supreme Court had a profound impact on the development of sex discrimination law. Of the six cases she argued before the justices, she was successful in five. She participated in *Reed v. Reed* (1971), *Frontiero v. Richardson* (1973), *Kahn v. Shevin* (1974), *Weinberger v. Wiesenfeld* (1975), and *Craig v. Boren* (1976).

In 1980 President Jimmy Carter nominated Ginsburg for the Court of Appeals for the District of Columbia. She was later joined on that court by Clarence Thomas and Antonin Scalia who would precede her to the Supreme Court. In thirteen years as a federal appellate judge, Ginsburg developed a reputation as an intelligent, highly competent jurist with a moderate political ideology.

Ginsburg's nomination to the Supreme Court met with broad, bipartisan approval. She received the highest rating of the American Bar Association. On August 3, 1993, by a vote of 96–3 the Senate confirmed Ruth Bader Ginsburg as the Supreme Court's 107th justice.

SOURCE: "Ruth Ginsburg: Carving a Career Path Through a Male-Dominated Legal World," *Congressional Quarterly Weekly Report*, July 17, 1993, 1876–7.

1971. In *Reed v. Reed* the justices considered the validity of an Idaho inheritance statute that used sex classifications. The statute was challenged on the grounds that it was in violation of the Equal Protection Clause of the Fourteenth Amendment. It was clear from the outset that the same requirements that had developed in race relations cases would apply here; that is, the statute's challenger would have to demonstrate both invidious discrimination and state action before a violation could be found.

What was not so clear was the standard of scrutiny the justices would use. In the racial discrimination cases, the Court had declared strict scrutiny the appropriate standard. Racial minorities were considered a suspect class, and, therefore, classifications based on race were presumed to be unconstitutional. The state had a heavy burden of proof if it wished to show that a law based on race was the least restrictive means to achieve a compelling state interest. Much of the success enjoyed by civil rights groups was due to this favorable legal status. The advocates of equal rights for women, especially ACLU attorneys such as Ruth Bader Ginsburg *(see Box 10-4)*, hoped the Court would adopt the same standard for sex discrimination claims.

===

Reed v. Reed

404 U.S. 71 (1971)

Vote: 7 (Blackmun, Brennan, Burger, Douglas, Marshall, Stewart, White)

0

Opinion of the Court: Burger

Richard Reed was the adopted child of Sally and Cecil Reed. He died March 29, 1967, in Ada County, Idaho, leaving no will. Richard's parents, who had separated before his death, became involved in a legal dispute over who should administer their son's estate. The estate was insignificant, consisting of a few personal items and a small savings account. The total value was less than $1,000. The probate court judge named Cecil Reed administrator of the estate, in accordance with Idaho law. Section 15-312 of the Idaho Code stipulated that when a person died intestate (without a will) an administrator would be appointed according to a list of priority relationships. First priority went to a surviving spouse, second priority to children, third to parents, and so forth. Section 15-314 of the statute stated that in the case of competing petitions from otherwise qualified individuals of the same priority relationship, "males must be preferred to females."

Sally Reed challenged the law as a violation of the Equal Protection Clause of the Fourteenth Amendment. The state district court agreed with her argument, but the Idaho Supreme Court reversed. With assistance of Ginsburg and other ACLU lawyers, Sally Reed took her case to the U.S. Supreme Court.

MR. CHIEF JUSTICE BURGER delivered the opinion of the Court.

Having examined the record and considered the briefs and oral arguments of the parties, we have concluded that the arbitrary preference established in favor of males by § 15-314 of the Idaho Code cannot stand in the face of the Fourteenth Amendment's command that no State deny the equal protection of the laws to any person within its jurisdiction.

Idaho does not, of course, deny letters of administration to women altogether. Indeed, under § 15-312, a woman whose spouse dies intestate has a preference over a son, father, brother, or any other male relative of the decedent. Moreover, we can judicially notice that in this country, presumably due to the greater longevity of women, a large proportion of estates, both intestate and under wills of decedents, are administered by surviving widows.

Section 15-314 is restricted in its operation to those situations where competing applications for letters of administration have been filed by both male and female members of the same entitlement class established by § 15-312. In such situations, § 15-314 provides that different treatment be accorded to the applicants on the basis of their sex; it thus establishes a classification subject to scrutiny under the Equal Protection Clause.

In applying that clause, this Court has consistently recognized that the Fourteenth Amendment does not deny to States the power to treat different classes of persons in different ways. The Equal Protection Clause of that amendment does, however, deny to States the power to legislate that different treatment be accorded to persons placed by a statute into different classes on the basis of criteria wholly unrelated to the objective of that statute. A classification "must be reasonable, not arbitrary, and must rest upon some ground of difference having a fair and substantial relation to the object of the legislation, so that all persons similarly circumstanced shall be treated alike." The question presented by this case, then, is whether a difference in the sex of competing applicants for letters of administration bears a rational relationship to a state objective that is sought to be advanced by the operation of §§ 15-312 and 15-314.

In upholding the latter section, the Idaho Supreme Court concluded that its objective was to eliminate one area of controversy when two or more persons, equally entitled under § 15-312, seek letters of administration and thereby present the probate court "with the issue of which one should be named." The court also concluded that where such persons are not of the same sex, the elimination of females from consideration "is neither an illogical nor arbitrary method devised by the legislature to resolve an issue that would otherwise require a hearing as to the relative merits . . . of the two or more petitioning relatives. . . ."

Clearly the objective of reducing the workload on probate courts by eliminating one class of contests is not without some legitimacy. The crucial question, however, is whether § 15-314 advances that objective in a manner consistent with the command of the Equal Protection Clause. We hold that it does not. To give a mandatory preference to members of either sex over members of the other, merely to accomplish the elimination of hearings on the merits, is to make the very kind of arbitrary legislative choice forbidden by the Equal Protection Clause of the Fourteenth Amendment; and whatever may be said as to the positive values of avoiding intrafamily controversy, the choice in this context may not lawfully be mandated solely on the basis of sex.

We note finally that if § 15-314 is viewed merely as a modifying appendage to § 15-312 and aimed at the same objective, its constitutionality is not thereby saved. The objective of § 15-312 clearly is to establish degrees of entitlement of various classes of persons in accordance with their varying degrees and kinds of relationship to the intestate. Regardless of their sex, persons within any one of the enumerated classes of that section are similarly situated with respect to that objective. By providing dissimilar treatment for men and women who are thus similarly situated, the challenged section violates the Equal Protection Clause. The judgment of the Idaho Supreme Court is reversed and the case remanded for further proceedings not inconsistent with this opinion.

Reversed and remanded.

The Court's unanimous decision in *Reed* applied two important principles to sex discrimination. First, the Court refused to accept Idaho's defense of its statute. The state had contended that it was inefficient to hold full court hearings on the relative merits of competing candidates to administer estates, especially small estates. Imposing arbitrary criteria saved court time and avoided intrafamily squabbles. The Supreme Court held that administrative convenience is no justification for violating the Constitution. Second, defenders of the Idaho law argued that the arbitrary favoring of males over females made sense because, in most cases, the male will have had more education and experience in financial matters than the competing female. In rejecting this argument, the justices said that laws containing overbroad, sex-based assumptions violate the Equal Protection Clause.

The *Reed* case also signaled that the justices were receptive to sex discrimination claims and would not hesitate to strike down state laws that imposed arbitrary sex classifications. While *Reed* was certainly good news for women's rights advocates, the standard used in the case was not. Chief Justice Burger clearly articulated the rational basis test, holding that laws based on gender classifications must be reasonable and have a rational relationship to a state objective. The Idaho law was sufficiently arbitrary to fail the rational basis test, but other laws and policies might well survive it.

Two years later, the Court heard another sex discrimination case, *Frontiero v. Richardson,* in which an attempt was made to convince the Court to adopt the strict scrutiny test. The case provided the first opportunity for two newly appointed justices, Powell and Rehnquist, to rule on a sex discrimination case. Note how the justices divide on which test is appropriate for sex discrimination cases. Also, keep in mind that, because this case involves a challenge to a U.S. military regulation, the governing constitutional provision is the Due Process Clause of the Fifth Amendment.

Frontiero v. Richardson

411 U.S. 677 (1973)
Vote: 8 (Blackmun, Brennan, Burger, Douglas, Marshall,
    Powell, Stewart, White)
    1 *(Rehnquist)*
Opinion announcing the judgment of the Court: Brennan
Concurring opinion: Powell

Sharron Frontiero was a lieutenant in the U.S. Air Force, and her husband, Joseph, was a full-time student at Huntingdon College in Mobile, Alabama. Sharron applied for certain dependent benefits for her husband, including medical and housing allowances. These benefits were part of the package the military offered to be competitive with private employers. To receive the benefits for her spouse, Sharron had to prove that Joseph was financially dependent upon her, which meant that she provided at least half of her husband's support.

According to the facts agreed to by the parties, Joseph's expenses amounted to $354 per month. He re-

ceived $205 (58 percent of his monthly expenses) from his own veterans' benefits. Consequently, Joseph was not considered financially dependent on his wife, and the benefits were denied. Sharron Frontiero objected to this treatment because male officers did not have to prove that their wives were financially dependent on them; such dependence was presumed. Supported by Ginsburg's amicus arguments for the ACLU, Frontiero challenged the regulations as a violation of the Due Process Clause on two grounds. First, females were required to provide evidence that males were not. Second, as a consequence, male officers could receive dependent benefits for their wives even if their spouses were not financially dependent, and female officers could not.

MR. JUSTICE BRENNAN announced the judgment of the Court....

At the outset, appellants contend that classifications based upon sex, like classifications based upon race, alienage, and national origin, are inherently suspect and must therefore be subjected to close judicial scrutiny. We agree and, indeed, find at least implicit support for such an approach in our unanimous decision only last Term in Reed v. Reed (1971).

In *Reed,* the Court considered the constitutionality of an Idaho statute providing that, when two individuals are otherwise equally entitled to appointment as administrator of an estate, the male applicant must be preferred to the female....

The Court noted that the Idaho statute "provides that different treatment be accorded to the applicants on the basis of their sex; it thus establishes a classification subject to scrutiny under the Equal Protection Clause." Under "traditional" equal protection analysis, a legislative classification must be sustained unless it is "patently arbitrary" and bears no rational relationship to a legitimate governmental interest.

In an effort to meet this standard, appellee contended that the statutory scheme was a reasonable measure designed to reduce the workload on probate courts by eliminating one class of contests. Moreover, appellee argued that the mandatory preference for male applicants was in itself reasonable since "men [are] as a rule more conversant with business affairs than ... women." Indeed, appellee maintained that "it is a matter of common knowledge, that women still are not engaged in politics, the professions, business or industry to the extent that men are." And the Idaho Supreme Court, in upholding the constitutionality of this statute, suggested that the Idaho Legislature might reasonably have "concluded that in general men are better qualified to act as an administrator than are women."

Despite these contentions, however, the Court held the statutory preference for male applicants unconstitutional. In reaching this result, the Court implicitly rejected appellee's apparently rational explanation of the statutory scheme, and concluded that, by ignoring the individual qualifications of particular applications, the challenged statute provided "dissimilar treatment for men and women who are ... similarly situated." The Court therefore held that, even though the State's interest in achieving administrative efficiency "is not without some legitimacy," "[t]o give a mandatory preference to members of either sex over members of the other, merely to accomplish the elimination of hearings on the merits, is to make the very kind of arbitrary legislative choice forbidden by the Constitution...." This departure from "traditional" rational-basis analysis with respect to sex-based classifications is clearly justified.

There can be no doubt that our Nation has had a long and unfortunate history of sex discrimination. Traditionally, such discrimination was rationalized by an attitude of "romantic paternalism" which, in practical effect, put women, not on a pedestal, but in a cage.... Our statute books gradually became laden with gross, stereotyped distinctions between the sexes and, indeed, throughout much of the 19th century the position of women in our society was, in many respects, comparable to that of blacks under the pre–Civil War slave codes. Neither slaves nor women could hold office, serve on juries, or bring suit in their own names, and married women traditionally were denied the legal capacity to hold or convey property or to serve as legal guardians of their own children. And although blacks were guaranteed the right to vote in 1870, women were denied even that right—which is itself "preservative of other basic civil and political rights"—until adoption of the Nineteenth Amendment half a century later.

It is true, of course, that the position of women in America has improved markedly in recent decades. Nevertheless, it can hardly be doubted that, in part because of the high visibility of the sex characteristic, women still face pervasive, although at times more subtle, discrimination in our educational institutions, in the job market and, perhaps most conspicuously, in the political arena.

Moreover, since sex, like race and national origin, is an immutable characteristic determined solely by the accident of birth, the imposition of special disabilities upon the members of a particular sex because of their sex would seem to violate "the basic concept of our system that legal burdens should bear some relationship to individual responsibility...." And what differentiates sex from such nonsuspect statuses as intelligence or physical disability, and aligns it with the recognized suspect criteria, is that the sex characteristic frequently bears no relation to ability to perform or contribute to society. As a result, statutory distinctions between the sexes often have the effect of invidiously relegating the entire class of females to inferior legal status without regard to the actual capabilities of its individual members.

We might also note that, over the past decade, Congress has itself manifested an increasing sensitivity to sex-based classifications. In Tit. VII of the Civil Rights Act of 1964, for example, Congress expressly declared that no employer, labor union, or other organization subject to the provisions of the Act shall discriminate against any individual on the basis of "race, color, religion, *sex,* or national origin." Similarly, the Equal Pay Act of 1963 provides that no employer covered by the Act "shall discriminate ... between employees on the basis of sex." And § 1 of the Equal Rights Amendment, passed by Congress on March 22, 1972, and submitted to the legislatures of the States for ratification, declares that "[e]quality of rights under the law shall not be denied or abridged by the United States or by any State on account of sex." Thus, Congress itself has concluded that classifications based upon sex are inherently invidious, and this conclusion of a coequal branch of Government is not without significance to the question presently under consideration.

With these considerations in mind, we can only conclude that classifications based upon sex, like classifications based upon race, alienage, or national origin, are inherently suspect, and must therefore be subjected to strict judicial scrutiny. Applying the analysis mandated by that stricter standard of review, it is clear that the statutory scheme now before us is constitutionally invalid.

The sole basis of the classification established in the challenged statutes is the sex of the individuals involved. Thus ... a female member of the uniformed services seeking to obtain housing and medical benefits for her spouse must prove his dependency in fact, whereas no such burden is imposed upon male members. In addition, the statutes operate so as to deny benefits to a female member, such as appellant Sharron Frontiero, who provides less than one-half of her spouse's support, while at the same time granting such benefits to a male member who likewise provides less than one-half of his spouse's support. Thus, to this extent at least, it may fairly be said that these statutes command "dissimilar treatment for men and women who are ... similarly situated."

Moreover, the Government concedes that the differential treatment accorded men and women under these statutes serves no purpose other than mere "administrative convenience." In essence, the Government maintains that, as an empirical matter, wives in our society frequently are dependent upon their husbands, while husbands rarely are dependent upon their wives. Thus, the Government argues that Congress might reasonably have concluded that it would be both cheaper and easier simply conclusively to presume that wives of male members are financially dependent upon their husbands, while burdening female members with the task of establishing dependency in fact.

The Government offers no concrete evidence, however, tending to support its view that such differential treatment in fact saves the Government any money. In order to satisfy the demands of strict judicial scrutiny, the Government must demonstrate, for example, that it is actually cheaper to grant increased benefits with respect to *all* male members, than it is to determine which male members are in fact entitled to such benefits and to grant increased benefits only to those members whose wives actually meet the dependency requirement. Here, however, there is substantial evidence that, if put to the test, many of the wives of male members would fail to qualify for benefits. And in light of the fact that the dependency determination with respect to the husbands of female members is presently made solely on the basis of affidavits rather than through the more costly hearing process, the Government's explanation of the statutory scheme is, to say the least, questionable.

In any case, our prior decisions make clear that, although efficacious administration of governmental programs is not without some importance, "the Constitution recognizes higher values than speed and efficiency." And when we enter the realm of "strict judicial scrutiny," there can be no doubt that "administrative convenience" is not a shibboleth, the mere recitation of which dictates constitutionality. On the contrary, any statutory scheme which draws a sharp line between the sexes, *solely* for the purpose of achieving administrative convenience, necessarily commands "dissimilar treatment for men and women who are ... similarly situated," and therefore involves the "very kind of arbitrary legislative choice forbidden by the [Constitution]...." We therefore conclude that, by according differential treatment to male and female members of the uniformed services for the sole purpose of achieving administrative convenience, the challenged statutes violate the Due Process Clause of the Fifth Amendment insofar as they require a female member to prove the dependency of her husband.

Reversed.

MR. JUSTICE POWELL ... concurring in the judgment.

I agree that the challenged statutes constitute an unconstitutional discrimination against servicewomen in violation of the Due Process Clause of the Fifth Amendment, but I cannot join the opinion of MR. JUSTICE BRENNAN, which would hold that all classifications based upon sex, "like classifications based upon race, alienage, and national origin, are inherently suspect and must therefore be subjected to close judicial scrutiny." It is unnecessary for the Court in this case to characterize sex as a suspect classification, with all of the far-reaching implications of such a holding. Reed v. Reed (1971), which abundantly supports our decision today, did not add sex to the narrowly limited group of classifications which are inherently suspect. In my view, we can and should decide this case on the authority of *Reed* and reserve for the future any expansion of its rationale.

There is another, and I find compelling, reason for deferring a general categorizing of sex classifications as invoking the strictest test of judicial scrutiny. The Equal Rights Amendment, which if adopted will resolve the substance of this precise question, has been approved by the Congress and submitted for ratification by the States. If this Amendment is duly adopted, it will represent the will of the people accomplished in the manner prescribed by the Constitution. By acting prematurely and unnecessarily, as I view it, the Court has assumed a decisional responsibility at the very time when state legislatures, functioning within the traditional democratic process, are debating the proposed Amendment. It seems to me that this reaching out to preempt by judicial action a major political decision which is currently in process of resolution does not reflect appropriate respect for duly prescribed legislative processes.

There are times when this Court, under our system, cannot avoid a constitutional decision on issues which normally should be resolved by the elected representatives of the people. But democratic institutions are weakened, and confidence in the restraint of the Court is impaired, when we appear unnecessarily to decide sensitive issues of broad social and political importance at the very time they are under consideration within the prescribed constitutional processes.

The *Frontiero* ruling was a clear victory for the supporters of equality of the sexes. The Court again condemned the imposition of sex classifications for administrative convenience, as well as the practice of incorporating overly broad, sex-based assumptions into the law. These two principles now seemed solidly woven into the fabric of constitutional law. But the result in *Frontiero* disappointed those who wanted the strict scrutiny test to be applied to such cases. Justice Brennan's opinion was a strong defense of such a position, but he was able to attract the support of only three of his colleagues. Explicitly opposed to the application of the strict scrutiny test were Powell, Burger, and Blackmun, although they found the military regulation challenged here to be unconstitutional even under the rational basis test. To their number we can add Rehnquist, who dissented from the Court's

judgment. With four justices in favor of the traditional rational basis test, and four supporting elevation to the strict scrutiny test, the deciding vote was held by Justice Stewart. But he failed to make his preferences known. In one line, Stewart indicated that he found the Air Force regulation unconstitutional without saying what standard he applied.

The question of an appropriate standard for sex discrimination cases was finally decided in 1976 in *Craig v. Boren*. Although the Court remained divided on the matter, the majority agreed to adopt an entirely new standard for sex bias cases. This intermediate test, known as the heightened scrutiny test, requires that laws that classify on the basis of sex be substantially related to an important government objective. It was originally suggested as a compromise solution by attorneys for women's rights groups who feared that the Court majority would remain committed to rational basis. Observe how Brennan, writing for the Court, justifies the new test as being consistent with *Reed* and how he treats the use of social science evidence. Also, read carefully Rehnquist's dissenting opinion rejecting the new test, especially as beneficially applied to males.

===

Craig v. Boren

429 U.S. 190 (1976)
Vote: 7 (Blackmun, Brennan, Marshall, Powell, Stevens,
        Stewart, White)
    2 (Burger, Rehnquist)
Opinion of the Court: Brennan
Concurring opinions: Powell, Stevens
Opinion concurring in judgment: Stewart
Opinion concurring in part: Blackmun
Dissenting opinions: Burger, Rehnquist

In 1972 Oklahoma passed a statute setting the age of legal majority for both males and females at eighteen. Before then, females reached legal age at eighteen and males at twenty-one. The equalization statute, however, contained one exception. Males could not purchase beer, even with the low 3.2 percent alcohol level, until they reached twenty-one; females could buy beer at eighteen. The state differentiated between the sexes in response to statistical evidence indicating a much greater tendency for males in the eighteen to twenty-one age bracket to be involved in alcohol-related traffic accidents, including fatalities. Curtis Craig, a male in the restricted age category, joined forces with a beer vendor to challenge the statute as a violation of the Equal Protection Clause. A three-judge district court found the statute valid under the rational basis test. With help from Ginsburg and the ACLU, Craig appealed.

MR. JUSTICE BRENNAN delivered the opinion of the Court.

Analysis may appropriately begin with the reminder that Reed emphasized that statutory classifications that distinguish between males and females are "subject to scrutiny under the Equal Protection Clause." To withstand constitutional challenge, previous cases establish that classifications by gender must serve important governmental objectives and must be substantially related to achievement of those objectives. Thus, in Reed, the objectives of "reducing the workload on probate courts" and "avoiding intrafamily controversy" were deemed of insufficient importance to sustain use of an overt gender criterion in the appointment of administrators of intestate decedents' estates. Decisions following Reed similarly have rejected administrative ease and convenience as sufficiently important objectives to justify gender-based classifications....

Reed v. Reed has also provided the underpinning for decisions that have invalidated statutes employing gender as an inaccurate proxy for other, more germane bases of classification. Hence, "archaic and overbroad" generalizations could not justify use of a gender line in determining eligibility for certain governmental entitlements. Similarly, increasingly outdated misconceptions concerning the role of females in the home rather than in the "marketplace and world of ideas" were rejected as loose-fitting characterizations incapable of supporting state statutory schemes that

were premised upon their accuracy. In light of the weak congruence between gender and the characteristic or trait that gender purported to represent, it was necessary that the legislatures choose either to realign their substantive laws in a gender-neutral fashion, or to adopt procedures for identifying those instances where the sex-centered generalization actually comported with fact.

In this case, too, "Reed, we feel, is controlling...." We turn then to the question whether, under Reed, the difference between males and females with respect to the purchase of 3.2% beer warrants the differential in age drawn by the Oklahoma statute. We conclude that it does not.

The District Court recognized that Reed v. Reed was controlling. In applying the teachings of that case, the court found the requisite important governmental objective in the traffic-safety goal proffered by the Oklahoma Attorney General. It then concluded that the statistics introduced by the appellees established that the gender-based distinction was substantially related to achievement of that goal.

... Clearly, the protection of public health and safety represents an important function of state and local governments. However, appellees' statistics in our view cannot support the conclusion that the gender-based distinction closely serves to achieve that objective and therefore the distinction cannot under Reed withstand equal protection challenge.

The appellees introduced a variety of statistical surveys. First, an analysis of arrest statistics for 1973 demonstrated that 18–20-year-old male arrests for "driving under the influence" and "drunkenness" substantially exceeded female arrests for that same age period. Similarly, youths aged 17–21 were found to be overrepresented among those killed or injured in traffic accidents, with males again numerically exceeding females in this regard. Third, a random roadside survey in Oklahoma City revealed that young males were more inclined to drive and drink beer than were their female counterparts. Fourth, Federal Bureau of Investigation nationwide statistics exhibited a notable increase in arrests for "driving under the influence." Finally, statistical evidence gathered in other jurisdictions, particularly Minnesota and Michigan, was offered to corroborate Oklahoma's experience by indicating the pervasiveness of youthful participation in motor vehicle accidents following the imbibing of alcohol....

Even were this statistical evidence accepted as accurate, it nevertheless offers only a weak answer to the equal protection question presented here. The most focused and relevant of the statistical surveys, arrests of 18–20-year-olds for alcohol-related driving offenses, exemplifies the ultimate unpersuasiveness of this evidentiary record. Viewed in terms of the correlation between sex and the actual activity that Oklahoma seeks to regulate—driving while under the influence of alcohol—the statistics broadly establish that .18% of females and 2% of males in that age group were arrested for that offense. While such a disparity is not trivial in a statistical sense, it hardly can form the basis for employment of a gender line as a classifying device. Certainly if maleness is to serve as a proxy for drinking and driving, a correlation of 2% must be considered an unduly tenuous "fit." Indeed, prior cases have consistently rejected the use of sex as a decisionmaking factor even though the statutes in question certainly rested on far more predictive empirical relationships than this.

Moreover, the statistics exhibit a variety of other shortcomings that seriously impugn their value to equal protection analysis. Setting aside the obvious methodological problems, the surveys do not adequately justify the salient features of Oklahoma's gender-based traffic-safety law. None purports to measure the use and dangerousness of 3.2% beer as opposed to alcohol generally, a detail that is of particular importance since, in light of its low alcohol level, Oklahoma apparently considers the 3.2% beverage to be "nonintoxicating." Moreover, many of the studies, while graphically documenting the unfortunate increase in driving while under the influence of alcohol, make no effort to relate their findings to age-sex differentials as involved here. Indeed, the only survey that explicitly centered its attention upon young drivers and their use of beer—albeit apparently not of the diluted 3.2% variety—reached results that hardly can be viewed as impressive in justifying either a gender or age classification.

There is no reason to belabor this line of analysis. It is unrealistic to expect either members of the judiciary or state officials to be well versed in the rigors of experimental or statistical technique. But this merely illustrates that proving broad sociological propositions by statistics is a dubious business, and one that inevitably is in tension with the normative philosophy that underlies the Equal Protec-

tion Clause. Suffice to say that the showing offered by the appellees does not satisfy us that sex represents a legitimate, accurate proxy for the regulation of drinking and driving. In fact, when it is further recognized that Oklahoma's statute prohibits only the selling of 3.2% beer to young males and not their drinking the beverage once acquired (even after purchase by their 18–20-year-old female companions), the relationship between gender and traffic safety becomes far too tenuous to satisfy *Reed*'s requirement that the gender-based difference be substantially related to achievement of the statutory objective.

We hold, therefore, that under *Reed*, Oklahoma's 3.2% beer statute invidiously discriminates against males 18–20 years of age.

MR. JUSTICE REHNQUIST, dissenting.

The Court's disposition of this case is objectionable on two grounds. First is its conclusion that *men* challenging a gender-based statute which treats them less favorably than women may invoke a more stringent standard of judicial review than pertains to most other types of classifications. Second is the Court's enunciation of this standard, without citation to any source, as being that "classification by gender must serve *important* governmental objectives and must be *substantially* related to achievement of those objectives." (Emphasis added.) The only redeeming feature of the Court's opinion, to my mind, is that it apparently signals a retreat by those who joined the plurality opinion in *Frontiero v. Richardson* (1973) from their view that sex is a "suspect" classification for purposes of equal protection analysis. I think the Oklahoma statute challenged here need pass only the "rational basis" equal protection analysis expounded in cases such as *McGowan v. Maryland* (1961) and *Williamson v. Lee Optical Co.* (1955), and I believe that it is constitutional under that analysis.

In *Frontiero v. Richardson*, the opinion for the plurality sets forth the reasons of four Justices for concluding that sex should be regarded as a suspect classification for purposes of equal protection analysis. These reasons center on our Nation's "long and unfortunate history of sex discrimination," which has been reflected in a whole range of restrictions on the legal rights of women, not the least of which have concerned the ownership of property and participation in the electoral process. Noting that the pervasive and persistent nature of the discrimination experienced by women is in part the result of their ready identifiability, the plurality rested its invocation of strict scrutiny largely upon the fact that "statutory distinctions between the sexes often have the effect of invidiously relegating the entire class of females to inferior legal status without regard to the actual capabilities of its individual members."

Subsequent to *Frontiero*, the Court has declined to hold that sex is a suspect class, and no such holding is imported by the Court's resolution of this case. However, the Court's application here of an elevated or "intermediate" level scrutiny, like that invoked in cases dealing with discrimination against females, raises the question of why the statute here should be treated any differently from countless legislative classifications unrelated to sex which have been upheld under a minimum rationality standard.

Most obviously unavailable to support any kind of special scrutiny in this case, is a history or pattern of past discrimination, such as was relied on by the plurality in *Frontiero* to support its invocation of strict scrutiny. There is no suggestion in the Court's opinion that males in this age group are in any way peculiarly disadvantaged, subject to systematic discriminatory treatment, or otherwise in need of special solicitude from the courts.

The Court does not discuss the nature of the right involved, and there is no reason to believe that it sees the purchase of 3.2% beer as implicating any important interest, let alone one that is "fundamental" in the constitutional sense of invoking strict scrutiny. Indeed, the Court's accurate observation that the statute affects the selling but not the drinking of 3.2% beer further emphasizes the limited effect that it has on even those persons in the age group involved. There is, in sum, nothing about the statutory classification involved here to suggest that it affects an interest, or works against a group, which can claim under the Equal Protection Clause that it is entitled to special judicial protection.

It is true that a number of our opinions contain broadly phrased dicta implying that the same test should be applied to all classifications based on sex, whether affecting females or males. However, before today, no decision of this Court has applied an elevated level of scrutiny to invalidate a statutory discrimination harmful to males, except where

the statute impaired an important personal interest protected by the Constitution. There being no such interest here, and there being no plausible argument that this is a discrimination against females, the Court's reliance on our previous sex-discrimination cases is ill-founded. It treats gender classification as a talisman which—without regard to the rights involved or the persons affected—calls into effect a heavier burden of judicial review.

The Court's conclusion that a law which treats males less favorably than females "must serve important governmental objectives and must be substantially related to achievement of those objectives" apparently comes out of thin air. The Equal Protection Clause contains no such language, and none of our previous cases adopt that standard. I would think we have had enough difficulty with the two standards of review which our cases have recognized—the norm of "rational basis," and the "compelling state interest" required where a "suspect classification" is involved—so as to counsel weightily against the insertion of still another "standard" between those two. How is this Court to divine what objectives are important? How is it to determine whether a particular law is "substantially" related to the achievement of such objective, rather than related in some other way to its achievement? Both of the phrases used are so diaphanous and elastic as to invite subjective judicial preferences or prejudices relating to particular types of legislation, masquerading as judgments whether such legislation is directed at "important" objectives or, whether the relationship to those objectives is "substantial" enough.

I would have thought that if this Court were to leave anything to decision by the popularly elected branches of the Government, where no constitutional claim other than that of equal protection is invoked, it would be the decision as to what governmental objectives to be achieved by law are "important," and which are not. As for the second part of the Court's new test, the Judicial Branch is probably in no worse position than the Legislative or Executive Branches to determine if there is *any* rational relationship between a classification and the purpose which it might be thought to serve. But the introduction of the adverb "substantially" requires courts to make subjective judgments as to operational effects, for which neither their expertise nor their access to data fits them. And even if we manage to avoid both confusion and the mirroring of our own preferences in the development of this new doctrine, the thousands of judges in other courts who must interpret the Equal Protection Clause may not be so fortunate.

The heightened scrutiny test was adopted by a narrow margin. Although six justices joined the opinion, Powell's and Stevens's concurring views indicated that their agreement with Brennan's new standard was qualified *(see Table 10-1)*. Nevertheless, the elevated level of scrutiny was established and since has been used in sex discrimination cases. The battle between strict scrutiny advocates and rational basis proponents thus ended with neither side able to claim victory. The strict scrutiny justices were forced to moderate their position just enough to capture sufficient votes to adopt an intermediate level test.

Heightened scrutiny was a compromise solution that did not fully please those who preferred strict scrutiny or those who favored the rational basis approach. Under such circumstances, the compromise may be temporary, lasting only as long as neither side has sufficient votes to adopt its preferences. In the sexual harassment case of *Harris v. Forklift Systems, Inc.* (1993) Justice Ginsburg signaled that the battle over appropriate standards for sex discrimination cases may be fought again. Consider the following statement contained in a footnote of Ginsburg's concurring opinion in that case:

Indeed, even under the Court's equal protection jurisprudence, which requires "an exceedingly persuasive justification" for a gender-based classification, it remains an open question whether "classifications based on gender are inherently suspect."

Her assertion that gender classification standards remain an *open question* is a clear indication that at least for Ginsburg the issue is not yet settled. The fact that she included this statement in her first published opinion as a Supreme Court justice may well reflect the importance of this issue to her. Recall that Justice Ginsburg was a prominent sex discrimination litiga-

TABLE 10-1 Court Division on Equal Protection Standards in Sex Discrimination Cases

Frontiero v. Richardson (1973)
Rational basis test:
Blackmun
Burger
Powell
Rehnquist
Strict scrutiny test:
Brennan
Douglas
Marshall
White
Undeclared:
Stewart
Craig v. Boren (1976)
Heightened scrutiny test:
Blackmun
Brennan
Marshall
Powell (with reservations)
Stevens (with qualifications)
White
Rational basis test:
Burger
Rehnquist
Undeclared:
Stewart

tor prior to her appointment as a federal judge, and had been involved as an attorney in *Craig v. Boren.*

Recognition of Sex Differences

All discrimination law, regardless of what standard of scrutiny courts impose, requires that claims of unequal treatment be based only on comparisons of persons "similarly situated." For example, female orderlies employed by a state-operated hospital could not validly claim sex discrimination if their pay was significantly less than that of male surgeons employed in the same hospital. Individuals in these two employment classifications are not similarly situated, and therefore comparisons between the two are inappropriate. If the hospital paid male orderlies significantly more than female orderlies, however, a sex discrimination claim would have greater merit.

In the area of sex discrimination law, the question persists whether the two sexes have inherently different traits that allow them to be treated differently under the law. In other words, are there some areas of human activity in which the sexes are not similarly situated? With respect to such activities, is it constitutional for the government to benefit or penalize one sex and not the other?

The Supreme Court tackled these questions in the next two cases we discuss. *Michael M. v. Superior Court of Sonoma County* (1981) focuses on the differences between males and females in sexual activity and reproduction. Although the opinion explaining its decision lacked majority support, the Court upheld the validity of a criminal law that applies only to males, but not without a spirited dissent registered by four justices.

Michael M. v. Superior Court of Sonoma County

450 U.S. 464 (1981)

Vote: 5 (Blackmun, Burger, Powell, Rehnquist, Stewart)
   4 (Brennan, Marshall, Stevens, White)

Opinion announcing judgment of the Court: Rehnquist
Concurring opinion: Stewart
Opinion concurring in judgment: Blackmun
Dissenting opinions: Brennan, Stevens

Around midnight on June 3, 1978, Michael M., a male aged seventeen, and two friends approached Sharon, who was sixteen, and her sister at a bus stop. Both Michael and Sharon had been drinking. During the course of their encounter, Michael and Sharon split off from the others. First they went into some bushes, where they hugged and kissed. Later, after Sharon's sister had left, Sharon and Michael walked

to a nearby park, laid down on a bench, and continued kissing. Michael tried to convince Sharon to remove her clothes and have sexual relations. When Sharon refused, Michael hit her in the face. Then, in Sharon's words, "I let him do what he wanted to do."

Michael M. was charged with a violation of Section 261.5 of the California penal code, which prohibits "an act of sexual intercourse accomplished with a female not the wife of the perpetrator, where the female is under the age of 18 years." This statutory rape law makes males alone criminally liable for the act of sexual intercourse. Michael M. moved to have the criminal prosecution dropped on the grounds that Section 261.5 invidiously discriminates on the basis of sex and therefore violates the Equal Protection Clause. California courts upheld the validity of the law.

JUSTICE REHNQUIST announced the judgment of the Court....

As is evident from our opinions, the Court has had some difficulty in agreeing upon the proper approach and analysis in cases involving challenges to gender-based classifications.... Unlike the California Supreme Court, we have not held that gender-based classifications are "inherently suspect" and thus we do not apply so-called "strict scrutiny" to those classifications. Our cases have held, however, that the traditional minimum rationality test takes on a somewhat "sharper focus" when gender-based classifications are challenged. In *Reed v. Reed* (1971), for example, the Court stated that a gender-based classification will be upheld if it bears a "fair and substantial relationship" to legitimate state ends, while in *Craig v. Boren*, the Court restated the test to require the classification to bear a "substantial relationship" to "important governmental objectives."

Underlying these decisions is the principle that a legislature may not "make overbroad generalizations based on sex which are entirely unrelated to any differences between men and women or which demean the ability or social status of the affected class." But because the Equal Protection Clause does not "demand that a statute necessarily apply equally to all persons" or require "'things which are different in fact ... to be treated in law as though they were the same,'" this Court has consistently upheld statutes where the gender classification is not invidious, but rather realistically reflects the fact that the sexes are not similarly situated in certain circumstances....

We are satisfied not only that the prevention of illegitimate pregnancy is at least one of the "purposes" of the statute, but also that the State has a strong interest in preventing such pregnancy. At the risk of stating the obvious, teenage pregnancies, which have increased dramatically over the last two decades, have significant social, medical, and economic consequences for both the mother and her child, and the State. Of particular concern to the State is that approximately half of all teenage pregnancies end in abortion. And of those children who are born, their illegitimacy makes them likely candidates to become wards of the State.

We need not be medical doctors to discern that young men and young women are not similarly situated with respect to the problems and the risks of sexual intercourse. Only women may become pregnant, and they suffer disproportionately the profound physical, emotional and psychological consequences of sexual activity. The statute at issue here protects women from sexual intercourse at an age when those consequences are particularly severe.

The question thus boils down to whether a State may attack the problem of sexual intercourse and teenage pregnancy directly by prohibiting a male from having sexual intercourse with a minor female. We hold that such a statute is sufficiently related to the State's objectives to pass constitutional muster.

Because virtually all of the significant harmful and inescapably identifiable consequences of teenage pregnancy fall on the young female, a legislature acts well within its authority when it elects to punish only the participant who, by nature, suffers few of the consequences of his conduct. It is hardly unreasonable for a legislature acting to protect minor females to exclude them from punishment. Moreover, the risk of pregnancy itself constitutes a substantial deterrence to young females. No similar natural sanctions deter males. A criminal sanction imposed solely on males thus serves to roughly "equalize" the deterrents on the sexes.

We are unable to accept petitioner's contention that the statute is impermissibly underinclusive and must, in order to pass judicial scrutiny, be *broadened* so as to hold the female as criminally liable as the male. It is argued that this statute is not *necessary* to deter teenage pregnancy because a gender-neutral statute, where both male and female would be subject to prosecution, would serve that goal equally well. The relevant inquiry, however, is not whether the statute is drawn as precisely as it might have been, but whether the line chosen by the California Legislature is within constitutional limitations.

In any event, we cannot say that a gender-neutral statute would be as effective as the statute California has chosen to enact. The State persuasively contends that a gender-neutral statute would frustrate its interest in effective enforcement. Its view is that a female is surely less likely to report violations of the statute if she herself would be subject to criminal prosecution. In an area already fraught with prosecutorial difficulties, we decline to hold that the Equal Protection Clause requires a legislature to enact a statute so broad that it may well be incapable of enforcement.

We similarly reject petitioner's argument that § 261.5 is impermissibly overbroad because it makes unlawful sexual intercourse with prepubescent females, who are, by definition, incapable of becoming pregnant. Quite apart from the fact that the statute could well be justified on the grounds that very young females are particularly susceptible to physical injury from sexual intercourse, it is ludicrous to suggest that the Constitution requires the California Legislature to limit the scope of its rape statute to older teenagers and exclude young girls.

There remains only petitioner's contention that the statute is unconstitutional as it is applied to him because he, like Sharon, was under 18 at the time of sexual intercourse. Petitioner argues that the statute is flawed because it presumes that as between two persons under 18, the male is the culpable aggressor. We find petitioner's contentions unpersuasive. Contrary to his assertions, the statute does not rest on the assumption that males are generally the aggressors. It is instead an attempt by a legislature to prevent illegitimate teenage pregnancy by providing an additional deterrent for men. The age of the man is irrelevant since young men are as capable as older men of inflicting the harm sought to be prevented.

In upholding the California statute we also recognize that this is not a case where a statute is being challenged on the grounds that it "invidiously discriminates" against females. To the contrary, the statute places a burden on males which is not shared by females. But we find nothing to suggest that men, because of past discrimination or peculiar disadvantages, are in need of the special solicitude of the courts. Nor is this a case where the gender classification is made "solely for . . . administrative convenience," or rests on "the baggage of sexual stereotypes." As we have held, the statute instead reasonably reflects the fact that the consequences of sexual intercourse and pregnancy fall more heavily on the female than on the male.

Accordingly, the judgment of the California Supreme Court is

Affirmed.

JUSTICE BRENNAN . . . dissenting.

It is disturbing to find the Court so splintered on a case that presents such a straightforward issue: Whether the admittedly gender-based classification bears a sufficient relationship to the State's asserted goal of preventing teenage pregnancies to survive the "midlevel" constitutional scrutiny mandated by *Craig v. Boren* (1976). Applying the analytical framework provided by our precedents, I am convinced that there is only one proper resolution of this issue: the classification must be declared unconstitutional. . . .

After some uncertainty as to the proper framework for analyzing equal protection challenges to statutes containing gender-based classifications, this Court settled upon the proposition that a statute containing a gender-based classification cannot withstand constitutional challenge unless the classification is substantially related to the achievement of an important governmental objective. This analysis applies whether the classification discriminates against males or against females. The burden is on the government to prove both the importance of its asserted objective and the substantial relationship between the classification and that objective. And the State cannot meet that burden without showing that a gender-neutral statute would be a less effective means of achieving that goal.

The State of California vigorously asserts that the "important governmental objective" to be served by § 261.5 is the prevention of teenage pregnancy. It claims that its statute furthers this goal by deterring sexual activity by males—the class of persons it considers more responsible for causing those pregnancies. But even assuming that prevention of teenage pregnancy is an important governmental objective and that it is in fact an objective of § 261.5, California still has the burden of proving that there are fewer teenage pregnancies under its gender-based statutory rape law than there would be if the law were gender neutral. To meet this burden, the State must show that because its statutory rape law punishes only males, and not females, it more effectively deters minor females from having sexual intercourse. . . .

Until very recently, no California court or commentator had suggested that the purpose of California's statutory rape law was to protect young women from the risk of pregnancy. Indeed, the historical development of § 261.5 demonstrates that the law was initially enacted on the premise that young women, in contrast to young men, were to be deemed legally incapable of consenting to an act of sexual intercourse. Because their chastity was considered particularly precious, those young women were felt to be uniquely in need of the State's protection. In contrast, young men were assumed to be capable of making such decisions for themselves; the law therefore did not offer them any special protection.

It is perhaps because the gender classification in California's statutory rape law was initially designed to further these outmoded sexual stereotypes, rather than to reduce the incidence of teenage pregnancies, that the State has been unable to demonstrate a substantial relationship between the classification and its newly asserted goal. But whatever the reason, the State has not shown that Cal. Penal Code § 261.5 is any more effective than a gender-neutral law would be in deterring minor females from engaging in sexual intercourse. It has therefore not met its burden of proving that the statutory classification is substantially related to the achievement of its asserted goal.

I would hold that § 261.5 violates the Equal Protection Clause of the Fourteenth Amendment, and I would reverse the judgment of the California Supreme Court.

Three months after Rehnquist's opinion in *Michael M.*, his opinion for the Court in *Rostker v. Goldberg* was announced. This case also dealt with male/female differences and the authority of the government to treat the sexes differently under the law. The *Rostker* dispute involved military service. Historically, males have had the primary responsibility and opportunity to serve in the armed forces. Physical differences between men and women led to this custom, which has been reinforced by the way society views sex roles.

The federal legislation challenged in this case continued the policy of distinguishing men and women with respect to military matters. The case also involved Congress's constitutional power to raise and regulate the armed forces. Traditionally, when the legislature has acted under this authority, the Court has accorded it great deference. In light of the subsequent military actions taken by the United States in Grenada, Panama, and the Persian Gulf, does the Court's position on the draft as expressed in *Rostker* have more or less validity than it did when it was announced?

Rostker v. Goldberg

453 U.S. 57 (1981)

Vote: 6 (Blackmun, Burger, Powell, Rehnquist,
        Stevens, Stewart)
    3 (Brennan, Marshall, White)

Opinion of the Court: Rehnquist
Dissenting opinions: Marshall, White

Under the Military Selective Service Act the president can require every male citizen and resident alien between the ages of eighteen and twenty-six to register for the draft. In 1971 several draft-age men filed suit in federal court in Pennsylvania against the director of the Selective Service System challenging the constitutionality of the registration law. Because draft registration was suspended in 1975, the suit became dormant. However, in 1980, in reaction to the Soviet

invasion of Afghanistan, President Jimmy Carter reactivated the draft registration program. Moreover, Carter asked Congress to amend the law to require females, as well as males, to register. Congress refused to change the law, and it appropriated only enough money to administer the registration of males. The long dormant suit was reactivated, and on July 18, 1980, three days before registration was to begin, the district court declared the law unconstitutional because its single-sex provisions violated the Due Process Clause of the Fifth Amendment. Bernard Rostker, director of Selective Service, appealed to the Supreme Court.

JUSTICE REHNQUIST delivered the opinion of the Court.

Whenever called upon to judge the constitutionality of an Act of Congress—"the gravest and most delicate duty that this Court is called upon to perform," the Court accords "great weight to the decisions of Congress."...

This is not, however, merely a case involving the customary deference accorded congressional decisions. The case arises in the context of Congress' authority over national defense and military affairs, and perhaps in no other area has the Court accorded Congress greater deference. In rejecting the registration of women, Congress explicitly relied upon its constitutional powers under Art. I, § 8, cls. 12–14.... This Court has consistently recognized Congress' "broad constitutional power" to raise and regulate armies and navies. As the Court noted in considering a challenge to the selective service laws: "The constitutional power of Congress to raise and support armies and to make all laws necessary and proper to that end is broad and sweeping."

Not only is the scope of Congress' constitutional power in this area broad, but the lack of competence on the part of the courts is marked....

None of this is to say that Congress is free to disregard the Constitution when it acts in the area of military affairs. In that area, as any other, Congress remains subject to the limitations of the Due Process Clause, but the tests and limitations to be applied may differ because of the military context. We of course do not abdicate our ultimate responsibility to decide the constitutional question, but simply recognize that the Constitution itself requires such deference to congressional choice. In deciding the question before us we must be particularly careful not to substitute our judgment of what is desirable for that of Congress, or our own evaluation of evidence for a reasonable evaluation by the Legislative Branch....

In this case the courts are called upon to decide whether Congress, acting under an explicit constitutional grant of authority, has by that action transgressed an explicit guarantee of individual rights which limits the authority so conferred. Simply labeling the legislative decision "military" on the one hand or "gender-based" on the other does not automatically guide a court to the correct constitutional result.

No one could deny that under the test of *Craig v. Boren,* the Government's interest in raising and supporting armies is an "important governmental interest." Congress and its Committees carefully considered and debated two alternative means of furthering that interest: the first was to register only males for potential conscription, and the other was to register both sexes. Congress chose the former alternative. When that decision is challenged on equal protection grounds, the question a court must decide is not which alternative it would have chosen, had it been the primary decisionmaker, but whether that chosen by Congress denies equal protection of the laws....

This case is quite different from several of the gender-based discrimination cases we have considered in that, despite appellees' assertions, Congress did not act "unthinkingly" or "reflexively and not for any considered reason." The question of registering women for the draft not only received considerable national attention and was the subject of wide-ranging public debate, but also was extensively considered by Congress in hearings, floor debate, and in committee. Hearings held by both Houses of Congress in response to the President's request for authorization to register women adduced extensive testimony and evidence concerning the issue. These hearings built on other hearings held the previous year addressed to the same question....

While proposals to register women were being rejected in the course of transferring funds to register males, Committees in both Houses which had conducted hearings on the issue were also rejecting the registration of women....

... [T]he decision to exempt women from registration was not the "'accidental by-product of a traditional way of thinking about females.'" In *Michael M.,* we rejected a similar argument because of action by the California Legislature considering and rejecting proposals to make a statute challenged on discrimination grounds gender-neutral. The cause for rejecting the argument is considerably stronger here. The issue was considered at great length, and Congress clearly expressed its purpose and intent.

Women as a group, ... unlike men as a group, are not eligible for combat. The restrictions on the participation of women in combat in the Navy and Air Force are statutory. Under 10 U.S.C. § 6015 (1976 ed., Supp. III), "women may not be assigned to duty on vessels or in aircraft that are engaged in combat missions," and under 10 U.S.C. § 8549 female members of the Air Force "may not be assigned to duty in aircraft engaged in combat missions." The Army and Marine Corps preclude the use of women in combat as a matter of established policy. Congress specifically recognized and endorsed the exclusion of women from combat in exempting women from registration....

The existence of the combat restrictions clearly indicates the basis for Congress' decision to exempt women from registration. The purpose of registration was to prepare for a draft of combat troops. Since women are excluded from combat, Congress concluded that they would not be needed in the event of a draft, and therefore decided not to register them.... This is not a case of Congress arbitrarily choosing to burden one of two similarly situated groups, such as would be the case with an all-black or all-white, or an all-Catholic or all-Lutheran, or an all-Republican or all-Democratic registration. Men and women, because of the combat restrictions on women, are simply not similarly situated for purposes of a draft or registration for a draft.

Congress' decision to authorize the registration of only men, therefore, does not violate the Due Process Clause. The exemption of women from registration is not only sufficiently but also closely related to Congress' purpose in authorizing registration. The fact that Congress and the Executive have decided that women should not serve in combat fully justifies Congress in not authorizing their registration, since the purpose of registration is to develop a pool of potential combat troops.... "[T]he gender classification is not invidious, but rather realistically reflects the fact that the sexes are not similarly situated" in this case. The Constitution requires that Congress treat similarly situated persons similarly, not that it engage in gestures of superficial equality....

... [W]e conclude that Congress acted well within its constitutional authority when it authorized the registration of men, and not women, under the Military Selective Service Act. The decision of the District Court holding otherwise is accordingly

Reversed.

Presumptions of Female Inferiority

Laws and government policies based on presumptions of female inferiority have been among the most objectionable to women's rights advocates and therefore the most subject to attack. Sometimes these laws limit the freedoms and opportunities of women. We have already looked at cases that challenged the presumptions that women are less qualified than men to manage estates and that women are financially dependent upon their husbands. Other laws and policies, however, provide benefits or protections to women that are not provided to men. Programs falling into this category are distasteful to women's rights advocates because they too are based upon presumptions that women are inferior and need special favors. While such laws provide certain short-term benefits, they may promote erroneous stereotypes that ultimately work to the detriment of women. Whatever position one takes on these issues, one fact is clear: such laws involve sex classifications that are subject to attack on equal protection grounds.

This section includes two Supreme Court decisions on state laws that provided special benefits or protections for women, one financial and the other educational. In each case the policies were challenged by males as violations of the Fourteenth Amendment. But the underlying issue was a presumption built into the laws that females are inferior. The first of these cases is *Orr v. Orr* (1979) which, like some other sex discrimination cases, grew out of a dispute between husband and wife. Family law historically has incorporated many sex-based notions, including female

dominance over custody and child care and male superiority in the area of financial support. Laws that accord rights and responsibilities based on such ideas are often criticized as out of step with modern social conditions. The *Orr* case involves a challenge to such a law, concerning marital support in Alabama.

Orr v. Orr

440 U.S. 268 (1979)

Vote: 6 (Blackmun, Brennan, Marshall, Stevens, Stewart, White)

3 (Burger, Powell, Rehnquist)

Opinion of the Court: Brennan

Concurring opinions: Blackmun, Stevens

Dissenting opinions: Powell, Rehnquist

On February 26, 1974, a final decree of divorce was entered by an Alabama court dissolving the marriage of William and Lillian Orr. As part of that decree, William was to pay Lillian $1,240 per month in alimony for her use and comfort for the rest of her life or until she remarried. In July 1976 Lillian began contempt proceedings against her former husband on the grounds that he had fallen behind in his alimony payments. He defended himself by claiming that the state alimony statute was unconstitutional. It was defective, according to his argument, because it allowed for wives to obtain alimony judgments against husbands, but did not permit husbands to receive alimony from wives. This Equal Protection Clause claim was denied by the Alabama trial court, and William was ordered to pay $5,524 in back alimony and attorney's fees. The Alabama appeals courts affirmed the judgment of the trial court.

MR. JUSTICE BRENNAN delivered the opinion of the Court.

In authorizing the imposition of alimony obligations on husbands, but not on wives, the Alabama statutory scheme "provides that different treatment be accorded ... on the basis of ... sex; it thus establishes a classification subject to scrutiny under the Equal Protection Clause," *Reed v. Reed* (1971). The fact that the classification expressly discriminates against men rather than women does not protect it from scrutiny. *Craig v. Boren* (1976). "To withstand scrutiny" under the Equal Protection Clause, "'classifications by gender must serve important governmental objectives and must be substantially related to achievement of those objectives.'" We shall, therefore, examine the three governmental objectives that might arguably be served by Alabama's statutory scheme.

Appellant views the Alabama alimony statutes as effectively announcing the State's preference for an allocation of family responsibilities under which the wife plays a dependent role, and as seeking for their objective the reinforcement of that model among the State's citizens. We agree, as he urges, that prior cases settle that this purpose cannot sustain the statutes. *Stanton v. Stanton* (1975) held that the "old notion" that "generally it is the man's primary responsibility to provide a home and its essentials," can no longer justify a statute that discriminates on the basis of gender. "No longer is the female destined solely for the home and the rearing of the family, and only the male for the marketplace and the world of ideas." If the statute is to survive constitutional attack, therefore, it must be validated on some other basis.

The opinion of the Alabama Court of Civil Appeals suggests other purposes that the statute may serve. Its opinion states that the Alabama statutes were "designed" for "the wife of a broken marriage who needs financial assistance." This may be read as asserting either of two legislative objectives. One is a legislative purpose to provide help for needy spouses, using sex as a proxy for need. The other is a goal of compensating women for past discrimination during marriage, which assertedly has left them unprepared to fend for themselves in the working world following divorce. We concede, of course, that assisting needy spouses is a legitimate and important governmental objective. We have also recognized "[r]eduction of the disparity in economic condition between men and women caused by the long history of discrimination against women ... as ... an important governmental objective." It only remains, therefore, to determine whether the classification at issue here is "substantially related to achievement of those objectives."

Ordinarily, we would begin the analysis of the "needy spouse" objective by considering whether sex is a sufficiently "accurate proxy" for dependency to establish that the gender classification rests "'upon some ground of difference having a fair and substantial relation to the object of the legislation.'" Similarly, we would initially approach the "compensation" rationale by asking whether women had in fact been significantly discriminated against in the sphere to which the statute applied a sex-based classification, leaving the sexes "*not* similarly situated with respect to opportunities" in that sphere.

But in this case, even if sex were a reliable proxy for need, and even if the institution of marriage did discriminate against women, these factors still would "not adequately justify the salient features of" Alabama's statutory scheme. Under the statute, individualized hearings at which the parties' relative financial circumstances are considered already occur. There is no reason, therefore, to use sex as a proxy for need. Needy males could be helped along with needy females with little if any additional burden on the State. In such circumstances, not even an administrative-convenience rationale exists to justify operating by generalization or proxy. Similarly, since individualized hearings can determine which women were in fact discriminated against vis-à-vis their husbands, as well as which family units defied the stereotype, and left the husband dependent on the wife, Alabama's alleged compensatory purpose may be effectuated without placing burdens solely on husbands. Progress toward fulfilling such a purpose would not be hampered, and it would cost the State nothing more, if it were to treat men and women equally by making alimony burdens independent of sex. "Thus, the gender-based distinction is gratuitous; without it, the statutory scheme would only provide benefits to those men who are in fact similarly situated to the women the statute aids," and the effort to help those women would not in any way be compromised.

Moreover, use of a gender classification actually produces perverse results in this case. As compared to a gender-neutral law placing alimony obligations on the spouse able to pay, the present Alabama statutes give an advantage only to the financially secure wife whose husband is in need. Although such a wife might have to pay alimony under a gender-neutral statute, the present statutes exempt her from that obligation. Thus, "[t]he [wives] who benefit from the disparate treatment are those who were ... nondependent on their husbands." They are precisely those who are not "needy spouses" and who are "least likely to have been victims of ... discrimination" by the institution of marriage. A gender-based classification which, as compared to a gender-neutral one, generates additional benefits only for those it has no reason to prefer cannot survive equal protection scrutiny.

Legislative classifications which distribute benefits and burdens on the basis of gender carry the inherent risk of reinforcing the stereotypes about the "proper place" of women and their need for special protection. Thus, even statutes purportedly designed to compensate for and ameliorate the effects of past discrimination must be carefully tailored. Where, as here, the State's compensatory and ameliorative purposes are as well served by a gender-neutral classification as one that gender classifies and therefore carries with it the baggage of sexual stereotypes, the State cannot be permitted to classify on the basis of sex. And this is doubly so where the choice made by the State appears to redound—if only indirectly—to the benefit of those without need for special solicitude.

Having found Alabama's alimony statutes unconstitutional, we reverse the judgment below and remand the cause for further proceedings not inconsistent with this opinion.

Reversed and remanded.

A second example of laws that run afoul of the Equal Protection Clause because of outdated sexual stereotypes is provided by *Mississippi University for Women v. Hogan* (1982). This suit, filed by a male who was denied admission to a nursing program, challenged state-operated, single-sex schools. While Mississippi argued that by creating a women's college the state expanded the choices and opportunities for females, the program was criticized for being based on an outmoded notion that women need an environment protected from men to succeed academically.

The case provided an opportunity for Justice O'Connor, the first woman appointed to the Supreme Court, to express her legal views on laws that classify according to sex. Is she on firm ground in arguing that the Mississippi program is repugnant to the Fourteenth Amendment because of its presumptions of the inferiority of women? Do the dissenting justices, through Justice Powell's opinion, make a valid point that the majority is imposing unwise uniformity and depriving women of educational choices and alternatives?

Mississippi University for Women v. Hogan

458 U.S. 718 (1982)
Vote: 5 (Brennan, Marshall, O'Connor, Stevens, White)
    4 (Blackmun, Burger, Powell, Rehnquist)
Opinion of the Court: O'Connor
Dissenting opinions: Blackmun, Burger, Powell

In 1884 the state legislature created the Mississippi Industrial Institute and College for the Education of White Girls of the State of Mississippi. Located in Columbus, the school evolved over the years to achieve the status of a fully accredited university. One of its characteristics, however, did not change: only women could be admitted as regular students.

Joe Hogan was a registered nurse working as a nursing supervisor in a medical facility in Columbus. In 1979 he applied for admission to the university to obtain a baccalaureate degree in nursing, which he did not have. Although he was otherwise fully qualified, Hogan was rejected on account of his sex. The university told him that he was free to audit courses, but could not take them for credit. Two other state institutions in Jackson and Hattiesburg provided the same degree program on a coeducational basis. But Hogan needed to keep his job in Columbus while pursuing the degree, and the closer of the two alternatives was 150 miles away. Hogan, therefore, filed suit in federal court attacking the single-sex admissions policy as a violation of the Equal Protection Clause. The district court upheld the state policies, but the court of appeals reversed.

JUSTICE O'CONNOR delivered the opinion of the Court.

We begin our analysis aided by several firmly established principles. Because the challenged policy expressly discriminates among applicants on the basis of gender, it is subject to scrutiny under the Equal Protection Clause of the Fourteenth Amendment. *Reed v. Reed* (1971). That this statutory policy discriminates against males rather than against females does not exempt it from scrutiny or reduce the standard of review. Our decisions also establish that the party seeking to uphold a statute that classifies individuals on the basis of their gender must carry the burden of showing an "exceedingly persuasive justification" for the classification. The burden is met only by showing at least that the classification serves "important governmental objectives and that the discriminatory means employed" are "substantially related to the achievement of those objectives."

Although the test for determining the validity of a gender-based classification is straightforward, it must be applied free of fixed notions concerning the roles and abilities of males and females. Care must be taken in ascertaining whether the statutory objective itself reflects archaic and stereotypic notions. Thus, if the statutory objective is to exclude or "protect" members of one gender because they are presumed to suffer from an inherent handicap or to be innately inferior, the objective itself is illegitimate.

If the State's objective is legitimate and important, we next determine whether the requisite direct, substantial relationship between objective and means is present. The purpose of requiring that close relationship is to assure that the validity of a classification is determined through reasoned analysis rather than through the mechanical application of traditional, often inaccurate, assumptions about the proper roles of men and women. The need for the requirement is amply revealed by reference to the broad range of statutes already invalidated by this Court, statutes that relied upon the simplistic, outdated assumption that gender could be used as a "proxy for other, more germane bases of classification" to establish a link between objective and classification.

Applying this framework, we now analyze the arguments advanced by the State to justify its refusal to allow males to enroll for credit in MUW's School of Nursing.

The State's primary justification for maintaining the single-sex admissions policy of MUW's School of Nursing is that it compensates for discrimination against women and, therefore, constitutes educational affirmative action. As applied to the School of Nursing, we find the State's argument unpersuasive.

In limited circumstances, a gender-based classification favoring one sex can be justified if it intentionally and directly assists members of the sex that is disproportionately burdened. However, we consistently have emphasized that "the mere recitation of a benign, compensatory purpose is not an automatic shield which protects against any inquiry into the actual purposes underlying a statutory scheme." The same searching analysis must be made, regardless of whether the State's objective is to eliminate family controversy, to achieve administrative efficiency, or to balance the burdens borne by males and females.

It is readily apparent that a State can evoke a compensatory purpose to justify an otherwise discriminatory classification only if members of the gender benefited by the classification actually suffer a disadvantage related to the classification....

In sharp contrast, Mississippi has made no showing that women lacked opportunities to obtain training in the field of nursing or to attain positions of leadership in that field when the MUW School of Nursing opened its door or that women currently are deprived of such opportunities. In fact, in 1970, the year before the School of Nursing's first class enrolled, women earned 94 percent of the nursing baccalaureate degrees conferred in Mississippi and 98.6 percent of the degrees earned nationwide. That year was not an aberration; one decade earlier, women had earned all the nursing degrees conferred in Mississippi and 98.9 percent of the degrees conferred nationwide. As one would expect, the labor force reflects the same predominance of women in nursing. When MUW's School of Nursing began operation, nearly 98 percent of all employed registered nurses were female.

Rather than compensate for discriminatory barriers faced by women, MUW's policy of excluding males from admission to the School of Nursing tends to perpetuate the stereotyped view of nursing as an exclusively woman's job. By assuring that Mississippi allots more openings in its state-supported nursing schools to women than it does to men, MUW's admissions policy lends credibility to the old view that women, not men, should become nurses, and makes the assumption that nursing is a field for women a self-fulfilling prophecy. Thus, we conclude that, although the State recited a "benign, compensatory purpose," it failed to establish that the alleged objective is the actual purpose underlying the discriminatory classification.

The policy is invalid also because it fails the second part of the equal protection test, for the State has made no showing that the gender-based classification is substantially and directly related to its proposed compensatory objective. To the contrary, MUW's policy of permitting men to attend classes as auditors fatally undermines its claim that women, at least those in the School of Nursing, are adversely affected by the presence of men.

MUW permits men who audit to participate fully in classes. Additionally, both men and women take part in continuing education courses offered by the School of Nursing, in which regular nursing students also can enroll. The uncontroversial record reveals that admitting men to nursing classes does not affect teaching style, that the presence of men in the classroom would not affect the performance of the female nursing students, and that men in co-educational nursing schools do not dominate the classroom. In sum, the record in this case is flatly inconsistent with the claim that excluding men from the School of Nursing is necessary to reach any of MUW's educational goals.

Thus, considering both the asserted interest and the relationship between the interest and the methods used by the State, we conclude that the State has fallen far short of establishing the "exceedingly persuasive justification" needed to sustain the gender-based classification. Accordingly, we hold that MUW's policy of denying males the right to enroll for credit in its School of Nursing violates the Equal Protection Clause of the Fourteenth Amendment.

In an additional attempt to justify its exclusion of men from MUW's School of Nursing, the State contends that MUW is the direct beneficiary "of specific congressional legislation which, on its face, permits the institution to exist as it has in the past." The argument is based upon the language of § 901(a) in Title IX of the Education Amend-

ments of 1972, 20 U.S.C. § 1681(a). Although § 901(a) prohibits gender discrimination in education programs that receive federal financial assistance, subsection 5 exempts the admissions policies of undergraduate institutions "that traditionally and continually from their establishment have had a policy of admitting only students of one sex" from the general prohibition. Arguing that Congress enacted Title IX in furtherance of its power to enforce the Fourteenth Amendment, a power granted by § 5 of that Amendment, the State would have us conclude that § 901(a)(5) is but "a congressional limitation upon the broad prohibitions of the Equal Protection Clause of the Fourteenth Amendment."

The argument requires little comment. Initially, it is far from clear that Congress intended, through § 901(a)(5), to exempt MUW from any constitutional obligation. Rather, Congress apparently intended, at most, to exempt MUW from the requirements of Title IX.

Even if Congress envisioned a constitutional exemption, the State's argument would fail. Section 5 of the Fourteenth Amendment gives Congress broad power indeed to enforce the command of the Amendment and "to secure to all persons the enjoyment of perfect equality of civil rights and the equal protection of the laws against State denial or invasion. . . ." Congress' power under § 5, however, "is limited to adopting measures to enforce the guarantees of the Amendment; § 5 grants Congress no power to restrict, abrogate, or dilute these guarantees." Although we give deference to congressional decisions and classifications, neither Congress nor a State can validate a law that denies the rights guaranteed by the Fourteenth Amendment.

The fact that the language of § 901(a)(5) applies to MUW provides the State no solace. . . .

Because we conclude that the State's policy of excluding males from MUW's School of Nursing violates the Equal Protection Clause of the Fourteenth Amendment, we affirm the judgment of the Court of Appeals.

It is so ordered.

JUSTICE POWELL . . . dissenting.

The Court's opinion bows deeply to conformity. Left without honor—indeed, held unconstitutional—is an element of diversity that has characterized much of American education and enriched much of American life. The Court in effect holds today that no State now may provide even a single institution of higher learning open only to women students. It gives no heed to the efforts of the State of Mississippi to provide abundant opportunities for young men and young women to attend coeducational institutions, and none to the preferences of the more than 40,000 young women who over the years have evidenced their approval of an all-women's college by choosing Mississippi University for Women (MUW) over seven coeducational universities within the State. The Court decides today that the Equal Protection Clause makes it unlawful for the State to provide women with a traditionally popular and respected choice of educational environment. It does so in a case instituted by one man, who represents no class, and whose primary concern is personal convenience.

It is undisputed that women enjoy complete equality of opportunity in Mississippi's public system of higher education. Of the State's 8 universities and 16 junior colleges, all except MUW are coeducational. At least two other Mississippi universities would have provided respondent with the nursing curriculum that he wishes to pursue. No other male has joined in his complaint. The only groups with any personal acquaintance with MUW to file *amicus* briefs are female students and alumnae of MUW. And they have emphatically rejected respondent's arguments, urging that the State of Mississippi be allowed to continue offering the choice from which they have benefited.

Nor is respondent significantly disadvantaged by MUW's all-female tradition. His constitutional complaint is based upon a single asserted harm: that he must *travel* to attend the state-supported nursing schools that concededly are available to him. The Court characterizes this injury as one of "inconvenience." This description is fair and accurate, though somewhat embarrassed by the fact that there is, of course, no constitutional right to attend a state supported university in one's home town. Thus the Court, to redress respondent's injury of inconvenience, must rest its invalidation of MUW's single-sex program on a mode of "sexual stereotype" reasoning that has no application whatever to the respondent or to the "wrong" of which he complains. At best this is anomalous. And ultimately the anomaly reveals legal error—that of applying a heightened equal protection standard, developed in cases of genuine sexual stereotyping, to a narrowly utilized state classification that

provides an *additional* choice for women. Moreover, I believe that Mississippi's educational system should be upheld in this case even if this inappropriate method of analysis is applied.

Coeducation, historically, is a novel educational theory. From grade school through high school, college, and graduate and professional training, much of the Nation's population during much of our history has been educated in sexually segregated classrooms. At the college level, for instance, until recently some of the most prestigious colleges and universities—including most of the Ivy League—had long histories of single-sex education.... Harvard, Yale, and Princeton remained all-male colleges well into the second half of this century....

The issue in this case is whether a State transgresses the Constitution when—within the context of a public system that offers a diverse range of campuses, curricula, and educational alternatives—it seeks to accommodate the legitimate personal preferences of those desiring the advantages of an all-women's college. In my view, the Court errs seriously by assuming—without argument or discussion—that the equal protection standard generally applicable to sex discrimination is appropriate here. That standard was designed to free women from "archaic and overbroad generalizations...." In no previous case have we applied it to invalidate state efforts to *expand* women's choices. Nor are there prior sex discrimination decisions by this Court in which a male plaintiff, as in this case, had the choice of an equal benefit.

The cases cited by the Court therefore do not control the issue now before us. In most of them women were given no opportunity for the same benefit as men. Cases involving male plaintiffs are equally inapplicable. In *Craig v. Boren* (1976), a male under 21 was not permitted to buy beer anywhere in the State, and women were afforded no choice as to whether they would accept the "statistically measured but loose-fitting generalities concerning the drinking tendencies of aggregate groups." A similar situation prevailed in *Orr v. Orr* (1979), where men had no opportunity to seek alimony from their divorced wives, and women had no escape from the statute's stereotypical announcement of "the State's preference for an allocation of family responsibilities under which the wife plays a dependent role...."

By applying heightened equal protection analysis to this

case, the Court frustrates the liberating spirit of the Equal Protection Clause. It prohibits the States from providing women with an opportunity to choose the type of university they prefer. And yet it is these women whom the Court regards as the *victims* of an illegal, stereotyped perception of the role of women in our society. The Court reasons this way in a case in which no woman has complained, and the only complainant is a man who advances no claims on behalf of anyone else. His claim, it should be recalled, is not that he is being denied a substantive educational opportunity, or even the right to attend an all-male or a coeducational college. It is *only* that the colleges open to him are located at inconvenient distances.

The Court views this case as presenting a serious equal protection claim of sex discrimination. I do not, and I would sustain Mississippi's right to continue MUW on a rational-basis analysis. But I need not apply this "lowest tier" of scrutiny. I can accept for present purposes the standard applied by the Court: that there is a gender-based distinction that must serve an important governmental objective by means that are substantially related to its achievement. The record in this case reflects that MUW has a historic position in the State's educational system dating back to 1884. More than 2,000 women presently evidence their preference for MUW by having enrolled there. The choice is one that discriminates invidiously against no one. And the State's purpose in preserving that choice is legitimate and substantial. Generations of our finest minds, both among educators and students, have believed that single-sex, college-level institutions afford distinctive benefits. There are many persons, of course, who have different views. But simply because there are these differences is no reason— certainly none of constitutional dimension—to conclude that no substantial state interest is served when such a choice is made available....

In sum, the practice of voluntarily chosen single-sex education is an honored tradition in our country, even if it now rarely exists in state colleges and universities. Mississippi's accommodation of such student choices is legitimate because it is completely consensual and is important because it permits students to decide for themselves the type of college education they think will benefit them most. Finally, Mississippi's policy is substantially related to its long-respected objective.

A distinctive feature of America's tradition has been respect for diversity. This has been characteristic of the peoples from numerous lands who have built our country. It is the essence of our democratic system. At stake in this case as I see it is the preservation of a small aspect of this diversity. But that aspect is by no means insignificant, given our heritage of available choice between single-sex and coeducational institutions of higher learning. The Court answers that there is discrimination—not just that which may be tolerable, as for example between those candidates for admission able to contribute most to an educational institution and those able to contribute less—but discrimination of constitutional dimension. But, having found "discrimination," the Court finds it difficult to identify the victims. It hardly can claim that women are discriminated against. A constitutional case is held to exist solely because one man found it inconvenient to travel to any of the other institutions made available to him by the State of Mississippi. In essence he insists that he has a right to attend a college in his home community. This simply is not a sex discrimination case. The Equal Protection Clause was never intended to be applied to this kind of case.

The *Hogan* decision would appear to settle the matter of government-operated single-sex schools— they violate the Constitution. By the time of the decision, most single-sex public colleges, including the U.S. military academies, had initiated coeducational admissions policies. However, state schools in Virginia (Virginia Military Institute) and South Carolina (The Citadel) refused to do so. Both claimed that the special mission of a military institution justified restricting admissions to males only. Female applicants sued the schools claiming a violation of the Constitution and federal law, and the schools responded with a spirited legal defense of their traditions. Ultimately, VMI compromised by joining a cooperative venture with Mary Baldwin College, a neighboring private women's college. The Citadel continued to press its position, but lost the first rounds in court. The Supreme Court may be called upon to settle the fate of both institutions.

ECONOMIC DISCRIMINATION

As with matters of race and gender, society's views on economic status have changed. In the early days of our nation, wealth was considered a reflection of individual worth. The poor were thought to be less deserving. The free enterprise philosophy that emphasized personal economic responsibility discouraged public policies designed to help the poor. The fact that people could be imprisoned for failure to pay debts (as opposed to today's more lenient treatment under the bankruptcy laws) reflects that period's hardline approach to economic failure. Even a sitting Supreme Court justice, James Wilson, was imprisoned in 1796 because of a failure to satisfy his creditors. In *City of New York v. Miln* (1837) the Court supported the power of the state to take "precautionary measures against the moral pestilence of paupers."

As our society has evolved, the plight of the poor has become a major public policy concern. Although opinions differ widely on the proper role of government in handling poverty, housing, and health care, our political system has developed social programs that would have been inconceivable to leaders during the nation's formative years. Moreover, economic disadvantage is no longer seen as a justification for denying a person full political and social rights. The Supreme Court has ruled in a number of areas with respect to economic status. For example, we have discussed cases in which the Court extended certain rights, such as government-provided attorneys, to indigent criminal defendants. In the next chapter, we will examine the Court's response to states' limiting the right to vote on the basis of economic status.

Included here are two Supreme Court decisions that deal directly with government policies affecting the poor. The first focuses on state welfare programs, the second on public education. These two public policy areas have a significant impact on the poor by providing direct assistance and opportunities for economic and social advancement. They also involve programs of great financial cost and inevitably raise questions about taxing and spending. The justices of the Supreme Court, like the nation as a whole, have had a difficult time coming to an agreement on how such questions should be answered.

Shapiro v. Thompson (1969) is one of a number of cases that have challenged the inequities within our social welfare programs. Although the infusion of federal funds into these programs has given the national government a role, for the most part, the states have retained substantial authority to set welfare policy. As a consequence, eligibility requirements and benefit schedules vary widely from state to state. This lack of uniformity often gives rise to charges of unequal treatment. The *Shapiro* case addresses the clash between a government's authority to establish regulations for its own welfare programs and its obligation to observe equal protection. It also concerns the danger of encroaching on the liberty of American citizens to move freely among the states. While reading this decision, note how little weight the majority gives to government arguments that fiscal interests should prevail over civil liberty considerations. Finally, note Justice Brennan's discussion of the appropriate standard to use in economic discrimination issues. While a rational basis standard normally would be appropriate, when a fundamental right also is involved (the right to interstate travel) the standard is elevated.

Shapiro v. Thompson

394 U.S. 618 (1969)
Vote: 6 (Brennan, Douglas, Fortas, Marshall, Stewart, White)
    3 (Black, Harlan, Warren)
Opinion of the Court: Brennan
Concurring opinion: Stewart
Dissenting opinions: Harlan, Warren

Vivian Marie Thompson was a nineteen-year-old unwed mother who was pregnant with her second child. In June 1966 she decided to move from Massachusetts and live with her mother in Hartford, Connecticut. After two months Thompson's mother was no longer able to support her and her son, and Thompson moved into an apartment of her own. Because of her pregnancy, she was unable to work or to enter a job training program. She applied for welfare benefits under the Aid to Families with Dependent Children (AFDC) program, but was denied assistance. Connecticut required a one-year residency to be eligible for financial assistance.

Thompson filed suit to challenge the constitutionality of the residency requirement on equal protection and freedom of travel grounds. A number of organized interests supported her case, including the Neighborhood Legal Services Program, the Center on Social Welfare Policy, the American Civil Liberties Union, the American Jewish Congress, and Legal Aid.

The AFDC program is jointly funded by Congress and the individual states. Federal requirements stipulated that no state regulations would be approved if residency requirements of more than one year were imposed. The lower federal court ruled in Thompson's favor, declaring the residency law unconstitutional. Similar suits challenging one-year residency requirements in Pennsylvania and the District of Columbia also were successful in the lower courts. The Supreme Court consolidated all three appeals for a single ruling in this case.

MR. JUSTICE BRENNAN delivered the opinion of the Court.

There is no dispute that the effect of the waiting-period requirement in each case is to create two classes of needy resident families indistinguishable from each other except that one is composed of residents who have resided a year or more, and the second of residents who have resided less than a year, in the jurisdiction. On the basis of this sole difference the first class is granted and the second class is denied welfare aid upon which may depend the ability of the families to obtain the very means to subsist—food,

shelter, and other necessities of life. In each case, the District Court found that appellees met the test for residence in their jurisdictions, as well as all other eligibility requirements except the requirement of residence for a full year prior to their applications. On reargument, appellees' central contention is that the statutory prohibition of benefits to residents of less than a year creates a classification which constitutes an invidious discrimination denying them equal protection of the laws. We agree. The interests which appellants assert are promoted by the classification either may not constitutionally be promoted by government or are not compelling governmental interests.

Primarily, appellants justify the waiting-period requirement as a protective device to preserve the fiscal integrity of state public assistance programs. It is asserted that people who require welfare assistance during their first year of residence in a State are likely to become continuing burdens on state welfare programs. Therefore, the argument runs, if such people can be deterred from entering the jurisdiction by denying them welfare benefits during the first year, state programs to assist long-time residents will not be impaired by a substantial influx of indigent newcomers.

There is weighty evidence that exclusion from the jurisdiction of the poor who need or may need relief was the specific objective of these provisions. In the Congress, sponsors of federal legislation to eliminate all residence requirements have been consistently opposed by representatives of state and local welfare agencies who have stressed the fears of the States that elimination of the requirements would result in a heavy influx of individuals into States providing the most generous benefits. The sponsor of the Connecticut requirement said in its support: "I doubt that Connecticut can and should continue to allow unlimited migration into the state on the basis of offering instant money and permanent income to all who can make their way to the state regardless of their ability to contribute to the economy.". . .

We do not doubt that the one-year waiting period device is well suited to discourage the influx of poor families in need of assistance. An indigent who desires to migrate, resettle, find a new job, and start a new life will doubtless hesitate if he knows that he must risk making the move without the possibility of falling back on state welfare assistance during his first year of residence, when his need may be most acute. But the purpose of inhibiting migration by needy persons into the State is constitutionally impermissible. This Court long ago recognized that the nature of our Federal Union and our constitutional concepts of personal liberty unite to require that all citizens be free to travel throughout the length and breadth of our land uninhibited by statutes, rules, or regulations which unreasonably burden or restrict this movement....

Thus, the purpose of deterring the in-migration of indigents cannot serve as justification for the classification created by the one-year waiting period, since that purpose is constitutionally impermissible. If a law has "no other purpose ... than to chill the assertion of constitutional rights by penalizing those who choose to exercise them, then it [is] patently unconstitutional."

Alternatively, appellants argue that even if it is impermissible for a State to attempt to deter the entry of all indigents, the challenged classification may be justified as a permissible state attempt to discourage those indigents who would enter the State solely to obtain larger benefits. We observe first that none of the statutes before us is tailored to serve that objective. Rather, the class of barred newcomers is all-inclusive, lumping the great majority who come to the State for other purposes with those who come for the sole purpose of collecting higher benefits. In actual operation, therefore, the three statutes enact what in effect are nonrebuttable presumptions that every applicant for assistance in his first year of residence came to the jurisdiction solely to obtain higher benefits. Nothing whatever in any of these records supplies any basis in fact for such a presumption.

More fundamentally, a State may no more try to fence out those indigents who seek higher welfare benefits than it may try to fence out indigents generally. Implicit in any such distinction is the notion that indigents who enter a State with the hope of securing higher welfare benefits are somehow less deserving than indigents who do not take this consideration into account. But we do not perceive why a mother who is seeking to make a new life for herself and her children should be regarded as less deserving because she considers, among other factors, the level of a State's public assistance. Surely such a mother is no less deserving than a mother who moves into a particular State in order to take advantage of its better educational facilities.

Appellants argue further that the challenged classification may be sustained as an attempt to distinguish between new and old residents on the basis of the contribution they have made to the community through the payment of taxes.... Appellants' reasoning would logically permit the State to bar new residents from schools, parks, and libraries or deprive them of police and fire protection. Indeed it would permit the State to apportion all benefits and services according to the past tax contributions of its citizens. The Equal Protection Clause prohibits such an apportionment of state services.

We recognize that a State has a valid interest in preserving the fiscal integrity of its programs. It may legitimately attempt to limit its expenditures, whether for public assistance, public education, or any other program. But a State may not accomplish such a purpose by invidious distinctions between classes of its citizens. It could not, for example, reduce expenditures for education by barring indigent children from its schools. Similarly, in the cases before us, appellants must do more than show that denying welfare benefits to new residents saves money. The saving of welfare costs cannot justify an otherwise invidious classification.

In sum, neither deterrence of indigents from migrating to the State nor limitation of welfare benefits to those regarded as contributing to the State is a constitutionally permissible state objective.

Appellants next advance as justification certain administrative and related governmental objectives allegedly served by the waiting-period requirement. They argue that the requirement (1) facilitates the planning of the welfare budget; (2) provides an objective test of residency; (3) minimizes the opportunity for recipients fraudulently to receive payments from more than one jurisdiction; and (4) encourages early entry of new residents into the labor force....

The argument that the waiting-period requirement facilitates budget predictability is wholly unfounded. The records in all three cases are utterly devoid of evidence that either State or the District of Columbia in fact uses the one-year requirement as a means to predict the number of people who will require assistance in the budget year.... The argument that the waiting period serves as an administratively efficient rule of thumb for determining residency similarly will not withstand scrutiny. The residence requirement and the one-year waiting-period requirement are distinct and independent prerequisites for assistance under these three statutes, and the facts relevant to the determination of each are directly examined by the welfare authorities. Before granting an application, the welfare authorities investigate the applicant's employment, housing, and family situation and in the course of the inquiry necessarily learn the facts upon which to determine whether the applicant is a resident.

Similarly, there is no need for a State to use the one-year waiting period as a safeguard against fraudulent receipt of benefits; for less drastic means are available, and are employed, to minimize that hazard. Of course, a State has a valid interest in preventing fraud by any applicant, whether a newcomer or a long-time resident. It is not denied, however, that the investigations now conducted entail inquiries into facts relevant to that subject....

Pennsylvania suggests that the one-year waiting period is justified as a means of encouraging new residents to join the labor force promptly. But this logic would also require a similar waiting period for long-term residents of the State. A state purpose to encourage employment provides no rational basis for imposing a one-year waiting-period restriction on new residents only.

We conclude therefore that appellants in these cases do not use and have no need to use the one-year requirement for the governmental purposes suggested. Thus, even under traditional equal protection tests a classification of welfare applicants according to whether they have lived in the State for one year would seem irrational and unconstitutional. But, of course, the traditional criteria do not apply in these cases. Since the classification here touches on the fundamental right of interstate movement, its constitutionality must be judged by the stricter standard of whether it promotes a *compelling* state interest. Under this standard, the waiting-period requirement clearly violates the Equal Protection Clause.

Affirmed.

San Antonio Independent School District v. Rodriguez (1973) was an economic discrimination case of enormous importance. First, the case involved the right of children to receive a public education, the surest way for the disadvantaged to improve their prospects for economic and social advancement. Second, the case attacked the constitutionality of the Texas method of funding public schools. Education is the most expensive of all state programs, and any change in the method of distributing these funds can have a tremendous impact. Third, the Texas system challenged here was similar to schemes used by most states in determining the allocation of education dollars. Whatever the Court decided, this case was going to be significant economically and socially.

At the heart of this case was the contention that the Texas system for funding schools discriminated against the poor. It was undeniable that children who lived in wealthy school districts had access to a higher quality education than children in poor districts. But does this difference violate the Constitution? In large measure, the answer to that question rests on which equal protection standard is used. Under strict scrutiny the Texas funding system almost certainly would fall. But before strict scrutiny can be applied, one of two requirements has to be met. Either the poor, like black Americans in the racial discrimination cases, would have to be declared a suspect class, or the right to an education would have to be declared a fundamental right. If the Court failed to support one of these positions, the rational basis test would control, and the state plan likely would stand. As you read Justice Powell's decision, think about his reasoning and conclusions on these two points.

San Antonio Independent School District v. Rodriguez

411 U.S. 1 (1973)
Vote: 5 (Blackmun, Burger, Powell, Rehnquist, Stewart)
   4 (Brennan, Douglas, Marshall, White)
Opinion of the Court: Powell
Concurring opinion: Stewart
Dissenting opinions: Brennan, Marshall, White

Demetrio Rodriguez and other Mexican-American parents whose children attended the public schools of the Edgewood Independent School District in San Antonio, Texas, were concerned about the quality of the local schools. The Edgewood district was about 90 percent Mexican-American and quite poor. Efforts to improve their children's schools were unsuccessful due to insufficient funding. Because the state formula for distributing education funds resulted in low levels of financial support for economically depressed districts, the parents filed suit to declare the state funding system in violation of the Equal Protection Clause. The funding program guaranteed each child in the state a minimum basic education by appropriating funds to local school districts through a complex formula designed to take into account economic variations across school districts. Local districts levied property taxes to meet their assigned contributions to the state program but could use the property taxing power to obtain additional funds.

The Edgewood district had an assessed property value per pupil of $5,960, the lowest in the San Antonio area. It taxed its residents at a rate of $1.05 per $100 in assessed valuation, the area's highest rate. This local tax yielded $26 per pupil above the contributions that had to be made to the state for the 1967–1968 school year. Funds from the state added $222 per pupil, and federal programs contributed $108. These sources combined for a total of $356 per pupil for the year. In the nearby Alamo Heights district, property values amounted to $49,000 per pupil, which was taxed at a rate of $.85 per $100 of assessed valuation. These property taxes yielded $333 additional available revenues per pupil. Combined with $225 from state funds and $36 from federal sources, Alamo Heights enjoyed a total funding level of $594 per pupil.

The suit filed by Rodriguez and the other parents was based on these disparities. Although the residents of Edgewood taxed themselves at a much higher rate, the yield from local taxes in Alamo Heights was almost thirteen times greater. To achieve equal property tax dollars with Alamo Heights, Edgewood would

Demetrio Rodriguez and other Mexican-American parents challenged the Texas public school financing system as discriminatory on the basis of economic status, but in 1973 the Supreme Court ruled against them.

have had to raise its tax rate to $13 per $100 in assessed valuation, but state law placed a $1.50 ceiling on such taxes. There was no way for the Edgewood parents to achieve funding equality.

A three-judge federal court agreed with the Rodriguez suit, finding that the Texas funding program invidiously discriminated against children on the basis of economic status. According to the federal court, the poor were a suspect class, and education was a fundamental right. The state appealed to the Supreme Court. Twenty-five states filed amicus curiae briefs supporting the Texas funding system. Groups such as the NAACP, the American Civil Liberties Union, and the American Education Association filed briefs backing Rodriguez.

MR. JUSTICE POWELL delivered the opinion
of the Court.

Texas virtually concedes that its historically rooted dual system of financing education could not withstand the strict judicial scrutiny that this Court has found appropriate in reviewing legislative judgments that interfere with fundamental constitutional rights or that involve suspect classifications. If, as previous decisions have indicated, strict scrutiny means that the State's system is not entitled to the usual presumption of validity, that the State rather than the complainants must carry a "heavy burden of justification," that the State must demonstrate that its educational system has been structured with "precision," and is "tailored" narrowly to serve legitimate objectives and that it has selected the "less drastic means" for effectuating its objectives, the Texas financing system and its counterpart in virtually every other State will not pass muster. The State candidly admits that "[n]o one familiar with the Texas system would contend that it has yet achieved perfection." Apart from its concession that educational financing in Texas has "defects" and "imperfections," the State defends the system's rationality with vigor and disputes the District Court's finding that it lacks a "reasonable basis."

This, then, establishes the framework for our analysis. We must decide, first, whether the Texas system of financing public education operates to the disadvantage of some suspect class or impinges upon a fundamental right explicitly or implicitly protected by the Constitution, thereby requiring strict judicial scrutiny. If so, the judgment of the District Court should be affirmed. If not, the Texas scheme must still be examined to determine whether it rationally furthers some legitimate, articulated state purpose and therefore does not constitute an invidious discrimination in violation of the Equal Protection Clause of the Fourteenth Amendment.

The District Court's opinion does not reflect the novelty and complexity of the constitutional questions posed by appellees' challenge to Texas' system of school financing. In concluding that strict judicial scrutiny was required, that court relied on decisions dealing with the rights of indigents to equal treatment in the criminal trial and appellate processes, and on cases disapproving wealth restrictions on the right to vote. Those cases, the District Court concluded, established wealth as a suspect classification. Finding that the local property tax system discriminated on the basis of wealth, it regarded those precedents as controlling. It then reasoned, based on decisions of this Court affirming the undeniable importance of education, that there is a fundamental right to education and that, absent some compelling state justification, the Texas system could not stand.

We are unable to agree that this case, which in significant aspects is *sui generis*, may be so neatly fitted into the conventional mosaic of constitutional analysis under the Equal Protection Clause. Indeed, for the several reasons that follow, we find neither the suspect-classification nor the fundamental-interest analysis persuasive.

The wealth discrimination discovered by the District Court in this case, and by several other courts that have recently struck down school-financing laws in other States, is quite unlike any of the forms of wealth discrimination heretofore reviewed by this Court. Rather than focusing on the unique features of the alleged discrimination, the courts in these cases have virtually assumed their findings of a suspect classification through a simplistic process of analysis: since, under the traditional systems of financing public schools, some poorer people receive less expensive educations than other more affluent people, these systems discriminate on the basis of wealth. This approach largely ignores the hard threshold questions, including whether it makes a difference for purposes of consideration under the Constitution that the class of disadvantaged "poor" cannot be identified or defined in customary equal protection terms, and whether the relative—rather than absolute—nature of the asserted deprivation is of significant consequence. Before a State's laws and the justification for the classifications they create are subjected to strict judicial scrutiny, we think these threshold considerations must be analyzed more closely than they were in the court below....

First, in support of their charge that the system discriminates against the "poor," appellees have made no effort to demonstrate that it operates to the peculiar disadvantage of any class fairly definable as indigent, or as composed of persons whose incomes are beneath any designated poverty level. Indeed, there is reason to believe that the poorest families are not necessarily clustered in the poorest property districts. A recent and exhaustive study of school districts in Connecticut concluded that ... the poor were clustered around commercial and industrial areas—those same areas that provide the most attractive sources of property tax income for school districts. Whether a similar pattern would be discovered in Texas is not known, but there is no basis on the record in this case for assuming that the poorest people—defined by reference to any level of absolute impecunity—are concentrated in the poorest districts.

Second, neither appellees nor the District Court addressed the fact that, unlike each of the foregoing cases, lack of personal resources has not occasioned an absolute deprivation of the desired benefit. The argument here is not that the children in districts having relatively low assessable property values are receiving no public education; rather, it is that they are receiving a poorer quality education than that available to children in districts having more assessable wealth. Apart from the unsettled and disputed question whether the quality of education may be determined by the amount of money expended for it, a sufficient answer to appellees' argument is that, at least where wealth is involved, the Equal Protection Clause does not require absolute equality or precisely equal advantages....

However described, it is clear that appellees' suit asks this Court to extend its most exacting scrutiny to review a system that allegedly discriminates against a large, diverse, and amorphous class, unified only by the common factor of residence in districts that happen to have less taxable wealth than other districts. The system of alleged discrimination and the class it defines have none of the traditional indicia of suspectness: the class is not saddled with such disabilities, or subjected to such a history of purposeful unequal treatment, or relegated to such a position of political powerlessness as to command extraordinary protection from the majoritarian political process.

We thus conclude that the Texas system does not operate to the peculiar disadvantage of any suspect class. But in recognition of the fact that this Court has never heretofore held that wealth discrimination alone provides an adequate basis for invoking strict scrutiny, appellees have not relied solely on this contention. They also assert that the State's system impermissibly interferes with the exercise of a "fundamental" right and that accordingly the prior decisions of this Court require the application of the strict standard of judicial review. It is this question—whether education is a fundamental right, in the sense that it is among the rights and liberties protected by the Constitution—which has so consumed the attention of courts and commentators in recent years.

In Brown v. Board of Education (1954) a unanimous Court recognized that "education is perhaps the most important function of state and local governments."... This theme, expressing an abiding respect for the vital role of education in a free society, may be found in numerous opinions of Justices of this Court writing both before and after *Brown* was decided.

Nothing this Court holds today in any way detracts from our historic dedication to public education. We are in complete agreement with the conclusion of the three-judge panel below that "the grave significance of education both to the individual and to our society" cannot be doubted. But the importance of a service performed by the State does not determine whether it must be regarded as fundamental for purposes of examination under the Equal Protection Clause....

Education, of course, is not among the rights afforded explicit protection under our Federal Constitution. Nor do we find any basis for saying it is implicitly so protected. As we have said, the undisputed importance of education will not alone cause this Court to depart from the usual standard for reviewing a State's social and economic legislation. It is appellees' contention, however, that education is distinguishable from other services and benefits provided by the State because it bears a peculiarly close relationship to other rights and liberties accorded protection under the Constitution. Specifically, they insist that education is itself a fundamental personal right because it is essential to the effective exercise of First Amendment freedoms and to intelligent utilization of the right to vote. In asserting a nexus between speech and education, appellees urge that the right to speak is meaningless unless the speaker is capable of articulating his thoughts intelligently and persuasively. The "marketplace of ideas" is an empty forum for those lacking basic communicative tools. Likewise, they argue that the corollary right to receive information becomes little more than a hollow privilege when the recipient has not been taught to read, assimilate, and utilize available knowledge....

We need not dispute any of these propositions. The Court has long afforded zealous protection against unjustifiable governmental interference with the individual's rights to speak and to vote. Yet we have never presumed to possess either the ability or the authority to guarantee to the citizenry the most *effective* speech or the most *informed* electoral choice. That these may be desirable goals of a system of freedom of expression and of a representative form of government is not to be doubted. These are indeed goals to be pursued by a people whose thoughts and beliefs are freed from governmental interference. But they are not values to be implemented by judicial intrusion into otherwise legitimate state activities....

It should be clear, for the reasons stated above and in accord with the prior decisions of this Court, that this is not a case in which the challenged state action must be subjected to the searching judicial scrutiny reserved for laws that create suspect classifications or impinge upon constitutionally protected rights.

We need not rest our decision, however, solely on the inappropriateness of the strict-scrutiny test. A century of Supreme Court adjudication under the Equal Protection Clause affirmatively supports the application of the traditional standard of review, which requires only that the State's system be shown to bear some rational relationship to legitimate state purposes. This case represents far more than a challenge to the manner in which Texas provides for the education of its children. We have here nothing less than a direct attack on the way in which Texas has chosen to raise and disburse state and local tax revenues. We are asked to condemn the State's judgment in conferring on political subdivisions the power to tax local property to supply revenues for local interests. In so doing, appellees would have the Court intrude in an area in which it has traditionally deferred to state legislatures. This Court has often admonished against such interferences with the State's fiscal policies under the Equal Protection Clause....

Thus, we stand on familiar grounds when we continue to acknowledge that the Justices of this Court lack both the expertise and the familiarity with local problems so necessary to the making of wise decisions with respect to the raising and disposition of public revenues. Yet, we are urged to direct the States either to alter drastically the present system or to throw out the property tax altogether in favor of some other form of taxation. No scheme of taxation, whether the tax is imposed on property, income, or

purchases of goods and services, has yet been devised which is free of all discriminatory impact. In such a complex arena in which no perfect alternatives exist, the Court does well not to impose too rigorous a standard of scrutiny lest all local fiscal schemes become subjects of criticism under the Equal Protection Clause.

In addition to matters of fiscal policy, this case also involves the most persistent and difficult questions of educational policy, another area in which this Court's lack of specialized knowledge and experience counsels against premature interference with the informed judgments made at the state and local levels. Education, perhaps even more than welfare assistance, presents a myriad of "intractable economic, social, and even philosophical problems." The very complexity of the problems of financing and managing a statewide public school system suggests that "there will be more than one constitutionally permissible method of solving them," and that, within the limits of rationality, "the legislature's efforts to tackle the problems" should be entitled to respect....

It must be remembered, also, that every claim arising under the Equal Protection Clause has implications for the relationship between national and state power under our federal system. Questions of federalism are always inherent in the process of determining whether a State's laws are to be accorded the traditional presumption of constitutionality, or are to be subjected instead to rigorous judicial scrutiny. While "[t]he maintenance of the principles of federalism is a foremost consideration in interpreting any of the pertinent constitutional provisions under which this Court examines state action," it would be difficult to imagine a case having a greater potential impact on our federal system than the one now before us, in which we are urged to abrogate systems of financing public education presently in existence in virtually every State.

The foregoing considerations buttress our conclusion that Texas' system of public school finance is an inappropriate candidate for strict judicial scrutiny. These same considerations are relevant to the determination whether that system, with its conceded imperfections, nevertheless bears some rational relationship to a legitimate state purpose....

In sum, to the extent that the Texas system of school financing results in unequal expenditures between children who happen to reside in different districts, we cannot say that such disparities are the product of a system that is so irrational as to be invidiously discriminatory. Texas has acknowledged its shortcomings and has persistently endeavored—not without some success—to ameliorate the differences in levels of expenditures without sacrificing the benefits of local participation. The Texas plan is not the result of hurried, ill-conceived legislation. It certainly is not the product of purposeful discrimination against any group or class. On the contrary, it is rooted in decades of experience in Texas and elsewhere, and in major part is the product of responsible studies by qualified people. . . .

These practical considerations, of course, play no role in the adjudication of the constitutional issues presented here. But they serve to highlight the wisdom of the traditional limitations on this Court's function. The consideration and initiation of fundamental reforms with respect to state taxation and education are matters reserved for the legislative processes of the various States, and we do no violence to the values of federalism and separation of powers by staying our hand. We hardly need add that this Court's action today is not to be viewed as placing its judicial imprimatur on the status quo. The need is apparent for reform in tax systems which may well have relied too long and too heavily on the local property tax. And certainly innovative thinking as to public education, its methods, and its funding is necessary to assure both a higher level of quality and greater uniformity of opportunity. These matters merit the continued attention of the scholars who already have contributed much by their challenges. But the ultimate solutions must come from the lawmakers and from the democratic pressures of those who elect them.

Reversed.

MR. JUSTICE MARSHALL . . . dissenting.

The Court today decides, in effect, that a State may constitutionally vary the quality of education which it offers its children in accordance with the amount of taxable wealth located in the school districts within which they reside. The majority's decision represents an abrupt departure from the mainstream of recent state and federal court decisions concerning the unconstitutionality of state educational financing schemes dependent upon taxable local wealth. More unfortunately, though, the majority's holding can only be seen as a retreat from our historic commitment to equality of educational opportunity and as unsupportable

acquiescence in a system which deprives children in their earliest years of the chance to reach their full potential as citizens. The Court does this despite the absence of any substantial justification for a scheme which arbitrarily channels educational resources in accordance with the fortuity of the amount of taxable wealth within each district.

In my judgment, the right of every American to an equal start in life, so far as the provision of a state service as important as education is concerned, is far too vital to permit state discrimination on grounds as tenuous as those presented by this record. Nor can I accept the notion that it is sufficient to remit these appellees to the vagaries of the political process which, contrary to the majority's suggestion, has proved singularly unsuited to the task of providing a remedy for this discrimination. I, for one, am unsatisfied with the hope of an ultimate "political" solution sometime in the indefinite future while, in the meantime, countless children unjustifiably receive inferior educations that "may affect their hearts and minds in a way unlikely ever to be undone." I must therefore respectfully dissent.

The decision in *Rodriguez* was a blow to civil rights advocates. It had a substantial impact on education by validating financing systems that perpetuated inequity. Several states, however, reacted by adjusting their financing schemes to reduce funding disparities, and a few state supreme courts even found unequal funding systems to be in violation of state constitutional provisions.

In terms of constitutional development, the ruling introduced problems for future litigation. The Court expressly held that the poor were not a suspect class. Unlike other groups, such as black Americans and aliens, that were granted such status, the poor were neither an easily identified group nor politically powerless; as a group they did not have a history of overt discrimination. The decision not to elevate the poor to suspect class status meant that a rational basis test would be used in economic discrimination cases. As we know, this test provides the government with an advantage in demonstrating that challenged laws are valid. In the years that followed, the Court, increasingly dominated by Reagan and Bush appointees, continued to refrain from expanding constitutional protections for the poor.

In addition, the Court in *Rodriguez* held that education was not a fundamental right under the Constitution. This holding also created potential problems for future cases. Civil rights advocates have concentrated their efforts on education because of its crucial role in human development. By not according it fundamental right status, the Court made litigation in the education field more difficult.

ALIEN DISCRIMINATION

The Supreme Court generally has sympathized with the rights of noncitizens, a position consistent with the country's relatively generous immigration and naturalization policies. Although aliens do not enjoy the full range of rights and liberties granted to American citizens, they are entitled to certain protections under the Constitution. The Court has a history of striking down state laws that unnecessarily discriminate against aliens. As early as *Yick Wo v. Hopkins* (1886) the justices held that a resident alien was entitled to equal protection guarantees. More recently, the Court has nullified laws that prohibit resident aliens from obtaining civil service employment, receiving financial aid for college, becoming a member of the bar, or even getting a fishing license.[4] In fact, the Court in *Graham v. Richardson* (1971), a challenge to the denial of public assistance to an alien, accorded suspect class status to noncitizens, explaining that:

[C]lassifications based on alienage, like those based on nationality or race, are inherently suspect and subject to close judicial scrutiny. Aliens as a class are a prime example of a "discrete and insular" minority ... for whom such heightened judicial solicitude is appropriate.

This position is based on the recognition that aliens who lawfully reside in the United States are politically powerless because they can neither vote nor

4. *Sugarman v. Dougall* (1973), *Nyquist v. Mauclet* (1977), *In re Griffiths* (1973), and *Takahashi v. Fish and Game Commission* (1948), respectively.

hold office. Yet they pay taxes, support the economy, serve in the military, and contribute to society in other ways, and, if they otherwise qualify for government benefits or opportunities, they should not be denied them on the basis of noncitizenship alone.

The favorable status granted to aliens, however, does not guarantee that in all situations they have the same rights as citizens. The Court, for example, has held that aliens may validly be excluded from the governing process. In *Foley v. Connelie* (1978) a divided Court concluded that the Constitution is not violated when a state denies an alien a job in law enforcement. Are there sufficient reasons, as the majority argues, to exclude aliens, or are the dissenters correct that such exclusions violate the Equal Protection Clause?

Foley v. Connelie

435 U.S. 291 (1978)
Vote: 6 (*Blackmun, Burger, Powell, Rehnquist, Stewart, White*)
  3 (*Brennan, Marshall, Stevens*)
Opinion of the Court: Burger
Concurring opinion: Stewart
Opinion concurring in result: Blackmun
Dissenting opinions: Marshall, Stevens

Edmund Foley was a legal resident alien of New York State who would become a naturalized citizen once the required waiting period was over. He wanted to become a state trooper, a position filled by competitive examination. But state officials refused to allow him to take the test because a New York statute held that "No person shall be appointed to the New York state police force unless he shall be a citizen of the United States." Foley filed suit in federal court to have the prohibition declared an unconstitutional violation of the Equal Protection Clause of the Fourteenth Amendment. The lower court upheld the validity of the law.

MR. CHIEF JUSTICE BURGER delivered the opinion of the Court.

Appellant claims that the relevant New York statute violates his rights under the Equal Protection Clause.

The decisions of this Court with regard to the rights of aliens living in our society have reflected fine, and often difficult, questions of values. As a Nation we exhibit extraordinary hospitality to those who come to our country, which is not surprising for we have often been described as "a nation of immigrants." Indeed, aliens lawfully residing in this society have many rights which are accorded to noncitizens by few other countries. Our cases generally reflect a close scrutiny of restraints imposed by States on aliens. But we have never suggested that such legislation is inherently invalid, nor have we held that all limitations on aliens are suspect. Rather, beginning with a case which involved the denial of welfare assistance essential to life itself, the Court has treated certain restrictions on aliens with "heightened judicial solicitude," *Graham v. Richardson* (1971), a treatment deemed necessary since aliens—pending their eligibility for citizenship—have no direct voice in the political processes....

It would be inappropriate, however, to require every statutory exclusion of aliens to clear the high hurdle of "strict scrutiny," because to do so would "obliterate all the distinctions between citizens and aliens, and thus depreciate the historic values of citizenship." The act of becoming a citizen is more than a ritual with no content beyond the fanfare of ceremony. A new citizen has become a member of a Nation, part of a people distinct from others. The individual, at that point, belongs to the polity and is entitled to participate in the processes of democratic decisionmaking. Accordingly, we have recognized "a State's historical power to exclude aliens from participation in its democratic political institutions," as part of the sovereign's obligation " 'to preserve the basic conception of a political community.' "

The practical consequence of this theory is that "our scrutiny will not be so demanding where we deal with matters firmly within a State's constitutional prerogatives." The State need only justify its classification by a showing of some rational relationship between the interest sought to be protected and the limiting classification. This is not intended to denigrate the valuable contribution of aliens who

benefit from our traditional hospitality. It is no more than recognition of the fact that a democratic society is ruled by its people. Thus, it is clear that a State may deny aliens the right to vote, or to run for elective office, for these lie at the heart of our political institutions. Similar considerations support a legislative determination to exclude aliens from jury service. Likewise, we have recognized that citizenship may be a relevant qualification for fulfilling those "important nonelective executive, legislative, and judicial positions," held by "officers who participate directly in the formulation, execution, or review of broad public policy." This is not because our society seeks to reserve the better jobs to its members. Rather, it is because this country entrusts many of its most important policy responsibilities to these officers, the discretionary exercise of which can often more immediately affect the lives of citizens than even the ballot of a voter or the choice of a legislator. In sum, then, it represents the choice, and right, of the people to be governed by their citizen peers. To effectuate this result, we must necessarily examine each position in question to determine whether it involves discretionary decisionmaking, or execution of policy, which substantially affects members of the political community.

The essence of our holdings to date is that although we extend to aliens the right to education and public welfare, along with the ability to earn a livelihood and engage in licensed professions, the right to govern is reserved to citizens.

A discussion of the police function is essentially a description of one of the basic functions of government, especially in a complex modern society where police presence is pervasive. The police function fulfills a most fundamental obligation of government to its constituency. Police officers in the ranks do not formulate policy, *per se*, but they are clothed with authority to exercise an almost infinite variety of discretionary powers. The execution of the broad powers vested in them affects members of the public significantly and often in the most sensitive areas of daily life. Our Constitution, of course, provides safeguards to persons, homes and possessions, as well as guidance to police officers. And few countries, if any, provide more protection to individuals by limitations on the power and discretion of the police. Nonetheless, police may, in the exercise of their discretion, invade the privacy of an individual in public places. They may under some conditions break down a door to enter a dwelling or other building in the execution of a warrant, or without a formal warrant in very limited circumstances; they may stop vehicles traveling on public highways.

An arrest, the function most commonly associated with the police, is a serious matter for any person even when no prosecution follows or when an acquittal is obtained. Most arrests are without prior judicial authority, as when an officer observes a criminal act in progress or suspects that felonious activity is afoot. Even the routine traffic arrests made by the state trooper—for speeding, weaving, reckless driving, improper license plates, absence of inspection stickers, or dangerous physical condition of a vehicle, to describe only a few of the more obvious common violations—can intrude on the privacy of the individual. In stopping cars, they may, within limits, require a driver or passengers to disembark and even search them for weapons, depending on time, place and circumstances. That this prophylactic authority is essential is attested by the number of police officers wounded or killed in the process of making inquiry in borderline, seemingly minor violation situations—for example, where the initial stop is made for a traffic offense but, unknown to the officer at the time, the vehicle occupants are armed and engaged in or embarked on serious criminal conduct.

Clearly the exercise of police authority calls for a very high degree of judgment and discretion, the abuse or misuse of which can have serious impact on individuals.... A policeman vested with the plenary discretionary powers we have described is not to be equated with a private person engaged in routine public employment or other "common occupations of the community" who exercises no broad power over people generally. Indeed, the rationale for the qualified immunity historically granted to the police rests on the difficult and delicate judgments these officers must often make.

In short, it would be as anomalous to conclude that citizens may be subjected to the broad discretionary powers of noncitizen police officers as it would be to say that judicial officers and jurors with power to judge citizens can be aliens. It is not surprising, therefore, that most States expressly confine the employment of police officers to citizens, whom the State may reasonably presume to be more familiar with and sympathetic to American traditions.

Police officers very clearly fall within the category of "important nonelective ... officers who participate directly in the ... *execution* ... of broad public policy." In the enforcement and execution of the laws the police function is one where citizenship bears a rational relationship to the special demands of the particular position. A State may, therefore, consonant with the Constitution, confine the performance of this important public responsibility to citizens of the United States.

Accordingly, the judgment of the District Court is

Affirmed.

MR. JUSTICE MARSHALL ... dissenting.

Almost a century ago, in the landmark case of *Yick Wo v. Hopkins* (1886), this Court recognized that aliens are "persons" within the meaning of the Fourteenth Amendment. Eighty-five years later, in *Graham v. Richardson* (1971), the Court concluded that aliens constitute a "'discrete and insular' minority," and that laws singling them out for unfavorable treatment "are therefore subject to strict judicial scrutiny." During the ensuing six Terms, we have invalidated state laws discriminating against aliens on four separate occasions, finding that such discrimination could not survive strict scrutiny.

Today the Court upholds a law excluding aliens from public employment as state troopers. It bases its decision largely on dictum from *Sugarman v. Dougall* [1973] to the effect that aliens may be barred from holding "state elective or important nonelective executive, legislative, and judicial positions," because persons in these positions "participate directly in the formulation, execution, or review of broad public policy." I do not agree with the Court that state troopers perform functions placing them within this "narrow ... exception" to our usual rule that discrimination against aliens is presumptively unconstitutional. Accordingly I dissent.

In one sense, of course, it is true that state troopers participate in the execution of public policy. Just as firefighters execute the public policy that fires should be extinguished, and sanitation workers execute the public policy that streets should be kept clean, state troopers execute the public policy that persons believed to have committed crimes should be arrested. But this fact simply demonstrates that the *Sugarman* exception, if read without regard to its context, "would swallow the rule." Although every state employee is charged with the "execution" of public policy, *Sugarman* unambiguously holds that a blanket exclusion of aliens from state jobs is unconstitutional.

Thus the phrase "execution of broad public policy" in *Sugarman* cannot be read to mean simply the carrying out of government programs, but rather must be interpreted to include responsibility for actually setting government policy pursuant to a delegation of substantial authority from the legislature. The head of an executive agency for example, charged with promulgating complex regulations under a statute, executes broad public policy in a sense that file clerks in the agency clearly do not. In short, as *Sugarman* indicates, those "elective or important nonelective" positions that involve broad policymaking responsibilities are the only state jobs from which aliens as a group may constitutionally be excluded.

In my view, the job of state trooper is not one of those positions.

Foley involved an alien who was lawfully residing in the United States and becoming a U.S. citizen. Of an entirely different class is the alien who is in the United States illegally. Undocumented aliens create difficult problems; their numbers cause economic, political, and social pressures, particularly in the Southwest. Their illegal status, combined with their economic and educational disadvantage, poses vexing social justice questions. Do such individuals, whose very presence is technically unlawful, merit the protection of the Constitution? May they be treated in a discriminatory manner by the states, or are they considered full persons under the meaning and protection of the Fourteenth Amendment?

In *Plyler v. Doe* (1982) the Supreme Court confronted these issues directly. To make the choices even more difficult, this case concerned not individuals who had knowingly entered the country illegally, but their minor children. In the majority and dissenting opinions how did the justices respond to the issues? What did they say on the proper role of the Court to set policy when the political branches have failed to solve a serious social problem?

Plyler v. Doe

457 U.S. 202 (1982)

Vote: 5 (Blackmun, Brennan, Marshall, Powell, Stevens)
    4 (Burger, O'Connor, Rehnquist, White)

Opinion of the Court: Brennan
Concurring opinions: Blackmun, Marshall, Powell
Dissenting opinion: Burger

In May 1975 the Texas legislature revised its laws to withhold from local school districts any state funds for the education of children who were not legal residents of the United States. The law also allowed local school districts to deny enrollment to any student who was an undocumented alien (Section 21.031 of the Texas Education Code).

In September 1977 a suit was filed on behalf of school-age children of Mexican origin who lived in Smith County, Texas. Because they could not prove their legal status, these children had been denied admission to the public schools of the Tyler Independent School District. The state defended its law by arguing that the increase in undocumented aliens and the children's educational deficiencies had placed a tremendous burden on the public schools. Providing free education for such children depleted the schools' resources and detracted from the quality of education available to citizens and legal residents. The trial court, however, was not convinced by these arguments, concluding instead that the state law violated the Equal Protection Clause of the Fourteenth Amendment. The judgments were affirmed by the appeals court, and the state asked the Supreme Court to reverse.

JUSTICE BRENNAN delivered the opinion of the Court.

The Equal Protection Clause directs that "all persons similarly circumstanced shall be treated alike." But so too, "the Constitution does not require things which are different in fact or opinion to be treated in law as though they were the same." The initial discretion to determine what is "different" and what is "the same" resides in the legislatures of the States. A legislature must have substantial latitude to establish classifications that roughly approximate the nature of the problem perceived, that accommodate competing concerns both public and private, and that account for limitations on the practical ability of the State to remedy every ill. In applying the Equal Protection Clause to most forms of state action, we thus seek only the assurance that the classification at issue bears some fair relationship to a legitimate public purpose.

But we would not be faithful to our obligations under the Fourteenth Amendment if we applied so deferential a standard to every classification. The Equal Protection Clause was intended as a restriction on state legislative action inconsistent with elemental constitutional premises. Thus we have treated as presumptively invidious those classifications that disadvantage a "suspect class," or that impinge upon the exercise of a "fundamental right." With respect to such classifications, it is appropriate to enforce the mandate of equal protection by requiring the State to demonstrate that its classification has been precisely tailored to serve a compelling governmental interest. In addition, we have recognized that certain forms of legislative classification, while not facially invidious, nonetheless give rise to recurring constitutional difficulties; in these limited circumstances we have sought the assurance that the classification reflects a reasoned judgment consistent with the ideal of equal protection by inquiring whether it may fairly be viewed as furthering a substantial interest of the State....

Sheer incapability or lax enforcement of the laws barring entry into this country, coupled with the failure to establish an effective bar to the employment of undocumented aliens, has resulted in the creation of a substantial "shadow population" of illegal migrants—numbering in the millions—within our borders. This situation raises the specter of a permanent caste of undocumented resident aliens, encouraged by some to remain here as a source of cheap labor, but nevertheless denied the benefits that our society makes available to citizens and lawful residents. The existence of such an underclass presents most difficult problems for a Nation that prides itself on adherence to principles of equality under law.

The children who are plaintiffs in these cases are special members of this underclass. Persuasive arguments support the view that a State may withhold its beneficence from those whose very presence within the United States is the product of their own unlawful conduct. These arguments do not apply with the same force to classifications imposing disabilities on the minor *children* of such illegal entrants. At the least, those who elect to enter our territory by stealth and in violation of our law should be prepared to bear the consequences, including, but not limited to, deportation. But the children of those illegal entrants are not comparably situated. Their "parents have the ability to conform their conduct to societal norms," and presumably the ability to remove themselves from the State's jurisdiction; but the children who are plaintiffs in these cases "can affect neither their parents' conduct nor their own status." Even if the State found it expedient to control the conduct of adults by acting against their children, legislation directing the onus of a parent's misconduct against his children does not comport with fundamental conceptions of justice....

Of course, undocumented status is not irrelevant to any proper legislative goal. Nor is undocumented status an absolutely immutable characteristic since it is the product of conscious, indeed unlawful, action. But § 21.031 is directed against children, and imposes its discriminatory burden on the basis of a legal characteristic over which children can have little control. It is thus difficult to conceive of a rational justification for penalizing these children for their presence within the United States. Yet that appears to be precisely the effect of § 21.031.

Public education is not a "right" granted to individuals by the Constitution. *San Antonio Independent School Dist. v. Rodriguez* (1973). But neither is it merely some governmental "benefit" indistinguishable from other forms of social welfare legislation. Both the importance of education in maintaining our basic institutions, and the lasting impact of its deprivation on the life of the child, mark the distinction. The "American people have always regarded education and [the] acquisition of knowledge as matters of supreme importance."...

In addition to the pivotal role of education in sustaining our political and cultural heritage, denial of education to some isolated group of children poses an affront to one of the goals of the Equal Protection Clause: the abolition of governmental barriers presenting unreasonable obstacles to advancement on the basis of individual merit. Paradoxically, by depriving the children of any disfavored group of an education, we foreclose the means by which that group might raise the level of esteem in which it is held by the majority. But more directly, "education prepares individuals to be self-reliant and self-sufficient participants in society."...

These well-settled principles allow us to determine the proper level of deference to be afforded § 21.031. Undocumented aliens cannot be treated as a suspect class because their presence in this county in violation of federal law is not a "constitutional irrelevancy." Nor is education a fundamental right; a State need not justify by compelling necessity every variation in the manner in which education is provided to its population. But more is involved in these cases than the abstract question whether § 21.031 discriminates against a suspect class, or whether education is a fundamental right. Section 21.031 imposes a lifetime hardship on a discrete class of children not accountable for their disabling status. The stigma of illiteracy will mark them for the rest of their lives. By denying these children a basic education, we deny them the ability to live within the structure of our civic institutions, and foreclose any realistic possibility that they will contribute in even the smallest way to the progress of our Nation. In determining the rationality of § 21.031, we may appropriately take into account its costs to the Nation and to the innocent children who are its victims. In light of these countervailing costs, the discrimination contained in § 21.031 can hardly be considered rational unless it furthers some substantial goal of the State.

It is the State's principal argument, and apparently the view of the dissenting Justices, that the undocumented status of these children *vel non* [or not] establishes a sufficient rational basis for denying them benefits that a State might choose to afford other residents.... Indeed, in the State's view, Congress' apparent disapproval of the presence of these children within the United States, and the evasion of the federal regulatory program that is the mark of undocumented status, provides authority for its decision to impose upon them special disabilities. Faced with an equal protection challenge respecting the treatment of aliens, we agree that the courts must be attentive to congressional policy; the exercise of congressional power might well affect the State's prerogatives to afford differential treatment to a particular class of aliens. But we are unable to find in the congressional immigration scheme any statement of policy that might weigh significantly in arriving at an equal protection balance concerning the State's authority to deprive these children of an education....

To be sure, like all persons who have entered the United States unlawfully, these children are subject to deportation. But there is no assurance that a child subject to deportation will ever be deported. An illegal entrant might be granted federal permission to continue to reside in this country, or even to become a citizen. In light of the discretionary federal power to grant relief from deportation, a State cannot realistically determine that any particular undocumented child will in fact be deported until after deportation proceedings have been completed. It would of course be most difficult for the State to justify a denial of education to a child enjoying an inchoate federal permission to remain....

Apart from the asserted state prerogative to act against undocumented children solely on the basis of their undocumented status—an asserted prerogative that carries only minimal force in the circumstances of these cases—we discern three colorable state interests that might support § 21.031.

First, appellants appear to suggest that the State may seek to protect itself from an influx of illegal immigrants. While a State might have an interest in mitigating the potentially harsh economic effects of sudden shifts in population, § 21.031 hardly offers an effective method of dealing with an urgent demographic or economic problem. There is no evidence in the record suggesting that illegal entrants impose any significant burden on the State's economy. To the contrary, the available evidence suggests that illegal aliens underutilize public services, while contributing their labor to the local economy and tax money to the state fisc. The dominant incentive for illegal entry into the State of Texas is the availability of employment; few if any illegal immigrants come to this country, or presumably to the State of Texas, in order to avail themselves of a free education. Thus, even making the doubtful assumption that the net impact of illegal aliens on the economy of the State is negative, we think it clear that "[c]harging tuition to undocumented children constitutes a ludicrously ineffectual attempt to stem the tide of illegal immigration," at least when compared with the alternative of prohibiting the employment of illegal aliens.

Second, while it is apparent that a State may "not ... reduce expenditures for education by barring [some arbitrarily chosen class of] children from its schools," appellants suggest that undocumented children are appropriately singled out for exclusion because of the special burdens they impose on the State's ability to provide high-quality public education. But the record in no way supports the claim that exclusion of undocumented children is likely to improve the overall quality of education in the State.... And, after reviewing the State's school financing mechanism, the District Court concluded that barring undocumented children from local schools would not necessarily improve the quality of education provided in those schools. Of course, even if improvement in the quality of education were a likely result of barring some *number* of children from the schools of the State, the State must support its selection of *this* group as the appropriate target for exclusion. In terms of education cost and need, however, undocumented children are "basically indistinguishable" from legally resident alien children.

Finally, appellants suggest that undocumented children are appropriately singled out because their unlawful presence within the United States renders them less likely than other children to remain within the boundaries of the State, and to put their education to productive social or political use within the State. Even assuming that such an interest is legitimate, it is an interest that is most difficult to quantify. The State has no assurance that any child, citizen or not, will employ the education provided by the State within the confines of the State's borders. In any event, the record is clear that many of the undocumented children disabled by this classification will remain in this country indefinitely, and that some will become lawful residents or citizens of the United States. It is difficult to understand precisely what the State hopes to achieve by promoting the creation and perpetuation of a subclass of illiterates within our boundaries, surely adding to the problems and costs of unemployment, welfare, and crime. It is thus clear that whatever savings might be achieved by denying these children an education, they are wholly insubstantial in light of the costs involved to these children, the State, and the Nation.

If the State is to deny a discrete group of innocent children the free public education that it offers to other children residing within its borders, that denial must be justified by a showing that it furthers some substantial state interest. No such showing was made here. Accordingly, the judgment of the Court of Appeals in each of these cases is

Affirmed.

CHIEF JUSTICE BURGER ... dissenting.

Were it our business to set the Nation's social policy, I would agree without hesitation that it is senseless for an enlightened society to deprive any children—including illegal aliens—of an elementary education. I fully agree that it would be folly—and wrong—to tolerate creation of a segment of society made up of illiterate persons, many having a limited or no command of our language. However, the Constitution does not constitute us as "Platonic Guardians" nor does it vest in this Court the authority to strike down laws because they do not meet our standards of desirable social policy, "wisdom," or "common sense." We trespass on the assigned function of the political branches under our structure of limited and separated powers when we assume a policymaking role as the Court does today.

The Court makes no attempt to disguise that it is acting to make up for Congress' lack of "effective leadership" in dealing with the serious national problems caused by the influx of uncountable millions of illegal aliens across our borders. The failure of enforcement of the immigration laws over more than a decade and the inherent difficulty and expense of sealing our vast borders have combined to create a grave socioeconomic dilemma. It is a dilemma that has not yet even been fully assessed, let alone addressed. However, it is not the function of the Judiciary to provide "effective leadership" simply because the political branches of government fail to do so.

The Court's holding today manifests the justly criticized judicial tendency to attempt speedy and wholesale formulation of "remedies" for the failures—or simply the laggard pace—of the political processes of our system of government. The Court employs, and in my view abuses, the Fourteenth Amendment in an effort to become an omnipotent and omniscient problem solver. That the motives for doing so are noble and compassionate does not alter the fact that the Court distorts our constitutional function to make amends for the defaults of others.

In a sense, the Court's opinion rests on such a unique confluence of theories and rationales that it will likely stand for little beyond the results in these particular cases. Yet the extent to which the Court departs from principled constitutional adjudication is nonetheless disturbing.

I have no quarrel with the conclusion that the Equal Protection Clause of the Fourteenth Amendment *applies* to aliens who, after their illegal entry into this country, are indeed physically "within the jurisdiction" of a state. However, as the Court concedes, this "only begins the inquiry." The Equal Protection Clause does not mandate identical treatment of different categories of persons.

The dispositive issue in these cases, simply put, is whether, for purposes of allocating its finite resources, a state has a legitimate reason to differentiate between persons who are lawfully within the state and those who are unlawfully there. The distinction the State of Texas has drawn—based not only upon its own legitimate interests but on classifications established by the Federal Government in its immigration laws and policies—is not unconstitutional....

Denying a free education to illegal alien children is not a choice I would make were I a legislator. Apart from compassionate considerations, the long-range costs of excluding any children from the public schools may well outweigh the costs of educating them. But that is not the issue; the fact that there are sound *policy* arguments against the Texas Legislature's choice does not render that choice an unconstitutional one.

The Constitution does not provide a cure for every social ill, nor does it vest judges with a mandate to try to remedy every social problem. Moreover, when this Court rushes in to remedy what it perceives to be the failings of the political processes, it deprives those processes of an opportunity to function. When the political institutions are not forced to exercise constitutionally allocated powers and responsibilities, those powers, like muscles not used, tend to atrophy. Today's cases, I regret to say, present yet another example of unwarranted judicial action which in the long run tends to contribute to the weakening of our political processes.

Congress, "vested by the Constitution with the responsibility of protecting our borders and legislating with respect to aliens," bears primary responsibility for addressing the problems occasioned by the millions of illegal aliens flooding across our southern border. Similarly, it is for Congress, and not this Court, to assess the "social costs borne by our Nation when select groups are denied the means to absorb the values and skills upon which our social order rests." While the "specter of a permanent caste" of illegal Mexican residents of the United States is indeed a disturbing one, it is but one segment of a larger problem, which is for the political branches to solve. I find it difficult to believe that Congress would long tolerate such a self-destructive result—that it would fail to deport these illegal alien families or to provide for the education of their children. Yet instead of allowing the political processes to run their course—albeit with some delay—the Court seeks to do Congress' job for it, compensating for congressional inaction. It is not unreasonable to think that this encourages the political branches to pass their problems to the Judiciary.

The solution to this seemingly intractable problem is to defer to the political processes, unpalatable as that may be to some.

DISCRIMINATION REMEDIES

Creating appropriate standards for interpreting the equal protection principles of the Constitution and determining when governments have engaged in impermissible discrimination are exceedingly difficult tasks. But even when they have been accomplished, the Court's business is not finished. In addition to condemning unconstitutional discrimination, the Court confronts the problem of remedies, which entails consideration of acceptable ways to eliminate the discrimination, to implement nondiscriminatory policies, and to compensate the victims of discrimination.

For some discrimination issues remedial action is minimal: often striking down a statute is sufficient. For example, nullifying Idaho's discriminatory inheritance statute in *Reed v. Reed* required no remedial action. The state simply had to decide future estate administration issues without regard to sex. Similarly, declaring Virginia's miscegenation law in violation of the Equal Protection Clause in the *Loving* decision did not demand any follow-up action. Virginia was plainly barred from any future prosecutions of such cases.

For other discrimination issues, however, the enforcement of the Court's orders can be a lengthy, complex process. Timetables for change, compliance standards, and methods of implementation pose troublesome choices, and conditions are exacerbated when the affected population resists the change. The integration of the public schools is an obvious and painful example.

The Supreme Court not only has created rules for implementing its own equal protection decisions, but also has heard cases challenging the antidiscrimination policies imposed by Congress and the state legislatures. Beginning in the late 1960s, many political bodies asserted that the Fifth and Fourteenth Amendments demanded more than just the elimination of overt discrimination; they also required positive actions taken by government to ensure that equality is achieved and the effects of past discrimination are eliminated. This policy gave rise to affirmative action and minority set-aside programs, which have been attacked as unconstitutional reverse discrimination. Questions of just how far Congress and state governments can go in developing remedies without violating the Constitution show up regularly on the Supreme Court's docket.

Issues of remedial action for discrimination are especially troublesome for the Court. The justices, like the nation generally, have been deeply divided over the appropriate actions to take. There is little agreement on what the Constitution requires and what it prohibits. In response to some questions, especially those involving affirmative action, the Court to date has not been very successful at building a consistent and coherent rule of law.

Racial Desegregation

Brown v. Board of Education (1954) is the clearest example of a judicial decision that required massive efforts for implementation. To agree that the racial separation in the public schools was unconstitutional was far easier than to decide how to end that practice and what would replace it. After all, areas that segregated the races did not enthusiastically embrace the idea of rapidly changing to fully integrated schools. When the justices issued their unanimous ruling, they instructed the attorneys in *Brown* and the accompanying cases to return the next year and argue the issue of remedies. The result, commonly referred to as *Brown II* (1955), set the stage for the public school desegregation battles that were to dominate the national agenda for the next quarter century and still linger in some districts.

The Court's ruling in *Brown II* focused on two basic questions. The first dealt with who was responsible for implementing desegregation, and here the justices held that the primary duty for ending segregation rested with local school boards. These political bodies carried out the general administration of the schools, and they should be responsible for implementing desegregation. The Court, however, was aware that many school boards would resist the change. After all, in most states, board members were elected by the people, and desegregation was very unpopular with the electorate.

To ensure that the school boards acted properly, the Court gave oversight responsibilities to the federal district courts, the trial courts of general jurisdiction for the federal system. Because they are the federal courts closest to the people, their judges understand local conditions. In addition, district court judges enjoy life tenure; they are appointed, not elected. When school boards failed to live up to the expectation of *Brown I*, district judges were instructed to use their equity jurisdiction to fashion whatever remedies were necessary to achieve desegregation. This grant of authority allowed the judges to impose plans especially tailored to meet the specific conditions of the district's schools.

The second question involved what desegregation schedule the Court would demand. Thurgood Marshall, the chief lawyer for those challenging the segregated schools, requested an immediate end to racial separation. Representatives of the federal government recommended a specific timetable for school boards to develop their desegregation plans. Attorneys for the southern states cited the substantial difficulties standing in the way of compliance and requested a gradual implementation. Chief Justice Warren, speaking for a unanimous Court, did not set a specific schedule, but instead ordered that desegregation take place "with all deliberate speed." This standard acknowledged that the situation in each district would determine how rapidly desegregation could progress. It was also a necessary compromise among the justices to achieve a unanimous ruling.

The combination of massive southern resistance, the vague with-all-deliberate-speed timetable, and the wide latitude granted to district judges in fashioning desegregation plans gave rise to many battles over implementing *Brown*. In each, the justices held steadfast in their desegregation goals. In 1958, for example, in *Cooper v. Aaron* the Court responded firmly to popular resistance in Arkansas by declaring that violence or threats of violence would not be allowed to slow the progress toward full desegregation. Some of the state legislatures and local governments were most creative in devising ways to evade integration. In *Griffin v. Prince Edward County School Board* (1964) the Court stopped a Virginia plan to close down public schools rather than integrate them. In *Green v. School Board of New Kent County* (1968) the justices struck down a "freedom of choice" plan as failing to bring about a nondiscriminatory school system. But, by the mid-1960s the justices had begun to lose patience. Justice Black remarked in his opinion for the Court in *Griffin* that "there has been entirely too much deliberation

and not enough speed" in enforcing *Brown*'s desegregation mandate. The Court made it increasingly clear that dilatory tactics would not be tolerated.[5]

The freedom given to district judges to approve desegregation plans led to a wide variety of schemes, some of which were criticized by school officials for going too far, and some by civil rights advocates for not going far enough. The specific methods of integration commonly were attacked for exceeding the powers of the district courts. To clear up the confusion, in 1971 the Supreme Court accepted an appeal, which it saw as a vehicle for the declaration of authoritative rules to govern the desegregation process. The case, *Swann v. Charlotte-Mecklenburg Board of Education*, involved challenges to a desegregation plan imposed by a district judge on North Carolina's largest city. In reading Chief Justice Burger's opinion for a unanimous Court, pay attention to the wide range of powers the Court approves for imposing remedies once a violation of the Constitution has been demonstrated.

Swann v. Charlotte-Mecklenburg Board of Education

402 U.S. 1 (1971)
Vote: 9 (Black, Blackmun, Brennan, Burger, Douglas, Harlan, Marshall, Stewart, White)

0

Opinion of the Court: Burger

This case resulted from a longstanding legal dispute over the desegregation of schools in Charlotte, North Carolina. As part of the efforts to bring the district into compliance, the Charlotte schools were consolidated with the surrounding Mecklenburg County schools. The combined district covered 550 square miles, with 107 schools with an enrollment of 84,000

5. See *Alexander v. Holmes County Board of Education* (1969).

children. Seventy-one percent of the students were white and 29 percent black.

As a result of a plan imposed by the courts in 1965, desegregation began in earnest, but the results were not satisfactory. Of the 21,000 black students in the city of Charlotte, two-thirds attended schools that were at least 99 percent black. All parties agreed that the plan was not working, but there was considerable controversy over what to do. When the school board failed to submit a suitable plan, the district court appointed John Finger, an educational consultant, to devise one. The minority members of the school board and the U.S. Department of Health, Education and Welfare also offered plans. After considerable legal maneuvering, the district court imposed the Finger plan, part of which was later approved by the court of appeals. Both the plaintiffs and the school board appealed to the Supreme Court.

MR. CHIEF JUSTICE BURGER delivered the opinion of the Court.

Nearly 17 years ago this Court held, in explicit terms, that state-imposed segregation by race in public schools denies equal protection of the laws. At no time has the Court deviated in the slightest degree from that holding or its constitutional underpinnings....

Over the 16 years since *Brown II*, many difficulties were encountered in implementation of the basic constitutional requirement that the State not discriminate between public school children on the basis of their race. Nothing in our national experience prior to 1955 prepared anyone for dealing with changes and adjustments of the magnitude and complexity encountered since then. Deliberate resistance of some to the Court's mandates has impeded the good-faith efforts of others to bring school systems into compliance. The detail and nature of these dilatory tactics have been noted frequently by this Court and other courts....

The problems encountered by the district courts and courts of appeals make plain that we should now try to amplify guidelines, however incomplete and imperfect, for the assistance of school authorities and courts. The failure of local authorities to meet their constitutional obligations ag-

gravated the massive problem of converting from the state-enforced discrimination of racially separate school systems. This process has been rendered more difficult by changes since 1954 in the structure and patterns of communities, the growth of student population, movement of families, and other changes, some of which had marked impact on school planning, sometimes neutralizing or negating remedial action before it was fully implemented. Rural areas accustomed for half a century to the consolidated school systems implemented by bus transportation could make adjustments more readily than metropolitan areas with dense and shifting population, numerous schools, congested and complex traffic patterns.

The objective today remains to eliminate from the public schools all vestiges of state-imposed segregation. Segregation was the evil struck down by *Brown I* as contrary to the equal protection guarantees of the Constitution. That was the violation sought to be corrected by the remedial measures of *Brown II*. That was the basis for the holding in *Green* [*v. County School Board*, 1968] that school authorities are "clearly charged with the affirmative duty to take whatever steps might be necessary to convert to a unitary system in which racial discrimination would be eliminated root and branch."

If school authorities fail in their affirmative obligations under these holdings, judicial authority may be invoked. Once a right and a violation have been shown, the scope of a district court's equitable powers to remedy past wrongs is broad, for breadth and flexibility are inherent in equitable remedies....

This allocation of responsibility once made, the Court attempted from time to time to provide some guidelines for the exercise of the district judge's discretion and for the reviewing function of the courts of appeals. However, a school desegregation case does not differ fundamentally from other cases involving the framing of equitable remedies to repair the denial of a constitutional right. The task is to correct, by a balancing of the individual and collective interests, the condition that offends the Constitution.

In seeking to define even in broad and general terms how far this remedial power extends it is important to remember that judicial powers may be exercised only on the basis of a constitutional violation. Remedial judicial authority does not put judges automatically in the shoes of school authorities whose powers are plenary. Judicial authority enters only when local authority defaults.

School authorities are traditionally charged with broad power to formulate and implement educational policy and might well conclude, for example, that in order to prepare students to live in a pluralistic society each school should have a prescribed ratio of Negro to white students reflecting the proportion for the district as a whole. To do this as an educational policy is within the broad discretionary powers of school authorities; absent a finding of a constitutional violation, however, that would not be within the authority of a federal court. As with any equity case, the nature of the violation determines the scope of the remedy. In default by the school authorities of their obligation to proffer acceptable remedies, a district court has broad power to fashion a remedy that will assure a unitary school system. . . .

We turn now to the problem of defining with more particularity the responsibilities of school authorities in desegregating a state-enforced dual school system in light of the Equal Protection Clause. Although the several related cases before us are primarily concerned with problems of student assignment, it may be helpful to begin with a brief discussion of other aspects of the process.

In *Green*, we pointed out that existing policy and practice with regard to faculty, staff, transportation, extracurricular activities, and facilities were among the most important indicia of a segregated system. Independent of student assignment, where it is possible to identify a "white school" or a "Negro school" simply by reference to the racial composition of teachers and staff, the quality of school buildings and equipment, or the organization of sports activities, a *prima facie* case of violation of substantive constitutional rights under the Equal Protection Clause is shown.

When a system has been dual in these respects, the first remedial responsibility of school authorities is to eliminate invidious racial distinctions. . . .

The construction of new schools and the closing of old ones are two of the most important functions of local school authorities and also two of the most complex. . . .

In ascertaining the existence of legally imposed school segregation, the existence of a pattern of school construction and abandonment is thus a factor of great weight. In devising remedies where legally imposed segregation has been established, it is the responsibility of local authorities and district courts to see to it that future school construction and abandonment are not used and do not serve to perpetuate or reestablish the dual system. When necessary, district courts should retain jurisdiction to assure that these responsibilities are carried out.

The central issue in this case is that of student assignment, and there are essentially four problem areas:

(1) to what extent racial balance or racial quotas may be used as an implement in a remedial order to correct a previously segregated system;

(2) whether every all-Negro and all-white school must be eliminated as an indispensable part of a remedial process of desegregation;

(3) what the limits are, if any, on the rearrangement of school districts and attendance zones, as a remedial measure; and

(4) what the limits are, if any, on the use of transportation facilities to correct state-enforced racial school segregation.

(1) Racial Balances or Racial Quotas.

The constant theme and thrust of every holding from *Brown I* to date is that state-enforced separation of races in public schools is discrimination that violates the Equal Protection Clause. The remedy commanded was to dismantle dual school systems. . . .

Our objective in dealing with the issues presented by these cases is to see that school authorities exclude no pupil of a racial minority from any school, directly or indirectly, on account of race; it does not and cannot embrace all the problems of racial prejudice, even when those problems contribute to disproportionate racial concentrations in some schools.

In this case it is urged that the District Court has imposed a racial balance requirement of 71%–29% on individual schools. . . .

As the voluminous record in this case shows, the predicate for the District Court's use of the 71%–29% ratio was twofold: first, its express finding, approved by the Court of Appeals and not challenged here, that a dual school system had been maintained by the school authorities at least until 1969; second, its finding, also approved by the Court of Appeals, that the school board had totally defaulted in its acknowledged duty to come forward with an acceptable plan of its own, notwithstanding the patient efforts of the District Judge who, on at least three occasions, urged the board to submit plans. As the statement of facts shows, these findings are abundantly supported by the record....

We see therefore that the use made of mathematical ratios was no more than a starting point in the process of shaping a remedy, rather than an inflexible requirement. From that starting point the District Court proceeded to frame a decree that was within its discretionary powers, as an equitable remedy for the particular circumstances. As we said in *Green*, a school authority's remedial plan or a district court's remedial decree is to be judged by its effectiveness. Awareness of the racial composition of the whole school system is likely to be a useful starting point in shaping a remedy to correct past constitutional violations. In sum, the very limited use made of mathematical ratios was within the equitable remedial discretion of the District Court.

(2) One-race Schools.

The record in this case reveals the familiar phenomenon that in metropolitan areas minority groups are often found concentrated in one part of the city. In some circumstances certain schools may remain all or largely of one race until new schools can be provided or neighborhood patterns change. Schools all or predominantly of one race in a district of mixed population will require close scrutiny to determine that school assignments are not part of state-enforced segregation.

In light of the above, it should be clear that the existence of some small number of one-race, or virtually one-race, schools within a district is not in and of itself the mark of a system that still practices segregation by law. The district judge or school authorities should make every effort to achieve the greatest possible degree of actual desegregation and will thus necessarily be concerned with the elimination of one-race schools. No *per se* rule can adequately embrace all the difficulties of reconciling the competing interests involved, but in a system with a history of segregation the need for remedial criteria of sufficient specificity to assure a school authority's compliance with its constitutional duty warrants a presumption against schools that are substantially disproportionate in their racial composition. Where

the school authority's proposed plan for conversion from a dual to a unitary system contemplates the continued existence of some schools that are all or predominately of one race, they have the burden of showing that such school assignments are genuinely nondiscriminatory. The court should scrutinize such schools, and the burden upon the school authorities will be to satisfy the court that their racial composition is not the result of present or past discriminatory action on their part....

(3) Remedial Altering of Attendance Zones.

The maps submitted in these cases graphically demonstrate that one of the principal tools employed by school planners and by courts to break up the dual school system has been a frank—and sometimes drastic—gerrymandering of school districts and attendance zones. An additional step was pairing, "clustering," or "grouping" of schools with attendance assignments made deliberately to accomplish the transfer of Negro students out of formerly segregated Negro schools and transfer of white students to formerly all-Negro schools. More often than not, these zones are neither compact nor contiguous; indeed they may be on opposite ends of the city. As an interim corrective measure, this cannot be said to be beyond the broad remedial powers of a court.

Absent a constitutional violation there would be no basis for judicially ordering assignment of students on a racial basis. All things being equal, with no history of discrimination, it might well be desirable to assign pupils to schools nearest their homes. But all things are not equal in a system that has been deliberately constructed and maintained to enforce racial segregation. The remedy for such segregation may be administratively awkward, inconvenient, and even bizarre in some situations and may impose burdens on some; but all awkwardness and inconvenience cannot be avoided in the interim period when remedial adjustments are being made to eliminate the dual school systems....

We hold that the pairing and grouping of noncontiguous school zones is a permissible tool and such action is to be considered in light of the objectives sought.... Conditions in different localities will vary so widely that no rigid rules can be laid down to govern all situations.

(4) Transportation of Students.

The scope of permissible transportation of students as

an implement of a remedial decree has never been defined by this Court and by the very nature of the problem it cannot be defined with precision. No rigid guidelines as to student transportation can be given for application to the infinite variety of problems presented in thousands of situations. Bus transportation has been an integral part of the public education system for years, and was perhaps the single most important factor in the transition from the one-room schoolhouse to the consolidated school. Eighteen million of the Nation's public school children, approximately 39%, were transported to their schools by bus in 1969–1970 in all parts of the country....

The importance of bus transportation as a normal and accepted tool of educational policy is readily discernible in this ... case.... The Charlotte school authorities did not purport to assign students on the basis of geographically drawn attendance zones until 1965 and then they allowed almost unlimited transfer privileges. The District Court's conclusion that assignment of children to the school nearest their home serving their grade would not produce an effective dismantling of the dual system is supported by the record.

Thus the remedial techniques used in the District Court's order were within that court's power to provide equitable relief; implementation of the decree is well within the capacity of the school authority.

The decree provided that the buses used to implement the plan would operate on direct routes. Students would be picked up at schools near their homes and transported to the schools they were to attend. The trips for elementary school pupils average about seven miles and the District Court found that they would take "not over 35 minutes at the most." This system compares favorably with the transportation plan previously operated in Charlotte under which each day 23,600 students on all grade levels were transported an average of 15 miles one way for an average trip requiring over an hour. In these circumstances, we find no basis for holding that the local school authorities may not be required to employ bus transportation as one tool of school desegregation. Desegregation plans cannot be limited to the walk-in school.

An objection to transportation of students may have validity when the time or distance of travel is so great as to either risk the health of the children or significantly impinge on the educational process. District courts must weigh the soundness of any transportation plan in light of what is said in subdivisions (1), (2), and (3) above. It hardly needs stating that the limits on time of travel will vary with many factors, but probably with none more than the age of the students. The reconciliation of competing values in a desegregation case is, of course, a difficult task with many sensitive facets but fundamentally no more so than remedial measures courts of equity have traditionally employed.

The Court of Appeals, searching for a term to define the equitable remedial power of the district courts, used the term "reasonableness."... On the facts of this case, we are unable to conclude that the order of the District Court is not reasonable, feasible and workable. However, in seeking to define the scope of remedial power or the limits on remedial power of courts in an area as sensitive as we deal with here, words are poor instruments to convey the sense of basic fairness inherent in equity. Substance, not semantics, must govern, and we have sought to suggest the nature of limitations without frustrating the appropriate scope of equity.

Order of District Court affirmed.

The Court's decision in *Swann* reaffirmed the broad powers of district courts in implementing desegregation. Plans imposed by the courts can affect teacher placement, school construction and maintenance, staff assignment, and funding equalization among schools within the district. Judges may use the overall racial composition of the district's students to set goals for racial balance in individual schools. Courts are empowered to use a wide arsenal of student placement strategies, including rearrangement of attendance zones and the politically unpopular imposition of forced busing.

In spite of the generally sweeping powers given to the district judges, a careful reading of Burger's opinion reveals certain limits. First, this judicial authority can be used only when the courts have determined that a particular district has violated the Constitution. These powers are remedial. Questions of school administration are to be left to local school officials unless unconstitutional discrimination has occurred and the districts have not made the necessary corrections. Second, the remedy imposed must be tailored to compensate for the violation. In Burger's terms, "The nature of the violation determines the scope of the remedy."

These limits have at times been obstacles to achieving effective integration, especially in large metropolitan areas in the North where many independent school districts may be in operation, and some may be composed of one race. True integration can take place only if multiple districts are brought into a single plan. But before a desegregation plan can be imposed on such a district, unconstitutional discrimination must be found to have occurred within that particular district. Violations are difficult to prove in northern cities where segregation laws never were in effect and segregated neighborhoods grew up without obvious government involvement.

That description fit Detroit, Michigan, in 1972. A district judge ordered a desegregation plan embracing Detroit and fifty-three suburban school districts. To achieve the integration of the predominantly black central city schools with the largely white suburbs, the judge ordered massive busing. The plan required the purchase of almost 300 school buses and the appropriation of millions of dollars to fund the transportation system. On appeal, the Supreme Court ruled in *Millikin v. Bradley* (1974) by a vote of 5 to 4 that the district court had exceeded its authority by imposing a desegregation plan on school districts for which there had been no finding of constitutional violations.

The scope and limits of judicial authority to impose remedies for racial segregation remain open and controversial. The desegregation of contemporary metropolitan areas may require overwhelming dislocation and staggering sums of money. District judges often are forced to impose orders that jurisdictions can ill afford. When judges see such desegregation plans as the only way to comply with the Constitution, disputes are likely.

A case in point is the 1989 decision in *Missouri v. Jenkins.* This suit arose out of attempts to attain satisfactory desegregation levels in the public schools of Kansas City, Missouri. The longstanding controversy focused on implementation of the district court's desegregation plan, at the heart of which was an expensive magnet school program. At various times the district judge had imposed spending orders to activate the plan, including $142.7 million for the magnet schools and $187.5 million for capital improvements. Because the state's law imposed certain property tax ceilings, the Kansas City school district could not raise its share of the money. The district judge, therefore, doubled the property tax rate. The state challenged his order, claiming that the district judge had abused his powers. The Supreme Court agreed that the district judge had exceeded his proper discretion, that he could not raise the taxes himself, but he could order city authorities to raise them.

Many school districts have been under court supervision since the early days of *Brown.* Judges still monitor all significant actions taken by these districts to ensure that desegregation efforts continue and that resegregation is not encouraged. How long should such judicial supervision continue and what standards must school districts meet to be free of it?

The Supreme Court provided a partial answer to these questions in *Board of Education of Oklahoma City Public Schools v. Dowell* (1991). The Oklahoma City schools had been under various levels of judicial supervision since the 1970s. As the 1980s drew to a close, it looked as if the school district was becoming resegregated. The supervising district judge ruled that the court's desegregation decree should be dissolved because the district was in compliance; any resegregation was due to residential patterns, not intentional actions taken by school officials. The court of appeals reversed, and the controversy over the appropriate standard came to the Supreme Court. A five-justice majority held that judicial supervision would be ended when, after considering every facet of school operations, the court finds that the elements of state-sanctioned discrimination have been removed "as far as practicable." This standard was attacked by the dissenters (Marshall, Blackmun, and Stevens) as too lenient; they thought districts should remain under court control until all feasible means of removing racial concentrations have been exhausted.

To many observers the Oklahoma City case was an indication that the Rehnquist Court was gradually reducing or perhaps eliminating close judicial supervision over the public schools on desegregation matters. This conclusion was reinforced one year later when the justices issued their ruling in *Freeman v. Pitts* (1992), a dispute concerning the extent to which the federal courts should maintain supervision over the public schools in DeKalb County, Georgia. The schools in this suburban Atlanta district had been under court supervision since 1969. In 1986 school officials petitioned the district court to release the school system from judicial supervision on the grounds that the county had made sufficient progress toward desegregation. The district court held that the county had achieved satisfactory desegregation in the areas of student assignments, transportation, physical facilities, and extracurricular activities.

The judge noted that the schools were becoming resegregated because of changing residential patterns, but found that such racial imbalances were the result of independent demographic changes unrelated to actions taken by the county. Based on these findings the judge declared that no additional remedial actions would be necessary in the areas where satisfactory progress had been made. However, the judge found inadequate progress in the areas of faculty assignments and resource allocation. Here, the district court refused to relinquish control and ordered additional remedial steps. The court of appeals reversed, holding that until full compliance is reached the district court must continue supervision of the entire school system.

On appeal, the Supreme Court upheld the authority of the district court to reduce supervision over desegregation efforts on an incremental basis. It was within the trial court judge's discretion to reduce or eliminate judicial control over areas in which the district had attained compliance with the principles of *Brown*, and retain control over those areas where compliance had not yet been achieved. The Court, therefore, rejected the more stringent enforcement called for by the appeals court. The vote in the case was unanimous, although in a strongly worded concurring opinion three justices, Blackmun, Stevens, and O'Connor, cautioned that the judiciary must not abdicate its responsibility to ensure that all state-sponsored racial segregation in the public schools be eliminated.

To many the Court's decision in *Freeman v. Pitts* was another example of the Rehnquist justices' backing away from the Court's longstanding commitment to racial equality. But just three months later, in *United States v. Fordice* (1992), the Court served notice that it was not removing itself from segregation controversies. In *Fordice* the Court confronted racial separation in Mississippi's public university system, which various parties alleged had failed to take the necessary steps to dismantle segregation.

United States v. Fordice

505 U.S. ___ (1992)
Vote: 8 (Blackmun, Kennedy, O'Connor, Rehnquist, Souter, Stevens, Thomas, White)
 1 (Scalia)
Opinion of the Court: White
Concurring opinions: O'Connor, Thomas
Opinion concurring in part and dissenting in part: Scalia

Mississippi founded its public university system in 1848 with the establishment of the University of Mississippi and over the years added seven institutions to the system. The universities operated on a racially segregated basis. Five schools were dedicated to the teaching of white students: University of Mississippi, Mississippi State University, Mississippi University for Women, University of Southern Mississippi, and Delta State University. Three institutions exclusively served black students: Alcorn State University, Jackson State University, and Mississippi Valley State University.

The state did not respond to the Supreme Court's decision in *Brown v. Board of Education.* The first black student did not enroll in the University of Mississippi until 1962, and then only under court order. Over the next twelve years, no meaningful desegregation occurred. For example, no white students attended Jackson State or Mississippi Valley, and only five whites enrolled at Alcorn State. The white schools remained almost totally white.

In 1969 the U.S. Department of Health, Education and Welfare began efforts to force the state to desegregate its universities. After several years of controversy, the university's board of trustees developed a desegregation plan, but the federal government found it inadequate. When no significant progress was made, private parties, later joined by the United States, filed suit in 1975 claiming that the university system was in violation of the Equal Protection Clause and the Civil Rights Act of 1964. For twelve years thereafter the parties attempted to reach consensus on a desegregation plan, but they were unsuccessful. In the mid-1980s, 99 percent of Mississippi's white college students attended the five "white" universities. Those schools were 80 percent to 91 percent white. The three "black" universities were 92 percent to 99 percent black.

Failing to reach an out-of-court agreement, the case went to trial in 1987. Seventy-one witnesses gave testimony, and the record included 56,700 pages of exhibits. The district court ruled in favor of the state, finding that it had imposed desegregation policies in good faith and had not violated federal law. The court of appeals affirmed, and the United States appealed to the Supreme Court.

JUSTICE WHITE delivered the opinion of the Court.

The District Court, the Court of Appeals, and respondents recognize and acknowledge that the State of Mississippi had the constitutional duty to dismantle the dual school system that its laws once mandated. Nor is there any dispute that this obligation applies to its higher education system. If the State has not discharged this duty, it remains in violation of the Fourteenth Amendment. *Brown v. Board of Education* and its progeny clearly mandate this observation. Thus, the primary issue in this case is whether the State has met its affirmative duty to dismantle its prior dual university system....

Like the United States, we do not disagree with the Court of Appeals' observation that a state university system is quite different in very relevant respects from primary and secondary schools. Unlike attendance at the lower level schools, a student's decision to seek higher education has been a matter of choice. The State historically has not assigned university students to a particular institution....

We do not agree with the Court of Appeals or the District Court, however, that the adoption and implementation of race-neutral policies alone suffice to demonstrate that the State has completely abandoned its prior dual system. That college attendance is by choice and not by assignment does not mean that a race-neutral admissions policy cures the constitutional violation of a dual system. In a system based on choice, student attendance is determined not simply by admissions policies, but also by many other factors. Although some of these factors clearly cannot be attributed to State policies, many can be. Thus, even after a State dismantles its segregative *admissions* policy, there may still be state action that is traceable to the State's prior *de jure* segregation and that continues to foster segregation.... If policies traceable to the *de jure* system are still in force and have discriminatory effects, those policies too must be reformed to the extent practicable and consistent with sound educational practices. We also disagree with respondents that the Court of Appeals and District Court properly relied on our decision in *Bazemore v. Friday* (1986). *Bazemore* neither requires nor justifies the conclusions reached by the two courts below.

Bazemore raised the issue whether the financing and operational assistance provided by a state university's extension service to voluntary 4-H and Homemaker Clubs was inconsistent with the Equal Protection Clause because of the existence of numerous all-white and all-black clubs. Though prior to 1965 the clubs were supported on a segregated basis, the District Court had found that the policy of segregation had been completely abandoned and that no evidence existed of any lingering discrimination in either services or membership; any racial imbalance resulted from the wholly voluntary and unfettered choice of private individuals. In this context, we held inapplicable the *Green* [*v. New Kent County School Bd.,* 1968] Court's judgment that a voluntary choice program was insufficient to dismantle a *de jure* dual system in public primary and secondary schools, but only after satisfying ourselves that the State had not fostered segregation by playing a part in the decision of which club an individual chose to join.

Bazemore plainly does not excuse inquiry into whether Mississippi has left in place certain aspects of its prior dual system that perpetuate the racially segregated higher education system. If the State perpetuates policies and practices traceable to its prior system that continue to have segregative effects—whether by influencing student enrollment decisions or by fostering segregation in other facets of the university system—and such policies are without sound educational justification and can be practicably eliminated, the State has not satisfied its burden of proving that it has dismantled its prior system. Such policies run afoul of the Equal Protection Clause, even though the State has abolished the legal requirement that whites and blacks be educated separately and has established racially neutral policies not animated by a discriminatory purpose. Because the standard applied by the District Court did not make these inquiries, we hold that the Court of Appeals erred in affirming the District Court's ruling that the State had brought itself into compliance with the Equal Protection Clause in the operation of its higher education system.

Had the Court of Appeals applied the correct legal standard, it would have been apparent from the undisturbed factual findings of the District Court that there are several surviving aspects of Mississippi's prior dual system which are constitutionally suspect; for even though such policies may be race-neutral on their face, they substantially restrict a person's choice of which institution to enter and they contribute to the racial identifiability of the eight public uni-

versities. Mississippi must justify these policies or eliminate them.

It is important to state at the outset that we make no effort to identify an exclusive list of unconstitutional remnants of Mississippi's *de jure* system.... With this caveat in mind, we address four policies of the present system: admission standards, program duplication, institutional mission assignments, and continued operation of all eight public universities.

We deal first with the current admissions policies of Mississippi's public universities. As the District Court found, the three flagship historically white universities in the system—University of Mississippi, Mississippi State University, and University of Southern Mississippi—enacted policies in 1963 requiring all entrants to achieve a minimum composite score of 15 on the American College Testing Program (ACT). The court described the "discriminatory taint" of this policy, an obvious reference to the fact that, at the time, the average ACT score for white students was 18 and the average for blacks was 7. The District Court concluded, and the en banc Court of Appeals agreed, that present admissions standards derived from policies enacted in the 1970's to redress the problem of student unpreparedness. Obviously, this mid-passage justification for perpetuating a policy enacted originally to discriminate against black students does not make the present admissions standards any less constitutionally suspect.

The present admission standards are not only traceable to the *de jure* system and were originally adopted for a discriminatory purpose, but they also have present discriminatory effects. Every Mississippi resident under 21 seeking admission to the university system must take the ACT. Any applicant who scores at least 15 qualifies for automatic admission to any of the five historically white institutions except Mississippi University for Women, which requires a score of 18 for automatic admission unless the student has a 3.0 high school grade average. Those scoring less than 15 but at least 13 automatically qualify to enter Jackson State University, Alcorn State University, and Mississippi Valley State University. Without doubt, these requirements restrict the range of choices of entering students as to which institution they may attend in a way that perpetuates segregation....

The segregative effect of this automatic entrance standard is especially striking in light of the differences in minimum automatic entrance scores among the regional universities in Mississippi's system. The minimum score for automatic admission to Mississippi University for Women (MUW) is 18; it is 13 for the historically black universities. Yet MUW is assigned the same institutional mission as two other regional universities, Alcorn State and Mississippi Valley—that of providing quality undergraduate education. The effects of the policy fall disproportionately on black students who might wish to attend MUW; and though the disparate impact is not as great, the same is true of the minimum standard ACT score of 15 at Delta State University—the other "regional" university—as compared to the historically black "regional" universities where a score of 13 suffices for automatic admission. The courts below made little if any effort to justify in educational terms those particular disparities in entrance requirements or to inquire whether it was practicable to eliminate them.

We also find inadequately justified by the courts below or by the record before us the differential admissions requirements between universities with dissimilar programmatic missions. We do not suggest that absent a discriminatory purpose different programmatic missions accompanied by different admissions standards would be constitutionally suspect simply because one or more schools are racially identifiable. But here the differential admission standards are remnants of the dual system with a continuing discriminatory effect, and the mission assignments "to some degree follow the historical racial assignments." Moreover, the District Court did not justify the differing admission standards based on the different mission assignments. It observed only that in the 1970's, the Board of Trustees justified a minimum ACT score of 15 because too many students with lower scores were not prepared for the historically white institutions and that imposing the 15 score requirement on admissions to the historically black institutions would decimate attendance at those universities. The District Court also stated that the mission of the regional universities had the more modest function of providing quality undergraduate education. Certainly the comprehensive universities are also, among other things, educating undergraduates. But we think the 15 ACT test score for automatic admission to the comprehensive universities, as compared with a score of 13 for the regionals,

requires further justification in terms of sound educational policy.

Another constitutionally problematic aspect of the State's use of the ACT test scores is its policy of denying automatic admission if an applicant fails to earn the minimum ACT score specified for the particular institution, without also resorting to the applicant's high school grades as an additional factor in predicting college performance. The United States produced evidence that the American College Testing Program (ATCP), the administering organization of the ACT, discourages use of ACT scores as the sole admissions criterion on the ground that it gives an incomplete "picture" of the student applicant's ability to perform adequately in college.... The record also indicated that the disparity between black and white students' high school grade averages was much narrower than the gap between their average ACT scores, thereby suggesting that an admissions formula which included grades would increase the number of black students eligible for automatic admission to all of Mississippi's public universities....

A second aspect of the present system that necessitates further inquiry is the widespread duplication of programs. "Unnecessary" duplication refers, under the District Court's definition, "to those instances where two or more institutions offer the same nonessential or noncore program. Under this definition, all duplication at the bachelor's level of nonbasic liberal arts and sciences course work and all duplication at the master's level and above are considered to be unnecessary." The District Court found that 34.6 percent of the 29 undergraduate programs at historically black institutions are "unnecessarily duplicated" by the historically white universities, and that 90 percent of the graduate programs at the historically black institutions are unnecessarily duplicated at the historically white institutions. In its conclusions of law on this point, the District Court nevertheless determined that "there is no proof" that such duplication "is directly associated with the racial identifiability of institutions," and that "there is no proof that the elimination of unnecessary program duplication would be justifiable from an educational standpoint or that its elimination would have a substantial effect on student choice."

The District Court's treatment of this issue is problematic from several different perspectives. First, the court appeared to impose the burden of proof on the plaintiffs to meet a legal standard the court itself acknowledged was not yet formulated. It can hardly be denied that such duplication was part and parcel of the prior dual system of higher education—the whole notion of "separate but equal" required duplicative programs in two sets of schools—and that the present unnecessary duplication is a continuation of that practice. *Brown* and its progeny, however, established that the burden of proof falls on the *State,* and not the aggrieved plaintiffs, to establish that it has dismantled its prior *de jure* segregated system. The court's holding that petitioners could not establish the constitutional defect of unnecessary duplication, therefore, improperly shifted the burden away from the State. Second, implicit in the District Court's finding of "unnecessary" duplication is the absence of any educational justification and the fact that some if not all duplication may be practicably eliminated. Indeed, the District Court observed that such duplication "cannot be justified economically or in terms of providing quality education." Yet by stating that "there is no proof" that elimination of unnecessary duplication would decrease institutional racial identifiability, affect student choice, and promote educationally sound policies, the court did not make clear whether it had directed the parties to develop evidence on these points, and if so, what that evidence revealed. Finally, by treating this issue in isolation, the court failed to consider the combined effects of unnecessary program duplication with other policies, such as differential admissions standards, in evaluating whether the State had met its duty to dismantle its prior *de jure* segregated system.

We next address Mississippi's scheme of institutional mission classification, and whether it perpetuates the State's formerly *de jure* dual system. The District Court found that, throughout the period of *de jure* segregation, University of Mississippi, Mississippi State University, and University of Southern Mississippi were the flagship institutions in the state system. They received the most funds, initiated the most advanced and specialized programs, and developed the widest range of curricular functions. At their inception, each was restricted for the education solely of white persons. The missions of Mississippi University for Women and Delta State University (DSU), by contrast, were more limited than their other all-white counterparts during the period of legalized segregation. MUW and DSU

were each established to provide undergraduate education solely for white students in the liberal arts and such other fields as music, art, education, and home economics. When they were founded, the three exclusively black universities were more limited in their assigned academic missions than the five all-white institutions. Alcorn State, for example, was designated to serve as "an agricultural college for the education of Mississippi's black youth.". . .

In 1981, the State assigned certain missions to Mississippi's public universities as they then existed. It classified University of Mississippi, Mississippi State, and Southern Mississippi as "comprehensive" universities having the most varied programs and offering graduate degrees. Two of the historically white institutions, Delta State University and Mississippi University for Women, along with two of the historically black institutions, Alcorn State University and Mississippi Valley State University, were designated as "regional" universities with more limited programs and devoted primarily to undergraduate education. Jackson State University was classified as an "urban" university whose mission was defined by its urban location.

The institutional mission designations adopted in 1981 have as their antecedents the policies enacted to perpetuate racial separation during the *de jure* segregated regime. . . . That different missions are assigned to the universities surely limits to some extent an entering student's choice as to which university to seek admittance. . . . We do not suggest that absent discriminatory purpose the assignment of different missions to various institutions in a State's higher education system would raise an equal protection issue where one or more of the institutions become or remain predominantly black or white. But here the issue is whether the State has sufficiently dismantled its prior dual system; and when combined with the differential admission practices and unnecessary program duplication, it is likely that the mission designations interfere with student choice and tend to perpetuate the segregated system. On remand, the court should inquire whether it would be practicable and consistent with sound educational practices to eliminate any such discriminatory effects of the State's present policy of mission assignments.

Fourth, the State attempted to bring itself into compliance with the Constitution by continuing to maintain and operate all eight higher educational institutions. The existence of eight instead of some lesser number was undoubtedly occasioned by State laws forbidding the mingling of the races. And as the District Court recognized, continuing to maintain all eight universities in Mississippi is wasteful and irrational. The District Court pointed especially to the facts that Delta State and Mississippi Valley are only 35 miles apart and that only 20 miles separate Mississippi State and Mississippi University for Women. It was evident to the District Court that "the defendants undertake to fund more institutions of higher learning than are justified by the amount of financial resources available to the state," but the court concluded that such fiscal irresponsibility was a policy choice of the legislature rather than a feature of a system subject to constitutional scrutiny.

Unquestionably, a larger rather than a smaller number of institutions from which to choose in itself makes for different choices, particularly when examined in the light of other factors present in the operation of the system, such as admissions, program duplication, and institutional mission designations. Though certainly closure of one or more institutions would decrease the discriminatory effects of the present system, based on the present record we are unable to say whether such action is constitutionally required. Elimination of program duplication and revision of admissions criteria may make institutional closure unnecessary. However, on remand this issue should be carefully explored by inquiring and determining whether retention of all eight institutions itself affects student choice and perpetuates the segregated higher education system, whether maintenance of each of the universities is educationally justifiable, and whether one or more of them can be practically closed or merged with other existing institutions.

Because the former *de jure* segregated system of public universities in Mississippi impeded the free choice of prospective students, the State in dismantling that system must take the necessary steps to ensure that this choice now is truly free. The full range of policies and practices must be examined with this duty in mind. That an institution is predominantly white or black does not in itself make out a constitutional violation. But surely the State may not leave in place policies rooted in its prior officially-segregated system that serve to maintain the racial identifiability of its universities if those policies can practically be eliminated without eroding sound educational policies....

Because the District Court and the Court of Appeals failed to reconsider the State's duties in their proper light, the cases must be remanded. To the extent that the State has not met its affirmative obligation to dismantle its prior dual system, it shall be adjudged in violation of the Constitution and Title VI and remedial proceedings shall be conducted. The decision of the Court of Appeals is vacated, and the cases are remanded for further proceedings consistent with this opinion.

It is so ordered.

In *Fordice* the Court clarified the standard states must meet to bring their systems into compliance with the Fourteenth Amendment. How states and lower courts use and apply the Court's mandate remains to be seen. *Fordice* will probably generate even more litigation, as other state university systems come under judicial scrutiny.

Segregated schools are not the only arena for battles over racial discrimination. Legal confrontations have occurred over housing,[6] employment,[7] admission policies in higher education,[8] and public accommodations.[9] In most of these areas federal civil rights statutes and the government's enforcement of them have played the dominant role, and, historically, the Supreme Court has supported congressional legislation to extend fair treatment to racial minorities. The Burger and Rehnquist Courts, however, handed down some rulings that members of Congress saw as excessively limiting the opportunities of blacks and other disadvantaged groups to assert their statutory rights. In response, Congress has passed or amended laws to counteract the Court's decisions.

6. See, for example, *Reitman v. Mulkey* (1967); *Village of Arlington Heights v. Metropolitan Housing Development Corporation* (1977); *Hills v. Gautreaux* (1976); *Spallone v. United States* (1990).

7. See, for example, *Sheet Metal Workers v. EEOC* (1986); *Wards Cove Packing Company v. Atonia* (1989); *Martin v. Wilks* (1989); *Patterson v. McLean Credit Union* (1989).

8. See, for example, *Regents of the University of California v. Bakke* (1978).

9. See, for example, *Heart of Atlanta Motel v. United States* (1964); *Katzenbach v. McClung* (1964).

Sex Discrimination Remedies

The discrimination suffered by women at the hands of government is different from that suffered by black Americans. Where state or federal laws unconstitutionally discriminated on the basis of sex, the elimination of the offending statutes often provided relief without additional court-imposed remedies. When such remedies were necessary, they could be much less comprehensive than those required to reverse the effects of slavery and segregation.

In the private sector, however, discrimination against women in employment, credit, and other areas of commerce has been common. Because private discrimination is beyond the reach of the Fifth and Fourteenth Amendments, the legislative branch must provide relief. Consequently, both Congress and the state legislatures have passed laws to remove sex-based bias from the economic marketplace. These laws have extended principles of nondiscrimination to hiring, credit, equal pay, higher education, sexual harassment, and related matters.[10]

In some areas of the private sector, true segregation of the sexes has been the practice. Private organizations of various kinds have prohibited women from becoming members. Some of these male-only organizations, while primarily social or fraternal, provide places for informal business contacts and meetings. Being excluded from such organizations can be an obstacle for women attempting to advance in the business world. Because of these economic considerations, as well as general objections to such exclusions based on sex, women's groups pressured the courts and the legislatures to open club membership to women. This goal was difficult to achieve. Private, voluntary organizations generally are protected by First Amendment rights to freedom of association, which preclude gov-

ernment from imposing membership requirements. But civil rights advocates pressed the argument that these organizations are commercial operations that should be regulated like any other business, and several states passed laws barring certain organizations from discriminating on the basis of sex. These laws drew fire from First Amendment advocates, setting up an inevitable court battle between freedom of association and the right to be free from discrimination. In *Roberts v. United States Jaycees* (1984) the Supreme Court responded to this conflict.

Roberts v. United States Jaycees

468 U.S. 609 (1984)
Vote: 7 (Brennan, Marshall, O'Connor, Powell, Rehnquist,
      Stevens, White)
       0

Opinion of the Court: Brennan
Opinion concurring in judgment: O'Connor
Not participating: Blackmun, Burger

The United States Jaycees was founded in 1920 as the Junior Chamber of Commerce. It was a nonprofit organization with headquarters in Tulsa, Oklahoma. The official purpose of the group was to develop young men's civic organizations to promote Americanism, civic involvement, personal achievement, and friendship among young men of all nations. Regular membership in the organization was limited to men between the ages of eighteen and thirty-five. Associate membership was open to women and older men. Associate members paid lower dues than regular members, but were prohibited from voting, holding office, or participating in a number of important organization activities. The association was made up of state organizations and local chapters, which sent delegates to the annual convention, the ultimate policy-making body of the national organization. At the time of this litigation, the Jaycees had 295,000 members in 7,400

---

10. As in the case of racial discrimination, the Supreme Court traditionally has supported such laws. When the Court interprets these statutes narrowly, however, Congress is not reluctant to respond. In 1988, for example, Congress passed the Civil Rights Restoration Act to counteract the Court's narrow interpretation of sex bias regulations in *Grove City College v. Bell* (1984).

local chapters. Associate members numbered 11,915, and women made up about 2 percent of total membership.

Beginning in 1974 the Minneapolis and St. Paul local chapters began admitting women as regular members in violation of the national organization's bylaws. The national Jaycees imposed certain sanctions on the Minnesota local chapters for admitting women and threatened to revoke their charters. Rather than comply, members of the two chapters filed a complaint with the Minnesota Department of Human Rights claiming that excluding women from regular membership violated the Minnesota Human Rights Act. That act prohibited denying "any person the full and equal enjoyment of the goods, services, facilities, privileges, advantages, and accommodations of a place of public accommodation because of race, color, creed, religion, disability, national origin, or sex." When the state commissioner of human rights ordered a full hearing on the issue, the U.S. Jaycees filed suit. The suit claimed that by requiring the organization to accept women, the act violated the regular members' constitutional rights of speech and association. The Jaycees lost in federal district court, but the court of appeals reversed, holding that the state's interest in eradicating discrimination was not sufficiently compelling to justify its interference with the Jaycees' constitutional right to freedom of association. Kathryn Roberts, the state's acting human rights commissioner, appealed to the Supreme Court.

JUSTICE BRENNAN delivered the opinion of the Court.

Our decisions have referred to constitutionally protected "freedom of association" in two distinct senses. In one line of decisions, the Court has concluded that choices to enter into and maintain certain intimate human relationships must be secured against undue intrusion by the State because of the role of such relationships in safeguarding the individual freedom that is central to our constitutional scheme. In this respect, freedom of association receives protection as a fundamental element of personal liberty. In another set of decisions, the Court has recognized a right to associate for the purpose of engaging in those activities protected by the First Amendment—speech, assembly, petition for the redress of grievances, and the exercise of religion. The Constitution guarantees freedom of association of this kind as an indispensable means of preserving other individual liberties.

The intrinsic and instrumental features of constitutionally protected association may, of course, coincide. In particular, when the State interferes with individuals' selection of those with whom they wish to join in a common endeavor, freedom of association in both of its forms may be implicated. The Jaycees contend that this is such a case. Still, the nature and degree of constitutional protection afforded freedom of association may vary depending on the extent to which one or the other aspect of the constitutionally protected liberty is at stake in a given case. We therefore find it useful to consider separately the effect of applying the Minnesota statute to the Jaycees on what could be called its members' freedom of intimate association and their freedom of expressive association.

The Court has long recognized that, because the Bill of Rights is designed to secure individual liberty, it must afford the formation and preservation of certain kinds of highly personal relationships a substantial measure of sanctuary from unjustified interference by the State. Without precisely identifying every consideration that may underlie this type of constitutional protection, we have noted that certain kinds of personal bonds have played a critical role in the culture and traditions of the Nation by cultivating and transmitting shared ideas and beliefs; they thereby foster diversity and act as critical buffers between the individual and the power of the State. Moreover, the constitutional shelter afforded such relationships reflects the realization that individuals draw much of their emotional enrichment from close ties with others. Protecting these relationships from unwarranted state interference therefore safeguards the ability independently to define one's identity that is central to any concept of liberty.

The personal affiliations that exemplify these considerations, and that therefore suggest some relevant limitations on the relationships that might be entitled to this sort of constitutional protection, are those that attend the creation and sustenance of a family—marriage, childbirth, the raising and education of children, and cohabitation with one's relatives. Family relationships, by their nature, involve deep attachments and commitments to the necessarily few other individuals with whom one shares not only a special community of thoughts, experiences, and beliefs but also distinctively personal aspects of one's life. Among other things, therefore, they are distinguished by such attributes as relative smallness, a high degree of selectivity in decisions to begin and maintain the affiliation, and seclusion from others in critical aspects of the relationship. As a general matter, only relationships with these sorts of qualities are likely to reflect the considerations that have led to an understanding of freedom of association as an intrinsic element of personal liberty. Conversely, an association lacking these qualities—such as a large business enterprise—seems remote from the concerns giving rise to this constitutional protection. Accordingly, the Constitution undoubtedly imposes constraints on the State's power to control the selection of one's spouse that would not apply to regulations affecting the choice of one's fellow employees.

Between these poles, of course, lies a broad range of human relationships that may make greater or lesser claims to constitutional protection from particular incursions by the State. Determining the limits of state authority over an individual's freedom to enter into a particular association therefore unavoidably entails a careful assessment of where that relationship's objective characteristics locate it on a spectrum from the most intimate to the most attenuated of personal attachments. We need not mark the potentially significant points on this terrain with any precision. We note only that factors that may be relevant include size, purpose, policies, selectivity, congeniality, and other characteristics that in a particular case may be pertinent. In this case, however, several features of the Jaycees clearly place the organization outside of the category of relationships worthy of this kind of constitutional protection.

The undisputed facts reveal that the local chapters of the Jaycees are large and basically unselective groups. At the time of the state administrative hearing, the Minneapolis chapter had approximately 430 members, while the St. Paul chapter had about 400. Apart from age and sex, neither the national organization nor the local chapters employ any criteria for judging applicants for membership, and new members are routinely recruited and admitted

with no inquiry into their backgrounds. In fact, a local officer testified that he could recall no instance in which an applicant had been denied membership on any basis other than age or sex. Furthermore, despite their inability to vote, hold office, or receive certain awards, women affiliated with the Jaycees attend various meetings, participate in selected projects, and engage in many of the organization's social functions. Indeed, numerous non-members of both genders regularly participate in a substantial portion of activities central to the decision of many members to associate with one another, including many of the organization's various community programs, awards ceremonies, and recruitment meetings.

In short, the local chapters of the Jaycees are neither small nor selective. Moreover, much of the activity central to the formation and maintenance of the association involves the participation of strangers to that relationship. Accordingly, we conclude that the Jaycees chapters lack the distinctive characteristics that might afford constitutional protection to the decision of its members to exclude women. We turn therefore to consider the extent to which application of the Minnesota statute to compel the Jaycees to accept women infringes the group's freedom of expressive association.

An individual's freedom to speak, to worship, and to petition the government for the redress of grievances could not be vigorously protected from interference by the State unless a correlative freedom to engage in group effort toward those ends were not also guaranteed. According protection to collective effort on behalf of shared goals is especially important in preserving political and cultural diversity and in shielding dissident expression from suppression by the majority. Consequently, we have long understood as implicit in the right to engage in activities protected by the First Amendment a corresponding right to associate with others in pursuit of a wide variety of political, social, economic, educational, religious, and cultural ends. In view of the various protected activities in which the Jaycees engages, that right is plainly implicated in this case.

Government actions that may unconstitutionally infringe upon this freedom can take a number of forms. Among other things, government may seek to impose penalties or withhold benefits from individuals because of their membership in a disfavored group; it may attempt to require disclosure of the fact of membership in a group seeking anonymity; and it may try to interfere with the internal organization or affairs of the group. By requiring the Jaycees to admit women as full voting members, the Minnesota Act works an infringement of the last type. There can be no clearer example of an intrusion into the internal structure or affairs of an association than a regulation that forces the group to accept members it does not desire. Such a regulation may impair the ability of the original members to express only those views that brought them together. Freedom of association therefore plainly presupposes a freedom not to associate. The right to associate for expressive purposes is not, however, absolute. Infringements on that right may be justified by regulations adopted to serve compelling state interests, unrelated to the suppression of ideas, that cannot be achieved through a means significantly less restrictive of associational freedoms. We are persuaded that Minnesota's compelling interest in eradicating discrimination against its female citizens justifies the impact that application of the statute to the Jaycees may have on the male members' associational freedoms.

On its face, the Minnesota Act does not aim at the suppression of speech, does not distinguish between prohibited and permitted activity on the basis of viewpoint, and does not license enforcement authorities to administer the statute on the basis of such constitutionally impermissible criteria. Nor does the Jaycees contend that the Act has been applied in this case for the purpose of hampering the organization's ability to express its views. Instead, as the Minnesota Supreme Court explained, the Act reflects the State's strong historical commitment to eliminating discrimination and assuring its citizens equal access to publicly available goods and services. That goal, which is unrelated to the suppression of expression, plainly serves compelling state interests of the highest order....

By prohibiting gender discrimination in places of public accommodation, the Minnesota Act protects the State's citizenry from a number of serious social and personal harms. In the context of reviewing state actions under the Equal Protection Clause, this Court has frequently noted that discrimination based on archaic and overbroad assumptions about the relative needs and capacities of the sexes forces individuals to labor under stereotypical notions that often bear no relationship to their actual abilities. It thereby both deprives persons of their individual dignity and denies society the benefits of wide participation in political, economic, and cultural life....

A State enjoys broad authority to create rights of public access on behalf of its citizens. Like many States and municipalities, Minnesota has adopted a functional definition of public accommodations that reaches various forms of public, quasi-commercial conduct. This expansive definition reflects a recognition of the changing nature of the American economy and of the importance, both to the individual and to society, of removing the barriers to economic advancement and political and social integration that have historically plagued certain disadvantaged groups, including women....

In applying the Act to the Jaycees, the State has advanced those interests through the least restrictive means of achieving its ends. Indeed, the Jaycees has failed to demonstrate that the Act imposes any serious burdens on the male members' freedom of expressive association.... There is ... no basis in the record for concluding that admission of women as full voting members will impede the organization's ability to engage in protected activities or to disseminate its preferred views. The Act requires no change in the Jaycees' creed of promoting the interests of young men, and it imposes no restrictions on the organization's ability to exclude individuals with ideologies or philosophies different from those of its existing members....

In claiming that women might have a different attitude about such issues as the federal budget, school prayer, voting rights, and foreign relations, or that the organization's public positions would have a different effect if the group were not "a purely young men's association," the Jaycees relies solely on unsupported generalizations about the relative interests and perspectives of men and women. Although such generalizations may or may not have a statistical basis in fact with respect to particular positions adopted by the Jaycees, we have repeatedly condemned legal decisionmaking that relies uncritically on such assumptions. In the absence of a showing far more substantial than that attempted by the Jaycees, we decline to indulge in the sexual stereotyping that underlies appellee's contention that, by allowing women to vote, application of the Minnesota Act will change the content or impact of the organization's speech.

In any event, even if enforcement of the Act causes some incidental abridgment of the Jaycees' protected speech, that effect is no greater than is necessary to accomplish the State's legitimate purposes. As we have explained, acts of invidious discrimination in the distribution of publicly available goods, services, and other advantages cause unique evils that government has a compelling interest to prevent—wholly apart from the point of view such conduct may transmit.... In prohibiting such practices, the Minnesota Act therefore "responds precisely to the substantive problem which legitimately concerns" the State and abridges no more speech or associational freedom than is necessary to accomplish that purpose.

Reversed.

The principles set in *Roberts* have been applied in subsequent decisions as well. In 1987 the Court unanimously enforced California's human rights law; the dispute concerned the Rotary Club International, which also excluded women from membership.[11] And in 1988 the justices, again without dissent, turned down a challenge to a New York City human rights law filed by a group of private clubs.[12] These rulings have reinforced the ability of state and local governments to combat private discrimination through the traditional powers to regulate commerce.

Affirmative Action

Few issues of constitutional law have prompted as much controversy as affirmative action. Based on the notion that the principles of the Equal Protection Clause cannot be achieved by simply terminating illegal discrimination, affirmative action programs direct government and private institutions to take positive measures to ensure that equality becomes a reality. This action is necessary, it is argued, because decades of race, sex, and ethnic discrimination have so held back certain segments of our population that special intervention is needed, at least temporarily, to level the playing field.

The affirmative action philosophy takes issue with Justice Harlan's assertion in his *Plessy v. Ferguson* dissent that the Constitution is "color blind," holding instead that characteristics associated with disadvantaged status must be considered and taken into account. Special programs and incentives for people from disadvantaged groups are warranted to eradicate and compensate for the effects of past discrimination. At its core, affirmative action is an attempt to help those who have suffered from longstanding, systematic bias.

Opponents of such special programs, however, see it very differently. Many valued goods and opportunities in society—jobs, promotions, and admission to education and training programs—are scarce. When factors such as race and sex are used (rather than merit alone) to determine who obtains these limited opportunities, the losers may themselves feel victimized and claim reverse discrimination. The principles of equal protection, affirmative action opponents assert, should prohibit discrimination against whites and males just as they prohibit discrimination against blacks and women. Those who have been negatively affected by it view affirmative action as inconsistent with the nation's commitment to equal opportunity.

Affirmative action programs have their roots in presidential orders, issued as early as the 1940s, that expanded government employment opportunities for blacks. These programs received their most significant boost, however, in 1965 when President Johnson issued Executive Order 11246 instructing the Labor Department to ensure that businesses contracting with the federal government were nondiscriminatory. To meet the requirements, government contractors altered their employment policies and recruited minority workers. Over the years, these requirements were strengthened and expanded. Failure to comply with the government's principles of nondiscriminatory em-

---

11. *Board of Directors of Rotary International v. Rotary Club of Duarte* (1987).
12. *New York State Club Association v. City of New York* (1988).

ployment was grounds for stripping any business or institution of its federal contract or appropriated funds. State and local governments adopted similar programs, many aggressively establishing numerical standards for minority participation. Some private businesses voluntarily adopted programs to increase the numbers of women and minorities, especially in positions where their numbers historically had been low. In addition, courts began imposing affirmative action plans on public employers.

Legal obstacles to affirmative action programs arise from two sources. The first is the Constitution. The Equal Protection Clause of the Fourteenth Amendment and the Due Process Clause of the Fifth could be interpreted to prohibit the government from giving special consideration to individuals because of their race, sex, or national origin. The second is the Civil Rights Act of 1964 and related statutes. For example, Title VII specifies, with respect to private employment, that race, color, religion, sex, and national origin cannot be used to discriminate against any employee. It further holds:

It shall be an unlawful employment practice for an employer ... to limit, segregate, or classify his employees or applicants for employment in any way which would deprive or tend to deprive any individual of employment opportunities or otherwise adversely affect his status as an employee, because of such individual's race, color, religion, sex, or national origin.

Title VI of the same statute contained similar provisions for state and local government programs that received federal funding. These provisions were originally intended to prohibit discrimination against members of groups that historically have been the victims of prejudice. Whether giving preference to such individuals, at the possible expense of others, also violates these constitutional or statutory provisions remained for the Supreme Court to determine.

Undoubtedly, the most significant decision in establishing the law of affirmative action was *Regents of the University of California v. Bakke* (1978), an Equal Protection Clause challenge to a public university's policy to admit a specific number of minority applicants. The stakes were high. For civil rights groups, the case represented a threat to the best way yet devised to eliminate the effects of past discrimination and promote minority students into professional positions. For opponents of affirmative action, it was an opportunity to overturn the growing burden of paying for the sins of the past and return to a system based on merit. Fifty-seven friend of the court briefs were filed by various organizations and interested parties.

The Supreme Court was deeply divided over this case. Four justices gave strong support to affirmative action programs, four others had serious reservations about them, and Justice Powell found himself in the middle. Portions of his opinion announcing the judgment of the Court were supported by one set of four justices, and other parts were joined by an entirely different group of four. As the "swing" justice in this case, Powell was effectively able to determine what the Constitution means with respect to affirmative action programs.

Regents of the University of California v. Bakke

438 U.S. 265 (1978)
Vote: 5 *(Burger, Powell, Rehnquist, Stevens, Stewart)*
    4 *(Blackmun, Brennan, Marshall, White)*
Opinion announcing the judgment of the Court: Powell
Opinion concurring in part and dissenting in part: Blackmun, Brennan, Marshall, White (jointly authored)
Separate opinion: White
Separate opinion: Marshall
Separate opinion: Blackmun
Opinion concurring in part and dissenting in part: Stevens

The medical school of the University of California at Davis began operations in 1968. In its first two years, it admitted only three minority students, all

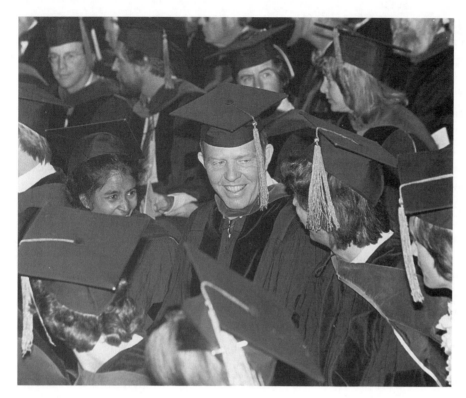

Twice rejected for admission to the medical school of the University of California at Davis, Allan Bakke (center) filed suit challenging school policy that admitted minority students with grades and test scores lower than his. Bakke's suit led to the Supreme Court's first major statement on the constitutionality of affirmative action programs. Bakke was awarded his medical degree from the university in 1982.

Asians. To improve minority participation, the school developed two admissions programs to fill the 100 seats in its entry class—a regular admissions program and a special admissions program. The regular admissions program worked in the customary way, in which applicants were evaluated on the basis of undergraduate grades, standardized test scores, letters of recommendation, extracurricular activities, and an interview. The special admissions program was for applicants who indicated that they were economically or educationally disadvantaged, or were black, Chicano, Asian, or Native American. Such applicants could choose to go through the regular admissions process or to be referred to a special admissions committee. Special admissions applicants were judged on the same characteristics as the regular applicants, but they competed only against each other. The school reserved sixteen seats to be filled from the special admissions pool. Many white applicants, claiming poverty, indicated a desire to be considered by the special admissions committee, but none was admitted. All specially admitted students were members of the designated minority groups.

Allan Bakke was a white male of Scandinavian descent. He graduated with honors in engineering from the University of Minnesota and was a Vietnam veteran. He worked for the National Aeronautics and Space Administration and received his master's degree in engineering from Stanford. Developing an interest in a medical career, Bakke took extra science courses and did volunteer work in a local hospital. At age thirty-three, he applied for admission to the 1973

TABLE 10-2 Admissions Data for the Entering Class of the Medical School of the University of California at Davis, 1973 and 1974

Class Entering in 1973

| | SGPA[a] | OGPA[b] | MCAT (Percentiles) | | | |
			Verbal	Quantitative	Science	Gen. Infor.
Bakke	3.44	3.46	96	94	97	72
Average of regular admittees	3.51	3.49	81	76	83	69
Average of special admittees	2.62	2.88	46	24	35	33

Class Entering in 1974

| | SGPA[a] | OGPA[b] | MCAT (Percentiles) | | | |
			Verbal	Quantitative	Science	Gen. Infor.
Bakke	3.44	3.46	96	94	97	72
Average of regular admittees	3.36	3.29	69	67	82	72
Average of special admittees	2.42	2.62	34	30	37	18

SOURCE: *Regents of the University of California v. Bakke* (1978).

NOTES: a. Science grade point average.

b. Overall grade point average.

entry class of the medical school at Davis. He was rejected. He applied in 1974 and was again rejected. Because applicants admitted under the special admissions program were, at least statistically, less qualified than he *(see Table 10-2)*, Bakke sued for admission, claiming that the university's dual admissions program violated the Equal Protection Clause of the Fourteenth Amendment.

The state trial court struck down the special program, declaring that race could not be constitutionally taken into account in deciding who would be admitted, but the court refused to order Bakke's admission. Both Bakke and the university appealed. The California Supreme Court found the special admissions program unconstitutional, holding that "no applicant may be rejected because of his race, in favor of another who is less qualified, as measured by standards applied without regard to race." The state supreme court's order to admit Bakke was stayed, pending the university's appeal to the U.S. Supreme Court.

MR. JUSTICE POWELL announced the judgment of the Court.

Petitioner does not deny that decisions based on race or ethnic origin by faculties and administrations of state universities are reviewable under the Fourteenth Amendment. For his part, respondent does not argue that all racial or ethnic classifications are *per se* invalid. The parties do disagree as to the level of judicial scrutiny to be applied to the special admissions program. Petitioner argues that the court below erred in applying strict scrutiny, as this inexact term has been applied in our cases. That level of review, petitioner asserts, should be reserved for classifications that disadvantage "discrete and insular minorities." Respondent, on the other hand, contends that the California court correctly rejected the notion that the degree of judicial scrutiny accorded a particular racial or ethnic classification hinges upon membership in a discrete and insular minority and duly recognized that the "rights established [by the Fourteenth Amendment] are personal rights."

En route to this crucial battle over the scope of judicial review, the parties fight a sharp preliminary action over the proper characterization of the special admissions program.

Petitioner prefers to view it as establishing a "goal" of minority representation in the Medical School. Respondent, echoing the courts below, labels it a racial quota.

This semantic distinction is beside the point: The special admissions program is undeniably a classification based on race and ethnic background. To the extent that there existed a pool of at least minimally qualified minority applicants to fill the 16 special admissions seats, white applicants could compete only for 84 seats in the entering class, rather than the 100 open to minority applicants. Whether this limitation is described as a quota or a goal, it is a line drawn on the basis of race and ethnic status.

The guarantees of the Fourteenth Amendment extend to all persons. Its language is explicit: "No State shall ... deny to any person within its jurisdiction the equal protection of the laws." It is settled beyond question that the "rights created by the first section of the Fourteenth Amendment are, by its terms, guaranteed to the individual. The rights established are personal rights." The guarantee of equal protection cannot mean one thing when applied to one individual and something else when applied to a person of another color. If both are not accorded the same protection, then it is not equal....

Racial and ethnic distinctions of any sort are inherently suspect and thus call for the most exacting judicial examination....

Although many of the Framers of the Fourteenth Amendment conceived of its primary function as bridging the vast distance between members of the Negro race and the white "majority," the Amendment itself was framed in universal terms, without reference to color, ethnic origin, or condition of prior servitude....

Petitioner urges us to adopt for the first time a more restrictive view of the Equal Protection Clause and hold that discrimination against members of the white "majority" cannot be suspect if its purpose can be characterized as "benign." The clock of our liberties, however, cannot be turned back to 1868. It is far too late to argue that the guarantee of equal protection to *all* persons permits the recognition of special wards entitled to a degree of protection greater than that accorded others. "The Fourteenth Amendment is not directed solely against discrimination due to a 'two-class theory'—that is, based upon differences between 'white' and Negro."...

If it is the individual who is entitled to judicial protection against classifications based upon his racial or ethnic background because such distinctions impinge upon personal rights, rather than the individual only because of his membership in a particular group, then constitutional standards may be applied consistently. Political judgments regarding the necessity for the particular classification may be weighed in the constitutional balance, but the standard of justification will remain constant. This is as it should be, since those political judgments are the product of rough compromise struck by contending groups within the democratic process. When they touch upon an individual's race or ethnic background, he is entitled to a judicial determination that the burden he is asked to bear on that basis is precisely tailored to serve a compelling governmental interest. The Constitution guarantees that right to every person regardless of his background....

We have held that in "order to justify the use of a suspect classification, a State must show that its purpose or interest is both constitutionally permissible and substantial, and that its use of the classification is 'necessary ... to the accomplishment' of its purpose or the safeguarding of its interest." The special admissions program purports to serve the purposes of: (i) "reducing the historic deficit of traditionally disfavored minorities in medical schools and in the medical profession"; (ii) countering the effects of societal discrimination; (iii) increasing the number of physicians who will practice in communities currently underserved; and (iv) obtaining the educational benefits that flow from an ethnically diverse student body. It is necessary to decide which, if any, of these purposes is substantial enough to support the use of a suspect classification.

If petitioner's purpose is to assure within its student body some specified percentage of a particular group merely because of its race or ethnic origin, such a preferential purpose must be rejected not as insubstantial but as facially invalid. Preferring members of any one group for no reason other than race or ethnic origin is discrimination for its own sake. This the Constitution forbids.

The State certainly has a legitimate and substantial interest in ameliorating, or eliminating where feasible, the disabling effects of identified discrimination. The line of school desegregation cases, commencing with *Brown*, attests to the importance of this state goal and the commitment of the judiciary to affirm all lawful means toward its attainment. In the school cases, the States were required by court order to redress the wrongs worked by specific instances of racial discrimination. That goal was far more focused than the remedying of the effects of "societal discrimination," an amorphous concept of inquiry that may be ageless in its reach into the past.

We have never approved a classification that aids persons perceived as members of relatively victimized groups at the expense of other innocent individuals in the absence of judicial, legislative, or administrative findings of constitutional or statutory violations. After such findings have been made, the governmental interest in preferring members of the injured groups at the expense of others is substantial, since the legal rights of the victims must be vindicated. In such a case, the extent of the injury and the consequent remedy will have been judicially, legislatively, or administratively defined. Also, the remedial action usually remains subject to continuing oversight to assure that it will work the least harm possible to other innocent persons competing for the benefit. Without such findings of constitutional or statutory violations, it cannot be said that the government has any greater interest in helping one individual than in refraining from harming another. Thus, the government has no compelling justification for inflicting such harm.

Petitioner does not purport to have made, and is in no position to make, such findings. Its broad mission is education, not the formulation of any legislative policy or the adjudication of particular claims of illegality.... Before relying upon these sorts of findings in establishing a racial classification, a governmental body must have the authority and capability to establish, in the record, that the classification is responsive to identified discrimination. Lacking this capability, petitioner has not carried its burden of justification on this issue.

Hence, the purpose of helping certain groups whom the faculty of the Davis Medical School perceived as victims of "societal discrimination" does not justify a classification that imposes disadvantages upon persons like respondent, who bear no responsibility for whatever harm the beneficiaries of the special admissions program are thought to have suffered. To hold otherwise would be to convert a remedy heretofore reserved for violations of legal rights into a privilege that all institutions throughout the Nation could grant at their pleasure to whatever groups are perceived as victims of societal discrimination. That is a step we have never approved.

Petitioner identifies, as another purpose of its program, improving the delivery of health-care services to communities currently underserved. It may be assumed that in some situations a State's interest in facilitating the health care of its citizens is sufficiently compelling to support the use of a suspect classification. But there is virtually no evidence in the record indicating that petitioner's special admissions program is either needed or geared to promote that goal....

Petitioner simply has not carried its burden of demonstrating that it must prefer members of particular ethnic groups over all other individuals in order to promote better health-care delivery to deprived citizens. Indeed, petitioner has not shown that its preferential classification is likely to have any significant effect on the problem.

The fourth goal asserted by petitioner is the attainment of a diverse student body. This clearly is a constitutionally permissible goal for an institution of higher education. Academic freedom, though not a specifically enumerated constitutional right, long has been viewed as a special concern of the First Amendment. The freedom of a university to make its own judgments as to education includes the selection of its student body....

The atmosphere of "speculation, experiment and creation"—so essential to the quality of higher education—is widely believed to be promoted by a diverse student body. As the Court noted in *Keyishian* [*v. Board of Regents of the University of the State of New York*, 1967] it is not too much to say that the "nation's future depends upon leaders trained through wide exposure" to the ideas and mores of students as diverse as this Nation of many peoples.

Thus, in arguing that its universities must be accorded the right to select those students who will contribute the most to the "robust exchange of ideas," petitioner invokes a countervailing constitutional interest, that of the First Amendment. In this light, petitioner must be viewed as seeking to achieve a goal that is of paramount importance in the fulfillment of its mission.

It may be argued that there is greater force to these views at the undergraduate level than in a medical school where the training is centered primarily on professional competency. But even at the graduate level, our tradition and experience lend support to the view that the contribution of diversity is substantial.... Physicians serve a heterogeneous population. An otherwise qualified medical student with a particular background—whether it be ethnic, geographic, culturally advantaged or disadvantaged—may bring to a professional school of medicine experiences, outlooks, and ideas that enrich the training of its student body and better equip its graduates to render with understanding their vital service to humanity.

Ethnic diversity, however, is only one element in a range of factors a university properly may consider in attaining the goal of a heterogeneous student body. Although a university must have wide discretion in making the sensitive judgments as to who should be admitted, constitutional limitations protecting individual rights may not be disregarded. Respondent urges—and the courts below have held—that petitioner's dual admissions program is a racial classification that impermissibly infringes his rights under the Fourteenth Amendment. As the interest of diversity is compelling in the context of a university's admissions program, the question remains whether the program's racial classification is necessary to promote this interest....

It may be assumed that the reservation of a specified number of seats in each class for individuals from the preferred ethnic groups would contribute to the attainment of considerable ethnic diversity in the student body. But petitioner's argument that this is the only effective means of serving the interest of diversity is seriously flawed. In a most fundamental sense the argument misconceives the nature of the state interest that would justify consideration of race or ethnic background. It is not an interest in simple ethnic diversity, in which a specified percentage of the student body is in effect guaranteed to be members of selected ethnic groups, with the remaining percentage an undifferentiated aggregation of students. The diversity that furthers a compelling state interest encompasses a far broader array of qualifications and characteristics of which racial or ethnic origin is but a single though important element. Petitioner's special admissions program, focused *solely* on ethnic diversity, would hinder rather than further attainment of genuine diversity.

Nor would the state interest in genuine diversity be served by expanding petitioner's two-track system into a multitrack program with a prescribed number of seats set aside for each identifiable category of applicants. Indeed, it is conceivable that a university would thus pursue the logic of petitioner's two-track program to the illogical end of insulating each category of applicants with certain desired qualifications from competition with all other applicants....

In such an admissions program, race or ethnic background may be deemed a "plus" in a particular applicant's file, yet it does not insulate the individual from comparison with all other candidates for the available seats. The file of a particular black applicant may be examined for his potential contribution to diversity without the factor of race being decisive when compared, for example, with that of an applicant identified as an Italian-American if the latter is thought to exhibit qualities more likely to promote beneficial educational pluralism. Such qualities could include exceptional personal talents, unique work or service experience, leadership potential, maturity, demonstrated compassion, a history of overcoming disadvantage, ability to communicate with the poor, or other qualifications deemed important. In short, an admissions program operated in this way is flexible enough to consider all pertinent elements of diversity in light of the particular qualifications of each applicant, and to place them on the same footing for consideration, although not necessarily according them the same weight. Indeed, the weight attributed to a particular quality may vary from year to year depending upon the "mix" both of the student body and the applicants for the incoming class.

This kind of program treats each applicant as an individual in the admissions process. The applicant who loses out on the last available seat to another candidate receiving a "plus" on the basis of ethnic background will not have been foreclosed from all consideration for that seat simply because he was not the right color or had the wrong surname. It would mean only that his combined qualifications, which may have included similar nonobjective factors, did not outweigh those of the other applicant. His qualifications would have been weighed fairly and competitively, and he would have no basis to complain of unequal treatment under the Fourteenth Amendment....

In summary, it is evident that the Davis special admissions program involves the use of an explicit racial classification never before countenanced by this Court. It tells applicants who are not Negro, Asian, or Chicano that they are totally excluded from a specific percentage of the seats in an entering class. No matter how strong their qualifications, quantitative and extracurricular, including their own potential for contribution to educational diversity, they are never afforded the chance to compete with applicants from the preferred groups for the special admissions seats. At the same time, the preferred applicants have the opportunity to compete for every seat in the class.

The fatal flaw in petitioner's preferential program is its disregard of individual rights as guaranteed by the Fourteenth Amendment. Such rights are not absolute. But when a State's distribution of benefits or imposition of burdens hinges on ancestry or the color of a person's skin, that individual is entitled to a demonstration that the challenged classification is necessary to promote a substantial state interest. Petitioner has failed to carry this burden. For this reason, that portion of the California court's judgment holding petitioner's special admissions program invalid under the Fourteenth Amendment must be affirmed.

In enjoining petitioner from ever considering the race of any applicant, however, the courts below failed to recognize that the State has a substantial interest that legitimately may be served by a properly devised admissions program involving the competitive consideration of race and ethnic origin. For this reason, so much of the California court's judgment as enjoins petitioner from any consideration of the race of any applicant must be reversed.

With respect to respondent's entitlement to an injunction directing his admission to the Medical School, petitioner has conceded that it could not carry its burden of proving that, but for the existence of its unlawful special admissions program, respondent still would not have been admitted. Hence, respondent is entitled to the injunction, and that portion of the judgment must be affirmed.

The *Bakke* decision held that absent a history of racial discrimination demanding a strong remedy, affirmative action programs that set quotas for particular racial or ethnic groups violate the Equal Protection Clause. But minority status may play a role in the ad-

missions process. Universities may seek a diverse student body by giving minority applicants special consideration. Race and ethnic background may permissibly be deemed a plus, but they cannot be the only factor determining admissions outcomes.

But what if a history of racial discrimination is present? Does the Constitution or federal law prohibit the use of racial classifications as a means of correcting the situation? One answer, in the private sector, was provided by *United Steelworkers of America v. Weber* (1979), decided just one year after *Bakke.* The case stemmed from an agreement between the steelworkers union and Kaiser Aluminum and Chemical Company. The agreement set up a training program for a Kaiser plant in Gramercy, Louisiana, for which half of the positions were reserved for blacks. The plan was voluntary, temporary, and a response to a history of discrimination against blacks in the craft unions. Almost no blacks worked in the skilled trades: in the area around the Gramercy plant, for example, 39 percent of the work force was black, but only 1.83 percent of the skilled craftworkers was black. Using lists of senior white workers and senior black workers, the union determined who would be offered positions in the training program, but only within racial groups.

Brian Weber, a white union member, was denied a position in the program, while less senior black workers were admitted. He filed suit to declare the program in violation of Title VII of the Civil Rights Act. The Supreme Court found no violations of the law, holding that this voluntary program, designed to remove discrimination from the workplace, was consistent with the spirit of the Civil Rights Act to "break down old patterns of racial segregation and hierarchy." The majority also cited the temporary nature of the plan and the fact that no white workers were discharged or absolutely barred from entering the training program. The minority thought the plan ran contrary to the act, a literal reading of which prohibited discrimination on the basis of race in job training programs, and contrary to the intent of Congress as expressed in legislative debates on the statute.

A second case in which the Court upheld the use of racial quotas to combat the effects of longstanding discrimination is *United States v. Paradise* (1987). This dispute centered on the hiring practices of the Alabama Department of Public Safety. In 1972 a district judge found the department in violation of the Equal Protection Clause: in the thirty-seven years since its inception, the department had not hired a single black state trooper. Blacks had been employed only as laborers. The district court imposed a strict 50 percent black hiring quota for all troopers and instructed the department to rid itself of all discriminatory practices, including those involving promotions. During the next twelve years, however, the department failed to achieve that goal. By 1984 only four blacks had been promoted to corporal, and none had been promoted to major, captain, lieutenant, or sergeant. In response to this lack of progress, the district court imposed a temporary 50 percent black quota for promotion to corporal and a similar, though conditioned, quota for promotions to the higher ranks.

The Reagan administration, opposed to the imposition of strict racial quotas, objected to the district court's order. Attempts to block the plan were unsuccessful at the court of appeals level, and the government asked the Supreme Court for review. In a 5–4 vote, the Court upheld the promotion quotas. The plurality opinion, issued by Justice Brennan, stressed the long history of discrimination by Alabama officials and the lack of progress made since the district court's first finding of constitutional violations. The remedy imposed here, according to the majority, was necessary given the extreme nature of the violations. The plan was temporary, flexible, and did not overly burden innocent parties. Writing for the dissenters, Justice O'Connor said that less extreme plans might have been just as effective and should have been considered before the imposition of quotas.

Johnson v. Transportation Agency of Santa Clara

County, California (1987) presented the justices with the issue of affirmative action programs focusing on sex discrimination. The plan challenged in this lawsuit imposed no rigid quotas, but carried an expectation that measurable progress would be made in the employment of women. Unlike the plans that had passed Supreme Court muster, this one was not explicitly temporary. The dispute arose when two people, a man and a woman, tried for the same job. The male applicant scored slightly higher on the competitive examination, but both were judged to be qualified. When affirmative action considerations were applied, the woman got the job.

Johnson v. Transportation Agency of Santa Clara County, California

480 U.S. 616 (1987)
Vote: 6 (Blackmun, Brennan, Marshall, O'Connor, Powell,
    Stevens)
    3 (Rehnquist, Scalia, White)
Opinion of the Court: Brennan
Concurring opinion: Stevens
Opinion concurring in judgment: O'Connor
Dissenting opinions: Scalia, White

In 1978 the Santa Clara County Transportation Agency adopted an affirmative action plan designed to attain equitable representation in its work force for minorities, women, and the handicapped. The plan allowed sex to be taken into account in deciding on promotions to positions in which women were significantly underrepresented. Women constituted 36.4 percent of the area labor market, but they occupied significantly lower percentages of the administrative, professional, and skilled craft positions in the agency. Females were overrepresented (76 percent) in office and clerical jobs. The agency's plan was designed to achieve "statistically measurable yearly improvement in hiring, training and promotion of minorities and women throughout the Agency in all major job classifications where they are underrepresented."

In December 1979 the agency announced a vacancy for a road dispatcher, a craftworker position. Of the 238 jobs in the craftworker category, none was held by a woman. Twelve employees applied for the promotion, including Paul Johnson and Diane Joyce. Both had sufficient training and experience to qualify for the position. After an evaluation of their records and two rounds of interviews, Johnson's score was 75 and Joyce's was 73. The selection panel recommended that Johnson receive the promotion. In the meantime, Joyce contacted the agency's affirmative action office and expressed a concern that her candidacy would not be treated fairly. After intervention by the affirmative action coordinator, Joyce got the job.

Johnson filed a complaint under the Civil Rights Act claiming that he had been denied promotion on account of sex. The federal district court ruled in his favor, finding that sex had been the determining factor in filling the position and that the agency's plan was defective because it was not temporary. The district court further found that although women were statistically underrepresented in various job categories, there was no evidence of agency discrimination as the cause of that imbalance. The court of appeals reversed, holding that the agency was free to correct the imbalances in its work force. The appeals court also held that the lack of a specific termination date for the plan was not sufficiently important to invalidate it, especially in the absence of strict quotas. Johnson then appealed to the Supreme Court.

JUSTICE BRENNAN delivered the opinion of the Court.

As a preliminary matter, we note that petitioner bears the burden of establishing the invalidity of the Agency's Plan. Only last term in *Wygant v. Jackson Board of Education* (1986), we held that "[t]he ultimate burden remains with the employees to demonstrate the unconstitutionality of an affirmative-action program," and we see no basis for a different rule regarding a plan's alleged violation of Title

VII.... Once a plaintiff establishes a prima facie case that race or sex has been taken into account in an employer's employment decision, the burden shifts to the employer to articulate a nondiscriminatory rationale for its decision. The existence of an affirmative action plan provides such a rationale. If such a plan is articulated as the basis for the employer's decision, the burden shifts to the plaintiff to prove that the employer's justification is pretextual and the plan is invalid....

The assessment of the legality of the Agency Plan must be guided by our decision in [*United Steelworkers of America v.*] *Weber* [1979]. In that case, the Court addressed the question whether the employer violated Title VII by adopting a voluntary affirmative action plan designed to "eliminate manifest racial imbalances in traditionally segregated job categories."...

We upheld the employer's decision to select less senior black applicants over the white respondent, for we found that taking race into account was consistent with Title VII's objective of "breaking down old patterns of racial segregation and hierarchy."...

We noted that the plan did not "unnecessarily trammel the interests of the white employees," since it did not require "the discharge of white workers and their replacement with new black hirees." Nor did the plan create "an absolute bar to the advancement of white employees," since half of those trained in the new program were to be white. Finally, we observed that the plan was a temporary measure, not designed to maintain racial balance, but to "eliminate a manifest racial imbalance."... Our decision was grounded in the recognition that voluntary employer action can play a crucial role in furthering Title VII's purpose of eliminating the effects of discrimination in the workplace, and that Title VII should not be read to thwart such efforts.

In reviewing the employment decision at issue in this case, we must first examine whether that decision was made pursuant to a plan prompted by concerns similar to those of the employer in *Weber*. Next, we must determine whether the effect of the plan on males and non-minorities is comparable to the effect of the plan in that case.

The first issue is therefore whether consideration of the sex of applicants for skilled craft jobs was justified by the existence of a "manifest imbalance" that reflected underrepresentation of women in "traditionally segregated job categories." In determining whether an imbalance exists that would justify taking sex or race into account, a comparison of the percentage of minorities or women in the employer's work force with the percentage in the area labor market or general population is appropriate in analyzing jobs that require no special expertise or training programs designed to provide expertise. Where a job requires special training, however, the comparison should be with those in the labor force who possess the relevant qualifications. The requirement that the "manifest imbalance" relate to a "traditionally segregated job category" provides assurance both that sex or race will be taken into account in a manner consistent with Title VII's purpose of eliminating the effects of employment discrimination, and that the interests of those employees not benefitting from the plan will not be unduly infringed....

It is clear that the decision to hire Joyce was made pursuant to an Agency plan that directed that sex or race be taken into account for the purpose of remedying underrepresentation. The Agency Plan acknowledged the "limited opportunities that have existed in the past" for women to find employment in certain job classifications "where women have not been traditionally employed in significant numbers." As a result, observed the Plan, women were concentrated in traditionally female jobs in the Agency, and represented a lower percentage in other job classifications than would be expected if such traditional segregation had not occurred.... The Plan sought to remedy these imbalances through "hiring, training and promotion of ... women throughout the Agency in all major job classifications where they are underrepresented."

As an initial matter, the Agency adopted as a benchmark for measuring progress in eliminating underrepresentation the long-term goal of a work force that mirrored in its major job classifications the percentage of women in the area labor market. Even as it did so, however, the Agency acknowledged that such a figure could not by itself necessarily justify taking into account the sex of applicants for positions in all job categories.... The Plan therefore directed that annual short-term goals be formulated that would provide a more realistic indication of the degree to which sex should be taken into account in filling particular positions. The Plan stressed that such goals "should not be construed as 'quotas' that must be met," but as reasonable

aspirations in correcting the imbalance in the Agency's work force....

As the Agency Plan recognized, women were most egregiously underrepresented in the Skilled Craft job category, since *none* of the 238 positions was occupied by a woman....

The Agency's Plan emphasized that the long-term goals were not to be taken as guides for actual hiring decisions, but that supervisors were to consider a host of practical factors in seeking to meet affirmative action objectives, including the fact that in some job categories women were not qualified in numbers comparable to their representation in the labor force....

Given the obvious imbalance in the Skilled Craft category, and given the Agency's commitment to eliminating such imbalances, it was plainly not unreasonable for the Agency to determine that it was appropriate to consider as one factor the sex of Ms. Joyce in making its decision. The promotion of Joyce thus satisfies the first requirement enunciated in *Weber*, since it was undertaken to further an affirmative action plan designed to eliminate Agency work force imbalances in traditionally segregated job categories.

We next consider whether the Agency Plan unnecessarily trammeled the rights of male employees or created an absolute bar to their advancement. In contrast to the plan in *Weber*, which provided that 50% of the positions in the craft training program were exclusively for blacks, the Plan sets aside no positions for women. The Plan expressly states that "[t]he 'goals' established for each Division should not be construed as 'quotas' that must be met." Rather, the Plan merely authorizes that consideration be given to affirmative action concerns when evaluating qualified applicants. As the Agency Director testified, the sex of Joyce was but one of numerous factors he took into account in arriving at his decision.... Similarly, the Agency Plan requires women to compete with all other qualified applicants. *No* persons are automatically excluded from consideration; *all* are able to have their qualifications weighed against those of other applicants.

In addition, petitioner had no absolute entitlement to the road dispatcher position. Seven of the applicants were classified as qualified and eligible, and the Agency Director was authorized to promote any of the seven. Thus, denial of the promotion unsettled no legitimate firmly rooted expectation on the part of the petitioner. Furthermore, while the petitioner in this case was denied a promotion, he retained his employment with the Agency, at the same salary and with the same seniority, and remained eligible for other promotions.

Finally, the Agency's Plan was intended to *attain* a balanced work force, not to maintain one. The Plan contains ten references to the Agency's desire to "attain" such a balance, but no reference whatsoever to a goal of maintaining it....

The Agency acknowledged the difficulties that it would confront in remedying the imbalance in its work force, and it anticipated only gradual increases in the representation of minorities and women. It is thus unsurprising that the Plan contains no explicit end date, for the Agency's flexible, case-by-case approach was not expected to yield success in a brief period of time. Express assurance that a program is only temporary may be necessary if the program actually sets aside positions according to specific numbers.... In this case, however, substantial evidence shows that the Agency has sought to take a moderate, gradual approach to eliminating the imbalance in its work force, one which establishes realistic guidance for employment decisions, and which visits minimal intrusion on the legitimate expectations of other employees. Given this fact, as well as the Agency's express commitment to "attain" a balanced work force, there is ample assurance that the Agency does not seek to use its Plan to maintain a permanent racial and sexual balance....

We therefore hold that the Agency appropriately took into account as one factor the sex of Diane Joyce in determining that she should be promoted to the road dispatcher position. The decision to do so was made pursuant to an affirmative action plan that represents a moderate, flexible, case-by-case approach to effecting a gradual improvement in the representation of minorities and women in the Agency's work force. Such a plan is fully consistent with Title VII, for it embodies the contribution that voluntary employer action can make in eliminating the vestiges of discrimination in the workplace. Accordingly, the judgment of the Court of Appeals is

Affirmed.

JUSTICE SCALIA ... dissenting.

With a clarity which, had it not proven so unavailing, one might well recommend as a model of statutory draftsmanship, Title VII of the Civil Rights Act of 1964 declares:

"It shall be an unlawful employment practice for an employer—

"(1) to fail or refuse to hire or to discharge any individual, or otherwise to discriminate against any individual with respect to his compensation, terms, conditions, or privileges of employment, because of such individual's race, color, religion, sex, or national origin; or

"(2) to limit, segregate, or classify his employees or applicants for employment in any way which would deprive or tend to deprive any individual of employment opportunities or otherwise adversely affect his status as an employee, because of such individual's race, color, religion, sex, or national origin." 42 U.S.C. § 2000e-2(a).

The Court today completes the process of converting this from a guarantee that race or sex will *not* be the basis for employment determinations, to a guarantee that it often *will*. Ever so subtly, without even alluding to the last obstacles preserved by earlier opinions that we now push out of our path, we effectively replace the goal of a discrimination-free society with the quite incompatible goal of proportionate representation by race and by sex in the workplace....

It is unlikely that today's result will be displeasing to politically elected officials, to whom it provides the means of quickly accommodating the demands of organized groups to achieve concrete, numerical improvement in the economic status of particular constituencies. Nor will it displease the world of corporate and governmental employers (many of whom have filed briefs as *amici* in the present case, all on the side of Santa Clara) for whom the cost of hiring less qualified workers is often substantially less—and infinitely more predictable—than the cost of litigating Title VII cases and of seeking to convince federal agencies by nonnumerical means that no discrimination exists. In fact, the only losers in the process are the Johnsons of the country, for whom Title VII has been not merely repealed but actually inverted. The irony is that these individuals—predominantly unknown, unaffluent, unorganized—suffer this injustice at the hands of a Court fond of thinking itself the champion of the politically impotent.

I dissent.

Minority Set-Asides

Minority set-aside programs are closely related to affirmative action plans and share underlying philosophies and goals. Minority set-asides attempt to enhance the prospects of disadvantaged groups by granting them special considerations in the awarding of government contracts and benefits. The justification for such programs is the long history of discrimination against minority-owned businesses in general commercial activity and in providing goods and services for the government. Set-asides are based on the principle that just eliminating discrimination in the letting of government contracts will not result in more business for minority-owned firms. Because of past discrimination, many minority businesses lack capital, management experience, and bonding eligibility. They cannot compete successfully with more solid, better-financed white firms. Consequently, minority set-aside programs propose for a time to reserve a percentage of government business and contracts for minority-owned enterprises.

Set-aside programs received their first significant review by the Court in 1980 in *Fullilove v. Klutznick.* The Court's deliberations reveal that the justices were no more able to reach consensus here than they had on affirmative action issues. *Fullilove* concerned the Public Works Employment Act passed by Congress in 1977. A provision of that law directed that in federally financed state public works projects 10 percent of the goods and services had to be procured from minority-owned businesses. A minority-owned business was defined as a company at least 50 percent owned by citizens of the United States who were black, Spanish-speaking, Asian, Native American, Eskimo, or Aleut. The constitutionality of the statute was attacked by a group of contractors who claimed economic injury due to its enforcement.

The Supreme Court upheld the validity of the law as a remedial action to correct a history of discrimination in government contracting. While the vote in the case was 6 to 3, the divisions among the justices were many and deep. Five different opinions were written, and no opinion garnered the support of more than three justices. Burger, Powell, and White held that the law was constitutional as a necessary means of advancing a compelling government interest. In their view, the law was a narrow and carefully tailored measure to eliminate a particular type of discrimination. Marshall, Brennan, and Blackmun also supported the law's validity. They adhered to their views expressed in *Bakke* giving strong support for the use of quotas as a means to alleviate discrimination. Stewart, Rehnquist, and Stevens dissented. Stewart wrote a strong opinion arguing that the Constitution should be hostile to all racial classifications.

Despite the divisions, six justices voted in *Fullilove* to uphold the federal set-aside program. This decision encouraged state and local governments that wanted to use the same kind of remedial approach. But in 1989 the Court reviewed such a plan enacted by the city of Richmond. The Richmond plan, like the federal program, set aside a certain proportion of city construction contracting business for minority-owned enterprises. The expressed purpose of the law was to correct the effects of past discrimination in the letting of city contracts and in the construction industry generally. In spite of its shared traits with the program approved in *Fullilove,* a majority of the justices found constitutional defects in the Richmond plan. As you read this case, consider whether the *Fullilove* precedent should control. Do the elements of the Richmond plan sufficiently distinguish it from the federal program to justify the Court's treating it differently?

City of Richmond v. J. A. Croson Co.

488 U.S. 469 (1989)

Vote: 6 (Kennedy, O'Connor, Rehnquist, Scalia, Stevens, White)

   3 (Blackmun, Brennan, Marshall)

Opinion of the Court: O'Connor

Concurring opinions: Kennedy, Stevens

Opinion concurring in the judgment: Scalia

Dissenting opinions: Blackmun, Marshall

In 1983 the Richmond City Council, consisting of five black and four white members, adopted the Minority Utilization Plan, which required the city's prime contractors to award subcontracts of at least 30 percent of the dollar amount of the total contract to one or more minority business enterprises (MBEs). Minority contractors were defined as businesses at least 51 percent owned by persons who were black, Spanish-speaking, Asian, Native American, Eskimo, or Aleut. The minority business did not have to be located in Richmond.

The plan was developed to correct the effects of racial discrimination. Richmond's population was 50 percent black, but between 1978 and 1983 only .678 percent of the city's construction business had been awarded to minority contractors. There was no specific finding that the city had discriminated in awarding contracts to minority businesses; the problem stemmed largely from a lack of minority-owned contracting businesses in the Richmond area.

The Croson company was the only bidder on a project to install plumbing fixtures at the city jail, but the company had difficulty finding a minority subcontractor to supply the materials. Once Croson located a qualified company willing to participate, the projected price was too high. Croson requested a waiver from the set-aside requirements or permission to raise the cost of the project. The city refused and elected to rebid the contract. Croson sued to have the set-aside program declared unconstitutional as a violation of the Equal Protection Clause of the Fourteenth Amendment. The company argued that set-aside programs should be allowed only to combat discrimination by the government. A plurality of the Court had supported such a position three years earlier in *Wygant v. Jackson Board of Education* (1986). Richmond, on the other hand, argued that *Fullilove v. Klutznick* should be interpreted to give state and local governments broad authority to combat the effects of discrimination.

JUSTICE O'CONNOR delivered the opinion of the Court....

In this case, we confront once again the tension between the Fourteenth Amendment's guarantee of equal treatment to all citizens, and the use of race-based measures to ameliorate the effects of past discrimination on the opportunities enjoyed by members of minority groups in our society....

The Equal Protection Clause of the Fourteenth Amendment provides that "[N]o State shall ... deny to *any person* within its jurisdiction the equal protection of the laws" (emphasis added). As this Court has noted in the past, the "rights created by the first section of the Fourteenth Amendment are, by its terms, guaranteed to the individual. The rights established are personal rights." The Richmond Plan denies certain citizens the opportunity to compete for a fixed percentage of public contracts based solely upon their race. To whatever racial group these citizens belong, their "personal rights" to be treated with equal dignity and respect are implicated by a rigid rule erecting race as the sole criterion in an aspect of public decisionmaking.

Absent searching judicial inquiry into the justification for such race-based measures, there is simply no way of determining what classifications are "benign" or "remedial" and what classifications are in fact motivated by illegitimate notions of racial inferiority or simple racial politics. Indeed, the purpose of strict scrutiny is to "smoke out" illegitimate uses of race by assuring that the legislative body is pursuing a goal important enough to warrant use of a highly suspect tool. The test also ensures that the means chosen "fit" this compelling goal so closely that there is little or no possibility that the motive for the classification was illegitimate racial prejudice or stereotype.

Classifications based on race carry a danger of stigmatic harm. Unless they are strictly reserved for remedial settings, they may in fact promote notions of racial inferiority and lead to a politics of racial hostility. We thus reaffirm the view expressed by the plurality in *Wygant* [*v. Jackson Board of Education*, 1986] that the standard of review under the Equal Protection Clause is not dependent on the race of those burdened or benefited by a particular classification....

In *Wygant*, four Members of the Court applied heightened scrutiny to a race-based system of employee layoffs. Justice Powell, writing for the plurality, again drew the distinction between "societal discrimination" which is an inadequate basis for race-conscious classifications, and the type of identified discrimination that can support and define the scope of race-based relief. The challenged classification in that case tied the layoff of minority teachers to the percentage of minority students enrolled in the school district. The lower courts had upheld the scheme, based on the theory that minority students were in need of "role models" to alleviate the effects of prior discrimination in society. This Court reversed, with a plurality of four Justices reiterating the view expressed by Justice Powell in [*Regents of the University of California v.*] *Bakke* [1978] that "[s]ocietal discrimination, without more, is too amorphous a basis for imposing a racially classified remedy."...

Like the "role model" theory employed in *Wygant*, a generalized assertion that there has been past discrimination in an entire industry provides no guidance for a legislative body to determine the precise scope of the injury it seeks to remedy. It "has no logical stopping point."...

Appellant argues that it is attempting to remedy various forms of past discrimination that are alleged to be responsible for the small number of minority businesses in the local contracting industry. Among these the city cites the exclusion of blacks from skilled construction trade unions and training programs. This past discrimination has prevented them "from following the traditional path from laborer to entrepreneur." The city also lists a host of nonracial factors which would seem to face a member of any racial group attempting to establish a new business enterprise, such as deficiencies in working capital, inability to meet bonding requirements, unfamiliarity with bidding procedures, and disability caused by an inadequate track record.

While there is no doubt that the sorry history of both private and public discrimination in this country has contributed to a lack of opportunities for black entrepreneurs, this observation, standing alone, cannot justify a rigid racial quota in the awarding of public contracts in Richmond, Virginia. Like the claim that discrimination in primary and secondary schooling justifies a rigid racial preference in medical school admissions, an amorphous claim that there has been past discrimination in a particular industry cannot justify the use of an unyielding racial quota.

It is sheer speculation how many minority firms there would be in Richmond absent past societal discrimination, just as it was sheer speculation how many minority medical students would have been admitted to the medical school at Davis absent past discrimination in educational opportunities. Defining these sorts of injuries as "identified discrimination" would give local governments license to create a patchwork of racial preferences based on statistical generalizations about any particular field of endeavor.

These defects are readily apparent in this case. The 30% quota cannot in any realistic sense be tied to any injury suffered by anyone. The District Court relied upon five predicate "facts" in reaching its conclusion that there was an adequate basis for the 30% quota: (1) the ordinance declares itself to be remedial; (2) several proponents of the measure stated their views that there had been past discrimination in the construction industry; (3) minority businesses received .67% of prime contracts from the city while minorities constituted 50% of the city's population; (4) there were very few minority contractors in local and state contractors' associations; and (5) in 1977, Congress made a determination that the effects of past discrimination had stifled minority participation in the construction industry nationally.

None of these "findings," singly or together, provide the city of Richmond with a "strong basis in evidence for its conclusion that remedial action was necessary." There is nothing approaching a prima facie case of a constitutional or statutory violation by *anyone* in the Richmond construction industry.

The District Court accorded great weight to the fact that the city council designated the Plan as "remedial." But the mere recitation of a "benign" or legitimate purpose for a racial classification is entitled to little or no weight. Racial classifications are suspect, and that means that simple legislative assurances of good intention cannot suffice. The District Court also relied on the highly conclusionary statement of a proponent of the Plan that there was racial discrimination in the construction industry "in this area, and the State, and around the nation." It also noted that the city manager had related his view that racial discrimination still plagued the construction industry in his home city of Pittsburgh. These statements are of little probative value in establishing identified discrimination in the Richmond construction industry. The fact-finding process of legislative bodies is generally entitled to a presumption of regularity and deferential review by the judiciary. But when a legislative body chooses to employ a suspect classification, it cannot rest upon a generalized assertion as to the classification's relevance to its goals.... The history of racial classifications in this country suggests that blind judicial deference to legislative or executive pronouncements of necessity has no place in equal protection analysis.

Reliance on the disparity between the number of prime contracts awarded to minority firms and the minority population of the city of Richmond is similarly misplaced. There is no doubt that "[w]here gross statistical disparities can be shown, they alone in a proper case may constitute prima facie proof of a pattern or practice of discrimination" under Title VII. But it is equally clear that "[w]hen special qualifications are required to fill particular jobs, comparisons to the general population (rather than to the smaller group of individuals who possess the necessary qualifications) may have little probative value."

In the employment context, we have recognized that for certain entry level positions or positions requiring minimal training, statistical comparisons of the racial composition of an employer's workforce to the racial composition of the relevant population may be probative of a pattern of discrimination. But where special qualifications are necessary, the relevant statistical pool for purposes of demonstrating discriminatory exclusion must be the number of minorities qualified to undertake the particular task.

In this case, the city does not even know how many MBEs in the relevant market are qualified to undertake prime or subcontracting work in public construction projects. Nor does the city know what percentage of total city construction dollars minority firms now receive as subcontractors on prime contracts let by the city....

The city and the District Court also relied on evidence that MBE membership in local contractors' associations was extremely low. Again, standing alone this evidence is not probative of any discrimination in the local construction industry. There are numerous explanations for this dearth of minority participation, including past societal discrimination in education and economic opportunities as well as both black and white career and entrepreneurial choices. Blacks may be disproportionately attracted to industries other than construction. The mere fact that black membership in these trade organizations is low, standing alone, cannot establish a prima facie case of discrimination.

For low minority membership in these associations to be relevant, the city would have to link it to the number of local MBEs eligible for membership. If the statistical disparity between eligible MBEs and MBE membership were great enough, an inference of discriminatory exclusion could arise. In such a case, the city would have a compelling interest in preventing its tax dollars from assisting these organizations in maintaining a racially segregated construction market.

Finally, the city and the District Court relied on Congress' finding in connection with the set-aside approved in *Fullilove* [*v. Klutznick*, 1980] that there had been nationwide discrimination in the construction industry. The probative value of these findings for demonstrating the existence of discrimination in Richmond is extremely limited. By its inclusion of a waiver procedure in the national program addressed in *Fullilove*, Congress explicitly recognized that the scope of the problem would vary from market area to market area.

Moreover, as noted above, Congress was exercising its powers under § 5 of the Fourteenth Amendment in making a finding that past discrimination would cause federal funds to be distributed in a manner which reinforced prior patterns of discrimination. While the States and their subdivisions may take remedial action when they possess evidence that their own spending practices are exacerbating a pattern of prior discrimination, they must identify that discrimination, public or private, with some specificity before they may use race-conscious relief....

In sum, none of the evidence presented by the city points to any identified discrimination in the Richmond construction industry. We, therefore, hold that the city has failed to demonstrate a compelling interest in apportioning public contracting opportunities on the basis of race. To accept Richmond's claim that past societal discrimination alone can serve as the basis for rigid racial preferences would be to open the door to competing claims for "remedial relief" for every disadvantaged group. The dream of a Nation of equal citizens in a society where race is irrelevant to personal opportunity and achievement would be lost in a mosaic of shifting preferences based on inherently unmeasurable claims of past wrongs.... We think such a result would be contrary to both the letter and spirit of a constitutional provision whose central command is equality.

The foregoing analysis applies only to the inclusion of blacks within the Richmond set-aside program. There is *absolutely no evidence* of past discrimination against Spanish-speaking, Oriental, Indian, Eskimo, or Aleut persons in any aspect of the Richmond construction industry. The District Court took judicial notice of the fact that the vast majority of "minority" persons in Richmond were black. It may well be that Richmond has never had an Aleut or Eskimo citizen. The random inclusion of racial groups that, as a practical matter, may never have suffered from discrimination in the construction industry in Richmond, suggests that perhaps the city's purpose was not in fact to remedy past discrimination.

If a 30% set-aside was "narrowly tailored" to compensate black contractors for past discrimination, one may legitimately ask why they are forced to share this "remedial relief" with an Aleut citizen who moves to Richmond tomorrow? The gross overinclusiveness of Richmond's racial preference strongly impugns the city's claim of remedial motivation.

As noted by the court below, it is almost impossible to assess whether the Richmond Plan is narrowly tailored to remedy prior discrimination since it is not linked to identified discrimination in any way. We limit ourselves to two observations in this regard.

First, there does not appear to have been any consideration of the use of race-neutral means to increase minority business participation in city contracting. Many of the barriers to minority participation in the construction industry relied upon by the city to justify a racial classification appear to be race-neutral. If MBEs disproportionately lack capital or cannot meet bonding requirements, a race-neutral program of city financing for small firms would, *a fortiori,* lead to greater minority participation. The principal opinion in *Fullilove* found that Congress had carefully examined and rejected race-neutral alternatives before enacting the MBE set-aside. There is no evidence in this record that the Richmond City Council has considered any alternatives to a race-based quota.

Second, the 30% quota cannot be said to be narrowly tailored to any goal, except perhaps outright racial balancing. It rests upon the "completely unrealistic" assumption that minorities will choose a particular trade in lockstep proportion to their representation in the local population.

Since the city must already consider bids and waivers on a case-by-case basis, it is difficult to see the need for a rigid numerical quota. As noted above, the congressional scheme upheld in *Fullilove* allowed for a waiver of the set-aside provision where an MBE's higher price was not attributable to the effects of past discrimination. Based upon proper findings, such programs are less problematic from an equal protection standpoint because they treat all candidates individually, rather than making the color of an applicant's skin the sole relevant consideration. Unlike the program upheld in *Fullilove,* the Richmond Plan's waiver system focuses solely on the availability of MBEs; there is no inquiry into whether or not the particular MBE seeking a racial preference has suffered from the effects of past discrimination by the city or prime contractors....

Under Richmond's scheme, a successful black, Hispanic, or Oriental entrepreneur from anywhere in the country enjoys an absolute preference over other citizens based solely on their race. We think it obvious that such a program is not narrowly tailored to remedy the effects of prior discrimination.

Nothing we say today precludes a state or local entity from taking action to rectify the effects of identified discrimination within its jurisdiction. If the city of Richmond had evidence before it that nonminority contractors were systematically excluding minority businesses from subcontracting opportunities it could take action to end the discriminatory exclusion. Where there is a significant statistical disparity between the number of qualified minority contractors willing and able to perform a particular service and the number of such contractors actually engaged by the locality or the locality's prime contractors, an inference of discriminatory exclusion could arise. Under such circumstances, the city could act to dismantle the closed business system by taking appropriate measures against those who discriminate on the basis of race or other illegitimate criteria. In the extreme case, some form of narrowly tailored racial preference might be necessary to break down patterns of deliberate exclusion....

Even in the absence of evidence of discrimination, the city has at its disposal a whole array of race-neutral devices to increase the accessibility of city contracting opportunities to small entrepreneurs of all races. Simplification of bidding procedures, relaxation of bonding requirements, and training and financial aid for disadvantaged entrepreneurs of all races would open the public contracting market to all those who have suffered the effects of past societal discrimination or neglect. Many of the formal barriers to new entrants may be the product of bureaucratic inertia more than actual necessity, and may have a disproportionate effect on the opportunities open to new minority firms. Their elimination or modification would have little detrimental effect on the city's interests and would serve to increase the opportunities available to minority business without classifying individuals on the basis of race. The city may also act to prohibit discrimination in the provision of credit or bonding by local suppliers and banks. Business as usual should not mean business pursuant to the unthinking exclusion of certain members of our society from its rewards.

In the case at hand, the city has not ascertained how many minority enterprises are present in the local construction market nor the level of their participation in city construction projects. The city points to no evidence that qualified minority contractors have been passed over for city contracts or subcontracts, either as a group or in any individual case. Under such circumstances, it is simply impossible to say that the city has demonstrated "a strong basis in evidence for its conclusion that remedial action was necessary."

Proper findings in this regard are necessary to define both the scope of the injury and the extent of the remedy necessary to cure its effects. Such findings also serve to assure all citizens that the deviation from the norm of equal treatment of all racial and ethnic groups is a temporary matter, a measure taken in the service of the goal of equality itself. Absent such findings, there is a danger that a racial classification is merely the product of unthinking stereotypes or a form of racial politics. "[I]f there is no duty to attempt either to measure the recovery by the wrong or to distribute that recovery within the injured class in an evenhanded way, our history will adequately support a legislative preference for almost any ethnic, religious, or racial group with the political strength to negotiate 'a piece of the action' for its members." Because the city of Richmond has failed to identify the need for remedial action in the awarding of its public construction contracts, its treatment of its citizens on a racial basis violates the dictates of the Equal Protection Clause. Accordingly, the judgment of the Court of Appeals for the Fourth Circuit is

Affirmed.

JUSTICE MARSHALL ... dissenting.

It is a welcome symbol of racial progress when the former capital of the Confederacy acts forthrightly to confront the effects of racial discrimination in its midst. In my view, nothing in the Constitution can be construed to prevent Richmond, Virginia, from allocating a portion of its contracting dollars for businesses owned or controlled by members of minority groups. Indeed, Richmond's set-aside program is indistinguishable in all meaningful respects from—and in fact was patterned upon—the federal set-aside plan which this Court upheld in *Fullilove v. Klutznick.*

A majority of this Court holds today, however, that the Equal Protection Clause of the Fourteenth Amendment blocks Richmond's initiative. The essence of the majority's position is that Richmond has failed to catalogue adequate findings to prove that past discrimination has impeded minorities from joining or participating fully in Richmond's construction contracting industry. I find deep irony in second-guessing Richmond's judgment on this point. As much as any municipality in the United States, Richmond knows what racial discrimination is; a century of decisions by this and other federal courts has richly documented the city's disgraceful history of public and private racial discrimination. In any event, the Richmond City Council *has* supported its determination that minorities have been wrongly excluded from local construction contracting. Its proof includes statistics showing that minority-owned busi-

CIVIL RIGHTS

nesses have received virtually no city contracting dollars and rarely if ever belonged to area trade associations; testimony by municipal officials that discrimination has been widespread in the local construction industry; and the same exhaustive and widely publicized federal studies relied on in *Fullilove*, studies which showed that pervasive discrimination in the Nation's tight-knit construction industry had operated to exclude minorities from public contracting. These are precisely the types of statistical and testimonial evidence which, until today, this Court had credited in cases approving of race-conscious measures designed to remedy past discrimination.

More fundamentally, today's decision marks a deliberate and giant step backward in this Court's affirmative action jurisprudence. Cynical of one municipality's attempt to redress the effects of past racial discrimination in a particular industry, the majority launches a grapeshot attack on race-conscious remedies in general. The majority's unnecessary pronouncements will inevitably discourage or prevent governmental entities, particularly States and localities, from acting to rectify the scourge of past discrimination. This is the harsh reality of the majority's decision, but it is not the Constitution's command....

The majority today sounds a full-scale retreat from the Court's longstanding solicitude to race-conscious remedial efforts "directed toward deliverance of the century-old promise of equality of economic opportunity." The new and restrictive tests it applies scuttle one city's effort to surmount its discriminatory past, and imperil those of dozens more localities. I, however, profoundly disagree with the cramped vision of the Equal Protection Clause which the majority offers today and with its application of that vision to Richmond, Virginia's, laudable set-aside plan. The battle against pernicious racial discrimination or its effects is nowhere near won. I must dissent.

The Court's condemnation of Richmond's minority set-aside program was a clear signal to other state and local governments that plans to increase business for minority-owned enterprises were going to be difficult to justify. The decision also gave encouragement to those majority-owned businesses that wanted to challenge such plans.

One year later, however, the Court heard another case involving the constitutionality of a plan to promote minority businesses, this one developed by the federal government. Its specific purpose was to encourage minority ownership of radio and television stations. Unlike most forms of commercial activity, the number of radio and television stations that can operate in a particular market is limited. Because of this constraint and the fact that broadcasters use the public air waves, the federal government—through the Federal Communications Commission—decides who is to be granted a license to broadcast. The process of obtaining a license can be highly competitive.

Once again, the Court addressed the difficult questions of minority preference, undue hardships on the majority, reserving benefits exclusively for minority businesses, stereotyping minority interests and behavior, and legitimate government interests. Here, unlike the Richmond decision, the Court upheld the minority preference policy. But again the justices were badly divided. Not only was the vote 5–4, but also the language of the dissenters indicated that the pro- and anti-minority preference blocs were growing farther apart.

Metro Broadcasting, Inc. v. FCC

497 U.S. 547 (1990)
Vote: 5 (Blackmun, Brennan, Marshall, Stevens, White)
    4 (Kennedy, O'Connor, Rehnquist, Scalia)
Opinion of the Court: Brennan
Concurring opinion: Stevens
Dissenting opinions: Kennedy, O'Connor

The Federal Communications Commission has two policies designed to promote minority ownership of broadcasting stations. The first policy concerns the process by which the FCC grants licenses after comparing the merits of the various competing applicants.

It identifies six clearly relevant criteria of judgment, but stipulates that applications of minority-owned businesses are to be enhanced. The "plus" granted to such applications is considered along with the six regular factors.

The second policy concerns FCC distress sales. Under FCC regulations, the owner of a radio or television station whose qualifications to broadcast in the public interest are formally questioned may not sell its broadcasting license until the FCC resolves the challenge. However, under its distress sale exception, the commission allows a challenged broadcasting company to sell its license before the FCC resolves the qualifications question if the sale is made to a qualified business that is minority owned and the sale price does not exceed 75 percent of fair market value. This policy, therefore, allows a reduced price, noncompetitive sale of a broadcasting license to a minority business.

This appeal involved two cases. In one, Metro Broadcasting challenged the minority preference policy. Metro was initially recommended among three competing firms to receive a license to operate a UHF television station in Orlando, Florida. Upon review, however, the license was granted to Hispanic-owned Rainbow Broadcasting, which had received a minority enhancement. In the other case, Shurberg Broadcasting attacked the distress sale policy. Shurberg wanted to operate a television station in Hartford, Connecticut. Faith Center, the holder of a Hartford license, was under FCC review. Shurberg hoped to be granted Faith Center's license, but, with FCC approval, Faith sold its license to Astroline Communications, a minority-owned enterprise.

JUSTICE BRENNAN delivered the opinion of the Court.

We hold that the FCC minority ownership policies pass muster under the test we announce today. First, we find that they serve the important governmental objective of broadcast diversity. Second, we conclude that they are substantially related to the achievement of that objective.

Congress found that "the effects of past inequities stemming from racial and ethnic discrimination have resulted in a severe underrepresentation of minorities in the media of mass communications." Congress and the Commission do not justify the minority ownership policies strictly as remedies for victims of this discrimination, however. Rather, Congress and the FCC have selected the minority ownership policies primarily to promote programming diversity, and they urge that such diversity is an important governmental objective that can serve as a constitutional basis for the preference policies. We agree.

We have long recognized that "[b]ecause of the scarcity of [electromagnetic] frequencies, the Government is permitted to put restraints on licensees in favor of others whose views should be expressed on this unique medium." *Red Lion Broadcasting Co. v. FCC* (1969)....

Against this background, we conclude that the interest in enhancing broadcast diversity is, at the very least, an important governmental objective and is therefore a sufficient basis for the Commission's minority ownership policies. Just as a "diverse student body" contributing to a "'robust exchange of ideas'" is a "constitutionally permissible goal" on which a race-conscious university admissions program may be predicated, *University of California Regents v. Bakke* (1978) (opinion of Powell, J.), the diversity of views and information on the airwaves serves important First Amendment values.... The benefits of such diversity are not limited to the members of minority groups who gain access to the broadcasting industry by virtue of the ownership policies; rather, the benefits redound to all members of the viewing and listening audience. As Congress found, "the American public will benefit by having access to a wider diversity of information sources."

We also find that the minority ownership policies are substantially related to the achievement of the Government's interest. One component of this inquiry concerns the relationship between expanded minority ownership and greater broadcast diversity....

The FCC has determined that increased minority participation in broadcasting promotes programming diversity....

Furthermore, the FCC's reasoning with respect to the minority ownership policies is consistent with longstanding practice under the Communications Act. From its inception, public regulation of broadcasting has been premised on the assumption that diversification of ownership will broaden the range of programming available to the broadcast audience. Thus, "it is upon *ownership* that public policy places primary reliance with respect to diversification of content, and that historically has proved to be significantly influential with respect to editorial comment and the presentation of news.". . .

Congress also has made clear its view that the minority ownership policies advance the goal of diverse programming. In recent years, Congress has specifically required the Commission, through appropriations legislation, to maintain the minority ownership policies without alteration. We would be remiss, however, if we ignored the long history of congressional support for those policies prior to the passage of the appropriations acts because, for the past two decades, Congress has consistently recognized the barriers encountered by minorities in entering the broadcast industry and has expressed emphatic support for the Commission's attempts to promote programming diversity by increasing minority ownership. . . .

As revealed by the historical evolution of current federal policy, both Congress and the Commission have concluded that the minority ownership programs are critical means of promoting broadcast diversity. We must give great weight to their joint determination.

The judgment that there is a link between expanded minority ownership and broadcast diversity does not rest on impermissible stereotyping. Congressional policy does not assume that in every case minority ownership and management will lead to more minority-oriented programming or to the expression of a discrete "minority viewpoint" on the airwaves. Neither does it pretend that all programming that appeals to minority audiences can be labeled "minority programming" or that programming that might be described as "minority" does not appeal to nonminorities. Rather, both Congress and the FCC maintain simply that expanded minority ownership of broadcast outlets will, in the aggregate, result in greater broadcast diversity. . . .

Although all station owners are guided to some extent by market demand in their programming decisions, Congress and the Commission have determined that there may be important differences between the broadcasting practices of minority owners and those of their nonminority counterparts. This judgment—and the conclusion that there is a nexus between minority ownership and broadcasting diversity—is corroborated by a host of empirical evidence. Evidence suggests that an owner's minority status influences the selection of topics for news coverage and the presentation of editorial viewpoint, especially on matters of particular concern to minorities. "Minority ownership does appear to have specific impact on the presentation of minority images in local news," inasmuch as minority-owned stations tend to devote more news time to topics of minority interest and to avoid racial and ethnic stereotypes in portraying minorities. In addition, studies show that a minority owner is more likely to employ minorities in managerial and other important roles where they can have an impact on station policies. . . .

. . . [T]he Commission established minority ownership preferences only after long experience demonstrated that race-neutral means could not produce adequate broadcasting diversity. The FCC did not act precipitately in devising the programs we uphold today; to the contrary, the Commission undertook thorough evaluations of its policies *three* times—in 1960, 1971, and 1978—before adopting the minority ownership programs. In endorsing the minority ownership preferences, Congress agreed with the Commission's assessment that race-neutral alternatives had failed to achieve the necessary programming diversity. . . .

The minority ownership policies are "appropriately limited in extent and duration, and subject to reassessment and reevaluation by the Congress prior to any extension or reenactment." Although it has underscored emphatically its support for the minority ownership policies, Congress has manifested that support through a series of appropriations acts of finite duration, thereby ensuring future reevaluations of the need for the minority ownership program as the number of minority broadcasters increases. In addition, Congress has continued to hold hearings on the subject of minority ownership. . . .

Finally, we do not believe that the minority ownership policies at issue impose impermissible burdens on nonminorities. Although the nonminority challengers in these cases concede that they have not suffered the loss of an already-awarded broadcast license, they claim that they have been handicapped in their ability to obtain one in the first instance. But just as we have determined that "[a]s part of this Nation's dedication to eradicating racial discrimination, innocent persons may be called upon to bear some of the burden of the remedy," we similarly find that a congressionally mandated benign race-conscious program that is substantially related to the achievement of an important governmental interest is consistent with equal protection principles so long as it does not impose *undue* burdens on nonminorities.

In the context of broadcasting licenses, the burden on nonminorities is slight. The FCC's responsibility is to grant licenses in the "public interest, convenience, or necessity," and the limited number of frequencies on the electromagnetic spectrum means that "[n]o one has a First Amendment right to a license." Applicants have no settled expectation that their applications will be granted without consideration of public interest factors such as minority ownership. Award of a preference in a comparative hearing or transfer of a station in a distress sale thus contravenes "no legitimate firmly rooted expectation[s]" of competing applicants.

Respondent Shurberg insists that because the minority distress sale policy operates to exclude nonminority firms completely from consideration in the transfer of certain stations, it is a greater burden than the comparative hearing preference for minorities, which is simply a "plus" factor considered together with other characteristics of the applicants. We disagree that the distress sale policy imposes an undue burden on nonminorities. By its terms, the policy may be invoked at the Commission's discretion only with respect to a small fraction of broadcast licenses—those designated for revocation or renewal hearings to examine basic qualification issues—and only when the licensee chooses to sell out at a distress price rather than to go through with the hearing. The distress sale policy is not a quota or fixed quantity set-aside. Indeed, the nonminority firm exercises control over whether a distress sale will ever occur at all, because the policy operates only where the qualifications of an existing licensee to continue broadcasting have been designated for hearing and no other applications for the station in question have been filed with the Commission at the time of the designation. Thus, a nonminority can prevent the distress sale procedures from ever being invoked by filing a competing application in a timely manner....

The Commission's minority ownership policies bear the imprimatur of longstanding congressional support and direction and are substantially related to the achievement of the important governmental objective of broadcast diversity. The . . . cases are remanded for proceedings consistent with this opinion.

It is so ordered.

JUSTICE O'CONNOR . . . dissenting.

At the heart of the Constitution's guarantee of equal protection lies the simple command that the Government must treat citizens "as *individuals*, not 'as simply components of a racial, religious, sexual or national class.'" Social scientists may debate how peoples' thoughts and behavior reflect their background, but the Constitution provides that the Government may not allocate benefits and burdens among individuals based on the assumption that race or ethnicity determines how they act or think. To uphold the challenged programs, the Court departs from these fundamental principles and from our traditional requirement that racial classifications are permissible only if necessary and narrowly tailored to achieve a compelling interest. This departure marks a renewed toleration of racial classifications and a repudiation of our recent affirmation that the Constitution's equal protection guarantees extend equally to all citizens. The Court's application of a lessened equal protection standard to congressional actions finds no support in our cases or in the Constitution. I respectfully dissent.

JUSTICE KENNEDY . . . dissenting.

Almost 100 years ago in *Plessy v. Ferguson* (1896), this Court upheld a government-sponsored race-conscious measure, a Louisiana law that required "equal but separate accommodations" for "white" and "colored" railroad passengers. The Court asked whether the measures were "reasonable," and it stated that "[i]n determining the question of reasonableness, [the legislature] is at liberty to act with reference to the established usages, customs and traditions of the people, and with a view to the promotion of their comfort." The *Plessy* Court concluded that the "race-conscious

The Supreme Court's affirmative action and minority set-aside decisions have been criticized for failing to develop a consistent and coherent set of legal principles. The unstable majorities that have controlled these cases surely have contributed to this result. The justices have not provided a rule of law in one clear test that would allow a reasonably accurate indicator of what is constitutionally defective. While there are no absolutes, there are certain characteristics that clearly make minority enhancement plans more acceptable.

An affirmative action or minority set-aside program is more likely to be found constitutional if it:

1. is a federal program, rather than a state or local program;

2. is enacted as a response to clear and demonstrable acts of unconstitutional or illegal discrimination;

3. is narrowly tailored to respond to acts of illegal discrimination or to the continuing effects of that illegal discrimination;

4. is designed to assist only those groups who have been the victim of illegal discrimination;

5. is not based on racial, ethnic, or gender stereotypes, or presumes the inferiority of such groups;

6. avoids the use of quotas and does not absolutely bar any group from competing or participating;

7. is temporary, with clear indicators of plan termination when certain thresholds are met;

8. seeks to eliminate racial imbalance, not maintain racial balance;

9. is based on data from relevant labor pools or other appropriate statistical comparisons;

10. does not trammel the rights of the majority;

11. seeks to achieve balance by providing new benefits to minorities rather than taking already earned benefits away from the majority;

12. serves an important governmental objective and is substantially related to the achievement of that objective;

13. is imposed by a federal court as a remedy for demonstrated constitutional violations.

measures" it reviewed were reasonable because they served the governmental interest of increasing the riding pleasure of railroad passengers. The fundamental errors in *Plessy*, its standard of review and its validation of rank racial insult by the State, distorted the law for six decades before the Court announced its apparent demise in *Brown v. Board of Education* (1954). *Plessy*'s standard of review and its explication have disturbing parallels to today's majority opinion that should warn us something is amiss here.

Today the Court grants Congress latitude to employ "benign race-conscious measures ... [that] are not ... designed to compensate victims of past governmental or societal discrimination," but that "serve important governmental objectives ... and are substantially related to achievement of those objectives." The interest the Court accepts to uphold the Commission's race-conscious measures is "broadcast diversity." Furthering that interest, we are told, is worth the cost of discriminating among citizens on the basis of race because it will increase the listening pleasure of media audiences. In upholding this preference, the majority exhumes *Plessy*'s deferential approach to racial classifications.

Once the Government takes the step, which itself should be forbidden, of enacting into law the stereotypical assumption that the race of owners is linked to broadcast content, it follows a path that becomes ever more tortuous. It must decide which races to favor. While the Court repeatedly refers to the preferences as favoring "minorities," and purports to evaluate the burdens imposed on "nonminorities," it must be emphasized that the discriminatory policies upheld today operate to exclude the many racial and ethnic *minorities* that have not made the Commission's list. The enumeration of the races to be protected is borrowed from a remedial statute, but since the remedial rationale must be disavowed in order to sustain the policy, the race classifications bear scant relation to the asserted governmental interest. The Court's reasoning provides little justification for welcoming the return of racial classifications to our Nation's laws.

I cannot agree with the Court that the Constitution permits the Government to discriminate among its citizens on the basis of race in order to serve interests so trivial as "broadcast diversity."...

The Court insists that the programs under review are "benign."...

Policies of racial separation and preference are almost always justified as benign, even when it is clear to any sensible observer that they are not. The following statement, for example, would fit well among those offered to uphold the Commission's racial preference policy: "The policy is not based on any concept of superiority or inferiority, but merely on the fact that people differ, particularly in their group associations, loyalties, cultures, outlook, modes of life and standards of development." See South Africa and the Rule of Law 37 (1968) (official publication of the South African Government)....

Though the racial composition of this Nation is far more diverse than the first Justice Harlan foresaw, his warning in dissent is now all the more apposite: "The destinies of the two races, in this country, are indissolubly linked together, and the interests of both require that the common government of all shall not permit the seeds of race hate to be planted under the sanction of law." *Plessy* (dissenting opinion). Perhaps the Court can succeed in its assumed role of case-by-case arbiter of when it is desirable and benign for the Government to disfavor some citizens and favor others based on the color of their skin. Perhaps the tolerance and decency to which our people aspire will let the disfavored rise above hostility and the favored escape condescension. But history suggests much peril in this enterprise, and so the Constitution forbids us to undertake it. I regret that after a century of judicial opinions we interpret the Constitution to do no more than move us from "separate but equal" to "unequal but benign."

Justice Brennan's majority opinion in *Metro Broadcasting* was his last after an illustrious career of thirty-four years on the Court. During that time, Brennan was a steadfast defender of liberal principles in constitutional interpretation. Brennan's 1990 retirement was followed the next year by Thurgood Marshall's stepping down. Like Brennan, Marshall consistently supported affirmative action programs. Given the close vote on most such appeals, and the nearly even division between liberal and conservative justices on an appropriate rule of law to govern these issues, the Brennan and Marshall retirements were a significant blow to those who supported minority enhancement programs. The affirmative action/minority set-aside controversy is far from settled. President Clinton's recent appointments to the Court have given hope to affirmative action supporters that some victories may still be possible. At the very least, it is safe to say that the Court has not heard its last minority preference case.

CONTEMPORARY DEVELOPMENTS IN DISCRIMINATION LAW

As they have since the Fourteenth Amendment was ratified in 1868, discrimination issues continue to evolve. Immigration brings new groups of people to the United States, and previously silent groups begin to organize and make their demands heard. Americans continually rethink concepts of equality and fair treatment, sometimes concluding that previously acceptable practices have discriminatory effects. Fluctuations in economic and political power alter the methods used to pursue equality demands. As such changes occur, the nature of the discrimination issues brought to the courts also changes, and so do the legal strategies used by those who pursue such claims.

Emerging Issues

In this chapter we have highlighted discrimination based on race, sex, economic condition, and alien status. We concentrated on these areas because historically they have provided the arena in which the Supreme Court has developed its most significant equal protection doctrines. The justices have used constitutional principles derived from the race cases, for example, to settle other discrimination claims.

While the justices have devoted enormous efforts

to the resolution of disputes in these traditional areas of discrimination law, perplexing issues have yet to be settled. Race and gender discrimination questions remain unresolved, especially in the area of employment rights, where charges of unequal treatment are common. The Court's handling of affirmative action questions has resulted in a confusing body of law. Racial and sexual harassment allegations are occurring more frequently. Highly publicized harassment charges have been lodged against members of Congress, a Supreme Court nominee, and even the president, demonstrating that claims of discriminatory treatment can touch the highest officeholders. Questions regarding equitable treatment of the poor with respect to education and other government services continue to arise. As legal and illegal immigration patterns change, new questions of discrimination based on alien status and national origin are inevitable. When these new residents place additional burdens on the states for government services, budget-conscious officials may adopt policies perceived as discriminatory.

Classes of individuals who were not organized have formed groups and are bringing discrimination issues to the judiciary. Gay and lesbian groups, for example, have become active in fighting discrimination against their members. Although the Supreme Court in *Bowers v. Hardwick* (1986) upheld Georgia's sodomy law, the justices have not yet dealt with the question of discrimination based on sexual orientation. Fierce battles over this issue have occurred at the state and local levels, making it inevitable that the Supreme Court will soon confront important equal protection questions regarding the treatment of homosexuals. The disabled also have become increasingly politicized and have demanded reforms from both the legislative and judicial branches. Claims of discrimination based on physical disability, mental handicap, and disease (cancer, AIDS, alcoholism, drug addiction) have become common and promise to escalate in number. As the nation's "baby boomers" age, creating the largest number of senior citizens in American history, age discrimination lawsuits are likely to be filed at significant rates.

Issue evolution characterizes the history of discrimination law, and there is no evidence that process will stop. Rather, it is inevitable that the Supreme Court's docket will include appeals asking the justices to consider new questions that arise from the changing socio-political environment.

Reliance on Statutory Law

The Equal Protection Clause of the Fourteenth Amendment and the Due Process Clause of the Fifth Amendment are the Constitution's primary provisions outlawing invidious discrimination. Despite their importance in the advancement of civil rights, these clauses have limited scope. They were designed to prohibit official discrimination, that is, discrimination to which the government is a party. In the formative years of the civil rights struggle, government-sponsored discrimination was the primary target. The legal battle against official discrimination was exceptionally successful: although issues of government-sponsored unequal treatment still arise, most discrimination occurs in the private sector.

Because the Equal Protection and Due Process Clauses were not intended to combat private discrimination, they offer little hope to those who suffer discrimination at the hands of nongovernmental parties. As we have learned, if there is no "state action," there is no violation of the Constitution. Today when discrimination occurs in areas such as employment, housing, and public accommodations, state action is rarely present. Congress has responded by passing a number of statutes to prohibit private sector discrimination. The most effective of these laws are based on Congress's authority to regulate interstate commerce, a power granted in Article I of the Constitution. The congressional role in regulating civil rights through the commerce power began with passage of the Civil Rights Act of 1964, which applies to all businesses engaged in interstate commerce. Among other things, this law prohibits discrimination based on race, color, religion, sex, or national origin in education, employment, and public accommodations (restaurants, theaters, hotels), and it gives the federal government broad enforcement authority. In *Heart of Atlanta Motel v. United States* (1964) the Supreme Court upheld the public accommodations provisions of the law, thereby giving constitutional approval for Congress to expand civil rights protections by using the commerce power.

Since then, Congress has expanded the scope of federal regulation over civil rights by passing amendments to the 1964 act and by enacting additional legislation *(see Box IV-2)*. For example, the Civil Rights Act of 1968 attempted to remove discrimination in the sale, rental, or financing of housing, and the Americans with Disabilities Act of 1990 extended federal protections to the disabled in employment, public services, and access to public places. As a result of such legislative actions, a large portion of federal civil rights law is based on congressional statutes rather than constitutional provisions.

Federal civil rights laws provide great opportunities for those who wish to challenge discriminatory behavior. Not only do these statutes regulate private-sector discrimination, but also they frequently impose thresholds of proof that are easier to satisfy than those the Supreme Court requires for constitutional challenges. For example, under the civil rights laws a worker claiming employment discrimination based on race may not have to establish discriminatory intent (a requirement for a violation of the Constitution), but may instead submit statistical evidence that the employer treats racial groups differently. Because of the growth of civil rights laws, the federal courts today hear many more cases involving alleged violations of civil rights statutes than those claiming a violation of the Constitution.

The problem of sexual harassment in the workplace provides an example. Title VII of the 1964 Civil Rights Act prohibits sex discrimination in employment. The law originally contemplated making it illegal for an employer to deny tangible benefits such as a job, a promotion, or fair compensation because of the employee's sex. As complaints of sexual harassment on the job increased, however, standards of appropriate behavior began to evolve. As a result, courts were asked to include the existence of a sex-based "hostile" or "abusive" job environment as a form of discrimination. Even the generally conservative Burger and Rehnquist Courts supported expanding the definition of illegal discrimination to encompass various forms of harassing behavior *(see Box 10-6)*. By interpreting the Civil Rights Act as prohibiting sexual harassment in the workplace, the Supreme Court encouraged additional complaints to be filed in federal court and signaled to the lower courts that such claims should be treated seriously. As a result of increased public attention and the possibility of costly lawsuits, employers began adopting more comprehensive policies to combat sexual harassment on the job.

The Supreme Court is more likely to be reversed by Congress when it interprets federal statutes than when it interprets the Constitution. If the Court reads a provision of a federal law in a manner unacceptable to Congress, the legislature can attempt to pass a new law that corrects the defect the Court found. However, if the Court interprets the Constitution in a way unacceptable to Congress, constitutional amendment may be the only way to reverse the Court's decision. Amending the Constitution requires not only a two-thirds vote in both houses of Congress, but also ratification by three-quarters of the states.

During the 1980s and 1990s Congress and the Court often clashed over statutory interpretations of civil rights laws. On most issues the Court took a more conservative position than Congress found acceptable. For example, in *Grove City College v. Bell* (1984) the Court narrowly interpreted the sex discrimination provision of a federal statute pertaining to educational assistance programs. Protests from civil

Congress has passed legislation to protect citizens against discrimination where constitutional prohibitions do not reach. An example is Title VII of the Civil Rights Act of 1964 that makes it "an unlawful employment practice for an employer ... to discriminate against any individual with respect to his compensation, terms, conditions, or privileges of employment, because of such individual's race, color, religion, sex, or national origin." When workers believe that their civil rights have been violated they may file lawsuits demanding that the situation be remedied. But the federal civil rights laws are only effective if the courts are willing to enforce them. Applying Title VII to discriminatory harassment has been one of the more controversial civil rights issues. Although the Burger and Rehnquist Courts have been criticized for failing to apply civil rights statutes vigorously, the justices have demonstrated special consideration for sexual harassment claimants. Here we summarize the two most important Supreme Court actions.

MERITOR SAVINGS BANK V. VINSON (1986)

Facts: In 1974 Mechelle Vinson began working for the Meritor Savings Bank. Her supervisor was bank vice president Sidney Taylor. Over a four-year period Vinson was promoted up the ranks from teller-trainee to assistant branch manager. All agree that these were merit-based promotions. In September 1978 Vinson took sick leave for an indefinite period, and two months later she was fired for abusing the leave policy. Vinson brought legal action against Taylor and the bank. She claimed she had been subject to constant sexual harassment. She said Taylor demanded sexual favors. After first resisting, she agreed because she feared losing her job. She estimated that she had sexual relations with Taylor between thirty and forty times. She also testified that Taylor fondled her in front of other employees, followed her into the restroom, where he exposed himself to her, and forcibly raped her on several occasions. Vinson did not report Taylor's advances to any of his supervisors or make use of established complaint procedures. The district court ruled in favor of the employer finding that much of the sexual relationship was voluntary, but the court of appeals reversed.

Outcome: By unanimous vote the justices supported Mechelle Vinson's claim. Justice Rehnquist wrote the majority opinion.

Ruling: The Court held that sexual harassment constitutes sex discrimination and is actionable under the 1964 Civil Rights Act. Sexual harassment litigants do not have to prove loss of any tangible or economic benefit. Noneconomic injury also violates the law. Harassment that creates a hostile work environment is sufficient cause to bring legal action. Sexual harassment may occur even if sexual activity is voluntary. The employer is not automatically immune nor automatically liable for the behavior of its supervising personnel. The question of employer responsibility must be considered separately in each case.

HARRIS V. FORKLIFT SYSTEMS, INC. (1993)

Facts: Teresa Harris worked as a manager at Forklift Systems, an equipment rental company in Tennessee, from 1985 to 1987. Charles Hardy was the company president. Throughout Harris's employment at Forklift, Hardy often insulted her because she was a woman and made her the target of unwanted sexual innuendoes. He would make statements such as, "You're a woman, what do you know" and "We need a man as the rental manager." He referred to her as "a dumb ass woman," and suggested that they "go to the Holiday Inn to negotiate [a] raise." Hardy would occasionally ask female employees to get coins from his front pocket. He threw objects on the ground in front of women and asked them to pick the objects up. He made sexually oriented comments about the clothing female employees wore. When Harris complained to Hardy about this conduct, he expressed surprise that she was offended and said that he was only joking. He apologized and promised to stop, but he soon returned to his former ways. Harris then sued Forklift, claiming that Hardy had created an abusive environment based on sex in violation of Title VII. The district court concluded that Hardy had engaged in offensive behavior, but not to the extent that he created an abusive environment that would interfere with job performance. The judge emphasized that Hardy's behavior was not so severe as to affect seriously Harris's psychological well-being. The court of appeals affirmed.

Outcome: By unanimous vote the justices supported Teresa Harris. Justice O'Connor wrote the majority opinion.

Ruling: A violation of Title VII occurs when the workplace is permeated with discriminatory behavior that is sufficiently severe or pervasive to create a hostile or abusive working environment. Harris need not prove that the offensive conduct seriously affected her psychological well-being. Whether an environment is "hostile" or "abusive" must be determined by examining all the circumstances rather than any single factor. Courts may look at the frequency of the offensive behavior, its severity, whether it was physically threatening or humiliating, and whether it reasonably interfered with an employee's work performance.

rights groups prompted the legislature to respond by passing the Civil Rights Restoration Act of 1988, which for most purposes reversed the *Grove City* ruling. Similarly, in 1989 the Supreme Court handed down a number of decisions interpreting federal civil rights laws relating to race and sex discrimination. Three of the more important were *Wards Cove Packing Co. v. Atonio, Martin v. Wilks,* and *Lorance v. AT&T Technologies.* These decisions, all by sharply divided votes, made it more difficult for civil rights claimants to win employment discrimination suits, and, in response, Congress passed the Civil Rights Act of 1991, which nullified the Supreme Court's interpretation of these statutory provisions. Not to be outdone, the Court in *Rivers v. Roadway Express* (1994) and *Landgraf v. USI Film Products* (1994) refused to apply the new law retroactively.

The Importance of the States

During the early years of the civil rights movement, many saw the federal courts as a reliable defender of minority interests, the most sympathetic agency of government on discrimination matters. State governments, on the other hand, were perceived as the enemy. After all, most of the laws that women and minorities found objectionable were enacted and enforced by the states. Terms such as "states' rights" were considered code words for discrimination.

After 1969 these perceptions began to change. As justices from the Warren era were replaced by more conservative jurists, observers noted that the Supreme Court was becoming more hostile to civil rights. In addition, conservative Reagan and Bush appointees to lower court judgeships transformed the image of the federal judiciary from accepting of discrimination claims to unsympathetic. These perceptions were not altogether unjustified. During the Burger and Rehnquist years, the courts handed down a number of civil rights decisions that gave little encouragement to parties bringing such lawsuits.

Concerned about possible unfavorable rulings from the federal courts, civil rights organizations and other liberal interest groups found a more sympathetic audience at the state level. Some states passed statutes that expanded civil rights protections. A number of the cases we have discussed in this chapter—for example, *Roberts v. United States Jaycees, Regents of the University of California v. Bakke,* and *City of Richmond v. J. A. Croson Co.*—focus on state and local laws intended to enhance the rights of women and minorities. The state judiciaries often granted civil rights litigants the relief they requested by applying state laws or state constitutional provisions.

Using the states to advance the civil rights agenda has its limitations. Obviously not all states have conditions favorable to expanded civil rights policies; and even if a state legislature or judiciary is amenable to discrimination claimants, the impact of any favorable action is confined to that state alone. Nevertheless, civil rights groups have increasingly turned to the states for help rather than risk unfavorable decisions in the federal courts. This trend likely will continue until the ideological complexion of the federal judiciary changes.

READINGS

Baer, Judith. *Equality Under the Constitution.* Ithaca, N.Y.: Cornell University Press, 1983.

Glazer, Nathan. *Affirmative Discrimination.* New York: Basic Books, 1975.

Goldstein, Leslie Friedman. *The Constitutional Rights of Women.* 2d ed. Madison: University of Wisconsin Press, 1988.

Graglia, Lino A. *Disaster by Decree: The Supreme Court's Decisions on Race and the Schools.* Ithaca, N.Y.: Cornell University Press, 1976.

Kluger, Richard. *Simple Justice.* New York: Knopf, 1976.

Mezey, Susan Gluck. *In Pursuit of Equality.* New York: St. Martin's Press, 1992.

Orfield, Gary. *Must We Bus? Segregated Schools and National Policy.* Washington, D.C.: Brookings Institution, 1978.

Rhode, Deborah L. *Justice and Gender.* Cambridge: Harvard University Press, 1989.

Ross, Susan Deller, and Ann Barcher. *The Rights of Women.* New York: Bantam Books, 1984.

Schwartz, Bernard. *Swann's Way: The School Busing Case and the Supreme Court.* New York: Oxford University Press, 1986.

Sindler, Allan P. *Bakke, DeFunis, and Minority Admissions.* New York: Longman, 1978.

Smith, Christopher E. *The Courts and the Poor.* Chicago: Nelson-Hall Publishers, 1991.

Vose, Clement E. *Caucasians Only: The Supreme Court, the NAACP, and the Restrictive Covenant Cases.* Berkeley: University of California Press, 1959.

Wilkinson, J. Harvie. *From Brown to Bakke: The Supreme Court and School Integration 1954–1978.* New York: Oxford University Press, 1979.

CHAPTER 11
VOTING AND REPRESENTATION

F OR ANY GOVERNMENT built on a foundation
of popular sovereignty, voting and representation are of critical importance. Through these
mechanisms the people express their political will and
ultimately control the institutions of government.
Representative democracy can function properly only
when the citizenry has full rights to regular and meaningful elections and when the system is structured so
that public officials act on behalf of their constituents.
If any segment of society is denied the right to vote or
is denied legitimate representation, the ideals of a republican form of government are not completely realized. Because elections and representation are the primary links between the people and their government,
it is not surprising that the history of American constitutional law is replete with disputes over rights of
political participation.

VOTING RIGHTS

When the Framers met at the Philadelphia Convention of 1787, the thirteen states already had elections systems, with their own voter qualification requirements and procedures for selecting state and
local officials. By European standards, the states were
quite liberal in extending the right to vote.[1] But suf-

frage was not universal. Ballot access generally was
granted only to free adult males, and in several states
only to those men who owned sufficient property.
Women, slaves, Indians, minors, and the poor could
not vote. Some states prohibited Jews and Catholics
from voting.

With state systems in place, the Framers saw no
reason to create a separate set of qualifications for participating in federal elections. Because there was little
uniformity from state to state and qualifications often
changed, the addition of a new body of federal voting
requirements could cause conflict. In addition, under
the Constitution drafted at Philadelphia, only one
agency of the new national government, the House of
Representatives, was to be elected directly by the
people, further reason why the federal government
need not develop its own voter rolls. So, the Constitution left voting qualifications to the states. Specifically,
in Article I, Section 2, the Constitution says with respect to House elections that "the Electors in each
State shall have the Qualifications requisite for Electors of the most numerous Branch of the State Legislature." If citizens were qualified to cast ballots in their
state's legislative elections, they were also qualified to
vote in congressional elections.

Only one constitutional provision gave the federal
government any regulatory authority over elections.

1. Melvin I. Urofsky, *A March of Liberty: A Constitutional History of
the United States* (New York: Knopf, 1988), 294.

Section 4 of Article I stipulates, "The Times, Places and Manner of holding Elections for Senators and Representatives, shall be prescribed in each State by the Legislature thereof; but the Congress may at any time by Law make or alter such Regulations, except as to the Places of chusing Senators." Congress took only modest advantage of this authority. In 1842 it passed a law requiring representatives to be elected from specific constituencies, rather than from the state at large; and in 1866 it clarified the procedures to be used in the selection of senators by the state legislatures. These statutes dealt essentially with procedural matters; they did not speak to the question of voter qualifications. During the first half of the nation's history, this authority remained in the hands of the states, where the electorate was expanding and barriers to suffrage gradually were being reformed. Following the Civil War, however, power over voting rights began steadily shifting toward the federal government.

Ratification of four constitutional amendments substantially limited the states' authority to restrict the right to vote. The first of these was the Fifteenth Amendment in 1870. Part of the Reconstruction package initiated by the Radical Republicans after the Civil War, the Fifteenth Amendment removed from the states the power to deny voting rights on the basis of race, color, or previous condition of servitude. It prohibits such discrimination by either the federal government or the states, but the obvious target was the South. Most members of the reconstructionist Congress reasoned that unless some action was taken to protect the political rights of the newly freed slaves, the majority white southerners would reinstitute measures to deny black citizens full participation.

Fifty years later the Constitution was again amended to expand the electorate. The Nineteenth Amendment, ratified in 1920, stipulated that the right to vote could not be denied on account of sex. Its acceptance represented decades of effort by supporters of female suffrage. Although a number of states had already modified their laws to allow women to vote, a change in the Constitution was necessary to extend that right uniformly across the nation. This amendment nullified the Supreme Court's unanimous 1875 decision in *Minor v. Happersett* in which the justices rejected Virginia Minor's contention that the Missouri constitution's granting of voting rights only to males violated the Privileges and Immunities Clause of the Fourteenth Amendment.

The third voter qualification amendment went into effect in 1964. The Twenty-fourth Amendment denied the federal government and the states the power to impose a poll tax as a voter qualification for federal elections. The levying of a tax on the right to vote was a common practice in the South and was identified by Congress as one of many tactics used to keep blacks from voting, and thereby circumventing the clear intent of the Fifteenth Amendment.

In 1971 the last of the voting rights amendments, the Twenty-sixth, was ratified. It set eighteen years as the minimum voting age for all state and federal elections. Before 1971 individual states determined the minimum voting age, which ranged from eighteen to twenty-one. Earlier, Congress had attempted to impose the eighteen-year minimum through legislation. The constitutionality of that act was challenged in *Oregon v. Mitchell* (1970). In a 5–4 vote, the justices held that Congress had the power under Article I to set a minimum age for voting in federal elections, but was without the constitutional authority to impose an age standard on state and local elections. Rather than face the possible confusion of conflicting sets of qualifications, Congress abrogated the impact of the *Mitchell* ruling by proposing the Twenty-sixth Amendment.

Each of these four constitutional changes altered the balance of authority over the establishment of voter qualifications. The states retained the basic right to set such qualifications, but with restrictions. States may no longer abridge voting rights by denying access to the ballot on the basis of race, sex, age or ability to pay a tax; any actions by the states affecting voting rights also are constrained by the Fourteenth Amendment's guarantee of equal protection of the laws.[2] In addition to limiting state power, the voting rights amendments increased congressional authority. The Fourteenth, Fifteenth, Nineteenth, Twenty-fourth, and Twenty-sixth Amendments declare: "The Congress shall have the power to enforce this article by appropriate legislation." These enforcement clauses grant Congress authority over an area that had been left entirely to the states.

Congress has not been reluctant to use its enforcement authority. Shortly after ratification of the Fourteenth and Fifteenth Amendments, it demonstrated the federal government's interest in extending the franchise to blacks by passing the Enforcement Act of 1870. This statute made it unlawful for state election officials to discriminate against blacks in the application of state voting regulations. It also made acts of electoral corruption, including bribery, violence, and intimidation, federal crimes. The following year Congress passed the Enforcement Act of 1871, which allowed for federal supervision of congressional elections. The federal government also intervened to stem the growing incidence of private intimidation of black voters with the Ku Klux Klan Act of 1871, which gave the president broad powers to combat conspiracies against voting rights.

The Supreme Court's response to these post–Civil War enforcement statutes was mixed. In some of its decisions the justices questioned the breadth of the congressional actions that regulated state elections beyond the specific racial purposes of the Fifteenth Amendment. For example, in *United States v. Reese* (1876) the justices declined to uphold the indictment of a Kentucky election official who refused to register a qualified black voter for a state election. The Court justified its conclusion on the ground that the Enforcement Act of 1870 was too broadly drawn. On the same day as *Reese,* and for the same reason, the Court in *United States v. Cruikshank* dismissed the federal indictments of ninety-six Louisiana whites who were charged with intimidating potential black voters by shooting them. The Court also was reluctant to approve sanctions under the Ku Klux Klan Act when the prosecution centered on purely private behavior (*United States v. Harris,* 1883). However, in *Ex parte Yarbrough* (1884) the justices gave strong support to federal enforcement actions against even private behavior when the right to vote in national elections was abridged. Similarly, in *Ex parte Clark* (1880), *Ex parte Siebold* (1880), and *United States v. Gale* (1883) the Court approved criminal charges against state officials who compromised the integrity of federal elections.

Although these enforcement measures had an impact on the South, their influence was short-lived. By the time the nation entered the 1890s, the zeal behind the Reconstruction efforts had waned. White southerners had regained control of their home states and began passing measures to restrict black participation in state and federal elections. The Jim Crow era had begun. The Civil War amendments officially had reduced the power of the states to discriminate and given regulatory authority to the federal government, but full voting rights were not a reality until after the civil rights movement of the mid-twentieth century.

Throughout the years, however, the Supreme Court was called upon to settle a number of important disputes over the constitutional right to vote. The specific issues brought to the Court involved state-imposed restrictions based on race, economics, residency, and criminal behavior. In spite of the wide-ranging subject matter, the underlying question remained the same: To what extent are the states free to determine voting qualifications?

2. The Fourteenth Amendment also contained a provision that stipulated that any state denying voting rights to any male citizens over the age of twenty-one could have its representation in the U.S. House reduced. This provision, however, has never had a practical impact and has been largely superseded by the ratification of the other voting rights amendments.

Race

In 1869, during the congressional debate over the Fifteenth Amendment, Sen. Waitman T. Willey, a Republican from West Virginia, proclaimed from the Senate floor:

This amendment, when adopted, will settle the question for all time of negro suffrage in the insurgent States, where it has lately been extended under the pressure of congressional legislation, and will preclude the possibility of any future denial of this privilege by any change in the constitutions of those States.

In retrospect, it would be hard to imagine a more overly optimistic prediction of the impact of the Fifteenth Amendment. While ratification meant that the states were constitutionally prohibited from engaging in racial discrimination in extending the right to vote, the southern states, once out from under the policies of Reconstruction, acted to keep blacks out of the voting booth.

One of their most notorious tactics was the white primary. This strategy was practiced in a number of southern states, but in none more vigilantly than in Texas. The white primary was based on the principle that the Fifteenth Amendment applied only to general elections. This view was given credence by the Supreme Court in an unrelated electoral corruption case, *Newberry v. United States* (1921), in which the justices held that primaries were the private affairs of political parties and were not included under the constitutional meaning of elections. In the post–Civil War South, however, the general election was virtually meaningless: given the region's resentment of Republican policies, it was not surprising that the overwhelming majority of whites supported the Democratic party. Republican presence was almost nonexistent throughout the South. Certainly, no viable Republican party organization played any meaningful role in southern politics, which meant that general elections in the South presented voters with only one true candidate for each office, the Democrat. The real political

contests, therefore, took place in the primary elections that determined who the Democratic nominees would be. Because the primary was not part of the election process covered by the Constitution, southern politicians believed them to be free from the constraints of the Fifteenth Amendment and any acts of Congress enforcing it. Consequently, they restricted primary election participation to white voters. If this view were to prevail, the Fifteenth Amendment would be rendered practically meaningless.

The battle over the Texas white primary became a constitutional ping-pong match in which the issue repeatedly bounced from Texas to the Supreme Court and back again. Each time the justices ruled, the state legislature and the Democratic party were sufficiently nimble to alter the voting regulations and sidestep the Court's holding. Thirty years passed before the issue was finally settled. The series of disputes began in 1923, when the state legislature enacted a statute declaring that "in no event shall a Negro be eligible to participate in a Democratic Party primary election in the State of Texas." L. A. Nixon, a black physician from El Paso County, who was otherwise qualified to vote, was denied a ballot in the Democratic primary on account of his race. With assistance provided by the NAACP, he filed suit against the state election judges, claiming a deprivation of his Fourteenth and Fifteenth Amendment rights. In *Nixon v. Herndon* (1927) the Supreme Court ruled in his favor. The justices avoided the issue of whether a primary election was covered by the Fifteenth Amendment, deciding the case on the basis of the Fourteenth Amendment claim. The state, the Court concluded, had denied Nixon equal protection of the laws by passing a statute discriminating on the basis of race.

The political powers in Texas were not about to accept the Court's ruling without a fight. The legislature revised its laws concerning political parties and primary elections by commanding that "every political party in this State through its State Executive

Committee shall have the power to prescribe the qualifications of its own members and shall in its own way determine who shall be qualified to vote."

In passing this revised statute the state legislature said in effect that if the Supreme Court ruled that as a government agency we cannot constitutionally discriminate on the basis of race, we will give permission to the Democratic party, a private organization, to do the discriminating for us. The state Democratic Executive Committee quickly passed a regulation restricting participation in its primary elections to white Democrats.

Once again, Nixon attempted to vote in a primary election and, when he was denied access to the ballot, once again he sued. The Court in *Nixon v. Condon* (1932) struck down the white primary, holding that, by officially granting the Democratic party the authority to discriminate on the basis of race, the state legislature made the party its representative. This act was sufficient state action under the Fourteenth Amendment and constituted a denial of Nixon's right to equal protection of the laws.

Texas Democrats were not disheartened by this defeat. Rather than relying on the state legislature or their own executive committee to act, members of the Democratic party met in convention and passed the following resolution: "Be it resolved that all white citizens of the State of Texas who are qualified to vote under the Constitution and laws of the state shall be eligible to membership in the Democratic Party and, as such, entitled to participate in its deliberations." By so doing, the members of the party themselves, without state intervention, authorized the continuation of the white primary.

After the resolution took effect, a black Texan filed suit. In *Grovey v. Townsend* (1935) a unanimous Supreme Court found no constitutional violation. Although discrimination based on race clearly had occurred, the justices could not find adequate state action to constitute a violation of the Equal Protection Clause. They reached this conclusion even though primary elections were otherwise regulated by the state and were required by state law. Nor did the Court alter the generally accepted view that primaries were not part of the official election system and, therefore, not controlled by the Fifteenth Amendment. Political parties were viewed as private organizations of like-minded individuals who associated for purposes of advancing their common political goals.

The *Grovey* ruling was a stinging defeat for civil rights advocates. The white primary continued in Texas, with those wishing to see it ended looking for some signal from the Supreme Court that would permit another attack on this discriminatory practice. The signal came in 1941, when the Court handed down its ruling in *United States v. Classic*. Classic, a Louisiana election commissioner, was charged by federal authorities with deliberately changing the votes of qualified electors in a Democratic primary to nominate a congressional candidate. Classic refuted the charges on the grounds that the federal government had no authority to regulate what occurred in a primary election. The Supreme Court rejected this argument, holding that the statutes of the state of Louisiana had made the primary election an integral part of selecting candidates for congressional seats and that the outcome of the primary election effectively determined who would be sent to Washington. Under these conditions, the justices ruled, the United States had the right to protect the integrity of the election and to ensure that the ballot of each voter is properly counted.

The *Classic* decision, coupled with the increasing presence of liberal New Deal justices, gave opponents of the white primary all the encouragement they needed to initiate new legal challenges to the Texas election system. In considering Justice Reed's majority opinion in *Smith v. Allwright* (1944), think about the Court's use of precedent. How did the recently decided *Classic* case affect the Court's judgment? And what did the justices do with the controlling precedent of *Grovey v. Townsend?*

========

Smith v. Allwright

321 U.S. 649 (1944)

Vote: 8 (Black, Douglas, Frankfurter, Jackson, Murphy, Reed, Rutledge, Stone)

   1 (Roberts)

Opinion of the Court: Reed

Dissenting opinion: Roberts

Lonnie E. Smith, a black resident of Harris County, Texas, was denied the right to vote in the Democratic primary election of July 27, 1940. The election was to select the party nominees for U.S. senator and representative, as well as for a number of state offices. Smith met all of the qualifications to vote in Texas, except race; the Texas Democratic party had adopted a resolution to limit voting to whites only. This same resolution had been upheld by the Supreme Court in *Grovey v. Townsend.* Based on the *Grovey* precedent, the district court denied the relief sought, and the court of appeals concurred. The U.S. Supreme Court accepted the case to resolve the apparent conflict between the precedents of *Grovey v. Townsend* and *United States v. Classic.* Smith's case was argued by two prominent civil rights attorneys who were associated with the NAACP Legal Defense Fund—Thurgood Marshall, who subsequently joined the Supreme Court, and William Hastie, who was later appointed by President Truman to the Court of Appeals for the Third Circuit.

MR. JUSTICE REED delivered the opinion of the Court.

Since *Grovey v. Townsend* and prior to the present suit, no case from Texas involving primary elections has been before this Court. We did decide, however, *United States v. Classic.* We there held that § 4 of Article I of the Constitu-

tion authorized Congress to regulate primary as well as general elections, "where the primary is by law made an integral part of the election machinery." Consequently, in the *Classic* case, we upheld the applicability to frauds in a Louisiana primary of §§ 19 and 20 of the Criminal Code. Thereby corrupt acts of election officers were subjected to Congressional sanctions because that body had power to protect rights of federal suffrage secured by the Constitution in primary as in general elections. This decision depended, too, on the determination that under the Louisiana statutes the primary was a part of the procedure for choice of federal officials. By this decision the doubt as to whether or not such primaries were a part of "elections" subject to federal control, which had remained unanswered since *Newberry v. United States,* was erased.... As the Louisiana statutes for holding primaries are similar to those of Texas, our ruling in *Classic* as to the unitary character of the electoral process calls for a reexamination as to whether or not the exclusion of Negroes from a Texas party primary was state action....

It may now be taken as a postulate that the right to vote in such a primary for the nomination of candidates without discrimination by the State, like the right to vote in a general election, is a right secured by the Constitution. By the terms of the Fifteenth Amendment that right may not be abridged by any State on account of race. Under our Constitution the great privilege of the ballot may not be denied a man by the State because of his color.

We are thus brought to an examination of the qualifications for Democratic primary electors in Texas, to determine whether state action or private action has excluded Negroes from participation.... Texas requires electors in a primary to pay a poll tax. Every person who does so pay and who has the qualifications of age and residence is an acceptable voter for the primary.... Texas requires by the law the election of the county officers of a party. These compose the county executive committee. The county chairmen so selected are members of the district executive committee and choose the chairman for the district. Precinct primary election officers are named by the county executive committee. Statutes provide for the election by the voters of precinct delegates to the county convention of a party and the selection of delegates to the district and state conventions by the county convention. The state convention selects the state executive committee. No convention may place in platform or resolution any demand for specific legislation without endorsement of such legislation by the voters in a primary. Texas thus directs the selection of all party officers.

Primary elections are conducted by the party under state statutory authority. The county executive committee selects precinct election officials and the county, district or state executive committees, respectively, canvass the returns. These party committees or the state convention certify the party's candidates to the appropriate officers for inclusion on the official ballot for the general election. No name which has not been so certified may appear upon the ballot for the general election as a candidate of a political party. No other name may be printed on the ballot which has not been placed in nomination by qualified voters who must take oath that they did not participate in a primary for the selection of a candidate for the office for which the nomination is made.

The state courts are given exclusive original jurisdiction of contested elections and of mandamus proceedings to compel party officers to perform their statutory duties.

We think that this statutory system for the selection of party nominees for inclusion on the general election ballot makes the party which is required to follow these legislative directions an agency of the State in so far as it determines the participants in a primary election. The party takes its character as a state agency from the duties imposed upon it by state statutes; the duties do not become matters of private law because they are performed by a political party. The plan of the Texas primary follows substantially that of Louisiana, with the exception that in Louisiana the State pays the cost of the primary while Texas assesses the cost against candidates. In numerous instances, the Texas statutes fix or limit the fees to be charged. Whether paid directly by the State or through state requirements, it is state action which compels. When primaries become a part of the machinery for choosing officials, state and national, as they have here, the same tests to determine the character of discrimination or abridgement should be applied to the primary as are applied to the general election. If the State requires a certain electoral procedure, prescribes a general election ballot made up of party nominees so chosen and limits the choice of the electorate in general elections for state offices, practically speaking, to those whose names appear on such a ballot, it endorses, adopts and enforces the discrimination against Negroes, practiced by a party entrusted by Texas law with the determination of the qualifications of participants in the primary. This is state action within the meaning of the Fifteenth Amendment.

The United States is a constitutional democracy. Its organic law grants to all citizens a right to participate in the choice of elected officials without restriction by any State because of race. This grant to the people of the opportunity for choice is not to be nullified by a State through casting its electoral process in a form which permits a private organization to practice racial discrimination in the election. Constitutional rights would be of little value if they could be thus indirectly denied.

The privilege of membership in a party may be, as this Court said in *Grovey v. Townsend,* no concern of a State. But when, as here, that privilege is also the essential qualification for voting in a primary to select nominees for a general election, the State makes the action of the party the action of the State. In reaching this conclusion we are not unmindful of the desirability of continuity of decision in constitutional questions. However, when convinced of former error, this Court has never felt constrained to follow precedent. In constitutional questions, where correction depends upon amendment and not upon legislative action, this Court throughout its history has freely exercised its power to reexamine the basis of its constitutional decisions. This has long been accepted practice, and this practice has continued to this day. This is particularly true when the decision believed erroneous is the application of a constitutional principle rather than an interpretation of the Constitution to extract the principle itself. Here we are applying, contrary to the recent decision in *Grovey v. Townsend,* the well-established principle of the Fifteenth Amendment, forbidding the abridgement by a State of a citizen's right to vote. *Grovey v. Townsend* is overruled.

Judgment reversed.

The *Smith* decision was a substantial victory for the civil rights movement. In overruling *Grovey,* the Court declared that the constitutional provisions of the Fourteenth and Fifteenth Amendments applied to

Prior to the 1970s southern states engaged in a number of tactics to keep black citizens from voting. In spite of threats and legal obstacles, black voters turned out in large numbers when given an opportunity. Blacks in Cobb County, Georgia, endured long lines to cast their ballots in the July 1946 Democratic primary elections.

party primary elections. Some states with white primaries complied with the Court's ruling. Any hopes that Texas Democrats were now prepared to allow full participation by blacks, however, were badly misplaced. Defeated in the Court, the members of the party went back to the drawing board to devise a way to circumvent the *Smith* ruling. They decided to rely on private county organizations or clubs, the most famous of which was the Jaybird Democratic Association of Fort Bend County.

The Jaybirds were a private organization founded in 1889. Membership was restricted to whites. The expressed purpose of the Jaybirds was to promote good government through a number of activities, including the endorsement of candidates running in Democratic primaries. Eventually, the association began to hold its own elections prior to any Democratic primary. Winners of the Jaybird election carried the organiza-

tion's support into the primary. So effective was this support that it almost assured victory in the party primary. As the Jaybirds' influence grew, candidates who failed to receive the association's approval usually dropped out. As a rule, winners of the Jaybird primary had no opponents in either the Democratic primary or the general election. Because black voters were excluded from the Jaybird elections, they had no real voice in county elections. It made little difference if the courts ordered that blacks be allowed to vote in the Democratic primary or the general election because the real decisions were made much earlier in the Jaybird contests.

Texas Democrats saw the Jaybird organization as a way to avoid granting blacks full participatory rights. The Jaybirds were a private organization without significant state recognition or official approval. If this model could be extended throughout the state, decisions such as *Classic* and *Smith* would have little impact. In fact, similar Democratic clubs were already functioning in many areas of the South.

Denied the right to participate in a Jaybird election, a group of black citizens from Fort Bend County filed suit March 16, 1950, claiming that they had been denied their Fourteenth and Fifteenth Amendment rights. They charged that the Jaybird organization was, in fact, a political party and that its discrimination on the basis of race sufficiently affected the ultimate outcome of elections so as to offend the Constitution. The Jaybirds countered that they were not a political party, but a private organization dedicated to good government. The district court decided in favor of the black plaintiffs, but the court of appeals reversed.

In *Terry v. Adams* (1953) the Supreme Court ruled against the Jaybirds. The Court held that the organization was functioning as a political party; in fact, it appeared to be an auxiliary of the Democratic party. As such, the Jaybirds materially affected the election process. When such conditions are met, the provisions of the Constitution apply, and the Fifteenth Amendment's prohibitions become self-executing. In announcing the judgment of the Court, Justice Black declared that the Fifteenth Amendment is violated whenever a state permits "the use of any device that produces an equivalent of the prohibited election." What the state cannot do directly, it cannot permit indirectly. The Court's ruling in *Terry* served notice that the white primary would not be tolerated in any shape or configuration.

Texas lost its battle to save the white primary, but, by conducting its legal jousting with the Supreme Court, the state had kept blacks from fully participating in the political process for more than thirty additional years. The white primary was only one tactic; other actions, formal and informal, were equally effective in discouraging black voting. Many of those strategies were ultimately tested before the Supreme Court.

Beginning in the 1960s the federal government undertook to reduce racial discrimination in voting. All three branches were involved: Congress passed legislation to enforce voting rights and remove legal barriers to the ballot box; the executive branch brought suits against state governments and election officials who deprived blacks of their rights; and the judiciary heard legal disputes over claims of voting discrimination. The opponents of political change tried another strategy—the "understanding test." As you read Justice Black's opinion for the Court in *Louisiana v. United States* (1965), pay close attention to his account of the many obstacles the state placed in the way of suffrage and how effective they were.

Louisiana v. United States

380 U.S. 145 (1965)
Vote: 9 (Black, Brennan, Clark, Douglas, Goldberg, Harlan,
   Stewart, Warren, White)

  0

Opinion of the Court: Black
Concurring opinion: Harlan

The U.S. government brought suit in the federal District Court for the Eastern District of Louisiana against the state of Louisiana and members of the state Board of Registration. The government charged the defendants with enforcing state laws denying black citizens the right to vote in violation of the Fourteenth and Fifteenth Amendments. The suit centered on the use of "interpretation" or "understanding" tests. These devices, commonly used throughout the South, required any citizens applying for voter registration to pass a test demonstrating a proper understanding of any section of the Louisiana or U.S. Constitution. The test had no objective standards: the local voting registrar selected the passage to be interpreted by the potential voter and determined whether sufficient understanding had been demonstrated. The state justified this requirement as a means of ensuring a well-informed, qualified electorate. The fact that the Board of Registration developed the interpretation test in cooperation with the state Segregation Committee indicated that other goals also were intended. The test was quite effective in denying blacks, even those with graduate and professional degrees, the right to vote. The district court ruled in favor of the federal government, and the state appealed.

MR. JUSTICE BLACK delivered the opinion of the Court.

The complaint alleged, and the District Court found, that beginning with the adoption of the Louisiana Constitution of 1898, when approximately 44% of all the registered voters in the State were Negroes, the State had put into effect a successful policy of denying Negro citizens the right to vote because of their race. The 1898 constitution adopted what was known as a "grandfather clause," which imposed burdensome requirements for registration thereafter but exempted from these future requirements any person who had been entitled to vote before January 1, 1867, or who was the son or grandson of such a person. Such a transparent expedient for disfranchising Negroes, whose ancestors had been slaves until 1863 and not entitled to vote in Louisiana before 1867, was held unconstitutional in 1915 as a violation of the Fifteenth Amendment, in a case involving a similar Oklahoma constitutional provision. Guinn v. United States. Soon after that decision Louisiana, in 1921, adopted a new constitution replacing the repudiated "grandfather clause" with what the complaint calls an "interpretation test," which required that an applicant for registration be able to "give a reasonable interpretation" of any clause in the Louisiana Constitution or the Constitution of the United States. From the adoption of the 1921 interpretation test until 1944, the District Court's opinion stated, the percentage of registered voters in Louisiana who were Negroes never exceeded one percent. Prior to 1944 Negro interest in voting in Louisiana had been slight, largely because the State's white primary law kept Negroes from voting in the Democratic Party primary election, the only election that mattered in the political climate of that State. In 1944, how-

ever, this Court invalidated the substantially identical white primary law of Texas, and with the explicit statutory bar to their voting in the primary removed and because of a generally heightened political interest, Negroes in increasing numbers began to register in Louisiana. The white primary system had been so effective in barring Negroes from voting that the "interpretation test" as a disfranchising devise had been ignored over the years. Many registrars continued to ignore it after 1944, and in the next dozen years the proportion of registered voters who were Negroes rose from two-tenths of one percent to approximately 15% by March 1956. This fact, coupled with this Court's 1954 invalidation of laws requiring school segregation, prompted the State to try new devices to keep the white citizens in control. The Louisiana Legislature created a committee which became known as the "Segregation Committee" to seek means of accomplishing this goal. The chairman of this committee also helped to organize a semiprivate group called the Association of Citizens Councils, which thereafter acted in close cooperation with the legislative committee to preserve white supremacy. The legislative committee and the Citizens Councils set up programs, which parish voting registrars were required to attend, to instruct the registrars on how to promote white political control. The committee and the Citizens Councils also began a wholesale challenging of Negro names already on the voting rolls, with the result that thousands of Negroes, but virtually no whites, were purged from the rolls of voters. Beginning in the middle 1950's registrars of at least 21 parishes began to apply the interpretation test. In 1960 the State Constitution was amended to require every applicant thereafter to "be able to understand" as well as "give a reasonable interpretation" of any section of the State or Federal Constitution "when read to him by the registrar." The State Board of Registration in cooperation with the Segregation Committee issued orders that all parish registrars must strictly comply with the new provisions.

The interpretation test, the court found, vested in the voting registrars a virtually uncontrolled discretion as to who should vote and who should not. Under the State's statutes and constitutional provisions the registrars, without any objective standard to guide them, determine the manner in which the interpretation test is to be given, whether it is to be oral or written, the length and complexity of the sections of the State or Federal Constitution to be understood and interpreted, and what interpretation is to be considered correct. There was ample evidence to support the District Court's finding that registrars in the 21 parishes where the test was found to have been used had exercised their broad powers to deprive otherwise qualified Negro citizens of their right to vote; and that the existence of the test as a hurdle to voter qualification has in itself deterred and will continue to deter Negroes from attempting to register in Louisiana.

Because of the virtually unlimited discretion vested by the Louisiana laws in the registrars of voters, and because in the 21 parishes where the interpretation test was applied that discretion had been exercised to keep Negroes from voting because of their race, the District Court held the interpretation test invalid on its face and as applied, as a violation of the Fourteenth and Fifteenth Amendments to the United States Constitution and of 42 U.S.C. § 1971(a). The District Court enjoined future use of the test in the State, and with respect to the 21 parishes where the invalid interpretation test was found to have been applied, the District Court also enjoined use of a newly enacted "citizenship" test, which did not repeal the interpretation test and the validity of which was not challenged in this suit, unless a reregistration of all voters in those parishes is ordered, so that there would be no voters in those parishes who had not passed the same test.

We have held this day in United States v. Mississippi that the Attorney General has power to bring suit against a State and its officials to protect the voting rights of Negroes guaranteed by 42 U.S.C. § 1971(a) and the Fourteenth and Fifteenth Amendments. There can be no doubt from the evidence in this case that the District Court was amply justified in finding that Louisiana's interpretation test, as written and as applied, was part of a successful plan to deprive Louisiana Negroes of their right to vote. This device for accomplishing unconstitutional discrimination has been little if any less successful than was the "grandfather clause" invalidated by this Court's decision in Guinn v. United States 50 years ago, which when that clause was adopted in 1898 had seemed to the leaders of Louisiana a much preferable way of assuring white political supremacy. The Governor of Louisiana stated in 1898 that he believed that the "grandfather clause" solved the problem of keeping Negroes from

voting "in a much more upright and manly fashion" than the method adopted previously by the States of Mississippi and South Carolina, which left the qualification of applicants to vote "largely to the arbitrary discretion of the officers administering the law." A delegate to the 1898 Louisiana Constitutional Convention also criticized an interpretation test because the "arbitrary power, lodged with the registration officer, practically places his decision beyond the pale of judicial review; and he can enfranchise or disfranchise voters at his own sweet will and pleasure without let or hindrance."

But Louisianans of a later generation did place just such arbitrary power in the hands of election officers who have used it with phenomenal success to keep Negroes from voting in the State. The State admits that the statutes and provisions of the state constitution establishing the interpretation test "vest discretion in the registrars of voters to determine the qualifications of applicants for registration" while imposing "no definite and objective standards upon registrars of voters for the administration of the interpretation test." And the District Court found that "Louisiana . . . provides no effective method whereby arbitrary and capricious action by registrars of voters may be prevented or redressed." The applicant facing a registrar in Louisiana thus has been compelled to leave his voting fate to that official's uncontrolled power to determine whether the applicant's understanding of the Federal or State Constitution is satisfactory. As the evidence showed, colored people, even some with the most advanced education and scholarship, were declared by voting registrars with less education to have an unsatisfactory understanding of the Constitution of Louisiana or of the United States. This is not a test but a trap, sufficient to stop even the most brilliant man on his way to the voting booth. The cherished right of people in a country like ours to vote cannot be obliterated by the use of laws like this, which leave the voting fate of a citizen to the passing whim or impulse of an individual registrar. Many of our cases have pointed out the invalidity of laws so completely devoid of standards and restraints. Squarely in point is Schnell v. Davis, in which we affirmed a district court judgment striking down as a violation of the Fourteenth and Fifteenth Amendments an Alabama constitutional provision restricting the right to vote in that State to persons who could "understand and explain any article of the Constitution of the United States" to the satisfaction of voting registrars. We likewise affirm here the District Court's holding that the provisions of the Louisiana Constitution and statutes which require voters to satisfy registrars of their ability to "understand and give a reasonable interpretation of any section" of the Federal or Louisiana Constitution violate the Constitution. And we agree with the District Court that it specifically conflicts with the prohibitions against discrimination in voting because of race found both in the Fifteenth Amendment and 42 U.S.C. § 1971(a) to subject citizens to such an arbitrary power as Louisiana has given its registrars under these laws.

Affirmed.

Although decisions such as *Louisiana v. United States* defined the constitutional rights of minority voters and condemned efforts by the states to depress black voting participation, court rulings alone were insufficient to prompt major changes. Too many alternative measures, many of them informal, were available to block or delay the effective exercise of the right to vote. The saga of the Texas white primary demonstrated how long relief could be delayed by relying on the judiciary to effect change. Registration numbers in the southern states highlight the fact that court victories did not necessarily translate into social change. According to Justice Department statistics, between 1958 and 1964 black voter registration in Alabama rose to 19.4 percent from 14.2 percent. From 1956 to 1965 Louisiana black registration increased only to 31.8 percent from 31.7 percent. And in Mississippi the ten years from 1954 to 1964 saw black registration rates rise to only 6.4 percent from 4.4 percent. In each of these states the registration rates for whites was fifty percentage points or more ahead of black rates. Figures such as these convinced Congress that its strategy of passing legislation to expand opportunities for taking civil rights claims to court had been ineffective and that a more aggressive policy was required. President Lyndon Johnson is reported to have in-

structed Attorney General Nicholas Katzenbach to "write the god-damnedest, toughest voting rights act that you can devise."[3] The result was the Voting Rights Act of 1965, the most comprehensive statute ever enacted by Congress to enforce the guarantees of the Fifteenth Amendment.

The provisions of the Voting Rights Act did not apply equally to all sections of the country. Instead, the act targeted certain areas. The coverage formula stipulated that the most stringent provisions of the statute would govern all states or counties that met the following criteria: (1) that a discriminatory test or device was in operation in November 1964; and (2) that less than 40 percent of the voting age population was registered to vote or voted in the 1964 presidential general election.

In 1965 the states covered were Alabama, Alaska, Georgia, Louisiana, Mississippi, South Carolina, and Virginia, as well as portions of North Carolina, Arizona, Hawaii, and Idaho. A state could be removed from coverage by convincing the District Court for the District of Columbia that no discrimination had been practiced for five years. The act's most significant provision authorized the U.S. attorney general to appoint federal examiners to supervise registration and voting procedures when the Justice Department determined that low black participation rates were likely due to racial discrimination. The law prohibited literacy tests and stipulated that any changes in state election laws had to be approved by the attorney general before they could take effect. The 1965 Voting Rights Act was Congress's most comprehensive intervention into the state's traditional powers over voter qualifications, and it was not surprising that it was almost immediately challenged as exceeding constitutional limits on federal power.

---

3. Howard Ball, "The Voting Rights Act of 1965," in *The Oxford Companion to the Supreme Court of the United States*, ed. Kermit L. Hall, James W. Ely, Jr., Joel B. Grossman, and William M. Wiecek (New York: Oxford University Press, 1992), 903.

South Carolina v. Katzenbach

383 U.S. 301 (1966)

Vote: 8 (Brennan, Clark, Douglas, Fortas, Harlan, Stewart,
Warren, White)
1 (Black)

Opinion of the Court: Warren

Opinion concurring in part and dissenting in part: Black

To gain a review of the Voting Rights Act, South Carolina instituted legal action against Attorney General Katzenbach, asking that he be enjoined from enforcing the act's provisions. Because the dispute involved a state suing a citizen of another state and because of the importance of the issues involved, the Supreme Court accepted the case under its original jurisdiction. The hearing before the Supreme Court involved not only South Carolina and the federal government but also other states invited by the Court to participate. Five states (all southern) appeared in support of South Carolina, and twenty-one states submitted legal arguments urging the Court to approve the act.

MR. CHIEF JUSTICE WARREN delivered the opinion of the Court.

The Voting Rights Act was designed by Congress to banish the blight of racial discrimination in voting, which has infected the electoral process in parts of our country for nearly a century. The Act creates stringent new remedies for voting discrimination where it persists on a pervasive scale, and in addition the statute strengthens existing remedies for pockets of voting discrimination elsewhere in the country. Congress assumed the power to prescribe these remedies from § 2 of the Fifteenth Amendment, which authorizes the National Legislature to effectuate by "appropriate" measures the constitutional prohibition against racial discrimination in voting. We hold that the sections of the Act which are properly before us are an appropriate means for carrying out Congress' constitutional responsibilities

and are consonant with all other provisions of the Constitution. We therefore deny South Carolina's request that enforcement of these sections of the Act be enjoined.

The constitutional propriety of the Voting Rights Act of 1965 must be judged with reference to the historical experience which it reflects. Before enacting the measure, Congress explored with great care the problem of racial discrimination in voting. The House and Senate Committees on the Judiciary each held hearings for nine days and received testimony from a total of 67 witnesses. More than three full days were consumed discussing the bill on the floor of the House, while the debate in the Senate covered 26 days in all. At the close of these deliberations, the verdict of both chambers was overwhelming. The House approved the bill by a vote of 328–74, and the measure passed the Senate by a margin of 79–18.

Two points emerge vividly from the voluminous legislative history of the Act contained in the committee hearings and floor debates. First: Congress felt itself confronted by an insidious and pervasive evil which had been perpetuated in certain parts of our country through unremitting and ingenious defiance of the Constitution. Second: Congress concluded that the unsuccessful remedies which it had prescribed in the past would have to be replaced by sterner and more elaborate measures in order to satisfy the clear commands of the Fifteenth Amendment....

The Voting Rights Act of 1965 reflects Congress' firm intention to rid the country of racial discrimination in voting. The heart of the Act is a complex scheme of stringent remedies aimed at areas where voting discrimination has been most flagrant. Section 4(a)-(d) lays down a formula defining the States and political subdivisions to which these new remedies apply. The first of the remedies, contained in § 4(a), is the suspension of literacy tests and similar voting qualifications for a period of five years from the last occurrence of substantial voting discrimination. Section 5 prescribes a second remedy, the suspension of all new voting regulations pending review by federal authorities to determine whether their use would perpetuate voting discrimination. The third remedy, covered in §§ 6(b), 7, 9, and 13(a), is the assignment of federal examiners on certification by the Attorney General to list qualified applicants who are thereafter entitled to vote in all elections.

Other provisions of the Act prescribe subsidiary cures for persistent voting discrimination. Section 8 authorizes the appointment of federal poll-watchers in places to which federal examiners have already been assigned. Section 10(d) excuses those made eligible to vote in sections of the country covered by § 4(b) of the Act from paying accumulated past poll taxes for state and local elections. Section 12(e) provides for balloting by persons denied access to the polls in areas where federal examiners have been appointed.

The remaining remedial portions of the Act are aimed at voting discrimination in any area of the country where it may occur. Section 2 broadly prohibits the use of voting rules to abridge exercise of the franchise on racial grounds. Sections 3, 6(a), and 13(b) strengthen existing procedures for attacking voting discrimination by means of litigation. Section 4(e) excuses citizens educated in American schools conducted in a foreign language from passing English-language literacy tests. Section 10(a)-(c) facilitates constitutional litigation challenging the imposition of all poll taxes for state and local elections. Sections 11 and 12(a)-(d) authorize civil and criminal sanctions against interference with the exercise of rights guaranteed by the Act....

These provisions of the Voting Rights Act of 1965 are challenged on the fundamental ground that they exceed the powers of Congress and encroach on an area reserved to the States by the Constitution....

The ground rules for resolving this question are clear. The language and purpose of the Fifteenth Amendment, the prior decisions construing its several provisions, and the general doctrines of constitutional interpretation, all point to one fundamental principle. As against the reserved powers of the States, Congress may use any rational means to effectuate the constitutional prohibition of racial discrimination in voting....

Section 1 of the Fifteenth Amendment declares that "[t]he right of citizens of the United States to vote shall not be denied or abridged by the United States or by any State on account of race, color, or previous condition of servitude." This declaration has always been treated as self-executing and has repeatedly been construed, without further legislative specification, to invalidate state voting qualifications or procedures which are discriminatory on their face or in practice.... [T]he Fifteenth Amendment expressly declares that "Congress shall have power to enforce this arti-

cle by appropriate legislation."... Accordingly, in addition to the courts, Congress has full remedial powers to effectuate the constitutional prohibition against racial discrimination in voting.

Congress has repeatedly exercised these powers in the past, and its enactments have repeatedly been upheld.... On the rare occasions when the Court has found an unconstitutional exercise of these powers, in its opinion Congress had attacked evils not comprehended by the Fifteenth Amendment.

The basic test to be applied in a case involving § 2 of the Fifteenth Amendment is the same as in all cases concerning the express powers of Congress with relation to the reserved powers of the States. Chief Justice Marshall laid down the classic formulation, 50 years before the Fifteenth Amendment was ratified:

"Let the end be legitimate, let it be within the scope of the constitution, and all means which are appropriate, which are plainly adapted to that end, which are not prohibited, but consist with the letter and spirit of the constitution, are constitutional." McCulloch v. Maryland.

The Court has subsequently echoed his language in describing each of the Civil War Amendments:

"Whatever legislation is appropriate, that is, adapted to carry out the objects the amendments have in view, whatever tends to enforce submission to the prohibitions they contain, and to secure to all persons the enjoyment of perfect equality of civil rights and the equal protection of the laws against State denial or invasion, if not prohibited, is brought within the domain of congressional power." Ex parte Virginia.

... We therefore reject South Carolina's argument that Congress may appropriately do no more than to forbid violations of the Fifteenth Amendment in general terms—that the task of fashioning specific remedies or of applying them to particular localities must necessarily be left entirely to the courts. Congress is not circumscribed by any such artificial rules under § 2 of the Fifteenth Amendment....

Congress exercised its authority under the Fifteenth Amendment in an inventive manner when it enacted the Voting Rights Act of 1965. First: The measure prescribes remedies for voting discrimination which go into effect without any need for prior adjudication. This was clearly a legitimate response to the problem, for which there is ample precedent under other constitutional provisions....

Second: The Act intentionally confines these remedies to a small number of States and political subdivisions which in most instances were familiar to Congress by name. This, too, was a permissible method of dealing with the problem. Congress had learned that substantial voting discrimination presently occurs in certain sections of the country, and it knew no way of accurately forecasting whether the evil might spread elsewhere in the future. In acceptable legislative fashion, Congress chose to limit its attention to the geographic areas where immediate action seemed necessary....

After enduring nearly a century of widespread resistance to the Fifteenth Amendment, Congress has marshalled an array of potent weapons against the evil, with authority in the Attorney General to employ them effectively. Many of the areas directly affected by this development have indicated their willingness to abide by any restraints legitimately imposed upon them. We here hold that the portions of the Voting Rights Act properly before us are a valid means for carrying out the commands of the Fifteenth Amendment. Hopefully, millions of nonwhite Americans will now be able to participate for the first time on an equal basis in the government under which they live. We may finally look forward to the day when truly "[t]he right of citizens of the United States to vote shall not be denied or abridged by the United States or by any State on account of race, color, or previous condition of servitude."

The bill of complaint is dismissed.

With the Court's approval of the Voting Rights Act, the federal government was free to launch a vigorous campaign to make the goals of the Fifteenth Amendment a reality. The executive branch actively enforced the law, and Congress periodically strengthened and extended its provisions. These efforts, coupled with large-scale voter registration drives conducted by civil rights organizations, have resulted in southern blacks being registered to vote at rates only slightly below that of whites. As the data in Table 11-1 depict, the final product has been widespread voting participa-

TABLE 11-1 Percentage of Eligible Blacks Registered to Vote, 1940–1984

Year	South	Peripheral South	Deep South
1940	3%	5%	1%
1947	12	17	8
1956	25	29	21
1964	43	52	30
1966	52	58	46
1968	62	67	57
1976	63	62	64
1984	59	58	59

SOURCE: Earl Black and Merle Black. *Politics and Society in the South* (Cambridge, Mass.: Harvard University Press, 1987), 137. Reprinted by permission.

NOTE: South: the eleven Peripheral and Deep South States. Peripheral South: Arkansas, Florida, North Carolina, Tennessee, Texas, Virginia. Deep South: Alabama, Georgia, Louisiana, Mississippi, South Carolina.

tion by minority citizens in the South—more than a full century after the ratification of the Fifteenth Amendment constitutionally declared voting equality.

Economics

In the early history of the United States it was not uncommon for the right to vote to be tied to economic status; suffrage frequently depended upon property ownership. A property holder was considered to have a sufficient stake in the community to be entitled to a voice in the political process. Because of their status and accomplishments, property owners also were presumed to be sufficiently involved and informed to cast intelligent votes. Gradually, property ownership qualifications lost favor and gave way to principles of universal suffrage.

In the 1960s the issue of property ownership as a requirement for voting again became an issue. With the postwar baby boom in full force and a growing need to improve education and other social programs, governments greatly expanded public services and raised taxes to pay for them. At the local level, the primary means of raising revenue was the property tax. Issuing various kinds of revenue bonds and increasing the property tax rate were the usual methods of raising revenue. Many states required such increases to be approved by the voters. Citizens opposed to tax increases were dismayed that individuals who would not have to pay the increased property taxes were allowed to vote in such elections. Obviously, these non-property holders would tend to favor increased facilities and services because the cost would be borne by others. Property owners considered this situation unfair, and some states passed laws restricting the right to vote in property tax and related elections to those who owned or rented real property.

Kramer v. Union Free School District (1969) arose as a challenge to such a law. Are property owners justified in being upset when their taxes are increased in part by voters who are not responsible for the tax bills? Or do individuals stand on solid ground when they claim that they should not be denied a vote on civic issues just because they do not own real property?

Kramer v. Union Free School District

395 U.S. 621 (1969)
Vote: 5 (Brennan, Douglas, Marshall, Warren, White)
　　　3 (Black, Harlan, Stewart)
Opinion of the Court: Warren
Dissenting opinion: Stewart

Section 2012 of the New York education law stipulated that in certain school districts residents who are otherwise qualified to vote in state and federal elections may vote in school district elections only if they (1) owned or leased taxable real property within the district, or (2) were parents or guardians of children enrolled in the local public schools. The state justified these restrictions on grounds that only two classes of residents have a direct interest in the schools: those who finance the schools through the property tax system and those who have children enrolled.

Morris H. Kramer was a resident of the Union Free School District No. 15. He was a thirty-one-year-old,

college-educated stockbroker, who had voted in state and federal elections since 1959. Kramer was a bachelor and lived with his parents. He had custody of no children enrolled in the local public schools, nor did he own or rent any taxable real property in the district. Because he failed to meet the special requirements, Kramer was denied the right to register for and vote in the school elections of 1965. He filed suit to have the special restrictions declared unconstitutional as a violation of the Equal Protection Clause, but a three-judge district court upheld the validity of the New York law. Kramer appealed.

MR. CHIEF JUSTICE WARREN delivered the opinion of the Court.

Besides appellant and others who similarly live in their parents' homes, the statute also disenfranchises the following persons (unless they are parents or guardians of children enrolled in the district public school): senior citizens and others living with children or relatives; clergy, military personnel, and others who live on tax-exempt property; boarders and lodgers; parents who neither own nor lease qualifying property and whose children are too young to attend school; parents who neither own nor lease qualifying property and whose children attend private schools.

Appellant asserts that excluding him from participation in the district elections denies him equal protection of the laws. He contends that he and others of his class are substantially interested in and significantly affected by the school meeting decisions. All members of the community have an interest in the quality and structure of public education, appellant says, and he urges that "the decisions taken by local boards ... may have grave consequences to the entire population." Appellant also argues that the level of property taxation affects him, even though he does not own property, as property tax levels affect the price of goods and services in the community.

We turn therefore to question whether the exclusion is necessary to promote a compelling state interest. First, appellees argue that the State has a legitimate interest in limiting the franchise in school district elections to "members of the community of interest"—those "primarily interested in such elections." Second, appellees urge that the State may reasonably and permissibly conclude that "property taxpayers" (including lessees of taxable property who share the tax burden through rent payments) and parents of the children enrolled in the district's schools are those "primarily interested" in school affairs.

We do not understand appellees to argue that the State is attempting to limit the franchise to those "subjectively concerned" about school matters. Rather, they appear to argue that the State's legitimate interest is in restricting a voice in school matters to those "directly affected" by such decisions. The State apparently reasons that since the schools are financed in part by local property taxes, persons whose out-of-pocket expenses are "directly" affected by property tax changes should be allowed to vote. Similarly, parents of children in school are thought to have a "direct" stake in school affairs and are given a vote.

Appellees argue that it is necessary to limit the franchise to those "primarily interested" in school affairs because "the ever increasing complexity of the many interacting phases of the school system and structure make it extremely difficult for the electorate fully to understand the whys and wherefores of the detailed operations of the school system." Appellees say that many communications of school boards and school administrations are sent home to the parents through the district pupils and are "not broadcast to the general public"; thus, nonparents will be less informed than parents. Further, appellees argue, those who are assessed for local property taxes (either directly or indirectly through rent) will have enough of an interest "through the burden on their pocketbooks, to acquire such information as they may need."

We need express no opinion as to whether the State in some circumstances might limit the exercise of the franchise to those "primarily interested" or "primarily affected." Of course, we therefore do not reach the issue of whether these particular elections are of the type in which the franchise may be so limited. For, assuming, *arguendo*, that New York legitimately might limit the franchise in these school district elections to those "primarily interested in school affairs," close scrutiny of the § 2012 classifications demonstrates that they do not accomplish this purpose with sufficient precision to justify denying appellant the franchise.

Whether classifications allegedly limiting the franchise to those resident citizens "primarily interested" deny those excluded equal protection of the laws depends, *inter alia*, on whether all those excluded are in fact substantially less interested or affected than those the statute includes. In other words, the classifications must be tailored so that the exclusion of appellant and members of his class is necessary to achieve the articulated state goal. Section 2012 does not meet the exacting standard of precision we require of statutes which selectively distribute the franchise. The classifications in § 2012 permit inclusion of many persons who have, at best, a remote and indirect interest, in school affairs and, on the other hand, exclude others who have a distinct and direct interest in the school meeting decisions.

Nor do appellees offer any justification for the exclusion of seemingly interested and informed residents—other than to argue that the § 2012 classifications include those "whom the State could understandably deem to be the most intimately interested in actions taken by the school board," and urge that "the task of . . . balancing the interest of the community in the maintenance of orderly school district elections against the interest of any individual in voting in such elections should clearly remain with the Legislature." But the issue is not whether the legislative judgments are rational. A more exacting standard obtains. The issue is whether the § 2012 requirements do in fact sufficiently further a compelling state interest to justify denying the franchise to appellant and members of his class. The requirements of § 2012 are not sufficiently tailored to limiting the franchise to those "primarily interested" in school affairs to justify the denial of the franchise to appellant and members of his class.

The judgment of the United States District Court for the Eastern District of New York is therefore reversed. The case is remanded for further proceedings consistent with this opinion.

MR. JUSTICE STEWART, with whom MR. JUSTICE BLACK, and MR. JUSTICE HARLAN join, dissenting.

Clearly a State may reasonably assume that its residents have a greater stake in the outcome of elections held within its boundaries than do other persons. Likewise, it is entirely rational for a state legislature to suppose that residents, being generally better informed regarding state affairs than are nonresidents, will be more likely than nonresidents to vote responsibly. And the same may be said of legislative assumptions regarding the electoral competence of adults and literate persons on one hand, and of minors and illiterates on the other. It is clear, of course, that lines thus drawn can not infallibly perform their intended legislative function. Just as "[i]lliterate people may be intelligent voters," nonresidents or minors might also in some instances be interested, informed, and intelligent participants in the electoral process. Persons who commute across a state line to work may well have a great stake in the affairs of the State in which they are employed; some college students under 21 may be both better informed and more passionately interested in political affairs than many adults. But such discrepancies are the inevitable concomitant of the line drawing that is essential to law making. So long as the classification is rationally related to a permissible legislative end, therefore—as are residence, literacy, and age requirements imposed with respect to voting—there is no denial of equal protection.

Thus judged, the statutory classification involved here seems to me clearly to be valid. New York has made the judgment that local educational policy is best left to those persons who have certain direct and definable interests in that policy: those who are either immediately involved as parents of school children or who, as owners or lessees of taxable property, are burdened with the local cost of funding school district operations. True, persons outside those classes may be genuinely interested in the conduct of a school district's business—just as commuters from New Jersey may be genuinely interested in the outcome of a New York City election. But unless this Court is to claim a monopoly of wisdom regarding the sound operation of school systems in the 50 States, I see no way to justify the conclusion that the legislative classification involved here is not rationally related to a legitimate legislative purpose.

The same day the Court issued its decision in *Kramer*, it also ruled on a Louisiana law that restricted voting in elections for the approval of municipal bonds to "property taxpayers" (*Cipriano v. City of Houma*, 1969). The justices found that this law also violated the Equal Protection Clause. In these and subsequent cases, the Court has held that it is not consti-

tutionally permissible to restrict the right to vote to property owners and renters for any election that can be considered to be of general interest or to have a general impact on the community. Such decisions have, for all practical purposes, eliminated the possibility of any significant voter qualifications based on property ownership.

Another form of the voting/economics relationship was the state-imposed tax on the privilege of casting a ballot. Where levied, the poll tax was for a nominal amount. States nonetheless claimed that the tax improved the quality of the electorate by weeding out those who did not sufficiently appreciate the right to vote and who probably would not be well informed on the issues and the candidates. In 1937, in *Breedlove v. Suttles*, the Supreme Court heard a challenge to the constitutionality of the poll tax. At that time, the justices rejected the idea that the Georgia poll tax violated the Equal Protection Clause of the Fourteenth Amendment.

With the rise of the civil rights movement two decades later, the poll tax began to attract increasing criticism. The poll-tax states were in the South, and many saw the tax as just another way of depressing black voting participation. Although large numbers of whites also forfeited the right to vote by failure to pay the poll tax, proportionately, the requirement hit blacks harder, and civil rights and other interest groups targeted the poll tax for elimination. In response, Congress proposed the Twenty-fourth Amendment outlawing the poll tax as a requirement for voting in any federal election. The amendment did not cover state elections because opposition by southerners in Congress and a number of states was judged sufficient to jeopardize its passage. Those who proposed the elimination of the tax were confident that if the requirement were removed as a condition for voting in federal elections, state elections would likely follow. It would be too costly and cumbersome, they reasoned, for the states to maintain two separate voting rolls. The amendment was ratified in 1964.

Shortly thereafter, all but four states rescinded the

poll tax on state elections. Alabama, Texas, and Virginia retained their poll taxes of $1.50, and Mississippi continued its $2 tax. Having failed to obtain a constitutional amendment that completely rid the nation of these taxes, opponents sought relief in the courts.

Harper v. Virginia State Board of Elections

383 U.S. 663 (1966)

Vote: 6 (Brennan, Clark, Douglas, Fortas, Warren, White)
  3 (Black, Harlan, Stewart)

Opinion of the Court: Douglas
Dissenting opinions: Black, Harlan

Annie E. Harper and other residents of Virginia filed suit in federal district court to have the Virginia poll tax declared unconstitutional as a violation of the Equal Protection Clause of the Fourteenth Amendment. The trial court ruled in favor of the state holding that the Supreme Court's precedent of *Breedlove v. Suttles* controlled the issue. Harper appealed. The Court confined its analysis to the economic discrimination inherent in the poll tax and did not confront the issue of racial discrimination and the right to vote.

MR. JUSTICE DOUGLAS delivered the opinion of the Court.

While the right to vote in federal elections is conferred by Art. I, § 2, of the Constitution, the right to vote in state elections is nowhere expressly mentioned. It is argued that the right to vote in state elections is implicit, particularly by reason of the First Amendment and that it may not constitutionally be conditioned upon the payment of a tax or fee. We do not stop to canvass the relation between voting and political expression. For it is enough to say that once the franchise is granted to the electorate, lines may not be drawn which are inconsistent with the Equal Protection Clause of the Fourteenth Amendment....

We conclude that a State violates the Equal Protection Clause of the Fourteenth Amendment whenever it makes the affluence of the voter or payment of any fee an electoral standard. Voter qualifications have no relation to wealth nor to paying or not paying this or any other tax. Our cases demonstrate that the Equal Protection Clause of the Fourteenth Amendment restrains the States from fixing voter qualifications which invidiously discriminate....

We say the same whether the citizen, otherwise qualified to vote, has $1.50 in his pocket or nothing at all, pays the fee or fails to pay it. The principle that denies the State the right to dilute a citizen's vote on account of his economic status or other such factors by analogy bars a system which excludes those unable to pay a fee to vote or who fail to pay.

It is argued that a State may exact fees from citizens for many different kinds of licenses; that if it can demand from all an equal fee for a driver's license, it can demand from all an equal poll tax for voting. But we must remember that the interest of the State, when it comes to voting, is limited to the power to fix qualifications. Wealth, like race, creed, or color, is not germane to one's ability to participate intelligently in the electoral process. Lines drawn on the basis of wealth or property, like those of race, are traditionally disfavored. To introduce wealth or payment of a fee as a measure of a voter's qualifications is to introduce a capricious or irrelevant factor. The degree of the discrimination is irrelevant. In this context—that is, as a condition of obtaining a ballot—the requirement of fee paying causes an "invidious" discrimination that runs afoul of the Equal Protection Clause. Levy "by the poll," as stated in Breedlove v. Suttles, is an old familiar form of taxation; and we say nothing to impair its validity so long as it is not made a condition to the exercise of the franchise. Breedlove v. Suttles sanctioned its use as "a prerequisite of voting." To that extent the *Breedlove* case is overruled.

We agree, of course, with Mr. Justice Holmes that the Due Process Clause of the Fourteenth Amendment "does not enact Mr. Herbert Spencer's Social Statics." Likewise, the Equal Protection Clause is not shackled to the political theory of a particular era. In determining what lines are unconstitutionally discriminatory, we have never been confined to historic notions of equality, any more than we have restricted due process to a fixed catalogue of what was at a given time deemed to be the limits of fundamental rights. Notions of what constitutes equal treatment for purposes of the Equal Protection Clause *do* change. This Court in 1896 held that laws providing for separate public facilities for white and Negro citizens did not deprive the latter of the equal protection and treatment that the Fourteenth Amendment commands. Plessy v. Ferguson. Seven of the eight Justices then sitting subscribed to the Court's opinion, thus joining in expressions of what constituted unequal and discriminatory treatment that sound strange to a contemporary ear. When, in 1954—more than a half century later—we repudiated the "separate-but-equal" doctrine of *Plessy* as respects public education we stated: "In approaching this problem, we cannot turn the clock back to 1868 when the Amendment was adopted, or even to 1896 when Plessy v. Ferguson was written." Brown v. Board of Education.

In a recent searching re-examination of the Equal Protection Clause, we held, as already noted, that "the opportunity for equal participation by all voters in the election of state legislators" is required. We decline to qualify that principle by sustaining this poll tax. Our conclusion is founded not on what we think governmental policy should be, but on what the Equal Protection Clause requires.

We have long been mindful that where fundamental rights and liberties are asserted under the Equal Protection Clause, classifications which might invade or restrain them must be closely scrutinized and carefully confined.

Those principles apply here. For to repeat, wealth or fee paying has, in our view, no relation to voting qualifications; the right to vote is too precious, too fundamental to be so burdened or conditioned.

Reversed.

MR. JUSTICE BLACK, dissenting.

It should be pointed out at once that the Court's decision is to no extent based on a finding that the Virginia law as written or as applied is being used as a device or mechanism to deny Negro citizens of Virginia the right to vote on account of their color. Apparently the Court agrees with the District Court below and with my Brothers HARLAN and STEWART that this record would not support any finding that the Virginia poll tax law the Court invalidates has any such effect. If the record could support a finding that the law as written or applied has such an effect, the law would of course be unconstitutional as a violation of the Fourteenth and Fifteenth Amendments and also 42 U.S.C. § 1971(a). . . . What the Court does hold is that the Equal Protection Clause necessarily bars all States from making payment of a state tax, any tax, a prerequisite to voting. . . .

A study of our cases shows that this Court has refused to use the general language of the Equal Protection Clause as though it provided a handy instrument to strike down state laws which the Court feels are based on bad governmental policy. The equal protection cases carefully analyzed boil down to the principle that distinctions drawn and even discriminations imposed by state laws do not violate the Equal Protection Clause so long as these distinctions and discriminations are not "irrational," "irrelevant," "unreasonable," "arbitrary," or "invidious." These vague and indefinite terms do not, of course, provide a precise formula or an automatic mechanism for deciding cases arising under the Equal Protection Clause. The restrictive connotations of these terms, however, . . . are a plain recognition of the fact that under a proper interpretation of the Equal Protection Clause States are to have the broadest kind of leeway in areas where they have a general constitutional competence to act. In view of the purpose of the terms to restrain the courts from a wholesale invalidation of state laws under the Equal Protection Clause it would be difficult to say that the poll tax requirement is "irrational" or "arbitrary" or works "invidious discriminations." State poll tax legislation can "reasonably," "rationally" and without an "invidious" or evil purpose to injure anyone be found to rest on a number of state policies including (1) the State's desire to collect its revenue, and (2) its belief that voters who pay a poll tax will be interested in furthering the State's welfare when they vote. Certainly it is rational to believe that people may be more likely to pay taxes if payment is a pre-requisite to voting. And if history can be a factor in determining the "rationality" of discrimination in a state law . . . then whatever may be our personal opinion, history is on the side of "rationality" of the State's poll tax policy. . . . Although I join the Court in disliking the policy of the poll tax, this is not in my judgment a justifiable reason for holding this poll tax law unconstitutional. Such a holding on my part would, in my judgment, be an exercise of power which the Constitution does not confer upon me.

Another reason for my dissent from the Court's judgment and opinion is that it seems to be using the old "natural-law-due-process formula" to justify striking down state laws as violations of the Equal Protection Clause. I have heretofore had many occasions to express my strong belief that there is no constitutional support whatever for this Court to use the Due Process Clause as though it provided a blank check to alter the meaning of the Constitution as written so as to add to it substantive constitutional changes which a majority of the Court at any given time believes are needed to meet present-day problems. Nor is there in my opinion any more constitutional support for this Court to use the Equal Protection Clause, as it has today, to write into the Constitution its notions of what it thinks is good governmental policy. If basic changes as to the respective powers of the state and national governments are needed, I prefer to let those changes be made by amendment as Article V of the Constitution provides. For a majority of this Court to undertake that task, whether purporting to do so under the Due Process or the Equal Protection Clause amounts, in my judgment, to an exercise of power the Constitution makers with foresight and wisdom refused to give the Judicial Branch of the Government....

... The Court gives no reason at all to discredit the long-standing beliefs that making the payment of a tax a prerequisite to voting is an effective way of collecting revenue and that people who pay their taxes are likely to have a far greater interest in their government. The Court's failure to give any reasons to show that these purposes of the poll tax are "irrational," "unreasonable," "arbitrary," or "invidious" is a pretty clear indication to me that none exist. I can only conclude that the primary, controlling, predominate, if not the exclusive reason for declaring the Virginia law unconstitutional is the Court's deep-seated hostility and antagonism, which I share, to making payment of a tax a prerequisite to voting.

The Court's justification for consulting its own notions rather than following the original meaning of the Constitution, as I would, apparently is based on the belief of the majority of the Court that for this Court to be bound by the original meaning of the Constitution is an intolerable and debilitating evil; that our Constitution should not be "shackled to the political theory of a particular era," and that to save the country from the original Constitution the Court must have constant power to renew it and keep it abreast of this Court's more enlightening theories of what is best for our society.

It seems to me that this is an attack not only on the great value of our Constitution itself but also on the concept of a written constitution which is to survive through the years as originally written unless changed through the

amendment process which the Framers wisely provided. Moreover, when a "political theory" embodied in our Constitution becomes outdated, it seems to me that a majority of the nine members of this Court are not only without constitutional power but are far less qualified to choose a new constitutional political theory than the people of this country proceeding in the manner provided by Article V.

Residency

Traditionally, the states have had the authority to restrict voting to individuals who were truly citizens and residents of the community, and state legislatures usually require individuals to be residents for a certain period of time before they can vote. States also normally require potential voters to register prior to election day. These restrictions have been based on the principle that only bona fide residents should have a voice in making political decisions for the community. They also prevent voter fraud: candidates cannot recruit large numbers of nonresident supporters to present themselves on election day and demand the right to vote. Although these limitations do not have the same connotations as restricting access to the ballot box on the basis of race or economic status, the Supreme Court has taken steps to ensure that they do not unreasonably deny the right to vote.

The Court, for example, has ruled that individuals moving into a community must have a reasonable opportunity to obtain resident status. *Carrington v. Rash* (1965) provides a good illustration. The Court struck down a Texas regulation that imposed too great a burden on military personnel. Texas, home to numerous military bases, feared that the large numbers of armed services personnel transferred into the state for relatively short assignments would have a disproportionate impact on local elections. The state argued that it was very difficult to determine whether these individuals were bona fide residents. Texas therefore imposed a blanket exclusion on service personnel, stipulating that members of the armed forces who moved into Texas could not vote so long as they remained in the military. The Court refused to accept such a burden being placed on an entire class of individuals, holding that the Equal Protection Clause demands a more precise test to determine those whose residence in the state is bona fide.

But the Court has never seriously questioned the authority of the state to limit voting to bona fide residents, and, in fact, many states require that individuals live in the state and the local community for a minimum period of time before they are eligible to vote. In 1970 Congress amended the Voting Rights Act to outlaw residency requirements longer than thirty days for voting in presidential elections. This change was based on the rationale that the length of time one lived in a particular state or locality had no reasonable connection to being qualified to vote for the federal executive. However, many states retained their time requirements for state and local elections. How reasonable such conditions are was a question presented to the Court in *Dunn v. Blumstein.* The majority takes a dim view of residency requirements that are longer than necessary to accomplish legitimate state interests. Based upon this decision, how long may a residency requirement be before the Court would find it an unreasonable burden on the right to vote?

Dunn v. Blumstein

405 U.S. 330 (1972)

Vote: 6 (Blackmun, Brennan, Douglas, Marshall, Stewart,
       White)
    1 (Burger)

Opinion of the Court: Marshall
Concurring opinion: Blackmun
Dissenting opinion: Burger
Not participating: Powell, Rehnquist

James F. Blumstein moved to Tennessee on June 12, 1970, to be an assistant professor of law at Vanderbilt University in Nashville. With primary and general elections scheduled for August and November, he went to register to vote on July 1, but was refused. Tennessee made voter eligibility dependent upon living in the state for a minimum of one year and in the county for at least three months. After exhausting his administrative remedies within the state, Blumstein filed suit against Gov. Winfield Dunn and other state officials to have the residency law declared unconstitutional. A three-judge district court struck down the requirement as impermissibly interfering with the right to vote, and the state appealed.

MR. JUSTICE MARSHALL delivered the opinion of the Court.

Durational residence laws penalize those persons who have traveled from one place to another to establish a new residence during the qualifying period. Such laws divide residents into two classes, old residents and new residents, and discriminate against the latter to the extent of totally denying them the opportunity to vote. The constitutional question presented is whether the Equal Protection Clause of the Fourteenth Amendment permits a State to discriminate in this way among its citizens....

In the present case, whether we look to the benefit withheld by the classification (the opportunity to vote) or the basis for the classification (recent interstate travel) we conclude that the State must show a substantial and compelling reason for imposing durational residence requirements....

Tennessee's durational residence laws classify bona fide residents on the basis of recent travel, penalizing those persons, and only those persons, who have gone from one jurisdiction to another during the qualifying period. Thus, the durational residence requirement directly impinges on the exercise of a second fundamental personal right, the right to travel....

We considered such a durational residence requirement in Shapiro v. Thompson [1969] where the pertinent statutes imposed a one-year waiting period for interstate migrants as a condition to receiving welfare benefits. Although in *Shapiro* we specifically did not decide whether durational residence requirements could be used to determine voting eligibility, we concluded that since the right to travel was a constitutionally protected right, "any classification which serves to penalize the exercise of that right, unless shown to be necessary to promote a *compelling* governmental interest, is unconstitutional."...

We turn, then, to the question of whether the State has shown that durational residence requirements are needed to further a sufficiently substantial state interest. We emphasize again the difference between bona fide residence requirements and durational residence requirements. We have in the past noted approvingly that the States have the power to require that voters be bona fide residents of the relevant political subdivision. An appropriately defined and uniformly applied requirement of bona fide residence may be necessary to preserve the basic conception of a political community, and therefore could withstand close constitutional scrutiny. But *durational* residence requirements, representing a separate voting qualification imposed on bona fide residents, must be separately tested by the stringent standard....

Tennessee tenders "two basic purposes" served by its durational residence requirements:

"(1) INSURE PURITY OF BALLOT BOX—Protection against fraud through colonization and inability to identify persons offering to vote, and

"(2) KNOWLEDGEABLE VOTER—Afford some surety that the voter has, in fact, become a member of the community and that as such, he has a common interest in all matters pertaining to its government and is, therefore, more likely to exercise his right more intelligently."

We consider each in turn.

Preservation of the "purity of the ballot box" is a formidable-sounding state interest. The impurities feared, variously called "dual voting" and "colonization," all involve voting by nonresidents, either singly or in groups. The main concern is that nonresidents will temporarily invade the State or county, falsely swear that they are residents to become eligible to vote, and, by voting, allow a candidate to win by fraud. Surely the prevention of such fraud is a legitimate and compelling government goal. But it is impossible to view durational residence requirements as necessary to achieve that state interest....

Fixing a constitutionally acceptable period is surely a matter of degree. It is sufficient to note here that 30 days appears to be an ample period of time for the State to complete whatever administrative tasks are necessary to prevent fraud—and a year, or three months, too much. This was the judgment of Congress in the context of presidential elections. And, on the basis of the statutory scheme before us, it is almost surely the judgment of the Tennessee lawmakers as well....

Our conclusion that the waiting period is not the least restrictive means necessary for preventing fraud is bolstered by the recognition that Tennessee has at its disposal a variety of criminal laws that are more than adequate to detect and deter whatever fraud may be feared. At least six separate sections of the Tennessee Code define offenses to deal with voter fraud....

The argument that durational residence requirements further the goal of having "knowledgeable voters" appears to involve three separate claims. The first is that such requirements "afford some surety that the voter has, in fact, become a member of the community." But here the State appears to confuse a bona fide residence requirement with a durational residence requirement. As already noted, a State does have an interest in limiting the franchise to bona fide members of the community. But this does not justify or explain the exclusion from the franchise of persons, not because their bona fide residence is questioned, but because they are recent rather than long-time residents.

The second branch of the "knowledgeable voters" justification is that durational residence requirements assure that the voter "has a common interest in all matters pertaining to [the community's] government...." By this, presumably, the State means that it may require a period of residence sufficiently lengthy to impress upon its voters the local viewpoint. This is precisely the sort of argument this Court has repeatedly rejected....

Finally, the State urges that a long-time resident is "more likely to exercise his right [to vote] more intelligently." To the extent that this is different from the previous argument, the State is apparently asserting an interest in limiting the franchise to voters who are knowledgeable about the issues. In this case, Tennessee argues that people who have been in the State less than a year and the county less than three months are likely to be unaware of the issues involved in the congressional, state, and local elections, and therefore can be barred from the franchise. We note that the criterion of "intelligent" voting is an elusive one, and susceptible of abuse. But without deciding as a general matter the extent to which a State can bar less knowledgeable or intelligent citizens from the franchise, we conclude that durational residence requirements cannot be justified on this basis....

It may well be true that new residents as a group know less about state and local issues than older residents; and it is surely true that durational residence requirements will exclude some people from voting who are totally uninformed about election matters. But as devices to limit the franchise to knowledgeable residents, the conclusive presumptions of durational residence requirements are much too crude. They exclude too many people who should not, and need not, be excluded. They represent a requirement of knowledge unfairly imposed on only some citizens. We are aware that classifications are always imprecise. By requiring classifications to be tailored to their purpose, we do not secretly require the impossible. Here, there is simply too attenuated a relationship between the state interest in an informed electorate and the fixed requirements that voters must have been residents in the State for a year and the county for three months. Given the exacting standard of precision we require of statutes affecting constitutional rights, we cannot say that durational residence requirements are necessary to further a compelling state interest.

Concluding that Tennessee has not offered an adequate justification for its durational residence laws, we affirm the judgment of the court below.

Affirmed.

The combined effects of constitutional amendments, federal enforcement legislation, and judicial decisions have taken away most of the states' discretion to determine qualifications for voting. The states retain responsibility for administering the voting process, but contemporary political and legal notions of universal suffrage have left them little else. The state may still deny individuals the right to vote if for legitimate considerations (for example, mental illness) they are demonstrably unqualified. The Court also has ruled that states may strip convicted felons of the right to vote. In some states, such bans last only until the convicted criminals complete all aspects of their sentences. In *Richardson v. Ramirez* (1974), however, the justices upheld a California law that forever disenfranchised individuals found guilty of felonies.

POLITICAL REPRESENTATION

Voting rights alone do not guarantee that people share equally in political influence. The United States is not a direct democracy; consequently, few public policy decisions are made in the voting booth. In a republican form of government, most political decisions are made by officials who are elected by the people from defined geographical districts. The duty of these officials is to represent the interests of their constituencies in the policy-making process.

How well and how equitably this representational process works depends in part on how the boundary lines of political units are drawn. These issues are not easy to resolve, as the history of our nation shows. Much of the debate at the Constitutional Convention centered on representation. The smaller states wanted representation in Congress based on statehood, with each of the thirteen states having equal voting powers. The larger states argued for legislative representation based on size of population. The convention compromised by accepting both ideas in a bicameral Congress.

Because district lines determine political representation, the authority to draw those boundaries carries with it a great deal of political power. Skillful construction of political subdivisions can be used to great advantage, and politicians have never been reluctant to use this power to advance their own interests. Since 1812 the art of structuring legislative districts to ensure political success has been known as gerrymandering. The term refers to the political maneuverings of Gov. Elbridge Gerry of Massachusetts, who convinced the state legislature to draw district lines so that his partisan supporters would have a high probability of reelection. Gerrymandered districts frequently are characterized by the rather strange geographical configurations necessary to achieve the desired political ends.

Establishing or modifying the district lines historically has been a political matter. Battles over drawing the boundaries of political subdivisions usually are fought within the halls of the state legislatures. However, serious legal or even constitutional questions may arise when officials use inappropriate criteria for drawing boundaries, or when the process results in the discriminatory treatment of certain groups of voters. In such cases the courts may be called upon to intervene in what is otherwise a legislative duty.

Gomillion v. Lightfoot (1960) is an example. C. G. Gomillion and other black citizens of Alabama filed suit against Phil Lightfoot, the mayor of Tuskegee, over a legislative act that redrew the city boundaries. Before 1957 Tuskegee city limits were in the shape of a square that covered the entire urban area. With the growing civil rights activism of the time and the increasing tendency of black citizens to vote, the white establishment in Tuskegee feared a loss of political control. Consequently, members of the Alabama legislature sympathetic to the city successfully sponsored a bill that changed the boundary lines. Instead of a square, the altered city limits formed, in Justice Felix Frankfurter's words, "an uncouth twenty-eight-sided figure." The effect of the redistricting was phenomenal. The law removed from the city all but 4 or 5 of its 400 black voters, but no white voters. The black plaintiffs, now former residents of Tuskegee, claimed that their removal from the city denied them the right to vote on the basis of race and, therefore, violated their Fifteenth Amendment rights. The city did not deny that race was at issue, but claimed that the state of Alabama had an unrestricted right to draw city boundaries as it saw fit and that the courts could not intervene to limit that authority. A unanimous Supreme Court ruled to the contrary, holding that when an otherwise lawful exercise of state power is used to circum-

In 1812 Elkanah Tinsdale lampooned the political maneuverings of Gov. Elbridge Gerry of Massachusetts, who deftly engineered the construction of constituency boundaries to aid in the election of a member of his own party. Because the district resembled a salamander in the cartoonist's illustration, the term *gerrymander* has come to mean the drawing of political district lines for partisan advantage.

vent a federally protected right, the courts may indeed intervene. A legislative act that removes citizens from the municipal voting rolls in a racially discriminatory fashion violates the Fifteenth Amendment.

The power to define political constituencies has given rise to a number of important legal questions. Under what conditions are the courts entitled to intervene in an activity normally left to the political process? Does the Constitution place limits on the relative size of representational districts? What criteria may a legislature take into account in deciding where to draw the boundaries of a political subdivision? How does the Constitution limit the legislature's freedom in shaping political units? Beginning in the 1960s the Supreme Court issued rulings on these and related issues of political representation.

The Reapportionment Controversy

In drafting Article I of the Constitution, the Framers clearly intended that representation in the lower house of Congress would be based upon population. Each state was allotted at least one representative, with additional seats based upon the number of persons residing within its boundaries.[4]

The Constitutional Convention wisely anticipated that the nation would undergo considerable growth and population mobility and consequently determined that the number of congressional seats allocated to each state would be reformulated every ten years following completion of the national census. States that grew in population would gain increased congressional representation, and those that lost population would lose representation. This process remains relatively unchanged today. The number of seats in the House of Representatives is fixed by federal law, currently at 435. Every ten years, when the Census Bureau completes its work, the allocation of those 435 seats among the states must be recalculated to reflect changes since the previous population count.

Following the census, each state is told the number of representatives it will have for the next decade. The state legislature then geographically divides the state into separate congressional districts, each of which elects a member of Congress. This scheme is known as the single-member constituency system of representation.[5] Political representation is equitable only if the state legislature constructs its congressional districts so that each contains approximately the same number of residents.

The process of devising the legislative districts is called apportionment. When the legislature creates equally populated districts, the system is properly apportioned. But when the districts are not in proper balance, when some districts are substantially larger than others, they are said to be malapportioned. A state can be malapportioned if the legislature does not draw the district lines properly or fails to adjust boundaries to keep pace with population shifts.

Representational districts are used not only for congressional seats but also for other government units. The state legislatures, for example, generally are based on a single-member constituency system, as are many county commissions and city councils. Even special purpose commissions, such as boards of education and public utility districts, often follow the same scheme. In each case, a legislative body must create districts from which representatives will be selected. The same apportionment concepts apply to these bodies as to congressional districts.

The constitutional issues regarding apportionment rose to the surface after World War II. Spurred by industrialization, two major wars, and an economic depression, major population shifts had occurred during the first half of the twentieth century. Large numbers of people moved from rural areas and small towns into larger urban centers. Cities grew rapidly and agricultural areas declined, but state legislatures failed to respond adequately to these migration patterns by reapportioning their congressional and state legislative districts. The more state legislatures came to be dominated by rural interests, the less incumbent legislators wished to consider redistricting. To apportion the districts properly would mean fewer legislative seats for the rural areas, and that meant abolishing some seats held by incumbents. At the midpoint of the century, many states had not reapportioned since the 1900 census.

The first major apportionment case to come before the Supreme Court was *Colegrove v. Green* (1946). Kenneth Colegrove and two others filed suit to challenge the constitutionality of the Illinois congressional district system. These plaintiffs lived in districts with dis-

4. Originally, population was determined by the number of free persons, including indentured servants, but excluding Indians not taxed, plus three-fifths of the slaves. This formula was changed with ratification of the Fourteenth Amendment in 1868 to define population as the whole number of persons, excluding Indians not taxed.

5. During the first half century of the nation's history it was common for the states to select their delegates to the House of Representatives on an at-large basis rather than using the single-member constituency plan.

proportionately large populations. They argued, among other points, that the Illinois districts were so badly malapportioned that they violated the constitutional guarantee of a republican form of government specified in Art. IV, § 4. Colegrove's factual case was a strong one. The Illinois legislature had not reapportioned its congressional districts since 1901, even though four census counts had occurred, documenting major population shifts into urban centers. When the plaintiffs filed their suit, the largest Illinois district had 914,053 residents and the smallest only 112,116. A resident in the smallest district had eight times more congressional representation than a citizen living in the largest district. In spite of these population disparities and legal provisions supporting redistricting, the Supreme Court, by a 4–3 vote, ruled that the question of reapportionment was a political, not legal, issue. The authority to draw district boundaries for congressional seats was given to the state legislatures, and the federal courts had no power to intervene. Justice Frankfurter, for the plurality, served notice that the Court "ought not to enter this political thicket," instead informing the complaining parties that their remedy was through the ballot box and legislative process rather than the courts.

The Court's admonishment presented an insurmountable problem for urban residents living in disproportionately large districts. Many states were so badly malapportioned and the dominant rural interests so opposed to change that electing enough state legislators sympathetic to reapportionment was almost impossible. But the Court maintained its position that reapportionment questions were outside the purview of judicial scrutiny. Meanwhile, the census figures for 1950 and 1960 indicated that the malapportionment problem was growing.

As the nation entered the 1960s, the Supreme Court's position began to soften. This change was prompted by a greater awareness of the problems associated with malapportionment and by significant personnel changes on the Court. Of the four votes

comprising the majority in *Colegrove,* only Justice Frankfurter remained on the bench. The justices, now under the leadership of Earl Warren, expressed a much greater willingness to accept rights violations claims.

In 1962 the Court decided *Baker v. Carr,* in which a group of urban residents from Tennessee challenged the way their state legislative districts were drawn. Although this case involved representation in the state assembly rather than in Congress, there were significant factual parallels between *Baker* and *Colegrove.* The central question in *Baker* was whether the federal courts have jurisdiction over apportionment cases. Rather than basing their jurisdictional claim on the Constitution's republican form of government guarantee, as Colegrove had done, the plaintiffs in *Baker* argued that the malapportioned Tennessee legislature violated the Fourteenth Amendment's Equal Protection Clause. If the Court did not alter its position that apportionment was a political question over which the federal courts had no say, urban residents would continue to find their representational voice diluted by legislatures dominated by rural interests. But a decision that granted federal court jurisdiction undoubtedly would set off an avalanche of litigation throughout the nation.

The justices considered the Baker case with extreme care.[6] The Court heard six hours of oral argument on two separate occasions. The justices deliberated at length in conference. The final opinions took up 163 pages in the *United States Reports,* and covered a wide range of subjects such as the political question doctrine, the Guarantee and Equal Protection Clauses, standing, and justiciability. In the excerpt of the *Baker* opinion reprinted here the Court discusses the power of the federal judiciary to hear reapportionment cases when a claim is made that legislative districting violates equal protection of the laws.

---

6. See J. W. Peltason, "Baker v. Carr," in *The Oxford Companion,* 56–59.

Baker v. Carr

369 U.S. 186 (1962)

Vote: 6 (Black, Brennan, Clark, Douglas, Stewart, Warren)
    2 (Frankfurter, Harlan)

Opinion of the Court: Brennan

Concurring opinions: Clark, Douglas, Stewart

Dissenting opinions: Frankfurter, Harlan

Not participating: Whittaker

Tennessee had experienced massive population migration to its urban areas during the first half of the twentieth century, but the state legislature had not redistricted since 1901. The result was a badly malapportioned state legislature in which the smallest district had nineteen times the representational power of the largest district. Charles Baker and other residents from Memphis, Nashville, and Knoxville sued Joseph C. Carr, the state secretary of state, requesting that the court declare the apportionment law unconstitutional and prohibit the state from conducting future elections under it. Feeling bound by the precedent of *Colegrove v. Green,* the district court dismissed the suit on grounds that legislative apportionment issues presented political questions over which the judiciary had no jurisdiction. The plaintiffs appealed to the U.S. Supreme Court.

MR. JUSTICE BRENNAN delivered the opinion of the Court.

Article III, § 2, of the Federal Constitution provides that "The judicial Power shall extend to all Cases, in Law and Equity, arising under this Constitution, the Laws of the United States, and Treaties made, or which shall be made, under their Authority...." It is clear that the cause of action is one which "arises under" the Federal Constitution. The complaint alleges that the 1901 statute effects an apportionment that deprives the appellants of the equal protection of the laws in violation of the Fourteenth Amendment. Dismissal of the complaint upon the ground of lack of jurisdiction of the subject matter would, therefore, be justified only if that claim were "so attenuated and unsubstantial as to be absolutely devoid of merit," *Newburyport Water Co. v. Newburyport,* or "frivolous," *Bell v. Hood.* That the claim is unsubstantial must be "very plain." *Hart v. Keith Vaudeville Exchange.* Since the District Court obviously and correctly did not deem the asserted federal constitutional claim unsubstantial and frivolous, it should not have dismissed the complaint for want of jurisdiction of the subject matter. And of course no further consideration of the merits of the claim is relevant to a determination of the court's jurisdiction of the subject matter. We said in an earlier voting case from Tennessee: "It is obvious ... that the court, in dismissing for want of jurisdiction, was controlled by what it deemed to be the want of merit in the arguments which were made in the complaint as to the violation of the Federal right. But as the very nature of the controversy was Federal, and, therefore, jurisdiction existed, whilst the opinion of the court as to the want of merit in the cause of action might have furnished ground for dismissing for that reason, it afforded no sufficient ground for deciding that the action was not one arising under the Constitution and laws of the United States." *Swafford v. Templeton.* "For it is well settled that the failure to state a proper cause of action calls for a judgment on the merits and not for a dismissal for want of jurisdiction." *Bell v. Hood.*

Since the complaint plainly sets forth a case arising under the Constitution, the subject matter is within the federal judicial power defined in Art. III, § 2, and so within the power of Congress to assign to the jurisdiction of the District Courts....

An unbroken line of our precedents sustains the federal courts' jurisdiction of the subject matter of federal constitutional claims of this nature. The first cases involved the redistricting of States for the purpose of electing Representatives to the Federal Congress. When the Ohio Supreme Court sustained Ohio legislation against an attack for repugnancy to Art. I, § 4, of the Federal Constitution, we affirmed on the merits and expressly refused to dismiss for want of jurisdiction "In view ... of the subject-matter of the controversy and the Federal characteristics which inhere in it...." *Ohio ex rel. Davis v. Hildebrant.* When the Minnesota

Supreme Court affirmed the dismissal of a suit to enjoin the Secretary of State of Minnesota from acting under Minnesota redistricting legislation, we reviewed the constitutional merits of the legislation and reversed the State Supreme Court. *Smiley v. Holm.* . . . When a three-judge District Court, exercising jurisdiction under the predecessor of 28 U.S.C. § 1343 (3), permanently enjoined officers of the State of Mississippi from conducting an election of Representatives under a Mississippi redistricting act, we reviewed the federal questions on the merits and reversed the District Court. *Wood v. Broom.* A similar decree of a District Court, exercising jurisdiction under the same statute, concerning a Kentucky redistricting act, was reviewed and the decree reversed. *Mahan v. Hume.*

The appellees refer to *Colegrove v. Green* as authority that the District Court lacked jurisdiction of the subject matter. Appellees misconceive the holding of that case. The holding was precisely contrary to their reading of it. Seven members of the Court participated in the decision. Unlike many other cases in this field which have assumed without discussion that there was jurisdiction, all three opinions filed in *Colegrove* discussed the question. Two of the opinions expressing the views of four of the Justices, a majority, flatly held that there was jurisdiction of the subject matter. MR. JUSTICE BLACK joined by MR. JUSTICE DOUGLAS and Mr. Justice Murphy stated: "It is my judgment that the District Court had jurisdiction . . . ," citing the predecessor of 28 U.S.C. § 1343 (3), and *Bell v. Hood.* Mr. Justice Rutledge, writing separately, expressed agreement with this conclusion. Indeed, it is even questionable that the opinion of MR. JUSTICE FRANKFURTER, joined by Justices Reed and Burton, doubted jurisdiction of the subject matter. . . .

Several subsequent cases similar to *Colegrove* have been decided by the Court in summary *per curiam* statements. None was dismissed for want of jurisdiction of the subject matter.

Two cases decided with opinions after *Colegrove* likewise plainly imply that the subject matter of this suit is within District Court jurisdiction. In *McDougall v. Green* the District Court dismissed for want of jurisdiction, which had been invoked under 28 U.S.C. § 1343 (3), a suit to enjoin enforcement of the requirement that nominees for state-wide elections be supported by a petition signed by a minimum number of persons from at least 50 of the State's 102 counties. This Court's disagreement with that action is clear since the Court affirmed the judgment after a review of the merits and concluded that the particular claim there was without merit. In *South v. Peters* we affirmed the dismissal of an attack on the Georgia "county unit" system but founded our action on a ground that plainly would not have been reached if the lower court lacked jurisdiction of the subject matter, which allegedly existed under 28 U.S.C. § 1343 (3). The express words of our holding were that "Federal courts consistently refuse to exercise their equity powers in cases posing political issues arising from a state's geographical distribution of electoral strength among its political subdivisions."

We hold that the District Court has jurisdiction of the subject matter of the federal constitutional claim asserted in the complaint.

We come, finally, to the ultimate inquiry whether our precedents as to what constitutes a nonjusticiable "political question" bring the case before us under the umbrella of that doctrine. A natural beginning is to note whether any of the common characteristics which we have been able to identify and label descriptively are present. We find none: The question here is the consistency of state action with the Federal Constitution. We have no question decided, or to be decided, by a political branch of government coequal with this Court. Nor do we risk embarrassment of our government abroad, or grave disturbance at home if we take issue with Tennessee as to the constitutionality of her action here challenged. Nor need the appellants, in order to succeed in this action, ask the Court to enter upon policy determinations for which judicially manageable standards are lacking. Judicial standards under the Equal Protection Clause are well developed and familiar, and it has been open to courts since the enactment of the Fourteenth Amendment to determine, if on the particular facts they must, that a discrimination reflects *no* policy, but simply arbitrary and capricious action.

This case does, in one sense, involve the allocation of political power within a State, and the appellants might conceivably have added a claim under the Guaranty Clause. Of course, as we have seen, any reliance on that clause would be futile. But because any reliance on the Guaranty

Clause could not have succeeded it does not follow that appellants may not be heard on the equal protection claim which in fact they tender. True, it must be clear that the Fourteenth Amendment claim is not so enmeshed with those political question elements which render Guaranty Clause claims nonjusticiable as actually to present a political question itself. But we have found that not to be the case here. . . .

We conclude that the complaint's allegations of a denial of equal protection present a justiciable constitutional cause of action upon which appellants are entitled to a trial and a decision. The right asserted is within the reach of judicial protection under the Fourteenth Amendment.

The judgment of the District Court is reversed and the cause is remanded for further proceedings consistent with this opinion.

Reversed and remanded.

In *Baker v. Carr*, with only Frankfurter and Harlan in dissent, the Court held that the federal judiciary has authority to hear challenges to state districting systems and that equal protection arguments do present justiciable issues not barred by the political question doctrine. Although the Court confined itself to these jurisdictional issues, the ruling in *Baker* opened the Supreme Court's doors to reapportionment cases; and there was little doubt that the justices were prepared to initiate significant changes in the nation's system of political representation.

The first major reapportionment case heard by the Supreme Court following *Baker* was *Wesberry v. Sanders* (1964), which involved a challenge to the way Georgia apportioned its congressional districts. Although this case involved only Georgia, the malapportionment there was typical of most states following the 1960 census and the 1962 congressional elections *(see Table 11-2)*. Justice Black's majority opinion in *Wesberry*, rich in history, places considerable importance on the intent of the Framers. Keep in mind the particular constitutional provision the Court is interpreting and the representational standard that must be achieved in order to satisfy the Constitution.

Wesberry v. Sanders

376 U.S. 1 (1964)

Vote: 6 (Black, Brennan, Douglas, Goldberg, Warren, White)
    3 (Clark, Harlan, Stewart)

Opinion of the Court: Black
Opinion dissenting in part and concurring in part: Clark
Dissenting opinions: Harlan, Stewart

This suit was filed by James P. Wesberry and other qualified voters of Georgia's Fifth Congressional District against Gov. Carl Sanders and other state officials. The plaintiffs claimed that the state's congressional districting system violated the federal Constitution. The Fifth (metropolitan Atlanta) was the largest of Georgia's ten congressional districts, with a population of 823,680. By comparison the Ninth District had only 272,154 residents, and the population of the average district was 394,312. This inequality meant that the Fifth District's legislator represented two to three times as many people as the other members of Congress from Georgia.

The districting scheme had been enacted by the state legislature in 1931, and no effort to bring the districts into balance had occurred since then. Wesberry claimed that this condition of significant malapportionment violated Article I, Section 2, of the Constitution, which says, "The House of Representatives shall be composed of Members chosen every second Year by the People of the several States."

Although agreeing that the Georgia districts were grossly inequitable, the district court dismissed the suit on the basis of the *Colegrove* ruling that congressional districting presented a political, and not legal, question. The Supreme Court accepted the case for review. It held that the precedent in *Baker v. Carr*, that state legislative malapportionment issues present justiciable questions, was also applicable to congressional districting, and then it discussed the substantive issues presented by the case.

TABLE 11-2 Congressional Malapportionment, 1964

State and Number of Representatives	Largest District	Smallest District	Difference Between Largest and Smallest Districts	State and Number of Representatives	Largest District	Smallest District	Difference Between Largest and Smallest Districts
Alabama (8)	——	——	——[1]	Montana (2)	400,573	274,194	126,379
Alaska (1)	——	——	——	Nebraska (3)	530,507	404,695	125,812
Arizona (3)	663,510	198,236	465,274	Nevada (1)	——	——	——
Arkansas (4)	575,385	322,844	242,541	New Hampshire (2)	331,818	275,103	56,715
California (38)	588,933	301,872	287,061	New Jersey (15)	585,586	255,165	330,421
Colorado (4)	653,954	195,551	458,403	New Mexico (2)	——	——	——[1]
Connecticut (6)	689,555	318,942	370,613	New York (41)	471,001	350,186	120,815
Delaware (1)	——	——	——	North Carolina (11)	491,461	277,861	213,600
Florida (12)	660,345	237,235	423,110	North Dakota (2)	333,290	299,156	34,134
Georgia (10)	823,680	272,154	551,526	Ohio (24)	726,156	236,288	489,868
Hawaii (2)	——	——	——[1]	Oklahoma (6)	552,863	227,692	325,171
Idaho (2)	409,949	257,242	152,707	Oregon (4)	522,813	265,164	257,649
Illinois (24)	552,582	278,703	273,879	Pennsylvania (27)	553,154	303,026	250,128
Indiana (11)	697,567	290,596	406,971	Rhode Island (2)	459,706	399,782	59,924
Iowa (7)	442,406	353,156	89,250	South Carolina (6)	531,555	302,235	229,320
Kansas (5)	539,592	373,583	166,009	South Dakota (2)	497,669	182,845	314,824
Kentucky (7)	610,947	350,839	260,108	Tennessee (9)	627,019	223,387	403,632
Louisiana (8)	536,029	263,850	272,179	Texas (23)	951,527	216,371	735,156
Maine (2)	505,465	463,800	41,665	Utah (2)	572,654	317,973	254,681
Maryland (8)	711,045	243,570	467,745	Vermont (1)	——	——	——
Massachusetts (12)	478,962	376,336	102,626	Virginia (10)	539,618	312,890	226,728
Michigan (19)	802,994	177,431	625,563	Washington (7)	510,512	342,540	167,972
Minnesota (8)	482,872	375,475	107,397	West Virginia (5)	422,046	303,098	118,948
Mississippi (5)	608,441	295,072	313,369	Wisconsin (10)	530,316	236,870	293,446
Missouri (10)	506,854	378,499	128,355	Wyoming (1)	——	——	——

SOURCE: *Wesberry v. Sanders,* 376 U.S. 1 at 49–50 (1964).

1. Representatives elected at large in 1962.

MR. JUSTICE BLACK delivered the opinion of the Court.

We agree with the District Court that the 1931 Georgia apportionment grossly discriminates against voters in the Fifth Congressional District. A single Congressman represents from two to three times as many Fifth District voters as are represented by each of the Congressmen from the other Georgia congressional districts. The apportionment statute thus contracts the value of some votes and expands that of others. If the Federal Constitution intends that when qualified voters elect members of Congress each vote be given as much weight as any other vote, then this statute cannot stand.

We hold that, construed in its historical context, the command of Art. I, § 2, that Representatives be chosen "by the People of the several States" means that as nearly as is practicable one man's vote in a congressional election is to be worth as much as another's. This rule is followed automatically, of course, when Representatives are chosen as a group on a statewide basis, as was a widespread practice in the first 50 years of our Nation's history. It would be extraordinary to suggest that in such statewide elections the votes of inhabitants of some parts of a State, for example, Georgia's thinly populated Ninth District, could be weighted at two or three times the value of the votes of people living in more populous parts of the State, for example, the Fifth District around Atlanta. We do not believe that the Framers of the Constitution intended to permit the same vote-diluting discrimination to be accomplished through the device of districts containing widely varied numbers of inhabitants. To say that a vote is worth more in one district than in another would not only run counter to our fundamental ideas of democratic government, it would cast aside the principle of a House of Representatives elected "by the People," a principle tenaciously fought for and established at the Constitutional Convention. The history of the Constitution, particularly that part of it relating to the adoption of Art. I, § 2, reveals that those who framed the Constitution meant that, no matter what the mechanics of an election, whether statewide or by districts, it was population which was to be the basis of the House of Representatives. . . .

The question of how the legislature should be constituted precipitated the most bitter controversy of the Convention. One principle was uppermost in the minds of many delegates: that, no matter where he lived, each voter should have a voice equal to that of every other in electing members of Congress. In support of this principle, George Mason of Virginia

"argued strongly for an election of the larger branch by the people. It was to be the grand depository of the democratic principle of the Govt."

James Madison agreed, saying "If the power is not immediately derived from the people, in proportion to their numbers, we may make a paper confederacy, but that will be all." Repeatedly, delegates rose to make the same point: that it would be unfair, unjust, and contrary to common sense to give a small number of people as many Senators or Representatives as were allowed to much larger groups—in short, as James Wilson of Pennsylvania put it, "equal numbers of people ought to have an equal no. of representatives . . ." and representatives "of different districts ought clearly to hold the same proportion to each other, as their respective constituents hold to each other."

Some delegates opposed election by the people. The sharpest objection arose out of the fear on the part of small States like Delaware that if population were to be the only basis of representation the populous states like Virginia would elect a large enough number of representatives to wield overwhelming power in the National Government. Arguing that the Convention had no authority to depart from the plan of the Articles of Confederation which gave each State an equal vote in the National Congress, William Paterson of New Jersey said, "If the sovereignty of the States is to be maintained, the Representatives must be drawn immediately from the States, not from the people; and we have no power to vary the idea of equal sovereignty." To this end he proposed a single legislative chamber in which each State, as in the Confederation, was to have an equal vote. A number of delegates supported this plan. . . .

The dispute came near ending the Convention without a Constitution. Both sides seemed for a time to be hopelessly obstinate. Some delegates threatened to withdraw from the Convention if they did not get their way. Seeing the controversy growing sharper and emotions rising, the wise and highly respected Benjamin Franklin arose and pleaded with the delegates on both sides to "part with some of their demands, in order that they may join in some accommodating proposition." At last those who supported representation of the people in both houses and those who supported it in neither were brought together, some expressing the fear that if they did not reconcile their differences, "some foreign sword will probably do the work for us." The deadlock was finally broken when a majority of the States agreed to what has been called the Great Compromise, based on a proposal which had been repeatedly advanced by Roger Sherman and other delegates from Connecticut. It provided on the one hand that each State, including little Delaware and Rhode Island, was to have two Senators. As a further guarantee that these Senators would be considered state emissaries, they were to be elected by the state legislature, Art. I, § 3, and it was specially provided in Article V that no State should ever be deprived of its equal representation in the Senate. The other side of the compromise was that, as provided in Art. I, § 2, members of the House of Representatives should be chosen "by the People of the several States" and should be "apportioned among the several States . . . according to their respective Numbers." While those who wanted both houses to represent the people had yielded on the Senate, they had not yielded on the House of Representatives. William Samuel Johnson of Connecticut had summed it up well: "in *one* branch the *people* ought to be represented; in the *other*, the *States*."

The debates at the Convention make at least one fact abundantly clear: that when the delegates agreed that the House should represent "people" they intended that in allocating Congressmen the number assigned to each State should be determined solely by the number of the State's inhabitants. The Constitution embodied Edmund Randolph's proposal for a periodic census to ensure "fair representation of the people," an idea endorsed by Mason as assuring that "numbers of inhabitants" should always be the measure of representation in the House of Representatives. The Convention also overwhelmingly agreed to a resolution offered by Randolph to base future apportionment squarely on numbers and to delete any reference to wealth. And the delegates defeated a motion made by Elbridge Gerry to limit the number of Representatives from newer Western States so that it would never exceed the number from the original States.

It would defeat the principle solemnly embodied in the Great Compromise—equal representation in the House for equal numbers of people—for us to hold that, within the States, legislatures may draw the lines of congressional districts in such a way as to give some voters a greater voice in choosing a Congressman than others. The House of Representatives, the Convention agreed, was to represent the people as individuals, and on a basis of complete equality for each voter. The delegates were quite aware of what Madison called the "vicious representation" in Great Britain whereby "rotten boroughs" with few inhabitants were represented in Parliament on or almost on a par with cities of greater population. Wilson urged that people must be represented as individuals, so that America would escape the evils of the English system under which one man could send two members to Parliament to represent the borough of Old Sarum while London's million people sent but four. The delegates referred to rotten borough apportionments in some of the state legislatures as the kind of objectionable governmental action that the Constitution should not tolerate in the election of congressional representatives....

Soon after the Constitution was adopted, James Wilson of Pennsylvania, by then an Associate Justice of this Court, gave a series of lectures at Philadelphia in which, drawing on his experience as one of the most active members of the Constitutional Convention, he said:

"[A]ll elections ought to be equal. Elections are equal, when a given number of citizens, in one part of the state, choose as many representatives, as are chosen by the same number of citizens, in any other part of the state. In this manner, the proportion of the representatives and of the constituents will remain invariably the same."

It is in the light of such history that we must construe Art. I, § 2, of the Constitution, which, carrying out the ideas of Madison and those of like views, provides that Representatives shall be chosen "by the People of the several States" and shall be "apportioned among the several States ... according to their respective Numbers." It is not surprising that our Court has held that this Article gives persons qualified to vote a constitutional right to vote and to have their votes counted. Not only can this right to vote not be denied outright, it cannot, consistently with Article I, be destroyed by alteration of ballots, or diluted by stuffing of the ballot box. No right is more precious in a free country than that of having a voice in the election of those who make the laws under which, as good citizens, we must live. Other rights, even the most basic, are illusory if the right to vote is undermined. Our Constitution leaves no room for classification of people in a way that unnecessarily abridges this right. In urging the people to adopt the Constitution, Madison said in No. 57 of The Federalist:

"Who are to be the electors of the Federal Representatives? Not the rich more than the poor; not the learned more than the ignorant; not the haughty heirs of distinguished names, more than the humble sons of obscure and unpropitious fortune. The electors are to be the great body of the people of the United States...."

Readers surely could have fairly taken this to mean, "one person, one vote."

While it may not be possible to draw congressional districts with mathematical precision, this is no excuse for ignoring our Constitution's plain objective of making equal representation for equal numbers of people the fundamental goal for the House of Representatives. That is the high standard of justice and common sense which the Founders set for us.

Reversed and remanded.

Wesberry clearly held that congressional districts within a state must be as equal in population as practicably possible, but it did not resolve the reapportionment controversy. A more difficult and politically charged issue centered on malapportionment within the state legislatures. It was one thing to command the state legislators to alter the boundaries of congressional districts, but still another to require them to reapportion their own legislative districts. Many states would regard such an action as an infringement of their sovereignty. In addition, the wholesale alteration of state legislative districts would mean that many state representatives would lose their districts or become politically vulnerable, and legislative power would shift from rural to urban interests. That the state legislatures were less than enthusiastic about such prospects is hardly surprising.

It did not take the Supreme Court long to address the dilemma of the state legislatures. Only four months after the *Wesberry* ruling, the Court announced its decision in *Reynolds v. Sims*. While *Reynolds* shares with *Wesberry* questions of representational equality, the legal basis for the two cases is very different. Article I, Section 2, of the Constitution, upon which the *Wesberry* outcome rested, deals only with the U.S. House of Representatives. Consequently, a challenge to state representational schemes had to be based on other grounds. In addition, all state legislatures except Nebraska's are bicameral, leaving open for dispute whether both houses of the state assembly must be population based. Notice in Chief Justice Warren's majority opinion in *Reynolds* how the Court reaches a conclusion consistent with *Wesberry* while using entirely different constitutional grounds. Also, consider the Court's holding on the issue of bicameralism. Is this ruling reasonable? Or should the states be

allowed to base representation in one house of the legislature on interests other than population alone? How compelling is Justice Harlan's dissent?

Reynolds v. Sims

377 U.S. 533 (1964)
Vote: 8 (Black, Brennan, Clark, Douglas, Goldberg, Stewart, Warren, White)
1 (Harlan)
Opinion of the Court: Warren
Concurring opinions: Clark, Stewart
Dissenting opinion: Harlan

Alabama's 1901 constitution authorized a state legislature of 106 House members and 35 senators. These legislators were to represent districts created generally on the basis of population equality. Although obliged to reapportion following each national census, the legislature had never altered the districts that were originally drawn following the 1900 census. Because of population shifts and a state constitutional requirement that each county, regardless of size, have at least one representative, Alabama had become severely malapportioned. For the state House of Representatives, the most populous legislative district had sixteen times the people as the least populous. Conditions in the state Senate were even more inequitable. The largest senatorial district had a population forty-one times greater than the smallest. As was the case in other states, rural areas enjoyed representation levels far in excess of what their populations warranted. For example, urban Jefferson County's single senator represented more than 600,000 residents, while rural Lowndes County had one senator for its 15,417 citizens.

Voters in urban counties filed suit to have the Alabama system declared unconstitutional as a violation of the Equal Protection Clause of the Fourteenth Amendment. Pressured by the threat of legal action in light of the Supreme Court's decision in *Baker v. Carr*, the state legislature offered two reapportionment plans to improve the situation. A three-judge district court declared the existing system unconstitutional and the proposed reforms inadequate. A temporary reapportionment plan was imposed by the trial court judges, and the state appealed to the Supreme Court. The *Reynolds* case was one of six state legislative reapportionment disputes the Supreme Court heard at the same time. The others came from Maryland, Delaware, Virginia, New York, and Colorado. The justices used the opinion in *Reynolds* as the primary vehicle for articulating the Court's position on the state redistricting issue.

MR. CHIEF JUSTICE WARREN delivered the opinion of the Court.

Legislators represent people, not trees or acres. Legislators are elected by voters, not farms or cities or economic interests. As long as ours is a representative form of government, and our legislatures are those instruments of government elected directly by and directly representative of the people, the right to elect legislators in a free and unimpaired fashion is a bedrock of our political system. It could hardly be gainsaid that a constitutional claim had been asserted by an allegation that certain otherwise qualified voters had been entirely prohibited from voting for members of their state legislature. And, if a State should provide that the votes of citizens in one part of the State should be given two times, or five times, or 10 times the weight of votes of citizens in another part of the State, it could hardly be contended that the right to vote of those residing in the disfavored areas had not been effectively diluted. It would appear extraordinary to suggest that a State could be constitutionally permitted to enact a law providing that certain of the State's voters could vote two, five, or 10 times for their legislative representatives, while voters living elsewhere could vote only once. And it is inconceivable that a state law to the effect that, in counting votes for legislators, the votes of citizens in one part of the State would be multiplied by two, five, or 10 while the votes of persons in another area would be counted only at face value, could be constitutionally sustainable. Of course, the effect of state legislative districting schemes which give the same number of representatives to unequal numbers of constituents is identical. Overweighting and overvaluation of the votes of those living here has the certain effect of dilution and undervaluation of the votes of those living there. The resulting discrimination against those individual voters living in disfavored areas is easily demonstrable mathematically. Their right to vote is simply not the same right to vote as that of those living in a favored part of the State. Two, five, or 10 of them must vote before the effect of their voting is equivalent to that of their favored neighbor. Weighting the votes of citizens differently, by any method or means, merely because of where they happen to reside, hardly seems justifiable. One must be ever aware that the Constitution forbids "sophisticated as well as simple-minded modes of discrimination."...

Logically, in a society ostensibly grounded on representative government, it would seem reasonable that a majority of the people of a State could elect a majority of that State's legislators. To conclude differently, and to sanction minority control of state legislative bodies, would appear to deny majority rights in a way that far surpasses any possible denial of minority rights that might otherwise be thought to result. Since legislatures are responsible for enacting laws by which all citizens are to be governed, they should be bodies which are collectively responsive to the popular will. And the concept of equal protection has been traditionally viewed as requiring the uniform treatment of persons standing in the same relation to the governmental action questioned or challenged. With respect to the allocation of legislative representation, all voters, as citizens of a State, stand in the same relation regardless of where they live. Any suggested criteria for the differentiation of citizens are insufficient to justify any discrimination, as to the weight of their votes, unless relevant to the permissible purposes of legislative apportionment. Since the achieving of fair and effective representation for all citizens is concededly the basic aim of legislative apportionment, we conclude that the Equal Protection Clause guarantees the opportunity for equal participation by all voters in the election of state legislators. Diluting the weight of votes because of place of residence impairs basic constitutional rights under the Fourteenth Amendment just as much as invidious discriminations based upon factors such as race or economic status....

We are told that the matter of apportioning representation in a state legislature is a complex and many-faceted one. We are advised that States can rationally consider factors other than population in apportioning legislative representation. We are admonished not to restrict the power of the States to impose differing views as to political philosophy on their citizens. We are cautioned about the dangers of entering into political thickets and mathematical quagmires. Our answer is this: a denial of constitutionally protected rights demands judicial protection; our oath and our office require no less of us.... To the extent that a citizen's right to vote is debased, he is that much less a citizen. The fact that an individual lives here or there is not a legitimate reason for overweighting or diluting the efficacy of his vote. The complexions of societies and civilizations change, often with amazing rapidity. A nation once primarily rural in character becomes predominantly urban. Representation schemes once fair and equitable become archaic and outdated. But the basic principle of representative government remains, and must remain, unchanged—the weight of a citizen's vote cannot be made to depend on where he lives. Population is, of necessity, the starting point for consideration and the controlling criterion for judgment in legislative apportionment controversies. A citizen, a qualified voter, is no more nor no less so because he lives in the city or on the farm. This is the clear and strong command of our Constitution's Equal Protection Clause. This is an essential part of the concept of a government of laws and not men. This is at the heart of Lincoln's vision of "government of the people, by the people, [and] for the people." The Equal Protection Clause demands no less than substantially equal state legislative representation for all citizens, of all places as well as of all races.

We hold that, as a basic constitutional standard, the Equal Protection Clause requires that the seats in both houses of a bicameral state legislature must be apportioned on a population basis. Simply stated, an individual's right to vote for state legislators is unconstitutionally impaired when its weight is in a substantial fashion diluted when compared with votes of citizens living in other parts of the State....

Legislative apportionment in Alabama is signally illustrative and symptomatic of the seriousness of this problem in a number of the States. At the time this litigation was commenced, there had been no reapportionment of seats in the Alabama Legislature for over 60 years. Legislative inaction, coupled with the unavailability of any political or judicial remedy, had resulted, with the passage of years, in the perpetuated scheme becoming little more than an irrational anachronism. Consistent failure by the Alabama Legislature to comply with state constitutional requirements as to the frequency of reapportionment and the bases of legislative representation resulted in a minority stranglehold on the State Legislature. Inequality of representation in one house added to the inequality in the other.... Since neither of the houses of the Alabama Legislature, under any of the three plans considered by the District Court, was apportioned on a population basis, we would be justified in proceeding no further. However, one of the proposed plans, that contained in the so-called 67-Senator Amendment, at least superficially resembles the scheme of legislative representation followed in the Federal Congress. Under this plan, each of Alabama's 67 counties is allotted one senator, and no counties are given more than one Senate seat. Arguably, this is analogous to the allocation of two Senate seats, in the Federal Congress, to each of the 50 States, regardless of population. Seats in the Alabama House, under the proposed constitutional amendment, are distributed by giving each of the 67 counties at least one, with the remaining 39 seats being allotted among the more populous counties on a population basis. This scheme, at least at first glance, appears to resemble that prescribed for the Federal House of Representatives, where the 435 seats are distributed among the States on a population basis, although each State, regardless of its population, is given at least one Congressman. Thus, although there are substantial differences in underlying rationale and results, the 67-Senator Amendment, as proposed by the Alabama Legislature, at least arguably presents for consideration a scheme analogous to that used for apportioning seats in Congress....

We agree with the District Court, and find the federal analogy inapposite and irrelevant to state legislative districting schemes. Attempted reliance on the federal analogy appears often to be little more than an after-the-fact rationalization offered in defense of maladjusted state apportionment arrangements. The original constitutions of 36 of our States provided that representation in both houses of the state legislatures would be based completely, or predominantly, on population. And the Founding Fathers clearly had no intention of establishing a pattern or model for the apportionment of seats in state legislatures when the system of representation in the Federal Congress was adopted....

The system of representation in the two Houses of the Federal Congress is one ingrained in our Constitution, as part of the law of the land. It is one conceived out of compromise and concession indispensable to the establishment of our federal republic. Arising from unique historical circumstances, it is based on the consideration that in establishing our type of federalism a group of formerly independent States bound themselves together under one national government....

Political subdivisions of States—counties, cities, or whatever—never were and never have been considered as sovereign entities. Rather, they have been traditionally regarded as subordinate governmental instrumentalities created by the State to assist in the carrying out of state governmental functions.... The relationship of the States to the Federal Government could hardly be less analogous.

Thus, we conclude that the plan contained in the 67-Senator Amendment for apportioning seats in the Alabama Legislature cannot be sustained by recourse to the so-called federal analogy. Nor can any other inequitable state legislative apportionment scheme be justified....

By holding that as a federal constitutional requisite both houses of a state legislature must be apportioned on a population basis, we mean that the Equal Protection Clause requires that a State make an honest and good faith effort to construct districts, in both houses of its legislature, as nearly of equal population as is practicable. We realize that it is a practical impossibility to arrange legislative districts so that each one has an identical number of residents, or citizens, or voters. Mathematical exactness or precision is hardly a workable constitutional requirement....

A State may legitimately desire to maintain the integrity of various political subdivisions, insofar as possible, and provide for compact districts of contiguous territory in designing a legislative apportionment scheme. Valid considerations may underlie such aims. Indiscriminate districting, without any regard for political subdivision or natural or historical boundary lines, may be little more than an open invitation to partisan gerrymandering. Single-member districts may be the rule in one State, while another State might desire to achieve some flexibility by creating multi-member or floterial districts. Whatever the means of accomplishment, the overriding objective must be substantial equality of population among the various districts, so that the vote of any citizen is approximately equal in weight to that of any other citizen in the State.

History indicates, however, that many States have deviated, to a greater or lesser degree, from the equal-population principle in the apportionment of seats in at least one house of their legislatures. So long as the divergences from a strict population standard are based on legitimate considerations incident to the effectuation of a rational state policy, some deviations from the equal-population principle are constitutionally permissible with respect to the apportionment of seats in either or both of the two houses of a bicameral state legislature. But neither history alone, nor economic or other sorts of group interests, are permissible factors in attempting to justify disparities from population-based representation. Citizens, not history or economic interests, cast votes. Considerations of area alone provide an insufficient justification for deviations from the equal population principle....

We find, therefore, that the action taken by the District Court in this case, in ordering into effect a reapportionment of both houses of the Alabama Legislature for purposes of the 1962 primary and general elections, by using the best parts of the two proposed plans which it had found, as a whole, to be invalid, was an appropriate and well-considered exercise of judicial power. Admittedly, the lower court's ordered plan was intended only as a temporary and provisional measure and the District Court correctly indicated that the plan was invalid as a permanent apportionment. In retaining jurisdiction while deferring a hearing on the issuance of a final injunction in order to give the provisionally reapportioned legislature an opportunity to act effectively, the court below proceeded in a proper fashion....

Affirmed and remanded.

MR. JUSTICE HARLAN, dissenting.

In these cases the Court holds that seats in the legislatures of six States are apportioned in ways that violate the Federal Constitution. Under the Court's ruling it is bound to follow that the legislature in all but a few of the other 44 States will meet the same fate. These decisions, with Wesberry v. Sanders, involving congressional districting by the States, and Gray v. Sanders, relating to elections for statewide office, have the effect of placing basic aspects of state political systems under the pervasive overlordship of the federal judiciary. Once again, I must register my protest.

Today's holding is that the Equal Protection Clause of the Fourteenth Amendment requires every State to structure its legislature so that all the members of each house represent substantially the same number of people; other factors may be given play only to the extent that they do not significantly encroach on this basic "population" principle. Whatever may be thought of this holding as a piece of political ideology—and even on that score the political history and practices of this country from its earliest beginnings leave wide room for debate ... I think it demonstrable that the Fourteenth Amendment does not impose this political tenet on the States or authorize this Court to do so.

The Court's constitutional discussion, found in its opinion in the Alabama cases, is remarkable ... for its failure to address itself at all to the Fourteenth Amendment as a whole or to the legislative history of the Amendment pertinent to the matter at hand. Stripped of aphorisms, the Court's argument boils down to the assertion that appellees' right to vote has been invidiously "debased" or "diluted" by systems of apportionment which entitle them to vote for fewer legislators than other voters, an assertion which is tied to the Equal Protection Clause only by the constitutionally frail tautology that "equal" means "equal."

Had the Court paused to probe more deeply into the matter, it would have found that the Equal Protection Clause was never intended to inhibit the States in choosing any democratic method they pleased for the apportionment of their legislatures. This is shown by the language of the Fourteenth Amendment taken as a whole, by the understanding of those who proposed and ratified it, and by the political practices of the States at the time the Amendment was adopted. It is confirmed by numerous state and congressional actions since the adoption of the Fourteenth Amendment, and by the common understanding of the Amendment as evidenced by subsequent

constitutional amendments and decisions of this Court before Baker v. Carr made an abrupt break with the past in 1962.

The failure of the Court to consider any of these matters cannot be excused or explained by any concept of "developing" constitutionalism. It is meaningless to speak of constitutional "development" when both the language and history of the controlling provisions of the Constitution are wholly ignored. Since it can, I think, be shown beyond doubt that state legislative apportionments, as such, are wholly free of constitutional limitations, save such as may be imposed by the Republican Form of Government Clause (Const., Art. IV, § 4), the Court's action now bringing them within the purview of the Fourteenth Amendment amounts to nothing less than an exercise of the amending power by this Court.

So far as the Federal Constitution is concerned, the complaints in these cases should all have been dismissed below for failure to state a cause of action because what has been alleged or proved shows no violation of any constitutional right.

Harlan's dissent in *Reynolds* predicting that the legislatures of all the states would be affected by the Court's one person, one vote principle proved to be accurate. At first, there was some disagreement with the Court's ruling. State advocates began a movement to amend the Constitution to provide states the authority to have at least one house of their legislatures based on factors other than population, but the proposal failed to garner sufficient support. As the states began the Court-imposed reapportionment process, opposition started to wane. Today, reapportionment of congressional and state legislative districts occurs each decade following the national census. The impact of the reapportionment rulings initially was to shift a significant amount of political power from the rural areas to the cities. In more recent years, consistent with demographic changes, the suburban areas have been the beneficiaries of the Court's redistricting policies. In the near future, increased representation for minority citizens, especially for the rapidly growing Hispanic population, undoubtedly will occur.

Upon his retirement, Chief Justice Warren said that, in his opinion, the reapportionment decisions were the most significant rulings rendered during his sixteen-year tenure. That statement was remarkable, considering that under his leadership the Court handed down landmark decisions on race relations, criminal justice, obscenity, libel, and school prayer. In spite of their significance, however, the initial redistricting decisions did not answer all of the relevant questions regarding the one person, one vote principle. For the next three decades, the Court faced additional perplexing constitutional issues flowing from *Baker, Wesberry,* and *Reynolds.*

Representational Equality: Applicability and Measurement

Although *Wesberry* and *Reynolds* made it clear that the Constitution demanded population-based representational units for the U.S. House of Representatives and both houses of state legislatures, the question of applying the one person, one vote principle to other governing bodies remained open. As early as 1963, when it struck down Georgia's county unit system of electing governors in *Gray v. Sanders,* the Supreme Court indicated a willingness to apply principles of population equality to political entities other than legislatures. It appeared quite possible that the justices would impose equal protection standards on the thousands of local government commissions, councils, and boards to which Americans regularly elect representatives. Most of these bodies were loosely based upon population, but they could not meet the exacting standards of the reapportionment rulings. Did the Constitution demand that these governing bodies be properly apportioned in the same manner as state legislatures? Supporters of representational equality sponsored numerous lawsuits asking the judiciary to extend one person, one vote to these local government units.

In *Avery v. Midland County* (1968) the Court ruled on a challenge to the representational system used to elect the county government. The seat of Midland County, Texas, contained more than 95 percent of the county's population but was only given 20 percent of the representatives on the governing commission. The Court struck down this scheme, holding that the equal protection principles that govern representation in the state legislature also control representation on elected local government bodies. In *Hadley v. Junior College District* (1970) the justices extended the same principles to elected special purpose boards that exercise legislative functions; and, as late as 1989, the Supreme Court unanimously struck down the system used for selecting members of New York City's Board of Estimate (*Board of Estimate of New York v. Morris),* which gave equal representation to each of the five New York boroughs even though they had substantially unequal populations. The Court's position has been relatively clear: the Equal Protection Clause demands that the principle of one person, one vote applies to local governing bodies that are elected and exercise legislative or general governing powers. The basic rule was articulated well in *Hadley:*

[W]henever a state or local government decides to select persons by popular election to perform governmental functions, the Equal Protection Clause of the Fourteenth Amendment requires that each qualified voter must be given an equal opportunity to participate in that election, and when members of an elected body are chosen from separate districts, each district must be established on a basis that will insure, as far as is practicable, that equal numbers of voters can vote for proportionally equal numbers of officials.

Exceptions have been made when the governing board exercises essentially administrative rather than general or legislative powers (see *Sailors v. Board of Education of Kent County,* 1967) and when the substantive authority of the commission is so narrow and so spe-

RURAL VOTE

RURAL VOTE

RURAL VOTE

ONE PERSON ONE VOTE RULING IN GEORGIA

RURAL VOTE

SUPREME COURT

BASSET

An editorial cartoon showing the loss of political power suffered by rural interests because of decisions such as *Gray v. Sanders*.

cialized as to justify representation based on factors other than population (see *Sayler Land Company v. Tulare Lake Basin Water Storage District*, 1973).

In its early apportionment decisions, the Supreme Court emphasized the need for population-based representational schemes. The justices used phrases such as "one person, one vote," "substantial equality," and "as equal as practicably possible" to refer to this standard. But the Court did not define what is meant by such equality. Although the justices regularly acknowledged that mathematical precision could not be expected, they failed to say what variation among districts would be constitutionally tolerated. Redistricting is an exceedingly complex process. Even with the

assistance of today's computer technology, drawing boundaries that create districts of nearly perfect equality is difficult. Adding to the burden are the demands of partisan, racial, ethnic, and economic interests for political power.

For the state legislatures involved in this process, it would be helpful for the Supreme Court to designate a minimum level of deviation that is constitutionally permissible. Such a *de minimis* standard would give legislators a guide as to what population equality means in practice. But in the Missouri congressional reapportionment case of *Kirkpatrick v. Preisler* (1969) the Supreme Court explicitly refused to provide any specified mathematical standard of equality. For the majority, Justice Brennan explained,

> We reject Missouri's argument that there is a fixed numerical or percentage population variance small enough to be considered *de minimis* and to satisfy without question the "as nearly as practicable" standard. The whole thrust of the "as nearly as practicable" approach is inconsistent with adoption of fixed numerical standards which excuse population variances without regard to the circumstances of each particular case.

In this decision, the Court declared Missouri's reapportionment plan to be unconstitutional in spite of the relatively small 1.6 percent average deviation from the ideal. The state had failed to convince the Court's majority that it had made a good faith attempt to achieve equality.

If size differences alone do not dictate constitutional standards for representational equality, what other factors do? *Karcher v. Daggett* (1983) helps answer this question. In his opinion for the Court, Brennan reaffirms the importance of states making good faith efforts to achieve equality among congressional districts and discusses some of the factors that may justify a degree of population disparity. Is Brennan's argument convincing, or is a more compelling position articulated in Justice White's dissent that the Court is imposing unreasonable standards on the state legislature?

Karcher v. Daggett

462 U.S. 725 (1983)

Vote: 5 (Blackmun, Brennan, Marshall, O'Connor, Stevens)
      4 (Burger, Powell, Rehnquist, White)

Opinion of the Court: Brennan
Concurring opinion: Stevens
Dissenting opinions: Powell, White

After completion of the 1980 census, the clerk of the U.S. House of Representatives informed the governor of New Jersey that the number of representatives to which the state was entitled had decreased from fifteen to fourteen. Not only would the New Jersey legislature have to redesign its congressional districts to take population mobility into account, but also it would have to eliminate one congressional district. In 1981 the legislature passed two congressional reapportionment bills. The first was vetoed by the governor. The second was signed into law, but became the target of considerable criticism because it diluted minority voting strength in Newark. Consequently, in January 1982 the legislature passed a revised reapportionment act, which became known as the Feldman Plan for the president pro tem of the state senate, who wrote the bill. Under this plan, the average congressional district contained 526,059 people. The mean variation from this average was 0.1384 percent, or 726 people. The difference between the largest and smallest of the fourteen districts was 3,674 people, or a disparity of 0.6984 percent. Before passing the Feldman Plan, the legislature considered other plans, one of which would have allowed a maximum population difference of only 2,375 people, or 0.4514 percent of the average district.

Shortly after the Feldman Plan became law, a group of individuals, including all incumbent Republican members of Congress from New Jersey, joined in a suit against Speaker Alan Karcher and other state officials to have the reapportionment law declared unconstitutional. The district court ruled in their favor, finding that the legislature had failed to engage in a good faith effort to achieve absolute population equality. The state appealed.

JUSTICE BRENNAN delivered the opinion of the Court.

Article I, § 2, "permits only the limited population variances which are unavoidable despite a good-faith effort to achieve absolute equality, or for which justification is shown." [*Reynolds v. Sims*, 1964.]

Thus two basic questions shape litigation over population deviations in state legislation apportioning congressional districts. First, the court must consider whether the population differences among districts could have been reduced or eliminated altogether by a good-faith effort to draw districts of equal population. Parties challenging apportionment legislation must bear the burden of proof on this issue, and if they fail to show that the differences could have been avoided the apportionment scheme must be upheld. If, however, the plaintiffs can establish that the population differences were not the result of a good-faith effort to achieve equality, the State must bear the burden of proving that each significant variance between districts was necessary to achieve some legitimate goal.

Appellants' principal argument in this case is addressed to the first question described above. They contend that the Feldman Plan should be regarded *per se* as the product of a good-faith effort to achieve population equality because the maximum population deviation among districts is smaller than the predictable undercount in available census data.

Kirkpatrick squarely rejected a nearly identical argument.... Adopting any standard other than population equality, using the best census data available, would subtly erode the Constitution's ideal of equal representation. If state legislators knew that a certain *de minimis* level of population differences was acceptable, they would doubtless strive to achieve that level rather than equality. In this case, appellants argue that a maximum deviation of approximately 0.7% should be considered *de minimis*. If we accept that argument, how are we to regard deviations of 0.8%, 0.95%, 1%, or 1.1%?

Any standard, including absolute equality, involves a certain artificiality. As appellants point out, even the census data are not perfect, and the well-known restlessness of the American people means that population counts for particular localities are outdated long before they are completed. Yet problems with the data at hand apply equally to any population-based standard we could choose. As between two standards—equality or something less than equality—only the former reflects the aspirations of Art. I, § 2....

The sole difference between appellants' theory and the argument we rejected in *Kirkpatrick* is that appellants have proposed a *de minimis* line that gives the illusion of rationality and predictability: the "inevitable statistical imprecision of the census." They argue: "Where, as here, the deviation from ideal district size is less than the known imprecision of the census figures, that variation is the functional equivalent of zero." There are two problems with this approach. First, appellants concentrate on the extent to which the census systematically undercounts actual population—a figure which is not known precisely and which, even if it were known, would not be relevant to this case. Second, the mere existence of statistical imprecision does not make small deviations among districts the functional equivalent of equality....

The District Court found that several other plans introduced in the 200th Legislature had smaller maximum deviations than the Feldman Plan. Appellants object that the alternative plans considered by the District Court were not comparable to the Feldman Plan because their political characters differed profoundly. We have never denied that apportionment is a political process, or that state legislatures could pursue legitimate secondary objectives as long as those objectives were consistent with a good-faith effort to achieve population equality at the same time. Nevertheless, the claim that political considerations require population differences among congressional districts belongs more properly to the second level of judicial inquiry in these cases, in which the State bears the burden of justifying the differences with particularity....

By itself, the foregoing discussion does not establish that the Feldman Plan is unconstitutional. Rather, appellees' success in proving that the Feldman Plan was not the product of a good-faith effort to achieve population equality means only that the burden shifted to the State to prove that the population deviations in its plan were necessary to achieve some legitimate state objective.... [W]e are willing to defer to state legislative policies, so long as they are consistent with constitutional norms, even if they require small differences in the population of congressional districts. Any number of consistently applied legislative policies might justify some variance, including, for instance, making districts compact, respecting municipal boundaries, preserving the cores of prior districts, and avoiding contests between incumbent Representatives. As long as the criteria are nondiscriminatory, these are all legitimate objectives that on a proper showing could justify minor population deviations. The State must, however, show with some specificity that a particular objective required the specific deviations in its plan, rather than simply relying on general assertions. The showing required to justify population deviations is flexible, depending on the size of the deviations, the importance of the State's interests, the consistency with which the plan as a whole reflects those interests, and the availability of alternatives that might substantially vindicate those interests yet approximate population equality more closely. By necessity whether deviations are justified requires case-by-case attention to these factors....

The District Court properly applied the two-part test of *Kirkpatrick v. Preisler* to New Jersey's 1982 apportionment of districts for the United States House of Representatives. It correctly held that the population deviations in the plan were not functionally equal as a matter of law, and it found that the plan was not a good-faith effort to achieve population equality using the best available census data. It also correctly rejected appellants' attempt to justify the population deviations as not supported by the evidence. The judgment of the District Court, therefore, is

Affirmed.

JUSTICE WHITE, with whom the CHIEF JUSTICE, JUSTICE POWELL, and JUSTICE REHNQUIST join, dissenting.

I respectfully dissent from the Court's unreasonable insistence on an unattainable perfection in the equalizing of congressional districts....

One must suspend credulity to believe that the Court's draconian response to a trifling 0.6984% maximum deviation promotes "fair and effective representation" for the people of New Jersey....

There can be little question but that the variances in the New Jersey plan are "statistically insignificant." Although the Government strives to make the decennial census as accurate as humanly possible, the Census Bureau has never intimated that the results are a perfect count of the American population. The Bureau itself estimates the inexactitude in the taking of the 1970 census at 2.3%, a figure which is considerably larger than the 0.6984% maximum variance in the New Jersey plan....

If today's decision simply produced an unjustified standard with little practical import, it would be bad enough. Unfortunately, I fear that the Court's insistence that "there are no *de minimis* population variations, which could practicably be avoided, but which nonetheless meet the standard of Art. I, § 2, without justification," invites further litigation of virtually every congressional redistricting plan in the Nation. At least 12 States which have completed redistricting on the basis of the 1980 census have adopted plans with a higher deviation than that presented here, and 4 others have deviations quite similar to New Jersey's. Of course, under the Court's rationale, even Rhode Island's plan—whose two districts have a deviation of 0.02% or about 95 people—would be subject to constitutional attack....

The only way a legislature or bipartisan commission can hope to avoid litigation will be to dismiss all other legitimate concerns and opt automatically for the districting plan with the smallest deviation. Yet no one can seriously contend that such an inflexible insistence upon mathematical exactness will serve to promote "fair and effective representation." The more likely result of today's extension of *Kirkpatrick* is to move closer to fulfilling Justice Fortas' prophecy that "a legislature might have to ignore the boundaries of common sense, running the congressional district line down the middle of the corridor of an apartment house or even dividing the residents of a single-family house between two districts." Such sterile and mechanistic application only brings the principle of "one man, one vote" into disrepute....

Although I am not wedded to a precise figure, in light of the current range of population deviations, a 5% cutoff appears reasonable. I would not entertain judicial challenges, absent extraordinary circumstances, where the maximum deviation is less than 5%. Somewhat greater deviations, if rationally related to an important state interest, may also be permissible. Certainly, the maintaining of compact, contiguous districts, the respecting of political subdivisions, and efforts to assure political fairness constitute such interests.

I would not hold up New Jersey's plan as a model reflection of such interests. Nevertheless, the deviation involved here is *de minimis*, and, regardless of what other infirmities the plan may have, constitutional or otherwise, there is no violation of Art. I, § 2—the sole issue before us. It would, of course, be a different matter if appellees could demonstrate that New Jersey's plan invidiously discriminated against a racial or political group.

It is important to keep in mind that in *Karcher v. Daggett* the Supreme Court is interpreting Article I, Section 2, of the Constitution which deals with the election of members to the U.S. House. The majority's rather strict approach to equality standards for congressional districts is not necessarily applicable to the apportionment of state and local governments, which is governed by the Equal Protection Clause of the Fourteenth Amendment. In fact, the Supreme Court has allowed the states much greater latitude in devising reapportionment plans and has tolerated much greater deviation from absolute equality than it has with creation of congressional constituencies.

In *Mahan v. Howell* (1973) the Supreme Court articulated the constitutional differences between congressional apportionment and state legislative apportionment. Compare the population variances approved by the Court in this suit over the Virginia state legislature with the deviations in congressional districts successfully challenged in *Karcher*. Does Justice Rehnquist provide a compelling argument for allowing less stringent standards for state legislatures than are imposed on congressional districts?

Mahan v. Howell

410 U.S. 315 (1973)

Vote: 5 (Blackmun, Burger, Rehnquist, Stewart, White)
*   3 (Brennan, Douglas, Marshall)*

Opinion of the Court: Rehnquist
Opinion dissenting in part and concurring in part: Brennan
Not participating: Powell

In 1971 the Virginia legislature reapportioned itself. The plan adopted for the House of Delegates, which this suit challenged, provided for representatives to be elected from fifty-two districts, some of which were single-member constituencies and others multimember districts. The average House member represented 46,485 constituents. The variance between the largest and smallest numbers of represented citizens was 16.4 percent, with a mean variation from the ideal of 3.89 percent. With the exception of Fairfax County, which was divided into two five-member districts, all of the reapportioned districts followed the existing city and county political boundaries. Henry Howell, Jr., and others brought suit against John Mahan, the secretary of the state board of elections, and other state officials to have the reapportionment plan for the House declared unconstitutional. Among other arguments, they contended that the plan's population deviations were too large to satisfy the principle of one person, one vote. Relying on *Kirkpatrick v. Preisler* (1969), which demanded good-faith efforts to attain absolute equality, the district court found the reapportionment plan to be in violation of the Constitution. The state appealed.

MR. JUSTICE REHNQUIST delivered the opinion of the Court.

This Court first recognized that the Equal Protection Clause requires both houses of a bicameral state legislature to be apportioned substantially on a population basis in Reynolds v. Sims. In so doing, it suggested that in the im-

plementation of the basic constitutional principle—equality of population among the districts—more flexibility was constitutionally permissible with respect to state legislative reapportionment than in congressional redistricting. Consideration was given to the fact that, almost invariably, there is a significantly larger number of seats in state legislative bodies to be distributed within a State than congressional seats, and that therefore it may be feasible for a State to use political subdivision lines to a greater extent in establishing state legislative districts than congressional districts while still affording adequate statewide representation. Another possible justification for deviation from population-based representation in state legislatures was stated to be:

"[T]hat of insuring some voice to political subdivisions, as political subdivisions. Several factors make more than insubstantial claims that a State can rationally consider according political subdivisions some independent representation in at least one body of the state legislature, as long as the basic standard of equality of population among districts is maintained. Local governmental entities are frequently charged with various responsibilities incident to the operation of state government. In many States much of the legislature's activity involves the enactment of so-called local legislation, directed only to the concerns of particular political subdivisions. And a State may legitimately desire to construct districts along political subdivision lines to deter the possibilities of gerrymandering...."...

By contrast, the Court in Wesberry v. Sanders recognized no excuse for the failure to meet the objective of equal representation for equal numbers of people in congressional districting other than the practical impossibility of drawing equal districts with mathematical precision. Thus, whereas population alone has been the sole criterion of constitutionality in congressional redistricting under Art. I, § 2, broader latitude has been afforded the States under the Equal Protection Clause in state legislative redistricting because of the considerations enumerated in Reynolds v. Sims. The dichotomy between the two lines of cases has consistently been maintained. In Kirkpatrick v. Preisler, for example, one asserted justification for population variances was that they were necessarily a result of the State's attempt to avoid fragmenting political subdivisions by drawing congressional district lines along existing political subdivision boundaries. This argument was rejected in the congressional context....

We conclude ... that the constitutionality of Virginia's legislative redistricting plan was not to be judged by the more stringent standards applicable to congressional reapportionment, but instead by the equal protection test enunciated in Reynolds v. Sims. We reaffirm its holding that "the Equal Protection Clause requires that a State make an honest and good faith effort to construct districts, in both houses of its legislature, as nearly of equal population as is practicable." We likewise reaffirm its conclusion that "[s]o long as the divergences from a strict population standard are based on legitimate considerations incident to the effectuation of a rational state policy, some deviations from the equal-population principle are constitutionally permissible with respect to the apportionment of seats in either or both of the two houses of a bicameral state legislature."...

We hold that the legislature's plan for apportionment of the House of Delegates may reasonably be said to advance the rational state policy of respecting the boundaries of political subdivisions. The remaining inquiry is whether the population disparities among the districts that have resulted from the pursuit of this plan exceed constitutional limits. We conclude that they do not....

... The relatively minor variations present in the Virginia plan contrast sharply with the larger variations in state legislative reapportionment plans that have been struck down by previous decisions of this Court.

Neither courts nor legislatures are furnished any specialized calipers that enable them to extract from the general language of the Equal Protection Clause of the Fourteenth Amendment the mathematical formula that establishes what range of percentage deviations is permissible, and what is not. The 16-odd percent maximum deviation that the District Court found to exist in the legislative plan for the reapportionment of the House is substantially less than the percentage deviations that have been found invalid in the previous decisions of this Court. While this percentage may well approach tolerable limits, we do not believe it exceeds them. Virginia has not sacrificed substantial equality to justifiable deviations.

The policy of maintaining the integrity of political subdivision lines in the process of reapportioning a state legislature, the policy consistently advanced by Virginia as a justification for disparities in population among districts that elect members to the House of Delegates, is a rational one.

It can reasonably be said, upon examination of the legislative plan, that it does in fact advance that policy. The population disparities that are permitted thereunder result in a maximum percentage deviation that we hold to be within tolerable constitutional limits. We, therefore, hold the General Assembly's plan for the reapportionment of the House of Delegates constitutional and reverse the District Court's conclusion to the contrary.

In a number of decisions, the Court has continued to follow the guidelines set in *Mahan*. For example, in *Gaffney v. Cummings* (1973) the justices upheld a Connecticut state legislative redistricting plan with a maximum 7.83 percent deviation from ideal equality, in part because the state provided evidence that the particular plan preserved political fairness. In *White v. Regester* (1973) a Texas state reapportionment scheme with a 9.9 percent maximum variation from the ideal was upheld, with the Court concluding that the threshold for a prima facie case of invidious discrimination had not been passed. On the same day, almost as if to emphasize the differences, the Court struck down the Texas congressional redistricting plan that contained substantially less deviation from perfect equality than did the state scheme the justices had upheld (*White v. Weiser*, 1973).

In developing state apportionment rules under the Equal Protection Clause, the Supreme Court has even accepted the *de minimis* position that it explicitly rejected in a number of congressional redistricting cases. In *Brown v. Thomson* (1983) Justice Powell, speaking for the Court, stated, "Our decisions have established, as a general matter, that an apportionment plan with a maximum population deviation under 10% falls within this category of minor deviations.... A plan with larger disparities in population, however, creates a prima facie case of discrimination and therefore must be justified by the State." The *Brown* case centered on a Wyoming redistricting plan that included a maximum deviation of 89 percent from perfect equality. This large variation was caused by the representation given to one isolated and sparsely populated county. The Court upheld the law, concluding that the state had provided convincing, nondiscriminatory reasons for allowing this exception to the one person, one vote rule. Ironically, *Brown* was handed down the same day that the Court in *Karcher v. Daggett* struck down New Jersey's congressional reapportionment with its maximum deviation of less than 1 percent and rejected a *de minimis* rationale for use in such cases.

So far we have discussed what is required when a state legislature draws district lines for itself or the state's congressional delegation. These intrastate actions give birth to the vast majority of reapportionment controversies. At the congressional level, however, there are occasional disputes over how seats are allocated *among* the states. Such a controversy reached the Supreme Court in the case of *United States Department of Commerce v. Montana* (1992).

Following the completion of the 1980 census, the federal government reallocated seats in the U.S. House of Representatives, taking into account the population shifts that had occurred over the previous ten years. The census concluded that the population of the fifty states was slightly more than 249 million people. If the population is divided by 435, the number of House seats, each congressional representative would serve 572,466 constituents. Such mathematical precision is not possible for several reasons. The most important is the requirement that each state have at least one member of the House. Some states, such as Wyoming, Alaska, and Vermont, have total populations of less than the ideal district size, and consequently have a disproportionate degree of congressional representation.

Over the years Congress has tried several different mathematical formulas for determining the number of seats that should be allocated to each state. The various formulas generally lead to similar results, but under certain conditions the particular method used

may slightly increase or decrease the number of seats assigned to a given state. The formula currently used, known as the "method of equal proportions," was adopted by Congress in 1941. Its application after the 1990 census led to increases in representation for California, Florida, and Texas, which had experienced population growth, and decreases in representation for other states.

One of the states that lost representation was Montana. Prior to 1990 Montana had two seats in the U.S. House, but following the census the state was informed that it would lose one representative. Montana went to federal court to contest the decision. With a total population of 803,655, Montana's single congressional district would be considerably larger than the 572,466 ideal. However, if Montana retained two congressional seats, each would represent an average of almost 402,000, a number closer to the ideal district size. Montana, therefore, claimed, and the district court agreed, that its allocation of only one seat ran contrary to the "one person, one vote" principle.

On appeal the Supreme Court unanimously reversed. The Court's opinion by Justice Stevens traces the history of disputes over allocation of House seats from 1790 to the present. It also examines the various formulas Congress tried in an attempt to make seat allocations as fair as possible. The Court concludes that the competing alternative methods are all sensible approaches to determining representational schemes, although none can guarantee a perfect fit with the Court's reapportionment principles. In the end, the justices deferred to Congress's determination of the best standard to use. Stevens concluded:

The decision to adopt the method of equal proportions was made by Congress after decades of experience, experimentation, and debate about the substance of the constitutional requirement. Independent scholars supported both the basic decision to adopt a regular procedure to be followed after each census, and the particular decision to use the method of equal proportions. For a half century the results of that method have been accepted by the States and the Nation. That history supports our conclusion that Congress had ample power to enact the statutory procedure in 1941 and to apply the method of equal proportions after the 1990 census.

Political Representation and Minority Rights

So long as the one person, one vote principle is observed, the Supreme Court generally has allowed the states freedom in constructing representational districts. That latitude, however, is not without limit. The Court always has been aware that representational schemes that satisfy standards of numerical equality may still offend basic constitutional principles. Plans that discriminate on the basis of race or ethnicity have been of particular concern. The justices have served notice that boundary lines cannot be drawn in a way that dilutes the political power of minorities.

Reducing the political participation rights of minorities can take forms other than Alabama's rather crude deannexation methods struck down in *Gomillion v. Lightfoot.* One representational form, the multimember district, has received considerable scrutiny because of its potential for abusing the rights of minority groups. Under a multimember arrangement, the districts are larger in population than the average constituency and are represented by more than one officeholder. For example, the state legislature may construct a district that is three times larger than the average single-member district and authorize the election of three representatives from that constituency. Normally under such a plan, there are three separate legislative seats with each voter casting a ballot in each of the three races. Once elected, all three legislators serve the same large constituency.

The Supreme Court consistently has held that multimember districts are not constitutionally defective per se and the states retain the right to use them as long as the representation is properly weighted according to population (*Burns v. Richardson,* 1966; *Whitcomb v. Chavis,* 1971). However, such districts run

afoul of the Equal Protection Clause if they are developed or maintained as intentional methods of minimizing, canceling out, or diluting the voting strength of racial or ethnic minorities. A multimember district can easily be designed to accomplish this purpose. Using our three-member legislative district example, assume that 40 percent of the district's population is found in a compact residential section made up of a particular minority group. If the district were divided into three single-member constituencies, the minority population would likely control one of those districts and be relatively assured of electing one of their own to the state legislature. With the multimember district scheme, however, the votes of the minority citizens would likely be insufficient to win any of the three at-large races. In *White v. Regester* (1973), for example, the Court found the use of some multimember districts in Texas to have politically disadvantaged black and Mexican-American voters in violation of the Equal Protection Clause.

Considerable controversy arose over what standards should be used in districting cases in which the diluting of minority voting power is alleged. In *Mobile v. Bolden* (1980) a badly divided Court ruled on claims that the at-large system for electing members of the Mobile, Alabama, city commission diluted the electoral strength of blacks to the extent that the Fourteenth and Fifteenth Amendments were violated. The Court held that to establish a violation of the Constitution the challengers must prove more than the fact that minority citizens were disadvantaged politically. It is required, the Court ruled, that racially discriminatory intent be demonstrated. If a governmental action is racially neutral on its face (as multimember districts and at-large election schemes almost always are), then a racially discriminatory purpose must be shown to prove a violation of the Constitution.

Proving discriminatory intent or purpose is quite difficult. Few government officials who want to implement racially discriminatory policies publicly admit it. Although the Court showed a willingness to infer discriminatory purpose when black political partici-pation was especially muted,[7] Congress, at the urging of civil rights groups, concluded that additional leg-islative action was necessary.

Short of proposing a constitutional amendment, Congress could do little to reverse the Court's position that discriminatory purpose must be shown before a violation of the Fourteenth or Fifteenth Amendment could be declared. Congress, however, was empow-ered to enforce voting rights through the normal leg-islative process. Consequently, in 1982 it amended the 1965 Voting Rights Act so that violations could be proven by discriminatory effects alone. Congress made clear that a demonstration of discriminatory purpose was not required. Whether intended or not, if a government action resulted in diluting black voting strength, Congress wanted black litigants to be able to use the legal process to put an end to it. This change in the voting rights law has made it easier for minority groups to win representational discrimina-tion cases. In 1986, for example, the Supreme Court in *Thornburg v. Gingles* struck down a North Carolina re-districting plan after minority voters were able to show the law's discriminatory effects. It is important to remember, however, that the amendment of the Voting Rights Act did not alter the requirements for providing a violation of the Constitution. To challenge the validity of a government act under the Fourteenth or Fifteenth Amendments, a party still must show dis-criminatory intent. Only with respect to alleged viola-tions of the Voting Rights Act is the demonstration of discriminatory effects or results sufficient.

The need to ensure that a reapportionment effort does not have the effect of diluting the electoral strength of certain minority groups has made redis-tricting a more complex task. Increasing representa-tion to one group almost always means decreasing the political influence of another. In a time when various racial and ethnic groups are competing for political power, no plan, even if drafted with good intentions, is likely to satisfy all parties. The result may be con-flict among competing communities, as *United Jewish Organizations of Williamsburgh v. Carey* demonstrates. Do the reapportionment criteria used by the state of New York appear reasonable? Or is Chief Justice Burger's dissenting opinion correct in asserting that the Court has turned away from the sound principles established since *Gomillion?*

United Jewish Organizations of Williamsburgh v. Carey

430 U.S. 144 (1977)
Vote: 7 (Blackmun, Brennan, Powell, Rehnquist, Stevens, Stewart, White)
　　 1 (Burger)
Opinion announcing the judgment of the Court: White
Concurring opinions: Brennan, Stewart
Dissenting opinion: Burger
Not participating: Marshall

To monitor compliance with the Voting Rights Act, Congress provided in Section 5 that the reapportion-ment plans of certain states be submitted to the U.S. attorney general or to the District Court for the Dis-trict of Columbia for approval prior to implementa-tion. Plans had to be judged not to have the purpose or effect of "denying or abridging the right to vote on account of race or color." States with histories of dis-crimination and low voter participation rates were obliged to submit to this procedure.

In 1972 New York State enacted congressional and state legislative reapportionment plans. Because cer-tain counties formerly had employed a discriminatory literacy test and had low voter participation levels, the state submitted the plans to the attorney general for clearance. The attorney general objected to the reap-

---

7. See, for example, *Rogers v. Lodge* (1982), in which the Court found discriminatory purpose in a county's representational system. Although 38 percent of the electorate was black, not a single black had been elected to the five-person county commission since the adoption of at-large elections in 1911.

portionment plan for the state legislature as it pertained to certain districts in Kings County covering the Bedford-Stuyvesant area of Brooklyn. The state responded in 1974 with a revised plan for the districts in this area. Under the 1972 plan, three senate districts in Kings County had nonwhite majorities of 91 percent, 61 percent, and 53 percent. The revised 1974 plan called for nonwhite majorities between 70 percent and 75 percent in all three districts. Under the 1972 plan, seven Assembly (lower house) districts had nonwhite majorities, with 52 percent being the smallest. The revised 1974 plan increased the black voting power in these districts, making the smallest nonwhite majority 65 percent. The clear purpose and effect of the revisions was to ensure black representation from these districts. According to evidence presented, the state was under the impression that to be assured of approval a plan needed to show a minimum nonwhite majority of 65 percent in the targeted districts. The plan left 70 percent of the county's legislative districts in the control of white majorities. The attorney general said he had no objections to the revised plan.

One of the communities adversely affected by the reapportionment plan was Williamsburgh, where about 30,000 Hasidic Jews lived. Under the 1972 plan, the Hasidic community was located entirely in a single Assembly and Senate district, as it had been for many years. To create substantial nonwhite majorities in the county, the 1974 revisions split the Hasidic community into two Assembly and two Senate districts. The United Jewish Organizations of Williamsburgh sued to block implementation of the plan, claiming that the Hasidic Jews had been assigned to electoral districts solely on the basis of race, and that this racial assignment diluted their voting power in violation of the Fourteenth and Fifteenth Amendments. The district court dismissed the complaint, ruling that the Hasidic community enjoyed no constitutional right as a separate entity in the reapportionment process and that taking racial considerations into ac-

count was permissible to correct past discrimination. The court of appeals affirmed.

MR. JUSTICE WHITE announced the judgment of the Court....

[T]he Constitution does not prevent a State subject to the Voting Rights Act from deliberately creating or preserving black majorities in particular districts in order to ensure that its reapportionment plan complies with § 5. That proposition must be rejected and § 5 held unconstitutional to that extent if we are to accept petitioners' view that racial criteria may never be used in redistricting or that they may be used, if at all, only as a specific remedy for past unconstitutional apportionments. We are unwilling to overturn our prior cases, however. Section 5 and its authorization for racial redistricting where appropriate to avoid abridging the right to vote on account of race or color are constitutional. Contrary to petitioners' first argument, neither the Fourteenth nor the Fifteenth Amendment mandates any *per se* rule against using racial factors in districting and apportionment. Nor is petitioners' second argument valid. The permissible use of racial criteria is not confined to eliminating the effects of past discriminatory districting or apportionment.

Moreover, in the process of drawing black majority districts in order to comply with § 5, the State must decide how substantial those majorities must be in order to satisfy the Voting Rights Act.... At a minimum and by definition, a "black majority district" must be more than 50% black. But whatever the specific percentage, the State will inevitably arrive at it as a necessary means to ensure the opportunity for the election of a black representative and to obtain approval of its reapportionment plan.... [A] reapportionment cannot violate the Fourteenth or Fifteenth Amendment merely because a State uses specific numerical quotas in establishing a certain number of black majority districts. Our cases under § 5 stand for at least this much....

There is no doubt that in preparing the 1974 legislation the State deliberately used race in a purposeful manner. But its plan represented no racial slur or stigma with respect to whites or any other race, and we discern no discrimination violative of the Fourteenth Amendment or any abridgment of the right to vote on account of race within the meaning of the Fifteenth Amendment.

It is true that New York deliberately increased the non-white majorities in certain districts in order to enhance the opportunity for election of nonwhite representatives from those districts. Nevertheless, there was no fencing out the white population from participation in the political processes of the county, and the plan did not minimize or unfairly cancel out white voting strength. Petitioners have not objected to the impact of the 1974 plan on the representation of white voters in the county or in the State as a whole. As the Court of Appeals observed, the plan left white majorities in approximately 70% of the assembly and senate districts in Kings County, which had a countywide population that was 65% white. Thus, even if voting in the county occurred strictly according to race, whites would not be underrepresented relative to their share of the population.

In individual districts where nonwhite majorities were increased to approximately 65%, it became more likely, given racial bloc voting, that black candidates would be elected instead of their white opponents, and it became less likely that white voters would be represented by a member of their own race; but as long as whites in Kings County, as a group, were provided with fair representation, we cannot conclude that there was a cognizable discrimination against whites or an abridgment of their right to vote on the grounds of race. Furthermore, the individual voter in the district with a nonwhite majority has no constitutional complaint merely because his candidate has lost out at the polls and his district is represented by a person for whom he did not vote. Some candidate, along with his supporters, always loses.

Where it occurs, voting for or against a candidate because of his race is an unfortunate practice. But it is not rare; and in any district where it regularly happens, it is unlikely that any candidate will be elected who is a member of the race that is in the minority in that district. However disagreeable this result may be, there is no authority for the proposition that the candidates who are found racially unacceptable by the majority, and the minority voters supporting those candidates, have had their Fourteenth or Fifteenth Amendment rights infringed by this process. Their position is similar to that of the Democratic or Republican minority that is submerged year after year by the adherents to the majority party who tend to vote a straight party line.

It does not follow, however, that the State is powerless to minimize the consequences of racial discrimination by voters when it is regularly practiced at the polls....

In this respect New York's revision of certain district lines is little different in kind from the decision by a State in which a racial minority is unable to elect representatives from multimember districts to change to single-member districting for the purpose of increasing minority representation. This change might substantially increase minority representation at the expense of white voters, who previously elected all of the legislators but who with single-member districts could elect no more than their proportional share. If this intentional reduction of white voting power would be constitutionally permissible, as we think it would be, we think it also permissible for a State, employing sound districting principles such as compactness and population equality, to attempt to prevent racial minorities from being repeatedly outvoted by creating districts that will afford fair representation to the members of those racial groups who are sufficiently numerous and whose residential patterns afford the opportunity of creating districts in which they will be in the majority....

The judgment is

Affirmed.

MR. CHIEF JUSTICE BURGER, dissenting.

The question presented in this difficult case is whether New York violated the rights of the petitioners under the Fourteenth and Fifteenth Amendments by direct reliance on fixed racial percentages in its 1974 redistricting of Kings County....

I begin with this Court's holding in *Gomillion v. Lightfoot* (1960), the first case to strike down a state attempt at racial gerrymandering. If *Gomillion* teaches anything, I had thought it was that drawing of political boundary lines with the sole, explicit objective of reaching a predetermined racial result cannot ordinarily be squared with the Constitution. The record before us reveals—and it is not disputed—that this is precisely what took place here. In drawing up the 1974 reapportionment scheme, the New York Legislature did not consider racial composition as merely one of several political characteristics; on the contrary, race appears to have been the one and only criterion applied....

The assumption that "whites" and "nonwhites" in the County form homogeneous entities for voting purposes is entirely without foundation. The "whites" category consists of a veritable galaxy of national origins, ethnic backgrounds, and religious denominations. It simply cannot be assumed that the legislative interests of all "whites" are even substantially identical. In similar fashion, those described as "nonwhites" include, in addition to Negroes, a substantial portion of Puerto Ricans. The Puerto Rican population, for whose protection the Voting Rights Act was "triggered" in Kings County, has expressly disavowed any identity of interest with the Negroes, and, in fact, objected to the 1974 redistricting scheme because it did not establish a Puerto Rican controlled district within the county.

Although reference to racial composition of a political unit may, under certain circumstances, serve as "a starting point in the process of shaping a remedy," *Swann v. Charlotte-Mecklenburg Bd. of Education* (1971), rigid adherence to quotas, especially in a case like this, deprives citizens such as petitioners of the opportunity to have the legislature make a determination free from unnecessary bias for or against any racial, ethnic, or religious group. I do not quarrel with the proposition that the New York Legislature may choose to take ethnic or community union into consideration in drawing its district lines. Indeed, petitioners are members of an ethnic community which, without deliberate purpose so far as shown on this record, has long been within a single assembly and senate district. While petitioners certainly have no constitutional right to remain unified within a single political district, they do have, in my view, the constitutional right not to be carved up so as to create a voting bloc composed of some other ethnic or racial group through the kind of racial gerrymandering the Court condemned in *Gomillion v. Lightfoot*....

The result reached by the Court today in the name of the Voting Rights Act is ironic. The use of a mathematical formula tends to sustain the existence of ghettos by promoting the notion that political clout is to be gained or maintained by marshaling particular racial, ethnic, or religious groups in enclaves. It suggests to the voter that only a candidate of the same race, religion, or ethnic origin can properly represent that voter's interests, and that such candidate can be elected only from a district with a sufficient minority concentration. The device employed by the State of New York and endorsed by the Court today, moves us one step farther away from a truly homogeneous society. This retreat from the ideal of the American "melting pot" is curiously out of step with recent political history—and indeed with what the Court has said and done for more than a decade. The notion that Americans vote in firm blocs has been repudiated in the election of minority members as mayors and legislators in numerous American cities and districts overwhelmingly white. Since I cannot square the mechanical racial gerrymandering in this case with the mandate of the Constitution, I respectfully dissent from the affirmance of the judgment of the Court of Appeals.

United Jewish Organizations, followed later by the Court's 1986 ruling in *Thornburg v. Gingles*, gave constitutional approval to the process of constructing political districts with the expressed purpose of ensuring the election of minority candidates. Civil rights groups and other liberal organizations had been advocating this practice as the only meaningful way to guarantee blacks and other minorities a fair share of legislative seats.

In promoting this cause, advocates of increasing the political power of minorities received significant support from the Justice Department under Presidents Reagan and Bush. Why would a Republican administration back efforts to increase the number of black representatives, especially since these legislators probably would be Democrats? The answer is simple. When lines are drawn to create districts with high concentrations of black voters, the other districts become more white and more Republican. In other words, by creating a few districts that are dominated by minorities, the state legislatures also fashion districts that are more likely to elect Republicans.

In many states the reapportionment battles that followed the 1990 census were not over one person, one vote issues; rather, they focused on drawing district boundary lines in a manner that would increase the number of minority officeholders. The successful

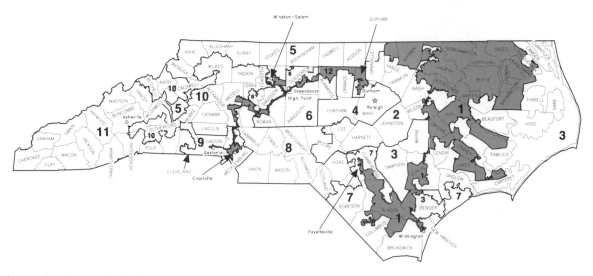

The irregular shapes of North Carolina's First and Twelfth Congressional Districts were challenged in *Shaw v. Reno*.

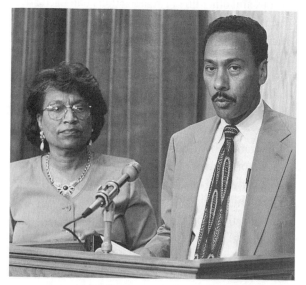

Rep. Eva Clayton of North Carolina's First Congressional District and Rep. Melvin Watt of the Twelfth. Clayton and Watt were elected in 1992 from legislative districts constructed to promote the election of minority representatives. Both legislators won their general elections by better than 2–1 margins. They became the first black members of the North Carolina congressional delegation since 1901.

creation of districts with heavy concentrations of racial and ethnic minorities had its intended effect. In the 1992 congressional elections, sixteen new black representatives were elected, bringing the total membership of the Black Caucus to forty. Eight newly elected Hispanic representatives also took their seats after the 1992 elections.

To draw these new "majority-minority" districts, state legislatures often had to engage in very creative districting methods. Critics contended that legislators went too far, frequently establishing district boundaries that were highly irregular in shape and possessing little compactness. It was one thing, they argued, to create districts that did not purposefully dilute minority voting strength, but a much different thing to base representational boundaries exclusively on race. As a consequence, lawsuits filed in Florida, Georgia, Louisiana, North Carolina, and Texas challenged the constitutionality of many new districts. The first appeal to reach the Supreme Court was *Shaw v. Reno* (1993), a challenge to two majority-minority congressional districts in North Carolina.

Shaw v. Reno

509 U.S. — (1993)

Vote: 5 (Kennedy, O'Connor, Rehnquist, Scalia, Thomas)
       4 (Blackmun, Souter, Stevens, White)

Opinion of the Court: O'Connor

Dissenting opinions: Blackmun, Souter, Stevens, White

As a result of the 1990 census, North Carolina gained one congressional seat, increasing its House membership to thirteen and requiring the state legislature to redraw the congressional districts. Because of previous racial discrimination, North Carolina fell under the provisions of the Voting Rights Act of 1965, which mandated that any redistricting plan adopted by the state legislature be submitted to the U.S. Justice Department or the District Court for the District of Columbia for approval. Such approval would be forthcoming only if the plan did not jeopardize minority representation.

North Carolina's initial reapportionment effort included one district purposefully constructed to have a majority of black voters. The Bush administration's Justice Department rejected this plan on the grounds that it gave blacks insufficient congressional representation. In response, the state legislature revised the plan in a way that created two districts (the First and the Twelfth) that would have a majority of black voters. The Justice Department accepted this revision.

The shapes of the two majority-black districts were quite controversial. The First District was somewhat hook-shaped, beginning in the northeastern part of the state and tapering down with fingerlike extensions almost to the South Carolina border. It included all or portions of twenty-eight counties. In the lower court record the district was said to resemble a Rorschach ink-blot test, and the *Wall Street Journal* claimed the district looked like a "bug splattered on a windshield." The Twelfth District received even harsher criticism. It was 160 miles long and generally corresponded to the Interstate 85 corridor. One of the lower court judges described it as winding in a snakelike fashion through tobacco country, financial centers, and manufacturing areas until it gobbled up enough enclaves of black neighborhoods to create a majority-black district. At some points the district was no wider than Interstate 85, prompting one state legislator to remark that if "you drove down the interstate with both car doors open, you'd kill most of the people in the district." It spite of such criticisms, the redistricting accomplished its goal. In the 1992 elections voters in both districts selected black representatives. They were the first blacks to represent North Carolina, a state with a 20 percent black population, since 1901.

Ruth Shaw and four other white North Carolina voters filed suit against the U.S. attorney general and various North Carolina officials, claiming that race-based redistricting violated, among other provisions, the Equal Protection Clause of the Fourteenth Amendment. A special three-judge district court dismissed the suit against both the attorney general and the state officials. Shaw appealed. Traditional civil rights groups—the NAACP Legal Defense Fund, Lawyers' Committee for Civil Rights Under Law, and the Mexican American Legal Defense Fund—submitted amicus curiae briefs in favor of the minority districts, and groups with long histories of opposition to quota programs—Washington Legal Foundation and the American Jewish Congress—argued against them. True to their ideological positions (but perhaps in spite of immediate partisan implications), the Democratic National Committee maintained that the minority districts were constitutional, and the Republican National Committee argued that they were not.

JUSTICE O'CONNOR delivered the opinion of the Court.

This case involves two of the most complex and sensitive issues this Court has faced in recent years: the meaning of the constitutional "right" to vote, and the propriety of race-based state legislation designed to benefit members of historically disadvantaged racial minority groups.... Appellants allege that the revised plan, which contains district boundary lines of dramatically irregular shape, constitutes an unconstitutional racial gerrymander. The question before us is whether appellants have stated a cognizable claim....

Appellants contended that the General Assembly's revised reapportionment plan violated several provisions of the United States Constitution, including the Fourteenth Amendment. They alleged that the General Assembly deliberately "create[d] two Congressional Districts in which a majority of black voters was concentrated arbitrarily— without regard to any other considerations, such as compactness, contiguousness, geographical boundaries, or political subdivisions" with the purpose "to create Congressional Districts along racial lines" and to assure the election of two black representatives to Congress....

"The right to vote freely for the candidate of one's choice is of the essence of a democratic society...." *Reynolds v. Sims* [1964]. For much of our Nation's history, that right sadly has been denied to many because of race. The Fifteenth Amendment, ratified in 1870 after a bloody Civil War, promised unequivocally that "[t]he right of citizens of the United States to vote" no longer would be "denied or abridged ... by any State on account of race, color, or previous condition of servitude."...

But it soon became apparent that guaranteeing equal access to the polls would not suffice to root out other racially discriminatory voting practices. Drawing on the "one person, one vote" principle, this Court recognized that "[t]he right to vote can be affected by a *dilution* of voting power as well as by an absolute prohibition on casting a ballot." *Allen v. State Board of Elections* (1969) (emphasis added). Where members of a racial minority group vote as a cohesive unit, practices such as multimember or at-large electoral systems can reduce or nullify minority voters' ability, as a group, "to elect the candidate of their choice." Accordingly, the Court held that such schemes violate the Fourteenth Amendment when they are adopted with a discriminatory purpose and have the effect of diluting minority voting strength. See, *e.g., Rogers v. Lodge* (1982); *White v. Regester* (1973). Congress, too, responded to the problem of vote dilution. In 1982, it amended § 2 of the Voting Rights Act to prohibit legislation that *results* in the dilution of a minority group's voting strength, regardless of the legislature's intent.

It is against this background that we confront the questions presented here. In our view, the District Court properly dismissed appellants' claims against the federal appellees. Our focus is on appellants' claim that the State engaged in unconstitutional racial gerrymandering. That argument strikes a powerful historical chord: It is unsettling how closely the North Carolina plan resembles the most egregious racial gerrymanders of the past.

An understanding of the nature of appellants' claim is critical to our resolution of the case. In their complaint, appellants did not claim that the General Assembly's reapportionment plan unconstitutionally "diluted" white voting strength. They did not even claim to be white. Rather, appellants' complaint alleged that the deliberate segregation of voters into separate districts on the basis of race violated their constitutional right to participate in a "color-blind" electoral process.

Despite their invocation of the ideal of a "color-blind" Constitution, see *Plessy v. Ferguson* (1896) (Harlan, J., dissenting), appellants appear to concede that race-conscious redistricting is not always unconstitutional. That concession is wise: This Court never has held that race-conscious state decisionmaking is impermissible in *all* circumstances. What appellants object to is redistricting legislation that is so extremely irregular on its face that it rationally can be viewed only as an effort to segregate the races for purposes of voting, without regard for traditional districting principles and without sufficiently compelling justification. For the reasons that follow, we conclude that appellants have stated a claim upon which relief can be granted under the Equal Protection Clause.

The Equal Protection Clause provides that "[n]o State shall ... deny to any person within its jurisdiction the equal protection of the laws." Its central purpose is to prevent the States from purposefully discriminating between individuals on the basis of race. *Washington v. Davis* (1976). Laws that explicitly distinguish between individuals on racial grounds fall within the core of that prohibition....

Classifications of citizens on the basis of race "are by their very nature odious to a free people whose institutions are founded upon the doctrine of equality." *Hirabayashi v. United States* (1943). They threaten to stigmatize individuals by reason of their membership in a racial group and to incite racial hostility....

These principles apply not only to legislation that contains explicit racial distinctions, but also to those "rare" statutes that, although race-neutral, are, on their face, "unexplainable on grounds other than race." *Arlington Heights v. Metropolitan Housing Development Corp.* (1977). As we explained in [*Personnel Administrator of Massachusetts v.*] *Feeney* [1979]:

"A racial classification, regardless of purported motivation, is presumptively invalid and can be upheld only upon an extraordinary justification. This rule applies as well to a classification that is ostensibly neutral but is an obvious pretext for racial discrimination."

Appellants contend that redistricting legislation that is so bizarre on its face that it is "unexplainable on grounds other than race," *Arlington Heights,* demands the same close scrutiny that we give other state laws that classify citizens by race. Our voting rights precedents support that conclusion....

... [W]e believe that reapportionment is one area in which appearances do matter. A reapportionment plan that includes in one district individuals who belong to the same race, but who are otherwise widely separated by geographical and political boundaries, and who may have little in common with one another but the color of their skin, bears an uncomfortable resemblance to political apartheid. It reinforces the perception that members of the same racial group—regardless of their age, education, economic status, or the community in which the live—think alike, share the same political interests, and will prefer the same candidates at the polls. We have rejected such perceptions elsewhere as impermissible racial stereotypes. By perpetuating such notions, a racial gerrymander may exacerbate the very patterns of racial bloc voting that majority-minority districting is sometimes said to counteract.

The message that such districting sends to elected representatives is equally pernicious. When a district obviously is created solely to effectuate the perceived common interests of one racial group, elected officials are more likely to believe that their primary obligation is to represent only the members of that group, rather than their constituency as a whole. This is altogether antithetical to our system of representative democracy. As Justice Douglas explained in his dissent in *Wright v. Rockefeller* nearly 30 years ago:

"Here t ̣ ̣ individual is important, not his race, his creed, or his color. The principle of equality is at war with the notion that District A must be represented by a Negro, as it is with the notion that District B must be represented by a Caucasian, District C by a Jew, District D by a Catholic, and so on.... That system, by whatever name it is called, is a divisive force in a community, emphasizing differences between candidates and voters that are irrelevant in the constitutional sense....

"When racial or religious lines are drawn by the State, the multiracial, multireligious communities that our Constitution seeks to weld together as one become separatist; antagonisms that relate to race or to religion rather than to political issues are generated; communities seek not the best representative but the best racial or religious partisan. Since that system is at war with the democratic ideal, it should find no footing here."

For these reasons, we conclude that a plaintiff challenging a reapportionment statute under the Equal Protection Clause may state a claim by alleging that the legislation, though race-neutral on its face, rationally cannot be understood as anything other than an effort to separate voters into different districts on the basis of race, and that the separation lacks sufficient justification. It is unnecessary for us to decide whether or how a reapportionment plan that, on its face, can be explained in nonracial terms successfully could be challenged. Thus, we express no view as to whether "the intentional creation of majority-minority districts, without more" always gives rise to an equal protection claim. We hold only that, on the facts of this case, plaintiffs have stated a claim sufficient to defeat the state appellees' motion to dismiss....

Racial classifications of any sort pose the risk of lasting harm to our society. They reinforce the belief, held by too many for too much of our history, that individuals should be judged by the color of their skin. Racial classifications with respect to voting carry particular dangers. Racial gerrymandering, even for remedial purposes, may balkanize us into competing racial factions; it threatens to carry us further from the goal of a political system in which race no longer matters—a goal that the Fourteenth and Fifteenth Amendments embody, and to which the Nation continues to aspire. It is for these reasons that race-based districting by our state legislatures demands close judicial scrutiny.

In this case, the Attorney General suggested that North Carolina could have created a reasonably compact second majority-minority district in the south-central to southeastern part of the State. We express no view as to whether appellants successfully could have challenged such a district under the Fourteenth Amendment. We also do not decide whether appellants' complaint stated a claim under constitutional provisions other than the Fourteenth Amendment. Today we hold only that appellants have stated a claim under the Equal Protection Clause by alleging that the North Carolina General Assembly adopted a reapportionment scheme so irrational on its face that it can be understood only as an effort to segregate voters into separate voting districts because of their race, and that the separation lacks sufficient justification. If the allegation of racial gerrymandering remains uncontradicted, the District Court further must determine whether the North Carolina plan is narrowly tailored to further a compelling governmental interest. Accordingly, we reverse the judgment of the District Court and remand the case for further proceedings consistent with this opinion.

It is so ordered.

JUSTICE SOUTER, dissenting.

Today, the Court recognizes a new cause of action under which a State's electoral redistricting plan that includes a configuration "so bizarre" that it "rationally cannot be understood as anything other than an effort to separate voters into different districts on the basis of race [without] sufficient justification" will be subjected to strict scrutiny. In my view there is no justification for the Court's determination to depart from our prior decisions by carving out this narrow group of cases for strict scrutiny in place of the review customarily applied in cases dealing with discrimination in electoral districting on the basis of race.

Until today, the Court has analyzed equal protection claims involving race in electoral districting differently from equal protection claims involving other forms of governmental conduct, and before turning to the different regimes of analysis it will be useful to set out the relevant respects in which such districting differs from the characteristic circumstances in which a State might otherwise consciously consider race. Unlike other contexts in which we have addressed the State's conscious use of race, see, *e.g., Richmond v. J. A. Croson Co.* (1989) (city contracting); *Wygant v. Jackson Bd. of Ed.* (1986) (teacher layoffs), electoral districting calls for decisions that nearly always require some consideration of race for legitimate reasons where there is a racially mixed population. As long as members of racial groups have the commonality of interest implicit in our ability to talk about concepts like "minority voting strength," and "dilution of minority votes," cf. *Thornburg v. Gingles* (1986), and as long as racial bloc voting takes place, legislators will have to take race into account in order to avoid dilution of minority voting strength in the districting plans they adopt. One need look no further than the Voting Rights Act to understand that this may be required, and we have held that race may constitutionally be taken into account in order to comply with that Act.

A second distinction between districting and most other governmental decisions in which race has figured is that those other decisions using racial criteria characteristically occur in circumstances in which the use of race to the advantage of one person is necessarily at the obvious expense of a member of a different race. Thus, for example, awarding government contracts on a racial basis excludes certain firms from competition on racial grounds. And when race is used to supplant seniority in layoffs, someone is laid off who would not be otherwise. The same principle pertains in nondistricting aspects of voting law, where race-based discrimination places the disfavored voters at the disadvantage of exclusion from the franchise without any alternative benefit.

In districting, by contrast, the mere placement of an individual in one district instead of another denies no one a right or benefit provided to others. All citizens may register, vote, and be represented. In whatever district, the individual voter has a right to vote in each election, and the election will result in the voter's representation. As we have held, one's constitutional rights are not violated merely because the candidate one supports loses the election or because a group (including a racial group) to which one belongs winds up with a representative from outside that group. It is true, of course, that one's vote may be more or less effective depending on the interests of the other individuals who are in one's district, and our cases recognize the reality that members of the same race often have shared interests. "Dilution" thus refers to the effects of districting decisions not on an individual's political power viewed in isolation, but on the political power of a group. This is the reason that the placement of given voters in a given district, even on the basis of race, does not, without more, diminish the effectiveness of the individual as a voter. . . .

There is thus no theoretical inconsistency in having two distinct approaches to equal protection analysis, one for cases of electoral districting and one for most other types of state governmental decisions. Nor, because of the distinctions between the two categories, is there any risk that Fourteenth Amendment districting law as such will be taken to imply anything for purposes of general Fourteenth Amendment scrutiny about "benign" racial discrimination, or about group entitlement as distinct from individual protection, or about the appropriateness of strict or other heightened scrutiny.

The Court appears to accept this, and it does not purport to disturb the law of vote dilution in any way. Instead, the Court creates a new "analytically distinct" cause of action, the principal element of which is that a districting plan be "so bizarre on its face" or "irrational on its face," or "extremely irregular on its face," that it "rationally cannot be understood as anything other than an effort to segregate citizens into separate voting districts on the basis of race without sufficient justification." Pleading such an element, the Court holds, suffices without a further allegation of harm, to state a claim upon which relief can be granted under the Fourteenth Amendment.

It may be that the terms for pleading this cause of action will be met so rarely that this case will wind up an aberration. The shape of the district at issue in this case is indeed so bizarre that few other examples are ever likely to carry the unequivocal implication of impermissible use of race that the Court finds here. It may therefore be that few electoral districting cases are ever likely to employ the strict scrutiny the Court holds to be applicable on remand if appellants' allegations are "not contradicted."

Nonetheless, in those cases where this cause of action is sufficiently pleaded, the State will have to justify its decision to consider race as being required by a compelling state interest, and its use of race as narrowly tailored to that interest. Meanwhile, in other districting cases, specific consequential harm will still need to be pleaded and proven, in the absence of which the use of race may be invalidated only if it is shown to serve no legitimate state purpose.

The Court offers no adequate justification for treating the narrow category of bizarrely shaped district claims differently from other districting claims. The only justification I can imagine would be the preservation of "sound districting principles," such as compactness and contiguity. But . . . we have held that such principles are not constitutionally required, with the consequence that their absence cannot justify the distinct constitutional regime put in place by the Court today. Since there is no justification for the departure here from the principles that continue to govern electoral districting cases generally in accordance with our prior decisions, I would not respond to the seeming egregiousness of the redistricting now before us by untethering the concept of racial gerrymander in such a case from the concept of harm exemplified by dilution. In the absence of an allegation of such harm, I would affirm the judgment of the District Court. I respectfully dissent.

The decision in *Shaw v. Reno* did not strike down the use of racial factors in the creation of legislative districts. However, Justice O'Connor's opinion clearly reflects considerable doubt about the validity of boundaries drawn the way they were in North Carolina. Reapportionment plans that can be understood only as the result of efforts to segregate voters on the basis of their race may well pose valid Equal Protection claims. Such plans can survive only if they are narrowly tailored to further a compelling government interest. While the final verdict on such districts is not yet in, initial lower court rulings applying the standards articulated in *Shaw* have held some minority districts to be in violation of the Fourteenth Amendment.

Efforts to create districts with high concentrations of minority voters have been criticized by some civil rights advocates as well. Various legal scholars have contended that majority-minority districts do not offer real opportunities for increased minority representation. Even if the number of minority representatives grew to approximate their proportion in the general population, they would still lack sufficient strength to pass legislation, and their opinions could still be effectively ignored by other legislators. Furthermore, while the creation of minority districts leads to a marginal increase in minority legislators, it also leads to the election of conservative white legislators from other districts, and these conservative gains may offset any minority gains. These critics argue that only through changes in representational and institutional rules can minorities achieve political influence beyond the local level.

These arguments, previously confined to law journals and other academic outlets, received national attention in 1993 when President Clinton nominated law professor Lani Guinier to head the Justice Department's Civil Rights Division. Guinier, who had worked for the NAACP Legal Defense and Educational Fund and had served as an assistant in the Civil Rights Division during the Carter administration, had written widely in the legal journals about alternative methods of enhancing minority representational strength. One of the reforms she suggested for discussion is "cumulative voting." Under a cumulative voting system, voters would select legislators from multimember districts. For example, a district might elect five legislators to represent it. Each voter would cast five votes and could spread those votes among several candidates or cast all five votes for the same candidate. Guinier argued that cumulative voting would allow minority citizens to concentrate votes on a few candidates who were supportive of minority interests thereby increasing their odds of election. Guinier also advocated changes in legislative rules, such as the use of "super majorities." If certain kinds of legislation were required to receive a two-thirds or three-fourths vote for passage, rather than a simple majority, legislators would have to pay greater attention to minority legislators.

Guinier's nomination provoked a strong reaction. Opponents used her academic writings to tag her as the "Quota Queen." Although Guinier responded that she had never advocated the use of quotas, the label stuck. The press portrayed her as a supporter of extreme affirmative action programs. Guinier argued that her critics had distorted her views beyond recognition, but opposition continued to mount. In response to the growing divisiveness, President Clinton withdrew the nomination before the Senate acted.

The political controversy over Guinier's nomination and the legal disputes over the creation of minority districts demonstrate that the debate over issues of minority representation is far from over. The Supreme Court added to the controversy with two 1994 decisions concerning the meaning of the 1965 Voting Rights Act. In *Holder v. Hall* the justices, by a 5–4 vote, held that the act did not prohibit Bleckley County, Georgia, from using a single commissioner form of government in which one officeholder exercised both legislative and administrative authority. The county's population was 22 percent black, and no minority candidate had ever been elected commissioner. The Court ruled that the act did not compel the county to adopt a multimember commission to increase the probability of black representation in government. In the second case, *Johnson v. De Grandy*, the justices rejected an argument that the Voting Rights Act required a legislature to draw district lines to maximize minority representation. The dispute centered on newly drawn legislative districts in Miami-Dade County, Florida. The lines could have been drawn to create eleven House districts and four Senate districts with Hispanic majorities, but the final reapportionment act contained only nine House and three Senate majority Hispanic districts. The justices concluded that as long as minority voters form effective voting majorities in a number of districts roughly proportional to their respective share of the voting-age population, the Voting Rights Act is not violated. Undoubtedly, all three branches of government will be forced to confront many of these questions over the next decade.

Partisan Gerrymandering

In spite of the Supreme Court's broadening of constitutional protections in the reapportionment process, the drawing of boundary lines for political districts has always been a distinctly political process. The political forces that control reapportionment can shape the political balance of the state for a decade. For this reason, the most important state legislative elections are those that coincide with the national census. The winning legislators approve the reapportionment of congressional and state legislative districts that will be in effect until the next census. While the decisions of the Supreme Court constrain the legislature, skillful districting still can be used to great political advantage. As district lines are adjusted, the political futures of both incumbents and challengers are affected, and the relative power of political parties, economic interests, and other forces are significantly altered.

Gaining partisan advantage through reapportionment has been a common goal for the major political parties. If a political party controls both houses of the state legislature, as well as the governor's mansion, little can stop it from constructing a reapportionment plan that provides it considerable advantage in future elections. Through the decennial redistricting ritual, the majority party can use the legislative process to construct barriers against the likelihood of significant gains by the minority party. Indeed, the power of reapportionment can be so great that the minority party has little chance of making inroads in congressional or state legislative politics.

When this occurs the minority political party is clearly the victim of purposeful discrimination, but the courts traditionally have held that this result is simply a matter of winners versus losers in the rough and tumble world of politics. Judges have not seen fit to expand the same constitutional rights accorded to racial and ethnic minorities to protect political parties that are out of power. In 1986, however, *Davis v. Ban-*

demer brought to the Supreme Court's doorstep the question of constitutional protections for minority political parties. A number of issues confronted the justices. Should the courts even rule on the issue, or should the justices leave these controversies to the political process? If the courts became involved in such cases, what criteria should be used to determine if a political party has been the victim of discrimination? These are difficult questions: they involve not only issues of justice, but also of the proper role of the courts in the internal political battles of the legislative branch. The Supreme Court had great difficulty arriving at clear agreement on these disputed points.

Davis v. Bandemer

478 U.S. 109 (1986)

Vote: 7 (Blackmun, Brennan, Burger, Marshall, O'Connor, Rehnquist, White)
  2 (Powell, Stevens)

Opinion announcing the judgment of the Court: White
Concurring opinions: Burger, O'Connor
Opinion concurring in part and dissenting in part: Powell

This suit challenged the 1981 reapportionment of the Indiana General Assembly, a bicameral state legislature with 50 seats in the Senate and 100 in the House. At the time of reapportionment, a Republican was governor, and the party controlled both houses of the legislature. The redistricting plan called for seven triple-member, nine double-member, and sixty-one single-member constituencies for the House and fifty single-member Senate districts. Population disparities were minimal and easily within the range normally accepted by the Supreme Court for state legislatures.

In early 1982 Irwin Bandemer and other Indiana Democrats filed suit against various state officials contending that the district lines and the mix of single-member and multimember districts were intended to and had the effect of violating the equal protection rights of Democratic voters. Before this suit went to trial, elections were held under the reapportionment plan. Democratic candidates received 51.9 percent of the statewide votes for the House, but captured only 43 of the 100 seats. For the twenty-five Senate seats up for election, Democrats gained 53.1 percent of the votes and won thirteen seats. In the multimember House districts of Marion and Allen counties, Democrats received 46.6 percent of the ballots, but won only three of twenty-one seats.

A divided three-judge district court ruled in favor of the Democratic plaintiffs. The court concluded that the reapportionment plan was based on an intentional effort to favor Republican candidates and to disadvantage Democratic voters. The plan "stacked" Democrats into districts with large Democratic majorities and split them in other districts so as to give Republicans safe but not excessive majorities. The district court found the reapportionment statute in violation of the Equal Protection Clause and invalidated it. The state officials appealed.

The Supreme Court was confronted with two important questions. First, does political gerrymandering constitute a justiciable issue, or should decisions about districting based purely on political factors remain with the political branches of government? Second, if political gerrymandering is a justiciable issue, does the reapportionment plan challenged here violate the Equal Protection Clause?

JUSTICE WHITE announced the judgment of the Court.

We address first the question whether this case presents a justiciable controversy or a nonjusticiable political question.... The appellees urge that this Court has in the past acknowledged and acted upon the justiciability of purely political gerrymandering claims. The appellants contend that we have affirmed on the merits decisions of lower courts finding such claims to be nonjusticiable.

Since *Baker v. Carr* (1962), we have consistently adjudicated equal protection claims in the legislative districting context regarding inequalities in population between districts. In the course of these cases, we have developed and enforced the "one person, one vote" principle....

The issue here is of course different from that adjudicated in *Reynolds* [*v. Sims*]. It does not concern districts of unequal size. Not only does everyone have the right to vote and to have his vote counted, but each elector may vote for and be represented by the same number of lawmakers. Rather, the claim is that each political group in a State should have the same chance to elect representatives of its choice as any other political group. Nevertheless, the issue is one of representation, and we decline to hold that such claims are never justiciable.

Our racial gerrymander cases such as *White v. Regester* and *Whitcomb v. Chavis* indicate as much. In those cases, there was no population variation among the districts, and no one was precluded from voting. The claim instead was that an identifiable racial or ethnic group had an insufficient chance to elect a representative of its choice and that district lines should be redrawn to remedy this alleged defect. In both cases, we adjudicated the merits of such claims, rejecting the claim in *Whitcomb* and sustaining it in *Regester*. Just as clearly, in *Gaffney v. Cummings*, where the districts also passed muster under the *Reynolds* formula, the claim was that the legislature had manipulated district lines to afford political groups in various districts an enhanced opportunity to elect legislators of their choice. Although advising caution, we said that "we *must* ... respond to [the] claims ... that even if acceptable populationwise, the ... plan was invidiously discriminatory because a 'political fairness principle' was followed...." We went on to hold that the statute at issue did not violate the Equal Protection Clause.

These decisions support a conclusion that this case is justiciable. As *Gaffney* demonstrates, that the claim is submitted by a political group rather than a racial group, does not distinguish it in terms of justiciability. That the characteristics of the complaining group are not immutable or that the group has not been subject to the same historical stigma may be relevant to the manner in which the case is adjudicated, but these differences do not justify a refusal to entertain such a case....

Having determined that the political gerrymandering claim in this case is justiciable, we turn to the question whether the District Court erred in holding that the appellees had alleged and proved a violation of the Equal Protection Clause....

We do not accept ... the District Court's legal and factual bases for concluding that the 1981 Act visited a sufficiently adverse effect on the appellees' constitutionally protected rights to make out a violation of the Equal Protection Clause. The District Court held that because any apportionment scheme that purposely prevents proportional representation is unconstitutional, Democratic voters need only show that their proportionate voting influence has been adversely affected. Our cases, however, clearly foreclose any claim that the Constitution requires proportional representation or that legislatures in reapportioning must draw district lines to come as near as possible to allocating seats to the contending parties in proportion to what their anticipated statewide vote will be.

The typical election for legislative seats in the United States is conducted in described geographical districts, with the candidate receiving the most votes in each district winning the seat allocated to that district. If all or most of the districts are competitive—defined by the District Court in this case as districts in which the anticipated split in the party vote is within the range of 45% to 55%—even a narrow statewide preference for either party would produce an overwhelming majority for the winning party in the state legislature. This consequence, however, is inherent in winner-take-all, district-based elections, and we cannot hold that such a reapportionment law would violate the Equal Protection Clause because the voters in the losing party do not have representation in the legislature in proportion to the statewide vote received by their party candidates. As we have said: "[W]e are unprepared to hold that district-based elections decided by plurality vote are unconstitutional in either single or multimember districts simply because the supporters of losing candidates have no legislative seats assigned to them." *Whitcomb v. Chavis.* This is true of a racial as well as a political group. It is also true of a statewide claim as well as an individual district claim....

In cases involving individual multimember districts, we have required a substantially greater showing of adverse effects than a mere lack of proportional representation to support a finding of unconstitutional vote dilution. Only where there is evidence that excluded groups have "less op-portunity to participate in the political processes and to elect candidates of their choice" have we refused to approve the use of multimember districts. In these cases, we have also noted the lack of responsiveness of those elected to the concerns of the relevant groups.

These holdings rest on a conviction that the mere fact that a particular apportionment scheme makes it more difficult for a particular group in a particular district to elect the representatives of its choice does not render that scheme constitutionally infirm. The conviction, in turn, stems from a perception that the power to influence the political process is not limited to winning elections. An individual or a group of individuals who votes for a losing candidate is usually deemed to be adequately represented by the winning candidate and to have as much opportunity to influence that candidate as other voters in the district. We cannot presume in such a situation, without actual proof to the contrary, that the candidate elected will entirely ignore the interests of those voters. This is true even in a safe district where the losing group loses election after election. Thus, a group's electoral power is not unconstitutionally diminished by the simple fact of an apportionment scheme that makes winning elections more difficult, and a failure of proportional representation alone does not constitute impermissible discrimination under the Equal Protection Clause.

As with individual districts, where unconstitutional vote dilution is alleged in the form of statewide political gerrymandering, the mere lack of proportional representation will not be sufficient to prove unconstitutional discrimination. Again, without specific supporting evidence, a court cannot presume in such a case that those who are elected will disregard the disproportionately underrepresented group. Rather, unconstitutional discrimination occurs only when the electoral system is arranged in a manner that will consistently degrade a voter's or a group of voters' influence on the political process as a whole.

Although this is a somewhat different formulation than we have previously used in describing unconstitutional vote dilution in an individual district, the focus of both of these inquiries is essentially the same. In both contexts, the question is whether a particular group has been unconstitutionally denied its chance to effectively influence the political process. In a challenge to an individual district, this inquiry focuses on the opportunity of members of the group to participate in party deliberations in the slating and nomination of candidates, their opportunity to register and vote, and hence their chance to directly influence the election returns and to secure the attention of the winning candidate. Statewide, however, the inquiry centers on the voters' direct or indirect influence on the elections of the state legislature as a whole. And, as in individual district cases, an equal protection violation may be found only where the electoral system substantially disadvantages certain voters in their opportunity to influence the political process effectively. In this context, such a finding of unconstitutionality must be supported by evidence of continued frustration of the will of a majority of the voters or effective denial to a minority of voters of a fair chance to influence the political process.

Based on these views, we would reject the District Court's apparent holding that *any* interference with an opportunity to elect a representative of one's choice would be sufficient to allege or make out an equal protection violation, unless justified by some acceptable state interest that the State would be required to demonstrate....

In sum, we hold that political gerrymandering cases are properly justiciable under the Equal Protection Clause. We also conclude, however, that a threshold showing of discriminatory vote dilution is required for a prima facie case of an equal protection violation. In this case, the findings made by the District Court of an adverse effect on the appellees do not surmount the threshold requirement. Consequently, the judgment of the District Court is

Reversed.

In the *Davis* decision the Court concluded that political gerrymandering controversies present justiciable issues under the Equal Protection Clause and may be brought to the courts for resolution. The degree of discrimination in Indiana's 1981 reapportionment plan was not found to be so extreme as to constitute a violation of the constitutional rights of the state's

Democrats, but the justices left the door open to future disputes. While the justiciability decision in *Davis* is unlikely to have the same dramatic impact as *Baker v. Carr*, the political gerrymandering ruling allows the federal judiciary to monitor another area of legislative activity for possible rights violations. It also serves notice on legislators that the use of apportionment powers to impose extreme and harsh restrictions on the political opportunities of the minority party may run afoul of the Constitution and not be tolerated by the courts.

READINGS

Alfange, Dean, Jr. "Gerrymandering and the Constitution: Into the Thorns of the Thicket at Last." *Supreme Court Review* (1986): 175–257.

Bullock, Charles S., and Charles M. Lamb. *Implementation of Civil Rights Policy.* Monterey, Calif.: Brooks/Cole, 1984.

Cortner, Richard C. *The Apportionment Cases.* Knoxville: University of Tennessee Press, 1970.

Dixon, Robert G. *Democratic Representation: Reapportionment in Law and Politics.* New York: Oxford University Press, 1968.

Grofman, Bernard. *Political Gerrymandering and the Courts.* New York: Agathon Press, 1990.

Hamilton, Charles V. *The Bench and Ballot: Southern Federal Judges and Black Voters.* New York: Oxford University Press, 1973.

Lewinson, Paul. *Race, Class and Party: A History of Negro Suffrage and White Politics in the South.* New York: Grosset and Dunlap, 1959.

Maveety, Nancy. *Representation Rights and the Burger Court Years.* Ann Arbor: University of Michigan Press, 1991.

Montague, Bill. "The Voting Rights Act Today." *ABA Journal* 74 (August 1988): 52–58.

Schuck, Peter H. "The Thickest Thicket: Partisan Gerrymandering and the Judicial Regulation of Politics." *Columbia Law Review* 87 (November 1987): 1325–84.

Thernston, Abigail. *Whose Votes Count?* Cambridge, Mass.: Harvard University Press, 1987.

REFERENCE MATERIAL

APPENDICES

CONSTITUTION OF THE UNITED STATES

We the People of the United States, in Order to form a more perfect Union, establish Justice, insure domestic Tranquility, provide for the common defence, promote the general Welfare, and secure the Blessings of Liberty to ourselves and our Posterity, do ordain and establish this Constitution for the United States of America.

ARTICLE I

Section 1. All legislative Powers herein granted shall be vested in a Congress of the United States, which shall consist of a Senate and House of Representatives.

Section 2. The House of Representatives shall be composed of Members chosen every second Year by the People of the several States, and the Electors in each State shall have the Qualifications requisite for Electors of the most numerous Branch of the State Legislature.

No Person shall be a Representative who shall not have attained to the age of twenty five Years, and been seven Years a Citizen of the United States, and who shall not, when elected, be an Inhabitant of that State in which he shall be chosen.

[Representatives and direct Taxes shall be apportioned among the several States which may be included within this Union, according to their respective Numbers, which shall be determined by adding to the whole Number of free Persons, including those bound to Service for a Term of Years, and excluding Indians not taxed, three fifths of all other Persons.][1] The actual Enumeration shall be made within three Years after the first Meeting of the Congress of the United States, and within every subsequent Term of ten Years, in such Manner as they shall by Law direct. The Number of Representatives shall not exceed one for every thirty Thousand, but each State shall have at Least one Representative; and until such enumeration shall be made, the State of New Hamp-

shire shall be entitled to chuse three, Massachusetts eight, Rhode-Island and Providence Plantations one, Connecticut five, New-York six, New Jersey four, Pennsylvania eight, Delaware one, Maryland six, Virginia ten, North Carolina five, South Carolina five, and Georgia three.

When vacancies happen in the Representation from any State, the Executive Authority thereof shall issue Writs of Election to fill such Vacancies.

The House of Representatives shall chuse their Speaker and other Officers; and shall have the sole Power of Impeachment.

Section 3. The Senate of the United States shall be composed of two Senators from each State, [chosen by the Legislature thereof,][2] for six Years; and each Senator shall have one Vote.

Immediately after they shall be assembled in Consequence of the first Election, they shall be divided as equally as may be into three Classes. The Seats of the Senators of the first Class shall be vacated at the Expiration of the second Year, of the second Class at the Expiration of the fourth Year, and of the third Class at the Expiration of the sixth Year, so that one third may be chosen every second Year; [and if Vacancies happen by Resignation, or otherwise, during the Recess of the Legislature of any State, the Executive thereof may make temporary Appointments until the next Meeting of the Legislature, which shall then fill such Vacancies.][3]

No Person shall be a Senator who shall not have attained to the Age of thirty Years, and been nine Years a Citizen of the United States, and who shall not, when elected, be an Inhabitant of that State for which he shall be chosen.

The Vice President of the United States shall be President of the Senate, but shall have no Vote, unless they be equally divided.

The Senate shall chuse their other Officers, and also a Presi-

---

1. The part in brackets was changed by section 2 of the Fourteenth Amendment.

2. The part in brackets was changed by the first paragraph of the Seventeenth Amendment.

3. The part in brackets was changed by the second paragraph of the Seventeenth Amendment.

dent pro tempore, in the Absence of the Vice President, or when he shall exercise the Office of President of the United States.

The Senate shall have the sole Power to try all Impeachments. When sitting for that Purpose, they shall be on Oath or Affirmation. When the President of the United States is tried, the Chief Justice shall preside: And no Person shall be convicted without the Concurrence of two thirds of the Members present.

Judgment in Cases of Impeachment shall not extend further than to removal from Office, and disqualification to hold and enjoy any Office of honor, Trust or Profit under the United States: but the Party convicted shall nevertheless be liable and subject to Indictment, Trial, Judgment and Punishment, according to Law.

Section 4. The Times, Places and Manner of holding Elections for Senators and Representatives, shall be prescribed in each State by the Legislature thereof; but the Congress may at any time by Law make or alter such Regulations, except as to the Places of chusing Senators.

The Congress shall assemble at least once in every Year, and such Meeting shall [be on the first Monday in December],[4] unless they shall by Law appoint a different Day.

Section 5. Each House shall be the Judge of the Elections, Returns and Qualifications of its own Members, and a Majority of each shall constitute a Quorum to do Business; but a smaller Number may adjourn from day to day, and may be authorized to compel the Attendance of absent Members, in such Manner, and under such Penalties as each House may provide.

Each House may determine the Rules of its Proceedings, punish its Members for disorderly Behaviour, and, with the Concurrence of two thirds, expel a Member.

Each House shall keep a Journal of its Proceedings, and from time to time publish the same, excepting such Parts as may in their Judgment require Secrecy; and the Yeas and Nays of the Members of either House on any question shall, at the Desire of one fifth of those Present, be entered on the Journal.

Neither House, during the Session of Congress, shall, without the Consent of the other, adjourn for more than three days, nor to any other Place than that in which the two Houses shall be sitting.

Section 6. The Senators and Representatives shall receive a Compensation for their Services, to be ascertained by Law, and paid out of the Treasury of the United States. They shall in all Cases, except Treason, Felony and Breach of the Peace, be privileged from Arrest during their Attendance at the Session of their respective Houses, and in going to and returning from the same; and for any Speech or Debate in either House, they shall not be questioned in any other Place.

No Senator or Representative shall, during the Time for which he was elected, be appointed to any civil Office under the Author-

ity of the United States, which shall have been created, or the Emoluments whereof shall have been encreased during such time; and no Person holding any Office under the United States, shall be a Member of either House during his Continuance in Office.

Section 7. All Bills for raising Revenue shall originate in the House of Representatives; but the Senate may propose or concur with Amendments as on other Bills.

Every Bill which shall have passed the House of Representatives and the Senate, shall, before it become a Law, be presented to the President of the United States; If he approve he shall sign it, but if not he shall return it, with his Objections to that House in which it shall have originated, who shall enter the Objections at large on their Journal, and proceed to reconsider it. If after such Reconsideration two thirds of that House shall agree to pass the Bill, it shall be sent, together with the Objections, to the other House, by which it shall likewise be reconsidered, and if approved by two thirds of that House, it shall become a Law. But in all such Cases the Votes of both Houses shall be determined by yeas and Nays, and the Names of the Persons voting for and against the Bill shall be entered on the Journal of each House respectively. If any Bill shall not be returned by the President within ten Days (Sundays excepted) after it shall have been presented to him, the Same shall be a Law, in like Manner as if he had signed it, unless the Congress by their Adjournment prevent its Return, in which Case it shall not be a Law.

Every Order, Resolution, or Vote to which the Concurrence of the Senate and House of Representatives may be necessary (except on a question of Adjournment) shall be presented to the President of the United States; and before the Same shall take Effect, shall be approved by him, or being disapproved by him, shall be repassed by two thirds of the Senate and House of Representatives, according to the Rules and Limitations prescribed in the Case of a Bill.

Section 8. The Congress shall have Power To lay and collect Taxes, Duties, Imposts and Excises, to pay the Debts and provide for the common Defence and general Welfare of the United States; but all Duties, Imposts and Excises shall be uniform throughout the United States;

To borrow Money on the credit of the United States;

To regulate Commerce with foreign Nations, and among the several States, and with the Indian Tribes;

To establish an uniform Rule of Naturalization, and uniform Laws on the subject of Bankruptcies throughout the United States;

To coin Money, regulate the Value thereof, and of foreign Coin, and fix the Standard of Weights and Measures;

To provide for the Punishment of counterfeiting the Securities and current Coin of the United States;

To establish Post Offices and post Roads;

To promote the Progress of Science and useful Arts, by securing for limited Times to Authors and Inventors the exclusive Right to their respective Writings and Discoveries;

4. The part in brackets was changed by section 2 of the Twentieth Amendment.

To constitute Tribunals inferior to the supreme Court;

To define and punish Piracies and Felonies committed on the high Seas, and Offences against the Law of Nations;

To declare War, grant Letters of Marque and Reprisal, and make Rules concerning Captures on Land and Water;

To raise and support Armies, but no Appropriation of Money to that Use shall be for a longer Term than two Years;

To provide and maintain a Navy;

To make Rules for the Government and Regulation of the land and naval Forces;

To provide for calling forth the Militia to execute the Laws of the Union, suppress Insurrections and repel Invasions;

To provide for organizing, arming, and disciplining, the Militia, and for governing such Part of them as may be employed in the Service of the United States, reserving to the States respectively, the Appointment of the Officers, and the Authority of training the Militia according to the discipline prescribed by Congress;

To exercise exclusive Legislation in all Cases whatsoever, over such District (not exceeding ten Miles square) as may, by Cession of particular States, and the Acceptance of Congress, become the Seat of the Government of the United States, and to exercise like Authority over all Places purchased by the Consent of the Legislature of the State in which the Same shall be, for the Erection of Forts, Magazines, Arsenals, dock-Yards, and other needful Buildings;-And

To make all Laws which shall be necessary and proper for carrying into Execution the foregoing Powers, and all other Powers vested by this Constitution in the Government of the United States, or in any Department or Officer thereof.

Section 9. The Migration or Importation of such Persons as any of the States now existing shall think proper to admit, shall not be prohibited by the Congress prior to the Year one thousand eight hundred and eight, but a Tax or duty may be imposed on such Importation, not exceeding ten dollars for each Person.

The Privilege of the Writ of Habeas Corpus shall not be suspended, unless when in Cases of Rebellion or Invasion the public Safety may require it.

No Bill of Attainder or ex post facto Law shall be passed.

No Capitation, or other direct, Tax shall be laid, unless in Proportion to the Census or Enumeration herein before directed to be taken.[5]

No Tax or Duty shall be laid on Articles exported from any State.

No Preference shall be given by any Regulation of Commerce or Revenue to the Ports of one State over those of another; nor shall Vessels bound to, or from, one State, be obliged to enter, clear, or pay Duties in another.

No Money shall be drawn from the Treasury, but in Conse-

5. The Sixteenth Amendment gave Congress the power to tax incomes.

quence of Appropriations made by Law; and a regular Statement and Account of the Receipts and Expenditures of all public Money shall be published from time to time.

No Title of Nobility shall be granted by the United States: And no Person holding any Office of Profit or Trust under them, shall, without the Consent of the Congress, accept of any present, Emolument, Office, or Title, of any kind whatever, from any King, Prince, or foreign State.

Section 10. No State shall enter into any Treaty, Alliance, or Confederation; grant Letters of Marque and Reprisal; coin Money; emit Bills of Credit; make any Thing but gold and silver Coin a Tender in Payment of Debts; pass any Bill of Attainder, ex post facto Law, or Law impairing the Obligation of Contracts, or grant any Title of Nobility.

No State shall, without the Consent of the Congress, lay any Imposts or Duties on Imports or Exports, except what may be absolutely necessary for executing it's inspection Laws: and the net Produce of all Duties and Imposts, laid by any State on Imports or Exports, shall be for the Use of the Treasury of the United States; and all such Laws shall be subject to the Revision and Controul of the Congress.

No State shall, without the Consent of Congress, lay any Duty of Tonnage, keep Troops, or Ships of War in time of Peace, enter into any Agreement or Compact with another State, or with a foreign Power, or engage in War, unless actually invaded, or in such imminent Danger as will not admit of delay.

ARTICLE II

Section 1. The executive Power shall be vested in a President of the United States of America. He shall hold his Office during the Term of four Years, and, together with the Vice President, chosen for the same Term, be elected, as follows

Each State shall appoint, in such Manner as the Legislature thereof may direct, a Number of Electors, equal to the whole Number of Senators and Representatives to which the State may be entitled in the Congress: but no Senator or Representative, or Person holding an Office of Trust or Profit under the United States, shall be appointed an Elector.

[The Electors shall meet in their respective States, and vote by Ballot for two Persons, of whom one at least shall not be an Inhabitant of the same State with themselves. And they shall make a List of all the Persons voted for, and of the Number of Votes for each; which List they shall sign and certify, and transmit sealed to the Seat of the Government of the United States, directed to the President of the Senate. The President of the Senate shall, in the Presence of the Senate and House of Representatives, open all the Certificates, and the Votes shall then be counted. The Person having the greatest Number of Votes shall be the President, if such Number be a Majority of the whole Number of Electors appointed; and if there be more than one who have such Majority, and have an equal Number of Votes, then the House of Representatives shall immediately chuse by Ballot one of them for President; and if no Person have a Majority, then from the five highest on the list the said House shall in like Manner chuse the President. But in chusing the President, the Votes shall be taken by States, the Representation from each State having one Vote; A quorum for this Purpose shall consist of a Member or Members from two thirds of the States, and a Majority of all the States shall be necessary to a Choice. In every Case, after the Choice of the President, the Person having the greatest Number of Votes of the Electors shall be the Vice President. But if there should remain two or more who have equal Votes, the Senate shall chuse from them by Ballot the Vice President.] [6]

The Congress may determine the Time of chusing the Electors, and the Day on which they shall give their Votes; which Day shall be the same throughout the United States.

No Person except a natural born Citizen, or a Citizen of the United States, at the time of the Adoption of this Constitution, shall be eligible to the Office of President; neither shall any Person be eligible to that Office who shall not have attained to the Age of thirty five Years, and been fourteen Years a Resident within the United States.

In Case of the Removal of the President from Office, or of his Death, Resignation, or Inability to discharge the Powers and Duties of the said Office,[7] the Same shall devolve on the Vice President, and the Congress may by Law provide for the Case of Removal, Death, Resignation or Inability, both of the President and Vice President, declaring what Officer shall then act as President, and such Officer shall act accordingly, until the Disability be removed, or a President shall be elected.

The President shall, at stated Times, receive for his Services, a Compensation, which shall neither be encreased nor diminished during the Period for which he shall have been elected, and he shall not receive within that Period any other Emolument from the United States, or any of them.

Before he enter on the Execution of his Office, he shall take the following Oath or Affirmation:-"I do solemnly swear (or affirm) that I will faithfully execute the Office of President of the United States, and will to the best of my Ability, preserve, protect and defend the Constitution of the United States."

Section 2. The President shall be Commander in Chief of the Army and Navy of the United States, and of the Militia of the several States, when called into the actual Service of the United States; he may require the Opinion, in writing, of the principal Officer in each of the executive Departments, upon any Subject relating to the Duties of their respective Offices, and he shall have Power to grant Reprieves and Pardons for Offences against the United States, except in Cases of Impeachment.

He shall have Power, by and with the Advice and Consent of the Senate, to make Treaties, provided two thirds of the Senators present concur; and he shall nominate, and by and with the Advice and Consent of the Senate, shall appoint Ambassadors, other public Ministers and Consuls, Judges of the supreme Court, and all other Officers of the United States, whose Appointments are not herein otherwise provided for, and which shall be established by Law: but the Congress may by Law vest the Appointment of such inferior Officers, as they think proper, in the President alone, in the Courts of Law, or in the Heads of Departments.

The President shall have Power to fill up all Vacancies that may happen during the Recess of the Senate, by granting Commissions which shall expire at the End of their next Session.

Section 3. He shall from time to time give to the Congress Information of the State of the Union, and recommend to their Consideration such Measures as he shall judge necessary and expedient; he may, on extraordinary Occasions, convene both Houses, or either of them, and in Case of Disagreement between them, with Respect to the Time of Adjournment, he may adjourn them to such Time as he shall think proper; he shall receive Ambassadors and other public Ministers; he shall take Care that the Laws be faithfully executed, and shall Commission all the Officers of the United States.

Section 4. The President, Vice President and all civil Officers of the United States, shall be removed from Office on Impeachment for, and Conviction of, Treason, Bribery, or other high Crimes and Misdemeanors.

ARTICLE III

Section 1. The judicial Power of the United States, shall be vested in one supreme Court, and in such inferior Courts as the Congress may from time to time ordain and establish. The Judges, both of the supreme and inferior Courts, shall hold their Offices during good Behaviour, and shall, at stated Times, receive for their Services, a Compensation, which shall not be diminished during their Continuance in Office.

Section 2. The judicial Power shall extend to all Cases, in Law and Equity, arising under this Constitution, the Laws of the United States, and Treaties made, or which shall be made, under their Authority;-to all Cases affecting Ambassadors, other public Ministers and Consuls;-to all Cases of admiralty and maritime Jurisdiction;-to Controversies to which the United States shall be a Party;-to Controversies between two or more States;-between a State and Citizens of another State;[8]-between Citizens of different States;-between Citizens of the same State claiming Lands under Grants of different States, and between a State, or the Citizens thereof, and foreign States, Citizens or Subjects.[8]

In all Cases affecting Ambassadors, other public Ministers and

---

6. The material in brackets has been superseded by the Twelfth Amendment.

7. This provision has been affected by the Twenty-fifth Amendment.
8. These clauses were affected by the Eleventh Amendment.

Consuls, and those in which a State shall be Party, the supreme Court shall have original Jurisdiction. In all the other Cases before mentioned, the supreme Court shall have appellate Jurisdiction, both as to Law and Fact, with such Exceptions, and under such Regulations as the Congress shall make.

The Trial of all Crimes, except in Cases of Impeachment, shall be by Jury; and such Trial shall be held in the State where the said Crimes shall have been committed; but when not committed within any State, the Trial shall be at such Place or Places as the Congress may by Law have directed.

Section 3. Treason against the United States, shall consist only in levying War against them, or in adhering to their Enemies, giving them Aid and Comfort. No Person shall be convicted of Treason unless on the Testimony of two Witnesses to the same overt Act, or on Confession in open Court.

The Congress shall have Power to declare the Punishment of Treason, but no Attainder of Treason shall work Corruption of Blood, or Forfeiture except during the Life of the Person attainted.

ARTICLE IV

Section 1. Full Faith and Credit shall be given in each State to the public Acts, Records, and judicial Proceedings of every other State. And the Congress may by general Laws prescribe the Manner in which such Acts, Records and Proceedings shall be proved, and the Effect thereof.

Section 2. The Citizens of each State shall be entitled to all Privileges and Immunities of Citizens in the several States.

A Person charged in any State with Treason, Felony, or other Crime, who shall flee from Justice, and be found in another State, shall on Demand of the executive Authority of the State from which he fled, be delivered up, to be removed to the State having Jurisdiction of the Crime.

[No Person held to Service or Labour in one State, under the Laws thereof, escaping into another, shall, in Consequence of any Law or Regulation therein, be discharged from such Service or Labour, but shall be delivered up on Claim of the Party to whom such Service or Labour may be due.][9]

Section 3. New States may be admitted by the Congress into this Union; but no new State shall be formed or erected within the Jurisdiction of any other State; nor any State be formed by the Junction of two or more States, or Parts of States, without the Consent of the Legislatures of the States concerned as well as of the Congress.

The Congress shall have Power to dispose of and make all needful Rules and Regulations respecting the Territory or other Property belonging to the United States; and nothing in this Constitution shall be so construed as to Prejudice any Claims of the United States, or of any particular State.

Section 4. The United States shall guarantee to every State in this Union a Republican Form of Government, and shall protect each of them against Invasion; and on Application of the Legislature, or of the Executive (when the Legislature cannot be convened) against domestic Violence.

ARTICLE V

The Congress, whenever two thirds of both Houses shall deem it necessary, shall propose Amendments to this Constitution, or, on the Application of the Legislatures of two thirds of the several States, shall call a Convention for proposing Amendments, which, in either Case, shall be valid to all Intents and Purposes, as Part of this Constitution, when ratified by the Legislatures of three fourths of the several States, or by Conventions in three fourths thereof, as the one or the other Mode of Ratification may be proposed by the Congress; Provided [that no Amendment which may be made prior to the Year One thousand eight hundred and eight shall in any Manner affect the first and fourth Clauses in the Ninth Section of the first Article; and][10] that no State, without its Consent, shall be deprived of its equal Suffrage in the Senate.

ARTICLE VI

All Debts contracted and Engagements entered into, before the Adoption of this Constitution, shall be as valid against the United States under this Constitution, as under the Confederation.

This Constitution, and the Laws of the United States which shall be made in Pursuance thereof; and all Treaties made, or which shall be made, under the Authority of the United States, shall be the supreme Law of the Land; and the Judges in every State shall be bound thereby, any Thing in the Constitution or Laws of any State to the Contrary notwithstanding.

The Senators and Representatives before mentioned, and the Members of the several State Legislatures, and all executive and judicial Officers, both of the United States and of the several States, shall be bound by Oath or Affirmation, to support this Constitution; but no religious Test shall ever be required as a Qualification to any Office or public Trust under the United States.

ARTICLE VII

The Ratification of the Conventions of nine States, shall be sufficient for the Establishment of this Constitution between the States so ratifying the Same. Done in Convention by the Unanimous Consent of the States present the Seventeenth Day of September in the Year of our Lord one thousand seven hundred and Eighty seven and of the Independence of the United States of America the Twelfth. IN WITNESS whereof We have hereunto subscribed our Names,

---

9. This paragraph has been superseded by the Thirteenth Amendment.

10. Obsolete.

George Washington, President and deputy from Virginia.

New Hampshire: John Langdon,
                   Nicholas Gilman.
Massachusetts: Nathaniel Gorham,
                   Rufus King.
Connecticut: William Samuel Johnson,
                   Roger Sherman.
New York: Alexander Hamilton.
New Jersey: William Livingston,
                   David Brearley,
                   William Paterson,
                   Jonathan Dayton.
Pennsylvania: Benjamin Franklin,
                   Thomas Mifflin,
                   Robert Morris,
                   George Clymer,
                   Thomas FitzSimons,
                   Jared Ingersoll,
                   James Wilson,
                   Gouverneur Morris.
Delaware: George Read,
                   Gunning Bedford Jr.,
                   John Dickinson,
                   Richard Bassett,
                   Jacob Broom.
Maryland: James McHenry,
                   Daniel of St. Thomas Jenifer,
                   Daniel Carroll.
Virginia: John Blair,
                   James Madison Jr.
North Carolina: William Blount,
                   Richard Dobbs Spaight,
                   Hugh Williamson.
South Carolina: John Rutledge,
                   Charles Cotesworth Pinckney,
                   Charles Pinckney,
                   Pierce Butler.
Georgia: William Few,
                   Abraham Baldwin.

[The language of the original Constitution, not including the Amendments, was adopted by a convention of the states on September 17, 1787, and was subsequently ratified by the states on the following dates: Delaware, December 7, 1787; Pennsylvania, December 12, 1787; New Jersey, December 18, 1787; Georgia, January 2, 1788; Connecticut, January 9, 1788; Massachusetts, February 6, 1788; Maryland, April 28, 1788; South Carolina, May 23, 1788; New Hampshire, June 21, 1788.

Ratification was completed on June 21, 1788.

The Constitution subsequently was ratified by Virginia, June 25, 1788; New York, July 26, 1788; North Carolina, November 21, 1789; Rhode Island, May 29, 1790; and Vermont, January 10, 1791.]

AMENDMENTS

Amendment I
(First ten amendments ratified December 15, 1791.)

Congress shall make no law respecting an establishment of religion, or prohibiting the free exercise thereof; or abridging the freedom of speech, or of the press; or the right of the people peaceably to assemble, and to petition the Government for a redress of grievances.

Amendment II

A well regulated Militia, being necessary to the security of a free State, the right of the people to keep and bear Arms, shall not be infringed.

Amendment III

No Soldier shall, in time of peace be quartered in any house, without the consent of the Owner, nor in time of war, but in a manner to be prescribed by law.

Amendment IV

The right of the people to be secure in their persons, houses, papers, and effects, against unreasonable searches and seizures, shall not be violated, and no Warrants shall issue, but upon probable cause, supported by Oath or affirmation, and particularly describing the place to be searched, and the persons or things to be seized.

Amendment V

No person shall be held to answer for a capital, or otherwise infamous crime, unless on a presentment or indictment of a Grand Jury, except in cases arising in the land or naval forces, or in the Militia, when in actual service in time of War or public danger; nor shall any person be subject for the same offence to be twice put in jeopardy of life or limb; nor shall be compelled in any criminal case to be a witness against himself, nor be deprived of life, liberty, or property, without due process of law; nor shall private property be taken for public use, without just compensation.

Amendment VI

In all criminal prosecutions, the accused shall enjoy the right to a speedy and public trial, by an impartial jury of the State and district wherein the crime shall have been committed, which district shall have been previously ascertained by law, and to be informed of the nature and cause of the accusation; to be confronted with the witnesses against him; to have compulsory process for obtaining witnesses in his favor, and to have the Assistance of Counsel for his defence.

Amendment VII

In Suits at common law, where the value in controversy shall exceed twenty dollars, the right of trial by jury shall be preserved, and no fact tried by a jury, shall be otherwise re-examined in any Court of the United States, than according to the rules of the common law.

Amendment VIII

Excessive bail shall not be required, nor excessive fines imposed, nor cruel and unusual punishments inflicted.

Amendment IX

The enumeration in the Constitution, of certain rights, shall not be construed to deny or disparage others retained by the people.

Amendment X

The powers not delegated to the United States by the Constitution, nor prohibited by it to the States, are reserved to the States respectively, or to the people.

Amendment XI

(Ratified February 7, 1795)

The Judicial power of the United States shall not be construed to extend to any suit in law or equity, commenced or prosecuted against one of the United States by Citizens of another State, or by Citizens or Subjects of any Foreign State.

Amendment XII

(Ratified June 15, 1804)

The Electors shall meet in their respective states and vote by ballot for President and Vice-President, one of whom, at least, shall not be an inhabitant of the same state with themselves; they shall name in their ballots the person voted for as President, and in distinct ballots the person voted for as Vice-President, and they shall make distinct lists of all persons voted for as President, and of all persons voted for as Vice-President, and of the number of votes for each, which lists they shall sign and certify, and transmit sealed to the seat of the government of the United States, directed to the President of the Senate;-The President of the Senate shall, in the presence of the Senate and House of Representatives, open all the certificates and the votes shall then be counted;-The person having the greatest number of votes for President, shall be the President, if such number be a majority of the whole number of Electors appointed; and if no person have such majority, then from the persons having the highest numbers not exceeding three on the list of those voted for as President, the House of Representatives shall choose immediately, by ballot, the President. But in choosing the President, the votes shall be taken by states, the representation from each state having one vote; a quorum for this purpose shall consist of a member or members from two-thirds of the states, and a majority of all the states shall be necessary to a choice. [And if the House of Representatives shall not choose a President whenever the right of choice shall devolve upon them, before the fourth day of March next following, then the Vice-President shall act as President, as in the case of the death or other constitutional disability of the President.-][11] The person having the greatest number of votes as Vice-President, shall be the Vice-President, if such number be a majority of the whole number of Electors appointed, and if no person have a majority, then from the two highest numbers on the list, the Senate shall choose the Vice-President; a quorum for the purpose shall consist of two-thirds of the whole number of Senators, and a majority of the whole number shall be necessary to a choice. But no person constitutionally ineligible to the office of President shall be eligible to that of Vice-President of the United States.

Amendment XIII

(Ratified December 6, 1865)

Section 1. Neither slavery nor involuntary servitude, except as a punishment for crime whereof the party shall have been duly convicted, shall exist within the United States, or any place subject to their jurisdiction.

Section 2. Congress shall have power to enforce this article by appropriate legislation.

Amendment XIV

(Ratified July 9, 1868)

Section 1. All persons born or naturalized in the United States, and subject to the jurisdiction thereof, are citizens of the United States and of the State wherein they reside. No State shall make or enforce any law which shall abridge the privileges or immunities of citizens of the United States; nor shall any State deprive any person of life, liberty, or property, without due process of law; nor deny to any person within its jurisdiction the equal protection of the laws.

Section 2. Representatives shall be apportioned among the several States according to their respective numbers, counting the whole number of persons in each State, excluding Indians not taxed. But when the right to vote at any election for the choice of electors for President and Vice President of the United States, Representatives in Congress, the Executive and Judicial officers of a State, or the members of the Legislature thereof, is denied to any of the male inhabitants of such State, being twenty-one years of age,[12] and citizens of the United States, or in any way abridged, except for participation in rebellion, or other crime, the basis of representation therein shall be reduced in the proportion which the number of such male citizens shall bear to the whole number of male citizens twenty-one years of age in such State.

Section 3. No person shall be a Senator or Representative in Congress, or elector of President and Vice President, or hold any office, civil or military, under the United States, or under any State, who, having previously taken an oath, as a member of Congress, or as an officer of the United States, or as a member of any

11. The part in brackets has been superseded by section 3 of the Twentieth Amendment.

12. See the Nineteenth and Twenty-sixth Amendments.

State legislature, or as an executive or judicial officer of any State, to support the Constitution of the United States, shall have engaged in insurrection or rebellion against the same, or given aid or comfort to the enemies thereof. But Congress may by a vote of two-thirds of each House, remove such disability.

Section 4. The validity of the public debt of the United States, authorized by law, including debts incurred for payment of pensions and bounties for services in suppressing insurrection or rebellion, shall not be questioned. But neither the United States nor any State shall assume or pay any debt or obligation incurred in aid of insurrection or rebellion against the United States, or any claim for the loss or emancipation of any slave; but all such debts, obligations and claims shall be held illegal and void.

Section 5. The Congress shall have power to enforce, by appropriate legislation, the provisions of this article.

Amendment XV

(Ratified February 3, 1870)

Section 1. The right of citizens of the United States to vote shall not be denied or abridged by the United States or by any State on account of race, color, or previous condition of servitude.

Section 2. The Congress shall have power to enforce this article by appropriate legislation.

Amendment XVI

(Ratified February 3, 1913)

The Congress shall have power to lay and collect taxes on incomes, from whatever source derived, without apportionment among the several States, and without regard to any census or enumeration.

Amendment XVII

(Ratified April 8, 1913)

The Senate of the United States shall be composed of two Senators from each State, elected by the people thereof, for six years; and each Senator shall have one vote. The electors in each State shall have the qualifications requisite for electors of the most numerous branch of the State legislatures.

When vacancies happen in the representation of any State in the Senate, the executive authority of such State shall issue writs of election to fill such vacancies: *Provided,* That the legislature of any State may empower the executive thereof to make temporary appointments until the people fill the vacancies by election as the legislature may direct.

This amendment shall not be so construed as to affect the election or term of any Senator chosen before it becomes valid as part of the Constitution.

Amendment XVIII

(Ratified January 16, 1919)

Section 1. After one year from the ratification of this article the manufacture, sale, or transportation of intoxicating liquors within, the importation thereof into, or the exportation thereof from the United States and all territory subject to the jurisdiction thereof for beverage purposes is hereby prohibited.

Section 2. The Congress and the several States shall have concurrent power to enforce this article by appropriate legislation.

Section 3. This article shall be inoperative unless it shall have been ratified as an amendment to the Constitution by the legislatures of the several States, as provided in the Constitution, within seven years from the date of the submission hereof to the States by the Congress.][13]

Amendment XIX

(Ratified August 18, 1920)

The right of citizens of the United States to vote shall not be denied or abridged by the United States or by any State on account of sex.

Congress shall have power to enforce this article by appropriate legislation.

Amendment XX

(Ratified January 23, 1933)

Section 1. The terms of the President and Vice President shall end at noon on the 20th day of January, and the terms of Senators and Representatives at noon on the 3d day of January, of the years in which such terms would have ended if this article had not been ratified; and the terms of their successors shall then begin.

Section 2. The Congress shall assemble at least once in every year, and such meeting shall begin at noon on the 3d day of January, unless they shall by law appoint a different day.

Section 3.[14] If, at the time fixed for the beginning of the term of the President, the President elect shall have died, the Vice President elect shall become President. If a President shall not have been chosen before the time fixed for the beginning of his term, or if the President elect shall have failed to qualify, then the Vice President elect shall act as President until a President shall have qualified; and the Congress may by law provide for the case wherein neither a President elect nor a Vice President elect shall have qualified, declaring who shall then act as President, or the manner in which one who is to act shall be selected, and such person shall act accordingly until a President or Vice President shall have qualified.

Section 4. The Congress may by law provide for the case of the death of any of the persons from whom the House of Representatives may choose a President whenever the right of choice shall have devolved upon them, and for the case of the death of any of the persons from whom the Senate may choose a Vice President whenever the right of choice shall have devolved upon them.

---

13. This Amendment was repealed by section 1 of the Twenty-first Amendment.

14. See the Twenty-fifth Amendment.

Section 5. Sections 1 and 2 shall take effect on the 15th day of October following the ratification of this article.

Section 6. This article shall be inoperative unless it shall have been ratified as an amendment to the Constitution by the legislatures of three-fourths of the several States within seven years from the date of its submission.

Amendment XXI

(Ratified December 5, 1933)

Section 1. The eighteenth article of amendment to the Constitution of the United States is hereby repealed.

Section 2. The transportation or importation into any State, Territory, or possession of the United States for delivery or use therein of intoxicating liquors, in violation of the laws thereof, is hereby prohibited.

Section 3. This article shall be inoperative unless it shall have been ratified as an amendment to the Constitution by conventions in the several States, as provided in the Constitution, within seven years from the date of the submission hereof to the States by the Congress.

Amendment XXII

(Ratified February 27, 1951)

Section 1. No person shall be elected to the office of the President more than twice, and no person who has held the office of President, or acted as President, for more than two years of a term to which some other person was elected President shall be elected to the office of the President more than once. But this Article shall not apply to any person holding the office of President when this Article was proposed by the Congress, and shall not prevent any person who may be holding the office of President, or acting as President, during the term within which this Article become operative from holding the office of President or acting as President during the remainder of such term.

Section 2. This article shall be inoperative unless it shall have been ratified as an amendment to the Constitution by the legislatures of three-fourths of the several States within seven years from the date of its submission to the States by the Congress.

Amendment XXIII

(Ratified March 29, 1961)

Section 1. The District constituting the seat of Government of the United States shall appoint in such manner as the Congress may direct:

A number of electors of President and Vice President equal to the whole number of Senators and Representatives in Congress to which the District would be entitled if it were a State, but in no event more than the least populous State; they shall be in addition to those appointed by the States, but they shall be considered, for the purposes of the election of President and Vice President, to be electors appointed by a State; and they shall meet in the District and perform such duties as provided by the twelfth article of amendment.

Section 2. The Congress shall have power to enforce this article by appropriate legislation.

Amendment XXIV

(Ratified January 23, 1964)

Section 1. The right of citizens of the United States to vote in any primary or other election for President or Vice President, for electors for President or Vice President, or for Senator or Representative in Congress, shall not be denied or abridged by the United States or any State by reason of failure to pay any poll tax or other tax.

Section 2. The Congress shall have power to enforce this article by appropriate legislation.

Amendment XXV

(Ratified February 10, 1967)

Section 1. In case of the removal of the President from office or of his death or resignation, the Vice President shall become President.

Section 2. Whenever there is a vacancy in the office of the Vice President, the President shall nominate a Vice President who shall take office upon confirmation by a majority vote of both Houses of Congress.

Section 3. Whenever the President transmits to the President pro tempore of the Senate and the Speaker of the House of Representatives his written declaration that he is unable to discharge the powers and duties of his office, and until he transmits to them a written declaration to the contrary, such powers and duties shall be discharged by the Vice President as Acting President.

Section 4. Whenever the Vice President and a majority of either the principal officers of the executive departments or of such other body as Congress may by law provide, transmit to the President pro tempore of the Senate and the Speaker of the House of Representatives their written declaration that the President is unable to discharge the powers and duties of his office, the Vice President shall immediately assume the powers and duties of the office as Acting President.

Thereafter, when the President transmits to the President pro tempore of the Senate and the Speaker of the House of Representatives his written declaration that no inability exists, he shall resume the powers and duties of his office unless the Vice President and a majority of either the principal officers of the executive department or of such other body as Congress may by law provide, transmit within four days to the President pro tempore of the Senate and the Speaker of the House of Representatives their written declaration that the President is unable to discharge the powers and duties of his office. Thereupon Congress shall decide the issue, assembling within forty-eight hours for that purpose if not in session. If the Congress, within twenty-one days after receipt of the latter written declaration, or, if Congress is not in session, within twenty-one days after Congress is required to assemble, determines by two-thirds vote of both Houses that the President is unable to discharge the powers and duties of his office, the Vice President shall continue to discharge the same as Acting President; otherwise, the President shall resume the powers and duties of his office.

Amendment XXVI

(Ratified July 1, 1971)

Section 1. The right of citizens of the United States, who are eighteen years of age or older, to vote shall not be denied or abridged by the United States or by any State on account of age.

Section 2. The Congress shall have power to enforce this article by appropriate legislation.

Amendment XXVII

(Ratified May 7, 1992)

No law varying the compensation for the services of the Senators and Representatives shall take effect, until an election of Representatives shall have intervened.

SOURCE: *United States Government Manual, 1993–94* (Washington, D.C.: Government Printing Office, 1993), 5–20.

U.S. PRESIDENTS

PRESIDENT	POLITICAL PARTY	TERM OF SERVICE
George Washington	Federalist	April 30, 1789–March 4, 1793
George Washington	Federalist	March 4, 1793–March 4, 1797
John Adams	Federalist	March 4, 1797–March 4, 1801
Thomas Jefferson	Democratic Republican	March 4, 1801–March 4, 1805
Thomas Jefferson	Democratic Republican	March 4, 1805–March 4, 1809
James Madison	Democratic Republican	March 4, 1809–March 4, 1813
James Madison	Democratic Republican	March 4, 1813–March 4, 1817
James Monroe	Democratic Republican	March 4, 1817–March 4, 1821
James Monroe	Democratic Republican	March 4, 1821–March 4, 1825
John Q. Adams	Democratic Republican	March 4, 1825–March 4, 1829
Andrew Jackson	Democrat	March 4, 1829–March 4, 1833
Andrew Jackson	Democrat	March 4, 1833–March 4, 1837
Martin Van Buren	Democrat	March 4, 1837–March 4, 1841
W. H. Harrison	Whig	March 4, 1841–April 4, 1841
John Tyler	Whig	April 6, 1841–March 4, 1845
James K. Polk	Democrat	March 4, 1845–March 4, 1849
Zachary Taylor	Whig	March 4, 1849–July 9, 1850
Millard Fillmore	Whig	July 10, 1850–March 4, 1853
Franklin Pierce	Democrat	March 4, 1853–March 4, 1857
James Buchanan	Democrat	March 4, 1857–March 4, 1861
Abraham Lincoln	Republican	March 4, 1861–March 4, 1865
Abraham Lincoln	Republican	March 4, 1865–April 15, 1865
Andrew Johnson	Republican	April 15, 1865–March 4, 1869
Ulysses S. Grant	Republican	March 4, 1869–March 4, 1873
Ulysses S. Grant	Republican	March 4, 1873–March 4, 1877
Rutherford B. Hayes	Republican	March 4, 1877–March 4, 1881
James A. Garfield	Republican	March 4, 1881–Sept. 19, 1881
Chester A. Arthur	Republican	Sept. 20, 1881–March 4, 1885

PRESIDENT	POLITICAL PARTY	TERM OF SERVICE
Grover Cleveland	Democrat	March 4, 1885–March 4, 1889
Benjamin Harrison	Republican	March 4, 1889–March 4, 1893
Grover Cleveland	Democrat	March 4, 1893–March 4, 1897
William McKinley	Republican	March 4, 1897–March 4, 1901
William McKinley	Republican	March 4, 1901–Sept. 14, 1901
Theodore Roosevelt	Republican	Sept. 14, 1901–March 4, 1905
Theodore Roosevelt	Republican	March 4, 1905–March 4, 1909
William H. Taft	Republican	March 4, 1909–March 4, 1913
Woodrow Wilson	Democrat	March 4, 1913–March 4, 1917
Woodrow Wilson	Democrat	March 4, 1917–March 4, 1921
Warren G. Harding	Republican	March 4, 1921–Aug. 2, 1923
Calvin Coolidge	Republican	Aug. 3, 1923–March 4, 1925
Calvin Coolidge	Republican	March 4, 1925–March 4, 1929
Herbert Hoover	Republican	March 4, 1929–March 4, 1933
Franklin D. Roosevelt	Democrat	March 4, 1933–Jan. 20, 1937
Franklin D. Roosevelt	Democrat	Jan. 20, 1937–Jan. 20, 1941
Franklin D. Roosevelt	Democrat	Jan. 20, 1941–Jan. 20, 1945
Franklin D. Roosevelt	Democrat	Jan. 20, 1945–April 12, 1945
Harry S. Truman	Democrat	April 12, 1945–Jan. 20, 1949
Harry S. Truman	Democrat	Jan. 20, 1949–Jan. 20, 1953
Dwight D. Eisenhower	Republican	Jan. 20, 1953–Jan. 20, 1957
Dwight D. Eisenhower	Republican	Jan. 20, 1957–Jan. 20, 1961
John F. Kennedy	Democrat	Jan. 20, 1961–Nov. 22, 1963
Lyndon B. Johnson	Democrat	Nov. 22, 1963–Jan. 20, 1965
Lyndon B. Johnson	Democrat	Jan. 20, 1965–Jan. 20, 1969
Richard Nixon	Republican	Jan. 20, 1969–Jan. 20, 1973
Richard Nixon	Republican	Jan. 20, 1973–Aug. 9, 1974
Gerald R. Ford	Republican	Aug. 9, 1974–Jan. 20, 1977
Jimmy Carter	Democrat	Jan. 20, 1977–Jan. 20, 1981
Ronald Reagan	Republican	Jan. 20, 1981–Jan. 20, 1985
Ronald Reagan	Republican	Jan. 20, 1985–Jan. 20, 1989
George Bush	Republican	Jan. 20, 1989–Jan. 20, 1993
William J. Clinton	Democrat	Jan. 20, 1993–

COURT ERA	CHIEF JUSTICES	DEFINING CHARACTERISTICS	MAJOR COURT CASES
Developmental Period (1789–1800)	John Jay (1789–1795) John Rutledge (1795) Oliver Ellsworth (1796–1800)	Low prestige: spotty attendance by justices, resignations for more "prestigious positions," hears about fifty cases Business of the Court: largely admiralty and maritime disputes Use of seriatim opinion practice	*Chisholm v. Georgia* (1793) *Ware v. Hylton* (1796) *Hylton v. United States* (1796)
The Marshall Court (1801–1835)	John Marshall (1801–1835)	Establishment of Court's role in governmental process Strong Court support for national powers (especially commerce) over states' rights Use of "Opinions of the Court," rather than seriatim practice Beginning of systematic reporting of Court opinions Despite the importance of its opinions interpreting the Constitution, the business of the Court continues to involve private law issues (maritime, property, contracts)	*Marbury v. Madison* (1803) *Fletcher v. Peck* (1810) *Dartmouth College v. Woodward* (1819) *McCulloch v. Maryland* (1819) *Cohens v. Virginia* (1821) *Gibbons v. Ogden* (1824)
Taney and Civil War Courts (1836–1888)	Roger Taney (1836–1864) Salmon Chase (1864–1873) Morrison Waite (1874–1888)	Continued assertion of federal power over states (with some accommodation for state police powers) Growing North–South splits on the Court Court showdowns with Congress at the onset and conclusion of the Civil War Growth of Court's caseload, with the majority of post–Civil War cases involving private law issues and war litigation Congress fixes Court size at nine	*Charles River Bridge v. Warren Bridge* (1837) *New York v. Miln* (1837) *Luther v. Borden* (1849) *Scott v. Sandford* (1857) *Ex parte Milligan* (1866) *Ex parte McCardle* (1869) *Civil Rights Cases* (1883)
Conservative Court Eras (1889–1937)	Melville Fuller (1888–1910) Edward White (1910–1921) William Howard Taft (1921–1930) Charles Evans Hughes (1930–1937)	But for a brief period reflecting progressivism, the Courts of this era tended to protect business interests over governmental police powers Court sets "civil rights" policy of "separate but equal"	*United States v. E. C. Knight* (1895) *Pollock v. Farmers' Loan* (1895) *Plessy v. Ferguson* (1896) *Allegeyer v. Louisiana* (1897) *Lochner v. New York* (1905)

COURT ERA	CHIEF JUSTICES	DEFINING CHARACTERISTICS	MAJOR COURT CASES
		Congress relieves justices of circuit-riding duty Congress, in 1925 Judiciary Act, gives Court greater discretion over its docket Despite Judiciary Act, Court's docket continues to grow, with many cases reflecting economic issues (e.g., congressional power under the Commerce Clause) Some important construction of Bill of Rights guarantees (protection of rights increases after WW I) Showdown with FDR over New Deal legislation: Court continues to strike down New Deal leading the president to propose a Court-packing plan	*Hammer v. Dagenhart* (1918) *Schenck v. United States* (1919) *Adkins v. Children's Hospital* (1923) *Near v. Minnesota* (1931) *Powell v. Alabama* (1932) *Schechter Poultry v. United States* (1935)
The Roosevelt and World War II Court Eras (1937–1953)	Charles Evans Hughes (1937–1941) Harlan Fiske Stone (1941–1946) Fred Vinson (1946–1953)	With the "switch in time that saved nine" the Court begins to uphold federal regulations under the Commerce Clause, as well as state use of police powers Expansion of rights and liberties, until WW II and ensuing cold war Increases in nonconsensual behavior (dissents and concurrences) among the justices	*NLRB v. Jones & Laughlin Steel* (1937) *United States v. Carolene Products* (1938) *Korematsu v. United States* (1944) *Dennis v. United States* (1951) *Youngstown Sheet & Tube v. Sawyer* (1952)
The Warren Court Era (1953–1969)	Earl Warren (1953–1969)	Expansion of rights, liberties, and criminal justice Establishment of the right to privacy Emergence of Court as national policy maker Continued increase in Court's docket, with steady growth in the number of *in forma pauperis* petitions Growth in the percentage of constitutional cases on Court's plenary docket First black (Marshall) appointed to the Court	*Brown v. Board of Education* (1954) *Roth v. United States* (1957) *Mapp v. Ohio* (1961) *Baker v. Carr* (1962) *Abington School District v. Schempp* (1963) *Gideon v. Wainwright* (1963) *Heart of Atlanta Motel v. United States* (1964) *New York Times v. Sullivan* (1964) *Griswold v. Connecticut* (1965) *Miranda v. Arizona* (1966)
Republican Court Eras (1969–)	Warren Burger (1969–1986) William Rehnquist (1986–)	Attempts in some areas (e.g., criminal law) to limit or rescind Warren Court rulings Expansion of women's rights, including right to abortion Some attempt to increase state power Legitimation of affirmative action policies Court increasingly called on to resolve intergovernmental disputes, involving separation of powers or the authority of one branch of government over another Appointment of first woman (O'Connor) to the Court	*Reed v. Reed* (1971) *New York Times v. United States* (1971) *Roe v. Wade* (1973) *Miller v. California* (1973) *United States v. Nixon* (1974) *Buckley v. Valeo* (1976) *Gregg v. Georgia* (1976) *Regents of the University of California v. Bakke* (1978) *United States v. Leon* (1984) *Garcia v. SAMTA* (1985) *Planned Parenthood of Southeastern Pennsylvania v. Casey* (1992) *R.A.V. v. City of St. Paul* (1992)

APPENDIX 4
THE JUSTICES

The justices of the Supreme Court are listed below in alphabetical order, with their birth and death years, state from which they were appointed, political party affiliation at time of appointment, educational institutions attended, appointing president, confirmation date and vote, date of service termination, and significant preappointment offices and activities.

Baldwin, Henry (1780–1844). Pennsylvania. Democrat. Yale. Nominated associate justice by Andrew Jackson; confirmed 1830 by 41–2 vote; died in office 1844. U.S. representative.

Barbour, Philip Pendleton (1783–1841). Virginia. Democrat. College of William and Mary. Nominated associate justice by Andrew Jackson; confirmed 1836 by 30–11 vote; died in office 1841. Virginia state legislator, U.S. representative, U.S. Speaker of the House, state court judge, federal district court judge.

Black, Hugo Lafayette (1886–1971). Alabama. Democrat. Birmingham Medical College, University of Alabama. Nominated associate justice by Franklin Roosevelt; confirmed 1937 by 63–16 vote; retired 1971. Alabama police court judge, county solicitor, U.S. senator.

Blackmun, Harry Andrew (1908–). Minnesota. Republican. Harvard. Nominated associate justice by Richard Nixon; confirmed 1970 by 94–0 vote; retired 1994. Federal appeals court judge.

Blair, John, Jr. (1732–1800). Virginia. Federalist. College of William and Mary; Middle Temple (England). Nominated associate justice by George Washington; confirmed 1789 by voice vote; resigned 1796. Virginia legislator, state court judge, delegate to Constitutional Convention.

Blatchford, Samuel (1820–1893). New York. Republican. Columbia. Nominated associate justice by Chester A. Arthur; confirmed 1882 by voice vote; died in office 1893. Federal district court judge, federal circuit court judge.

Bradley, Joseph P. (1813–1892). New Jersey. Republican. Rutgers. Nominated associate justice by Ulysses S. Grant; confirmed 1870 by 46–9 vote; died in office 1892. Private practice.

Brandeis, Louis Dembitz (1856–1941). Massachusetts. Republican. Harvard. Nominated associate justice by Woodrow Wilson; confirmed 1916 by 47–22 vote; retired 1939. Private practice.

Brennan, William Joseph, Jr. (1906–). New Jersey. Democrat. University of Pennsylvania, Harvard. Received recess appointment from Dwight Eisenhower to be associate justice 1956; confirmed 1957 by voice vote; retired 1990. New Jersey Supreme Court.

Brewer, David Josiah (1837–1910). Kansas. Republican. Wesleyan, Yale, Albany Law School. Nominated associate justice by Benjamin Harrison; confirmed 1889 by 53–11 vote; died in office 1910. Kansas state court judge, federal circuit court judge.

Breyer, Stephen G. (1938–). Massachusetts. Democrat. Stanford, Oxford, Harvard. Nominated associate justice by William Clinton; confirmed 1994 by 87–9 vote. Law professor; chief counsel, Senate Judiciary Committee; federal appeals court judge.

Brown, Henry B. (1836–1913). Michigan. Republican. Yale, Harvard. Nominated associate justice by Benjamin Harrison; confirmed 1890 by voice vote; retired 1906. Michigan state court judge, federal district court judge.

Burger, Warren Earl (1907–). Minnesota. Republican. University of Minnesota, St. Paul College of Law. Nominated chief justice by Richard Nixon; confirmed 1969 by 74–3 vote; retired 1986. Assistant U.S. attorney general, federal appeals court judge.

Burton, Harold Hitz (1888–1964). Ohio. Republican. Bowdoin College, Harvard. Nominated associate justice by Harry Truman; confirmed 1945 by voice vote; retired 1958. Ohio state legislator, mayor of Cleveland, U.S. senator.

Butler, Pierce (1866–1939). Minnesota. Republican. Carleton College. Nominated associate justice by Warren G. Harding; confirmed 1922 by 61–8 vote; died in office 1939. Minnesota county attorney, private practice.

Byrnes, James Francis (1879–1972). South Carolina. Democrat. Privately educated. Nominated associate justice by Franklin Roosevelt; confirmed 1941 by voice vote; resigned 1942. South Carolina local solicitor, U.S. representative, U.S. senator.

Campbell, John Archibald (1811–1889). Alabama. Democrat. Franklin College (University of Georgia), U.S. Military Academy. Nominated associate justice by Franklin Pierce; confirmed 1853 by voice vote; resigned 1861. Alabama state legislator.

Cardozo, Benjamin Nathan (1870–1938). New York. Democrat. Columbia. Nominated associate justice by Herbert Hoover; confirmed 1932 by voice vote; died in office 1938. State court judge.

Catron, John (1786–1865). Tennessee. Democrat. Self-educated. Nominated associate justice by Andrew Jackson; confirmed 1837 by 28–15 vote; died in office 1865. Tennessee state court judge, state chief justice.

Chase, Salmon Portland (1808–1873). Ohio. Republican. Dartmouth. Nominated chief justice by Abraham Lincoln; confirmed 1864 by voice vote; died in office 1873. U.S. senator, Ohio governor, U.S. secretary of the Treasury.

Chase, Samuel (1741–1811). Maryland. Federalist. Privately educated. Nominated associate justice by George Washington; confirmed 1796 by voice vote; died in office 1811. Maryland state legislator, delegate to Continental Congress, state court judge.

Clark, Tom Campbell (1899–1977). Texas. Democrat. University of Texas. Nominated associate justice by Harry Truman; confirmed 1949 by 73–8 vote; retired 1967. Texas local district attorney, U.S. attorney general.

Clarke, John Hessin (1857–1945). Ohio. Democrat. Western Reserve University. Nominated associate justice by Woodrow Wilson; confirmed 1916 by voice vote; resigned 1922. Federal district judge.

Clifford, Nathan (1803–1881). Maine. Democrat. Privately educated. Nominated associate justice by James Buchanan; confirmed 1858 by 26–23 vote; died in office 1881. Maine state legislator, state attorney general, U.S. representative, U.S. attorney general, minister to Mexico.

Curtis, Benjamin Robbins (1809–1874). Massachusetts. Whig. Harvard. Nominated associate justice by Millard Fillmore; confirmed 1851 by voice vote; resigned 1857. Massachusetts state legislator.

Cushing, William (1732–1810). Massachusetts. Federalist. Harvard. Nominated associate justice by George Washington; confirmed 1789 by voice vote; died in office 1810. Massachusetts state court judge, electoral college delegate.

Daniel, Peter Vivian (1784–1860). Virginia. Democrat. Princeton. Nominated associate justice by Martin Van Buren; confirmed 1841 by 22–5 vote; died in office 1860. Virginia state legislator, state Privy Council, federal district court judge.

Davis, David (1815–1886). Illinois. Republican. Kenyon College, Yale. Nominated associate justice by Abraham Lincoln; confirmed 1862 by voice vote; resigned 1877. Illinois state legislator, state court judge.

Day, William Rufus (1849–1923). Ohio. Republican. University of Michigan. Nominated associate justice by Theodore Roosevelt; confirmed 1903 by voice vote; resigned 1922. Ohio state court judge, U.S. secretary of state, federal court of appeals judge.

Douglas, William Orville (1898–1980). Connecticut. Democrat. Whitman College, Columbia. Nominated associate justice by Franklin Roosevelt; confirmed 1939 by 62–4 vote; retired 1975. Law professor, Securities and Exchange Commission.

Duvall, Gabriel (1752–1844). Maryland. Democratic/Republican. Privately educated. Nominated associate justice by James Madison; confirmed 1811 by voice vote; resigned 1835. Maryland state legislator, U.S. representative, state court judge, presidential elector, comptroller of the U.S. Treasury.

Ellsworth, Oliver (1745–1807). Connecticut. Federalist. Princeton. Nominated chief justice by George Washington; confirmed 1796 by 21–1 vote; resigned 1800. Connecticut state legislator, delegate to Continental Congress and Constitutional Convention, state court judge, U.S. senator.

Field, Stephen J. (1816–1899). California. Democrat. Williams College. Nominated associate justice by Abraham Lincoln; confirmed 1863 by voice vote; retired 1897. California state legislator, California Supreme Court.

Fortas, Abe (1910–1982). Tennessee. Democrat. Southwestern College, Yale. Nominated associate justice by Lyndon Johnson; confirmed 1965 by voice vote; resigned 1969. Counsel for numerous federal agencies, private practice.

Frankfurter, Felix (1882–1965). Massachusetts. Independent. College of the City of New York, Harvard. Nominated associate justice by Franklin Roosevelt; confirmed 1939 by voice vote; retired 1962. Law professor, War Department law officer, assistant to secretary of war, assistant to secretary of labor, War Labor Policies Board chairman.

Fuller, Melville Weston (1833–1910). Illinois. Democrat. Bowdoin College, Harvard. Nominated chief justice by Grover Cleveland; confirmed 1888 by 41–20 vote; died in office 1910. Illinois state legislator.

Ginsburg, Ruth Bader (1933–). New York. Nominated

associate justice by William Clinton; confirmed 1993 by 96–3 vote.   Professor, federal court of appeals judge.

Goldberg, Arthur J. (1908–1990).   Illinois.   Democrat. Northwestern.   Nominated associate justice by John Kennedy; confirmed 1962 by voice vote; resigned 1965.   Secretary of labor.

Gray, Horace (1828–1902).   Massachusetts.   Republican. Harvard.   Nominated associate justice by Chester A. Arthur; confirmed 1881 by 51–5 vote; died in office 1902.   Massachusetts Supreme Court.

Grier, Robert Cooper (1794–1870).   Pennsylvania.   Democrat.   Dickinson College.   Nominated associate justice by James Polk; confirmed 1846 by voice vote; retired 1870.   Pennsylvania state court judge.

Harlan, John Marshall (1833–1911).   Kentucky.   Republican.   Centre College, Transylvania University.   Nominated associate justice by Rutherford B. Hayes; confirmed 1877 by voice vote; died in office 1911.   Kentucky attorney general.

Harlan, John Marshall (1899–1971).   New York.   Republican.   Princeton, Oxford, New York Law School.   Nominated associate justice by Dwight Eisenhower; confirmed 1955 by 71–11 vote; retired 1971.   Chief counsel for New York State Crime Commission, federal court of appeals.

Holmes, Oliver Wendell, Jr. (1841–1935).   Massachusetts. Republican.   Harvard.   Nominated associate justice by Theodore Roosevelt; confirmed 1902 by voice vote; retired 1932.   Law professor, justice, Supreme Judicial Court of Massachusetts.

Hughes, Charles Evans (1862–1948).   New York.   Republican.   Colgate, Brown, Columbia.   Nominated associate justice by William Howard Taft; confirmed 1910 by voice vote; resigned 1916; nominated chief justice by Herbert Hoover; confirmed 1930 by 52–26 vote; retired 1941.   New York governor, U.S. secretary of state, Court of International Justice judge.

Hunt, Ward (1810–1886).   New York.   Republican.   Union College.   Nominated associate justice by Ulysses S. Grant; confirmed 1872 by voice vote; retired 1882.   New York state legislator, mayor of Utica, state court judge.

Iredell, James (1751–1799).   North Carolina.   Federalist. English schools.   Nominated associate justice by George Washington; confirmed 1790 by voice vote; died in office 1799.   Customs official, state court judge, state attorney general.

Jackson, Howell Edmunds (1832–1895).   Tennessee. Democrat.   West Tennessee College, University of Virginia, Cumberland University.   Nominated associate justice by Benjamin Harrison; confirmed 1893 by voice vote; died in office 1895. Tennessee state legislator, U.S. senator, federal circuit court judge, federal court of appeals judge.

Jackson, Robert Houghwout (1892–1954).   New York. Democrat.   Albany Law School.   Nominated associate justice by Franklin Roosevelt; confirmed 1941 by voice vote; died in office 1954.   Counsel for Internal Revenue Bureau and Securities and Exchange Commission, U.S. solicitor general, U.S. attorney general.

Jay, John (1745–1829).   New York.   Federalist.   King's College (Columbia University).   Nominated chief justice by George Washington; confirmed 1789 by voice vote; resigned 1795.   Delegate to Continental Congress, chief justice of New York, minister to Spain and Great Britain, secretary of foreign affairs.

Johnson, Thomas (1732–1819).   Maryland.   Federalist. Privately educated.   Nominated associate justice by George Washington; confirmed 1791 by voice vote; resigned 1793.   Delegate to Annapolis Convention and Continental Congress, governor, state legislator, state court judge.

Johnson, William (1771–1834).   South Carolina.   Democratic/Republican.   Princeton.   Nominated associate justice by Thomas Jefferson; confirmed 1804 by voice vote; died in office 1834.   South Carolina state legislator, state court judge.

Kennedy, Anthony McLeod (1936–   ).   California.   Republican.   Stanford, London School of Economics, Harvard. Nominated associate justice by Ronald Reagan; confirmed 1988 by 97–0 vote.   Federal appeals court judge.

Lamar, Joseph Rucker (1857–1916).   Georgia.   Democrat. University of Georgia, Bethany College, Washington and Lee. Nominated associate justice by William Howard Taft; confirmed 1910 by voice vote; died in office 1916.   Georgia state legislator, Georgia Supreme Court.

Lamar, Lucius Quintus Cincinnatus (1825–1893).   Mississippi.   Democrat.   Emory College.   Nominated associate justice by Grover Cleveland; confirmed 1888 by 32–28 vote; died in office 1893.   Georgia state legislator, U.S. representative, U.S. senator, U.S. secretary of the interior.

Livingston, Henry Brockholst (1757–1823).   New York. Democratic/Republican.   Princeton.   Nominated associate justice by Thomas Jefferson; confirmed 1806 by voice vote; died in office 1823.   New York state legislator, state court judge.

Lurton, Horace Harmon (1844–1914).   Tennessee.   Democrat.   University of Chicago, Cumberland.   Nominated associate justice by William Howard Taft; confirmed 1909 by voice vote; died in office 1914.   Tennessee Supreme Court, federal court of appeals judge.

McKenna, Joseph (1843–1926).   California.   Republican. Benicia Collegiate Institute.   Nominated associate justice by William McKinley; confirmed 1898 by voice vote; retired 1925. California state legislator, U.S. representative, federal court of appeals judge, U.S. attorney general.

McKinley, John (1780–1852).   Alabama.   Democrat.   Self-educated.   Nominated associate justice by Martin Van Buren; confirmed 1837 by voice vote; died in office 1852.   Alabama state legislator, U.S. senator, U.S. representative.

McLean, John (1785–1861).   Ohio.   Democrat.   Privately educated.   Nominated associate justice by Andrew Jackson; confirmed 1829 by voice vote; died in office 1861.   U.S. representative, Ohio Supreme Court, commissioner of U.S. General Land Office, U.S. postmaster general.

McReynolds, James Clark (1862–1946).   Tennessee.   Democrat.   Vanderbilt, University of Virginia.   Nominated associate justice by Woodrow Wilson; confirmed 1914 by 44–6 vote; retired 1941.   U.S. attorney general.

Marshall, John (1755–1835).   Virginia.   Federalist.   Privately educated, College of William and Mary.   Nominated chief justice by John Adams; confirmed 1801 by voice vote; died in office 1835.   Virginia state legislator, minister to France, U.S. representative, U.S. secretary of state.

Marshall, Thurgood (1908–1993).   New York.   Democrat.   Lincoln University, Howard University.   Nominated associate justice by Lyndon Johnson; confirmed 1967 by 69–11 vote; retired 1991.   NAACP Legal Defense Fund, federal court of appeals judge, U.S. solicitor general.

Matthews, Stanley (1824–1889).   Ohio.   Republican.   Kenyon College.   Nominated associate justice by Rutherford B. Hayes; no Senate action on nomination; renominated associate justice by James A. Garfield; confirmed 1881 by 24–23 vote; died in office 1889.   Ohio state legislator, state court judge, U.S. attorney for southern Ohio, U.S. senator.

Miller, Samuel Freeman (1816–1890).   Iowa.   Republican.   Transylvania University.   Nominated associate justice by Abraham Lincoln; confirmed 1862 by voice vote; died in office 1890.   Medical doctor, private law practice, justice of the peace.

Minton, Sherman (1890–1965).   Indiana.   Democrat.   Indiana University, Yale.   Nominated associate justice by Harry Truman; confirmed 1949 by 48–16 vote; retired 1956.   U.S. senator, federal court of appeals judge.

Moody, William Henry (1853–1917).   Massachusetts.   Republican.   Harvard.   Nominated associate justice by Theodore Roosevelt; confirmed 1906 by voice vote; retired 1910.   Massachusetts local district attorney, U.S. representative, secretary of the navy, U.S. attorney general.

Moore, Alfred (1755–1810).   North Carolina.   Federalist.   Privately educated.   Nominated associate justice by John Adams; confirmed 1799 by voice vote; resigned 1804.   North Carolina legislator, state attorney general, state court judge.

Murphy, Francis William (1880–1949).   Michigan.   Democrat.   University of Michigan, London's Inn (England), Trinity College (Ireland).   Nominated associate justice by Franklin Roosevelt; confirmed 1940 by voice vote; died in office 1949.   Michigan state court judge, mayor of Detroit, governor of the Philippines, governor of Michigan, U.S. attorney general.

Nelson, Samuel (1792–1873).   New York.   Democrat.   Middlebury College.   Nominated associate justice by John Tyler; confirmed 1845 by voice vote; retired 1872.   Presidential elector, state court judge, New York Supreme Court chief justice.

O'Connor, Sandra Day (1930–   ).   Arizona.   Republican.   Stanford.   Nominated associate justice by Ronald Reagan; confirmed 1981 by 99–0 vote.   Arizona state legislator, state court judge.

Paterson, William (1745–1806).   New Jersey.   Federalist.   Princeton.   Nominated associate justice by George Washington; confirmed 1793 by voice vote; died in office 1806.   New Jersey attorney general, delegate to Constitutional Convention, U.S. senator, governor.

Peckham, Rufus Wheeler (1838–1909).   New York.   Democrat.   Albany Boys' Academy.   Nominated associate justice by Grover Cleveland; confirmed 1895 by voice vote; died in office 1909.   New York local district attorney, city attorney, state court judge.

Pitney, Mahlon (1858–1924).   New Jersey.   Republican.   Princeton.   Nominated associate justice by William Howard Taft; confirmed 1912 by 50–26 vote; retired 1922.   U.S. representative, New Jersey state legislator, New Jersey Supreme Court, Chancellor of New Jersey.

Powell, Lewis Franklin, Jr. (1907–   ).   Virginia.   Democrat.   Washington and Lee, Harvard.   Nominated associate justice by Richard Nixon; confirmed 1971 by 89–1 vote; retired 1987.   Private practice, Virginia State Board of Education, American Bar Association president, American College of Trial Lawyers president.

Reed, Stanley Forman (1884–1980).   Kentucky.   Democrat.   Kentucky Wesleyan, Yale, Virginia, Columbia, University of Paris.   Nominated associate justice by Franklin Roosevelt; confirmed 1938 by voice vote; retired 1957.   Federal Farm Board general counsel, Reconstruction Finance Corporation general counsel, U.S. solicitor general.

Rehnquist, William Hubbs (1924–   ).   Arizona.   Republican.   Stanford, Harvard.   Nominated associate justice by Richard Nixon; confirmed 1971 by 68–26 vote; nominated chief justice by Ronald Reagan; confirmed 1986 by 65–33 vote.   Private practice, assistant U.S. attorney general.

Roberts, Owen Josephus (1875–1955).   Pennsylvania.   Republican.   University of Pennsylvania.   Nominated associate justice by Herbert Hoover; confirmed 1930 by voice vote; resigned 1945.   Private practice, Pennsylvania local prosecutor, special U.S. attorney.

Rutledge, John (1739–1800).   South Carolina.   Federalist.   Middle Temple (England).   Nominated associate justice by George Washington; confirmed 1789 by voice vote; resigned 1791.   Nominated chief justice by George Washington August 1795 and served as recess appointment; confirmation denied and service terminated December 1795.   South Carolina legislator, state attorney general, governor, chief justice of South Carolina, delegate to Continental Congress and Constitutional Convention.

Rutledge, Wiley Blount (1894–1949).   Iowa.   Democrat.   Maryville College, University of Wisconsin, University of Colorado.   Nominated associate justice by Franklin Roosevelt; confirmed 1943 by voice vote; died in office 1949.   Law professor, federal court of appeals judge.

Sanford, Edward Terry (1865–1930).   Tennessee.   Republican.   University of Tennessee, Harvard.   Nominated associate justice by Warren G. Harding; confirmed 1923 by voice vote; died in office 1930.   Assistant U.S. attorney general, federal district court judge.

Scalia, Antonin (1936–   ).   District of Columbia.   Republican.   Georgetown, Harvard.   Nominated associate justice by Ronald Reagan; confirmed 1986 by 98–0 vote.   Assistant U.S. attorney general, federal court of appeals judge.

Shiras, George, Jr. (1832–1924).   Pennsylvania.   Republican.   Ohio University, Yale.   Nominated associate justice by Benjamin Harrison; confirmed 1892 by voice vote; retired 1903.   Private practice.

Souter, David Hackett (1939–   ).   New Hampshire.   Republican.   Harvard, Oxford.   Nominated associate justice by George Bush; confirmed 1990 by 90–9 vote.   New Hampshire attorney general, state court judge, federal appeals court judge.

Stevens, John Paul (1920–   ).   Illinois.   Republican.   Chicago, Northwestern.   Nominated associate justice by Gerald Ford; confirmed 1975 by 98–0 vote.   Federal court of appeals judge.

Stewart, Potter (1915–1985).   Ohio.   Republican.   Yale, Cambridge.   Received recess appointment from Dwight Eisenhower to be associate justice in 1958; confirmed 1959 by 70–17 vote; retired 1981.   Cincinnati city council, federal court of appeals judge.

Stone, Harlan Fiske (1872–1946).   New York.   Republican.   Amherst College, Columbia.   Nominated associate justice by Calvin Coolidge; confirmed 1925 by 71–6 vote; nominated chief justice by Franklin Roosevelt; confirmed 1941 by voice vote; died in office 1946.   Law professor, U.S. attorney general.

Story, Joseph (1779–1845).   Massachusetts.   Democratic/Republican.   Harvard.   Nominated associate justice by James Madison; confirmed 1811 by voice vote; died in office 1845.   Massachusetts state legislator, U.S. representative.

Strong, William (1808–1895).   Pennsylvania.   Republican.   Yale.   Nominated associate justice by Ulysses S. Grant; confirmed 1870 by voice vote; retired 1880.   U.S. representative, Pennsylvania Supreme Court.

Sutherland, George (1862–1942).   Utah.   Republican.   Brigham Young, University of Michigan.   Nominated associate justice by Warren G. Harding; confirmed 1922 by voice vote; retired 1938.   Utah state legislator, U.S. representative, U.S. senator.

Swayne, Noah Haynes (1804–1884).   Ohio.   Republican.   Privately educated.   Nominated associate justice by Abraham Lincoln; confirmed 1862 by 38–1 vote; retired 1881.   Ohio state

legislator, local prosecutor, U.S. attorney for Ohio, Columbus city council.

Taft, William Howard (1857–1930).   Ohio.   Republican.   Yale, Cincinnati.   Nominated chief justice by Warren G. Harding; confirmed 1921 by voice vote; retired 1930.   Ohio local prosecutor, state court judge, U.S. solicitor general, federal court of appeals judge, governor of the Philippines, secretary of war, U.S. president.

Taney, Roger Brooke (1777–1864).   Maryland.   Democrat.   Dickinson College.   Nominated associate justice by Andrew Jackson; nomination not confirmed 1835; nominated chief justice by Andrew Jackson; confirmed 1836 by 29–15 vote; died in office 1864.   Maryland state legislator, state attorney general, acting secretary of war, secretary of the Treasury (nomination later rejected by Senate).

Thomas, Clarence (1948–   ).   Georgia.   Republican.   Holy Cross, Yale.   Nominated associate justice by George Bush; confirmed 1991 by 52–48 vote.   Department of Education, Equal Employment Opportunity Commission, federal appeals court judge.

Thompson, Smith (1768–1843).   New York.   Democratic/Republican.   Princeton.   Nominated associate justice by James Monroe; confirmed 1823 by voice vote; died in office 1843.   New York state legislator, state court judge, secretary of the navy.

Todd, Thomas (1765–1826).   Kentucky.   Democratic/Republican.   Liberty Hall (Washington and Lee).   Nominated associate justice by Thomas Jefferson; confirmed 1807 by voice vote; died in office 1826.   Kentucky state court judge, state chief justice.

Trimble, Robert (1776–1828).   Kentucky.   Democratic/Republican.   Kentucky Academy.   Nominated associate justice by John Quincy Adams; confirmed 1826 by 27–5 vote; died in office 1828.   Kentucky state legislator, state court judge, U.S. attorney, federal district court judge.

Van Devanter, Willis (1859–1941).   Wyoming.   Republican.   Indiana Asbury University, University of Cincinnati.   Nominated associate justice by William Howard Taft; confirmed 1910 by voice vote; retired 1937.   Cheyenne city attorney, Wyoming territorial legislature, Wyoming Supreme Court, assistant U.S. attorney general, federal court of appeals judge.

Vinson, Frederick Moore (1890–1953).   Kentucky.   Democrat.   Centre College.   Nominated chief justice by Harry Truman; confirmed 1946 by voice vote; died in office 1953.   U.S. representative, federal appeals court judge, director of Office of Economic Stabilization, secretary of the Treasury.

Waite, Morrison Remick (1816–1888).   Ohio.   Republican.   Yale.   Nominated chief justice by Ulysses S. Grant; confirmed 1874 by 63–0 vote; died in office 1888.   Private practice, Ohio state legislator.

Warren, Earl (1891–1974). California. Republican. University of California. Recess appointment as chief justice by Dwight Eisenhower 1953; confirmed 1954 by voice vote; retired 1969. California local district attorney, state attorney general, governor.

Washington, Bushrod (1762–1829). Virginia. Federalist. College of William and Mary. Nominated associate justice by John Adams; confirmed 1798 by voice vote; died in office 1829. Virginia state legislator.

Wayne, James Moore (1790–1867). Georgia. Democrat. Princeton. Nominated associate justice by Andrew Jackson; confirmed 1835 by voice vote; died in office 1867. Georgia state legislator, mayor of Savannah, state court judge, U.S. representative.

White, Byron Raymond (1917–). Colorado. Democrat. University of Colorado, Oxford, Yale. Nominated associate justice by John Kennedy; confirmed 1962 by voice vote; retired 1993. Deputy U.S. attorney general.

White, Edward Douglass (1845–1921). Louisiana. Democrat. Mount St. Mary's College, Georgetown. Nominated associate justice by Grover Cleveland; confirmed 1894 by voice vote; nominated chief justice by William Howard Taft; confirmed 1910 by voice vote; died in office 1921. Louisiana state legislator, Louisiana Supreme Court, U.S. senator.

Whittaker, Charles Evans (1901–1973). Missouri. Republican. University of Kansas City. Nominated associate justice by Dwight Eisenhower; confirmed 1957 by voice vote; retired 1962. Federal district court judge, federal appeals court judge.

Wilson, James (1742–1798). Pennsylvania. Federalist. University of St. Andrews (Scotland). Nominated associate justice by George Washington; confirmed 1789 by voice vote; died in office 1798. Delegate to Continental Congress and Constitutional Convention.

Woodbury, Levi (1789–1851). New Hampshire. Democrat. Dartmouth, Tapping Reeve Law School. Nominated associate justice by James Polk; confirmed 1846 by voice vote; died in office 1851. New Hampshire state legislator, state court judge, governor, U.S. senator, secretary of the navy, secretary of the Treasury.

Woods, William B. (1824–1887). Georgia. Republican. Western Reserve College, Yale. Nominated associate justice by Rutherford B. Hayes; confirmed 1880 by 39–8 vote; died in office 1887. Ohio state legislator, Alabama chancellor, federal circuit court judge.

NATURAL COURTS

Natural court[a]	Justices[b]	Dates	U.S. Reports[c]
Jay 1	Jay (*o* October 19, 1789), J. Rutledge (*o* February 15, 1790), Cushing (*o* February 2, 1790), Wilson (*o* October 5, 1789), Blair (*o* February 2, 1790)	October 5, 1789–May 12, 1790	2
Jay 2	Jay, Rutledge (*r* March 5, 1791), Cushing, Wilson, Blair, Iredell (*o* May 12, 1790)	May 12, 1790–August 6, 1792	2
Jay 3	Jay, Cushing, Wilson, Blair, Iredell, T. Johnson (*o* August 6, 1792; *r* January 16, 1793)	August 6, 1792–March 11, 1793	2
Jay 4	Jay (*r* June 29, 1795), Cushing, Wilson, Blair, Iredell, Paterson (*o* March 11, 1793)	March 11, 1793–August 12, 1795	2–3
Rutledge 1	J. Rutledge (*o* August 12, 1795; *rj* December 15, 1795), Cushing, Wilson, Blair (*r* January 27, 1796), Iredell, Paterson	August 12, 1795–February 4, 1796	3
No chief justice	Cushing, Wilson, Iredell, Paterson, S. Chase (*o* February 4, 1796)	February 4, 1796–March 8, 1796	3
Ellsworth 1	Ellsworth (*o* March 8, 1796), Cushing, Wilson (*d* August 21, 1798), Iredell, Paterson, S. Chase	March 8, 1796–February 4, 1799	3
Ellsworth 2	Ellsworth, Cushing, Iredell (*d* October 20, 1799), Paterson, S. Chase, Washington (*o* February 4, 1799)	February 4, 1799–April 21, 1800	3–4
Ellsworth 3	Ellsworth (*r* December 15, 1800), Cushing, Paterson, S. Chase, Washington, Moore (*o* April 21, 1800)	April 21, 1800–February 4, 1801	4
Marshall 1	Marshall (*o* February 4, 1801), Cushing, Paterson, S. Chase, Washington, Moore (*r* January 26, 1804)	February 4, 1801–May 7, 1804	5–6
Marshall 2	Marshall, Cushing, Paterson (*d* September 9, 1806), S. Chase, Washington, W. Johnson (*o* May 7, 1804)	May 7, 1804–January 20, 1807	6–7
Marshall 3	Marshall, Cushing, S. Chase, Washington, W. Johnson, Livingston (*o* January 20, 1807)	January 20, 1807–May 4, 1807	8
Marshall 4	Marshall, Cushing (*d* September 13, 1810), S. Chase (*d* June 19, 1811), Washington, W. Johnson, Livingston, Todd (*o* May 4, 1807)	May 4, 1807–November 23, 1811	8–10

Natural court[a]	Justices[b]	Dates	U.S. Reports[c]
Marshall 5	Marshall, Washington, W. Johnson, Livingston, Todd, Duvall (*o* November 23, 1811)	November 23, 1811–February 3, 1812	11
Marshall 6	Marshall, Washington, W. Johnson, Livingston (*d* March 18, 1823), Todd, Duvall, Story (*o* February 3, 1812)	February 3, 1812–February 10, 1824	11–21
Marshall 7	Marshall, Washington, W. Johnson, Todd (*d* February 7, 1826), Duvall, Story, Thompson (*o* February 10, 1824)	February 10, 1824–June 16, 1826	22–24
Marshall 8	Marshall, Washington (*d* November 26, 1829), W. Johnson, Duvall, Story, Thompson, Trimble (*o* June 16, 1826; *d* August 25, 1828)	June 16, 1826–January 11, 1830	25–27
Marshall 9	Marshall, W. Johnson (*d* August 4, 1834), Duvall (*r* January 14, 1835), Story, Thompson, McLean (*o* January 11, 1830), Baldwin (*o* January 18, 1830)	January 11, 1830–January 14, 1835	28–33
Marshall 10	Marshall (*d* July 6, 1835), Story, Thompson, McLean, Baldwin, Wayne (*o* January 14, 1835)	January 14, 1835–March 28, 1836	34–35
Taney 1	Taney (*o* March 28, 1836), Story, Thompson, McLean, Baldwin, Wayne	March 28, 1836–May 12, 1836	35
Taney 2	Taney, Story, Thompson, McLean, Baldwin, Wayne, Barbour (*o* May 12, 1836)	May 12, 1836–May 1, 1837	35–36
Taney 3	Taney, Story, Thompson, McLean, Baldwin, Wayne, Barbour, Catron (*o* May 1, 1837)	May 1, 1837–January 9, 1838	36
Taney 4	Taney, Story, Thompson, McLean, Baldwin, Wayne, Barbour (*d* February 25, 1841), Catron, McKinley (*o* January 9, 1838)	January 9, 1838–January 10, 1842	37–40
Taney 5	Taney, Story, Thompson (*d* December 18, 1843), McLean, Baldwin (*d* April 21, 1844), Wayne, Catron, McKinley, Daniel (*o* January 10, 1842)	January 10, 1842–February 27, 1845	40–44
Taney 6	Taney, Story (*d* September 10, 1845), McLean, Wayne, Catron, McKinley, Daniel, Nelson (*o* February 27, 1845)	February 27, 1845–September 23, 1845	44
Taney 7	Taney, McLean, Wayne, Catron, McKinley, Daniel, Nelson, Woodbury (*o* September 23, 1845)	September 23, 1845–August 10, 1846	44–45
Taney 8	Taney, McLean, Wayne, Catron, McKinley, Daniel, Nelson, Woodbury (*d* September 4, 1851), Grier (*o* August 10, 1846)	August 10, 1846–October 10, 1851	46–52
Taney 9	Taney, McLean, Wayne, Catron, McKinley (*d* July 19, 1852), Daniel, Nelson, Grier, Curtis (*o* October 10, 1851)	October 10, 1851–April 11, 1853	53–55
Taney 10	Taney, McLean, Wayne, Catron, Daniel, Nelson, Grier, Curtis (*r* September 30, 1857), Campbell (*o* April 11, 1853)	April 11, 1853–January 21, 1858	56–61
Taney 11	Taney, McLean (*d* April 4, 1861), Wayne, Catron, Daniel (*d* May 31, 1860), Nelson, Grier, Campbell (*r* April 30, 1861), Clifford (*o* January 21, 1858)	January 21, 1858–January 27, 1862	61–66
Taney 12	Taney, Wayne, Catron, Nelson, Grier, Clifford, Swayne (*o* January 27, 1862)	January 27, 1862–July 21, 1862	66
Taney 13	Taney, Wayne, Catron, Nelson, Grier, Clifford, Swayne, Miller (*o* July 21, 1862)	July 21, 1862–December 10, 1862	67

Natural court[a]	Justices[b]	Dates	U.S. Reports[c]
Taney 14	Taney, Wayne, Catron, Nelson, Grier, Clifford, Swayne, Miller, Davis (*o* December 10, 1862)	December 10, 1862– May 20, 1863	67
Taney 15	Taney (*d* October 12, 1864), Wayne, Catron, Nelson, Grier, Clifford, Swayne, Miller, Davis, Field (*o* May 20, 1863)	May 20, 1863– December 15, 1864	67–68
Chase 1	S. P. Chase (*o* December 15, 1864), Wayne (*d* July 5, 1867), Catron (*d* May 30, 1865), Nelson, Grier (*r* January 31, 1870), Clifford, Swayne, Miller, Davis, Field	December 15, 1864– March 14, 1870	69–76
Chase 2	S. P. Chase, Nelson (*r* November 28, 1872), Clifford, Swayne, Miller, Davis, Field, Strong (*o* March 14, 1870), Bradley (*o* March 23, 1870)	March 14, 1870– January 9, 1873	76–82
Chase 3	S. P. Chase (*d* May 7, 1873), Clifford, Swayne, Miller, Davis, Field, Strong, Bradley, Hunt (*o* January 9, 1873)	January 9, 1873– March 4, 1874	82–86
Waite 1	Waite (*o* March 4, 1874), Clifford, Swayne, Miller, Davis (*r* March 4, 1877), Field, Strong, Bradley, Hunt	March 4, 1874– December 10, 1877	86–95
Waite 2	Waite, Clifford, Swayne, Miller, Field, Strong (*r* December 14, 1880), Bradley, Hunt, Harlan I (*o* December 10, 1877)	December 10, 1877– January 5, 1881	95–103
Waite 3	Waite, Clifford, Swayne (*r* January 24, 1881), Miller, Field, Bradley, Hunt, Harlan I, Woods (*o* January 5, 1881)	January 5, 1881– May 17, 1881	103
Waite 4	Waite, Clifford (*d* July 25, 1881), Miller, Field, Bradley, Hunt, Harlan I, Woods, Matthews (*o* May 17, 1881)	May 17, 1881– January 9, 1882	103–104
Waite 5	Waite, Miller, Field, Bradley, Hunt (*r* January 27, 1882), Harlan I, Woods, Matthews, Gray (*o* January 9, 1882)	January 9, 1882– April 3, 1882	104–105
Waite 6	Waite, Miller, Field, Bradley, Harlan I, Woods (*d* May 14, 1887), Matthews, Gray, Blatchford (*o* April 3, 1882)	April 3, 1882– January 18, 1888	105–124
Waite 7	Waite (*d* March 23, 1888), Miller, Field, Bradley, Harlan I, Matthews, Gray, Blatchford, L. Lamar (*o* January 18, 1888)	January 18, 1888– October 8, 1888	124–127
Fuller 1	Fuller (*o* October 8, 1888), Miller, Field, Bradley, Harlan I, Matthews (*d* March 22, 1889), Gray, Blatchford, L. Lamar	October 8, 1888– January 6, 1890	128–132
Fuller 2	Fuller, Miller (*d* October 13, 1890), Field, Bradley, Harlan I, Gray, Blatchford, L. Lamar, Brewer (*o* January 6, 1890)	January 6, 1890– January 5, 1891	132–137
Fuller 3	Fuller, Field, Bradley (*d* January 22, 1892), Harlan I, Gray, Blatchford, L. Lamar, Brewer, Brown (*o* January 5, 1891)	January 5, 1891– October 10, 1892	137–145
Fuller 4	Fuller, Field, Harlan I, Gray, Blatchford, L. Lamar (*d* January 23, 1893), Brewer, Brown, Shiras (*o* October 10, 1892)	October 10, 1892– March 4, 1893	146–148
Fuller 5	Fuller, Field, Harlan I, Gray, Blatchford (*d* July 7, 1893), Brewer, Brown, Shiras, H. Jackson (*o* March 4, 1893)	March 4, 1893– March 12, 1894	148–151
Fuller 6	Fuller, Field, Harlan I, Gray, Brewer, Brown, Shiras, H. Jackson (*d* August 8, 1895), E. White (*o* March 12, 1894)	March 12, 1894– January 6, 1896	152–160

Natural court[a]	Justices[b]	Dates	U.S. Reports[c]
Fuller 7	Fuller, Field (r December 1, 1897), Harlan I, Gray, Brewer, Brown, Shiras, E. White, Peckham (o January 6, 1896)	January 6, 1896–January 26, 1898	160–169
Fuller 8	Fuller, Harlan I, Gray (d September 15, 1902), Brewer, Brown, Shiras, E. White, Peckham, McKenna (o January 26, 1898)	January 26, 1898–December 8, 1902	169–187
Fuller 9	Fuller, Harlan I, Brewer, Brown, Shiras (r February 23, 1903), E. White, Peckham, McKenna, Holmes (o December 8, 1902)	December 8, 1902–March 2, 1903	187–188
Fuller 10	Fuller, Harlan I, Brewer, Brown (r May 28, 1906), E. White, Peckham, McKenna, Holmes, Day (o March 2, 1903)	March 2, 1903–December 17, 1906	188–203
Fuller 11	Fuller, Harlan I, Brewer, E. White, Peckham (d October 24, 1909), McKenna, Holmes, Day, Moody (o December 17, 1906)	December 17, 1906–January 3, 1910	203–215
Fuller 12	Fuller (d July 4, 1910), Harlan I, Brewer (d March 28, 1910), E. White, McKenna, Holmes, Day, Moody, Lurton (o January 3, 1910)	January 3, 1910–October 10, 1910	215–217
No chief justice	Harlan I, E. White (p December 18, 1910), McKenna, Holmes, Day, Moody (r November 20, 1910), Lurton, Hughes (o October 10, 1910)	October 10, 1910–December 19, 1910	218
White 1	E. White (o December 19, 1910), Harlan I (d October 14, 1911), McKenna, Holmes, Day, Lurton, Hughes, Van Devanter (o January 3, 1911), J. Lamar (o January 3, 1911)	December 19, 1910–March 18, 1912	218–223
White 2	E. White, McKenna, Holmes, Day, Lurton (d July 12, 1914), Hughes, Van Devanter, J. Lamar, Pitney (o March 18, 1912)	March 18, 1912–October 12, 1914	223–234
White 3	E. White, McKenna, Holmes, Day, Hughes, Van Devanter, J. Lamar (d January 2, 1916), Pitney, McReynolds (o October 12, 1914)	October 12, 1914–June 5, 1916	235–241
White 4	E. White, McKenna, Holmes, Day, Hughes (r June 10, 1916), Van Devanter, Pitney, McReynolds, Brandeis (o June 5, 1916)	June 5, 1916–October 9, 1916	241
White 5	E. White (d May 19, 1921), McKenna, Holmes, Day, Van Devanter, Pitney, McReynolds, Brandeis, Clarke (o October 9, 1916)	October 9, 1916–July 11, 1921	242–256
Taft 1	Taft (o July 11, 1921), McKenna, Holmes, Day, Van Devanter, Pitney, McReynolds, Brandeis, Clarke (r September 18, 1922)	July 11, 1921–October 2, 1922	257–259
Taft 2	Taft, McKenna, Holmes, Day (r November 13, 1922), Van Devanter, Pitney (r December 31, 1922), McReynolds, Brandeis, Sutherland (o October 2, 1922)	October 2, 1922–January 2, 1923	260
Taft 3	Taft, McKenna, Holmes, Van Devanter, McReynolds, Brandeis, Sutherland, Butler (o January 2, 1923)	January 2, 1923–February 19, 1923	260
Taft 4	Taft, McKenna (r January 5, 1925), Holmes, Van Devanter, McReynolds, Brandeis, Sutherland, Butler, Sanford (o February 19, 1923)	February 19, 1923–March 2, 1925	260–267
Taft 5	Taft (r February 3, 1930), Holmes, Van Devanter, McReynolds, Brandeis, Sutherland, Butler, Sanford, Stone (o March 2, 1925)	March 2, 1925–February 24, 1930	267–280
Hughes 1	Hughes (o February 24, 1930), Holmes, Van Devanter, McReynolds, Brandeis, Sutherland, Butler, Sanford (d March 8, 1930), Stone	February 24, 1930–June 2, 1930	280–281
Hughes 2	Hughes, Holmes (r January 12, 1932), Van Devanter, McReynolds, Brandeis, Sutherland, Butler, Stone, Roberts (o June 2, 1930)	June 2, 1930–March 14, 1932	281–285

Natural court[a]	Justices[b]	Dates	U.S. Reports[c]
Hughes 3	Hughes, Van Devanter (r June 2, 1937), McReynolds, Brandeis, Sutherland, Butler, Stone, Roberts, Cardozo (o March 14, 1932)	March 14, 1932–August 19, 1937	285–301
Hughes 4	Hughes, McReynolds, Brandeis, Sutherland (r January 17, 1938), Butler, Stone, Roberts, Cardozo, Black (o August 19, 1937)	August 19, 1937 January 31, 1938	302–303
Hughes 5	Hughes, McReynolds, Brandeis, Butler, Stone, Roberts, Cardozo (d July 9, 1938), Black, Reed (o January 31, 1938)	January 31, 1938–January 30, 1939	303–305
Hughes 6	Hughes, McReynolds, Brandeis (r February 13, 1939), Butler, Stone, Roberts, Black, Reed, Frankfurter (o January 30, 1939)	January 30, 1939–April 17, 1939	306
Hughes 7	Hughes, McReynolds, Butler (d November 16, 1939), Stone, Roberts, Black, Reed, Frankfurter, Douglas (o April 17, 1939)	April 17, 1939–February 5, 1940	306–308
Hughes 8	Hughes (r July 1, 1941), McReynolds (r January 31, 1941), Stone (p July 2, 1941), Roberts, Black, Reed, Frankfurter, Douglas, Murphy (o February 5, 1940)	February 5, 1940–July 3, 1941	308–313
Stone 1	Stone (o July 3, 1941), Roberts, Black, Reed, Frankfurter, Douglas, Murphy, Byrnes (o July 8, 1941; r October 3, 1942), R. Jackson (o July 11, 1941)	July 3, 1941–February 15, 1943	314–318
Stone 2	Stone, Roberts (r July 31, 1945), Black, Reed, Frankfurter, Douglas, Murphy, R. Jackson, W. Rutledge (o February 15, 1943)	February 15, 1943–October 1, 1945	318–326
Stone 3	Stone (d April 22, 1946), Black, Reed, Frankfurter, Douglas, Murphy, R. Jackson, W. Rutledge, Burton (o October 1, 1945)	October 1, 1945–June 24, 1946	326–328
Vinson 1	Vinson (o June 24, 1946), Black, Reed, Frankfurter, Douglas, Murphy (d July 19, 1949), R. Jackson, W. Rutledge, Burton	June 24, 1946–August 24, 1949	329–338
Vinson 2	Vinson, Black, Reed, Frankfurter, Douglas, R. Jackson, W. Rutledge (d September 10, 1949), Burton, Clark (o August 24, 1949)	August 24, 1949–October 12, 1949	338
Vinson 3	Vinson (d September 8, 1953), Black, Reed, Frankfurter, Douglas, R. Jackson, Burton, Clark, Minton (o October 12, 1949)	October 12, 1949–October 5, 1953	338–346
Warren 1	Warren (o October 5, 1953), Black, Reed, Frankfurter, Douglas, R. Jackson (d October 9, 1954), Burton, Clark, Minton	October 5, 1953–March 28, 1955	346–348
Warren 2	Warren, Black, Reed, Frankfurter, Douglas, Burton, Clark, Minton (r October 15, 1956), Harlan II (o March 28, 1955)	March 28, 1955–October 16, 1956	348–352
Warren 3	Warren, Black, Reed (r February 25, 1957), Frankfurter, Douglas, Burton, Clark, Harlan II, Brennan (o October 16, 1956)	October 16, 1956–March 25, 1957	352
Warren 4	Warren, Black, Frankfurter, Douglas, Burton (r October 13, 1958), Clark, Harlan II, Brennan, Whittaker (o March 25, 1957)	March 25, 1957–October 14, 1958	352–358
Warren 5	Warren, Black, Frankfurter, Douglas, Clark, Harlan II, Brennan, Whittaker (r March 31, 1962), Stewart (o October 14, 1958)	October 14, 1958–April 16, 1962	358–369
Warren 6	Warren, Black, Frankfurter (r August 28, 1962), Douglas, Clark, Harlan II, Brennan, Stewart, B. White (o April 16, 1962)	April 16, 1962–October 1, 1962	369–370
Warren 7	Warren, Black, Douglas, Clark, Harlan II, Brennan, Stewart, B. White, Goldberg (o October 1, 1962; r July 25, 1965)	October 1, 1962–October 4, 1965	371–381

Natural court[a]	Justices[b]	Dates	U.S. Reports[c]
Warren 8	Warren, Black, Douglas, Clark (r June 12, 1967), Harlan II, Brennan, Stewart, B. White, Fortas (o October 4, 1965)	October 4, 1965– October 2, 1967	382–388
Warren 9	Warren (r June 23, 1969), Black, Douglas, Harlan II, Brennan, Stewart, B. White, Fortas (r May 14, 1969), T. Marshall (o October 2, 1967)	October 2, 1967– June 23, 1969	389–395
Burger 1	Burger (o June 23, 1969), Black, Douglas, Harlan II, Brennan, Stewart, B. White, T. Marshall	June 23, 1969– June 9, 1970	395–397
Burger 2	Burger, Black (r September 17, 1971), Douglas, Harlan II (r September 23, 1971), Brennan, Stewart, B. White, T. Marshall, Blackmun (o June 9, 1970)	June 9, 1970– January 7, 1972	397–404
Burger 3	Burger, Douglas (r November 12, 1975), Brennan, Stewart, B. White, T. Marshall, Blackmun, Powell (o January 7, 1972), Rehnquist (o January 7, 1972)	January 7, 1972– December 19, 1975	404–423
Burger 4	Burger, Brennan, Stewart (r July 3, 1981), B. White, T. Marshall, Blackmun, Powell, Rehnquist, Stevens (o December 19, 1975)	December 19, 1975– September 25, 1981	423–453
Burger 5	Burger (r September 26, 1986), Brennan, B. White, T. Marshall, Blackmun, Powell, Rehnquist (p September 26, 1986), Stevens, O'Connor (o September 25, 1981)	September 25, 1981– September 26, 1986	453–478
Rehnquist 1	Rehnquist (o September 26, 1986), Brennan, B. White, T. Marshall, Blackmun, Powell (r June 26, 1987), Stevens, O'Connor, Scalia (o September 26, 1986)	September 26, 1986– February 18, 1988	478–484
Rehnquist 2	Rehnquist, Brennan (r July 20, 1990), B. White, T. Marshall, Blackmun, Stevens, O'Connor, Scalia, Kennedy (o February 18, 1988)	February 18, 1988– October 9, 1990	484–498
Rehnquist 3	Rehnquist, B. White, T. Marshall (r October 1, 1991), Blackmun, Stevens, O'Connor, Scalia, Kennedy, Souter (o October 9, 1990)	October 9, 1990– October 23, 1991	498–
Rehnquist 4	Rehnquist, B. White (r July 1, 1993), Blackmun, Stevens, O'Connor, Scalia, Kennedy, Souter, Thomas (o October 23, 1991)	October 23, 1991– August 10, 1993	
Rehnquist 5	Rehnquist, Blackmun (r August 3, 1994), Stevens, O'Connor, Scalia, Kennedy, Souter, Thomas, Ginsburg (o August 10, 1993)	August 10, 1993– August 3, 1994	
Rehnquist 6	Rehnquist, Stevens, O'Connor, Scalia, Kennedy, Souter, Thomas, Ginsburg, Breyer (o August 3, 1994)	August 3, 1994	

SOURCE: Lee Epstein, Jeffrey A. Segal, Harold J. Spaeth, Thomas G. Walker, *The Supreme Court Compendium: Data, Decisions, and Developments* (Washington, D.C.: Congressional Quarterly, 1994), Table 5-2.

NOTES: The term *natural court* refers to a period of time during which the membership of the Court remains stable. There are a number of ways to determine the beginning and end of a natural court. Here a natural court begins when a new justice takes the oath of office and continues until the next new justice takes the oath. When two or more justices join the Court within a period of fifteen or fewer days, we treat it as the beginning of a single natural court (for example, Marshall 9, Chase 2, White 1, and Stone 1).

a. Numbered sequentially within the tenure of each chief justice.

b. The name of the chief justice appears first, with associate justices follow-

ing in order of descending seniority. In addition, the date a justice left the Court, creating a vacancy for the next justice to be appointed, is given, as well as the date the new justice took the oath of office. *o*=oath of office taken, *d*=died, *r*=resigned or retired, *rj*=recess appointment rejected by Senate, *p*=promoted from associate justice to chief justice.

c. Volumes of *United States Reports* in which the actions of each natural court generally may be found. Because of the way decisions were published prior to the twentieth century, these volume numbers may not contain all of the decisions of a given natural court. They do, however, provide a general guide to the location of each natural court's published decisions. Natural courts of short duration may have little business published in the reports.

THE AMERICAN LEGAL SYSTEM

FEDERAL COURTS	STATE COURTS
HIGHEST APPELLATE COURT	
U.S. Supreme Court	State Supreme Court[1]
INTERMEDIATE APPELLATE COURTS	
U.S. Court of Appeals	Courts of Appeals[2]
Court of Appeals for the Federal Circuit	
TRIAL COURTS OF GENERAL JURISDICTION	
U.S. District Courts	District Courts[3]
TRIAL COURTS OF LIMITED JURISDICTION	
Examples include:	*Examples include:*
Rail Reorganization Court	Juvenile Court
Court of Federal Claims	Family Court
Court of International Trade	Traffic Court
Tax Court	Small Claims Court
	Justice of the Peace
	Magistrate Court

1. Sometimes called Supreme Judicial Court or Court of Appeals.
2. These courts exist in about two-thirds of all states. They are sometimes called Superior or District Courts.
3. Sometimes called circuit courts, superior courts, or supreme courts.

THE PROCESSING OF CASES

OCCURS THROUGHOUT TERM

Court Receives Requests for Review (4,000-6,000)
• appeals (e.g., suits under the Civil Rights and Voting Rights Acts)
• certification (requests by lower courts for answers to legal questions)
• petitions for writ of certiorari (most common request for review)
• requests for original review

OCCURS THROUGHOUT TERM

Cases Are Docketed
• original docket (cases coming under its original jurisdiction)
• appellate docket (all other cases)

OCCURS THROUGHOUT TERM

Justices Review Docketed Cases
• Chief justice, in consultation with the associate justices and their staffs, prepares discuss lists (approximately one quarter of docketed cases)
• Chief justice circulates discuss lists prior to conferences

FRIDAYS

Conferences
• selection of cases for review, for denial of review
• Rule of Four: Four or more justices must agree to review most cases

BEGINS MONDAYS AFTER CONFERENCE

Announcement of Action on Cases

Clerk Sets Date for Oral Argument
• usually not less than three months after the Court has granted review

Attorneys File Briefs
• appellant must file within forty-five days from when Court granted review
• appellee must file within thirty days of receipt of appellant's brief

SEVEN TWO-WEEK SESSIONS, FROM OCTOBER THROUGH APRIL ON MONDAYS, TUESDAYS, WEDNESDAYS

Oral Arguments
• Court typically hears four cases per day, with each case receiving one hour of Court's time

WEDNESDAY AFTERNOONS, FRIDAYS

Conferences
• discussion of cases
• tentative votes

Assignment of Majority Opinion

Drafting and Circulation of Opinions

Issuing and Announcing of Opinions

Reporting of Opinions
• U.S. Reports (U.S.) (official reporter system)
• Lawyers' Edition (L.Ed.)
• Supreme Court Reporter (S.Ct.)
• U.S. Law Week (U.S.L.W.)
• electronic reporter systems (WESTLAW, LEXIS)
• Project Hermes (accessed though bitnet, internet, or National Public Telecomputing Network)

SOURCE: Lee Epstein, Jeffrey A. Segal, Harold J. Spaeth, Thomas G. Walker, *The Supreme Court Compendium: Data, Decisions, and Developments* (Washington, D.C.: Congressional Quarterly, 1994), Figure 1-1.

APPENDIX 8
SUPREME COURT CALENDAR

Activity	Time
Start of Term	First Monday in October
Oral Argument Cycle	October–April: Mondays, Tuesdays, Wednesdays in seven two-week sessions
Recess Cycle	October–April: two or more consecutive weeks after two weeks of oral argument; Christmas, Easter holidays
Conferences	Wednesday afternoon following Monday oral arguments (discussion of four Monday cases)
	Friday following Tuesday, Wednesday oral arguments (discussion of eight Tuesday–Wednesday cases; certiorari petitions)
	Friday before two-week oral argument period
Majority Opinion Assignment	Following oral arguments/conferences
Opinion Announcement	Throughout term with bulk coming in spring/summer
Summer Recess	Late June/early July until first Monday in October
Initial Conference	Late September (resolve old business, consider certiorari petitions from the summer)

BRIEFING SUPREME COURT CASES

1. **What is the name of the case?**
   The name is important because it *generally* reveals which party is asking the Court to review the case. The name appearing first is usually (but not always) the appellant/petitioner, the party that lost in the court below.

2. **In what year did the Supreme Court decide the case?**
   The year is important because it will help to put the case into a legal and historical context. See Thumbnail Sketch of Supreme Court History for more detail.

3. **What circumstances triggered the dispute?**

4. **What statute or action triggered the dispute?**

5. **What provision of the Constitution is at issue?**

6. **What is the basic legal question(s) the Court is being asked to address?**

7. **What was the outcome of the dispute?**

8. **How did the majority reach its decision? What was its legal reasoning?**

9. **What legal doctrine, standards, or policy did the majority announce?**

10. **What other views (dissents, concurrences) were expressed?**

AN EXAMPLE: *Texas v. Johnson* (1989)

1. Case Name: *Texas v. Johnson*
2. Year Case Decided by Supreme Court: 1989
3. Facts that Triggered the Dispute. While the Republican National Convention was meeting in Dallas, Texas, in 1984, Gregory Johnson took part in a demonstration, protesting policies of the Reagan administration. During the demonstration, Johnson burned an American flag, and Dallas police arrested him.
4. Statute. Johnson was arrested and subsequently convicted under a Texas law that made it a criminal activity to desecrate a "venerable" object, including a state or national flag.
5. Provision of the Constitution. Johnson alleged that his conviction, under the Texas state law, violated First Amendment guarantees of freedom of expression.
6. Legal Question. Is flag burning, in the context of this dispute, an activity protected by the First Amendment?
7. Outcome. In a 5–4 ruling, the Court held for Johnson.

8. Legal Reasoning of the Majority. In delivering the opinion of the Court, Justice William J. Brennan, Jr., held that:
   a. Johnson's action constituted expressive conduct, allowing him to raise a First Amendment claim.
   b. Although governments have a "freer hand" in restricting "conduct" (as opposed to pure speech or writing), they still must demonstrate a sufficiently important governmental interest in regulating the activity in question.
   c. Texas's stated interests—preventing breaches of the peace and preserving the flag as a symbol of national unity—are insufficient to prohibit Johnson's expressive conduct.
9. Legal Doctrine. The majority:
   a. set policy in an area of the law that was previously murky. States may not "foster" their own view "of the flag by prohibiting expressive conduct relating to it."
   b. reaffirmed past precedents, suggesting that in such cases the

Court will not only consider the nature of the expression (whether it is verbal or nonverbal), but the governmental interest at stake.

c. reaffirmed a general commitment to the fundamental nature of the First Amendment: "If there is a bedrock principle underlying the First Amendment, it is that the Government may not prohibit the expression of an idea simply because society finds that idea itself offensive or disagreeable."

10. Other Points of View.

a. Justice Kennedy concurred: while the flag "holds a lonely place of honor," the Constitution mandates the outcome expressed by the majority. In short, sometimes justices "make decisions" they do not "like." But they make them "because they are right."

b. Chief Justice Rehnquist (joined by White and O'Connor) dissented: freedom of expression is not absolute: conduct may be pro-

hibited in light of legitimate governmental interests. Here, those interests outweigh the expression.

i. Johnson's conduct had the tendency to incite a breach of the peace.

ii. the American flag is a "visible symbol embodying our Nation"; it does not represent a political idea or philosophy, nor is it just "another symbol."

c. Justice Stevens dissented: the question of flag desecration is unique. Cases involving other forms of symbolic expression are not dispositive of it. Our nation's flag symbolizes those values—liberty and equality—that "are worth fighting for." As such it cannot be "true that the flag . . . is not itself worthy of protection from unnecessary desecration."

GLOSSARY

A fortiori With greater force or reason.

Abstention A doctrine or policy of the federal courts to refrain from deciding a case so that the issues involved may first be definitively resolved by state courts.

Acquittal A decision by a court that a person charged with a crime is not guilty.

Advisory opinion An opinion issued by a court indicating how it would rule on a question of law should such a question come before it in an actual case. Federal courts do not hand down advisory opinions, but some state courts do.

Affidavit A written statement of facts voluntarily made under oath or affirmation.

Affirm To uphold a decision of a lower court.

Aggravating circumstances Conditions that increase the seriousness of a crime but are not a part of its legal definition.

Amicus curiae "Friend of the court." A person (or group), not a party to a case, who submits views (usually in the form of written briefs) on how the case should be decided.

Ante Prior to.

Appeal The procedure by which a case is taken to a superior court for a review of the lower court's decision.

Appellant The party dissatisfied with a lower court ruling who appeals the case to a superior court for review.

Appellate jurisdiction The legal authority of a superior court to review and render judgment on a decision by a lower court.

Appellee The party usually satisfied with a lower court ruling against whom an appeal is taken.

Arguendo In the course of argument.

Arraignment A formal stage of the criminal process in which the defendants are brought before a judge, confronted with the charges against them, and they enter a plea to those charges.

Arrest Physically taking into custody or otherwise depriving freedom of a person suspected of violating the law.

Attainder, Bill of A legislative act declaring a person or easily identified group of people guilty of a crime and imposing punishments without the benefit of a trial. Such legislative acts are prohibited by the United States Constitution.

Bail A security deposit, usually in the form of cash or bond, which allows those accused of crimes to be released from jail and guarantees their appearance at trial.

Balancing test A process of judicial decision making in which the court weighs the relative merits of the rights of the individual against the interests of the government.

Bench trial A trial, without a jury, conducted before a judge.

Bicameral A legislature, such as the U.S. Congress, with two houses.

Bona fide Good faith.

Brandeis brief A legal argument that stresses economic and sociological evidence along with traditional legal authorities. Named after Louis Brandeis, who pioneered its use.

Brief A written argument of law and fact submitted to the court by an attorney representing a party having an interest in a lawsuit.

Case law Law that has evolved from past court decisions, as opposed to law created by legislative acts.

Case or controversy rule The constitutional requirement that courts may only hear real disputes brought by adverse parties.

Case A legal dispute or controversy brought to a court for resolution.

Certification A procedure whereby a lower court requests that a superior court rule on specified legal questions so that the lower court may correctly apply the law.

Certiorari, Writ of An order of an appellate court to an inferior court to send up the records of a case that the appellate court has elected to review. The primary method by which the U.S. Supreme Court exercises its discretionary jurisdiction to accept appeals for a full hearing.

Circuit courts of appeal The intermediate level appellate courts in the federal system having jurisdiction over a particular region.

Civil law Law that deals with the private rights of individuals (e.g., property, contracts, negligence), as contrasted with criminal law.

Class action A lawsuit brought by one or more persons who represent themselves and all others similarly situated.

Collateral estoppel A rule of law that prohibits an already settled issue from being relitigated in another form.

Comity The principle by which the courts of one jurisdiction give respect and deference to the laws and legal decisions of another jurisdiction.

Common law Law that has evolved from usage and custom as reflected in the decisions of courts.

Concurrent powers Authority that may be exercised by both the state and federal governments.

Concurring opinion An opinion that agrees with the result reached by the majority, but disagrees as to the appropriate rationale for reaching that result.

Consent decree A court-ratified agreement voluntarily reached by parties to settle a lawsuit.

Constitutional court A court created under authority of Article III of the Constitution. Judges serve for terms of good behavior and are protected against having their salaries reduced by the legislature.

Contempt A purposeful failure to carry out an order of a court (civil contempt) or a willful display of disrespect for the court (criminal contempt).

Contraband Articles that are illegal to possess.

Criminal law Law governing the relationship between individuals and society. Deals with the enforcement of laws and the punishment of those who, by breaking laws, commit crimes.

Curtilage The land and outbuildings immediately adjacent to a home and regularly used by its occupants.

De facto In fact, actual.

De jure As a result of law or official government action.

De minimis Small or unimportant. A de minimis issue is considered one too trivial for a court to consider.

De novo New, from the beginning.

Declaratory judgment A court ruling determining a legal right or interpretation of the law, but not imposing any relief or remedy.

Defendant A party at the trial level being sued in a civil case or charged with a crime in a criminal case.

Demurrer A motion to dismiss a lawsuit in which the defendant admits to the facts alleged by the plaintiff but contends that those facts are insufficient to justify a legal cause of action.

Deposition Sworn testimony taken out of court.

Dicta; Obiter dicta Those portions of a judge's opinion that are not essential to deciding the case.

Directed verdict An action by a judge ordering a jury to return a specified verdict.

Discovery A pretrial procedure whereby one party to a lawsuit gains access to information or evidence held by the opposing party.

Dissenting opinion A formal written expression by a judge who disagrees with the result reached by the majority.

Distinguish A court's explanation of why a particular precedent is inapplicable to the case under consideration.

District courts The trial courts of general jurisdiction in the federal system.

Diversity jurisdiction The authority of federal courts to hear cases in which a party from one state is suing a party from another state.

Docket The schedule of cases to be heard by a court.

Double jeopardy The trying of a defendant a second time for the same offense. Prohibited by the Fifth Amendment to the Constitution.

Due process Government procedures that follow principles of essential fairness.

En banc An appellate court hearing with all the judges of the court participating.

Enjoin An order from a court requiring a party to do or refrain from doing certain acts.

Equity Law based on principles of fairness rather than strictly applied statutes.

Error, Writ of An order issued by an appeals court commanding a lower court to send up the full record of a case for review.

Ex parte A hearing in which only one party to a dispute is present.

Ex post facto law A criminal law passed by the legislature and made applicable to acts committed prior to passage of the law. Prohibited by the U.S. Constitution.

Ex rel Upon information from. Used to designate a court case instituted by the government but instigated by a private party.

Ex vi termini From the force or very meaning of the term or expression.

Exclusionary rule A principle of law that illegally gathered evidence may not be admitted in court.

Exclusive powers Powers reserved for either the federal government or the state governments, but not exercised by both.

Federal question A legal issue based on the U.S. Constitution, laws, or treaties.

Felony A serious criminal offense, usually punishable by incarceration of one year or more.

Grand jury A panel of twelve to twenty-three citizens who review prosecutorial evidence to determine if there are sufficient grounds to issue an indictment binding an individual over for trial on criminal charges.

Guilty A determination that a person accused of a criminal offense is legally responsible as charged.

Habeas corpus "You have the body." A writ issued to determine if a person held in custody is being unlawfully detained or imprisoned.

Harmless error An error occurring in a court proceeding that is insufficient in magnitude to justify the overturning of the court's final determination.

In camera A legal hearing held in the judge's chambers or otherwise in private.

Indictment A document issued by a grand jury officially charging an individual with criminal violations and binding the accused over for trial.

Information A document, serving the same purpose as an indictment, but issued directly by the prosecutor.

In forma pauperis "In the form of a pauper." A special status granted to indigents that allows them to proceed without payment of court fees and to be exempt from certain procedural requirements.

Injunction A writ prohibiting the person to whom it is directed from committing certain specified acts.

In re "In the matter of." The designation used in a judicial proceeding in which there are no formal adversaries.

In rem An act directed against a thing and not against a person.

Immunity An exemption from prosecution granted in exchange for testimony.

Incorporation The process whereby provisions of the Bill of Rights are declared to be included in the due process guarantee of the Fourteenth Amendment and made applicable to state and local governments.

Infra Below.

Interlocutory decree A provisional action that temporarily settles a legal question pending the final determination of a dispute.

Inter alia Among other things.

Judgment of the court The final ruling of a court, independent of the legal reasoning supporting it.

Judicial activism A philosophy that courts should not be reluctant to review and if necessary strike down legislative and executive actions.

Judicial restraint A philosophy that courts should defer to the legislative and executive branches whenever possible.

Judicial review The authority of a court to determine the constitutionality of acts committed by the legislative and executive branches and to strike down acts judged to be in violation of the Constitution.

Jurisdiction The authority of a court to hear and decide legal disputes and to enforce its rulings.

Justiciable Capable of being heard and decided by a court.

Legislative court A court created by Congress under authority of Article I of the Constitution to assist in carrying out the powers of the legislature.

Litigant A party to a lawsuit.

Magistrate A low level judge with limited authority.

Mandamus "We command." A writ issued by a court commanding a public official to carry out a particular act or duty.

Mandatory jurisdiction A case that a court is required to hear.

Marque and reprisal An order from the government of one country requesting and legitimizing the seizure of persons and property of another country. Prohibited by the Constitution.

Merits The central issues of a case.

Misdemeanor A less serious criminal act, usually punishable by less than one year of incarceration.

Mistrial A trial that is prematurely ended by a judge because of procedural irregularities.

Mitigating circumstances Conditions that lower the moral blame of a criminal act, but do not justify or excuse it.

Moot Unsettled or undecided. A question presented in a lawsuit that cannot be answered by a court either because the issue has resolved itself or conditions have so changed that the court is unable to grant the requested relief.

Motion A request made to a court for a certain ruling or action.

Natural law Laws considered applicable to all persons in all nations because they are thought to be basic to human nature.

Nolle prosequi The decision of a prosecutor to drop criminal charges against an accused.

Nolo contendere No contest. A plea entered by a criminal defendant in which the accused does not admit guilt but submits to sentencing and punishment as if guilty.

Opinion of the court An opinion announcing the judgment and reasoning of a court endorsed by a majority of the judges participating.

Order A written command issued by a judge.

Original jurisdiction The authority of a court to try a case and to decide it, as opposed to appellate jurisdiction.

Per curiam An unsigned or collectively written opinion issued by a court.

Per se In and of itself.

Petitioner A party seeking relief in court.

Petit jury A trial court jury to decide criminal or civil cases.

Plaintiff The party who brings a legal action to court for resolution or remedy.

Plea bargain An arrangement in a criminal case in which the defendant agrees to plead guilty in return for the prosecutor reducing the criminal charges or recommending a lenient sentence.

Plurality opinion An opinion announcing the judgment of a court with supporting reasoning that is not endorsed by a majority of the justices participating.

Police powers The power of the state to regulate for the health, safety, morals, and general welfare of its citizens.

Political question An issue more appropriate for determination by the legislative or executive branch than the judiciary.

Precedent A previously decided case that serves as a guide for deciding a current case.

Preemption A doctrine under which an area of authority previously left to the states is, by act of Congress, brought into the exclusive jurisdiction of the federal government.

Prima facie "At first sight." A case that is sufficient to prevail unless effectively countered by the opposing side.

Pro bono publico "For the public good." Usually refers to legal representation done without fee for some charitable or public purpose.

Pro se A person who appears in court without an attorney.

Quash To annul, vacate, or totally do away with.

Ratio decidendi A court's primary reasoning for deciding a case the way it did.

Recuse The action of a judge not to participate in a case because of conflict of interest or other disqualifying condition.

Remand To send a case back to an inferior court for additional action.

Res judicata A legal issue that has been finally settled by a court judgment.

Respondent The party against whom a legal action is filed.

Reverse An action by an appellate court setting aside or changing a decision of a lower court.

Ripeness A condition in which a legal dispute has evolved to the point where the issues it presents can be effectively resolved by a court.

Selective incorporation The policy of the Supreme Court to decide incorporation issues on a case-by-case, right-by-right basis.

Solicitor general Justice Department official whose office represents the federal government in all litigation before the U.S. Supreme Court.

Standing; standing to sue The right of parties to bring legal actions because they are directly affected by the legal issues raised.

Stare decisis "Let the decision stand." The doctrine that once a legal issue has been settled it should be followed as precedent in future cases presenting the same question.

State action An action taken by an agency or official of a state or local government.

Stay To stop or suspend.

Strict construction Narrow interpretation of the provisions of laws.

Subpoena An order compelling a person to testify or to produce evidence before a court, legislative hearing, or grand jury.

Sub silentio "Under silence." A court action taken without explicit notice or indication.

Summary judgment A decision by a court made without a full hearing or without receiving briefs or oral arguments.

Supra Above.

Temporary restraining order A judicial order prohibiting certain challenged actions from being taken prior to a full hearing on the question.

Test A criterion or set of criteria used by courts to determine if certain legal thresholds have been met or constitutional provisions violated.

Three-judge court A special federal court made up of appellate and trial court judges created to expedite the processing of certain issues made eligible for such priority treatment by congressional statute.

Ultra vires Actions taken that exceed the legal authority of the person or agency performing them.

Usus loquendi The common usage of ordinary language.

Vacate To void or rescind.

Vel non "Or not."

Venireman A juror.

Venue The geographical jurisdiction in which a case is heard.

Voir dire "To speak the truth." The stage of a trial in which potential jurors are questioned to determine their competence to sit in judgment of a case.

Warrant A judicial order authorizing an arrest or search and seizure.

Writ A written order of a court commanding the recipient to perform or not to perform certain specified acts.

CASE INDEX

ILLUSTRATION CREDITS